THE ROUTLEDGE INTERNATIONAL HANDBOOK OF FEMINISMS IN SOCIAL WORK

This handbook highlights innovative and affect-driven feminist dialogues that inspire social work practice, education, and research across the globe. The editors have gathered the many (at times silenced) feminist voices and their allies together in this book which reflects current and contested feminist landscapes through 52 chapters from leading feminist social work scholars from the many branches and movements of feminist thought and practice. The breadth and width of this collection encompasses work from diverse socio-political contexts across the globe including Central and South America, Africa, Asia, the Middle East, Europe, North America, Aotearoa New Zealand and Australia.

The book is divided into six parts as follows:

- Decoloniality, Indigeneity and Radical Theorising
- Feminist Social Work in Fields of Practice
- Academy and Feminist Research
- The Politics of Care
- Allyship, Profeminisms and Queer Perspectives
- Social Movements, Engaging with the Environment and the More-than-Human

The above sections present the diverse feminisms that have influenced social work which provides a range of engaging, informative and thought-provoking chapters. These chapters highlight that feminists still face the battle of working towards ending gender-based violence, discrimination, exploitation and oppression, and therefore it is urgent that we feature the many contemporary examples of activism, resistance, best practice and opportunities to emphasise the different ways feminisms remain central to social work knowledge and practice.

It will be of interest to all scholars and students of social work and related disciplinary areas including the social and human sciences, global and social politics and policy, human rights, environmental and sustainability programmes, citizenship and women's studies.

Carolyn Noble, PhD, is a former Associate Dean and Foundation Professor of Social Work at Australian College of Applied Professions in Sydney, Australia.

Shahana Rasool, PhD, is a Professor and Head of the Social Work Department at the University of Johannesburg, South Africa.

Linda Harms-Smith, PhD, is an Associate Professor of Social Work at the University of Pretoria, South Africa.

Gianinna Muñoz-Arce, PhD, is an Associate Professor and Director of the University of Chile Department of Social Work.

Donna Baines, PhD, is a Professor and Former Director of the University of British Columbia School of Social Work, Vancouver, Canada.

ROUTLEDGE INTERNATIONAL HANDBOOKS

ROUTLEDGE HANDBOOK OF HOMICIDE STUDIES
Edited by Kyle A. Burgason and Matt DeLisi

THE ROUTLEDGE HANDBOOK OF THE POLITICAL ECONOMY OF HEALTH AND HEALTHCARE
Edited by David Primrose, Rodney Loeppky and Robin Chang

THE ROUTLEDGE HANDBOOK ON KARL POLANYI
Edited by Michele Cangiani and Claus Thomasberger

THE ROUTLEDGE HANDBOOK OF POSTCOLONIAL DISABILITIES STUDIES
Edited by Tsitsi Chataika and Dan Goodley

THE ROUTLEDGE INTERNATIONAL HANDBOOK OF DISABILITY AND GLOBAL HEALTH
Edited by Lieketseng Ned, Minerva Rivas Verlade, Satendra Singh, Leslie Swartz and Karen Soldatić

THE ROUTLEDGE HANDBOOK OF LGBTQ IDENTITY IN ORGANIZATIONS AND SOCIETY
Edited by Julie A. Gedro and Tonette S. Rocco

THE ROUTLEDGE INTERNATIONAL HANDBOOK OF FEMINISMS IN SOCIAL WORK
Edited by Carolyn Noble, Shahana Rasool, Linda Harms-Smith, Gianinna Muñoz-Arce and Donna Baines

THE ROUTLEDGE INTERNATIONAL HANDBOOK OF FEMINISMS IN SOCIAL WORK

*Edited by Carolyn Noble, Shahana Rasool,
Linda Harms-Smith, Gianinna Muñoz-Arce
and Donna Baines*

LONDON AND NEW YORK

Designed cover image: © Getty Images
This is an image of Molas (decorative embroidered cloth panels) made by Kuna women of the San Blas Islands, Panama. In this instance, as a woven textile (often regarded as a product of 'women's work'), it represents diversity, relatedness and the interconnected patterns of various feminisms, foregrounding voices from the South.

First published 2024
by Routledge
4 Park Square, Milton Park, Abingdon, Oxon OX14 4RN

and by Routledge
605 Third Avenue, New York, NY 10158

Routledge is an imprint of the Taylor & Francis Group, an informa business

© 2024 selection and editorial matter, Carolyn Noble, Shahana Rasool, Linda Harms-Smith, Gianinna Muñoz-Arce and Donna Baines; individual chapters, the contributors

The right of Carolyn Noble, Shahana Rasool, Linda Harms-Smith, Gianinna Muñoz-Arce and Donna Baines to be identified as the authors of the editorial material, and of the authors for their individual chapters, has been asserted in accordance with sections 77 and 78 of the Copyright, Designs and Patents Act 1988.

All rights reserved. No part of this book may be reprinted or reproduced or utilised in any form or by any electronic, mechanical, or other means, now known or hereafter invented, including photocopying and recording, or in any information storage or retrieval system, without permission in writing from the publishers.

Trademark notice: Product or corporate names may be trademarks or registered trademarks, and are used only for identification and explanation without intent to infringe.

British Library Cataloguing-in-Publication Data
A catalogue record for this book is available from the British Library

Library of Congress Cataloging-in-Publication Data
Names: Noble, Carolyn, editor. | Rasool, Shahana, editor. | Harms-Smith, Linda, editor. | Muñoz-Arce, Gianinna, editor. | Baines, Donna, 1960– editor.
Title: The Routledge international handbook of feminisms in social work / edited by Carolyn Noble, Shahana Rasool, Linda Harms-Smith, Gianinna Muñoz-Arce and Donna Baines.
Description: Abingdon, Oxon; New York, NY: Routledge, 2024. | Series: Routledge international handbooks | Includes bibliographical references and index.
Identifiers: LCCN 2023054879 (print) | LCCN 2023054880 (ebook) | ISBN 9781032327600 (hardback) | ISBN 9781032329260 (paperback) | ISBN 9781003317371 (ebook)
Subjects: LCSH: Social service. | Feminist theory. | Gender-based violence.
Classification: LCC HV40 .R68476 2024 (print) | LCC HV40 (ebook) | DDC 361.3—dc23/eng/20240111
LC record available at https://lccn.loc.gov/2023054879
LC ebook record available at https://lccn.loc.gov/2023054880

ISBN: 978-1-032-32760-0 (hbk)
ISBN: 978-1-032-32926-0 (pbk)
ISBN: 978-1-003-31737-1 (ebk)

DOI: 10.4324/9781003317371

Typeset in Sabon
by codeMantra

To all the participants and co-researchers who shared their ideas, research, lives and her-stories with us.
To our mothers, sisters (including each other), children, partners, friends, colleagues who supported and carried us as we brought this collection to fruition.
To all the women, girls, trans, non-binary and queer people dealing with multiple discriminations and injustices around the world.
To the women who play so many care roles in the home and community. We salute you ALL for your strength and persistence in keeping communities and families thriving against all odds.

CONTENTS

List of figures	xv
List of tables	xvi
About the editors	xvii
List of contributors	xx
Preface	xxxv
Acknowledgements	xl

    Introduction   1
*Carolyn Noble, Shahana Rasool, Linda Harms-Smith,
Gianinna Muñoz-Arce and Donna Baines*

SECTION 1
Decoloniality, indigeneity and radical theorising   7

1 Feminisms in social work practice   9
   Carolyn Noble

2 Locating African feminism, womanisms, and nego-feminism –
   possibilities for social work   21
   Shahana Rasool

3 Colored demarcations in postcolonial feminism:
   Can the subalterned social worker now speak?   33
   Melinda Madew

Contents

4 Reversing a one-track history: Listening to minority voices at the intersections of gender, race and intellectual disability 45
Patience Udonsi

5 Privileging Indigenous knowledge and wisdom as Feminist social work practitioners 55
Péta Phelan and Bindi Bennett

6 Tensions and dialogues between intersectional and decolonial feminist contributions to Latin American social work 68
Lelya Troncoso-Pérez, Karina Pinto G. and Rocío Gallardo Aranguren

7 Social work and marxism: Unitary perspective in the anti-racist, feminist, and anti-imperialist struggle 80
Marina Machado-Gouvêa and Camila Carduz-Rocha

8 Social work, indigenous feminisms and decolonisation of public policies in Chile 92
Alicia Rain Rain

9 The intersectionality body-territory-daily life in Mayan-Xinka community feminism. Its importance for social work 102
Silvana Martínez and Juan Agüero

10 Feminism, politics, and social work 111
Ruth Phillips

SECTION 2
Feminist social work in fields of practice 123

11 Gender empowerment in youth work in Palestine: A missing link 125
Abeer Musleh

12 A critical race feminist rights (CRFR) social work approach to trafficking of women in South Africa 138
Ajwang' Warria

13 #Reporting worries: Narratives of sexual harassment and intersecting inequalities in Swedish social work 151
Mona B. Livholts, Sanna Stenman, and Louise Thorén Lagerlöf

14 Nego-feminist practices adopted by senior women traditional leaders in Kwazulu-Natal, South Africa to address women abuse — 164
Tanusha Raniga and Gladys Nkareng Klaas-Makolomakwe

15 Feminist social work practice and efforts towards gender equality in Australia — 175
Elizabeth Orr, Louise Morley, Wendy Bunston, Carrie Maclure and Louise Whitaker

16 The impact of Patriarchy on premarital relationships in Nigeria — 189
Augusta Y. Olaore, Oluwatobiloba Bello and Oluwafikayomi O. Banjo

17 Where do I belong? Feminism, social work, and women with intellectual disabilities — 203
Kelley Johnson, Emily Ardley and Alisha Gilliland

18 An intersectional feminist analysis of Australian print media representations of sexual violence by Indian men: Implications for social work — 215
Jillian Barraud, Carole Zufferey and Helena de Anstiss

19 Commentary - Resisting carcerality, embracing abolition implications for feminist social work practice — 228
Beth E. Richie and Kayla M. Martensen

20 Feminisms and social work: The development of an emancipatory practice — 233
Jeannette Bayisenge

SECTION 3
Academy and feminist research — 245

21 Knowing subjects? Feminist epistemologies, power struggles and social work research — 247
Stephen Hicks

22 Feminist participatory action research with breast cancer survivors in China — 258
Yuk Yee Lee and Hok Bun Ku

23 Feminist research in social work: Epistemological-methodological
    keys from the South   272
    María Eugenia Hermida and Yanina Roldán

24 Feminist queries: Exploring feminist social work research questions   281
    Stéphanie Wahab, Ben Anderson-Nathe and Christina Gringeri

25 Academia and gender disparities: A critical historical analysis
    of academic careers of Chilean social workers from a
    feminist-intersectional approach   292
    *Gabriela Rubilar Donoso, Catherine LaBrenz, Paz Valenzuela
    Rebolledo and Gianinna Muñoz-Arce*

26 Creating space for critical feminist social work pedagogy   305
    Sarah Epstein, Norah Hosken and Sevi Vassos

27 Feminist leadership and social work: The experience of women
    leaders in Palestinian universities   317
    Najwa Sado Safadi

28 The contributions of Latin American feminisms to social work
    undergraduate academic training in Argentina   328
    *Melisa Campana Alabarce, Laura Lorena Leguizamón
    and Maria Belén Verón Ponce*

SECTION 4
The politics of care   339

29 Life-sustaining communitarian weavings: Feminist interpellations
    of the approach of community social work   341
    Javiera Cubillos-Almendra

30 Incubators of the future: Motherhood, biology and pre-birth
    social work in feminist practice   350
    Eileen Joy and Liz Beddoe

31 Parenting through mental health challenges: Intersections of gender,
    race, class and power   360
    Rochelle Hine and Hanna Jewell

32 Social work and two types of maternalism: Supporting single
    mothers through strategic maternalism   373
    Toshiko Yokoyama

33 Matricentric feminist social work: Towards an organising conceptual framework and practice approach to support empowered mothering 384
   Sarah Epstein and Pippa Mulley

34 Feminized care work, social work and resistance in the context of late neoliberalism 394
   Donna Baines

SECTION 5
Allyship, profeminisms and queer perspectives 405

35 Social work reckons with cisnormativity & the gender binary 407
   Jama Shelton and Courtney Virginia Fox

36 *Marica* and *Travesti* interpellations to conservative social work practices 415
   Alejandra Gutiérrez Saracho and Claudio Barbero

37 Generation old and proud: No going back in the closet 426
   Teresa Savage and Jude Irwin

38 Heteropatriarchy and child sexual abuse: Contemplating profeminist practice with men victim-survivors 440
   Alankaar Sharma and Amelia Wheeler

39 Making men allies in stopping men's violence via processes of intersectional identification: A study of Swedish profeminist men 451
   Keith Pringle, Anna-Lena Almqvist and Linn Egeberg Holmgren

40 Men, feminist welfare, and allyship in social work education 462
   Goetz Ottmann and Iris Silva Brito

41 'Men' as social workers: Professional identities, practices and education 473
   Fiachra Ó Súilleabháin and Alastair Christie

42 Ally work at the intersections: Theorising for practice and practicing for theory 485
   Glenda Kickett, Antonia Hendrick and Susan Young

43 Beyond alternative masculinities and men's allyship: Troubling men's engagement with feminisms in social work and human services practice   498
Bob Pease

SECTION 6
Social movements, engaging with the environment, and the more-than-human   511

44 Deliberate democracy and the MeToo movement: Examining the impact of social media feminist discourses in India   513
Akhila K. P. and Jilly John

45 "We can't just sit back and say it's too hard": Older women, social justice, and activism   526
Tina Kostecki

46 Feminist social work responses to intersectional oppression faced by ethnic minority women in Japan   536
Osamu Miyazaki

47 The contribution of feminist new materialism to social work   547
Vivienne Bozalek

48 Eco-femagogy: A red-green perspective for transforming social work education in the post-covid world   560
Susan Hillock

49 Intersectionality, feminist social work, animals and the politics of meat   573
Heather Fraser and Nik Taylor

50 Ecofeminism and the popular solidarity economy in Latin American social work: Resistance to the patriarchal and capitalist system   587
Juana Narváez Jara

51 The futures of writing *with* posthuman feminism in social work   598
Mona B. Livholts and Fanny Södergran

52 Eco-feminist responses to climate change and its gendered impacts   614
Leah Holdsworth and Jennifer Boddy

Index   625

FIGURES

42.1	A framework for ally work in an intersectional setting	488
42.2	Ethical Practice: Allyship	491
49.1	Animals, meat and social work	573
51.1	Photograph of Oodi Library, Helsinki, Finland	599
51.2	Cloudberry blossoms in tractor ruts	604
51.3	Barley	605
51.4	Bark skin/*Barkhud*/*Kuoren iho*. Stockholm, Sweden, 2020	606
51.5	Exhausted Things/*Utmattade saker*/*Uupuneet asiat*, Stockholm, Sweden, 2020	608

TABLES

28.1	Critical feminist scholarly contributors	334
32.1	Comparison of essentialist maternalism and strategic maternalism	379
48.1	Applying eco-femagogy	567
49.1	Vegan-friendly, "real-world" intersectional examples	582

ABOUT THE EDITORS

This book, *Routledge International Handbook of Feminisms in Social Work* has gathered feminist scholars from across the globe to highlight feminist conversations, arguments, practices, education, and research that inspire feminist social work across its spheres of influence. In gathering the many chapters listed in this handbook, we showcase innovative local, national, regional, and international practices that position feminist social work as critical to addressing the growing misogynistic, patriarchal, male-dominated authoritarianism that persists across the world. The editors think this aim is crucial, for while most social workers would acknowledge that feminism has played a significant part in the development of social work, its theory and its many and varied approaches to practice, research and education, its ideas and impact have not been adequately captured in one significant volume. This handbook has been developed to redress this omission.

The editors of the handbook bring a combination of academic, activist and practice experience from our collective commitment to feminist scholarship and the profession. This handbook will be of interest to all social work students, practitioners, and academics, as well as a much wider audience concerned with social and environmental justice not only for women, trans, non-binary, and gender diverse people but for all human and non-human species as well as the planet.

Carolyn Noble, PhD, is a Former Associate Dean and Foundation Professor of social work at Australian College of Applied Professions in Sydney, Emerita Professor of social work at Victoria University, Melbourne and Research Associate, Johannesburg University, South Africa. She has been an academic since 1984, and mental health and child protection practitioner before that in Sydney and London. She has taught and developed undergraduate and postgraduate programmes in social work, counselling and psychotherapy, social science, mental health and professional supervision; all with a critical lens. She is active in Australian, Asia Pacific and International Schools of social work Associations and has held executive positions in each of these organisations. Her research interests include social work theory, work-based learning and professional supervision. Further areas of research include gender democracy, right-wing populism, and post-Covid-19 welfare state. She has published widely in her areas of research and continues to present her work nationally and internationally. She is Editor-in-Chief of open-access social issues magazine for IASSW www.socialdialogue.online.

Shahana Rasool is a Rhodes Scholar who obtained a Masters and Doctorate from the University of Oxford (UK), Department of Social Policy. She is a Full Professor and Head of the Department at the University of Johannesburg (UJ). Her research has focused extensively on gender-based violence and gender inequality. More recently she extended her work to Decoloniality in social work education. Shahana has various partnerships both regionally and internationally and coordinates the social policy course in the joint master programme with the University of West Indies. She is a Vice President of the Association for Schools of Social Work in Africa (ASSWA) and the African representative of the International Association of Schools of Social Work (IASSW). Shahana is Chair of the International Conference on Gender and Sexuality and recently edited a special issue in the *Journal of Gender Issues*. At UJ, Shahana is a member of the Senate academic freedom committee. She has published and presented at many local and international conferences on gender in/equality, gender-based violence, Decoloniality, and help-seeking. She is committed to transformation and social justice both within academia and beyond.

Linda Harms-Smith is an Associate Professor of Social Work at the University of Pretoria, South Africa, previously at Robert Gordon University, Scotland from 2015 to 2021 and before that from 2000 until 2015, at the University of the Witwatersrand, Johannesburg. Her career as a community social worker began during the era of racist Apartheid, which shaped a commitment to social justice and radical social work. She obtained her PhD at the University of the Witwatersrand (2013) on social work and social change; a Master's in Social Science at Rhodes University in Grahamstown, a Social Science (Hons) (Psychology) at UNISA; and a BA in Social Work (Hons) University of Stellenbosch. Her scholarship and research focuses on Decoloniality and anti-colonialism, 'race' and anti-racism, radical social work, Fanonian practices, social work theory, social movements, Feminisms in social work and qualitative research. She is the chairperson of the editorial board of the *Critical and Radical Social Work Journal* (Africa regional editor), member of the Editorial Board of *International Social Work Journal*, Steering committee member of Social Work Action Network (SWAN), and a founding member of the Social Work Action Network, South Africa.

Gianinna Muñoz-Arce holds a PhD in Social Work from Bristol University (UK). She is an Associate Professor and Head of Department of Social Work University of Chile. Her research interests are critical theory, social intervention, and social work. She teaches Social Work Theoretical Approaches in several PhD programmes in Social Work (La Plata University, Argentina, and Alberto Hurtado University, Chile). She is Primary Researcher of the project 'Professional resistances in frontline social programmes implementation" (Grant N°1201685, National Agency for Research and Development, Chilean Government). Her recent publications include 'Decolonising community social work: Contributions of frontline professional resistances from a Mapuche perspective' (*Critical and Radical Social Work*) and 'Decolonial feminism and practices of resistance to sustain life: Experiences of women social workers implementing mental health programmes in Chile' (*Affilia*). She is member of the Social Work Action Network (SWAN-I), the Chilean Social Work Research Network, and the Latin American Decolonial Social Work Network.

About the editors

Donna Baines is a Professor and Former Director of the University of British Columbia School of Social Work. She teaches and writes on anti-oppressive practice and theory, paid and unpaid care work, and austerity. Her work focuses on anti-oppressive and decolonising approaches to theory and practice, paid and unpaid care work, and social policy and austerity. She has published recently in *British Journal of Social Work*, *Work in the Global Economy*, and the fourth edition of Doing Anti-Oppressive Social Work: Rethinking Theory and Practice (with Clark, N. and Bennett, B. 2023, Fernwood Publishing). She has joined many social justice movements across her life and draws on anti-oppressive, feminist, intersectional, anti-racist, decolonising, and Marxist approaches.

CONTRIBUTORS

Juan Agüero is a Master and PhD in Social Work, Licentiate and PhD in Administration, Research Professor Category 1, Director of the Master in Social Policies, and Co-Director of the G-TEP Social Theory, Decolonial Studies and Critical Thinking Group of the National University of Mar del Plata, Argentina.

Melisa Campana Alabarce obtained a Bachelor degree and PhD in Social Work (National University of Rosario). Melisa Campana Alabarce is an Associated Researcher at CONICET, Principal Professor at National University of Rosario, Director of the Research Centre on Governmentality and State (CIGE-PEGUES), Researcher at Complutense University of Madrid, MSCA-UNA4CAREER fellow. Her research interests include social work, social policy, social assistance, and neoliberalism.

Anna-Lena Almqvist is an Associate Professor/Senior Lecturer in Social Work at Mälardalen University, Sweden. Her research interests include families/family policy, young people in vulnerable life situations, as well as men's anti-violence work and she has published internationally on these issues. She is Co-author of 'Men's Activism to End Violence Against Women: Voices from Spain, Sweden and the UK', Policy Press, 2021.

Ben Anderson-Nathe is a Professor of Child, Youth, & Family Studies at Portland State University. He holds Master's degree in Social Work and Public Policy, a graduate certificate in disability policy and services, and a PhD in community education and youth studies from the University of Minnesota. Ben has worked with youth in therapeutic foster and group care, community mental health, juvenile corrections, homeless and street settings, community education, sexuality education, and recreation/camping. His teaching and scholarship focus on youth and youth work; critical, queer, and post-structural epistemologies; and gender, sexuality, and queerness.

Rocío Gallardo Aranguren is a Social Worker. Aranguren obtained Master in Gender Studies, Culture and Humanities at University of Chile, Member of R&D Nucleus 'Diversity and Gender: Intersectional Feminist Approaches'.

Contributors

Emily Ardley is a performing artist, self-advocate and woman living with intellectual disability. Emily is the founder of (it is no) drama, a movement and physical theatre group for people with and without disability based in South Gippsland, Victoria (Australia). Emily worked as a peer educator in the Sexual Lives & Respectful Relationships programme from 2010 to 2018 and continues to contribute to this work through research and storytelling.

Oluwafikayomi O. Banjo, PhD, is a Senior Lecturer in the Department of Social Work, Babcock University, Nigeria. She holds a Doctor of Philosophy in Education with specialisation in Social Welfare from the University of Ibadan. She has served in various service capacities such as the Head of the Psychosocial Unit at the University's Student Support Center. She is a member of several professional and academic bodies including but not limited to Association of Social Work Educators in Nigeria (ASWEN), Nigeria Association of Social Workers (NASOW), Counselling Association of Nigeria (CASSON), International Federation of Social Worker (IFSW) and Positive Psychology Association of Nigeria (PPOAN).

Claudio Barbero is a Sexuality activist, and a Professor in Philosophy and Educational Sciences, Bachelor of Social Work (National University of Córdoba, Argentina), Specialist in Education (Professional Association in Social Service of the Province of Córdoba, CPSSPC), Higher Diploma in Human Rights and Sexual Diversity (CLACSO/Argentine Federation of Lesbians, Gays, Bisexuals and Trans), doctoral student in Social and Human Sciences (National University of Luján, Argentina), Researcher (National University of Mar del Plata, Argentina), Head of the Commission on Gender and Sexual Diversity of the CPSSPC (2018–2022) and member of the Federal Forum on Gender and Sexual Diversity of the Argentine Federation of Professional Associations of Social Service, FAAPSS (2019–2022).

Jillian Barraud is a social work first-class honours graduate in Justice & Society, University of South Australia. She was the 2021 recipient of the Zonta Club of Adelaide Community Development Awards at the University of South Australia. She is now a practitioner in the field working with children and children.

Jeannette Bayisenge is an Associate Professor of Gender Studies at the University of Rwanda's Centre for Gender Studies. She has a PhD in social work from the University of Gothenburg, Sweden, and earned her Master's in development cooperation with a specialisation in women and development from Ewha Womans University in South Korea. Her academic pursuits and published research are in the fields of gender, women's empowerment, and women's land rights.

Liz Beddoe is a Professor of Social Work at the University of Auckland in New Zealand. Her professional background was in women's health. Her interests include reproductive justice, critical social work, student hardship in social work education, and the experiences of migrant social workers. Liz has published widely in international journals and written several books.

Oluwatobiloba Bello, MSW, University of Ibadan is a licensed Social Worker and certified Family Systems Engineering Practitioner based in Nigeria. She holds a Master of Social Work degree from the University of Ibadan and specialises in premarital counselling and sexuality education. She currently serves as the Lead Social Worker at the Paroche Reach Out Foundation, a Substance Abuse Awareness Non-Governmental Agency.

Contributors

Bindi Bennett, PhD, is a Gamilaraay woman, mother, and social worker. She is committed to improving and growing cultural responsiveness; re-Indigenising Western spaces; understanding and exploring Indigenous Knowledge Systems; and exploring the human-animal bond.

Jennifer Boddy is an internationally recognised Researcher with expertise in Climate Violence. Most recently she has focused on the intersections between domestic violence and climate change and examined alternative approaches to working with male perpetrators of violence that are situated within the natural environment. Her work is grounded in a commitment to social and environmental justice, and through her research, she seeks to create safe and sustainable environments free from violence.

Vivienne Bozalek is an Emerita Professor in Women's and Gender Studies at the University of the Western Cape and Honorary Professor in the Centre for Higher Education Research, Teaching and Learning (CHERTL) at Rhodes University. Her most recent books include *In conversation with Karen Barad: Doings of Agential Realism* with Karin Murris (Routledge 2023), *Posthuman and Political Care Ethics for Reconfiguring Higher Education* with Michalinos Zembylas and Joan Tronto (Routledge, 2021), *Post-Anthropocentric Social Work: Critical Posthuman and New Materialist Perspectives*, with Bob Pease (Routledge, 2021), *Higher Education Hauntologies: Living with Ghosts for a Justice-to-Come* with Michalinos Zembylas, Siddique Motala, and Dorothee Hölscher (Routledge, 2021). She is the editor-in-chief of the open source online journal *Critical Studies in Teaching and Learning*.

Iris Silva Brito is at Federation University, Berwick. Iris Silva Brito is a Lecturer in Social Work at the Australian College of Applied Professions (ACAP). She chairs Live and Learn Environmental Education's Board and is a Director of ATEC Biodigesters International. Iris is passionate about social work education, social policy, and community development. Born in Brazil, Iris draws her search for and appreciation of knowledge from both her parents who have dedicated their lives to the education of children living in poverty, and scholars such as Paulo Freire who combined education with social and political consciousness raising.

Hok Bun Ku holds a PhD degree from the Department of Anthropology and Sociology at SOAS, University of London. Now he is a Professor, the Programme Leader of DSW and Sociology Panel Chair in the Department of Applied Social Sciences at The Hong Kong Polytechnic University. He is also an Honorary Professor at China Youth University for Political Science. He serves as the Director of China and Global Development Network and Co-Director of the Peking University-The Hong Kong Polytechnic University China Social Work Research Centre. He is currently an Associate Editor of *China Journal of Social Work*.

Wendy Bunston, PhD, is an International Author, Presenter, Researcher, and Clinician who specialises in working therapeutically with infants, children, and families who are impacted by family violence. She is a social worker, family therapist, infant mental practitioner, and adjunct lecturer at La Trobe University, Victoria, Australia.

Camila Carduz-Rocha is an Economist and social worker (PUC/SP-Brasil), MD in Social Work (UFRJ-Brasil) and PhD candidate in Social Work (PUC/SP-Brasil), and holds a CNPQ research grant.

Contributors

Alastair Christie is an Emeritus Professor of Applied Social Studies at University College Cork, Ireland. His research interests draw on both social work and social policy, and focus on how social work is constructed/provided within patriarchal and racialised contexts. He is a member of the *Critical Social Policy* editorial collective and a number of activist community projects including the Cork Traveller Visibility Group.

Javiera Cubillos-Almendra is a Research Associate (UK)/Associate Professor (US) at the School of Sociology, Catholic University of Maule, and Director of the Center for Urban and Territorial Studies (CEUT), in Chile. Javiera is an MSc in Gender Equality and Social Sciences and PhD in Political Science, both awarded by the Complutense University of Madrid, Spain. Research interests include feminist theory, gender studies, Intersectionality, decolonial Feminism, communities, public policies, sexual and reproductive rights. ORCID: 0000-0001-8080-4049

Helena de Anstiss, PhD, has an established academic career as well as 20 years professional experience in the area of social policy development and analysis, service planning, development and evaluation, and industry development and capacity building. She is currently Co-CEO of Multicultural Youth South Australia (MYSA).

Gabriela Rubilar Donoso is the Director in the Department of Social Work at the University of Chile, and Researcher on the project ANID/CONICYT/Fondecyt 1190257 and 1230605. Her lines of research focus on a biographical approach, research trajectories, longitudinal qualitative research, and social work and public policy.

Sarah Epstein, PhD, is a Senior Lecturer in Social Work at Deakin University. Her work experience has focused on supporting victim/survivors of violence. Sarah's doctorate examined feminist mothers' experiences of raising sons and the potential for feminist maternal practice to build gender equality. Her research interests involve examining ways to re-qualify maternal knowledge in social work, developing feminist social work pedagogy and considerations of hope in social work practice.

Courtney Virginia Fox (they/they) is a licensed social worker and advocate for queer youth. Their work focuses on identity exploration, relationship building, and the prevalence of eating disorders in the LGBTQ+ community. They is a graduate of the Silberman School of Social Work (MSW) and the University of Virginia School of Education (MEd).

Heather Fraser is an Associate Professor Faculty of Health, School of Public Health and Social Work, Queensland University of Technology. Heather is a critical social worker of more than three decades. She completed her PhD at Monash University in 2002 and has coordinated the Master of Social Work at QUT since 2018. Heather specialises in animal social work, narrative methods and co-design, and teaches units in health and wellbeing, and crisis, trauma, and addiction.

Alisha Gilliland (B App Sci, B Health Sci, MBA) has a background working in local government, the not-for-profit sector and academia, mostly in Gippsland (Victoria, Australia) and always with the intent of building a healthier, safer, fairer, and more inclusive community. Currently, Alisha works at Gippsland Centre Against Sexual Assault as an educator where her work has a focus on gender equity and violence prevention and includes the Sexual Lives & Respectful Relationships programme.

Christina Gringeri, PhD, MSW, is a Professor at the College of Social Work, University of Utah. Her research has focused on the working lives of low-income women, examining the nexus of social support and quality of life. Additional research has examined the nexus of adverse childhood experiences, adult social support, and quality of health and mental health. More recent projects include exploring ways social work education links field and classroom education, and a narrative project examines the intersections of spirituality, feminist social change, and patriarchy in institutional religion. All projects utilise qualitative data collection and analytic methods, principally from critical, feminist, and constructivist perspectives.

Antonia Hendrick is a Wadjella (white) woman born on Whadjuk Nyungah boodja (Swan Valley, Western Australia). Given her work takes place across the many nations of Australia and with its violent history and stolen lands, she actively seeks to foreground the gifts, wisdom, and generosity of Aboriginal and Torres Strait Islander peoples in all her work. Antonia graduated with a BSW (1st class Hons.) in 1997. She has held various appointments before completing her PhD in 2010. Over the last 15 years, Antonia has worked as an academic and is currently a Senior Lecturer at UWA in the Social Work and Social Policy programme. Her research interests include working to decolonise the social work curriculum and develop culturally responsive policies towards systemic change. Antonia has several publications on decolonial theory and practice. This work intersects with her interest in seeking to collaborate with Lived Experience Educators (LEE) in the tertiary system.

María Eugenia Hermida is a social worker and education specialist, PhD in Social Work, Professor and Researcher at the Faculty of Health Sciences and Social Work, Universidad Nacional de Mar del Plata (Argentina), Postgraduate Professor at different universities in Argentina and Chile. Her research topics include feminism, Decoloniality, affective turn, and public policies.

Stephen Hicks is a Senior Lecturer in Social Work at the University of Manchester (UK), where he teaches research issues to postgraduate social work students and supervises a number of doctoral candidates. He was involved in research and activism on LGBTQ foster care and adoption for many years and published *Lesbian, Gay and Queer Parenting: Families, Intimacies, Genealogies* in 2011. He is a member of the Morgan Centre for Research into Everyday Lives and is currently co-investigator on a National Institute for Health & Care Research (NIHR) School for Social Care Research funded project on the social care assessment of older LGBTQ people.

Susan Hillock is a Professor of Social Work at Trent University in Oshawa, Ontario, Canada. Her education and research methods stem from, and build upon, experiential, liberation, and anti-oppressive perspectives including eco-femagogy, feminist, Indigenous, critical race, structural social work, and queer theories. She was recently the successful recipient of Trent University's Award for Educational Leadership and Innovation. Previous edited books include *Greening Social Work Education: Caring Sustainability* (UoT Press, 2023);

Teaching About Sex and Sexuality(ies) in Higher Education (UoT Press, 2021); *Teaching Social Work: Pedagogy & Practice* (UoT Press, 2021); and *Queering Social Work Education* (UBC Press, 2016).

Rochelle Hine, PhD, is a social worker and academic living and working on GunaiKurnai County in rural Victoria, with over 25 years of practice experience in a range of sectors including mental health, women's health promotion, child protection and research. Rochelle's research is grounded in social justice and identifying and addressing inequality, focusing predominantly on critical qualitative approaches to exploring the circumstances of people's lives, collaborating with lived experience experts and other stakeholders.

Leah Holdsworth is a practicing social worker and researcher. Working in the field, she is experiencing first-hand the ongoing effects of a natural disaster on mental health and vulnerable populations, currently supporting her local community after a recent natural disaster. Leah is passionate about examining the effects of natural disasters on women, in particular. Her research focuses on ecofeminist approaches to climate change and natural disasters, as well as the benefits that natural environments can have on women recovering from trauma.

Linn Egeberg Holmgren obtained PhD in Sociology and is a Senior Lecturer in Social Work at Uppsala University, Sweden. Her research focus includes the role of men in social work and the theoretical/empirical understanding of pro-feminism about which she has published internationally. She is co-author of *'Men's Activism to End Violence Against Women: Voices from Spain, Sweden and the UK'*, Policy Press, 2021.

Norah Hosken, PhD, is a Senior Lecturer in Social Work Edith Cowen University, WA with 30 years' experience as a practitioner and educator in social work, community work, welfare, and women's sectors. Norah has worked alongside, and learned with individuals, groups and communities who have been highly discriminated against, in urban, regional, rural and remote locations. Norah has published in national and international refereed journals, co-edited a book about critical social work, and contributed to edited books in areas including poverty and class, cross-cultural research, social work education, and social work supervision.

Jude Irwin, PhD, is an Emeritus Professor of Social Work and Social Justice at the University of Sydney. The focus of her work is on challenging structural and systemic inequalities of groups and communities who live with marginalisation, including LGBTIQ+ communities and individuals.

Juana Narváez Jara, PhD in Social Work, Master in Educational Management, Research Professor at the Ibero-American Network of Intercultural and Interdisciplinary Studies, Member of the Decolonial and Intercultural Social Work Network-Fabrics of Latin American and Caribbean Social Work, and Ecofeminist and social activist.

Hanna Jewell is a social worker and Family Therapist who lives on Bunurong land. She is currently the Statewide Coordinator for the Victorian FaPMI (Families where a parent has a mental illness) programme. She works at The Bouverie Centre-Latrobe University, an integrated practice-research organisation promoting relationships in families, organisations, and communities. She has extensive experience working as a mental health social worker, clinical family therapist, clinical supervisor, family practice consultant, workforce trainer, manager, and implementation specialist. Her work has focused on ways to improve mental health services' response to families affected by mental health issues.

Jilly John, PhD, is an Assistant Professor in the Department of Social Work, School of Social Sciences at Central University of Kerala, Kasaragod, India. She has more than 20 years of teaching experience. She was a parallel speaker in the 9th International Conference in Health and Mental Health at York University, England in 2019. She has publications in reputed journals and research paper presentations in national and international conferences. Her research areas include mental health, child care, family health, and gender studies.

Kelley Johnson, Professor (Hon), BA, MA, PhD, is an internationally recognised scholar in the fields of disability, institutional closure, social inclusion, rights, and gender. She currently holds honorary professorships at Deakin University and UNSW in Australia. She has researched extensively in the field of disability with particular focus on undertaking inclusive research with people with learning disabilities. This involves people with disabilities as active researchers undertaking research about issues which are important to them. It aims to support people with disabilities to have a heard voice and to work for change in policy, practice, and advocacy.

Eileen Joy is a Professional Teaching Fellow at the University of Auckland in Aotearoa New Zealand. Her interests include feminism, intersectional social work, child protection, gender and sexuality, and decolonising social work education and practice. Her doctoral work involved a critical examination of the role that early prevention sciences play in child protection social work policy and practice.

Glenda Kickett is a Whadjuk and Ballardong Nyungah woman from the South West of Western Australia. She has a Social Work degree from the University of Western Australia (UWA), a Master of Arts from Curtin University in Indigenous Research and Development, and in the final stages of a PhD in Social Work at UWA. Glenda is the CEO of Karla Kuliny Aboriginal Corporation, an organisation which supports Aboriginal Carers to care for Aboriginal and Torres Strait Islander children and young people in Out of Home Care. She has worked in Out of Home Care supporting Carers and advocating for the children and young people's care needs, and family support and reunification programmes with government and non-government organisations for nearly 30 years. She is also a Senior Lecturer in the School of Social Work in the unit, Aboriginal and Torres Strait Islander Knowledges and Worldviews in Social Work learning and practice.

Gladys Nkareng Klaas-Makolomakwe is a social work professional and holds a Doctorate in Social Work. She has joined the University of Mpumalanga as a Social Work lecturer. She worked as a researcher for the Department of Cooperative Governance and Traditional Affairs in KwaZulu-Natal province of South Africa. Her role entailed conducting research on vast issues affecting municipalities and the institution of traditional leadership. She is an ambitious scholar whose growing pedagogic interests are grounded within the Nego-feminist and Afrocentric theories. She is continuously publishing and presenting at conferences.

Contributors

Tina Kostecki, PhD, is State-wide Field Education Coordinator in Social Work at the University of Tasmania, Australia. Her work as a social work practitioner/manager/coordinator has been primarily in the women's services sector addressing violence against women. Tina's research interests are aligned to social justice issues and include critical gerontology, feminism, and the application of critical theory perspectives to inform social work practice.

Catherine LaBrenz is an Assistant Professor at the University of Texas at Arlington School of Social Work. She received her PhD from the University of Texas at Austin Steve Hicks School of Social Work and her Master's in Social Work with Families from the Pontificia Universidad Católica de Chile. Her research focuses on family and community resilience and child maltreatment prevention.

Louise Thorén Lagerlöf, Drama Pedagogue and Bachelor of Science in Social Work (Swedish: socionom) from Linköping University in Sweden. She has worked as a drama pedagogue in Hässleholm and Malmö in Sweden with diverse projects during seven years. She is currently working as social worker in the Deaconess Center for Children and Youth Activities, Norrköping.

Laura Lorena Leguizamón holds Bachelor degree in Social Work and PhD in Social and Human Sciences (National University of Quilmes). She is a Researcher and Professor at the Institute of Gender Studies of the Museum of Anthropological and Natural Sciences (National University of La Rioja). Her studies are linked to Human Sciences, from a Latin American, decolonial and gender perspective. Her work prioritises situated social studies, seeking to dialogue the intersections between feminism, gender, and rurality.

Mona B. Livholts is a Professor of Social Work in the Department of Social Sciences, affiliated with INEQ-Inequality studies, at the University of Helsinki, Finland; Executive Member and Secretary the European Association of Schools of Social Work (EASSW); Founder of the Network for Reflexive Academic Writing (RAW) 2008–2017. Current research focuses on situated writing as creative resistance, narratives of sexual violence, gender space and memory, monuments and narrative inequality, exhaustion and environmental justice. Latest books are *Situated Writing as Theory and Method, The Untimely Academic Novella* (2019); *The Body Politics in Glocal Social Work, Essays on the Post-Anthropocentric Condition* (2023).

Marina Machado-Gouvêa is a Professor at Universidade Federal do Rio de Janeiro (ESS/UFRJ-Brasil), Economist, PhD in International Political Economics, Researcher at the 'World Economy and Crisis' workgroup of the Latin American Council of Social Sciences (CLACSO) and at the 'Marxist Theory of Dependency' workgroup of the Brazilian Political Economy Society (GT-TMD/SEP), Director of the Society for Political Economy and Critical Thought in Latin America between 2016 and 2022.

Carrie Maclure, BSW, has been a social worker for 25 years in statutory and clinical settings in the UK and Australia, largely working with children who have experienced abuse-related trauma. In 2018, Carrie joined the tertiary sector, and works as an academic, supervisor, and programme manager. She is passionate about school social work.

Contributors

Melinda Madew, EdD, is a Professor in international social work at the Protestant University of Applied Sciences Ludwigsburg, Germany. She lectures on postcolonial themes in various European universities where she brings her Global South perspective in social work practice and theory. She is a Research Associate of the University of Johannesburg and member of the board for the European Social Work Research Association. Her commitment to radical social work and postcolonial advocacy developed from her years of community work with Indigenous women in the Philippines.

Kayla M. Martensen is a PhD candidate (ABD) in the Department of Criminology Law and Justice, University of Illinois Chicago. Under the supervision of Dr. Beth E. Richie, Kayla is using an anti-carceral feminist lens to explore the detainment of Latinx/a girls and young women in various residential placements, including juvenile detention centres.

Silvana Martínez is PhD in Social Sciences, Licentiate, and Master in Social Work, Research Professor Category 1, Director of the Doctorate in Social Work and Director of the G-TEP Social Theory, Decolonial Studies and Critical Thinking Group of the National University of Mar del Plata, Argentina.

Osamu Miyazaki (they/them) is an Associate Professor of Social Work at Meiji Gakuin University in Japan. They obtained their PhD from Hokusei Gakuen University. Their research interests lie in understanding how social differences, including race, ethnicity, gender, and sexuality; contribute to exclusion and oppression, and the role of social work in addressing these issues. Their work draws influence from critical theories such as postcolonialism, anti-oppressive practice, anti-racism, feminism, and queer theory. They prioritise learning from minority communities.

Louise Morley, PhD, is a Lecturer in Social Work at the University of New England in Armidale, Australia. Throughout her social work career, she has focused on the systematic impacts of inequality on rural and remote communities. Her doctoral research examined the deeply personal issues for child welfare workers in a highly contested political and policy environment.

Pippa Mulley works as a social worker providing support for people experiencing family violence and for parents needing assistance with the care and wellbeing of children and young people. Pippa is a PhD candidate investigating the influence of feminism on children assigned male at birth in order to consider its potential as a location for violence prevention work.

Abeer Musleh is an Assistant Professor at Bethlehem University – Palestine, and the Chairperson of the Department of Social Sciences. She is a youth worker in practice and researcher in youth engagement and development. Her research interest is focused on youth engagement and community development within the Arab countries, with a special focus on youth collective agency, alternative models of action, and mobilisation for change with special focus on young women and youth in colonised contexts. As the VP of RC34 Sociology of youth in the International Sociological Association, she aims at working with a network of Arab researchers on enhancing critical youth research in the region, and to advance youth research in the Arab countries. Her latest article is related to youth agriculture cooperatives in Palestine.

Contributors

Augusta Y. Olaore is a Social Work Educator, Practitioner, and Administrator. She earned an MSW degree from the University of California, Los Angeles, and her Doctorate degree from the University of South Africa. She is the Pioneer Chair Emeritus of the Social Work Department of Babcock University Nigeria and a past member of the Board of Directors for the International Association of Schools of Social Work. She currently serves as the Executive Director of Savaye LLC, a relationship education organisation in Stockton California as well as being a Senior Research Associate with the University of Johannesburg.

Elizabeth Orr, PhD, is a First Nations ally with 40 years' experience in community and social work activism for gender and health equality. She is a Senior Lecturer in Social Work at the University of New England Armidale and works alongside communities to implement prevention strategies to end violence, teach action research and qualitative evaluation skills.

Fiachra Ó Súilleabháin is the Vice-Head of School of Applied Social Studies, University College Cork, Ireland. A professionally qualified, CORU registered Social Worker since 2002, he researches and teaches on gender and sexualities, LGBT+ matters, social services and welfare practice, child sexual abuse, child protection and welfare, and social work practice. He is the Programme Director of the PhD in Social Work and a Coordinator of the Master in Social Work programme. Prior to working UCC, he was the manager of a regional multi-disciplinary child sexual abuse assessment unit within the Child and Family Agency (TUSLA).

Goetz Ottmann, PhD, is a Senior Lecturer at Federation University. He is the author of several books, book chapters, and numerous peer-reviewed journal articles. His research interests include critical social theory, authoritarian 'welfare', social policy, and aged and disability care. His latest co-authored books include *Post-Pandemic Welfare and Social Work: Reimagining the 'New Normal'* and *The Challenge of Right-wing Nationalist Populism for Social Work* (both with Carolyn Noble) published by Routledge.

Akhila K P is an Assistant Professor in the Department of Social Work Acharya Institute of Graduate Studies, Acharya Institutes, Bangalore, India and holds a PhD in Social Work from Central University of Kerala, and an MSW in Medical & Psychiatry, Family Child Welfare Social Work. She has involved in several government projects, including the Evaluation of Policies on Empowerment of Women at Grass Root Level in Collaboration with National Commission for Women, India. With over seven years of social work field. Research and Teaching experience, she has published many Research Articles in Scopus indexed, Web of Science, UGC care group journals. She owned a Patent and edited a book and also published chapters in National and International edited books. Her fields of interest are women and gender studies, research methodology, medical & psychiatry, mental health, child rights and human rights, academic research and training.

Bob Pease is an Adjunct Professor in the School of Social Sciences at the University of Tasmania and Honorary Professor in the School of Humanities and Social Sciences at Deakin University in Australia. His most recent books are *Facing Patriarchy: From a Violent Gender Order to a Culture of Peace* (Zed Books, 2019), *Post-Anthropocentric Social Work: Critical Posthuman and New Materialist Perspectives* (co-editor, Routledge, 2021), *Undoing Privilege: Unearned Advantage and Systemic Injustice in an Unequal World* (second edition, Zed, 2022) and *Posthumanism and the Man Question: Beyond Anthropocentric Masculinities* (co-editor, Routledge, 2023).

Péta Phelan is a Koorie lesbian with a disability, with family connections to the Riverina region of South-West NSW, Australia. A rehabilitation counsellor, and social and emotional wellbeing practitioner, her work is embedded in Indigenous intersectional knowledge and practices.

Ruth Phillips is an Associate Professor in the Social Work and Policy Studies programme at the University of Sydney. As a social justice researcher, Ruth does research on social policy, the third sector (civil society) and feminism and feminist practice. Ruth argues a critical connection between feminism and social work and, after 20 years of teaching future social workers, has seen the positive results of ensuring students graduate with strong theoretical frameworks to apply to their practice. As well as having supervised over 25 PhDs to completion. She has recently published a monograph with Routledge UK, *Practising Feminism for Social Welfare: A Global Perspective* (2023), which reflects her wide-ranging interests are social policy, human services, and feminism.

Karina Pinto G. is a social worker at the University of Chile. Master © in gender studies, culture, and humanities at the University of Chile. Member of R&D Nucleus 'Diversity and Gender: intersectional feminist approaches'.

Maria Belén Verón Ponce holds a Bachelor's degree in Social Work and in Social Communication (National University of Catamarca); PhD in Social Work (National University of Rosario); Director of the Specialisation in Public Policy on Gender and Gender Violence at the Faculty of Humanities (National University of Catamarca); Director of the project on colonial and patriarchal violence and resistance from a situated geopolitical perspective. She is a member of the Southern Political Ecology Team (IRES-CONICET-UNCA). Her studies refer to extractivism, feminism, gender, and social policy.

Keith Pringle is a Professor Emeritus in the Department of Sociology, Uppsala University, Sweden. In the course of his career he has been professor, variously, of sociology, social policy, or social work in Denmark, Sweden, and the UK. His research focus is on intersectional forms of oppression associated with 'race', gender and younger age, about which he has published extensively including 12 authored/edited books.

Alicia Rain Rain is an Assistant Professor in the Department of Social Work at the Alberto Hurtado University in Chile.

Tanusha Raniga is the Interim DST/NRF Chair for welfare and social development at the University of Johannesburg. She is a C2 NRF Rated Researcher. She is actively involved in research primarily in the area of social protection policy, feminisation of poverty and sustainable livelihoods. She has published widely in national and international journals and has presented at numerous social work conferences. Her teaching areas include social policy, development management, and integrated social and economic development.

Paz Valenzuela Rebolledo is a social worker who received her degree from the University of Chile. Her professional roles have been related to human rights and social work research.

Currently, she is a public policy analyst with the Subsecretary of Human Rights with the Ministry of Justice and Human Rights.

Beth E. Richie is the Head of the Department of Criminology, Law and Justice and Professor of African American Studies, Sociology, and Gender and Women's Studies. Holding an MSW, her research focused on gender violence and abolition. Dr. Richie is a founding member of INCITE!: Women of Color Against Violence and is the author of the proclaimed book, *Arrested Justice: Black Women, Violence, and America's Prison Nation*.

Yanina Roldán is a social worker (Universidad Nacional de Mar del Plata, Argentina) and specialist in methods and techniques in social research (Latin American Council of Social Sciences, CLACSO); Master's in Social Politics (in progress) and PhD in Social Work (in progress); Research Fellow; Specialist in Human Rights and Gender (Universidad Nacional de Mar del Plata, Argentina). Her research topics are Latin American Feminisms, social policies, and social work.

Najwa Sado Safadi, PhD, is an Associate Professor in Social Work Department at Al-Quds University. She received her PhD in Social Work from Boston College with concentration in poverty and social policy. She earned her Master's degree in Social Work (community organising) from McGill University in Canada. She has been the principal investigator on six major research projects on topics related to social workers wellbeing, domestic violence, and social protection policies. Her research has appeared in a number of peer-reviewed journals. In addition, Dr. Safadi has several years of experience in teaching and social work practice in Jerusalem and West Bank.

Alejandra Gutiérrez Saracho is an activist for the rights of travestis and trans people, Bachelor of Social Work (National University of Catamarca, Argentina), Professor of the subjects 'Social and Cultural Anthropology' and 'Mental Health' of the degree in Social Work (Faculty of Humanities, National University of Catamarca, Argentina). He is studying Specialisation in Social Anthropology (Faculty of Philosophy and Humanities, National University of Córdoba, Argentina).

Teresa Savage (she/her) lives and works on the land of the Wangal people (now known as the Inner West of Sydney, Australia.) She is a semi-retired consultant working on projects and submissions which advocate for the wellbeing of older LGBTIQ+ people.

Alankaar Sharma, PhD, (he/him) is a Senior Lecturer in Social Work at the University of Wollongong, Australia. Alankaar's academic interests are in the areas of critical studies of men and masculinities, sexual violence and child sexual abuse, and sexuality and sexual rights. He has worked in Australia, India, the United States, and South and Southeast Asia. His research and teaching are inspired by social justice, (pro)feminism, and critical social work. Confronting and ending oppression against marginalised people is at the heart of his social justice-oriented social work practice.

Jama Shelton (they/them) is an Associate Professor at the Silberman School of Social Work at Hunter College and the Associate Director of the Silberman Center for Sexuality and Gender. Dr. Shelton's programme of research focuses on cisgenderism in social services and social work education, as well as LGBTQ+ youth homelessness and structural inequity.

In particular, they are interested in identifying and addressing systemic barriers rooted in hetero/cisgenderism and the binary gender system that frequently constrain the successful transition into stable housing for transgender, non-binary and gender expansive youth and limit the efficacy of social service responses to homelessness.

Fanny Södergran is a licensed Social Worker and a Doctoral Researcher in Social Sciences at the University of Helsinki, Finland. Södergran has a special interest in posthuman theory developments within the social work field. In her doctoral research, she focuses on how environmental movements make meaning of how circumstances mediated by space, time and materiality, generate unequal possibilities for wellbeing and social justice in the climate crisis. She is currently working as a researcher social worker within a collaboration between the City of Helsinki, the Mathilda Wrede-Institute and the Helsinki Practice Research Centre, that emphasises social work practice developments.

Sanna Stenman holds Bachelor of Science in Social Work (Swedish Socionom) from Linköping University, Sweden. She currently works as a Social Worker with children and youth in The Social Services for Children, Youth and Family, Norrköping, Sweden. She wrote her candidate essay and published research in Swedish on #Metoo and sexual harassment in Swedish social work with Mona Livholts and Louise Thorén Lagerlöf 2019.

Nik Taylor, Professor, is a critical and public sociologist whose research focuses on mechanisms of power and marginalisation expressed in/through human relations with other species and is informed by critical/ intersectional feminism. Nik is currently the Co-Director of the New Zealand Centre for Human-Animal Studies at the University of Canterbury, New Zealand, where she also teaches topics in the Human Services programme that focus on human-animal violence links; scholar-advocacy; social change, and crime and deviance, particularly domestic violence and animal abuse. Nik's latest books include *Queer Entanglements* (Cambridge University Press, with Damien Riggs, Heather Fraser and Shoshana Rosenberg) and *Rescuing Me, Rescuing You: Companion Animals and Domestic Violence* (Palgrave, 2019, with Heather Fraser).

Lelya Troncoso-Pérez, Feminist Social Psychologist, is an Assistant Professor in the Department of Social Work, University of Chile. She is the Co-coordinator of the R&D Nucleus 'Diversity and Gender: intersectional feminist approaches'. She holds a PhD in Psychology (University of Chile) and a Master's in Gender Studies (Lund University). Her research and teaching areas are Feminist studies, critical social psychology, gender and memory, sexuality, Intersectionality, and feminist coalitions.

Patience Udonsi holds the position of Lecturer in Learning Disabilities Nursing and Social Work at the University of Salford, England, UK. Patience has an extensive background in professional practice, as a Community Learning Disability Nurse and a Mental Health Social Worker. Her research interests include promoting equity for individuals with intellectual disabilities who are neurodivergent and anti-racist practice within the context of Health and Social Care practice.

Sevi Vassos, PhD, is a Senior Lecturer in Social Work and Academic Lead for Social Work Field Education at Deakin University. Her research interests are in the areas of critical feminist approaches in social work education, and more specifically practice-based learning.

Her teaching interests are in direct practice skill development, critical policy analysis, and organisational practice.

Stéphanie Wahab, PhD, MSW, is a Professor at Portland State University's School of Social Work, and Honorary Research Associate Professor at the University of Otago, Social and Community Work in New Zealand. She teaches courses focused on social justice, philosophies of science, qualitative inquiry, and intimate partner violence. Her research and scholarship tend to occur at the intersections of individual and state-sanctioned violence including, but not limited to, intimate partner violence, systemic racism, militarisation, and occupation. She is a co-editor of *Feminisms in Social Work Research: Promise and Possibilities for Justice-Based Knowledge.*

Ajwang' Warria is an Associate Professor in the Faculty of Social Work at the University of Calgary (Canada). She has published more than 50 peer-reviewed journal papers and book chapters in the areas of child protection, transnational migration, and intervention research. When she is not writing, you can find her thrifting, watching cooking shows, and exploring nature.

Amelia Wheeler, PhD, (she/her) is a Lecturer in Social Work at the Australian Catholic University in Canberra. Amelia has worked in the fields of child protection, domestic violence and family law. Amelia has held research positions with the Gendered Violence Research Network at the University of New South Wales and the Australian Institute of Relationship Studies at Relationships Australia NSW. Her research interests include the relationships between theory and practice, the inclusion of children and young people in social services, anti-racist and decolonising social work and ethics in everyday professional life.

Louise Whitaker, PhD, worked in mental health, women's health, Legal Aid, and cancer workforce development before joining academe in 2012. Her practice-based research examines social work with people impacted by mental distress, and she fosters transformative mental health and the social inclusion of women from refugee backgrounds.

Toshiko Yokoyama is a Professor in the Faculty of Humanities, Sapporo Gakuin University, PhD, and a certified mental health social worker. Her areas of expertise include social work theory, family/women's social work, mental health social work, and qualitative research methods. In recent years, she has explored alternatives to maternal and family norms in Japan from the perspective of gender and feminism.

Susan Young is an English migrant whose journey to 'being' in this land has encompassed learnings from the generous teachings of Aboriginal and Torres Strait Islander peoples leading to her continued work in social work education to encourage allyship as a practice. A qualified social worker, with the BSW and PhD gained from the University of Western Australia (UWA), Susan spent some years in practice mainly with Aboriginal and Torres Strait Islander peoples. She now teaches social work at UWA, Perth where she has worked for 30 years. Many changes have occurred during that time, significantly the greater attention paid to learning about more culturally responsive ways to work with Aboriginal and Torres Strait Islander peoples. Susan writes and researches mainly in the area of decolonising practice which has led her to incorporate this thinking in her feminist practice.

Contributors

Yuk Yee Lee, PhD, is a highly experienced professional in the field of social work, holding Doctor of Social Work degree from the Hong Kong Polytechnic University. Currently, she serves as an Assistant Professor at UOW College Hong Kong, specialising in mental health, macro social work, social policy, and narrative practice. With expertise in these areas, Dr. Lee has successfully supervised various participatory research projects in Hong Kong and China, with a specific focus on feminist issues and health policy.

Carole Zufferey is a Senior Lecturer in Social Work, University of South Australia (Justice & Society). She has published extensively in the fields of social work, Intersectionality, gender, and homelessness. She has published one sole authored book Zufferey, C. (2017) *Homelessness and Social Work: An Intersectional Approach* and two edited books with Routledge, Zufferey, C. & Yu, N. (Eds) (2018) *Faces of Homelessness in the Asia Pacific Region* and Zufferey, C. & Buchanan, F. (2020) (Eds) *Intersections of Mothering: Feminist Accounts*. As well as Franzway, S., Wendt, S., Moulding, N., Zufferey, C. & Chung, D. (2019). *The Sexual Politics of Gendered Violence and Women's Citizenship*. Policy Press, UK.

PREFACE

Our stories: The personal is the political

Carolyn

I went to university in 1968! What a time of upheaval and the promise of change. I was almost delirious when presented with the prospective of a new politics that challenged the conservative politics of the family, gender stereotypes and women's invisibility from public life. Even as a young 18 year old it was obvious, at least to me, that male domination in the world needed to be challenged and alternatives found. It was not women's fault that we found ourselves on the margin of public life. I was positioned on the threshold of the promise of great revolution informed by the beginnings of feminist politics. Women across the globe were rising to the challenge, not only to fight for equal rights but to actively work with other women to demystify and interrogate men's privilege and power. Oh! such excitement. Such new ways of looking at the world. The opening up of new pathways to a new freedom to explore life fully and without restraints.

To this end feminist literature has remained my constant literary companion and source of insight and strength throughout my personal and professional life. It opened my mind to rich and enticing alternatives to the patriarchy and suggested that it was possible to have children, study for PhD, enter academe and eventually achieve a Professorship in Social Work. Working in higher education gave me the opportunity to frame my teaching and research with a gender lens. To advocate for women's space in the public arena. But above all it was my women colleagues and students who gave me the inspiration to find my feminist voice in academia and university governance. To find my activist voice for social justice with my international colleagues and to continue to fight for a world where women can flourish through ongoing conversations, dialogue, argument, activism, teaching and writing. This book is a testament to the power of feminist and profeminist theory and practice, across generations, cultures and experiences. I am so happy to be a part of it.

Shahana

I am an African woman and proudly feminist. Sometimes I wonder if I was born a Feminist. Long before I learnt about feminist theory – which I immediately connected with – I had many questions about the differential access that men had to certain spaces; the differential expectations of women and men; and the preferential treatment men received. I remember for example wondering why in a township with multiple mosques, I was unable to enter one to pray. In the same way, I was disallowed from entering specific spaces, using certain beaches, or attending certain schools, because I am Black.

In my first Sociology class, I encountered Prof. Jacklyn Cock. I will never forget the first lecture in which she questioned why boy children are almost always dressed in blue clothes and baby girls in pink clothes- still it is almost impossible to find less gendered clothes for babies. Feminist theories and later, African feminist theories helped me name so many of my lived experiences. I resonated with the ideas and concepts. African feminism helped me explain my experiences and observations of gender inequality and how these intersect with race, class, and other dimensions. My lived experiences of being an African woman growing up in a township with working-class parents under apartheid in South Africa have profoundly shaped my feminist activism and quest to make a difference in the world and challenge all types of inequalities. It led me to want to work in the field of gender for my social work internship as a student, which led me to engage in organizations working against violence against women. My first social work experience was in an organization that provided support and shelter to abused women. This led to the core of my research work on women abuse and gender inequality.

My passion for achieving gender inequality and attaining social justice for all remains at the core of my engagements. This energy is currently concerned with issues of Decoloniality in Africa and beyond, whilst still raining my concerns from a feminist orientation. Social work provided me with the tools and knowledge base for understanding and tackling injustices and inequalities. The issues colonial occupation is still present today through neo-colonialism of French Africa for example and most vividly in the Palestinian occupation.

At present, I am distraught that as a world we are watching a 'cataclysmic assault on the occupied Gaza strip' (Amnesty International, 20 October 2023). The collective punishment of civilian Palestinians who are being denied food, water, fuel, and other necessities is horrendous. The deafening silence of the international social work community on the extensively documented human rights violations in Palestine – including the targeting and bombing of schools and hospitals- is shameful. As social workers who claim in our global definitions and agendas to be concerned with human rights and social justice, it's astonishing that we remain silent or argue for stances of neutrality in the case of Palestine, and not Ukraine. We have also learnt that many academics and others who are standing in solidarity with Palestinians are being censored and punished for their views – the silencing of a social justice stance is frightening and a violation of academic freedom. The ongoing Western-dominated colonial biases embedded in some social work discourses and engagements are concerning and need to be addressed. As feminists, we are concerned with dismantling the colonial, patriarchal, racist nexus that dominates and perpetuates structural inequality wherever it exists in the world and amongst ourselves. I have learned this in engagements with so many amazing feminists, decolonial theorists, anti-racist and anti-colonial theorists – and I am committed to building a world with those concerned with social justice to end inequality and violence.

I can't begin to name all the people who contributed to who I am, but you know who you are. However, I have to mention my maternal grandmother who was kind, loving, and passionate about education and provided me with a solid foundation. She passed her passion for education onto my mum who was an inspirational teacher who loved her children and contributed not only to their knowledge but to addressing the everyday issues of poverty they faced. Many of my uncles have also influenced my life and created the space for me to grow and continue to support my aspirations and dreams. So many women friends and colleagues have strengthened and supported me through many complex and challenging times. With these phenomenal women we shared our various lived experiences – such as dealing with issues of divorce, domestic violence, maintenance courts, and childcare. My feminist sisters all over the world who work together on the co-producing knowledge, and ideas, I cannot thank you enough for your contributions to my life and for supporting me through various ups and downs. We have been together in sisterhood and found ways of dealing with life at every level to make a difference in the lives of those 'othered'. Through these engagements, together we imagine and work towards a better and more socially just world for all. I am committed to this vision and a feminist imaginary that contributes to activism and Research that is transformational and life giving. We shall overcome! Aluta Continua!

Linda

Growing up in South Africa during Apartheid, I felt, but could not understand, the strangeness, silences, taboos, and proscriptions that characterised my 'white' world. That is, until I came to see the violence and brutality hidden in plain sight by Apartheid's spatiality and engineered oblivion. Not only did it racially stratify society into those that have and those that do not, but achieved this through land expropriation and exploitative, extractive racial capitalism, inferiorising and dehumanising Black South Africans. This was the continuity of settler Colonialism.

Other than in family conversations, critical questions such as about privileged living in white suburbia, brutal and racist violence, outrageous legislated race-based inequality, compulsory military conscription for violent Apartheid repression, or the 'outsourcing' of the care burden to slave waged, Black 'nannies', were silenced. A first critical conscientisation encounter while visiting Dutch family and strolling down an Amsterdam side-street, was an Anti-Apartheid sanctions poster against importing 'outspan oranges' depicting metaphoric 'squeezing' of a Black person's head on an orange juicer.

My journey into social work and later, into academia, included a political consciousness arising from 'philosophers have hitherto only interpreted the world in various ways, the point, however, is to change it'. As I understood more about the colonial past and the neoliberal racial capitalist present, I realised that women's oppression is a feature of both, and so the liberation of women is inextricably part of working towards a better world. I am inspired by colleague-friends of various traditions of feminism, such as Shahana Rasool; Tessa Hochfeld (1972–2019); Suryia Nayak; and Gianinna Muñoz-Arce and similarly, by colleagues and contributors to this volume. Theorist activists such as Rosa Luxemburg, Angela Davis, Maria Lugones, Sylvia Federici, Shose Kessi; Amina Mama; and Pumla Dineo Gqola provide rich sources of learning.

However, those who have inspired me most, are those women gathered in late night candlelit township meetings, planning community interventions or political protests; a woman leading the singing for a women's march, seeking justice for murdered Marikana miners; and the storytellers, poets and praise-singers, those truth-keepers and proclaimers of hope and justice. They demonstrate women's strength, agency and voice, and hope.

And yet right now, the horror of what is happening in Gaza. The illegal blockade of the Palestinian territories since 2007, the ongoing violent oppression of its people, and now the Israeli military's unprecedented onslaught with 'damning evidence of war crimes leaving nowhere safe for civilians to seek shelter' (Amnesty International, 23 November 2023), must end. Blocking humanitarian aid leading to starvation, lack of water, fuel, medicine, and basic medical care as a tactic of war against the Palestinian people, seems an impossible crime against humanity in our age. What will be said about this generation for allowing such an atrocity? The millions of voices of ordinary people, including those of Jewish people, are being heard across the globe, and yet world leaders do not respond. We cannot remain silent, not as social workers, not as women, not as people.

Gianinna

The first time I spoke about feminism was a few years ago on a live programme. When I was asked when I started being a feminist, I felt several things: on the one hand, I felt a lot of fear and shame, because maybe I wasn't 'feminist enough'. I hadn't read enough books on feminism, I thought. On the other hand, I felt discomfort, because I had always felt that 'feminism' (as I knew it at the time) did not represent me. From my perspective, the barriers to my personal and professional development had much more to do with my social class, the colour of my skin or where I was born.

With time and my own life experiences -being a mother, being a migrant, accompanying my husband in his fight against cancer, having had the privilege of studying for a doctorate in England and then having a position in a public university in my country, having formed a precious circle of friends where mutual support has been unconditional, having experienced the fruits of teaching social work from a 'pedagogy of tenderness', among so many other experiences- has taught me that feminism is read, but above all, it is a lived experience: every day, in every action, in every detail. The conceptual contributions of Gayatri Spivak and María Lugones, among other authors who have moved through Marxism, Derrida's deconstruction, northern and southern Feminisms, and 'subaltern' and 'border' approaches linked to Intersectionality, have allowed me to understand that struggles, like oppressions, are articulated. And when struggles are articulated, they are more powerful. Today I can say that I am a feminist, without fear and without feeling indebted: because feminism also means renouncing the pretension of absolute knowledge and positioning oneself from humility and openness to the knowledge of the other. And because, above all, it means not living the struggle alone, but always with others, in acts where reciprocity becomes a form of resistance to the onslaught of individualism and competitiveness promoted by the neoliberal rationality.

Donna

Though I was invited into this project after the initial steps had taken place, I am always happy to contribute to projects that deepen international exchange, and advance critical feminist and knowledges, compassion and peaceful solutions on our complex and troubled planet.

Many years ago when my daughter was a baby and my older child was still young, I flew from Toronto to Washington, DC for one day to give a paper at an important feminist conference. I only went for a single day because my kids seemed too small to leave for longer. But, I so wanted to be part of the conference: meeting people, building social movements and having a big life full of exciting ideas and social justice struggle. I gave my paper, went to every workshop possible, networked, chatted, bonded and bought a souvenir T shirt that said "THIS IS WHAT A FEMINIST LOOKS LIKE" (cost: $10).

Upon my return to Canada, I dutifully filled out my Customs and Immigration form, noting my $10 purchase. I was eager to get home and hoped I could race through the hoops of re-entry to Canada. As a youngish, middle class white woman, I fit the stereotype of a cross-border shopper and the declaration of only $10, meant I was pulled out of line and sent to the backrooms of Customs. Two bored looking young, Black women were on duty and, in a disinterested way, they told me to show them the "$10 T Shirt." Almost in tears, I told them I'd been at a feminist conference and held up my new shirt. They started laughing and shooed me away, saying "go on, get out of here" with warmth and humor.

This story captures the complexity of the feminism I love: trying to change the world in the context of endless in-balances of care, paid work and unpaid work; living and understanding Intersectionality in all its variations; finding and protecting a big place for women in public life and knowledge building; cross border solidarity and working for global social justice; as well as expected and unexpected moments of warmth, connection and humor. A postscript to this story is that the T shirt now fits my daughter, who carries on these traditions, continuing to push back at patriarchy, racism, capitalism and the other social relations that shape our longing for equity and ongoing struggle for social justice.

I am humbled to be part of the international coming together of feminist and pro-feminist scholars in this handbook. It presents another important way to engage with feminist complexities and knowledge, and to expand emancipatory opportunities.

ACKNOWLEDGEMENTS

A handbook this comprehensive does not come together without a wonderful group of colleagues committed to the process of gathering feminist scholarship across the globe. We thank all the contributors for their contributions, keeping to tasks and timelines and for their innovative and fruitful ideas, research and conversations encased in this handbook. We acknowledge the added difficulty of working across time zones, work cultures and demands and the complexities of family life. It was an amazing achievement.

We thank Professor Bob Pease who suggested that a book devoted to feminist thought, praxis and education was a missing resource in the Routledge International Handbook collection. Little did we know what a mammoth task we set ourselves but we thank him for helping set the structure and framework so we could embark on this project with some confidence.

We thank Professor Donna Baines who joined the project midway and stepped up to the challenge with all her commitment, diligence, good humor, expertise and dedication to feminist politics.

We thank special colleagues- Claire Jarvis for supporting the project through the review process, Sully Evans and Uma Maheswari for their editorial support and guidance, Razina Munshi for language support and editing and IASSW for special funds for project development.

We thank each other for our collaborative effort, support and patience and for a rewarding working partnership in getting an edited book to fruition. We faced several hurdles as life's complexities and demands drained our time, but we are thankful to have built up strong support and respect for each other in our shared love of feminist scholarship, research and writing.

Finally, we thank all current and future social workers working in difficult times and that this edited handbook provides you with inspiration and a feminist lens that answers; 'what is feminism?', 'what is a feminist?' and 'how feminism can guide our work?'.

Carolyn Noble, *Australian College of Applied Professions Sydney, Australia (Emerita)*
Shanana Rasool, *University of Johannesburg*
Linda Harms-Smith, *University of Pretoria*
Gianinna Muñoz-Arce, *Universidad de Chile*
Donna Baines, *University of British Columbia*

INTRODUCTION

*Carolyn Noble, Shahana Rasool, Linda Harms-Smith,
Gianinna Muñoz-Arce and Donna Baines*

This book *Routledge International Handbook of Feminisms in Social Work* has been developed to highlight the innovation and activism, and affect-driven feminist dialogue, practices and research that inspire feminist social work across its broad sphere of influence. In this Handbook, the editors have gathered leading feminist scholars from the many branches and movements of feminist thought and practice from Central and South America, Africa, Asia, the Middle East, Europe, North America, Australia and New Zealand to present the diverse Feminisms that have influenced social work. In gathering the many (at times silenced) feminist voices and their allies together, the editors aimed to create an opportunity where current and contested feminist landscapes can be discussed, acknowledged, respected and critiqued. Feminists still face the battle of working towards ending gender-based violence, discrimination, exploitation and oppression, and therefore, it is urgent that we highlight the many contemporary examples of activism, resistance, best practice and opportunities to emphasise the different ways Feminisms remain central to social work knowledge and practice (Wendt & Moulding, 2016, p. 303).

The editors contend that these feminist perspectives offer social work an analysis of interlocking oppressions. They provide contemporary examples of resistance, empowerment and voices that aim at opposing the patriarchal, neocolonial, capitalist and structural social disadvantage, violence, marginalisation and the ubiquitous gender inequities. In gathering the many chapters encapsulated in this Handbook, we have showcased innovative local, national and international practices that position feminist social work as critical to addressing the growing societal misogynistic, patriarchal, male-dominated authoritarianism that persists across the world. While most social workers would acknowledge that Feminisms have played a significant part in the development of social work, its impact has not been adequately captured in one significant volume. This collection of various forms of Feminisms and profeminist works aims to redress this omission.

Feminisms in social work

Since its early days, social work has been a predominantly women's profession – not always feminist, but often practised by women as providers and in the service of women as users of various programmes and services. From the 1960s, however, feminist voices, debates and theories have assumed a crucial space in highlighting and addressing the complex dynamics of gender relations in society and 'how they play out in the many problems of living that social work deals with' (Wendt & Moulding, 2016, p. 3). Applying feminist theory in social work inspired a wealth of scholarship discourse and political activism, across many decades.

Broadly, we argue that feminist debates within social work highlight the ongoing tensions between individualist explanations and responses to women's needs and problems and those providing a critical lens on the structural dynamics of oppressive society with gendered power relations that marginalise diverse groups oppressed by patriarchy and the gender binary. Feminist theories offer a specific lens for social workers and their male allies to advocate for social justice, empowerment and social, political, economic and cultural change. Feminist politics and theory remain critical in contemporary societies and more specifically to social work, since social work is concerned with social justice, human rights, environmental justice and social change. Despite feminist social work's contradictory relationship with patriarchy, capitalism, Coloniality and the neoliberal state, it remains positioned to influence change both from its practice within and outside the state and by engaging with policy and services in communities by advocacy and social mobilisations for change (e.g., #metoo movement) (Dominelli, 2002; Rasool, 2019; Hermida, 2020).

Why this book on Feminisms in social work?

It is now common to talk about Feminisms because it is too difficult to come up with a linear and definitive definition, especially as there are many strands of thought and practice, built up over many decades of examination, argument, reflection and political action. Feminists have struggled for centuries to find explanations and theoretical and political analysis to stem and correct the gender injustices and inequality including dealing with sexism, misogyny and gender binaries. These many strands of thought include intersectional, non-identitarian, poststructuralist, postcolonial, decolonial, postmodernist, new materialist, posthuman, post-anthropocentric, profeminist, Black, womanist, indigenist, and African Feminisms, as well as queer, transfeminist, Marxist and radical feminist theories. These myriad approaches that have been used in rising social, political, cultural and environmental inequities especially those that have a gender underpinning are theoretically sophisticated and innovative as well as emotionally and ethically challenging (Dominelli, 2002; Mama, 2011; Wendt & Moulding, 2016; Noble, 2021). How these thoughts have been incorporated into social work education, knowledge, research and practice are addressed in some measure in this Handbook.

It is unacceptable that there is still extensive gender inequality worldwide, which is further exacerbated by class, race, ethnic, sexuality and (dis)ability oppressions. In the Handbook, the editors have gathered contemporary social work scholars and practitioners of Feminisms, whose work and scholarship have been devoted to developing and enacting innovative and complex social and political analysis. These scholars and practitioners aim at addressing the continued oppression and marginalisation of women whose experience of oppression is multi-faceted, locally specific and differentiated across multiple social divisions. This aim presents unique challenges for all women and non-binary people, not just those involved in feminist social work policy, politics and practice.

This Handbook then has been compiled to honour and document the thick, complex and at times contradictory histories of the relationship between various Feminisms and

Introduction

social work as engagement with diverse feminist perspectives has and continues to play a dynamic and central role in contemporary social work, nationally, regionally and internationally. Their broad influences across the Global North and Global South, their successes and difficulties, their challenges, resistances and critiques need to be highlighted and this compilation of chapters does just that.

The Handbook is divided into six sections

Section 1: Decoloniality, indigeneity and radical theorising

This section addresses critical and radical theorising for feminist social work, in postcolonial and settler contexts. It excavates so-called Indigenous knowledges, visibilises silenced voices, incorporates perspectives of Decoloniality, interrogates and resists knowledges, discourses and theories based on capitalist, colonial and patriarchal rationalities; and rejects Western scholars' dismissal of non-Western epistemologies as naïve, immature or 'indigenous' and proposes revolutionary discourses for revolutionary feminist social work praxis. Theoretical contributions are presented, such as those found in ancient Feminisms of Australia, surviving despite the violence of colonisation; of complex African philosophical traditions of Ubuntu as situated in Africana womanisms; and of those inscribed in the cosmogeny of Community Feminisms of Bolivia and Guatemala, specifically the contribution of the Mayan-Xinka Feminism of Guatemala.

Proposals are made for collective feminist dissent and oppositional knowledges; anti-colonial, anti-racist and anti-capitalist practice; Black feminism, Intersectionality and postcolonial social work; a situated, decolonial, feminist and emancipatory social work; a departure from Feminisms serving the interests of whiteness; critical, constructive dialogue to resolve tensions in differing feminist discourses; political participation and lively women's movements; African Feminisms and womanism; and a Marxist perspective for revolutionary feminist praxis.

Section 2: Feminist social work in fields of practice

This section critically analyses the way in which social work practices address oppressions and inequalities affecting women and other feminised bodies. Human trafficking, sexual violence, physical and psychological abuse, marginalisation and stigmatisation reproduced in social norms, legal apparatuses and in the very social workers' practices, are discussed from feminist, decolonial and intersectional perspectives. Professional approaches and skills that contribute to promote human rights, social justice, respect, safety and dignity in practice are also analysed from previous research and professional experiences.

Section 3: Academy and feminist research

This section engages with debates concerning feminist epistemologies and methods, and their implications for feminist social work and its expressions in research, publication, teaching and leadership in social work departments. Gender gaps and epistemic injustices associated with the geopolitics of knowledge are recognised as the cornerstones of cognitive capitalism and the basis of the 'neoliberal university'. Hierarchical structures, androcentric power relationships, accelerated demands for production, prioritisation of positivist frameworks, competitive and individualistic approaches are discussed and challenged from a variety of expressions of feminism, in order to imagine and co-produce social work knowledge otherwise.

Section 4: Feminisms and the politics of care

This section explores Feminisms and the politics of care, in particular the way that social constructions of femininity have been used to bind women tightly to caring roles replete with contradictory meanings, complex but subordinate practices of power, high levels of economic and emotional exploitation and exclusion from equity and full social and political participation. The editors draw on a range of critical theories to explore the ways that social constructions of femininity are inextricably linked to the naturalised identities and social expectations for women including compulsory motherhood and mother work, and the expectation that women will care and provide care work endlessly regardless of the conditions of care work. The chapters also highlight resistance strategies and ways that social work can deepen its emancipatory practice in these important areas.

Section 5: Allyships, profeminisms and queer perspectives

This section provides important insights on LGBTQI+ and queer theories that challenge feminism to stretch beyond the boundaries of the male-female binaries. It also engages with the complex ground of profeminist allyship from men, particularly around issues of violence against women, as well as the deeply important insights provided by LGBTQI+ insights, and queer theories that challenge Feminisms to stretch beyond the boundaries of the male-female binary. This section also includes a very useful ally framework for feminists engaging in decolonising work in this era of rising calls for re-Indigenisation and reconciliation with Indigenous peoples. Contributions to Part 5 show how these important perspectives can work with or within Feminisms to resist multiple oppressions and generate more liberatory and equitable world in partnership with allies.

Section 6: Social movements, engaging with the environment and more-than-human

This section deals with responses to the climate catastrophe and environmental degradation, through perspectives of communality, solidarity and the relatedness of humans, other animals and nature. These perspectives are described through descriptions of women's activism in India; activism among older women; the analysis of oppressions of Japan's leading subalternised ethnic minority group, Zainichi Korean women; the importance of Popular Solidarity Economy amongst the women of Abya Yala; and addressing environmental degradation and impacts of climate change on vulnerable people through ecofeminism and its role in moving beyond the Anthropocene.

These perspectives include Post-humanism; Feminist new materialism; Green-red environmental and left politics; animal oppression within intersectional oppressions; politics of meat production and consumption; Eco-feminism; a post-human feminist worldview in postcolonial work; a relational ontology of personhood and relationships; and the centring of indigenist, eco-feminist, critical race and socialist/Marxist knowledges.

Introduction

To conclude

This exciting collection of scholarship on Feminisms and social work is ground-breaking and addresses various facets of social work practice, research, policy, advocacy and lobbying. Working on this book with various authors from a range of contexts was an incredible privilege and learning experience for us as editors. The relationships formed and knowledge exchanged across various knowledge fields and discourses allowed us as editors to reflect on our practice, pedagogy, writing and engagement from a feminist social work perspective. The process was much like weaving a tapestry of ideas and knowledge together to further the feminist imagination for social change and transformation both within and without the complexity of living a feminist life.

References

Dominelli, L. (2002). *Feminist Social Work Theory and Practice*. Palgrave: Basingstoke.
Hermida, M.E. (2020). La tercera interrupción en Trabajo Social: descolonizar y despatriarcalizar. [The third interruption in social work: Decolonise and depatriarchalise]. *Libertas 20*(1), 94–119.
Mama, A. (2011). *The Power of Feminist Pan-African Intellect*. Special Editorial, Feminist Africa, 1–15.
Noble, C. (2021). Ecofeminism to feminist materialism: Implications for Anthropocene feminist social work. In V. Bozalek, & B. Pease (Eds.). *Post-Anthropocentric Social Work*. Routledge: Oxon and NY, 95–107.
Rasool, S. (2019). Heterogeneity of social movements addressing the intersections of gender and race: A reflection on feminisms and womanisms emerging from African women. In T. Kleibl, R. Lutz, N. Noyoo, B. Bunk, A. Dittmann, & B.K. Seepamore (Eds.). *The Routledge Handbook of Post-Colonial Social Work*. Routledge: Oxon, 127–137.
Wendt, S., & Moulding, N. (2016). *Contemporary Feminisms in Social Work Practice*. Routledge: Oxon and NY.

SECTION 1

Decoloniality, indigeneity and radical theorising

1
FEMINISMS IN SOCIAL WORK PRACTICE

Carolyn Noble

Introduction

This chapter explores several major ideas underpinning feminist theories and their implications for feminist social work scholarship and practice. It elucidates feminism's historical development and changes to feminist scholarship over time from early second-wave feminism and its many diversities to recent challenges posed by anti-genderist and anti-feminist sentiments challenging contemporary applications. In reviewing social work scholarship and practice through a feminist lens over time, it seeks contemporary applications that will sustain social work practitioners and scholars continually having to defend feminist practice.

Feminist theorising: searching for understanding

Having gained women's suffrage under the first wave, second-wave feminism emerged after the Second World War as women began to grapple with their exclusion from social and political power and representations based on gender rather than ability. In highlighting unequal power relations, they drew attention to the way in which social structures reinforced women's inferior status to men across cultures and centuries (Dominelli, 2002; Hyde, 2022). Rooted in the realities of women's lives and in ways of knowing flowing directly from women's personal experiences, feminist theorising sought to understand the sociocultural, political, and economic dynamics leading to the marginalisation and oppression of women in European society. In so doing, it sought recognition of women's rights.

While Western feminism set the critical standpoint for progressive feminist politics, it was not enough in itself. Black African, Latin American, and Indigenous feminists set a trajectory that would serve their own and global needs – all producing a plethora of theoretical inquiries – in the subjective, collective, social, cultural, and political spheres. Despite different beginnings, feminists called out the subordination, discrimination, and oppression of women in all spheres of culture and society, noting how gender differences structured power relations, privileging men in positions of power and influence. Women's voices demanded a democratic and emancipatory response. It was not just about understanding the world of male privilege and entitlement but also about trying to change oppressive structures through theoretically driven feminist activism (Kim, Zelnick, & Goodkind, 2021).

Liberal feminism

Liberal feminist scholars and activists sought to construct a women friendly politics that challenged the patriarchal construction of society and recognised women's capacities for intimacy, connectedness, reciprocity, and relational self-definition. They prioritised their concerns about women's equality, promoted an ethics of care, and foregrounded discussions of motherhood, maternal thinking, and peacemaking in a revitalised public sphere, where women and men could participate equally, with the same level of influence and power (Dietz, 2003). They called for the transformation and transfiguration of the cultural and socio-political spheres to redress power imbalances between men and women (Hicks, 2014; Hyde, 2022). Where gender differences were obvious, they sought the introduction of policies to address discrimination. Enriching feminist politics and scholarship, liberal feminists argued for the recognition of women's equal moral worth and rights. They called for women friendly social policies that reflected women's interests and concerns, surrounding equal pay for equal work, affirmative action to redress imbalances, childcare and maternity leave to enhance women's labour participation, reproductive health services, and free and safe abortions to improve women's wellbeing. In sections below, I outline some of the influential feminist theories that changed the socio-political landscape in favour of listening to women.

Radical feminism

Radical feminists drew attention to *social differences* of ethnicity, class, race, age, and sexuality that characterised women's experience, in this way undermining the essentialist notion of a singular female identity based on innate features of womanhood. They constructed new responses based on sociological understandings of difference and the diversity of women's experience. They mounted a universal call for society to address political, social, cultural, moral, ethical, and philosophical injustices against women (Dominelli, 2002; Hyde, 2022). They took a collective rather than an individualistic view, arguing that social structures, such as education, healthcare, the family, legal systems, the economy, and religion, collectively played a role in maintaining discrimination against, and the subordination of, women in society (Gray & Boddy, 2010; Hicks, 2014). Radical feminists criticised dominant constructions of the nuclear family, highlighted women who were caught in low-paid jobs, and that family and childcare was regarded as women's work, as well as the impact of the denial of women's reproductive rights. They highlighted that these were societal concerns rather than individual women's issues. They argued that patriarchy underpinned the socio-political system and that that was where feminists should focus their attention. The 'personal is political' became the catchcry of radical feminists. They encouraged women to question notions like 'a woman's place is in the home' and 'care of children and older people is women's work'. The problem was political with dominant discourses sustaining gendered ideas about the role of women. They saw them as oppressive, especially since men dominated the public sphere, made policy, and created the dominant discourse.

Socialist feminism

Socialist feminists focused on the political economy and social inequalities resulting from capitalism, especially the unjust distribution of social resources. They called for a redistribution of wealth, arguing that women's oppression resulted from class interests, politics, and economic globalism. They opened up new sites of struggle, including racial difference, homophobia, ideology, and culture (Dietz, 2003; Gray & Boddy, 2010). Swanson (2005) introduced Gramsci's theory of hegemony as a useful device to identify the diverse structural practices creating economic, political, social, and cultural injustices. This gave a sharper focus to feminist debates.

Poststructural and postmodern feminism

Poststructural and postmodern theories questioned feminist notions of identity as personal and political and that knowledge was based on lived experience, positing instead that language or discourse is what constructs reality, where reality is open to diverse interpretation and meaning (Pease & Fook, 1999; Hicks, 2014). As an offshoot of deconstruction, postmodern feminism adopted Foucault's (1977) idea of power as fluid, not fixed, and present in all social interactions. All knowledge was subjective and relative, produced through powerful discourses that subjugated women's and Indigenous ways of knowing (Hicks, 2014; Noble, 2004). Identity is socially constructed so it is possible to deconstruct and reconstruct discourse, knowledge, and social relationships. Critical reflection was one tool. These diverse interpretations gave rise to the concepts of intersectionality and performativity.

Intersectionality

The notion of intersectionality (Crenshaw, 1989) took the political stage to name and explain the diversity of woman's lived experiences as being created by structures and institutions that perpetuated gender discrimination, male privilege, and entitlement. Williams Crenshaw (2017), credited as the originator of the term intersectionality, argued, successfully at the time, that Intersectionality is the lens that highlights how power comes and collides with gender, race, class, sex, and ability issues and create a hierarchical structure of power relations that affected women's experience (Crenshaw, 1989, 2017; Harris & Bartlow, 2015). Intersectional scholars highlighted the commonality of experience of all women similarly affected by structural disadvantage and oppressive power relations. The LGBTQIA+ community similarly argued that they, too, endured discrimination based on sexuality and sexual preferences and were joined by non-binary and queer people fight for rights and recognition. This recognition of difference and diversity produced a multifaceted kaleidoscope of women's experience of oppression and exclusion from the legislature, military, religious, and civic state apparatuses and drew stark attention to women's marginalisation and discrimination, across class, race, sexuality, politics, culture, and gender.

Performativity

Butler's (1990) thesis that gender was inflected with power and privilege and regulated through political procedures and disciplinary practices gave rise to her idea of performative rather than fixed or foundational gender roles. It provided yet another lens through which to examine gender relations (Butler, 1990). Gender is performative in conservative, traditionalist ways ascribed for men and women and exists only insofar as performed ritualistically and repetitively in social interaction. Everyday gendered experiences constructed gender. Butler's (1990) notion of performativity led to a view of gender as fluid and unstable; it created possibilities for performing gender in new and transgressive ways by going against stereotypical gender roles (Lee & Logan, 2019). The emphasis on understanding women's oppression as fluid, local, and contextual drew attention to operations of power and gender that created a fixed and binary category, one that undermined women's agency, identify, and notions of selfhood (Lee & Logan, 2019). There were multiple sites of domination and meaning making. The notion of performativity called on women to embrace ambiguity, complexity, and particularity. It became the rallying call of 'post-theorists'. Its appeal was that it challenged a homogeneous view of gender and fixed notions of power and oppression. It drew attention to the complexity of experience, valuing difference and diversity and multiple social positionings.

Black, womanist feminism

Combining the postmodern appreciation of difference, diversity, and deconstruction with Black, womanist feminism, working class and Black women 'advocated for their rights to overcome relations of domination and white privilege and move the focus of racism beyond (white) self-examination' (Gray & Boddy, 2010, 13). Hemmed in by male-dominated left-wing ideology and the civil rights movement, Black feminists found it necessary to adopt a separate stance to highlight the exploitation and abuse of working-class and Black women (hooks, 2000). It was not possible to eradicate sexism and racism until the capitalist economic system and patriarchal power structures that produced them had been erased (Gray & Boddy, 2010; Hill Collins, 1990).

Black feminists argued that white women paid lip service to diversity by excluding Black women from their scholarship and politics of resistance (Brewer, 2021; hooks, 2000; Nash, 2019). To highlight their differences with mainstream feminism, Black women referred to their stance as 'womanist', drawing attention to the lived experience of Black women, defined by Black culture and a value of self-determination. Womanism highlighted the way in which culture, spirituality, localism, power, and racism collectively defined Black women's experience with resistance, positionality, reflection, theorisation, and social justice as core aspects of Black women's activism (Brewer, 2021; Nash, 2019 also see Rasool, Chapter 2 in this volume).

Overlooked Indigenous and decolonial Feminisms and social work

Indigenous voices

Gray, Coates, and Yellow Bird (2008) reminded us that contemporary social work, despite its intentions to be inclusive and capture diversity, still preferred modernist, Euro-American paradigms that defined rules for acceptable knowledge and practice. The criticism from Indigenous voices is that social work curricula reinforced colonial tendencies and promoted Western hegemony. In particular, Aboriginal and Torres Strait Islanders people in Australia, Māori tribes in Aotearoa New Zealand, First Nations, Metis and Inuit, people of Canada faced challenges arising from Colonialism and attempts to assimilate Indigenous people into European (Western) white society and culture through the imposition of colonial administration, social systems, and laws and the removal of Indigenous children into state or religious care. The colonial gaze overlooked and undermined tradition and culture, prohibiting Indigenous language and cultural practices. Coates, Gray, and Hetherington (2006) suggested an 'ecospiritual' perspective to capture social work's acceptance and embrace of Indigenous voices. Indigenous social work emphasises that human survival and environmental sustainability flow from humans' ability to live in harmony with nature and non-human species. Contemporary discourse on *ubuntu* in social work highlights religious and cultural heritage as key features of an Indigenous Black African perspective (Bennet et al., 2013; Green, 2017).

Decolonisation

Decolonisation is a response to the persistence of Western theories and approaches that dominated social work programs as they developed across the world, mostly with the influence of Western countries (particularly USA) (Gray, 2017; Gray et al., 2013). Like feminism, decolonisation is partisan; it promotes an anticolonial response and privileges the voice and ways of knowing of Indigenous Peoples that emphasise relational connections, including the relationship between spirituality, nature, land, and environment (Green, 2017; Nash, 2019). More specifically, decolonising feminism involves engaging with debates pertaining to Coloniality – the set of attitudes, values, ways of knowing, and power structures upheld as normative by Western colonising societies and serving to rationalise and perpetuate Western dominance. This includes debates on modernisation, patriarchy, and concepts of Indigenous identity and gender in the Global North and South. It creates a space for previously 'othered' women's voices and experiences to be heard. It requires that decolonial voices take their place in knowledge production in the Global North adding to the richness and complexity of feminist debates and form an alignment with the social and economic struggles of women in the Global South (Makoni, et al., 2022; Nash, 2019). Many of these 'othered' women live in the in-between spaces of lived experiences and the contemporary social and cultural life constructed by modernity, Coloniality, and patriarchy.

Indigenous and decolonial feminisms ask the racial gaze to be turned on epistemological frameworks that underpin social work curricula, professional knowledge, values, and skills (Green, 2017; Green & Baldry, 2008). Ecofeminist and new feminist materialism is likewise linked with Indigenous knowledge on the relationship between human survival and environmental sustainability (Bozalek & Pease, 2021; Noble, 2021).

Ecofeminism and feminist new materialism

Most feminists incorporated aspects of patriarchy in their analysis. However, ecofeminists were the first to draw attention to male exceptionalism and dominance in the natural and non-natural worlds (Casselot, 2016; Gaard, 2017). Early pioneers of environmental activism criticised patriarchal capitalism as normalising man's dominance over the natural world, just as they had normalised violence and oppression against women; capitalist patriarchy was a threat to the environment *and* women (Gaard, 2017; Mies & Shiva, 1994/2014; Noble, 2021). They highlighted the synergy between environmental justice and the sustainability movement, introducing the notion of 'womannature', foregrounding women and nature in contemporary socio-political, patriarchal thought as the missing piece in contemporary feminist theory's emphasis on the social constructs of race, class, and gender (Gaard, 2017; Noble, 2021). Ecofeminists' concern with nature and their call for re-evaluating and reimagining non-patriarchal, non-linear structures, along with their view of nature as a source of inspiration and healing, gave new meaning to the global fight for environmental justice. Humans were biological and sociocultural beings with an ecological heritage coterminous with nature (Salleh, in Pellow, 2017). By advocating for a geocentric feminism, ecofeminist perspectives advanced social and environmental justice, human and environmental rights, and women's liberation, to gain a fuller understanding of women's lives in patriarchal capitalist societies while hoping to save the planet as well.

Feminist materialism, like ecofeminism, is interested in the corporeality of the body and 'how gender and other embodied differences, such as class, ability, race and sex structure our experience of the environment' (Casselot, 2016, 82) and expose the social and ethical blind spots of oppressive constructs and political practices. In particular, it wants to transverse the dualisms of nature-culture, man-woman, and mind-body characteristic of modernist thought by breaking down inherent power differences and redistributing power relations so humans, non-humans, and other-than-human actors form a single assemblage and life force – arguing that the protection of all life forces is crucial to planetary survival (Bozalek & Pease, 2021; Braidotti, 2013). It envisions a post human ethics and a world where human and non-humans work towards mutual co-existence and survival. It draws culture and nature into one effective composition, letting go of anthropocentric privileges to keep the planet and all species healthy (Noble, 2021).

Green social work links the degradation of the planet with the continued oppression of women, Indigenous Peoples, poor people, and marginalised groups, such as migrants, asylum seekers, and refugees, positioning them in conflict with one another. It refigures critical theory by also embedding environmental justice with social justice emphasising the connection between animate and inanimate realities and the need to protect and safeguard all living and non-living things to maintain a healthy planet and fair and just society (Dominelli, 2018; Noble, 2016).

Contemporary debates: feminism at a crossroad

Though still searching for an adequate explanation of women's oppression, feminists agree that a unilateral, universal solution is no longer tenable, given the diversity of women's experience and theoretical perspectives and social locations. Further, the popularist and right wing backlash has forced feminists to re-evaluate current theories and find new ways to incorporate the women's equity agenda into mainstream politics.

Anti-feminism and gender populism

Anti-feminism and anti-genderism propagated by populist, right-wing male leaders flaunting misogynistic attitudes and behaviours have all but undone previously discredited stereotypes of women's roles, sexual prejudices, predatory sexual violence, and legal and cultural oppression, sending feminist theory back several decades. This perspective challenges the ontological position that only changes in gendered power relations (to be made more equal) can remove power imbalances and inequalities between men and women.

Eschewing the 'battle of the sexes', anti-feminism and anti-genderism accept that men and women have complementary roles and social positions and seek to preserve gender differences at all costs. It is essentially a concerted fight against feminists' demand for gender equality and is a public defence of patriarchy, the importance of promoting traditional family values and roles and criticising diverse family compositions and gender preferences (Caberzas, 2022). Extreme anti-feminist rhetoric has branded progressive feminists as 'feminazis', who are wasting public resources on imposing their political gender ideology on society. For example, there were accusations that, following a strike in 2018 and 2019, feminists in Spain had imposed an ideological burka on Spanish society (Caberzas, 2022). Grzebalska (2016) linked women's anti-feminist stance to their general dissatisfaction with liberal (soft left) democratic values of freedom, equality, and religious tolerance.

Believing that feminists had achieved the goal of gender equality, Paglia (2008) described the gender war as unproductive and divisive. Faludi (2010) attributed the feminist backlash to radical and progressive feminists' failure to entertain and embrace the views of women, who valued traditional gender roles; wanted to stay home and parent; disagreed on heterosexual encounters as rape; opposed abortion; and resisted feminist claims that they were victims of patriarchy and male oppression. While agreeing on some issues, like equal pay and gender equality, many women found the aggressive political platform of radical feminists off putting. Many ascribed to conservative politics that served their religious and traditional interests. Some appropriated masculine traits to negotiate their way through culturally dominant ideas of masculinity and femininity and achieve some degree of empowerment (Caberzas, 2022).

Persistent neoliberalism

There have been criticisms of social work's inability to transcend the aggressive neoliberal governmentality of the last three decades that has spawned increased economic inequalities and poverty; employment insecurity, flexibility, and precarity; and the blaming of individuals for structural problems (Garrett, 2018). To minimise resistance to growing dissatisfaction, governments increased their surveillance of, and intrusion into, the lives of the oppressed and welfare-dependent people through diligent austerity measures and punitive sanctions for so called troublesome groups and those viewed as disposable under the aegis of neoliberalism (Giroux, 2011; Morley et al., 2020). Along with other marginalised groups, women have suffered under austerity policies, cuts to public spending, and low wage-growth strategies (mainly in female-dominated industries). The promotion of family values and traditional gender roles by the broader anti-gender movement of the new right, as well as the free loading of women's reproductive labour, such as child, family, and age care, has exacerbated the situation (Gender & Development Network, 2018). Indeed, feminism also changed through its engagement with neoliberalism. Facebook Chief Operating Officer Sheryl Sandberg's (2013) *Lean In* that called on women to embrace their ambitions is an example of uncritical engagement with neoliberal capitalism and the conservative agenda normalising an individualistic focus on women's aspirations; white, class privilege; and heteronormativity. Many criticised her application of individual-focused solutions to the systemic issues holding back women in the workplace, especially women of colour and low-income women.

Problems within contemporary Feminisms

These vibrant theoretical discourses are a reminder that we still do not live in a postgendered world, despite extensive feminist scholarship and political activism. In many ways, this is unsurprising, as there was never a linear, unifying epistemology; many voices existed in a crowded and, at times, politically wrought environment that positioned women against women. The wars about trans-inclusive feminism and non-binary or gender-queer politics are contemporary examples of discriminatory discourses continuing to oppress and marginalise these groups, resulting in increasing individual, family, and structural violence and in many ways fostering a real disjuncture in feminist politics (Shaw, 2023).

Despite this disjuncture juncture, intersectional feminism still holds sway and the struggle for women's equality, safety, recognition, and inclusion remains real and pressing for many across the globe, particularly for left-wing academics in the context of the dominance of neoliberal economic rationalism and globalisation.

The challenge is finding ways to balance the voices of diverse groups and their respective interests, and to centre on the question of *difference* and recognition of ways in which ethnicity, socioeconomic, religion, ability, and sexuality differentiate and divide women while maintaining solidarity to achieve a collective feminist politics of resistance, with women as the primary focus. A more feminist practice might help refocus feminist politics and engage with more contemporary issues. Let's look at feminist scholarship first, then feminist theory and social work practice.

Feminist critical scholarship, education, and the academy

Feminism seeks to de-gender education and promote a pro-feminist stance in scholarship and the academy. As argued throughout this chapter, repositioning women from the periphery to the centre of social analysis is the central task for feminist theorists; feminist scholarship challenges the masculinist order of knowledge and epistemologies and posits a feminist pedagogy (Abakedi & Egbai, 2020). Many favour Giroux's (2011) critical pedagogy that critically questions power and authority in the classroom; challenges hegemonic structures through critical refection and analysis; develops a critical consciousness, to disrupt hegemonic views; and gives voice to the voiceless. These ideas permeate feminist pedagogy, based on the belief that principles of critique and action can set in place conditions for resistance, struggle, and emancipation from oppressive power relations enabling women to flourish free from oppression (Morley, Ablett, Noble, Cowden, 2020 Abakedi & Egbai, 2020; hooks, 2000, 2003).

Social work education influences how social workers act and informs their ability to facilitate progressive social change through activist practice beyond the classroom or maintain the status quo. A feminist pedagogy offers students a counteroffensive to the increasingly technicist approach. For bell hooks (2003), it was about taking classroom teaching into the community, positioning social workers in the marginalised spaces, where disadvantage flourishes and the invisibility of oppressed groups continues unabated (Noble, 2020).

Dovetailing with Freire's (1972) critical pedagogy of conscientisation, the teaching of critical literacy inhered in the power to speak and criticise. A forerunner in feminist pedagogy, bell hooks' (2003, 2010) writings on Black women's oppression in educational institutions drew attention to the white, mostly male, authority figures that perpetuated class privilege and imperialist politics. Her confronting, candid critique of the imperialist, white supremacist capitalist patriarchy, at the time, had no contemporary feminist parallel. Feminists across race, class, and educational lines could read her account of the gendered educational system.

A feminist practitioner needs a critically informed pedagogy to navigate her practice. Critically informed questions shape the basis of critical scholarship: the where, when, who, what, and how of unjust circumstances and injustices (Noble, 2020; Noble, Gray, & Johnston, 2016). Critical pedagogy for feminist practice seeks to:

- Engage in forms of reasoning that challenge the social, political, and economic order that maintains women's oppression.
- Work towards solidarity and collective organisation, unmasking the unequal flow of power in women's lives and communities.
- Challenge the all-pervasive effects of oppressive ideologies and embrace an alternative vision for a better world by seeking social change (Noble, Gray & Johnston, 2016, 129).

Feminist theory and social work practice

Feminist theory is integral to social work practice from micro (individual) to macro (social movements and change) seeking to find ways to counteract the prejudices, biases, oppressive practices, marginalisation, violence, and discrimination women face. Feminist theory and its application names and identifies the nature of the problem and ways to address it (Phillips, 2022). Feminist perspectives bring a critical lens to women's continued oppression and a rich scholarship and activist practice to enable feminist social workers to promote social justice, a social change agenda, and challenge the domination of men and the subordination of women (Noble, 2020). A gendered lens speaks specifically to understanding the power dynamics generated by gender norms, expectations, and behaviours; it unpacks the entrenched discriminatory and oppressive practices that directly affect women and girls. Feminist social work calls for the end of male privilege, opens public and private spaces to name and address women's issues, and encourages awareness of the social worker's and other women's experiences through stories of their lives and their hopes and aspirations for the future (Naples, 2021). Connectivity and collaboration are foundational tenets of feminist practice (UN Women, 2021).

Feminist social work is steeped within a critical tradition. Social workers are using feminist theories and stories to acknowledge the multiple oppressions; unequal, hierarchical relationships between the genders; and social structures that disempower women and maintain men's entitlement, control, and privilege over the social, economic, legal, and political world (Dominelli & Ioakimidis, 2016). Feminism Feminist social work is about social change and putting theory into practice. This is central to its rationale and meaning – theory and practice are in conversation with one another (Phillips, 2022). Feminist social workers respond to the most complex social problems, including domestic violence, rape and sexual assault, homelessness, poverty, child trafficking, aging, disability, and their impact on the lives of women and young girls (Wendt & Moulding, 2016). Feminist politics focuses on social justice, human rights, and women's liberation and women 'at the front line fighting against toxic dumps, nuclear power, water contamination, global warming, expansion of resource extraction industries, growth in materialism and global capitalist expansion at the expense of local ecosystems and planet survival' (Noble, 2021, 102).

Feminist social work is pro women; it seeks to improve the lives of women, non-binary and queer peoples, and girls. It seeks to give voice to their struggle against sexism, homophobia, colonialism, patriarchy, and environmental destruction. It seeks, at its best, to unite women, queer, and non-binary peoples in a collective struggle for dignity, equity, fairness, solidarity, diversity, inclusivity, and gender justice (Noble, 2021). Politically Walker, Taylor, and Habibs (2013) ask white women to rethink their privilege, more specifically how their whiteness influences their practices and conversations with Indigenous and Black women. While a herculean task, it is a challenge white, non-Indigenous feminists need to address to enhance their accountability for their actions and opinions and their implication.

Feminism provides a sophisticated knowledge base to approach large-scale challenges and develop innovative practices to guide intervention. Historical and contemporary core principles of feminist social work practice exert a powerful influence on working to end disadvantage and exclusion. They include a gendered lens that links the personal with the political, facilitates democratised structures and processes, advocates inclusivity and diversity, and sees the elimination of social, political, cultural, and economic oppression of women as part of the feminist transformative vision. It has become a significant means to frame social work advocacy across practice, education, research, and policy. Feminist theory provides a much-needed politicised context for social work and critical scholarship for innovative feminist social work that seeks to improve the conditions in which women live, work, and flourish, calls for an end of male privilege, and continues to open up public spaces, where marginalised women voices can be heard. Feminist practice forms links with social movements and social change politics, positing a politics of hope for a changed future (Noble, 2021, 81).

Conclusion: way forward

This chapter has drawn together diverse, sometimes contradictory, feminisms, in the process identifying sites of backlash and ways to incorporate theoretical understanding into feminist praxis. The breadth and scope of diverse feminist politics and struggles are changing continually, in response to the challenges of anti-gender, rhetoric, and environmental sustainability. Feminist social workers have a choice to work, for a changed future by finding a common ground for women and people of other genders to lead lives unencumbered by gender oppressions and exclusions. It is a commitment women have made over many decades and one for which feminist social work, with its focus on political and cultural and environment activism, is well equipped, as feminist social workers continue to work towards a just society.

References

Abakedi, D., & Egbai, M. (2020). Introducing feminist epistemology. In D. Abakedi, D. Oluwagbemi-Jacob, M. Egbai, & A. Effiong (Eds.), *A general introduction to feminism and feminist philosophy: Studies in feminist philosophy 1* (rev. ed.). CreateSpace Independent Publishing Platform. Retrieved from https://www.researchgate.net/publication/346240686_Introducing_Feminist_Epistemology

Bennet, B., Green, S., Gilbert, S., & Bessarab, D. (2013). *Our voices: Aboriginal and Torres Strait social work.* Palgrave Macmillan.

Bozalek, V., & Pease, B. (Eds.). (2021). *Post-anthropocentric social work: Critical posthuman and new materialist perspectives.* Routledge.

Braidotti, R. (2013). *Posthuman knowledge.* Polity Press.

Brewer, R. (2021). Black feminism and womanism. In N. A. Naples (Ed.), *Companion to feminist studies.* John Wiley & Sons. 91–104.

Butler, J. (1990). *Gender trouble: Feminism and the subversion of identity.* Routledge.

Caberzas, M. (2022). Silencing feminism? Gender and the rise of the nationalist far right in Spain. *Signs: Journal of Women in Culture and Society, 47*, 2, 319–345.

Casselot, M.-A. (2016). Ecofeminist echoes in the new materialism? *PhaenEx, 11*, 1, 73–96. Retrieved from https://philpapers.org/rec/CASEEI-2

Coates, J., Gray, M., & Hetherington, T. (2006). An 'ecospiritual' perspective: Finally, a place for Indigenous approaches. *British Journal of Social Work, 36*, 3, 381–399. https://doi.org/10.1093/bjsw/bcl005

Crenshaw, K. (1989). *Demarginalizing the intersection of race and sex: A black feminist critique of antidiscrimination, doctrine, feminist theory and antiracist policies.* University of Chicago Press. 139–167.
Crenshaw, K. (2017). *On intersectionality: Essential writings.* The New Press.
Dietz, M. (2003). Current controversies in feminist theory. *Annual Review of Political Science, 6,* 399–431. https://doi.org/10.1146/annurev.polisci.6.121901.085635
Dominelli, L. (2002). *Feminist social work: Theory and practice.* Palgrave Macmillan.
Dominelli, L. (2018). (Ed) *The Routledge handbook of Green Social Work.* Routledge.
Dominelli, L., & Ioakimidis, V. (2016). The challenges of realising social justice in 21st century social work. *International Social Work, 59,* 6. https://doi.org/10.1177/0020872816665981
Faludi, S. (2010). *Backlash: The undeclared war against women.* Vintage Books.
Pease, B. & Fook, J., (1999). *Transforming social work practices: Postmodern critical perspectives.* Routledge.
Foucault, M. (1977). *Discipline and punish: The birth of the prison.* Penguin.
Freire, P. (1972). *Pedagogy of the oppressed.* Penguin.
Gaard, G. (2017). *Critical ecofeminism.* Lexington Books.
Garrett, M. (2018). *Social work and social theory, making connections.* Bristol University Press. Retrieved from https://doi.org/10.51952/9781447341925.ch005
Gender & Development Network (2018). *The impact of austerity on women.* Gender & Development Network. Retrieved from https://www.ohchr.org/sites/default/files/Documents/Issues/Development/IEDebt/WomenAusterity/GenderDevelopmentNetwork.pdf
Giroux, H. (2011). *On critical pedagogy.* Continuum.
Gray, M. (Ed.). (2017). *The Routledge handbook of social work and social development in Africa.* Routledge.
Gray, M., & Boddy, J. (2010). Making sense of waves: Wipeout or still riding high? *Affilia, 25,* 4, 368–389. https://doi.org/10.1177/0886109910384069
Gray, M., Coates, J., & Yellow Bird, M. (2008). *Indigenous social work around the world: Towards culturally relevant education and practice.* Routledge.
Gray, M., Coates, J., Yellow Bird, M., & Hetherington, T. (Eds.). (2013). *Decolonizing social work.* Routledge.
Green, J. (2017). (Ed) *Making space for Indigenous feminism.* Fernwood Publishing.
Green, S., & Baldry, E. (2008). Building indigenous social work. *Australian Social Work, 61,* 4, 389–402. https://doi.org/10.1080/03124070802430718
Grzebalska, W. (2016). Militarizing the nation: Gender politics and the Warsaw uprising. In A. Altinay & A. Pető (Eds.), *Gendered wars, gendered memories: Feminist conversations on war, genocide and political violence.* Routledge. 141–154.
Harris, A., & Barlow, S. (2015). Intersectionality, race, gender, sexuality and class. In J. DeLamater & R. Plante (Eds.), *Handbook of the sociology of sexualities.* Springer. 261–271.
Hicks, S. (2014). Social work and gender: An argument for practical accounts. *Qualitative Social Work, 14,* 4, 471–487. https://doi.org/10.1177/1473325014558665
Hill Collins, P. (1990). *Black feminism thought.* Routledge.
hooks, b. (2000). *Feminist theory form margin to centre.* South End Press.
hooks, b. (2003). *Teaching community: A pedagogy of hope.* Routledge.
hooks, b. (2010). *Teaching critical thinking.* Routledge.
Hyde, C. (2022). Feminist macro social work practice. *Encyclopedia of Social Work.* https://doi.org/10.1093/acrefore/9780199975839.013.151
Kim, M. E., Zelnick, J. R., & Goodkind, S. (2021). Pandemics, protest and feminist politic of resistance. *Affilia, 36,* 1, 5–9. https://doi.org/10.1177/0886109920982094
Lee, C., & Logan, A. (2019). Women's agency, activism and organization. *Women's History Review, 28,* 6, 831–834. https://doi.org/10.1080/09612025.2017.1346880
Makoni, S., Madany-Saá, M., Anita, B., & Gomes, R. (2022). *Decolonial, voices, language and race.* Multilingual Matters.
Mies, M., & Shiva, V. (1994/2014). *Ecofeminism.* Zed Books.
Morley, C., Ablett, P., Noble, C., & Cowden, S. (Eds.). (2020). *The Routledge handbook of critical pedagogies for social work.* Routledge.
Naples, N. A. (2021). *Companion to feminist studies.* John Wiley & Sons.
Nash, J. (2019). *Black feminism reimagined.* Duke University Press.

Noble, C. (2004). Postmodern thinking: Where is it taking social work? *Journal of Social Work, 4*, 3. https://doi.org/10.1177/1468017304047747

Noble, C. (2016). Green social work–the next Frontier for action. *Social Alternatives Journal, 35*, 4, 14–19.

Noble, C. (2020). bell hooks trilogy: Pedagogy for social work supervision. In C. Morley, P. Ablett, C. Noble, & S. Cowden (Eds.), *The Routledge handbook of critical pedagogies for social work*. Routledge. 501–511.

Noble, C. (2021). Ecofeminism to feminist materialism: Implications for anthropocentric social work. In V. Bozalek & B. Pease (Eds.), *Post-anthropocentric social work: Critical posthuman and new materialist perspectives*. Routledge. 95–107.

Noble, C., Gray, M., & Johnston, L. (2016). *Critical supervision for the human services: A social model to promote learning and value-based practice*. Jessica Kingsley.

Paglia, C. (2008). Feminism past and present: Ideology, action and reform. *Arion: A Journal of Humanities and the Classics 16*, 1, 1–18. Retrieved from https://www.jstor.org/stable/29737373

Pellow, D. N. (2017). Review of ecofeminism as politics: Nature, Marx and the postmodern by Ariel Salleh. 2017. (2nd ed.). Zed Books. *Journal of World-Systems Research, 24*, 2, 478–482. Retrieved from https://jwsr.pitt.edu/ojs/jwsr/article/view/864/1166

Phillips, R. (2022). *Practising feminism for social welfare*. Routledge.

Sandberg, S. (2013). *Lean in: Women, work and the will to lead*. Alfred A. Knopt.

Shaw, D. (2023). A tale of two feminisms: Gender critical feminism, trans inclusive feminism and the case of Kathleen Stock. *Women's History Review, 32*, 5, 768–780. https://doi.org/10.1080/09612025.2022.2147915

Swanson, J. (2005). Recognition and redistribution: Rethinking culture and economic. *Theory, Culture & Society, 22*, 4, 87–118. https://doi.org/10.1177/0263276405054992

United Nations (2021). *New feminist activism, waves and generations*. UN Women. Retrieved from https://www.unwomen.org/en/digital-library/publications/2021/05/discussion-paper-new-feminist-activism-waves-and-generations

Walker, M., Taylor, S., & Habibs, D. (2013). How white is Australian social work. *Austrian Social Work, 64*, 11, 6–19. https://doi.org/10.1080/0312407X.2010.510892

Wendt, S., & Moulding, N. (Eds.). (2016). *Contemporary feminisms in social work practice*. Routledge.

2
LOCATING AFRICAN FEMINISM, WOMANISMS, AND NEGO-FEMINISM – POSSIBILITIES FOR SOCIAL WORK

Shahana Rasool

Introduction

Varying strands of feminism have arisen over time in response to various historical, social, and political developments that have been aligned with the various waves of feminism (Mokgwathi, 2023). The various strands of feminism range from liberal feminism, the first strand of feminism to be explicitly articulated in the West, to African strands that are relevant to those of us who live and work in Africa, but which also provide important theoretical contributions to the global context of Feminisms. Some Feminisms emerged because of women's experiences of oppression in religious/spiritual contexts – such as Jewish, Islamic, Christian, or Wiccan Feminisms; whilst other Feminisms emerged in particular continents, such as Latin American, Caribbean, or Indian Feminisms, which speak to the issues in specific regions of the world. Yet, other Feminisms emerged out of socio-political and historical events/movements such as Marxist, eco, queer, or trans-national Feminisms (some of these types of Feminisms are discussed in this collection). Hence, it is very difficult to have one all-encompassing definition of feminism. However, early Feminisms articulated that the relationships among men and women in society are unequal and that women are oppressed, because of their gender. More later post-structuralist feminists challenged the notion of gender as a fixed, immutable category and argued that it is rather a process that is constantly being reconstituted (Begoña, 2017). As Imam, (1997, p. 2) states, "Gender identities are situated in both time and place, with the context of masculinities and femininities changing over time." In more recent years, Feminisms have evolved to challenge heteronormativity and respond to the fluidity of gender as a spectrum (Liljeström, 2019).

Feminisms are constantly evolving in relation to women and queer experiences of oppression based on their lived experiences in varied socio-historical contexts, as well as the various resistances to feminism. Payne (2005, p. 257) contends, "The resistance to feminism seems to lie in the refusal of male institutions, including marriage, employment, and social work agencies, to give up power." Further, as conceptions of women's oppression deepen, Feminisms evolve, and as women share their varying life experiences, more strands of feminism or womanism emerge – all of which cannot be covered here (such as township, Bantu, Chicana, and Transatlantic Feminisms). Thus, the term Feminisms (plural) instead of feminism (singular) is used in this chapter to accentuate that even within each type of feminism, there is heterogeneity.

Each strand of feminism understands and theorises gender relations in a unique way, and each strand provides different solutions for tackling the oppression of women (Stanley & Wise, 1983), which provides different options for social practices at the micro-, meso-, and macro levels. Hence, Feminisms are not just theoretical perspectives but are also social, cultural, political, and economic movements for asserting women and non-binary people's rights and interests. Critically, feminism provides social workers with a lens from which to consider the ways in which women and non-binary people are oppressed and discriminated against. This discrimination leads to women and queer people being denied equal opportunities, resources, and access. Social workers need to address gender discrimination and engage in activities that enable women and queer people access to opportunities and resources in various contexts. Feminisms provide different knowledge bases, approaches, and strategies to guide social workers in creating a socially just world. There are also theoretical viewpoints from women in Africa that do not align themselves politically with the concept feminism but are concerned with women's interests and activism such as womanism, nego-feminism, snail-sense feminism, township feminism, and motherism.

In this chapter, my focus is on some approaches to dealing with gender inequality that emerged in Africa, since it is these Feminisms and womanisms that speak most closely to the experiences of African women and non-conforming communities racialised as Black[1] that align most closely with Decoloniality. This chapter engages with anti-, ante-, post-, and decolonial Feminisms as a context for specific approaches to dealing with gender oppression relevant to Africa from a 'think like Black' perspective – namely, African feminism (AF), womanism, and nego-feminism. The descriptions of AFs and womanisms below are merely a summary of the salient aspects of these strands, rather than a comprehensive account of the various theoretical nuances that inform these perspectives. It is important to note that even within the different strands of feminism, there are divergent views and some overlap. Each of these perspectives provides social worker with opportunities to think and act based on different knowledge bases informed by the African context.

Waves of Feminisms

There are various waves of Feminisms that represent important shifts in the historical development of feminism. Suffragettes are synonymous with the first wave of Feminisms (Rampton, 2015). Their struggle for women's political power during the nineteenth and early 20th centuries in the USA and UK is deemed to be central to the birth of the first wave of Feminisms (Rampton, 2015). To expand the feminist movement beyond political transformation, the second wave of Feminisms emerged between the 1960s and 1980s. The second wave extended the fight for transformation to women's social and cultural domains and proclaimed that "the personal is political" (Hanisch, 1970). However, first- and second-wave feminists were seen as representing the interests of White, middle-class, and heterosexual women only.

In response to the limitations of the second wave of Feminisms, which ignored issues of race, sexuality, ethnicity, location, and other social divisions, a third wave of Feminisms emerged. hooks' (2014) seminal book, 'Ain't I a woman,' is often considered iconic to the third wave of feminists since she highlighted the exclusionary nature of earlier Feminisms that omitted the lived experiences of women of Colour. The third wave of feminism was influenced by post-colonial and decolonial thought and thus deconstructed the perception of universal womanhood – which has been influential to the work presented in this chapter. The third wave is also characterised by an extensive backlash, challenging "artificial categories of identity, gender, and sexuality" (Rampton, 2015, para 12).

The fourth wave of feminism emerged through the extension of feminist activism in the online domain (Munro, 2013). Rampton (2015, para 19) states that the internet plays an important role in "gender-bending and levelling hierarchies." The internet creates the space for young and historically marginalised women to play a significant role in shaping feminist thought and politics (Munro, 2013.). While the various waves appear as analytically separate stages in history, they are rather extensions of each other, as activism in all areas remains ongoing domains of struggle and contestation.

However, it seems that many historical accounts assume that feminism only started in Europe and America during the 19th and 20th centuries, and some refer to Greece and the medieval world as possible sources of feminism (Rampton, 2015). These accounts have ignored the struggles and resistance of women in the Global South (Lugones, 2010). It invisibilises the ways in which gender was dealt with in pre-colonial and non-Western societies. It seems that women's role and contributions to the liberation of women prior to and during the 19th century is not encompassed in these articulations.

Ante-colonial, anti-colonial, post-colonial, and decolonial Feminisms

The role of women in societies prior to the first wave of feminism and resistance to male domination and sexual discrimination in the global South has been invisible for a long time (Lugones, 2010; Mohanty, 1991). Perhaps this is because of the perception that African women and women in the global South had not amassed a political movement to represent women's interests. An additional explanation for their invisibility may be linked to the way history has been written based on imperialist and colonial viewpoints that render the contribution of women and people in the South invisible (Lugones, 2010). Whilst post-colonial and decolonial Feminisms are seen as a response to 'western' feminists and colonial imposition, many women in the global South have been active and resistant to forms of Patriarchy long before colonisation (Ntombovuyo, 2016). Perhaps the agenda for ante-, post-, and decolonisation may change the gaze of history to more actively highlight the role of women in various societies prior to the suffragettes. Some of these histories, rather her-stories, are being re-discovered and written about in some parts of the world (Ranmuthugala, 2018).

Post-colonial and decolonial feminists highlight the impact of the relationship between race, gender, Colonialism, and imperialism on women's oppression (Lewis, 2001; Lugones, 2010). Post-colonial and decolonial thought resulted in varying forms of post-colonial/decolonial feminism, including AFs, Latina Feminisms, Indian Feminisms, Caribbean Feminisms, and other Feminisms from the global South, all of which are diverse in their approaches, based on their locationality (Lewis, 2001). It has been argued that decolonial thought emerged largely from South America, whilst post-colonial thought emerged from the Middle East and South Asia (Bhambra, 2014).

In my discussions here, I prefer anti-colonial Feminisms, rather than post-colonial or decolonial Feminisms, as the latter two are a response to Colonialism and thus may inadvertently not account for Feminisms in Africa and the global South prior to colonisation. However, some feminist writers are addressing these concerns (Thebe, 2023).

It is important to highlight the roles women played and the struggles and challenges that women engaged with in pre-colonial and colonial times in response to Patriarchy and gender power hierarchies. In Africa, for example, oral traditions pre-dominated, so women's narratives and struggles are not necessarily recorded in written form (Kuba, 2018). However, women from the global South may have constructed, reconstructed, and negotiated Patriarchy in the way that they related stories in their communities and to their children (Sheik, 2018). Moreover, women have contributed to many areas of social, political, and economic life pre-colonisation and during colonisation. Thus, as Mokgwathi (2023) argues, African women are agentive and are not in need of rescuing from the West.

In many African pre-colonial societies such as Ancient Nubia, Berber, and Egypt, women occupied leadership positions (Kuba, 2018; Monges, 1993; Ntombovuyo, 2016). Some examples of women leaders are Queen Amina of the Hausa who was a warrior; Akyaawa Yikwan, an Asante Royal, who was "described as one of the best diplomats and negotiators of the nineteenth century;" and Yaa Anantewana who was the queen mother of Edweso in 1877, who was known to believe that "men were not fences for any woman to lean against" (Kuba, 2018, pp. 3 & 10). There were also "several matrilineal societies in Africa like the Akan, the Nyanja, the Chew" and some matriarchal societies (Musingafi, 2023, p. 18). Moreover, in some societies, women were also represented in cosmology as Gods. For example, in the ancient Egyptian religion of Kemet, there were both female and male deities and both were equally important (Monges, 1993). In ancient Kemet society, non-royal women owned land and were priestesses (Monges, 1993). Adjepong (2015, p. 5) asserts that

> African women's history shows that before the establishment of European colonial rule in Africa, women in many African societies enjoyed considerable freedom of action and were less dependent on their male counterparts. These studies establish that African women participated in mainstream political activities with relatively few restrictions.

Hence, women's relationships with Patriarchy prior to and during colonisation in the global South may have been different, and many her-stories may not be documented or are ignored and invisibilised (Mtombeni, 2020).

Moreover, many women were active in various liberation struggles across Africa, including "Yaa Asantewaa (Ghana), Charwe Nyakasikana (Zimbabwe), Mrs. Theodosia Salome Okoh (Ghana)" (Kuba, 2018, p. 159) and the multitude of women in South Africa as represented in the 1956 March against the pass laws (Hassim, 1991). Women in Nigeria also provide strong evidence of active resistance over the years, as Ada (2011) states,

> The Feminist Movement started subtly and unconsciously in Nigeria in 1929 during the Aba women's riot. Over the years, remarkable growth has been recorded which is evident in the noticeable presence of women in all spheres of life in Nigeria.

Women from the global South have been writing her-stories and contributing to challenging colonial impositions on their identity, subjectivities, and experiences (Sheik, 2018), which is evident in ante-, anti-, post-, and decolonial work.

Anti-, post-, and decolonial Feminisms and, by extension, AFs emerged as a critique of the way in which 'Western' feminists mainstreamed the experiences of 'Western' women at the expense of women 'racialised as Black' from other parts of the world (Fennell & Arnot, 2009; Mohanty, 1991). Lyons (2000) contends that there have been very few attempts in mainstream 'Western' feminism to understand the strengths of social systems from the global South. Due to the mainstreaming of the experience and views of 'Western' women, ante-, post-, and decolonial Feminisms argue that the struggles of women from the global South against oppressive systems have largely been ignored because their social status is generally viewed as subordinate in 'Western' literature (Lyons, 2000). 'Western' feminist movements have thereby lost opportunities to learn from the resistance methods employed by women in the global South in fighting Patriarchy and other systems of oppression (Mohanty, 1991). Moreover, the examples of equality in leadership, representation, and access to land ownership and other resources that were evident in some ancient African cultures are lost opportunities for learning (Monges, 1993).

Anti-, post-, and decolonial Feminisms are concerned with looking at local knowledges and challenging imperialist, colonial, racist, and patriarchal discourses about women in the global South. Thus, they are concerned with the decentralisation of gender philosophies to include the cultures, point of reference, and experiences of women 'racialised as Black' and/or women from the global South. Although the various Feminisms that hailed from the global South are important, due to space constraints and my location in Africa, only some types of Feminisms that are promonent in African, such as AF, Africana womanism, and nego-feminism will be discussed below, as these are often decentred. Whilst there are many others that are equally important and relevant such as township feminism, stiwanism, etc. it is not possible to include them all here.

African Feminisms

AFs challenged the ways in which 'Western' feminists depicted African women and are concerned with accentuating the concerns and interests of African women. However, since Africa is a huge continent, African feminist thinking and activism is as diverse as Africa itself. Nevertheless, AF creates the space for the lived experiences of African women to be foregrounded, thus giving life to feminist theorisation by women in Africa (Nnaemeka, 2004). This perspective reinforces that Africans, and particularly African women, are not merely subjects of research, but actors in their worlds and they can, and do, define their own engagements and world views (Nnaemeka, 2004).

AF provides the space for African norms and values to be recognised, but this does not necessarily mean it is concerned with valorising the traditional, since Ake (1988, p. 19) indicates that "there is no fossilized existence of the African past available for us to fall back on." Ake (1988, p. 19) suggests that Indigenous is, "whatever the people consider important to their lives, whatever they regard as an authentic expression of themselves…" AFs also engage with those aspects of culture that may be oppressive to women; not in a way that is denigrating but rather in ways that recognise that women from different locations may engage and experience cultural practices differently (Coleman, 2013). Hence, AFs have resulted in "strategies and approaches that are sometimes complementary and supportive, and sometimes competing and adversarial" (Nnaemeka, 1998, p. 5).

For African women, motherhood in African society is not a subordinate position, but it is embedded with power (Mekgwe, 2003). In pre-colonial Zulu society for example, "the importance of women's labour, as well as their reproductive responsibilities, gave women crucial rights and obligations, especially as they aged" (Mekgwe, 2003, p. 75). Hence, AF argues that women within African societies play an important role in the sustenance and maintenance of the home, which they contend is a central place in African society (Ntombovuyo, 2016). African feminists further argues that women are afforded power by being the centre of the home (Mekgwe, 2003), which differs from the arguments made by some 'Western' feminists, that suggests motherhood confines women to the domestic sphere and contributes to their oppression.

Some African women are however not comfortable aligning themselves with the term feminist and have problematised AF and Black feminist thought as being contained within a feminist framework that has marginalised African women (Hudson-Weems, 1993). Hence, some African women prefer to call themselves African womanists.

Africana womanism

In response to the need for African women to self-actualise, self-identify, and self-name, Clenora Hudson-Weems, an African American feminist, coined the term Africana womanism in 1987 (Phillips, 2006). Africana womanism is an ideology that aims to reflect the unique histories and needs of African women, with its roots firmly established in African culture. It is not AF but rather an ideology grounded in the African culture, which focusses specifically on the unique; multi-layered; experiences of African women (Reed, 2001). Hudson-Weems (1993) suggests that Africana womanism is centrally based on the insider perspective, and hence African women themselves need to identify their priorities and find solutions to social issues affecting them. Yaa Asantewaa Reed (2001) confirms that women with first-hand experience are the most reliable sources of information for theorising both African experiences and possible solutions. She further argues that the solutions to the oppression of African women are present in African social systems, such as tribal councils and African philosophies e.g. Ubuntu (discussed later) which foregrounds communalism, as a way to address social issues in African communities.

Hudson-Weems (1993) further asserts that many types of Feminisms are not applicable to African women, since the background and experiences of whites, as well as Blacks from other contexts, are vastly different from Black women located in Africa. She contends that African women experience "forms of oppression that are not necessarily a part of the overall white women's experiences" (Hudson-Weems, 1989, p. 42), because of the complex issues that result from racial oppression. The African woman or 'Africana' woman is confronted by triple oppression: racism, classism, and sexism (Ogunyemi, 1985), and hence the different forms of victimisation experienced by African women need to be prioritised and addressed (Hudson-Weems, 1993). However, she suggests that sexism is a result of racism and classism, and sexism is therefore a secondary problem (Coleman, 2013), which is different to what many African feminists would articulate.

Africana womanism, like womanism, contends that instead of alienating Africana men, 'Africanans' must work hand-in-hand with African men for a renegotiation of roles (Hudson-Weems, 1993). Ladner (1971) articulates that Black women do not necessarily perceive Black men as enemies but suggests that social structures also subjugate Black men, women, and children. They further assert that racialised manhood stigmatises and punishes Black men, and thus working with men as part of the community is essential (Gaines, 2016). The Southern African concept of *Ubuntu*, which translates to 'I am because we are' (Goduka, 2000), aligns with an Africana womanist perspective since it is drawn from African culture and values a communal-based view of humanity. This perspective gives precedence to the community over the individual (Oyewumi, 1998) which is juxtaposed with some types of 'Western' Feminisms that are argued to give precedence to the individual.

Some African writers (Makaudze, 2014; Ntiri, 2001) have shown how Africana womanism is applied in the African context. For example, Makaudze (2014) conducted research in Zimbabwe in which the games children played were analysed from an Africana womanist perspective. Through this research, it was argued that Shona girls are taught qualities that have strong Africana womanist foundation such as family-centeredness, respect for elders, and nurturing (Makaudze, 2014). Hence, African womanism is very embedded in African culture and perspectives and works with men to find solutions to gender and other issues in the community, which is related to nego-feminism in this respect.

Nego-feminism

Nnaemeka (2004), a Nigerian woman, conceptualised nego-feminism as a feminism that allows for negotiation with and within the patriarchal system. Aligned with African conceptions of shared values, compromise, and balance it disengages from egotism (Mengistu, 2021). Nego-feminism incorporates negotiation, not only with respect to giving and taking but also to 'go-around' Patriarchy. Nnaemeka (2004, p. 380) contends that "African women working for social change build on the Indigenous by defining and modulating their feminist struggle in deference to cultural and local imperatives." So in effect, nego-feminism accounts for the contexts in which African women negotiate with, or 'go-around' Patriarchy to contribute to stability in the system, instead of the 'Western' approaches to feminism that advocate for challenging and over-throwing a system of Patriarchy (Muhammad & Rosli, 2014).

Nego-feminism highlights the locatedness of feminism in relation to the real context in which women live where negotiations with systems of power, like Patriarchy, is the lived reality of African women. Nnaemeka (2004) provides the example of Burkina Faso, where women save some of their household financial allocation until they have enough to open a small shop or kiosk in or near their house to sustain themselves and their families whilst still maintaining their care roles. In this way, they 'go-around' Patriarchy to acquire capital and negotiate the public/public spaces in non-confrontational ways to be involved in production, without compromising their reproductive roles. In this collection, Klaas-Makolomakwe and Raniga also provide insights on how traditional leaders adopted nego-feminist practices in dealing with women abuse.

Nego-feminism also asserts that in interactions between West and the rest, learning is mutual (Nnaemeka, 2004). Nnaemeka (2004) contends that colonialists and people from the West can learn values such as connectedness, community, and family from African people, as much as Africans learn individualism from the West. Hence, culture is dynamic and mutually influenced by global engagements and the transfer of knowledge and information. Therefore, nego-feminism contends that 'Western' Feminisms can learn from Southern Feminisms. It also articulates how women negotiate and work around patriarchal structures, rather than actively confronting them. Hence, approaches to gender equality in Africa diverge in some respects from Western Feminisms and draw on African culture and notions of people's embeddedness in commuity.

Conclusions

Feminism is not a homogenous concept and has developed over time in different contexts in response to social, political, and cultural moments. It is a controversial theory that is contested both within feminist circles and by those womanists who feel it alienates men. However, it provides a useful lens for social workers from which to unpack gender oppression in society and areas to consider for challenging systems of discrimination at various levels in the ecosystem. Ante-, post-, and decolonial feminists highlight women's oppression, particularly in the Global South, which they argue was obscured and ignored by first- and second-wave Western feminists. African feminists particularly reflect on the differential experiences of African women, because of their location in Africa and the multiple oppressions they experience, which provides different possibilities for working as social workers in the African context.

AF provides the space for African women to articulate their needs and interests and find ways to address them. Africana womanism was developed by women who do not align with the notion of feminism which they found to be too challenging and exclusionary of men but are still concerned with raising the voices of African women on the ground. Nego-feminism emerged to reflect the real lived experiences of women in which they need to negotiate with Patriarchy in order to survive. These African feminist/womanist perspectives are more inclusive of men and specific cultural requirements in an attempt to indigenise and decolonise women's experiences of oppression, which provides social workers with opportunities to engage men in ending gender oppression and violence against women. African feminist/womanist approach also emphasises that as social workers, we should recognise that African women can articulate and provide solutions for managing their lives.

This chapter reflects on African feminist and womanist 'thought from Black.' That is, it engages with theories that are an expression of African and Black women's lives and experiences with racism, and the historical legacy of Western Colonialism, which influenced the ways in which women mediated their relationships with men. In many instances, White women could be concerned with overthrowing Patriarchy, as they did not have to deal with systemic racial discrimination, colonial and imperial legacies that most African and Black women confront. These dimensions change the nature and ways in which African women and those racialised as Black navigate Patriarchy, which is important for social workers to recognise. Some African and Black women see Feminism as a Western import that does not represent their lived experiences of racism and Colonialism, and they prefer not to have adversarial relationships with men but rather work with them to address multiple oppressions. Black women's lives are besieged with legacies of imperialism, Colonialism, and ongoing racism, which often means protecting themselves and Black men from colonial and racist oppressive structures that sometimes overshadow their own gender oppression, which is something critical to take note of in working with oppressed communities as social workers. This has been seen in domestic violence situations, where women are reluctant to seek help, as this exposes Black men to racist and colonial authoritarian structures that use these instances as opportunities for violating Black men. Thus, social workers need to recognise that help-seeking and help-provision from social workers and other referral sources could be potentially dangerous and exposing for some client groups and our response strategies need to account for these since the criminal justice system may not present marginalised groups with justice and support. Hence, for womanists and nego-feminists men are seen as partners in the fight against oppression, rather than adversaries, as the racist and colonial structure could not be trusted to deal justly or fairly with Black men who are demonised and othered as violent, etc. Thus, many African and Black women have chosen to negotiate and work around Patriarchy instead of work towards dismantling it.

Sadly, some Black men have bought into Colonial gender discrimination and benefit from the patriarchal dividend. Some men, in particular those who ascribe to Abrahamic religions, have used religious texts to justify Patriarchy and gender discrimination. In these religions, historically men had most of the power as priests, imams, or Rabbis, unlike African spiritual religions, which have a strong place for women where many women are Sangomas. Understanding the role of alternative health and spiritual care in African communities is critical for social workers who work with African women on many aspects of their lives including reproductive health matters.

It is also important to recognise that Older women in particular have a high status in many African societies, as they become wise matriarchs who are repositories of social and ecological knowledge (Mokgwathi, 2023, p. 59), thus in negotiating access to communities as social workers and working within them, these roles need to understood and respected. Moreover, some African women have reclaimed the domains of care and motherhood as powerful status symbols rather than as symbols of oppression. This is not to valorise African societies as non-patriarchal. However, gender relations differed from the dominant Western models and women though often still invested in differing roles, had power in many more domains. Hence, gender relations differed and the possibilities for different gender imaginaries existed and still exist, which could be engaged with in social work practice to create affirming care for all people under the spirit of Ubuntu, including non-binary communities.

Hence, as social workers located in Africa, we need to consider the specific and unique socio-cultural, spiritual, and religious issues that African women encounter, that may be different for women in other contexts. Because of our professional status as social workers, we have power to actively challenge gender discrimination. We can either maintain or challenge the status quo that contributes to women's oppression. As practitioners, we could practice in ways that reinforce gender, class, and racial oppression or challenge it. Some theorists argue that it is only through feminist consciousness that women can attain deeper levels of empowerment (Kabeer, 2001). Feminist consciousness is not something that "oppressed groups can claim automatically" but rather something that must be achieved through struggle utilising both science and politics (Harding, 2004, p. 8). To fight gender oppression in its various forms at micro-, meso-, and macro levels, social workers can assist communities in connecting with their feminist consciousness and desires to challenge all forms of oppression, through various empowerment programs. There has been recognition of the need to work with men and boys in many spheres as articulated by womanists and nego-feminist, which his critical if gender inequality is to be achieved, this can be driven by social workers.

To challenge gender hierarchies and other power hierarchies as social workers, when doing research or practice from a feminist social work approach, we need to create space in the work we are doing to tackle gender inequality with men, women, girls, boys, and non-binary communities. We need to engage communities about how they see the world and what is important to them in order to work with them from their worldview, which may be substantially different to our worldview, to co-create gender equality. So being aware of power relations not only in society, but also in our individual interactions with individuals, groups, and communities in practice, education, and research becomes critical as feminist or womanist social workers.

Acknowledgements

- Funders: Oppenheimer memorial trust, South African National Research Foundation.
- Research assistant: Many thanks to my research assistants Innocent Mwatsiya and Rose Kibaara for their assistance.
- This chapter is an adapted version of a chapter entitled Feminisms produced In *Theories for decolonial social work practice in South Africa*. It is reproduced with permission of Oxford University Press South Africa © Oxford University Press 2019.

Note

1 Whilst I, like others, reclaim the term Black as a powerful construct as articulated by Biko (1987) in the Black consciousness sense and to include people of Colour, I also recognise that Black is a social construct that has been imbibed with negativity, hence the use of the notion 'racialised as Black.' As Ahmed (2002, p. 46) argues, "…racialization involves a process of *investing skin* colour with meaning, such that 'black' and 'white' come to function, not as descriptions of skin colour, but as racial identities. The term 'racialized bodies' …suggests that that we cannot understand the production of race without reference to embodiment: if racialization involves multiple processes, then these processes involve the marking out of bodies as the *site* of racialization itself."

References

Ada, F.G. (2011). A Critical Survey of Selected Texts on the Growth of Feminism in Nigeria. *LWATI: A Journal of Contemporary Research*, 8(3), 50–60.

Adjepong, A. (2015). The role of women in the political development of pre-colonial Africa. In S. A. Ajayi & J. K. Ayantayo (Eds.), *Women in development yesterday and today: Essays in memory of Professor Dorcas Olubanke Akintunde* (pp. 17–40). John Archers Publishers Limited.

Ahmed, S. (2002). Racialized bodies. In M. Evans & E. Lee (Eds.), *Real bodies* (pp. 46–63). Palgrave. https://doi.org/10.1007/978-0-230-62974-5_4

Ake, C. (1988). Building on the indigenous. In P. Frühling (Ed.), *Recovery in Africa: A challenge for development cooperation in the 1990s* (pp. 19–22). Swedish Ministry of Foreign Affairs.

Begoña, S. T. (2017). Future perspectives of feminism: The way towards queer feminism. In J. R. Velasco (Ed.), *Feminism: Past, present and future perspectives* (pp. 119–127). NOVA Science Publishers.

Bhambra, G. K. (2014). Postcolonial and decolonial dialogues. *Postcolonial Studies*, 17(2), 115–121. https://doi.org/10.1080/13688790.2014.966414

Biko, S. (1987). *I write what I like*. Heinemann.

Coleman, M. A. (Ed.). (2013). *Ain't I a womanist, too? Third wave womanist religious thought*. Fortress Press.

Fennell, S., & Arnot, M. (2009). Decentring hegemonic gender theory: The implications for educational research. *Research Consortium on Educational Outcomes and Poverty* (Working Paper no. 21). Development Studies and Faculty of Education, University of Cambridge.

Gaines, R. (2016). Critical negotiations and black lives: An Africana womanist analysis to raise consciousness. *Cultural Studies Critical Methodologies*, 16(3), 324–332. https://doi.org/10.1177/1532708616634838

Goduka, I. N. (2000). African or indigenous philosophies: Legitimizing spiritually centered wisdoms within the academy. In P. Higgs, N. C. G. Vakalisa, T. V. Mda, & N. T. Assie-Lumumba (Eds.), *African voices in education* (pp. 63–83). Juta.

Hanisch, C. (1970). The personal is political. In S. Firestone, & A. Koedt, (Eds.), *Notes from the second year: Women's liberation: Major writings of the radical feminists* (pp. 82–85). Radical Feminism.

Harding, S. G. (Ed.). (2004). *The feminist standpoint theory reader: Intellectual and political controversies*. Routledge.

hooks, B. (2014). *Ain't I a woman: Black women and feminism*. Routledge.

Hudson-Weems, C. (1989). Cultural and agenda conflicts in academia: Critical issues for africana women's studies. *Western Journal of Black Studies*, 13(4), 185. https://www.proquest.com/openview/be54263a70294d12d692695e6335ee60/1?pq-origsite=gscholar&cbl=1821483

Hudson-Weems, C. (1993). *Africana womanism: Reclaiming ourselves*. Bedford.

Imam, A.M. (1997). Engendering African social sciences: An introductory essay. In A. M. Imam, F. Sow, & A. Mama (Eds.), *Engendering African Social Sciences CODESRIA*, Dakar, Senegal (pp. 1–30). Also in French as Sexe, Genre Et Société: Engendrer Les Sciences Sociales Africaines CODESRIA/Karthala 2004.

Kabeer, N. (2001). Conflicts over credit: Reevaluating the empowerment potential of loans to women in rural Bangladesh. *World Development*, 29(1), 63–68. https://econpapers.repec.org/RePEc:eee:wdevel:v:29:y:2001:i:1:p:63-84

Kuba, A. (2018). Women nationalists in nineteenth and twentieth century Ghana and Zimbabwe: Case studies of Charwe Nehanda Nyakasikana and Yaa Asentewaa. *Journal of International Women's Studies*, 19(2), 159–171. https://vc.bridgew.edu/jiws/vol19/iss2/10/

Ladner, J. A. (1971). Racism and tradition: Black womanhood in historical perspective. In F. C. Steady (Ed.), *The black woman cross-culturally*. Schenkman Books.

Lewis, D. (2001). Introduction: African feminisms. *Agenda: Empowering Women for Gender Equity* (50), 4–10. http://www.jstor.org/stable/4066401

Liljeström, M. (2019). Feminism and queer temporal complexities. *SQS–Suomen Queer-Tutkimuksen Seuran Lehti*, 13(1–2), 23–38. https://doi.org/10.23980/sqs.89127

Lugones, M. (2010). Toward a decolonial feminism. *Hypatia*, 25(4), 742–759. http://www.jstor.org/stable/40928654

Lyons, L. T. (2000). Disrupting the center: Interrogating an 'Asian feminist' identity. *Communal/Plural: Journal of Transnational and Crosscultural Studies*, 8(1), 65–79. https://doi.org/10.1080/13207870050001466

Makaudze, G. (2014). Africana womanism and Shona children's games. *The Journal of Pan African Studies*, 1.6(10), 128–143. https://www.jpanafrican.org/docs/vol6no10/6.10-10-Makaudze.pdf

Mekgwe, P. (2003). Theorizing African feminism(s) the 'colonial' question. *An African Journal of Philosophy/Revue Africaine de Philosophie*, 10(20), 11–22. https://quest-journal.net/Quest_XX_2006.pdf#page=11

Mengistu, M. T. (2021). Chameleon imagery as a strategy of women survival in Valiare Tagwira's novel, the uncertainty of hope: A nego feminist approach. *Turkish Online Journal of Qualitative Inquiry*, 12(9), 3963–3974. https://www.tojqi.net/index.php/journal/article/view/6414/4569

Mohanty, C. (1991). Under Western eyes: Feminist scholarship and colonial discourses. In C. Mohanty, A. Russo, & L. Torres (Eds.), *Third world women and the politics of feminism* (pp. 51–80). Indiana University Press.

Mokgwathi, K. (2023). "I am because we are": A historical conceptualisation of African feminism(s) and womanism. In M. Musingafi (Ed.), *Women empowerment and the feminist agenda in Africa* (pp. 111–124). IGI Global.

Monges, M. M. (1993). Reflections on the role of female deities and queens in ancient Kemet. *Journal of Black Studies*, 23(4), 561–570. https://doi.org/10.1177/002193479302300408

Mtombeni, B. (2020). Women in pre-colonial Africa: Southern Africa. In O. Yacob-Haliso & T. Falola (Eds.), *The Palgrave handbook of African women's studies* (pp. 1185–1202). Palgrave Macmillan.

Muhammad, A., & Rosli, T. (2014). Feminism reimagined. Recoded. *Journal of Language and Communication*, 1(1), 85–97. http://psasir.upm.edu.my/id/eprint/50354/1/Feminism%20reimagined.%20Recoded..pdf

Munro, E. (2013). Feminism: A fourth wave? *Political Insight*, 4(2). https://doi.org/10.1111/2041-9066.12021

Nnaemeka, O. (1998). Introduction: Reading the rainbow. In O. Nnaemeka (Ed.), *Sisterhood, feminisms, and power: From Africa to the diaspora* (pp. 1–35). Africa World Press.

Nnaemeka, O. (2004). Nego-feminism: Theorizing, practicing, and pruning Africa's way. In F. Lionnet, O. Nnaemeka, S. H. Perry, & C. Schenck (Eds.), *Signs 29, special issues- development cultures: New environments, new realities, new strategies* (pp. 357–385). http://www.jstor.org/stable/10.1086/378553

Ntiri, D. W. (2001). Reassessing Africana womanism: Continuity and change. *The Western Journal of Black Studies, 25*(3), 163–167. https://www.proquest.com/docview/200389466/fulltextPDF/89A1F17460474C2DPQ/1?accountid=13425#

Ntombovuyo, L. (2016). *Gender equality and women empowerment for Africa's renewal: Existing influences and future considerations.* https://www.mbeki.org/2018/06/01/gender-equality-and-women-empowerment-for-africas-renewal-existing-influences-and-future-considerations/. Accessed 4 June 2018.

Ogunyemi, C. O. (1985). Womanism: The dynamics of the contemporary Black female novel in English. *Signs, 11*(1), 63–80. https://www.jstor.org/stable/3174287

Oyewumi, O. (1998). Deconfounding gender: Feminist theorizing and Western culture. *Signs: Journal of Women in Culture and Society, 23*(4), 1049–1062. https://www.jstor.org/stable/3175203

Payne, M. (2005). *Modern social work theory* (3rd ed.). Palgrave MacMillan.

Phillips, R. (2006). Undoing an activist response: Feminism and the Australian government's domestic violence policy. *Critical Social Policy, 26*(1), 192–219. https://doi.org/10.1177/0261018306059771

Rampton, M. (2015: para 12). *Four waves of feminism.* Pacific Magazine. https://www.pacificu.edu/about/media/four-waves-feminism

Ranmuthugala, M. E. P. (2018). *Widows and concubines: Tradition and deviance in the women of Kanthapura.* Paper presented at the 4th World Conference on Women's Studies 03-05 May 2018: Colombo, Sri Lanka.

Reed, P. Y. A. (2001). African womanism and African feminism: A philosophical, literacy, and cosmological dialect on family? *Western Journal of Black Studies 25*(3), 168–176. https://www.proquest.com/docview/200317038?pqorigsite=gscholar&fromopenview=true

Sheik, A. (2018). The more than beautiful woman – African folktales of female agency and emancipation. *Agenda, 32*(4), 45–53. https://doi.org/10.1080/10130950.2018.1535094

Stanley, L., & Wise, S. (1983). *Breaking out feminist consciousness and feminist research.* Routledge.

Thebe, S. (2023). Retracing her story: Imperialism and the African woman. In M. C. C. Musingafi & C. Hungwe (Eds.), *Women empowerment and the feminist agenda in Africa* (pp. 40–57). IGI Global.

3
COLORED DEMARCATIONS IN POSTCOLONIAL FEMINISM
Can the subalterned social worker now speak?

Melinda Madew

The subjugated voice

In this chapter, we examine many voices raised together to bring attention to those thoughts long silenced, in subverted dissention. The purpose is neither to seek retribution nor comfort from a feminist community but rather to uncover ways that accumulated knowledge may be traced back to its owners and whereby emergent knowledges are able to flourish within a movement. Subjection is insidious in many ways because the misappropriation of knowledge is a hegemonic practice committed against the subalterned.

To the subalterned, the search for knowledge is parallel with the search for wholeness and belonging because the structures of our daily lives compel us to recognize different realities (Davis, 1981). This searching takes us to non-normative spaces where we interpret experience and evolve insights from once untested paradigms. On one hand is the recreation of learning experiences, and on the other is the need to acknowledge lessons that reveal the integrity of our wholeness.

The recovery of self-knowledge cannot be separated from the reclaiming of a collective consciousness, because the individual is always set in the context of group identification. There cannot be an I without the we. With permission from those whose voices are echoed here, the I would be intermittently shifting to the we (Wright et al., 2021).

Ours is an oppositional view, a mode of seeing and knowing that is unknown to those who do not identify with our oppression (hooks, 1984). These voices rise from the ranks of social workers resisting various institutionalized practices that negate their agency through the imposition of power demarcations and racialized categories of hegemonic control and colonization. This writing intends to contribute to the assertion that it is imperative that the decolonization of social work is juxtaposed with the decolonization of the feminist movement.

This chapter is a gathering of voices coming together as we define where we stand, the reason for standing and for how long we hold our ground together. Writing is not our element because we have lived much from the spoken words of elders who tried to reach and teach us, if only we could have listened more humbly. Many times our lack of written language drives us mad (Andreotti, 2011). However, spoken words that resonate in cadential meaning are known and owned by those who speak and by those who render uncoerced capacity for listening. So often, the subalterned is the coerced listener and the silenced observer.

Emotion can be intoned in a manner that the written word could not. But yet again, we have often been admonished by those who do not know us, to rein in emotionality, to have it stilled and quietened down, so that the supposed objectivity of true knowledge can find its place. Among us, both as the owners and the disowned of language and speech, we claim these pages for our subjected voices. It is a call on the willingness and a responsibility among those who care, to take as many perspectives as possible, and include the positions of those whose existences are questioned and their voices dismissed as dispensable and insignificant (Du Bois, 1986).

Who is the subalterned?

We use the active verb sublaterned to denote an imposed state of being minoritized and othered. This chapter borrows from postcolonial feminist thought and Spivakian subalternity in attempting to articulate and represent the lived reality of those of us who are rarely asked to speak (Spivak, 2017). Spivak's subalternity locates the self in a subjected position of exclusion from established structures of politics and a culture. Exclusion is not self-willed; it is an imposed positionality of subservience.

This piece was written with the consent of the owners of voices that are echoed in the ensuing pages.[1] These are voices raised in resistance to a subalterned condition. Postcolonial feminism can find location in the Spivakian positioning of race, class, culture and religion operating in an overlapping manner in subalternity (Spivak, 2017). The Spivakian subalternity references Gramsci's notion of the disenfranchised underclass proletariat whose only means of survival is to trade labor capacity to the owners of capital in exchange for wages. The proletariat surrenders agency to speak (Gramsci, 2012), because the very act of claiming voice is an act of subversion that cannot be countenanced by the wielders of hegemonic power. Gramsci's notion of the subaltern is one whose position in a hierarchical constellation is subverted by a higher authority such as a fascistic military order. The subalterns are the displaced peasants, dispossessed workers and lumpen proletariat who among others consigned to the inhumanities of life within a fascistic regime (Gramsci, 2012). The subaltern is forced not to exercise discerning judgment and to surrender agency to a controlling hierarchy.

This chapter claims space for other ways of defining experience and deriving situated knowledge away from the dominant lines of Western epistemology and historiography which dismiss other forms of knowing as marginal, anecdotal narrations, so lacking in evidential, scientific foundations (Lewis, 1996). Because of this, the subaltern's lived reality as her wellspring of knowing is rejected and regarded as frivolous and irrelevant. The Spivakian and Gramscian characterization of the subaltern takes into account those who to this day inherit the vestiges of Colonialism in a reality of cultural dislocation, economic divestment and political disenfranchisement.

Yet, that brazen ability to name and proclaim a subalterned status is an act of subversion itself because naming one's reality demands speaking in a knowledged voice that can define identity within a lived reality. It comes with Spivak's assertion that when this happens, the subaltern begins transcending their subordinated status (Spivak, 2017). The very act of naming one's worldly situatedness is subversive as it is liberative (Paulo Freire, 2007).

Such knowledged interrogation is dangerous to those who benefit from a relationship that marginalizes and reduces others to the seeming powerlessness of silence.

Social work is not an innocent profession despite all attempts to a claim, a sacrosanct historical narrative of human dignity and belief in the inviolability of human rights (Ife, 2012; Lavalette et al., 2015; Lorenz, 2006). The profession swears to these aspirational ideals, but there are intruding voices within our ranks who demand the application of ideals into actual practice. There are dissenting voices demanding the tearing down of illusory pedestals of power occupied by members who perpetuate social symbols that guarantee the privilege of dispensing power over others (Wright et al., 2021).

The "whitewashing" of social work history to this very day is an all confining structure from which dissenting voices still emerge. How would subalterned voices find counter-representations within a hegemonic narrative? In asserting a counter-narrative, the subalterned social worker will occupy that excluded space as the seat of oppositional knowledge. Exclusion becomes positionality because epistemological representations are also legitimized at the margins of social movements (Fricker, 2007).

The Spivakian subaltern emerges from the excluded spaces, and it is from these margins that the epistemology of relations will be organized by the subalterned social worker. This is an epistemology that refuses obliteration because it demands a rethinking of obsolete supremacist patterns, which when not challenged will render the social work profession irrelevant and inconsequential (Rogowski, 2020). The subalterned social worker speaks, not from the center, but from the margins (hooks, 1984) by reclaiming power residing in ghettoed spaces.

Locating the subalterned ghetto

The subaltern ghetto is not an imagined space, it is a lived reality that women of color in social work contend within their daily working lives. The ghetto is recognizable to those who are shunted there. In this ghetto are different relational reactions in contending with privilege and oppression. Those who do not experience it do not know it (hooks, 1984).

The subalterned ghetto as lived location has no set territoriality. As a shared and lived experience, it is recognizable to those who belong to it. For women of color in social work, there is that sense of deep knowing what and how it is to live and work in locations where the self has to find that safe crevice to unfold, regenerate and re-collect. In events such as international conferences or any other professional gatherings, women of color representing dominantly white organizations and institutions do exchange stories of personal struggles (Pierro, 2022). When there is chance for voices to converge, stories are told aplenty. Not in bitterness but more in the reflective realization over how our own social work community uses demarcations of color to exclude others in a competitive professional field. Despite the profession's spoken avowals of inclusivity, the academe is awash with vicious covert and overt competition even when the rewards are so low and so little such as the number of publications and mentions in academic references. There is a complex mode of domination in our organizations and institutions, where ambition, influence and publicized performance are the currencies in relationships.

> I will always be treated as a migrant from the South living in the affluent North. I have always been an academic worker in my country. I was respected for this. That respect

is absent where I am now. I am expected to speak and think along the contours of someone representing my imagined place of origin. This was like an enforced mantle of subjection I wore on my body until I realized how it crippled my everyday walk. I must not show how good I am at something, lest I offend someone higher in the hierarchy. I eventually discovered how the results of my work were callously appropriated by white women without misgivings. Having experienced their bullying and demeaning treatment, discovering this hurt deeply.[2]

There is no denying the existing subjection of the migrant social worker (Obasi, 2022). Hegemonic practice in the workplace insidiously enforces submission to a racialized culture where essentialized skin color determines the pecking order. The questions remain as to how that imposed subordinated status could be disrupted. There are critical debates among ourselves, as there is much to discover on how we can break away from an entrenched system that easily relegates our capacity to know and acquire knowledge as suspect. In Spivak's geographies of postcolonialism (Morris and Spivak, 2010), she cites Western scholars' dismissal of non-Western knowledge as immature and fundamentally flawed in its scientific moorings. African, Asian and Middle Eastern patterns of knowing are consigned to the corner of anecdotal imagination. For those who succeed at gaining entrance into the inner sanctums of the social work academic community, there is that pain resulting from the many forms of self-betrayal when one must adapt to the Western way of knowing, speaking and reasoning in the process of carving a location of visibility and influence. The demarcations of color bleed out to many other demeaning reminders that even when the subaltern may have merited access to some position of privilege, there is still no escaping the status of the "othered". The othered is set against a grading system where she passes through an unrecognizable sieve of affirmation or disaffirmation.

> There are questions asked of me that no other colleague in the department would be asked. Where do you originally come from? Considering where you come from, you speak really good English, so how did you get that accent? Where did you earn your credentials? Then the final question - did you do your own hair?[3]

These are not innocuous questions because however these are answered, there are signifiers of class background, academic privileges, geographic advantage and cultural habits that are connotative of value or disvalue to the interrogator. Every woman of color navigating a white society carries the demarcations of value or disvalue on her body as a set of characterizations the world imposess on her. While confirming or repudiating such impositions, she exposes the context of her cultural, political and economic background. The interrogator constructs an imagined narrative around the subalterned to evaluate if the privilege accorded her is at all deserved.

There is the gratuitous adherence to the tokenism of diversity and interculturality as catchy neoliberal jargon in the welfare system. Albeit condescending and patronizing of women of color in the workplace, these serve the purpose of lending credibility to an organization's tokenistic commitment to diversity and interculturality. How often would organizations install a diversity officer for an anti-discrimination desk led by white women who if not complicit are oblivious of systemic racism despite their intonations about inclusivity

Colored demarcations

and diversity. How many careers have been launched on the backs of colored women (Moraga and Anzaldúa, 2015)? One research assistant recounted:

> Being my direct manager, she explicitly forbade me to use her self-assigned scientific terminology describing her supposed expertise in diversity and intercultural studies. I later found out how she used my projects to lend prominence to her name when bidding for external funding for her own projects. While sabotaging my effort to deliver results, she was using my project results to prop her name. It struck like a double-edged dagger, because on one side was my person lending legitimacy to the organization's progressive credentials as an employer of a woman of color in the academe, and on the other, was the bullying and eventual misuse of my work. Diversity as a term is reduced to jargonistic embellishment on a slick business card and catchy email signature.[4]

The subaltern ghetto is where discrimination takes immense toll on social workers, who when reporting racist, homophobic, sexist and classists slurs are subjected to the backlash of increased harassment and bullying. Discrimination by colleagues, supervisors and service users are pervasive because this goes unchecked (National Association of Social Workers [NASW], 2021; UK Community Care, 2018). The subalterned would have to muster resources and personal courage to pursue a racist case that when not dismissed would take years to merit a token formal apology without addressing the need to engage in institutional change. In Europe and North America, studies have been conducted to expose homophobic and racist attacks by colleagues and service users against social workers (Lin et al., 2018; Pierro, 2022). However, the cases under study do not mirror the totality of experience in other parts of the world where social workers do not always have access to legal or organizational resources that could effectively address discriminatory practices in the workplace.

The Intersectionality of disvalued characteristics and background is a reality in the social work ghetto where colored women navigate their working lives, at times with ease, at times with a watchful wisdom that survival within an organization requires one to weather veiled racial slurs almost on daily basis in the workplace. Diversity and interculturality are conflated jargon – neither of these concepts is transformative, nor do these address the status quo of domination and subalternity.

But yet again, organizations continue to employ women of color, explicitly for the purpose that social workers of migration background bring added-value to the work they do (Popescu and Libal, 2018). Research explore the reasons why migrant social workers are hired reveal interesting reasons. They have a higher ability to engage in emotional connections; they serve as role models among families; they are cultural mediators and interlocutors; they have an openness to other cultures; they are sensitive to the power imbalances with their clients; they are able to deal with clients' resistance; they serve as cultural brokers for colleagues and agencies even as they expose themselves to community and agency discrimination (Lin et al., 2018). Social work has become a niche profession for young people with migration backgrounds. The social worker of migration background has employable assets. They put down their heads and work. There is the multilingual competence. There is a patience to navigate the welfare bureaucracy. They are persevering and appreciative. They have empathy for those who are in a similar situation to their own families. Given these characteristics, social workers of migration backgrounds report being given more difficult caseloads with the perception that they are better equipped to deal with ethnic minorities, refugees and migrant families (Lin et al., 2018; SASW, 2021).

Social workers of migration background and women of color from all over the world are increasingly important to the social care sector in many affluent countries (Baltruks et al., 2017). They have earned their academic qualifications under the most onerous of circumstances, and once qualifying for a job, there is appreciation and respect for the work they do, even when they often run the risk of job exploitation and discrimination. Here is an excerpt from a conversation between the author and her former student:

> I am the first in my extended family to achieve formal university qualification. As a student, I then lived with my family in social housing where neighbors in our Turkish community would send their young children to me when they needed help with their homework. So today, they look up to me as a replicable success story for children living in the Brenntpunkt[5] of social housing. Now I am the social worker, the one who helps families in similar situation as my own in the past.[6]

The subalterned social worker has a claim to a life-history set in contemporary postcolonial reality and global neoliberalism. Diasporic communities in the West can predominantly claim a generational pattern of migration to escape the ravages of a colonized land and damaged culture, for the promises of the European metropolis. Postwar neoliberal governments needed migrant labor to fuel the economic miracles of Europe in the 1950s. Cheap migrant labor jump-started the postwar economic miracles of Europe's nation-states. Not only did migrants from former colonies arrive, so did the extended families of workmen from countries still wracked by political upheavals such as Greece, Italy, Turkey and Spain. In the university where she teaches, this author[7] could safely estimate that 10–20% of all new entrants in social work every semester, lay claim to a Gastarbeiter[8] ancestry that had powered Germany's juggernaut industry for generations. The grandsons and granddaughters of guest workers who even as they are racially white still carry the markings of their supposed disadvantaged class, ethnicity and migration background. These categories of subjection demarcate them further down the "white but not quite" segment of the European population (Kalmar, 2022).

Reclaiming the ghetto – dissention from the ranks

There is a resurgent resistance in the ghetto defining itself within a profession that seems oblivious to its complicity in systemic racism. This complicity is regarded by many young social workers today as white supremacism in the form of knowledge misappropriation, the imposition of colored hierarchies, and the dismissal of the distinct contributions that colored women bring to the workplace (Tuhiwali Smith, 2012). The social work profession sits comfortably on a hegemonic narrative promoting how rich privileged white women inspired a scientific practice of social care, negating the contributions of Black, Indigenous and other people of color who labored collectively to uphold the survival of their communities despite the hostile and often violent system of repression they had to endure (Wright et al., 2021). Such a hegemonic narrative is a perpetuation of the myth about white people's manifest destiny to colonize and subjugate as a means of redeeming the poor and the weak from themselves.

There is no generalized intention to homogenize colored women in social work as subalterned in status the world over, nor is social work inspired alone by a white supremacist ideology. In recent years, there are even louder calls from social work organizations to clear the ranks of racism in the workplace. Published reports document job-related discriminatory practices experienced by women of color and persons of migration background as they assume important responsibilities in social work organizations (NASW, 2021; Pierro, 2022; SASW, 2021). They are specifically assigned in public or private agencies serving marginalized sectors such as migrant groups, displaced individuals, refugees and all other ethnically diverse communities. Discriminatory practices happen at agency and community levels from managers, colleagues, students and service users, prompting social work networks to release statements calling for institutional change (Pierro, 2022). NASW (2021) released commitments to end racism in social work, calling for the dismantling of systems of oppression and fight racism within social work. This was followed by a statement in June 17, 2021 apologizing for racist practices in American social work throughout US history. In England, a study done in 2022 revealed how over a quarter of social workers face racism from colleagues or managers (Pierro, 2022). The Scottish Association of Social Workers (SASW, 2021) reported how racism is embedded in the work system calling to end the belief that racism does not exist in social work. Evidence is documented in a system where preferences, priorities and policies are made by decision makers representing the white majority putting minoritized ethnic social workers at a disadvantage (SASW, 2021).

The social work community has taken steps to acknowledge the situation of racism within its own ranks admitting that white supremacy exists in social work (Obasi, 2022; Wright et al., 2021). It concedes that the social work profession has made mistakes in its perpetuation of racist systems by not acting to directly confront racism on individual and institutional levels. The NASW raises what it calls the virus of racism and states that social workers who are expressing racist thoughts and feelings towards Black Americans or other racial groups should do some "soul searching" to humanize Black, Latinx and Indigenous people by "treating them with the same respect you treat people who look like you" (NASW, 2020). The purpose is not so much name calling and shaming but more to uncover the multitude of ways where the process of othering takes place among ourselves and within institutions burdened by an "indifference to difference" (Ghandi, 2019).

The above are some examples of social work networks, the predominantly white membership of which close ranks with women of color to end systemic discrimination in the workplace. These good intentions while valued and respected fall short of an earnest engagement in institutionalized strategies on a systemic scale to address a white supremacist culture within our profession. Effective institutional policies that promote equality from the perspective of women of color hardly exist, nor are measures to sanction white supremacism firmly in place. Racism as a form of white supremacism is a political phenomenon that needs to be understood before it can be addressed (Lavalette and Penketh, 2014). This should not be from the perspective of concerned onlookers, but from the standpoint of those who contend with the daily consequences of a subalterned status.

To many among us who feel removed from our own communities of belonging having been subjects of intergenerational miseducation and systemic discrimination, there is a longing to create restorative and affirming communities. At the same time we have to distance ourselves from those still arrogate their histories, race and class background to expand privilege as unquestioned entitlement (Wright et al., 2021). This is a pervasive mindset among those who consciously or unconsciously derive benefits from empire building (Escobar, 2011), proving how the colonizing project succeeds in multi-pronged ways. Colonialism in its many "post" forms asserts in oblique and direct ways its hidden hegemonic modes of power in the minds and bodies of individuals as well as in the institutions they represent. Postcolonial actuality permeates the relational complexity of our lived reality as feminists in the field of social work education and practice. The interrogation that subalternity compels is in fact a process of decolonization by its very effort of naming and resisting an on-going condition of subordinated situationality (Lugones, 2010). The subalterned condition is a sociological experience (Piu, 2023) with the qualifying actuality that not all oppressed people are subalterned, because not all have been subject to colonial history. Not all silenced social workers are submitted to a colonial legacy traced back to an ancestral histography of oppression and its obtaining resurrection in neocolonial and neoliberal global reality.

The situation of subalterned women remains an unexplored terrain where knowledge about struggle and resistance can be gained. The subalterned social worker embodies the markings of an intergenerational experience of Colonialism etched in her body, where her physicality reveals a narrative of her background; her speech becomes a measure of her geographic origin; her walk is the bearing of agency or lack of it; and the choices she makes at work and personal relationships are proof of her value moorings. The subalterned is constantly read along these and many other demarcations set by a colonial past and present, which assign her and the people she represents to the realm of the other. She operates within a hegemonic system that still considers her inferior to her peers and appraises her on the bases of her embodied demarcations. On the one hand is her colonial historicity, and on the other is her being a woman, albeit at times the only colored woman in a particular work setting. She interrogates a colonial past and present, acknowledging that she is a bearer of past oppressions that are resurrected in a hegemonic order. This hegemonic order must not only be endured, it must be resisted and destabilized.

Embodied demarcations operate sharply with consequential impacts on the individual and the collective lives of those shunted to the subalterned ghetto. But here at the far margins of the white feminist movement is the very site of revolutionary dissension. In the demarcated ghetto are seditious acts that destabilize much of established gender theory in social work practice. Women in the South reject the claim that feminism started in the West as new histographies emerge about how anti-patriarchal and anti-colonial movements have been led by Black, Indigenous, Asian and Latin American women (Martínez-Cairo and Buscemi, 2021). Their contributions have been reduced and ignored, given their demarcated embodiment as the subalterned women of African ancestry, peasant class, Indio origin, slaves, unschooled and poor.

The subaltern ghetto is the site of oppositional knowledge

Social work functions as an "Othering" profession when theory and practice are instrumentalized against its own professionals. It happens when those who situate themselves outside the realm of Eurocentric hegemony are relegated as the minoritized and ethnicized subaltern. Postcolonial social work interrogates this by bringing forward a complexity of questions, starting from the colonialist education that social workers the world over are persistently subjected to (Kleibl et al., 2020). To this day, the vestiges of Colonialism cannot be erased while evidence surfaces that at every critical point in history, social work can be indicted for its complicity in supporting fascist dictators; its participation in genocidal campaigns; its enslavement of vulnerable women; its practice of tearing apart families at risk; its generational abuse of forcibly institutionalized children – all these are but a few examples calling for the urgent examination of our past and present social order. This examination cannot be arrogated by a white supremacist professional culture, nor could this be at the initiation of those whose comfortable inertia have long cocooned them in entitled privilege.

To the Western ethnocentric thinker, gender and Patriarchy are the subjects of feminism. To the postcolonial feminist, however, the condition of Coloniality is the reason for a resistance that is never static in so far as the process of Coloniality is ongoing (Mignolo and Walsh, 2018). Postcolonial theory is a response to the condition of Coloniality. New trajectories in postcolonial feminism demythologize the innocence of social work, much in the same way that the critical de-Europeanization of social work practice could be restorative of epistemic justice. In this way, knowledge will be affirmed from where it is source and flourish where it is most needed (Fricker, 2007).

The subaltern ghetto is the site of oppositional knowledge. The dynamic of dissidence happening here forces the decolonization of social work knowledge at the instigation of those whose lived experiences are a rewriting of postcolonial feminism in the history of social work professionals. Postcolonial theory is the non-coercive dialog with the subalterned other, by acknowledging her as the knowing subject who can account for knowledge and assume power over objective reality (Gandhi, 2019). It implies the undoing of hierarchical structures of race, gender, class and heteropatriarchy that continue to control the lives and knowledge sources of the subalterned, who must now contemplate these demarcations in order to claim positionality (Collins, 2009).

When the colonial subject is the other in feminist theory

Today a thoughtful examination must be undertaken regarding feminism's commitment to the decolonial movement. There must also be reflection on why Global South feminists repudiate the popular call that "no woman is free until all women are free" as the messianic mission of Western feminists. They arrogate the liberation of the downtrodden Global South sisters for themselves to fulfill (Lugones, 2010; Moraga and Anzaldúa, 2015). This seems to replicate the time when the British colonial government in India outlawed the practice of Suttee with their triumphalist declaration that it takes white men to save brown women from their brown men (Spivak, 2017). In postcolonial period, white women in a supremacist, saviourist arrangement claim the moral burden of freeing those Global South women who have no agency over their own liberation. The paternalistic arrogation of agency in the messianic guise of liberating the othered is after all an insidious hegemonistic construct.

Decolonized feminism can be a movement in full dynamic maturation when it questions the very Coloniality of power. That Coloniality of power is also the Coloniality of knowledge. When knowledge comes home to its very source, this epistemic homing is freed of racialization and demarcated territoriality (Mignolo, 2011). It does not cancel, threaten or obscure. It recognizes the sound of constitutive longing to be reconciled to its source, which are the lived realities of the subalterned. For women of color living in white societies, we are the Southerns[9] in the world. We are pitted against a postcolonial world where oppression does not recognize geographic borders. The Southerns can only be at the forefront of history in interrogating hegemonic feminism as a decolonizing project (Martínez-Cairo and Buscemi,

2021) in every society where oppression is normality. There is that longing among women in the Global South to have our sources of knowledge reconstituted and acknowledged as our ownership. After all, feminism is more than a phenomenon, it is an episteme. Our participation in centuries of struggle against Colonialism and neocolonialism will continue to serve as the seedbed of knowledge and community belonging (Lugones, 2010).

Conclusion: the many souths in the world

The decolonization of the social work profession is a non-static resistance movement led by those of us who carry the many markings of Coloniality. Categories of differentiation such as race, biography, class origin and history that mark our lives as social workers had justified the many forms of systemic exclusion experienced within a work culture organized around Eurocentric or Western valuation. These categories continue to legitimize the hegemonic colonizing project. As subalterned women in social work, we are the Southerns in the world, who wage resistance against subalternity as a decolonizing process in our institutions. This process of decolonization will not be in linear trajectory because the conditions of subjection are complex and interlocking given that these are nuanced in insidiousness. The colonized subaltern succeeds at finding positionality within an affirming community. Breaking out of subalternity is an insurgent practice never done alone. The many Southerns in the world when shunted into the subalterned ghettoes will rise and rise again. So often was history written not from the center, but from the ghettoed margins. Ghettoes are where strategies in collective resistance are tried, tested and tempered for strength. Such resistance may yet flourish into fresh forms of revolutionary feminist expression.

Notes

1 As protection against potential backlash, women who lent their voices preferred not to be named, nor their organizations mentioned.
2 Social Worker in Germany, 2022.
3 Filipino social work educator while studying in the United States, 2022.
4 Social Worker, Germany, conversation in a counselling session, 2022.
5 Brenntpunkt or hotspot refers to inner city areas.
6 Former student recounting her story with the author, 2021.
7 While leading a university-wide project called Migrants in Campus (MicCa).
8 Gastarbeiters translates to guest workers, who were expected to return home upon expiration of work contracts.
9 Walter Mignolo first used the phrase 'the many Souths of the North'.

References

Andreotti, V. (2011). *Actionable postcolonial theory in education. Postcolonial studies in Education Ser*. Palgrave Macmillan. http://site.ebrary.com/lib/alltitles/docDetail.action?docID=10518189

Baltruks, D., Hussein, S., & Lara Montero, A. (2017). *Investing in the social services workforce*. Brighton: European Social Network. https://www.esn-eu.org/sites/default/files/publications/Investing_in_the_social_service_workforce_WEB.pdf

Collins, P. H. (2009). *Black feminist thought: Knowledge, consciousness, and the politics of empowerment* (2nd ed.). Routledge classics. Routledge.

Community Care UK. https://www.communitycare.co.uk/2022/03/18/one-third-of-social-workers-faced-racism-from-colleagues-or-managers-in-past-year-finds-survey/

Davis, A. (1981). *Women, race & class*. The Women's Press.

Du Bois, W. E. B. (1986). *Writings: The suppression of the African slave trade, the souls of black folk, Dusk of dawn, essays and articles* (Ninth print). Library of America series: Vol. 34. Viking Press.

Escobar, A. (2011). *Anthropology encountering development: The making and unmaking of the third world. Princeton studies in culture/power/history, 1: Vol. 1*. Princeton University Press.

Fricker, M. (2007). *Epistemic injustice: Power & the ethics of knowing*. Oxford University Press.

Gandhi, L. (2019). *Postcolonial theory: A critical introduction* (2nd ed.). Columbia Univeristy Press.

Gramsci, A. (2012). *Selections from cultural writings* (D. Forgacs, & G. Nowell-Smith, Eds.). Haymarket.

hook, b. (1984) 2000). *Feminist theory: From margin to center* (2nd ed.). *South End Press classics: V 5*. South End Press. https://www.taylorfrancis.com/books/9781315743172 https://doi.org/10.4324/9781315743172

Ife, J. (2012). *Human rights and social work: Towards rights-based practice*. Cambridge University Press.

Kalmar, I. (2022). *White but not quite: Central Europe's illiberal revolt*. Bristol Univeristy Press.

Kleibl, T., Lutz, R., Noyoo, N., Bunk, B., Dittmann, A., & Seepamore, B. (Eds.). (2020). *Routledge international handbooks. The routledge handbook of postcolonial social work*. Routledge, Taylor & Francis Group. https://www.taylorfrancis.com/books/e/9780429468728

Lavalette, M., & Penketh, L. (2014). *Race, racism and social work: Contemprorary issues and debates*. Bristol.

Lavalette, M., & Penketh, L. (2015). *Race, racism and social work: Contemporary issues and debates* (2nd ed.). Policy Press.

Lewis, G. (1996). Situated voices: 'Black women's experience' and social work. *Feminist Review* (53), 24. https://doi.org/10.2307/1395660

Lin, C.-H., Chiang, P. P., Lux, E. A., & Lin, H.-F. (2018). Immigrant social worker practice: An ecological perspective on strengths and challenges. *Children and Youth Services Review*, 87, 103–113. https://doi.org/10.1016/j.childyouth.2018.02.020

Lorenz, W. (2006). *Perspectives on European social work: From the birth of the nation state to the impact of globalisation*. Barbara Budrich Verlag. https://ebookcentral.proquest.com/lib/kxp/detail.action?docID=5719462

Lugones, M. (2010). Toward a decolonial feminism. *Hypatia*, 25(4), 742–759. https://doi.org/10.1111/j.1527-2001.2010.01137.x

Martínez-Cairo, B., & Buscemi, E. (2021). Latin American decolonial feminisms: Theoretical perspectives and challenges. *Amérique Latine Histoire Et Mémoire*. Advance online publication. https://doi.org/10.4000/alhim.10153

Mignolo, W. D. (2011). *The dark side of western modernity: Global futures, decolonial options*. Duke University Press.

Mignolo, W. D., & Walsch, C. E. (2018). *On decoloniality: Concepts, analytics, praxis*. Duke University Press.

Moraga, C., & Anzaldúa, G. (Eds.). (Copyright 2015). *This bridge called my back: Writings by radical women of color* (4th ed.). SUNY Press.

Morris, R. C., & Spivak, G. C. (Eds.). (2010). *Can the subaltern speak? Reflections on the history of an idea*. Columbia University Press. http://swb.eblib.com/patron/FullRecord.aspx?p=895096

National Association of Social Workers [NASW] (2020, April 21). *Social workers must help dismantle systems of oppression and fight racism with the social work profession* [press release]. USA.

National Association of Social Workers [NASW] (Ed.). (2021). Undoing racism thorugh social work: NASW report to the profession on racial justice priorities and action [special issue], 2021. USA.

Obasi, C. (2022). Black social workers: Identity, racism, invisibility/hypervisibility at work. *Journal of Social Work*, 22(2), 479–497. https://doi.org/10.1177/14680173211008110

Paulo Freire. (2007). Pedagogy of the oppressed: Pedagogy of the oppressed. In P. Kuppers & G. Robertson (Eds.), *The community performance reader* (pp. 24–27). Routledge. https://doi.org/10.4324/9781003060635-5

Pierro, L. (Ed.). (2022). *Workforce: We must become a more anti-racist profession* [special issue]. Social Work Leaders, 2022. England. British Association of Social Workers.

Piu, P. (2023). The journey of subalternity in Gayatri Spivak's work: Its sociological relevance. *The Sociological Review*, 71(6), 1258–1276. https://doi.org/10.1177/00380261231194495

Popescu, M., & Libal, K. (2018). Social work with migrants and refugees. *Advances in social work*, *18*(3), i–x. https://doi.org/10.18060/22600

Rogowski, S. (2020). *Social work: The rise and fall of a profession*. Policy Press.

SASW (Ed.). (2021). *Racism in Scottish social work – A 2021 snapshot* [special issue]. Scottish Association of Social Workers, 2021. Scotland.

Spivak, G. C. (2017). *Can the subaltern speak*. Afterall Books.

Tuhiwali Smith, L. (2012). *Decolonizing methodologies: Research and indigenous peoples* (2nd ed.). ZED Books.

Wright, K. C., Carr, K. A., & Akin, B. A. (2021, September 23). The whitewashing of social work history: How dismantling racism in social work education begins with an equitable history of the profession. *Advances in social work*, 21(1 und 2). https://journals.iupui.edu/index.php/advancesinsocialwork/article/view/23946

4
REVERSING A ONE-TRACK HISTORY

Listening to minority voices at the intersections of gender, race and intellectual disability

Patience Udonsi

Introduction

An intellectual disability (ID) can be defined as a reduced intellectual ability and difficulty with everyday activities (MENCAP, 2022). People with an ID may take longer to assimilate new information and may need support to develop new skills or understand abstract, complex information (MENCAP, 2022). In some geographical regions such as England and Wales within the United Kingdom, the term Learning Disability may be used synonymously with the term ID. The term disability evokes ideas about people having deficits which require some form of intervention from professionals and those who are perceived to be more able (Spitzer & Endicott, 2018). There is a risk of unnecessary, misaligned or outrightly oppressive professional interventions where women with IDs are assessed through the lens of deficits. In the year 2017–2018, 10% of all adults who were the subject of safeguarding enquiries in England had IDs (Public Health England, 2020). It is evident that people with IDs may be at risk of multiple forms of abuse. Whilst it is noted that there may be occasions when people with IDs require social work intervention to protect them from harm, the nature of any intervention must be enabling, empowering, anti-discriminatory and anti-oppressive.

Intellectually disabled, racialized and minoritized women are particularly at risk of being harmed by ill-informed professionals and members of the public. Cho et al. (2013), in explaining Intersectionality, underline that people may be disadvantaged by multiple sources of oppression based on markers such as race, disability, gender, identity, religion and culture. "Intersectionality successfully exposes *these* [emphasis added] socially constructed borders of experience and goes on to detail the destructive negative consequences of separated categories (Nayak, 2015:90)." In this chapter, the impact of racist and disablist processes will be deconstructed, exposing the need for an intersectional approach in anti-racist social work. It is worth noting that an intersectional approach that focuses on the categories of difference outside geo-political context and positionality is inadequate in shifting the interests of those in positions of power. Intersectionality when applied as a totalizing theoretical construct falls into the fallacy of binaries which functions as a tool for regulation and control of those in subject positions (Nayak et al., 2019).

Case study part 1

An Integrated Health and Social Care Team has allocated a Social Worker and an Intellectual Disability Nurse to work with a family following a referral from the Forced Marriage Unit. The Forced Marriage Unit is a British Border Agency unit which leads on the government's forced marriage policy, outreach and casework. The Social Worker and Intellectual Disability Nurse are informed of the following.

Rahia is a 21-year-old woman with intellectual disabilities who lives with her mother Shagufta and 12-year-old younger brother Amjad. Rahia has been assessed by a court appointed Clinical Psychologist as having a severe intellectual disability with an Intelligence Quotient (IQ) score of 34. She has also been assessed as being unable to consent to marriage. She was referred to the Forced Marriage Unit following an application made to the British Border Agency for a Spousal Visa for the man whom she married following a recent holiday to Pakistan. The courts have requested that an assessment be carried out to determine Rahia's understanding regarding the acts of marriage. Rahia and Shagufta both cannot speak English, a Mirpuri interpreter is required when working with them. They have both been relying on Amjad to read letters sent to the family home. There is a history of professionals arriving at the home for pre-arranged appointments and being unable to gain access into the home. Shagufta has declined an offer for Rahia to attend a day service for people with intellectual disabilities. Rahia and Shagufta's passports have been confiscated by order from the courts to safeguard Rahia from the likelihood of being taken to Pakistan to meet the man she married. The Anti-Social Behaviour, Crime and Policing Act (2014) made it a criminal offence in England, Wales and Scotland to force someone to marry, with a possible prison sentence of up to seven years. According to the United Kingdom's Foreign, Commonwealth & Development Office (2022), the definition of Forced Marriage includes:

- taking someone overseas to force them to marry (whether or not the forced marriage takes place)
- marrying someone who lacks the mental capacity to consent to the marriage (whether they are pressured to or not).

Intersections of gender, disability and race

Rahia had been assessed by a court appointed Clinical Psychologist as having a severe ID with an IQ score of 34. This score suggested that she lacked the mental capacity to consent to marriage, thereby placing her marriage under the category of a forced marriage. The Mental Capacity Act (2005) dictates that assessments of mental capacity be decision specific, as such if Rahia desired to get married again in the future, another assessment of her mental capacity would be conducted. In the United Kingdom ID is diagnosed using normed, standardized tests which are geared towards people with a Eurocentric background (Udonsi, 2022). The outcome of these tests may have a lasting impact on an individual's life for the rest of their lives as once a diagnosis is given, it is rarely ever revised. The diagnosis of an ID hinges on the definition of intelligence, of which there is no universally agreed standard. Intelligence is measured and described in diverse ways according to cultural interpretations and prevalent thinking within a particular time (Sternberg et al., 2001). Sternberg et al. (2001) caution that although IQ scores can be a useful indicator of academic ability, an IQ score cannot be used to predict a person's ability in other aspects of their lives. Tuffrey-Wijne (2013) recommends that an assessment of a person's ID should be situated within their usual contexts, social environment, culture and what is typical for their peers in similar contexts. Rodgers and Namaganda (2005) echo these recommendations and further state that a person's capacity to understand information being presented to them will be influenced by their life experiences and whether they are interested in the assessment process. Rahia's IQ assessment was undertaken by a stranger who did not understand her cultural context, nor the type of education that she had received in her country of birth. It is important to note that a person with ID can develop functionally over time when exposed to appropriate support. There are assumptions that IDs cause mental incompetence which in turn leads to physical incompetence, thereby justifying the need to control and regulate disabled people (Phillips, 2007). There is a notable lack of bespoke, personalized relationships and sexuality education which leads to a lack of self-determination for women with IDs (Fish, 2017).

> Rahia eventually learnt about the female anatomy, relationships, sexually transmitted infections and how to exercise her rights and choices in the expression of her sexuality.

If this education intervention had not been commenced by two racialized women, she would have been harmed by a racist system through IQ testing which was not suitable for her cultural paradigm. Rahia's assigned Clinical Psychologist and other professionals around her would have been appalled at the suggestion that she was experiencing racism at their hands. Racism is not necessarily always made manifest as personal, overt prejudice. Critical race theory suggests that because racism is defined so narrowly, "white people have little to no language to discuss racism as a systematic and widespread ideology (Wesp et al., 2018:321)." It is therefore crucial to bear witness, call out racism and sit with the discomfort of the realization that one may be part of a system that is causing harm to racialized people as part of the global system of post-colonialism (Harrison, 2022).

Post-colonial feminism combines anti-racist post-colonial and feminist theories to challenge political, economic and social environments that continue to oppress women (Wesp et al., 2018). There is an acknowledgement that historical colonial systems continue to disempower women globally. Rahia was born with a speech impediment which affected the fluency of her speech. Her IQ assessment was administered by a white male Clinical Psychologist with the support of an Urdu interpreter. Rahia and her family however spoke Mirpuri which is a different dialect from Urdu. Furthermore, as the Clinical Psychologist and the interpreter were not familiar with Rahia's particular speech pattern and disfluency, they were not able to accurately interpret her verbal responses. There may be a discrepancy in a person's expressive and receptive communication skills. Rahia had excellent receptive skills but difficulties with expressive communication because of a speech impediment. Assumptions were then made about the severity of her ID. There was no use of accessible forms of communication which is a recommendation when working with people with IDs (Van der Gaag, 1998). Total Communication is a recommended strategy which uses complementary signs, symbols, pictures, photographs, objects of reference and speech to enhance verbal comprehension and improve expressive language ability (Van der Gaag, 1998). Total Communication may be extended to the use of information technology, drama, mime, art and other forms of visual communication. The absence of a Total Communication approach in Rahia's assessment amounted to disability discrimination.

Rahia experienced fear and distress triggered by the communication from the Forced Marriage Unit and adult social care services that her mother may have broken the law and was at a risk of incarceration. As minoritized immigrants, Rahia and her family may have already been carrying intergenerational fear. Ellis (2021) points to the theory of implicit memories whereby trauma is transmitted from historical colonial oppression. Eckhart Tolle (as cited in Amen, 2020) explains,

> there is such a thing as an old emotional pain living inside of you. It is an accumulation of painful life experience that was not fully faced and accepted in the moment it arose. It leaves behind an energy form of emotional pain.
>
> *(82)*

Humans operate on a three-system Model of Emotions, the threat, drive and soothing systems (Beaumont et al., 2022). The threat system is triggered whenever one feels threatened (Beaumont et al., 2022). This results in physiological changes in the brain and body in readiness for dealing with the perceived threat. Neuroscience research has proven that thoughts and feelings occur not just in the brain but in almost every system of the body (Pert, 1997). Emotional memories are consolidated better than neutral memories (Payne et al., 2012). As such, careful attention must be paid to the fact that every encounter of oppression and intersectional racism potentially leaves racialized people traumatized. Trauma is often characterized by helplessness and loss of control whereby people become objects rather than subjects of unpredictable, stressful situations (Sar & Ozturk, 2006). These circumstances prevent the person from successfully processing and resolving the trauma without skilled intervention. The unprocessed traumatic experience leads to polarized behaviours ranging from unresponsiveness to excessive reactivity (Sar & Ozturk, 2006). In Rahia's case, she and her mother stopped opening the door to professionals. When offered a day service to ensure she had meaningful day time activities, Rahia and her mother declined. This was interpreted in some circles as further evidence that Rahia was a victim of abuse at home. Yuval-Davis (2006) notes that for a migrant family to feel like they belong in any country, they must first feel safe in that environment. When you are threatened by legal processes that seem to vilify your cultural beliefs and choices, it becomes impossible to feel like you are welcome in that community. Once women with IDs are frightened and no longer feel safe, only trauma informed, post-colonial feminist, anti-racist interventions will make a positive difference to their lives.

Rahia and her family had arrived in the United Kingdom when she was 16 years old. Soon after arrival, her father had died leaving her mother to raise her and her brother as a lone parent reliant on welfare benefits. As a migrant family, they did not have a network of support to lean on or reach out to for confidential advice. By the time they became known to Social Services and the courts they had already experienced a considerable number of losses. Barnes and Rowe (2008) explain loss as the experience of separation from a person or something of significant value. Rahia lost her full citizenship status when her family migrated to the UK. Furthermore, the diagnosis of an ID meant the loss of her self-determination and right to marry without being questioned. For women with IDs, each life change they experience is usually accompanied by losses which require internal and external adaptations (Murray, 2001). This suggests that both psychological and social adjustments are required to cope with their losses. Furthermore, the significance of a loss is subjectively determined by the affected individual and not external sources (Murray, 2001). The impact of what carers and professionals may deem to be a small loss might in fact result in devastating grief reactions. In Rahia's context, she had lost her father, the family bread winner and source of wisdom on how to navigate the new cultural context of the United Kingdom. At the point of her involvement with adult social care, she lost the right to self-determination and the right to a private family life. It is acknowledged that Social Workers have a crucial role in the safeguarding of women and young people especially as related to immigration contexts and harmful practices such as forced marriage or gender-based violence (Siddiqui & Thiara, 2019). However, Social Workers may at times be used as agents of the United Kingdom's border agency and state oppression (Siddiqui & Thiara, 2019). As such Intersectionality as a practice theory must always be acknowledged and applied to practice scenarios by Social Workers (Siddiqui & Thiara, 2019).

Case study part 2

Rahia is allocated to Community ID Nurse Noma who sends a letter to the family home introducing herself. An appointment letter is also sent out in English. Noma is aware that Mirpuri is not a written language and as such the appointment letter cannot be translated into Mirpuri. She asks a colleague who speaks the Mirpuri dialect to telephone Shagufta to explain the referral and proposed ID Team involvement. Shagufta agrees for a visit to take place in the family home. Noma requests for a Mirpuri interpreter, specifically stating that a female Mirpuri speaking worker was required. Two days before the arranged appointment, the Interpreter Services manager emails to say there are a limited number of Mirpuri-speaking women as such a male worker would be allocated. Noma replies that a male worker would not be acceptable for the visit. On the day of the visit, an Urdu-speaking worker is assigned by the Interpreter Services manager as most Mirpuri speakers would be able to understand Urdu. Noma refuses to proceed with the visit and requests for her Mirpuri-speaking colleague to explain to the family that the appointment needs to be re-arranged. Eventually, a Mirpuri-speaking interpreter is assigned. The Nurse works with the same interpreter for the duration of the intervention to ensure consistency and the building of rapport with Rahia and her family. The interpreter has the same cultural background as Rahia, whilst the Nurse is from another racially minoritized context.

The practice of routinely sending people letters in the English language even when it is known that they speak a different language is an example of the lack of acknowledgement of minoritized people in the UK. Furthermore, Health and Social Care services as well as the Criminal Justice System discriminated against Rahia and her mother by denying them access to an interpreter who could speak their language. They were left bewildered and anxious by court processes, unable to fully comprehend the trajectory of the legal proceedings. The devastating results of oppression are usually hidden to those who hold more power and privilege (Afuape, 2011).

Rahia and her family were able to feel safe and to articulate their views to the two minoritized women who were working as their Nurse and interpreter. It is important to have collective knowledge from communities of women coming together to initiate the painful and often traumatic conversations about racism (Hon-Sing Wong, 2019; Harrison, 2022). No further divisions should be created between women, instead there should be an acknowledgement that interlocking oppressions are the result of common historical and political processes (Collins, 2000). The dynamics of the power shifted for Rahia compared to when she was allocated people who were not attentive to her cultural context. Cultural fluency refers to the understanding and use of elements from different cultures for the purpose of communication (Carter & Carter, 2021). It enables the communicator to convey meaning across cultures, and the receiver to understand messages as they are intended (Carter & Carter, 2021).

Case study part 3

Noma (female ID Nurse) and Farah (female Mirpuri interpreter) visit Rahia and Shagufta at home. Noma booked Farah for two hours so that they could spend the first hour discussing the referral, including culturally appropriate ways for discussing relationships and sexuality. Farah explains to Noma that what is referred to as Mirpuri in the United Kingdom is known as the Pahari-Pothwari language by the Mirpuri community. It is the second largest mother tongue in the United Kingdom. Farah explains that culturally women do not discuss sex and sexuality in the detail which the courts would like Rahia to be assessed for. Farah explains that certain English words which describe parts of the female anatomy have no direct translation in Pahari-Pothwari. Shagufta and Rahia express their joy at meeting Farah who speaks the same dialect as them. They recount how they have not met an interpreter throughout the meetings that they have had with services who was able to speak their dialect. They could not understand many of the things that had been said to them so far. They are frightened as their passports have been confiscated. Shagufta's 92-year-old mother is extremely ill in Azad Kashmir. Shagufta would have wanted to go and visit her before she dies. They don't know if they will ever get their passports back. They are happy that Noma and Farah are going to be supporting them throughout the court process. Rahia has a speech impediment but can express herself when given enough time to speak. She is looking forward to learning about relationships and sexuality as she never went to school much as a young child. Shagufta's warns that sexually explicit discussions would be sinful according to her Islamic faith.

Disabling, racist environments

There are legal and policy stipulations that mandate public services to ensure that reasonable adjustments are made to environments to ensure that they are accessible to disabled people. In England, the Equality Act (2010) enshrines these principles in law. Public Health England (2020) reiterates this and extends the guidance to encourage forward planning so that potential oppressive, disabling barriers are anticipated and addressed without disadvantaging disabled people. In the context of the case study under review, the question arises as to the accessibility of the court processes. Rahia was assessed whilst in a state of what Mantell and Clark (2008) term "information deprivation," whereby she had no access to the information which she needed to make important life choices. Furthermore, this deprivation led to wrong labels being given to her, thereby limiting her life experiences even further.

Modern scholars are often in agreement on the fact that race is a social construct that has no biological basis (Ellis, 2021). Racism can be defined as "the local and global power system structured and maintained by persons who classify themselves as white, whether consciously or sub-consciously determined; this system consists of patterns of perception, logic, symbol formation, thought, speech, action and emotional response (Welsing 1991:2)." These patterns of perception that perpetuate the marginalization of racialized people may not be discernible to the person with IDs; however, they cause their environments to become more disabling and oppressive (Udonsi, 2022). Rahia could not discern that being given an interpreter she could not fully understand was discriminatory, oppressive and unjust. Ellis (2021:76) observes that "by design, the race construct also dials down empathy towards people of colour and, the darker you are, the more empathy is dialled down." As a Muslim woman of Asian heritage, Rahia was seen as a victim of an oppressive culture and thereby needing state intervention (Bibi, 2019). There is a paradoxical scenario whereby in seeking to save Muslim women from their perceived oppression, they are oppressed and denied their personhood (Bibi, 2019). Once Rahia was given an interpreter who spoke her dialect, respected her cultural perspectives and an ID Nurse who was able to teach her accessible relationships and sexuality content, it became apparent that she did not have a severe ID. Professionals who work with people with IDs ought to be conscious of the extent of the power that they wield over the people they are assessing. The incorrect labelling of Rahia as being severely disabled had the potential to sentence her to the prison of being treated as a perpetual child with no capacity to engage in intimate relationships or live as a full citizen. Often people who are intellectually disabled are treated as asexual and having no desire or right to seek out non-platonic relationships.

It is essential that Social Workers do not engage in surface-level interventions where assumptions remain unpicked and interlocking oppressions remain unchallenged (Hon-Sing Wong, 2019). There must be an acknowledgment that social work is built upon sociopolitical structures that favour the maintenance of white privilege (Tascon & Gatwiri, 2020). As such, every social work intervention must be seen as an opportunity for actively contributing to the pulling down of racist, oppressive structures. Cultural humility is essential in anti-racist, anti-oppressive social work. Tervalon and Murray-García (1998:123) define cultural humility as "a lifelong commitment to self-evaluation and critique, to redressing power imbalances and to developing mutually beneficial and non-paternalistic partnerships with communities on behalf of individuals and defined populations." An emancipatory approach is advisable whereby there is a respect for diversity in values, traditions and practices when working within minoritized communities (Wesp et al., 2018). Müller (2021), commenting on the European Union's anti-racism action plan for 2020–2025, notes the devaluing of racialized people through stereotyping based on prejudice. It is imperative to maintain a continuous recognition that encounters with individuals from a particular cultural group do not justify generalizations about the lived experiences of the entire cultural group to which they belong.

Conclusion

Disabled women may encounter instances of injustice perpetuated by well-intentioned health and social care professionals when presumptions are made regarding their perceived incompetence (Fish, 2017). The intersecting forms of oppression become particularly apparent among impoverished women, a group that often includes women with IDs due to their limited opportunities for income generation and wealth accumulation (Zack, 2005). It is crucial to move beyond neoliberal ideologies that fail to recognize the essential non-marketized roles that intellectually disabled women fulfil within their communities (Goodley & Runswick-Cole, 2011). A person-centred and nuanced approach is necessary to shift the barriers of prejudice, eugenics, ableism and inflexible assessment processes, which obstruct a comprehensive understanding of the impact of racism on women with IDs.

References

Afuape, T. (2011). *Power, Resistance and Liberation in Therapy with Survivors of Trauma: To Have Our Hearts Broken*. Taylor & Francis Group. Retrieved from https://ebookcentral.proquest.com/lib/salford/detail.action?docID=735289

Amen, D. G. (2020). *The End of Mental Illness*. Tyndale House Publishers.

Anti-Social Behaviour, Crime and Policing Act (2014). Retrieved March 28, 2023 from https://www.legislation.gov.uk/ukpga/2014/12/contents/enacted

Barnes, M., & Rowe, J. (2008). *Child, Youth and Family Health: Strengthening Communities* (2nd Edition). Chatswood: Elsevier Australia.

Beaumont, E., Irons, C., & McAndrew, S. (2022). A Qualitative Study Exploring the Impact the Self-Compassion App Has on Levels of Compassion, Self-Criticism, and Wellbeing. *OBM Integrative and Complementary Medicine*, 7(3), 23. Retrieved from https://lidsen.com/journals/icm/icm-07-03-045

Bibi, R. (2019). Gendered Islamophobia – Intersectionality, Religion and Space for British South Asian Muslim Women. In Nayak, S. & Robbins, R. (Eds.), *Intersectionality in Social Work: Activism and Practice in Context*. Abingdon: Routledge, pp. 63–76.

Carter, L., & Carter, A. (2021). Serving Adult Learners from International Backgrounds at Two Canadian Universities. In *Advances in Educational Technologies and Instructional Design* (pp. 107–131). IGI Global. https://doi.org/10.4018/978-1-7998-4360-3.ch006

Cho, S., Crenshaw, K. W., & McCall, L. (2013). Toward a Field of Intersectionality Studies. Theory, Applications, and Praxis. *Signs*, 38(4), 785–810. https://doi.org/10.1086/669608

Collins, P. H. (2000). Gender, Black Feminism, and Black Political Economy. *The Annals of the American Academy of Political and Social Science*, 568(1), 41–53. https://doi.org/10.1177/000271620056800105

Ellis, E. (2021). *The Race Conversation – An Essential Guide to Creating Life-Changing Dialogue*. Confer Books.

Equality Act (2010). Retrieved March 28, 2023 from https://www.legislation.gov.uk/ukpga/2010/15/contents

Fish, R. (2017). *A Feminist Ethnography of Secure Wards for Women with Learning Disabilities: Locked Away*. Taylor & Francis Group.

Foreign, Commonwealth & Development Office (2022). Forced Marriage – How to Protect, Advise and Support Victims of Forced Marriage – Information and Practice Guidelines for Professionals. Retrieved March 28, 2023 from https://www.gov.uk/guidance/forced-marriage

Goodley, D., & Runswick-Cole, K. (2011). The Violence of Disablism. *Sociology of Health and Illness*, 33(4), 602–617. https://doi.org/10.1111/j.1467-9566.2010.01302.x

Harrison, P. (2022). Sitting with Discomfort: Experiencing the Power of Racism and Working to Imagine Ways Forward? *Critical and Radical Social Work*, 10(2), 193–201. https://doi.org/10.1332/204986022X16248398429332

Hon-Sing Wong, E. (2019). The Detachment of Intersectionality from Its Black Feminist Roots – A Critical Analysis of Social Service Provision Training Material Based in Ontario. In S. Nayak & R. Robbins (Eds.), *Intersectionality in Social Work: Activism and Practice in Context*. Routledge, pp. 37–51.

Mantell, A., & Clark, A. (2008). Making Choices: The Mental Capacity Act 2005. In A. Mantell & T. Scragg (Eds.), *Safeguarding Adults in Social Work*. Learning Matters, pp. 44–59.

MENCAP. (2022). What Is a Learning Disability? Retrieved March 28, 2023 from https://www.mencap.org.uk/learning-disability-explained/what-learning-disability

Mental Capacity Act, 2005. Retrieved March 28, 2023 from https://www.legislation.gov.uk/ukpga/2005/9/contents

Müller, C. (2021). Anti-Racism in Europe: An Intersectional Approach to the Discourse on Empowerment through the EU Anti-Racism Action Plan 2020–2025. *Social Sciences*, 10, 137. https://doi.org/10.3390/socsci10040137

Murray, J. A. (2001). Loss as a Universal Concept: A Review of the Literature to Identify Common Aspects of Loss in Diverse Situations. *Journal of Loss & Trauma*, 6(3), 219–241. https://doi.org/10.1080/108114401753201679

Nayak, S. (2015). *The Activism of Black Feminist Theory: Race, Gender and Social Change*. Abingdon: Routledge.

Nayak, S. (2019). Black Feminist Diaspora Spaces of Social Work Critical Reflexivity. In R. A. Maglajlic, R. Larkin, & L. Wroe (Eds.), *Social Work with Asylum Seekers, Refugees and Undocumented People: Going the Extra Mile*. London: Jessica Kingsley Publishers, pp. 41–56.

Nayak, S., Montenegro, M., & Pujol, J. (2019). Conclusion: Contextual Intersectionality – A Conversation. In S. Nayak, & R. Robbins (Eds.), *Intersectionality in Social Work – Activism and Practice in Context*. London: Routledge Taylor & Francis Group, pp. 230–250.

Payne, J. D., Chambers, A. M., & Kensinger, E. A. (2012). Sleep Promotes Lasting Changes in Selective Memory for Emotional Scenes. *Frontiers in Integrative Neuroscience*, 6, Article 108. https://doi.org/10.3389/fnint.2012.00108

Pert, C. B. (1997). *Molecules of Emotion – Why You Feel the Way You Feel*. London: Simon and Schuster UK Ltd.

Phillips, D. (2007). Embodied Narratives: Control, Regulation and Body Resistance in the Life Course of Older Women with Learning Difficulties. *European Review of History – Revue Europeenne d'Histoire*, 14, 503–524.

Public Health England (2020). *People with Learning Disabilities in England – Safeguarding*. London. Retrieved March 28, 2023 from https://www.gov.uk/government/publications/people-with-learning-disabilities-in-england/chapter-3-safeguarding

Rodgers, J., & Namaganda, S. (2005). Making Information Easier for People with Learning Disabilities. *British Journal of Learning Disabilities*, 33, 52–58. https://doi-org.salford.idm.oclc.org/10.1111/j.1468-3156.2005.00341.x

Sar, V., & Ozturk, E. (2006). What Is Trauma and Dissociation? *Journal of Trauma Practice*, 4(1–2), 7–20. https://doi.org/10.1300/J189v04n01_02

Siddiqui, H., & Thiara, R. K. (2019). Returning Home – Intersectionality, Social Work and Violence against BME Women and Girls in the UK. In S. Nayak, & R. Robbins (Eds.), *Intersectionality in Social Work: Activism and Practice in Context*. Abingdon: Routledge, pp. 23–36.

Spitzer, R. L., & Endicott, J. (2018). Medical and Mental Disorder: Proposed Definition and Criteria. *Annales Médico-psychologiques, revue psychiatrique*, 176(7), 656–665. https://doi.org/10.1016/j.amp.2018.05.009

Sternberg, R. J., Grigorenko, E. L., & Bundy, D. A. (2001). The Predictive Value of IQ. *Merrill-Palmer Quarterly*, 47(1), 1–41. Retrieved from https://www.jstor.org/stable/23093686

Tascon, S., & Gatwiri, K. (2020). Towards Cultural Humility: Theorising Cultural Competence as Institutionalised Whiteness. *Beyond "Cultural Competency": Confronting Whiteness in Social Work*, 3(1), 1–16. Retrieved from https://openjournals.library.sydney.edu.au/SWPS/article/view/14406

Tervalon, M., & Murray-Garcia, J. (1998). Cultural Humility Versus Cultural Competence: A Critical Distinction in Defining Physician Training Outcomes in Multicultural Education. *Journal of Health Care for the Poor and Underserved*, 9(2), 117–125. Retrieved from https://nhchc.org/wp-content/uploads/2020/01/Cultural-Humility-vs-Cultural-Compentence.pdf

Tuffrey-Wijne, I. (2013). *How to Break Bad News to People with Intellectual Disabilities – A Guide for Carers and Professionals*. London: Jessica Kingsley Publishers.

Udonsi, P. (2022). Young, Gifted and Black: The Intersectionality of Race, Intellectual Disability and Neurodivergence. *Critical and Radical Social Work*, 10(2), 226–241. Retrieved September 30, 2022 from https://bristoluniversitypressdigital.com/view/journals/crsw/10/2/article-p226.xml

Van der Gaag, A. (1998). Communication Skills and Adults with Learning Disabilities: Eliminating Professional Myopia. *British Journal of Learning Disabilities*, 26, 88–93. Retrieved from https://onlinelibrary-wiley-com.salford.idm.oclc.org/doi/abs/10.1111/j.1468-3156.1998.tb00057.x?casa_token=6f9TwnqOh9IAAAAA:CBVg0EF4ywj9wCmx1vSzEMH3zK6YYGAD4NwVCKq7qRevCByJfCoemNoqU8u9w6iY9FoWfD_GEvUKvSs

Welsing, F. C. (1991). *The Isis Papers: The Keys to the Colours*. Chicago, IL: Third World Press.

Wesp, Scheer, V., Ruiz, A., Walker, K., Weitzel, J., Shaw, L., Kako, P. M., & Mkandawire-Valhmu, L. (2018). An Emancipatory Approach to Cultural Competency: The Application of Critical Race, Postcolonial, and Intersectionality Theories. *Advances in Nursing Science*, 41(4): 316–326. https://doi.org/10.1097/ANS.0000000000000230

Yuval-Davis, N. (2006) Belonging and the Politics of Belonging. *Patterns of Prejudice*, 40(3). Retrieved from https://static1.squarespace.com/static/5ad0d247af209613040b9ceb/t/5dfab3c7d013c3671da814e2/1576711111979/document-7.pdf

Zack, N. (2005). *Inclusive Feminism: A Third Wave Theory of Women's Commonality*. Lanham, MD: Rowman & Littlefield Publishers, Inc.

5
PRIVILEGING INDIGENOUS KNOWLEDGE AND WISDOM AS FEMINIST SOCIAL WORK PRACTITIONERS

Péta Phelan and Bindi Bennett

Introduction

Colonial Feminism exists within inherent proximity to and reliance upon the Colonial Patriarchy, from which it has always drawn much of its position and power. Colonial patriarchal structures, systems, and modes of operation – the centring, privileging, and enforcement of white supremacist, cisgendered, heteronormative, ableist, and capitalist knowledges, worldviews, and existences – ensure that the perspectives and wisdom of Indigenous Peoples is denied, included only as an afterthought, dismissed as novelty, or ignored and excluded altogether (Fredericks, 2010). In cases where Indigenous knowledge *is* prioritised, it is almost exclusively done so as an act of mining, extraction, appropriation, and exploitation, from which the colonial agent derives social and/or economic benefit. Imperative to the pursuit of *authentic* social justice as foundational to the social work profession, is the centring and privileging of Indigenous Feminist and intersectional narratives, perspectives, and wisdoms as primary mechanism of progressive and ethical disciplinary practice.

Since the late 1980s and into the 1990s, Feminist theory has begun to recognise how nationality, race, class, sexuality, and ethnicity form intersections of differentiation for women (Suzack et al., 2010). In Australia, Feminism has been used to label a wide range of political views with the goal of empowering women from Patriarchy, sexism, and male domination. However, it has been grounded in white, middle-classed, privileged, ableist, cisgendered thought (Moradi & Grzanka, 2017). The oppressions of Bla(c)k women are not interchangeable with that of dominant, privileged white women. As white women seek to struggle against (and overthrow) male domination and Patriarchy, the tenants of Bla(c)k/Blak[*1] Feminism are a return to 'traditional', 'native', or Indigenous ways of knowing, doing, and being (Martin & Mirraboopa, 2003). This wisdom, in existence for over 80,000 years and replete with Indigenous cultural values and systems (Grey, 2004), essentially demands the re-structuring of colonisation and all that it represents.

Indigenous women, their lives, and experiences are still unrecognised or obscured in overwhelmingly dominant contemporary Feminist theory. "Women have been a footnote in [a] male-defined system. And if women are the footnote, then Aboriginal women are the footnote to the footnote" (Patricia Monture, as cited in Boulton, 2003: par. 4). Indigenous women and peoples with multidimensional identities such as those that are (i) queer (e.g., lesbian, bisexual, pansexual, asexual), (ii) gender diverse (e.g., intersex, transgender, non-binary, genderqueer), (iii) have a disability (e.g., intellectual, physical, sensory, psychological), and (iv) other factors (e.g., class, religion, 'criminality') are even further marginalised, oppressed, and omitted. This chapter seeks to fortify *already existent* conversations in and of the dismantling and re-writing of Feminism; one considerate, allied, and inclusive of Indigenous Peoples, Feminisms, and wisdoms, and, in unrelenting pursuit to decolonise Feminism, social work, and the colonies.

Indigenous Feminisms

Indigenous Feminisms exist uniquely and separately, beyond Western patriarchal perceptions, location, or grasp, despite the intentioned and meticulous interference by colonisation and its agents. Anciently conscious and animate in Australia, and at least 80,000 years in its development and practice (Ingman & Gyllensten, 2003; Larnach, 1974), they locate personhood in relationship to a complex paradigm of existence; kinship, community, Country, and culture (Martin & Mirraboopa, 2003). Indigenous Feminism is inherently anti-colonial and anti-patriarchal, anchoring it in anti-white supremacist, anti-racist, anti-cisheteronormative, anti-ableist, and anti-capitalist practices by all who operate from within this paradigm. These practices are amongst the oldest in human communities and are rooted in cosmology, a way of life that deems all beings as relations, or the concept that *we are all related* (Arabena, 2008; Graham, 1999).

Indigenous worldviews are wholistic, with each element/being existent within, considered deeply interconnected and interdependent (Graham, 1999). This contrasts significantly with Western Eurocentric paradigms that are conceived and mechanised in fundamentally dualistic ways, where the *natural world* and all that exists and operates within is constructed into separate and mutually antagonistic pairs (e.g., human/nature, body/mind, rational/emotional, male/female, light/dark, life/death, active/passive, individual/society). Within this framework, every element is in *opposition* to its counterpart, and, ranked within a hierarchy, each dominant/superior element of the dualistic pair perceives itself as without any dependence on the submissive/inferior pair (Plumwood, 2002). In this pursuit to categorise and rank, the dualistic worldview produces and sustains domination and competition between individuals and social classes, and between humanity and its environment (Ruuska et al., 2020). It is in the unyielding alignment, sustainment, and progression of this worldview that harms are not only righteously validated, affirmed, and justified but deeply authorised and enforced as essential in the pursuit of legitimate *civilisation* and *human* evolution.

Indigenous worldviews offer the potential to reilluminate, reauthorise, and centre wisdom that has been concealed or erased by universally dominating, destructive/harmful, *power-over* patriarchal modes of being. Indigenous wisdom provides consciousness and *being* that inspires examination, re-imagining, and transformation of communities and societies that have long accepted, sustained, and replicated, self-injurious and self-destructive patriarchal modes of existing. Indigenous wisdom must be seen as metamorphic, informing, advisory, and necessary in the new wave of Feminism, to empower the generation of significant impact in subverting the Colonial Patriarchy and revolutionising the World.

Colonialism and Patriarchy are interconnected systems that have influenced and reinforced each other throughout history, including contemporarily (Arvin et al., 2013; Spencer-Wood, 2016). While they are distinct forms of oppression, they have operated overwhelmingly in tandem and mutually reinforced one another (Baskin, 2020; Moane, 1999). Under The Doctrine of Discovery, which established and validated a religious, political, and legal justification for colonisation, the seizure and dispossession of land not inhabited by Christians, patricentric religion played a dominant and momentous role in colonisation around the world (Behrendt, 2010; Watson, 2010). Indigenous Feminism has arisen from Indigenous women's activism from and within their culture and has been aimed at securing social justice and equity for Indigenous women (Moreton-Robinson, 2021). Indigenous women share the experience of the collusion between the (overwhelmingly Christian) Patriarchy and colonisation, where worldwide it has removed Indigenous women from positions of power and taken and exerted control over Indigenous women's bodies and roles (Suzack et al., 2010). It has historically and continues to remove, abduct, exploit, rape, incarcerate, and murder Indigenous women, and all whom it deems *non-male*. This includes not only those whom it *traditionally* identifies and categorises as girls and women, but people who exist as transgender, non-binary, and homosexual (Holmes et al., 2015; Lugones, 2016). Indigenous Feminism seeks to root out systems of Colonialism, cisheteropatriarchy, and racism that serve settler nations and societies, with poignant implications for Indigenous, Bla(c)k, women/people of colour, and those with other marginalised identities (Arvin et al., 2013).

Although we have presented a neat couple of paragraphs about Indigenous Feminism, colonisation tends to want ideas to fit into nice small, digestible portions. We argue that there are hundreds of multiple, varied, complex ideas, realities, and experiences of Indigenous Feminism. As social work allies, to be bound with Indigenous Feminism, social workers must investigate and educate themselves about the (i) local and national history of the area they live and work, (ii) Indigenous social, political, cultural, and spiritual lives, and (iii) multidimensional identities of Indigenous women, and those they may know as colleagues and friends. Only then can we raise them to accurately represent their views.

The historic and continued colonial project, Feminism, and social work

Alongside a myriad of other human-centred services professions (i.e., medicine, law, education), social work has a long-standing history of violence towards Indigenous Peoples (Fejo-King, 2014). Deployment of these professional disciplines has done inexplicable harm to Indigenous populations through the enforcement, sustainment, and perpetuation of weaponised practices, forged in the fires of colonial ideology (Phelan & Oxley, 2021). Social work has also contributed to and endorsed a universalised women's experience, when in fact, Indigenous women are at far greater risk of marginalisation, criminalisation, violence, and death than non-Indigenous women (Drever, 2022; McGuire & Murdoch, 2022). Additionally, social work itself has not engaged well (or at all) with the vast complexities of *Intersectionality*; where the interlocking of minority identities compounds in individuals or groups to produce further marginalisation and harm (Seng et al., 2012). Expanding upon the assumption that Intersectionality is only about identity, the theory and practice extends into broader spheres such as relationality, social context, power relations, complexity, social justice, and inequalities (Hopkins, 2019). Predominantly inhabited by white women, social work has likewise not found an answer to *white fragility* and *white victimhood*

(Phipps, 2021) and the harm of such dominating and pervasive *colonial* liabilities found within its profession. What, then, does social work need to do to redeem any of this?

Sandy Grande (2003) describes 'Indigena' as a public life and standpoint that presumes decolonisation as a central tenet of Indigenous Feminism. What does decolonisation mean to Feminists? Does it mean radical theoretical, value, and skill intervention? Critical interrogation and discursive structures? Recreation of Feminist knowledge production? Attacking neo-colonial ideas? Is decolonisation possible in a colonised country such as Australia, where the settlers are unlikely to go *home*? What happens to Feminism when Indigenous peoples are collective and not individual? Given this, is decolonisation a buzzword? Is it useful for social work? Is it the concept in Australia?

In a neoliberal country like Australia, does the catchphrase 'the political is personal' have a role in Indigenous Feminism? Language is always important. First Nations Peoples are focussed on core values of relational reciprocity and inclusion of all ages and genders. Indigenous Feminist scholarship calls into question notions of tradition that originate from and bolster colonial settler intents. Indigenous sociologists and Indigenous Feminist scholars address connections between racialisation, Colonialism, disenfranchisement, and Patriarchy as foundational to understanding reproductions of unequal social relations (Arvin et al., 2013; Meissner & Whyte, 2017).

The ideas of 'matriarchal' and 'patriarchal' are Western frameworks and thus not helpful in describing the nuanced gender relations in Aboriginal societies (Grey, 2004). Colonisation is intentionally structured to attack the links/bonds/structures between Indigenous men and women (via prison, suicide, untimely and early deaths, and Stolen Generations, portraying all Aboriginal men as paedophiles; see the Northern Territory Intervention [Altman, 2018]) which leads to ongoing marginalisation, systemic racisms, alienation, and inequities. These structures shape our psychological attitudes towards women, creating situations where First Nations Peoples are taken from their autonomy, cultural supports, and connections and fed into mistreatment and other secondary effects (i.e., prison, domestic violence, substance use/dependencies) (Fernandez, 2003; Martin-Hill, 2003).

For many years, social work has been guilty of imposing pervasive and unrelenting colonial existential immersion within its *program*. When social work and Feminism are theorised and constructed from within the Western colonising universe, they can only ever replicate, perpetuate, and sustain what they are built and animated from. Regardless of moderate (or even radical) positioning by white/colonial Feminism – away from, in defiance of, or antagonistic to the Western Patriarchy – the substance and materiel of social work remain innately *colonially* constructed. Consequently, Western Eurocentric Feminism within social work is inherently flimsy and susceptible to co-option, manipulation, and weaponisation by the Patriarchy, and that which, or those whom, are powerfully positioned at its pinnacle. To begin to undo this damage, it is vital to expose the intrinsic reproduction of colonial Western Eurocentric theories and practices; those that "establish a sociopolitical structure of affects that (it) positions as universal, concrete, and true" (Garcia-Rojas, 2017, p. 255).

Gender, sexuality, disability, criminality, and Feminism

Meekosha (2011, p. 671) states that the "fundamental business of colonisation involved structural, cultural, economic and political domination". It directs this power via the *bodies* (physical, psychological, spiritual, environmental) of Indigenous Peoples, by "displacing them, alienating them, dispossessing them from their native lands, commodifying them, regulating them, extracting their labor, killing them, and using them as a means for colonisers' ends" (Manjapra, 2020, p. 201). To inform, validate, and absolve such widespread and devastating abuses, colonisation brought a *moral* strategy and coinciding frameworks, built on perceived *unshakable* foundations of religious doctrine (Miller, 2010; Tuck & Yang, 2021). These ideologies intentionally categorise and restrict peoples into binaries of gender and sexuality, ability, civility, production, and *humanness*, replete with consequent acts of *all-encompassing*, violent enforcement (Moreton-Robinson, 2011). Embedded with social and institutional mechanisms of self-replication, and deployed as assimilatory processes, colonising practices have been unceasing in their resolve to deform, replace, and erase cultural ways of knowing, doing, and being (Day, 2021; O'Sullivan, 2021).

The sites of colonial incursion have interfaced with every aspect of Indigenous cultures. Yet, despite the historical and ongoing brutality, violence, and genocide/s, Indigenous cultures (including elements of gender, sexuality, and functional embodiment) have and continue to resist translation as much as they resist erasure (Picq & Tikuna, 2019). If language is the essence of culture, within an Australian context, before 1788, there were approximately 250 languages and 800 dialects spoken (Nicholls, 2001). Non-Indigenous Feminism must acknowledge, understand, and reconcile with the wisdom embodied in Indigenous languages, many thousands of years old. Indigenous languages conceive a world without Western patriarchal coding and categorisation, illuminating sites, spaces, ways of being and existing that Western/white Feminism continues to struggle with. Like many Indigenous languages around the world (Picq & Tikuna, 2019) in Australia, "many, if not all, Aboriginal languages ... do not have gendered third-person pronouns" (Coleman, 2020).

Aldrich et al. (1993) provide valuable insights into the incongruence and incompetency of early colonial accounts of gender and sexuality in Australian Aboriginal societies. Garcia-Rojas (2017) speaks to the presence and significance of lesbian and queer women of colour Feminists, affirming their powerful theoretical and activist contributions to the unsettling refusal of colonial Feminism. Unlike Western Eurocentric Feminism, Indigenous Feminisms encapsulate an understanding of gender that is radically anti-colonial.

> First Nations cultures worldwide have always recognised and celebrated diverse genders that do not conform to colonial understandings of gender. Trans and gender-diverse people have been and continue to be a part of every First Nations population worldwide, including here in so-called '*Australia*'.
>
> *(Moon, 2020, n.p.)*

'Mainstream' Feminisms are historically founded in and operate from a male/female gender binary, with 'whitestream' cisheteronormative Feminism, having been entirely theorised and established by cisgender white women from the Global North (Weerawardhana, 2018). This paradigmatic position is comprehensively dislocated from Indigenous ways of knowing, doing, and being – existences *beyond* the colonial obsession with binary.

Although there is currently a dearth of Indigenous transgender, non-binary, or genderqueer, Feminist (institutional) scholarly literature published, powerful narratives from Indigenous women weave through, strengthen, and galvanise Indigenous Feminisms. In her essay 'Aboriginal Feminism and Gender', Noongar woman Claire Coleman writes

> We have no direct evidence that cultural transgenderism or homosexuality existed in Australia when white people came and missionaries enforced their notions of gender

and sexuality, nor have we evidence that such a thing did not exist. Cultural and religious prejudices shared by the people recording the information would have ensured that anything not fitting in with their prejudices would never have been collected.

(Coleman, 2020, n.p.)

Noongar sistergirl, Aunty Vanessa, speaks to her own experiences existing as Indigenous, *beyond* colonial philosophies of gender and sexuality, stating

> my understanding and acceptance of who and where I come from as an Indigenous Person first and foremost, of the fact that I am descended from the oldest surviving civilisations on Earth. I understand that my people have been through struggle and turmoil. I am able to acknowledge, just 200 hundred plus years old culture as opposed to our survival of 40, 60 or 100,000 years and that I can survive if I chose to, my struggle is a part of a bigger struggle – that is who we are as a race of people.
>
> *(Transhub, 2021, n.p.)*

Coultard-Dare (2022) speaks of the persistence and power of Indigenous trans women, particularly in the unwavering presence of colonial violence, "It's hard, but we live with it – Aboriginal and Torres Strait Islanders have been fighting for our rights since 1788, and we've been warriors all our lives" (n.p.). Existing at the intersections of race, and gender diversity, she expresses the impacts this struggle has on her life; "Living as an Indigenous person is hard. Living as a woman is hard. Living as a trans woman is hard…then putting all these together and having to face racism, sexism and transphobia is extremely tiring and mentally exhausting" (Coultard-Dare, 2022, n.p.). Clarke (2017) speaks of Indigenous trans women's presence, resistance, and of the re-telling and reclaiming of culture; "we were told to conform and forget, resulting in negative perceptions onto our existence, which we are fighting hard now to correct, (to) enhance our beautiful space in culture" (n.p.). Indigenous Feminism includes the exposure and dismantling of indoctrinated and insidiously dispersed colonial ideologies (i.e., cisheteronormativity) that can pervade and perpetuate violence in Indigenous communities "Aboriginal and queer communities need to work together to reduce stigma and decolonise our understandings of gender and sexualities" (Clarke, 2017).

Disability too was and is perceived by Indigenous Peoples' counter to colonial constructions of *body, function, and production*. Gilroy and Donelly (2016) conclude that "the generic concepts of 'disability' or 'impairment' were not recognised by any Australian Indigenous community before European colonisation" (p. 547). This is consistent with other Indigenous Peoples across the globe with Ineese-Nash (2020, p. 29) stating that "many Indigenous languages of Turtle Island (North America) have no word describing the concept of disability". Ariotti (1999) argues that different abilities are accepted, celebrated, and seen as examples of the natural diversity of humans by Australian Indigenous communities. Colonial fabrications of *disability*, therefore, are deeply considered and interrogated in Indigenous Feminist thought, practice, and activism.

Indigenous Peoples and cultures globally have been interrupted, surveyed, and examined through an unqualified and deficient *colonial* gaze, in an arrogant yet futile attempt to observe, interpret, and situate into its worldview that which it cannot recognise, perceive, or comprehend. With colonisation, came the disruption and erasure of complex Indigenous traditional law/lore, and the introduction of an imperialist criminal justice system (Staines & Scott,

2020). This legal system, a colonial arsenal built on the genocide and dispossession of Indigenous Peoples, has been designed and operated as a brutal mechanism to maintain a racist, patriarchal, and capitalist order, to violate, control, regulate, and dispose of Indigenous lives and bodies (Ananda, 2022; Mbembé & Meinjes, 2003). Foundational to this system, and critical to upholding social domination and power, has been the establishment, execution, and perpetuation of colonial violence through the prison-industrial complex (PIC). The PIC, defined as "overlapping interests of government and industry that uses surveillance, policing, and imprisonment as solutions to economic, social and political problems" (Critical Resistance, 2022, n.p.), represents the wilful collusion between colonial authorities and other powerful vested commercial interests in order to profit from the incarceration, violation, and exploitation of Bla(c)k (and other) bodies and lives it deems both productive and/or disposable (Delia Deckard, 2017; Sudbury, 2002).

Protractedly, the (white) Feminist movement has endorsed and leveraged these deeply violent structures to advocate for and enact a sense of *Feminist* justice. 'Carceral Feminism' sustains "a reliance on policing, prosecution, and imprisonment to resolve gendered or sexual violence" (Press, 2018, n.p.). Abolition Feminism, conversely, takes an intersectional and structural approach to analysing and dismantling systems of oppression. It maintains that violence, both interpersonal and structural, must be concurrently confronted to achieve social transformation, rather than commission and utilise punishment for social control (Ananda, 2022). Indigenous women and girls across the globe are imprisoned at alarming rates (Aroha Rule et al., 2021; Kendall et al., 2019). Within Australia, it is Indigenous women, trans, and non-binary people who not only "shine a light on a form of violence that carceral Feminism continues to overlook" (Watego et al., 2021, n.p.) but also lead the abolitionist movement with great endurance and ferocity. Oxley (2020, n.p.) states, "defunding the police, prison abolition, and dismantling the systems that created and continue the ongoing oppression, violence, discrimination, and the 'othering' of this country's Aboriginal and Torres Strait Islander people, is not a radical idea". In her 2022 presentation 'Abolishing the colonial carceral state is anti-racism', Lean (2022) spoke to colonial justice systems and the PIC as an elite weapon of oppression and violence, devised and wielded uncompromisingly by the colonial patriarchal State. Lean calls for a dismantling of the systems that are holding colonisation up.

> What I am proposing, is a creative process where we can sit together and imagine another world. I'm opening a portal of possibility, a space for us to dream collectively. Like the little white rabbit beckoning Alice to follow him down a rabbit hole, I'm asking you to take that step into the dreaming space with me, but in doing so you need to know that like Alice you're going to see some things that make your head spin - some things that puzzle you and some things that make you outright uncomfortable. Because for many of you, you're going to have to confront the reality that you are entirely complicit in the atrocities committed against people by the State, and many of you are beneficiaries of it also.
>
> *(Lean, 2022)*

We make the point that Indigenous Lore is not the same as colonial law. Indigenous Lore did have punishment, but it was also based in reciprocity and kinship with clear limits and boundaries to punishment that did not drain the community. Colonised systems of law are instead controlling and aimed to destroy the human, we argue.

Lean argues that many in this colonial system have (naively or unintentionally) been masters of upholding and perpetuating these exact systems (i.e., those working in child protection, prison systems, and policing systems). She argues that many of us in these systems (attesting to the inclusion of social work university lecturers) are part of the means of colonisation's controlling power. Punishment and violent machinations deliberately designed and deployed to uphold white supremacy. Thus, as social workers, to avoid complicity with such functions, Lean argues we must actively engage in resistance against the State, and its sanctioned and state-sponsored harm to truly be unified with human rights and social justice. Lean urges us to "radically rethink the place and purpose of your role as state actors" and to cease contributing to the violent responses by the state and structural social problems inflicted on Indigenous Peoples, including women and girls. Finally, she argues that we have a choice, "a choice to remain a slave to the machine, slave to the death squads that disappear my people, slave to those that seek to harm us, or you can join us in fucking shit up" (Lean, 2022). Although Lean's call is to abolish the *criminalising* structures and system, the authors call for further dismantling of all colonial systems of violence.

Anti-exploitative practice for social work

What does it mean when the tools of a racist patriarchy are used to examine the fruits of that same patriarchy? It means that only the most narrow perimeters of change are possible and allowable.

(Lorde, 2012, n.p.)

Anti-exploitative practice inherently understands and asserts that humans, and the communities they are a part of, do not exist as a 'resource' (Neely & Lopez, 2022). That *human* and/or *community* is not the entity upon which research is undertaken, to whom (upon) which practice is performed, or *subject* engaged within (colonially defined) 'equitable' transfer of knowledge or resource. Within colonised geographies/nations, any semblance of equity is simply colonial mythology; wilful deceit is desperately generated and expressed from within white supremacist machinery. Like Indigenous People and their authentic sovereignty and self-determination, '*equity*' was violated, decimated, massacred, and dispossessed.

It is from within this Western colonising patriarchal framework that Indigenous women's knowledges and experiences have been so voraciously pursued, extracted, and exploited by non-Indigenous researchers and practitioners alike (Kilian et al., 2019; Skille, 2021). From outsider standpoints – positioned and embedded in non-Indigenous, colonial, and patriarchal socialisation and existential frameworks – the distortion, dilution, engulfment, and appropriation of Indigenous women's knowledges are attained. In possession of these 'echoed knowledges' under the (colonial) premise of *valid* proprietorship and entitlement by means of *labour* and/or *authorship*, Indigenous women's existential wealth can be transplanted and commodified for the benefit and advantage of colonial Feminism and social work practice.

Feminism has never been severed from the white gaze. Consequently, the pervading 'Feminism' of discourse and activism is only ever recognised, summoned, and materialised to fulfil the measures and priorities of whiteness (Zakaria, 2022, p. 11). Feminism within social work practice requires further transformation, to cast off these disciplinary legacies that weigh it down and underpin the harms it continues to perpetuate on marginalised and oppressed communities. Rather than continuing to nourish itself in colonial patriarchal paradigms, the privileging of Indigenous wisdoms provides a site of unlearning where new ways to think and work can be perceived and constructed. To do this, the discipline, and its non-Indigenous actors (practitioners, educators, institutions), must commit to anti-exploitative practice.

In collaborating humbly and effectively with Indigenous Peoples, non-Indigenous social work practitioners and researchers must acknowledge the imperative to understand how Eurocentric ideologies generate and maintain colonial relationships and undermine self-determination (Max, 2005). Deeply nuanced, critical self-reflection by professionals on their own positions of privilege and power – including the frequently uninterrogated cultivation and indoctrination by, and alliance to, the ideals and operations of colonial Patriarchy – provide an opportunity to access and embody greater self-wisdom (Bennett, 2021). This, in turn, enables one to contribute from a more enlightened position, one where solidarity and collaboration is elevated and centred, respect and safety is paramount, and all forms of extractive or exploitative practice are obliterated.

Conclusion

Indigenous Feminisms are ancient, continuous *despite* the violent disruption. They exist beyond the extraordinarily limited colonial constructions of gender and sexuality, ability, civility, and production and hold within them the significant potential of transformation for all peoples, including social workers, so that social workers start imagining beyond colonial paradigms.

Nayuka Gorrie speaks truth to the power of Indigenous Feminism when they state:

> I don't owe white people anything. I don't owe men anything. I don't owe strangers anything. It is the luxury of the privileged to expect things, to feel entitled to things. Cis men often expect people to put out. White settlers expect Bla(c)k people to not remind them of invasion. Rich people expect poor people to get out of their way. Heterosexuals expect queers to not make them feel uncomfortable with their hot queer love. People in power expect everyone else to be grateful for scraps.
> *(Gorrie, 2017, n.p.)*

When we began to write this chapter, we were cognisant that we do not represent Indigenous Feminism or social work. We do represent our own lived realities of Aboriginal women in the colony. In notes to each other about the purpose of the chapter, we argued that we must do more than simply elevate Indigenous women's voices, and instead transform them through true Indigenous governance, real connection to First Lore (Graham, 1999) and links to social justice and human rights. We celebrate a transnational Feminism of the future, with true and real dialogues with Indigenous Peoples occurring not only with collaboration, but *action*. Developing a unified women's movement requires recognising the manifold implications of the continuing racial divide. Developing a unified stance *is* a move from the status quo. Failure to confront continued colonisation creating subdivides of class and racism just adds to the status quo. Lastly, our notes summed up this chapter with one idea. Revolution! As social workers, women, and people of the world, we need to decolonise ourselves, our profession, and the systems we work in.

Note

1* Bla(c)k or Blak is used to remove the c which denotes the removal of colonial/coloniser. See https://www.reconciliation.org.au/blak-black-blackfulla-language-is-important-but-it-can-be-tricky/

References

Aldrich, R., Hodge, D., Lee, G., & Milera, E. J. (1993). *Gay Perspectives II*. Department of Economic History with the Australian Centre for Gay and Lesbian Research, University of Sydney.

Altman, J. (2018). The Howard Government's Northern Territory Intervention: Are Neo-Paternalism and Indigenous Development Compatible? *Centre for Aboriginal Economic Policy Research 16(2007)*. Retrieved from https://openresearchrepository.anu.edu.au/bitstream/1885/148959/1/Altman_AIATSIS_0%20(1).pdf

Ananda, K. (2022, July 21). What is abolition Feminism and why do we need it now? Non Profit Quarterly. Retrieved from https://nonprofitquarterly.org/what-is-abolition-Feminism-and-why-do-we-need-it-now/

Arabena, K. (2008). *Indigenous epistemology and wellbeing: Universe-referent citizenship*. Canberra: Australian Institute of Aboriginal and Torres Strait Islander Studies.

Ariotti, L. (1999). Social construction of an Angu disability. *Australian Journal of Rural Health*, 7(4), 216–222.

Arvin, M., Tuck, E., & Morrill, A. (2013). Decolonizing Feminism: Challenging connections between settler colonialism and heteropatriarchy. *Feminist Formations*, 25(1), 8–34.

Baskin, C. (2020). Contemporary Indigenous women's roles: Traditional teachings or internalized colonialism? *Violence against Women*, 26(15–16), 2083–2101.

Behrendt, L.Y. (2010). The doctrine of discovery in Australia, In: R.J. Miller, *Discovering Indigenous Lands: The Doctrine of Discovery in the English Colonies* (pp. 171–186). Oxford University Press.

Bennett, B., McMinn, S., Millgate, N., & Morse, C. (2021). Mistakes and misunderstandings: Why are social workers still not getting it right? In B. Bennett (Ed.), *Aboriginal fields of practice* (pp. 304–321). Red Globe Press.

Boulton, M. (2003). Monture takes advocacy for aboriginal women to national stage on person's day. *University of Saskatchewan on Campus News*, 11(6), 9–22.

Clarke, E. (2017). This is yours, this is who you are. Woman's Way – A collection of stories, poems, and short essays by First Nations women. *NITV*. Retrieved from https://www.sbs.com.au/nitv/creative/womans-way-a-collection-of-stories-poems-and-short-essays-by-first-nations-women/dupwiwmic#estelle-clarke-70390

Coleman, C. (2020, April 9). Aboriginal Feminism and gender. *National Gallery of Victoria*. https://www.ngv.vic.gov.au/essay/aboriginal-Feminism-and-gender/

Coultard-Dare, C. (2022, July 11). (Roberts, G.) First Nations, transgender woman and broadcaster Charlotte Coulthard-Dare fights for visibility. ABC. Retrieved from https://www.abc.net.au/news/2022-07-11/charlotte-proud-first-nations-and-transgender-woman/101222198

Critical Resistance. (2022). The prison industrial complex. Retrieved from https://criticalresistance.org/mission-vision/not-so-common-language/

Day, M. (2021). Remembering Lugones: The critical potential of heterosexualism for studies of so-called Australia. *Genealogy*, 5(3), 71. https://doi.org/10.3390/genealogy5030071

Delia Deckard, N. (2017). Prison, coerced demand, and the importance of incarcerated bodies in late capitalism. *Social Currents*, 4(1), 3–12. https://doi.org/10.1177/2329496516670186

Drever, M. (2022). The gendered disposability of Indigenous women across time and space. *INvoke*, 7. https://doi.org/10.29173/invoke49009

Fejo-King, C. (2014). "Indigenism and Australian social work". In C. Noble, H. Strauss & B. Littlechild (Eds), *Global social work: Crossing borders, blurring boundaries (pp. 55–68)*. Sydney University Press.

Fernandez, C. (2003). Coming full circle: A young man's perspective on building gender equity in Aboriginal communities. In K. Anderson & B. Lawrence (Eds), *Strong Women Stories: Native Vision and Community Survival* (pp. 242–260).

Fredericks, B. (2010). Re-empowering ourselves: Australian Aboriginal women. *Signs: Journal of Women in Culture and Society*, 35(3), 546–550. https://doi.org/10.1086/648511

Garcia-Rojas, C. (2017) (Un)disciplined futures: Women of color Feminism as a disruptive to white affect studies. *Journal of Lesbian Studies, 21*(3), 254–271.

Gilroy, J., & Donelly, M. (2016). Australian indigenous people with disability: Ethics and standpoint theory. In *Disability in the global south* (pp. 545–566). Springer, Cham. Retrieved from https://link.springer.com/chapter/10.1007/978-3-319-42488-0_35

Gorrie, N. (2017, February 14). Things that are not my job. *Victorian Women's Trust*. Retrieved from https://www.vwt.org.au/things-not-job/

Graham, M. (1999). Some thoughts about the philosophical underpinnings of Aboriginal worldviews. *Worldviews: Global Religions, Culture, and Ecology, 3*(2), 105–118.

Grande, S. (2003). Whitestream Feminism and the colonialist project: A review of contemporary feminist pedagogy and praxis. *Educational Theory, 53*(3), 329–346. Retrieved from https://nycstandswithstandingrock.files.wordpress.com/2016/10/grande-2003-educational_theory.pdf

Grey, S. (2004). Decolonising Feminism: Aboriginal women and the global 'Sisterhood'. *Enweyin: The Way We Speak, 8*(1), 9–22.

Holmes, C., Hunt, S., & Piedalue, A. (2015). Violence, colonialism and space: Towards a decolonizing dialogue. *ACME: An International Journal for Critical Geographies, 14*(2), 539–570. https://acme-journal.org/index.php/acme/article/download/1102/992

Hopkins, P. (2019). Social geography I: Intersectionality. *Progress in Human Geography, 43*(5), 937–947.

Ineese-Nash, N. (2020). Disability as a colonial construct: The missing discourse of culture in conceptualizations of disabled indigenous children. *Canadian Journal of Disability Studies, 9*(3), 28–51. Retrieved from https://cjds.uwaterloo.ca/index.php/cjds/article/view/645/898

Ingman, M., & Gyllensten, U. (2003). Mitochondrial genome variation and evolutionary history of Australian and New Guinean aborigines. *Genome Research, 13*(7), 1600–1606.

Kendall, S., Lighton, S., Sherwood, J., Baldry, E., & Sullivan, E. (2019). Holistic conceptualizations of health by incarcerated aboriginal women in New South Wales, Australia. *Qualitative Health Research, 29*(11), 1549–1565. https://doi.org/10.1177/1049732319846162

Kilian, A., Fellows, T. K., Giroux, R., Pennington, J., Kuper, A., Whitehead, C. R., & Richardson, L. (2019). Exploring the approaches of non-Indigenous researchers to Indigenous research: A qualitative study. *Canadian Medical Association Open Access Journal, 7*(3), E504–E509. https://doi.org/10.9778/cmajo.20180204

Larnach, S. L. (1974). The origin of the Australian Aboriginal. *Archaeology & Physical Anthropology in Oceania, 9*(3), 206–213.

Lean, T. (2022, November 29). Abolishing the colonial carceral state is anti-racism [Video]. Media Futures NSW. YouTube.com. https://www.youtube.com/watch?v=WUKYh16V5tc&t=13s

Lorde, A. (2012). *Sister outsider: Essays and speeches*. Crossing Press.

Lugones, M. (2016). The coloniality of gender. In *The Palgrave handbook of gender and development* (pp. 13–33). Palgrave Macmillan, London. https://link.springer.com/chapter/10.1007/978-1-137-38273-3_2

Manjapra, K. (2020). Body. In *Colonialism in global perspective* (pp. 200–214). Cambridge University Press, Cambridge. https://doi.org/10.1017/9781108560580.011

Martin, K. L., & Mirraboopa, B. (2003). Ways of knowing, being and doing: A theoretical framework and methods for indigenous and indigenist re-search. Journal of Australian Studies, 27, 203–214.

Martin-Hill, D. (2003). She no speaks and other colonial constructs of the "traditional woman". In K. Anderson & B. Lawrence (Eds), *Strong Women Stories: Native Vision and Community Survival* (pp. 106–120).

Max, K. (2005). Chapter four: Anti-colonial research: Working as an Ally with Aboriginal peoples. *Counterpoints, 252*, 79–94.

Mbembé, J. A., & Meintjes, L. (2003). Necropolitics. *Public Culture, 15*(1), 11–40. https://muse.jhu.edu/article/39984

McGuire, M. M., & Murdoch, D. J. (2022). (In)-justice: An exploration of the dehumanization, victimization, criminalization, and over-incarceration of Indigenous women in Canada. *Punishment & Society, 24*(4), 529–550. https://doi.org/10.1177/14624745211001685

Meekosha, H. (2011). Decolonising disability: Thinking and acting globally. *Disability & Society, 26*(6), 667–682. https://doi.org/10.1080/09687599.2011.602860

Meissner, S. N., & Whyte, K. (2017). Theorizing indigeneity, gender, and settler colonialism. In P. Taylor, L. Alcoff, & L. Anderson (Eds), *The Routledge companion to philosophy of race* (pp. 152–167). Routledge.

Miller, R. J. (2010). Christianity, American Indians, and the Doctrine of Discovery. https://ssrn.com/abstract=1803674

Moane, G. (1999). Hierarchical systems: Patriarchy and colonialism. In *Gender and colonialism*. Palgrave Macmillan, London. https://doi.org/10.1057/9780230279377_2

Moon, H. (2020, July 20). Brotherboys and sistergirls: We need to decolonise our attitude towards gender in this country. Retrieved from https://junkee.com/brotherboy-sistergirl-decolonise-gender/262222

Moradi, B., & Grzanka, P. R. (2017). Using Intersectionality responsibly: Toward critical epistemology, structural analysis, and social justice activism. *Journal of Counseling Psychology*, 64(5), 500. https://psycnet.apa.org/doi/10.1037/cou0000203

Moreton-Robinson, A. (2011). Virtuous racial states: The possessive logic of patriarchal white sovereignty and the United Nations declaration on the rights of Indigenous peoples. *Griffith Law Review*, 20(3), 641–658. https://doi.org/10.1080/10383441.2011.10854714

Moreton-Robinson, A. (2021). *Talkin' up to the white woman: Indigenous women and feminism*. University of Minnesota Press.

Neely, A. H., & Lopez, P. J. (2022). Toward healthier futures in post-pandemic times: Political ecology, racial capitalism, and Bla(c)k feminist approaches to care. *Geography Compass*, 16(2), e12609. https://doi.org/10.1111/gec3.12609

Nicholls, C. (2001). Reconciled to what? Reconciliation and the Northern Territory's bilingual education program, 1973–1998. In J. L Bianco & R. Wickert (Eds), *Australian Policy Activism in Language and Literacy*— (pp. 327–345).

O'Sullivan, S. (2021). The colonial project of gender (and everything else). *Genealogy*, 5(3), 67. https://doi.org/10.3390/genealogy5030067

Oxley, R. (2020, September 23). Defunding the police and abolishing prisons are not radical ideas. IndigenousX. Retrieved from https://indigenousx.com.au/defunding-the-police-and-abolishing-prisons-are-not-radical-ideas/

Phelan, P., & Oxley, R. (2021). Understanding the social and emotional wellbeing of Aboriginal LGBTIQ(SB)+ youth in Victoria's youth detention. *Social Inclusion*, 9(2), 18–29. https://doi.org/10.17645/si.v9i2.3770

Phipps, A. (2021). White tears, white rage: Victimhood and (as) violence in mainstream Feminism. *European Journal of Cultural Studies*, 24(1), 81–93. https://doi.org/10.1177/1367549420985852

Picq, M. L., & Tikuna, J. (2019). Indigenous sexualities: Resisting conquest and translation. *Sexuality and Translation in World Politics*, 57. https://www.e-ir.info/wp-content/uploads/2019/08/Sexuality-and-Translation-in-World-Politics-%E2%80%93-E-IR.pdf#page=68

Plumwood, V. (2002). Decolonisation relationships with nature. *Philosophy Activism Nature* (2), 7–30. https://search.informit.org/doi/10.3316/informit.761776856886629

Press, A. (2018). #MeToo must avoid "carceral Feminism". *Vox*. Retrieved from https://www.vox.com/the-big-idea/2018/2/1/16952744/me-too-larry-nassar-judge-aquilina-Feminism

Rule, L.A., Brown, L., & Ironfield, N. (2021). Incarceration Nation exposes the racist foundations of policing and imprisonment in Australia, but at what cost? The Conversation (August 30, 2021) https://theconversation.com/incarceration-nation-exposes-the-racist-foundations-of-policing-and-imprisonment-in-australia-but-at-what-cost-165951

Ruuska, T., Heikkurinen, P., & Wilén, K. (2020). Domination, power, supremacy: Confronting anthropolitics with ecological realism. *Sustainability*, 12(7), 2617. https://doi.org/10.3390/su12072617

Seng, J. S., Lopez, W. D., Sperlich, M., Hamama, L., & Reed Meldrum, C. D. (2012). Marginalized identities, discrimination burden, and mental health: Empirical exploration of an interpersonal-level approach to modeling Intersectionality. *Social Science & Medicine (1982)*, 75(12), 2437–2445. https://doi.org/10.1016/j.socscimed.2012.09.023

Skille, E. Å. (2021). Doing research into Indigenous issues being non-Indigenous. *Qualitative Research*, 0(0). https://doi.org/10.1177/14687941211005947

Spencer-Wood, S. M. (2016). Feminist theorizing of patriarchal colonialism, power dynamics, and social agency materialized in colonial institutions. *International Journal of Historical Archaeology*, 20, 477–491.

Staines, Z., & Scott, J. (2020). Crime and colonisation in Australia's Torres Strait Islands. *Australian & New Zealand Journal of Criminology*, 53(1), 25–43. https://doi.org/10.1177/0004865819869049

Sudbury, J. (2002). Celling Bla(c)k bodies: Black women in the global prison industrial complex. *Feminist Review*, 70(1), 57–74.

Suzack, C., Huhndorf, S. M., Perreault, J., & Barman, J. (Eds.) (2010). *Indigenous women and Feminism: Politics, activism, culture*. UBC Press.

Transhub. (2021). Trans mob. Retrieved from https://www.transhub.org.au/trans-mob

Tuck, E., & Yang, K. W. (2021). Decolonization is not a metaphor. *Tabula Rasa* (38), 61–111. https://doi.org/10.25058/20112742.n38.04

Watego, C., Macoun, A., Singh, D., & Strakosch, E. (2021). Carceral Feminism and coercive control: When Indigenous women aren't seen as ideal victims, witnesses or women. *The Conversation*.Retrievedfromhttps://theconversation.com/carceral-Feminism-and-coercive-control-when-indigenous-women-arent-seen-as-ideal-victims-witnesses-or-women-161091

Watson, B. A. (2010). The impact of the American Doctrine of Discovery on native land rights in Australia, Canada, and New Zealand. *Seattle University Law Review*, 34, 507.

Weerawardhana, C. (2018). Profoundly decolonizing? Reflections on a transfeminist perspective of international relations. *Meridians*, 16(1), 184–213. https://doi.org/10.2979/meridians.16.1.18

Zakaria, R. (2022). *Against white Feminism*. Penguin Random House, UK.

6
TENSIONS AND DIALOGUES BETWEEN INTERSECTIONAL AND DECOLONIAL FEMINIST CONTRIBUTIONS TO LATIN AMERICAN SOCIAL WORK

Lelya Troncoso-Pérez, Karina Pinto G. and Rocío Gallardo Aranguren

Introduction

Latin American social work has constructed critical and complex theoretical understandings of social reality, acutely aware of how epistemic locations always inform our profession (even if they are not explicitly stated), while also promoting other forms of professional practice and social intervention (Hermida & Meschini, 2017; Matus, 2018; Muñoz-Arce et al., 2017). Critical social work questions many underlying assumptions in the discipline, such as (1) the neoliberalization of social work (Mussot, 2018); (2) dichotomous understandings of theory and practice that promote metaphysical, essentialist, and individualist understandings of social phenomena (Matus, 2018); and (3) the depoliticized implementation of social programs and the supposed presumption of neutrality in social intervention (Muñoz-Arce, 2018; Mussot, 2018). It also emphasizes the need to incorporate historical perspectives, recognizing the power-knowledge relationships that operate in these action frameworks (Falla, 2016).

During the last decade, interest in incorporating feminist perspectives into the theory and practice of Latin American social work has increased, and this awareness is certainly fostered by the massiveness and diversification of feminist social movements in Latin America during this period (Riveiro, 2019). Feminist discussions have contributed to debates on epistemic positioning in social work, enhancing ethical and political horizons of social research and intervention.

In Chile, there has been increasing engagement with intersectional and decolonial feminist contributions that are having a significant impact in Social Sciences, Humanities, and, particularly, social work. Such contributions connect critical concerns about the effects of Capitalism, Neoliberalism, Colonialism, among others, with complex feminist discussions that go beyond unidimensional "women", "gender", and "patriarchy" questions. This is particularly relevant considering that social work is devalued in the Social Sciences in a way similar to that of Gender and Feminist Studies (Harding & Mendoza, 2021; Troncoso et al., 2019). Additionally, Social Science intellectuals have often dismissed feminist perspectives. Those on the right do so due to conservative ideologies, while those on the left tend to oversimplify and make false associations between feminism and liberal, separatist, and bourgeois interests (Lamas, 2020). It is therefore still very challenging to incorporate, promote, and value feminist knowledge production in higher education. However, recent commitments to non-sexist education in Chilean universities, following massive feminist student mobilizations in 2018, are promising, in the sense that now feminist theories, epistemologies, methodologies, and pedagogies are beginning to be recognized as a fundamental component of critical higher education (Hiner & Troncoso, 2021; Troncoso et al., 2019).

In this chapter, we will critically assess the relationship between intersectional and decolonial Feminisms to deepen understandings not necessarily explored in social work. We propose a constructive dialogue between both perspectives; however, it is not our intention to assimilate these views, and it is important to acknowledge the disagreements and tensions that have arisen between both currents, which are themselves heterogeneous and intellectually diverse fields of research and praxis (Cho et al., 2013).

Embarking upon this constructive dialogue, we start by presenting key tensions and points of confluence between intersectional and decolonial perspectives. Then, we focus on how a critical constructive dialogue between these approaches can strengthen feminist social work in three ways: by making more robust our contextualized and situated analyses; by problematizing our categories; and, finally, by promoting coalitional politics. We conclude by emphasizing some aspects that advance the collective construction of discourses, perspectives, and practices of feminist, intersectional, and decolonial social work.

Tensions between decolonial and intersectional perspectives

We propose that the relationship between these perspectives is one of productive tensions (Velez, 2019), as decolonial and intersectional feminist perspectives share a trajectory of productive dialogues and common resonances in the development of frameworks that have been critical of white hegemonic Feminisms and Eurocentric paradigms. Both have problematized universal and ahistorical conceptualizations of Patriarchy and share a mutual interest in disputing the political subject category of "woman", focusing on processes of differentiation (Cubillos, 2015). Centering the causes and the consequences of colonial domination in Latin America, decolonial feminists have defended the need for decolonization and depatriarchalization (Galindo 2013; Harding and Mendoza, 2021, p. 110). Intersectional perspectives, however, operate as a critical approach and as an analytical tool for studying, understanding, and addressing the ways in which different axes of power are articulated in specific historical contexts. In this way, they are enmeshed in concrete experiences and relationships of oppression and privilege; social inclusion; and exclusion (Troncoso et al., 2019). They seek to articulate a way of "understanding and analyzing complexities in the world, in people, and in human experiences" (Hill Collins & Bilge, 2016, p. 2).

When discussing decolonial and intersectional feminist contributions, it is important to take North/South power relations and respective tensions into account, where Intersectionality has been associated mainly with the North and decolonial feminism with the South, and with Abya Yala[1]/Latin America specifically (Harding & Mendoza, 2021; Kurtiş & Adams, 2017). The Aymara sociologist Silvia Rivera Cusicanqui (2010) has emphasized that Northern universities do not follow or interact with Andean and Southern debates in any significant way. She has been very critical of some authors and strands of decolonial scholarship, particularly those associated with, or stemming from, the area of "Latin American subaltern studies", and calls for a "political economy" of knowledge, because the so-called geopolitics of knowledge are not always considered by many Global North decolonial scholars. In that sense, these scholars contradict themselves through the recolonization of Southern imaginaries and intellectuality. Rivera Cusicanqui proposes that North American postcolonial discourse is not just an economy of ideas but also an economy of salary, comfort, and privilege, one which certifies value through titles, scholarships, teaching invitations, and publishing opportunities.

At the same time, we must also recognize that Global North scholarship seems to be mostly unaware of what happens beyond its borders, "even when colonialist power relations within the U.S. academy are perceived and critiqued" (Pérez & Radi, 2019, p. 9). This includes not only U.S. and Canadian scholars but also European scholars, as European critical thought has paid little attention to Latin America (Guerrero, 2021). Southern scholarship is mainly informed through dialogue with Northern productions, which could lead to a poor understanding of our own reality (Pérez & Radi, 2019). If we are interested in promoting North/South dialogues, we need to be critically aware of these power dynamics. This outlook is also important to further South/South dialogues, between South America and Africa, for example, because we are similarly subjected to internal Colonialism (Rivera Cusicanqui, 2010).

There has been some distrust concerning Intersectionality's popularity in some Latin American academic and feminist circles (Kurtiş & Adams, 2017). Currently, some renowned decolonial and anti-racist feminists in the South associate Intersectionality with the North, liberal diversity politics and privileged academic settings, positing that decolonial contributions are more relevant and revolutionary and that they have more political emancipatory potential. One of the most outspoken critics of Intersectionality is Ochy Curiel, an Afro-Dominican feminist activist and academic, who works at a Colombian university and is one of the most influential decolonial, anti-racist feminists in Latin America. She is suspicious of Intersectionality's popularity stating that

> The concept of intersectionality has had the most success in feminist research and proposals to understand oppression, and it is not by chance because, in the end, it is a liberal and modern proposal, even if it was proposed by an African American.
> *(Curiel, 2014, pp. 54–55)*

There has been a problematic association linking Intersectionality mainly with Kimberlé Crenshaw's work, even though many genealogies of Intersectionality have questioned this reductionist view (de los Reyes, 2021; Hill-Collins & Bilge, 2016; Lykke, 2010; Viveros, 2016). A long and diverse tradition of social movement politics, activists and intellectuals used complex and intersectional frameworks before the term was "coined", often in Black and Latina Feminist contexts far outside the legal scholarship of Crenshaw. For example, the Colombian anthropologist Mara Viveros (2016) has highlighted the activism and intellectual work of women who belonged to the Brazilian Communist Party in the 1960s, as well as the work of Lelia González, Sueli Carneiro, and other Afro-Brazilian women who promoted the theory of the "race-class-gender" triad of oppressions in South America. These genealogies are still being rewritten, identifying relevant authors in different latitudes, and helping to move beyond merely citing Crenshaw's influential article from 1991. In this same vein, Hill-Collins and Bilge (2016) ask themselves: "how do certain histories about Intersectionality's origins become authoritative at the expense of others?" (p. 64). They critically reflect on the impact of naming a field, which has helped legitimize a kind of scholarship "by making it more compatible with academic norms of discovery, authorship and ownership" (p. 80).

These are very colonial norms we would add, and the consequences of Intersectionality as an umbrella term seem contradictory. It has promoted not only legitimacy in academia, but also institutional amnesia: valuing Black feminist and social justice projects drawn from social movement sensibilities while, at the same time, neoliberal universities "suppressed the transformative and potentially disruptive dimensions of these critical projects" (Bilge, 2014 cited in Hill-Collins & Bilge, 2016, p. 85). It is important to note, as well, that decolonial criticisms of Intersectionality are actually quite similar to many intersectional criticisms of Intersectionality, in the sense that intersectional intellectuals and activists within the field of Intersectionality studies also profoundly engage with these same perceived problems in their field (Cho et al., 2013; Gandarias, 2017).

At a recent talk at the University of Santiago de Chile about the contributions and limitations of Intersectionality, Ochy Curiel (2021) insisted that Intersectionality was promoting a liberal, multicultural politics of inclusion, seeing categories of difference as separate, pre-existing, and intersecting, which leads to its focus on recognizing difference and ignoring that these differences are produced through oppressive structural forces and hierarchies of power. In a similar spirit, Yuderkys Espinosa (2019) has criticized Intersectionality as a perspective that reaffirms identity categories instead of questioning their historical and social conditions of production. According to Curiel, Intersectionality cannot offer a liberatory politics, because it only offers a politically correct position from which self-identified intersectional feminists can claim that they are including all women (Black, Indigenous, lesbian, etc.). She also adds that Intersectionality has been mostly useful for NGOs and governmental institutions interested in diversity politics, rather than revolutionary politics.

Curiel and Espinosa's criticisms address some key political debates and concerns in both decolonial and intersectional studies. Even though we share these apprehensions, we think it is problematic to criticize Intersectionality as an abstract and unitary theoretical perspective or associate it only with Crenshaw's work, which would make us complicit with the same erasure we are trying to question. What we mean is that this way of referring to Intersectionality overlooks the fact that Intersectionality studies are an extremely heterogeneous field (Cho et al., 2013) that has been in a process of consistent expansion globally and which signifies an ongoing process of transformation and diversification. When we question "intersectionality" in an abstract manner, we are focusing on what we think Intersectionality is, stabilizing (fixing) its meaning, and disregarding the rich internal and inter, trans, and post-disciplinary debates (Lykke, 2010) that have been discussing these same issues that supposedly define its failures. We do not want to idealize Intersectionality, but it seems more productive and rigorous to focus on what Intersectionality does, rather than what it is (or what it is supposed to be) (Cho et al., 2013).

At the same time, it is also important to emphasize that both intersectional and decolonial feminist currents constitute heterogeneous and complex fields of study, where neither the decolonial nor the intersectional can be understood as static, monolithic, or deterministic concepts. Just as different understandings of the relationship between gender and Coloniality are argued within decolonial feminist approaches (Lugones, 2008; Rivera Cusicanqui, 2018; Segato, 2011), there is also a wide diversity of theoretical and methodological proposals and internal differences in the field of intersectional studies (Cho et al., 2013) and decolonial studies, which can be understood as part of the complex "distinctiveness of Latin American anti-colonial thought" (Harding & Mendoza, 2021).

We want to promote a critical and constructive dialogue between intersectional and decolonial feminist perspectives and politics because we believe that they can complement each other in important ways, as they are mutually concerned with analyses of complex power relations, inequality, social injustice, and political praxis. This means recognizing that problematic interpretations and the depoliticization of Intersectionality have also been widely discussed and analyzed by feminist theorists who position their studies from this perspective. These feminist scholars underscore how we need to problematize the simplistic reification of the intersectional, addressing the challenge of re-politicizing its uses through making its theoretical frameworks more complex and not losing sight of the fact that this current is not static and that it is in a constant process of construction (Carastathis, 2019; Rodó-Zárate, 2021). Alexander-Floyd (2012) and Bilge (2013) are cited by McKinzie and Richards (2019, pp. 1–2) who state:

> Despite its expansive influence, a number of problems have been identified in relation to intersectional research, theorizing, and practice. Perhaps most importantly, a great deal of scholarship purports to be intersectional but highlights difference without paying attention to power. Such work emphasizes intersectional identities without highlighting how structures and institutions operate intersectionally to shape people's life chances. In addition, the move for intersectionality to be inclusive of the intersectional subjectivities of all people has led to the concern that intersectionality has become depoliticized, moving away from the Black feminist standpoint in which it originated

Following these same ideas, we propose that the relation between decolonial feminism and Intersectionality should be one of *productive tensions* (Velez, 2019). Decolonial and intersectional Feminisms have been deeply influenced by the critical legacies of Black and Chicana feminist authors, such as bell hooks, Audre Lorde, Sojourner Truth, Angela Davis, Gloria Anzaldúa, and Chela Sandoval. Their work is heavily cited in both decolonial and intersectional feminist texts.

We want to highlight the importance of not collapsing these perspectives into themselves or ordering them into a dichotomous relationship or hierarchy. Rather, we seek to broaden the scope of these interconnected, decolonial-intersectional discussions. We will focus on three aspects that are intimately related, although, of course, far from exclusive. We propose this discussion as an invitation to mutually rewarding dialogues within feminist, anti-racist, and anticolonial theorization and practice.

Constructive dialogues between intersectional and decolonial Feminisms for social work

The importance of robust, contextualized, and situated analyses

According to Yuderkys Espinosa (2016), Afro-Dominican philosopher, decolonial feminism looks to critically re-interpret History and modernity in Latin America/Abya Yala, by focusing not only on their inherent androcentrism and misogyny, as classical feminist epistemology has done, but also their deep and ongoing racism and Eurocentrism, usually referred to as "Coloniality" in these studies. To construct critical genealogies and reinterpretations of History has been paramount for feminist criticisms of white, hegemonic feminist discourses. It is impossible to refer to *one feminism* not only because of the diverse experiences of women, and the problematic ways in which European and North American colonial feminist discourses have defined what it means to be a "woman", but also due to the feminist, construction of "Third-world" women (or Black, Latina, Asian, First Nations, etc.) as "others" (Lozano, 2010).

In Abya Yala/Latin America, Colonialism and Coloniality should be inescapable dimensions of contextualized feminist analysis in social work. And we should also ask ourselves if it is possible to critically understand any structural and transnational power dynamics without taking Colonialism into account. Siobhan Guerrero (2021) critically addresses Hispanic Feminisms and the important role that decolonial knowledge production in Abya Yala plays in producing more complex understandings of the relationship between Latin America and Spain. She reminds us of how Maria Lugones insisted that Intersectionality should be read from a decolonial point of view. Guerrero (2021) states that Intersectionality is not a mere exercise in contrasting identities or thinking about interlocking oppressions but rather requires a historical perspective on the ways in which the world and different bodies are made, declaring certain subjects as legitimate while others become abject, alongside forms of government and violence that place us in certain categories. Vrushali Patil (2013) has also pointed out that "applications of Intersectionality also continue to be shaped by the geographies of colonial modernity" (p. 853), identifying its failure to "interrogate how transnational dynamics of colonialism, imperialism and neoliberalism structure and constrain life prospects through processes of racialization and gendering" (Cho et al., 2013, p. 805).

We have emphasized the importance of Colonialism as a structural and historical force shaping current power relations in relation to decolonial and intersectional Feminisms and social work. We would now like to highlight the challenges of contextualizing and situating feminist analyses and social interventions in social work, a crucial practice that is easier said than done.

McKinzie and Richards (2019) present key arguments for a "context-driven intersectionality" that would avoid many of the pitfalls identified by criticisms of Intersectionality

> We suggest that a focus on context—historical, social, economic, geographic, and political—is critical to conducting robust intersectional work. In doing so, we emphasize how much earlier work reveals the importance of historical, political, economic, and social context to intersectional analyses and also present examples of more recent literature that exemplifies this approach.
>
> *(p. 2)*

Afro-Colombian author Mara Viveros (2016) also addresses the risk of intersectional theory falling into capitalist academicism and commercial use, which means being stripped of its context and History and, therefore, its political power. Intersectionality should always critically interrogate the articulation of power structures and avoid treating them as ahistorical and pre-existing. In this manner, Intersectionality will continually evaluate situated effects in the materialization of social relationships, subjectivities, and concrete experiences of privilege, domination, exclusion, and inclusion (Troncoso et al., 2019, p. 5).

A "context-driven intersectionality" is, according to McKinzie and Richards (2019), critically important to our commitment to praxis, because:

> The goal of intersectional thought has been to start with real experiences of injustice to develop an understanding of the intersectional structural conditions that enable injustice to thrive and then to challenge and eventually dismantle those conditions. Starting with context should also lay bare the urgency of the inequalities the framework reveals, thus compelling researchers to act in favor of social justice. That is, focusing on context reminds us that intersectionality is not only about observing parts of people's identities but about changing structural conditions.
>
> *(p. 6)*

McKinzie and Richards (2019) also argue that "context-driven intersectionality" is crucial to resisting depoliticization, and its neoliberal trappings. This is not inherent to Intersectionality but occurs, rather, when we lose sight of structural systems of power and their interactions. Focusing on context means maintaining a radical focus on institutions and power structures and problematizing "the association of intersectionality with identity alone that has led to its depoliticization" (p. 7).

Dean Spade (2013) also clearly resists depoliticized and decontextualized uses of Intersectionality and considers anti- Colonialism as a crucial aspect of struggles for social justice. He refers to *intersectional resistance*, informed by anticolonial and antiracist feminist resistance, and highlights the importance of genealogies of violence to break with dominant narratives and critically explore "genealogies of racialized-gendered control and exploitation" (p. 1044) that will make more complex political demands possible.

It is important to discuss the ethical and political implications of contextualizing our feminist research and praxis. How do we contextualize our own views and arguments and how do we "think about social inequality, relationality, and power relations in a social context?" (Hill-Collins & Bilge, 2016, p. 28). And how do we focus on context in a way that helps us to identify relevant inequalities, oppressions, and privileges? (McKinzie & Richards, 2019). These are important questions if we wish to resist the neoliberalization and depoliticization of feminist social work research.

The problematization of categories

How we approach analytical categories such as gender, class, ethnicity, disability, and sexuality has been a huge concern in feminist theorizing and social work (Pombo, 2019). In line with intersectional perspectives, we must also consider how we analyze the contested relationships between categories that have been characterized as mutually constituted, articulated, intermeshed, interacting, and interconnected (Cho et al., 2013). This discussion is still ongoing and, currently, different ways of "doing intersectionality" continue to co-exist.

This issue is intimately connected to previous concerns with contextualization, because as stated by McKinzie and Richards (2019) "context-driven intersectionality (...) is critical to conducting robust intersectional analyses that avoids reification of social categories and inequalities" (p. 1).

Intersectional approaches have sought to go beyond additive models of analysis (Yuval-Davis, 2006), because they attend to the inseparability of categories such as gender, class, race, and sexuality (among others) that cannot be understood in isolation from each other (Hill-Collins & Chepp, 2013). The problem with reification is that it makes categories appear as separate and physical objects (Rodó-Zárate, 2021). This has led to many debates about other useful metaphors, and how to better conceptualize interconnectedness without leading to notions of separateness. María Lugones (2005) has taken up this critique of Intersectionality and categories being considered separate elements that intersect at certain points and proposed the need to move toward an overlapping understanding of categories as intermeshed and fused. Others have also problematized the scope of Lugones' critique, as it supposes a rather nominative critique that does not necessarily consider the diverse and complex uses of Intersectionality where the metaphor of intersection is not taken literally (Velez, 2019, p. 395) and that criticism can even reproduce forms of epistemic violence and weaken possible alliances between both currents (Thomas, 2020).

However, intersectional and decolonial perspectives have problematized categories in different ways, as pointed out by Emma Velez (2019)

> Posing the "intersectionality question" to feminist theorizing and praxis, thinkers like Kimberlé Crenshaw and Patricia Hill-Collins unveil the essentializing and universalizing assumptions that lie at the core of categories like "woman" and "race." In an effort to further the analyses of oppression given by intersectionality theory, decolonial feminism additionally asks the "Coloniality question" of feminist theories and practices in order to unveil how Coloniality buttresses the oppressive categorial logics that intersectionality identifies.
>
> (p. 392)

This points out how Decoloniality is not incompatible with Intersectionality, and that it makes sense for both theories to work together to change and resist dominant frameworks (Thomas, 2020). Velez (2019) takes up the pivotal Combahee River Collective Statement to argue for the need to argue for *intersectional* and *fusion* understandings of oppression as complimentary and intertwined. As this Collective posited in the late 1970s, we need an "integrated analysis and practice based upon the fact that the major systems of oppression are interlocking. The synthesis of these oppressions creates the conditions of our lives" (p. 395). She emphasizes that to resist and dismantle the structures of oppression shaping our lives, we will have to recognize "*both* the inner workings and operations of the categories of oppression, that is, as intersecting and interlocked, *and* the simultaneity of the experience of these oppressions, that is, as intermeshed and fused" (Velez, 2019, p. 395).

The promotion of coalition politics

Finally, we want to emphasize this last aspect because it connects feminist social work with its political implications and praxis. Recently in Chile, we have been facing many social upheavals, such as the 2019 Social Revolts known as *estallido social*, and the 2018 feminist student mobilizations, that have made it clear that it is urgent for different social movements to work together in order to dismantle heteropatriarchal, colonial, capitalist, and neoliberal systems of power and oppression. Coalition building based on the recognition of power relations and the interdependence of the struggles for emancipation has been at the center of both feminist intersectional and decolonial theorizing for decades (Lugones, 2021 [2003]; Mohanty, 2003; Reagon, 2000). When we go beyond unidimensional perspectives and recognize how Colonialism, heteropatriarchy, and capitalism, among other structures of inequality, interact and intermesh, the urgency to struggle for social justice in a broad and complex sense is undeniable (Troncoso et al., 2019).

Lugones' work (2021 [2003]) has emphasized the processes by which our struggles and resistances become interdependent. She argues that to generate multidimensional social transformations based on coalitions implies the recognition of different contextualized practices of resistance that different actors carry out daily when confronting the interconnection of axes of oppression in their situated lives. Therefore, people do not form alliances just to share and optimize resources, but, rather, to transform their relationships with each other, as well as recognize and "see" each other in this interconnectedness.

Many feminist reflections on coalition building are very moving and heartfelt. In our daily political struggles, we face constant obstacles and frustrations and this can promote empathy, consciousness-raising, and feminist organization. However, we can also often encounter a form of "oppression Olympics" (Hancock, 2011), that is, a competition to see "who has it worse", marked by individualism, violence, fragmentation, and many complicated and exhausting conflicts that have us fighting to find hope. We need the kind of solidarity that critically engages with decolonial and intersectional feminist perspectives, aware of power relations and inequalities, open to decolonizing narratives of freedom "where we accept that our Western ways of measuring truth in the world are not superior to forms of assessment grounded in different epistemologies" (Méndez, 2018, p. 18). Velez (2019) argues that focusing on productive tensions furthers "the 'deep' coalitional politics emphasized by decolonial Feminisms, especially between Black women and Latinas" (p. 62). We agree that it is important to promote further critical constructive dialogue and alliances between decolonial and intersectional feminists and theories if we wish to strengthen our liberatory struggles within and outside of university and social work settings.

Conclusions

We have reviewed intersectional and decolonial feminist contributions, focusing on tensions and constructive criticism. We have sought to highlight how both perspectives can complement each other and work together to inspire complex and liberatory feminist analyses and political praxis in social work, and beyond. We have underscored theoretical and political feminist contributions that are relevant for social work and Social Sciences in general. We believe that the issues and discussions that we have presented here are important for the development of socially committed practices of social justice, as they also invite us to face complex challenges.

> This means we must have the courage to engage in difficult conversations; those that actively make transparent the influences of power, privilege, oppression, and the disparate effects of the economy of academia. We must have honest conversations about our personal identities in relation to our work and how these interact with institutional power. In essence, we must build a culture of communication over time and across varied relationships. This work is not easy, particularly given that the neoliberal, Western, masculinist culture of academia does not often encourage a culture of transparency or open communication. However, it is our view that working toward this with a vision of culturally relevant, feminist, collaborative work across diverse social positionalities is important to feminist and critical scholarship within our field.
> *(Beltrán & Mehrotra, 2015, p. 110)*

Acknowledgments

The research project "FONDECYT Iniciación N 11200226: Memorias de activismo feminista en Chile (2010–2020): un análisis interseccional de experiencias, diferencias y coaliciones en la praxis política" was funded by a Chilean-state ANID Fondecyt de inicio grant, whose main researcher is Lelya Troncoso Pérez (Social Work Department, University of Chile).

Note

1 Latin-American anti-colonial thought has criticized the term "Latin America" because it was imposed and excludes Indigenous and afro-descendent peoples, and many consider that Abya Yala is a better way to name this region, as referred to by the Kuna of Panama and Colombia (Harding & Mendoza, 2021).

References

Alexander-Floyd, N. G. (2012). Disappearing acts: Reclaiming intersectionality in the social sciences in a post-Black feminist era. *Feminist Formations, 24*, 1–25. https://doi-org.uplib.idm.oclc.org/10.1353/ff.2012.0003

Beltrán, R. & Mehrotra, G. (2015). Honoring our intellectual ancestors: A feminist of color treaty for creating allied collaboration. *Affilia: Journal of Women and Social Work, 30*(1), 106–116. https://doi.org/10.1177/0886109914531958

Bilge, S. (2013). Intersectionality undone: Saving intersectionality from feminist intersectionality studies. *Du Bois Review, 10*(2), 405–424. https://doi-org.uplib.idm.oclc.org/10.1017/S1742058X13000283

Carastathis, A. (2019). *Intersectionality: Origins, contestations, horizons.* University of Alberta Libraries.

Cho, S., Crenshaw, K. W., & McCall, L. (2013). Toward a field of intersectionality studies: Theory, applications, and praxis. *Signs, 38*(4), 785–810. https://doi.org/10.1086/669608

Cubillos, J. (2015). La importancia de la interseccionalidad para la investigación feminista [The importance of intersectionality for feminist research]. *Oxímora: revista internacional d'Ètica i Política, 7*, 119–137. https://revistes.ub.edu/index.php/oximora/article/view/14502

Curiel, O. (2014). Construyendo metodologías feministas desde el feminismo decolonial [Building feminist methodologies from decolonial feminism]. In I. Mendia Azkue, M. Luxán, M. Legarreta, G. Guzmán, I. Zirion, & J. Azpiazu (Eds.), *Otras formas de (re)conocer. Reflexiones, herramientas y aplicaciones desde la investigación feminista* (pp. 45–60). UPV/EHU.

Curiel, O. [Universidad de Santiago de Chile] (2021, April 23). *Clase Magistral "Aportes y Límites de la Interseccionalidad"* [Master Class "Contributions and limits of intersectionality"] [Video]. Youtube. https://www.youtube.com/watch?v=TYvNOQlwt0c

de los Reyes, P. (2021). Apuntes (des)confinados. Sobre las contribuciones de la interseccionalidad a los desafíos del Covid-19 [(De)confined notes. On the contributions of intersectionality to the challenges of Covid-19]. *Propuestas Críticas en Trabajo Social, 1*(2), 31–49. https://doi.org/10.5354/2735-6620.2021.61524

Espinosa Miñoso, Y. (2016). De por qué es necesario un feminismo descolonial: diferenciación, dominación co-constitutiva de la modernidad occidental y el fin de la política de identidad [Why a decolonial feminism is necessary: Differentiation, co-constitutive domination of Western modernity, and the end of identity politics]. *Solar, 12*(1), 141–171. https://doi.org/10.20939/solar.2016.12.0109

Espinosa Miñoso, Y. (2019). Superando el análisis fragmentado de la dominación: una revisión feminista descolonial de la perspectiva de la interseccionalidad [Overcoming the fragmented analysis of domination: A decolonial feminist revision of the intersectionality perspective]. In X. Leiva (Ed.), *Cuerpos en resistencia y rebeldía en tiempos de guerra* (pp. 273–293). Editorial Retos.

Falla, U. (2016). La intervención como forma de poder en el trabajo social [Intervention as a form of power in social work]. *Tabula Rasa, 24*, 349–368. https://doi.org/10.25058/20112742.69

Galindo, M. (2013). *No se puede Descolonizar, sin Despatriarcalizar*. Mujeres Creando.

Gandarias Goikoetxea, I. (2017). ¿Un neologismo a la moda?: Repensar la interseccionalidad como herramienta para la articulación política feminista [A buzzword?: Rethinking intersectionality as a tool for feminist political articulation]. *Investigaciones Feministas*, 8(1), 73–93. https://doi.org/10.5209/INFE.54498

Guerrero, S. (2021). Los feminismos de la hispanidad [The feminisms of Hispanicity]. In C. Serra, C. Garaizábal, & L. Mácaya (Eds.), *Alianzas rebeldes: un feminismo más allá de la identidad* (pp. 209–216). Bellaterra Ediciones.

Hancock, A. M. (2011). *Solidarity politics for millennials: A guide to ending the oppression Olympics*. Palgrave Macmillan.

Harding, S.& Mendoza, B. (2021). Latin American decolonial feminist philosophy of knowledge production. In S. Crasnow & K. Intemann (Eds.), *The Routledge handbook of feminist philosophy of science* (pp. 104–116). Routledge. https://doi.org/10.4324/9780429507731

Hermida, M. & Meschini, P. (2017). *Trabajo Social y Descolonialidad. Epistemologías insurgentes para la intervención en lo social* [Social work and Decoloniality. Insurgent epistemologies for social intervention]. Editorial de la Universidad Nacional de Mar del Plata.

Hill-Collins, P. & Bilge, S. (2016). *Intersectionality*. Polity Press.

Hill-Collins, P. & Chepp, V. (2013). Intersectionality. In G. Waylen, K. Celis, J. Kantola, & S. L. Weldon (Eds.), *The Oxford handbook of gender and politics* (pp. 57–87). Oxford Handbooks. https://doi.org/10.1093/oxfordhb/9780199751457.013.0002

Hiner, H. & Troncoso, L. (2021). LGBTQ+ Tensions in the 2018 Chilean feminist tsunami. *The Bulletin of Latin American Research*, 4(5), 679–695. https://doi.org/10.1111/blar.13331

Kurtiş, T. & Adams, G. (2017). Decolonial intersectionality: Implications for theory, research, and pedagogy. In K. A. Case (Ed.), *Intersectional pedagogy: Complicating identity and social justice* (pp. 46–59). Routledge. https://doi.org/10.4324/9781315672793

Lamas, M. (2020). Debate feminista: ¿una revista de izquierda? [Feminist debate: A left-wing magazine?]. In J. Cadena-Roa y M. López (Eds.), *Las izquierdas mexicanas hoy: las vertientes de la izquierda* (pp. 151–178). UNAM.

Lozano, B. (2010). El feminismo no puede ser uno porque las mujeres somos diversas. Aportes a un feminismo negro decolonial desde la experiencia de las mujeres negras del Pacífico Colombiano [Feminism cannot be single because women are diverse. Contributions to a Decolonial Black Feminism stemming from the experience of black women of the Colombian Pacific]. *La Manzana de la discordia*, 5(2), 7–24. https://doi.org/10.25100/lamanzanadeladiscordia.v5i2.1516

Lugones, M. (2005). Multiculturalismo radical y feminismos de mujeres de color [Radical multiculturalism and feminisms of women of color]. *Revista internacional de filosofía política 25*, 61–76.

Lugones, M. (2008). Colonialidad y género [Coloniality and gender]. *Tabula Rasa*, 9, 73–101. https://revistas.unicolmayor.edu.co/index.php/tabularasa/article/view/1501

Lugones, M. (2021 [2003]). *Peregrinajes. Teorizar una coalición contra múltiples opresiones* [Pilgrimages/peregrinajes: Theorizing coalition against multiple oppressions]. Ediciones del Signo.

Lykke, N. (2010). *Feminist studies. A guide to intersectional theory, methodology and writing*. Routledge. https://doi.org/10.4324/9780203852774

Matus, T. (2018). *Punto de Fuga: imágenes dialécticas de la crítica en el Trabajo Social contemporáneo. Tomo I* [Vanishing point: Dialectical images of criticism in contemporary social work. Volume I]. Editorial Espacio.

McKinzie, A. & Richards, P. (2019). An argument for context-driven intersectionality. *Sociology Compass*, 13, e12671, 1–14. https://doi.org/10.1111/soc4.12671

Méndez, M. J. (2018). "The river told me": Rethinking intersectionality from the world of Berta Cáceres. *Capitalism Nature Socialism*, 29(1), 7–24. https://doi.org/10.1080/10455752.2017.1421981

Mohanty, C. T. (2003). *Feminism without borders: Decolonizing theory, practicing solidarity*. Duke University Press.

Muñoz-Arce, G. (2018). Contra la exclusión: Lugar de enunciación e intervención social en la primera línea [Against exclusion: Locus of enunciation and frontline social intervention]. *Polis, Revista Latinoamericana*, 17(49), 259–278. https://doi.org/10.4067/S0718-65682018000100259

Muñoz-Arce, G., Hernández-Mary, N., & Véliz-Bustamante, C. (2017). La relación entre investigación e intervención social: voces desde el trabajo social chileno [The relationship between research and social intervention: Voices from chilean social work]. *Trabajo Social Global, Revista de Investigaciones en Intervención Social, 7*(12), 3–24. https://doi.org/10.30827/tsg-gsw.v7i12.5573

Mussot, M. (2018). Intervención social en tiempos de neoliberalismo en América Latina [Social intervention in times of neoliberalism in Latin America]. *Revista Trabajo Social, 20*(2), 19–52. https://doi.org/10.15446/ts.v20n2.74304

Patil, V. (2013). From patriarchy to intersectionality: A transnational feminist assessment of how far we've really come. *Signs, 38*(4), 847–867. https://doi.org/10.1086/669560

Pérez, M. & Radi, B. (2019). Current challenges of north/south relations in gay-lesbian and queer studies. *Journal of Homosexuality, 67*(7), 965–989. https://doi.org/10.1080/00918369.2019.1582218

Pombo, G. (2019). La interseccionalidad y el campo disciplinar del trabajo social: Topografías en diálogo [Intersectionality and the disciplinary field of social work: Topographies in dialogue]. In L. Riveiro (Ed.), *Trabajo Social y feminismos. Perspectivas y estrategias en debate* (pp. 149–176). Colegio de Asistentes Sociales o Trabajadores Sociales de la Provincia de Buenos Aires.

Reagon, B. J. (2000). Coalition politics: Turning the century. In B. Smith (Ed.), *Homegirls: A Black feminist anthology* (pp. 356–368). Kitchen Table, Women of Color Press.

Riveiro, L. (2019). *Trabajo Social y feminismos. Perspectivas y estrategias en debate* [Social work and feminisms. Perspectives and strategies on debate] Colegio de Asistentes Sociales o Trabajadores Sociales de la Provincia de Buenos Aires.

Rivera Cusicanqui, S. (2010). *Ch'ixinakax utxiwa. Una reflexión sobre prácticas y discursos descoloniales* [Ch'ixinakax utxiwa. A reflection on decolonial practices and discourses]. Tinta Limón/Retazos.

Rivera Cusicanqui, S. (2018). *Un mundo ch'ixi es posible. Ensayos desde un presente en crisis* [A ch'ixi world is possible. Essays from a present in crisis]. Tinta Limón.

Rodó-Zárate, M. (2021). *Interseccionalidad. Desigualdades, Lugares y Emociones* [Intersectionality. Inequalities, places and emotions]. Bellaterra Ediciones.

Segato, R. (2011). Género y colonialidad: en busca de claves de lectura y de un vocabulario estratégico descolonial [Gender and Coloniality: In search of reading keys and a decolonial strategic vocabulary]. In K. Bidaseca & V. Vásquez (Eds.), *Feminismos y Poscolonialidad. Descolonizando el feminismo desde y en América Latina* (pp. 17–48). Ediciones Godot.

Spade, D. (2013). Intersectional resistance and law reform. *Signs, 38*(4), 1031–1055. https://doi.org/10.1086/669574

Thomas, K. B. (2020). Intersectionality and epistemic erasure: A caution to decolonial feminism. *Hypatia, 35*(3), 509–523. https://doi.org/10.1017/hyp.2020.22

Troncoso, L., Follegati, L., & Stutzin, V. (2019). Más allá de una educación no sexista: aportes de pedagogías feministas interseccionales [Going beyond non-sexist education: Contributions from intersectional feminist pedagogies]. *Pensamiento Educativo, 56*(1), 1–15. https://doi.org/10.7764/PEL.56.1.2019.1

Velez, E. D. (2019). Decolonial feminism at the intersection: A critical reflection on the relationship between decolonial feminism and intersectionality. *Journal of Speculative Philosophy, 33*(3), 390–406. https://doi.org/10.5325/jspecphil.33.3.0390

Viveros, M. (2016). La interseccionalidad: una aproximación situada a la dominación [Intersectionality: A situated approach to dominance], *Debate Feminista, 52*, 1–17. https://doi.org/10.1016/j.df.2016.09.005

Yuval-Davis, N. (2006). Intersectionality and feminist politics. *European Journal of Women's Studies, 13*(3), 193–209. https://doi.org/10.1177/1350506806065752

7
SOCIAL WORK AND MARXISM
Unitary perspective in the anti-racist, feminist, and anti-imperialist struggle

Marina Machado-Gouvêa and Camila Carduz-Rocha

Our standpoint: Marxism, social work, crisis, and the totality of social reproduction

In Brazil, Marxism became the predominant perspective in the technical-operative, ethical-political, and theoretical-methodological social work Guidelines during the 1990s. This happened due to the struggle against the corporate-military dictatorship (1964–1985) and the contradictory nature of the Latin American Reconceptualisation Movement, which emerged during the 1960s, intending to accommodate the professional changes for social workers arising from capitalist expansion in previous decades, when Social Policy was first consolidated as State Policy (Alayon, 2005; Iamamoto, 1998, 2017; Netto, 1991, 2005).

Boosted by the social struggles in the region, and especially by the Cuban Revolution, this process led to the questioning of the role of social work in the social division of labour, as well as the antithetic role of Social Policy in capitalist development (Iamamoto, 1998, 2017; Netto, 1991, 2005). In Brazil, a critical perspective towards social work was defended by the Catholic University Social Work School in Belo Horizonte and became victorious in the 1979 Brazilian social workers Congress. This victory paved the way for the hegemony of a critical approach to social work during the debates of the Brazilian New Constitution in the 1980s.

An initial dispute between an openly conservative view and a developmentalist-conservative view was thus gradually overcome by a critical approach, one carried out by professionals and intellectuals that embraced historical-dialectical materialism (Iamamoto, 2017). By the end of the 1970s, the Critical social work perspective began to defeat developmentalism (Iamamoto, 1998, 2017).

The achievements of Critical social work in Brazil reflect the possibilities and limits of the struggle for rights within a capitalist society and were enshrined in the Federal Constitution of 1988 (Constituição, 1988). At the same time, they advocate for a future of overcoming capitalism as the sole means to guarantee a broader range of rights.

At the core of this process was the reconceptualisation of the notion of 'social issue'. In the documents *Diretrizes Gerais Para o Curso de Serviço Social* (Brazilian General Guidelines for Professional Training in social work) (ABPESS, 2021) and *Código de Ética do/a*

Assistente Social (Brazilian Social Workers Ethical Code) (CFESS, 1993/2019), issues traditionally labelled 'social problems', such as hunger or lack of housing, are no longer viewed in isolation nor as mere consequences of *scarcity*. On the contrary, they *sprout from the same root* – the antagonistic contradiction between an increasingly collective mode of production and increasingly private appropriation (ABEPSS, 1996/2021; CFESS, 1993/2019). In the Guidelines (ABEPSS, 1996/2021), this contradiction is identified as the root of the 'social issue'. It is entrenched within the structural and formative aspects of capitalism, and it constantly evolves within the dynamics of class struggle (Iamamoto, 2001; Ianni, 1989; Netto, 2001; Yasbek, 2001).

This, for us, is the most important point of contact between social work and Marxism. The so-called social issue does not originate in scarcity. In fact, in capitalist societies, there is plenty of food, housing, clothing, and other assets. However, capitalist relations of production obstruct an equitable distribution of goods and rights, as the working class has no possibility of accessing most of the existing means of production (Marx, 1867/1992). This critical perspective marks a departure from the philanthropic perspective in social work, previously dominant throughout Brazil. Moreover, this reconceptualisation of the 'social issue' has evolved further, as social work in Brazil acknowledges the need to consider the 'social issue' in a concrete way: it recognises that the working class is intrinsically gendered and racialised (Abepss, 2018; Gonçalves, 2018; Irineu et al., 2021).

Acknowledging that the working class does not exist in an 'abstract' sense contributes to the constant changes to which Marxism is subjected. This recognition is imperative for establishing a robust connection between theory and practice, facilitating a truly materialist understanding of the world. Reality does not exist 'in layers' but should always be understood as a totality. Historical-dialectical materialism proposes that practice is always the foundation, the criterion, and the purpose of theory (Sánchez-Vázquez, 1967/1977). Marx understood theory as part of history and considered conceptual categories as determinants of reality that need to be recognised properly to inform our actions more adequately. He perceived reality itself as an inseparable and concrete unity (Kosik, 1963/2012; Lukács, 1967/2012, 1976/2013; Sánchez-Vázquez, 1967/1977, 1967/2010).

Our times require that critical thinking reconsiders the whole of social reproduction as a *totality*. This totality is conditioned by the material reproduction of human life, which breeds, reproduces, and changes the values of a given time. When aiming to transform society, this perspective of totality is paramount to apprehend the indestructible unity among the universal, the particular, and the singular.

The contemporary capitalist organic crisis that has evolved since 2007 is unfolding as an economic, political, geopolitical, sanitary, and a climate crisis (Machado-Gouvêa, 2020a, 2020b). It encompasses a crisis of social reproduction so deep that the contradictions of capitalist modernity and the limits of capitalism for human survival can be felt as never before. Dialectically, this moment has spurred the resurgence of struggles by women, Black people, and native peoples, among others, questioning the modern notion of a 'universal subject' and challenging the utilitarian relationship with nature. This resurgence emphasises the need for reproductive work and care as indispensible aspects of human survival.

Conversely, the crisis presents itself as an open attack of the ruling class against the working classes and the peoples of the world. As such, it carries the potential for a reconfiguration of capitalism and of the widening of neoliberalism (Machado-Gouvêa, 2020b), understood here as the form assumed by capitalist reproduction after the 1965–1979 crisis and the collapse of the Socialist Camp. As such, neoliberalism is not just a set of economic, social, and foreign policies we can choose to use or not. Instead, it represents the very structure of capitalist reproduction, and its widening and deepening continue to unravel the commodification of life itself. If this unravelling exposes the antagonistic contradictions within capitalism, it also leaves the space open for the rise of conservatism, given the limitations of class conciliation pacts in times of crisis (Machado-Gouvêa, 2020a, 2020b).

This scenario demands the recognition of the role of reproductive work in the process of social reproduction. It is not only important to scrutinise who carries out this reproductive work, but also the conditions under which it is performed. We argue that racialisation, binary gendering, and territorialisation are inseparable dimensions of the social division of labour (Machado-Gouvêa, 2020c, 2022; Machado-Gouvêa & Carduz-Rocha, 2021). Hence, it is important to understand that the category 'class' does not singularly determine 'race' or 'gender', even though the category 'labour' significantly influences the material reproduction of life.

This concreteness of the working class is often left aside in essentialist understandings of class contradictions common within Marxism. In response to this problem, a common point of view is that it is necessary to overcome Marxism. This reactionary point of view assumes that all Marxist analyses inherently essentialise class, which is false, given the examples of the contrary. The work of Frantz Fanon, Angela Davis, Eugene DuBois, Clóvis Moura, George Jackson, and Heleieth Saffiotti, among others, provides non-essentialist perspectives within the Marxist tradition. This view deems Marxism insufficient, Eurocentric, mainstream, and even 'civilising'.

Such perspectives can lead to assuming the centrality of race and/or gender, without understanding them as the basis of an integrative ontology that encompasses all dimensions of the social division of labour. However, this tendency remains prevalent within the field of feminist studies, whether through an autonomist understanding that considers social reproduction as a whole (e.g. Federici, 2017, 2019) or from a perspective that regards racism and Patriarchy as separate systems intersecting from capitalism (e.g. Lerner, 1986, see also Akotirene, 2019) or consubstantiated with it (e.g. Delphy, 1977; Kergoát, 2010).

It is vital to note that no single or hegemonic understanding exists in any of the perspectives mentioned above. The process of theoretical reflection is complex and carries the risk of omission or error. It evolves through critique, negation, and affirmation of previous viewpoints. The history of social thought is always based on a confrontation of distinct perspectives, all materially based on distinct interests and in the contradictions of the social reproduction itself.

Concerning feminist studies, a critique of the above-mentioned perspectives is made by the theorists of Social Reproduction Theory (SRT). SRT is one of the approaches that advocate for an integrative ontology based on a perspective of totality. In other words, it considers social production and reproduction as a contradictory and dialectical unity, while considering oppressions as structural and formative elements in the process of capital accumulation (Arruzza, 2013, 2014; Arruzza et al., 2019; Bhattacharya, 2013, 2017; Ferguson, 2016; Fraser, 2016; Vogel, 2013. See also Ruas, 2021). SRT entails the study of value production/circulation in capitalist accumulation, including the share of these that are directly related to the reproduction of labour power. Additionally, it investigates the study of reproductive labour, which often remains unrecognised in our society. It proposes that all the labour required for the reproduction of collective social labour power is part of the accumulation of capital, exerting a determining influence of all aspects of life. SRT presents itself as a tool for understanding and transforming reality, as it recognises conflicts surrounding social reproduction as key in the dispute between capital and labour within the broader dynamics of class struggle (Carduz-Rocha, 2021).

Another decisive critique of the aforementioned non-totality perspectives, although not directly aimed at them, is offered through the integrative scholarship of brilliant Marxist intellectual Angela Davis (1981, 1990, 2015, among others). Davis explores race, gender, and class as a unity, by means of studying the past and present history of capitalism and the many faces of class struggle. Her work is part of the distinguished field of Black Marxism and she is an important author within multiple currents of Black Feminism.

We believe that revolutionary praxis must arise from contributions such as the radical and multiple fecundities of Black Marxism, the SRT, the Marxist Theory of Dependence, the experiences of originary peoples who strive for a life in plenitude, and the reclaiming of Marxism as a *philosophy of praxis*. A Marxist perspective based on the concreteness of social reproduction is indispensable to contemporary revolutionary praxis. It is also key to deepening the reconceptualisation of the category 'social issue'. This standpoint inspires some of the following reflections.

The racial, binary-gendered, and territorial division of labour as inseparable dimensions of the social division of labour in capitalism

The working class does not exist in isolated, 'abstract' form neither does the dominant class. People embodying social classes carry a multitude of factors, including race, gender, territory, sexual orientation, age, and more. The connections between these determinations are not external to capitalism, but an inseparable part of its existence. To interact theoretically with the working class purely in abstract terms is to assume a philosophical idealism, to postulate a reality that does not exist (Machado-Gouvêa, 2017; Machado-Gouvêa and Mastropaolo, 2019).

In capitalism, commodification is the most fundamental trace of both individual and social life reproduction. In order to consume goods, we must be alive, and to stay alive, we must consume and produce goods, and commodities. This, in turn, necessitates access to money. For those who lack sufficient access to the means of production, the alternative is to sell one's own labour power as a commodity, to be able to obtain the means to acquire necessities and remain alive.

However, as the collective social workforce reproduces, there is a need for quantities of non-commodified labour. In a mode of production where value is determined by commodification, these quantities of non-commodified labour are not socially recognised as labour (for a debate on what is considered labour in capitalism, see Marx, 1867/1992, 2023. Also see Bhattacharya, 2017; Carcanholo, 2007; Marini, 1998/2008). This is what we term 'invisible reproductive labour' which is an integral part of capitalist reproduction. The facts that it is mainly performed by women of colour and that it is ethically devalued, is intertwined with the perception of whiteness as ethically superior to non-whiteness. It also relates to the ethical valuation of masculinity over the feminine, in a binary-gendered norm. These concrete social constructs play a reciprocal role in how the labour force is valued. Together with performing invisible reproductive labour, populations that are looked down on by the capitalist ethical system are those whose labour force prices and exchange values are drastically devalued when sold directly. Racialisation, binary gender roles, and territorialisation are linked to the ethical assessment of a particular social group over others. This favoured group – white, cisgendered, and metropolitan – becomes the reference point for social recognition. It is the group whose interests are most universalised by coercion and consensus. It constitutes the image of the 'universal subject', ideologically passed on to all of us. Ultimately, only a small group of people genuinely align with the liberal notion of the 'individual' that we typically internalise. The individuals that can truly be socially recognised as fully entitled 'individuals' are only white, cisgendered, and heterosexual men, from the capitalist core countries who also own the means of production.

This is a historical ethical construct, which imposes itself beyond our individual will and can only be collectively transformed. In the course of human praxis, we are guided by ethical values. We reproduce values and we generate new values. Our actions exert an influence on the entirety of society's value system, and this impact extends to the quantitative dimension of the value of labour power – its exchange value (Machado-Gouvêa, 2022).

We base our analysis on three findings drawn from our previous work (Machado-Gouvêa, 2020c; Machado-Gouvêa and Carduz-Rocha, 2021). We assert that it is due to this ethical system, inevitably produced with the capitalist reproduction of life, that leads to the following outcomes: (a) individuals of colour and those who do not conform to masculine norms experience the devaluation and underpricing of their labour based on race and gender; (b) non-commodified reproductive work is not recognised as value-producing, and disproportionately burdens coloured people and women; and (c) this, in turn, reinforces and exacerbates the dehumanisation of these groups, based on race, gender, sexual orientation, disabilities, age, and more. This cycle of dehumanisation contributes to higher rates of violence and a continuous threat to these bodies and lives.

When selling their labour power, the value and price of labour for different groups of the population are determined in a particular way

In Latin America and the Caribbean, poverty disproportionately affects women, Indigenous Peoples, and Black communities. In 2019, there were 13.3% more women than men living in poverty in *Nuestra America*, the term used by Cuban poet José Martí to refer to Latin America and the Caribbean (Eclac, 2022). In the same year, in Brazil, the poverty rate was 11.5% among the white population and 25.5% for the Black population. In Colombia, it stood at 27.7% for white people and 40.8% for Black people; in Ecuador, the rates were 19.5% for white people and 31.5% for Black people; in Peru, 9.9% for white people and 19.6% for Black people; and in Uruguay, it was 2.7% for white people and 7.5% for Black people (Eclac, 2021).

In Brazil in 2019, for a white woman to earn the same as a white man when selling her labour power, she had to work an average of 17% more (Dieese, 2019). A Black man had to work 75% more than a white man, and a Black woman 92% more. These disparities are on rise, exacerbated by economic crisis and the actions of the dominant class, who use racism and misogyny to increase profit margins. In 2022, the average income of Black women in Brazil was 46% of the average income of white men (Ibge, 2023). Between 2014 and 2019, the average real income of non-Black people fell by 6.8%, and that of Black people fell by 13% (Dieese, 2019). This means a decrease in purchase power (fewer or lower quality commodities – goods and services), and less access to rights.

Women and those racialised as people of colour are most likely to find themselves part of the reserve army of labour, either as the unemployed or in latent or floating forms of this relative surplus population. On a global scale, women make up 60% of the unemployed population (or the stagnant form of the reserve army of labour, in Marxist terms) and have higher rates of informality (Oxfam, 2020). This is directly related to systematic gender violence and to the idea that women have less time for work, stemming from the notion that women bear the primary responsibility for caregiving. As a result, women tend to have 'multiple shifts' and employers tend to fear the possibility of their cisgendered women employees becoming pregnant and consequently accessing labour rights (Oxfam, 2020).

In pre-pandemic Brazil, prior to the worsening of the global crisis caused by the pandemic (a period during which the Bolsonaro government failed to generate sufficient data), unemployment for Black people was 12% and 8.2% for non-Black people. The unemployment rate for Black women was notably higher at 16.7% and for non-Black women at 11% (Dieese, 2019; Ibge, 2019). During the initial six months of the pandemic, the unemployment rate surged to 13.8% for Black men and 17.6% for Black women (Ibge-pnad-covid, 2020).

This data shows a difference in labour power pricing based on race and gender. We argue that there might also be a difference in the values of exchange of this labour force.

Within the framework of capitalism, it is not socially recognised that a woman holds the same value as a man or that a Black person holds the same value as a white person (Fanon, 1952/2008; González & Hasenbalg, 1982/2022; hooks, 1981/2014; Moura, 1977/2021; Nascimento, 1976). Similarly, it is also not recognised that a person from dependent regions has the same value as a person coming from central regions (a distinction that is often linked to racialisation).

There is also a lack of social recognition that the reproduction of a woman's life and her labour power require the consumption of the same quantity of commodities as that of a man. Likewise, it is not acknowledged that the reproduction of the life and the labour power of those racialised as people of colour require the consumption of the same amount of abstract human labour as the reproduction of the lives of people racialised as white. Finally, the reproduction of the life and labour power of someone from a dependent region is not recognised as requiring the same consumption of abstract human labour as that of someone from a central region.

Furthermore, the recognition of the basket of goods and services (in the form of social rights or commodities) that must be consumed for the reproduction of the labour power changes according to the specialisation or qualification of the work performed (Machado-Gouvêa, 2020c, 2022).

In our society, particular types of work are disqualified as *women's work* (see Oxfam, 2020). The association of women with the work of caring, cleaning, cooking, teaching, treating, and attending to people, among others, is deeply ingrained in our society, yet it is fundamentally a historical construct. Similarly, there are types of work that are stigmatised as *slave work* (Almeida, 2019; González & Hasenbalg, 1982/2022; Moura, 1977/2021; Nascimento, 1976), as a result of the displacement, dispossession, and forced enslavement of populations from Africa and the Americas. This marginalisation contributed to policies of whitening and to the physical and cultural genocide of Black and native people. The association of Black and native people with kinds of work that are less healthy, more physically demanding, and with the work of caregiving and domestic work has been amplified by ideological currents such as scientific racism and fascism which sought to dehistoricise and naturalise these associations. For Black and native women, some of the ethical constraints concerning work in our society are particularly distressing, as the notions of 'women's work' and 'slave work' intersect.

We argue that the labour power qualified for jobs involving reproductive work is undervalued. In general, the sale of labour power by women and people of colour is confined to these sectors, further diminishing their exchange value and pricing. For example, in Latin America and the Caribbean, hired domestic work is one of the most undervalued occupations, a product of sexism and slavery (González, 1984; Preta-Rara, 2019). In 2021, in Brazil, 92% of domestic workers were women and 65% were Black women (Ibge, 2022). They typically receive less than the minimum wage and are employed under informal working conditions (Ibge, 2022). Worldwide, 80% of hired domestic workers are women, and nine out of ten cannot access labour rights (Oxfam, 2020).

In dependent countries, the effect of these determinants could also contribute to the structural tendency of overexploitation of labour power as a form of compensating the transfer of value in dependent countries (see Fagundes, 2022; Sabino, 2020; Soares, 2022).

Women, particularly those racialised as people of colour, bear the heaviest burden of invisible domestic and care workload, which often goes unrecognised as legitimate labour

When we approach social reproduction as a totality, the invisible portion of domestic and care workload is not 'external' to capitalism. On the contrary, we can see capitalist relations of production both in their past and present historical development. This kind of labour contributes to capital accumulation, as it contributes to the production of labour power as a commodity (Bhattacharya, 2017). It relates, however, to a kind of labour that does not create or exchange any other commodities apart from labour power itself. As such, it is not socially recognised as labour, despite being an integral part of capitalist accumulation.

Only labour that produces commodities is the type of labour that can be socially recognised as necessary for the reproduction of labour power in capitalism. This happens when these commodities are also recognised as necessary for the reproduction of labour power. For example, the total amount of socially required abstract labour to produce one pound of rice as a commodity is recognised as an amount of labour socially necessary for the reproduction of the labour force itself, once this rice is bought by workers to reproduce their lives (Marx, 1992/1867). The same happens with the direct or indirect commodification of leisure, services, and other elements.

However, the amount of labour needed for these same workers to cook this rice at home is not recognised as necessary for the reproduction of labour power. Its only when the rice is bought already cooked, in a restaurant for instance, the socially required abstract labour to cook it becomes part of its exchange value and is recognised as necessary to the reproduction of these workers' labour power.

The basket of goods and services socially recognised as necessary for the reproduction of labour power is different for each group, according to race and gender and according to the nature of the work performed. In some professions, the need to buy reproductive work as a commodity is socially recognised, composing the ongoing labour force exchange value in these professions. That is the case of some middle-class wages, which reflect a social recognition of the need to buy food in restaurants or to hire someone else to do the cleaning.

These better valued and/or more qualified occupations are not equally accessible to differently racialised and gendered people. Consequently, coloured women are the most overloaded by an invisible amount of reproductive labour.

In Latin America and the Caribbean, an Eclac survey concluded that women spend an average of 37 hours a week on unpaid domestic and care work, compared to 13 hours for men (SEPLA, 2019). In Colombia, women do unpaid domestic and care work for 34.1

hours/week, compared to 18.4 hours for men (DANE & UN-Women, 2018). In Brazil, women dedicated 21.3 hours to domestic chores in 2018, about twice as many hours as men (Neto, 2019).

Women are the majority in all forms of reproductive work, waged and unwaged. The ethical conditioning that leads them to bear the greatest burden of invisible reproductive labour are the same constraints that restrict the selling of their own labour power to jobs related to the reproduction of labour force in general (on which they suffer the impacts shown in the previous section).

According to Oxfam International (2020), women perform 75% of the world's unwaged domestic and care work. Regarding waged care work, women constitute 60% of the world's workforce (Oxfam, 2020). In healthcare, 70% of positions are filled by women, and they are often in positions most subject to unprotected contact with patients – which had a significant impact on their health during the Covid-19 pandemic.

Invisible reproductive labour is essential to capitalist accumulation. However, since it goes unrecognised as labour, the actual labour it represents does not contribute to the formation of the exchange value of labour power. Consequently, it can be entirely appropriated by the dominant class in the form of surplus labour or surplus value, effectively expropriating it from the population that performs this labour and increasing the exploitation of labour power in general (Machado-Gouvêa, 2020a, 2022).

This invisibilisation impacts the exchange value of labour power for the entire working class by altering the quantity of abstract labour socially considered as necessary for the reproduction of labour power (Machado-Gouvêa, 2020a, 2022).

Women and populations racialised as Black or Indigenous experience heightened levels of violence under capitalism in Latin America and the Caribbean

This ethical subordination of some parts of humanity compared to others is connected to their relative dehumanisation. It is linked to the persistent, unacknowledged perpetuation of everyday micro-aggressions, as well as to the normalisation of historically constructed practices, including torture, sexual violence, spatial segregation, and selective hunting.

Adult women and girls account for 72% of the world's victims of human trafficking. More than 80% of human traffic victims are women, and nearly 75% of them are girls (Unodoc, 2018). Regrettably, this aligns with one of the most fundamental North-South dynamics, alongside the overexploitation of undocumented immigrant labour.

For 13 years, Brazil has witnessed the highest number of murders of transgender people (Transrespect, 2021). In the region, countries with high rates of transgender murders include Mexico, Colombia, and Ecuador (Transrespect, 2022).

Racist state violence also claims hundreds of thousands of lives, a fact downplayed by the portion of Brazilian population considered white. In Brazil, 6,416 people were murdered by the police in 2020, 79% of them were Black (FBSP, 2021). Between 2007 and 2017, Black homicides grew by 33.1%, while non-Black homicides grew by only 3.3% (FBSP, 2019). The probability of a young Black person being a victim of homicide is 2.7 times higher than if they were not Black, even though, officially, the Black population comprises less than 0.25 times their proportion of the total population. Three-quarters of people murdered by police officers in Brazil in 2017–2018 were Black and 51.7% of police deaths were also Black, represented in only 34% of the police force (FBSP, 2019).

Motherhood is frequently denied to Black and Indigenous women by the state. Throughout history, Black women have had their children uprooted and enslaved for the production of commodities (Davis, 2016). They also had to bear forced sterilisation processes (Cruz, 2018; Stabile, 2022) and the murder of their children due to state violence (Passos, 2023). It's important to note that abortion by choice is illegal for most Latin American and Caribbean women, which affects the poor (racialised as Black or Indigenous), who do not have access to quality clandestine clinics (Diniz, Medeiros & Madeiro, 2017).

Consistent with this data, femicide rates make Latin America and the Caribbean the deadliest region in the world for women (UN-women, 2019). In 2018, more than 3,500 femicides were recorded, being more than nine per day (UN-women, 2019). These figures are likely an underestimation. For instance, in Mexico, the feminist movement reported an average of ten femicides per day in 2020 (Amnistía Internacional, 2021).

Gender-based violence is often perpetrated by people close to the victims, and often within the household (UN-women, 2019), contradicting the neoconservative discourse that the family would protect children and women from 'external' violence. The World Health Organisation found that in 15 countries within the region 69% of women reported experiencing violence at the hands of their partners, 53% of women said they had suffered physical or sexual violence by an intimate partner during their lifetime, and 47% of women said they were victims of at least one sexual assault (SEPLA, 2019). The situation is worse at lower income brackets. The majority of rape victims are girls. In Brazil, in 2018, 66,000 women were victims of rape, marking a record since the beginning of the research in 2007. Of this group, 53.8% were girls up to 13 years old (FBSP, 2019).

Black women die more frequently and more violently. They were 66% of female murder victims and 61% of femicide victims in Brazil in 2017 (FBSP, 2019). The murder rate among Black women grew by 30% between 2007 and 2017, compared to 4.5% among non-Black women. In addition, Black women are more likely to be attacked in public spaces (32% of Black women vs. 23% of white women), more harassed (40.5% of Black women vs. 34.9% of white women), and seek fewer official bodies to report violence (FBSP, 2019).

These multiple violences are not just products of so-called original capitalist accumulation, even though the ethical devaluation of Black or Indigenous racialised people in capitalism began with colonial slavery and forced labour. Structural racism and structural misogyny are integral components of capitalist accumulation and of the racial and binary-gendered division of labour itself.

Conclusions

The data presented indicate that (i) female workers, particularly those racialised as Black and Indigenous and/or immigrants, are the most overexploited portion of the labour force in the region; (ii) they are the most overloaded with reproductive, socially unappreciated work; and (iii) they are subject to multiple forms of oppression and violence.

The data speaks for itself and is even recognised by liberal perspectives. From a Marxist perspective, it is necessary to understand those determinations within the context of the totality of social reproduction, investigating the material reproduction of life as a whole, in its concrete determinations and overdeterminations.

This political and theoretical point of view must assume practice as the foundation, the criterion, and the purpose of theory. It aims to interpret reality as a totality to inform praxis. This perspective is especially crucial for social work, where Marxist perspectives – including the contributions of SRT, Black Marxism, the Marxist Theory of Dependence, and the reclaiming of Marxism as a philosophy of praxis – are invaluable. Social workers operate at the expressions of various aspects of the 'social issue', where they mediate the conditions in which labour power reproduces.

Recognising the inseparable dimensions of the racial, binary-gendered and the territorial division of labour within capitalism is essential to deepen reconceptualisation of the category 'social issue'. This is indispensable to better understand the dynamics of the reproduction of labour power and impact the education and professional practice of social workers. We believe that a Marxist perspective based on the concreteness of social reproduction as a totality is key.

An anti-racist, feminist, anti-imperialist, and anti-capitalist perspective is necessary to investigate capitalism as a social totality and to overcome it.

References

Associação Brasileira de Ensino e Pesquisa em Serviço Social (ABEPSS) (2018). *Subsídios para o debate sobre a questão étnico-racial na formação em serviço social*. Associação Brasileira de Ensino e Pesquisa em Serviço Social.

Associação Brasileira de Ensino e Pesquisa em Serviço Social (ABEPSS) (2021). *Diretrizes gerais para o curso de serviço social* (Commemorative trilingual ed.). Associação Brasileira de Ensino e Pesquisa em Serviço Social (Original work published 1996). https://www.abepss.org.br/arquivos/textos/documento_20230302165042293900.pdf

Akotirene, C. (2019). *Interseccionalidade*. Pólen.

Alayon, N. (Ed.) (2005). *Trabajo social latino-americano. A 40 años de la reconceptualización*. Espacio Editorial.

Almeida, S. (2019). *Racismo estrutural*. Pólen.

Amnistía Internacional (2021). Juicio a la Justicia. https://amnistia.org.mx/contenido/wp-content/uploads/2021/09/Informe-Juicio-a-la-Justicia-Amnist%C3%ADa-Internacional-M%C3%A9xico.pdf

Arruzza, C. (2013). *Dangerous liaisons: The marriages and divorces of Marxism and feminism*. The Merlin Press.

Arruza, C. (2014). *Remarks on gender*. Viewpoint Magazine.

Arruzza, C., Bhattacharya, T., & Fraser, N. (2019). *Feminism for the 99%: A manifesto*. Verso.

Bhattacharya, T. (2013, September 10). What is social reproduction theory? *Socialist Worker*.

Bhattacharya, T. (Ed.) (2017). *Social reproduction theory: Remapping class, recentering oppression*. Pluto Press.

Carcanholo, R. (2007). *O Trabalho Produtivo Na Teoria Marxista*. Mimeo. https://www.unicamp.br/cemarx/anais_v_coloquio_arquivos/arquivos/comunicacoes/gt1/sessao7/Reinaldo_Carcanholo.pdf

Carduz-Rocha, C. (2021). La división social del trabajo en la (re)producción capitalista en tiempos de la pandemia del Covid-19. *Plaza Pública*, 14(25), 5–23

Constituição (1988). *Constituição da República Federativa do Brasil*. Constitution of the Federative Republic of Brazil.

Cruz, E. A. (2018). *O caso Janaína me lembrou que o Brasil já fez esterilização em massa, com apoio dos EUA*. Intercept Brasil. https://bit.ly/44ipoGq

DANE (National Administrative and Statistics Department) and UN-Women (2018). Progress of women in Columbia 2018: Transforming the economy to guarantee rights. ONU Mujeres https://www.dane.gov.co/files/investigaciones/genero/publicaciones/INVESTIGAS_innova_estadisticas_genero.pdf

Davis, A. (1981). *Women, race & class*. Vintage Books.

Davis, A. (1990). *Women, culture & politics*. Vintage Books.

Davis, A. (2015). *Freedom is a constant struggle: Ferguson, Palestine, and the foundations of a movement*. Haymarket.

Davis, A. Y. 2016. *Freedom is a constant* struggle, F. Barat (Ed). Haymarket Books.

Delphy, C. (1977). *The main enemy*. Women's Research and Resources Centre Publications.
Dieese (2019). Análise PED, diversas regiões metropolitanas. https://bit.ly/3y5gAWp
Diniz, D., Medeiros, M., & Madeiro, A. (2017). Pesquisa Nacional de Aborto 2016. *Revista Ciência e Saúde Coletiva*, 22(2), 653–660
Eclac (2021). *Síntese: Afrodescendentes e a matriz da desigualdade social na América Latina*. Desafios para a inclusão. https://bit.ly/3OpAnp1
Eclac (2022). Cepalstat. https://oig.cepal.org/pt/indicadores/indice-feminidade-da-pobreza
Fagundes, G. (2022). *Superexploração e racismo no Brasil: diálogos e questões*. Ed. Appris.
Fanon, F. (2008). *Black skin, white masks*. Groove Press. (Original work published 1952).
FBSP (2019). Anuário brasileiro de segurança pública, 13. https://bit.ly/3QsdO4V
FBSP (2021). Anuário brasileiro de segurança pública, 15. https://bit.ly/3HE2PkI
Federal Council of Social Services (CFESS) (1993/2019). *Código de Ética do/a Assistente Social* [Code of Ethics of the Social Worker, Brazil] https://www.cfess.org.br/arquivos/2019CfessCEP-Trilingue-Site.pdf
Federici, S. (2017). Notes on gender in Marx's Capital. *Continental Thought & Theory: A Journal of Intellectual Freedom*, 1(4), 19–37
Federici, S. (2019). *Re-enchanting the world: Feminism and the politics of the commons*. PM Press.
Ferguson, S. (2016). Intersectionality and social-reproduction feminisms: toward an Integrative ontology. *Historical Materialism*, 24 (2), 38–60.
Fraser, N. (2016). Contradictions of capital and care. *New Left Review*, 99–117.
Gonçalves, R. (2018). Quando a questão racial é o nó da questão social. *Revista Katálysis*, 21(03), 514–522. https://doi.org/10.1590/1982-02592018v21n3p514
González, L. (1984). *Racismo E Sexismo Na Cultura Brasileira*. Revista Ciências Sociais Hoje, Anpocs, 1984.
González, L. & Hasenbalg, C. (2022). *Lugar de negro*. Zahar. (Original work published 1982).
hooks, b. (2014). *Ain't I a woman?* Routledge. (Original work published 1981).
Iamamoto, M. (1998). *Serviço Social na contemporaneidade: trabalho e formação profissional*. Cortez.
Iamamoto, M. (2001). A questão social no capitalismo. ABEPSS. *Revista Temporalis*, 2(3), 9–32.
Iamamoto, M. (2017). 80 anos do Serviço Social no Brasil: a certeza na frente, a história na mão. *Serviço Social e Sociedade*, 128, 13–38. https://doi.org/10.1590/0101-6628.091
Ianni, O. (1989). A questão social. *Revista Usp*, 3, 145–154.
Ibge (2019). Pesquisa Nacional por Amostra de Domicílios. Retrieved March, 2020, from www.ibge.gov.br
Ibge (2022). Pesquisa Nacional por Amostra de Domicílios. Retrieved April, 2023, from www.ibge.gov.br
Ibge (2023). Pesquisa Nacional por Amostra de Domicílios. Retrieved April, 2023, from www.ibge.gov.br
Ibge-Pnad-Covid (2020). Pesquisa Nacional por Amostra de Domicílios COVID-19. Retrieved September, 2021, from www.ibge.gov.br
Irineu, B., Silva, L., Cantalice, L., Brettas, T. & Closs, T. (2021). Crise capitalista, questão social no Brasil e diretrizes curriculares da Abepss. *Revista Temporalis*, 21(42), 6–15.
Kergoát, D. (2010). Dinâmica e consubstancialidade das relações sociais. *Revista Novos Estudos CEBRAP*, 86, 93–103.
Kosik, K. (2012). *Dialetics of the concrete. A study on problems of man and world*. Dordrecht. (Original work published 1963).
Lerner, G. (1986). *The creation of patriarchy*. Oxford University Press.
Lukács, G. (2012). *Para uma ontologia do ser social*, v.1. Boitempo. (Original work published 1976).
Lukács, G. (2013). *Para uma ontologia do ser social*, v.2. Boitempo. (Original work published 1976).
Machado-Gouvêa, M. (2018). Marxismo, questão social e capitalismo dependente. *Anais do XVI Encontro Nacional de Pesquisa e Ensino em Serviço Social*. ABEPSS (Proceedings of the XVI National Meeting of Research and Teaching in Social Work), 1–16. https://periodicos.ufes.br/abepss/article/view/22121
Machado-Gouvêa, M. (2020a). A culpa da crise não é do vírus. In Moreira, E., et al. (Eds.), *Em tempos de pandemia. Propostas para defesa da vida e de direitos sociais*. Edufrj, 19–28. http://www.cress-es.org.br/wp-content/uploads/2020/05/1_5028797681548394620.pdf

Machado-Gouvea, M. (2020b). Estamos vivendo uma reconfiguração da tecitura capitalista. *Revista Margem Esquerda*, 35.
Machado-Gouvêa, M. (2020c). Lendo o Capital na quarentena. Aula 8: Classe Trabalhadora e Divisão Racial, Binariogenerificada e Territorial do trabalho [vídeo file]. YouTube. https://bit.ly/3bCzeML
Machado-Gouvêa, M. (2022). Reclaiming Marx's surplus value: racial, gendered and geographical divisions of labour today, in context of the capitalist crisis [Manuscript submitted for publication].
Machado-Gouvêa, M. & Carduz-Rocha, C. (2021). Trabajo social y lucha antirracista, antipatriarcal y anti-imperialista: una actitud política necesaria. *Eleuthera*, 23(1), 261–282.
Machado-Gouvêa, M. & Mastropaolo, J. (2019). Capitalismo, racismo, patriarcado, dependência: por uma teoria unitária materialista, histórico-dialética. *Anais do Congresso Internacional Marx e o Marxismo*. NIEP-UFF. August 2019, Niterói, Rio De Janero. https://www.niepmarx.blog.br/MM/MM2019/AnaisMM2019/MC27/MC271.pdf
Marini, R. M. (2008). *El concepto de trabajo productivo*. Nota Metodológica. Clacso Editorial. (Original work published 1998).
Marx, K. (1992). *The capital. Critique of political economy*. Vol. 1. Penguin. (Original work published 1867).
Marx, K. (2023). *Manuscritos de 1863–1867*. Capítulo 6, inédito. Boitempo.
Moura, C. (2021). *O negro: de bom escravo a mau cidadão?* Dandara. (Original work published 1977).
Nascimento, B. (1976). A mulher negra no mercado de trabalho. *Jornal A Última Hora*. https://bit.ly/3Li7N8Z
Neto, J. (2019). *Mulheres dedicam quase o dobro do tempo dos homens em tarefas domésticas*. Agência IBGE. https://bit.ly/3tNOEns
Netto, J. P. (1991). *Ditadura e serviço social: uma análise do serviço social no Brasil pós-64*. Cortez.
Netto, J. P (2001). Cinco notas a propósito da 'questão social'. *Revista Temporalis*, 2(3), 41–50.
Netto, J. P. (2005). O Movimento de Reconceituação: 40 anos depois. *Revista Serviço Social e Sociedade*, 84 (26), 5–20.
Oxfam (2020). Tempo de cuidar: o trabalho de cuidado não remunerado e mal pago e a crise global da desigualdade. https://www.oxfam.org.br/publicacao/tempo-de-cuidar-o-trabalho-de-cuidado-nao-remunerado-e-mal-pago-e-a-crise-global-da-desigualdade/
Passos, R. G. (2023). *Na mira do fuzil: a saúde mental das mulheres negras em questão*. Hucitec.
Preta-Rara (2019). *Eu, empregada doméstica: a senzala moderna é o quartinho da empregada*. Letramento.
Ruas, R. (2021). Teoria da Reprodução Social: apontamentos para uma perspectiva unitária das relações sociais capitalistas. *Revista Direito e Práxis*, 12(01), 379–415.
Sabino, C. (2020). *Racismo e luta de classes na América Latina: as veias abertas do capitalismo dependente*. Hucitec.
Sánchez-Vázquez, A. (1977). *The philosophy of praxis*. Humanities Press. (Original work published 1967).
Sánchez-Vázquez, A. (2010). *O conceito de essência humana em Marx*. Anexo. In Sánchez Vázquez, A., *Filosfia da Práxis*. Expressão Popular. (Original work published 1967).
SEPLA (2019). La lucha por el socialismo debe ser antirracista y antipatriarcal, o no será victoriosa [comunicado de prensa]. www.sepla21.org
Soares, M. (2022). *Escravidão e dependência: opressões e superexploração da força de trabalho*. Lutas Anticapital.
Stabile, A. (2022). Quem são as mulheres submetidas a laqueadura no Brasil. *Jornal O Estado de São Paulo*. https://bit.ly/3LJhNd5
Transrespect (2021). Trans Murder Monitoring Project (TMM). TVT TMM Update: Trans day of remembrance 2021.
Transrespect (2022). Trans Murder Monitoring Project (TMM). Map. https://bit.ly/3OxIq3n
Unodoc (2018). Global Report on Trafficking in Persons 2018. https://bit.ly/39CcLyA
Un-women (2019). Hechos y cifras: Acabar con la violencia contra mujeres y niñas. https://bit.ly/3udqBi5
Vogel, L. (2013). *Marxism and the oppression of women: Toward a unitary theory*. Brill.
Yasbek, C. (2001). Pobreza e exclusão social: expressões da questão social no Brasil. *Revista Temporalis*, 2(3), 33–40.

8
SOCIAL WORK, INDIGENOUS FEMINISMS AND DECOLONISATION OF PUBLIC POLICIES IN CHILE

Alicia Rain Rain

Introduction

This chapter is intentionally written in plural in order to recognise that it is collective knowledge and not individual knowledge, and since the author herself is a Mapuche woman with experience in the field of social work in Chile.

The Spanish conquest in the current country of Chile and Argentina led to a series of warlike confrontations, where the Mapuche people managed to resist through various cultural practices based on territorial political alliances and the forging of socio-familial relationships, such as polygamy. Therefore, the Spanish army adapted to the above-mentioned practices to negotiate with the Mapuche people and, mainly, to seek new practices of conquest (Boccara, 2007; Zavala, 2008). In this context, one of the most representative institutions of the 17th century was the parliament, which gave way to peace treaties. Thus, the Mapuche people gained their territorial and political independence on January 6, 1641 (Pichinao, 2012; Zavala, 2008).

Mapuche territorial and political autonomy (Pichinao, 2012) were compromised by 'integration strategies', through Spanish educational and religious institutions (Zavala, 2008). Therefore, the 17th century was a period that combined warfare with integration strategies in a scenario of 'apparent' peace (Zavala, 2008). These integration strategies were systematically pursued by the Chilean state in the context of its independence from the Spanish Crown (Pichinao, 2012). This is what is known as social and political whitening (Mariman, 2006).

In the second half of the 20th century, a military campaign based on violence was implemented to expropriate the lands of the Mapuche people and dispossess the Mapuche people of their political agency (Mariman, 2006; Pichinao, 2012). The public policies that have prevailed in Chile have been policies based on colonial dispossession. In addition, they have been intentionally integrationist policies, since white and Western values, practices and ways of conceiving the world and life have prevailed, which do not value what the First Nations claim (Bolados, 2012; Pichinao, 2012).

Integrationist and colonial dispossession policies have coexisted with neoliberal and patriarchal practices for the last 200 years (Cumes, 2014; Guerra, 2014). Hence, the social and/or political situation and contributions of racialised women have mattered little in political agendas (García-Mingo, 2017; Richards, 2016). Thus, a multidimensional demand emerges. It is about the recognition and valuation of the political actors of the nations, but also of the processes of depatriarchalising and struggle against the capitalist project, which has driven appropriation by dispossession (Harvey, 2007).

These multidimensional demands challenge social work, as a discipline and profession, to critically analyse the public policies implemented in Chile. A framework to support this necessary concern is that social work adopts a clear position, which can be seen in its global definition which promotes respect for diversity and valuing the knowledge of First Nations, which was approved by the IASSW General Assembly and the IFSW General Meeting in 2014 (International Federation of Social Workers, 2014).

In this chapter, we propose to reflect on the colonial and patriarchal rationality of public policies in Chile and to show the contributions of Indigenous Feminisms and the visibilisation of non-hegemonic knowledge that have been excluded in the policy-making process. In the first part, we address the logics that prevail in the design and implementation of 'monocultural' public policies, which underlies an idea of social development that excludes racialised people, particularly women. Subsequently, we present a review of the main contributions that Mapuche women have built in Chile, in their daily experiences or within their processes of organisation and political participation, particular forms of resistance, since we belong to that collective. Finally, we present some strategic guidelines to contribute to the process of decolonisation and depatriarchalisation of public policies, which we consider to be central challenges to approach the construction of a decolonial social work with a situated gender perspective.

Monoculturalist and patriarchal logics of public policies in Chile

Some of the writings of Spanish chroniclers gave an account of the biases regarding gender relations in Mapuche society. Evidence of this are Jorge Juan and Antonio Ulloa, who in the 17th century dismissed Mapuche defensive tactics against the weaponry and power of the Spanish Army (Zavala, 2008). The expressions of sexuality and the relationships that single women established with different partners are some of the examples (Calfío, 2012). In this regard, at the time of the first menstruation of Mapuche girls, collective celebrations were held, which was questioned by representatives of the Catholic Church (Calfío, 2012; Castillo-Muñoz & Mora-Guerrero, 2020).

The Catholic Church, together with the education system, exerted significant transformations in the way of conceiving the world, but also in the meanings of certain events and practices regarding sexuality, family formation, among others (Calfío, 2012; Zavala, 2008). After these colonial contacts, the ceremony of the onset of puberty for women was no longer a source of pride, but a shameful event. From that historical moment on, the Mapuche woman came to be seen as a figure of family and community distrust. Patriarchal ideologies are installed, as Mapuche women are seen as synonymous with sin and as the cause of male and family dishonour (Calfío, 2012; García-Mingo, 2017).

Colonial relations have had far-reaching socio-historical and political repercussions, such as the establishment of monoculturalism and Western cultural dominance at the level of public policies related to education, health or justice (Marimán, 2006). In this way, all knowledge, meaning and practice of what has been understood as education, generated through Mapuche traditions, has been replaced by Western knowledge guided by people outside the *lof*, – Mapuche territories of belonging –, and transmitted in a language that is foreign and dominant, such as Spanish (Marimán, 2006). Likewise, another instance of colonisation has been the way of understanding, but also the way of approaching health and disease, by means of a policy that denies socio-cultural and territorial particularities, in this case of the Mapuche people.

Reproductive health is a field of colonial disciplining, but it also shows an androcentric approach, which relegates women's corporealities to a space of biological intervention, of maximum control and isolation. Hence, a sort of social, emotional and collective fracture is produced in the experiences of some Mapuche women, especially those who live in the Mapuche territory, *Wallmapu* (Alarcón & Nahuelcheo, 2008).

The conception of pregnancy in the Mapuche people is understood as a biological fact and not as a fact of mystical order, as it happens with other native peoples of Latin America. However, the process of accompanying women, childbirth and puerperium are endowed with meanings that relate people to animals and spiritual forces that inhabit things and spaces (Alarcón & Nahuelcheo, 2008). Therefore, Mapuche women who are pregnant or have given birth require family and community accompaniment, which not only refers to facilitating practical chores but also requires care in the use of time and space. In fact, the daily practices and action/rest, the permanence or not in certain spaces, depends on the adequate adjustment of time according to the sun (Grebe, 1987). For example, some of the care that has been reported in studies carried out with Mapuche women are related to ensure that women do not exert physical forces that could contract the uterus, as this could lead to miscarriage. Also, care must be taken that women's diets are balanced between extreme cold and extreme heat, as this can also affect the uterus. As for childbirth and puerperium, a permanent family accompaniment is relevant, because the loneliness of the woman, and her daughter or son, can lead to the invasion of spiritual forces that may harm them physically or spiritually (Alarcón & Nahuelcheo, 2008). Hence, childbirth in a formal health centre, surrounded by people outside the family and with a high biological manipulation, has nothing to do with this socio-cultural view that involves the emotional, the spiritual and the territorial.

We observe that public policies have been designed and implemented with a clear intention to silence the diversities present in the current country called Chile, since what has been sought is to generate a Western and hygienist social, cultural and political domination. In this sense, the brown, the Indigenous is undervalued in a monocultural model, where only one nation prevails, the Chilean nation, which is predominantly Western and Spanish through ongoing Coloniality (Mariman, 2006; Richards, 2016). In this monocultural model of public policies, we observe that disciplinary practices have been markedly patriarchal, since women's corporealities are the object of attention and action from state policies. A particularly striking area to carry out the control of female corporealities has been the health field, where different acts of obstetric violence have been generated, and which have come to be classified as natural and routine in various formal health centres (Rodríguez, 2019). In these acts of obstetric violence, the biological takes precedence over the emotional, women are not consulted about invasive procedures, and they are taken away from their families to intervene in childbirth as if it were a disease.

Mapuche women's acts of resistance

The struggles of Mapuche women have been historical and diverse in terms of political expressions and meanings. Some of the highlights of their daily resistance occurred in the context of the post-colonial dispossession that took place in Chile, after the military campaign wrongly named 'Pacification of Araucania'. This campaign was so-called for the main purpose of colonial invasion and dispossession, under the idea that the Mapuche people are savage and need to be violently subjugated and silenced. The 'Pacification of Araucania' was carried out in the second half of the 19th century and led to a process of massive impoverishment of the Mapuche people, as they were violently dispossessed of their lands and their political status as a people with an autonomous territory (Nahuelpan, 2013; Pichinao, 2012).

Under the context of colonial dispossession, the forced displacement of an entire people from south to north took place, mainly, having as its centre of attention the *füta warria* – the great city of Santiago. In these displacements, there is a fact that is not properly recognised, the displacement and settlement of Mapuche women in the city of Santiago, whose main purpose was the exercise of service and care work. In the displacement experiences of Mapuche women, the strong link they maintain with their *lof*, where the *reyñma*, – the family –, is their centre of attention, acquires relevance. This is due to the felt need to maintain a material collaboration for the subsistence of fathers, mothers, sisters and brothers. But also, by affective needs, sense of belonging and Mapuche identification, as can be seen in different studies (Alvarado, 2016; Millaleo, 2011; Nahuelpan, 2013; Rain, Llombart, & Mora-Malo, 2020).

The expressions of political resistance by Mapuche women have not always achieved public notoriety, although they have been present in different historical moments of the Mapuche struggle. In this regard, Margarita Calfío (2009) highlights the political participation in the first half of the 20th century of one of the women who formed part of the board of the Araucanian Federation, Herminia Aburto Colihueque, who was also a candidate in the municipal elections of 1935. Not far from this event was the creation of the Araucanian Women's Society Yafluayin, and a year after its creation, Herminia Aburto herself assumed its presidency (Calfío, 2009). An issue to highlight about this Association is that it was the first of its kind, its composition was only of women, who, although claiming struggles for the autonomy and recognition of the Mapuche people, sought their own space to strengthen their political participation as women in the city and make their actions visible in the public arena. To do this, they used writing, a particular and rare issue for that time within the Mapuche political movement (Calfío, 2009). Despite all these actions and contributions, Margarita Calfío (2009) analyses, social and academic recognition has been almost non-existent.

It is important to highlight that in 1935, the same year in which the Araucanian Women's Association Yafluayin was created, the Movement for the Emancipation of Chilean Women, – MEMCH – was created. This Movement carried out a campaign in support of Mapuche women artisans who sold their products on public streets at Temuco city (Calfío, 2009). These gestures can be interpreted as instances that contributed to the generation of bridges for dialogue between the movements of Chilean women's and Mapuche women's gender demands. Some decades later, the presence of Mapuche women in the public arena grew in terms of demands for human and collective rights. This, within the context of the military dictatorship, where there were violations with a marked racist accent, as the 'fence runs' and revenge related to the recovery of lands won during the Agrarian Reform (Rodenkirchen, 2015) were promoted, both for foreign landowners and for Chileans from the south of the *Wallmapu*.

All of the above was combined with the military action carried out in Araucanía, where violence against Mapuche leaders was mixed with revenge for land recoveries, according to the Rettig Report (Correa, 2021). The serious violations of rights and the violence experienced by many of the families in the *Wallmapu* gave rise to a lack of justice, since in general they did not dare to denounce these events (Correa, 2021; Durán, Basic, & Pérez, 1998). Something similar was experienced by the families of the detained-disappeared and politically tortured. It was a kind of exclusion and rejection inside and outside of their village, since in some *lof* the exclusion and rejection of other families, who did not agree with embracing political struggles considered outsiders, was generated. Both exclusion and rejection were also felt due to the lack of solidarity from organisations and relatives of non-Mapuche detained-disappeared persons (Durán et al., 1998).

During the period of military dictatorship in Chile, different women generated a series of mobilisations and support actions for access to justice. They were Ide Reuque, Ana Llao, Elisa Avendaño and Lucy Traipe, who were from different organisations, and at the same time united by their participation in Ad-Mapu, were able to unveil facts of injustice and urge organisation (García-Mingo, 2017; Richards, 2016). Later, during the process of return to democracy, these same women promoted the access to State reparation processes. Here it is worth mentioning the work of other Mapuche women, such as María Elena Calfuquir, who worked as a Human Rights Worker, and together with other people elaborated the register of affected families, to support them in paperwork and in the psychosocial field, among other matters.

During the first decades of the return to democracy in 1990, the problems of land restitution, the struggle for territorial autonomy and the recognition of the Mapuche nationhood were a source of conflict with the Chilean State. These same facts and conflict have been present to this day. In this regard, it should be noted that an emblematic issue has been the implementation of the State's Internal Security Law, created during the Chilean military dictatorship to be applied to political opponents. However, it has been repeatedly applied to Mapuche people politically mobilised for the recovery of lands in *Wallmapu*. In this conflictive scenario, it has been recurrent to observe, in different media, the political negotiations of people called 'Mapuche political prisoners', where their public representations have been mostly present in the spokespersons of women, who publicly represent the Mapuche people under investigation. Ingrid Conejeros, for example, was the spokesperson for the *machi* – a person who by family inheritance, or by dreams, intervenes to balance a person's physical, emotional or spiritual health – Francisca Linconao, accused in the murder case of the German settler couple who died burnt to death in their home in the south of the *Wallmapu* (Richards, 2016). Francisca Linconao was found not guilty by the Temuco Criminal Court in May 2018. Natividad Llanquileo was also the spokesperson for the Mapuche political prisoners of the Coordinadora Arauco Malleco from 2009 to 2011 (Aguilera, 2011). Also, in professional roles of support to the Mapuche people, Mapuche women lawyers have been present, some of these women are Rosa Catrileo, Gloria Painemilla, Natividad Llanquileo, María Del Rosario Salamanca Huenchullán, Pamela Nahuelcheo Queucupura, among others.

Another area of resistance or defiance relates to gender violence against Mapuche women. Recently and due to a political scenario marked by the demands related to gender equality, at a global and national level, a current and unresolved debate has emerged within the Mapuche political movements. This debate focuses on the discussion of what corresponds to the public or private world, an issue already analysed in Feminisms. It is about gender violence experienced within a couple's relationship. In this regard, for example, a Mapuche feminist woman, Ana Millaleo, states that the situation of violence experienced by Mapuche women needs to be publicly revealed through the 'funa' – social exposure of repudiation, in different open media, which exposes the aggressor of women, as a political tool.

Within these Mapuche feminist movements, the male aggressors have been called 'Mapumachos' (Millaleo, 2009), men who attack women in different ways who, under the need to sustain the social prestige of their families, do not dare to denounce. We are faced with an act of rupture that seeks to overcome situations of violence within the Mapuche world, which needs to be overcome both within Chilean society and elsewhere.

Decolonial proposals and depatriarchalisation of public policies for social work

It is necessary to make Mapuche women visible as active political subjects and agents in the vindication of Mapuche collective rights, but at the same time, it is necessary to generate processes of transformation in terms of gender relations within Mapuche organisations (Richards, 2016). This struggle also needs to be directed towards demands for responses situated within public policies on collective rights, and towards the visibilisation of the intersectionalities that particularly affect racialised women (García-Mingo, 2017; Richards, 2016).

In line with the above-mentioned, the interpellations about the particular demands of Mapuche women in Chile are an issue to be addressed in a deeper way within feminist movements, which do not always manage to generate bridges of encounter with the mobilisations of women belonging to native peoples and Afro-descendants, since the struggles of the latter focus on aspects of self-determination, autonomy, land and territory, which exceed feminist struggles in general (Tapia, 2018). An example of this is the struggles of Black and Chicana feminists, who have brought into the public arena the multiple discriminations they suffer in labour, political and everyday spaces, which could be understood as Intersectionality of oppressions acting in concert, which are produced/supported by structural mechanisms underpinned by colonial-patriarchal capitalism rationality (Anzaldúa & Moraga 1981; Combahee River Collective 2012 [1977]; Crenshaw 1989; Cumes, 2014; Curiel, 2007; Davis, 1981, 2005; hooks, 2020).

The situation of Mapuche women, as part of the racialised women of Chile, shows that history is not a past but a continuity in terms of the conditions of inequality they live in, and in relation to other non-racialised women. This is the particular case of the exclusions that inhabit Chilean society and Mapuche society itself, where Mapuche women are fixed in a place of inferiority. As an example, it is possible to mention domestic work, which although it is an issue that affects all women (Federici, 2018), in the case of Mapuche women, obeys a colonial continuity. In colonial contacts, Mapuche women, girls and boys, were captured to perform domestic work and slave service, along with girls and boys in the haciendas (Boccara, 2007; Zavala, 2008). This fixation of an inferior place is characteristic of the stripping of value that such work has in Chilean society (Millaleo, 2011).

This historisation of an unequal reality for Mapuche women, in the world of work, is a condition present today as indicated by statistical measurement instruments, such as the Social Characterization Survey [CASEN]. In fact, the 2017 CASEN survey shows that the vast majority of Mapuche women occupy paid domestic and care work. Similarly, another group of Mapuche women, settled in rural areas, occupy non-regular trade work, through the sale of vegetables, for example. For their part, professional Mapuche women represent a smaller number, but they are also the ones who for similar work, always obtain lower salaries than other professionals (Blanco, Rain & Julián, 2022).

The afore-mentioned is relevant, since statistics shows a reality that has been historically configured, and that allows affirming that Chilean society is structurally unequal for Mapuche men and even more unequal for Mapuche women. Hence, in unequal societies, racialised women are expected to occupy workplaces that are always of service to white society (Cumes, 2014). But it is also worth remembering that the conditions and situations of labour precariousness have been accompanied by various acts of colonial disciplining of Mapuche women, which has led to emotional, physical and material abuses that have configured labour biographies of suffering (Alvarado, 2016; Millaleo, 2011; Nahuelpan, 2013; Rain, 2020). In this context, social work situated as a profession and as a discipline in a scenario of inequalities needs to respond to its professional *ethos* in search of social justice, but in order to address these demands in a situated way, it needs to recognise a long memory (Paredes, 2010). This means bringing Colonialism, capitalism and Patriarchy into focus as webs that simultaneously intersect racialised women (Anzaldúa & Moraga, 1981; Combahee River Collective, 2012[1977]; Crenshaw, 1989; Davis, 2005).

It is important not to confuse that, although the depatriarchalisation of social policies is urgent, it is necessary to put decolonisation at the centre, since Colonialism reigns and transversalises oppressions towards racialised women (Cumes, 2014; Paredes, 2010; Tapia, 2018). For this reason, their mobilisations and struggles are never easy to understand within the white feminist movement. At the centre of the mobilisations and struggles of Mapuche women is the collective view, the belonging to a people, to a nation, although they also present themselves in a questioning way when it comes to claiming other struggles, such as the struggle for gender equality (Paredes, 2010; Tapia, 2018). The struggles for gender demands are necessarily accompanied by class and race struggles. Thus, understanding racialised women who experience gender violence has sometimes been complex, as Crenshaw (1989) has shown in the case of African American women, who rarely denounced white authorities for fear of exposing their communities to prevailing racism.

Final reflections

In order to think about decolonial and situated public policies, social work requires keeping in mind the colonial, patriarchal and class history that constitutes Chilean society as a whole, and its relationship with the other nations with which they co-inhabit and relate on a daily basis. But, above all it requires a critical position in the face of social realities that have come to be naturalised, such as the precarious labour conditions of Mapuche women, the prevailing monoculturalism within public policies and the particular attention to the claims they generate to address social inequalities, where the understanding and approach of the intersectionalities that cross them cannot be fragmented.

Monoculturalism has been installed and updated in public policies, since the quest of Chilean society and the State has been social and political whitening. Hence, the military and political actions that were carried out during the second half of the 20th century, and that have continued, have focused on a race for social integration and not for the recognition and valuation of socio-cultural diversity and the rights to dignity and humanisation, given the inequality, lack of socio-economic justice and oppression, and even less, for the recognition of Mapuche territorial autonomy. All these facts have been highly detrimental to Mapuche institutions in the areas of health, education and justice. Likewise, among the most affected groups are women, who have been deprived of social value, with visible effects on the recognition of the social value of their work, inside and outside the home, but also on the autonomy of their bodies, which have been trapped in a political institutionality that objectifies, excludes and oppresses them.

Early social work requires putting at the centre of professional training the listening and understanding of the intersectional oppressions that affect racialised women, and the strategies they design and implement to address them. Hence, Indigenous feminist struggles are key, since the knowledge of the native nations themselves is what contributes to generate decolonial and situated public policies. In this regard, in this work, we have wanted to show the great variety of strategies that Mapuche women have deployed at different historical moments, to not only confront their oppressions and Chilean society, but also to confront Mapuche society itself, when their contributions as political subjects have not been adequately valued. Therefore, the invitation for social work is the recognition of these struggles, but also the generation of collaborative, participatory, cross-cutting work, since they are political actors and not passive subjects in the face of public policies. It is worth remembering here that the Indigenous feminist movements themselves have demanded this central place in the transformations of their own situations and conditions.

Finally, social work as a profession and in order to contribute to the relevant design of public policies, sensitive to the socio-cultural diversity of racialised women, requires a historical perspective. This historical perspective needs to observe the present and question the past, in order to make it possible to situate the social discomforts and oppressions experienced by racialised women.

References

Aguilera, R. (2011, April 22). Natividad Llanquileo deja la vocería de los Presos Políticos Mapuche por temas académicos. Biobío Chile, 2 de diciembre del 2011. https://www.biobiochile.cl/noticias/2011/12/02/natividad-llanquileo-deja-la-voceria-de-los-presos-politicos-mapuche-por-temas-academicos.shtml

Alarcón, A. & Nahuelcheo, Y. (2008). Creencias sobre el embarazo, parto y puerperio en la mujer mapuche: Conversaciones privadas. *Chungará*, 40(2), 193–202. https://doi.org/10.4067/S0717-73562008000200007

Alvarado, C. (2016). Silencios coloniales, silencios micropolíticos. Memorias de violencias y dignidades mapuche en Santiago de Chile. *Aletheia*, 6(12), 1–17. http://www.memoria.fahce.unlp.edu.ar/art_revistas/pr.7286/pr.7286.pdf

Anzaldúa, G. & Moraga, C. (1981). *This Bridge Called My Back: Writings by Radical Women of Color*. Persephone Press.

Blanco, O., Rain, A., & Julián, D. (2022). Precariedades, racialización e interseccionalidad. Segmentos y perfiles laborales de mujeres mapuche residentes en La Araucanía, Chile. *Revista mexicana de ciencias políticas y sociales*, 67(245), 331–369. http://doi.org/10.22201/fcpys.2448492xe.2022.245.78829

Boccara, G. (2007). *Los Vencedores. Historia del Pueblo Mapuche en la Época Colonial*. Línea Editorial IIA. Universidad Católica del Norte.

Bolados, P. (2012). Neoliberalismo multicultural en el Chile postdictadura: la política indígena en salud y sus efectos en comunidades mapuches y atacameñas. *Chungará, revista de antropología chilena*, 44(1), 135–144. https://doi.org/10.4067/S0717-73562012000100010

Calfío, M. (2009). Mujeres mapuche, voces y acciones en dictadura (1978–1989). *Nomadías*, 9, 93–112. https://doi.org/10.5354/n.v0i9.12299

Calfío, M. (2012). Peküyen. En CHM, *Ta iñ fijke xipa rakizuameluwün. Historia, colonialismo y resistencia desde el País Mapuche* (pp. 279–296). Ediciones Comunidad de Historia Mapuche.

Castillo-Muñoz, A. and Mora-Guerrero, G. (2020). ¿Pensar el cuerpo femenino como diálogo de Saberes? *Revista Estudios Feministas, Florianópolis,* 29(1), e65893. https://doi.org/10.1590/1806-9584-2021v29n165893

Combahee River Collective. 2012 [1977]. Un manifiesto feminista negro. In L. Platero (Ed.), *Intersecciones: Cuerpos y sexualidades en la encrucijada* (pp. 75–86). Ediciones Bellaterra.

Correa, M. (2021). *La historia del despojo. El origen de la propiedad particular en el territorio mapuche.* Ceybo Ediciones & Editorial Pehuén.

Crenshaw, K. (1989). Demarginalizing the intersection of race and sex: A black feminist critique of antidiscrimination doctrine, feminist theory and antiracist politics. *University of Chicago Legal Forum* (1), 139–167. https://chicagounbound.uchicago.edu/cgi/viewcontent.cgi?article=1052&context=uclf

Cumes, A. (2014). *La "india" como "sirvienta": Servidumbre doméstica, colonialismo y patriarcado en Guatemala* (Doctoral Thesis). Centro de Investigaciones y Estudios Superiores en Antropología Social, CIESAS. Ciudad de México, México. http://repositorio.ciesas.edu.mx/bitstream/handle/123456789/283/D259.pdf?sequence=1&isAllowed=y

Curiel, O. (2007). Crítica poscolonial desde las prácticas políticas del feminismo antiracista. *Revista Nómadas* (26), 92–101. https://www.redalyc.org/pdf/1051/105115241010.pdf

Davis, A. (1981). *Women, race and class.* Vintage Books, Random House

Davis, A. (2005). *Mujeres, raza y clase.* Editorial Akal.

Durán, T., Basic, R., & Pérez, P. (1998). *Muerte y desaparición forzada en La Araucanía: Una aproximación étnica. Efectos psicosociales e interpretación sociocultural de la represión política vivida por los familiares de los detenidos-desaparecidos y ejecutados mapunches y no mapunches. IX Región, Chile (1973–90).* LOM Ediciones.

Federación Internacional de Trabajadores Sociales (2014). *Global statement of the ethical principles of social work. Ethical principles of social work.* Accessed January 30, 2023, https://www.ifsw.org/declaracion-global-de-los-principios-eticos-del-trabajo-social/

Federici, S. (2018). *El patriarcado del salario: críticas feministas al marxismo. Críticas feministas al marxismo.* Tinta Limón Ediciones.

García-Mingo, E. (2017). *Zomo Newen. Relatos de vida de Mujeres Mapuche en su lucha por los derechos indígenas.* LOM Ediciones.

Grebe, M. (1987). La concepción del tiempo en la cultura mapuche. *Revista Chilena de Antropología,* 6, 59–74. https://revistadeantropologia.uchile.cl/index.php/RCA/article/view/17625

Guerra, L. (2014). *La Ciudad Ajena: Subjetividades de Origen Mapuche en el Espacio Urbano.* Ediciones Ceibo.

Harvey, D. (2007). *Una breve historia del neoliberalismo.* Editorial Akal.

hooks, bell (2020). *Teoría feminista: De los márgenes hacia el centro.* Traficantes de Sueños.

Marimán, P. (2006). Los mapuche antes de la conquista militar chileno-argentina. In P. Marimán, S. Caniuqueo, J. Millalen & R. Levil (Eds.). *¡…Escucha Winka…! Cuatro Ensayos de Historia Nacional Mapuche y un epílogo sobre el futuro* (pp. 53–127). LOM Ediciones.

Millaleo, A. (2009). La FUNA: algo huele mal en el Wallmapu y hay que gritarlo #NuncaMasSinNosotras. Mapuexpress, 9 de marzo del 2020. https://www.mapuexpress.org/2020/03/09/la-funa-algo-huele-mal-en-el-wallmapu-y-hay-que-gritarlo-nuncamassinnosotras/

Millaleo, A. (2011). *Ser 'Nana' en Chile: Un imaginario cruzado por el género e identidad étnica* [Unpublished Doctoral Dissertation]. University of Chile. http://146.83.150.183/bitstream/handle/10533/76519/MILLALEO_ANA_1610M.pdf?sequence=1

Nahuelpan, H. (2013). Las "zonas grises" de las historias mapuche. Colonialismo internalizado, marginalidad y políticas de la memoria. *Revista de historia social y de las mentalidades,* 17(1), 11–33. https://www.revistas.usach.cl/ojs/index.php/historiasocial/article/view/1552

Paredes, J. (2010). Hilando fino desde el feminismo indígena comunitario. In Y. Espinosa (Ed.), *Aproximaciones críticas a las prácticas teóricas políticas del feminismo latinoamericano* (pp. 117–120). En la Frontera.

Pichinao, J. (2012). Los parlamentos hispano-Mapuche como escenario de negociación simbólico-político durante la colonia. In H. Nahuelpán, H. Huinca, & P. Marimán (Eds.), *Ta iñ fijke xipa rakizuameluwün: Historia colonialismo y resistencia desde el país mapuche* (pp. 25–42). Comunidad de Historia Mapuche.

Rain, A., Llombart, M., & Mora-Malo, E. (2020). Mujeres mapuche en la diáspora y el retorno al Wallmapu: Entre micro-resistencias de género y despojos coloniales. *Chungará, 52*(2), 347–360. https://doi.org/10.4067/S0717-73562020005001004

Richards, P. (2016) *Racismo: El modelo chileno y el multiculturalismo neoliberal bajo la Concertación, 1990–2010*. Pehuén Editores.

Rodenkirchen, A. (2015). Memorias Mapuche en la continuidad colonial: experiencias durante la dictadura militar chilena (1973–1990). In E. Antileo, L. Cárcamo-Huechante, M. Calfío & H. Piutrin (Eds.), *Awukan ka kuxankan zugu Wajmapu Meu. Violencias coloniales en Wajmapu* (pp. 239–270). Ediciones Comunidad de Historia Mapuche.

Rodríguez, P. (2019). Educación popular y violencia obstétrica: un encuentro en la perspectiva de género. In Pol-Len & Dona LLum (Eds.). *Mirades a la violencia obstétrica* (pp. 121–137).

Tapia, A. (2018). *Mujeres indígenas en defensa de la tierra*. Ediciones Cátedra.

Zavala, J. (2008). *Los Mapuche del Siglo XVIII. Dinámica Interétnica y Estrategias de Resistencia*. Ediciones Universidad Bolivariana.

9
THE INTERSECTIONALITY BODY-TERRITORY-DAILY LIFE IN MAYAN-XINKA COMMUNITY FEMINISM. ITS IMPORTANCE FOR SOCIAL WORK

Silvana Martínez and Juan Agüero

Introduction

Community Feminisms constitute a political and theoretical movement that emerged from the Aymara peoples of Bolivia in the early 1990s and spread to Guatemala in the early 2000s. For Adriana Guzmán (2019), these Feminisms emerge from the need for political struggle against Patriarchy, capitalism and neoliberalism. Also because of the need to decolonize thought and resignify the words, categories and concepts of Western feminism. They have their origin in the revolutionary struggle of the native Bolivian peoples against neoliberalism and North American imperialism in Latin America. As a political movement, in the year 2003, it supports the need to build a new plurinational state and a new non-patriarchal order. In this sense, it proposes a revolutionary struggle that includes Indigenous men, but questioning their privileges in the communities and in politics. In other words, it is an anti-patriarchal struggle of men and women in community.

These Feminisms recover the wisdom and long memory of the original peoples. They raise the need to build a social theory that accounts for multiple oppressions and provides tools for the transformation of the patriarchal-colonial-capitalist order. This need is based on the fact that existing theories – Marxism, Christianity, Indianism, indigenism, Colonialism, among others do not make visible or explain the multiple oppressions. Nor do they serve as tools to build a new social order. For these Feminisms, this task constitutes a political, historical and ethical responsibility to their ancestors and to all Indigenous women who have died in resistance. They consider the resistance of native peoples to be valuable. However, they argue that this resistance is not enough and that a proposal for action is necessary.

From this political, historical and ethical responsibility, community Feminisms reconceptualize the very definition of feminism. They also reconceptualize Patriarchy, community, bodies, territory and daily life, among others. For Guzmán (2019), feminism is the struggle of any woman, anywhere in the world and at any time in history, who fights, rebels and proposes in the face of a Patriarchy that oppresses or pretends to oppress her. For this author, the European definition of Patriarchy as a system of domination, oppression and exploitation of men against women is not sufficient. Therefore, she proposes to define Patriarchy as "the" system historically built on the body of women, of all oppressions, all discriminations and all violence that humanity (men, women, intersex people, bodies and non-genders) and nature live and suffer.

The community feminism of Bolivia emphasizes the community and that of Guatemala the territory. Both coincide in the rejection of Patriarchy and Coloniality. They recover the long memory of native peoples and women ancestors. They reinterpret history from their own stories, beliefs and ancestral practices. They recover the centrality of the body as a place of memory, beliefs, feelings and expression of all oppressions, discriminations and violence. They recover the form of life and community social organization and the unity between the body, the territory, mother earth and the community.

All these contributions and resignifications are fundamental for a feminist social work, rooted in Latin America and the Caribbean. In this chapter, we are interested in focusing specifically on the contributions of Maya-Xinka community feminism in Guatemala. In the first part, we highlight the theoretical contributions of this feminism. In the second, we analyze the contributions linked to the Intersectionality between Body-Territory-Daily Life. Finally, in the third part, we focus on the implications that this Intersectionality has for research/intervention in a situated, decolonial and emancipatory social work.

Maya-Xinka community feminism

In Guatemala, community feminism emerged at the beginning of the 21st century, from the collective and territorial work developed by the Xinka women members of the Association of Indigenous Women of Santa María in the Xalapán mountain. This feminism constitutes a proposal born from the indignant bodies of native women with the purpose of reinterpreting themselves from the multiple oppressions, but also from their emancipations. It is therefore a proposal that neither arises nor comes from the academic spheres.

For Lorena Cabnal (2018), community feminism is a proposal that has built several elements of analysis to be able to interpret the historical-structural oppression of women. For this interpretation, it brings elements of ancestral Patriarchy and ethnic fundamentalisms within the communities themselves. She also brings to consciousness today, here and now, the memory of the original women transgressors. This author rejects the idea of Indigenous women passively victimized by the colonial system. In this sense, she rescues the struggles and resistances of women ancestors, who have provided life and energy.

In order to understand the historical subjugation of Indigenous women, this author proposes to start from what she calls the cosmogony of suspicion. This is a way of interpreting life in the Indigenous world, understanding that every native people has its own cosmogony as a unit of meaning. In other words, this feminism recreates and reinterprets Maya-Xinka cosmogonic thought in a feminist key, in order to account for the long memory, the ancestral historical construction and the daily life of Indigenous women.

For these feminists, there is an ancestral original Patriarchy that oppresses Indigenous women from their own heterosexual cosmogony as a norm, both for women and men, and for men in relation to the cosmos. This ancestral original Patriarchy is reinforced by the new order installed by patriarchal, racist and capitalist Colonialism. From this new order, the Indigenous are born with racialized bodies in a hierarchical and symbolic order. In this order, the superior is the white European man and the inferior all Indigenous men and women.

Lorena Cabnal (2010) criticizes ethnic essentialism. For this author, there is an original cosmogonic heterosexuality installed as a norm. She establishes that all relations of humanity and of humanity with the cosmos are based on principles and values such as complementarity and heterosexual duality for the harmonization of life. There are hegemonic spirituality practices where the feminine is dependent and complementary to the masculine. This perpetuates the oppression of women in their heterosexual relationship with nature. This is the basis of Sumak Kawsay or Good Living. Sumak is an Ecuadorian Quichua term meaning good life in itself. Kawsay is a Bolivian Aymara term that alludes to the communitarian.

From the cosmogony of suspicion, Cabnal proposes to question the "situated historical victimization" in order to transcend internalized racism. Moreover, in order to make it visible and question it from its own cultural construction. In this sense, community feminism proposes the need to recover the body as the first territory. It is an emancipatory political act based on "the personal is political" and "what is not named does not exist". Assuming the individual corporeality as one's own and unrepeatable territory allows strengthening the sense of affirmation of the existence of being and being in the world. From this act, self-consciousness is generated. The different manifestations of Patriarchy and all the oppressions derived from them are perceived in the body. In this way, the process of transformation of Indigenous women into thinking and acting political subjects begins, both individually and collectively, with their own liberating and emancipating thought (Martínez, 2018).

For Lorena Cabnal (2018), the cosmogony of suspicion implies a first moment in which an answer is sought to the question of why the situation of oppression of native women. Why native women are the ones who suffer the greatest oppressions. Even in relation to other women who are also oppressed, but who do not come from native peoples. These questions lead to indignation and this in turn leads to the search for new answers. It is a search based on feeling rather than thinking. The act of feeling constitutes a vital act of epistemic recovery in the bodies. Feeling and putting the body in experience leads to building a relational thread with the long memory of the oppression of the original ancestral Patriarchy, which is expressed and manifested differently from colonial Patriarchy.

In Cabnal's (2018) proposal, the concept of acuerpamiento is also fundamental. It is a concept that should be understood as mutual physical and spiritual support among Indigenous women. It constitutes a process of emotional and spiritual recovery of Indigenous women who defend ancestral territories in the face of the problems of criminalization and judicialization, and who fight for life in their communities. The author sustains the need for healing in the face of illness, sadness, stigmatization and displacement experienced by Indigenous women and their families. For this feminism, it is necessary to account for the original ancestral Patriarchy and the territorial disputes and the bodies of Indigenous women before Colonialism. This constitutes an act of cosmogonic political vindication of the original women, with the epistemic authority that implies having lived these violences in their bodies. These violences constitute a complexity that disharmonizes life, but which in turn comes with a proposal that reweaves from emancipation.

This feminism also proposes a political conception of the body. The conception of the body as a political body allows us to visualize the body not only as an object of violation, expropriation, violence or manipulation, but also as a subject of resistance, autonomy, freedom and emancipation. In addition, it allows visualizing the body as episteme and as a place of expression of Intersectionality. As Virginia Vargas puts it, "By affirming its political existence [...] the body politic opens a political and theoretical kaleidoscope that can contain an immeasurable dimension of democratization of everyday coexistence" (Vargas, 2019, p. 188).

Intersectionality Body-Territory-Daily Life as a theoretical category

Intersectionality as a concept refers to multiple systems of domination and oppression that interrelate and mutually empower each other simultaneously, complexifying the homogenizing gaze of social inequalities. It also alludes to the need to heterogenize the subjects of knowledge that are embodied in singular and collective histories that condense structural inequalities of race, gender and class, among others (Migliaro González et al., 2020).

As these authors argue, "intersectionality has no date of birth or precise affiliation. Moreover, if we were to mention any, we would silence the voices that from different times and geographies have risen to name the dominations" (Migliaro González et al., 2020, p. 69). In other words, Intersectionality, before being a concept, is constructed in the struggles against the multiple oppressions that Indigenous women, women of color, Black women of African descent and slaves experienced simultaneously in their bodies. These oppressions were not visible or were seen as independent of each other.

As a concept, Intersectionality was first raised in 1989 by the Black American lawyer Kimberlé Crenshaw, in the defense of Black women in a labor dismissal lawsuit. Its purpose was to demonstrate the discrimination based on sex and race that these women suffered simultaneously (Crenshaw, 1989). Subsequently, this author founded Intersectionality as a theoretical and political category (Crenshaw, 1991).

In Guatemala, the Maya-Kaqchikel feminist Aura Cumes focuses her research on how Indigenous women experience the overlapping of oppressions. She criticizes the reductionism of the analytical-political visions of the Indigenous movement and the feminist movement by focusing on a single axis of demands. It also rejects the ethnic essentialism of ethnocentric hegemonic feminism, when referring to "indigenous women". Likewise, it rescues the principles of complementarity, duality, difference and identity, present in the Mayan cosmovision, but resignifying them in order to make visible the existing relations of oppression (Cumes, 2009).

Mayan-Xinka feminists emphasize the Intersectionality of body-territory-daily life and propose to recover the territory-body and the body as territory. This political-epistemic bet is proposed as a tool of struggle against ancestral Patriarchy and colonial Patriarchy. From these systems of oppression, women's bodies have historically been the disputed territory that made it possible for these systems to perpetuate oppression.

In this sense, these feminists propose to recover the body-territory as the first place of enunciation, as bodily and historical memory, since in the body-territory inhabits the history of colonial expropriation, but also of the struggles for liberation and emancipation. In turn, the body-territory is connected to the territory-land and is interrelated with the long memory of the peoples, where there is also the sign of expropriation and colonial violence (Martínez, 2021).

For the Maya-Xinka feminist Lorena Cabnal, "Feminist proposals that call for the emancipation of bodies against Patriarchy and do not call for the depatriarchalization of nature, as a territory in dispute by the current neoliberal model, lack political sustainability" (Cabnal, 2019, p. 122). These proposals are expressed in slogans of struggle in an intersectional key such as "defense and recovery of the body-earth territory", "healing as a cosmic-political path", "healing of bodies for liberation and emancipation", "from my body as my first territory of defense", "from the earth as the historical and meaningful place where life is recreated", "reclaiming joy without losing indignation because life is worth living", "without depatriarchalization there is no decolonization", "depatriarchalization of the territory-body and territory-earth", among others.

For this communitarian feminism, a territory is much more than a plot of land. It is a cultural, symbolic and historical living space. To understand the body as territory is to understand it as a living, complex and integral system. It is constituted by multiple relationships in which all living beings and natural assets such as water, land and mountains participate. This implies thinking of our individual and collective bodies as part of a community and a constitutive part of territories. Territory-body-land is more than the corporeal and physical. They are shared feelings, perceptions and experiences. They are safe spaces in which Indigenous women can feel at ease and free to choose.

Adopting this perspective, the Intersectionality of body-territory-daily life provides a greater depth of understanding than the more simplistic view of an intertwining of multiple oppressions of class-race-gender. Firstly, it includes not only oppressions, but also resistances, struggles and emancipatory processes. Secondly, it focuses on the body-territory-daily life and this allows us to inscribe Intersectionality in the long memory of peoples and in broader historical processes.

Gender, raciality, class, among other dimensions, are experienced in the body. However, this body is not in the air as an entelechy. Nor is it a contingency, but has history and memory. It is a body rooted and imbricated in millenary historical processes. This Intersectionality has therefore a greater scope, breadth and epistemic potential than the conceptualization developed by Kimberlé Crenshaw.

The proposal of this communitarian feminism integrates the historical and daily struggle of native peoples to recover their lands as a concrete space where the life of bodies is manifested. In this sense, it does not separate the historical struggle for the recovery of their territories from the struggle for the defense and recovery of the body-territory. This feminism recognizes that there has been progress in terms of the uprisings of native peoples to recover their territories. However, it also warns and denounces that Indigenous women are still under a system of oppression and sexual, symbolic and economic violence. This clearly demonstrates that the body-territory of women is still expropriated and in the power of men.

In order to understand violence against women in the communities, Mayan-Xinka feminists do not use the category gender. They consider that it is a colonial Spanish word that many women in the communities do not speak. Instead, they use as an interpretative element the idea of disharmonization of the web of life. This disharmony is felt in the body through the traces of multiple oppressions and forms of violence. It is from this bodily experience that the interpretations of the unequal power relations that are totally naturalized are constructed.

The process of denaturalization and construction of another way of thinking implies, therefore, necessarily starting from the evidence and verification of the bodily traces of the multiple oppressions of the original women. That is to say, it is necessary to intentionally start from the pain of multiple oppressions, in order to initiate a process of liberation and emancipation. This process enables women to desire the denied, more harmonious relationships, to know other places, to be more in touch with nature, to know other women, other experiences, to study, to read, among others. In this way, the body becomes the vital space of verification, both of oppression and emancipation. It is a situated sentipensar-doing (Martínez, 2021).

Implications for a feminist, decolonial and emancipatory social work

The theoretical and political contributions of Maya-Xinka community feminism are key for an emancipatory social work as proposed by Martínez and Agüero (2008, 2014). This constitutes a political, epistemic, theoretical and methodological proposal of a situated, feminist, decolonial and anti-capitalist Social Work, which rescues the richness and epistemic value of popular and native peoples' knowledge.

The Intersectionality body-territory-daily life implies for Social Work to take into account the personal experiences and the individual and collective historical experiences of the social subjects with whom it works. In addition, it makes visible the importance of everyday life as a vital space where multiple oppressions are expressed, but also the various forms of resistance and collective struggles for liberation and emancipation.

For feminist and decolonial Social Work, this Intersectionality provides a unity of meaning that enables the construction of processes of self-awareness and historical consciousness. At the same time, it constitutes a powerful tool to set in motion processes of power construction oriented towards liberation and popular emancipation. In this sense, the cosmogony of suspicion proposed by Lorena Cabnal (2018) becomes a powerful heuristic tool.

As a heuristic tool, the cosmogony of suspicion allows Social Work to identify, understand and interpret the traces of the multiple oppressions lodged in women's bodies. From these traces and from the feeling of indignation that they generate in women, arise the interpellations, the research/intervention questions and the search for answers to walk the path of social transformation.

The idea of body-territory-land, contributed by Maya-Xinka feminism, is also key to travel this path of search and construction of processes of liberation and mancipation. It allows the construction of democratic and horizontal social relations, without race-class-gender hierarchies. It allows us to think of political bodies, not only from the multiple oppressions, but also as subjects of resistance, autonomy, freedom and emancipation. That is to say, it opens the theoretical-political-epistemic possibility of democratization of coexistence in the daily life of the subjects, of the community and of the social movements and organizations.

Daily life with nature, proposed by this feminism, has its correlate in the conception of the world of life as an experience of daily life. Here, everything lived with others takes on meaning and significance, as a material and immaterial, singular and collective, natural and cultural totality. Moreover, as a web of meanings and life experiences, this enables an understanding of a world as given and modified by the subjects themselves.

The idea of autonomy of the body-territory provides a concrete path for Social Work. It points out a path along which to advance in the construction of processes of liberation and emancipation. The decision about one's own body as an inviolable territory delimits a concrete space of autonomy and self-determination of social subjects. In this sense, it sets limits not only to patriarchal domination and oppression, but also to the exploitation of the body-territory and territory-land as vital spaces.

For feminist and decolonial Social Work, the great collective struggles for liberation and emancipation begin with the daily struggle for women's autonomy and self-determination over their own bodies as the first territory of dispute. Without this real and effective possibility of deciding over one's own body as an inviolable territory, collective struggles are empty of content and lose meaning. They have no raison d'être, whatever the motive or the banner of struggle that is raised.

In this sense, one of the fundamental and priority tasks of feminist and decolonial Social Work is precisely the depatriarchalization and decolonization of social relations and power devices. This includes not only the knowledge and practices involved in social intervention, but also the knowledge produced and reproduced in academic research and professional training. It also includes social movements, institutions, social organizations and the professional organizations of Social Work themselves.

The great task of depatriarchalization and decolonization of social relations and power devices aims – firstly – to make visible the multiple oppressions built from the capitalist-patriarchal-colonial social order; secondly, not to reproduce racist, ethnocentric and patriarchal logics; thirdly, not to fragment the struggles either by gender, class, race or other conditions.

Final reflections

The contributions of Mayan-Xinka community Feminisms constitute a profound epistemic rupture with the postulates of modern Western science and its canonical epistemology. Indeed, the cosmogony of suspicion proposed by Lorena Cabnal (2018) poses a direction in the complete opposite direction to the Cartesian cogito, ergo sum. The starting point proposed by the author is the body, understood as territory, is a vital, integral and complex space, constituted by multiple relationships of living beings with nature. A space loaded with shared experiences, memories, experiences, life stories and social meanings. It is a body, understood as a unit of sense that feels-thinks-acts. That is to say, feeling fulfills an epistemic function, since it generates the conditions for thinking, and this thinking leads to concrete actions.

For Social Work it is a situated feeling-thinking-doing, which has an enormous political importance. Indeed, it is a positioning that rescues and unifies the struggle of peoples against Patriarchy as the main ancestral and colonial system that summarizes and condenses all the discriminations, oppressions and violences historically built on women's bodies. This system not only oppresses and harms women but also men, children, the elderly and nature. In this sense, the struggle against Patriarchy is the struggle for free and egalitarian human communities and also for the preservation of nature and the human habitat.

For feminist, decolonial and emancipatory Social Work, it is fundamental to recover the historically silenced voices, the scorned knowledge, the denied bodies and the forms of social organization razed by the colonizers. It is also essential to recover the long memory of the peoples, because it not only contains the violence and multiple oppressions, but also the resistance, the struggles and the enormous experience and potential to carry out processes of liberation and emancipation.

In times of civilizational crisis, where nature is devastated, life is despised, bodies are annihilated and social relations are commodified, the Intersectionality body-territory-daily life becomes an enormous ethical-political imperative for Social Work. It is a way of understanding life and the world from another non-commercial logic, not subjugating nature, not annihilating bodies and life on the planet. It is a logic of hope and a powerful political-epistemic banner of struggle for another possible world, more just, more humane, more democratic and, fundamentally, without oppression and domination.

In times of neoliberalism, individualism, competitiveness, meritocracy, every man for himself, don't get involved, anomie, alienation, it is more necessary than ever to recover the idea of "acuerpamiento" proposed by Maya-Xinka feminism. These are spaces of containment, shelter, solidarity, affection and embrace. Without these spaces, it is impossible to think of alternative ways of life and other possible worlds.

The accord breaks the idea of society as a sum or aggregate of individuals. On the contrary, it implies intersubjectivity, closeness, recognition of the other, construction of social ties and collective life projects. It implies living in community, weaving stories in common with others, building a common destiny and feeling part of a social collective, of a political body.

Maya-Xinka community feminism proposes as a political-epistemic project very concrete actions of struggle against the patriarchal-capitalist-colonial order. It proposes, from the Intersectionality body-territory-daily life, a path to liberation and emancipation. It is a project and a political aspiration of enormous importance that those of us who support and fight for a feminist, decolonial and emancipatory Social Work share.

It is, without a doubt, a wonderful and challenging ethical-political option. It is a way of thinking and doing Social Work. It is a political-strategic bet to build historical conscience, collective conscience and pluriverse critical thinking. It is a challenge to build rooted and collective subjectivities, alliances, cooperation and social bonds. It is a powerful call to accompany and promote political, economic, social, cultural and affective processes of power building and popular emancipation.

References

Cabnal, L. (2010). Approach to the construction of the proposal of epistemic thinking of indigenous feminist community women of Abya Yala. In L. Cabnal, and A. L. Segovias (Comp). *Diverse feminisms: community feminism* (pp. 11–25). ACSUR-Las Segovias.

Cabnal, L. (2018). Tzk'at, ancestral healing networks of community feminism from Iximulew-Guatemala. *Revista EcologíaPolítica*, 54, pp. 100–104. https://www.ecologiapolitica.info/?p=10247

Cabnal, L. (2019). The story of violence from my body-earth territory. In X. Leyva and R. Icaza (Coords.). *In times of death: bodies, rebellions, resistances* (pp. 113–116). Coedition CLACSO-Cooperativa Editorial Retos. https://biblioteca-repositorio.clacso.edu.ar/handle/CLACSO/15453

Crenshaw, K. (1989). Demarginalizing the intersection of race and sex: A Black feminist critique of antidiscrimination doctrine, feminist theory and antiracist politics. University of Chicago. *Legal Forum*, 1989(1), Article 8, 139–167. http://chicagounbound.uchicago.edu/uclf/vol1989/iss1/

Crenshaw, K. (1991). Mapping the margins: Intersectionality, identity politics, and violence against women of color. *Stanford Law Review* 43 (6) (July 1991), pp. 1241–1299.

Cumes, A. (2009). Multiculturalism, gender, and feminisms: Diverse women, complex struggles. In A. Pequeño (comp.). *Participation and politics of indigenous women in Latin America*. FLACSO.

Guzmán, A. (2019). *Decolonizing memory*. Decolonizing feminisms. Llojeta.

Martínez, S (2021). Raizal-indisciplined spistemology as heuristic potentiality of Social Work in feminist key. In S Martínez, J. Agüero and P. Meschini (Coords.) *Spitemological frameworks in Social Work. Contributions for a feminist, decolonial and intercultural situated sentipensar-doing*. Editorial Fundación La Hendija

Martínez, S. (2018). Feminismo Comunitario. A theoretical and political proposal from Abya Yala. *Servicios Sociales y Política Social* XXXV (118) (December 2018), pp. 25–34.

Martínez, S. and Agüero, J. (2008). *The political-ideological dimension of Social Work. Keys for an emancipatory Social Work*. Editorial Dunken.

Martínez, S. and Agüero, J. (2014). *Emancipatory Social Work: from discipline to indiscipline*. Editorial Fundación La Hendija.

Martinez, S. (2021). Power, politics and social work: The need to reinvent social work around the world. In: Jacques Boulet and Linette Hawkins (Eds.). *Practical and contextual approaches to recontextualising social work* (pp. 229–240). IGI Global. DOI: 10.4018/978-1-7998-6784-5.ch012

Migliaro González, A. and others (2020). Intersectionalities in the body-territory. In D. Cruz Hernández and M. Bayón Jiménez (coord.). *Cuerpos, Territorios y Feminismos. Latin American compilation of theories, methodologies and political practices*. Ediciones Abya Yala.

Vargas, V. (2019). The body as a political category and potential for struggle from diversity. In X. Leyva and R. Icaza (Coords.). *In times of death: bodies, rebellions, resistances*. Coedition CLACSO-Cooperativa Editorial Retos.

10
FEMINISM, POLITICS, AND SOCIAL WORK

Ruth Phillips

Introduction

Social work and social policy are inseparable. Although not the focus of this chapter, social policy is, in its development and in its functioning in a welfare state, highly political. This is regardless of how it is organised or defined by government. Social work practice rarely sits beyond the domain of social policy. Even in the private sector, it is monitored or determined by some level of government regulation or funding arrangements and where there is government and assertions of power, there is politics. Effective feminist social work requires recognition and understanding of how politics defines development and implementation of social policy. Given the hegemonic power of neoliberalism in contemporary politics, social policies are bounded by the dominance of the market and ideologies that disengage individuals from social rights and social solidarity. Further, neoliberalism intrinsically denies layers of intersectional complexities experienced by many people in their everyday lives as its primary goals are rooted in economisation and economic growth (Laruffa, 2022). Social justice in its role as a universal framework for defining social work and as a central objective for practice (Hosken et al., 2020; Pease and Nipperess 2016) acts to counter the negative aspects of neoliberalism in both practical and political ways. This chapter highlights the importance of feminist frameworks and action for social work practice and focuses on its necessary political role and nature.

Feminist social work

Although there is a wide diversity of feminist theory and feminist identities, all Feminisms and feminist practices also have the primary objective of achieving social justice (Phillips, 2023; Wendt and Moulding, 2017). This relies on the shared intent of ending sexism and achieving gender equality. Like feminism, social justice is inherently political as it is concerned with how power is applied and exercised as either a means of exercising oppression or exclusion or through emancipation from oppression (Herrero & Charnley, 2021; Watts & Hodgson, 2019). How power is used or exerted can have resource, economic, personal, and social consequences for individuals, families, communities, and even nations. For more than a century of historical recognition as a social movement, Feminisms have, in both theory and practice, engaged and resisted those with power to seek and gain justice for women and other marginalised groups (Phillips, 2023). Feminisms are also part of critical social theory, which is essentially based on the pursuit of emancipation from oppression (Kellner, 1990; Pease and Nipperess, 2020; Steinberg, and Kincheloe, 2010). However, as noted by Steinberg and Kincheloe, '[m]any feminists ... raise the concern that emancipation has often been conceptualised as the pursuit of autonomy and self-direction' (2010, p. 143). These features, they maintain, must be balanced by 'a view of emancipation that allows for new forms of connectedness with others' (2010, p. 143) or, if in the African context, practicing the principles of Ubuntu (Chigangaidze et al., 2023). This understanding of emancipation is linked to broader visions for a connectedness between citizenship rights and diverse voices in pluralist democracies.

The pursuit of emancipatory practices and citizens' rights in democracies are defined and constrained by the ideology and policies of governments and by societal 'norms' that are essential influences affecting contexts for social work practice. For example, feminists concerned with women's labour have highlighted how domestic labour, including the reproductive labour of care, has been left out of wider economic and political considerations and fought to make domestic work visibly connected to the additional load of working outside the home (Crenshaw, 1991; Hill Collins, 1993). This focus also drew attention to systems of power, including an understanding of feminised work, work that has often been poorly paid, casualised, and precarious. Feminists from across the world, particularly the Global South, have made and continue to make important contributions to understanding how oppression occurs through gender, class, and race and have provided an analytical frame for women's risks and experiences of poverty (Nazneen et al., 2019a, 2019b; Rasool, 2020).

Although it may not be evident in all social work education, administration, or services, there are important synergies and alignments between critical social work theory, practice, and feminism. However, critical social work is by no means a universal approach as social work has been increasingly dominated by a 'therapeutic turn' where a psychological lens is applied that invites more professionals into the services to *do* social work (McLaughlin, 2008, p. vii). The individualising tendency of psychology leads increasingly to pathologising or medicalised responses and in doing so diminishes the agency and subjectivity of clients through the separation it creates between people and their familial, personal, community, or national context – their connectedness. Extracting an individual from their social context and 'responsibilisng' them for their condition or situation (Schram, 2019) also works against intersectional understandings (Crenshaw, 1991; Steinmetz, 2020) that are now central to effective feminist practice. From a broad political perspective, individualisation is also evidence of how successfully neoliberal values of individualism (Schram, 2019) have made inroads via the growth and dominance of marketisation of human services that promote the idea of individual choice.

As McLaughlin (2008) points out, we are in an era that has moved along from the heady influence of radical social work of the 1970s to the era of intense political interrogation of social work that was closely aligned with radical feminism. Although there has been a recent upsurge in interest in Feminisms across the world, and a consistent level of interest within specific fields of social work scholarship and practice, it has often slipped to the margins in social work education and research (Phillips, 2015). Citing Jones et al.'s (2019) research on the contemporary status of gender in Australian social work, Beddoe noted that 'gender is under-researched in Australia and feminist literature is largely siloed in specialist journals such as Affilia' (2022, p. 7).

Lena Dominelli and Eileen McLeod (1989) described the end of the 1980s as a time when feminist social work was coming into its own. For them, the central principle of feminism was gender equality and inclusivity. Feminist social work included resistance to 'other social divisions which reflect dominance and subordinate', such as race, class, heterosexism, ageism, and 'able-bodiedism' (1989, p. 2). Inclusivity has always been a central aspect of the principle of social justice inherent in feminism and is often reframed in a popularised idea of 'intersectional feminism' as a practice and an identity. However, Intersectionality was never intended to be an identity-related feminism but rather a lens for understanding layers of structural oppression imposed on Black and other women of colour, therefore it is best applied as a lens and is unfitting as an identity or form of practice (Steinmetz, 2020; Yuval-Davis, 2006) as it can fail to account for structural oppressions.

It is arguable that social work, with its complex, unjust historical complicities and abuses of power within the state, struggles to meet the emancipatory goals of feminism. However, critical social work, through its political project for social justice, sought to uncouple social work from its negative history and develop a discipline and a practice that sought to engage with the politics of disadvantage. This is most evident in the growing field of decolonising social work research and practice (Rasool and Harms-Smith, 2021). Social work perspectives that have been influenced by feminist social justice and emancipatory principles will certainly be engaged in work towards social justice. As noted by Dominelli (1998, p. 4), 'those endorsing an emancipatory approach to social work have an explicit commitment to social justice and to engage in overt challenges to the welfare system if it is seen to thwart this goal'.

The political nature of social work

Contemporary social work's alignment with what conservative politics sees pejoratively as 'wokeness' demonstrates that not only is social work highly political but that concerns of social work now inform many political debates in the public sphere as well as within social policy development (Zavattarro and Bearfield, 2022). The positive term 'woke' is derived from the idea of being awake to racial oppression, which emerged in the 1960s civil rights movement in the USA (Zavattarro and Bearfield, 2022). Acts of wokeness have become largely diminished by being marketed through consumer brands 'that are perceived to have appropriated social justice rhetoric and representations in pursuit of profit' (Sobande, 2019, p. 2724). Critiques of this appropriation highlight how neoliberal marketing led to a diminishing of courageous movements seeking to highlight racist and gendered oppressions and how this process created a means of its use as a pejorative by conservatives cynically labelling all progressive acts as woke (Sobande, 2019). Despite that it becoming a politicised term affecting political debates and policy decisions, its widespread association with positive social change and empathy with causes such as the 'Me Too' movement and 'Black Lives Matter' has led to popular support for such causes and in some contexts a positive association with being woke (Zavattarro and Bearfield, 2022). This was clearly demonstrated in a survey conducted in Australia in 2022 that showed 'more Australians assign a positive definition to the term woke than a negative one (48% vs 30%)' and that it was widely understood to be related to key issues such as understanding white privilege and action on climate change (Browne, 2022). This suggests that in the Australian context at least social work is on the right side of social and political transformations.

Social work's long history as agents of the state in removing children and imposing non-Indigenous culture on First Nations peoples, although now possibly acting as advocates against the state for those same communities, has embroiled social work in the highly political 'culture wars'. The culture wars are not only an extension of conservative anti-woke attacks but also attempt to maintain a positive narrative of colonisation. For social work, learning to listen to First Nations peoples and supporting the need to recognise the impact of colonisation on generations of First Nations peoples has led to a powerful and critical shift towards trauma-informed services and support from social workers. Further, UK researcher Joanne Warner (2015), in her exploration of the emotional politics of social work and child protection, alludes to how the concerns of social work in child protection enter the public sphere in the reporting of cases and the demonisation of both failed mothers and failed social workers as well as the negative moralisation around poverty and people living in poverty. A similar analysis in the Australian context demonstrated how the media focuses on failed child protection practices (Goddard and Saunders, 2001). Added to this are inherent racist biases that have formed historically in Australia and the UK where white superiority framed early child protection practices.

As noted by Okpokiri (2021), such biases in social work continue in attitudes towards Nigerian immigrants' parenting in the UK. Okpokiri conducted research aimed at decolonising 'parenting knowledges linked to chauvinistic sensibilities that sustain Western perceptions' (2021, p. 428). This process is also directly related to neoliberal governance by market-oriented deregulation that has resulted in a predominantly conservative media in countries such as the UK and Australia. Further, in South Africa, for example, dominant news outlets are under white ownership, which affects perceptions of people in poverty. However, bias in the media is most evident in relation to domestic and sexual violence (SV) against women, which is at extremely high levels in South Africa (Falkof, 2019). As observed by Falkof, the

> visibility of the female victim coupled with the invisibility of the male perpetrator in South African news coverage of violence against women is part of a rhetorical structure that allows public discourse to avoid broadly discussing the social consequences of masculine violence.
>
> *(2019, p. 161)*

Biased media has led to the popularisation of negative attitudes to welfare, which supports an open critique of social work practice and social justice-oriented policies (Binder, 2013; Neimanns, 2023).

Another example of politically potent social work is the now widely accepted practice around supporting LGBTQI children in their self-identity and understanding as a field of positive intervention for children's safety and mental health (Poirier et al., 2014). Anti-woke forces in the public sphere and within conservative political parties across English-speaking countries have used the prevailing professional supportiveness of children's claiming of their sexual identity in education, mental health, and social work as a deliberate promotion of non-heteronormative society and a transgression against religious beliefs and 'norms'. This example places social workers, who work with children requiring support in relation to their sexual identity, at the centre of a political storm of debate between political parties, religious institutions, social movements, and government.

The same could be said in relation to many of the responsibilities of social work practice, particularly in relation to changes in government policies related to social services, allocation of resources, and social and civil rights. Governments' social policies determine the effectiveness of a welfare state and therefore how people survive poverty, homelessness, unemployment, disasters, sexual and family violence, neglect and abuse of children, elder care, and so on. Politically determined social policies directly affect social work practice on the frontline of services. Equally, social work advocacy can influence political decisions about human needs and services. Advocating for the interests of individuals, families, and communities is a political activity both within government services and within the rapidly growing non-governmental sector, where many services are now delivered (Goodwin and Phillips, 2015). There is of course wide diversity amongst non-government sector services, reflecting both restrictive religious missions that would share the anti-woke agenda to services created by feminists to support women's other gender identities, particularly in relation to refuges providing protection from domestic violence.

This interface of the political nature of social work and the politics of the county in which it is practiced has been demonstrated throughout its professional history. For example, Quintero (2021) accounts for historical and contextual aspects of social work's development across Latin America. He described the role of the Catholic Church in establishing social work, the rise of radical social work, in student movements heavily influenced by Marxism, a struggle with conservative Catholicism and, importantly, women's movements, and then the modifying influence of Liberation Catholicism. This occurred over time when adjusting to Latin America's widespread evolution as capitalist economies was occurring and poverty of the working classes was a core focus for social work practice (Quintero, 2021).

Reproductive rights have been central to human rights social work, especially since the early 2000s (Alzate, 2009). After many years of struggle, particularly from a legislative perspective (Petchesky, 2003), feminists won the battle to decriminalise abortion in Columbia in 2022, a critical issue for poor women in Columbia and hence a significant political achievement for human rights and social justice for women (FOS Feminista, 2022). Regardless of social workers' direct involvement in the Causa Justa feminist group that ran a long campaign for reproductive justice, this movement reflects the importance and influence of feminist action on the role of social work in Columbia. This feminist victory, which spread across several Latin American countries, occurred during a time when the clock on women's reproductive rights in the USA was being wound back – denying access to women's reproductive rights in politically conservative states (Phillips, 2023). Summed up by the international feminist alliance, 'FOS Feminista' and this is an achievement clearly related to core social work fields of practice:

> Together with more than 135 local organizations across the globe, we engage in healthcare, education, and advocacy to advance our agenda. This includes providing sexual and reproductive health services and implementing community-based strategies that make sexual and reproductive healthcare more accessible to women, girls, and others at the margins... We stand alongside our partners in the streets, in the courts, and in other advocacy spaces as an unapologetically feminist voice, resisting injustice and advocating for gender equality and reproductive rights locally and globally.
>
> *(2022)*

Beddoe (2022) and Liddell (2018) noted that reproductive rights and fertility have not been a focus of social work research and practice and are sometimes presented as a problem for social work related to pregnancy and child protection. Beddoe further observed that '[i]n some programmes set up to support women who have children in care, accepting long-acting contraception is a requirement ... and contraceptive prescribing may be shaped by racist assumptions and other biases of health professionals' (2022, p. 8). The field of child protection has indeed been an area of feminist social work critique and struggles for the rights of 'problematised mothers' and reproductive rights are at the centre of the politics about access to contraception and abortion. Beddoe supported an intersectional approach to position 'reproductive health as a dimension of health in which multiple intersecting identities and social locations – gender, race, class, sexualities, geography, culture, health and disabilities – situate some people in a precarious position' (2022, p. 9). She also noted that social work can be seen to 'fence-sit' regarding reproductive rights as some publications have included pro-life social work papers and chapters, written by male social workers. For example, Marson (2019) noted:

> These [three chapters] have clearly been chosen to represent a range of views, but it can be argued that in doing so, client self-determination and reproductive justice are again cast as expendable, and women's rights are made subject to moral policing by male social work academics. Most social work journals and edited works strive to avoid inclusion of material that is sexist or racist, or that promotes stigma and oppressive practice.
>
> *(as cited in Beddoe, 2022, p. 12)*

This demonstrates not only that critical social work is not the dominant paradigm for social work, but an absence of feminist sensibility in some Global North contexts in a field that is a resounding global human rights issue (United Nations, 2020).

Political action by feminists has been highly visible in action against sexual assault across most cultures as rape and sexual exploitation and the failure of justice for women victims continues as one of the deepest forms of gendered oppression (Phillips, 2023). Violence against women relied on feminist action to become a public issue, pushed out of the secrecy of the private sphere onto social policy agendas, is a central field of social work practice (Nazneen et al., 2019a, 2019b; Weeks and Gilmore, 2020). There are numerous ways that the politics of domestic and family violence (DFV) and SV can be viewed in contexts where social work is at the centre of support for women who have experienced gendered violence. These contexts are at once highly personal and highly political. The impact of violence against women unleashes domino effects on those who experience it once they seek to stop it or report it (Nazneen et al., 2019a, 2019b). These effects involve multiple systems and institutions that can be supportive and emancipatory or in more formal contexts oppressive and fail to protect the rights and justice for women. Both DFV and SV can begin with police interactions that can be judgemental, cavalier, intrusive, sexist, and dismissive, or, if they act in the interests of women (and their children), highly supportive and protective. In addition, other interactions can be with agencies such as the health and criminal justice systems, child protection services as well as with refugee services and social housing. Processes required to engage with institutions and services are always mediated by decisions made by governments of the day, which, in a democracy, are affected by prevailing culture, political interests, advocacy, and budgets.

Highlighting the Intersectionality of experiences of violence, Zufferey et al.'s (2016) Australian study of how women found housing after leaving a violent relationship, found that most women from diverse socio-economic backgrounds suffered due to their already established inequality. They noted:

> However, the effects of IPV [DVF] on women's housing exacerbate the gendered inequality women already experience. Access to safe and affordable housing, respect, recognition, financial security, and feelings of belonging to a safe home are fundamental to women's well-being. Yet, women escaping IPV experience limited access to social justice and basic human rights, which is a central concern for social work and feminism ....
>
> *(Zufferey et al., 2016, p. 473)*

Zufferey et al.'s study provided evidence that men's violence had eroded 'women's citizenship by disrupting their access to housing rights and constraining their agency in their public and private lives' linking it to limited women's fundamental social and human rights (2016, p. 473). The extensive engagement of social workers in services for women who have experienced DFV and SV means that social work is in a critical advocacy role for women's equal citizenship.

A further example of how social work is political is within social work pedagogy. Pushing back against the increasingly neoliberal university context and in recognition of tensions it creates with collectivist feminist practice, a group of Australian researchers sought to recalibrate the synergy of being feminists and social work educators and administrators (Hosken et al., 2020). Their project recognised the inherently political nature of social work education. They pursued the idea that, as a pedagogy, social work must include theorisations and practice understandings of power, particularly how the power of political decisions and how government policies affect social work practice contexts. Learning to do social work and the practice of doing social work are indivisible in relation to the need to recognise and understand the impact of power. This was affirmed by feminist social worker educators, Hosken et al., when they stated that '[w]hat we have learned is that feminist social work pedagogy involves enacting social work practice' (2020, p. 311). They expressed an obligation 'to engage in human rights advocacy within the academy' and 'demand recognition and equity for marginalised and non-traditional students in the curriculum, assessment and in their daily life as students' (Hosken et al., 2020, p. 311). Their support for feminist goals in pedagogy was manifested in administrative action through advocacy for social work students that were clearly counter to the efficiency demands of a neoliberal context.

The impact of politics on social work practice

As described above, Latin American struggles for basic reproductive rights occurred in contexts where women experienced high levels of inequality and change required mass protest and action. Further examples can be found in India and several countries in the African continent (Phillips, 2023). Rush and Keenan (2014), in an analysis of the social politics of social work, found that even though 21st-century social work across the Global North is mostly framed by a broad adherence to forms of anti-oppressive practice, the capacity of social workers to achieve this is constrained or enabled by the welfare state model within which they work, which differs across countries. In other words, social democratic states, such as Denmark and Sweden, where there are strong social citizenship rights and universal services, are better contexts for anti-oppressive social work than the liberal welfare states such as the UK, Australia, and the USA. Welfare state models are directly related to the prevailing politics of governments in power and directly affect women's rights and access to resources. Even though there are stated emancipatory and anti-oppressive global values for international social work (International Federation of Social Workers [IFSW], 2023), they're impossible to achieve if the government's social policies are punitive, socially controlling and driven by a neoliberal agenda placing the market above citizen welfare. As noted by Dominelli (1998), the way the UK welfare state emerged and slowly became a highly residual system was an ideological and political response determined by neoliberalism asserting that welfare issues could be best addressed by economic growth and free market capitalism.

Canadian social work researchers (Pollack and Rossiter, 2010) describe their concerns about the impact of neoliberalism on social work practice and in particular 'on social movements such as feminism and with the concomitant rejection of a notion of the collective public good in favour of an individualised entrepreneurial subject' (2010, p. 157). They and others also expressed concern about the appropriation of feminist discourses as forms of neoliberal commodification that de-politicises feminist objectives for gender equality through individualisation that overshadows the meaning of equality for women (Phillips and Cree, 2014; Pollack and Rossiter, 2010).

Understanding neoliberalism is important in social work and feminism because it has become the dominant governmental framework for most nations of the Global North and Global South due to the work of institutions such as the World Bank and the International Monetary Fund. The key tensions within neoliberalism for feminism are also the key tensions for social work. The operation of a contemporary neoliberal economy relies on individualism and a rejection of collectivist values. Collectivist values, those that are the interests of groups, communities, identities, and nations, are central to social justice and more socially just communities. As mentioned above, the sense of working collectively is a way of being in African cultures understood as Ubuntu, more suited to African 'womanism', a specific agency for many African feminists (Rasool, 2020).

Accounting for diversity and difference, feminism broadly relies on collective action to address collective, not individual, needs. Social work also aims to facilitate collective change, beginning within families and their extended relations, to communities and society in general. Feminist and social work aspirations seek to build a more equal society, more gender equal, more educationally equal, more equal access to welfare, employment, health, secure housing, and appropriate level of welfare assistance. For both feminists and social workers, this requires both political engagement and political action.

Globally, social workers are engaging in feminist causes and actions, for example in the USA there have been ongoing conflicts related to justice outcomes for women. The following is from a USA social work organisation *SWHelper* website:

> Feminism continues to be a fraught issue with fractures within the community of feminists, as well as women in general. Yet, feminism is more crucial than ever given the diversity of challenges women are now facing. Feminism has become a focal point again recently largely as a result of the Presidential election and the response from it.

This is clearly important for social workers as well, from the perspective of human rights and social justice, as well as from a policy perspective.

(Ringler-Jayanthan, 2022)

The political context in the USA during and since the Trump presidency is misogynistic, with the rise to power of populist politics and fundamentalist Christians, eager to deny women reproductive rights and allowing high-profile SV to go unpunished (Ringler-Jayanthan, 2022) resulting in women in many US states losing rights. It is also when racism and health and welfare failures saw people of colour, particularly transgender women of colour, attacked and vilified (Human Rights Campaign [HRC], 2019). Evidence of this was particularly stark in statistics about who suffered most from the COVID-19 pandemic but also the rise in maternal mortality for African American women (Yusef et al., 2020). The USA example is valuable for understanding how the context for social work practice is framed and affected by the prevailing political climate as, despite being the richest nation in the world, it has extreme inequalities and large scale, multiple layers of intersectional disadvantage.

Conclusion

This chapter has illuminated the importance of an understanding of the political nature of both feminism and social work and demonstrated the important connections between them. This relates to recognition of assertions of power as the core basis of politics and a key concern for both feminism and social work. The social policies and operation of governments in the context of a global dominance of the neoliberal framework of individualism challenge the desirable 'collectivities' of feminist advocacy and social work practice. Although apparently marginalised in social work research and pedagogy, feminism offers universal critical responses to core issues of concern for social work. Examples of reproductive rights and the widespread incidence of gendered domestic and SV serve to establish the importance of feminist activism and social work practice to address women's unequal and unjust experiences.

The primary goal that merges feminism with objectives of social work, social justice, is essentially political. Effective social work is emancipatory, seeking to address the abuse of power over excluded and less equal people, this is a political struggle as well as a material one. Feminist activists and feminist social workers are at the centre of these engagements and struggles in how they seek to provide services, change, and critique social policies and ultimately seek equal social justice in their communities.

References

Alzate, M. M. (2009). The role of sexual and reproductive rights in social work practice. *Affilia: Journal of Women and Social Work*, 24(2), 108–119. Doi: 10.1177/0886109909331695

Beddoe, L. (2022). Reproductive justice, abortion rights and social work. *Critical and Radical Social Work*, 10(1), 7–22.

Binder, D. (2013). *Attitudes towards Welfare and Welfare Recipients Are Hardening*. London School of Economics and Political Science. https://blogs.lse.ac.uk/politicsandpolicy/scrounging-off-the-state-hardening-attitudes-toward-welfare-and-its-recipients/

Browne, B. (2022). 'Woke up call': Australian attitudes to and perceptions of 'wokeness'. *Research Paper*, Australia Institute. https://australiainstitute.org.au/wp-content/uploads/2022/08/P1243-Woke-up-call-Web.pdf

Chigangaidze, Mafa I., Simango, T. G., & Mudehwe, E. (2023). Establishing the relevance of the Ubuntu philosophy in social work practice: Inspired by the Ubuntu World Social Work Day, 2021 celebrations and the IFSW and IASSW's (2014) Global Definition of Social Work. *International Social Work*, 66(1), 6–20.

Crenshaw, K. (1991). Mapping the margins: Intersectionality, identity politics, and violence against women of colour. *Stanford Law Review*, 43(6), 1241–1299.

Dominelli, L. (1998). Anti-oppressive practice in context. In Adams, R., Dominelli, L., & Payne, M. (Eds.), *Social Work, Themes, Issues and Critical Debates*. London: Macmillan, pp. 3–22.

Dominelli, L. & McLeod, E. (1989). *Feminist Social Work*. Houndmills, Basingstoke, Hampshire and London: MacMillan Education.

Falkof, N. (2019). Patriarchy and power in the South African news: Competing coverage of the murder of Anene Booysen 1. In Carter, C., Steiner, L., & Allan, S. (Eds.), *Journalism, Gender and Power* (1st ed.). Routledge, pp. 159–173. https://doi.org/10.4324/9781315179520

FOS Feminista (2022). Fòs feminista applauds Colombian Court ruling to decriminalize abortion, February 22, 2022. https://fosfeminista.org/media/fos-feminista-applauds-colombian-court-ruling-to-decriminalize-abortion/

Goddard, C. & Saunders, B. J. (2001). Child abuse and the media. In *Policy and Practice Paper*. Canberra: Australian Institute of Health and Welfare. https://aifs.gov.au/resources/policy-and-practice-papers/child-abuse-and-media

Goodwin, S. & Phillips, R. (2015). Policy capacity in the community sector. In Head, B. & Crowley, K. (Eds.), *Policy Analysis in Australia*. Sydney: Policy Press Australia, pp. 245–258.

Hill Collins, P. (1993). Toward a new vision: Race, class, and gender as categories of analysis and connection. *Race, Sex and Class*, 1(1), 25–45.

Hosken, N., Vassos, S., & Epstein, S. (2020). Feminist social work pedagogy: Personal, cultural and structural advocacy in the academy. *Social Work Education*, 40(3), 302–314. https://doi.org/10.1080/02615479.2020.1774533

Human Rights Campaign (HRC) (2021) *Fatal Violence Against the Transgender and Gender Non-Conforming Community in 2021*. HRC Foundation. https://www.hrc.org/resources/fatal-violence-against-the-transgender-and-gender-non-conforming-community-in-2021

International Federation of Social Workers (IFSW) (2023) *Global Definition of Social Work*. https://www.ifsw.org/what-is-social-work/global-definition-of-social-work/

Jones, M., Mlcek, S. H. E., Healy, J. P., & Bridges, D. (2019). Gender dynamics in social work practice and education: A critical literature review. *Australian Social Work*, 72(1), 62–74.

Keck, M. E. & Sikkink, K. (2014). *Activists beyond Borders: Advocacy Networks in International Politics*. Ithaca, NY: Cornell University Press.

Kellner, D. (1990). Critical theory and the crisis of social theory. *Sociological Perspectives*, 33(1), 11–33.

Laruffa, F. (2022). Neoliberalism, economization and the paradox of the new welfare state. *European Journal of Sociology*, 63(1), 131–163.

Liddell, J. L. (2018). Reproductive justice and the social work profession: Common grounds and current trends. *Affilia*, 34(1), 99–115.

Marson, S. M. (Ed.) (2019). *Routledge Handbook of Social Work Ethics and Values*. New York: Routledge.

McLaughlin, K. (2008). *Social Work, Politics and Society, from Radicalism to Orthodoxy*. Bristol: Policy Press.

Nazneen, S., Hickey, S., & Sifaki, E. (Eds.) (2019a). *Negotiating Gender Equity in the Global South, the Politics of Domestic Violence Policy*. Oxon and New York: Routledge.

Nazneen, S., Hossain, N., & Chopra, D. (2019b). Introduction: Contentious women's empowerment in South Asia. *Contemporary South Asia*, 27(4), 457–470.

Neimanns, E. (2023). Welfare states, media ownership and attitudes towards redistribution. *Journal of European Public Policy*, 30(2), 234–253.

Okpokiri, C. (2021). Parenting in fear: Child welfare micro strategies of Nigerian parents in Britain. *The British Journal of Social Work*, 51(2), 427–444.

Pease, B. & Nipperess, S. (2016). Doing critical social work in the neoliberal context: Working on the contradictions. In Pease, B., Goldingay, S., Hosken, N., & Nipperess, S. (Eds.), *Doing Critical*

Social Work: Transformative Practices for Social Justice. Milton Park, Abingdon, Oxon and New York: Routledge, pp. 3–25.

Pease, B., & Nipperess, S. (2020). *Doing Critical Social Work Inn the Neoliberal Context: Woreking on the Contradictions*. Taylor and Francis.

Petchesky, R. (2003). *Global Prescriptions: Gendering Health and Human Rights*. New York: Zed Books; Geneva: United Nations Research Institute for Social Development.

Phillips, R. (2015). Feminist research and social work. In Wright, J. D. (Editor-in-chief), *International Encyclopedia of the Social & Behavioral Sciences* (2nd ed.). Vol. 8. Oxford: Elsevier, pp. 935–941.

Phillips, R. (2023). *Practising Feminism for Social Welfare, a Global Perspective*. Oxon, New York: Routledge.

Phillips, R. & Cree, V. E. (2014). What does the "fourth wave" mean for teaching feminism in 21st century social work? *Social Work Education: The International Journal*, 33(7), 930–943.

Poirier, J. M., Fisher, S. K., Hunt, R. A., & Bearse, M. (2014). *A Guide for Understanding, Supporting, and Affirming LGBTQI2-S Children, Youth, and Families*. Washington, DC: American Institutes for Research. https://www.socialworkers.org/LinkClick.aspx?fileticket=jjq0-NcZlU0%3D&portalid=0

Pollack, S. & Rossiter, A. (2010). What happened to feminism in social work? Qu'en est-il advenu du féminisme en service social? *Canadian Social Work Review/Revue Canadienne de Service Social* 27(2), 155–169.

Quintero, S. (2021). The influence of Catholicism on social work: From classic conservatism to critical renewal. *Critical and Radical Social Work*, 9(1), 97–112.

Rasool, S. (2020). Heterogeneity of social movements addressing the intersections of gender and race: A reflection on feminisms and womanisms emerging from African women. In Kalbi, T., Lutz, R., Noyoo, N., Bunk, B., Dittmann, A., & Seepamore, B. K. (Eds.), *The Routledge Handbook of Post-Colonial Social Work*. Oxon: Routledge, pp. 127–137.

Rasool, S. & Harms-Smith, L. (2021). Towards Decoloniality in a social work programme: A process of dialogue, reflexivity, action and change. *Critical African Studies -Decolonizing African Studies, Part 2*, 13(1), 56–72.

Ringler-Jayanthan, E. (2022). Why feminism is still important for social workers. *SWHelpers*. https://swhelper.org/2017/04/12/feminism-still-important-social-workers/

Rush, M. & Keenan, M. (2014). The social politics of social work: Anti-oppressive social work dilemmas in twenty-first-century welfare regimes. *British Journal of Social Work*, 44(6), 1436–1453.

Schram, S. F. (2019). Neoliberal relations of poverty and the welfare state. In Webb, S. (Ed.), *The Routledge Handbook of Critical Social Work*. Routledge, pp. 15–23.

Sobande, F. (2020). Woke-washing: "Intersectional" femvertising and branding "woke" bravery. *European Journal of Marketing*, 54(11), 2723–2745.

Steinberg, S. R. & Kincheloe, J. L. (2010). Power, emancipation, and complexity: Employing critical theory. *Power and Education*, 2(2), 140–151.

Steinmetz, K. (2020). She coined the term 'intersectionality' over 30 years ago. Here's what it means to her today. *Time*, February 20. https://time.com/5786710/kimberle-crenshaw-intersectionality/

United Nations (2020). *Information Series on Sexual and Reproductive Health and Rights, Abortion*. Geneva: UN Human Rights, Office of the High Commission. https://www.ohchr.org/sites/default/files/Documents/Issues/Women/WRGS/SexualHealth/INFO_Abortion_WEB.pdf

Warner, J. (2015). *The Emotional Politics of Social Work and Child Protection*. University of Bristol, Bristol: Policy Press.

Watts, L. & Hodgson, D. (2019). *Social Justice Theory and Practice for Social Work*. Singapore: Springer Nature.

Weeks, W. & Gilmore, K. (2020). How violence against women became an issue on the national policy agenda. In Dalton, T., Draper, M., Weeks, W., & Wiseman, J. (Eds.), *Making Social Policy in Australia: An Introduction* (1st ed.). Routledge, Taylor & Francis Group, pp. 141–153

Wendt, S. & Moulding, N. (2017). The current state of feminism and social work. *Australian Social Work*, 70(3), 261–262.

Yusuf, K. K., Dongarwar, D., Ibrahimi, S., Ikedionwu, C., Maiyegun, S. O., & Salihu, H. M. (2020). Expected surge in maternal mortality and severe morbidity among African-Americans in the Era of COVID-19 pandemic. *International Journal of Maternal and Child Health and AIDS*, 9(3), 386–389.

Yuval-Davis, N. (2006). Intersectionality and feminist politics. *The European Journal of Women's Studies*, *13*(3), 193–209.

Zavattaro, S. M. & Bearfield, D. (2022). Weaponization of wokeness: The theatre of management and implications for public administration. *Public Administration Review*, *82*(3), 585–593.

Zufferey, C., Chung, D., Franzway, S., Wendt, S., & Moulding, N. (2016) Intimate partner violence and housing: Eroding women's citizenship. *Affilia*, *31*(4), 463–478.

SECTION 2

Feminist social work in fields of practice

11
GENDER EMPOWERMENT IN YOUTH WORK IN PALESTINE

A missing link

Abeer Musleh

Introduction and context

Young people in Palestine have been described as both change agents as well as a problem for the government and general population (Salih et al., 2017). At the same time, the ability of governments to control the bodies, energies, and intentions of young people in the Arab world has declined (Comaroff & Comaroff, 2005, p. 22). During the 1960s and the first intifada (uprising in the occupied territories in 1987), youth were perceived as political activists and protectors of the Palestinian people from Israeli colonisation (Collins, 2004). However, after the signing of the Oslo Peace Accord between the Palestinians and Israelis,[1] the image of young people as activists shifted from that of social change agents to victims of the conflict (Collins, 2004). The perception of youth as a social construct changed from being a social asset to a group that needed to be empowered. This shift in status has had consequences for opportunities available to young people in general, and young women in particular, to effect change.

Adopting a deficit model working with young people – instead of addressing the structural issues affecting them – resulted in them being perceived as problematic (Musleh, 2015a). Working from this approach, youth programmes fail to challenge the socioeconomic and political structures responsible for marginalising young people. In fact, these programmes tend to separate political and civic engagement, thus restricting the range of activities available to young people to acquire the skills essential for active citizenship (Watts & Flanagan, 2007).

Youth programmes tended to replicate existing social power relations, especially pre-existing gender roles and power imbalances. They were also influenced by the social values held by the organisations' founders, particularly regarding the role of women, relations between genders, and their overall world views. Leftist organisations, however, seemed more likely to promote equal relationships between young women and men, providing more space for young women's involvement. Still, gender roles were not challenged (Musleh, 2016).

Youth programmes within most other organisations seemed to ignore the differences and power dynamics among various groups of young people based on gender, class, and locality. Locality is an important consideration, due to colonisation and the implications of the Oslo Accord, which significantly altered the rights of Palestinians and their living conditions according to the places in which they live, the identity that they held, and their political affiliation.

Youth empowerment efforts were influenced by inclusion/exclusion discourse embedded in binary distinctions such as public/private, religious/modern, and Arabised/westernised, which also had gendered implications. Okin (1991) describes how "patriarchy is served by confining women to the private sphere, restricting their representation in the public realm, and obscuring the resulting oppression of women by the claim that the two spheres are of equal importance" (Moller Okin, 1991, as cited in Rasool-Bassadien & Hochfeld, 2005). The religious/Western divide frames women's rights as a Western practice that not only contradicts religious belief but actively opposes it. This has influenced the access of individuals and groups (especially for young women) to resources, spaces available for engagement, and acceptable forms of engagement (Salih et al., 2017).

Studies on youth in Arab countries and Palestine, in particular, have highlighted that social policies are generally insensitive to young people and their gender. These policies reinforce the exclusion of young people and limit their opportunities (Marzo, 2016; Musleh, 2015b; Salih et al., 2017). Furthermore, neoliberal policies tend to increase socioeconomic inequalities amongst marginalised young people. Such policies seek individual solutions to problems and fail to address the structural roots of youth marginalisation. "Thus, one of the major trends in Arabic social structures consolidates differences based on economic criteria, occupation and authority, similar to those established in Western societies under neoliberal rules promoted by global economic institutions" (Sanchez-Montijano & Sanchez-García, 2019).

Youth literature also paid minimal attention to the influence of gender structure on youth development and engagement (Gordon, 2008). Gender shapes the social development of young people including their sense of commitment, forms of engagement, and positions in the public sphere (Gordon, 2008). Programmes and policies that adopt a gender-neutral approach unintentionally reinforce existing gender relations and reproduce the structures that marginalise young women (Greenberg, 2018). These programmes, led by adults, tend to define what "normal" gendered behaviour of young people should be (Ghannam, 2013). While youth organisations provide various interventions to enhance the status of young people, they treat young people as a homogeneous group and do not build on their assets (Musleh, 2015a). Programmes working with young people acknowledged that gender is a major factor impacting youth participation, yet gender dynamics were not tackled (Musleh, 2016). As a result, young people's roles shifted from being community decision-makers to mere participants in programmes (Hamammi, 2000; Musleh, 2015a).

Empowerment

The discourses of inclusion/exclusion and empowerment are important and are strongly linked to social change (Tremblay & Gutberlet, 2010). Youth development literature sees empowerment as a strategy for youth inclusion. However, while youth development models focus on pushing boundaries of exclusion of young people, they fail to tackle structural marginalisation, with no focus on gender at all (Watts & Flanagan, 2007). Youth development models should adopt an empowerment approach which utilises conscientisation processes (Watts & Flanagan, 2007) which develops a critical understanding of context and way of living, through the process of action and reflection (Freire, 1970). Young people may then collectively understand gender dynamics and connect this to the larger social context. They can then better understand their practices through a critical analysis of the sociopolitical factors that influence their group. As they acquire this knowledge, they develop new ways of taking action and new attitudes to their collective and individual power (Abu Nahele et al., 2003). Context plays an essential role in shaping identity, capability, and engagement, yet the impact of gender on youth is not widely explored (Yates & Youniss, 1998).

Inclusion/exclusion discourse in the context of Palestinian youth illustrates the extent to which young people are excluded from social policies (Musleh, 2015b). This means young women face double marginalisation due to social barriers such as cultural perceptions about women's roles and restrictions to domestic spaces (Musleh, 2015b; Salih & Welchman, 2017). Discourse around youth inclusion in Arab countries is also shaped by neoliberal policies aimed at enhancing opportunities for market access. Youth empowerment has primarily revolved around skills development, which is problematic because it fails to address the impact of colonisation and socioeconomic factors marginalising young people (Musleh, 2015b).

The concept of empowerment shifted over time. In the 1970s, it was seen as a transformative force, but by the 1990s it had evolved into a more individualised notion of economic production (Bisnath & Elson, 2000). It also changed from being a tool to reinforce social justice through transformative sociopolitical structures (Townsend et al., 1999), to a focus on individual participation in decision-making, and access to resources. Empowerment practices therefore lost their transformative characteristics that had previously enabled marginalised people to critically analyse their context and to work together to create change (Abu Nahleh et al., 2003).

Kabeer (1994) emphasises that empowerment of women is embedded in structures of power, often perceived as individual concerns impacting decision-making or contributing to social change. However, this perspective does not consider how factors such as the economy and political systems impact the status of youth and young women in particular (Börner, Kraftl, & Giatti, 2021). According to Sika (2021), public policies and socioeconomic structures influence young peoples' opportunities and statuses, while their practices and actions in turn influence the same social, political, and economic structures. This reflects the dynamic nature of youth agency and power.

It is important to recognise the interdependence of individual and structural change within the context of empowerment. This interplay affects individual decisions, choices, and objectives. The marginalisation of young women results from the combined effects of structural factors arising from age and gender. Empowerment as a process enables both individuals and communities to take power and act effectively in gaining greater control, efficacy, and social justice in changing their lives and their environment (Rappaport, 1981).

In this chapter, I argue that youth programmes in post-Oslo Accord Palestine reinforce existing gender hierarchies among young people. Youth programmes utilised a neutral strategy towards equality which fails to tackle binaries of public/private, religious/modernity, and the interventions designed to empower youth. While young women were individually empowered, in order to engage they had to shift away from the traditional roles and expectations of women in Palestinian/Arab society. Youth workers' perceptions about empowerment limited possibilities of empowering young women and impinged gender dynamics of youth groups.

Research methods

This study used a qualitative approach, examining three youth groups active in three organisations in Bethlehem and Jerusalem. These organisations ran youth programmes on economic and social empowerment, and youth groups' participation varied in programmes based on their enrolment. The groups had been active for more than three years.

Interviews were conducted with 12 group leaders (Castro, Harger, & Swauger, 2017) of which six were female), and three youth workers (one male and two females) working with them. As the researcher is a youth worker, it was easy to recruit organisations and gain their acceptance.

Despite organisational consent, participation was voluntary and youth workers had the liberty to accept or reject inclusion in the study with no repercussions. Youth workers played a role in nominating suitable youth leaders to reduce risk of harm, and all prospective participants were told that nomination to participate does not require participation. Four youth leaders were selected from each programme. All participants were over 18 years, and youth leaders exercised their voice and agency in deciding whether to participate or not (Best, 2007). Participants were assured of confidentiality and they were given the freedom to choose a comfortable location for the interviews.

Youth leaders who agreed to participate were interviewed in person in semi-structured interviews of between 45 and 60 minutes. Interview transcripts were shared with participants, and they approved the texts before the data analysis began.

Results and discussion

Influence of the family on youth engagement

Family expectations have a more significant influence on the form and level of participation of young women than on men. All the participants said parental support was essential for determining the extent and intensity of young women's participation.

> My parents did not want me to stay late or go to activities in the refugee camp. For them my studies are the most important, and they did not want me to stay out with male youth that they did not know. So many times, I had to get into conflict with them to participate in activities. With activities they supported, participation was easier, at least I did not have an additional fight to worry about.
>
> *(Interview #6, 2021)*

Young women had to negotiate with their families around the time of their return from activities, and for permission to participate in events, especially outside the governorate, or city boundaries (Interview #5, 2021). Young men did not face the same restrictions and were less concerned about opposing their parents' wishes. While a supportive home environment is essential for youth engagement, young women are more affected by their parent's opinions and control over their movements compared to young men, who have more freedom of movement. Men are more likely to be harassed by the military and are seen as a bigger threat (Interview #4, 2021).

Youth workers were aware of the pressures young women faced but hesitated to engage with the families or to empower young women to challenge their parents. To avoid potential conflict about returning home late, project activities were arranged at earlier times.

Some youth workers expressed empathy for the young women's struggles, but offered only verbal solidarity, without working to create a more supportive environment. Patriarchal structures can jeopardise young people's access to youth activities when there is an absence of a supportive home (Coe et al., 2013).

Gender hierarchies in youth work (when equality causes marginalisation)

The programmes inadvertently reinforced customary practices, gender hierarchies, and power imbalances by using an equality-focused strategy rather than challenging existing structures. This was evident in statements by youth workers.

> We try to treat both genders the same. They have the same rights and responsibilities, we try to have them in the same numbers. We allow them to choose the tasks they want freely.
>
> *(Interview #2, 2021)*

The notion of equality was limited to numerical representation but did not extend to roles and responsibilities. Although some young women had access to the programmes, their role remained marginal. With such strategies, youth programmes failed to challenge social structures that limit women's roles and development of their capabilities.

Although youth workers were aware of the limitations of women's participation, they did not take measures to enhance participation in activities.

> We knew that young women are facing more challenges than young men. Being with the opposite sex, staying late, and commuting between various communities, were challenges they faced. Young women had to deal with pressures from their parents or culture, sometimes they can fight it and sometimes they do not.
>
> *(Interview #4, 2021; male)*

While youth workers demonstrated an understanding of the challenges women faced with their families, their reluctance to intervene in these dynamics placed young women's inclusion at risk. Only minor adaptations were made to programme activities such as redistribution of responsibilities and adjusting activity hours. In general, working with families and the community is not seen as being part of youth work (Watts & Flanagan, 2007).

By treating young people as a homogenous group, programmes were not sensitised towards diversity. For example, they did not consider challenges faced by women who are married or have children. This perpetuates discrimination, where young women cannot access services (Interview #2, 2021), and replicates socioeconomic policies in Palestine that are not youth or gender-sensitive (Musleh, 2015b).

In keeping with gender role expectations, male youth perceived themselves as protectors of young women and often acted on their behalf when challenges arose. For example, during an activity in a rural community, local male youth surrounded young women who were leading an activity, which was culturally inappropriate behaviour. To address this, the activity was moved indoors, but the young women refused this solution. Nevertheless, blame for the incident was placed upon the women, because of their choice of clothes – jeans and blouses – and not all wore a head scarf, which deviates from the diversity of Palestinian society (Interview #6, 2021).

The public/private and Western/religious divide was clear in this interaction. Organisations form a safe zone for young people to be socialised into new activities (Delgado & Staples, 2007), where genders can play equal roles, and tasks are based on capabilities and needs. However, when faced with intense social pressure, young people will revert to socially acceptable practices. The masculine and feminine divide was perpetuated by blaming the victim for their choice of dress, which was acceptable in their own city (Coe et al., 2013). Young men's view of women's dress reflects a religious/Western binary where women's dress code is seen as inappropriate. Moving young women indoors ensured minimum public interaction.

Gender role expectations were reinforced by youth workers, and at times they hindered young women's attempts to challenge these traditional roles.

> When I started moving chairs and heavy things from one place to another, I was told by Mr. Ahmad [pseudonym], that I should leave the heavy lifting for the guys, still I kept on lifting the heavy things, I did not understand why he didn't want me to do it.
> *(Interview #7, 2021)*

Youth workers do not always support young women's attempts to break from traditional hierarchies. This may be attributed to a lack of gender training and their own alignment with entrenched patriarchal stereotypes and expectations.

Young people in these organisations are mostly educated and some are already part of the labour market. As mentors, youth workers set the boundaries for what is deemed acceptable (Delgado & Staples, 2007) and wield the authority to allow or prevent specific actions. The economy and community participation impact women empowerment (Kabeer, 1994) and their previous experiences and capabilities also impact their engagement (Mische, 2008). For example, women leaders indicated that with support from organisations, and a track record of involvement, they were more inclined to negotiate the forms of engagement and roles they would play within groups (Interview #2, 2001).

Furthermore, rigidity of gender norms was the strongest consideration influencing cipation, and this was evident in parental control as the quote below illustrates: around such issues.

> My parents were not happy with the places where we do our activities, they wanted me to stay at home instead, they wanted me to leave and come back at specific times, which they did not ask my brother to do.
> *(Interview #7, 2021)*

No restrictions were imposed on male youth participation and mobility. They had to take on the tasks requiring mobility or staying out late, associated mainly with building networks and coordination.

> When we had an assignment, we knew that the 'girls' will not be able to stay late, but still we have to ensure that everything is ready on time, so we took over these tasks, in a way we are the one who will go from one place to another, check the site, and finish all necessary arrangements.
> *(Interview #9, 2021)*

Not all women faced parental restrictions. Their history of involvement, age, and the type and location of activities influenced their ability to negotiate their participation. Young women who were involved in many activities were better able to negotiate their participation with their parents. This aligns with findings by McAdam (1992) and Whittier (1997) about activists' backgrounds being a determinant of their level of participation and engagement.

> My parents were not happy that I will participate in activities in the refugee camp. For them it was all about what risks I will be in; the refugee camp was, for them, a totally different social setting. Not having any other place to practice our sport did not leave them with a choice. Every time I wanted to go, I had to fight for it. When they saw that we won awards they became more accepting.
>
> *(Interview #6, 2021)*

Young women noted that youth workers understood the challenges that they faced. However, they did not intervene to address these challenges. A few youth workers attempted to raise awareness about potential community impact as a strategy to relieve pressure from parents. However, these strategies only provided women with moral support (Interview #8, 2021). The fear of creating a conflict when tackling the public/private binary limited the possibilities for empowerment.

Political context reinforcing gender hierarchies

Youth organisations that maintained an apolitical status ignored the influence of colonisation in reinforcing gender roles and hierarchies. For example, parents' restrictions on young women's mobility were exacerbated by the fear of arrest, injury, and mobility restrictions imposed by Israeli forces, such as at checkpoints (Interview #4, 2021). Although mobility restrictions are applied to both genders, women are perceived as more at risk of sexual and other types of violence. Hence, cultural values intertwined with the political context reinforce gender hierarchies and further limit women's mobility.

Offering young people with the opportunity to take leadership roles was a vital component in building their power and a way for them to realise their self-worth, make decisions, and create change.

> We encouraged them all the time to take action, and to believe in themselves and their abilities.
>
> *(Interview #2, 2021)*

Building self-esteem is vital; however, youth empowerment remains constrained because it does not affect underlying social structures (Musleh, 2016). Personally, young women are becoming stronger, more skilled, and outspoken, yet at a community level social structures were not impacted.

Young women leaders as power figures

The presence of women leaders in each group was vital for younger women. For the younger cohort, the female leader served as a mentor to talk to, to look up to, and to give them a voice.

> When newcomers joined our group, it was important that we [the group] had me and Maha 'sabaya' [Young women], when the younger women started, they were shy, and

they were not comfortable in speaking in meetings and expressing themselves. It was easier for them to talk to us before or after the meeting to ensure that their voice is taken into consideration, it was a way to ease them into the group.
(Interview #4, 2021 youth leader)

This highlights the importance of peer-to-peer empowerment and diversity brought by age and level of experience. Younger female members could build trust and connections with mentor and learn that it is safe to voice their concerns. With this, we see that if leaders do not have consciousness about gender, they reproduce pre-existing gender roles. In a youth group with strong women leaders since its formation, younger women had a better status (Interview #2, 2021). This shows how leaders play a role in setting group culture and how groups may be more sensitised to the needs of female youth (Coburn, 2011).

Having women leaders in the core team of a programme was essential for engaging younger women and encouraging them to participate, express themselves, and find a mentor.

Having a youth leader as part of the core team meant there is someone we can talk to, follow, and allows us to discuss issues easily. It is not the same when she is not around.
(Interview #6, 2021)

Women leaders provided support and guidance and encouraged the utilisation of available opportunities. They were also the voice for those who were not yet comfortable speaking. Voicing concerns as a collective was essential in building women's voices in the group. Knowing that they were not alone and that other women had survived the same challenges was essential for their agency.

When in the community and teenage boys gathered around us, and the "Shabab" male youth in our group tried to force us to move inside, we refused together. Knowing it is not me alone, but all of us having the same challenge, made me stronger.
(Interview #4, 2021)

The power of "we" is vital when challenging binaries such as the public/private divide. It shows that a young woman is not an outlier, but rather, when faced with shared injustices, they possess a common interest in creating change, achieved by standing in solidarity. "Power with" is vital as it recognises the collective. It reflects collaboration, respect, and mutual support beyond differences. This leads to collective action and the ability to act together (Mathie et al., 2017).

Achieving their objectives led to a sense of accomplishment. Young people are sometimes perceived as a problem, so shifting this perception to view them as "doers" provides them with trust in themselves as individuals, groups, and communities (Delgado & Staples, 2007). Accomplishment and developing capabilities are important for both genders. This leads to agency and opens a space for young women in the public sphere, enabling them to challenge social structures that prevent both sexes from working together.

Activities of resistance and challenge

Young people had a clear understanding of challenges they faced due to colonisation. The issues they tackled, such as preserving heritage or providing stationary for marginalised school children, were chosen to keep them off the Israeli radar. Youth indicated that their activities should not be seen to be political to avoid the risk of arrest. Accordingly, their activities would seem to relate more to community development or recreation, such as hiking or biking or even sitting in groups at the steps of the Damascus Gate in the old city of Jerusalem.

However, such initiatives were actually an important strategic challenge and resistance against gender hierarchies as well as colonisation, infused with a youth culture twist.

> Joining a biking trail is fun, we can easy have young people join us, still it is not customary for young women to ride a bike. It is considered for "boys". Additionally, she will be riding a bike with boys and she will be outdoors. We have to secure the bikes for participants which cost some money, so not anyone can join, also they need to know how to ride, and only a few girls learned how to ride a bike. We go to demolished villages, and we visit places in different locations of Palestine, places that we will never reach otherwise.
>
> *(Interview #12, 2021)*

With this activity, young people can reestablish their reconnect with Palestinian locations from which Palestinians were forcibly displaced in 1948. Keeping the memory of a place alive is considered a form of resistance. At the same time, the activity is recreational, which protects them from being considered political and gives them a feeling of safety.

This type of activity challenges traditional gender expectations regarding recreational activities for young women. It aligns with events like the gathering at the Damascus Gate steps in the Old City of Jerusalem, where young people invite others to join them.

Young people use social networks to gather, to eat "Kaaek" (traditional bread), and to participate in activities. This initiative became more frequent after the Israeli army reinforced new surveillance restrictions on the steps. It drew in more diverse groups of young people, and utilised a tradition well-known among Palestinians in Jerusalem. Young people therefore enacted a powerful collective response to colonial policies in Jerusalem.

The shared experience of daily humiliation, surveillance, and Israeli control contributed to their participation in activities like sitting at the steps as a form of resistance. It allowed them to reclaim a sense of control over their public space (Ihmoud, 2019). For young women, being part of a collective endeavour to protect Jerusalem (considering its political and religious significance) and displaying solidarity reaffirmed the Palestinian presence in the city, resulting in a feeling of empowerment and a departure from the social restrictions around their presence in public.

Ihmoud (2019) describes a related action, the presence of the "Murabitat", a group of older women who remain at the Al Aqsa Mosque as a sacred duty of protection. These older women also gain power in their private lives, leading to a change in their roles within their families as a direct result of their role in resisting colonisation.

These examples demonstrate agency and resistance and present new ways of practicing popular sovereignty (Bishara, 2017) in which people reclaim a space denied by colonisation. Historically, resisting colonisation has granted Palestinian women status (Hamammi, 2000; Jad, 2007). In essence, women are allowed in public spaces to show resistance to occupation even though there are efforts to restrict their presence in such spaces.

Abeer Musleh

Empowerment as practice: pushing boundaries vs reproducing structures

Participation for empowerment

According to participants, organisations provided young people with a place to meet, and exposed them to training and workshops on topics such as leadership, life skills, and sometimes gender (Interview #8, 2021). Youth groups aimed to equip youth with skills and knowledge, supporting them to implement their skills. Participation is viewed as a pathway to empowerment, giving the marginalised a voice (Akchurin & Lee, 2013).

Participation makes youth visible as doers in the community.
(Interview #10, 2021)

While youth group members were recognised as active actors by their communities, this did not mean they were consulted on community issues. The programmes did not challenge the internal dynamics and gender hierarchies of these groups, even though they provided a place to meet, find resources, and provide community support, which provided legitimacy. Youth groups were seen as an entity marginalised only because of their age (Interview #2, 2021).

Task divisions in youth groups

The division of tasks was based on gender expectations. Coordination tasks were assigned to males (Interview #4, 2021) while interventions aimed at supporting local communities were given to women. The youth allocated tasks among themselves, based on convenience and success of the group. They claimed they were free to choose any task but did not analyse the meaning of what they selected from a gender perspective (Interview #8, 2021).

The awareness about the division of responsibilities only became evident during interviews when youth leaders reflected on their role divisions. They realised that task related to contacting community leaders, needed late hours of work, or commuting, was assigned to males, while communication tasks such as phoning or printing, working with children, or organising a space were assigned to women. The youth still gained confidence and collective power, but young women's roles remained unchanged.

The influence and authority of a woman leader were dependent on her traits, skills, and access to networks. The role she assumed in the group from when she joined was essential to developing authority. Leadership is related not only to personal traits but also to the backgrounds and experiences of young people (Musleh, 2015a; Whittier, 1997).

Lack of outreach to marginalised young people

Youth selection in programmes can be described as gender insensitive since organisations did not actively approach young people – especially those marginalised, but instead mostly worked with those who reached out to them. This means there was no outreach to youth who lacked opportunities and may have had difficulties going out, such as young women. Most organisations are situated in cities and in the centre of the West Bank (Rabah, 2009), which may exclude young women from villages, as well as those who are married or have children. These difficulties stemmed from social or political constraints on their mobility. Participants said the involvement of young women came to a halt after marriage (Interview

#2, 2021; Interview #4, 2021) as they were expected to take on new role as adults, as if community engagement is considered appropriate only for single women.

As Kabeer (1994, p. 2) noted, institutional bias can constrain people's ability to make strategic choices. This bias can lead subordinate groups to accept inequality. Programmes can lack a multicultural perspective and are not always tailored towards groups like young women. Additionally, programmes devote energy to young people and not the structures limiting their participation.

> It will bring a lot of opposition for the organisation to tackle gender hierarchy.
> *(Interview #4, 2021)*

Gender equality is often framed within the context of the Western/religious binary, with changes seen as externally introduced by donors. This tension, combined with "gender blindness", limits organisations' ability to tackle structural biases impacting young women.

Additionally, the turnover of young women in these groups has a negative impact on the development of knowledge and skills. Losing group leaders reduces the scope of engagement for younger women. Leaders were not only seen as role models that could "show them the ropes" but were also individuals who understood them, lived similar experiences, and achieved success despite the odds against them (Interview #6, 2021).

The challenge associated with losing women leaders after marriage, or due to social pressure, redefined what young women perceived they could achieve. Empowerment and agency are closely tied to the meanings and values that legitimise inequality (Kabeer, 1994). Delgado and Staples (2007) present the importance of mentorship in youth work and describe how one-to-one interaction between more experienced young people and newer members is empowering. Mentorship provides youth with skills, meaningful connections, and ultimately empowering them. The bond between older and younger women in the group was important, as the older gave the younger women a voice, either through collaboration to solve challenges or by working with younger women to become active group members (Interview #11, 2021).

Conclusion

Utilising neutral perspectives and approaches towards gender dynamics merely reproduces existing Patriarchy and social structures of unequal gender power. The empowerment of young women cannot be considered in isolation from broader oppressive structures of colonisation, Patriarchy, and the market. While young women themselves must challenge patriarchal systems and systems of ongoing colonisation, it is also necessary that those engaging in work with young women should engage in critical reflection and action to enable this to happen. In youth work, it is not only important to facilitate individual achievements but also to ensure that this occurs within a context of collective power and solidarity.

The power of "we" is cultivated in groups through mentorship, through development of skills and achievements, and by collectively resisting colonisation, gender hierarchies, Patriarchy, and occupation. Additionally, being part of broader society, and expanding the meaning of engagement from the binary of private/public to community resilience, may provide a wider lens and space for young women's empowerment to take place. Even small achievements, such as leading a meeting, or having the ability to say "no" when necessary, contribute to the agency of young women and their capacity to engage in public spaces.

To empower young women, youth workers must be acutely aware of and address the internal dynamics of a group as it is formed and developed. This can occur by becoming conscious of the division of labour and roles played by group members. Youth workers need to be sensitised to challenges faced by diverse groups as well as gender asymmetries that limit women's participation in public spaces. In this way, inclusive programmes can be developed.

Fostering adult-youth partnerships with a gender perspective can facilitate changes within the community and various structures of society. Even programmes claiming to be apolitical need to engage critically with the impact of colonisation on youth and on gender dynamics. By working with youth towards critical conscientisation about what it means to be living under colonisation and Patriarchy, youth programmes can help contribute to a praxis of youth work aimed at challenging structural oppressions.

Note

1 The Palestinian Authority (PA) was established as a result but after 25 years it has still not been implemented.

References

Abu-Nahla et al. (2003). *Women empowerment: the development of frame and concept "Tamkin Almara: Tatawor Almafhom w Itar Nathari"*. Institute of Women Studies, Birzeit University, Palestine.

Akchurin, M., & Lee, C. S. (2013). Pathways to empowerment: repertoires of women's activism and gender earnings equality. *American Sociological Review*, 78(4), 679–701. http://www.jstor.org/stable/23469232

Best, A. L. (Ed.). (2007). *Representing Youth: Methodological Issues in Critical Youth Studies*. NYU Press. http://www.jstor.org/stable/j.ctt9qg0pf

Bishara, A. (2017). Sovereignty and popular sovereignty for Palestinians and beyond. *Cultural Anthropology*, 32(3), 349–358.

Bisnath, S., & Elson, D. (2000). Women's empowerment revisited. In Progress of the World's Women: A New Biennial Report. http://www.undp.org/unifem/progressww/empower.html

Börner, S., Kraftl, P., & Giatti, L.L. (2021). *Blurring the '-ism' in youth climate crisis activism: everyday agency and practices of marginalized youth* in the Brazilian urban periphery, *Children's Geographies*, 19(3), 275–283, DOI: 10.1080/14733285.2020.1818057

Castro, I. E., Harger, B., & Swauger, M. (2017). *Researching children and youth: methodological issues, strategies, and innovations*. First edition. Emerald Publishing Limited.

Comaroff, J. & Comaroff, J. (2005). Reflections on youth: From the past to the postcolony in Africa. In A. Honwana & De Boeck (Eds.), *Makers & Breakers: Children & Youth in Postcolonial Africa* (pp. 19–30). Africa World Press.

Coburn, A. (2011). Building social and cultural capital through learning about equality in youth work. *Journal of Youth Studies*, 14(4), 475–491. https://doi.org/10.1080/13676261.2010.538041

Coe, A. B., Goicolea, I., & Öhman, A. (2013). How gender hierarchies matter in youth activism: young people's mobilising around sexual health in Ecuador and Peru. *Journal of Youth Studies*, 16(6), 695–711. https://doi.org/10.1080/13676261.2012.744815

Collins, J. (2004). *Occupied by memory the Intifada generation and the Palestinian state of emergency*. New York University Press.

Delgado, M., & Staples, L. (2007). *Youth-led community organising: theory and action*. Oxford University Press.

Freire, P. (1970). *Pedagogy of the oppressed*. (Translated by Myra Bergman Ramos). Continuum.

Ghannam, F. (2013). *Live and die like a man: gender dynamics in urban Egypt*. Stanford University Press.

Gordon, H. R. (2008). Gendered paths to teenage political participation: parental power, civic mobility, and youth activism. *Gender & Society*, 22(1), 31–55. https://doi.org/10.1177/0891243207311046

Greenberg, M. A. (2018). Empowerment in a controlling place: youth program facilitators and resistance to school discipline. *Sociological Perspectives*, 61(4), 610–625. https://www.jstor.org/stable/26580590

Hammami, R. (2000). Palestinian NGOs since Oslo: from NGO politics to social movements? *Middle East Report*, Spring (214), 16–48.

Ihmoud, S. (2019). Murabata: the politics of staying in place. *Feminist Studies*, 45(2–3), 512–540. https://doi.org/10.15767/feministstudies.45.2-3.0512

Jad, I. (2007). NGOs: between buzzwords and social movements. *Development in Practice*, 17(4/5).

Kabeer, N. (1994). *Reversed realities: gender hierarchies in development thought*. Verso.

Marzo, P. (2016). Why youth empowerment can sustain Tunisia's democratic consolidation. Istituto Affari Internazionali (IAI). http://www.jstor.org/stable/resrep09847

Mathie, A., Cameron, J., & Gibson, K. (2017). Asset-based and citizen-led development: using a diffracted power lens to analyse the possibilities and challenges. *Progress in Development Studies*, 17(1), 1–13. https://doi.org/10.1177/1464993416674302. Available from http://journals.sagepub.com/doi/abs/10.1177/1464993416674302

McAdam, D. (1992). Gender as a mediator of the activist experience: the case of freedom summer. *American Journal of Sociology*, 97(5), 1211–1240.

Mische, A. (2008). *Partisan publics: communication and contention across Brazilian youth activist networks*. Princeton University Press.

Musleh, A. (2015a). The change of the field of youth engagement and development in the oPt: a comparison across three eras. Available from Dissertations & Theses at Brandeis University; ProQuest Dissertations & Theses Full Text; ProQuest Dissertations & Theses Global.

Musleh, A. (2015b). The shortfall of development policies to address youth issues in Palestine. Power 2 Youth, WP2, Paris, France. http://power2youth.iai.it/system/resources/W1siZiIsIjIwMTYvMDcvMTQvMTNfNDdfNDhfNDE1X3AyeV8xMS5wZGYiXV0/p2y_11.pdf

Musleh, A. (2016). Roles of organisations in socialisation of youth leaders in the occupied Palestinian territory (oPt) after Oslo, Revista de Estudios Internacionales Mediterráneos, 19, 91–111. https://doi.org/10.15366/reim2015.19.006

Rabah, J. (2009). *Mapping of organisations working with youth in the oPt*. United Nations Development Program.

Rappaport, J. (1981). In praise of paradox: a social policy of empowerment over prevention. *American Journal of Community Psychology*, 9(1), 1–25. https://doi.org/10.1007/BF00896357

Rasool-Bassadien, S., & Hochfeld, T. (2005). Across the public/private boundary: contextualising domestic violence in South Africa, *Agenda*, 19(66), 4–15. DOI: 10.1080/10130950.2005.9674640

Salih, R., Welchman, L., & Zambeli, E. (2017). Gender intersectionality and youth civic and political engagement. An analysis of the meso-level factors of youth exclusion/inclusion in the south and east Mediterranean region. Power2Youth, WP.#24. Paris, France.

Sánchez-Montijano, E., & Sánchez-García, J. (2019). Youth demarginalisation strategies in the Arab Mediterranean countries. In Sánchez-Montijano, E., & Sánchez-García, J. (Eds). *Youth at margins*. Routledge, pp. 266–276.

Sika, N. (2021). Beyond the Impasse? Dynamics of youth agency in times of crisis. *Mediterranean Politics*, 26(3), 273–284. https://doi.org/10.1080/13629395.2020.1749803

Townsend, J. et al. (1999). *Empowerment matters: understanding power*. Women and Power. Zed Books.

Tremblay, C., & Gutberlet, J. (2010). Empowerment through participation: assessing the voices of leaders from recycling cooperatives in Sao Paulo, Brazil. *Community Development Journal*, 47, 282–302. https://doi.org/10.1093/cdj/bsq040

Watts, R. J., & Flanagan, C. (2007). Pushing the envelope on youth civic engagement: a developmental and liberation psychology perspective. *Journal of Community Psychology*, 35(6), 779–792.

Whittier, N. (1997). Political generations, micro-cohorts, and the transformation of social movements. *American Sociological Review*, 62(5), 760–778.

Yates, M., & Youniss, J. (1998). *Roots of civic identity: international perspectives on community service and activism in youth*. Cambridge University Press.

12
A CRITICAL RACE FEMINIST RIGHTS (CRFR) SOCIAL WORK APPROACH TO TRAFFICKING OF WOMEN IN SOUTH AFRICA

Ajwang' Warria

Introduction

Trafficking in persons (TIP) is a crime, a form of gender-based violence (GBV) (Watson & Silkstone, 2006), and a human rights violation (Sidun & Flores, 2020) that has also been widely documented globally and in South Africa. It is often marked by extreme forms of violence and exploitation against individuals – including marginalization and stigmatization. GBV is a driver of trafficking and a tool used to manipulate, control, and exploit people (Watson & Silkstone, 2006), with Burke et al. (2019) arguing that sex trafficking is structural GBV. The exploitative nature of a person's trafficking experience is a multi-staged process of cumulative pain and suffering. In overlapping phases of trafficking, victims suffer a diminished quality of life, autonomy, and independence – with consequences (Herman, 2001; Warria, 2017, 2022). Trafficking removes agency from trafficked persons, resulting in infantilization (Matzke-Fawcett, 2006).

The inclusion of well-developed feminist (Payne, 2005, p. 254), rights-based (Ife, Soldatić & Briskman., 2022) and critical race lenses (Constance-Huggins et al., 2022) in social work curricula is increasing. Yet contributions to improve TIP advocacy, policy, and practice are limited in feminist social work orientation (Lobasz, 2009; Sidun & Hume, 2018) and from a Critical Race Theory (CRT) perspective (Butler, 2015). Although the application of these lenses is growing (Kolivoski, Weaver & Constance-Huggins, 2014), their combined practice application to TIP is almost non-existent. Therefore, social work practice along a continuum, i.e., from prevention to reintegration of trafficked persons, may not be guided by an integrated critical perspective.

The research question guiding this study is: *What are the experiences of Black and Coloured victims of TIP, and is policy and practice shaped to reflect their voices?* In answering this question, elements of a qualitative intersectional positioned methodology for TIP scholarship by Twis and Preble (2020, p. 418) are adopted because

> (a) the individual's standpoint is critical to understanding oppression, (b) structural obstacles in political and social systems lead to further oppression, (c) oppressed persons' storytelling and lived experiences are critical, and (d) any knowledge about

oppressed groups obtained through qualitative inquiry ought to be applied to [micro-] macrosystems to create change.

The adoption of this methodology moves away from social work's predominant reliance on general systems theory which is descriptive and focuses on the here-and-now situation without explanations and links with oppressive structures (Mullaly, 2009). Intersectionality, therefore, talks to the multidimensionality, intersections, and complexities of experiences.

This chapter draws on a critical race feminist rights (CRFR) lens, with attention to Intersectionality, social construction, and lived experiences to discuss data collected from a trafficking study in South Africa. I argue that social workers are positioned to address these conditions rather than reinforce narratives that devalue survivors. In conclusion, considerations should be made to the social constructions in the politics and dance of representation for trafficked persons – as these can perpetuate stereotypes, exploitation, marginalization, and harm rather than empower. This chapter aims to create dialogue about the intentionality of service provision to diverse trafficked persons and their inclusion of survivor voices (Lockyer, 2022).

My translocational positionality: I write from the position of a Black African female-identifying survivor, with current Global North geographic and academic privilege. I did not live through the actual reality of colonization, or during Apartheid in South Africa and my positionality does not make claim to that, i.e., absolute understanding of colonization, Apartheid, and/or of trafficking experiences. My social work training and practice experiences in South Africa related to trafficking often occurred in white, heteronormative social contexts or with colleagues who were taught under Apartheid. I put on different hats - all which allow me different reflexive lenses to challenge myself and to question the norms and accepted practices in counter-trafficking work. This chapter does not promise to have exhausted potential decolonized and/or survivor-centred interventions, rather I hope it will stir conversations and debates into complexities aligned to unacknowledged biases and an intersectional lens.

Literature review

Overview of exploitation and human trafficking

Trafficking is a crime where people are compelled or coerced to give labour or other services or to engage in commercial sex acts. The United Nations Convention Against Transnational Organised Crime Protocol to Prevent, Suppress and Punish Trafficking in Persons, Especially Women and Children (2000) provides a comprehensive definition of trafficking. The definition of trafficking in the Palermo Protocol implies that TIP is multidimensional. Pourmokhtari (2015, p. 156) reports that the "causes and consequences [*of trafficking*] are as manifold as they are complex." According to the Global Estimates of Modern Slavery report, fifty million people (28 million in forced labour and 22 million in forced marriages) were trapped in modern slavery in 2021 (ILO, Walk Free & IOM, 2022). While much focus is on women and girls, it is imperative to note that men and boys are also trafficked and subjected to forced marriages (ILO et al., 2022).

Trafficking is referred to as a "gendered crime" with females being mostly identified across contexts. Watson and Silkstone (2006) argue that trafficking is a form of GBV. Sixty-five per cent of all trafficking victims globally are girls and women – with more than

90% being sexually exploited, i.e., for every ten victims detected, about five were adult women and two were girls (UNODC, 2020, p. 9).

Sustainable Development Goal 5 on gender equality recognizes trafficking as a form of violence against women. Although there is a need for further studies to explore and better understand the nexus between GBV and TIP, the limited evidence points to GBV as a driver in feminine risks to trafficking. This relationship cannot be ignored based on increasing numbers of trafficked women with underlying GBV-based narratives and backstories. The risk factors associated with GBV towards women in South Africa such as poverty, poor education and employment opportunities, and gender discrimination are like those that push or pull them to trafficking (Botha & Warria, 2020).

Trafficking of girls and women in South Africa

Trafficking as an offence is committed for the purpose of exploitation, but it can also be committed irrespective of exploitation taking place. Piecemeal legislation was previously being used in South Africa to prosecute trafficking perpetrators leading to a fragmented approach to tackling trafficking.

The South African Constitution (Act 7 of 1996) clearly states that everyone is entitled to freedom – including the right to be free from all forms of violence. This was complemented by South Africa's ratification of the Palermo Protocol in 2004. Eventually, in 2013, the first inclusive law that directly targets TIP, namely the Prevention and Combating of Trafficking in Persons (PACOTIP) Act, No. 7 of 2013, was enacted. The Act only came into effect in 2015 and is often critiqued from rights-based and socio-economic standpoints regarding its effectiveness in the South African context.

Racial discrimination is linked to trafficking risk. From South Africa's Apartheid history that privileged Whiteness in the racial hierarchy, it is critical that counter-trafficking initiatives consider an intersectional approach in their responses. Socio-economic factors such as gender, race, and lack of opportunities have persisted since Apartheid era and they can be linked to human trafficking from a cultural deprivation theory. From a CRT perspective, race in South Africa has been a salient factor in how Black, Indian, and Coloured people experienced and continue to experience spaces. The post-Apartheid developmental concerns persisting are linked to poverty, unemployment and inequality, systemic failures, and moderating economic dominance by few elitist Black individuals or by white-run or owned companies (Scott, 2019; Sguazzin, 2021).

The socio-economic issues have not only led to tensions, but they have also facilitated settings which make TIP thrive. South Africa has statutory and common law legislations and policies that target trafficking, but they rarely target the root causes of trafficking. For example, PACOTIP criminalizes human trafficking, deters potential criminals, and protects victims in South Africa but it is quiet on the environmental conditions that make South Africa lucrative for trafficking. Bello and Olutola (2022, p. 5) criticized legal responses associated with trafficking in post-Apartheid South Africa. Indeed, legal reforms alone are not enough to tackle trafficking (Warria, 2019) and political and socio-economic development must be considered too. Pertinent structural and underlying issues, which perpetuate trafficking, should be tackled alongside policy reforms.

Select trafficking studies in South Africa, focusing on women and girls, have addressed the following issues: trafficking and exploitation of women (Sambo & Spies, 2020), and exploring the vulnerability of migrant women to trafficking (Walker & Oliviera, 2015).

According to Motseki and Mofokeng (2022) and Bello and Olutola (2022), trafficking is multifaceted and therefore challenging to determine a specific cause. The existing power structures perpetuate inequalities and further support women's subordinate positions which prevent them from meeting their needs, protecting themselves, and making decisions (Govender, 2023). Black women in South Africa subsequently end up as victims of both sexist and racist subjugation – a unique double intersectional burden for them making them prone to trafficking (Zulu, 2021).

The problem of trafficking of women and girls is known in South Africa – evident when profound patterns of marginalization are examined (Zulu, 2021). However, links between trafficking and the vulnerability of Black and Coloured women remain unchanged, misunderstood, underreported, and unchallenged. These women remain on the margins due to the violence perpetrated against them and as they face further trials in their identification, recognition, and referral for psychosocial and health care services and for criminal justice interventions. This tends to harm and further marginalize them as they continue to be invisible in trafficking debates, policy, and practice. According to Duhaney (2022), the situational contexts, systemic and institutional racism create unique and risky challenges for Black women in the perpetration of violence.

Lens of approach: CRFR theory

A rights-based approach is crucial in understanding TIP as a multiple human rights violation. The fundamental engagement with vulnerable populations including victims of trafficking lies in the principles of social justice and human rights. Thus, the rights framework provides an ethical basis for practice and policy development (Warria, 2022).

The feminist rights-based approach (FRBA) views trafficking through a "gender lens." The FRBA does not negate trafficking legitimacy; rather, it takes a human rights and gendered approach to conceptualizing, theorizing, and addressing the practice. Like the study by Pourmokhtari (2015, p. 157), an FRBA is highly sensitive to complexities and power imbalances in trafficking as linked to profiteering.

CRT deconstructs, reconstructs, and subsequently constructs equitable and socially just relations of power. The tenets of CRT that are aligned to this chapter are:

i Intersectionality (recognition of the complex and multiple ways in which systems of subordination merge at the same time);
ii social constructionism (i.e., race is a social construct, and it shapes outcomes for racialized people);
iii race is endemic (i.e., racism is a daily experience for racialized people, which is also reproduced in structures, laws, and customs – thus defining experiences); and
iv (counter-)storytelling, there is an acknowledgement that "the stories of marginalised individuals provide insights into existing inequalities and function as counter-narratives to the normative hegemonic discourse that has largely silenced their views" (Mohammed, Ramadan & Riaz, 2021, p. 3).

The aim of CRT on the other hand is to change the relationship that exists between race and power. As a critique, the application of CRT solely to analyse trafficked women and girls is an incomplete framework. This is because the exploration of marginalization and exploitation exclusively through a race lens fails to explain structural inequalities faced by Black and Coloured women and their exclusion by feminist scholarship.

According to Butler (2015, p. 106), critical race feminism offers an alternative framework to consider how race and other factors intersect to increase women's vulnerability to exploitation. The narratives of trafficked persons must be heard in ways that acknowledge their context (Razack & Jeffery, 2002, p. 262). The researcher is proposing a combination, i.e., CRFR theory, which holds greater identification, examination, and understanding and ongoing contestations of how trafficking of Black and Coloured women is a form of structural oppression. A CRFR lens informs our understanding of how traditional feminist discourse about trafficking "has not fully considered the role of race, structural racism, and intersectional oppression in both the scholarly and policy discourse" (Cook, Le & García, 2022, p. 1).

A glance into methods

A qualitative research approach was applied in this exploratory study. Purposive sampling was used with the specific purpose of tapping into the victims' lived experiences. Unique case examples were selected that are especially informative, and because trafficked victims are a difficult-to-reach population partnerships were established with community-based organizations to identify, recruit, and access study participants (i.e., "experiential experts"). This was an essential and multifaceted step that assisted the researcher to overcome mistrust based on the nature of trafficking and ensure a sense of safety. A semi-structured interview schedule was developed for this study, in English language. The principle of "Voice" applied to this study ensured that the persons who were trafficked were given opportunities to participate and comment on service provision (Ashby, 2011; Bogdan & Biklen, 1998).

The study adhered to the World Health Organization Ethical and Safety Recommendations for Interviewing Trafficked Women. Pseudonyms were chosen to ensure anonymity and the names of the shelters are not shared in this chapter to protect the victims, their families, and the practitioners who work with them. The study participants were interviewed, individually, in a private room at the shelter where they were staying, to further ensure confidentiality and safety (Xin & Meshelemiah, 2021). The duration of the interviews varied. The data was analysed using thematic analysis.

Presentation of findings and discussion

In the presentation of the findings, the study participants are referred to as experiential experts to foreground their stories as linked to their lived experiences.

(De)valued storytelling: labels and silenced narratives

The voices of the experiential experts that contributed to this study indicate knowledge based on lived encounters – with stories which contribute to fresh attributes, a nuanced social reality and positive outlook. When asked which term they would like used when referring to them, i.e., victims or survivors, it was evident that what they chose reduced their own internal judgement and somewhat legitimized their voices and narratives and countered those of the oppressor thus becoming a tool for empowerment. While they acknowledged that they were trafficked and their human rights violated, they felt uncomfortable being referred to as victims. One experiential expert wanted to be referred to as a *survivor.... I think survivor is right ... Because you are a survivor*. To counter the narratives of those who oppressed them and continue to do so unknowingly and contributing towards narratives being tools for empowerment another experiential expert said that they wanted to be referred to as a survivor

> because I'm a survivor. But I'm no longer a victim, I was a victim, but I'm not still a victim. And a victim mentality is not the kind of mentality I want to live with, you know what I mean. I want to live as someone who has been through it but is now through it. You know what I mean? I'm not still there.

Two-fold fear, i.e., their own and family safety was a challenge during help-seeking. As such, they indicated that they could not share their stories with their families or close relatives as they were concerned about their safety and did not want them to also live in fear. One expert said *I didn't tell her because I didn't want her to be afraid… You don't want to tell anybody these stories; it would make them scared and shock them. They'd be horrified.* Yet another one echoed similar sentiments by saying *…absolutely not. Yeah. So, I wouldn't tell my family … [because] it'll just traumatise them. And then they don't deserve that.*

These narratives speak to the selflessness of the study participants and the heavy load that they carry because they are unable to fully share their trafficking experiences. In this way, they are not only (emotional) protectors to their families but also the relationship breakdown is evident because of trafficking. Fear was also relationships based and due to lack of trust in the frontline service providers, and a setback in service provision. One experiential expert revealed that lack of trust is hopeless. When asked if she would go to the police if she had a problem, she indicated that she would not and she said *No … I'd kill whoever it is [perpetrators] [reflective pause].*

This mistrust and inability to share their trafficking backstory despite viewing themselves as survivors can be a form of entrapment and show the long-term impact of trafficking. From a CRFR framework, these women are being "penalized for behaviors they engaged in even when the behaviors are logical extensions of their racialized gender identities, their culturally expected gender roles, and the violence" from trafficking (Richie, 1996, p. 5). The implications for this mistrust, fragmented relationships, isolation, and inability to talk about concerns sometimes lead to Black and Coloured girls and women not being acknowledged as victims. This lack of recognition can be linked to absence of interventions by social workers and other practitioners with power to intervene. However, when identified as victims, they get condemned for the trafficking crime committed against them. If this inconsistent response and flawed formal but limited evidence-based knowledge go unchallenged, it is bound to affect service provision and policy implementation and perpetuate marginalization further.

Intersectionality

The findings indicate that the experiential experts had complicated lived experiences due to their multiple social identities. The interconnected factors of age, gender, and poverty played out in several of the participant's narratives. In these cases, interpersonal marginalization captures aspects of structural intersectional marginalization. For example, when I inquired from one experiential expert if she thought that her brother and father would have trafficked her if they were employed and held better-paying jobs, she replied that they wouldn't have. Another example is of the young, experiential expert who later used substances and tested positive for HIV. She said that her friends advised her to go with her perpetrator who was a much older Nigerian man because

> ... he pays good ... [but] he locked me up for four days ...he took the keys ... we would have sex then he goes ... he would bring back food and alcohol and he always left 'cat' [Methcathinone] on the table ... I always looked at it afraid to take drugs at that time ... when he let me go, he gave me R6000 ... you should know that was a lot of money for a 16-year-old.

This quotation seems consistent with Intersectionality and marginalization, yet how the survivor of trafficking is disadvantaged is much more than the racism and sexism combined. This is because gender inequalities are racialized, and racial inequalities are gendered – contributing to well-being being gendered and racialized. The quotation above indicates that socio-economic resources protect the well-being of Black women less. This case is complex. As narrated to the researcher, at this point there was no third-party trafficker or pimp as she was operating somewhat independently, with agency, and she did not see herself as a victim but as a willing participant. According to Phillips (2015, in Constance-Huggins et al., 2022, p. 68),

> this concept of "survival sex" is not included in the service and policy discourse of Commercial Sexual Exploitation of Children (CSEC), and therefore does not capture the socio-economic vulnerabilities and pathways of Black, [Asian, and Coloured] girls into sex trafficking.

This further explicates the relationship between interpersonal and structural intersectional marginalization previously mentioned.

Several experiential experts who were interviewed were infected with STI including HIV whilst in the trafficking situation. From most survivor-victim narratives, they have suspicions of when they might have contracted the HIV but were not fully certain. This speaks to those chaotic life periods in captivity, coercively working, and dissociation. Inadequate health care, where and how to access it perpetuated the paradigm of pre-disposed economic disadvantage. Therefore, social stratification is a determinant of the experiential experts' general well-being. This economic coercion in racialized women is often misinterpreted as consent, but in an actual sense it is a generation and reproduction of social stratification (Prins et al., 2021).

Traumatic childhood experiences, gender, and family relations influenced trafficking. Abuse emerged as one of the main ways the experiential experts were susceptible to trafficking and family-facilitated exploitation increased the survivors' vulnerability to trafficking. When reflecting on her backstory, one experiential expert noted that

> it was really messed up. Because um, because I got sexually abused by my uncle when I was very young. And I was always selling drugs from very young age... He [uncle] stayed with us in my granny's home... she knew about it.

In narrating her ordeal, she further highlighted that the abuse endured was also regarded as a way of teaching her sexual lessons that were important in her experience of sex trafficking. She further said

> she [granny] also used to teach me lessons. Like, she would, sometimes she would hit me, but she'd mostly get my uncle to teach me a lesson. It wasn't really like; it was like a sexual lesson. He would rape me so that things are ... You know what I mean? So that I shut up? Or that I do whatever they tell me to do.

These childhood traumatic experiences clearly indicate how some children, especially girls born in toxic environments, are vulnerable to trafficking or violence as children and later in life as adults (Till-tentschert, 2017). Over time, these experiences are normalized and become increasingly difficult during identification of victims and prosecution of perpetrators.

Social construction

Gendered socialization feeds into the social construction dance making it easy to recruit and exploit victims. The oppression that girls feel, know, are exposed to, and go through and the hyper-sexualized and hyper-fertile roles assigned to them may make them susceptible to sex trafficking. That is, the negative social construction of Black and Coloured girls, how their bodies are policed, and the gendered socialization processes may lead to them being seen and equally treated as willing participants and as more knowledgeable on sex.

As part of her backstory, one experienced expert highlighted how oppressive gender norms and poverty made her susceptible to sex trafficking as she was expected to perform all chores, including sleeping with her mother's clients in exchange for money – she was dehumanized and aged-up (adultification) in the process. She shared that

> boys and girls are not treated the same. Like I was the only girl and I had to do all the work, all the chores, all the everything...Boys were not. They could do whatever they want...So it was very, just very oppressing, you know? But that becomes your way of life. It becomes your way of life that you know, you just do what you have to do.

This in turn feeds into the recruitment patterns by perpetrators. This is not only limited to female victims of trafficking but males too, i.e., the gendered norms that link women with sexual gratification make them vulnerable to trafficking while the norms around masculinity make men susceptible to labour trafficking. In this study, victimhood is intimately associated with traditional notions of womanhood – a social construct which normalizes negative portrayal of and acceptance of violence and that which deprives victim status and protection to Black women (Duhaney, 2022, p. 2778).

The negative portrayal of Black women as willing participants in their trafficking is evident in the technology-facilitated sex trafficking too. Most experiential experts that I interviewed shared that their images were posted online. One of them said

> So they call, then a photographer will come to our house. And then the person will take the pictures. And then after that, they'll edit them, and then they'll put it online. So, then you use a fake name also. So, they'll write your name there and then write your own blog in there and then with your pictures, and then your numbers will be there. Then guys that are seeing those pictures [with exotic Black girls] then they will call the number – which is your number – then make a booking with you.

This quotation does not mean that the woman is excited, chooses to be freely present, and engage in trafficking acts being perpetrated, but it acknowledges notions of coercion, inability to exercise rights, and vulnerability to exploitation when trafficked. Race and gender and their intersections, and the images in media, perpetuate negative myths about Black women. This finding supports that of Butler (2015, p. 130) on racialized sexual stereotypes influencing the modern commercial sex industry and trafficking through the racialized fetishes which drive the demand for Black sex trafficked females.

When racism is reproduced and used to explain experiences, and Black and other racialized women are decentred, viewed, and treated as worthless and threatening, there can be wounds to the spirit as manifestations of marginalization and oppression (Butler, 2015, p. 129). Spirit injury can also be linked to trafficking and substance use. One experiential expert, who was trafficked by her mother, highlighted this about the use of recreational drugs

> Yeah it was ... It took all my emotions away ... It somehow numbed me; it was like I fell in love with crystal meth because it just made me feel nothing. Ya, you know, just growing up. You know, like if your own mother doesn't love you, who's gonna love you. If you own mother's sells you know, you grow up and ... you just know that you are worthless .... Can I get a tissue please? [sobbing].

The relationship between trafficking and substance use is complex. Findings from this study revealed that survivors of trafficking resorted to substance use as a mechanism that partially numbed the misery and pain that they experienced. Women's involvement in trafficking relates to internalized oppression, their gendered social positioning; their sense of agency and also how their choices are influenced by structural Intersectionality from micro to macro levels.

Implications for social work practice

TIP is complex, and it is intertwined with other crimes such as drug trafficking and cybercrime and intersecting factors such as gender, age, and poverty. These form the root causes of the crime, and unless these and other intersecting factors and their nuances are recognized, known, understood, and addressed, social work and other counter-trafficking interventions will continue to fall short (Bello & Olutola, 2022). It is also crucial to understand barriers to accessing services for Black and Coloured victims (Chadambuka & Warria, 2022). Promoting counter-trafficking policy development calls for a solid data base. From an Intersectionality perspective, researchers must also gather data on race and ethnicity to examine these complex and intersecting relationships in trafficking cases. This becomes the building block of a gender-race-rights transformative policy response.

Social workers are offered an enhanced understanding and means of engaging with Black, Coloured, and other racialized victims and survivors through the CRFR lens. This improved understanding of experiences must contribute to better designed practice approaches to address their unique needs and disrupt structures in society that perpetuate oppression. This calls for social workers to identify destructive beliefs and practices and reclaim practice intervention – a (re-)framing that draws attention to lived experiences and includes other critical perspectives. Select reflective and progressive ways of how this and its adoption by social workers across micro-macro divide (Constance-Huggins, Moore & Slay, 2022; Cook et al., 2022; Kavoliski et al., 2021) and select examples are briefly presented next.

Social workers as gatekeepers on how voices of victims are framed, supported, or distorted can be oppressive, foregrounders of *-isms* and leave discriminatory systems intact (Chikadzi & Warria, 2022; Warria, 2022). Although many clinical social workers engaging with racialized victims are white, privileged, and social work subject-matter experts by training, the trafficked person remains an expert of their back, current and future narratives. Their lived experiences matter, and they should be given enough space and pace to voice these stories in the ways they know best. This would enable some understanding of the complexities around historical and current Intersectionality of race and gender within their context of trafficking. Considering this, clinical assessments should be informed by the appraisal of intersecting factors (visible and invisible, personal, and structural) adding to an increased empathic and trauma-informed understanding of Black and Coloured women's vulnerabilities.

Rights, race, and gender are important aspects that affect the lives of those who are oppressed through trafficking. Story circles can be used to advance the voice of the trafficked persons – and their unique experiences brought about by their intersecting and marginalized identities. These stories can reveal those layers of oppression which are often more devastating than any single aspect of their identity. From a relational theory, and informed by an Africentric approach, focusing on the fundamental cultural competency elements of respect, curiosity, and relationship building can contribute to improved interventions. These call for sensitivity and a transformative relational based practice when engaging with racialized trafficked persons and being cognizant of their unique needs that are influenced by personal and structural race-based stereotypes and dominant cultures. CRFR allows social work practitioners to see and act on race and gender in prevention interventions (Walker, Michener, & Ieva, 2022) and as contributory factors in widening gaps in resource allocation. Embracing this race-gender-rights–based perspective therefore provides opportunities for more effective and holistic interventions and in pursuit of social transformation.

Limitation: challenge of implementing the CRFR

Whilst I am proposing CRFR as a framework for analysis and intervention within social work, it is worthwhile also thinking about the additional *burden* of adopting and adapting such a framework within the already stretched workloads of social workers practising in this field in South Africa. Like in the study by Constance-Huggins (2012) on incorporating CRT into social work curricula, the anecdotal responses I have received talking about this chapter to practitioners is the lack of time, space, skill set, and/or the presence of other critical social classifications to be tackled.

The contribution of this chapter is to emphasize the relationship among race, gender, and rights within trafficking – and not ignoring other forms of marginalization. In support of Mullaly's (2009, p. 21) argument, "progressive social work today recognizes that fundamental social change cannot occur without fundamental personal change also occurring." Indeed, social justice should not be seen as an option but as an integral part of continuous professional development through integrated social work macro-micro practice.

Conclusion

This chapter examined exploitation and trafficking of girls and women in South Africa. In understanding the narratives of Black and Coloured women whose pathways into trafficking mainly started when they were children, I drew from CRT and FRBA theories to give rise to the proposed CRFR as a lens of approach. An important finding, holding critical implications for practice and policy, is that well-being of trafficking survivors is undermined by intersecting structural inequalities. Therefore, interventions must also target overlapping systems of marginalization at structural levels. A response emphasizing the individual only and not the structural and/or vice versa is not sustainable. If social work is committed towards dismantling social injustices, embracing CRFR raises critical awareness of the relationship between personal versus structural discrimination when considering issues around race, gender, rights, and resources and their intersections with trafficking.

The study contributes to globalized understanding of race, gender, and rights within trafficking scholarship. Unlearning Eurocentrism and adopting a CRFR lens in social work practice with trafficked Black and Coloured women can be challenging but a necessary step in ensuring effective and sustainable responses, positive and transformative shifts, and reflective spaces for thinking, feeling, and action. This chapter advances the calls by other researchers (see Homan et al., 2021) who have highlighted synthesizing intersectional and structural approaches.

Acknowledgement

This study was made possible through support from United States Agency for International Development (USAID) and the South African Department of Science and Innovation, as a supplement to a USAID Cooperative Agreement #7200AA18CA00009 (LASER-PULSE) to Purdue University. Opinions expressed are those of the author.

References

Ashby, C. (2011). Mediated communication/whose "voice" is it anyway?: Giving voice and qualitative research involving individuals that type to communicate. *Disability Studies Quarterly, 31*(4). https://dsq-sds.org/index.php/dsq/article/view/1723/1771

Bello, P.O. & Olutola, A.A. (2022). Effective response to human trafficking in South Africa: Law as a toothless bulldog. *SAGE Open, 12*(1). https://doi.org/10.1177/21582440211069379

Bogdan, R. & Biklen, S.K. (1998). *Qualitative Research for Education: An Introduction to Theory and Method.* Boston, MA: Allyn & Bacon.

Botha, R. & Warria, A. (2020). Social service provision to adult victims of trafficking at shelters in South Africa. *Practice, 32*(1), 3–20. https://doi.org/10.1080/09503153.2019.156770

Burke, M.C., Amaya, B., & Dillon, K. (2019). Sex trafficking as structural gender-based violence: Overview and trauma implications. In: J. Winterdyk & J. Jones (Eds.), *The Palgrave International Handbook of Human Trafficking.* Cham: Palgrave Macmillan. https://doi.org/10.1007/978-3-319-63192-9_22-1

Butler, C.N. (2015). A critical race feminist perspective on prostitution & sex trafficking in America. *Yale Journal of Law and Feminism.* https://ht-radar.com/wp-content/uploads/2020/07/SSRN-id2642976.pdf

Chadambuka, C. & Warria, A. (2022). Intimate partner violence: Understanding barriers in seeking formal support services in a rural area in Zimbabwe. *Journal of Family Violence, 37*(3), 521–532.

Chikadzi, V., & Warria, A. (2022). Social work as an unwitting enabler of oppression and disenfranchisement of the masses: A Freirean analysis of social workers' perspectives on the government of Zimbabwe's COVID-19 response. In: M.C.S. Gonçalves, R. Gutwald, T. Kleibl, R. Lutz,

N. Noyoo & J. Twikirize (Eds.), *The coronavirus crisis and challenges to social development* (pp. 307–321). Cham: Springer. https://doi.org/10.1007/978-3-030-84678-7_26.

Constance-Huggins, M. (2012). Critical race theory in social work education: A framework for addressing racial disparities. *Critical Social Work, 13*(2), 1–16. https://doi.org/10.22329/csw.v13i2.5861

Constance-Huggins, M., Moore, S., & Slay, Z.M. (2022). Sex trafficking of Black girls: A CRT approach to practice. *Journal of Progressive Human Services, 33*(1), 62–74. https://doi.org/10.1080/10428232.2021.1987755

Cook, M.C., Le, P.D., & García, J.J. (2022). Addressing racism in the domestic minor sex trafficking of Black girls: The role of public health critical race praxis. *Public Health Reports, 137*(1_suppl), 10S–16S.

Duhaney, P. (2022). Criminalized Black women's experiences of intimate partner violence in Canada. *Violence against Women, 28*(11), 2765–2787. https://doi.org/10.1177/10778012211035791

Govender, I. (2023). Gender-based violence – An increasing epidemic in South Africa. *South African Family Practice, 65*(1), 5729. https://doi.org/10.4102/safp.v65i1.5729

Herman, J.L. (2001). *Trauma and Recovery: From Domestic Abuse to Political Terror*. London: Pandora/Basic Books.

Homan, P., Brown, T.H., & King, B. (2021). Structural intersectionality as a new direction for health disparities research. *Journal of Health and Social Behavior, 62*(3), 350–370.

Ife, J., Soldatić, K., & Briskman, L. (2022). *Human Rights and Social Work: Towards Rights-Based Practice* (4th ed.). Cambridge: Cambridge University Press. doi:10.1017/9781108903868

ILO, Walk Free & OM. (2022). *Global estimates of modern slavery: Forced labour and forced marriage*. https://www.ilo.org/wcmsp5/groups/public/---ed_norm/---ipec/documents/publication/wcms_854733.pdf

Kolivoski, K., Weaver, A., & Constance-Huggins, M. (2014). CRT: Opportunities for application in social work practice. *Families in Society: The Journal of Contemporary Social Services, 95*(4), 269–276. https://doi.org/10.1606/1044-3894.2014.95.36

Lobasz, J.K. (2009). Beyond border security: Feminist approaches to human trafficking. *Security Studies, 18*(2), 319–344, DOI: https://doi.org/10.1080/09636410902900020

Lockyer, S. (2022) Beyond inclusion: Survivor-leader voice in anti-human trafficking organizations. *Journal of Human Trafficking, 8*(2), 135–156.

Matzke-Fawcett, A. (2006). Communication with muted groups: The case of human trafficking. A thesis submitted to the faculty of Old Dominion University in partial fulfillment of the requirements of the degree of Master of Arts Lifespan and Digital Communication.

Mohammed, K., Ramadan, I., & Riaz, N. (2021). A brief introduction to CRT. https://www.advance-he.ac.uk/sites/default/files/2021-10/3%20Introduction%20to%20Critical%20Race%20Theory.pdf

Motseki, M.M., & Mofokeng, J. (2022). An analysis of the causes and contributing factors to human trafficking: A South African perspective. *Cogent Social Sciences, 8*(1), 2047259, https://doi.org/10.1080/23311886.2022.2047259

Mullaly, B. (2009). *Challenging Oppression and Confronting Privilege* (2nd ed.). Canada: Oxford University Press.

Payne, M. (2005). *Modern Social Work Theory* (3rd ed.). Basingstoke: Palgrave Macmillan.

Pourmokhtari, N. (2015) Global human trafficking unmasked: A feminist rights-based approach. *Journal of Human Trafficking, 1*(2), 156–166. https://doi.org/10.1080/23322705.2014.1000078

Prins, S.J., McKetta, S., Platt, J., Muntaner, C., Keyes, K.M., & Bates, L.M. (2021). The serpent of their agonies: Exploitation as structural determinant of mental illness. *Epidemiology, 32*(2), 303–309. https://doi.org/10.1097/EDE.0000000000001304

Razack, N. & Jeffery, D. (2002). Critical race discourse and tenets for social work. *Canadian Social Work Review/Revue canadienne de Service Social, 19*(2), 257–271.

Richie, B. E. (1996). *Compelled to Crime: The Gender Entrapment of Battered Black Women*. New York: Routledge

Sambo, J. & Spies, G. (2020). Consequences experienced by women survivors of human trafficking in South Africa. *Social Work, 56*(1), 78–87. https://doi.org/10.15270/52-2-791.

Scott, K. (2019). South Africa is the world's most unequal country. 25 years of freedom have failed to bridge the divide. https://www.cnn.com/2019/05/07/africa/south-africa-elections-inequality-intl/index.html

Sguazzin, A. (2021). South Africa wealth gap unchanged since Apartheid, Says World Inequality Lab. https://time.com/6087699/south-africa-wealth-gap-unchanged-since-apartheid/

Sidun, N.M. & Flores, Y.G. (2020). Human trafficking: Vulnerabilities, human rights violations, and psychological consequences. In N.S. Rubin & R.L. Flores (Eds.), *The Cambridge Handbook of Psychology and Human Rights* (pp. 273–287). Cambridge University Press. https://doi.org/10.1017/9781108348607.019

Sidun, N.M. & Hume, D.L. (2018). *A Feminist Perspective on Human Trafficking of Women and Girls: Characteristics, Commonalities and Complexities.* Oxon & New York: Taylor & Francis & Routledge.

Twis, M.K. & Preble, K. (2020). Intersectional standpoint methodology: Toward theory-driven participatory research on human trafficking. *Violence and Victims, 35*(3), 418–439.

UNODC (2020). *Global Report on Trafficking in Persons.* Vienna: UNODC.

Walker, N., Michener, C., & Ieva, K. (2022). Do you see us?: The need for school-based sex trafficking prevention programs for Black girls. *Journal of African American Women and Girls in Education, 2*(1), 82–100. https://doi.org/10.21423/jaawge-v2i1a36.

Walker, R., & Oliveira, E. (2015). Contested spaces: Exploring the intersections of migration, sex work and trafficking in South Africa. *Graduate Student Journal of Social Science, 11*(2), 129–153.

Warria, A. (2017). Challenges in assistance provision to child victims of trafficking. *European Journal of Social Work, 21*(5), 710–723. https://doi.org/10.1080/13691457.2017.1320534

Warria, A. (2019). Child marriages, child protection and sustainable development in Kenya: Is legislation enough? *African Journal of Reproductive Health, 23*(2), 121–133. http://www.bioline.org.br/pdf?rh19028.

Warria, A. (2022). Trafficking and exploitation of children in fragile environments: Is prevention possible? *Intervention, 20*(1), 5–13.

Warria, A. (2022). Decolonizing trafficking responses: Reflections on social work practice and training. *Social Dialogue, 26,* 32–36.

Watson, J. & Silkstone, C. (2006). Human trafficking as a form of gender-based violence – Protecting the victim. *Agenda, 20*(70), 110–118.

Xin, Y. & Meshelemiah, J.C.A. (2021). Safety issues for social workers engaging in anti-trafficking work. *Social Work, 66*(4), 369–371. https://doi.org/10.1093/sw/swab039

Zulu, N.T. (2021). The struggles and the triumphs of South African black women professors. *South African Journal of Higher Education, 35*(6), 239–257. https://doi.org/10.20853/35-6-4272

13
#REPORTING WORRIES

Narratives of sexual harassment and intersecting inequalities in Swedish social work

Mona B. Livholts, Sanna Stenman, and Louise Thorén Lagerlöf

Setting the scene

Reporting worries [Swedish: #Orosanmälan] is a call for social workers with experiences of being read as women[1], and is against sexism, sexual harassment and sexual abuse within the profession. Sexual abuse, harassment and sexism also exist among social workers and it is now time to come together and show that we do not accept this!

(Jangland et al., 2019, 99)

This introductory quote is collected from the #MeToo #Reporting worries (Swedish: #Orosanmälan), where Swedish social workers give voice to stories about sexual harassment from academia, education and organisations such as social services, prison care and homes for residential care. They constitute fragments in a global context of the #MeToo movement founded in 2006 by the New York women's rights activist Tarana Burke to support Black women in underprivileged areas as survivors of sexualised violence. In connection with accusations against film producer Harvey Weinstein in 2017, actress and activist Alyssa Milano started a #MeToo campaign on Twitter, which became a digital feminist movement with more than 1.7 million users in 85 countries (Hearn, 2018).

Historically, MacKinnon (1979, 1) defined sexual harassment of working women as "The undesirable situation of sexual demands in a context of unequal power relations". Sexual harassment, for example, could take the form of men in superior positions expecting sexual interaction from a woman in order to keep her job. However, women could also be subjected to repeated sexual abuse or "invitations" that were not linked to a benefit. Ahmed (2017, 140) reminds us that the word harass derives from the French word harasser, "tire out". She describes harassment not only as a situation where loss of relations to people, but also material resources like references, work tasks and feelings of guilt and shame is "how someone is stopped by being worn down". MacKinnon (1979) demanded that sexual harassment should be recognised as discrimination and a violation of human rights and called for changes in the law. An international research overview by Bondestam and Lundqvist (2018) shows how complexity regarding definitions and reporting of sexual harassment prevails. Thus, there is an important role for social workers in assisting survivors of sexual harassment report and deal with the impact, thereof, as well as contribute to advocacy and policy changes in this sphere.

Sexual harassment is underreported due to the fear of not being believed and feelings of guilt and shame. The focus on individual- and positivist-oriented studies in law, criminology and psychology justifies the need for further studies across disciplines to study the complex notion of sexual harassment in social research. Birinxhikaj and Guggisberg (2017) show that women's agency to call attention to sexual harassment is related to vulnerability in the life situation in general. Carstensen (2016) mentions that women's subjective experience seems to be taken seriously when it is confirmed by others. Holland and Cortina (2013) examined how women were subjected to gender-based treatment and sexual harassment as feminists and activists. They found that those who self-identified as feminists experienced more exposure to sexual harassment. Possibly awareness of power relations enabled them to identify sexual harassment. They also showed that self-identified feminists had more experience of both gender-based treatment and sexual harassment. It was more likely for men to "sexually harass (i.e., send pornography or sexist jokes to) feminist women than women with traditional attitudes" (p. 2). Women who identified as feminist activists challenged normative views on women as "vulnerable" and were often perceived as "powerful" and a threat to men in gender hierarchical organisations (p. 11).

There is limited research on sexual harassment in social work. O'Reilly and Garett (2017, 115) highlight the complexity that sexual harassment has in a field such as social work, which includes many kinds of activities where gender and power interact. Women social workers can, for example, be subjected to sexual harassment by men as colleagues and clients, which is made possible by regarding such actions as part of "acceptable masculinity". Wood and Moylan (2017) state that sociology students who were trained in how to act in cases of sexual harassment felt more confident and prepared when they entered working life and that training should therefore be included in social work education to deal with sexual violence (see also Mansfield et al., 2017).

We situate our study within feminist research that shows how collective organisation in digital spaces has strengthened women's resistance towards violence (Jackson & Banaszczyk, 2016; Milan, 2015; Lievrouw, 2011). Lievrouw (2011) emphasises that social media has contributed to dissolving boundaries between individual and collective, and local and global levels allowing subordinate groups to mobilise resistance against inequality and oppression. Jackson and Banaszczyk (2016) point out that many personal stories affect the social construction of "women", so that such stories can no longer be considered a person's isolated experience but are intertwined with many similar stories.

Zarkov and Davies (2018) raise questions about who is allowed to speak and how we can understand #MeToo as a collective movement. They discuss the shift from the founding of #MeToo's focus on Black women's exposure to sexual violence to primarily giving voice to influential women in the film and media industry and the consequent risk of a growing focus on individual men. Hearn (2018) points out that #MeToo initially focused on professions with a focus on famous men, while professions where mainly women work have so far been underreported. We find this aspect important for the field of social work, where women are in the majority although intersecting inequalities of power still prevail (O'Reilly and Garett, 2017; Sewpaul, 2013).

The aim of this chapter is to visualise, analyse and critically reflect on narratives of sexual harassment and intersecting inequalities of power in social work organisations in Sweden. The study focuses on women in working life but acknowledges sexual harassment as a widespread phenomenon that affects women in different life situations, institutional contexts and personal lives. The chapter draws on a previously published study in the Swedish journal of gender studies (Jangland et al., 2019) and has been rewritten for an international English-speaking audience in social work. We removed text about the history of Swedish social work, extended the literature review and reframed the study by using diffraction as a methodological tool to analyse intersecting inequalities in situations of sexual harassment.

Diffractive Intersectionality as a narrative methodological tool in social work

Feminist postcolonial scholarship has developed complex understandings about interlocking relations of power and methodologies of *doing* Intersectionality analysis (Ahmed, 2017; Crenshaw, 1991). Ahmed (2017, p. 119) writes about Intersectionality as "messy and embodied" and argues for analytical attention towards unstable and rapidly shifting relations of power in individual life situations as they are shaped by the history of Patriarchy and Colonialisms. An important departure for our study is to critically analyse rapidly changing situations when sexual harassment occurs. In social work, the practice-based aspect of Intersectionality as a tool for critical analysis and anti-oppressive practice has been emphasised (Mattsson, 2014; Mehrotra, 2010; Sewpaul, 2013). As Mattsson (2014, 9) writes, critical reflexivity is "a way for the social worker to develop awareness of how she and social work practice uphold oppression as part of an unreflective, everyday practice".

In this study, we suggest that diffraction adds value as a narrative tool for analysing intersecting inequalities by offering an alternative critical reflexive practice that attends to how embodiment, speech acts, ways of seeing and spatial power dimensions are entangled in narrative memories. Bozalek and Zembylas (2017, 8) describe the difference between reflexivity and diffraction in the following way: "In reflexivity, there is a researcher as an independent subject who is actually the locus of reflection, whereas in diffraction there is no such distinction as subjects and objects are always already entangled". Diffraction was developed by Haraway (2000) as a critique of the limitations of reflexivity to reproduce more of sameness over diversity. Inspired by Haraway, Barad (2007, 71) developed diffraction as a research practice of reading by "attending to and responding to the details and specificises of relations of difference and how they matter". Barad (2014, 168–169) emphasises diffraction as a tool to analyse how we can trouble dichotomies rather than erasing them by using the notion of "thick moments", which promotes a dynamic understanding of time entangled with lived experiences and contexts. We contend that the written memories in #Reporting worries constitute what Barad (2014) names "thick moments", where each memory is entangled with bodies, actions, voices, people and movements, across space and time (see also Ahmed, 2017).

Motivated by the fact that #Reporting worries is a call for social workers with "experience of being read as women" to disclose their experiences of sexual violence, our analysis of these disclosures focus on gender and heteronormativity, age and racialisation as they are actualised in the stories. We use Butler's (1990) analytical conceptualisations of performativity, heteronormativity and subversion to analyse gender as performative based on societal norms in relation to which a person is perceived to embody gender through social practices of stylised body acts. Gender norms are maintained when people act in accordance with them, but since they are *dependent on repetition* there is a subversive force in the possibility that gender norms can be set aside by failed or parodic repetition (Butler, 1990, 192).

The sexualisation of bodies emerges through diffractive entanglement with age and racialisation. Krekula (2007) has criticised the theoretical silence about age in feminist theory in a Western context and discusses how gender and heteronormativity are supported by representations of the family, mainly through a focus on young women's parenting of young children. The relationship between sexism and ageism means the objectification and sexualisation of younger women and invisibility of older women. In a revisiting of Intersectionality, Brah and Phoenix (2004) turn their attention to women's biographies and resistance to oppression to problematise the category of women linked to ageism, racism, sexism and classism. They make visible the discursive counter-narrative power related to subjective constructions of femininities that force Black women's bodies to bear an imposed silence. Brah and Phoenix (2004, 7) argue for "the historical power of the political subject to challenge coercive subordinates and thereby also create new visions". hooks (1989) emphasises the liberating power of oppressed and colonised subjects to resist and speak back through written stories. In the forthcoming section, we outline our narrative approach, describing the possible transformative narrative power of digital stories, as well as emphasising the importance of listening to stories, which we return to in the concluding section of this chapter.

Material, method and ethical considerations

This study is based on 100 testimonies published on the #Orosanmälan website via the public blog platform Tumblr (retrieved 2018-03-18) numbered in ascending order from 1 to 100. They are published by individuals whose inputs vary from a few words to detailed descriptions, and they are also available as video recordings with actors to anonymise the author. We chose only written stories, as verbal and visual narratives contribute other dimensions of storytelling that we cannot address here. The nature of the material means that we do not know how the persons themselves would use pronouns, gender or other identities. We used Georgakopoulou's (2015) poststructuralist narrative analytics of short stories on social media, which acknowledged non-linear or multilinear and forward-looking narratives, co-constructed in relation to actors and audiences. They often emerged as counter-narratives to dominant narratives, violating expectations of what could be said in a specific situation and place and relying on the recipient's ability to listen (cf. Lafrance & McKenzie-Mohr, 2014).

Georgakopoulou's (2015) emphasises that small stories in social media have the potential to be read by many and build forward-looking stories that promote social justice. For our analysis, we identified three areas of exploration: (1) how and what is told and how action is created; (2) the physical context of the situation and the production of social space and (3) narrators as actors and characters in their own stories expressing thoughts, hopes, desires and fears. The study used ethical guidelines for internet research (Association of Internet Researchers, 2012). A central ethical issue concerned the researcher's access to social network communities. #Orosanmälan is a public online community and we did not inform the administrators or we could not obtain consent from the people who had written the stories. We discussed risk and unintended consequences, the relationship between private and public and dignity and respect throughout the research. We did not include detailed descriptions and information about events, people and places where we thought there could be a high risk of recognition.

The staging of sexual fantasies and sexual violence: pregnant, young and racialised bodies

In the first part of the analysis, we show how pregnant, young, racialised and heteronormative bodies are primarily in focus for the staging of sexual fantasies in various work-related contexts of unequal power relations in social work.

> A colleague reacted when I showed up pregnant at work. He said he was aroused by pregnant girls and I was among the sexiest he's seen. He told me more about his sex life. I asked him to stop when I became uncomfortable and he left, but he soon came back. Then he said he must touch me.
>
> *(23)*

The story shows how the pregnant body is focused on. It begins with verbal harassment by the man saying that he "gets aroused by pregnant girls" and forces the woman to listen to a description of his "sex life". There is a brief interruption in the harassment when the woman articulates being "uncomfortable" and asks him to stop, but he returns with the intention of physically touching her and taking the harassment to another level. In several stories, social workers describe young clients using sexualising and abusive language even when other colleagues are present. In one situation, a man in his 50s who works in a home for care and housing comments on a 15-year-old client's "newly purchased thong" (17). The colleague who witnessed the situation writes:

> The story goes that almost all the girls in the home had difficulty with boundaries, since they had often been exploited or otherwise had used their sexuality at a young age as a way of relating to and getting attention from men. This was something that the rest of us staff worked on a lot. My colleague had to tone down his behaviour.
>
> *(17)*

Reading the memories as thick moments and attending to detail (e.g., Barad, 2014) reveal emerging and shifting entanglements between using abusive language, spatial power, as well as objects, such as clothing to construct sexual harassment. A diffractive analytical understanding of how a woman's body is read in the staging of sexual harassment through a sexualising gaze, sexualised speech and physical harassment is what Butler calls the surface of stylised body acts. Body contours, expressions and gestures "create the illusion of a gendered self", as Butler (1990, 200) writes. Age is also central, and Krekula (2007) emphasises that it is often young women's bodies that are the main focus of sexualised practices, while older women are rendered invisible. The 50-year-old man who comments on a 15-year-old client's thong and the man who makes the statement about young clients looking "cheap" use their superior position and power hierarchies of gender and age vis-à-vis a client to sexually harass them and, further, subject women colleagues to being witnesses.

In other stories, racist and homophobic sexual fantasies and violations occur. A man in the staff of a home for care and housing tells colleagues and clients that he plans to "import" a wife into Sweden from the Global South. In the evenings, he shows pictures of women to his clients. He assesses the appearance and bodies of the women in the pictures, encouraging clients to do the same and asking for their opinions. It would appear that the man believes that this "activity" becomes increasingly more fun when, on a number of occasions, a colleague points out that it is unsuitable, especially for a social worker since it violates the values and ethics of social work (30).

Another situation occurs when a woman living in a same-sex relationship is subjected to sexual harassment by a man at her workplace, who uses her relationship as a sexualised dream scenario. The woman had told some colleagues in confidence that she lives with another woman and describes how she was exposed to sexual harassment by one of the men at the workplace: "One of them then started approaching me as soon as we were alone. He said things like "he'd always dreamed of sleeping with a lesbian couple". He showed me pictures of his genitals and insisted on meeting my partner" (74).

As Brah and Phoenix (2004) highlight that racialising practices are made possible by devaluing women in terms of class and race in a geopolitical globalised context. Such colonising discourses make it possible for a man to talk about "importing" a wife as a normalised exoticising act. When the high-ranked staff member mentioned in the first case above shows the other employees' pictures, he makes them complicit in the sexualisation of Black women's bodies, which are objectified, racialised and dehumanised by being referred to as a commodity. Similarly non-binary bodies are being forced into thinking that is saturated by heteronormativity. The second scene with the woman living in a same-sex relationship shows how the hierarchy of heterosexual masculinity is created based on power relations of superiority and subordination. It further adopts a heteronormative assumption of a mandatory heteronormativity (Butler, 1990).

Through a diffractive framework of critical reflexivity, it is possible to see how sexual harassment emerges in diverse situations as performative acts that create social spaces through the telling, seeing, feeling and thinking of various actors. In one situation, the narrator experiences the course of events as "inappropriate, offensive and unpleasant" (16). In both stories, images are used to reinforce the objectification of womens' bodies and to reinforce masculine and heteronormative superiority. Research shows that the many stories in #MeToo challenge the binary and oppressive norms used to legitimise sexual harassment (see, for example, Jackson & Banaszczyk, 2016; Lievrouw, 2011). Our analysis also shows how men can become defensive and aggressive when women show resistance and rejection or tell others.

Out of a total of 100 stories, it appears that only two men had to leave their jobs on the grounds of sexual harassment. In one case, a man sexually harassed several women colleagues: "He was not fired until a couple of men colleagues heard him talk about a woman colleague with whom he wanted to have sex" (3). In several stories, we can see how women sought support from colleagues and that collective resistance grew when it was shown that other colleagues had been subjected to harassment from the same man. In several stories, women say that they had reported the harassment to the manager, union or the police and that they would do the same if they were harassed again. We understand the increased tendency to report sexual harassment both because of being exposed to harassment multiple times and due to the collective resistance emerging in #MeToo. Holland and Cortina (2013) show that being exposed to sexual harassment multiple times and awareness of gendered relations of power increase the agency of survivors to label these acts of violence as sexual harassment and to report them. In the context of #MeToo, telling, writing, reading and sharing stories became a powerful collective process of knowledge building, which promoted courage to report sexual harassment (e.g., Zarkov & Davies, 2018).

Cultures of violence and silence: sexualising jargon, threats and fear

This part of the analysis deepens knowledge about how gender norms and organisational culture legitimise sexual harassment by normalising sexualising jargon and how threats and fear keep gender norms in place. This is apparent in the following two situations, the first in a one-to-one situation and the second at a festive event.

> One winter day I was dry around the mouth. A colleague started joking that it looked like dried semen and said he was happy to help teach me in other ways as well. With a twinkle in his eye of course. I felt embarrassed but still laughed along.
>
> *(64)*

> I go to the social administration's Christmas party for the first time. When I'm about to leave, I stand at the short side of the table, lean forward, and say a few words of farewell to my colleagues. Then a man stands behind one of my colleagues and smiles. "That looks good," he says, looking at my breasts. When I'm just about to go, he grabs my arm, leads me back to the short side of the table, goes back to where he stood before and says "lean forward like that again". I'm completely taken aback by the situation. None of my colleagues (who have heard and seen everything) react or say anything.
>
> *(58)*

In the first story, the man insinuates that the woman has performed oral sex and from a dominant position of age and gender he suggests that he can "teach" her. The second situation takes place among colleagues at a social services Christmas party. Here, both speech and physical force are used to place the woman's body into a sexualising position. As Butler (1990) points out, heteronormative sexuality is created through stylised performative social practices. In the situations we described above, specific parts of the body are associated with sexuality in a way that disciplines women to be subordinate and obedient. The first situation describes how the woman is "embarrassed" but "laughs along" with the others, and in the second situation the woman is "surprised" and describes how none of the colleagues react or intervene. As research has shown, the general culture of silence at the workplace and the silence of colleagues and other people present in an environment enable sexual harassment (Bondestam & Lundqvist, 2018). Rasool (2012, 156) shows that similar patterns are evident in cases of domestic violence and writes that even if the violence is "constructed as a private matter, it is in fact known by family, friends, relatives and community members".

Narratives of sexual harassment in the Swedish #Reporting worries demonstrate how the private and the public are entangled spheres of oppression both at work and at home. One example is a woman who talks about how a colleague had fantasies about hurting or killing her when she came to work on the following day, and although this information was reported to the manager, the woman received no help:

> A colleague comes to work and tells me that he has been thinking all night about whether he should hurt me; he states that he has even thought about killing me.

I bring this up with my manager who looks at me and says "you're really important to him, he really cares about you". While she says it, she smiles.

(67)

This situation reveals how leaders protect perpetrators and thereby expose women to further sexual violation and secondary victimisation by minimising and invisibilising the violence as an act of caring rather than violence.

Sexual harassment can also be used to exercise power over a person who wants to apply for a new job. Another woman writes how she is forced to find strategies to get away from her boss, who expects "payment" after she has been given an "extra assignment": she reveals:

As a young woman, I was selected for an extra assignment. I was very happy and honoured about it. But one day it dawned on me that my boss expected "payment" because he "was kind". I managed to break away from him. I was constantly forced after that to try and stay far away from him in a room and always tried to avoid being alone with him. After a couple of months, I resigned. I did not say anything to anyone because it was my boss who would sign my work certificate and give me a reference for my next job.

(70)

Several situations demonstrate how unequal gender relations are reproduced by those who expose women to harassment, but also how instances of harassment are made possible when colleagues and managers are complicit and in many cases the perpetrators. In the situation where a young woman has been selected for an extra assignment by her boss, he legitimises sexual harassment as "payment" because he was "kind". The dependency situation of giving a reference for a new job entails a threat of punishment if the woman resists, says no or reports the incident. In several stories, women leave their employment, as they feel they have no other option. It is evident how age intersects with gender for many of the women in #Reporting worries through the telling of memories of sexual harassment that occurred in the past or when the women were young.

Cultures of violence and silence also occur in social work education. A student describes how a teacher used his position of power in the context of the students establishing a feminist group. The teacher is described as having an "obvious position of power", but wants to attend a meeting of the group. In connection with the meeting, he states that "women say no when they mean yes" (57). Another student writes that a person in a leadership position in social work education tried to prevent her group's work, which used a feminist perspective, from being presented: "The head of the school was very upset about our work. [...] My dream of a doctoral position eventually died then and I have hated academia ever since" (52).

Holland and Cortina (2013) draw attention to how women's involvement in feminist issues and activism can affect their vulnerability as well as resilience to sexual harassment. The stories above show how students' interest in feminist perspectives or starting feminist groups leads to harassment. Being present at the group meeting and making sexist stereotypical statements that "women say no when they say yes" undermines the feminist knowledge project and justifies sexual violence. In both situations, students with a feminist interest in knowledge were violated and disciplined.

Studies in social work (O'Reilly & Garett, 2017; Pease, 2011) highlight the tension that exists in social work around gender and feminism. Offensive comments can be related to negative expectations about what a woman can expect in the future: "When I had been employed for a few weeks, one of the men managers says: you know that you're the prettiest one here, right? That's why you were hired" (27). Another person reports that managers at group meetings said that "it should actually be men who work in our sector as clients don't respect women" (20).

The narratives provide insights into different organisational contexts of a culture of violence and silence where colleagues and managers see or have knowledge of sexual harassment without intervening and in the first two cases act as perpetrators and use their power for sexual harassment. Carstensen (2016) addresses the difficulty in proving that sexual harassment has occurred. However, #Reporting worries show how sexual harassment, both verbal and physical, can take place openly and in front of other colleagues, managers or student groups in classrooms at university, as in this next case. Sexualising speeches are made visible in the way in which the future wage situation for women is conveyed by a teacher at the university:

> [that women] could not expect either appreciation or high pay in our future profession. To clarify the contrasts, he talked about a director who was a man director who earned 60,000 Swedish crowns a month. I raised my hand and claimed that one day I would certainly earn 60,000. The teacher's offensive response was that it might be possible if I became a prostitute.
>
> (92)

In a classroom context in front of a group of students, a student was exposed to sexual harassment. Getting help is complex in these situations, as often these types of remarks are minimised or normalised, rather than considered as sexual harassment. Previous research indicates that difficulties in defining and labelling sexual harassment can be an obstacle to prevention and intervention in Sexual harassment (Bondestam & Lundqvist, 2018). Carstensen (2016) states that the lack of a general definition creates ambiguity about what behaviour is regarded as sexual harassment and this affects the likelihood of reporting and getting help. Birinxhikaj and Guggisberg (2017) suggest that there can be sexual undertones in a workplace, from flirting to pronounced sexual harassment, and as Wood and Moylan (2017) point out that reactions to these experiences can vary between silence, reporting or resigning, as have been evidenced in the cases presented above.

However, in most contexts, there are definitions of sexual harassment. In Sweden, several laws regulate preventive measures and unlawful behaviour of sexual harassment. According to the Discrimination Act (Diskrimineringslag, 2008, 567, 1§5), sexual harassment is defined as a "conduct of a sexual nature that violates someone's dignity" and all universities have policies for prevention, reporting and handling situations of sexual harassment. However, we believe that there is a low likelihood of someone taking a case as the above further, due to the risk that it would be dismissed as once off, a joke, or minimised. Ahmed (2017, 140) explains sexual harassment as:

> a network that stops information from getting out, [...] a set of alliances that come alive to stop something; that enable a complaint to be held up or to become confidential, so that it never comes out into the public domain.

Sexual harassment, diffractive intersectionality and the power of stories to promote change

Based on the first 100 stories in the Swedish #MeToo call to social workers, the aim of this chapter has been to visualise, analyse and critically reflect on narratives of sexual harassment and intersecting inequalities of power in social work organisations in Sweden. Our study shows how sexual harassment can be understood as performative body acts towards pregnant, young, Black and lesbian women's bodies in diverse situations and organisational contexts in social work. This is made possible by speech acts and physical abuse, often expressed as threatening fantasies and (dream) scenarios supported by heteronormative oppression. The range of stories demonstrates how sexual harassment occurs in many situations and in multiple ways and needs to be understood within a larger context of sexualised violence (Hearn, 2018). Women in social work are forced to find strategies to deal with threats, endure harassment for fear of losing their jobs or receiving negative references. Exposure to sexual harassment also occurred in the context of social work education (Holland & Cortina, 2013).

We wish to emphasise that the contribution to new knowledge that our study makes comes from *within* organisations of social work. We have shown how intersecting inequalities emerge through the creation of *social spaces* and organisational cultural practices that build on power differentials of Patriarchy, capitalism and Coloniality. Butler (1990) argues that heteronormative sexuality is created through stylised performative social practices and that such norms need to be interrupted and displaced. The methodology of a small story approach (Georgakopoulou, 2015) has been applied, in this study to provide important knowledge about the complex and rapidly changing situations where men as perpetrators in the workplace continue to abuse their positions of power by applying violence through speech acts and physical assault, often in the presence of colleagues and management to create *the social spaces* that make sexual harassment possible.

We propose that diffraction (Barad, 2014; Haraway, 2000) is used as a critical intersectional narrative methodology to better understand the entanglements of complex processes of speech acts, embodiment and the agency of multiple actors such as perpetrator and the role of colleagues and management in specific places and situations where sexual harassment occurs. Diffraction offers a form of critical reflexivity that is both embodied and visual and encourages multiple ways of reading, listening and seeing differences in the same situation and includes humans, objects and spaces. Our understanding is that each case of sexual harassment constitutes a thick memory (Barad, 2014), from which multiple effects and dynamics occur that troubles dichotomies. Each of the stories shows how structural conditions of inequality create the basis for sexual harassment to occur, but also that institutional settings impact on how spatial power relations are set into practice. Perpetrator, colleague, manager or university teacher emerges as a network of different positions that builds on the structural relations of power related to gender, age and racialisation (compare Ahmed, 2017). A close reading of cases shows how both women and men, victims and colleagues, speech and images and clothes are used for setting the scene of sexual harassment. Thick memories of sexual harassment led the way to better understand time as complex as written memories stretch over decades in a non-linear collage in #MeToo. Thus, diffraction opens a dynamic understanding of memory, time and difference not only as a "now" but also as being entangled with many different aspects of embodiments, places and contexts across the present, the past and transformative agency for the future.

Feminist postcolonial scholarship has pointed towards the power of written autobiographical stories to promote change (hooks, 1989; Lafrance & McKenzie-Mohr, 2014). One of the key aspects of creating change is the courage to write stories of oppression and another is to find recipients who will listen and spaces where they can be heard. However, creating equality and freedom from all forms of oppression requires that stories about sexual harassment, including the stories of those experiencing other forms of oppression, such as Black women, or marginalised groups like social work clients or young girls and non-binary people, are also taken seriously. It requires that those who do the emotional work of writing and sharing these stories are listened to as a first step and then options for action are created in order to create equality and freedom from all forms of oppression. Our study challenges the discourse of social work in Sweden as an academic discipline and profession that always supports the values of human rights, social justice, respect and dignity by examining sexual harassment from an insider's perspective within this discipline. We hope that it will awaken interest among readers to conduct further research about sexual harassment from within diverse social work organisations.

Note

1 The expression "being read as a woman" is used in #Orosanmälan to acknowledge the diversity of ways in which acts of sexual harassment are directed towards the embodied appearance of a person who is seen as "a woman" by the offender despite their own self-identification regarding pronoun, gender identity or sexual orientation.

References

Ahmed, S. (2017). *Living a feminist life*. Durham and London: Duke University Press.
AOIR (Association of Internet Researchers) (2012). *Ethical decision-making and internet research*. Recommendations from the AoIR Ethics Working Committee (Version 2.0). https://aoir.org/reports/ethics2.pdf [Retrieved 2019-03-29].
Barad, K. (2007). *Meeting the universe half-way: Quantum physics and the entanglement of matter and meaning*. Durham, NC: Duke University Press.
Barad, K. (2014). Diffracting diffraction: Cutting together-apart. *Parallax*, 20(3), 168–187. https://doi.org/10.1080/13534645.2014.927623
Birinxhikaj, M., Guggisberg, M. (2017). The wide-ranging impact of sexual harassment in the workplace: An Australian pilot study. *International Journal of Employment Studies*, 25(1), 6–26.
Bondestam, F., & Lundqvist, M. (2018). *Sexuella trakasserier i akademin: en internationell forskningsöversikt*. [*Sexual harassment in academia: An international research review*.] Stockholm: Vetenskapsrådet.
Bozalek, V. & Zembylas, M. (2017). Diffraction or reflection? Sketching the contours of two methodologies in educational research. *International Journal of Qualitative Studies in Education*, 30(2), 111–127.
Brah, A., & Phoenix, A. (2004). Ain't I a woman? Revisiting intersectionality. *Journal of International Women's Studies*, 5(3), 75–86. https://vc.bridgew.edu/jiws/vol5/iss3/8
Butler, J. (1990). *Gender trouble: Feminism and the subversion of identity*. New York and London: Routledge.
Carstensen, G. (2016). Sexual harassment reconsidered: The forgotten grey zone. *NORA: Nordic Journal of Feminist and Gender Research*, 24(4), 267–280. https://doi.10.1080/08038740.2017.1292314

Crenshaw, K. (1991). Mapping the margins: Intersectionality, identity politics, and violence against women of color. *Stanford Law Review*, 43, 1241–1299.

Diskrimineringslag (2008). [Discrimination Act 2008: 567]. https://www.riksdagen.se/sv/dokument-och-lagar/dokument/svensk-forfattningssamling/diskrimineringslag-2008567_sfs-2008-567/ [Retrived 20.2.2024]

Georgakopoulou A. (2015). Small stories research: Methods – analysis – outreach. In: de Fina, A. & Georgakopoulou, A. (eds.), *The handbook of narrative analysis*. (pp. 255–271). Chichester: John Wiley & Sons.

Haraway, D. (2000). *How like a leaf: An interview with Thyrza Nichols Goodeve*. New York: Routledge.

Hearn, J. (2018). You, them, us, we, too? … Online–offline, individual–collective, forgotten-remembered, harassment–violence. *European Journal of Women's Studies*, 25(2), 228–235. https://doi.org/10.1177/1350506818765286

Holland, K. J., & Cortina, L. M. (2013). When sexism and feminism collide: The sexual harassment of feminist working women. *Psychology of Women Quarterly*, 37(2), 192–208. https://doi.org/10.1177/0361684313482873

hooks, b. (1989). *Talking back: Thinking feminist, thinking Black*. Boston, MA: South End Press.

Jackson, S. J., & Banaszczyk, S. (2016). Digital standpoints: Debating gendered violence and racial exclusion in the feminist counter public. *Journal of Communication Inquiry*, 40(4), 391–407. https://doi.org/10.1177/0196859916667731

Jangland, S., Thorén Lagerlöf, L., & Livholts, M. B. (2019). #Metoo: Motståndsberättelser om sexuella trakasserier i(nifrån) socialt arbete i Sverige. [#Metoo: Resistance stories on sexual harassment from within social work in Sweden]. *Tidskrift för genusvetenskap [Journal of Gender Studies]* 40(2), 98–118.

Krekula, C. (2007). The intersection of age and gender: Reworking gender theory and social gerontology. *Current Sociology*, 55(2), 155–171. https://doi.org/10.1177/0011392107073299

Lafrance, M. M., & McKenzie-Mohr, S. (Eds.) (2014). *Women voicing resistance: Discursive and narrative explorations*. London and New York: Routledge.

Lievrouw, L. (2011). Alternative and activist new media: Digital media and society series. *Contemporary Sociology*, 41(3), 387–388.

MacKinnon, C. (1979). *Sexual harassment of working women*. New Haven, CT and London: Yale University Press.

Mansfield, K. C., Beck, A. G., Fung, K, Montiel, M. and Goldman, M. (2017). What constitutes sexual harassment and how should administrators handle it? *Journal of Cases in Educational Leadership*, 20(3), 37–55.

Mattsson, T. (2014). Intersectionality as a useful tool: Anti-oppressive social work and critical reflection. *Affilia: Journal of Women and Social Work*, 29(1), 8–17. https://doi.org/10.1177/0886109913510659

Mehrotra, G. (2010). Toward a continuum of intersectionality theorizing for feminist social work scholarship. *Affilia: Journal of Women and Social Work*, 25, 417–430. https://doi.org/10.1177/0886109910384190

Milan, S. (2015). From social movements to cloud protesting: The evolution of collective identity. *Information, Communication & Society*, 18(8), 887–900. https://doi.org/10.1080/1369118X.2015.1043135

O'Reilly, A., & Garett, P. M. (2017). "Playing the Game?": The sexual harassment of female social workers across professional workspaces. *International Social Work*, 62(1), 105–118. https://doi.org/10.1177/0020872817706410

Orosanmälan: upprop för socialarbetare. https://www.metoo-orosanmalan.nu [Retreived: 2019-08-20].

Pease, B. (2011). Men in social work: Challenging or reproducing an unequal gender regime? *Journal of Women and Social Work*, 26(4), 404–418. https://doi.org/10.1177/0886109911142428207

Rasool, S. (2012). Do we accept the unacceptable? The privatisation of women abuse by informal networks in South Africa. *Journal of Gender and Religion in Africa*, 18(2), 143–149.

Sewpaul, V. (2013). Inscribed in our blood: Challenging the ideology of racism and sexism. *Affilia: Journal of Women and Social Work*, 28(2), 116–125. https://doi.org/10.1177/0886109913485680

Tumblr. https://www.metoo-orosanmalan.nu [Retreived 2018-03-18].

Wood, L., & Moylan, C. (2017). "No One Talked About It": Social work field placements and sexual harassment. *Journal of Social Work Education*, 53(4), 714–726. https://doi.org/10.1080/10437797.2017.1283270

Zarkov, D., & Davies, K. (2018). Ambiguities and dilemmas around #MeToo: #ForHowLong and #WhereTo? *European Journal of Women's Studies*, 25(1), 3–9. https://doi.org/10.1177/1350506817749436

14
NEGO-FEMINIST PRACTICES ADOPTED BY SENIOR WOMEN TRADITIONAL LEADERS IN KWAZULU-NATAL, SOUTH AFRICA TO ADDRESS WOMEN ABUSE

Tanusha Raniga and Gladys Nkareng Klaas-Makolomakwe

Introduction

Global statistics attest that violent attacks on women remain rampant such that 26% (one in four women) aged 15 years and above have at least once in their lifetime experienced acts of physical and/or sexual violence at the hands of their intimate male partners (World Health Organisation, 2022). South Africa is in an unenviable position among the Global South countries having reached epidemic levels of women abuse that result in heightened fear among women (Moleko, 2019). On 26 March 2020, when the country imposed lockdown restrictions that curtailed peoples' movement to curb the spread of the Coronavirus, incidents of women abuse increased sharply and police recorded a total of 2300 cases in just nine days (Amnesty International, 2021). In a space of two months from April to June 2022, 855 women were murdered in South Africa (Cele, 2022).

Ensuring that women have adequate access to services intended to curb the spread of women abuse in all communities is essential. However, rural areas in South Africa typically lack service delivery compared to urban areas. Arguably, the distances of rural areas make it easy to justify staggered, inadequate and biased allocation of resources compared to an easily accessible services network plethora in urban areas (Treffry-Goatley, Wiebesiek and Moletsane, 2016). A report released by the Human Sciences Research Council in 2008 revealed that rural social worker ratios in provinces with large rural populations were inadequate (Nicci, 2008). KwaZulu-Natal (KZN) is largely rural and among the provinces struggling to maintain the number of social workers needed to service its population. Rural areas in KZN are defined by "scattered settlement pattern which did not develop according to predetermined systems and procedures but emerged in the context of social identity and livelihood strategies" (Trade and Investment KwaZulu-Natal, 2020, p. 21). These rural areas fall under the authority of and are governed by traditional leaders (Trade and Investment KwaZulu-Natal, 2020) wherein African traditional communities observe culture and tradition. For the purpose of this chapter, reference is made to rural African traditional communities to advance discussions relating to traditional leadership as it is vastly located within rural areas of KZN.

The shortage and lack of employment of social workers has become a political dilemma in South Africa (Gray & Lombard, 2023) and, as such, challenge to release accurate statistics on the allocation of social workers within provinces like KZN. The Portfolio Committee on Social Development (2020, p. 1) was briefed that "budget cuts, a lack of tools of trade, a shortage of vehicles to transport social workers to remote areas and office space" remained obstacles hampering even the employment of social work graduates in the province. Although KZNDSD projected a five-year target between 2021 and 2026 to increase employment of social services professionals from 2475 to 2599 (inclusive of social workers), the Department regressed to a lower level of 2442 due to budget cuts (KZNDSD, 2021/2022). This implies that increasing the number of social workers in the province remains stagnant and subsequently suggests a serious lack within rural areas of KZN. This occurs despite social workers falling within the formal system of significant role players in the provision of services to abused women (Rasool, 2012, 2015, 2017). In the meantime, communities residing in rural areas have generally witnessed all kinds of criminal and violent activities in South Africa, including acid attacks being mostly experienced by women and girls within and outside their homes (Kapur, 2019).

One resource that can augment the gap of delivering services to abused women within rural areas in South Africa is the institution of traditional leadership. The institution of traditional leadership, among other functions, is charged with the preservation of African culture and traditions (Ray, 2003). According to Idang (2015), culture embraces various human characteristics and values that when commonly shared by people, distinctly mark them out from others. Although there is great diversity among groupings of African peoples, there are also many commonalities in their belief systems and values such as the spirit of Ubuntu which is regarded as uniquely cultural and traditional (Idang, 2015) across many African countries.

As the immediate authority within traditional African communities, traditional leaders are mandated by the Constitution of the Republic of South Africa (Act 108 of 1996 as amended) to take the necessary actions to curb incidents of violence and to promote peaceful relations among community members. Whereas government is mandated to ensure adequate provision of all services within provinces, provision is often concentrated within urban areas resulting in many rural residents relying on traditional leaders to bridge the gap of inaccessible government services. In KZN for instance, 35% of land area coverage is under traditional leaders' custody as compared to that under the municipal custody (Trade and Investment KwaZulu-Natal, 2020). These areas are largely located in "very mountainous areas, and isolated in terms of distance and access" (Trade and Investment KwaZulu-Natal, 2020, p. 24) and thus traditional leaders are more likely to be accessible to rural communities, even though they may be consulted by urban dwellers as well.

When women experience abuse, traditional leaders are key stakeholders who "have an important role to play in the social protection of women who disclose abuse" (Rasool, 2015, p. 9). However, not much research is available on the role that traditional leaders play in women's early disclosures of abuse (Rasool, 2011). Part of this omission is attributed to historical patriarchal marginalisation of women that has dominated the institution of traditional leadership in both South Africa and Africa more broadly. Ngobese (2016) aptly states that, because leadership positions within the institution were previously premised on male primogeniture, there have been historical failures to document the leadership of African women in society. Considering these concerns, this chapter highlights unique Nego-feminist practices based on empirical evidence from a study with 21 senior women traditional leaders (SWTL). Using Nego-feminism as a theoretical framework, the study aimed to gain greater insight to women abuse and gender relations in addressing the abuse of women within rural African traditional communities. Nego-feminism is a theory that shares a close conceptual synergy with African feminism, acclaiming that Africa is shaped by its unique cultural context and that the solutions to its problems require a no-ego approach where men and women negotiate without competing with one another (Nnaemeka, 2004). In relation to the abuse of women, Nego-feminism advocates for emancipatory strategies that women need to adapt and work around Patriarchy. The empirical evidence highlights how SWTL used their agency and leadership positions to challenge hegemonic attitudes within the institution of traditional leadership to address abuse of women.

The central premise of this chapter is that Nego-feminist practices can be integrated by SWTL within the institution of traditional leadership to mitigate the abuse of women. Moreover, since the provision of social work services is staggered within rural areas of South Africa, it is critical for social workers to acknowledge the work being done by SWTL and seek collaboration to promote the cause of abused women.

Patriarchy as a learnt pathological remnant of eurocentrism and maintainer of women abuse within African communities

The colonial and apartheid systems forcefully distorted, erased or undermined African cultural systems, and thus prohibited the discovery of suitable culturally appropriate solutions to the scourge of women abuse in South Africa and especially within rural African traditional communities. Enaifoghe, Dlelana, Durokifa and Dlamini (2021, p. 123) argue that "the high rate of violence against women in South Africa can be attributed to the inherited policies of the past" that introduced the patriarchal disorder at the core of women abuse. Patriarchal views have been blamed for having maintained over time that women are subspecies with less capability than men (Sampselle, 1992). Enaifoghe (2019, p. 15) highlighted that "a man-controlled society is a social and political framework that regards men to be better than women" and therefore constraining the ability of women to self-protect or fully enjoy public participation among other things. Consequently, men gained freedom to exercise cruelty against women (Enaifoghe, 2019). Favouring men, Patriarchy has therefore facilitated the denial and violation of women's rights (Sigsworth and Kumalo, 2016; Rasool, 2021). Patriarchy remained transmissible within African communities when it was strategically located within homes, which are nucleuses and critical elements of shaping identities, belonging and economic prowess.

Nego-feminism in the context of the study

There is no doubt that all feminist movements centralise and give prominence to the well-being of women and challenge societal incongruities that maintain the vulnerability of women. However, there are significant contributions that highlight the importance of context-specific Feminisms and being cautious not to assume the universal dominance of Western feminism (Mohanty, 1984; Rasool, 2020). Warnings are issued for social workers to be cognisant of the difference between the African and Western worldviews (Mabvurira and Makhubele, 2018) in their approach to empowering African communities. With Africa being a culture-driven continent, Nego-feminism offers an alternative feminist perspective as it advocates for negotiated rather than confrontational approach to achieve gender justice (Muhammad, Talif, Kaur and Bahar, 2019). Nego-feminism was conceptualised to negotiate the agency of women and provide solutions through navigating Patriarchy and the strong cultural African belief systems without causing an upheaval, thus being welcoming to both men and women (Alkali, Talif and Jan, 2013). Nego-feminism differs with other feminism streams that promote being confrontational in order to overthrow Patriarchy (Ezenwa-Ohaeto, 2015). While Nego-feminism acknowledges male domination as detrimental to the well-being of women, it is premised around the principles of facilitated communication where African shared values of negotiation, give and take, compromise and balance form the basis of seeking solutions to gender injustices (Nnaemeka, 2004). Nego-feminism offers that co-existence and "no-ego" can yield better results as men and women take upon themselves, the equal responsibility to redress the abuse of women (Nnaemeka, 2004).

The linkages between social work practice and Nego-feminist practices cannot be ignored. In its global statement, the social work profession reaffirms its position on respecting the various cultures of people. Gray and Coates (2010, p. 615) suggest that the application of knowledge within social work needs to "arise from within culture, reflect local behaviours and practices, be interpreted within a local frame of reference and thus be locally relevant." It is therefore critical that the social work profession seeks relevance and ground itself in accordance with Indigenous cultural practices. In seeking relevance, it is important to realise the relations that exist between Nego-feminism and social work practice through the application of negotiation that this framework stresses. While social work encompasses the ability to negotiate and advocate for compromise between conflicting parties towards a win-win solution (Watson and West, 2006), Nego-feminism aims for negotiation, reconciliation and cooperation between men and women specifically (Muhammad, Mani, Talif and Kaur, 2017). Thus, Nego-feminism is fundamentally different from other streams of Feminisms which aim to unseat Patriarchy rather than negotiate with it (Rasool, 2020).

Methodology

This chapter draws from the findings of a doctoral study by Klaas-Makolomakwe (2019) (the 2nd author), conducted in the KZN province of South Africa. Purposive sampling was used to select women occupying senior traditional leader positions that by virtue of protocol within the institution of traditional leadership presided over traditional courts and dealt with cases of women abuse. Semi-structured interviews were conducted with 21 SWTL. Semi-structured interviews provided advantage for the exploration of issues spontaneously raised by participants (Ryan, Coughlan and Cronin, 2009).

Subsequent to obtaining permission and ethical clearance from the ethics committee of the University of KwaZulu-Natal, interviews were conducted by the researcher following an interview schedule with questions relating to how the abuse of women was being addressed. The researcher made contact with each participant to schedule appointments on participants' preferred dates, times and venues. As suggested by Adhabi and Anozie (2017), the researcher ensured that interviews became conversations dominated by participants in order to learn as much from their lived leadership experiences. The five central tensions and structures of decolonial research identified by Keikelame and Swartz (2019) were also observed. To this effect, the researcher ensured that (i) power to knowledge production remained with SWTL, (ii) trust was built and respect was accorded to SWTL both in their positions of seniority within rural African traditional communities and as research participants in the study, (iii) culture and cultural competence where the researcher was familiar with protocol and appropriate conduct to be observed when engaging with traditional leader, (iv) respectful and legitimate research practice where cultural appropriateness such as the kind of language appropriate for use when conversing with traditional leaders was applied (i.e., "siyabonga Nkosi Yesizwe"/ thank you leader of the nation or "Inkosi yase Ndlunkulu"/Your royal highness) and (v) recognition of individual and communities' assets where the role of SWTL was significantly observed throughout the study processes. Owor (2022) recommends that researchers should always acknowledge that participants in research are always knowledgeable in their field. To this effect, the experiences of SWTL in this study remained significant and the researcher ensured that issues relating to trustworthiness such as confirmation of transcribed data with SWTL occurred.

Information on the study was shared and participants were made aware of their right to voluntary participation and withdrawal at any time. Confidentiality was assured and permission to record interviews was obtained. To enhance trustworthiness, interviews were conducted in English and/or isiZulu languages depending on the choice of participants. Translations into English were later performed when transcribing for purposes of reporting and thematic analysis was performed. It must be acknowledged that some meaning may have been lost when translating from one language to another. However, rich, detailed descriptions are provided to ensure authentic transferability of the findings (Ryan, Coughlan and Cronin, 2009). The next section highlights the findings and the names used to refer to participants in this chapter are pseudonyms.

Presentation of findings

According to Statistics South Africa (2017), the violation of women and their human rights happens without discriminating amongst their socioeconomic status, race, age and religion. In this study, SWTL attested to not being immune themselves to experiencing incidents of abuse within their families and communities. Central to this study was how SWTL's own experiences of abuse contributed to their unique comprehension of abuse when abuse was experienced by other women and as cases were brought to their attention. In the sections below, two analytical principles connected to Nego-feminist practice namely commitment to African feminist identity and analysis of community structures of oppression are presented. Nnaemeka (2004, p. 361) identifies Nego-feminism as an African feminism, "a practice of feminism in Africa." According to Atanga (2013), "there is no single 'African feminism' and to claim so is problematic." As a result, Amaefula (2021) identifies Nego-feminism among other strands of African Feminisms such as Snail-sense Feminism, or African Womanism, while highlighting their distinct features that are however rooted in the African environment. Thus, the principle of commitment to African identity gains support from Nnaemeka (2004, p. 380) that unlike Western feminism which "challenge, disrupt, deconstruct, blow apart..., African feminism challenges through negotiation, accommodation, and compromise."

Commitment to African feminist identity

Leadership qualities demonstrated by SWTL in the study suggested entrenched Nego-feminist commitment and attentiveness to African cultural value system. The foundational arguments of Nego-feminism are that culture "should not be dismissed as a negative or neutral factor in development; rather, attempts should be made to find out in what ways culture is a positive force that can serve development well" (Nnaemeka, 2004, p. 375). African cultural value system demands for priority to be given to the well-being of other humans therefore exercising care, protection and offering assistance (Isike and Uzodike, 2011). The study established that SWTL took queues from the initial state of desperation presented by women who experienced abuse and responded promptly. As suggested by Nnaemeka (2004), African women practice culture and will not only negotiate and compromise in situations influenced by Patriarchy but also have the ability to strategise and know when to exercise moral responsibility of ensuring the well-being of others. In the below narratives in which SWTL react to situations when women have been abused, it is suggested that Nego-feminism offers the notion of paying attention and prioritising the well-being of individuals while also seeking to collaborate and complement other available services. The following responses were obtained:

Inkosi Danile: She gets assistance, to the extent that if there is no other way, you keep her at your home, until you get a solution. Sometimes that is what I do to make sure a woman is safe.

Inkosi Rawula: In cases of rape, they are of course vulnerable in those situations. But then you try and comfort them, for them not to be scared. We assure them that the perpetrator won't be near them, that social workers and medical care would be available.

Inkosi Dedela: When a woman comes crying, naked, I become quick in attending to her. Just as she comes, she is trusting and is hurting. I am supposed to put on gloves and rush to her, get something and quickly cover her up. I call the police after I have done that...I have done that to those that had been raped, as they come crying and running to komkhulu.[1]

At the centre of the above narratives are the responses of SWTL to ensure provision of care and safety for abused women. Attending to the well-being of fellow women and preserving their dignity were done without delay. SWTL were swift to identify and acknowledge states of vulnerability and emergencies that women presented. The manner in which SWTL received women who had been violated was cathartic and resonated immediately with the here and now situation following violent ordeals. Such actions resonate with Nego-feminism in its Indigenous form of what is culturally regarded as genuine expression of care and recognition of others in their entire form as humans (Nnaemeka, 2004). The qualities offered in the approach of SWTL here including acknowledging other service providers demonstrate how Nego-feminism is rooted within the African culture of inclusivity and collaboration with others. Therefore, in its Indigenous nature, Nego-feminism appeals to the African shared values of reciprocal care and protection of other fellow human beings. These are qualities of Ubuntu which according to Mayaka, van Breda, Uwihangana and Mugumbate (2023, p. 12) "is both social (the connections between people that constitute community and shared humanity) and ethical (the quality of our interactions with others, such as respect and care)."

Analysis of community structures of oppression and negotiation skills

One of the tenants of Nego-feminism is the call for negotiating even during difficult times. As Nnaemeka (2004, p. 380) puts it, "African women's willingness and readiness to negotiate with and around men even in difficult circumstances is quite pervasive." The perpetual and complex patriarchal and cultural contexts within which SWTL addresses the abuse of women facilitate these difficult times. In other words, SWTL operate within environments where Patriarchy is misconstrued as culture and tradition and thus rendering women vulnerable to abuse. Nnaemeka (2004) implies that Nego-feminism acknowledges the abilities of women and the tactics they employ to respond to cultural practices that expose them to vulnerability and render them weak. Intervention approaches of SWTL started with separating and advocating for an understanding of what the original cultural practices were as opposed to cultural practices that were distorted by colonial and apartheid regimes. The findings of this study showed that SWTL created harmonious platforms that enabled men and women to express their feelings and relate the context in which harm occurred. This highlights in relation to Nego-feminism, the involvement of men in seeking solutions unlike other feminism streams that encourage banishing of men. SWTL capitalised on negotiation and used their leadership positions to facilitate conflict resolution between men and women. Inkosi Zabantu shared how she centralised her position and allowed partners to narrate each other's behaviours that warranted abusive reactions towards one another. She facilitated their communication through herself and shared that:

Inkosi Zabantu: A man had hit a woman, and when I asked her what the cause was; she said that it was because of money... I summoned the man to come see me. I explained to him that the woman was hurting and made it clear she does have a right to be unhappy about the situation. So we discussed and the man said wife was disrespectful towards him in how she asked for money... saying hey you, this so-called money of yours... Then I [participant] said...nxese [sorry]...it was a mistake... she got carried away but didn't mean that... and it was resolved... They got out of here happy and life went on.

The ability to negotiate is an African skill that manifests successfully when interests of aggrieved parties are equally acknowledged (Ademowo, 2015). Those who intervene seek to harmonise the interests of all and restore the morals (Ademowo, 2015) of co-existence. Clearly money took the centre stage in fuelling the abuse. However, Inkosi Zabantu worked with both parties to establish what went wrong, where it all started and how things unfolded towards finding amicable solution and acknowledging both their weaknesses towards finding happiness. Inkosi Zabantu was able to strike the balance in driving the intervention towards a compromised position where harmony was reached through both parties feeling heard.

Traditional Africans are also driven by innate foundational desires of ensuring commitment, selflessness, tolerance and sharing in their relations with others (Isike and Uzodike, 2011). Participants worked towards reigniting these embedded qualities and subtly reminding conflicted parties of their indebtedness to each other given that traditional African co-existence and sense of togetherness are reciprocity (Kariuki, 2015). Inkosi Benkosi shared that

Inkosi Benkosi: If a husband fights with his wife, I am supposed to approach him so that he will calm down. I would begin to show the wife the importance of respecting her husband and the husband will be told that he needs to humble himself before his wife...people would stop breaking up and be able to reconcile.

In the narrative, Inkosi Benkosi highlighted the importance of negotiating for calm and, in this way, negotiating for a win-win situation. Inkosi Benkosi related how she would identify and verbalise actions that strain relationships. Evident in the narrative is the husband experiencing disrespect from wife while the wife experienced arrogance from her husband. Inkosi Benkosi also related how in passing her opinion she would identify and negotiate around respect and humility as areas to work on as partners in ensuring that they both approach one another better. Reaching the point of not breaking up and the ability to reconcile subsequent to the intervention by SWTL imply that the abusive behaviour was arrested. As cultural context also dictates, people within traditional areas avoid being summoned to the traditional courts because it is seen as damaging to family names and the royal house. Often times, matters are not repeatedly addressed because the final word given by an Inkosi is respected. However, this does not mean that an abused woman would not be allowed to present a case should the behaviour be repeated. It is also worthy to highlight the leadership quality presented by Inkosi Benkosi in not assuming a dominant position of providing solutions but rather negotiating towards reconciliation.

The above demonstrated the ability of SWTL to negotiate for harmonious relationships between men and women in the approaches they undertook to address women abuse.

Conclusions and recommendations

The experiences of SWTL in this study emphasise the special qualities and focused interventions when addressing the abuse of women within rural African traditional communities of KZN. Although Patriarchy took central stage as highlighted in the narratives of participants, SWTL were able to assert their roles as women leaders and where appropriate, negotiated peaceful relations between perpetrators and victims using a Nego-feminist approach. The narratives of SWTL provided evidence that post their intervention, conflicted partners pardoned each other and reached amicable solutions. It is important to however acknowledge that SWTL are stakeholders playing a role in addressing the abuse of women towards its elimination and the long-term outcomes of SWTL approaches are not known in relation to ensuring the non-repeat of abuse. Participants' narratives indicated how they manoeuvre patriarchal spaces and apply Nego-feminist approaches to negotiate with masculinity in their communities. The special Nego-feminist abilities of SWTL are what social workers need to adopt as practical approaches when addressing male hegemonic behaviour in rural African traditional communities. This can be done through partnering with traditional leaders to work together towards helping to deal with the situation and implementing interim measures to eliminate the abuse of women and enabling the reporting and referral of cases. Much work in utilising the traditional and cultural structures to augment social work services and address the abuse of women in rural African traditional communities is imperative.

Acknowledgements

This work is based on the PhD research work supported by the National Institute for the Humanities and Social Sciences.

Note

1 A term used to refer to the residence area of Inkosi which is respected by community members and is pluralistic in nature to acknowledge that traditional leadership does not belong to the individual on the throne but serves as the core place for all community members (the living and dead).

References

Ademowo, A. J. (2015). *Conflict management in traditional African society*. Retrieved August 19, 2019, from https://www.researchgate.net/publication/281749510

Adhabi, E., & Anozie, C. B. (2017). Literature review for the type of interview in qualitative research. *International Journal of Education, 9(3)*, 86–97.

Alkali, M., Talif, R., & Jan, J. M. (2013). Violence and sexual harassment in Nigerian novels: The Nego-Feminist option. *Research on Humanities and Social Sciences, 3(9)*, 10–14.

Amaefula, R. C. (2021). African Feminisms: Paradigms, problems and prospects. *Feminismo/s, 37*, 289–305.

Amnesty International (2021). *"Treated like furniture" Gender-based violence and Covid-19 response in Southern Africa*. London: Amnesty International Ltd Retrieved March 7, 2021, from Amnesty.org

Atanga, L. L. (2013). African feminism? In Atanga, L. L., Ellece, S. E., Litosseliti, L., & Sunderland, J. (Eds.), *Gender and language in sub-Saharan Africa. Tradition, struggle and change* (pp. 301–314). Amsterdam: John Benjamins Publishing Company.

Cele, B. (2022). *Quarter one crime statistics 2022/2023*. Retrieved January 15, 2023, from https://www.gov.za

Department of KZN Social Development (2021). Annual Report for Financial Year 2021/2022. Province of KwaZulu-Natal.

Enaifoghe, A. O. (2019). South Africa gender based violence and the global gendered viewpoint approach mechanisms in building a peaceful world. *Journal of Social and Development Sciences, 10(2)*, 15–25.

Enaifoghe, A. O., Dlelana, M., Durokifa, A. A., & Dlamini, N. (2021). The prevalence of gender-based violence against women in South Africa: A call for action. *African Journal of Gender, Society and Development, 10*, 121–150. https://doi.org/10.31920/2634-3622/2021/v10n1a6

Ezenwa-Ohaeto, N. (2015). Fighting patriarchy in Nigerian cultures through children's literature. *Canadian Academy of Oriental and Occidental Culture, 10(6)*, 59–66.

Gray, M., & Coates, J. (2010). 'Indigenisation' and knowledge development: Extending the debate. *International Social Work, 53(5)*, 613–627.

Gray, M., & Lombard, A. (2023). Progress of the social service professions in South Africa's developmental social welfare system: Social work, and child and youth care work. *International Journal of Social Welfare, 32(4)*, 429–441. https://doi.org/10.1111/ijsw.12562 Idang, G. E. (2015). African culture and values. *Phronimon, 16(2)*, 97–111.

Isike, C., & Uzodike, U. O. (2011). Towards an indigenous model of conflict resolution: Reinventing women's roles as traditional peace-builders in neo-colonial Africa. *African Journal of Conflict Resolution, 11(2)*, 32–58.

Kapur, R. (2019). Problems and Challenges in Rural Areas. Retrieved June 13, 2022, from https://www.researchgate.net/publication/332187494

Kariuki, F. (2015). Conflict Resolution by Elders in Africa: Successes, Challenges and Opportunities. Paper was delivered at the Chartered Institute of Arbitrators Centenary Conference "Learning from Africa" on 15th July 2015 at the Victoria Falls Convention Centre, Livingstone, Zambia.

Keikelame, M. J., & Swartz, L. (2019). Decolonising research methodologies: Lessons from a qualitative research project, Cape Town, South Africa. *Global Health Action, 12(1)*, 1561175. https://doi.org/10.1080/16549716.2018.1561175

Klaas-Makolomakwe, G. N. (2019). *The experiences of senior women traditional leaders in addressing women abuse in Kwazulu-Natal, South Africa: An afrocentric and Nego-feminist approach.* Unpublished PhD thesis, University of KwaZulu-Natal. Durban, South Africa.

Mabvurira, V., & Makhubele, J. C. (2018). Afrocentric methodology: A missing pillar in African social work research, education and training. In Shokane, A. L., Makhubele, J. C., & Blitz, L. V. (Eds.), *Issues around aligning theory, research and practice in social work education: Knowledge pathing: Multi-, inter- and trans-disciplining in social sciences series* (pp. 11–26). Cape Town: AOSIS.

Mayaka, B., van Breda, A. D., Uwihangana, C., & Mugumbate, R. (2023). The Ubuntu practitioner in historical and contemporary contexts. In Mayaka, B., Uwihangana, C., & van Breda, A. D. (Eds.), *The Ubuntu practitioner: Social work perspectives* (pp. 4–30). Rheinfelden: The International Federation of Social Workers.

Mohanty, C. T. (1984). Under Western eyes: Feminist scholarship and colonial discourses. On humanism and the university, I: The discourse of humanism. *Boundary 2, 12(3),* 333–358.

Moleko, N. (2019). Do we have the tracking tools to monitor the National Gender Machinery? In Bosch, A. (Ed.), *South African board for people practices women's report* (pp. 17–23). Weltevredenpark: SABPP.

Muhammad, U. A., Mani, M., Talif, R., & Kaur, H. (2017). Nego-Feminism as a bridge between patriarchy and matriarchy in Zaynab Alkali's the stillborn and the virtuous woman. *Journal of Language and Communication, 4(1),* 125–133.

Muhammad, N. U., Talif, R., Kaur, H., & Bahar, I. B. (2019). Establishing the female voice in contemporary Nigerian narrative through Nego-feminism: A study of Abubakar Gimba's Sacred apples. *Journal of Language and Communication (Jlc), 3(2),* 195–202.

Ngobese, D. (2016). Women power: A contribution to the role of African women during and after Anglo-Zulu conflicts of the 19th century and beyond. *Gender & Behaviour, 14(2),* 7419–7425.

Nicci, E. (2008). Social work as a scarce and critical profession. Scarce & Critical Skills Research Project. Research commissioned by Department of Labour South Africa. Human Sciences Research Council.

Nnaemeka, O. (2004). Nego- feminism: Theorizing, practicing, and pruning Africa's way. In Lionnet, F., Nnaemeka, O., Perry, S. H., & Schenck, C. (Eds.), *Signs 29, Special issues – Development cultures: New environments, new realities, new strategies* (pp. 357–385). www.jstor.org/ stable/ 10.1086/ 378553 (Accessed November 18, 2014).

Owor, A. (2022). Researching the ethics of data collection in post-conflict acholiland (Northern Uganda): The good, the bad, and the ugly. *International Journal of Qualitative Methods, 21(1),* 1–13. https://doi.org/10.1177/16094069221120342

Portfolio Committee on Social Development (2020). Update on Employment of Social Workers and Foster Care Backlog. Retrieved from https://pmg.org.za

Rasool, S. (2011). *Help-seeking by abused women in South Africa.* Unpublished doctoral dissertation, University of Oxford, England.

Rasool, S. (2012). Abused women's experiences with social workers and shelters. The social work practitioner-researcher. *Research Gate, 24(1),* 103–119.

Rasool, S. (2015). Helping abused women access a protection order: The role of religious, traditional and community leaders. *Journal of Gender & Religion in Africa, 21(1),* 9–26.

Rasool, S. (2017). Adolescent reports of experiencing gender based violence: Findings from a cross-sectional survey from schools in a South African city. *Gender and Behaviour, 15(2),* 9109–9121.

Rasool, S. (2020). Heterogeneity of social movements addressing the intersections of gender and race: A reflection on feminisms and womanisms emerging from African women. In Kleibl, T. Lutz, R., Noyoo, N., Bunk, B., Dittmann, A., & Seepamore, B. K. (Eds.), *The Routledge handbook of post-colonial social work* (pp. 127–137). Oxon: Routledge.

Rasool, S. (2021). The implications of a patriarchal culture for women's access to "formal" human rights in South Africa: A case study of domestic violence survivors. In Sewpaul V., Kreitzer L., & Raniga T. (Eds.), *The tensions between culture and human rights: Emancipatory social work and afrocentricity in a global world* (pp. 147–164). Alberta: University of Calgary Press.

Ray, D. I. (2003). Rural local governance and traditional leadership in Africa and the afro-caribbean: Policy and research implications from Africa to the Americas and Australasia. In Ray D. I., & Reddy, P. S. (Eds.), *Grassroots governance? Chiefs in Africa and the afro-caribbean* (pp. 1–30). Calgary: University of Calgary Press.

Republic of South Africa. The Constitution of the Republic of South Africa Act, 108, 1996 (as amended).
Ryan, F., Coughlan, M., & Cronin, P. (2009). Interviewing in qualitative research: The one-to-one interview. *International Journal of Therapy and Rehabilitation, 16(6)*, 309–314.
Sampselle, C. M. (Ed.) (1992). *Violence against women.* New York: Hemisphere Publishing.
Sigsworth, R., & Kumalo, L. (2016). Women, peace and security: Implementing the Maputo Protocol in Africa. *Institute for Security Studies Paper, 295*, 1–24.
Statistics South Africa (2017). *Victims of crime survey 2016/17.* Statistical Release P0341.
Trade and Investment KwaZulu-Natal (2020). KwaZulu-Natal rural and township economies revitalisation strategy: Situation analysis report. Department of Economic Development, Tourism and Environmental Affairs. South Africa.
Treffry-Goatley, A. J., Wiebesiek, L., & Moletsane, R. (2016). Using the visual to address gender-based violence in rural South Africa: Ethical considerations. *Learning Landscapes, 10(1)*, 341–359.
Watson, D., & West, J. (2006). *Social work process and practice: Approaches, knowledge and skills.* New York: Palgrave Macmillan.
World Health Organisation (2022). World health statistics 2022: Monitoring health for the SDGs, sustainable development goals. Retrieved January 2023, from http://www.who.org.int

15
FEMINIST SOCIAL WORK PRACTICE AND EFFORTS TOWARDS GENDER EQUALITY IN AUSTRALIA

Elizabeth Orr, Louise Morley, Wendy Bunston, Carrie Maclure and Louise Whitaker

Introduction

This chapter aims to show how individual feminist social work practices have contributed to the overall political struggle for justice for women in mainstream Australian society. Referring to social work practice, the concept of "homemade" social work was put forward by Fran Crawford (2014). It denotes everyday intuitive practices that are interpretative, involve local knowledge, are responsive to time and place, and are generated from the lived experience of the practitioner and their clients. Such practices are often overlooked, under-rated or ignored. They come from contextual lived experience rather than meta theories or rationalist models of intervention. Using an "autoethnographic" reflection on social work practice, we describe how our local approaches to social work practice are informed by feminist principles, insider knowledge, and the engagement of people in the common ground of their lives. Examples from the practice of the co-authors of this chapter illustrate how such "homemade" feminism has a central place in the social work struggle for gender-based equality and justice in Australia. We contend that the sharing of stories of practice empowers social workers to evaluate outcomes for women and can build bridges between past, current, and future feminist social work practice.

The dominant standpoint and positionality of the co-authors are discussed and the strengths and limitations of how the chapter was brought together are described. Feminist literature that the five co-authors identify as key influences in their practice are summarised and then practice experience of the authors is presented. Working with women-specific groups, the creation of employment and education pathways for refugee and immigrant women, challenges of teaching feminism and social work in current times and examples of good, and not so good supervision and its outcomes are the topics discussed.

Social constructivism and homemade feminist social work practice

Western feminism's mantra, "the individual is collective, the personal is political, and the private is public", governed the women's movements of the 1980s and 1990s. This mantra reiterates the connection between what sociologist C. Wright Mills (1959) referred to as personal troubles and public issues and then feminist sociologist, Dorothy Smith (1987), refined. Smith (1987) advocates that gender is an essential lens through which to undertake any analysis of the structural inequalities and ruling relations. We concur and add that decolonising and intersectional lenses are also critical if we are to achieve equality and justice for all (Bennett & Green, 2019; Crenshaw, 1989; Muller, 2007).

As gendered social beings, our personal experience of the world and our social work identities and actions are shaped by history, culture, and the social and economic structures into which we are born and live. Expanding this understanding of position through the concept of "intersectionality" (Chen, 2017), we see that our personal and professional identities and actions are also grounded in lived experiences of race, class, ability, ethnicity, ecology, sexuality, and status. Our ability to reflect on our experience of these worlds assists us to transform our ideas into action (Archer, 2007).

Collective action, exemplified in second-wave feminism in Australia, rallied women to bring into the public arena what had been personal and private issues, such as wage inequality, caring for infants and elders, and sexual and domestic violence. Those actions led to political debate and real change. Specific changes such as anti-discrimination and no-fault divorce legislation, and service and policy responses to develop women's health and centres against violence during that era in Australia are well documented (e.g., Sawyer, 1987; Weeks, 2003).

Wendy Weeks (1994), an Australian social work educator, specifically documented stories of feminist social and community work practice from women's health, violence against women, community development, and education. Similar to bell hooks, who "eschews academic language ... to use autobiography and storytelling as teaching tools" (Noble, 2020, p. 503), Weeks documented a wide range of "insider" women's narratives of social work practice during the 1990s. Crawford (2014) compliments that approach and promotes such insider knowledge of social work practices calling them "homemade". The five authors in this chapter share such homemade insider knowledges. Our stories of homemade practice demonstrate a dialogical dynamic between the personal and political in feminist social work practice and show how we have been influenced by, and in turn influence, feminist activism and feminist practice in Australian settings.

The chapter is written in the first person: the terms "we", "us", and "our" are used to denote our collective views and actions. Italics are used to denote first voice where authors are referring to their own experience and practice.

Positionality and privilege

Our collective position is that of dominant middle-aged white Anglo-Celtic and now middle-class women. Our standpoint (Harding, 2004) and aspirations are to be allies to the First Nations and non-hetero-binary, diversely abled, refugee, and diverse ethnic population groups we work alongside (Land, 2012). The "likeness" of the authors is not only a significant limitation of this chapter, but it is also an authentic dominant profile of social workers in Australia.

Feminist Intersectionality (Chen, 2017), which aims to include the full diversity of women in the overall project to achieve equality, continues as work in progress in Australia. Allyship, which refers to working alongside groups that experience discrimination and disadvantage, is also a privileged and ongoing project. We do not shy away from the power afforded to us as professional white women. However, personal experiences of poverty, regional and remote living, lived experiences of disasters and unsafe relationships, and heterosexual and lesbian backgrounds are also part of our intersectional experiences and positionalities.

The intersectional and "whiteness" (Moreton-Robinson, 2000) critique required to fully unpack the nature of power relations in social work in Australia (Bennett and Green, 2019) is an ongoing and deeper project than we are not fully able to address in this chapter. As non-First Nations women, we aim to find our place with decolonising practices (Muller, 2007) but respectfully acknowledge that because all the co-authors are non-Indigenous, we can only speak as allies who seek to promote the rights of First Nations women to represent themselves in the world. Readers are referred to the extensive and growing scholarship by First Nations social work scholars (e.g., Arabena, 2015; Bennett & Green, 2019; Bessarab & Ng'Andu, 2010; Bnads et al., 2021; Moreton-Robinson, 2000).

Methodology

A broad call out via email and word of mouth was made for stories of feminist practice and the five co-authors produced a brief story of their social work experience using a template designed by the lead author. A key area of practice was identified in each and then across the combined stories. The template design and analysis of data were informed by feminist (Dominelli, 2002; Stanley & Wise, 1993) and Indigenous (Chilisa, 2012; Martin, 2008; Smith, 1999) qualitative methodologies. A draft of the chapter was then shared with all contributors for further input or changes, and then submitted.

Meet the participants and some key feminist texts

Each author shared some of the literature that shaped our feminism(s). This section does not constitute an academic review or analysis.

Liz Orr: Senior Lecturer in Social Work University of New England.

> Early written material that influenced my social work practice focused on the subjugation of women in domestic and public life in Australia and the Western world. That included Anne Summers (1975) "Damned Whores and God's Police", Kay Hargraves (1982) "Women and Work", Lyn Richards (1985) "Having Families", from the UK, Elizabeth Wilson's (1977) "Women and the Welfare State", and from the USA, Susan Brownmiller's (1975) "Against Our Will", and bell hooks (1983) "Aint I a Woman: Black Women and Feminism". The fortnightly Women's Liberation Newsletter published in Melbourne during the 1970s and 1980s and sent via subscription was also a source of local knowledge and theoretical and political discussion. Aileen Moreton-Robinson's (2000) "Talkin up to the White Woman" influenced my journey to becoming a conscious ally for justice for First Nations peoples.

Louise Morley: Lecturer in Social Work, University of New England, Australia.

The feminist readings that have influenced me are mostly from my undergraduate studies in philosophy. Simone de Beauvior's (1972) "The Second Sex" helped me understand the nuanced, gendered power dynamics in everyday interactions. There were other texts that helped me further comprehend why male power and domination is so powerful and difficult to turn around (see, for example, Faludi, 1993 and French, 1992). My favourite text was, and continues to be, Val Plumwood's (1993) "Feminism and the Mastery of Nature". This text shows how ingrained the Western binaristic thinking is, and how this lays the foundations for colonialist thinking and a disregard for First Nations people, women, and nature. Such a critique assisted me to understand how the personal and political have come to be hyperseparated, and in so doing, has prompted me to honour feminist values such as caring for one another.

Wendy Bunston: Private Practitioner and Consultant in Australia.

Feminist thinking has been instrumental in developing my ability to use critical thinking to deconstruct the use and misuse of power in my work with infants and children in families where there is violence. I was profoundly impacted by the work of feminist social workers and family therapists Virginia Goldner (Goldner, 1992; Goldner et al., 1990) and Deborah Luepnitz (1988). Their work comprehensively challenged male privilege but within the context of intimate relationships, and they worked to therapeutically overt and then grow respectful reciprocity within family systems. My direct work with infants and children taught me the rest.

Carrie MacLure: Social Work in Schools Coordinator, University of New England, Australia.

Naomi Wolf's (1993) "The Beauty Myth" encouraged me as a social work student to seek out other feminist texts. Kimberley Crenshaw's (1989) work critiqued the feminist movement and the lack of an intersectional lens. I use the concept of intersectionality to ensure that the interplay between gender and other forms of discrimination is acknowledged. Roxanne Gay's (2014) "Bad Feminist" explores the complexities of the feminist label and highlights the importance of using intersectionality and inclusion in teaching. My direct social work practice focused on trauma-informed interventions through a feminist lens, and was shaped by some of Judith Herman's (1997) work. My most recent read is "Not Now, Not Ever" (Gillard, 2022), which explores patriarchal systems, the gendered nature of domestic violence, and the need for structural change.

Louse Whitaker: Senior Lecturer in Social Work, Southern Cross University, Australia.

Dale Spender's (1985) description of male dominance in publishing opened my eyes to the silencing of women's voices. As a new graduate in mental health social work I also noticed the care provided by women went unacknowledged. Gilligan (2016) "In A Different Voice", and books that discuss the unseen social factors that contribute to women's depression (Crowley, 1991), the glass ceiling (Baxter & Wright, 2000), and the silencing of women in meetings with colleagues made me yearn for a more nurturing work environment. The publication "Women Working Together" (Weeks, 1994) spoke of the social work practice world into which I had found my way, and postmodernist literature such as "Volatile Bodies" (Grosz, 1994) and "The Orchard" (Modjeska, 1994) revealed ways of thinking about women and our well-being. Also, witnessing women from the global south advocating with women from the global north at the 1995 Fourth World Conference on Women in Beijing made the global context of sexism and intersectionality very real.

Including queer and LGBTI + perspectives (Kumashiro, 2015) and promoting First Nations teachings (Bennett & Green, 2019) are further contemporary texts we feel might refocus feminist social work back into ways of working for solidarity and community.

Women-specific groups

Feminist groupwork was named by three co-authors, Liz, Wendy, and Louise W. It is described as growing from direct practice work with women, and with women and the infants and children of women leaving family violence. Feedback from the participants in each of the groups was used to guide the groupwork and created a "practice-based evidence" about its efficacy.

Wendy notes that

> The practice principles of the interventions being implemented were co-designed by the group members. This work requires the ability to explore, discover, and grow relational opportunities for each unique individual who makes up each unique group.
> *(Wendy)*

Liz described a young women's group in the 1980s that *"started where the women were at"*. The group was in a lower socio-economic suburb in outer Melbourne:

> We had a room, some paid and supported childcare, access to refreshments, and a regular meeting time. The group members created session plans or things they would like to do during the three hours a week set aside for the meetings. The group was open to women between the ages of 15 and 23, with or without children, and interested in looking for work or further study.
> *(Liz Orr, 2021)*

Two female facilitators gained group access to transport, supported childcare, and opportunities for participants to meet with other young women. Topics included information about social security payments, housing, employment, and education pathways. Networks of friendship and support grew for many of the women who attended with some women joining into broader women's movement events such as the International Women's Day march. Louise Whitaker worked to establish similar groups with women in Queensland around this same time.

Wendy spoke of the groupwork she did with Djerriwarrh Health Services in developing feminist-informed children and mothers' groupwork interventions (Bunston, 2001, 2008; Bunston & Pavlidis, 2021):

> ...addressing the impacts of family violence on the child and mother's relationship led to developing an infant/mother groupwork intervention called *The Peek a Boo Club* (Bunston, Eyre, et al., 2016) and a group specifically for women's shelters. Further to this, we developed another specialist groupwork intervention for fathers who had completed a men's behaviour change program (Bunston, 2013). The intervention emerged from the ground up, was guided by the children and mothers themselves, and has been run in collaboration with multiple organisations both within Australia and overseas. The derivatives of this work and PARKAS(parents accepting responsibility – kids are safe) itself have influenced many other groupwork interventions to address family violence that have been developed within Australia. PARKAS and *The Peek a Boo Club*™ (2005) are still being delivered today.

The scaffold upon which the above feminist groupwork grows involved:

- being co-led by the group
- making time for a thorough assessment that prioritises engagement
- adequate time and number of facilitators to run the group
- appropriate group size (8–10 participants)
- weekly reflective supervision for facilitators
- provision of a safe, welcoming, protected, and consistent space
- reciprocal feedback sessions post group
- group reunion

Feminist groupwork approaches continue to evolve and our personal groupwork continuously builds on the work that precedes it. One of Wendy's groups recently celebrated 25 years of sustainable practice.

Feminist activism in social work practice

In the late 1980s in Victoria, feminist social work activism focussed on health policy and a review of sexual assault services (Orr, 1997). Again Louise Whitakernoted similar developmental work in Queensland where she volunteered on a board to apply feminist management principles.

As the project officer employed to develop a service model for a service against sexual assault in the Western region of Melbourne, Liz outlined how this work was significantly influenced by feminist and community development principles, such as:

- Listening to, and responding to, women's experience of the world.
- Engaging a diversity of women in the discussion, design, and delivery of services and policies aimed to address sexual violence.
- Using a community-driven process that would keep women informed of the progress and outcomes of the project.

- Using a feminist lens to analyse the issue of sexual violence, naming the gendered nature and individual and collective impact of creating fear, and understanding how power is used in diverse ways, rather than focusing on a narrow definition of the physical act of rape and sexual assault.
- Including women community workers and women community leaders in the planning of consultation and decision-making forums.
- Developing an ongoing, inclusive, and transparent communication and engagement strategy to engage women living and working in the geographic communities as the primary stakeholders in the project.
- Providing interpreters and translating key documents and consultation messages to encourage active engagement by women from non-English-speaking backgrounds.
- Facilitating forums in suitable, accessible venues, and providing transport, childcare, and food to create an inclusive and friendly environment for all participants (Orr, 2021).

That project was supported by a group of social work students who arranged the venues with childcare, transport, and, in one location, the employment of several interpreters to share the forum information in community languages.

The PARKAS groupwork that Wendy facilitated was also used in public advocacy and teaching during the 2000s. As Wendy states:

> The publications about this body of work were entered into the evidence submitted to the *Victorian Royal Commission into Family Violence* (2016). I was also called as an expert witness to address the commission about my findings resulting from this work (State of Victoria, 2016). These different interventions to address family violence have also been cited as examples of good practice.
>
> *(Humphreys et al., 2015).*

This feminist social work practice outlined by Wendy also won multiple national awards including three Australian Crime and Violence Prevention Awards and two Gold Awards from The Mental Health Services Conference Inc. of Australia and New Zealand.

Diverse women's voices and feminist services

Excited about the possibilities of feminist management countering Colonialism, Louise Whitaker joined the Women's Justice Network in the late 1990s and early 2000s in Queensland (Whitaker, 2001). Web-based technologies were employed by the Women's Justice Network to link rural and Indigenous women to legal services. Relationships of trust and transparency were the hallmark of the Women's Justice Network and empowering processes brought women together to work on conscientisation, interpretation, identity, mobilisation, political action, and change (Summarson-Carr, 2003). They mobilised by creating a service network that honoured and addressed the diverse experiences of women at that time. Less explicit or visible, Louise W reports that the feminist knowledge and experience from this network informed her social work with a group of immigrant and refugee women called *3Es to Freedom: Education, Empowerment, Employment*.

As Louise W notes, feminism:

- held my attention on the ways we relate to one another. Taking the time to build relationships and document the various voices of women involved with the project, we aimed to embody the respect, equality, and welcoming of diversity that the project promoted.
- encouraged creativity beyond binaries. Our research team comprised a social worker, a sociologist, and social geographer who worked with women from refugee backgrounds, practitioners, and managers to drive new ways of working the project.
- invited participatory management structures. Through participation on the programme steering committee, the design and development of the programme moved towards fostering social capital and social networks with the women, away from the didactic approach to knowledge and skill development that was originally envisaged.
- promoted critical reflection, making the implicit, explicit. By facilitating reflective practice with staff, we revealed the details of their approach to practice.

The 3 E's project held community exhibitions, displaying creative works that provided insights into participants' lived experiences, in the communities where the women lived. The project also investigated women's experience of engaging in community arts (Hughes et al., 2021) and the practice of staff in fostering social inclusion (Whitaker et al., 2021). It was **for women, by women, and with women** although feminism was not explicitly acknowledged as a guiding framework for the project. Documentation of the programme outputs through films, a book, reports, and academic publications brought recognition of the richness of the work and lives of the women and staff. This programme has also won awards and was a finalist in the Australian Migration and Settlement Awards in 2019 and received the 2019 Southern Cross University Impact Award for Social Justice.

The above three small examples of social workers group and policy change activism demonstrate a collective agency and connectedness of women that can be celebrated. Knowledge of local women's networks, student needs for learning opportunities, and a ground swell of the women's movement, "breaking the silence about sexual violence", are strong feminist values that enabled the achievement of the Western Region Service Against Sexual Assault. Growing a parent's programme like PARKAS from the ground up with women who have survived violence fosters respect and agency at a critically important time in their lives. Giving voice and agency to marginalised refugee women through the 3 E's project has opened pathways and helped to shape services that this group would use.

Feminism and teaching social work

From micro- to macro-level practice, feminist frameworks highlight the impacts of gender inequality from birth till death (Workplace Gender Equality Agency 2022) and avenues to challenge oppression. Feminist frameworks helped Carrie critically review policies, consider implicit gendered power relations, and integrate anti-oppressive approaches into her teaching. Furthermore, utilising feminist frameworks offered a lens through which to ensure that the processes and structures that impact on the lived experience are considered within a political context (Alston, 2018).

The 2000s saw a reduction in arts and humanities courses and, in many Australian Universities, this also meant a decline in feminist publishing and women's studies courses (Spongberg, 2010). Social work educators such as Carrie and Louise M. noticed a reluctance on the part of female students to identify as a feminist. Carrie recalls quietness and awkward glances in the classroom when she asked social work students "who would consider themselves a 'feminist'?". While some social work students identified as a feminist, Carrie was surprised at the number of students who did not feel that way. She wonders if: *"students may be a feminist in practice, but not in identity?"*. Some female students expressed fear about not wanting to be seen as a "man hater" or worried that being seen as a feminist could be stigmatising. Some students also raised concerns about a lack of intersectionality as a critique of feminism(s). There was also ambivalence or confusion expressed about feminism by students from different standpoints. This could be explained by what Gill (as cited in Banet-Weiser et al., 2020) identified as the contradictions of the 1990s, when women began to experience a stronger sense of female agency and autonomy – "girl power" – which contrasted with the hostile scrutiny of women in the public arena. Feminist media and cultural studies scholars, Banet-Weiser et al. (2020), find similar issues when they reflect on their teaching of feminism in this period:

> Year after year, I would teach undergraduates who insisted – vehemently – that they were not feminists – and nor did they need to be, as political and economic obstacles to gender equality had apparently been overcome.

Lazar Charter (2021) conducted a study of 116 Master of Social Work students in the USA. The study examined perceptions of feminism and whether students self-identified as feminist. "Of the 116 students who participated in this study, 42% self-identified as feminist, whereas 58% did not" (Lazar Charter, 2021, p. 82). They found an increase in identification with feminism when students were given a clear definition, which suggests a need for further learning opportunities to build a greater understanding. Lazar Charter (2021) theorised that the pervasive impacts of internalised oppression may also lead to an internal normalisation of gender inequality, leading to a rejection of feminist ideals. We ask, why is identifying as a feminist in Western society appearing to be making some students feel uneasy? The rallying cry of second-wave feminism, "the personal is political", appears to have lost the "personal" for some.

The conversations about feminism in Australian universities have taken place in the context of the Me-Too# movement and the experiences of Brittany Higgins and Grace Tame, who are two high-profile Australian survivors of sexual violence, and as Wendt and Moulding (2017) note,

> while social work students may often question the relevance of feminism to contemporary life, when sexual politics is recognised, it becomes clear why feminism remains critical not only in contemporary societies but also, more specifically, in social work.
> *(p. 261)*

Teaching the shared value base of feminism and social work's commitment to social justice is critical because gender inequality, oppression, and discrimination remain embedded in Australian systems with devastating consequences. Violence against women is described as being of "epidemic proportions" in Australia (OurWatch, 2021). Also, the *2021–2022 Personal Safety Survey* (Australian Bureau of Statistics, 2023) shows that one in four women experience violence from an intimate partner, and Serpell et al. (2022) report that one woman in Australia is murdered by an intimate partner every ten days.

Furthermore, students need to know about how systemic racist and gendered discrimination are reflected in the overincarceration of First Nations women (Kendall et al., 2020) in the female prison population of Australia. For example, First Nations women comprise one-third (36%) of the prison population (Australian Bureau of Statistics, 2020, as cited in Anthony et al., 2021), while the general adult female population is only 1.29%. Gender inequality is pervasive in Australia in the individual, social, and political systems. The Global Gender Gap index considers gender parity across four dimensions: economic participation and opportunity, educational attainment, health and survival, and political empowerment. In 2022, Australia was ranked 43rd in the global gender gap, coming a long way behind New Zealand (3rd), South Africa (20th), the United Kingdom (22nd), and the USA (27th) (World Economic Forum, 2022).

Providing learning experiences that question stereotypes, challenge myths, and link feminist theory to practice interventions offers contemporary relevance and highlights the need for feminist social work approaches both in the classroom and in practice.

Supervision where the personal can become political

Social work supervision is where both the internalisation and externalisation of gender inequality need to be explored. Teaching an understanding of gendered oppression and trauma in academe needs to be complimented by ongoing supervision for reflective practice about gender inequality and circumventing resistances.

Co-authors have experiences of supervision as being both supportive or a hindrance to practice. Inevitably, the personal experience of supervision involves considering the public and political contexts of being women in social work practice in a male-dominated world.

Louise M notes that the challenges involved in putting feminist principles into practice can be related to the often masculinised workplace environments that surround many academics and social workers. Academics are under continual pressure to do more with less and it is easy to slip into being short and sharp with colleagues and students and to deny people the space to talk and articulate their concerns. Yet giving people the space to express themselves can mean falling behind in work and working in the evenings or weekends to catch up. Dealing with this dilemma requires evaluation of how to navigate the tension between responding to personal needs and the needs of others and finding time for collective action. The role of caring, for the young, the old, and those more vulnerable, continues to fall unequally at the feet of women.

Reflection and visualising our existence not in terms of an individual self but as a part of the collective whole supports feminist action about caring roles. Even though it is still challenging within the workplace, such a conceptualisation assists. Finding solidarity in the workplace may not always be possible, but supervision and support in the academy as well as in direct work can be of assistance for maintaining or growing our feminist practice.

Informed about the issues raised by young women in the young women's group described above, Liz reports that her supervisor encouraged her to participate in a regional housing network. The network was a public housing advocacy group, and in addition to monitoring housing waitlists, it submitted data and achieved major policy reforms such as Tenancy Law Reform. This network advocated for women's rights through submitting local statistics and "case studies" about women experiencing housing strain due to family violence.

Louise M's reflection on her social work lived experience also led to action. Sharing her frustrations about the cruelty of the child protection system with a supervisor manager, she had broken some unwritten rules of interaction. She had felt angry and upset about the way in which a specific investigation was carried out. Expressing her feelings in a supervision session, she recalls being told to "take some time off", with the strong message to her that it was she "not the system" that was at fault. Moved by this personal work experience, Louise M looked closely at Airlie Hochschild's (1983) concept of emotional labour in her thesis. She found that the work done in managing our emotions in the public space of paid employment in social work can help lessen the burden of emotional labour by allowing the space for honest reflection. In that understanding, Louise M suggests that practitioners' own lived experience needs to be valued so that they can find that "fabulous zone" (Reynolds, 2019) for practice.

Conclusion

"Homemade" feminist social work practices exemplify the links between everyday action with broader struggles for women's rights. Our stories reveal how feminist social work practice can transform personal ideas, principles, and political intentions into actions that disrupt oppressive gender status quo(s). They also signpost the need for diverse and evolving Feminisms in Australia to engage with holistic Indigenous social work practices to address the challenges of all inequalities. The international social justice charter and ethics of the social work profession require a continuing embedding of gender analysis in social work education, practice, and research. Sharing stories of practice is a valuable way to consider the continuities and changes in feminists' social work practices, teaching, and research. We encourage the growing of homemade feminist social work practice and sharing stories of those disruptive practices into the future.

References

Alston, M. (2018). Working with women: Gender-sensitive social work practice. In M. Alston, S. McCurdy, & J. McKinnon (Eds.), *Social work: Fields of practice* (3rd ed., pp. 3–18). Oxford University Press.
Anthony, T., Sentance, G., & Behrendt, L. (2021). "We're not being treated like mothers": Listening to the stories of First Nations mothers in prison. *Laws, 74,* 1–18. https://doi.org/10.3390/laws1003007
Arabena, K. (2015). *Becoming Indigenous to the universe.* Australian Scholarly Publishing.
Archer, M. (2007). *Making our way in the world: Human reflexivity and social mobility.* Cambridge
Australian Bureau of Statistics (2023). 2021-2022 Financial Year Personal Safety Survey ttps://www.abs.gov.au/statistics/people/crime-and-justice/personal-safety-australia/latest-release (Accessed 22/02/2024).
Banet-Weiser, S., Gill, R., & Rottenberg, C. (2020). Postfeminism, popular feminism and neoliberal feminism? Sarah Banet-Weiser, Rosalind Gill and Catherine Rottenberg in conversation. *Feminist Theory, 21*(1), 3–24. https://doi.org/10.1177/1464700119842555
Baxter, J., & Wright, E. (2000). The glass ceiling hypothesis: A comparative study of the United States, Sweden, and Australia. *Gender & Society, 14.* https://doi.org/10.1177/089124300014002004
Bennett, B., & Green, S. (2019). *Our voices: Aboriginal social work* (2nd ed., pp. 1–281). Red Globe Press.
Bessarab, D., & Ng'Andu, B. (2010). Yarning about yarning as a legitimate method in Indigenous research. *International Journal of Critical Indigenous Studies, 3*(1), 37–50.

Bnads, H., Orr, E., & Clements, J. (2021). Improving the service to Aboriginal and Torres Strait Islanders through innovative practices between Aboriginal hospital liaison officers and social workers in hospitals in Victoria, Australia. *British Journal of Social Work, 51*(1), 77–95. https://doi.org/10.1093/bjsw/bcaa032

Brownmiller, S. (1975). *Against our will*. Simon and Schuster.

Bunston, W. (2001). *PARKAS: Parents accepting responsibility kids are safe*. Royal Children's Mental Health Service, Victoria.

Bunston, W. (2008). Baby lead the way: Mental health groupwork for infants, children and mothers affected by family violence. *Journal of Family Studies, 14*(2–1), 334–341.

Bunston, W. (2013). "What about the fathers?" Bringing'Dads on Board™' with their infants and toddlers following violence. *Journal of Family Studies, 19*(1), 70–79.

Bunston, W., Eyre, K., Carlsson, A., & Pringle, K. (2016). Evaluating relational repair work with infants and mothers impacted by family violence. *Australian & New Zealand Journal of Criminology, 49*(1), 113–133. https://doi.org/10.1177/0004865814559925

Bunston, W., & Pavlidis, T. (2021). *'Child led' groupwork & family violence: PARKAS plus*. RCH-MH.

Chen, J. (2017). *Intersectionality matters: A guide to engaging immigrant and refugee communities in Australia*. Multicultural Centre for Women's Health, Melbourne.

Chilisa, B. (2012). *Indigenous research methodologies*. Sage.

Crawford, F. (2014). Homemade social work starting in the ontological. *Advances in Social Work & Welfare Education, 16*(1), 22–35.

Crenshaw, K. (1989). Demarginalizing the intersection of race and sex: A black feminist critique of antidiscrimination doctrine. *Feminist Theory and Antiracist Politics, University of Chicago Legal Forum, 1*(8), 139–167.

Crowley, J. D. (1991). *Silencing the self: Women and depression*. Harvard University Press.

De Beauvior, S. (1972) *The Second Sex*. Penguin.

Dominelli, L. (2002). *Anti-oppressive social work theory and practice*. Palgrave Macmillan.

Faludi, S. (1993). *Backlash: The undeclared war against women*. Random House.

French, M. (1993). *The war against women*. Ballantine Books.

Gay, R. (2014). *Bad feminist: Essays*. Harper Perennial.

Gillard, J. (2022). *Not now, not ever: Ten years on from the mysogyny speech*. Penguin Random House.

Gilligan, C. (2016). *In a different voice: Psychological theory and women's development*. Harvard University Press.

Goldner, V. (1992). Making room for both/and. *Family Therapy Networker, March/April, 16*, 55–61.

Goldner, V., Penn, P., Sheinberg, M., & Walker, G. (1990). Love and violence: Gender paradoxes in volatile attachments. *Family Process, 29*(4), 343–364. https://doi.org/10.1111/j.1545-5300.1990.00343.x

Grosz, E. (1994). *Volatile bodies*. Routledge.

Harding, S. ed. (2004). *The feminist standpoint theory reader*. Routledge.

Hargraves, K. (1982). *Women at work*. Penguin.

Herman, J. (1997). *Trauma and recovery: The aftermath of violence - from domestic abuse to political terror*. BasicBooks.

Hochschild, A. (1983). *The managed heart: Commercialization of human feeling*. University of California Press.

hooks, b. (1983). *ain't i a woman: black women and feminism*. Pluto Press.

Hughes, M., Whitaker, L., & Rugendyke, B. (2021). "Yesterday I couldn't see. Tomorrow's sun shines now": Sharing migrant stories through creative arts practice to foster community connections and promote wellbeing'. *Journal of Intercultural Studies, 6*(42), 541–560. DOI:10.1080/07256868.2021.1971170.

Humphreys, C., Thiara, R. K., Sharp, C., & Jones, J. (2015). Supporting the relationship between mothers and children in the aftermath of domestic violence. In N. Stanley & C. Humphreys (Eds.), *Domestic violence and protecting children: New thinking and approaches* (pp. 130–147). Jessica Kingley Pubishers.

Kendall, S., Lighton, S., Sherwood, J., Baldry, E., & Sullivan, E. A. (2020). Incarcerated Aboriginal women's experiences of accessing healthcare and the limitations of the 'equal treatment' principle. *International Journal for Equity in Health, 19*, 48.

Kumashiro, K. (2015). *Against common sense: Teaching and learning about social justice* (3rd ed.). Routledge.
Land, C. (2012). *The politics of solidarity with Indigenous struggles in southeast Australia* [Unpublished PhD thesis]. Deakin University, Victoria, Australia.
Lazar Charter, M. (2021). Exploring the importance of feminist identity in social work education. *Journal of Teaching in Social Work*, 41(2), 117–134. https://doi.org/10.1080/08841233.2021.1895404
Luepnitz, D. A. (1988). *The family interpreted: Feminist theory in clinical practice*. Basic Books.
Martin, K. L. (2008). *Please knock before you enter: Aboriginal regulation of outsiders and the implication for researchers*. Post Pressed.
Mills, C.W. (1959). *The Sociological Imagination*. Oxford University Press.
Modjeska (1994). *The Orchar*. Pan Macmillan, Picador.
Moreton-Robinson, A. (2000). *Talkin' up to the white woman*. University of Queensland Press.
Muller, L. (2007). Decolonisation: Reflections and implications for social work practice. *Communities, Children and Families Australia*, 13(1), 13.
Noble, C. (2020). bell hooks trilogy: Pedagogy for social work supervision. In C. Morley, P. Ablett, C. Noble, & S. Cowden (Eds.), *The Routledge handbook of critical pedagogies for social work* (pp. 501–511). Routledge.
Orr, L. (1997). Women's interests and the Australian State. *Violence against Women*, 5, 34–43.
Orr, E., (2021). Feeling the felt: Reflections on feminist social and community practices. In Boulet, J., & Hawkins, L., (Eds.), *Practical and political approaches to recontexualising social work* (pp. 89–110). IGI Global.
OurWatch. (2021). *Change the story: A shared framework for the primary prevention of violence against women in Australia* (2nd ed.). https://media-cdn.ourwatch.org.au/wp-content/uploads/sites/2/2021/11/18101814/Change-the-story-Our-Watch-AA.pdf
Plumwood, V. (1993). *Feminism and the Mastery of Nature*. Routledge.
Reynolds, V. (2019). Zone of Fabulousness. https://www.youtube.com/watch?v=qnTDUCkYby0
Richards, L. (1985). *Having families: Marriage, parenthood and social pressures in Australia*. Penguin.
Sawyer, M., (1987). *Sisters in Suits: women and public policy in Australia*.
Serpell, B., Sullivan, T., & Doherty, L. (2022). *Homicide in Australia 2019–20*. Statistical report no. 39. Australian Institute of Criminology. https://doi.org/10.52922/sr78511
Smith, D. (1987). *The everyday world as problematic: A feminist sociology*. Open University Press.
Smith, L. T. (1999). *Decolonising methodologies*. Zed Books.
Spender, D. (1985). *Man made language*. HarperCollins.
Spongberg, M. (2010). Feminist publishing in a cold climate? "Australian feminist studies" and the new ERA of research. *Feminist Review*, 95, 99–110.
Stanley, L., & Wise, S. (1993). *Breaking out again: Feminist ontology and epistemology*. Routledge.
State of Victoria. (2016). *Royal commission into family violence: Summary and recommendations*. https://www.rcfv.com.au/MediaLibraries/RCFamilyViolence/Reports/RCFV_Full_Report_Interactive.pdf
Summarson-Carr, S. (2003). Rethinking empowerment theory using a feminist lens: The importance of process. *Affilia*, 18(1) (Spring 2003), 8–20. https://doi.org/10.1177/0886109902239092/
Summers, A. (1975). *Damned whores and God's police: The colonisation of women in Australia*. Penguin.
Weeks, W. (1994). *Women working together: Lessons from feminist women's services*. Longman Cheshire.
Weeks, W. (2003). Women: Developing feminist practice in women's services. In J. Allan, B. Pease, & L. Briskman (Eds.), *Critical social work: An introduction to theories and practices* (pp. 107–123). Allan & Unwin.
Wendt, S., & Moulding, N. (2017). The current state of feminism and social work. *Australian Social Work*, 70(3), 261–262.
Whitaker, L. (2001). The women's justice network. *Alternative Law Journal*, 26(2), 91–92
Whitaker, L., Hughes, M., & Rugendyke, B. (2021). Capturing practice wisdom: Advancing the empowerment of women from refugee and migrant backgrounds. *British Journal of Social Work*, 51(4), 1296–1313. https://doi.org/10.1093/bjsw/bcab038
Wilson, E. (1977). *Women and the welfare state*. Routledge.

Wolf, N. (1993). *The beauty myth: How images of beuty are used against women.* Vintage Arrow.
Workplace Gender Equality Agency (2022). *Women's economic security in retirement.* https://www.wgea.gov.au/sites/default/files/documents/Women%27s%20economic%20security%20in%20retirement.pdf
World Economic Forum. (2022). *Global gender gap report.* https://www3.weforum.org/docs/WEF_GGGR_2022.pdf

16
THE IMPACT OF PATRIARCHY ON PREMARITAL RELATIONSHIPS IN NIGERIA

Augusta Y. Olaore, Oluwatobiloba Bello and Oluwafikayomi O. Banjo

Introduction

Nigeria is a country with a rich and diverse cultural history spread across more than 350 ethnic groups (Offiong & Uduigwomen, 2021). Each ethnic group has its own language, culture, beliefs, and heritage. The patriarchal system of administration, where men dominate and run the affairs of communities, is the dominant socio-political structure. In most Nigerian communities, women are disadvantaged due to entrenched Patriarchy that, as Anele (2010) describes, is a "well-oiled socio-cultural machine" that reinforces the authority of men over women. Patriarchy as a social construct is common to most ethnic groups. The National Gender Policy (Federal Ministry of Women Affairs and Social Development, 2006) states that Nigeria is a highly patriarchal society that prefers male children over female children. The influence of the mother and the father is particularly significant in shaping and perpetuating Patriarchy (Federal Ministry of Women Affairs and Social Development, 2006, p. 6).

Patriarchy and colonization

While male dominance was indeed present in Nigeria in the pre-colonial era, it differed significantly from the Patriarchy introduced by colonization (Dogo, 2014). Pre-colonial gender relationships in Nigeria were devoid of subjugation, oppression, and male privilege. Women played significant roles politically and economically, contributing in meaningful ways to their communities (Ogun and Martins, 2010). Jaiyeola and Aladegbola (2020, p. 9) posited that, though women featured prominently in the socio-political arena and had an active role in community affairs, there were some boundaries designated by patriarchal domination that women could not cross. However, Amoah-Boampong and Agyeiwaa (2020, p. 1) argue, "women contested, negotiated, complemented, and transformed their societies through their diverse roles in the political, social, religious, and economic realities of pre-colonial life in West Africa".

Britain colonized Nigeria in 1884 and this had a significant impact on the subjugation of women. Women were removed from civic positions and the focus of Western education was directed upon men. Badru (2005) also highlights that colonial policy, which restricted active participation in public affairs to men, was an aggressive reinforcement of the pre-colonial antecedence of a lesser form of Patriarchy in Nigeria.

The practice of Patriarchy

Hunnicutt (2009, p. 553) defines Patriarchy as "systems of male dominance and female subordination. It also symbolizes normative values and judgments, which center on biological variances between males and females, and provide for opportunities, privileges, and division of labor between women and men based on gender". Chereji and King (2015) note that Patriarchy places emphasis on male authority and sons are preferred over daughters. In a patriarchal society, such as the Ogoni people of Nigeria, young men have the freedom to marry whom they wish, but young women face restrictions. This contributes to the prevalence of forced or early marriages in parts of Nigeria (Amzat, 2020). These patriarchal practices have led to socio-cultural attitudes which have been discriminatory and reinforced economic inequalities (Offiong, 2019). Studies such as Enfield (2019), Adeosun and Owolabi (2021) and Mushfiqu et al. (2018) reveal that stereotypical gender expectations and norms in Nigerian society position men as providers, while women are subordinated and dependent on men. Even when women compete equally in the labor force, they have the primary care of the home, and children are socialized into a system of rigid gender roles (Ogunola, 2018), which are then carried into dating relationships.

Ntoimo and Isiugo-Abanihe (2014) observed that women are often dissuaded from pursuing professions associated with power, such as the police, which might defy gender stereotypes and ideas of womanhood. Women who challenge the status quo through their education, profession, or a desire to rise above such subservience are viewed as being uncultured, disrespectful, and proud. Such attitudes may affect their marriage prospects. Instead, women are expected to be self-sacrificing and give up their careers and goals to maintain the patriarchal structure and meet societal gender expectations (Ajayi et al., 2019).

Male privilege is a consequence of Patriarchy (Thomas, 2017) and manifests in various ways, including social acceptance of infidelity only for men, as well as a lack of sexual freedom and recognition of women's sexual autonomy (Chung & Liu, 2018; Uma, 2021). Olaore and Agwu (2020) argue that cultural traditions promote men's hierarchical roles in sexual relationships, which contribute to the practice of polygamy in Africa and tend to excuse infidelity among African men. It is also assumed that African women are indifferent to infidelity as expected in the patriarchal and polygamy-permissive culture (Olaore & Agwu, 2020).

Patriarchy and premarital relationships

Male privileges and the superiority of Patriarchy inform unhealthy power dynamics in premarital relationships. These patriarchal postures permit men to do whatever they choose as a result of their perceived "power" (Ekoh et al., 2019; Kim et al., 2019).

In the Nigerian context, Patriarchy not only influences power dynamics but also plays a role in intimate partner violence (IPV) (Aihie, 2009; Ifeanyichukwu et al., 2017). It serves as a socio-political system relying on gendered physical and sexual violence to maintain the subordinated status of women (Quek, 2019). In their analysis of Asian countries, Cala and Soriano-Ayala (2021) said girls in patriarchal cultures were vulnerable to teen dating violence. In Nigeria, a bride who is found not to be a virgin – if they do not bleed on the wedding night – is shamed by her husband's family who claim she was "not met at home". Her own family is thus forced to refund all or part of the bride price, regardless of whether she was a victim of sexual violence. Adegboyega et al. (2015) observed that male virginity is of no concern, but women are exposed to intrusive virginity tests that may be injurious to their reproductive health. In Nigeria, a man is defined by his perceived strength and authority and is socialized to use violence, aggression, or dominance. A woman is raised to be passive, agreeable, and quiet (Aborisade, 2021). At an extreme level, among the Tiv-speaking people of Nigeria, wife beating is regarded as a display of love which women have been conditioned to accept. This is carried into dating relationships (Oyediran & Isiugo-Abanihe, 2005).

Patriarchal socialization

Culture is the medium through which males and females are socialized to internalize values such as Patriarchy (Para-Mallam, 2010). Guhin et al. (2021) argue that norms and values are instilled and enforced within group socialization, through the asymmetry of power, historicity, and transferability. These asymmetries of power produce structures of oppression and control. Gansen (2017) used gendered sexual socialization theory to explain how children in families learn that boys hold power over girls' bodies.

Religion is a key agent of socialization and reinforces norms and values (Alifa, 2022). While Nigeria is constitutionally a secular state, Salahu (2023) describes it as a multi-nation state with strong religious traditions. Christianity, Islam, and traditional religions each have their own variant of male dominance and feminine subjugation (Dogo, 2014; Salahu 2023). Patriarchy has therefore been further perpetuated through religious socialization (Klingenberg & Sjö, 2019).

Patriarchy, culture, and power

A patriarchal system is characterized by unequal power relations (Ekpenyong et al., 2018) where women are systematically disadvantaged and oppressed. Akanwa (2023) submitted that Nigerian women are "ingloriously" portrayed in literature as weak and powerless against the back drop of male dominance and their contributions are overlooked.

The political, economic, social, and personal interests of women are often underrepresented and undervalued (Henderson & Jeydel, 2010) In addition to women being undervalued, Mbah and Oti (2013) posited that a patriarchal mentality discriminates against women and excludes them from political leadership by infering that their "femaleness" makes them weak and feeble and therefore ineligible for political leadership like their male counterparts.

Akanwa, (2023) further observed that, " Nigerian—women, like their African sisters, have constantly been confronted with a plethora of limiting factors ranging from colonialism, neocolonialism, and suppression by a cultural ideology that sees women as subordinates, incapable of assuming serious roles independent of the men" (p. 319). It is the composite of this cultural ideology that fuels the patriarchal mentalities that is demonstrated in the everyday living, beliefs and languages of the Nigerian culture. The goal of this chapter is to shed light on how Patriarchy as a culture of male dominance, male privilege, and female subjugation influences the dynamics of premarital relationships for Nigerian women.

Methodology

This qualitative study collected data from virtual discussion group conversations and an online questionnaire. Our sampling method was purposive, and the study was carried out using digital research data collection via two closed WhatsApp groups and a Google Form. To collect data using the Google Form, the research questionnaire was shared on one of the researcher's WhatsApp statuses. This was made available for voluntary participation, and 55 participants completed this form.

The first closed WhatsApp group comprised five participants (all female), recruited by placing an invitation on the researcher's WhatsApp status to people on her contact list. This group was created to discuss the research questions. Group Two, with eight participants (seven females and one male), was recruited from a broader WhatsApp network to which both the researchers belong, called the "Family Systems Engineering" group (FSE). The FSE is composed of 126 male and female family life coaches and practitioners. The research study was introduced to the FSE, and its members were asked to indicate interest in joining the newly created WhatsApp group. Group Three comprised seven participants (five females and two males) who were members of the "Puresexuals" WhatsApp network of 49 members, to which the researchers belong. Puresexuals is a group of male and female graduates and undergraduates of a faith-based university in Nigeria, who are committed to practicing premarital sexual abstinence. The research questions were posted on the Puresexuals group, and members were invited to respond.

Two broad research questions were asked in each of the digital platforms. These questions facilitated discussions through sharing of responses in the form of texts and voice notes (short audio recordings). Participants ranged in age from 18 to 45 years, and the gender distribution across the three WhatsApp discussions was 15% male and 85% female. For those using the Google Form, confidentiality was maintained. However, in the WhatsApp groups, participants were aware of one another, similar to the dynamics of a focus group. Participation was voluntary, and participants were free to exit the group at any time. Responses from all the participants were meticulously documented and systematically analyzed by identifying emergent themes, patterns, interconnections, and consistency. The data was collected over a period of one month in 2022. The following research questions formed the basis for the group discussions as well as for the completion of the Google Form:

1. What are some Nigerian cultural beliefs about what a woman can or cannot do in a dating relationship?
2. What behaviors or practices are permissible for men but not women in dating relationships?

Results

The overall themes identified were male leadership in dating relationships; women having to prove their own marriageability; inconsistent fidelity expectations; aggressive or violent behavior that is excused for men; and economic marginalization of women.

Male leadership in dating relationships

Various sub-themes emerged within the theme of male leadership in dating relationships.

The impact of patriarchy

Men initiate the dating relationship

It was clear that women were not expected to propose to men:

> It is believed that only the man should initiate an interest towards dating a woman. It is a taboo according to culture for a woman to express her love interest in a man or worse still, propose marriage to a man.

The intentions of a woman initiating contact with a potential love interest were questionable:

> A woman who initiates a relationship can also be perceived to want sex.

Women are labeled promiscuous if they approach a man they are interested in. The patriarchal social system assigns leadership to a man even in dating relationships and socialization prescribes what society expects of a woman (Para-Mallam, 2010). These unwritten rules of behavior drive the mutual gender expectations such as who initiates a dating relationship. Deviation by reversing the roles is met with steep resistance, with consequences such as stigmatization as being promiscuous. This can have dire social consequences, including being disowned by parents, public flogging, loss of educational opportunities, body mutilations, and sometimes death (Okobia, 2015; Smith, 2010).

Men determine the pace of the relationship

Participants agreed that, culturally, men determined how relationships developed, including how fast or slow the relationships progressed:

> Women should not dictate the pace of a relationship.
>   He (the man) controls the relationship and determines how it goes.
>   They (women) have no say so.
>
> *(having no voice)*

This means that a woman cannot slow the pace of the relationship even if she may not feel ready for the permanence of marriage. Similarly, they are not able to speed up its progression if the man is not making efforts to formalize the relationship. Comments by participants corroborate the findings of Ekoh et al. (2019) and Kim et al. (2019), Patriarchy gives men the freedom to do whatever they choose in a dating relationship as a result of the "power" and privilege their culture has given to them, while women are limited in their freedom of expression and action.

Inequality between women and men in the dating relationship

Overall, women felt that they are seen as second-class citizens and as such men are given the right to express power and control over them:

> Women can't propose interest in a man or be seen as equals with their male partners in the relationship, taking only a submissive role and losing their autonomy.

Women should not assume equality with a man in a relationship. The woman doesn't have a say on issues affecting both parties in the relationship and the decisions are made by the man.

Once a woman consents to a romantic relationship, it implies they consent to a subservient role in relation to the man. Ajayi et al. (2022) posited that women assume an inferior role to men because of beliefs around the superiority of the men in the household which are tied to their role as the breadwinner and decision-maker. Women "cannot be seen" as equal to their male partners even if they are equal in other aspects of life. Consequently, women find themselves pressured to conform to societal expectations of submissiveness in the premarital relationship.

Men make the decisions and determine the pace of the relationship, but it is worth noting that the responsibility for keeping the relationship healthy rests on the woman. This often means that if the relationship does not last, the woman is blamed. Adisa et al. (2021a, 2021b) submitted that while women are expected to be responsible for the care of the home, they are also expected to cater to men's sexual satisfaction and are blamed if men choose to have extra marital affairs (Dosekun, 2023). A post in one of the discussion groups corroborates this in the following statement:

Men are told to expect sex from their partners at all times, regardless of what she thinks. That's why men can say they want to have sex with a woman who just delivered a baby and is not fully recovered, and they will tell her if she says no, he will 'look out'.

Female submission

Several participants mentioned that it is expected that a woman be submissive at all costs. If she is perceived otherwise, she is at risk of losing the relationship:

A woman can only be submissive while the man makes the decision.
Women should not talk back, they should be submissive. Women should lose themselves and forget their dreams and aspirations.

This corroborates the findings of Ajayi et al. (2019) that women are expected to be self-sacrificing and give up on their careers and goals to maintain the patriarchal structure. Fakunmoju et al. (2018) and Oyediran and Isiugo-Abanihe (2005) posit that women may also be blamed for the violent behavior of their partners when they do not submit sexually to him. This is social blackmail and sexual coercion.

Women have to prove marriageability

The dating period is presumed as a time to prepare for marriage. Women are expected to do everything to prove their marriageability to the man as well as his relatives.

Some even expect that you do those household chores, cook and some other stuff before they find or consider you worthy of their son.
Even the first time you visit your partner's mother, they can tell you to wash plates and pound yam all in the name of testing you to see if you are fit for their son.

This was the norm in some families. A woman who fails the test of domesticity is seen as unfit and lacking in home training. Men are not expected to prove marriageability:

> The day your partner visits your parents, they will give him food and worship him and they will not even let him lift a finger. I have not seen a future son-in-law wash plates or cloth or wash cars, all in the name of testing or seeing if he is a good fit for their daughter." "Some families want to be sure you are fertile before they consider you marriageable.
>
> I hear some families endorse pregnancy before accepting the woman as a wife in the family, for reasons known to them.

A woman may be asked to cohabit with her would-be husband to prove that she is fertile. In other cases, she may be required to carry out medical tests to prove her fertility or virginity. Men are not required to prove their fertility. Keredei (2022) observed that parents place greater value on their daughters' marriage prospects than on their physical or medical health. This informs the practice of female genital mutilation in some Nigerian communities. Okeke-Ihejirika (2004) stated that the Igbo tribe of the southeastern part of Nigeria diligently grooms their daughters to gain social acceptance as potential brides. Finding a husband takes priority over other forms of social recognition. However, if after cohabiting with the man a woman does not become pregnant, she stands the risk of the man ending the relationship.

Inconsistent fidelity expectations

Many responses implied that while it is socially acceptable for a man to practice infidelity, it is unacceptable for a woman:

> He (man) can have one or multiple sex partners, but she should keep herself as her value is in her purity.
>
> It is because men are presumed to be polygamous in nature, that is why fidelity is excused for them.
>
> It is permissible and forgivable for men to have multiple partners at once, but an abomination for a woman to do the same. There is a saying "A bee can go from flower to flower, to flower, but a flower cannot go from bee to bee, to bee".

The irony of the bees and flowers metaphor mentioned by the participant is that while bees (men) can excusably go from one flower, (woman) to another, don't flowers then have to accept more than one bee? We may ask, why are flowers(women) penalized for accepting more than one bee (men) if bees 'naturally' go from flower to flower? Fakunmoju et al. (2021) highlights this inconsistent patriarchal informed standard by stating that young Nigerian women are socialized to adhere to acceptable standards of sexual behavior and purity, while young men are believed to be sexually indiscriminate and do not receive the same level of purity socialization. Smith (2010) observed that, among the Igbo tribe, men often engage in relationships with women who society regards as "promiscuous", and they may marry them. Nevertheless, they ex-pect their wives to be faithful to them irrespective of their prior sexual history. Layefa and Ezenagu (2019) maintain that, despite strong religious influences in Nigeria that condemn infidelity, stricter levels of condemnation are meted out to women.

Aggressive or violent behavior is excused for men

Participants mentioned that men were aggressive and violent toward women in various ways such as beating, lying, and shouting.

> Some people believe a man can hit a woman even while dating, but a woman can't.
> Some men become aggressive towards their women when they assume she is being disobedient to their instructions, or she comes home late regardless of her reasons.

Violence against women in dating relationships can be analyzed through the lens of gendered sexual socialization theory. According to Gansen (2017), this theory suggests children in families learn that boys have power over girl's bodies. If women are expected to be submissive and tolerate abusive behaviors, children in that home witness their mothers enduring abuse, which can lead them to accept violence as normalized behavior. Such beliefs can also stem from religious doctrines promoting superiority of men, which can be exerted by disciplining women as subordinates (Fakunumoju & Rasool 2018). Children are therefore socialized into these patriarchal postures of the culture that condones aggressive behavior against women in homes, which is then perpetuated when these children grow up and start dating.

Economic marginalization

Women are sometimes forced to choose between a relationship and a successful career pursuit. Marxist theory describes Patriarchy as a power structure in which women are oppressed by the capitalist system in order to serve and do reproductive work in the family. This dynamic further enables men to wield financial control over women (Thomas, 2017):

> Men will tell you if you take on so and so career, they can't continue with you because how will you be a good wife and mother to the unborn kids.
> I have heard stories of people saying my partner said when we get married, I will have to stop doing so and so, quit my job and do XYZ, or not even pursue a particular career because of whatever stupid reason.

Responses by participants reflect the prevailing belief that a woman's primary assignment in life is to take care of the home. Layefa and Ezenagu (2019) state that the husband or potential suitors' insistence on women choosing between family and career is rooted in the traditional view of men as the breadwinners responsible for the household finances.

However, the prevailing trend in contemporary Nigerian society is witnessing women pursuing careers and excelling in them, challenging these deeply ingrained stereotypes. This shift can have a profound impact (Adisa et al., 2021a, 2021b; Gillard & Okonjo-Iweala, 2021). Nigerian society will need to reorientate toward an egalitarian approach to work-life balance and revise its expectations of women in dating relationships. Women should be able to pursue their desired career paths without fear of rejection by suitors (Adejugbe & Adejugbe, 2018; Layefa & Ezenagu, 2019; Mushfiqur et al., 2018).

Discussion

The study sheds light on how Patriarchy affects social interactions between men and women in Nigeria, which informs the dynamics of both premarital and marital relationships. Patriarchy as a system of male dominance, male privilege, female economic marginalization, and inequalities (Hunnicutt, 2009) informed participants' opinions on dating relationships. However, the post-structural feminist perspective argues that all gendered relationships are socially constructed, and that Patriarchy can be dismantled through a revolutionary restructuring of society (Thomas, 2017). As such, there is a need to adjust societal expectations to acknowledge and appreciate the contributions women make to society outside the home in addition to their reproductive roles.

Socio-cultural norms that reinforce the idea of men as leaders discourage women from taking the lead to initiate an intimate relationship. When a woman does approach someone, it is met with disapproval, and she is likened to "a bee who approaches a flower", which is culturally a typically masculine role.

Women are also denied the ability to determine the pace of the relationship by increasing or slowing its progression, as this is seen to be the prerogative of men (Anele, 2010). Participants also shared that some men exert control over their partners by dictating what they should wear, and how they look and act in public. This domination leaves women feeling restricted and devoid of the freedom to express themselves. Ajayi et al. (2022) highlighted how religion contributes to a belief in subjugated behavior in dating relationships where the female is socialized to believe that it is her duty to submit her body to her suitor or prospective husband.

Some women are eager to pursue their careers while also fulfilling marital obligations, and others wait until after childbirth and child-rearing. In general, participants expressed the view that women should not pursue a career that outpaces that of their partners. If a woman is successful, earns more, or becomes the sole provider, it is perceived as a threat to masculinity. Participants reported that women find themselves compelled to choose between a career or a well-paying job and a dating relationship. They are taught not to "outshine" their partners.

Nonetheless, some Nigerian women have achieved success and have become socio-economic leaders, excelling in roles within politics, academia, and finance. Contemporary African feminist perspectives may explain how these women have managed to succeed. These perspectives offer non-confrontational, conflict management postures through cooperation, accommodation, and tolerance to challenge the harsh patriarchal nature of Nigerian society. Examples of this approach include Nnaemeka's (2004) Nego-feminism, Adimora-Ezeigbo's (2012) Snail-sense Feminism, and Acholonu's (1995) Motherism, which gives women a proverbial seat at the negotiating table to advocate for equity (Okafor in Rasool & Harms-Smith, 2022).

Data from our study indicates that negotiation rights are earned once the woman is married. Being single carries a stigma for Nigerian women which, as stated by Okeke-Ihejirika (2004, p. 41), increases the pressure to marry. In this cultural context, a single woman finds it challenging to navigate the landscape of male superiority and dominance. Nego-feminism and other perspectives could be a plausible bridge between matriarchy and Patriarchy (Muhammad et al., 2017), even within the context of premarital relationships.

The gendered socialization of male ownership of the female body for sex and the religious socialization for women to submit to their husbands sexually as a religious duty predispose women to IPV in dating relationships (Ajayi et al., 2022; Gasan, 2017). Participants stated that a woman has no right to refuse sex in relationships with men. One in four women in Nigeria has experienced spousal violence (Owoo, 2020). There are also differences in IPV prevalence at regional and state levels due to variations in cultural norms and modern agency that contradict women's subjugation (Oyediran, 2021). However, when some women seek help and report cases of violence, they are subjected to questioning and blamed for the violence they endured. These women may internalize self-blame for the actions of men, who are then left unaccountable.

Male privilege is also manifested in dating relationships through gendered responses to infidelity. It is acceptable for men to have multiple dating partners, yet women are expected to remain monogamous. A more egalitarian approach to fidelity holds both partners equally responsible for upholding monogamy.

The findings indicated that, culturally, the success of a relationship is the woman's responsibility, and she is expected to prove her suitability for marriage. Daughters are groomed and subjected to invasive examinations to confirm their adherence to social expectations of sexual purity as a means of proving their eligibility for marriage. In contrast, sons are not (Keredei, 2022). It was expressed that young men are welcomed and celebrated by women's families without necessarily possessing matrimonial skills. Marriageability for men is usually determined by age rather than a demonstration of sexual purity or household skills (Okunlola et al., 2023).

Conclusion and recommendations

The categorization of Nigeria as a patriarchal nation, as affirmed by the Federal Ministry of Women Affairs (2006), can be traced back to the colonial capitalist expeditions by Islamic and Judeo-Christian colonizers (Dogo, 2014; Nwalutu & Nwalutu, 2019). These colonial influences prioritized male superiority and dominance while subjugating women in economic and political arenas. Patriarchal practices like designing men as breadwinners, public leaders, and the suppression of education of girls have become foundational in Nigerian families through gendered and religious socialization.

This study has shed light on the reality of Patriarchy within premarital relationships. Patriarchal norms shape the dynamics of dating and perpetuate inequalities such as male leadership in initiating and determining the pace of the premarital relationship; the burden of female proof of marriageability; gendered fidelity expectations; excused aggressive or violent behavior from men; and economic marginalization of women through the restriction of careers opportunities, forcing them to fulfill homemaking and reproductive labor demands.

Addressing Patriarchy during dating relationships in Nigeria requires a multi-pronged approach. The social work profession, as a catalyst for social change, should challenge detrimental patriarchal attitudes through psychoeducational programs. In keeping with principles of Nego-feminism and other African perspectives on feminism, young women can be empowered with relationship skills to navigate patriarchal hurdles. Recognizing how early socialization perpetuates these norms, social workers should partner with schools and religious institutions to redefine relationship norms and promote respectful dating behaviors through family and community engagements. Children's books and novels may be utilized for deconstructing existing patriarchal cultural norms.

Moreover, Nigerian dating websites should also be re-engineered with algorithms that match couples based on non-patriarchal criteria. Men with male privilege and power should be encouraged to take on an advocacy role to promote equity for women. This multifaceted approach can contribute to dismantling patriarchal structures within dating relationships and fostering a more equitable and respectful dating culture.

Limitation of study

Data was collected from participants who were able to engage in a social media-hosted group and Google Form, who had access to the Internet and who were comfortable with using online platforms. Individuals who were not active on social media or lacked such access were excluded from the study. Nevertheless, this methodology did prove beneficial by allowing for the inclusion of individuals from different geographical locations. To improve future research, it is recommended that multiple platforms are made available for participants to share their views, which will ensure broader representation.

In our survey, we did not include gender in the Google Form so participants could not indicate their gender. As such, we were unable to analyze the role of gender in the responses. It is recommended that further studies include the gender of participants as a data point.

Additionally, although participants indicated that their home country was Nigeria, we did not request information on the specific region of Nigeria they were from. This information would have contributed to greater understanding about variations in perspectives based on cultural, tribal, and ethnic groupings or dialects. Including it in future research would yield a more comprehensive analysis.

References

Aborisade, R. A. (2021). Untold stories of violence experienced by female students in cohabitation relationships on Nigerian university campuses. *Partner Abuse*, 12(4), 409–431.

Adegboyega, L. O., Oniye, A. O., & Abdulkareem, S. (2015). Virginity among youths: Implications for sexual health and marital counseling. *The Counsellor*, 34(2), 32–38.

Adejugbe, A., & Adejugbe, A. (2018). Women and discrimination in the workplace: A Nigerian perspective. Available at SSRN 3244971.

Adeosun, O. T., & Owolabi, K. E. (2021). Gender inequality: determinants and outcomes in Nigeria. *Journal of Business and Socio-economic Development*, 1(2), 165–181.

Acholonu, C. O. (1995). *Motherism: An Afro-Centric Alternative to Feminism.* Owerri: Afa Publications.

Adimora-Ezeigbo, A. (2015) Snail-Sense Feminism: Building on an Indigenous
Model. Lagos; Wealthsmith; Books, Print.

Adisa, T. A., Gbadamosi, G., & Adekoya, O. D. (2021a). Gender apartheid: The challenges of breaking into "man's world". *Gender, Work & Organisation*, 28(6), 2216–2234.

Adisa, T. A., Mordi, C., Simpson, R., & Iwowo, V. (2021b). Social dominance, hypermasculinity, and career barriers in Nigeria. *Gender, Work & Organization*, 28(1), 175–194.

Aihie, O. (2009). Prevalence of domestic violence in Nigeria: Implication for counseling. *Edo Journal of Counseling*, 2(1), 1–8. https://doi.org/10.4314/ejc.v2i1.52648

Ajayi, C. E., Chantler, K., & Radford, L. (2022). The role of cultural beliefs, norms, and practices in Nigerian women's experiences of sexual abuse and violence. *Violence against Women*, 28(2), 465–486.

Ajayi, L. A., Olanrewaju, F. O., Olanrewaju, A., & Nwannebuife, O. (2019). Gendered violence and human rights: An evaluation of widowhood rites in Nigeria. *Cogent Arts & Humanities*, 6(1), Article: 1676569, 1–17,

Akanwa, E. (2023) Women in the Nigerian Civil War Literature: Facing the Politics of Representation. *International Journal of Latest Research in Humanities and Social Science (IJLRHSS)*, 6(6), 317–324.

Alifa, S. (2022). Religious issues in national unity and development. *Nnamdi Azikiwe Journal of Philosophy*, 13(1).

Amoah-Boampong, C., & Agyeiwaa, C. (2020). Women in pre-colonial Africa: West Africa. In Yacob-Haliso, O. & Falola, T. (eds.), *The Palgrave handbook of African women's studies*. London: Palgrave MacMillan. 1–13.

Amzat, J. (2020). Faith effect and voice on early marriage in a Nigerian state. *Sage Open*, 10(2), 2158244020919513.

Anele, K. A. (2010). Patriarchy and institutionalised sexism in the Nigerian university system: The case of the University of Port Harcourt. *African Anthropologist*, 17(1–2), 63–80.

Badru, F. A. (2005). Patriarchy and constraints of democratic political space of women in Nigeria. *Unilag Journal of Politics*, 2(2), 77–101.

Cala, V. C., & Soriano-Ayala, E. (2021). Cultural dimensions of immigrant teen dating violence: A qualitative metasynthesis. *Aggression and Violent Behavior*, 58, 101555. https://doi.org/10.1016/j.avb.2021.101555

Chereji, C. R., & King, C. W. (2015). Aspects of traditional conflict management practices among the Ogoni of Nigeria. *Conflict Studies Quarterly*, 10, 56–68.

Chung, J. J., & Liu, J. (2018). The abolition of the adultery law in South Korea: A critique. *Asian Journal of Women's Studies*, 24(2), 205–223.

Dogo, S. A. (2014). The Nigerian patriarchy: when and how. *Cultural and Religious Studies*, 2(5), 263–275.

Dosekun, S. (2023). The problems and intersectional politics of "#BeingFemaleinNigeria". *Feminist Media Studies*, 23(4), 1429–1445.

Ekoh, C., Agha, A. A., & Ejimakaraonye C. (2019). Unhealthy romantic relationships among young persons: Implication for social work practice in Nigeria. *Nigerian Journal of Psychological Research*, 15(2019), 33–38.

Ekpenyong, V. O., Tawo, C. N., & Oboqua, E. D. (2018). Non-formal education for empowering adults in Nigeria for sustainable development. *Adult Education in Nigeria*, 23(II), 120–127.

Enfield, S. (2019). *Gender Roles and Inequalities in the Nigerian Labour Market. K4D Helpdesk Report*. Brighton: Institute of Development Studies. May 21, 2019.

Fakunmoju, S. B., Abrefa-Gyan, T., & Maphosa, N. (2018). Confirmatory factor analysis and gender invariance of the revised IRMA scale in Nigeria. *Affilia: Journal of Women and Social Work*. Advance online publication. https://doi.org/10.1177/0886109918803645

Fakunmoju, S. B., Abrefa-Gyan, T., Maphosa, N., & Gutura, P. (2021). Rape myth acceptance: Gender and cross-national comparisons across the United States, South Africa, Ghana, and Nigeria. *Sexuality & Culture*, 25, 18–38.

Fakunmoju, S. B., & Rasool, S. (2018). Exposure to gender-based violence and beliefs about violence against women among high school students in Nigeria and South Africa. In *Special Issue: Reproductive Health in Sub-Saharan Africa*. Sage Open, 8(4), 1–17.

Federal Ministry of Women Affairs and Social Development (2006). National gender policy. http://www.aacoalition.org/national_policy_women.htm

Gansen, H. M. (2017). Reproducing (and disrupting) heteronormativity: gendered sexual socialisation in preschool classrooms. *Sociology of Education*, 90(3), 255–72.

Gillard, J., & Okonjo-Iweala, N. (2021). *Women and leadership: Real lives, real lesson*. Cambridge: MIT Press.

Guhin, J., Calarco, J. M., & Miller-Idriss, C. (2021). Whatever happened to socialisation? *Annual Review of Sociology*, 47, 109–129.

Henderson S. L., & Jeydel A. S. (2010). *Women and politics in a global world*. New York: Oxford University Press.

Hunnicutt, G. (2009). Varieties of patriarchy and violence against women: Resurrecting "patriarchy" as a theoretical tool. *Violence against Women*, 15(5), 553–573.

Ifeanyichukwu, O., Christopher, P., & Kizito, D. (2017). The emerging trend in culture of domestic violence in Nigeria: Causes, theoretical assumptions and implications. *Research Journal of Humanities, Legal Studies & International Development*, 2(1), 53–63.

Jaiyeola, E. F., & Aladegbola, A. I. (2020). Patriarchy and colonisation: The "brooder house" for gender inequality in Nigeria. *Journal of Research on Women and Gender*, 10(1), 3–22.

Keredei, R. (2022). The effects of female genital mutilation among teenage girls and young women in Nigeria. Masters thesis. Linnaeus University.

Kim, J. J., Visserman, M. L., & Impett, E. A. (2019). Power in close intimate relationships. In C. R. Agnew & J. J. Harman (eds.), *Power in close relationships*. Cambridge: Cambridge University Press, 192–224.

Klingenberg, M., & Sjö, S. (2019). Theorising religious socialisation: A critical assessment. *Religion*, 49(2), 163–178.

Layefa, G., & Ezenagu, N. (2019). Career, marriage and family life: Engaging the theme of culture change in "Best of both world". *NTAtvc Journal of Communication*, 3(2), 84–94.

Mbah, C. S., & Oti, E. O. (2013). Patriarchy and women's political leadership position in Nigeria: Issues, challenges and prospects. *The Nigerian Journal of Sociology and Anthropology*, 13(1), 13–33.

Muhammad, U. A., Mani, M., Talif, R., & Kaur, H. (2017). Nego-feminism as a bridge between patriarchy and matriarchy in Zaynab Alkali's the stillborn and the virtuous woman. *Language & Communication*, 4(1), 124.

Mushfiqur, R., Mordi, C., Oruh, E. S., Nwagbara, U., Mordi, T., & Turner, I. M. (2018). The impacts of work-life-balance (WLB) challenges on social sustainability: The experience of Nigerian female medical doctors. *Employee Relations*, 40(5), 868–888.

Nnaemeka, O. (2004). Nego-feminism: Theorising, practicing, and pruning Africa's way. *Signs: Journal of Women in Culture and Society*, 29(2), 61–74, 357–385.

Ntoimo, L. F., & Isiugo-Abanihe, U. (2014). Patriarchy and singlehood among women in Lagos, Nigeria. *Journal of Family Issues*, 35(14), 1980–2008.

Nwalutu, M. O., & Nwalutu, F. I. (2019). The shifting feminine statuses among indigenous peoples: Rethinking colonization and gender roles among the WeppaWanno people of Mid-Western Nigeria. *Sociology Mind*, 9(03), 168.

Offiong, E. E. (2019). Language and discourse in Nigerian education: Historic implication of gender issues. *Society Register*, 3(4), 37–56.

Offiong, E. E., & Uduigwomen, G. A. (2021). Sociocultural values and children's rights in Calabar. *Society Register*, 5(2), 13–30.

Ogun, A., & Martins, U. (2010). Patriarchy and women under-representation in Nigeria: A case sudy of Buchi Emecheta's the joys of Motherhood, and Ngozi Chimamanda Adichie's Purple Hibiscus as lens into the live experiences of women. *Journal of Sociology, Psychology and Anthropology in Practice: International Perspective*, 2(1–3), 96–107.

Ogunola, A. A. (2018). Socialisation and the Nigerian child: Context and implications. *East African Journal of Education, Humanities and Literature*, 1, 40–46.

Okeke-Ihejirika, P. E. (2004). *Negotiating power and privilege: Igbo career women in contemporary Nigeria*. Vol. 82. Ohio University Press, Columbus, OH

Okobia, F. N. (2015). Curbing promiscuous habits among Nigerians through religious studies. *UNIZIK Journal of Religion and Human Relations*, 7(1), 167–175.

Okunlola, D. A., Makinde, O. A., & Babalola, S. (2023). Socio-economic correlates of marital status and marriage timing among adult men in Nigeria. *Journal of Family Issues*, 44(6), 1508–1524.

Olaore, A., & Agwu, P. (2020). Women in African marriages: Voice, visibility and value. In *The Palgrave handbook of African women's studies*. https://doi.org/10.1007/978-3-319-77030-7_29-1

Owoo, N. S. (2020). Occupational prestige and women's experience of intimate partner violence in Nigeria. *Feminist Economics*, 26(4), 56–88.

Oyediran, K.A. (2021). Intimate partner violence in Nigeria. In: Stith, S.M., & Spencer, C.M. (eds.), *International Perspectives on Intimate Partner Violence*. AFTA SpringerBriefs in Family Therapy. Springer, Cham. https://doi.org/10.1007/978-3-030-74808-1_10

Oyediran, K. A., & Isiugo-Abanihe, U. C. (2005). Perceptions of Nigerian women on domestic violence: Evidence from 2003 Nigeria demographic and health survey. *African Journal of Reproductive Health*, 9(2), 38–53.

Para-Mallam, F. J. (2010). Promoting gender equality in the context of Nigerian cultural and religious expression: Beyond increasing female access to education. *Compare*, 40(4), 459–477.

Quek, K. (2019). Patriarchy. In Shepherd, L. J. (ed.), *Handbook on gender and violence*. Edward Elgar Publishing, Northampton, MA.

Rasool, S., & Harms-Smith, L. (2022). Retrieving the voices of Black African womanists and feminists for work towards Decoloniality in social work. *Southern African Journal of Social Work and Social Development*, 34(1), 1–30.

Salahu, M. O. (2023). Politics, religion and electoral outcomes in Nigeria: The 2023 presidential election in perspective. *Journal of Administrative Science*, 20(1), 213–233.

Smith, D. J. (2010). Promiscuous girls, good wives, and cheating husbands: Gender inequality, transitions to marriage, and infidelity in southeastern Nigeria. *Anthropological Quarterly*, 83(1), 1–20.

Thomas, K. (2017). *S Masculinities in contemporary American culture: An intersectional approach to the complexities and challenges of male identity*. Routledge, New York.

Uma, S. (2021). Fidelity, male privilege and the sanctity of marriage: Examining the decriminalisation of adultery in India. *Women & Criminal Justice*, 33(1), 28–45.

17
WHERE DO I BELONG? FEMINISM, SOCIAL WORK, AND WOMEN WITH INTELLECTUAL DISABILITIES

Kelley Johnson, Emily Ardley and Alisha Gilliland

Introduction

Feminism, social work, disability are three complex and inter-related discourses which have, individually and together, affected the lives of women with intellectual disabilities differentially over time. In this chapter, we explore how changes in knowledge, values, and power in each of these discourses have impacted on the relationships and sexual lives of women with intellectual disabilities. We then go on to describe and analyse two integrated projects, based in Australia, Living Safer Sexual Lives (LSSL) and Sexual Lives & Respectful Relationships (SL&RR), which have aimed to support people with intellectual disabilities in developing and having safe and fulfilling sexual lives. We focus in this chapter particularly on the impact of these projects for women. We do this through the life stories of three women – a researcher (Kelley), a project facilitator (Alisha), and a peer educator (Emily) – whose lives and work intersected in the context of sexuality rights for people with intellectual disabilities. In conclusion, we discuss the learnings from the projects which are relevant in a consideration of feminism, social work, and women with intellectual disabilities.

In preparing this chapter we have considered the terminology used in relation to women with intellectual disability. We are very conscious that the 'label' given to this group of women varies in different cultures. We are using the term "intellectual disabilities" as it is the term used by Disabled Persons Organisations and self-advocates in Australia. However, other terms are used by other countries, e.g., learning disabilities in the UK. We have followed the social model of disability (Barnes, 2012) which informs the UN Convention on the Rights of Persons with Disabilities (CRPD) where a distinction is made between disability, which focuses on the responsibility of society to be accessible and inclusive, and impairment, which refers to a characteristic of a person.

Feminism and women with intellectual disabilities

Feminism, 40 years ago, was criticised as focusing on and reflecting the lives, interests, rights, and needs of white, middle-class women. Consequently, and as part of a broader feminist movement towards inclusion and diversity, women with disabilities were slowly acknowledged as one of the marginalised or excluded groups within feminist thought and research (Asch & Fine, 1992; Morris, 1996). It took a long time for women with intellectual disabilities to be included within the feminist discourse, and they did not have a heard voice in feminist writing until the late 1990s when some researchers and self-advocates began to assert their voices (Atkinson et al., 2000; McCarthy, 1999; Traustadottir & Johnson, 2000). Ironically, the lack of rights and experiences of oppression expressed by some women with intellectual disabilities were often contrary to the central rights being canvassed by the broader feminist movement at the time, such as challenging and escaping from the stereotypical roles of women as wives and mothers and exploring women's rights to equality in employment and society. The heard voices of women with intellectual disabilities demanded the right to have adult sexual relationships, including marriage, to have children and to be parents (Dhanda, 2008). Having a family or an adult sexual relationship was often very difficult, with accounts of oppressive social, family, and medical pressure and action preventing these women from pursuing relationships and families (Johnson et al., 2001; McCarthy, 1999; Monk & Townson, 2015; Traustadottir & Johnson, 2000).

At the same time, as women with intellectual disabilities were obtaining a heard voice in feminist literature, there was gradual recognition of the general lack of economic, social, political, and cultural rights of people with disabilities and of the difficulties they experienced in achieving them. This led to an international movement impelling the UN to initiate and develop the CRPD (United Nations, 2006). The need to consider specifically the rights of women with disabilities as separate from a consideration of the rights of people with a disability was raised in the discussions leading to the CRPD (Dhanda, 2008). The CRPD, in its final form, included some which were specifically directed at the rights of women (Article 3). Among the nations involved, issues of sexuality were highly contentious and the only article directly referring to them concerned the rights to marriage and to have children (Article 23). Notably, this did not include provisions in relation to sexual rights outside of marriage (Dhanda, 2008). The right to sexual relationships outside of marriage is a feminist issue for many women in various contexts, however, due to societal attitudes and disability service practices women with intellectual disabilities face a greater challenge (O'Shea & Frawley, 2020).

Social work and women with intellectual disabilities

Social work has been conceptualised as journeying with a tension that exists between two aims: that of "assuaging individual suffering" and achieving social justice (Maylea, 2021; Orme, 2003; Zaviršek, 2009). In relation to people with disabilities, the social work journey focused historically on care for individuals. Although this remains a necessary practice emphasis, social work has evolved to have a stronger focus on rights and societal change to remove the barriers of discrimination, negative attitudes, and practices which prevent people with intellectual disabilities from engaging in community life fully and in ways of their choosing. Historically, people with intellectual disabilities were considered as "patients", as unable to participate in community life, as vulnerable to exploitation or abuse, and, under the theory of eugenics, constituting a genetic threat to the community, should they have children (Walmsley et al., 2015). These perceptions were encapsulated in what has been called the "medical model". Social workers and medical professionals saw institutions as the place where people with intellectual disabilities belonged and, while support was offered to them in such institutions, their rights as citizens were rarely recognised (Johnson, 1998).

However, the latter half of the 20th century saw a movement to the social model, which makes a distinction between an impairment which an individual may have, and the failure of society to remove barriers to the individual's participation as a citizen in society (Barnes, 2012). This model is an important underpinning to the CRPD and places an emphasis on social work practice to focus on the rights of those with whom they work and on achieving positive societal change to create an environment where people with disabilities can enact those rights (Zaviršek, 2009).

For people with intellectual disabilities, issues of sexuality and intimate relationships remain an area of concern in social work practice, both in relation to working with individuals and in seeking to create a more just society. Turner and Crane (2016) note that previous research demonstrates that the sexual rights of people with intellectual disabilities have not been acknowledged or supported strongly by social workers and that further education of social workers and other professionals working with people with intellectual disabilities is required to address this. Sexual rights are particularly pertinent issue for women with intellectual disabilities as they are more likely to experience sexual violence or abuse than other women (McCarthy, 1999). Further, they experience the intersectional discrimination of being a woman and having intellectual disabilities (Didi et al., 2016), characteristics which may be complicated by cultural issues, minority group membership, or refugee status (Kakoullis & Johnson, 2020). Feminist social work practice provides a way of acknowledging and working with such intersectionality through recognition of the complexity of gender diversity and power inequalities, engagement with the intersectionality of gender with other identities such as class, race, ethnicity, disability, and age and with "a commitment to social justice, the importance of a critical and reflective stance on social work and the valuing of personal experience as political" (Wendt & Moulding, 2017, p. 261). However, some research also indicates a stronger need for social workers to include positive aspects of sexuality (desire, pleasure, identity) rather than conflating sexuality with abuse or the incapacity to be sexual (Wilson et al., 2019).

Feminism and social work in practice with women with intellectual disabilities

The next section of this chapter explores how feminist and social work values and knowledge have been used in research and community development in two integrated approaches to sexuality and relationships of women with intellectual disabilities. This section documents the involvement of the three authors of this chapter in two Australian projects, LSSL and SL&RR, to support women with intellectual disabilities to have safer and more respectful sexual lives.

Methodology

Participants

Alisha, Emily, and Kelley have known each other for several years, through their work in sexuality and disability rights. Kelley is an academic who has researched, advocated, written, and taught people with disabilities for more than 20 years in universities both in her home country, Australia, and internationally. Kelley's work informed the development of the LSSL and SL&RR projects in which Emily and Alisha worked together, for around eight years, and through which they forged a strong personal and professional connection. Emily is a performer and self-advocate and identifies as a woman living with an intellectual disability. Alisha identifies as a woman and works in paid and unpaid roles to build inclusive, respectful, and safer communities.

Life stories

Life stories are peoples' reminiscences or memories about past experiences as told to another person or persons at various points in time (Atkinson, 2018). They express who we are as individuals and how we got that way. Life stories are also cultural artefacts that provide in-depth accounts of how times, places, and experiences impact upon people's lives. We decided to base this chapter on life stories of our involvement in the LSSL and SL&RR projects in Australia because we felt this would effectively show how feminism, social work, and disability were interwoven in the work of the project. The stories reflect the ways in which our lives informed and motivated this work, with feminism and social work practice being explicitly discussed.

Ethics

The three of us (Kelley, Emily, and Alisha) are authors and participants in this chapter. This is a project that we all consented to and Emily, as a self-advocate, chose to discuss both the project and the chapter with trusted support people. Nothing in this chapter is published without the informed consent of all three participants.

Life stories

The start of the journey – living safer sexual lives: Kelley Johnson

I began doing research on people with disability more than 30 years ago and have since been involved with them as an advocate, researcher, teacher, and, most of all, a learner. My work with women with intellectual disabilities began with my PhD studies in social work which involved me in a feminist ethnographic study of the lives of 22 women in a locked ward in an Australian institution for people with intellectual disabilities. During the time of my study, the institution was being closed and decisions were being made about the women's futures (Johnson, 1998). The process of closure did not focus on the women's rights and although they were formally consulted, their voices were not heard.

As part of my research, I visited the UK, and a researcher there asked me what kind of sexual lives the women in the locked ward had experienced. I realised I had not given this issue any focus in my PhD, and, during my remaining fieldwork, I explored this issue in more detail. This led me to discover how important some women's sexual experiences were in decisions that were made about them being placed in a locked ward (Johnson, 1998). For example, two women were there because of the possibility they were being sexually assaulted by other residents when they lived in open wards in the institution. Two others were moved to a locked ward because they were perceived to be forming sexual relationships with someone, either in the community or in other open units in the institution. The great fear of staff in the institution was that a woman with intellectual disability might become pregnant, either through consensual relationships or abuse, and precautions were taken to ensure this did not happen, primarily by excluding contact with men who were residents, though male staff were not included in this prohibition.

After finishing my PhD, I decided to look more closely at what kind of lives women with intellectual disabilities had in relation to adult intimate and sexual relationships. I discovered that, at that time, there was little research in Australia on this issue and I, with colleagues at La Trobe University, gained funding to carry out a study which would explore how people with intellectual disabilities saw their experiences of sexuality and relationships. We undertook an inclusive research study which was called LSSL (Johnson et al., 2001). Before we started the research, self-advocates with intellectual disabilities were consulted at meetings about the usefulness and importance of undertaking this research. They were unanimous in thinking it was very important as they felt they did not have a heard voice in relation to their sexuality. A reference group of people with intellectual disabilities, government representatives and advocacy organisations were established to advise and work with the researchers who undertook the task of gathering 25 life histories of people with intellectual disabilities; 12 of the people were men and 13 were women. People in the reference group did not undertake the interviews as it was likely that they may have known the participants in the research. However, they advised on how and where the interviews should occur, helped develop questions using accessible language, were involved in analysing the life stories, and acted in films which made the life stories more accessible.

LSSL was funded not only as research but to create a practical way to share the findings, with the aim of supporting people with intellectual disabilities to lead safer and more positive sexual lives. A series of workshops was developed for people with learning disabilities, families, and service providers which used life stories to inform people about the lives of people with intellectual disabilities, their sexual rights, and issues. The workshops were used in Australia and internationally (Frawley et al., 2002). As a result of being involved in this research, people with intellectual disabilities who had been on the reference group became part of an advisory group to the Victorian (state) government, leading to a change in the law relating to the sexuality of people with disabilities which recognised more clearly their rights.

LSSL began with a concern about the lack of rights and power over their lives experienced by women with intellectual disabilities and the failure to consider their lives or their issues in feminist writing or campaigns. It also began because of concerns revealed by other research about the extent of sexual abuse experienced by people with intellectual disabilities. The study drew from feminist research and literature available at the time (McCarthy, 1999; Morris, 1996). It reflected social work values which give primacy to the rights of individuals and the needs for careful consultation with them about their values and desires. The study showed the value of undertaking research which involved people with disabilities from its beginnings. Their input both as participants and as paid members of the reference group for the study was integral to its relevance and usefulness. This study and its conclusions were carried forward and developed by some of the original researchers (including people with intellectual disabilities) into the research and action described by Emily and Alisha. This project led me to recognise the value of involving people with intellectual disabilities in research about their lives and the powerful force that their voices have in leading to change at both individual and societal levels.

Collaboration, growth, and friendship: Alisha Gilliland

This story is about the experience that I have had working alongside women with intellectual disability in relation to their sexuality rights and the prevention of violence, and the reciprocal meaning that this has had for me in my life.

I am a cis-gendered, able-bodied, healthy, educated, privileged, and married white woman. As a woman, I have had some challenges and many opportunities. I have experienced the great privileges of motherhood, education, and doing work that I choose and enjoy and am paid for. I acknowledge that many women with intellectual disability, some of whom I know, have not had the opportunity to choose to bear and raise children, to undertake rewarding paid work, or to freely explore and inhabit their sexuality.

I have also experienced violence, control, and abuse from a past male partner. Knowing what I do now about the dynamics of power and control, I don't believe that would have happened to me if I were not a woman. I don't believe I would have stayed as long as I did and put up with as much as I did, if I were not a woman. Learning what I did, in part through my work with women with intellectual disabilities, provided me with the insights and impetus that I needed to leave and never allow that pattern to repeat in my life. I feel that my experiences of violence and control contribute to the work that I have done and continue to do in the prevention of gendered violence, including women with intellectual disabilities in the SL&RR programme (Frawley et al., 2011, 2019).

The SL&RR programme is a sexuality rights and respectful relationships programme for people with intellectual disabilities. Building on findings from LSSL and undertaking further research with people with intellectual disabilities with a focus on their rights and strategies to prevent or deal with sexual abuse or violence, the programme uses a peer education model where educators with intellectual disabilities (with the support of sector professionals including social workers) deliver the programme to an audience of their peers. The development of peer education and community networks was an extension beyond the original LSSL project and is an important component of the current approach.

I found out about this programme through my workplace as a training opportunity resulting from the first National Action Plan to Reduce Violence against Women and their Children: First Action Plan 2010–2013 (Australian Government, 2009). I already knew Emily (co-author), but the SL&RR training is where we first connected as colleagues. I was interested as I had recently started a job – Building Inclusive Communities Officer in local government – that involved working alongside people with disabilities as colleagues and collaborators and, not having done this before, I wanted to build my skills in working in this way. The training was conducted over four days, with researchers and educators with intellectual disabilities engaging us – people with disabilities and sector professionals – through stories, activities, and discussions about the sexual lives of people with intellectual disabilities. The stories were real stories told by actors with disability, and they were used as a basis for conversations about key messages relevant to sexuality, sexual assault and violence, choice, safety, consent, and respectful relationships.

These workshops, in both approach and content, were a revelation to me. I had only a limited insight around the issue of gendered violence and no knowledge about how this played out in the lives of women with intellectual disability. I had no concept of the degree of exclusion, marginalisation, violence, and abuse that were experienced by women with intellectual disabilities and the degree to which they were disallowed their human rights in this context. I also learned to work alongside women (people) with intellectual disabilities, seeing them as collaborators, peers, and experts. This was not a way of working that I had been previously exposed to, and it was a game changer for me in terms of how this – and other work – could be done.

Initially, I undertook this training to build my skills, but once I'd been exposed to the injustice that exists for women with disability in terms of sexual rights and safety, I felt I needed to continue to work in this programme. This involved convening the Gippsland SL&RR network – a network of peer educators and self-advocates with intellectual disabilities, and workers from government, disability, health, and community sectors – with encouragement and ongoing support from the Deakin University team. The network members worked together to co-deliver SL&RR programmes across Gippsland. Gippsland is a large and predominantly rural region, so we met centrally at Gippsland Centre Against Sexual Assault (GCASA), also a founding member of the Gippsland SL&RR network, in Morwell, Victoria.

I chaired and undertook the administration for the network for ten years. The network met six to ten times a year, and we would deliver one or two SL&RR programmes per year to people with intellectual disabilities. The programme would involve four sessions of around three hours each and run over the course of four weeks, for example, each Tuesday afternoon. We used the same real-life stories and method (peer educators supported by sector professionals) as we did with our initial training. In Gippsland, we partnered with GCASA which enabled us to have a counsellor/advocate present at all sessions. This was valuable for the group and to support any additional conversations or referrals that needed to happen outside of the sessions. The network is now supported through a partnership of GCASA and New Wave Gippsland – a Gippsland-wide organisation of self-advocates who identify with having an intellectual or cognitive disability or acquired brain injury. Under the current arrangement, both the network and the programme are going from strength to strength.

To me, the wonderful things about this programme are its basis in human rights and social justice, and the use of a peer education model. It is so powerful to see the lived experience connection between peer educators and programme participants. I have often been reminded how important this is, particularly for people with intellectual disabilities who are not often positioned as experts or educators. I have also observed how a peer educator approach informs the work of sector professionals who utilise this insight into the lived experience of people with intellectual disabilities in their practice and who are committed to working with people with intellectual disability in an inclusive and empowering way.

Emily has been a colleague and friend for 14 years. We've worked together quite closely at times, on projects including "(it's no) drama" (Emily's current project and passion) and a job-share role at Deakin University, working in the SL&RR programme in Sydney. The latter involved a lot of travel, opportunity, and responsibility and was challenging for both of us, not only because of the amount of work and being away from home but also because of the focus on sexuality rights and violence prevention. When we work on people with intellectual disabilities, we know that most people in the room have had some with not on experience of control and violence, including sexual violence. Talking about this can be difficult and triggering, for both participants and programme facilitators. We are mindful of this and support everyone by working with GCASA, by debriefing and supporting each other and by getting more support (clinical supervision) when and if we need it.

GCASA currently have funding through the National Disability Insurance Agency to deliver this programme, facilitate the network, and train peer educators and sector professionals, and I continue to do this with them. Being involved in this work has brought many challenges – both professional and personal – but, as discussed later in this chapter, it has also been a source of great collaboration, growth, and friendship.

Standing up as a woman for our rights: Emily Ardley

Some people from Deakin University came and talked with some of us at the day centre I go to about sexuality and respectful relationships and people with intellectual disabilities. They were running workshops and one of my friends and I went to some of them. I wanted to learn more about standing up for myself and more about relationships. We learned about having safe sex and how not to be pressured into having sex and being comfortable with ourselves about sexuality and relationships. I think the honesty in the group and because what we said was seen as confidential was important. I am fortunate to have a close relationship with my family (my sisters and my parents) and an ongoing relationship with my counsellor, so I had previously talked with them but that was really the first time I had been able to talk openly about my own sexual relationships in a group.

At the end of the workshop, the people from Deakin asked if we were interested in working with people with intellectual disabilities about sex and relationships. I was interested and so were some other people. I decided to become a peer educator in the programme because I was really passionate about helping people with intellectual disabilities to talk about their experiences and to give avenues where they could get help. This was when I met Alisha who was helping to set up a group in our area. We started our own group in the district where I live. We did a session and we talked about what we might do in a group and what people might want to do. We planned what we were going to do. We then had a lot of training in Melbourne and Geelong which was run by people at Deakin University with some self-advocates who had done the workshop before us and who were working as peer educators. The training was about how to run a group about safe sex and respectful relationships, and we learned how to use the manual for the programme (Frawley et al., 2011) and to talk about the films that had been made and that we used in the workshops. We learned as peer educators how to listen to other people's stories about their experiences. Sometimes the work was really difficult because the stories were terrible, and they sometimes triggered memories and feelings from my own experience. I had a counsellor, friends, and family to help me with these things. Deakin University would help if we needed counselling, but I had people of my own.

I was a peer educator for eight years. I worked in my local area to support the network and we ran programmes for people with intellectual disabilities and services people to give them information and to support them. We asked self-advocates if they wanted to become educators and a number did the training and worked with the network. But we also went to Hawaii to talk about the programme at a conference, and we worked interstate in Australia to introduce and to teach peer educators. During my work as a peer educator, I learned about the very difficult lives a lot of women with intellectual disabilities have. They may not be allowed to have relationships, some things that they should know are put underneath the carpet and some rights have been taken away from them; things like paid work and equal and friendly work relationships, having sexual relationships that they want, and responsibilities as a woman like having children. A lot of women also experience abuse, and they think it is ok but it is not. Finding these things out made me want to stand up as a woman for our rights.

The good thing about this work was that I met new people and saw their faces light up when they were really happy, respecting everyone's identity and space. I learned a lot of different things. I found there were lots of different workshops run at Deakin where I learned confidence in giving speeches and how to work with people who might be upset. Working with Alisha as a team was really good because we were able to take turns and we knew when one of us was upset. We were always there for each other. I got paid for the work I did as a peer educator. However, it was hard to keep leaving my family and travelling was so tiring. I remember Alisha had to drive home one time and it was really, really late but we took our time and got home safely. Sometimes it was really draining working with people who were very upset about their experiences, especially when they had been abused. That was hard. But I would still do it again if I could. But I have moved on.

In the end, I found that the travelling wore me out and both Alisha and I felt that we had done enough. In my acting career, which I am doing now, I use the passion and responsibility and respect for each other that I learned from being part of the SL&RR programme. I lift people up when they are having a bad day and they come back and feel better. I learned these things through being a peer educator. I dreamt of being a famous drummer. One time, I remember thinking "why me" why do I have this disability, why couldn't it be anyone else? Now I'm happy being me because I'm awesome.

Reflection and conclusion

This chapter has focused on the stories of three women's contributions, from the interwoven perspectives of research, community development, and self-advocacy to the work and struggle relating to sexuality rights for women with intellectual disabilities. We have examined these through the lens of the LSSL/SL&RR programmes, and in the context of the social constructs and disciplines of feminism social work and disability.

Developing the life stories about our experiences through this lens was a powerful learning experience for each of us. We were awakened to the importance of people having information that is meaningful and accessible and to the power of hearing women's voices in getting change to happen. On reading and discussing these stories, they revealed themes about the impact of feminism and social work in relation to sexuality and relationships of women with intellectual disabilities. We discuss these briefly in this section.

Changing discourses

The life stories reveal the changes and the interconnectedness of the three discourses of feminism, social work, and disability theory and practice during the life of LSSL and SL&RR. The stories demonstrate the evolving relationship of people with disability, their families and support people, and of service providers in understanding and acknowledging the rights of people with intellectual disabilities to have relationships, to be sexual beings, and to have access to information and services that are inclusive of them and responsive to their needs.

LSSL began with a concern about the lack of rights and power experienced by women with intellectual disabilities over their lives and the failure to consider their lives or their issues in feminist writing or campaigns. It also began because of concerns revealed by other research about the extent of sexual abuse experienced by people with intellectual disabilities. The study drew from feminist research and literature available at the time which emphasised the importance of hearing women's voices on matters of concern to them, information about the abuse of women with intellectual disabilities, and the failure to consider their sexual desires and needs. It reflected social work values which give primacy to the rights of individuals and the needs for careful consultation with them about their values and desires. The study showed the value of undertaking research which involved people with disabilities from its beginning: their input both as participants and as paid members of the reference group was integral to its relevance and usefulness.

SL&RR has gone further; women with intellectual disabilities now work as paid peer educators to educate social workers and other service providers about their needs and rights and form collaborative relationships with them. These shifts, taking place within one long-term project, are a microcosm of those required to increase the rights of women with intellectual disabilities across society. Our stories speak to an evolution, through this work and similar work around the world of positioning those with lived experience as central in the changing discourses of social work, feminism, and disability.

The importance of mutual learning

While LSSL developed accessible workshops in which women with intellectual disabilities had a role in preparing films and resources, they were not active educators. However, SL&RR has made peer education central to the work. This has increased the power of women with intellectual disabilities through having paid work, and facilitating sexual rights education with other women with intellectual disabilities, supported by social workers and other professionals (Frawley & O'Shea, 2020; James et al., 2022). This impact is evidenced in Emily and Alishas' accounts of their collaboration, learnings, and friendship which have had positive impacts on both their personal and professional lives. Significantly, SL&RR involves the development of local regional networks of service providers (including social workers) and people with intellectual disabilities who support each other and work together for change. Our stories are also a reflection of the way our lives have intersected in a space of social justice through our involvement in the LSSL and SL&RR projects. We have aimed to use our own personal experiences and convictions to support the sexual rights of women with intellectual disabilities and to work for positive social change.

Individual learning

From the life stories, it became apparent that the learnings from working together on the LSSL and SL&RR projects were important for all three of us at both a personal level and in relation to our work. Emily has taken her learning as a peer educator into a career in drama, through her increased confidence and knowledge of how to support and work with others on difficult issues. Alisha sees her work in the project as informing the way she sees her own life as a woman and how she undertakes her work supporting women who have experienced sexual abuse and educating the community to prevent gendered violence. Kelley learned the value of including people with intellectual disabilities in undertaking research about them.

Continuing challenges

Challenges, however, remain. The life stories developed in LSSL 20 years ago remain powerful accounts of people's lives today and are still being used. This is a sad reminder that change towards safer and more fulfilling sexual and other relationships is slow to occur. Women with intellectual disabilities are still more likely to experience sexual violence than other women in our communities (Frawley & O'Shea, 2020) and the need for stronger heard voices of women about their rights and power in their lives remains an important issue (Celorio, 2022). From both the research evidence, and our own experiences, we believe that peer education has a critical role to play in changing life outcomes for people with intellectual disability in the context of their sexuality rights and safety. Peer education has been shown to increase the power and confidence of women employed in these positions, and the impact of the discussions and workshops as participants – both peers and sector workers – relate to the lived experience of peer educators. This is particularly powerful where people with intellectual disability are positioned as experts and educators and where sensitive topics are discussed.

Conclusion

In summary, feminism, social work, and disability are three complex discourses, the values, knowledge, and power of each having impact on the ways that women with intellectual disabilities are constituted by those around them. Despite the developments in feminism, social work, and self-advocacy movements in the last 40-plus years, there remain challenges to women with intellectual disabilities being able to fully participate in these and their communities and to lead good lives. These challenges are particularly evident in issues which are culturally and personally sensitive, such as sexuality and intimate relationships. However, the life stories in this chapter provide one model to facilitate positive change at an individual and community level by involving women with intellectual disabilities as peer educators and developing networks which bring them together with service providers in a learning situation.[1]

Note

1 LSSL and SL&RR included both men and women with intellectual learning disabilities. However, in this chapter, we focus particularly on the ways in which the projects aimed to support women.

References

Asch, A., & Fine, M. (1992). Beyond pedestals: Revisiting the lives of women with disabilities. In Fne, M. (ed.), *Disruptive voices: The possibilities of feminist research*. Ann Arbor: University of Michigan Press, pp. 25–36.
Atkinson, D. (2018). *An auto/biographical approach to learning disability research*. don: Routledge.
Atkinson, D., McCarthy, M., Walmsley, J., Cooper, M., Rolf, S., Aspis, S., Barette, P., Coventry, M., & Ferris, G. (2000). *Good times, bad times: Women with learning difficulties telling their stories*. Kidderminster: BILD Publishing.
Australian Government. (2009). *National plan to reduce violence against women and children*. Canberra: Department of Families, Housing, Community Services and Indigenous Affairs.
Barnes, C. (2012). Understanding the social model of disability: Past, present, and future. In Watson, N., Roulstone, A., & Thomas, C. (eds.), *Routledge handbook of disability studies*. Abingdon: Routledge, pp. 12–29.
Celorio, R. (2022). *Women and international human rights in modern times. A contemporary casebook*. London: Edward Elgar Publishing.

Dhanda, A. (2008). A sameness and difference: Twin track empowerment for women with disabilities. *Indian Journal of Gender Studies, 15*(2), 209–232.

Didi, A., Soldatic, K., Frohmader, C., & Dowse, L. (2016). Violence and women with disabilities in Australia: Is Australia meeting its human rights obligations. *Australian Journal of Human Rights, 22*(1), 159–177.

Frawley, P., Johnson, K., Hillier, L., & Harrison, L. (2002). *Living safer sexual lives: Workshop manual.* Brighton: Pavilion Publishing.

Frawley, P., Slattery, J., Stokoe, L., Houghton, D., & O'Shea, A. (2011). *Living safer sexual lives: Respectful relationships. Peer educator and co-facilitator manual.* Melbourne: Australian Research Centre in Sex, Health & Society, La Trobe University.

Frawley, P., & O'Shea, A. (2020). Nothing about us without us: Sex education by and for people with intellectual disability. *Sex Education, 20*(4), 413–424.

Frawley, P., O'Shea, A., SL&RR Review Team, & Wellington, M. (2019). *Sexual lives & respectful relationships training manual.* Deakin University. Geelong.

James, M., Porter, J., Kattel, S., Prokopiv, V., & Hopwod P. (2022). Peer educators in the facilitation of sexuality and respectful relationship education for people with an intellectual disability: A scoping review and narrative synthesis. *Sexuality and Disability, 40*(3), 487–502.

Johnson, K. (1998). *Deinstitutionalising women: An ethnographic study of institutional closure.* Melbourne: Cambridge University Press.

Johnson, K., Hillier, L., Harrison, L., & Frawley, P. (2001). *Living safer sexual lives: Final report.* Melbourne: Australian Research Centre in Sex, Health & Society, La Trobe University.

Johnson, K., Traustadóttir, R., Harrison, L., Hillier, L., & Sigurjónsdóttir, H. B. (2001). The possibility of choice: women with intellectual disabilities talk about having children. *Disability and the Life Course: Global Perspectives.* Cambridge: Cambridge University Press, England, pp. 206–218.

Kakoullis, E., & Johnson, K. (eds). (2020). *Recognising human rights in different cultural contexts. The United Nations convention on the rights of persons with disabilities.* Singapore: Palgrave Macmillan.

Maylea, C. (2021). The end of social work. *The British Journal of Social Work, 51*(2), 772–789.

McCarthy, M. (1999). *Sexuality and women with learning disabilities.* London: Jessica Kingsley Publishers.

Monk, L., & Townson, L. (2015). Intimacy and oppression: A historical perspective: *Sexuality and relationships in the lives of people with intellectual disabilities: Standing in my shoes.* London: Jessica Kingsley Publishing, pp. 46–54.

Morris, J. (1996). *Encounters with strangers: Feminism and disability.* London: Women's Press.

Orme, J. (2003). It's feminist because I say so!' feminism, social work and critical practice in the UK. *Qualitative Social Work, 2*(2), 131–153.

O'Shea, A., & Frawley, P. (2020). Gender, sexuality and relationships for young Australian women with intellectual disability. *Disability & Society, 35*(4), 654–675.

Traustadóttir, R., & Johnson, K. (2000). *Women with intellectual disabilities: Finding a place in the world.* London: Jessica Kingsley Publishers, pp. 9–23.

Turner, G., & Crane, B. (2016). Sexually silenced no more, adults with learning disabilities speak up: A call to action for social work to frame sexual voice as a social justice issue. *The British Journal of Social Work, 46*(8), 2300–2317. https://doi.org/10.1093/bjsw/bcw133

United Nations. (2006). *United Nations convention on the rights of persons with disabilities. (CRPD).* New York: UN

Walmsley, J., Ingham, N., Mee, S., Hamilton, C., Harrison, S., Chapman, R., ... & Docherty, D. (2015). Far more people were able to have sex lives: Sexual relationships and reproductive control in institutional care. In *Sexuality and relationships in the lives of people with intellectual disabilities: Standing in my shoes.* London: Jessica Kingsley Publishers, pp. 173–184.

Wendt, S., & Moulding, N. (2017). The current state of feminism and social work. *Australian Social Work, 70*(3), 261–262.

Wilson, N. J., Frawley, P., Schaafsma, D., O'Shea, A., Kahonde, C. K., Thompson, V., McKenzie, J., & Charnock, D. (2019). Issues of sexuality and relationships. In J. Matson (Ed.), *Handbook of intellectual disabilities: Integrating theory, research, and practice.* London: Springer, pp. 989–1010.

Zaviršek, D. (2009). Social work with adults with disabilities: An international perspective. *British Journal of Social Work, 39*(7), 1393–1405.

18
AN INTERSECTIONAL FEMINIST ANALYSIS OF AUSTRALIAN PRINT MEDIA REPRESENTATIONS OF SEXUAL VIOLENCE BY INDIAN MEN

Implications for social work

Jillian Barraud, Carole Zufferey and Helena de Anstiss

Introduction

This chapter discusses an intersectional feminist social work research project that explored Australian print media discourses about sexual violence in India. Using Carol Bacchi's 'What's the Problem Represented to be?' (WPR) approach, it examined how Indian men who perpetrate sexual violence against Indian women are represented in Australian print media, commencing with the 'Nirbhaya Delhi gang rape' in 2012. It is important for social workers to examine media discourses because they have underpinning assumptions and problematic representations of 'reality' and 'truth claims' which shape public perceptions of social issues such as gendered violence (Couldry & Hepp, 2016; Danaher, Schirato & Webb, 2000; McIntosh & Cuklanz, 2015), which in turn shape community responses. Media discourses are ideas or statements about taken-for-granted truths and knowledges (Danaher, Schirato & Webb, 2000). This chapter argues that it is a feminist social work imperative to support culturally safe and sensitive responses to gendered violence and to interrogate intersecting unequal gender, race and colonial power relations that shape media discourses about sexual violence in Indian communities.

The theorising of patriarchy by 'western, radical, second-wave' feminists as being universal, irrespective of historical and cultural nuances, has been criticised by Black, African and intersectional feminists who incorporate race, capitalism and Colonialism in their analyses (Bain & Arik, 2017, p. 1). The concept of Patriarchy is used in this research to describe hierarchical power and gender relations, where masculinity is privileged, permitting men's domination and the oppression and exploitation of women, contributing to the development of masculinised social structures (Bain & Arik, 2017).

Intersectionality was first introduced by legal scholar Kimberlé Crenshaw to highlight the marginalisation of African American women in anti-discrimination law and feminist theory and politics (Crenshaw, 1989; Romero, 2018). Intersectionality has been expanded in social work to examine how multidimensional and intersecting systems of power and oppression simultaneously privilege some and disadvantage others (Hulko, 2009). The intersectionality of Colonialism, gender, race, class and nationality (Hunnicutt, 2009) imbues society and the media. Media representations of sexual violence are manifested in complex intersecting gendered, racist and colonial discourses.

However, it must be noted that intersectionality has also been critiqued for the way in which oppressions are 'equalised' and minimised for the sake of a unified feminist approach that denies a critical understanding that all oppressions serve the interests of the ruling classes/elite in capitalist socioeconomic systems (Foley, 2018). As well, despite the scholarly contributions of Black African feminists, their voices are often excluded in social work debates about decolonisation and racism, they need to be included with the intent to disrupt the Coloniality of gender and Patriarchy (Rasool & Smith, 2022). Black feminist theorists often find that they are 'speaking into the void' (Crenshaw, 2011, p. 228) because 'power asymmetries and dominant imaginaries converge in the act of interpretation (or co-optation) of intersectionality' (May, 2014, p. 94).

Media research and the Nirbhaya case

The research reported on in this chapter examined Australian print media representations of Indian men who use sexual violence against Indian women, commencing with the Nirbhaya Delhi gang-rape case (2012–2017). In December 2012, a 23-year-old female physiotherapy student was gang-raped, beaten and tortured by six male passengers and the driver on a private bus as it navigated the streets of India's capital, New Delhi. She died from her injuries two days later. The attack gave rise to an uproar in India and around the world because of its horrific details, and the reported frequency of sexual violence in India (Himabindu, Arora & Prashanth, 2014; Kaur, 2017; Phillips et al., 2015). To protect the identity of the victim, the incident was dubbed the 'Nirbhaya Delhi gang-rape' (herein referred to as the 'Nirbhaya case'). Media coverage of the Nirbhaya case and other incidents of violence against women in India resulted in public activism and global protests (Hart & Gilbertson, 2018; Phillips et al., 2015; Roychowdhury, 2013).

Colonial discourses in the media

Violence against women exists across the world and the West, along with other racist forms of violence (Bain & Arik, 2017; Hart & Gilbertson, 2018; Ismail, 2020). However, colonial media discourses and ideas of orientalism perpetuate a narrative that it is 'cultural to use gendered violence' in India and that their 'uncivilised', 'third world' values are different to 'western', 'Anglo' ideologies (Hart & Gilbertson, 2018, p. 4). Orientalism is the process of 'othering' that results in oppression through lines of separation, differentiation, discrimination and the exclusion of individuals who are perceived to belong to an Othered group (Said, 1978). Colonialism is related to foreign invasions and the positioning of locals as socially, economically and legally 'inferior' through the assertion of 'superior' cultural assumptions and dominance (Reinhard, 2019, p. 6). As Adrija Dey (2019, p. 357) argues in her intersectional analysis of the Nirbhaya rape case, class, caste, religion and geography influence perceptions of gendered violence and victims and perpetrators in India. Previous studies have found that in the global context of asserting Western superiority and the institutionalisation of Patriarchy and racism, women are positioned as subordinate to men, as the property of men, and, at times, as 'deserving' of men's violence (Bain & Arik, 2017; Hart & Gilbertson, 2018; Ismail, 2020; Phillips et al., 2015).

Gendered discourses in the media

Gendered discourses about sexual violence, especially by Black men, can represent the perpetrators as being 'sub-human' figures who are incapable of being anything other than the product of their circumstances, reducing their individual responsibility and accountability (Anderson, Doherty & Ussher, 2008, pp. 81–82) and, thus, ignoring systemic injustices. As well, it has been noted that there are two dominant media portrayals of an Indian woman who is a 'victim' of violence in Indian society; either she is 'honourable' and 'virtuous' (but only when accompanied by a husband or male companion) or she is 'provocatively' dressed, 'out late at night' and 'behaving in a suggestive way', which invites violence (Himabindu, Arora & Prashanth, 2014, p. 3). However, Nirbhaya was predominantly portrayed as being an 'everyday woman' in terms of her middle-class status, whose behaviour was 'within the limits of normative femininity' (Hart & Gilbertson, 2018, p. 8), which arguably contributed to the global visibility and reporting of the case. Scholars such as Roychowdhury (2013) argued that media coverage of the Nirbhaya case presented the problem of violence against women as a battle between the 'new and modern' and 'old and backward' Indian culture. Violence was positioned as symptomatic of the backward 'culture' and systemic gender inequality in Indian society and assumed that 'gender progressivism' is 'rooted in the West and in normative middle-class Australian society' (Hart & Gilbertson, 2018, p. 3). These media representations of the Nirbhaya case in both Australian and the US media render invisible the prevalence and effects of sexual violence against women globally and the need for men's accountability for that violence (Durham, 2015; Hart & Gilbertson, 2018). As evidenced by the #MeToo Movement, gendered power relations exist in all countries and shape responses to sexual violence, which are reinforced by the media.

Methodology

This study makes a unique contribution to intersectional feminist social work literature by applying Carol Bacchi's (2009) WPR framework to examine Australian print media representations of Indian men who use sexual violence against Indian women. The WPR approach has primarily been used to investigate how social problems are represented in social policy and how governing by state institutions takes place through these policies, highlighting the politics involved in policy making processes (Bacchi, 2009; Beasley & Bletsas, 2012). The WPR questioning framework has also proven useful in analysing media discourses of social problems, for example, about homelessness (Zufferey, 2014). The WPR questioning framework asks six interrelated questions to interrogate policy or media assumptions: What is the problem represented to be? What are the underlying presuppositions or assumptions? How have these representations come about? What is left unproblematic? What are the silences? How can the problem be thought of differently? What effects (discursive, subjectification, lived) are produced by this representation of the problem? How and where has this representation of the problem been produced, disseminated and defended? (Bacchi, 2009, p. 2). This analysis commenced by asking: How is the problem of sexual violence perpetrated by Indian men against Indian women represented in Australian print media?

Sample

This study used purposive sampling (Gentles et al., 2015) to source relevant Australian national and state newspaper articles about the Nirbhaya case (2012), using the search terms 'Nirbhaya' or 'Delhi rape' or 'gang rape' and 'Delhi'. An extensive search of the *NewsBank* and *ProQuest* databases located 508 and 171 newspaper articles respectively. The search was narrowed to 22 national and state newspapers with the highest readership, which resulted in a total of 547 articles, which were about sexual violence in India more broadly. It is noteworthy that Australian media did focus so extensively on violence against women in India. After excluding duplicate articles and those unrelated to the Nirbhaya case, and filtering articles for relevance to the research question, a total of 16 key articles, published from 2012 to 2017, were included in the study. The media articles examined and focused on the specifics of the incident, including details about the perpetrators and victims.

The media articles and content were collated, categorised, sorted and, then, analysed using Bacchi's WPR approach (Walter, 2014, p. 255). The articles were subjected to a discourse analysis drawing on the first four questions of Bacchi's (2009) six-question WPR framework, namely: How is the problem of sexual violence perpetrated by Indian men represented in Australian print media? What are the underlying presuppositions or assumptions? How has this representation come about? What is left unproblematic? What are the silences? How can the problem be thought of differently? This chapter was confined to the first four questions of Bacchi's (2009) framework due to practical limitations such as word length.

The next section discusses the analysis and underlying colonial and gendered assumptions in the print media and how they came about. It then outlines what is left invisible or silent in these media representations, before suggesting how the problem can be thought of differently, to create a space for change and highlight considerations for social work.

Findings and discussion

This analysis particularly found that media discourses positioned gendered sexual violence as being prevalent within Indian culture and society. As social work scholars Rasool and Smith (2022, p. 3) note 'Decoloniality' means 'the complete transformation of structures of material inequality, discrimination, oppressive power relations, inferiorisation, and Western-centric and colonial epistemologies that also perpetuate patriarchy'. It is important for social work research to make visible colonial, classed, gendered and racialised media representations that ignore structural and systemic inequalities and the individual choices that men make to use violence, holding female victims and the entire nation responsible.

How is the problem of sexual violence perpetrated by men in India represented in the Australian print media?

This first question identifies and deconstructs the 'implicit problem representation' in media reporting (Bacchi, 2009; Beasley & Bletsas, 2012, pp. 21–22). The question is

An intersectional feminist analysis

intended to clarify and highlight what is being 'problematised', which invokes particular reactions and responses (Bacchi, 2009, pp. 2–3).

Colonial discourses about Indian culture

This analysis found that sexual violence in the context of the Nirbhaya case was represented in the media to be a cultural problem specific to India, where systemic 'sexism and misogyny' underpins the treatment of women, and the 'horrific violence against women' in India (Wallbridge, 2012, p. 19). Media articles also reported that India's 'degrading customs' (Dhillon, 2014, p. 18) were the cause of the violence which 'is a feature of daily life for [it's] women' (Elliott, 2013, p. 8) and prevents the country from 'hold[ing] its head up in the civilised world' (Purves, 2013, p. 10). When describing the events of the incident, phrases such as 'national soul-searching' (Dhillon, 2014, p. 18) were used to imply that the entire nation needed to reflect on, and refrain from, perpetrating sexual violence against women. This generalises the actions of the entire country's population and renders invisible the accountability of the perpetrators who were convicted of the violence.

When discussing the reporting of another high-profile perpetrator case of sexual assault in India, one journalist explained violence against women in India by drawing on essentialist ideas about patriarchal Indian culture:

> The culture still values boys above girls. The former are pampered and placed on a pedestal from birth. With exceptions, women are taught to be obedient and long-suffering, and to follow tradition ...Why their culture treats women so badly... why it produces men who dominate and control their wives... why women are blamed if they are raped.... why the male sense of entitlement is so powerful...why degrading customs such as female foeticide and dowry persist?
>
> *(Dhillon, 2014, p. 18)*

This explanation suggested that Indian 'tradition' and 'culture', rather than Patriarchy and the perpetrators themselves, should be condemned for the violence. When discussing systemic Patriarchy, this news article asserted that the situation in India has changed because women are more confident to report sexual violence, as indicated in the rise in reported rapes in Delhi from 706 cases in 2012 to 1330 in 2013. After the Nirbhaya case, associated with changes to sexual harassment legislation in the workplace and the policing of gendered violence, there was an increase in reported rapes. Although rape within marriage is still not a crime (Dhillon, 2014), the shame of reporting persists.

However, another news article by Doherty (2012a, p. 6) suggests that 'rape is seen less as a crime than a risk girls run growing up', especially in rural parts of India, implicating geographical location for the violence. This resonates with previous media studies that also highlight constructing these intersections between rural culture, 'tradition' and violence, which ignores the violence that exists in 'normative White society and culture' (Hart & Gilbertson, 2018, p. 3). In India, there are numerous intersections that may influence a woman's sense of shame and self-blame associated with reporting male violence, including other axes of discrimination such as class, caste and religion (Hart & Gilbertson, 2018).

Previous research has found that in the context of sexual violence by Indian men against Indian women, the notion of 'honour' can underpin media conversations, highlighting the extent of institutional Patriarchy in India where women are often held responsible for maintaining the honour and reputation of the community (Ismail, 2020, p. 52). Two news media articles by Dhillon (2014, p. 18; 2017, p. 26) suggested that gendered violence is associated with 'regressive' 'traditional' Indian culture associated with family honour, as exampled by:

> Regressive attitudes towards women are rooted in India's deeply traditional and conservative culture, in which women embody a family and community's izzat, or honour.
> *(Dhillon, 2017, p. 26)*

Akin to findings of other studies that examine legal discourses about izzat (honour) in India, these media representations position women as the 'subordinate counterparts' and the 'property' of men (Ismail, 2020, p. 52). Media representations about culture being the source of the problem are constructed as a 'truth' and 'fact'. For example, when referring to rape, police indifference, abduction and trafficking of women in India, Purves (2013, p. 10) stated, 'there is unignorable, statistical evidence of this cultural rottenness', which ignores institutional Patriarchy. Deficit media discourses about culture and violence draw on colonial discourses that can further encourage the 'discrimination and exclusion' of already marginalised and 'Othered' groups and communities and attaches 'moral codes of inferiority' to racial and classed differences (Krumer-Nevo & Sidi, 2012, p. 300). When referring to the current female leader and her colleagues in the Indian ruling party, Purves (2013) positions blame and 'shame' on women in elite positions by saying: 'They should be mired in bitter shame at their failure to make a difference to women below their own social and professional level', which again, renders invisible the accountability of perpetrators and systemic and institutionalised Patriarchy that absolves male leaders from responsibility.

Media discourses are based on assumptions that 'mainstream Western women' are not subjected to violence as are 'Third World women' (Hart & Gilbertson, 2018, pp. 3–4), and Western women are not positioned by the media as existing within a 'culture' or a patriarchal system. For example, in reporting on the Nirbhaya case, Purves (2013, p. 10) states, 'we in the West have the luxury of fretting about feminist issues such as magazine images, rude remarks and men not doing housework', while India's 'shame' is in the 'reality' that it oppresses its women, which resonates with discourses associated with violence against Muslim and Black women (Rasool & Suleman, 2016). However, the prevalence of violence against women is of global concern and patriarchal Western countries also oppress women. As an example, in the Australian context, the statistics on violence against women are concerning, with one in three women experiencing physical violence since the age of 15, one in five experiencing sexual violence (ABS, 2017) and, on average, one woman is killed by an intimate partner every ten days (Serpell, Sullivan & Doherty, 2022). Yet, this violence is not attributed to Australian cultural practices except when referring to the culture of Indigenous communities, again coming from a colonial lens. These misconceptions must be challenged, since violence against women is not inherent to traditional Aboriginal or Torres Strait Islander cultures (Our Watch, 2018).

An intersectional feminist analysis

Gendered discourses about sexual violence

When considering gender discourses about violence against women in the media, media representations imply that female victims of sexual violence are responsible because they are 'ambitious' and 'loose' (Elliott, 2013, p. 8), and 'too western':

> In the male Indian mind, a woman is "loose" if she has a lover... the sexually available woman is the foreign woman... the belief that Western women who are accustomed to living in what the men regard as a debauched and hyper-sexualised culture are fair game.
>
> *(Dhillon, 2014, p. 18)*

As bell hooks (2004a) argues, within neo-colonial white supremacist capitalist Patriarchy, the Black male body is perceived to be the embodiment of violence and this media representation about male violence in India reinforces representations of Black and brown men as aggressors of violence who are targeting Western women. Representations of violence against women in India also occur within specific colonial discourses that imagine 'brown women' needing saving from 'brown men', through intervention from an 'enlightened' West (Spivak, 1988, p. 91). These notions in the media of the 'male Indian mind' and women being 'fair game' illustrate how colonial and gendered discourses are simultaneously drawn on in media accounts of sexual violence in India, essentialising Indian culture and all Indian men, while rendering invisible broader systemic and structural power relations.

These media representations also imply that sexual violence perpetrated by Indian men is understandable because it is reported that India is 'a country steeped in foetus-to-funeral patriarchy' (Dhillon, 2014, p. 18). Colonial and patriarchal discourses intersect in media representations when discussing the 'crisis of male identity' in India, including when noting that Indian parents groom 'a sense of masculinity and male privilege' in their sons 'to have a feeling of entitlement' (Elliott, 2012, p. 8). Thus, media reporting about violence against women in India positions this violence within Indian 'culture' rather than as a man's responsibility, by relating this to their 'mentality' and upbringing (No Author [NA], 2013, p. 7). This idea that women's empowerment has contributed to men being 'in crisis' blames women and feminists for men's behaviour and draws on broader debates about social constructions of masculinity, where men are also perceived to be harmed by Patriarchy (hooks, 2004b).

Victim blaming occurs when the responsibility for sexual violence is placed on the woman herself (Ismail, 2020, p. 51). In the print media articles examined, the perspectives of 'experts' with 'knowledge' such as senior policemen and lawyers were drawn on, to highlight that women are blamed for being victims:

> Senior police are regularly quoted in the Indian press as saying women who are raped are to blame for their attacks - for being out at night, for talking to men, or for wearing jeans.
>
> *(Doherty, 2012b, p. 6)*

Another article reporting on the perspectives of the lawyers representing the perpetrators:

> The lawyer representing three of the men charged with the gang rape and murder of a medical student aboard a moving bus has blamed the victims for the assault, saying he has never heard of a "respected lady" being raped in India.
> *(No Author (NA), 2013, p. 7)*

This news article illustrates how victim blaming discourses persist in legal proceedings and noted that the defence lawyer said that the male companion was 'wholly responsible' for the murder of the 23-year-old because an unmarried couple should not be out on the streets at night (No Author [NA], 2013). These media articles highlight debates about the culpability of rape victims in India and the tactics used by the perpetrators and their lawyers to avoid the perpetrators being held accountable for that rape and murder.

In summary, the Australian print media generates and maintains colonial, gendered and racialised assumptions that, in India, it is 'cultural to use gendered violence' because it is an 'uncivilised' and 'backward' culture (Hart & Gilbertson, 2018, p. 4). Furthermore, colonial discourses are reinforced when the media asserts that 'Australia must help' India to become 'civilised' and change its attitudes towards women, assuming racial and cultural superiority (Wallbridge, 2012, p. 19). This 'othering' type of media representation does not acknowledge colonial contexts and violence against women and the colonial brutality against First Nations peoples within Australia (Our Watch, 2018), where similar representations are made of Indigenous communities. This analysis is important because media and policy discourses can shape social work practices and colonising assumptions can contribute to the systemic oppression of the Indian and other immigrant and Indigenous communities in Australia, which has implications for how comfortable Indian Australians and other Black and brown women may feel about reporting violence and seeking help more generally.

What are the underlying presuppositions or assumptions? How has this representation come about?

This second question from Bacchi's WPR framework teases out 'the conceptual premises' and deep-seated assumptions that underpin taken-for-granted knowledge and discourses about sexual violence, by tracing their origins, identifying practices that sustain them and considering their consequences (Bacchi & Goodwin, 2016, p. 17). This analysis found that Australian media representations drew on intersecting colonial and gendered discourses that essentialise Indian culture and assume that gendered violence is inherent to India. This chapter argues that these culturally essentialising media discourses are important to make visible for improving social work understanding and responses to gendered violence.

Colonial discourses

In the context of an extensive history of the European colonisation of India, these media representations of Indian culture can be linked to Said's (1978) concept of Orientalism, which includes the 'inferior' positioning of 'the colonised' in legal, social, and economic social institutions (Reinhard, 2019, p. 6). The colonial agenda was built on notions of 'racial purity and superiority', thereby justifying the discriminatory and oppressive actions of colonising countries (Reinhard, 2019). These colonial assumptions about India have a long history that assumed that the development of institutions and civilisation would be provided by the British to the Indians who were 'historically inferior' and incapable of ruling themselves (Dey, 2019). This colonial history contributes to the process of 'othering' all Indian people based on 'moral codes' attached to racial differences (Krumer-Nevo & Sidi, 2012, p. 300).

Gendered discourses

These media discourses have also perpetuated the notion that sexual violence is an issue only in the 'Third World', rendering invisible prevalence and effects of sexual violence in Australia and other Western countries (Hart & Gilbertson, 2018, pp. 3–4). Victim blaming and men's entitlement are perceived to be embedded in Indian culture, which perpetuates a generalised perception that all Indian women are victims of gendered violence at the hands of all Indian men. Nirbhaya was presented as a 'westernised' individual who focused on her education and was career-oriented, embracing a 'secular Western woman' lifestyle. She was becoming liberated from Indian 'culture', as opposed to having 'traditional' values or behaviours that are 'expected of a woman' (Hart & Gilbertson, 2018, p. 4). Thus, she was positioned as being partially responsible for her own death in the Australian media because she was perceived to be modern and respectable, but also, challenging traditional gendered and cultural norms in India. In contrast, Nirbhaya's attackers were described as 'newly urbanised [Indians]' coming 'from villages still almost medieval' who considered sexual harassment 'their male birth-right' (Roychowdhury, 2013, p. 283). This representation deflected attention from their accountability for the violence committed. This social work research shows how the history of Western colonial dominance combined with patriarchal power relations that reinforce male entitlement and the naturalising of sexual violence imbues Australian print media representations of sexual violence in India.

What is left unproblematic? What are the silences?

This WPR question aims to develop a 'sharpened awareness' of dominant power relations while identifying and scrutinising gaps in public and policy representations of social issues (Beasley & Bletsas, 2012, pp. 22–23). What is left invisible in these media representations is that violence against women and girls is not limited to India but is rather a global social problem existing in all countries and geographical locations. Colonial media representations of sexual violence as the consequence of a 'traditional', 'uncivilised' (often rural) culture and society imply that women in 'white, liberal and developed' geographical spaces (Hart & Gilbertson, 2018) and 'cosmopolitanism of Western cities' (Roychowdhury, 2013, p. 283) are safer, which is not the reality for most metro and urban spaces. If the blame for sexual violence is placed on rural geographies, cultures and victims, men's accountability for that violence will not be addressed. As well, patriarchal and colonial systems of power are not accounted for in media representations of violence against women. It is important for social work research to make these invisibilities apparent in its quest to analyse how race, class and gender interlock and increase consciousness about structural issues and power dynamics in all levels of society (Rasool & Smith, 2022).

How can the problem be thought of differently?

This question invites a critical analysis of 'pervasive and authoritative' assumptions in media representations (Beasley & Bletsas, 2012, p. 23), with the intention to create a space for reflection, resistance and change (Bacchi & Goodwin, 2016, pp. 23–24). This involves advocating for social work research and practice to acknowledge that colonial discourses and unequal gender and power relations contribute to excusing men's violence. Sexual violence is perpetrated in all societies and cultures, with women coming forward with their experiences of violence from countries around the world. WHO (2021) reports found almost one third (27%) of women aged 15–49 years who have been in a relationship have been subjected to physical and/or sexual violence by their intimate partner. There are important localised anti-violence advocacy and community-based initiatives being undertaken in Australia that could have been made more visible in the media, including by Indian Australian communities, such as the Australia India Society of Victoria (2021) Taskforce against Domestic Violence (2009–2013). Consistent with our ethics of human rights and social justice, it is important for social workers to make visible gender and power inequalities in society, in policy, practice and the media and to initiate and participate in social and community activism that address violence against all women. It is evident from the findings of this study that feminist social workers need to have a stronger voice in the media and provide accurate analyses that hold men accountable for their violence, to challenge media representations attributing violence to race and culture.

Implications for intersectional feminist social work

Social work activism across the world requires colonial practices and misogyny in society to be challenged, and that colonial Patriarchy to be made more visible. The Indian community is currently the third-largest migrant population group in Australia (ABS, 2020), the second largest in the USA and the largest ethnic minority group in the UK. These media representations contribute to the 'social humiliation' (Reinhard, 2019, pp. 5–6) of Indian communities because of their assumed violence and cultural 'inferiority' that apparently perpetuates violence against women (Krumer-Nevo & Sidi, 2012, p. 300). When a culture is unfavourably represented in the media, women may be reluctant to seek support to avoid bringing shame on themselves and their communities (Cramp & Zufferey, 2020). The shaming and stigmatising of women and men in public media discourses contributes to the underreporting of intimate partner and sexual violence (Stewart & Chandra, 2017). It is crucial that social workers are engaged in culturally responsive practices that challenge dominant media discourses that denigrate Indian culture as being inherently violent and inferior.

An intersectional feminist analysis enables social workers to challenge how colonial and gendered discourses intersect in media-influenced societal perceptions of Indian men, culture and women. Social work scholarship highlights that colonial state policies produce contested views about ethical practice and knowledge making in social work as a profession that reflects its white colonial legacy (Clarke, 2022). Given the media's influence on social perceptions of 'reality' (Couldry & Hepp, 2016), it is important for social workers to challenge colonising social practices that contribute to the production of particular types or categories of 'persons' or 'subjects' (Bacchi & Goodwin, 2016, pp. 13–26), which are constructed within historical and political contexts (Heyes, 2010, p. 159). For example, the 'subject' categories in these media representations include the 'violent Indian man' and the 'passive compliant Indian woman', which has discursive, subjective and lived effects (Bacchi 2009). Social workers can draw on alternative anti-oppressive discourses to challenge disempowering representations of violence against women (Piippo et al., 2022), to ensure that service provision is empowering, culturally safe, sensitive and responsive (AASW, 2020). It is also important to acknowledge intersecting unequal power relations (Tsantefski et al., 2018, p. 202), including how they shape media discourses about sexual violence in Indian communities. Further research about the perspectives of social workers and Indian Australian women and men, and their responses to these media representations, would build on the findings of this research.

Conclusion

There are conflicting discourses about the position of India in the Western imaginary where the mainstream media often associates India with 'colour, chaos and spirituality, where tourists flock to in their droves' (Poskitt, 2013, p. 21), while simultaneously likening it with 'a deeply conservative, patriarchal rural society' with ingrained misogyny (Doherty, 2012a, p. 6). This research has highlighted that the latter perception is prevalent in Australian print media representations of Indian men's use of violence, shifting the responsibility for sexual violence from the perpetrators to 'Indian culture'. This study has important implications for all minority groups, including the Australian Indian community, because media representations compounded existing language, cultural and systemic barriers to accessing victim/survivor and perpetrator support services. While acknowledging that white Australian social workers and social work are also embedded in institutionalised racist practices (Zufferey, 2013), social workers can challenge these media representations, advocate for social change and support culturally safe responses to gendered violence. The interrogation of Western media discourses is critical for social work advocacy, and to develop a culturally safe space for women victims/survivors who need access to services and supports.

References

Anderson, I., Doherty, K., & Ussher, J. (2008). *Accounting for rape: Psychology, feminism and discourse analysis in the study of sexual violence.* Taylor & Francis.
Australian Association of Social Workers (AASW) (2020). *Code of ethics.* AASW.
Australian Bureau of Statistics (ABS) (2017). *2016 Personal Safety Survey (PSS).* ABS.Australian Bureau of Statistics (ABS) (2020). *Migration, Australia.* ABS.
Bacchi, C. (2009). *Analysing policy: What's the problem represented to be?* Pearson Education.
Bacchi, C., & Goodwin, S. (2016). *Poststructural policy analysis: A guide to practice.* Palgrave Macmillan.
Bain, A. L., & Arik, H. (2017). Patriarchy. In D. Richardson, N. Castree, M. F. Goodchild, A. Kobayashi, W. Liu, & R. A. Marston (eds.), *International encyclopedia of geography: People, the Earth, environment and technology* (pp. 1–2). Wiley.
Beasley, C., & Bletsas, A. (2012). *Engaging with Carol Bacchi: Strategic interventions and exchanges.* University of Adelaide Press.
Clarke, K. (2022). Reimagining social work ancestry: Toward epistemic decolonization. *Affilia, 37*(2), 266–278.
Couldry, N., & Hepp, A. (2016). *The mediated construction of reality.* Polity Press.
Cramp, K. J., & Zufferey, C. (2020). The removal of children in domestic violence: Widening service provider perspectives. *Affilia, 36*(3), 406–425.
Crenshaw, K. (1989). Demarginalizing the intersection of race and sex: A Black feminist critique of antidiscrimination doctrine, feminist theory and antiracist politics. *University of Chicago Legal Forum* (pp. 139–167). http://chicagounbound.uchicago.edu/uclf/vol1989/iss1/8.

Crenshaw, K. (2011). Postscript. In H. Lutz, M. Teresa Herrera Vivar, & L. Supik (eds.), *Framing intersectionality: Debates on a multi-faceted concept in gender studies* (pp. 221–235). Ashgate.

Danaher, G., Schirato, T., & Webb, J. (2000). *Understanding Foucault*. SAGE.

Dey, A. (2019). 'Others' within the 'Others': An intersectional analysis of gender violence in India. *Gender Issues*, 36(4), 357–373.

Dey, D. (2019). India: The context of its current internal colonialism. In D. Schorkowitz, J. R. Chavez, & I. W. Schroder (eds.), *Shifting forms of continental colonialism: Unfinished struggles and tensions* (pp. 249–72). Palgrave Macmillan.

Dhillon, A. (2014, February 13). The women who've had enough. *The Age*, p. 18.

Dhillon, A. (2017, December 10). Beliefs failing women of India. *The Sunday Age*, p. 26.

Doherty, B. (2012a, December 31). Silence in tribute to India's daughter. *The Sydney Morning Herald*, p. 6.

Doherty, B. (2012b, December 24). Police under fire from furious protesters in India's 'rape capital'. *The Sydney Morning Herald*, p. 6.

Durham, M. G. (2015). Scene of the crime. *Feminist Media Studies*, 15(2), 175–191.

Elliott, F. (2012, December 22). Bus gang rape reveals India's misogyny epidemic. *Weekend Australian*, p. 10.

Elliott, F. (2013, January 10). Jyoti's ordeal needs 'to wake up India'. *The Australian*, p. 8.

Foley, B. (2018). Intersectionality: A Marxist Critique. *Science & Society*, 82(2), 269–275.

Gentles, S. J., Charles, C., Ploeg, J., & McKibbon, K. A. (2015). Sampling in qualitative research: Insights from an overview of the methods literature. *The Qualitative Report*, 20(11), 1772–1789.

Hart, C., & Gilbertson, A. (2018). When does violence against women matter? Gender, race and class in Australian media representations of sexual violence and homicide. *Outskirts*, 39, 1–31.

Heyes, C. J. (2010). Subjectivity and power. In D. Taylor (ed), *Michel Foucault: Key concepts*, (pp. 159–172). Acumen Publishing.

Himabindu, B. L., Arora, R., & Prashanth, N. S. (2014). Whose problem is it anyway? Crimes against women in India. *Global Health Action*, 7(1), pp. 1–6. https://doi.org/10.3402/gha.v7.23718

hooks, b. (2004a). *We real cool*. Routledge.

hooks, b. (2004b). *The will to change: Men, masculinity, and love*. Washington Square Press.

Hulko, W. (2009). The time- and context-contingent nature of intersectionality and interlocking oppressions. *Affilia*, 24(1), 44–55.

Hunnicutt, G. (2009). Varieties of patriarchy and violence against women: Resurrecting "patriarchy" as a theoretical tool. *Violence Against Women*, 15(5), 553–573.

Ismail, Z. (2020). The communal violence bill: Women's bodies as repositories of communal honour. *Journal of International Women's Studies*, 21(3), 50–63.

Kaur, R. (2017). Mediating rape: The Nirbhaya effect in the creative and digital arts. *Signs: Journal of Women in Culture and Society*, 42(4), 945–976.

Krumer-Nevo, M., & Sidi, M. (2012). Writing against othering. *Qualitative Inquiry*, 18(4), 299–309.

May, V. (2014). "Speaking into the void"? Intersectionality critiques and epistemic backlash. *Hypatia*, 29(1), 94–112.

McIntosh, H., & Cuklanz, L. M. (2015). *Documenting gendered violence, representations, collaborations, and movements*. Bloomsbury.

No Author (NA) (2013, January 11). Rape victim blamed: India – around the globe. *The Age*, p. 7.

Our Watch (2018). *Changing the picture: A national resource to support the prevention of violence against Aboriginal and Torres Strait Islander women and their children*. https://www.ourwatch.org.au/

Phillips, M., Mostofian, F., Jetly, R., Puthukudy, N., Madden, K., & Bhandari, M. (2015). Media coverage of violence against women in India: A systematic study of a high profile rape case. *BMC Womens Health*, 15. https://doi.org/10.1186/s12905-015-0161-x

Piippo S., Notko M., Husso M., & Carter A. J. (2022). Framing social work discourses of violence against women. Insights from Finland and India. *Affilia*, 37(3), 487–504.

Poskitt, L. (2013, January 6). Gang rape digs up can of worms – should it take a loss of life to say that other women should not have been subjected to abuses? *The Examiner*, p. 21.

Purves, L. (2013, January 1). Gang-rape shame could drag India into 21st century. *The Australian*, p. 10.

Rasool, S., & Smith, L. H. (2022). Retrieving the voices of Black African womanists and feminists for work towards decoloniality in social work. *The Social Work Practitioner-Researcher*, 34(1), 1–30.

Rasool, S., & Suleman, M. (2016). Muslim women overcoming marital violence: Breaking through 'structural and cultural prisons' created by religious leaders. *Agenda*, 30(3), 39–49. https://doi.10.1080/10130950.2016.1275199

Reinhard, W. (2019). Empires, modern states, and colonialism(s): A preface. In D. Schorkowitz, J. R. Chavez, & I. W. Schroder (eds.), *Shifting forms of continental colonialism: Unfinished struggles and tensions* (pp. 1–21). Palgrave Macmillan.

Romero, M. (2018). *Introducing intersectionality*. Polity.

Roychowdhury, P. (2013). "The Delhi Gang Rape": The making of international causes. *Feminist Studies*, 39(1), 282–292.

Said, E. (1978). *Orientalism: Western conceptions of the orient*. Routledge.

Serpell, B., T Sullivan, T., & Doherty, L. (2022). *Homicide in Australia 2019-20*, Statistical Report no. 39, Australian Institute of Criminology (AIC), https://doi:10.52922/sr78511.

Spivak, G. C. (1988). "Can the subaltern speak?. In Nelson, C. (ed.), *Marxism and the interpretation of culture* (pp. 67–109). Macmillan Education.

Stewart, D. E., & Chandra, P. S. (2017). WPA International competency-based curriculum for mental health providers on intimate partner violence and sexual violence against women. *World Psychiatry*, 16(2), 223–224.

The Australian India Society of Victoria (2021). *Achieving family harmony: addressing family violence, Australian Indian Community*. https://www.aisv.org.au/domestic-violence-project.php.

Tsantefski, M., Wilde, T., Young, A., & O'Leary, P. (2018). Inclusivity in interagency responses to domestic violence and child protection. *Australian Social Work*, 71(2), 202–214.

Wallbridge, E. J. (2012, 26 December). The beast in Delhi's belly. *The Age*, p. 19.

Walter, M. (2014). *Social research methods*. Oxford University Press.

World Health Organisations (WHO) (9th March 2021). Violence against women. Violence against women (who.int)

Zufferey C. (2013). 'Not knowing that I do not know and not wanting to know': Reflections of a white Australian social worker. *International Social Work*, 56(5), 659–673.

Zufferey, C. (2014). Questioning representations of homelessness in the Australian print media. *Australian Social Work*, 67(4), 525–536.

19
COMMENTARY - RESISTING CARCERALITY, EMBRACING ABOLITION IMPLICATIONS FOR FEMINIST SOCIAL WORK PRACTICE[1]

Beth E. Richie and Kayla M. Martensen

Commentary—anti-carceral feminism: imaging a world without prisons

Few social dynamics have altered the landscape of communities in the United States as profoundly as the buildup of a Prison Nation and the expansion of the carceral state. In this chapter, we will use the terms "carceral expansion," "carceral state," and "buildup of a Prison Nation" interchangeably. As the discussion will show, these concepts refer to the ways that ideology, economic policy, and legal/legislative initiatives have supported the growth of legal apparatuses associated with punishment. We have witnessed dramatic shifts in how this country understands, uses, responds to, and, in some sense, creates "crime" in contemporary society, from massive financial investments in law enforcement and surveillance technology; the amplification of deep ideological commitments to retributive justice; aggressive punishment regimes (including preemptive arrests); the swell in the number of the facilities that imprison over 7 million people (for longer periods of time, in harsher conditions) to the co-optation of major reform efforts, these shifts are comprehensive and well-documented. The impact of this shift affects the communities that have been the focus of social work attention for decades; those that have been the most disadvantaged by historical patterns of discrimination and social policies of exclusion.

Scholars, legal theorists, and community activists have used various conceptual frames to characterize this expansion of the carceral state. Included among those widely used and which have made it into professional discourse are the "prison industrial complex," "mass incarceration or imprisonment," and "hyper-criminalization." While there are slight distinctions between these concepts, there are three core elements of carceral expansion that are generally agreed upon.

First is the critical understanding that the buildup of a Prison Nation does not correspond, necessarily, to changes in patterns of crime. That is, the investment in *responses* to crime does not correspond to *actual shifts* in what is considered "illegal behavior," and in

DOI: 10.4324/9781003317371-22

some eras we have seen crime rates go down but the allocation of resources to punishment go up. This inconsistency is important because it helps to show how carcerality actually operates as a set of political commitments that are independent from data about actual occurrences of lawbreaking. Similarly, responses to immigration at the United States, Mexico border, the creation of punitive immigration law and the increased policing, surveillance, and captivity of (im)migrants do not correlate to actual migration data. In this way, the buildup of a Prison Nation, and its extensions, is as much a sign of our society's deep commitment to social regulation as it is to public safety.

Important to a critique of the expansion of the carceral state hinges on an understanding of how crime is more of a social construction rather than an absolute phenomenon. What is considered a crime is fluid, not static. Major examples of this include the legalization and decriminalization of marijuana, while countless people remain incarcerated or under state surveillance for marijuana crimes. With this, the simultaneous racialized rhetoric of drug addiction to more serious substances needing medical attention versus previous decades of criminal attention. From this perspective, crime can be understood as a social artifact that reflects political and social impulses, as much as it is something "real." With minimal effort or contestation, new laws are passed that criminalize previously legal behaviors, intrusive policing techniques are implemented, and harsh and/or mandatory sentences are constructed, rendering crime policies fodder for social control by power elites. Examples of this are found in discussions of the different treatment of powder cocaine and crack cocaine charges in the 1980s, the ways that nuanced crimes emerged in response to gentrification efforts in the 1990s, such as that related to broken windows policing, and how new laws and criminal legal policies emerged in response to attack on the United States by governments from around the world. A rigorous examination of what is considered "illegal" reveals patterns that suggest in many ways law and legal policies serve as an instrument of social control of marginalized groups rather than some neutral mechanism for encouraging safety and social order. Therefore, criminologists and other social critics discuss crime as a political artifact rather than something that is either absolute or consistently logical.

Second, the expansion of the carceral state is associated with a simultaneous divestment of resources from programs and services that would otherwise strengthen communities with their most significant needs. There has been considerable attention given to the ways that investment in punishment correlates with divestment in social services and human needs. When economic and ideological capital are directed toward punishment, surveillance, and control, then funding for health and mental health services, schools and other youth-oriented programs, transportation infrastructure, community-based service organizations, parks, and other public services decline in the communities that need them most. To this point, it is important to consider the role of privatization that is rooted in neoliberal politics, and how the state constructs relationships with private investors to help ease the cost of a punishment regime. This issue is both a basic financial question of where resources are allocated as well as a more nuanced understanding of what it means to fund *some* kinds of services—those that are linked to social control and punishment—rather than others that are geared toward expanding opportunity or creating equity.

Finally, and perhaps most importantly, "mass incarceration," which is sometimes used to describe the buildup of a Prison Nation, is actually a misnomer because the expansion of the carceral state is targeted, not random. It affects different groups in the population differently, with a clear predisposition to aggressively target socially vulnerable groups and those that politically threaten the system controlled by power elites. Race and class disparities are very well established when one looks closely at how punishment is applied across the population. In fact, there are few places where one can better observe the lingering legacy of institutionalized racism and settler Colonialism than in the carceral state (Davis, 2000). Continued carceral expansion to capture (im)migrants, transgender and gender-non-conforming people, people with disabilities, young people, and people with physical and mental health challenges illustrate both the power of carceral expansion *and* the ways that the carceral state is motivated by political instincts to control groups that threaten the status quo. This framing allows for attention to be given to the relationship between the buildup of a Prison Nation and heteropatriarchy, able-bodism, and class exploitation such that we see new laws targeting people who depend on state resources, the criminalization of gender non-conformity and the arrest, and detention of undocumented people in record numbers. The targeting includes the harsh punishments and unforgiving administrative policies, and the lifelong disenfranchisement or what some scholars have called "civil death."

Due to a long history of co-optation of social movements and resistance strategies that destroy efforts of true liberation, in the short and long term, it is important to emphasize our efforts must bear in mind *all* of the aforementioned characteristics of the buildup of a Prison Nation (1) that carceral expansion is not related to crime rates, (2) that the investment in punishment is directly related to divestment in other aspects of society that create equitable opportunity, and (3) that it is targeted toward the literal capture and metaphorical containment of Black and other people of color, Indigenous peoples, transgender and gender-non-conforming people, young people from poor communities, people with mental health issues, and other groups who are disadvantaged by institutionalized oppression, and as such, it is an artifact of social control and exclusion. Importantly, these three characteristics of carceral expansion make the work against the buildup of a Prison Nation ripe for feminist social work attention. It is the case that, increasingly, social services are adopting the logics of the Prison Nation and progressively building a relationship with the carceral state. Appropriately, we identify these services as *carceral services* that replicate the control, surveillance, and punishment of the Prison Nation, and thus punitive and social services can become indistinguishable. It is important to highlight the surveillance element of carceral expansion as it relates to carceral services. Perhaps well-intentioned, social services, and social workers who conspire with the punishment system assist the carceral state in the excessive surveillance that fuels mass incarceration. Accordingly, the distinction between well-intentioned feminist social work and anti-carceral feminist social work should be made. Indeed, some anti-carceral feminist social workers have been at the forefront of the struggle against the expansion of the carceral state, a struggle that has deep roots in a disciplinary critique of society's tendency toward social exclusion and ideological commitments to race, class, gender, and other forms of oppression. Taken up as a systemic critique, some feminist social workers have engaged to resist the buildup of the carceral state. A growing cohort has been working to organize community-based intervention services, advocate for community accountability projects, work in coalitions to build a broader systematic justice movement, and provide individual crisis intervention, restorative justice, and harm reduction services in cases where harm has occurred.

In the remainder of this commentary, we will bring forth the notion of "feminist abolition" and describe how the aspirational political concept has concrete, real-time implications for the work that social workers are called to do. Here, we will review the basic tenants of abolition praxis and point to ways that feminist social workers can work at the individual, community, administrative, or systematic level to embrace a more liberatory understanding of our work.

Feminist abolition praxis is a way of thinking about social justice that takes seriously the damaging power of the three aspects of carceral expansion previously described. It calls forth the need for an analysis of the criminal legal system that understands how it serves to create oppression rather than safety or protection. At the level of direct services, an abolition praxis means that intervention programs and advocacy initiatives must avoid even the most subtle or indirect reliance on the punishment industry as a way to restore equilibrium to individuals or groups. Alternative approaches must be developed that are not built on carceral logic and do not, even inadvertently, buildup the Prison Nation. Attention must be paid to those most affected *as well as* the larger network or community who experience secondary consequences of carceral expansion, so that social work intervention does not position "helping some get protection" against "creating risk" for others who are similarly situated. Self-determination and centering the lives of those most impacted by the work we do is crucially important when advocating and building alliances with the communities targeted by the Prison Nation.

At the level of systems advocacy and institutional change, feminist social workers working from the framework of abolition need to prioritize the work against the buildup of a Prison Nation. Prisons are not feminist,[2] and service is not liberation. Any work at the individual level must have a concomitant social change component that focuses on resisting the profoundly powerful carceral state. This mandate results from the analysis shared at the beginning of this chapter that shows how issues that social workers are typically preoccupied with educational access, health, and mental health services, ensuring safe public spaces, food justice, safe, and affordable housing, and so on, *in addition to the larger questions* of racial justice, gender equity, community empowerment, and the like, which are all threatened by the pernicious expanding carceral state. That is, the specific goals that we have as feminist social workers as well as the larger principles that guide our work are critically threatened if we do not engage with resistance to the buildup of a Prison Nation. It is here that we must begin any attempt to create safety, expand opportunity, or deliver on the promise of justice that we are called and obligated to do, and abolition of the carceral state and investing in the liberation of people and the power of communities will advance our work almost more than anything else that we can do.

And finally, it is critical that as social workers we embrace the philosophy of feminism, especially women of color Feminisms, that offers so much guidance on how to do our work. Being led by those most affected, understanding the intersectionality of oppression, resisting participation in structures of oppression as short-term reform compromises, and working at both the micro- and macrolevel will surely advance our cause. The chapters in this series are guided by these feminist abolition ideals. When feminist social workers are influenced by an understanding of the ways and the reason carcerality has been so prominent in the course of continued oppression, then the path toward a feminist abolition future is possible.

Notes

1 Permission has been granted by Sage and the authors to reproduce this article first published in SAGE *Affilia Journal of Women and Social Work* (2020) Vol. 35 (1), 12–16. DOI: 10.1177/0886109919897576

2 *Prisons are not Feminist* as a proclamation is graciously gifted to us all by the legendary Marianne Kaba.

Reference

Davis, A.Y. (2000). From the convict lease system to the super-max prison. In: James, J. (eds) *States of Confinement*. New York: Palgrave Macmillan. https://doi.org/10.1007/978-1-137-10929-3_6

20
FEMINISMS AND SOCIAL WORK
The development of an emancipatory practice

Jeannette Bayisenge

Gender and feminist perspectives on social work: theory and practice

This chapter aims to explore the contribution of feminist perspectives to social work theory and practice. To fully grasp this contribution, it's crucial to acknowledge the extensive and intricate history of feminism, spanning centuries and continents. Feminism is not a singular, monolithic ideology; instead, it constitutes a diverse and continuously evolving movement with various branches, perspectives, and schools of thought. Key developments in the history of feminism have revolved around different waves or stages. Chamallas (1999/2012), for example, outlines three generations of feminism: the Generation of Equality (1970s), the Generation of Difference (1980s), and the Generation of Complex Identities (1990s to the present). The latter encompasses emerging substantive areas such as intersectionality, autonomy, postmodern feminism, transgender issues, sex trafficking, and reproductive justice, among others. Contemporary feminism is characterised by its rich diversity, which plays a pivotal role in shaping its body of knowledge and approaches.

The critiques that one group of feminists has directed towards another have spurred new developments, including various Black African feminist and womanist perspectives (Rasool, 2020). Just as with feminism in general, African feminists and womanists are incredibly diverse. There are no homogenous Black African women across Africa and in the diaspora; their diversity is extensive (Rasool & Harms-Smith, 2022; Byrne, 2020). In reality, they may not be as distinct or separate as articulated in theory. Sometimes their agendas overlap and various women may come together to work on common goals, despite aspects of difference (Hyde, 2022; Rasool, 2020).

The purpose of this chapter is not to provide an exhaustive account of how every aspect of feminism has impacted social work. With the diversity of feminist perspectives, it is impractical to comprehensively discuss each variety and its contribution to social work within the scope of this work, although various other chapters in this collection address this (Rasool & Noble for example). Instead, it aims to explore how their shared objective of achieving gender equality and justice has contributed to social work theory and practice, with a particular focus on diversity and intersectionality rooted in Black feminism scholarship. In a general sense, feminists universally assert that women experience political, economic, and social oppression, but they diverge on the sources of this oppression and strategies to address it (Chamallas, 1999/2012; Dominelli, 2002; Levit & Verchick, 2006). Feminist schools of thought have developed a wide range of theories to understand gender relations and other forms of social oppression, addressing various socio-economic and political issues related to gender equality and justice over the years. This extensive body of work has significantly influenced social work theory and practice in its pursuit of social justice (Jackson et al., 2022).

A number of feminist practitioners and scholars have drawn on feminist theories and practice to place gender on the social work map (Dominelli, 2002) and to highlight its interwoven nature with other social identities such race, ethnicity, social class, disability, religious belief, age, and more (Bagilhole, 2009; Brewer, 2021; Collins et al., 2021; Livingstone, 2018; Rasool & Harms-Smith, 2022). They have recognised the diversity and intersectionality of women's experiences across social identities. Indeed, they advocate centring women's voices and agency in the process of social change and empowerment and expanding the scope of social work issues to include sexual violence, reproductive rights, pay equity, mental health, and more (Hyde, 2022).

It is clear that feminists in general and, in particular, feminist social work scholars and practitioners both from the global north and global south have played a major role articulating complex systems of oppression and proposing various strategies to resist it (Brewer, 2021; Caron & Ou Jin Lee, 2020; Rasool, 2020). They have provided alternative and contextualised approaches for social workers to consider regarding the realities faced by diverse groups of women and the solutions they generate for themselves that align with their specific contexts (Rasool, 2020).

To explore the relationship between social work and feminist's approaches, this chapter discusses the gendered nature of social work construction which cannot be understood without considering the complex social, unequal, and power relations of parties involved (Payne, 2014). In doing so, the chapter explores gender and interlocking social identities of both privileged and oppressed individuals and how their interconnectedness impacts their self-perception. It also looks at how they are viewed and treated by other individuals, groups, institutions, and by society at micro, mezzo, and macro levels (Livingstone, 2018).

Secondly, the chapter endeavours to shed light on the importance of women's lives as a source of knowledge. It also makes a general commitment to equal and fair gender relations with the idea that the daily experiences of all people matter (Siltanen & Doucet, 2008). Feminism has helped social work to focus on the issues of women discrimination as a starting point and advocated for a social order based on the notion that the well-being of people should be at the heart of the social agenda. Lastly, this chapter highlights the challenges that hamper the implementation of feminists' perspective in social work.

Feminist perspectives have brought insights in social work which influenced the theory and practice in many ways. The exploration of feminism as a critical perspective to social work has gained space in the literature especially since Lena Dominelli and Eileen McLeod published the book *Feminist Social Work* in 1999, and the process of exploration and development is still ongoing (Cubillos & Zarallo, 2021). The following subsections provide a summary of these contributions by focusing on how feminism has shed light on the gendered nature of social work (Foster, 2018; Hyde, 2022) and on how relationships within social work extend beyond the gender binaries to embrace the interwoven complexities of social identities (Bagilhole, 2009; Livingstone, 2018). The discussion will also touch upon how Feminisms have expanded social workers ways of knowing and understanding the social world and contribute to the reconceptualisation of the private-public divide. Through this paper we amplify the voices of women in the process of social change and empowerment.

Looking beyond the gendered nature of social work construction

Gender and feminist perspectives have been critical to social work, considering how social work is constructed as a discipline and a profession; the people and organisations involved; and the theories that inform the practice (Payne, 2014). Social work is socially constructed through interactions with all those involved and through the social context in which it operates (Payne, 2014). Dominelli (2002, p. 97) states that gender dynamics impact upon three key social work relationships: (1) practitioners and clients; (2) working colleagues; (3) employees and their employers. I can add social work researchers and research subjects, and social work faculty members and students to this list.

According to Dominelli (2002), the constant and dynamic interchange between these individuals continuously shapes one's ideas. As a result, this mutual influence makes social work reflexive and ready to respond to the societal concerns of clients. In turn, clients gain agency over their emotions and lifestyles (Payne, 2014). Furthermore, feminist social workers have underlined that discrimination and oppression extend beyond interpersonal interactions, permeating institutions such as the family, school, church, among others, as well as patriarchal cultural systems (Dominelli, 2002). The latter makes it difficult to permanently dismantle the subjugation of women and change structures of unequal power relations (Bueno et al., 2021; Connell, 2009; Rasool & Harms-Smith, 2022; Siltanen & Doucet, 2008).

By concentrating only on personal relationships, the construction of the problem ignores the role of internalised and institutionalised discrimination as well as systematised patriarchal relations on contextualising practice and shaping the experiences and expectations of men and women, whether as practitioners, researchers, or clients (Dominelli, 2002; Livingstone, 2018).

Indeed, feminist scholarship has examined the contexts in which social work practice occurs within the global framework of patriarchal social structures (Dominelli, 2002; Rasool & Harms-Smith, 2022). It urges a departure from assumptions about social categories and the associated characteristics attributed to individuals within them. Instead of endorsing preconceived misconceptions and stereotypes, it advocates for a critical approach that empowers practitioners to form judgements through a careful evaluation of the unique realities in a given situation. For instance, Payne (2014) illustrates this by cautioning against assuming that women are inherently caregivers for children while men are not, based solely on women's biological role in childbirth.

The feminist perspective provides a vital critique of ingrained societal beliefs as it challenges how gendered social assumptions affect relationships and social institutions. It steadfastly refuses to take the current social order for granted. Dominelli's work (2002) shows that by deconstructing gender binaries, social workers can concentrate on the intricate and fluid identities of women and men within various social divisions across time and space. Cubillos and Zarallo (2021) further argue that understanding social work intervention as a complex, constructed, and situated process opens the door to insights from feminist perspectives. These insights can provide interesting clues to address the complexities of social problems where many times standardised prescriptions and patterns of action are insufficient.

The intersectionality and diversity of women's experiences

Unequal power dynamics may appear straightforward when examining gender relations alone. However, the complexity deepens when considering intersectionality. This involves an examination of additional social divisions, with each intersection influencing and being influenced by other social identities such as gender, race, disability, sexual orientation, religion or belief, age, sex, socio-economic status, health, language, profession, education, and much more (Bagilhole, 2009; Brewer, 2021; Collins et al., 2021; Livingstone, 2018; Rasool & Harms-Smith, 2022). Over time, identity labels may change or be eliminated altogether, making some social identities fixed while others remain fluid (Livingstone, 2018).

Black feminists have emphasised the simultaneous nature of oppressions and the multiplicative effects of various social identities, critiquing additive thinking and parallelist tendencies (Brewer, 2021, p. 97). In the framework of intersectionality, the essence lies not in the sum of these social categories or multiple identities but in their interwoven nature and how they can mutually strengthen or weaken each other (Crenshaw, 1989; Pellegrino, 2009). These are not independent of one another. Instead, they are interconnected, multiple, interdependent, simultaneous, and mutually constitutive forms of oppression that manifest in various forms of discrimination (Bowleg, 2012; McCall, 2005). As stated by Caron and Ou Jin Lee (2020), it is important to recognise that when gender is mediated by these varied forms of identity, the effects and meanings can vary significantly.

Intersectionality stands out as a cornerstone in feminist scholarship (Davis, 2008). It serves as the primary analytical tool that feminist and anti-racist scholars deploy for theorising identity and oppression (Nash, 2008). Its relevance to social work is evident, given that social work is grounded in principles of respect for the equality, worth, and dignity of all people with the aim to meet their needs and develop their potential (Bueno et al., 2021; Cubillos & Zarallo, 2021).

The respect for diversity embedded in the concept of intersectionality has become one of the key principles in social work in recent years, reflecting its increasing significance in social practices, underscoring the pressing need to accommodate and understand differences. Consequently, intersectionality became an important tool for social work, amplifying the voices of those who are marginalised and capturing their unique experiences (Norris et al., 2013). It invites social workers to understand the complex interactions between different structures of inequality, to make them explicit and discuss them openly.

Analysing the distribution of power and its impact on social relations assists social work to formulate plans of action that eliminate the privileges and oppressions. Social workers should acknowledge the hierarchical social relations among all participants to avoid silencing, re-victimisation, the reproduction of stereotypes, and impositions during the intervention process (Cubillos & Zarallo, 2021). The recognition of diversity helps to understand and address the intersectionality of social identities, ensuring that support is provided in ways that are sensitive and relevant to the unique experiences of each individual (Orme, 1998).

Therefore, understanding the web of social relationships which interact over time and in a power context is of utmost importance. Understanding the creation and recreation of power relations within social relationships is essential for social workers' theorisation of oppression and privilege, as well as the development of alternative ways of organising daily experiences. Equally crucial is the identification of an individual's behaviours, attitudes, and positions as socially constructed (Dominelli, 2002).

Expanding upon the ways of knowing and understanding the social world

Feminist and decolonial theorists have played a crucial role in redefining the source of knowledge in social work, by challenging and subverting traditional notions of what counts as knowledge (Byrne, 2020). Particularly, feminists from the global south have interrogated positivist epistemological and ontological paradigms, reviewing and contesting established and reliable ways of knowing and understanding the social world (Brewer, 2021).

In this regard, African women highlight the imperative to integrate the voices of Black African feminists and womanists who have often been excluded in research and scholarship in the social work program (Caron & Ou Jin Lee, 2020; Rasool & Harms-Smith, 2022).

The various approaches to African Feminisms and womanisms, as described by Rasool (2020), are dedicated to embracing the knowledge production of African women, especially to generate self-defined understandings rooted in their daily lived experiences. Rasool and Harms-Smith (2022) emphasise the importance of identifying everyday lived experiences as sites of knowledge production and recognising the value of the everyday struggles, needs, and capacities of Black African women to overcome their oppression at various levels. The notion that women are the generators of knowledge has been a subject of discourse among Black feminist scholars (Twikirize, 2014). It acknowledges their ability to resist and navigate oppression across different levels and manifestations (Rasool & Harms-Smith, 2022; Twikirize & Spitzer, 2019). Knowledge, in this context, is co-constructed and emerges through a collaborative process of collective daily lived experiences, illustrating how women navigate and resist hegemonic oppressive power structures (Payne, 2014). This flexible and participatory approach to gaining knowledge, while being attentive to power imbalances, fosters openness, where stories and narratives are constructed and interpreted which is used as a source of knowledge to improve people's well-being (Belenky et al., 1997; Reinharz, 1992).

In the realm of research, feminist scholars have confronted traditional and conventional research methods that presume a neutral observer looking at a social situation from outside. Instead, they advocate for research methods that incorporate the lived experiences of active participants, involving them as collaborators in the research process. This requires researchers to build interpersonal relationships with the people being researched, rather than maintaining a stance as a neutral observer (Dominelli, 2002).

This new approach to creating knowledge challenges traditional understandings of professionalism that relied on the use of expert knowledges privileged as objective (Belenky et al., 1997; Dominelli, 2002). In traditional models, clients are considered having a lesser or inferior knowledge and their experiences become devalued, invalid, and less important. This perpetuates an inequitable dynamic within helping relationships. Feminist social work, in contrast, has sought to engage "clients" as key partners in the decision-making process, alongside professional workers. This aims to foster self-determination and ensure the objectives of social justice (Dominelli, 2002).

This feminist perspective rejects the conventional psychodynamic view according to which clients are driven by irrational and unreasonable needs, rendering them incapable of overcoming oppression or effecting change. Hence, the patients, clients, service users, citizens, research subjects, learners must be seen as crucial actors in achieving whatever outcomes are desired in the social work process (Dominelli, 2002; Payne, 2014). Furthermore, feminists have challenged the perpetuation of a singular narrative of abuse that portrays women solely as helpless victims, neglecting the multifaceted ways in which women come to make meaning of, resist, and negotiate their positioning (Rasool & Harms-Smith, 2022)

In numerous instances, the field of social work has inadvertently perpetuated Eurocentric perspectives which lead to the devaluation of local knowledge and practices. These knowledge systems and associated discourses often carry an undercurrent of conservative ideologies, effectively sustaining existing colonial power dynamics (Twikirize, 2014; Twikirize & Spitzer, 2019). As pointed out by Masson and Harms-Smith (2020), this dynamic contributes to the ongoing maintenance of Coloniality. To address this, feminist scholars advocate for a shift towards a decolonial feminist social work framework. This is not simply a recognition of diversity but an attempt to shift social work paradigms, research methodologies and practice strategies to facilitate a profound shift in how we understand issues and how we take actions, all while incorporating Indigenous ways of knowing (Caron & Ou Jin Lee, 2020; King et al., 2017; Twikirize & Spitzer, 2019; Uwihangana et al., 2020).

The core features of the decolonial feminist approach to social work education and practice encompass, among others things, the co-construction of knowledge to mobilise strategies that directly impact people through dialogue and often long-term relationship-building (Caron & Ou Jin Lee, 2020). To acknowledge African women's contributions to knowledge creation, Rasool and Harms-Smith (2022, p. 10) propose prioritising and embracing Black feminist epistemological strategies that challenge Western-centric dominance in authentic knowledge production. These strategies involve recognising the agency of Black women in knowledge generation, valuing lived experiences as significant sites of analysis and emphasising creativity and imagination. These approaches are particularly essential in social work, a discipline that frequently reinforces the status quo (Rasool & Harms-Smith, 2022).

Amplifying women's voices and agency in the process of social change and empowerment

The foundational contributions of feminism to social work aim to establish a more inclusive, equitable, and supportive environment for women. This is achieved by addressing the unique challenges women face and by recognising the value of their diverse perspectives and experiences. However, it is evident that the voices of women from inclusive social categories have not been given priority (Rasool & Harms-Smith, 2022). The experiences and voices of Black women scholars are still notably absent in the literature, despite their continuous and significant contribution to social work (Jackson et al., 2022).

African feminist and womanist movements, both within Africa and among African women in the diaspora, have emerged to spotlight the lived experiences of African women that have been obscured, erased, ignored, or muted, while prioritising specific notions of womanhood as universal (Rasool, 2020). They have challenged discourses that pretend to be universal such as the notions of "sisterhood" and a common oppression of women as this thinking masks and invisibilises privileges (Jackson et al., 2022). Deidere (2020) proposed ethical principles of solidarity, ally-hood, and respect as key alternatives to the unsatisfactory term and vague assumption of sisterhood. These movements create a platform for advocating the interests and concerns of African women and amplifying their voices.

Amplifying the voices of the marginalised should be done through a process of conscientisation that develops the confidence to break the culture of silence. Furthermore, it should encompass the unveiling of hidden narratives and experiences expressed through alternative forms that may be used when the lived realities, struggles, and suffering are represented. This could find expression through song, dance, and even through silence, dreams, gestures, tears, and so on (Rasool & Harms-Smith, 2022). It is by elevating, centring, and elucidating non-academic and everyday voices of these subaltern voices that entrenched power structures will be disrupted. To align with its ethical vision of social justice, social work must consider the cultures, points of reference, and experiences of varying groups of women (Rasool, 2020).

Furthermore, feminist and gender perspectives have contributed to the reconceptualisation of the public-private divide by linking women's personal difficulties, untold stories and social struggles to the public sphere. This shift has redefined private matters as issues of public concern (Dominelli, 2002). For years, the abuse of women and children in the family setting was considered a private matter seen as personal and not warranting public intervention (Rasool & Harms-Smith, 2022, p. 13). However, the private sphere cannot be considered just and neutral as it portrays how social structures operate and perpetuate inequalities at various levels – domestic, family organisational and societal levels of health, welfare, legal, educational, and other systems – which subjugate women's interests and often ignore their needs (Rasool & Harms-Smith, 2022). The perpetuation of violence against women as a problem confined to the private sphere and the notion that reporting it breaches privacy reproduced the silence of women. It also places blame on them by making the issue visible in the external scenario (Bueno et al., 2021) which makes the process to bring the principles of justice into the private sphere impossible (Cubillos & Zarallo, 2021).

In their study, Cubillos and Zarallo (2021, p. 24) emphasise the absence of fixed boundaries between the public and private spheres. They argued that the public and private are interconnected because the domestic sphere holds political significance and is of public interest, while the public space cannot disregard the unique aspects and interdependent relationships among individuals. Indeed, feminists have highlighted the gendered and intersectional nature of social relations in everyday life, encompassing private or family-based relationships and the public arena. Conclusively, feminists advocate for drawing on women's lives to recount their suffering, and document their stories, thus converting private troubles into public issues.

Reproduction and persistence of unequal power relations in social work

The International Federation of Social Workers (IFSW) according to Ornellas et al. (2018), defines social work as a discipline and a profession anchored by social justice, human rights, collective responsibility, and respect for diversities. While there exists a rich history of commitment to social justice, radical transformation, and social action, social work and numerous other social science disciplines have often been seen as instruments of Coloniality. They have, through their discourse and knowledge, perpetuated and sustained colonial racism and structural dominance originally established by Western civilisation (King et al., 2017; Masson & Harms-Smith, 2020; Uwihangana et al., 2020).

The historical roots of social work in the global north are intrinsically tied to global legacies of Colonialism, racism, hegemonic power, and imperialism (Caron & Ou Jin Lee, 2020; Harms-Smith & Rasool, 2020; Rasool & Harms-Smith, 2021). The debate about whether social work continues to be informed by and contribute to colonial logics is still ongoing within the profession (Caron & Ou Jin Lee, 2020). Feminists have pointed out numerous instances where social work, as a discipline, has been perceived as an oppressive domesticating tool for social control and an extension of Colonialism in various contexts and countries. In these cases, social work often failed to address destructive power dynamics within its own domain and in society at large, contributing to the preservation of existing structural dominance and power imbalances (Ferguson et al., 2018; Masson & Harms-Smith, 2020).

Feminists have played a pivotal role in challenging and deconstructing discourses, concepts and practices that purport to be universally applicable. Such discourses often mask, perpetuate, and fortify relationships of control and subjugation, ultimately leading to the marginalisation of particular social groups (Cubillos & Zarallo, 2021). They highlight the risk social workers face in creating "False Equality Traps" where women are assumed to have similar experiences of patriarchal oppression and access to the same opportunities as well as similar ways of knowing and states of being. This misconception may occur within social work or outside of it and can be perpetrated inadvertently by any individual, whether woman or man (Dominelli, 2002). Avoiding false equality traps requires feminists to reconceptualise power on various levels and consider the diverse power relations that can exist among and between women. Being aware of the conditions that create false equality traps is essential for feminist social workers.

Although the priorities, vision, and principles of feminist social work for a just and inclusive society may be justified and clear, the reality is that it may be difficult for social workers themselves to intervene to challenge and change oppression. Foster (2018) explained how even committed feminist social workers found themselves grappling with guilt over their perceived failure to consistently practise feminist social work. Despite subscribing to a theory and practice that endorses egalitarianism, well-intentioned professional feminist social workers can still inadvertently support oppressive social relations and perpetuate existing power dynamics and inequalities. This can contribute to the subsequent reproduction of oppression and unequal relations through their work, thereby hindering the attainment of justice (Cubillos & Zarallo, 2021; Dominelli, 2002; Payne, 2014).

The above dilemma results from unequal systems of multiple forms of discrimination, social division, and oppressive behaviours that are constructed, internalised, institutionalised, and normalised in both private and public spheres (Cubillos & Zarallo, 2021; Siltanen & Doucet, 2008). Individuals with oppressed identities and those with privileged identities can sometimes inadvertently contribute to their own oppression or perceive themselves as superior. This socialisation begins in early childhood and is shaped by social institutions, including family, school, mass media, churches, and state. Further complicating the situation is the fact that women often internalise ideas of their subordination and consider them the norm (West & Fenstermaker, 1993). For example, at the micro level, women may socialise children into gendered views that endorse the superiority of boys over girls from childhood to adulthood (Dominelli, 2002).

Feminists have also highlighted another significant aspect related to the diversity of behaviour. The notion that women are always oppressed and never the oppressor may not always hold true, as women can, in certain circumstances, perpetuate oppression among themselves. This oppression may not solely occur along gender lines but can also manifest across other social divisions such as race, ethnicity, age, and disability (Collins et al., 2021; Payne, 2014).

Expanding on the previous discussion, it is not unexpected for social workers to inadvertently perpetuate oppression, given that they are products of the societies in which they were born, raised, and in which they live. Consequently, they may occasionally fall short of their ideals when implementing social work principles of social justice. Like other members of their communities, feminists have been socialised to endorse social and gender unequal relations and challenging this socialisation became a struggle. It is important to reemphasise that the patriarchal system is powerful, hindering the easy application of feminist principles (Payne, 2014). In her work, Livingstone (2018) states that the formulation of feminist insights into social work might have overlooked the realities of the global systems of unequal gender relations in which social work operates. Social work theory and practice are constructed in an unequal and patriarchal system, making it challenging to embrace feminist insights and effect transformation and change in the oppressive social order.

In her research, White (2006) interviewed women social workers to explore how they identify themselves in relation to feminism. Four stances emerge: (1) A small group of women identified and aligned themselves with feminism and valued their identification with a specific school of thought; (2) Some saw themselves as feminist with reservations, seeing feminism as validating the importance of valuing women's perspectives in their practice, while not associating with political or radical connotations that feminist might have (3) Others saw themselves as not being feminist but drew on feminist principles in their practice. (4) The last group is for women social workers who did not consider themselves to be feminists and did not see themselves as drawing on feminist principles. This could be because their life experiences didn't emphasise this as a primary concern or because they believed that feminism didn't adequately address the different aspects of oppression. For instance, this is evident in the case of some African women who were concerned about women's issues and struggles, but didn't feel comfortable associating with feminism, perceiving it as Western, discriminatory, adversarial, unrepresentative of their experiences and perspectives, and a framework that had marginalised and alienated African men (Byrne, 2020; Rasool, 2020).

Furthermore, the examination of social work institutions reveals that the unequal social relationships, which feminists have critically scrutinised for an extended period, have not significantly evolved, even though feminist ideas were not directly contested by the discipline or these institutions. For example, despite the tendency to define social work as a women's profession (Caron & Ou Jin Lee, 2020), women do not control it. Criticisms of the lack of women in senior positions in social work organisations in proportion to the number of women in the organisation and in universities, in ongoing. However, this remains commonplace in almost all workplaces (Dominelli, 2002). In their article "Taking Back the Narrative: Gendered Anti-Blackness in Predominantly White Schools of Social Work", Jackson et al. (2022) and her colleagues narrated how the representation of Black women is still not prioritised. They continue to be underrepresented both as students and faculty. They face numerous challenges stemming from their multiple marginalised statuses related to race and gender. As research shows, in many organisations, decision-making processes and policy formulation remain firmly under men's control, while women are left with caring responsibilities as the commanding heights of managerial hierarchies are still dominated by men (Dominelli, 2002; White, 2006).

While acknowledging the described challenges, it is important to recognise that social work has the potential to position itself as a discipline that generates knowledge and practical skills capable of reducing discrimination. It can actively engage in the reconstruction and transformation journey toward social justice. Social workers can strengthen their role as allies by acknowledging the systemic nature of problems, actively listening to and working with those in need, and forming partnerships with collective movements that challenge unequal systems and harmful policies (Deepak, 2020).

Conclusion

Reflecting on the discussion about feminism's contributions to social work theory and practice, it becomes evident that social work is a socially constructed field. Recognising this contribution necessitates an understanding of the diversity within the body of feminist knowledge and how this diversity operates in the field of social work. Feminism, with its multifaceted strands, has significantly influenced social work by highlighting and addressing different sources of inequalities and oppression present in both theories and practice. The challenges and contributions posed by feminists have been particularly intriguing and vital because they often align with values and principles of social work related to social justice.

Feminists have championed the recognition of private matters as social problems, challenging the rigid public-private divide. They have been instrumental in amplifying the voices and narratives of marginalised women, contributing to a more comprehensive understanding of the insidious nature of unequal gender relations. They advocated for a redefinition of a profession and discipline, valuing lived experiences as a source of knowledge and embracing anti-oppressive approaches in practice. These feminist critiques have exerted a significant influence on the development of social work theory, reshaping the sources of knowledge, practice, and research towards more egalitarian and power-sharing orientations. In this transformation, feminists have played a central role by placing gender relations prominently on the social work agenda and emphasising the interconnections with other social identities. They also call for the acknowledgement of the broader social context and the dominant narratives of white supremacy and Patriarchy that perpetuate disparities.

Furthermore, the significant contributions of Black women to the field of social work still need to be recognised as their voices and experiences are often marginalised. This neglect has had adverse effects on the career paths and experiences of Black women. Although feminists have introduced innovative concepts to the social work profession and discipline, the implementation of substantial changes has been sluggish. Integrating these insights has encountered obstacles due to the entrenched structural inequalities within which social work is rooted and operates.

Transformative change and empowering women to take control of their lives and make their voices heard must involve challenging patriarchal structures, dismantling complex systems of discrimination, and deconstructing gender and social identity categories related to oppression and privilege. The feminist debate has allowed for the development of emancipatory practices that provide a more nuanced understanding of intervention contexts, moving away from standardised discourses and their uncritical application. It is my hope that these reflections will continue to foster more critical perspectives, ultimately leading to anti-oppressive, inclusive, and emancipatory forms of social work that ensure justice for all, leaving no one behind.

References

Bagilhole, B. M. (2009). For diversity against discrimination: From gender mainstreaming, through multiple discrimination, to intersectionality. In Franken, M., Woodward, A., Cabó, A., & Bagilhole, B. M. (Eds.), *Teaching intersectionality: Putting gender at the centre* (pp. 45–52). Utrecht, Athena: Zuidam Uithof Drukkerijen.

Belenky, M., Clinchy, B. M., Goldberger, N. R., & Tarule, J. M. (1997). *Women's ways of knowing: The development of self, voice, and mind.* New York: Basic Books.

Bowleg, L. (2012). The problem with the phrase women and minorities: Intersectionality – an important theoretical framework for Public Health. *American Journal of Public Health, 102*(7), 1267–1273. doi: 10.2105/AJPH.2012.300750

Brewer, M. R. (2021). Black feminism and womanism. In Naples, N. A. (Ed.), *Companion to feminist studies* (pp. 91–104). Wiley-Blackwell, 1st edition. West Sussex: The Atrium, Southern Gate.

Bueno, A. M., Florián, M., & Chinchilla, D. (2021). Feminist reflections on social work intervention with women experiencing violence in Bogota. *Propuestas Críticas en Trabajo Social – Critical Proposals in Social Work, 1*(2), 139–163. https://doi.org/10.5354/2735-6620.2021.64323

Byrne, D. (2020). Decolonial African feminism for white allies. *Journal of International Women's Studies, 21*(7), 37–46. Available at: https://vc.bridgew.edu/jiws/vol21/iss7/4

Caron, R. & Ou Jin Lee, E. (2020). Towards a decolonial feminist approach to social work education and practice. In Kleibl, T., Lutz, R., Noyoo, N., Bunk, B., Dittmann, A., & Seepamore, B. (Eds.), *The Routledge handbook of post-colonial social work* (pp. 71–87). Oxon: Routledge.

Chamallas (1999/2012). *Introduction to feminist legal theory* (3rd ed.). New York: Aspen Publishers, Inc, Legal Education Division.

Collins, P. H., da Silva, E. C. G., Ergun, E., Furseth, I., Bond, K. D., & Martinez-Palacios, J. (2021). Intersectionality as critical social theory. *Contemporary Political Theory, 20*(3), 690–725. https://doi.org/10.1057/s41296-021-00490-0

Connell, R. (2009). *Gender: Short introductions* (2nd ed.). Cambridge: Polity Press.

Crenshaw, K. (1989). Demarginalizing the intersection of race and sex: A black feminist critique of antidiscrimination doctrine. *Feminist Theory and Antiracist Politics*, University of Chicago Legal Forum, *1*(8), 139–167.

Cubillos, A. J. & Zarallo, V. C. (2021). Feminist counterpoints in the ethical debate and its possibilities for social work. *Propuestas Críticas en Trabajo Social – Critical Proposals in Social Work, 1*(2), 10–30. https://doi.org/10.5354/2735-6620.2021.60952

Davis, K. (2008). Intersectionality as buzzword: A sociology of science perspective on what makes a feminist theory successful. *Feminist Theory, 9*(1), 67–85.

Deepak, A. C. (2020). Orientations from social movements: A postcolonial feminist social work perspective on human trafficking. In Kleibl, T., Lutz, R., Noyoo, N., Bunk, B., Dittmann, A., & Seepamore B. (Eds.), *The Routledge handbook of post-colonial social work* (pp. 102–112). Oxon: Routledge.

Dominelli, L. (2002). *Feminist social work theory and practice*. New York: Palgrave Publishers.

Ferguson, I., Ioakimidis, V. & Lavalette, M. (2018). *Global social work in a political context; Radical perspectives*. Bristol: Bristol University Press.

Foster, J. (2018). Key feminist theoretical orientations in contemporary feminist practice. In Butler-Mokoro, S. & Grant, L. (Eds.), *Feminist perspectives on social work practice: The intersecting lives of women in the twenty- first century* (pp. 33–58). Madison Avenue, NY: Oxford University Press.

Hyde, C. (2022). *Feminist macro social work practice*. Encyclopedia of social work. https://doi.org/10.1093/acrefore/9780199975839.013.151

Jackson, F. K., Mitchell, M. F., Nwabuzor Ogbonnaya, I., Mackey, C., Crudup, C., & Turnlund Carver, A. (2022). Taking back the narrative: Gendered anti-Blackness in predominantly white schools of social work. *Affilia: Feminist Inquiry in Social Work, 37*(4), 565–584. https://doi.org/10.1177/08861099221099322

King, U. R., Bokore, N., & Dudziak, S. (2017). The significance of indigenous knowledge in social work responses to collective recovery: A Rwandan case study. *Journal of Indigenous Social Development, 6*(1), 37–63.

Levit, N. & Verchick, R. (2006). *Feminist legal theory: A primer*. New York and London: New York University Press.

Livingstone, A. (2018). Privilege, oppression, and the intersections: The many faces of gender and identity. In Butler-Mokoro, S. & Grant, L. (Eds.), *Feminist perspectives on social work practice: The intersecting lives of women in the twenty- first century* (pp. 59–83). Madison Avenue, NY: Oxford University Press.

Masson, F. & Harms-Smith, L. (2020). Colonisation as collective trauma: Fundamental perspectives for social work. In Kleibl, T., Lutz, R., Noyoo, N., Bunk, N., Dittmann, A., & Seepamore, B. (Eds.), *The Routledge handbook of post-colonial social work* (pp. 13–26). Oxon: Routledge.

McCall, L. (2005). The complexity of intersectionality. *Signs: Journal of women in Culture and Society, 30*(3), 1771–1800.

Nash, C. J. (2008). Re-thinking intersectionality. *Feminist Review, 89*, 1–15.

Norris, A., Murphy-Erby, Y., Green, A., Willis, K., & Jones, T. (2013). An intersectional exploration: The experiences of southern, rural, Black and white women participating in an empowerment-based entrepreneurial program. *Intersectionalities: A Global Journal of Social Work Analysis, Research, Polity, and Practice, 2*, 88–106.

Orme, J. (1998). Feminist social work. In Adams, R., Dominelli, R. L., Payne, M., & Campling, J. (Eds.), *Social work* (pp. 218–228). London: Palgrave. https://doi.org/10.1007/978-1-349-14400-6_18

Ornellas, A., Spolander, G., & Engelbrecht, L. K. (2018). The global social work definition: Ontology, implications and challenges. *Journal of Social Work, 18*(2), 222–240. https://doi.org/10.1177/1468017316654606

Payne, M. (2014). *Modern social work theory* (4th ed.). Oxford University Press. Original work published in 1991.

Pellegrino, G. (2009). An Intersectional Approach to Gender and Communication: Beyond the 'Media Gaze'? In Franken, M., Woodward, A., Cabó, A., & Bagilhole, B. M. (Eds.), *Teaching Intersectionality: Putting Gender at the Centre* (pp. 89–100). Utrecht, Athena: Zuidam Uithof Drukkerijen.

Rasool, S. (2020). Heterogeneity of social movements addressing the intersections of gender and race: A reflection on feminisms and womanisms emerging from African women. In Kleibl, T., Lutz, R., Noyoo, N., Bunk, B., Dittmann, A., & Seepamore, B. (Eds.), *The Routledge handbook of post-colonial social work* (pp. 127–136). Oxon: Routledge.

Rasool, S. & Harms-Smith, L. (2022). Retrieving the voices of Black African womanists and feminists for work towards decoloniality in social work. *Southern African Journal of Social Work and Social Development, 34*(1), 1–30.

Rasool, S., & Harms-Smith, L. (2021). Towards decoloniality in a social work programme: A process of dialogue, reflexivity, action and change. *Critical African Studies –Decolonizing African Studies, 13*(1), 56–72.

Reinharz, S. (1992). *Feminist methods in social research*. Oxford: Oxford University Press.

Siltanen, J. & Doucet, A. (2008). *Gender relations in Canada: Intersectionality and beyond*. Toronto: Oxford University Press.

Twikirize J. M. (2014). Indigenisation of social work in Africa: Debates, prospects and challenges. In: Spitzer, H., Twikirize, J. M., & Wairire, G. G. (Eds.), *Professional social work in East Africa. Towards social development, poverty reduction and gender equality* (pp. 75–90). Kampala: Fountain.

Twikirize, J. M. & Spitzer, H. (2019). *Social work practice in Africa Indigenous and innovative approaches*. Fountain Publishers. ISBN: 978-9970-617-92-0

Uwihangana, C., Hakizamungu, A., Rutikanga, C., Bangwanubusa, T., & Kalinganire, C. (2020). *Social work practice in rwanda: Indigenous and innovative models of problem solving*. Kampala: Fountain Publishers.

West, C. & Fenstermaker, S. (1993). Power, inequality and accomplishment of gender: An ethnomethodological view. In England, P. (Ed.), *Theory on gender. Feminism on theory* (pp. 151–174). New York: Aldine De Gruyter.

White, V. (2006). *The state of feminist social work*. New York: Routledge-Taylor & Francis.

SECTION 3
Academy and feminist research

21
KNOWING SUBJECTS? FEMINIST EPISTEMOLOGIES, POWER STRUGGLES AND SOCIAL WORK RESEARCH

Stephen Hicks

Introduction

Why should epistemological questions matter to social workers and to feminist social work research? Are the debates about what counts as knowledge really so important? And what does 'epistemology' mean? According to Stanley, epistemology 'deals with foundational issues in knowing, including who knows, under what conditions, using what criteria, with what challenges and counter-claims, and whether certain or absolute knowledge of the social world can be gained' (2019, p. 96). Such questions are important to feminist social work because they consider where knowledge comes from and seek to challenge the potentially oppressive nature of 'common sense' views (Bell, 2014; Clarke, 2022; Trinder, 2000). In addition, these provocations apply not only to evidence produced through social work research but also, methodologically, to how that research is carried out.

This chapter asks what a feminist account of knowledge production might look like but, rather than looking for *a* definition, the discussion focuses on debates since it 'would be a mistake…to believe that there is a unique and agreed-upon feminist epistemology' (Tanesini, 1999, p. 4). This is something also highlighted in arguments about 'evidence' in social work, where the nature and origin of knowledge is subject to much debate rather than settled (Mäntysaari & Weatherley, 2010). The chapter considers the contested basis of feminist knowledge, focusing on questions of difference, experience, values, and reflexivity and pays significant attention to epistemic injustice. Having outlined these debates, the chapter also considers their implications for feminist social work research, focusing on both epistemological and methodological issues.

Feminist epistemologies and feminist research

An 'epistemology' is a framework or theory for specifying the constitution and generation of knowledge about the social world; that is, it concerns how to understand the nature of 'reality'. A given epistemological framework specifies not only what 'knowledge' is and how to recognise it, but who are 'knowers' and by what means someone becomes one, and also the means by which competing knowledge claims are adjudicated.

(Stanley & Wise, 1993, p. 188)

Given Stanley and Wise's definition of epistemology, it is not surprising that there is no one feminist version of the concept: 'the term does not have a single referent and…it may never' (Alcoff & Potter, 1993, p. 1). Anderson has suggested that a feminist epistemology 'investigates the influence of *socially constructed conceptions and norms of gender and gender-specific interests and experiences* on the production of knowledge' (1995, p. 54). Even this definition is controversial because, for many feminist thinkers, it is not *solely* gender that influences knowledge production but also race, class, sexuality, disability, and trans issues, for example (Bey, 2022; Collins, 2000; Mohanty, 2003; Narayan, 2004; Shelton et al., 2022). But, crucially, it is both the origins and forms of knowledge that concern the work of those focused on feminist epistemologies.

These questions are central to feminist enquiry because any account of knowledge is an account of power relations too. Early interventions into debates about feminist research, for example, challenge supposedly universal or 'malestream' forms of knowledge that are actually by and about men (Du Bois, 1983; Mies, 1993; Tanesini, 1999). Relatedly, feminist thinkers scrutinize evidence for potentially oppressive effects, partly because they are working towards the various emancipatory aims of feminism.

These epistemological questions have taken on a particular significance, in part because many suggest that the *feminism* of feminist research lies not within particular methods but, rather, is about a way of thinking (Letherby, 2007; Stanley and Wise, 1993; Wahab et al., 2015). That is, those who argue for the significance of feminist *epistemologies* are concerned with asking what counts as knowledge, where it comes from, and whose knowledge counts. In addition, they argue that knowledge is a critical tool for rethinking hierarchies, so that those who have been sidelined may challenge those that are dominant. A key point here is that feminist epistemologies argue not just for opposition to gender oppression, in part because an adequate feminism does not focus solely on gender. Rather, as with other critical theoretical perspectives it has sometimes drawn upon (such as Marxism, ethnomethodology, decolonial or liberation pedagogies), feminism attends closely to knowledge production processes and contributes emancipatory versions. This it does via epistemological commitments to: anti-foundational and situated forms of knowledge; moving beyond a focus solely on gender oppression; questions of injustice; and reflexive forms of theorizing, all of which this chapter now moves on to consider.

What do feminist epistemologies look like?

A feminist epistemology is anti-foundational

Foundational forms of knowledge suggest that there are secure evidential bases for epistemological claims and, further, that these precede any research since they are already agreed. An example would be the notion that it is possible for research to be carried out in an objective manner, one which sees the social world as a seamless 'reality' entirely external to issues of power or the influence of the researcher. Feminists, however, usually theorize and research from an anti-foundational position (Hawkesworth, 2006) since all knowledge is situational (see next section). Further, feminists dispute the notion that a single social reality since, at the very least, views of the world are fractured along gendered lines.

Wise and Stanley, however, have proposed 'feminist fractured foundationalism', which rejects 'the normative/realist versus the anti-foundationalist binaries' (2006, p. 446). Their approach operates an epistemological 'double take' (2006, p. 448) since they wish to locate knowledge-making within both everyday usage and its interpretation by the feminist researcher. In this sense, feminist fractured foundationalism recognizes both the material grounding of knowledge and that different groups (of women, for example) have very different views of 'reality'. For Wise and Stanley, this implies that feminist researchers will need to grapple with the interpretation of data in ways that do not automatically privilege their views over those of research subjects.

For feminist social work research, the implications of anti-foundationalism are likely to include a critical and conscious attention to knowledge production, of the sort that may also be found where questions are raised about reliance upon 'evidence-based' research and practice (Trinder, 2000). This would also imply attempting to address power imbalances within 'evidence' and research processes, challenging the exclusion from the record of some voices or working towards anti-oppressive forms of inquiry. Here, then, there is no straightforward or unfractured 'reality' that social work research can easily access and, relatedly, a feminist focus on whose accounts are privileged will also be crucial.

A feminist epistemology draws upon situated knowledge

Haraway's argument for situated knowledges is 'against various forms of unlocatable, and so irresponsible, knowledge claims' (1988, p. 583). In feminist epistemologies, the knower is not a 'featureless abstraction' (Code, 1991, p. 1). Instead, knowledge emerges from a particular location, is a practical achievement, and one that derives from the author's values. Feminists have further argued that knowledge is a collective endeavor (Du Bois, 1983), not something that belongs solely to an individual. Collins, for example, in discussing Black feminist epistemologies, has noted that these are undergirded by an 'experiential, material base...namely, collective experiences and accompanying worldviews' of Black women (2000, p. 256).

It is here, perhaps, that 'standpoint theory' comes to the fore, since this suggests that location offers a particular view on social relations. Harding, for example, argues that women's experiences of a 'dominated situation enables the production of distinctive kinds of knowledge' (2004, p. 7) and Hartsock suggests that this offers a 'privileged vantage point on male supremacy' (2004, p. 36). Nevertheless, it is important to acknowledge some caveats here: Hartsock's account of a feminist standpoint emphasizes that this is not automatic. It is something that must be struggled for through collective action. Second, some have also cautioned that a standpoint based upon shared gender oppression is, in itself, a foundationalist stance (Fawcett and Hearn, 2004, p. 206), and one that may elide differences among women. This dilemma is perhaps illustrated by Hartsock's statement:

> I propose to lay aside the important differences among women across race and class boundaries and instead search for central commonalities...Still, I adopt this strategy with some reluctance, since it contains the danger of making invisible the experience of lesbians or women of color.

(2004, p. 41)

Hartsock makes this point to emphasize that a standpoint emerges not from an individual identity, but from material and collective relations. Yet, her attempt to 'lay aside' race and class fails to acknowledge these as part of gender relations or as dynamics that not only pose questions about any collective based upon gender but, also, might transform it. Collins' (2000) argument for a Black women's collective, not homogeneous, standpoint echoes Hartsock's views, but it objects to the notion that race may somehow be put to one side. For example, leaving out questions of race would put a very different slant on Hartsock's notion of epistemic *privilege*, highlighting the ways in which whiteness is problematically privileged in accounts that suggest that race or class are somehow less important than questions of gender.

Here, then, is perhaps the most controversial issue debated within feminist standpoint theories; that is, whether this offers epistemic advantage. For, while some have argued that it does (Harding, 2004; Hartsock, 2004), adding that it produces less biased, more critical forms of knowledge, others have raised objections to this notion. Narayan, for example, offers caution concerning this 'doctrine of "double vision" – the claim that oppressed groups have an epistemic advantage and access to greater critical conceptual space' (2004, p. 223). The word 'doctrine', here, ought to offer us considerable pause when thinking about feminist accounts of knowledge as power, since Narayan is suggesting that epistemic privilege is in danger of becoming an unquestioned tenet of some standpoint theories.

Mirza also notes that designating epistemic privilege amongst Black women would 'be to assume a naive essentialist universal notion of a homogeneous Black womanhood, no better in its conception of the self and the nature of power than that embodied in the authoritative discourses we seek to challenge' (1997, p. 5). Given women's experiences are also subject to powerful gender relations, the interpretation of those experiences cannot offer any simple and reliable basis for knowledge claims. Trinder, for example, notes that, while representing the subject's voice is crucial in feminist research, this cannot be based upon naïve claims to authenticity. That would, at the very least, avoid important questions about how 'voice' is constructed through social relations and research processes, a 'smoothing out [of] complexity' (Trinder, 2000, p. 48).

For feminist social work research, the notion of situated knowledge implies attention, not just to competing perspectives but also to both material and collective forms, such as those raised by Black and Indigenous theorists against the 'colonizing institution of knowledge' (Smith, 2012, p. x). But, this would also imply some caution regarding the emergence of 'authentic' voices within social work, meaning that feminists may also need to ask who may be speaking for communities and why it would be dangerous to treat any voice as unmediated. Feminist researchers must not only acknowledge epistemic difference, but they should also be cautious about the notion of privilege. There is no objective, value free or, indeed, 'innocent' evidence here, including that produced by feminist social work researchers. As Stanley and Wise succinctly put it, feminist researchers cannot have 'empty heads' (1990, p. 22) either.

A feminist epistemology is not solely based on women's experiences of gender

Social location is not only about experiences of gender oppression but is also about class, disability, race, sexuality or trans issues, for example. Lewis' research on Black women in social work reminds us that gender and race are mutually, not separately, constituted and that their meanings are not already given (2000). White applies this latter point to the feminist social worker/researcher, an identity which may be 'fluid, sometimes fragile or even non-existent' (2006, p. 3), with others noting that feminism itself is often ambivalent and/or contested (Cree and Dean, 2015). Further, Mohanty argues that to 'define feminism purely in gendered terms assumes that our consciousness of being "women" has nothing to do with race, class, nation, or sexuality, just with gender' (2003, p. 54). For others, decolonial or transnational Feminisms are also part of a struggle for epistemic justice, in which the prioritization of white, Western forms of knowledge is questioned (Alexander and Mohanty, 1997; Brah, 2022; Khader, 2018; Phillips, 2023).

Collins refers to Black feminist thinking as 'subjugated knowledge' (2000, p. 251) and reminds us that epistemological debates point to powerful designations, not only of what but also who is credited as a knower. She is also, in part, responding to problematic claims by some feminists that women's shared experience of gender oppression forms the basis of feminist epistemology. A feminist epistemology that does not take race seriously is a partial one. Yet, for Collins, Black women's status as 'outsider-within' (2000, p. 268) also accounts for the creativity of a Black feminist epistemology, even though she does not see this as privileged.

Bey has argued that Black trans-feminist perspectives produce 'renegade knowledge' (2022, p. 51) because they trouble the idea of 'gender' and 'race' as easily knowable. Trans names a movement across, and a questioning of, socially defined boundaries, with the category 'women' having been:

critiqued by Black and Women of Color feminists as a category that continuously fails, fails to articulate clearly what it is that makes some women, who are not white, who are not middle class, illegible as the imagined universalized representative subject.
(Green and Bey, 2017, p. 441)

Another problematic aspect of shared experiences of gender oppression is the question of *experience* as a basis for knowledge. Lazreg argues that this epistemic fallacy allocates experience 'ontological status, and [is] a form of methodological individualism whereby reality is seen as analysable in terms of individual experiences' (1994, p. 58). Several writers have offered cautions about the suggestion that research offers direct access to faithful accounts of experience. Scott, for example, suggests that it is 'historical processes that, through discourse, position subjects and produce their experiences. It is not individuals who have experience, but subjects who are constituted through experience' (1992, pp. 25–26).

Yet, here, it seems important to recall that many have argued for an account of knowledge that is not individually derived but, rather, collective. A feminist epistemology thus retains some basis in how gendered categories are made sense of and in experiences of ontological difference. However, this does not rely upon an essential/biological version of gender. As Stanley and Wise have noted, 'a defining element in all feminist theorizing is its treatment of gender as socially constructed and of feminism as the remaking of a changeable and non-essentialist gender order' (1993, p. 211). They further stress that experience is relevant to any feminist epistemology, since a deontological version is not possible. Others, such as Butler, have added that asking questions about experience as the basis for any epistemological stance does not negate subjectivity. This is not 'a conspiracy against women and other disenfranchised groups who are now only beginning to speak on their own behalf', but it does remind us that some experiences have been accorded more status than others since 'the subject' has been used as 'an instrument of Western imperialist hegemony' (Butler, 1992, p. 14).

For feminist social work research, this implies that such theories are not, and should not be, solely about gender, linked to writings that note feminist practice is not just about shared gender oppression either (Bryant, 2016; Wise, 1990). In addition, while acknowledging the importance of differing experiences, feminists ought also to exercise caution concerning the notion that experience allows an automatic or authentic access to 'reality'. That would, at the very least, elide questions not only of interpretation of experience by both researchers and subjects but also the role of language as a powerful and partial constructor of meaning (Park, 2005).

A feminist epistemology is concerned with epistemic injustice

A key argument here has been that knowledge is never value-free but, rather, always a political endeavor that may wish to challenge forms of oppression. In that sense, for feminist epistemologies, the question is not just about what counts as knowledge but, crucially, whose knowledge counts. Valuing the perspectives of those ordinarily excluded, for example, attempts to right what Spivak terms 'epistemic violence' (1988, p. 76). Thus, one way in which a feminist epistemological stance may attempt to right injustices is via:

> the building of situated knowledge from the perspectives of those who previously had little voice or power in the creation of such knowledge in order to influence change to the social conditions and structures which produce and sustain marginalization and exclusion.
>
> *(Drummond and Brotman, 2022, p. 190)*

Fricker's work on 'epistemic injustice' is helpful here, as this suggests a person may be 'wronged specifically in her capacity as a knower' (2007, p. 20) via denial of testimonial capacity. Black women, for example, may be subject to processes that exclude their knowledge or downplay its status, suggesting a lack of credibility. As Collins has noted, epistemological rules reproduce social inequalities, since 'the substance of the rules themselves foster social injustice' (2019, p. 127).

Earlier discussions of epistemologies of the oppressed also challenge universalistic accounts of women's experience. Collins also argues for a framework that 'analyzes heterosexism as a system of oppression, but also conceptualizes its links to race, class, and gender as comparable systems of oppression' (2000, pp. 128–129). Stanley and Wise, similarly, in a discussion of Black and lesbian feminist epistemologies, note that different ontologies feed into epistemological positions. Black feminists oppose the colonizing role of white, universal feminism with hooks objecting to the phenomenon whereby 'developing theory... has been a task particularly subject to the hegemonic dominance of white academic women' (2000, p. 32). For lesbians, too, 'difference' within the context of a heteronormative world produces the kinds of ontological particularities that have 'epistemological consequentiality' (Stanley and Wise, 1993, p. 226).

For feminist social work research, attention to forms of knowledge that have been excluded from the archive is vital. Mies refers to this as attempting to access the 'view from below' (1993, p. 68), a reminder that feminist research ought not to serve domination. For social work, this also chimes with concerns to produce evidence that challenges oppression, something which cannot be achieved, however, 'in a kind of "add and stir" manner' (Shelton et al., 2022, p. 177). That is, merely adding in the voices of the excluded to an otherwise unchallenged paradigm reinforces 'difference' and leaves traditional and powerful epistemologies untouched. It is possible to highlight situations where feminists have shifted discourse significantly – think of how theories regarding sexual violence and abuse have emerged . Yet, still there remain limitations regarding, for example, the potential whiteness and cis/heteronormativity of such interventions, something that is central to feminist work that rethinks understandings that are, in fact, based upon ongoing forms of racial, sexual, and colonial domination (Jaleel, 2021; Roy, 2022).

A feminist epistemology is reflexive

Referring to an approach that asks how a particular version of events has come about, how that account has been achieved and by what claims to knowledge, 'reflexivity' means subjecting knowledge claims to analysis and demonstrating how a particular account has been arrived at. This is because reflexivity also refers 'fundamentally to the fact that…the very act of observing or measuring constitutes the phenomena being described' (Whitaker and Atkinson, 2021, p. 18). Reflexivity asks us to account for how we know things and so, for feminist epistemologies, this implies 'the researcher locating herself in the written accounts of the research and acknowledging that all accounts should be seen as representations of reality' (Letherby, 2007, p. 76).

Feminist epistemologies have proposed a reflexivity that is concerned with ethical knowledge, with accountable forms of evidence that reflect upon the researcher's stance, and with demonstrating how conclusions have been formulated. This, of course, poses some necessary questions about all aspects of participatory research, since co-production processes, the involvement of participants, accessing the voices of the 'silenced', or 'taking research back' to respondents are all epistemologically informed moves, yet, not ones that easily resolve power struggles. As Gunaratnam and Hamilton have noted, feminists ought to be wary of 'naïve investment in collective research as by definition ethical or politically radical – more "feminist" perhaps' (2017, pp. 9–10).

Whitaker and Atkinson suggest that reflexivity ought not to be mistaken for reflection and 'should *not* be equated with introspection or autobiographical "confession"…' (2021, p. 6). Instead, analytical reflexivity asks us to account for how we produce theories or claims rooted in our own experiences of researching social life. Drawing on Gouldner's comment that the 'aim of the reflexive sociologist is not to remove his [*sic*] influence on others, but to *know* it' (1973, p. 77), Stanley argues analytical reflexivity '…is concerned with the act of knowing and the claim to possess 'knowledge about' things' (2004, p. 9).

For feminist social work research, this implies reflexivity regarding both the processes by which knowledge or evidence are produced as well as how those various claims work (Taylor and White, 2000). This means going further than mere reflection on practice and research, since there is a danger in treating such accounts as 'factual', whereas the active construction of social work concepts and the role of a situated self with particular values, ethics and theories require critical attention. As Harrell et al. have noted:

> Feminist principles in social work research challenge us to build knowledge that renders these processes and their effects visible and pushes practitioners and academics toward a politic of resistance and disruption within oppressive systems.
>
> *(2022, p. 63)*

Further implications of feminist epistemologies for social work research

Leotti and Muthanna have argued that feminist social work research is a 'small act of resistance' needed to avoid 'epistemological unconsciousness' (2015, p. 184). While it would certainly be possible to argue that social work's avoidance of epistemological questions is more than just 'unconscious', Self has echoed their point, suggesting that reliance upon modernist/positivist research agendas may lead to ignorance of 'undergirding epistemologies' (2015, p. 254) in social work.

Feminist epistemological debates indicate a desire to think through the complexities of ethics, power and reflexivity in relation to knowledge concerning gendered forms of oppression (and not 'just gender' too). Even so, where social work research does focus on gender at all, it often treats this as an agreed category that explains social processes, rather than something which, itself, is subject to epistemological complexity and debate (Hicks, 2015; Trinder, 2000). Feminist epistemologies have taught us that knowledge is situated in a material context and is not 'more feminist' simply by virtue of 'shared gender oppression'. They have also highlighted that accounts of power/knowledge ought to treat race, class, sexuality, disability and trans issues as central; problematize easy notions of the authenticity of 'experience'; seek epistemic justice; and bring out into the open the processes by which knowledge is arrived at. Bell has argued that, since groups that experience oppression seek to resist dominance, '[s]ocial work research located in such pockets of resistance has potential to redress epistemic injustice' (2014, p. 173), something that may also contribute to the decolonization of existing normative frameworks (Clarke, 2022; Gatwiri and Tusasiirwe, 2022; Rasool and Harms-Smith, 2021).

Such important epistemological questions, therefore, ought to find a place in any feminist social work research agenda, since these are essentially about the status of evidence within practice, theory and policy. However, in addition, feminist epistemological concerns also suggest that what counts as knowledge and, indeed, whose knowledge counts are vital decisions that ought to be transparent. Further, feminist social work research must highlight the ways in which power dynamics are an intimate aspect of knowledge production and ought to acknowledge that evidence-making processes may rest upon decisions that exclude some. This is an important epistemological point that social work research should take seriously and it implies a feminist praxis that challenges such dynamics. And, while endorsing the point that 'a specifically feminist epistemology doesn't exist' (Harrell et al., 2022, p. 70) in the sense that there is no *one* feminist account, this chapter has highlighted the debates about various feminist epistemological stances, so that we might encourage research practices more attuned to knowledge/power dynamics and to the potential for praxis that avoids the reproduction of dominance.

References

Alcoff, L., & Potter, E. (1993). Introduction: When feminisms intersect epistemology. In L. Alcoff & E. Potter (Eds.), *Feminist epistemologies* (pp. 1–14). Routledge.

Alexander, M.J., & Mohanty, C.T. (Eds.). (1997). *Feminist genealogies, colonial legacies, democratic futures*. Routledge.

Anderson, E. (1995). Feminist epistemology: An interpretation and a defense. *Hypatia, 10*(3), 50–84. https://doi.org/10.1111/j.1527-2001.1995.tb00737.x

Bell, K. (2014). Exploring epistemic injustice through feminist social work research. *Affilia, 29*(2), 165–177. https://doi.org/10.1177/0886109913516457

Bey, M. (2022). *Black trans feminism*. Duke University Press.
Brah, A. (2022). *Decolonial imaginings: Intersectional conversations and contestations*. Goldsmiths Press.
Bryant, L. (2016). Repositioning social work research in feminist epistemology, research and praxis. In S. Wendt & N. Moulding (Eds.), *Contemporary feminisms in social work practice* (pp. 82–97). Routledge.
Butler, J. (1992). Contingent foundations: Feminism and the question of 'postmodernism'. In J. Butler & J.W. Scott (Eds.), *Feminists theorize the political* (pp. 3–21). Routledge.
Clarke, K. (2022). Reimagining social work ancestry: Toward epistemic decolonization. *Affilia, 37*(2), 266–278. https://doi.org/10.1177/08861099211051326
Code, L. (1991). *What can she know? Feminist theory and the construction of knowledge*. Cornell University Press.
Collins, P.H. (2000). *Black feminist thought: Knowledge, consciousness, and the politics of empowerment* (2nd ed.). Routledge.
Collins, P.H. (2019). *Intersectionality as critical social theory*. Duke University Press.
Cree, V.E., & Dean, J.S. (2015). Exploring social work students' attitudes towards feminism: Opening up conversations. *Social Work Education, 34*(8), 903–920. https://doi.org/10.1080/02615479.2015.1081884
Drummond, J.J., & Brotman, S. (2022). Exploring the intersection of queer disability as life story: A feminist narrative approach to social work research and practice. In C. Cocker & T. Hafford-Letchfield (Eds.), *Rethinking feminist theories for social work practice* (pp. 189–206). Springer International Publishing.
Du Bois, B. (1983). Passionate scholarship: Notes on values, knowing and method in feminist social science. In G. Bowles & R.D. Klein (Eds.), *Theories of women's studies* (pp. 105–116). Routledge & Kegan Paul.
Fawcett, B., & Hearn, J. (2004). Researching others: Epistemology, experience, standpoints and participation. *International Journal of Social Research Methodology, 7*(3), 201–218. https://doi.org/10.1080/13645570210163989
Fricker, M. (2007). *Epistemic injustice: Power and the ethics of knowing*. Oxford University Press.
Gatwiri, K., & Tusasiirwe, S. (2022). Afrocentric feminism and Ubuntu-led social work practice in an African context. In C. Cocker & T. Hafford-Letchfield (Eds.), *Rethinking feminist theories for social work practice* (pp. 123–139). Springer International Publishing.
Gouldner, A.W. (1973). *For sociology: Renewal and critique in sociology today*. Allen Lane.
Green, K.M., & Bey, M. (2017). Where black feminist thought and trans* feminism meet: A conversation. *Souls, 19*(4), 438–454. https://doi.org/10.1080/10999949.2018.1434365
Gunaratnam, Y., & Hamilton, C. (2017). The wherewithal of feminist methods. *Feminist Review, 115*(1), 1–12. https://doi.org/10.1057/s41305-017-0023-5
Haraway, D. (1988). Situated knowledges: The science question in feminism and the privilege of partial perspective. *Feminist Studies, 14*(3), 575–599. https://doi.org/10.2307/3178066
Harding, S. (2004). Introduction: Standpoint theory as a site of political, philosophic, and scientific debate. In S. Harding (Ed.), *The feminist standpoint theory reader: Intellectual and political controversies* (pp. 1–15). Routledge.
Harrell, S., Anderson-Nathe, B., Wahab, S., & Gringeri, C. (2022). Feminist research and practice: Reorienting a politic for social work. In C. Cocker & T. Hafford-Letchfield (Eds.), *Rethinking feminist theories for social work practice* (pp. 59–76). Springer International Publishing.
Hartsock, N.C.M. (2004). The feminist standpoint: Developing the ground for a specifically feminist historical materialism. In S. Harding (Ed.), *The feminist standpoint theory reader: Intellectual and political controversies* (pp. 35–53). Routledge.
Hawkesworth, M. (2006). *Feminist inquiry: From political conviction to methodological innovation*. Rutgers University Press.
Hicks, S. (2015). Social work and gender: An argument for practical accounts. *Qualitative Social Work, 14*(4), 471–487. https://doi.org/10.1177/1473325014558665
hooks, b. (2000). *Feminist theory: From margin to center* (2nd ed.). Pluto Press.
Jaleel, R.M. (2021). *The work of rape*. Duke University Press.
Khader, S.J. (2018). *Decolonizing universalism: A transnational feminist ethic*. Oxford University Press.

Lazreg, M. (1994). Women's experience and feminist epistemology: A critical neo-rationalist approach. In K. Lennon & M. Whitford (Eds.), *Knowing the difference: Feminist perspectives in epistemology* (pp. 45–62). Routledge.

Leotti, S.M., & Muthanna, J.S. (2015). Troubling the binary: A critical look at the dualistic construction of quantitative/qualitative methods in feminist social work research. In S. Wahab, B. Anderson-Nathe, & C. Gringeri (Eds.), *Feminisms in social work research: Promise and possibilities for justice-based knowledge* (pp. 170–186). Routledge.

Letherby, G. (2007). *Feminist research in theory and practice*. Open University Press.

Lewis, G. (2000). *'Race', gender, social welfare: Encounters in a postcolonial society*. Polity Press.

Mäntysaari, M., & Weatherley, R. (2010). Theory and theorizing: Intellectual contexts of social work research. In I. Shaw, K. Briar-Lawson, J. Orme, & R. Ruckdeschel (Eds.), *The Sage handbook of social work research* (pp. 180–194). Sage.

Mies, M. (1993). Towards a methodology for feminist Rresearch. In M. Hammersley (Ed.), *Social research: Philosophy, politics and practice* (pp. 64–82). Sage.

Mirza, H.S. (1997). Introduction: Mapping a genealogy of Black British feminism. In H.S. Mirza (Ed.), *Black British feminism: A reader* (pp. 1–28). Routledge.

Mohanty, C.T. (2003). *Feminism without borders: Decolonizing theory, practicing solidarity*. Duke University Press.

Narayan, U. (2004). The project of feminist epistemology: Perspectives from a nonwestern feminist. In S. Harding (Ed.), *The feminist standpoint theory reader: Intellectual and political controversies* (pp. 213–224). Routledge.

Park, Y. (2005). Culture as deficit: A critical discourse analysis of the concept of culture in contemporary social work discourse. *Journal of Sociology & Social Welfare, 32*(3), 11–33. https://scholarworks.wmich.edu/jssw/vol32/iss3/3

Phillips, R. (2023). *Practising feminism for social welfare: A global perspective*. Routledge.

Rasool, S., & Harms-Smith, L. (2021). Towards decoloniality in a social work programme: A process of dialogue, reflexivity, action and change. *Critical African Studies, 13*(1), 56–72. https://doi.org/10.1080/21681392.2021.1886136

Roy, S. (2022). *Changing the subject: Feminist and queer politics in neoliberal India*. Duke University Press.

Scott, J.W. (1992). 'Experience'. In J. Butler & J.W. Scott (Eds.), *Feminists theorize the political* (pp. 22–40). Routledge.

Self, J. (2015). Critical feminist social work and the queer query. In S. Wahab, B. Anderson-Nathe, & C. Gringeri (Eds.), *Feminisms in social work research: Promise and possibilities for justice-based knowledge* (pp. 240–258). Routledge.

Shelton, J., Dunleavy, M., & Kroehle, K. (2022). The transformative potential of transfeminist social work practice. In C. Cocker & T. Hafford-Letchfield (Eds.), *Rethinking feminist theories for social work practice* (pp. 175–187). Springer International Publishing.

Smith, L.T. (2012). *Decolonizing methodologies: Research and indigenous peoples* (2nd ed.). Zed Books.

Spivak, G.C. (1988). Can the subaltern speak? In C. Nelson & L. Grossberg (Eds.), *Marxism and the interpretation of culture* (pp. 66–111). Macmillan.

Stanley, L. (2004). A methodological toolkit for feminist research: Analytical reflexivity, accountable knowledge, moral epistemology and being 'a child of our time'. In H. Piper & I. Stronach (Eds.), *Educational research: Difference and diversity* (pp. 3–29). Ashgate.

Stanley, L. (2019). Epistemology. In J.M. Ryan (Ed.), *Core concepts in sociology* (pp. 96–97). John Wiley & Sons.

Stanley, L., & Wise, S. (1990). Method, methodology and epistemology in feminist research processes. In L. Stanley (Ed.), *Feminist praxis: Research, theory and epistemology in feminist sociology* (pp. 20–60). Routledge.

Stanley, L., & Wise, S. (1993). *Breaking out again: Feminist ontology and epistemology* (2nd ed.). Routledge.

Tanesini, A. (1999). *An introduction to feminist epistemologies*. Blackwell.

Taylor, C., & White, S. (2000). *Practising reflexivity in health and welfare: Making knowledge*. Open University Press.

Trinder, L. (2000). Reading the texts: Postmodern feminism and the 'doing' of research. In B. Fawcett, B. Featherstone, J. Fook & A. Rossiter (Eds.), *Practice and research in social work: Postmodern feminist perspectives* (pp. 39–61). Routledge.

Wahab, S., Anderson-Nathe, B., & Gringeri, C. (2015). Conclusion. In S. Wahab, B. Anderson-Nathe & C. Gringeri (Eds.), *Feminisms in social work research: Promise and possibilities for justice-based knowledge* (pp. 276–281). Routledge.

Whitaker, E.M., & Atkinson, P. (2021). *Reflexivity in social research*. Palgrave Macmillan.

White, V. (2006). *The state of feminist social work*. Routledge.

Wise, S. (1990). Becoming a feminist social worker. In L. Stanley (Ed.), *Feminist praxis: Research, theory and epistemology in feminist sociology* (pp. 236–249). Routledge.

Wise, S., & Stanley, L. (2006). Having it all? Feminist fractured foundationalism. In K. Davis, M. Evans & J. Lorber (Eds.), *Handbook of gender and women's studies* (pp. 435–456). Sage.

22
FEMINIST PARTICIPATORY ACTION RESEARCH WITH BREAST CANCER SURVIVORS IN CHINA

Yuk Yee Lee and Hok Bun Ku

Background of the study

In 2006, the Chinese government articulated its strong support for the social work profession by announcing plans to "build up a strong team of social workers to help in the development of a harmonious society." A system of national qualification examinations for various levels of social work professionals was introduced in 2007. An objective of "setting up regular posts for 2 million well-trained social work professionals by 2015 and 3 million by 2020" was further proposed in the National Medium and Long-term Talent Development Plan by the State Council in May 2010. Although the National Health and Family Planning Commission and State Administration of Traditional Chinese Medicine published an Action Plan for Further Improvement of Medical Services (2018–2020) in 2020, medical social work in Mainland China remains at an early stage of development. The medical social workforce is limited and mostly concentrated in public hospitals located in big cities such as Beijing, Shanghai, and Foshan. A survey undertaken by local well-known newspaper, the Southern Metropolis Daily, published in Guangzhou City of Guangdong Province in 2011 showed that 68% of respondents (patients) were unaware of the existence of medical social workers in their area (Nandu.com, 2014), thus demonstrating the need to develop and promote medical social services for hospital patients in Tier 3 cities of China.[1]

In 2017, the authors were invited by Wuyi University and a breast cancer hospital in Jiangmen City, which is a Tier 3 city in Guangdong Province, to develop an action research project to improve hospital medical social service for women with breast cancer. We set up our research with local partners to explore: 1. What are the treatment experiences of women with breast cancer and the causes of their suffering? 2. What services or support should be contained in a transdisciplinary intervention framework for Chinese women with breast cancer, through a lens sensitive to gender, societal, cultural, and illness experiences of women with breast cancer? 3. What are the implications of this study for policy and medical social work practice in general?

Women, illness, and medical social work

According to 2020 global cancer burden data released by the World Health Organization's International Agency for Research on Cancer, 10 million people died from cancer in 2020. Most notably, breast cancer surpassed lung cancer for the first time to become the most common cancer in the world, accounting for about 11.7% of all new cancer cases (Office of the International Agency for Research on Cancer, 2020). As in other countries, "cancer" in Mainland China is not just a medical problem but also a social and cultural problem, impacting patients' psychological, emotional well-being, as well as how women make medical decisions. Women with breast cancer experience psychological stress, self-stigma, and social exclusion. Bodily disfigurement impacts breast cancer survivors' experiences of change in personal and sexual relationships. According to Yusuf et al. (2013), women in Asia are powerless in medical decisions because one of the barriers they face in breast cancer screening is their "inability to act without husband's permission" (p. 3695). In China, women with breast cancer not only have no right to participate in making medical decisions, but Chinese cultural beliefs suggest that family issues that area considered shameful must not be spread, which often lead women with breast cancer to avoid interactions or limit disclosure to others and they are thus less likely to seek help and social support (Wellisch et al., 1999). Breast cancer hospitals in many Chinese cities have no formal provision of medical social work or self-help organizations to support breast cancer patients and their caregivers during their medical treatment and rehabilitation. Few doctors and other health professionals providing breast cancer services in China have received any gender-sensitive or culture-sensitization training. Thus, gender-centered practice and the "ethics of care" are undervalued in the medical setting. Given this background, the authors and research team adopted an action research approach aiming to develop a culture- and gender-sensitive medical service model for breast cancer patients and their families in Jiangmen City, Guangdong Province.

Breast cancer is a common gynecological illness. However, a gender-centered perspective is absent from all treatment stages in Mainland China, and the dominant cultural conception in breast cancer care is the so-called wholeness of women's bodies, i.e., "two-breasted femininity" (Potts, 2000, pp. 8–9). Women with breast cancer see themselves as embodying visible "discredited traits", and thus camouflage their appearances to reduce the possibility of being stigmatized (Suwankhong & Liamputtong, 2016). Even worse, breast cancer doctors tend not to facilitate or well-inform the breast cancer patients' rights to choose medical treatment. According to existing literature, breast cancer survivors report that when they are well-informed about the disease, related treatment and prognosis enable them to develop adequate coping strategies at different stages of the disease, while diminution of their quality of life is highly correlated with their levels of anxiety, depression, feelings of social isolation, and fear of cancer recurrence (Stanton et al., 2002; Stanton & Snider, 1993). Therefore, it is worth reflecting critically on the urgency of integrating feminist perspectives into healthcare services, on the one hand to empower women through self-help group and finally transform them from victim to peer supporter for other breast cancer patients; on the other hand, to let breast cancer doctors listen to the voices of the women and be willing to transform their practice to be able to disclose bad news to women with breast cancer and their families in a gender-sensitive manner.

It has been demonstrated that if patient-centered medical services are available, then the illness experience of many cancer survivors may improve (Stanton et al., 2006).

This may be evident in, for example, improvements in social relations, a greater appreciation for life, a changed sense of priorities, a greater feeling of personal strength and beneficial spiritual changes (Wen et al., 2017), gratitude for survival and hope (Venter, 2008), and greater social support (Tedeschi & Calhoun, 1995). However, according to Li and Lambert (2007), the predominant coping strategy employed by Chinese women with breast cancer is problem-focused. Wang et al. (2014) reported that breast cancer patients in China received less social support due to the self-isolation, and at least one-third suffered higher psychological distress. Influenced by the mainstream discourse, the women perceived breast cancer as a terrible and disgusting disease that was embarrassing for themselves and their families (Suwankhong and Liamputtong, 2016). Therefore, they isolated themselves.

Cixous and Clement (1986) also contend that the oppression of women with breast cancer is rooted in everyday language, such as "you are victim," "patient," or "service recipient." Green (2012) well demonstrates how everyday language use materially harms woman. Thus, this participatory action research project will adopt feminist perspective to uncover the hidden voices of Chinese female breast cancer patients, identify their needs, and make meaning of women's illness. It will also challenge the dominant discourse on breast cancer and empower the women to voice out their voices and become our partner in the action research process and finally become the peer supporters for other breast cancer patients.

Research design and methods

Feminist participatory action research as methodology

According to Ponic et al. (2010), the women's health research movement has grown in response to women's exclusion from traditional research settings. Historically, healthcare research has assumed "gender-neutrality" that has not adequately considered the ways women's health is affected by sex, gender, social differences, and diversity. Healthcare research in China continues to be dominated by positivist science (Yu & Liu, 2007) and its successors of medical hegemony. It considers that "personal experience" should not be considered "reliable knowledge." Our research was highly influenced by feminism which emphasizes "an ethics of care" epistemology (Gilligan, 1982). Women are active actors who are parts of knowledge construction, and their voices have to be included in the process. It will consider how the medical system disregards the needs of female in the treatment process, and constructs the oppression of women with breast cancer through the distribution of power and privilege, the feminist perspective will uncover the oppressed voices of women with breast cancer and understand their needs in medical settings in Mainland China since feminist practice emphasizes the transformation of women's identity through narrative or storytelling and the reconstruction of counter-discourse against dominant hegemony (McLaren, 2003). Feminist Participatory Action Research integrates the theoretical and methodological accomplishments of both feminist research and participatory action research as a gender-centered intervention framework, both theoretically and practically (Coghlan & Brydon-Miller, 2014). Feminist Participatory Action Research specifically considers how gender embeds itself in power structures, institutions, and interpersonal relations in ways that oppress women (Green, 2012). Participatory action research has been described as "a democratic process concerned with developing practical knowledge in the pursuit of worthwhile human purposes" (Schneider, 2012, p. 2) for the improvement of women's lives. It brings together action and reflection, theory and practice (Baldwin, 2012). Participatory action research combines three activities: research, education, and action (Small, 1995). Its primary goal is "to lead to a more just society through transformative social change" (Kwok & Ku, 2008, p. 266). Therefore, the central value of this project was to let women's suppressed voices be heard, invite them to participate in research process, including the needs identification, action planning, and evaluation. We tentatively promoted the ideal of "women listening to women" (Ku, 2011), with the same experiences. First, we established an action research team consisting of a local social work teacher, two local social workers, and a psychologist. The research team trained breast cancer survivors to interview women with breast cancer through oral history; creating space to enable them to generate research questions which is meaningful to women's unique cancer experience. Another importance of "women listening women" was to enhance the solidarity among the breast cancer survivors and women with breast cancer and form the women mutual supporting network. Feminist Participatory Action Research generally includes a spiral process as other kinds of action research: (1) planning for change, (2) acting and observing, (3) reflecting on the processes and consequences, and (4) beginning the process again through re-planning (Mertler, 2017). As in many action research projects, these stages are not always linear and often overlap.

Sampling and data collection

The research was undertaken in co-operation with the Jiangmen Maternity and Child Health Care Hospital (JMCHCH). Six core action team members, a caregiver, and 14 participants who were outpatients who had received chemotherapy, radiation, or medication at JMCHCH were recruited, and informed consent was obtained. This research was approved by the University's Ethics Committee, throughout the research process, guided by the principle of PAR, we tried our best to transform our relationship with the women as partners, to ensure that the FPAR project was open and inclusive, and to avoid generating oppression and disempowerment of the participants. WE also tried to maintain anonymity and confidentiality; all interviews, reflection meeting notes, and group materials were audio-recorded and transcribed verbatim in Cantonese. This study adopted qualitative research methods in different stages of the action research, which was more user-friendly. In Action Stage I, the research team trained the women as interviewers, and the research team and action team conducted interviews with other breast cancer survivors using oral history and participatory observation methods. In Action Stage II, we worked with the women to collect materials such as drawings, songs, poetry, and handicrafts as data. In Action Stages III and IV, we collected data through storytelling, observation of Hong Kong study trip, and public speeches. Researchers' reflection notes in all action stages also served as important data. This chapter mainly used the data from Stage I and II.

Findings and discussion

Listening to the voices of women with breast cancer at each treatment stage

We began our journey with oral history a total of six women with breast cancer. Following a discussion with the members of the action research team, we classify the treatment stages into four stages.

At Stage I, where breast cancer was suspected, the women felt very stressed and helpless, because formal and informal support networks were unknown. Such support is vital, as health professionals' positive attitudes exert a great influence on the willingness of women with breast cancer to receive cancer treatment. Women with breast cancer and their families who are well-informed about their illness, its treatment, and prognosis are less likely to refuse cancer treatment. Like Ah Lin and Ah Zhi, they narrated.

> When I tried to express or clarify more, he (doctor) would ask me to shut up, I don't know what he used to lift up my T-shirt for the (breast) examination, but it was in such a rude manner.
>
> *(Ah Lin)*

> Every time I told the doctor that I was not going back. The doctor told me, 'Now you go for the treatment, you will have no regrets. However, if you don't go now, you may have irreversible regrets. It will just pass.' Every time she was telling me the same thing to encourage me, ……I finally passed through all treatments.
>
> *(Ah Zhi)*

At Stage II, the diagnosis stage, the biggest impact on women and their families is the fear of harm that cancer is causing to their bodies, during this stage, body image is one of the biggest barriers to undergoing a mastectomy. Like Ah Ying narrated:

> He (doctor) said that lymphatic clearance was needed. I said I wouldn't do it. I would definitely not do it because I cannot accept because you cut it all off (meaning I have got no breasts).
>
> *(Ah Ying)*

At Stage III, treatment and prognosis, the risk factors are suffering from treatment side effects, being ashamed of changes in their health and physical appearance and lack of personal family care during hospitalization. Like Ah Lai narrated:

> I came for chemotherapy myself. I cook for myself. Others say that I serve myself…, I went home and saw my husband was sleeping all day. He didn't care…., so I cooked for myself.
>
> *(Ah Lai)*

> My husband doesn't come to visit, and no one pays attention to me. Do you think I'll become disheartened and lose enthusiasm this way? I'm all alone. My two sons are too young to take care of me.
>
> *(Ah Hao)*

Protective factors that can cultivate the resilience of women with breast cancer are including spousal; children and peer support are crucial for supporting women with breast cancer to continue with cancer treatment.

> My husband always supports me and backs me up. He accompanies me wherever I go, both my husband and my daughter are my big support.
>
> *(Ah Ying)*

If you are going through something, it is unlikely for you to talk to nobody. Instead, you would talk to those who have the same experience as you. So, you can share relevant information and resources with one another interactively.

(Ah Xiu)

Her bed was next to mine, so we talked, and she said, 'I have the illness for seven years now, there has been no problems.' then I told myself that I would be fine as well.

(Ah Zhi)

Another protective factor is for those who need to shoulder the caring responsibilities for older parents and children. This dual caregiving role can be challenging and demanding, but it also serves as a source of resilience and power for these women.

I have to stand up and hold on. I'm not afraid of death, but I can't die before my dad...... Because I am very important to them, and I want to support the whole family.

(Ah Ying)

In Stage IV, rehabilitation and integration, we found that women with breast cancer worried more about social exclusion, not finding a job, and risk to their livelihoods than the illness itself.

(the employer) discovered my wig. I was wearing a wig and that was considered to be having (breast) cancer, the person (women with breast cancer) is not a good person... Actually, it was just the second day and the employer complained that I cooked badly and told me to find another job.

(Ah Lin)

Relationships

The study supported previous literature that women with breast cancer experienced changes that affected their entire lives (Yusuf et al., 2013); changes in their social roles, body and personal image, and personal relationships may be either positive or negative.

The research revealed that breast cancer in China is perceived as a shameful disease.

I don't want to disclose my illness to others as it is not just having a fever or a flu. Cancer has been considered an incurable disease. (It may be stigmatized/not acceptable in society).

(Ah Zhi)

Everyone (patient). Because I have this disease, I always feel embarrassed, so I feel afraid of others to pity you.

(Ah Lai)

When I heard the word "cancer", I would already feel horrible.

(Ah Lin)

The dominant pathologizing and cultural discourses in China construct women with breast cancer as "bringing bad luck and disgrace to the family and village," and thus, they are the recipients of negative stigmatizing attitudes. The women with breast cancer in this study chose not to talk about their illness with their children.

Body image

Body image includes psychological, physical, and social dimensions (Yang, 2003). Below, we examine body image in women with breast cancer in terms of scars (body), self-concept (psychological), and intimate sexual (social) contacts. It considers how society understands how breast-conserving surgery may lead to barriers in social interaction, changes in the psychological and physical conditions of women with breast cancer, and related gender issues.

Physical level – mastectomy scar

The interviews revealed that seeing wounds is a very difficult moment for women with breast cancer. Some were even more afraid of family members and their husbands seeing or touching their wounds. According to feminist theorists, men's perspective on what constitutes a woman's physical beauty can lead to the domestication of the female body, which in turn affects women's interactions with society and can result in discrimination and gossip (Fournier, 2002; Gatens, 1996; Yang, 2003; Young, 1990). To analyze the strategies, they adopted during body domestication; women who lose their breasts are perceived as deformation, imperfect, and incomplete.

> I dared not look at the wound even when I was in the bathroom alone. It was quite disgusting indeed.... It was hard to see because (breast) was gone... I find it difficult to accept.
>
> (Ah Xiu)

> I really mind. I feel incomplete, unattractive, and imperfect. I feel like I am defective.
>
> (Ah Ying)

> I just mind, I mind my deformation of bodies.
>
> (Ah Lai)

Psychological level – self-identity

Women with breast cancer commonly avoid looking in the mirror and experience common sentiments, including decreased self-worth and attractiveness, feeling deformed, inadequate, sad, embarrassed, frustrated, and having a sense of loss. Women with breast cancer who had a mastectomy commonly doubted whether they were "real women." Women with breast cancer seem to fall into the trap of binary gender thinking, which is understandable in a society that is very gendered. The women said:

> Unattractive and imperfect, I just feel that I am defective that I cannot accept it. As you are a woman, breasts are so important.
>
> (Ah Ying)

Without her breasts, a woman seems unlike a woman. ...I didn't want anyone to know, ... And I think, when going swimming or to hot springs in the future, I would be so ugly if there is no breast on one side.

(Ah Xiu)

Social level intimate relationships

Decreased or lack of sexual desire of both parties after cancer treatment was commonly experienced.

> He doesn't touch me (having sex). He said that he will not touch me (having sex), it is because you are not feeling well (having breast cancer). I told him that I don't need you to touch.
>
> *(Having sex) (Ah Hao)*

> Of course, we have desire (sex desire), he definitely does (having sex desire). But sometimes he feels like he doesn't want to because of the way I am.
>
> *(Ah Lai)*

> Often times my husband is accommodating (I rejected to have sex), I am so lucky to have him.
>
> *(Ah Ying)*

> As there were wounds on my back and chest, I did not think about having sex. Of course, [husband] would have the thought (having sex) after abstinence for quite a while.
>
> *(Ah Xiu)*

> When having sex before, I was naked but now I can't...Yes, I mind, I don't want him to see my scars.
>
> *(Ah Lin)*

> I am too young to be like this to (breast removed), I am no longer a complete woman. How do I face my husband in the future?
>
> *(Ah Zhi)*

Women's oral histories revealed that breast cancer resulted in body changes that were referred to as "feeling deformed," and "unattractive" in contrast to idealized discourses of feminine youth and beauty. Moreover, breasts are usually seen a particularly feminine and idolized and sexualized by men and media. These women tended to position their bodies in terms of a loss of femininity. Losing a breast can also affect a woman's interactions with society. It became a way of domesticating the body through discriminatory eyes or others' gossip; merely perceived as someone who lost a breast. Arguably, women are trapped in common stereotypic ideas of what two-breast femininity is through the FPAR's process, empowering women with breast cancer to regain their power to make medical decisions and lifestyle choices were central. In view of this, the action team has proposed that while empowering individual women is important, the real changes need to be structural so that other breast cancer survivors don't go through the same thing. Thus, feminist consciousness education or gender-sensitive education with healthcare workers, as well as at individual and community level, is advocated. Community education should be central to the intervention framework for breast cancer.

Oppression experience on traditional culture about "bad luck"

As mentioned earlier in this chapter, women with breast cancer in our study revealed the oppressive experience of the women; breast cancer in Mainland China is perceived as a shameful disease. The dominant cultural discourses in Mainland China construct them as "bringing bad luck and disgrace," and thus, they are treated with negative stigmatizing attitudes. They encountered traumatic experiences. Moreover, as parents they often chose to deceive their children having breast cancer, some of child was told mother in hospital, until their death, only revealing the fact that their mother died of breast cancer at this time; making it difficult for children to accept that their mother died of breast cancer.

> When I first saw my mother, I actually cried. I did not expect my mother to be in this condition (look so sick). She could still react to me when I was talking with her. I was glad that she still nodded. I knew that my mother might leave me and sometimes my mother needed a rest. I like to run to the two ends outside the hospital room.
>
> *(Xiaoli)*

> My son didn't know about my illness. I just told him that there was something wrong with my health and surgery was needed.
>
> *(Ah Zhi)*

> We were so shocked when we talked to her husband as he did not arrange for her daughter to visit her in the hospital. She did not know how her mother was in the hospital and she was unprepared for her to leave.
>
> *(Researcher)*

Bringing bad luck to other relatives

Ah Liang's stories revealed that cancer for a woman could be a "hidden taboo-bringing bad luck" to the family; in this connection, they are treated badly after diagnosing breast cancer. She revealed that her husband also passed away from cancer. She suffered discrimination from her mother-in-law and husband's younger brother, which was rooted in Chinese culture. When diagnosed with breast cancer, her husband's family members remained cold toward her, as she did not adhere to traditional customs. She directly told her son about her cancer, without any regrets.

> It was the Chinese New Year, the beginning of another year, the tradition was to avoid any bad or unpleasant matters, which are considered to bring bad luck. Not many relatives or friends were notified about the news. So, it was entirely deserted in the

funeral. I have been blaming myself for allowing this to happen... I know how others see us (breast cancer patients), not coming close to us for they are scared to see us as if seeing ghosts.

(Ah Liang)

The older Chinese generation must be understanding that going to these places (breast cancer ward) just feels unlucky...going to this place will bring bad luck (Dà jílì shì.) to the visitors.

(Ah Liang)

This disease (breast cancer), they are all very discriminatory. We all feel unlucky to have this disease/illness and they will detour even after passing through my door. If you say there is no discrimination, this is deceiving.

(Ah Yuk)

Women with breast cancer in our study encountered traumatic experiences such as marginalized and discrimination in the community, because of traditional cultural norms. Dominant cultural discourse of breast cancer in Mainland China as "disgraceful" made them afraid to disclose their cancer for fear of others getting to know about it. Children are not informed to see the "last face" of their mother because it is believed to bring bad luck to the offspring, the family, and the village. This belief is disrespectful to the mother and puts women with breast cancer in a low and disgraceful position. The right to grieve should be advocated as an essential part of hospice care.

Women empowerment via storytelling

In telling their stories, the women with breast cancer were filled with very problematic self-illness narratives. However, in the process, the research team tried to facilitate a process for them to rediscover the "power bank (gains from the cancers experiences)" to turn their negative illness experience into asset that can be used to help others. For example, in Ah King's narrative, she told us how she learned from this illness experience

> I want to be a peer counselor; my opinion on how to well prepared and equipped the peer counselors, such as personal care after the surgery, the condition of the breast, the nursing care, diet, wound care and emotional support, both Chinese and Western medicine is useful for quality caring.
>
> *(Ah Yun)*

Because in the future, comrades in arms, in fact our people come from comrades in arms. Is it (establish those mutual assistance, companionship, peer support)?

(Ah Yuk)

It's the same when it comes to relaxing. In fact, it is important to regularly organize some activities or some rehabilitation activities.

(Ah Xia)

In fact, we need to learn some knowledge. For example, health knowledge, we don't have enough health knowledge (to help the new patient).

(Ah Liang)

In this study, we also formed a peer-support group to enable breast cancer survivors to provide each other with peer support. This was an effective way to facilitate breast cancer survivors discovering commonalities in their lived stories; they found they were not alone. Through the process, raising their gender consciousness of the oppression of the dominant discourse was important, and we showed them how they could re-author their illness experience in fighting back against "Breast Cancer." The women told us they gained a lot in the process:

I will cherish more, I will love this (my) life more and cherish my days and life in the coming future.

(Ah King)

Because of my illness, there are a lot more people to care for me, I feel really grateful. I am satisfied with this feeling now.

(Ah Liang)

I think the most important thing in life is to live happily, don't make yourself unhappy.
(Ah Yuk)

I feel it's a new me, I'll treat myself good and to love myself more.

(Ah Xia)

Now I can say that I am free and there is nothing to worry about, I like to have fun and enjoy life whenever I want.

(Ah Xia)

Based on the peer support group, the action team drafted an intervention framework to advocate empowering medical social work services for breast cancer survivors and their families. Capacity building for the peer support group was the next step. The action team organized a study tour in Hong Kong for the women to learn about peer support networks and other supportive services for women with breast cancer. This enabled the women to explore how peer support would be helpful for women with breast cancer to reintegrate into the community, the importance of empowering women to aware the gender binary so that they can reclaim their power, and the importance of developing gender sensitive and anti-oppressive practices in the care of breast cancer survivors.

Conclusion

In this action research, we found that each stage of treatment in hospitals in China, pre-treatment, diagnosis, treatment (surgery, chemotherapy), and rehabilitation, lacked gender-sensitivity. Caring is essential to the experience of women with breast cancer. The concepts of care and responsibility are primary to Chinese women's constructions of their moral domain (Gilligan, 1982), as demonstrated by the notion that women are the primary caregivers in the home, caring for children and other family members, such as older parents (Walker & Thompson, 1983), but often don't receive care themselves in situations such as these. It was illuminated in this study that caring duties are one of the protective factors for women with breast cancer that enabled them to continue treatment and fight cancer. When "caregivers" were very sick, they were concerned about who could replace their role in the family? The stories of these women with breast cancer revealed that in Chinese culture, they do not encourage their children to get involved in the treatment process and malign them. They do not involve anyone in basic caring duties even when they face death in the terminal stage of cancer. Do children of women with breast cancer have the right to grieve? How can these children become involved in bereavement counseling? How can they be allowed more time with their mother during the end stage of breast cancer? Grief is a normal and natural response to loss, and we often expect to grieve the death of a family member. Knowing a parent is sick and may potentially die is difficult, but better than not knowing as children are given the opportunity to spend more time with the parent, care for the parent, and say goodbye.

The stories of these women uncovered their hidden voices and disclosed the dominant cultural discourse of breast cancer in Mainland China as "shameful" and resulting in women feeling unfeminine. They are not only suffering from the wounded body – breast scar – but also suppressed by the discriminative discourse. These findings remind us that we don't only need gender-sensitive medical practice but that there is a need to challenge the dominant gender discourse in society that creates cancer stigma, suppresses women's bodily experiences, lets them experience disrespectful treatment, prevents them from obtaining social support, and increases their exposure to the discrimination. We thus advocate for policy and structural change in the medical system for women with breast cancer, but more importantly societal stigma needs to be challenged. There is a need to strengthen culture and gender-sensitive training in the medical and health professions. It is critical to put in place mutual support opportunities for breast cancer survivors to be able to support each other, due to the huge cultural stigma that prevents them disclosing their health to others in their environment who could potentially be a support. There is a greater need for challenging the societal discrimination of cancer survivors and the feminist consciousness education should be advocated, so that options for community and family support become a reality for survivors of breast cancer.

Acknowledgments

We would like to thank Dr. Fang Lang for supporting the women with breast cancer who participated in this project and members of the action team, Dr. Xu Huan-ling, Dr. Wan Chi-man Wan, Ms. Ms Liang Jian-ling, Miss Chen Jing-ya, Miss Fang-xi, and Miss Tracy Cheung, who provided their generous support. We dedicate this chapter to the women who took part in the study; we learned a lot from your life stories.

Note

1 The tiers of cities in China usually refer to key characteristics of the city, including its economic development, provincial GDP, advanced transportation systems and infrastructure, and historical and cultural significance. Third-tier cities are typically medium-sized cities within each province. Tier 3 cities and lower show promising prospects due to local government support fostering innovation.

References

Baldwin, M. (2012). Participatory action research. In M. Gray, J. Midgley, & S. A. Webb (Eds.), *The Sage handbook of social work* (pp. 467-481). London: Sage Publications Ltd.

Cixous, H., & Clement, C. (1986). *The newly born woman* (trans. B. Wing). Minneapolis: University of Minnesota Press.

Coghlan, D., & Brydon-Miller, M. (2014). *The Sage encyclopedia of action research*. London: Sage Publications.

Fournier, V. (2002). Fleshing out gender: Crafting gender identity on women's bodies. *Body & Society*, 8(2), 55–78.

Gatens, M. (1996). *Imaginary bodies: Ethics, power and corporeality*. London: Routledge.

Gilligan, C. (1982). *In a different voice: Psychological theory and women's development*. Cambridge, MA: Harvard University Press.

Green, L. (2012). 'Non-sporty' girls take the lead: A feminist participatory action research approach to physical activity. (Doctoral dissertation, Brunel University, London). Retrieved from https://bura.brunel.ac.uk/handle/2438/7554

Kwok, J. Y.-C., & Ku, H. B. (2008). Making habitable space together with female Chinese immigrants to Hong Kong. *Action Research (London, England)*, 6, 261–283. https://doi.org/10.1177%2F1476750308094131

Ku, H. B. (2011). Gendered suffering: Married Miao women's narratives on domestic violence in southwest China. *China Journal of Social Work*, 4, 23–39. https://doi.org/10.1080/17525098.2011.563944

Li, J., & Lambert, V. A. (2007). Coping strategies and predictors of general well-being in women with breast cancer in the People's Republic of China. *Nursing & Health Sciences*, 9, 199–204. https://doi.org/10.5993%2FAJHB.41.4.1

McLaren, M. (2003). *Feminism, foucault, and embodied subjectivity*. Albany: State University of New York Press.

Mertler, C. A. (2017). *Action research: Improving schools and empowering educators*. Thousand Oaks, CA: Sage Publications.

Nandu.com. (2014). Qī chéng shòu fǎng zhě bù zhīdào shénme shì yīwù shèhuì gōngzuò. *Southern Metropolis Daily*. Retrieved from http://news.ifeng.com/gundong/detail_2014_03/21/34992506_0.shtml

Office of the International Agency for Research on Cancer. (2020, December 17). Latest global cancer data: Cancer burden rises to 19.3 million new cases and 10.0 million cancer deaths in 2020 [Press release]. https://www.iarc.who.int/news-events/latest-global-cancer-data-cancer-burden-rises-to-19-3-million-new-cases-and-10-0-million-cancer-deaths-in-2020/

Ponic, P., Reid, C., & Frisby, W. (2010). Cultivating the power of partnerships in feminist participatory action research in women's health. *Nursing Inquiry*, 17, 324–335. https://doi.org/10.1111/j.1440-1800.2010.00506.x

Potts, L. (2000). Introduction: Why ideologies of breast cancer? Why feminist perspectives? In L. Potts (Ed.), *Ideologies of breast cancer: Feminist perspectives* (pp. 1–11). London: Macmillan.

Schneider, B. (2012). Participatory action research, mental health service user research, and the Hearing (our) Voices projects. *International Journal of Qualitative Methods*, 11, 152–165. http://dx.doi.org/10.1177/160940691201100203

Small, S. A. (1995). Action-oriented research: Models and methods. *Journal of Marriage and Family*, 57, 941–955. https://doi.org/10.2307/353414

Stanton, A. L., Bower, J. E., & Low, C. A. (2006). Posttraumatic growth after cancer. In L. G. Calhoun & R. G. Tedeschi (Eds.), *Handbook of posttraumatic growth: Research and practice* (pp. 138–175). Mahwah, NJ: Lawrence Erlbaum Associates.

Stanton, A. L., Danoff-Burg, S., & Huggins, M. E. (2002). The first year after breast cancer diagnosis: Hope and coping strategies as predictors of adjustment. *Psycho-Oncology*, 11, 93–102. https://doi.org/10.1002/pon.574

Stanton, A. L., & Snider, P. R. (1993). Coping with a breast cancer diagnosis. *Health Psychology*, 12, 16–23. https://psycnet.apa.org/doi/10.1037/0278-6133.12.1.16

Suwankhong, D., & Liamputtong, P. (2016). Breast cancer treatment: Experiences of changes and social stigma among Thai women in southern Thailand. *Cancer Nursing*, 39, 213–220. https://doi.org/10.1097/ncc.0000000000000255

Tedeschi, R., & Calhoun, L. G. (1995). *Trauma and Transformation: Growing in the Aftermath of Suffering* (1st edition.). Thousand Oaks, CA: SAGE Publications, Incorporated. https://doi.org/10.4135/9781483326931

Venter, M. (2008). *Cancer patients' illness experiences during a group intervention.* [Unpublished Masters dissertation, North West University]. Retrieved from https:www.v-des-win3.nwu.ac.za/handle/10394/4154

Walker, A. J., & Thompson, L. (1983). Intimacy and intergenerational aid and contact among mothers and daughters. *Journal of Marriage and the Family, 45,* 841–849. https://psycnet.apa.org/doi/10.2307/351796

Wang, F., Liu, J., Liu, L., Wang, F., Ma, Z., Gao, D., Zhang, Q., & Yu, Z. (2014). The status and correlates of depression and anxiety among breast-cancer survivors in Eastern China: A population-based, cross-sectional case-control study. *BMC Public Health, 14,* 326. https://doi.org/10.1186/1471-2458-14-326

Wellisch, D., Kagawa-Singer, M., Reid, S. L., Lin, Y-I., Nishikawa-Lee, S., & Wellisch, M. (1999). An exploratory study of social support: A cross-cultural comparison of Chinese-, Japanese-, and Anglo American breast cancer patients. *Psycho-Oncology (Chichester, England), 8,* 207–219. https://doi.org/10.1002/(sici)1099-1611(199905/06)8:3%3C207::aid-pon357%3E3.0.co;2-b

Wen, K-Y., Ma, X. S., Fang, C., Song, Y., Tan, Y., Seals, B., & Ma, G. X. (2017). Psychosocial correlates of benefit finding in breast cancer survivors in China. *Journal of Health Psychology, 22,* 1731–1742. https://doi.org/10.1177/1359105316637839

Yang, J. (2003). Fantastic costume: The female breast cancer patients, gender performance, and body image. *Taiwan: A Radical Quarterly in Social Studies, 49,* 49–95.

Young, I. M. (1990). Breasted experience: The look and the feeling. In L. J. Nicholson (Ed.), *Feminism/postmodernism* (pp. 189–209). Bloomington: Indiana University Press.

Yu, H., & Liu, J.P. (2007). A review of international clinical trial registration. *Zhong Xi Yi Jie He Xue Bao 5,* 234–242 (in Chinese).

Yusuf, A., Ab Hadi, I., Mahamood, Z., Ahmad, Z., & Keng, S. (2013). Understanding the breast cancer experience: A qualitative study of Malaysian women. *Asian Pacific Journal of Cancer Prevention, 14,* 3689–3698. https://doi.org/10.7314/apjcp.2013.14.6.3689

23
FEMINIST RESEARCH IN SOCIAL WORK
Epistemological-methodological keys from the South

María Eugenia Hermida and Yanina Roldán

Introduction: cartographies of Feminisms

To think about the contributions of Feminisms to Social Work, we stand outside the genealogies of white liberal feminism and next to the contributions of Southern Feminisms. We wish to highlight the contributions of different perspectives. Decolonial feminism (Espinosa Miñoso, 2017; Lugones, 2008; Segato, 2015) denounces the imbrication between Coloniality and Patriarchy. Postcolonial feminism links the idea of alterity not only to race but also to gender, class, sexuality (Bidaseca, 2016; Spivak, 1981). The struggles of Latin American women are recovered to overcome the separation between academia and activism (Alvarado, 2020; Alvarado & Fischetti, 2018). Communitarian and Indigenous Feminisms (Cabnal, 2010; Millan, 2017) introduce the notion of body-land-territory to discuss the nature-culture divide and recover the value of ancestral knowledge. Black feminism and intersectional feminism (Crenshaw, 1991; Gonzalez, 2018; Hill Collins, 2000; hooks, 2017; Lorde, 1978) denounce the differences within the category of women, and the subordinate place of Black women. Brown feminism and popular feminism (Colectivo Ayllu & Rivadeneira, 2020; Korol & Castro, 2016) highlight the intersection between class and race and the oppression experienced by mestizo women. Transfeminist and queer/cuir Feminisms (Butler, 2011; flores, 2013; Preciado, 2011; Shock, 2011) point out that not only gender but also sex is a social construction and denounces cis-heterocentrism and violence towards gender-sex non-conforming people. Various texts expand the description of these approaches (Disch & Hawkesworth, 2016; Roldán, 2022). Focusing on the contributions, they make to Social Work research; these Feminisms share a series of dimensions to be addressed[1]:

1 The ethical-political dimension, prioritising and shedding light upon the patriarchal wound and its multiple intersections. This implies the ethical stance of being affected and involving ourselves in the struggle against gender and sexual inequalities while registering the inscriptions that class, race, age and abilities have in these processes. The ethical dimension implies horizontality and the consideration of feminist movements' agenda in research and methodological decisions, as to avoid academic extractivism.

2 The political-epistemological dimension: it signifies sexual difference as eminently political (as opposed to a biological or cultural phenomenon). Political interventions involve strategies to suture the academia vs activism or literate knowledge vs popular knowledge divide, among other issues.
3 The theoretical-epistemological dimension recognises the cis-hetero-androcentric normativity of knowledge. It intertwines the Coloniality of gender – a systemic conception of gender used to destroy cosmologies and communities – and the Coloniality of knowledge – the ways in which social sciences in Latin America negotiate, accept or resist the influences of the Global North. It proposes various strategies to reinvent epistemological practice with feminist validity criteria and contests spaces of power in the scientific field.
4 The theoretical-methodological dimension: understanding that there is no "what" without a "how". It involves reviewing the patriarchal biases in the so-called universal scientific methods for research (e.g., in the selection of subjects and objects, resources and techniques, both for collection and processing information).

These shared dimensions should not lead us to think that these perspectives are homogeneous. Decolonial feminism, for example, differs from postcolonial feminism on several points. In epistemological terms, postcolonial feminism makes use of European categories – like "deconstruction" (Derrida) and subalternity (Gramsci) – while decolonial feminism recovers Latin American traditions according to authors like Curiel (2014) and Lugones (2008). Black feminist epistemology points to the potential binarism and essentialism of Harding's feminist epistemology. Decolonial feminism criticises Black feminism's notion of intersectionality (Crenshaw, 1991) – between race, social class, gender, sexuality, ethnicity and age in matrices of oppression – and proposes the idea of consubstantiality (Lugones, 2008) of race or gender as indivisible processes. In other words, there are multiple differences but, unlike androcentric positivist epistemology, we envision a Ch'ixi (Rivera Cusicanqui, 2018) epistemology in which knowledge is built upon divergences, articulating tensions and agreements, enriching our reflexive practices. Ch'ixi refers to grey as a colour in which Black and white do not merge but antagonise and complement each other. This Ch'ixi perspective will allow us to interweave contributions from the different feminist perspectives mentioned above to enrich research practices in Social Work and think about different ways of constructing social knowledge.

Contributions of situated Feminisms to Social Work research

In this section, we go over the dimensions mentioned above to put them in dialogue with Social Work research. To this end, we propose an ethical-political-epistemological and a theoretical-political-methodological perspective. These feminist perspectives allow us to reinvent research practices in Social Work. The turn they propose is radical, as they offer different criteria and tools for each moment of the research process. They allow us to recreate the answers to questions such as for what, for whom and with whom do we do research; how can we produce valid and useful knowledge in social work; where and how are androcentric practices reproduced in research and how can they be eradicated.

The ethical-political-epistemological perspective

Harding (1986) denounces the androcentric bias of science, stating that science is both sexist and androcentric. It establishes the white, Northern, heterosexual male as the privileged knowledge-producing subjectivity and considers the male vision as universal. Hegemonic epistemology has sought to expel everything considered feminine (emotional and subjective) from the production of scientific knowledge as threatening to academic quality. Feminisms and the affective turn criticised this vision derived from naïve positivist realism. Ahmed (2017) suggests that "theory can do more the closer it gets to the skin" (p. 10), alluding to the fact that the knowledge-producing subject is always affected in its corporeality. To write close to the skin is to think that the personal is not only political but also theoretical, and reason is always mediated by affect: making these links explicit allows us to construct powerful theoretical tools.

About situated knowledge and neutrality, Spivak (1981) stated that "Unless one is aware that one cannot avoid taking a stand, unwitting stands get taken" (p. 174). The Social Work researcher does so from a standpoint that refers to concepts and practices around knowledge. This locus of enunciation (Mignolo, 1995) refers to a geographical area, traversed by economic and racial relations of power-knowledge, and to the body itself, upon which systems such as heterosexism and cissexism intersect.

On the political dimension, Hill Collins (2000) postulates a Black feminist epistemology focused on the production of knowledge upon lived experiences. Dialogue is postulated as opposed to the contradictory debate characteristic of the androcentric hypothetical-deductive method, which claims that knowledge advances only when one argument defeats the other. The use of dialogue involves at least two subjects which, rather than being absent in the process, form a central and present part of the text. Its ethics of care – for which knowledge and the validity of arguments must be assessed on the basis of empathy, compassion and emotion – aims to remedy the binary split between emotion and intellect. Black feminist epistemology considers that all knowledge is based on opinions/beliefs and that opinion/belief implies personal responsibility. These epistemic positions should function as guides for multiple decisions in Social Work research, facilitating the necessary creation of new ways of knowledge construction.

In this regard, an essential point in any study is the construction of the theoretical framework. We must point out the eminently political nature of the theoretical corpus construction that will guide our research, questions and interpretations. Latin American and Southern Feminisms remind us of this aspect: as Urania Ungo claimed, quoting is a political fact. Latin American feminists do not quote ourselves in our writings: we resort to external authority to justify our thinking. But authority is always political (Gargallo, 2004, as cited in Alvarado & Fischetti, 2018, p. 92). A major research task is to review our bibliographic search criteria so as not to reproduce the silencing of the voices of women and sexual and gender dissidents, to promote South-South dialogues, drawing on the advances of our colleagues who have been constructing other forms of knowledge.

The ethical, political and epistemological dimensions are not merely declamatory: they materialise in each of the methodological decisions we make in research. In the process of constructing knowledge, the formulation of the research problem emerges as a nodal element, as an epistemological and methodological construct. Is not the foundation that makes a study justifiable both political and epistemological? Are not the agendas that give entity to certain questions to the detriment of other politics? Does it not imply an ethical debate to ask ourselves why we are going to prioritise a topic/problem, or why we are going to insert ourselves into a territory or community to investigate it? That is why we believe that the first great contribution of Feminisms to Social Work research is to ask ourselves about the ethical, political and epistemological foundations of the research problem.

We cannot dissociate such questions from the dialogue with feminist agendas, nor from the subjects involved in the processes addressed in the fieldwork.

Finally when we consider the political and epistemological relevance of the research problem from a feminist perspective, we are not only talking about the topic and its convergence with the topics of interest to social collectives but mainly the form, manner or perspective upon which we build this topic as a research problem. At this point, and as we move on to the methodological dimension, we turn to the contributions of Azpiazu Carballo (2014), who affirms the need for new feminist methodological strategies: these elements will allow us to offer a different perspective on the issues under research, rather than investigating different issues (of feminist interest) through the same perspective (p. 121).

The theoretical-political-methodological perspective

If we look at the epistemological advances of Feminisms, we can point to various methodological approaches to feminist research in Social Work. The first one is to recognise the need to build strategies so that the construction of the research problem can be articulated with the agendas, struggles and disputes that various collectives have been campaigning in order to resist the patriarchal, colonial, capitalist system in its multiple facets and expressions. It is about building useful knowledge in terms of its potential direct application but mainly about enabling processes that contribute to reflection, the emergence and visibility of other histories, other sensibilities, other corporealities, other futures.

This point is associated with the recovery of lived experience as a source of knowledge proposed by Hill Collins (2000). Not limited to the fieldwork phase, the subject's participation can also be considered relevant in the initial phases of the design of the research project. This means reclaiming our professional inscription in the everyday life processes of the popular sectors. Positivism has insisted that connection with the object biases research processes. Quite the opposite, feminism proposes to think of it as an opportunity to engage in dialogical processes with the subjects affected by the patriarchal, colonial wound to co-create situated knowledge questions and objectives.

The epistemological postulate of dialogue leads us to the methodological proposals of co-labour (Araya & Chávez, 2022) and feminist activist research (Araiza Díaz & González García, 2017). These strategies propose an economy of knowledge/power that is utterly different from classical asymmetrical power approaches, where the researcher is the subject who has the theory and the *researched* individuals or groups are objects holding the information to be collected. These contributions recover elements from the Latin American perspectives of Participatory Action Research (Fals Borda) and popular education (Freire) adding to their claim against gender inequalities reproduced by androcentric research's technical reductionism in knowledge production processes.

Critical of the *research object* idea, Ochy Curiel (2014) brings a decolonial feminist perspective to feminist methodology. To this end, she revisits Hill Collins (2000) in reference to the experiences of Black women as main source of knowledge, suggesting that if the experience of Black women allows a better interpretation of their reality, they should be the ones doing the research. Curiel (2014) is not saying that only those who have suffered oppression have the capacity to understand and research it, but that there is an important epistemic privilege (Hill Collins, 2000) to be considered in the production of knowledge, and that means moving from being objects to subjects (p. 54). Such political commitment humanises Black women as producers of knowledge and displaces white male as the privileged subject of knowledge processes.

On her part, Biglia (2014) argues that a feminist methodology implies a particular focus not only on the topics of study and the cognitive subjects but also on the processes of knowledge production. This means that the shift from women as objects of study to women as subjects of study leads to a non-discriminatory redefinition of the processes of knowledge production, which implies implementing a methodology of interpretation of reality based on non-heteropatriarchal logics. A feminist approach does not mean that the data collection and analysis techniques that have been used so far have to be discarded, but that we are committed to a research practice consistent with feminist postulates, redesigned according to the specificities of the research, its context, its purpose, and the feminist position undertaken (p. 26).

This is how we find approaches to a collaborative methodology from a feminist ethnographic perspective. Such is the case of Araya and Chávez (2022), who report on the use of qualitative techniques – like life narratives, ethnographic photography and women's writing – and the political-epistemological position they imply, including the evaluation that the communities and women involved in the research designs make of the use of such methodologies. The incorporation of the perspectives, emotions and visions of the collaborators regarding the methodologies used in this participatory process was part of an evaluation of this type of ethnographic practices, oriented towards collaboration and the annulment of the exclusivity of the allegedly authorised voice of researchers (p. 25).

Biographical and narrative approaches are another nodal contribution of feminist research. Re-signifying centuries-old social sciences traditions, studies with a gender and situated perspective emphasise that recovering the perspective of the subject from a narrative logic – drawing upon the oral histories and storytelling traditions of Indigenous communities – can help us understand and transform historical and social processes, acknowledging significant value to experience rather than generalisation. Methodological proposals, such as self-interviewing (Rubilar Donoso, 2015), auto-biography and feminist corpo-biography (Rodríguez, 2018), appear as a decolonial tool. Writing in the first person – as suggested by Hill Collins (2000) – the recognition of the cognitive potential of bodily experience: such efforts to strengthen a methodological strategy provide textual form and consciousness to the body, shaking the traditional discursive foundations of science, and presenting protective measures against methodological plundering and epistemic/cognitive extractivism (Rodríguez, 2018, p. 1).

Indeed, one of the major phenomena that feminist methodology seeks to combat is "cognitive extractivism" (Simpson & Klein, 2017) as colonial capitalist nature-plundering extractivism ally, fostering assimilation, the theft of ancestral knowledge and the accumulation of power/knowledge in the institutional structures of the white, lettered city. Co-building the research objective by observing the agendas of the popular sectors is an ethical, political and methodological step away from extractivist logic. Our results must contribute to the disputes over access to rights. Fieldwork must be valuable to the collectives we work with, fostering meaningful and respectful experiences that allow us to generate ties and share learnings, within a logic of dialogues among knowledges (De Sousa Santos et al., 2007, p. 20). The subjects who participate in these processes should be strengthened by their journey through our research.

Regarding fieldwork analysis, we refer to the proposal of Azpiazu Carballo (2014) for an analysis of feminist discourse that involves revising the principles of critical discourse analysis as to account for power inequalities in terms of gender but also the possibility of thinking about collaborative strategies when working on the deconstruction of meaning entailed in working with discourses. Finally, concerning what Samaja (2010) called the instance of expository validation of the results, we believe in the relevance of incorporating the ethical question of authorship and access to knowledge into the research processes. Different strategies are put in place to acknowledge the authorial character of the people who participate in our studies. The unspoken criterion of fieldwork participants' anonymity is revised: it is about people being able to agree and decide what privacy they would like to have, rather than the exercise of expert power and the hierarchical imposition of academic modes of doing (Rodríguez & Da Costa, 2020, p. 25). Decolonial feminism proposes that we ask ourselves whether there is something of the extractivist logic of making those who produce knowledge invisible hidden behind the alleged ethical pretence of preserving the identity of those who have participated in our interviews. One strategy we have learned from social worker Gabriela Rubilar Donoso (2015) is that of researchers and interviewees working in co-labour processes in the editing of recorded interviews to produce and publish co-authored texts. With neoliberalism encouraging the commodification of academic work, it is important to consider where we publish: open-access journals and websites, Creative Commons copyright licenses, allow us to think about formats that enable the inclusive circulation of knowledge, sharing what we have produced outside market logic. Thinking of knowledge as a right and not as a commodity is central from this perspective. Social Work research groups from various Argentine universities (Universidad Nacional de Mar del Plata; Universidad de Buenos Aires; Universidad Nacional de Rosario, Universidad Nacional de La Plata, Universidad Nacional de San Juan) have been incorporating elements of these methodologies in their research as a way of making visible the struggles of social groups and reducing academic extractivism.

Conclusion

In this chapter, we have set out to explore the contributions of situated Feminisms to research in Social Work. To do so, we began by mapping the situated Feminisms to establish four dimensions: an ethical-political dimension affected by and involved in the struggle against gender and sexual inequalities, a political-epistemological dimension in which strategies are conjured up to overcome the academy/activism or literate knowledge/popular knowledge divide, a third theoretical-epistemological dimension recognising the cis-hetero-androcentric bias of knowledge production and a theoretical-methodological dimension reviewing the patriarchal biases of scientists.

The contributions of situated Feminisms to research in Social Work deal with the ethical-political-epistemological and the theoretical-political-methodological dimensions. On the one hand, we present the contributions of Feminisms on the epistemological-political-ethical level, recognising the sexist biases of science (Harding, 1986) and that all knowledge is positioned (Spivak, 1981). On the other hand, in the theoretical-political-methodological dimension, we recover the political commitment of Hill Collins (2000) to a Black feminist epistemology, enriched by decolonial feminism (Curiel, 2014), highlighting the sexist and racist nature of knowledge production.

These inputs allow us to envisage a shift in the way we do research: not only in our fieldwork but also from the very beginning of the construction of the problem, seeking strategies to articulate our research with feminist agendas and struggles. We also recognise the relevance of making the productions of Latin American feminist colleagues visible in our theoretical framework, fostering dialogues among knowledges. Moving forward on this path, Biglia (2015) posited the utmost importance of feminist methodologies. A corpus of diverse authors helped us explore methodological strategies to materialise this perspective: such as feminist narrative biographical approaches, auto-corpo-biography, collaborative methodologies, strategies against cognitive extractivism, feminist activist research and feminist discourse analysis, among others.

Feminist research in Social Work encompasses theoretical, political, epistemological and methodological dimensions, recognising the place of women and gender diversity in the scientific field, while creating conditions of possibility for them to produce such knowledge. Above all, it questions the ways in which knowledge is validated. In this sense, it is not enough to contest what already exists: the challenge is to redefine the processes of scientific knowledge by implementing reality interpretation methodologies based on a non-heteropatriarchal logic. This does not mean discarding all pre-existing production and analysis techniques but rather trying out Social Work research based on feminist postulates and redesigned according to the specificity, context and purpose of each research. Last, such definition, as Curiel (2014) points out, must deconstruct heteropatriarchal postulates.

In summary, Social Work feminist research implies:

- co-building the research problem with those involved;
- to incorporate the production of women and gender-sex non-conforming people in the theoretical framework of our research;
- a horizontal and dialogical methodology that does not generate symbolic violence;
- strategies to avoid academic extractivism;
- prioritising time with the community over academic administrative obligations;
- promoting new achievements in the gender agenda based on the contributions of our research;
- generating synergy between academic Social Work research and professional intervention in social services and institutions.

Recovering feminist proposals for social research makes us wonder how Social Work knowledge is produced today. We believe that although feminist epistemology and methodology still have a low impact on the social sciences in general, there are advances. Social Work is a feminised profession with a long tradition of addressing the gender perspective. We find some publications proposing and exercising a feminist perspective in Social Work research (Guzzetti and Zunino, 2019; Martínez and Hermida, 2022; Riveiro, 2019). But there is still a long way to go.

Note

1 Dimensions 1 and 2 are addressed in the section "The ethical-political-epistemological perspective", while 3 and 4 are addressed in the section "The theoretical-political-methodological perspective".

References

Ahmed, S. (2017). *Living a feminist life*. Duke University Press. https://doi.org/10.2307/j.ctv11g9836
Alvarado, M. (2020). *Feminismos del Sur: Recorridos, Itinerarios, Junturas* [Southern feminisms: Journeys, itineraries, junctures]. Prometheus.

Alvarado, M. & Fischetti, N. (2018). Feminismos del Sur. Alusiones / Elusiones / Ilusiones [Southern feminisms. Allusions / elusions / illusions]. *Pléyade, 22*, 87–105. https://doi.org/10.4067/S0719-36962018000200087

Araiza Díaz, A. & González García, R. (2017). La Investigación Activista Feminista. Un diálogo metodológico con los movimientos sociales [Feminist activist research. A methodological dialogue with social movements]. *EMPIRIA: Revista de Metodología de Ciencias Sociales, 38*, 63–84. https://doi.org/10.5944/empiria.38.2018.19706

Araya, I., & Chávez, N. (2022). Metodologías Colaborativas: etnografía feminista con mujeres afrodescendientes e indígenas en Arica (Chile) [Collaborative methodologies: feminist ethnography with Afro-descendant and Indigenous women in Arica (Chile)]. *Antropologías Del Sur, 9*(17), 19–38. https://doi.org/10.25074/rantros.v9i17.2008

Azpiazu Carballo, J. (2014). Análisis crítico del discurso con perspectiva feminista. In Azkue, M. L., Matxalen Legarreta, G., Guzmán, I. & Zirion, J. (Eds.), *Otras formas de (re)conocer. Reflexiones, herramientas y aplicaciones desde la investigación feminista.* [Other forms of (re)cognition. Reflections, tools and applications from feminist research] (pp. 111–124). Hegoa.

Bidaseca, K. (2016). *Feminismo y Poscolonialidad 2* [Feminism and postcoloniality 2]. Godot.

Biglia, B. (2014). Avances, dilemas, y retos de las epistemologías feministas en la investigación social. In Azkue, M. L., Matxalen Legarreta, G., Guzmán, I. & Zirion, J. (Eds.), *Otras formas de (re)conocer. Reflexiones, herramientas y aplicaciones desde la investigación feminista.* [Other forms of (re)cognition. Reflections, tools and applications from feminist research] (pp. 21–44). Hegoa.

Butler, J. (2011). *Bodies that matter: On the discursive limits of sex.* Routledge. https://doi.org/10.4324/9780203828274

Cabnal, L. (2010). *Feminismos diversos: el feminismo comunitario* [Diverse feminisms: Community feminism]. ACSUR - Las Segovias.

Colectivo Ayllu & Rivadeneira, E. (2020). Afectividades marrones y negras: conversación con el colectivo Ayllu -Migrantes transgresorxs del Reino de España [Brown and Black affects: a dialogue with colectivo Ayllu - Kingdom of Spain's transgresor migrants]. *post(s), 6*(1). https://doi.org/10.18272/post(s).v6i1.2098

Crenshaw, K. W. (1991). Mapping the margins: Intersectionality, identity politics, and violence against women of color. *Stanford Law Review, 43*(6), 1241–1299.

Curiel, O. (2014). Construyendo Metodologías Feministas desde el feminismo decolonial. In Azkue, M. L., Matxalen Legarreta, G., Guzmán, I. & Zirion, J. (Eds.), *Otras formas de (re)conocer. Reflexiones, herramientas y aplicaciones desde la investigación feminista.* [Other forms of (re)cognition. Reflections, tools and applications from feminist research]. Hegoa.

De Sousa Santos, B., Nunes, J. A., & Meneses, M. P. (2007). Opening up the canon of knowledge and recognition of difference. In De Sousa Santos, B. (Ed.), *Another knowledge is possible: Beyond northern epistemologies* (pp. 19–62). Verso.

Disch, L. J., & Hawkesworth, M. E. (Eds.). (2016). *The Oxford handbook of feminist theory.* Oxford University Press. https://doi.org/10.1093/oxfordhb/9780199328581.001.0001

Espinosa Miñoso, Y. (2017). De por qué es necesario un feminismo descolonial: diferenciación, dominación co-constitutiva de la modernidad occidental y el fin de la política de identidad [On why decolonial feminism is necessary: Differentiation, co-constitutive domination of western modernity and the end of identity politics]. *Solar: revista de filosofía iberoamericana, 12*(1), 146–171.

flores, v. (2013). *Interruqciones, ensayos de poética activista. Escritura, política, pedagogía* [Interruqtions, essays on activist poetics. Writing, politics, pedagogy]. La Mondonga Dark. https://www.bibliotecafragmentada.org/interrupciones/

Gargallo, F. (2004). *Las ideas feministas latinoamericanas* [Feminist ideas from Latin America]. Desde abajo.

Gonzalez, L. (2018). Racismo y sexismo en la cultura brasileña. In Brasil, A. & Bringel, B. (Eds.), *Antología del pensamiento crítico brasileño contemporáneo* [Anthology of contemporary Brazilian critical thought]. CLACSO, 565–582.

Guzzetti, L. & Zunino, E. (Eds.) (2019) *Feminismos y Trabajo Social* [Feminisms and social work]. Espacio Editorial.

Harding, S. G. (1986). *The science question in feminism.* Cornell University Press.

Hill Collins, P. (2000). *Black feminist thought: Knowledge, consciousness, and the politics of empowerment.* Routledge. https://doi.org/10.4324/9780203900055

hooks, b. (2017). *Feminism is for everybody: Passionate politics.* Routledge, 2014.
Korol, C. & Castro, C. (2016). *Feminismos populares: pedagogías y políticas. Aprendizajes compartidos y voces desobedientes de Colombia, Argentina, Brasil, Venezuela, Paraguay, Palestina y Cuba* [Popular feminisms: pedagogies and politics. Shared learning and disobedient voices from Colombia, Argentina, Brazil, Venezuela, Paraguay, Palestine and Cuba]. La fogata.
Lorde, A. (1978). *Uses of the erotic: The erotic as power.* Out & Out Books.
Lugones, M. (2008). Colonialidad y Género [Coloniality and gender]. *Tabula Rasa, 9,* 73–101.
Martínez, S. & Hermida, M. E. (2022). *Los Feminismos del Sur e intervención social: genealogías, diálogos y debates.* Espacio.
Mignolo, W. (1995). La razón postcolonial: herencias coloniales y teorías postcoloniales [Postcolonial reason: Colonial legacies and postcolonial theories]. *Revista chilena de literatura, 47,* 91–114.
Millan, M. (2017). Mujer Mapuche: explotación colonial sobre el territorio corporal. In de Santiago Guzmán, A., Caballero Borja, E. & Gonzalez Ortuño, G (Eds.), *Mujeres intelectuales: feminismos y liberación en América Latina y el Caribe* [Women intellectuals: feminisms and liberation in Latin America and the Caribbean] (pp. 141–148). CLACSO.
Preciado, P. (2011). *Manifiesto contrasexual* [Countersexual manifesto]. Anagrama.
Riveiro, L. (2019). *Trabajo Social y feminismos. Perspectivas y estrategias en debate* [Social Work and feminisms. Perspectives and strategies in debate]. Colegio de asistentes sociales o trabajadores sociales de la provincia de Buenos Aires.
Rivera Cusicanqui, S. (2018). *Un mundo ch'ixi es posible. Ensayos desde un presente en crisis* [A Ch'ixi world is possible. Essays from a present in crisis]. Tinta Limón.
Rodríguez, R. (2018). *De la auto-biografía a la corpo-biografía feminista: Herramientas descoloniales contra el saqueo metodológico* [From auto-biography to feminist corpo-biography: Decolonial tools against methodological plundering]. VI Encuentro Latinoamericano de Metodología de las Ciencias Sociales (ELMeCS). Innovación y creatividad en la investigación social: Navegando la compleja realidad latinoamericana. Universidad de Cuenca.
Rodríguez, R. P. & da Costa, S. (2020). Descolonizar las herramientas metodológicas. Una experiencia de investigación feminista [Decolonising methodological tools. A feminist research experience]. *MILLCAYAC - Revista Digital de Ciencias Sociales, 11,* 13–30.
Roldán, Y. (2022). Feminismos del Sur y Trabajo Social: cruces, relevos y aportes [Feminismos del Sur e intervención social: genealogías, diálogos y debates]. Espacio.
Rubilar Donoso, G. (2015). Prácticas de memoria y construcción de testimonios de investigación. Reflexiones metodológicas sobre autoentrevista, testimonios y narrativas de investigación de trabajadores sociales [Practices of memory and the construction of research testimonies: A methodological reflection about self-interviewing, testimonies, and social workers' accounts of their research]. *Forum Qualitative Social Research, 16*(3). https://doi.org/10.17169/fqs-16.3.2257
Samaja, J. (2010). *Epistemología y metodología. Elementos para una teoría de la investigación científica* [Epistemology and methodology. Elements for a theory of scientific research]. Eudeba.
Segato, R. (2015). *La crítica de la colonialidad en ocho ensayos. Y una antropología por demanda* [The critique of coloniality in eight essays. And an anthropology on demand]. Prometeo.
Shock, S. (2011). *Poemario Trans pirado* [Trans pired poems]. Nuevos tiempos.
Simpson, L. & Klein, N. (2017). Dancing the world into being: A conversation with idle-no-more's Leanne Simpson. *Yes Magazine.*
Spivak, G. C. (1981) French Feminism in an International Frame. *Yale French Studies Feminist Readings: Frencha Texts/American Contexts, 62,* 154–184.

24
FEMINIST QUERIES
Exploring feminist social work research questions

Stéphanie Wahab, Ben Anderson-Nathe and Christina Gringeri

Introduction

We began our explorations of feminist social work research (FSWR) in 2010 (Gringeri, Wahab, & Anderson-Nathe, 2010) and have maintained the interest, concern, and excitement since. In fact, the current "dangerous times" (Park, Wahab, & Bhyan, 2017) marked by the dominance of far-right politics, the climate crisis, intensified attacks on feminist and critical scholarship (Park, Bhuyan, & Wahab, 2019; Staller, 2019), and the 2022 United States' Supreme Court decision to overturn federal protections for abortions through Roe v. Wade have emboldened and motivated us to continue calling attention to social work feminist inquiry. Consequently, this chapter is born of our commitments to feminist praxis and our curiosity about the current landscape of FSWR as seen through the questions posed by researchers. Given the emphasis we place on teaching students about the significance of a robust research question, we sought to analyze what research questions in published feminist inquiry can tell us about FSWR in general. With a 20-year history of editorial relationships and responsibilities to social work's only explicitly feminist academic journal, *Affilia: Feminist inquiry in social work*, we've had front row seats to social work feminist scholarship and research. Since our initial research attempts to map the landscape of feminist inquiry (2010, 2012, 2013), we have observed that, while social work scholars have produced knowledge about feminist ethics (Bozalek, 2016), practice (Eyal-Lubling & Krumer-Nevo, 2016; Wendt & Moulding, 2016), and teaching (Epstein, Hosken, Vassos, 2018), very few scoping reviews, essays, analyses, or commentaries have been published (outside of *Affilia*) on the broader landscape of feminist social work theory or research. Feminist research remains in the margins, rather than in the center, of social work scholarship.

The past ten years of FSWR

Feminisms and social work journals

Unfortunately, there continues to be a dearth of feminist research evident in social work textbooks (Bryant, 2016; Gringeri et al., 2010; Rubin & Babbie, 2014; Shaw, 2010; Thyer, 2010), and broadly referenced English-language social work academic journals.

The marginalization of feminist inquiry consequently limits and precludes access to the scope of creative solutions to social problems and social work practice, policy, and teaching as well as limits access to the counternarratives to hegemonic social work knowledge. We have argued elsewhere that feminist research holds the potential to interrupt: (1) neoliberalism's embrace of individual change at the expense of social change; (2) an overreliance on objectivist epistemologies; and (3) perpetuation of carceral and policing logics that uphold white supremacy and reinscribe social workers' roles as agents of state control (Harrell et al., 2022, p. 3). We further believe that social work has much to gain from feminist research outside of social work, as well as much to contribute:

> A more robust engagement with feminist research might help us recognize the knowledge-building capacity of social activism and the astonishing capacity of human solidarity. Feminist research can also help us find and assert our voices to dismantle the silence and complicity of social work in the face of systems of oppression by centering the margins, and those who are quietly doing the work of rejecting institutional norms that oppress and erase. Feminist research might help us see the centrality of social and economic inequality, and the degradation of the environment as radical causes of physical and mental illness. This could spur us to develop new and rich collaborations with far-reaching transformative impacts. Perhaps more than ever, social work can lean on feminist research to dream a new social work, one that rejects complicity with systems of oppression once and for all.
>
> *(Harrell et al., 2022, p. 13)*

Our critique of the continued marginalization of FSWR in social work scholarship however should not obscure the fact that creative, theory-engaged, robust FSWR does exist and in the Global North is typically published in the only academic journal specifically dedicated to feminist knowledge and praxis, *Affilia: Feminist inquiry in social work*, with occasional appearances in more broadly defined journals such as *Qualitative Social Work*. The latter case is significant in that it may signal the material outcomes of the conceptual, methodological, and often values alignment between Feminisms and qualitative modes of inquiry. While it is beyond the scope of this chapter to theorize why so few explicitly feminist articles are published in more mainstream social work journals in the U.S. and Canada, we do note this finding as significant when it comes to the landscape for our work as it suggests that feminist social work scholarship in the Global North is largely siloed. We are troubled by this continued siloing of feminist scholarship given the epistemic implications that gendered, queer, critical ways of knowing are not worthy of attention and engagement at the center of social work research and education. The marginalization of feminist inquiry consequently limits and precludes access to the scope of creative solutions to social problems and social work practice, policy, and teaching as well as limits access to the counternarratives to hegemonic social work knowledge.

Nevertheless, feminist scholars engage a broad and nuanced range of epistemologies and methodologies (Ackerly & True, 2010; Hesse-Biber, 2007; Olesen, 2000), calling attention to the *seventh moment in social work* (Denzin, 2002) as focused on "previously silenced voices, a turn to performance texts, and an abiding concern with moral discourse, with conversations about democracy, politics, race, gender, nation, freedom and community" (p. 26). Three recent contributions to social work feminist research worth mentioning in this context include Rasool and Harms-Smith (2022)'s article highlighting the often ignored

Black African and womanist decolonial contributions to social work knowledge, Bryant's (2016) chapter on epistemology in feminist research, and the editorial in *Affilia* (Goodkind et al., 2021).

Rasool and Harms-Smith (2022) place Black African and womanist scholarship in conversation with principles of Decoloniality for social work that includes

> positioning Afrika as the centre; accounting for power dynamics in structures, systems, and relationships; confronting the oppressive hierarchies of race, class, and gender; adopting a structural perspective to uncover oppressive and inequitable social structures; critical conscientisation as a precursor to foregrounding the "voice" of those who are marginalized.
>
> *(p. 2)*

Bryant (2016) offers an expansive and hopeful analysis of recent FSWR by presenting an overview of the dominant methodologies engaged by feminist scholars, including those grounded in intersectionality, narrative, and Foucauldian analyses. At the core of this project is an exploration of the uniquely social work contributions to feminist inquiry, including "the ways we practice research, the way we work alongside our co-researchers to implement social transformation at the individual, community and societal level" (p. 92).

The other contribution, relevant to our epistemological grounding, is *Affilia*'s editorial board's discussion of the principles and practices grounding critical feminist inquiry. The editorial board, comprising leading feminist scholars in social work, offers three categories of principles for feminist inquiry and praxis: conceptual, epistemological, and political. While a discussion of the numerous principles embedded within these three categories extends beyond the scope of our chapter, we appreciate their engagement with neoliberalism as a significant force shaping not just social work research, but FSWR as well. Our previous scholarship in this area did not engage with the impacts of neoliberalism and *Affilia*'s editorial extends previous analyses of FSWR in very important ways. We underscore the authors' caution that social work feminist scholars be mindful of the ways neoliberalism has coopted Feminisms through "choice feminism" to reinforce rather than challenge and resist status quo power structures. Because we believe that feminist research, rooted in a complex, historicized, and dynamic power analysis, has much to contribute to social work theory, practice, policy, and research, we look to research questions as one indicator of how published FSWR approaches this potential.

Researching the questions

There is scant research, if any, analyzing the questions scholars pose to better understand what research questions might tell us about the direction, or landscape of disciplinary scholarship. Yet research questions are an influential guidepost in conducting a scholarly project; the questions we pose may reveal our philosophical or paradigmatic worldview, lead to the selection of methods, compatible theories, analytic strategies, and the focus of our discussions. As Trede and Higgs (2009, p. 13) note, research is the "pursuit of knowledge through questioning." Our questions, as found in published research, may highlight different aspects of the knowledge we choose to develop. Finally, the questions we ask reveal much about what knowledge is disciplinarily validated, particularly salient in the professions, where research is assumed to drive professional practice.

Interestingly, most research texts devote little time to the process of developing a good research question; the standard instructions are to review the relevant literature, identify unasked questions that may contribute to the scholarly conversation, and develop the project – much easier said than done! Such scant attention to the process and the questions may lead one to mistakenly assume that good questions are easy to come by and do not contribute substance to the project. We differ; in this chapter, we examine the questions feminist social work scholars pose to see what they teach us about social work's pursuit of feminist knowledge over the past decade.

Research questions can be broadly grouped into four types: descriptive, explanatory, prescriptive, and emancipatory. While disciplines pose questions of all types, the STEM (so-called natural sciences) fields tend to pose positivist questions aimed at prediction and explanation, the social science questions fall within the first three types with some in the last category, and the critical theory approaches across disciplines emphasize emancipatory aims in research (Trede & Higgs, 2009, p. 17). Feminist inquiry is a branch of critical approaches, and the use of a feminist research ethic (Ackerly & True, 2010) grounds feminist scholarship in particular ways that attend to power dynamics, especially those within the discipline; frames the scholarly endeavor from the perspective of "concrete and located experiences" (p. 94); and relies upon the reflexivity and humility of the researchers. We note that while no particular set of methods makes research feminist, ethical approaches attending to power, relationality, positionality, and reflexivity are frequently recognized as impacting constructions of gender, and gender relations that shape inquiry.

Ackerly and True (2010) underscore the importance of the research question by highlighting its potential to expose what we often assume, raise up voices silenced by structures and norms, and center topics and analyses marginalized by our disciplines. Equally important for social work is that feminist research questions have the power to foreground institutional practices and processes that are normatively accepted or unquestioned within the profession; that is, feminist scholars may raise questions about social work interventions, processes, and structures that may contribute to or undermine equity, equality, and inclusion. Social work scholars need to be well-versed in a broad range of theoretical and interdisciplinary literature so that we can examine the silences and neglected topics in our field.

Research questions may also be generated by observing gaps or inadequacies in the literature; Sandberg and Alvesson (2011) refer to this as "gap-spotting." In their review of research questions in organizational literature, this was the most common strategy authors used to justify the research question. The gap-spotting approach did not tend to lead to scholarship that developed new theories or explanations; rather, it seemed to contribute to descriptive understandings within accepted disciplinary terrain. Less frequently, authors found that scholars generated questions that challenged the assumptions and approaches in their field, which was more likely to contribute to theoretical developments and new lines of inquiry.

Methods

Sample

We sought to understand what can be gleaned from an examination of published FSWR questions. To generate a list of articles in which researchers located their work explicitly in the language of social work and Feminisms, we conducted a literature search of

English-language articles published between 2011 and 2020 that included both *social work* and *feminis** in their abstract, keywords, or article title. Using the asterisk after "feminis" signals the search engine to include associated terms such as feminism, feminisms, or feminist. We selected 2011 as the starting year as our previous research analyzed social work feminist research spanning 2000–2010. To further refine the search, we analyzed all articles identified in this first round to assure that they presented findings from research (of any explicit method or methodology). In total, we arrived at a sample of 98 FSWR articles from this process. Of these, the majority (n = 63) were published in *Affilia*; other journals included *Qualitative Social Work* (n = 12), *British Social Work* (n = 7), *Social Work* (n = 6), *Australian Social Work* (n = 3), *the Journal of Social Work* (n = 3), and a handful of others with fewer than three articles each. While these articles reflected scholarship conducted in a variety of geographies, including the USA (n = 53), Australia (n = 13), Canada (n = 8), the Middle East (n = 7), Asia (n = 6), Europe (n = 6), Africa, (n = 4), and South America (n = 1), the sample is more representative of the Global North and Middle East. We acknowledge the limitations of our sample and note that our keyword search does not capture feminist scholarship that did not use social work and *feminis** in the keywords, abstract, or article. Future research in this area may explore a broader range of keywords that feminist social work scholars use to identify their work as well as look at research that is read as feminist yet not explicitly named as such by the authors.

Data collection and analysis

Informed by our review of the current literature and our previous work on Feminisms in social work research (Anderson-Nathe, Gringeri, & Wahab, 2013; Gringeri, Wahab, & Anderson-Nathe, 2010; Wahab, Anderson-Nathe, Gringeri, 2012), we created a data collection instrument to identify features of each article salient to our overall aim of understanding the contemporary context of FSWR. This template included questions related to the articles' stated research question or purpose, substantive topical area, populations of focus, stated theoretical foundations, methods, and authors' stated contributions to social work.

Our initial analysis consisted of first selecting two articles to be read by all members of the research team. This first read helped the research team to calibrate the template, pointing to areas of alignment and misalignment in how we interpreted and applied it to the sample. After clarifying items in the template, we selected four additional articles, which all researchers read to arrive at final agreement on the use of the template. We distributed the remaining articles among the research team, coded them with the template, and discussed them in full-team conferences to arrive at agreement and consistency in coding. We then excerpted all analytic categories from the template related to research questions and conducted a thematic analysis of the language of the questions themselves (or in some cases, where research questions weren't explicitly indicated, on the stated purpose of the research) for the following categories: population of focus; substantive area of the research; and indications of epistemology evident in the framing of the question.

Findings and discussion

Despite their centrality in conceptualizing and formulating research projects, research questions appear to occupy a position of slightly less prominence in published articles than we had anticipated. The questions reflect researchers' attempts to distill their investigations and truncate their studies' aims down to a form that is easily and succinctly articulated for a given publication. Still, examining the questions within this context reveals interesting and valuable observations about FSWR.

Question or purpose

Most manuscripts in the sample explicitly state the research question or purpose guiding the inquiry; nearly half (n = 55) the articles offer a clear research question, 41 articulate some statement of purpose for the research (but do not include the exact question), and only 2 manuscripts offer neither a question nor a purpose. Given the importance we've placed in our project attending to research questions, as well as the emphasis we place on formulating a strong research question in the research courses we teach, we find it noteworthy that most authors do provide the question or purpose guiding the inquiry. Further, we suspect that those articles in which the research question was omitted in favor of a statement of purpose may point to the pressures of the publication environment, in which full studies guided by comprehensive questions may be reduced out of necessity to brief summaries of purpose rather than comprehensive questions. We speculate, as well, that there may be an epistemological component to this observation. Post-positivist research includes hypothesis testing, which lends itself particularly well to explicit and discrete research questions. The common alignment of feminist research to interpretive and constructivist methods and apparent neglect of post-positivist methods may therefore contribute to many researchers in our sample defaulting to summaries of purpose. Nevertheless, in the case of both explicit research questions and statements of research purpose, little information can be gleaned about the individual articles' underlying theoretical or epistemological stance.

Women and "women's issues"

The majority of the research questions in our sample focus on women and girls (n = 79), and a smaller minority on gender (n = 42) more broadly, with some studies framing women and gender interchangeably. The focus and subjects of study – either implicitly or explicitly – center cis-women, with two studies in the sample focusing on transgender or gender non-binary participants. Two studies focused specifically on men or masculinities. This finding suggests that FSWR continues to center cis-women, girls, and topics that are of traditional interest to cis-women (mothering, care work, violence, victimization, children, power, and empowerment), and that FSWR generally still does not trouble the category woman in any consistent or systematic fashion. As the category woman remains largely unsettled in FSWR, so does the gender binary.

Gap-spotting and challenges

We categorized the research questions in terms of how authors posed them: how, what, or why, using these words as proxies for the knowledge claims being made (e.g., descriptive, explanatory, or predictive). The overwhelming majority of our sample (n = 79) asked "how" or "what" questions, typically associated with questions of research participants' descriptions of experience or interpretations of phenomena. Only one article in the sample asked a "why" question; a handful of articles did not have a clearly stated research question but had a generalized aim to describe phenomena. Thus, more than three-fourths of all feminist social work publications posed questions or stated aims that led to descriptive research. In line with the observations of Sandberg and Alvesson (2011), we examined the research questions further to determine whether authors generated their questions based on a noted gap in the existing literature or as a way to challenge assumptions in the substantive area. We found that 67% of the research questions were generated by gap-spotting in the literature, and 33% explored questions that challenged assumptions.

Overall, feminist social work publications are predominantly descriptive projects that aim to address a gap in the literature and, in doing so, seek to add to or deepen understanding of the experiences and contexts of the lives of women and girls. The minority (33%) of FSWR raises questions that challenge normative or theoretical assumptions as a way to problematize dominant academic narratives on the lives of women and girls. These types of research questions open new avenues of study that hold the potential to turn the researchers' gaze toward systems and structures, as well as toward strengths and areas of resistance, disruption, and empowerment. Feminist work that challenges assumptions tends to be more explanatory in its aims and may be more likely to make theoretical contributions. Both descriptive and explanatory research are needed to develop knowledge in the field of social work; however, explanatory work is more likely to lead to developments in feminist interventions and practice approaches.

Turning the gaze on social work

Thirty-one studies in our sample turn the research gaze onto social work itself, including social work education, research, scholarship/publication, and practice. Thirty of these studies engaged a descriptive or exploratory research question, with a stated purpose to better understand particular social work domains. Precisely 4 of these 31 manuscripts present a research purpose rather than explicit research question, complicating our ability to assess the type of question guiding the inquiry. Still, authors of these 31 studies explored and often simultaneously unsettled discourses (including but not limited to language, policy, politics, and assumptions) present in social work and social service settings. For example, researchers explored how service providers perceive and theorize sex workers in practice (Anasti, 2018), how feminist social workers claim Feminisms in practice (Eyal-Lubling & Krumer-Nevo, 2016), the role of pathologizing discourses in clinical practice with survivors of domestic violence (Hahn & Scanlon, 2016), how social workers in India define Feminisms in their practice (Mitra, 2011), and the role of care ethics for merging anti-oppressive, social justice practice in gerontology (Ward & Barnes, 2016).

While these examples are not exhaustive, they offer a glimpse into the ways feminist social work researchers may simultaneously seek to explore undertheorized or under-researched arenas of practice while troubling taken for granted assumptions about social work theory and practice. One study by Bergen and Abji (2020) explores how carceral logics underpin child protection, immigration, and criminal systems while simultaneously troubling social work's complicity in carceral logics and systems. Hereth and Bouris (2020) explicitly frame their research as a challenge to the Social Work Grand Challenge to address mass incarceration through smart decarceration initiatives. Another study by Hudson and Richardson (2016) asks,

> In what ways is attention to emotion an integral aspect of teaching and practicing social work research? How can teaching and practicing qualitative inquiry grant access to emotional and experiential information and knowledges otherwise often left untapped, buried, or deemed problematic, flawed, undesirable, or ancillary?
>
> (p. 416)

Their question is exploratory in its aim to better understand how emotional labor functions in the teaching of research in social work, while simultaneously troubling the taken for granted assumption that emotional labor is inconsequential and not valued as legitimate labor, or an aspect of labor across normative metrics of production.

Implications and recommendations

In our review of published FSWR, we noted patterns related to articulation of the research questions or purpose, the centering of cis-women and related issues, the tendency toward gap-spotting and descriptive work, and works by authors in which they troubled assumptions within social work. Most authors offered a research question (56%), and slightly under half articulated a purpose (41%). Most authors focused on cis-women and related issues, taking for granted the category of "woman" and the lived experiences of those within that category; there was little that troubled the gender binary. We recognize the value and utility of the category "woman" in many contexts, and at the same time, we suggest that feminist social work's reliance on this category limits our engagement with feminist scholarship which has broadened to include analyses of gender as a construct. We recommend that feminist social work researchers demonstrate more conscious engagement with the constructs of sex, gender, and the binary, inclusive of but not limited to the category of "woman." A majority of studies posed descriptive questions that addressed gaps in the literature and aimed to deepen understanding of women's or girls' experiences; research that explicitly engages with theory to help move feminist work beyond description is needed. Finally, we noted a few examples of works that turned the gaze on social work to raise questions about commonly held assumptions.

Authors' focus on micro-, or lived experiences leads to consistent application of constructivist methods, neglecting macro issues examined in larger data using post-positivist or critical methods of analysis. We recommend that feminist social work researchers additionally recognize the potential contributions post-positivist and critical research methods and analysis of larger data can make to social work Feminisms. Such research can examine larger social patterns of discrimination, exclusion, and oppression that would augment understanding of micro-level experiences by substantiating links to macro issues, policies, and programs. Centering cis-women reinscribes the gender binary, narrowing and distorting a fuller range of experiences of concern to feminists. Such reliance on the gender binary requires conscious disruption and expansion by feminist researchers so that published works avoid reinforcing assumptions that align social work research, education, and practice with binary constructs of sex and gender.

We recognize that the academy's push for increased publications is one factor that may underlie the reliance of feminist researchers on constructivist methods utilizing small samples and focused on micro-experiential issues. This may be compounded by doctoral-level training that equates feminist work with the personal at the expense of the political. We recommend that feminist social work researchers reclaim our profession's focus on the intertwined issues at the micro-, mezzo-, and macro levels so that we do not neglect the political in efforts to understand the personal.

Limitations and conclusion

While we'd hoped to learn more about FSWR from studying research questions, we are admittedly disappointed that even if mentioned and clearly stated in the manuscript (which isn't always the case), standing alone, research questions are significantly decontextualized from the philosophy, epistemology, and methodology of the research and consequently not legible in terms of their greater substance. While research questions give us a hint of the substantive focus of the research and therefore may alert us to some of the trends and interests capturing our attention and energy, ultimately, to make sense of a research question, we believe it needs to be explored in conversation with, or in relationship with the rest of the manuscript, including discussions about theory, philosophy, methodology, rational, and methods. Digesting research questions without the context of the study and its assembling parts is rather limiting and may perpetuate a way of thinking about research that actually works against our (the three of us) collective value of theory as a scaffolding for knowledge production. Examining questions as disconnected from their relationship to epistemology for example perpetuates a focus on methods (tools) over methodology (the theory of the tools) that we've written against in our previous work.

Developing a research question is a dynamic process that tends to occur over time, rather than a static one-time event in the course of scholarly work (Wahab, Mehrotra, & Myers, 2022). Researchers may start out with a general question, collect data that then raises new questions, which leads to further data collection, and so forth. In a published article or chapter, the research question may be narrowed to what can be discussed in the given space, depending on the audience, the publication venue, and the author's purposes. Coloniality and racism also influence these decisions; scholars from the Global South are often encouraged to publish in English-language venues, which inflates the positioning of the Global North and West as sites of knowledge production. Consequently, authors' and editors' decisions around what does and doesn't get published about a research project is, in part, shaped by the business of publishing, in addition to the other factors we've discussed above. In the process of revising and editing our chapter, we acknowledge the ways our English-language sampling privileges work from the Global North and West and reinscribes colonial epistemics. While we are disappointed in what we can learn from studying research questions alone and angry at the continued exclusion of scholarly voices constrained by these factors, we are reaffirmed in our belief that theory matters, that feminist inquiry holds potential for unsettling taken for granted assumptions around power, gender, resistance, and social change. Finally, research questions serve multiple purposes. They function, perhaps first and foremost, as a guide for researchers to structure the process and the focus of inquiry. They also serve as a signal to reviewers, readers, and other audiences what the researchers are leaning into with the project, even if this micro communication is limited in scope or depth.

References

Ackerly, B. & True, J. (2010). *Doing feminist research in political and social science.* Palgrave Macmillan.

Anasti, T. (2018). Survivor or laborer: How human service managers perceive sex workers. *Affilia: Women and Social Work, 33*(4), 453–476. https://doi.org/10.1177/0886109918778075

Anderson-Nathe, B., Gringeri, C., & Wahab, S. (2013). Nurturing "critical hope" in teaching feminist social work research. *Journal of Social Work Education, 49*(2), 277–291. https://doi.org/10.1080/10437797.2013.768477

Bergen, H., & Abji, S. (2020). Facilitating the carceral pipeline: Social work's role in funneling newcomer children from the child protection system to jail and deportation. *Affilia: Women and Social Work, 35*(1), 34–48. https://doi.org/10.1177/0886109919866165

Bozalek, V. (2016). The political ethics of care and feminist posthuman ethics: Contributions to social work. In R. Hugman & J. Carter (Eds.), *Rethinking values and ethics in social work* (pp. 80–96). Palgrave MacMillan.

Bryant, L. (2016). Repositioning social work research in feminist epistemology, research and praxis. In S. Wendt & N. Moulding (Eds.), *Contemporary feminisms in social work practice* (pp. 82–97). Routledge.

Denzin, N. K. (2002). Social work in the seventh moment. *Qualitative Social Work, 1*(1), 25–38. https://doi.org/10.1177/147332500200100102

Epstein, S. B., Hosken, N., & Vassos, S. (2018). Theoretical research: Creating space for critical feminist social work pedagogy. *Aotearoa New Zealand Social Work, 30*(3), 8–18. https://doi.org/10.11157/anzswj-vol30iss3id489

Eyal-Lubling, R., & Krumer-Nevo, M. (2016). Feminist social work: Practice and theory of practice. *Social Work, 61*(3), 245–254. https://doi.org/10.1093/sw/sww026

Goodkind, S., Kim, M. E., Zelnick, J. R., Bay-Cheng, L. Y., Beltrán, R., Diaz, M., Gibson, M. F., Harrell, S., Kanuha, K., Moulding, N., Mountz, S., Sacks, T. K., Simon, B. L., Toft, J., & Walton, Q. L. (2021). Critical feminisms: Principles and practices for feminist inquiry in social work. *Affilia: Women and Social Work, 36*(4), 481–487. https://doi.org/10.1177/08861099211043166

Gringeri, C., Wahab, S., & Anderson-Nathe, B. (2010). What makes it feminist? Mapping the landscape of social work feminist research. *Affilia: Women and Social Work, 25*(4), 390–405. https://doi.org/10.1177/0886109910384072

Hahn, S. A. & Scanlon, E. (2016). The integration of micro and macro practice: A qualitative study of clinical social workers' practice with domestic violence survivors. *Affilia: Women and Social Work, 31*(3), 331–343. https://doi.org/10.1177/0886109915578730

Harrell, S., Anderson-Nathe, B., Wahab, S., & Gringeri, C. (2022). Feminist research and practice: Reorienting a politic for social work. In T. Hafford-Letchfield & C. Cocker (Eds.), *Feminist theories for social work practice,* (pp. 59–76). Palgrave.

Hereth, J., & Bouris, A. (2020). Queering smart decarceration: Centering the experiences of LGBTQ+ young people to imagine a world without prisons. *Affilia: Women and Social Work, 35*(3), 358–375. https://doi.org/10.1177/0886109919871268

Hesse-Biber, S.N. (2007). Handbook of feminist research: Theory and praxis. SAGE.

Hudson, K. D., & Richardson, E. J. (2016). Centering power, positionality, and emotional labor in a Master of Social Work research course: Perspectives from a student and instructor. *Qualitative Social Work, 15*(3), 414–427. https://doi.org/10.1177/1473325015625761

Mitra, A. (2011). To be or not to be a feminist in India. *Affilia: Women and Social Work, 26*(2), 182–200. https://doi.org/10.1177/0886109911405493

Olesen, V. (2000). *Feminisms and qualitative research at and into the millennium.* In N. K. Denzin, & Y. S. Lincoln (Eds.), Handbook of qualitative research (pp. 215–256). SAGE.

Park, Y., Wahab, S., & Bhuyan, R. (2017). Feminisms in these dangerous times. *Affilia: Women and Social Work, 32*(1), 5–9. https://doi.org/10.1177/0886109916686271

Park, Y., Bhuyan, R., & Wahab, S. (2019). Reclaiming the space of contestation. *Affilia: Women and Social Work, 34*(1), 1–3. https://doi.org/10.1177/0886109918822652

Rasool, S., & Harms-Smith, L. (2022). Retrieving the voices of Black African womanists and feminists for work towards decoloniality in social work. *Southern African Journal of Social Work and Social Development, 34*(1), 1–30. https://doi.org/10.25159/2708-9355/9011

Rubin, A., & Babbie, E. R. (2014). *Research methods for social work*. Brooks/Cole.
Sandberg, J., & Alvesson, M. (2011). Ways of constructing research questions: gap-spotting or problematization? *Organizations, 18*(1), 23–44. https://doi.org/10.1177/1350508410372151
Shaw, I. (2010). *The Sage handbook of social work research*. Sage.
Staller, K. (2019). Stitching tattered cloth: Reflections on social justice and qualitative inquiry in troubled times. In N. Denzin & M. Giardina (Eds.), *Qualitative inquiry at a crossroads: Political, performative, and methodological reflections*. Routledge.
Thyer, B. A. (Ed.) (2010). *The handbook of social work research methods*. Sage.
Trede, F., & Higgs, J. (2009). Framing research questions and writing philosophically. In J. Higgs, D. Horsfall, & S. Grace (Eds.), *Writing qualitative research on practice* (pp. 13–25). Sense Publishers.
Wahab, S., Anderson-Nathe, B., & Gringeri, C. (2012). Joining the conversation: Social work contributions to feminist research. In S. Hesse-Biber (Ed.), *Handbook of feminist research* (pp. 455–474). Sage.
Wahab, S., Mehrotra, G. R., Myers, K. E. (2022). Slow scholarship for social work: A praxis of creativity and resistance. *Qualitative Social Work, 21*(1), 147–159. https://doi.org/10.1177/1473325021990865
Ward, L., & Barnes, M. (2016). Transforming practice with older people through an ethic of care. *The British Journal of Social Work, 46*(4), 906–922. https://doi.org/10.1093/bjsw/bcv029
Wendt, S., & Moulding, N. (2016). *Contemporary feminisms in social work practice*. Routledge.

25
ACADEMIA AND GENDER DISPARITIES
A critical historical analysis of academic careers of Chilean social workers from a feminist-intersectional approach

*Gabriela Rubilar Donoso, Catherine LaBrenz,
Paz Valenzuela Rebolledo and Gianinna Muñoz-Arce*

Introduction: trajectories in academia and the gender gap

Academic social work has been analyzed and studied over the past century. In recent times, academic capitalism has impacted universities and rewarded the trajectories of those who produce the most (Simbürger & Guzmán, 2019). Academic capitalism reflects the global flow of power; specifically, how intellectual property, concentration of knowledge, and forms of social reproduction shape the production of socially useful knowledge (D'Amico, 2016). Thus, knowledge is proffered on the research market, leading to a new phase of capitalist accumulation, where knowledge occupies a central place. Academic capitalism has colonized the sphere of knowledge production by installing market logic across the board: establishing research productivity indicators, generating publication incentive bonuses, encouraging individual work to the detriment of collaboration, and reinforcing competition between academics (Sisto, 2017).

In this context, female academics are confronted daily with evaluative systems and standards that measure their scientific productivity and require management of their own work, without considering gender differences or disparities. Researchers have found that women tend to publish less, receive fewer promotions, and have more interruptions in their careers than men (Murgia & Poggio, 2018; Winslow & Davis, 2016; Woodward, 2007). In parallel, models of organization of work have evidenced a dichotomization of the teaching-administration track and research-publication track in academia (Ríos et al., 2017; Sánchez, 2002).

Slightly more than one-third of knowledge producers in academic research are women (Ministerio de Ciencia y Tecnología, 2022). When entering academia, they face a gender gap and disparities such as socioeconomic segregation, disparities in academic achievements, and differences in functions and tasks (López et al., 2021). These disparities, in turn, force them to evaluate whether they want to stay in academia. Specific to Chile, recent studies have

DOI: 10.4324/9781003317371-29

explored women's experiences and perspectives on academia. Researchers have analyzed career trajectories and how women obtain diverse positions, including higher ranking roles within the university space (Martínez & Bivort, 2014; Suárez-Ortega & Sepúlveda-Zapata, 2022; Undurraga & Simbürger, 2018; Zapata-Sepúlveda & Suárez-Ortega, 2022). These studies have identified academic spaces as socially contradictory for women, considering that the proportion of women decreases as the level or prestige of a position increases (Araneda-Guirriman & Sepúlveda-Páez, 2021; Martínez & Bivort, 2014). In parallel, the experiences of women who have succeeded as academics are often ignored. This perpetuates disparities and a gender gap, as women who have been promoted within academia often face increased workload, precarious work conditions, and fewer opportunities to conduct research than their male peers (Undurraga & Simbürger, 2018).

It is crucial to recognize gender bias and disparities that are present across diverse stages of academic trajectories. At the beginning of their careers, women tend to have more difficulties in networking internationally, given barriers to traveling and establishing cross-national networks (McAlpine et al., 2014). These barriers can be understood from an intersectional approach. The concept of intersectionality emerged from Black feminists, who recognized that inequality and oppression could not be addressed in isolation. Rather, intersectionality recognizes the importance of considering multidimensional experiences and identities that reflect diverse systems of domination and oppression (Platero, 2012). Since its emergence in feminist theory, intersectionality has expanded to understand how different forms of inequality can lead to discrimination and oppression. Instead of a rigid theoretical framework, intersectionality provides a perspective to understand social phenomena as complex and constantly transforming. Therefore, intersectionality can guide studies such as this one, to explore gender disparities within academia, considering: "what women share is a concrete position based on their sex, which leads to shared experiences of discrimination, inequality, or violence based not only on their sex but other identities and the contexts in which they develop" (Rodó-Zarate, 2021, 100).

Within the academic space, women in the mid-career stage tend to take on more duties related to administration and teaching, which can impede research and scholarship, further exacerbating gender gaps that may negatively impact their promotion (Vásquez-Cupeiro & Elston, 2006). In later stages of academic careers, only a low percentage of women retire as full professors or with high-ranking positions within university leadership (Wolfinger et al., 2009), which highlights the under-representation of women academics in positions of power (Saracostti, 2006).

Key concepts have been coined to describe the barriers women face, such as the glass ceiling, gate keepers, sticky floor, rush hours, glass escalator, and imposter syndrome, all of which can be used to analyze horizontal and vertical gender disparities (Acker, 1994; Chodorow, 2007; Martínez & Bivort, 2014). Thus, horizontal gender disparities have been linked to the concentration of women in traditionally feminized fields, such as degrees related to care, compared to the smaller concentration of women in traditionally masculine fields such as hard sciences, technology, engineering, and mathematics (STEM). A metaphor for this horizontal gender disparity is "sticky floor", which illustrates the difficulty women have to propel their careers as these tend to align with undervalued traditional gender stereotypes (Martínez & Bivort, 2014).

In contrast, vertical disparities are connected to symbolic difficulties and structures that women have had to face to obtain positions of power (Sanhueza Díaz et al., 2020). In this case, the concept of "glass ceiling" is a metaphor for vertical gender disparities and has been used to explain gender disparities in higher-up positions. The concept of the glass ceiling can help explain organizational imbalances in high-up positions of management and power (Fundación PRODEMU, 2021; Gaete-Quezada, 2015; Red Feminista, 2023).

These metaphors illustrate the gender gap and reflect barriers women face in securing vertical promotions, inserting themselves in academic spaces, and interrupting traditional structures. While these concepts have been used to explain organizational barriers at a broader level, they are also applicable within academia to analyze trajectories of female academics, as they each contain elements that may slow down or interrupt promotion processes and contribute to the lack of visibility of gender biases in academia.

Among prior studies of trajectories of women in science (Burstin & Arora, 2021; Paludi, 2022; Rubilar, 2022), there are two main lines of research related to gender gaps: the first includes literature that analyzes trajectories from a gendered perspective as a tool to understand inequities. The second encompasses studies that conceptualize gender as a symbolic order that permeates organizations (including universities), through which researchers study processes of subjectification of academics. Both of these lines of research view gender as binary. While this makes it easier to compare situations and interpretations, it also imposes a hegemonic norm through which other genders or gender identities are kept invisible. In this chapter, we subscribe to a different approach to analyze trajectories followed by Chilean social workers in the context of research policies underpinned by academic capitalism (Araneda-Guirriman & Sepúlveda-Páez, 2021; D'Amico, 2016; Sisto, 2017), integrating a feminist and intersectional lens (Harding, 1986; Hill & Bilge, 2019; Platero, 2012).

This approach allows for a cross-cutting approach that includes multiple social identities beyond the feminine-masculine binary. Following Butler's (1997) readings on sexual division of work as a performative act, we understand gender gaps as shaped by repetitions that have been ritualized and normalized, producing a social illusion of essentialism. Notably, social work has been conceptualized in some instances as an extension of caregiving, which in part may have contributed to the overrepresentation of females in the field. An intersectional approach to social work studies expands critical discussion to include identities such as generational status, ethnicity, sex/genderized differences, and socioeconomic backgrounds, among other hierarchies of oppression that act as markers of positionality and explores how these intersect in the process of social work knowledge production within the dynamics and demands of academic capitalism (Araneda-Guirriman & Sepúlveda-Páez, 2021; Muñoz & Rubilar, 2021). By focusing on multiple, intersecting identities in critical analyses of gender in academia, we transcend the binary norms to understand cumulative advantage and disadvantage beyond "masculine" and "feminine" individuals.

Gender disparities in Chilean universities – feminist May

Women in academia continue to face challenges. In Chile, females are participating in higher education at increasing rates – surpassing male enrollment among undergraduate students (51.2% female – 48.8% male). Yet, while their participation in higher education at the undergraduate level may be equal to or slightly higher than males (CNED, 2020), the proportion of females declines as the level of study increases. Thus, gender gaps widen at the doctoral and post-doctoral level. This pattern of decreasing rates of participation is part of the vertical gap that affects women in academia. Further evidence was provided by the most recent study of the Ministry of Science y Tecnología (2022), which found women to make up 43% of students enrolled in doctoral programs, 37% of students graduating with a doctorate, and only 34% of researchers at institutions of higher education. Even more concerning, only 20% of full professors in Chile are women, for whom the average time to promotion was significantly longer than their male peers, a phenomenon present in other countries as well (Winslow & Davis, 2016).

Over the last decade, in Chile, there have been three distinct turning points in the debate about gender disparities within academia. In 2013, Andrade published the book *Del biombo a la catedra* that examined gender inequities in academia from a historical perspective. The first historical milestone presented in this book was in the 19th century, when Eloísa Díaz became the first female student to study and graduate in Medicine in South America in 1886 and is recognized today as one of the contributors to the first wave of feminism in Chile. Key feminist figures in academia such as Amanda Labarca and Elena Caffarena, who advocated for women's suffrage and access to higher education, were also presented in the book. These figures led the Association of University Women in 1931 and later spearheaded the Movement for Emancipation of Women in Chile (MEMCH).

In May 2018, in conjunction with international movements against gendered violence, there was a feminist movement that directly challenged Chilean universities and demanded concrete action to combat patriarchal structures. It emerged with feminist voices and leaders of organizations that were connected to the student movement (of 2006 and 2011) and who, one decade later, held representative positions (ministers) within the government. These events specific to Chile intersected with global phenomena such as #Niunamenos, #Metoo, and #8M (Hiner & López-Dietz, 2021).

Formal reports of sexual harassment of women within academia (students and faculty) have increased since 2015 (Bernardo, 2021; Hiner & López-Dietz, 2021). In response, universities developed action protocols and procedures related to sexual harassment and violence; nonetheless, there were challenges in implementing and enforcing the protocols given bureaucratic and cultural barriers. The movement that began in May 2018 formally denounced this situation and led to students questioning systemic sexism in academia, particularly in how the universities had responded to sexual violence. In parallel, the construction of knowledge and lack of inclusion of feminist perspectives within universities was highlighted through the movement (Muñoz-García, 2020).

This movement was dubbed Feminist May and, in addition to criticizing the impacts of academic capitalism in Chile, it encompassed reports of harassment, sexual abuse, and abuse of power within university systems. As a result of Feminist May, several protocols related to gender in academic trajectories were developed, including the enactment of Law 21,369 in 2021 that provided protection against harassment, violence, or discrimination based on gender. Moreover, this movement gained traction at a national level with other initiatives to promote gender equity in research and in knowledge production, such as the Network of Researchers (REDI, created in May 2016) that promotes the inclusion of women in scientific careers.

In May 2021, the first female Rector of the University of Chile was elected, after 176 years of exclusively male leaders. The recent election of Rosa Devés as Rector of the main university of the country (period 2022–2026) has led to more discussion about the glass ceiling and gender biases that women are faced with in academia. Topics related to the exercise of power and protection from gendered discrimination are especially relevant when considering that in Chile there are more than 40 universities, yet only eight women have served as university rectors, comprising at most 10% of all rectors within the country at any point in time.

Gender disparities and social work in Chile

Gender disparities in Chilean social work education are also notable, with key turning points within the evolution of formal social work at universities. In May 1925, the first generation of students entered the School of Social Service, which emerged as a response to demands for female participation in higher education. As the first school of social services, it had a secular imprint, largely influenced by the social hygiene movement and laid the foundations for social sciences in Chile (Rubilar, 2013). Some alumni of this first Social Service School obtained further specialization abroad and traveled around Latin America, founding other schools of social services. This has led to a secular, progressive, and feminist tradition of social services in Latin America (Illanes, 2012; Matus, 2008).

While interest in further specialization and development of academic careers within social work has existed since the initial formal school, it has largely been invisible within typical discourse of the profession (Matus, 2008). To study the prevalence of doctoral studies among Chilean social workers, in May 2015, there was an official registry created of social workers with a doctoral degree. The project initially identified 70 workers (Rubilar, 2015). Subsequently, a Network for Social Work Researchers was developed and launched (Muñoz et al., 2021) to support academic trajectories. The purpose of the Network is to promote collaboration as a way of countering academic capitalism, under which individual trajectories are often privileged. As of May 2022, the initial registry had been expanded to over 150 social workers with doctoral degrees (68% female; 32% male). While this reflects a large proportion of women with advanced social work degrees, there is still a vertical gap, considering that among undergraduate social work students in Chile, 80% are female and 20% are male.

Among social work academics with a doctoral degree, gender disparities are also present in title and rank. There are fewer than a dozen female social work academics who are at the full professor or tenured rank; those who have achieved tenure and promotion are faced with other barriers. In addition to gender disparities, there are also biases within universities about the status of social work as a discipline. Currently, only three female academics have held or are currently holding a deanship position within larger colleges of social sciences (from 2016 to 2022). Even within schools of social work, there is a higher proportion of male deans than females, giving more weight to the argument that the glass escalator (e.g., challenges in being promoted internally) still exists for certain positions of power.

Intersectional analysis of social work academic trajectories in Chile

We now present the results of a longitudinal study from 2008 to the present on trajectories of social workers. To date, there have been 72 participants. This study was led by the first author of this chapter; since 2019, the co-authors have joined as co-investigators and part of the Project team. The project will continue until 2025. As a longitudinal study spanning almost two decades, its analysis encompasses the centenary of social work in Chile. Thus, it is a study that is currently underway (funded by projects ANID/CONICYT/FONDECYT 11130401, 1190257 and 1230605).

The analysis here has been conducted as part of a cycle of biographical interviews carried out with social workers who participated in a longitudinal study on research trajectories and transitions. It includes interviews that were conducted with 16 academics employed at Chilean universities. Six of the participants completed two to three interviews over the course of a decade, whereas the other ten participants were interviewed two to three times within a shorter time frame of five to six years. A total of 14 women and two men participated. Together, this allows us to observe trajectories over time (diachronically).

All interviews were conducted and analyzed by the authors of this chapter. As part of the interview process, all interviewees read and signed an informed consent document, and the study was vetted and approved by the Institutional Review Board at the sponsoring institutions. Interviews were guided by a semi-structured interview guide that focused on trajectories and transitions experienced in academic or research duties.

Participants included academics of distinct generations who had advanced their careers at regional or national universities. Interviewees had occupied diverse roles and levels of hierarchy at their institutions. Among the sample, there were three deans of Schools of Social Sciences, three directors of specialized centers, three directors of Social Work Departments, two early career researchers, two mid-career researchers, two researchers who were retired, and one at the end of their career.

Results

In the results from the qualitative analysis, we found that female academics tend to spend time early on in their career trajectory on activities related to administration and teaching, which has a negative impact on their research productivity, leaving them at a disadvantage in the face of the accelerated demands of academic capitalism (D'Amico, 2016; Sisto, 2017). The little importance placed on these activities in promotion guidelines affects their promotion later on, which has a direct impact on their ability to reach higher university positions.

The old men's club in academia: different tasks and expectations

This theme is expressed by one interviewee, who is currently a mid-career researcher:

> I've been confronted with a machista logic at the university. It is basically an old men's club. There are very few female Deans. There is also a lack of female directors and at the central administration there are none. There are only men […] It has been difficult for me to sacrifice what I want to do, and to focus on this project of faculty involvement within the school.
>
> *(Interviewee 33, August 2019)*

When considering intersectional identities, age and generation of formation also impact how participants perceive academic work. Particularly among younger generations, there is a growing critique of the lack of women in positions of power. A greater recognition of demands of academic competition, individual freedom, and neoliberalism across universities in Chile has led to younger generations being more alert to the tension between administration/teaching/research. Despite the more sacrificial stance of female academics from older generations, the older generations tend to follow career trajectories that are more individualized instead of participating in collective work.

Gendered bodies: production and reproduction

Another theme that emerged from this analysis was related to the distribution of gendered bodies across universities and their intersections with motherhood and care. Notably, the majority of interviewees in our study reported experiences that symbolized motherhood and care during their academic trajectories, such as

> The speed bumps on the academic career are connected and not detached from childcare, having children, experiencing separations, etc.
>
> *(Interviewee 9, May 2022)*

Across narratives, the notion of "waiting" appears frequently, in which trajectories of their male peers (partners or work colleagues) tend to be prioritized over their own. In their narratives, female academics mention waiting for a raise, a promotion, etc. The few who follow non-traditional "feminine" trajectories express a contradictory sentiment, one that comes with holding a position that is not common among their peers. One participant expressed it as:

> ...I dealt with a lot of family issues in the doctoral program. This led to me sometimes feeling guilty about being at the university while my husband was at home, things that are very ingrained in gender roles.
>
> *(Interviewee 35, November 2019)*

The differences in salary between men and women academics were another issue that those who seek higher positions confronted, advocating and critiquing gender gaps in pay for similar roles and titles. One University Dean commented on her experience with salary negotiation:

> And I remember that I told him (the Rector) [...] First, gender equity. I'm not going to accept anything less than what the previous Dean got, nor any of the Deans before them. Two—I said—I'm going to lead based on the guidelines of my discipline and that means that sometimes I may not be in agreement with you and we are going to have to resolve any issues collectively.
>
> *(Interviewee 17, May 2022)*

Among public universities, as a result of policies requiring salary transparency, these differences tend to be more subtle and may be more evident in incentives or rewards that are negotiated "behind closed doors". In contrast, at private universities, the salaries are less visible. Policies related to transparency in academia emerged as something interviewees actively advocated for and attempted to activate across their own trajectories.

Slim bodies of female academics, robust bodies of male academics

Another theme that emerged from the interviews was related to the "voice" of the interviewees in relation to their male peers. This theme encompassed inequities in how initiatives were proposed, developed, planned, and accepted by academics that identified with another sex/gender.

In general, interviewees reported that proposals spearheaded by women tended to collectivize quickly and wound up being appropriated by everyone, whereas proposals led by men tended to include their name, which led to constant recognition and validation in public spaces. Phenomena such as mansplaining and hepeating were mentioned frequently by interviewees. One department director explained her experience with this in relation to her male peers:

> I spoke privately with one of them and we came up with a list of topics that we would explore in upcoming meetings. We observed how many times his ideas were immediately considered and recognized versus those that I proposed, which were quickly made collective and not considered. It was so apparent that after some meetings, he called me on the phone and apologized, because he thought I was exaggerating.
> *(Interviewee O, May 2020)*

Again, the question of public versus private appears as one of the critical points to address gendered differences and disparities. Through these spaces, the centering of female academics' voices in research and knowledge production is key to being heard, made visible, and recognized. The interviewees also reported experiencing subtle microaggressions, through which female social work researchers were perceived as less important. This occurred when decisions were already made in research collaborations or departments, which perpetuated disadvantage compared to their male counterparts or their peers in other disciplines. Through these processes, disciplinary subordination occurred.

On occasion, female academics in administration faced microaggression from female colleagues, some of whom complained about their leadership or did not actively recognize their authority. Several of the interviewees reported having to masculinize themselves so that others would listen to them. In some cases, even their female peers reproduced these same behaviors, acting as gate keepers to spaces of power. Therefore, female academics in leadership reported the need to constantly prove their knowledge and abilities to others, which created an exhausting and demanding process that was often not sustainable over time.

With respect to masculinization, there were differences by generation. Women closer to retirement or at the senior career stage of their trajectory tended to report more masculinization in positions of power. Younger generations tended to develop other strategies for resistance that included: (1) variations in the access and duration of positions; (2) placing themselves in less visible positions of power; and/or (3) shortening periods of administrative leadership as that could impact their research trajectory. Among the younger generations of social work academics, there was also a more active outreach to form alliances and collaborations with peers to develop a more collective administrative leadership and more explicitly ask for support.

Burnout and the final exit

Another salient theme that was transversal across interviews was extreme exhaustion or depletion. Academic life is constantly busy, synonymous with a lack of personal time, and can result in incoherence in one's overall purpose. Interviewees navigated this through ruptures and resignations of significant parts of their private and public lives. Within the academic context, this sometimes resulted in "the final exit".

Within academic spaces, dynamics have been generated that reinforce stereotypes of researchers as masculine and working independently, therefore reproducing masculinized images of power and hierarchy in laboratories where research is conducted. Social workers who have positions of hierarchical power have had to manage these stereotypes and engage in different ways of forming relationships. That is how one interviewee, a recently elected Dean, expressed it:

[I have] the firm belief that transformation will come from collective projects that involve strong communities. It is also important to understand these secret ties among generations. I am proud to belong to social network of great women that, at the beginning of the 20th century, opposed the war, fought for women's suffrage [...] they opened new, inventive ways of rebelling.
(presentation of candidate_Interviewee 2, May 2022)

That makes me more sensitive to things that keep appearing. I mean, in 2012 I had no idea that we would be living through the current situation [...] never in my life did I think that we would be able to put together a collective project to coordinate the department. For me, it was just as incredible as if they had told me in 2012 that we would be reopening social work at the University of Chile.
(Interviewee 2, March 2022)

Discussion and conclusion

Findings from our study align with prior literature on gender gaps in academia, and specifically across social work careers in higher education, which exacerbates the tensions and pressures that impact academics in general. Gender gaps reinforce the deeper dimensions of inequality that underpin academic capitalism. Although the glass ceiling may be broken in certain cases, it remains in others. Therefore, it is important to address perceived barriers to female achievement and advancement in academia.

Through our analysis, some questions also arise about academic and research development that is stagnated by administrative duties, or paused due to trajectories of care (children, family, or even teams at work). Intersectional feminist perspectives contribute to our observation of care beyond blood connections and can extend to university communities and their members. Indeed, "mentorships" and other significant service expectations related to supporting others in their department were reported frequently among interviewees.

In parallel, under the framework of academic capitalism, there is an individual responsibility of organization and regulation of one's own academic trajectory (Sisto, 2017). There is tension between this responsibility and collaborative practices in constructing multiple, heterogeneous trajectories. Tension is also present in corporality of governance. Within the intersectional feminist approach, social work researchers have highlighted the role of female bodies within academic institutions and the disparate impact of the COVID-19 pandemic on them resulting from a triple shift (Rubilar et al., 2021). Results from our study build upon this by examining how female academics must govern their own lives and self-regulate their careers based on individual competition, responsibility, and performance.

Expanding the feminist approach to include intersectionality, we also critically question the notion of "individual freedom" as a subtle form of hiding gender inequities and other markers of positionality presented in this chapter. Findings from our study question the over-valuation of one pure type of individual trajectory, one which often perpetuates masculinity and constant, non-stopping competition.

Through narrations of the trajectories of female academics, we observe a construction of subjectivity that is articulated in three main axes: (i) a subjectivity tied to the overall structure, which maintains precarious and competitive work conditions that characterize academic capitalism; (ii) a subjectivity tied to the private sphere, encompassing domestic life and care; and (iii) a connection to biographical dimensions with the unique experiences and history of each female academic given their own generational status and sociohistorical contexts they have lived.

The bodies of women academics transform not only with time and experiences of maternity (Rubilar et al., 2021) but also based on their experiences within the university from the start of their early career start until their exit. Contributions from feminism and intersectional analyses allow us to not only examine intersections of sex and university position but also links between these and possible tensions and transformations within larger structures that have historically reinforced the principles of individualism, competition, and quantification of success 155 years after the enrollment of the first woman at the University of Chile and 100 years after the creation of formal social work in Chile and Latin America, we can affirm that the discipline is positioned within this current framework and from this symbolic location will continue to evolve over the next century. It will not be an easy road, even less so in a country with a high penetration of neoliberal capitalism like Chile; however, the possibilities of challenging the entrepreneurial perspectives in the production of knowledge and power in academia are broad and are in full development. This gives us hope that female academic social workers will continue to dispute and conquer material and symbolic spaces in the times to come.

In addition to conquering material and symbolic spaces, women can conquer academic capitalism and liberalism through the collaborative practices and actions described in this chapter. Nationally, work such as that done by the Network of Social Work Researchers and feminist groups has brought together women researchers and academics across disciplines. These exchanges have led to discussions in congress about laws for gender equity in academia and addressing harassment in universities. At the micro and meso level, there have been strategies such as workshops for girls and young women in science, peer mentorship and female empowerment in science. Liza Taylor (2018) refers to these actions as feminism in coalition, which we highlight at the end of this chapter as resources that foster new ways of social organization. Coalition politics can be a key feature of an intersectional feminist perspective. Through an intersectional lens, coalition politics can foster collective reflection, which can begin to counter the hegemonic, capitalistic logic inherent in academia.

Acknowledgments

We would like to acknowledge the support of project ANID/CONICYT/Fondecyt N°1190257, Longitudinal study of research trajectories and transitions among Chilean social workers, and ANID/CONICYT/Fondecyt N°1230605, Centenary travels and trajectories of ideas. Geopolitics, knowledge production, and research agendas in social work which has financed the study presented in this chapter.

References

Acker, S. (1994). *Género y educación. Reflexiones sociológicas sobre mujeres, enseñanza y feminismo*. Nance.
Andrade, C. (2013). Del biombo a la cátedra igualdad de oportunidades de género en la Universidad de Chile. *Oficina de Igualdad de Género*. Universidad de Chile. http://web.uchile.cl/archivos/VEX/BiomboCatedra/files/assets/basic-html/index.html#3
Araneda-Guirriman, C., & Sepúlveda-Páez, G. (2021). Reflexiones sobre los desafíos que enfrentan las académicas en el contexto del capitalismo académico. *Formación universitaria*, 14(5), 75–84. https://doi.org/10.4067/S0718-50062021000500075
Bernardo, A. (2021). *Acoso #Metoo em la ciencia española*. Pamplona: Next Door Publishers.
Burstin, H. R., & Arora, V. M. (2021). Gender disparities in journal citations—another metric of inequity in academia. *JAMA Network*, 4(7), E2114787.https://doi.org/10.1001/jamanetworkopen.2021.14787
Butler, J. (1997). *The psychic life of power: Theories in subjection*. Stanford University Press.
Chodorow, N. (2007). Techo de cristal, pisos pegajosos y muros de hormigón: Barreras internas y externas para el trabajo y la realización de la mujer. In: M. Elizade & B. Zeeling B (eds.), *El techo de cristal: Perspectivas psicoanalíticas sobre las mujeres y el poder* (pp. 29–43). Lumen.
Consejo Nacional de Educación CNED. (2020). Informe tendencias de estadística de educación superior por sexo. https://www.cned.cl/sites/default/files/2020_informe_matricula_por_sexo_0.pdf/
D'Amico, M. (2016). Presentación. In: Sierra, F. (Coord.) (ed.), *Capitalismo cognitivo y economía social del conocimiento. La lucha por el código* (pp. 432–436). Ciespal.
Fundación PRODEMU. (2021). Glosario de Género. Educando en Género. https://www.prodemu.cl/educando-en-genero/
Gaete-Quezada, R. (2015). El techo de cristal en las universidades estatales chilenas. Un análisis exploratorio. *Revista iberoamericana de educación superior*, 6(17), 3–20. https://doi.org/10.1016/j.rides.2015.06.001
Harding, S. (1986). *The science question in feminism*. Cornell University Press.
Hill, P., & Bilge, S. (2019). *Interseccionalidad*. Morata.
Hiner, H., & López-Dietz, A. (2021). Movimientos feministas y LGBTQ+: de la transición pactada a la revuelta social, 1990–2020. In: Gálvez, A., Hiner, H., Toro, M. S., López, A., Cerda, K., Alfaro, K., & Inostroza, G. (eds.), *Históricas. Movimientos feministas y de mujeres en Chile* (pp. 1850–2020). LOM.
Illanes, M. A. (2012). Sus cuerpos mutuos. La "pedagogía crítica" de los trabajadores sociales en Chile de los sesenta y setenta. In: J. Pinto (ed.), *Mujeres. Historias chilenas del siglo XX.* (pp. 9–33). LOM.
López, M., Silvestre, M., & García, I. (2021). Igualdad de género en instituciones de educación superior e investigación. *Investigaciones Feministas*, 12(2), 263–270. https://doi.org/10.5209/infe.76643/
Martínez, S., & Bivort, B. (2014). Procesos de producción de subjetividad de género en el trabajo académico: Tiempos y espacios desde cuerpos femeninos. *Psicoperspectivas*, 13(1), 15–22.
Matus, T. (2008). Las pioneras del trabajo social en Chile. In: S. Montecino (ed.), *Mujeres chilenas fragmentos de una historia* (pp. 219–234). Catalonia.
McAlpine, L., Amundsen, C., & Turner, G. (2014). Identity-trajectory: Reframing early career academic experience. *British Educational Research Journal*, 40(6), 952–969. https://doi.org/10.1002/berj.3123/
Ministerio de Ciencia y Tecnología. (2022). Segunda Radiografía de género en ciencia, tecnología conocimiento e innovación. Oficina de Estudios y Estadísticas. División de Políticas Públicas. https://www.minciencia.gob.cl/uploads/filer_public/9a/c4/9ac46c03-ecb0-473c-a070-34e3f6488df5/radiografia_genero_2022.pdf
Muñoz, G., & Rubilar, G. (2021). Social work research in Chile: Tensions and challenges under the 'knowledge economy' and managerialist research agendas. *The British Journal of Social Work*, 51(7), 2839–2856. https://doi.org/10.1093/bjsw/bcaa132
Muñoz G., Rubilar G., Matus T., & Parada P. (2021). ¿Qué nos dicen las revistas y redes de investigación en trabajo social? Expresiones y concepciones en torno a la construcción de conocimiento disciplinar. *Propuestas Críticas En Trabajo Social-Critical Proposals in Social Work*, 1(1), 145–162. https://doi.org/10.5354/2735-6620.2021.61241/

Muñoz-García, A. L. (2020). Reflexiones feministas para otra investigación posible. *Cuadernos de Teoría Social*, 6(12): 14–40. https://cuadernosdeteoriasocial.udp.cl/index.php/tsocial/article/view/106

Murgia, A., & Poggio, B. (2018). *Gender and precarious research careers. A comparative analysis*. Routledge. https://doi.org/10.4324/9781315201245/

Paludi, M. (2022). *Mujeres y Ciencia en Chile: relatos autobiográficos de investigadoras del siglo XXI*. Universidad Mayor.

Platero, L. (2012). *Intersecciones: cuerpos y sexualidades en la encrucijada*. Bellaterra.

Red Feminista. (2023). Estrategias para la promoción de una academia digna y feminista en las ciencias sociales. https://redfeministaccss.com/

Ríos González, N., Mandiola Cotroneo, M., Varas Alvarado, A. (2017). Haciendo género, haciendo academia: Un análisis feminista de la organización del trabajo académico en Chile. *Psicoperspectivas. Individuo y Sociedad*, 16(2), 114–124. http://www.psicoperspectivas.cl/index.php/psicoperspectivas/article/viewFile/1041/668

Rodó-Zárate, M. (2021). *Interseccionalidad. Desigualdades, lugares y emociones*. Bellaterra.

Rubilar, G. (2013). Repertorios y aproximaciones biográfico-narrativas. Testimonios y análisis de prácticas investigativas en trabajadores sociales. *Forum Qualitative Sozialforschung / Forum: Qualitative Social Research*, 14(2). http://nbn-resolving.de/urn:nbn:de:0114-fqs130229/

Rubilar, G. (2015). Trabajo social e investigación social ¿Cómo hacen investigación los trabajadores sociales? Memoria y testimonios de cuatro generaciones de profesionales chilenos. Tesis para optar al grado de doctor Universidad Complutense de Madrid. https://eprints.ucm.es/id/eprint/34467/1/T36729.pdf

Rubilar, G. (2022). Transiciones y trayectorias de trabajadoras y trabajadores sociales: Biografías y encuentros con las ciencias y la investigación. ANID/CONICYT/ FONDECYT 1190257.

Rubilar, G., Galaz, C., & LaBrenz, C. (2021). Academic and family disruptions during the COVID-19 pandemic: A reflexive from social work. *Qualitative Social Work*, 20(1–2), 587–594. https://doi:10.1177/1473325020973293/

Sánchez, M. J. A. (2002). Las académicas. Profesorado universitario y género. *Revista de Educación*, 328, 465–475.

Sanhueza Díaz, L., Fernández Darraz, C., & Montero Vargas, L. (2020). Segregación de género: narrativas de mujeres desde la academia. *Polis (Santiago)*, 19(55), 310–334. https://doi.org/10.32735/s0718-6568/2020-n55-1453

Saracostti, M. (2006). Mujeres en la alta dirección de educación superior: Posibilidades, tensiones y nuevas interrogantes. *Calidad en la Educación*, 25, 243–259. https://doi.org/10.31619/caledu.n25.261

Simbürger, E., & Guzmán, C. (2019). Framing educational policy discourse in neoliberal contexts: Debates around the public university in a Chilean newspaper. *Journal of Higher Education Policy and Management*, 25. https://doi.org/10.1080/1360080X.2019.1687267

Sisto, V. (2017). Gobernados por números: El financiamiento como forma de gobierno de la universidad en Chile. *Psicoperspectivas*, 16(3), 64–75. https://doi.org/10.5027/psicoperspectivas-vol16- issue3-fulltext-1086

Suárez-Ortega, M., & Zapata-Sepúlveda, P. (2022). Professional development in academia: Co-performing voices from feminist research. *International Review of Qualitative Research*. https://doi.org/10.1177/19408447211068199

Taylor, L. (2018). *Feminism in coalition thinking with US women of color feminism*. Duke University Press.

Undurraga, R., & Simbürger, E. (2018). Género y políticas institucionales en universidades chilenas: un desierto con incipientes oasis estatales. In: C. Mora, A. Kottow, V. Osses, M. Ceballos (eds.), *El género furtivo: la evidencia interdisciplinaria del género en el Chile actual* (pp. 239–257). LOM.

Vásquez-Cupeiro, S., & Elston, M. A. (2006). Gender and academic career trajectories in Spain: From gendered passion to consecration in a sistema endogmico? *Employee Relations*, 28(6), 588–603. https://doi.org/10.1108/01425450610704515

Winslow, S., & Davis, SN. (2016). Gender inequality across the academic life course. *Sociology Compass*, 10(5), 404–416. https://doi.org/10.1111/soc4.12372

Wolfinger, N. H., Mason, M. A., & Goulden, M. (2009). Stay in the game: Gender, family formation and alternative trajectories in the academic life course. *Social Forces, 87*(3), 1591–1621.

Woodward, D. (2007). Work-life balancing strategies used by women managers in British 'modern' universities. *Equal Opportunities International, 26*(1) 6–17. https://doi.org/10.1108/02610150710726507

Zapata-Sepúlveda, P., & Suárez-Ortega, M. (2022). Qualitative female researchers in academia: Challenges and contradictions. *Cultural Studies - Critical Methodologies.* https://doi.org/10.1177/15327086221093417/

26
CREATING SPACE FOR CRITICAL FEMINIST SOCIAL WORK PEDAGOGY[1]

Sarah Epstein, Norah Hosken and Sevi Vassos

Introduction

Social work is a profession with a stated commitment to the principles and goals of social justice and human rights. Critical social workers take up these principles by casting a lens on the way that power is constructed, used and reproduced. Critical feminist social workers foreground women's diverse experiences of personal, cultural and structural injustice, aiming to make visible women's diverse lived experiences to form the core knowledge base from which to work towards socially just practice. Critical feminist social work pedagogy, shaped by these ideas of what social work is, commits to circulating knowledge about the effects of power. The goal is to enable an ongoing, mutual (re)construction and sharing of the knowledge and skills required to imagine and enact socially just practice. However, the practice and teaching of social work are not context-free; therefore, the profession at large is conditioned by the "social structures, discourses and systems in which it is placed" (Macfarlane, 2016, p. 326). As such, the current and dominant context in which social work education is conditioned is the standardising outcome-based measures of the neoliberal university system. The neoliberal paradigm regulates differences (Burke, 2015), obscures the particular and devalues process. These impacts leave social work education at risk of being complicit in a system that is not capable of accounting for the multiplicity of knowledge and diversity of lived experience, let alone the nuances of the pedagogical process. This article represents an attempt at non-compliance with neoliberal hegemony. We (the authors) choose to highlight the particulars of a critical feminist social work pedagogy that aims to make visible the relations of power that condition the lived experiences of educators, students and service users.

Based on an examination of relevant literature and the use of a reflective, inductive approach, we explore and analyse observations made about efforts to engage with a subversive pedagogy whilst surviving in the neoliberal academy. The aim is to provide a way of thinking about the processes involved in co-creating a community of learning and practice situated in critical feminist social work pedagogy. The article is structured as follows. First, we introduce and locate ourselves as the collaborative authors of this article. Second, we situate the aims of this article within Australian and international critical feminist social work pedagogy and the ideology and practices of neoliberalism within the higher education context. We draw on anecdotal and structured observations from our learning and practice throughout the article to elucidate understandings of the constraints and challenges we have routinely faced in imagining, co-constructing, enacting and improving ways to engage in the communal relationality of critical feminist pedagogy.

Acknowledging and exploring the benefits of intersectionality

In positivist, scientific epistemology there is an emphasis on the importance of a neutral, objective stance as a method to eliminate subjective interpretations from the pursuit of knowledge. In contrast, feminist researchers, writers and academics generally contest the assumption that an objectivity free of social context is possible. Further, feminists assert this claim to objectivity often serves to conceal a privileged, dominant, white masculine bias (Smith, 1987). In line with other feminists, rather than striving for objectivity in this article and our work, we commit to practise ongoing critical reflexivity aiming to recognise, examine and understand how our own social locations can influence the construction of knowledge (Hesse-Biber, 2014).

As the three authors of this article, we locate ourselves within our contexts to provide the reader with this information to consider its relevance to our discussion and the arguments we make. We share some similarities: being non-Indigenous, Euro settler-background, middle-aged, mothers and social work educators who are living, teaching and learning on the lands of the First Nation people of Australia, the Aboriginal and Torres Strait Islander people.

Following significant periods of direct service work, we each completed PhDs as mature-aged students and became social work educators. An interest in critical social work, Feminisms, difference, collaboration, situatedness, relationality, complementarity, and survival in the university system, brought us together. We are curious and constantly seek to learn more about our differences across lived experiences of religion, spirituality, ethnicity, class, sexual orientation, health, socialisation, personality, knowledge and skill sets.

In the next section, we situate the purpose of this article, developing a tentative outline for thinking about the processes involved in co-creating a critical feminist pedagogical practice within an examination of relevant national and international literature. Following Wickramasinghe (2009, p. 112), the engagement with the literature is presented as a "distinctly epistemic project ... a subjective process of knowledge production and meaning-making ... reliant on the [authors'] ...subjectivity and standpoint", rather than an account of all available scholarly research on the topics. Each discussion of a section of the literature is followed by reflective observations explaining how we engage with, and try to enact, the ideas from the literature.

Social work education within the neoliberal context

Academic life in a neoliberal university is fast-paced and every move the academic makes must be tracked, measured and capable of fitting into standardised data sets and the allocated fields of numerous forms (Clegg & David, 2006; David, 2015; Hosken, 2017; Kovacs, Hutchison, Collins, & Linde, 2013; McCusker, 2017; Mountz et al., 2015). The neoliberal paradigm of competency-based outcomes focuses on measuring individual (teacher and student) outputs and standardising teaching outcomes (Clegg & David, 2006). The pedagogical relationship between teacher and student, as well as the learning relationships between and among class cohorts, are devalued and diminished (McCusker, 2017; Mountz et al., 2015). Within this context, it is increasingly difficult to make visible a pedagogical process grounded in the way that lived experiences (of teacher, student and service user) reflect the multiple systems of oppression and privilege. This is particularly important for the social work pedagogue who tries to embody socially just social work practice.

Feminist social work pedagogues argue that the current neoliberal paradigm represents the antithesis of critical pedagogies, including feminism. Critical pedagogies place priority on recognising the role that social locations and processes play in the ongoing production of knowledge and relations of oppression and privilege (Luke, 1996; Macfarlane, 2016; McCusker, 2017; Mountz et al., 2015). This matters to the teaching of social work practice because the focus of social work, whether it be traditional, radical, progressive, case management focused or grounded in critical theory, is that the client must be considered in light of the social, cultural, political, economic context in which they are positioned (Fook, 2012).

Without the ability or incentive to work with context, the joint social work and feminist goal of transforming society is replaced with the reproduction of "oppressive social arrangements" (Kovacs et al., 2013, p. 234). Feminist pedagogy aims to destabilise the status quo (Crabtree & Sapp, 2003) to work towards social change. This positions both the feminist educator and, potentially, her students in opposition to dominant and powerful structures and practices. Therefore, it is not in the best interests of the neoliberal university to support feminist pedagogical goals (Crabtree & Sapp, 2003). However, the authors of this article believe it is the responsibility of feminist social work pedagogy to work out ways to do so. Asserting the production of knowledge as the core business of university education, this article reveals the privileging of lived experiences as a core critical feminist social work pedagogy.

Lived experience pays attention to who determines which knowledge shape the understanding and response in social work practice, and whose knowledge are reflected in the laws, policies and practices that restrict the lives of non-dominant groups including social work service users. The views from these standpoints of lived experience are not considered as pure windows to truth or reality but rather a place to start an investigation (Smith, 1987). Smith's (2005) and Sprague's (2005, p. 52) reading of standpoint theory is adopted in this article as that "which builds strategically on contrasting social locations" to explore the implications of both material realities and fluidities. We aim to take up Collin's (2009, p. xi) challenge to "place the social structural and interpretative/narrative approaches to social reality in dialogue with one another". Feminist and Indigenist perspectives recognise that, by actively including, indeed centring or foregrounding, the experiences and knowledge of those who have been marginalised, we generate fuller accounts of knowledge. The greater the involvement of people who have been discriminated against, the higher the possibility that pedagogy and curriculum can include lived experiences and other forms of knowledge. Pedagogy and curriculum that are inclusive of diverse experiences and knowledge improve how social work students engage in critical self-reflection, learn to work with others and contribute to democratising the generation of knowledge (Finn & Jacobson, 2003).

Reflection: the need for imagination and community

Collectively our experience in the university has taught us that the measure of success in the neo-liberal academy is not determined by deeply thought through pedagogical decision-making and practices of the academic. Nor is success measured by including diverse and collaborative co-constructions of knowledge. How well a teaching team talks to each other about what it is they do in the classroom and why they have chosen to do it has no subject line in a course review.

Instead, success in the academic system is determined via individual metrics of performance and achievement of standardised and universal outcomes. Attached to this are timelines for handing in cohort statistics and tracking percentages that require us to think about our students and ourselves as measurable units. In the meantime, using a calculator and spread sheet to account for a whole term of teaching steals time from us.

The entirety of neoliberal policy, procedure and social relations conditions our work selves and our work lives closing down space for discussion and critique of the university (Blackmore, 2007; Hil, 2012; Hosken, 2017). Formal attempts to speak out about the impacts of neoliberalism that preclude the provision of considered, quality teaching have, as elsewhere (Bessant, 2014), been met with disregard, reprimand and ridicule.

We have been working together for over three years now and as the pressure built, we began talking, at first informally, off campus, over food and wine and by the sea. We needed the space to think deeply, to test ideas, to argue about feminism, about social work, about the best ways to reflect socially just social work practice inside the academy. We needed time to identify the social, cultural, political and economic context of the workplace, of the world in which our students lived and where their future clients come from. We met to make visible the particularities of who we felt we were and who we thought we wanted to become. We needed an environment where we could test out our own transformative potential before we could justify making these demands of our students. If we were to teach students to respect the similarities and differences in the lived experiences of clients' lives, we needed to immerse ourselves in a space where we bore witness to, and validated, each other's lives.

These informal meetings solidified the impetus to create a space where we could be immersed in context to work out how to change it, to work in ways that foster "critical hope" (Leonard, 1979, cited in Pease, Goldingay, Hosken, & Nipperess, 2016) and where we could imagine what collaboration looked like. Paying attention to each other's lived experiences of working in the university made us aware of the criticality of working out ways to do this not only with ourselves but also with our students and so we decided to come in from the margins. This mutual, critical sociological imagination (Mills, 1959) is subversive in countering the ideological rhetoric discourse of "there is no other alternative" to the individualism inherent in neoliberalism. Now, formally we meet, discuss, share, and develop teaching and research ideas and we have made ourselves visible as Critical Edge Women (CrEW).

Feminisms

Understanding what feminist pedagogy means in the higher education teaching and learning context starts with identifying what feminism means in the 21st century. Contemporary feminist analysis recognises that gender cannot be the sole analytical category if we are to truly recognise and understand the multiple social locations in which women are positioned (Gray & Boddy, 2010). However, the personal is political feminist statement remains as salient and useful as ever. This is because feminist analysis seeks to understand the complex cultural discourses and multiple structural systems that women interact with and through which women's lived experiences are shaped (Clegg & David, 2006).

The feminist cause is also about identifying opportunities for agency and equality at both the individual but also the social and collective levels (Clegg & David, 2006; Dore, 1994; Gray & Boddy, 2010). This is a key reason why feminist academics consider the learning and teaching context as a viable, legitimate and important location for activism. The integration of activism in pedagogical activity affords students opportunities to engage experientially with the practice of socially just social work with service users.

Reflection: CrEW as a space for feminist activism

As CrEW we meet formally on a regular basis in the university workplace. While gender is not the sole analytic category we employ to make sense of our lived experiences in the teaching and learning space, the personal as political is the starting point for identifying the complex discourses and structural systems that condition our academic selves. Ensuring that there are regular and substantial amounts of time allocated for critical collective discussion provides reprieve from the isolated siloing that is a function of the neoliberal paradigm. In this space, we are not sole practitioners making teaching and learning choices. Instead, we assume relational positions as critical friends in discussion with a view to supporting each other to sharpen our thinking and improve the depth and quality of our work.

Collectively we occupy different cultural, class and religious social locations. We have arrived at academia via different theoretical and feminist avenues. Our social work practice experiences come from health systems, community organisations, feminist collectives and the violence against women sector. Some of us work full time and one works part-time. We live regionally and in urban environments. We are all carers with differently aged children in fluid stages of love, resentment and hope for the world, our partners, our children and our lives. We argue, and we rage, and we rely on our differences to hold each other accountable to our assumptions, partial understandings and biases. These discussions carry through into our wider interactions, the questions we ask, the curriculum choices we make and the shape of our interactions with students.

As a social and collective space, CrEW creates opportunities for us to identify the potential for agentic activity; that is, what do we want to change, how are we positioned in ways to be able to enact change and what would this activity look like? The first step was to legitimate collective, formal space to take time back and create opportunities for understanding and co-construction of knowledge. Primarily, CrEW is an attempt to work out all of the ways the university as a teaching and learning space can be a location for our feminist activism.

Feminisms and social work

There is a strong argument for the place of feminism in social work education that is about more than the disproportionate overrepresentation of women in the profession and the service user populations (Morley, 2009; Payne, 2014). Feminist practice in Australian social work was first articulated in the 1970s and was an attempt to address the gender blindness of social work (Morley, 2009). Feminism and social work share fundamental principles and indeed reflect shared philosophies and goals (Dore, 1994). Both the Australian Association of Social Workers and the International Federation of Social Workers identify human rights and social justice as core values and objectives. Violence against women and girls, economic disadvantage and patriarchal culture and politics all pose a significant threat to women's human rights and obstruct social justice. Gender equity issues that impact the lives of service users who identify as female is consequently core business for social work. Further, in the recent compilation of Contemporary Feminism in Social Work Practice, the editors assert that feminism is indeed fundamental to both social work ethics and values but also professional identity and practice (Wendt & Moulding, 2016).

Reflection: collective nourishment to imagine, hope and be imperfect

In the CrEW discussions and space, we provided and felt the healing protection of loyalty and care in a community. This provided safety, nourishment and the "capacity to imagine something rooted in the challenges of the real world yet capable of giving birth to that which does not yet exist" (Lederach, 2005, p. ix). Inspired by Audre Lorde (2007), we longed for something different

> The possible shapes of what has not been before exist only in that back place where we keep those unnamed, untamed longings for something different and beyond what is now called possible, and to which our understanding can only build roads.
> *(Lorde, 2007, p. 121)*

As we learned and explored more about each other's social locations we felt more knowledgeable. Ideas were shared for creating relational spaces with students where their lived experiences and diverse social locations become part of creating the pedagogy and content of the subjects we taught. Often, straight after the excitement of sharing ideas, we came up against the realisation that enacting this relational space with students would be invisible, unvalued and unpaid work in the academy; work that often stole time away from us and our families. We would oscillate between feeling hopeless and feeling critical hope (Leonard, 1979, cited in Pease et al., 2016). Encouragement and strength were gained from reading and sharing the works of other feminist academics about their efforts to resist neoliberalism, particularly by the calls for "collectivity" and "slow scholarship" (Mountz et al., 2015). Discussions about the inevitable imperfection of trying to embody the values and beliefs of feminist social work within the worst of neoliberal times not only made us sad but also enabled us to be less judgemental about others and ourselves. Openness about our strategic, or just exhausted, complicity in neoliberal organisational values and practices allowed us to consider the material reality of the dominance of neoliberalism. Rather than setting ourselves up as heroic feminist social work activists, we allowed ourselves to imagine and imperfectly try to resist or transform, often in small ways. Humility came from awareness of the privilege of aspects of our own situations. This privilege included having a relatively high wage generating disposable income and good housing as compared to the lives of many of our female identifying students, and the service users they worked with on placement, as they lived in poverty, juggled the demands of caring, and faced discrimination and micro-aggressions without the protections afforded by a secure income. These disadvantages we framed as human rights concerns and in the CrEW space we began to map out the gender equity issues and intersecting systems of oppression that faced both our students and their social work clients.

Critical feminist social work

Critical social work sits within the tradition of progressive social work and is informed by critical theory. Macfarlane (2016, p. 327) defines critical social work as: ...

...A social work lens that acknowledges and addresses: structural inequalities and inequitable power dynamics; the impact of discourse on lived experience; the importance of diverse knowledge systems, social work values and ethics; and critical reflection for progressive practice.

In essence, this means that critical social work seeks to understand the way that power is constructed, used and reproduced. Some of the ways that critical social workers do this include: questioning assumptions about truth and knowledge that are taken for granted; seeking information from multiple sources to deepen understandings of lived experiences; recognising that the personal is political and our everyday actions are political in nature; and acknowledging that language is powerful in both reflecting and reproducing discourse as well as capable of introducing alternative discourses.

Critical social workers have a longstanding interest in the emancipation of the oppressed as well as an interest in the ways in which oppressed groups exercise agency and personal power. More recently, critical social work has turned the focus on relations of power towards the machinations of privilege to redress and understand the marginalising and othering effects of objectifying oppressed groups, communities, cultures and people (Pease et al., 2016). This attention to the behaviours of those who benefit from discrimination aims to re-distribute responsibility for change.

Critical social work has been influenced by feminist principles and goals (Allan et al., 2009). Many critical social workers argue that enacting critical social work practice demands consideration of gender inequality and the intersections at which clients who identify as women are positioned in ongoing ways (Allan, Briskman, & Pease, 2009; Fook, 2012; Pease et al., 2016). Critical feminist social work seeks to understand how women's experiences engage with other systems of oppression to understand discrimination and disadvantage at the intersections of race, class, culture, age, ability and sexuality (Briskin & Coulter, 1992; Shrewsbury, 1998; Webber, 2006). Critical feminist social work takes stock of what gender equality and social justice look like and considers the role that social work can play in achieving them.

A critical feminist social work approach suggests there are some unifying principles that are used to co-create a critical feminist pedagogy and practice that is informed by, and suited to, the local context. In Australia, critical feminist pedagogy has to be informed by the history and ongoing realities of colonisation, invasion and whiteness, and the need to foreground the works of Aboriginal social work academics.

Reflection: interrogating the whiteness of Australian social work and foregrounding the works of Aboriginal social work academics

Drawing on the work of Aboriginal and Torres Strait Islander scholars and their allies (Bennett, 2013, 2015; Bennett, Green, Gilbert, & Bessarab, 2013; Bennett, Redfern, & Zubrzycki, 2017; Green & Baldry, 2008, 2013; Land, 2015; Zubrzycki et al., 2014), we aimed to learn and prioritise the processes of problematising and decolonising ourselves and our teaching. Examples of this included contributing to efforts to increase the diversity of the social work teaching team to better reflect the demographic of social work students and service users. Another example is situating the works of Aboriginal and Torres Strait Islander scholars in positions of prominence in curriculum alerting students to the cutting-edge nature of this knowledge for social work, rather than Indigenous content being a discrete add-on topic at the end of units of study. We have built on the work of others to adapt and develop ways to engage with students in a process of exploring the intersectionality of oppression and privilege in our lives and social work practice.

Critical feminist social work pedagogy

The teaching of women's studies, the advent of self-identified feminist academics and the articulation of feminist pedagogy is approximately 50 years young (David, 2015). Despite this, feminist academics have been prolific contributors to both research and the scholarship of teaching and learning. Feminist pedagogy has come to be a priority for feminists in the academy (Baiada & Jensen-Moulton, 2006). However, there is not one singular approach as feminist pedagogy also reflects the diversity of the feminist academic cohort (Webber, 2006).

The feminist scholarship of teaching and learning offers a critique of traditional pedagogy (Cuesta & Witt, 2014). Overall, the feminist pedagogical project focuses on resistance to phallocentric knowledge (Luke, 1996; Ylöstalo & Brunila, 2017) understanding gendered relations of power and making these power arrangements visible (Briskin & Coulter, 1992; Webber, 2006). Feminist pedagogues argue that traditional pedagogy and phallocentric knowledge obscure women's lived experiences, histories, achievements, concerns and entitlements. Feminist pedagogy is a driving force that shifts the focus of study towards understanding the lived experiences of women (Borshuk, 2017; Chung, 2016; Cuesta & Witt, 2014; David, 2015; Dore, 1994; Forrest & Rosenberg, 1997; Kovacs et al., 2013; McCusker, 2017). Gender and its intersections with race, class, culture, age, ability and sexuality, is the core analytic category that distinguishes feminist pedagogy from other forms of critical pedagogical theories (Briskin & Coulter, 1992).

Feminist pedagogy is complex because it is informed by, and interacts with, theory and practice connected to broader feminist struggle, therefore the pedagogical goal is concerned with contributing to change in gender relations on a societal level. Critical feminist social work pedagogy also bears in mind the service users' own gendered positioning. Further, it looks at pedagogical strategies for ensuring accountability to the client for the production of knowledge and descriptions of her experience that reproduce problematic categories of identity. In so doing, feminist critical social work pedagogy works with knowledge that reveal the personal, cultural and structural contexts within which the service user is positioned. It also privileges lived experience in efforts to bring her in from the margins and promote social work practice that does not bother her. Critical feminist social work pedagogy aligns with the centrality of women's lived experiences in "understanding and the development of knowledge" (David, 2004, p. 103). This is the hallmark of feminist pedagogy.

Reflection: bridging the gap through collective action

As early career academics, we have often felt overwhelmed by the publish-or-perish culture that permeates the neoliberal academy. Our ideal is to contribute well to social work scholarship in ways that align coherently with our critical feminist social work ethos.

Our practical reality is the institutional push to continually demonstrate our value in terms of the number and impact of our research publications. The credibility gap between our ideal and our reality was often the main theme in our early discussions as the CrEW. Through these discussions, we started to become aware of how we had actively committed to a process of mutual engagement, at a level that was deeper than the professional relationships we had established in our work with other groups within the neoliberal academy. Most importantly, in line with our critical feminist values, we were continually negotiating issues of power, collegiality, competition and trust as part of our mutual engagement. We were starting to build a shared repertoire of practices, language and history that enabled a collective approach to meaning-making. Ultimately, we were carving out a space within which we could start visualising different ways to respond to the neoliberal metrics defining our expected work outputs, whilst simultaneously resisting neoliberal ways of working.

The next step was to join up our individual work goals and position ourselves to capitalise on the power of collectivity. More specifically, we committed to joining as the CrEW in our research and advocacy work around women and social work pedagogy. At the time of making this commitment, we were all working on different research and writing projects individually. Although we each had a basic understanding of each other's work, it was not until the decision to join up around some of this work that we started to more fully appreciate the differences in our thinking models and approaches to the work in this space. We discovered that homogeneity of individual work goals is not a precondition for achieving a joined-up approach to our work. Rather, we experience our differences as a productive force. It is the ongoing process of collective negotiation around these differences that propels our shared accountability and coherence as a community of learning.

We currently have three projects that we are working on. The first project is our reflection on the development of CrEW as a community of learning situated within a critical feminist social work pedagogy. The second draws together reflections on how we use critical hope and knowledge co-creation as pedagogical strategies to resist and disrupt the neoliberal discourses and regimes of the higher education system. The third is a mixed methods study that seeks to deepen understanding of the lived experience of social work students with caring responsibilities on placement. Our aim is to co-author all articles and co-lead the advocacy activities emerging from this joint work.

Conclusion

Social workers are in a privileged and unique position to bear witness to women's storied lives. Feminist social work pedagogues therefore have the opportunity to learn with and teach each other, and students, about the importance of these stories to understand the conditions in which women live. In this article, we have engaged with the literature and our own observations to sketch out some of the principles and processes we are using to co-create practices situated in critical feminist social work pedagogy, from our social locations in the Australian context. Our work started with conversations that sought to place social structural and interpretative/narrative approaches to social reality whilst also acknowledging and exploring the benefits of intersectionality. These conversations fuelled the desire to create a space for community and collective nourishment to imagine, hope and be imperfect. During our conversations, we continually acknowledged the normality of oscillation between feeling hopeless and feeling critical hope in the imperfect process of trying to resist the metrics of individualism within neoliberalism. We also interrogated the whiteness of Australian social work and foregrounded the works of Aboriginal social work academics. The work continued by joining up our work goals, collaborating and sharing our work efforts ultimately for the benefit of the students and service users we work with. The next step for us will be explicitly exploring with students how to improve our attempts at feminist pedagogical practice. We share these experiences, processes and principles as part of contribution to a conversation and, in the hope they may have relevance for others to adapt to other social locations and contexts.

Note

1 This chapter is reproduced with permission of editor and authors from *Aotearoa New Zealand Social Work*, 30(3), 8–18 (August, 2018). doi:10.11157/anzswj-vol30iss3id489.

References

Allan, J., Briskman, L., & Pease, B. (Eds) (2009). *Critical social work: Theories for a socially just world* (2nd ed.). Crows Nest: Allen & Unwin.
Baiada, C., & Jensen-Moulton, S. (2006). Building a home for feminist pedagogy. *Women's Studies Quarterly*, 34(3/4), 287–290.
Bennett, B. (2013). The importance of Aboriginal and Torres Strait Islander history for social work students and graduates. In B. Bennett, S. Green, S. Gilbert, & D. Bessarab (Eds.), *Our voices: Aboriginal and Torres Strait Islander social work* (pp. 1–22). South Yarra: Palgrave Macmillan.
Bennett, B. (2015). "Stop deploying your white privilege on me!" Aboriginal and Torres Strait Islander engagement with the Australian Association of Social Workers. *Australian Social Work*, 68(1), 19–31.
Bennett, B., Green, S., Gilbert, S., & Bessarab, D. (2013). *Our voices: Aboriginal and Torres Strait Islander social work*. South Yarra: Palgrave Macmillan.
Bennett, B., Redfern, H., & Zubrzycki, J. (2017). Cultural responsiveness in action: Co-constructing social work curriculum resources with Aboriginal Communities. *The British Journal of Social Work*, 48(3), 808–825.
Bessant, J. (2014). "Smoking guns": Reflections on truth and politics in the university. In M. Thornton (Ed.), *Through a glass darkly: The social sciences look at the neoliberal university* (pp. 463–516). Canberra: Australian National University Press.
Blackmore, J. (2007). Equity and social justice in Australian education systems: Retrospect and prospect. In W. Pink, & G. Noblit (Eds.), *International handbook of urban education* (pp. 249–264). Dordrecht: Springer.
Borshuk, C. (2017). Managing student disclosure in class settings: Lessons from feminist pedagogy. *Journal of the Scholarship of Teaching and Learning*, 17(1), 78–86.
Briskin, L., & Coulter, R. (1992). Feminist pedagogy: Challenging the normative. *Canadian Journal of Education*, 17(3), 247–263.
Burke, P. (2015). Re/imagining higher education pedagogies: Gender, emotion and difference. *Teaching in Higher Education*, 20(4), 388–401. doi:10.1080/13562517.201 5.1020782
Chung, Y. (2016). A feminist pedagogy through online education. *Asian Journal of Women's Studies*, 22(4), 372–391.
Clegg, S., & David, M. (2006). Passion, pedagogies and the project of the personal in higher education. *Twenty-First Century Society*, 1(2), 149–165. doi:10.1080/17450140600906989
Collins, P. H. (2009). Foreword: Emerging intersections, building knowledge and transforming institutions. In B. Dill & R. Zambana (Eds.), *Emerging intersections: Race, class and Gender in theory, policy and practice* (pp. VII–XIII). New Brunswick: Rutgers UP.
Crabtree, R., & Sapp, D. (2003). Theoretical, political, and pedagogical challenges in the feminist classroom: Our struggles to walk the walk. *College Teaching*, 51(4), 131–140.
Cuesta, M., & Witt, K. (2014). How gender conscious pedagogy in higher education can stimulate actions for social justice in society. *Social Inclusion*, 2(1), 12–23.

David, M. (2004). Feminist sociology and feminist knowledges: Contribution to higher education pedagogies and processional practices in the knowledge economy. *International Studies in Sociology of Education*, 14(2), 99–124. doi:10.1080/0962021040020121

David, M. (2015). Gender & education association: A case study in feminist education? *Gender and Education*, 27(7), 928–946. doi:10.1080/09540253.2015.1096923.

Dore, M. (1994). Feminist pedagogy and the teaching of social work practice. *Journal of Social Work Education*, 30(1), 97–106.

Finn, J. L., & Jacobson, M. (2003). Just practice: Steps toward a new social work paradigm. *Journal of Social Work Education*, 39(1), 57–78.

Fook, J. (2012). *Social work: A critical approach to practice* (2nd ed.). London: SAGE Publications.

Forrest, L., & Rosenberg, F. (1997). A review of the feminist pedagogy literature: The neglected child of feminist psychology. *Applied & Preventive Psychology*, 6(1), 179–192.

Gray, M., & Boddy, J. (2010). Making sense of the waves: Wipeout or still riding high? *Affilia*, 25(4), 368–189.

Green, S., & Baldry, E. (2008). Building indigenous Australian social work. *Australian Social Work*, 61(4), 389–402.

Green, S., & Baldry, E. (2013). Indigenous social work education in Australia. In B. Bennett, S. Green, S. Gilbert, & D. Bessarab (Eds.), *Our voices: Aboriginal and Torres Strait Islander social work* (pp. 166–177). South Yarra: Palgrave Macmillan.

Hesse-Biber, S. (2014). *Feminist research practice: A primer* (2nd ed.). Los Angeles, CA: Sage Publications.

Hil, R. (2012). *Whackademia: An insider's account of the troubled university*. Sydney: NewSouth Publishing.

Hosken, N. (2017). Exploring the organisation of social injustice in Australian social work education (Unpublished doctoral thesis). University of Tasmania, Tasmania.

Kovacs, P., Hutchison, E., Collins, K., & Linde, L. B. (2013). Norming or transforming: Feminist pedagogy and social work competencies. *Affilia: Journal of Women and Social Work*, 28(3), 229–239.

Land, C. (2015). *Decolonizing solidarity: Dilemmas and directions for supporters of indigenous struggles*. London: Zed Books.

Lederach, J. (2005). *The moral imagination: The art and soul of building peace*, Vol. 3. New York: Oxford University Press.

Lorde, A. (2007). *Sister outsider*. New York: Crown Publishing Group.

Luke, C. (1996). Feminist pedagogy theory: Reflections on power and authority. *Educational Theory*, 46(3), 283–302.

Macfarlane, S. (2016). Education for critical social work: Being true to a worthy project. In B. Pease, S. Goldingay, N. Hosken, & S. Nipress (Eds.), *Doing critical social work: Transformative practices for social justice* (pp. 301–315). Crows Nest: Allen & Unwin.

McCusker, G. (2017). A feminist teacher's account of her attempts to achieve the goals of feminist pedagogy. *Gender and Education*, 29(4), 445–460. doi:10.1080/09540253.2017.1290220

Mills, C. (1959). *The sociological imagination*. New York: Oxford University Press.

Morley, C. (2009). Using critical reflection to improve feminist practice. In J. Allan, L. Briskman, & B. Pease (Eds.), *Critical social work: Theories and practices for a socially just world* (2nd ed., pp. 149–159). Crows Nest: Allen & Unwin.

Mountz, A., Bonds, A., Mansfield, B., Loyd, J., Hyndman, J., Walton-Roberts, M., ... Hamilton, T. (2015). For slow scholarship: A feminist politics of resistance through collective action in the neoliberal university. *ACME: An International Journal for Critical Geographies*, 14(4), 1235–1259.

Payne, M. (2014). *Modern social work theory* (4th ed.). Basingstoke: Palgrave Macmillan.

Pease, B., Goldingay, S., Hosken, N., & Nipperess, S. (2016). *Doing critical social work: Transformative practices for social justice*. Crows Nest: Allen & Unwin.

Shrewsbury, C. (1998). What is feminist pedagogy? In M. Rogers (Ed.), *Contemporary feminist theory* (pp. 167–171). Boston, MA: McGraw-Hill.

Smith, D. E. (1987). *The everyday world as problematic: A feminist sociology*. Toronto: University of Toronto Press.

Smith, D. (2005). *Institutional ethnography: A sociology for people*. Lanham, MD: AltaMira Press.

Sprague, J. (2005). *Feminist methodologies for critical researchers: Bridging differences*. Lanham, MD: AltaMira.

Webber, M. (2006). Transgressive pedagogies? Exploring the difficult realities of enacting feminist pedagogies in undergraduate classrooms in a Canadian university. *Studies in Higher Education*, 31(4), 453–467. doi:10.1080/03075070600800582

Wendt, S., & Moulding, N. (2016). *Contemporary feminisms in social work practice*. New York: Routledge. https://www.routledge.com/Contemporary-Feminisms-in-Social-Work-Practice/Wendt-Moulding/p/book/9781138494534

Wickramasinghe, M. (2009). *Feminist research methodology: Making meanings of meaning-making*. London: Routledge.

Ylöstalo, H., & Brunila, K. (2017). Exploring the possibilities of gender equality pedagogy in an era of marketization. *Gender and Education*, 30(7), 917–933. doi:10.1080/09540253.2017.1376042

Zubrzycki, J., Green, S., Jones, V., Stratton, K., Young, S., & Bessarab, D. (2014). *Getting it right: Creating partnerships for change: Integrating Aboriginal and Torres Strait Islander knowledges in social work education and practice: Teaching and Learning Framework*. Sydney: Australian Government Office for Learning and Teaching.

27
FEMINIST LEADERSHIP AND SOCIAL WORK

The experience of women leaders in Palestinian universities

Najwa Sado Safadi

Introduction

Although Palestinian women constitute half of the society (49.2%), only a small percentage of women were able to take an important role in the labor market, in political life, and in occupying high administrative positions. For example, the percentage of women's participation in the labor force for the year 2017 was 19.2% compared to males (71.6%). Similarly, as for administrative positions, the percentage of women who held senior management positions in 2018 was only 17.4% (Palestinian Central Bureau of Statistics, 2020). This low prevalence also applies to the administrations of social work departments in Palestinian universities. Since their establishment in the late 1970s and early 1980s (Blome & Safadi, 2016), these departments have been run predominantly by male faculty. The delay in women's access to leadership positions in Palestine was linked to the political, social and cultural factors that constituted an obstacle to women's investment in education and employment. Living under occupation has required that the family remain cohesive to confront the Israeli arbitrary measures such as cases of arrests, killings and land confiscation displacement (Institute of Women's Studies, UN Women & Promundo, 2017). Palestinian women have played a central role in preserving the cohesion of the family as a form of resistance. Yet, Palestinian women within the family and other communal institutions do not enjoy gender equality, and the societal view of woman's role inside the home still exists despite some changes in people's perceptions on this subject (Institute of Women's Studies, UN Women & Promundo, 2017). Nevertheless, a number of female social workers (as well as women in other disciplines) have been able to complete their studies and become an active part of the leadership and teaching competencies in social work programs. Most, if not all, of these women hold the position of Head of the social work department at a Palestinian university and have the ability to influence others and institutions' policies and practices.

Scholars from various disciplines including leadership and feminism have emphasized the need to pay attention to exploring women's leadership experiences and including gender as a concept in leadership research (Blackmore, 2017; Griffin et al., 2017; Lazzari et al.,

2009; Northouse, 2016). It has been argued that the prevailing theories of leadership such as trait, behavioral, charismatic and transformational reflect the viewpoint of a part of society, as the knowledge produced in this field was based on the experiences of people who were in leadership positions, and these were men (Blackmore, 2017; Dunn et al., 2014; Northouse, 2016; Sinclair, 2014). However, women's experiences are diverse because they have been influenced by factors other than gender, such as colonialism, class, race, and ethnicity (Hyde, 2022; Rasool, 2020; Tylor et al., 2009). This requires drawing attention to women's unique experiences as well as to the commonalities. Therefore, this study focuses on exploring the unique experiences of women's leadership in the Palestinian academic field; where women struggle for gender equality and national liberation (Elia, 2017; Kuttab, 2009). Specifically, this study aims to explore: (1) the characteristics of women's leadership styles, (2) the perceptions of women leaders about gender differences in leadership styles, and (3) the effectiveness of women's leadership. It is envisaged that this study will contribute to adding new knowledge and insights to leadership perspectives as well as changing our perceptions of social realities and relations (Blackmore, 2017; Hesse-Biber & Leavy, 2007; Tylor et al., 2009).

Literature review

Feminist social work theory

Feminism refers to a philosophical perspective that analyzes gender inequality in a society and seeks to end women's oppression (Dominelli, 2002; Rasool, 2020; Tylor et al., 2009). Yet, feminism is not one model but includes a set of theories that arose out of the differences in the political, social and historical realities of women such as liberal, radical, African, and Marxist and socialist feminisms (Dominelli, 2002; Lay & Daley, 2007; Rasool, 2020). Despite the diversity among feminists, there are several commonalities, including a commitment to analyzing and eliminating gender inequality and women's oppression, taking into consideration that women's suffering is not just personal but political, an interest in raising people's consciousness, and paying attention to women's unique experiences as well as addressing commonalities (Dominelli, 2002; Lay & Daley, 2007; Tylor et al., 2009)

Social work scholars accentuated the importance of integrating feminist viewpoints into the social work profession. It has been argued that this perspective provides social workers with new insights for analyzing gender inequality, exploitation and injustice (Dominelli, 2002; Hyde, 2022; Mehrotra, 2010; Rasool, 2020; Turner & Maschi, 2015). Moreover, using a feminist perspective helps women clients to understand the reasons for their oppression and participate in various actions for social change and justice (Turner & Maschi, 2015; Wendt & Moulding, 2017). Ultimately, such an approach enables social work practitioners and researchers to participate in ending women's suffering, informing social work practice (Anderson-Nathe et al., 2013; Lazzari et al., 2009; Mehrotra, 2010; Turner & Maschi, 2015), and building new knowledge and theory (Anderson-Nathe et al., 2013; Mehrotra, 2010). Therefore, feminist social work can be defined as a sort of social work practice that starts from the experience of women and stresses that responding to women's needs by addressing structural inequalities, and combats all forms of oppression (Dominelli, 2002).

Guided by feminism and feminist social work perspectives, this study shows interest in giving a voice to women leaders in social work departments at Palestinian universities to talk about their experiences. The hope is that this study will be part of scientific efforts that contribute to the construction of new knowledge about leadership by paying attention to the half of society that has been ignored for many years in prevailing leadership theories and studies.

Feminist social work in the Palestinian context

The eventual goal of feminist perspectives is to end inequality, violence, and oppression and to reach social justice. Guided by this vision, feminism and feminist social work in Palestine have given central importance to the Palestinian struggle against the ongoing violence, brutal measures and the confiscation of Palestinian lands by the Israeli occupation (Elia, 2017; Shalhoub-Kevorkian et al., 2022). It argues that "justices are indivisible" (Elia, 2017), in that any separation between the struggle for gender equality and the struggle for national liberation reflects a narrow understanding of women's oppression and Patriarchy. Therefore, it insists on the necessity of realizing the causes of the Palestinian crisis, represented in the Israeli occupation of the West Bank and Gaza Strip, the policy of apartheid and its violation of Palestinian rights (Elia, 2017; Lloyd, 2014; Shalhoub-Kevorkian et al., 2022).

Feminist theory of leadership

Power, influence and authority are key concepts in leadership as presented in the mainstream of leadership theories (Griffin et al., 2017; Northouse, 2016). Leaders use the power to influence followers to reach specific goals (Griffin et al., 2017; Northouse, 2016). Several scholars claim that all ideas in leadership theories are constructed based on men's experience and thus reflect masculine characteristics (Blackmore, 2017; Griffin et al., 2017; Lazzari et al., 2009; Northouse, 2016). Therefore, a number of researchers in social sciences including social work profession advocate the use of feminist perspectives in the leadership domain (Blackmore, 2017; Christensen, 2011; Lazzari et al., 2009). They argue that there is a need to end patriarchal ideologies and hegemonic relations (Lazzari et al., 2009; Sinclair, 2014), whether within the family institution or the institutions of society (Lazzari et al., 2009). This entails replacing power over the other with the concept of empowering others, to avoid repeating the relationships of domination–subordination in leadership (Blackmore, 2017; Lazzari et al., 2009; Sinclair, 2014), and makes all members of organization accountable to all (Hyde, 2022; Lazzari et al., 2009).

Yet, exercising this type of leadership requires adherence to several principles including participatory and shared decision-making, reduction or elimination of hierarchies, collective control of resources, open governance, and the production of new knowledge (Blackmore, 2017; Hyde, 2022; Lazzari et al., 2009). Another principle is a recognition that the "personal is political," and paying attention to how individuals' personal lives and work environments affect each other (Lazzari et al., 2009). In addition, human diversity must be considered. This entails analyzing how gender intersects with other factors such as race, class, and age, and affects the distribution of power, resources, and status among different groups of men and women (Chin, 2007; Lazzari et al., 2009; Tylor et al., 2009). Therefore, encouraging all social groups to actively participate in decision-making, and respecting all opinions is a necessity to ensure inclusiveness (Chin, 2007; Hyde, 2022; Lazzari et al., 2009). Finally, a feminist leader is committed to creating a safe work environment free from violence resulting from abuse of power such as unfair distribution of resources, exploitations, and exclusion (Lazzari et al., 2009.

Therefore, the use of feminist leadership perspective provided a new insight and lens for analyzing and understanding the leadership style of Palestinian women and comparing it with the dominant-male leadership model. Further discussion of the dominant masculine leadership model will be in the next section.

Perceptions toward women leaders

Scholars stressed the need to go beyond only the numbers of women in leadership positions, and rather focus on the perceptions towards women in leadership roles (Blackmore, 2017; Griffin et al., 2017; Northouse, 2016). Phelan and Rudman (2010) argued that how women are perceived in the workplace is associated with gender stereotypes about gender roles, characteristics and acceptable behaviors. In addition, scholars pointed out that the desirable expectations for leadership correspond to the masculine characteristics of assertiveness, competitiveness, and self-confidence (agentic characteristics), which differ from the traditional female role and characteristics (e.g. communal characteristics) (Blackmore, 2017; Eagly & Karau, 2002; Phelan & Rudman, 2010). If a woman works according to communal characteristics, she is considered less qualified for a leadership position. But when a woman possesses agentic qualities, although considered eligible, she experiences rejection and prejudice from both male and female because she violates the traditional gender role (Blackmore, 2017; Eagly & Karau, 2002; Phelan & Rudman, 2010). This may lead to difficulty in accessing leadership positions for women and difficulty in recognizing their success and effectiveness (Eagly & Carli, 2003; Eagly & Karau, 2002).

In the Palestinian context, the results of an opinion poll in 2017 showed that despite the positive changes in attitudes towards gender equality, opinions about the role of gender are still unfair (Institute of Women's Studies, UN Women & Promundo, 2017). For example, a high percentage of women (59%) and men (80%) considered domestic work to be a woman's task, while 48% of women and 80% of men said that the man should have the last word at home. Moreover, the results indicated that only 59% of women and 42% of men agreed that women should reach political positions, and 80% of women and 63% of men said that a woman can do her job as well as a man if she has the required qualifications (Institute of Women's Studies, UN Women & Promundo, 2017).

Method

A qualitative approach was used to conduct in-depth interviews with women who held leadership positions (N = 7) in the social work departments at Palestinian universities. In addition, a comprehensive review of the literature on the topic of feminism, feminist social work, and feminist leadership within the global and Palestinian context was conducted. The purpose was to answer three main questions: (1) to what extent do Palestinian women leaders in social work repeat the dominant male patterns in leadership rather than having their own style of leadership? (2) what are the perceptions of Palestinian women leaders about the gender differences in leadership styles? (3) to what extent are women's leadership styles in social work departments effective?

Sampling, data collection and participants

A purposeful sample with a snowballing technique (Woodley & Lockard, 2016) was used to collect data from women who had experience leading social work departments in three universities in the West Bank and Jerusalem. Two of these universities have bachelor's and master's degrees in social work and one has only a BA program. Data was collected through semi-structured interviews using phone calls which lasted between 45 and 90 minutes. Open-ended questions were utilized and the interviews were recorded by handwriting in Arabic, which is the first language of the researcher and participants. To ensure the accuracy of the handwriting recording, each interview transcript was typed and returned to each participant for review and make any necessary modifications. Then, the main statements, categories and selected quotes have been translated into English by the author and reviewed by an English language specialist.

Background information about the participants was collected through a short questionnaire that included nine questions. The results showed that most of the participants were aged 40–49 years old (N = 5), single (N = 4), had Ph.D. (N = 5), held an assistant professor position (N = 5) and all of them had more than six years of experience at the respective universities. Moreover, most of the participants had three to four years of experience as a head of the department, while one had five years, and one had one year.

Data analysis

This study utilized within-participants and across-participants approaches to analyze the data (Ayres et al., 2003). The aim was to identify the unique experiences of each participant as well as the shared experiences of all participants. In the beginning, the researcher read the interview transcripts several times to understand each woman's leadership experience and to identify the keywords and sentences. After that, common categories were formulated from the same main words and sentences, which reflect commonalities. Then a comparison of the common categories of the participants' experiences was made to find commonalities.

Results

Leadership style of women in leadership in social work departments

Motivation and vision

Findings revealed that all participants had the desire, incentive and vision for the position of Head of Department (HOD) because they wanted to be part of change and development, and influence decision-making. One leader pointed out "I had a vision and ... motivation to lead the department... I had the desire to change the department's leadership style, my former colleague [HOD] was temperamental, dictatorial and not democratic in the department's management" (# 2). Other participants considered this position as a stage of academic development or as an opportunity for learning and development.@@@@@@ In addition, when asked about readiness to lead, all the answers were positive, "for me the readiness was high" (# 7), "I have always had the readiness to lead even in my personal life" (# 3), "I was ready to accept the challenge" (# 6). Yet, each woman leader had her own view on the source of readiness including previous leadership experience, belief in her qualifications and ability to lead, and exercising leadership in her personal life.

Women's leadership style

The findings indicated that the main style of leadership is consistent with transformational leadership, which is participatory and cooperative, but the discussion about inequality in the hierarchical structure and power relationship was almost absent (Lazzari et al., 2009). Participants stated: "the most important feature of our work, me and my former colleague, is the use of the participatory method" (# 1), "I relied on consultation, respected people's experiences, respected their specializations, and gave space for movement" (# 7), Moreover, participants' answers revealed that there was a rejection of the arrogance and controlling manner in leadership, "I did not use a single word, but there were always meetings and dialogues" (# 2), "I am not superior because I am always in the field among people ... I do not have an authoritarian approach" (# 6).

In addition, when asked about the leadership orientation of the women leaders, whether it is towards relationships or accomplishing tasks, most participants emphasized that the most important were relationships, despite noting the need to combine relationships and the accomplishment of tasks. One participant said: "I believe that good relations between the manager and others will give a greater possibility for the success of the work and this is reflected on the whole organization" (# 5). Yet, two participants gave equal weight to both models, "I was trying to combine them because integration is important, but there were times I focused on tasks when I felt that relationships would be used against work or personally exploited" (# 7).

Even though all the women leaders emphasized that the successful leadership style is participatory, they accentuated their ability to make critical decisions when needed, "If there was a need to make a decision for the interest of the work, students ... [and] institution, I would have made the decision," (# 7), "it is important to have firmness because there are regulations and laws that must be applied, but without giving orders or directing" (# 2).

The experiences of women in leadership about others' view

The experience of women leaders in this study varied from positive to negative or both. In some cases, the dominant features of a positive view of women in leadership positions by others are those of respect, trust and support, "a lot of respect [from] both males and females because the nature of our department is different from other departments" (# 2). Another positive experience was described as being that "there was no form of disapproval, the look was respectful and appreciative" (# 5). Other participants said they had both positive and negative experience regardless of the gender factor, as one participant noted: "I cannot generalize, sometimes there was an acceptance of women in leadership, other times there was resistance from both sides, male and female" (# 7).

However, three participants said that the experience was full of conflict, disrespect, and lack of acceptance as participants stated: "men did not accept that a woman was in charge of them"(# 4), "[people] said that I looked at them from above and that I was very serious" (# 1), "their view of me became as if I was aggressive/or having a temper ... I became evil in their eyes," (# 6), "in the first period, they tried to promote the idea that I am an unmarried, strong and tomboyish woman in university" (# 4). These answers illustrate the backlash that challenges women's career stages (Blackmore, 2017; Eagly & Karau, 2002; Phelan & Rudman, 2010).

Yet, leadership position was a challenge for all participants and led them to focus on mastering the tasks of the Department Head to prove to themselves and others that they were capable of leadership and taking responsibility. Participants stated: "I did not like to have a high rate of error, I must be up to this task and responsibility" (# 3), "I faced a look of doubt and my colleagues were wondering if I could lead or not ... my colleagues' view of me made me challenge myself that I could (# 6).

Reasons for the negative perceptions toward women in leadership

The majority of participants reported that stereotypical gender attitudes were the reason behind the negative views of women in leadership positions, "societal views of women are that their place is the home" (# 3), "because I am a woman ... men do not accept that a woman is in charge of them" (# 4), "a man is always seen as a leader, no one describes a man as a broken man, but rather a person who fills his position" (# 1). In addition, several participants provided further information about reasons for the non-acceptance and sometimes conflict, "one of the reasons was their expectations that you would be like them [as women] and that you would overlook their mistakes" (# 2), "sometimes they had another philosophy, different priorities and interests" (# 7), "a woman's resistance came from a woman who was incapable, or if she had personal problems and did not want to work" (# 7).

Perceptions of the gender differences in leadership style

Most participants believed that the difference in leadership style had nothing to do with being a man or a woman, but rather based on the understanding of the meaning of leadership. Participant stated: "I did not feel that they differed ...it depends on how well a person understands the position she/he is in, her/his role, and the role of the department members" (# 2), "I think that the environment in which we were in was a masculine environment and the feminine aspects were less important" (# 5), "in many places, a man's leadership was better than a woman's ... when a woman adopted a patriarchal style of leadership" (# 6).

Yet, some of these participants returned and talked during the interview about a number of differences, one said: "I imagine, yes, in a certain part. I think that the male model cares less about details and human relationships" (# 5), same participant added, "because I am a woman, the leadership model can be strict and firm ... [but] I do not know if men stand these positions" (# 5). Others indicated: "women prefer cooperative or group work; women's ability to listen is more than men" (# 3), "decision-making for women is not easy. I study the subject a lot, review, and repeat and repeat, but the man takes decisions more quickly" (# 3). Only one participant indicated that women leaders are more understanding of the reproductive and nurturing roles of working women than men, she said: "not all men are aware of gender ... women leaders are more flexible in this aspect and give more space to female students because we know the requirements of our role well as women" (# 1). These answers reflect the awareness of the participants that women have distinct talents and skills that add to the characteristics of effective leadership (Blackmore, 2017).

Effectiveness and impact

The view of the effectiveness of the leadership experience for each woman differed. The answers included supporting colleagues, professional development, graduating social workers familiar with the feminist dimension, dealing with challenges and making achievements, maintaining a good relationship with students, solving students' problem, modifying program plans, improving the department's vision and developing some courses. Participants' statements "it was effective ... leading a department with males and females of varying degrees, I had to give space for the department members to ... develop themselves" (# 2), "I was able to lead the department ...dealing with challenges, making achievements, maintaining good relations with others" (# 6), I was effective in influencing the university's decisions regarding the department (# 4). In addition, one participant said that a leadership position was an opportunity to change the stereotypical view about women's roles, "woman who is given the opportunity to assume leadership positions ... must prove her presence with all her strength to change the stereotypical view in society about women and the leadership roles" (# 3).

Discussion

This study explored the experience of leadership women in the schools of social work in the Occupied Palestinian Territories, where women suffer from multiple forms of oppression including the Patriarchy system and colonialism. Yet, the results of this study showed that some women were able to resist the barriers they faced due to the expected role of women and succeeded in their struggle to obtain an advanced level of education that enabled them to occupy senior administrative positions in Palestinian universities. This finding is consistent with the liberal feminist argument that the lack of opportunities for women to gain qualifications and experience is the cause of gender inequality and discrimination, rather than any inherent qualities (Dominelli, 2002; Rasool, 2020), and with feminist proposals that deal with women as active actors who can control their lives and resist their circumstances (Dominelli, 2002; Tylor et al., 2009). The findings also indicated that all participants were active actors within the university, as they had a vision, motivation and enthusiasm to influence decision-making and make important changes, whether in the leadership style, existing programs or developing other programs.

In addition, the results revealed that a collaborative participatory approach, shared decision-making, and respect were the main features of women's leadership in schools of social work reflecting transformational leadership (Griffin et al., 2017; Lazzari et al., 2009; Northouse, 2016). Only one of the participants indicated that a feminist dimension should be present in their work and spoke about the hierarchical structure and the power over relationships in choosing people for senior positions, "the institution plays a major role in choosing who is allowed to participate in decision-making". This view is consistent with the assumptions of feminist leadership as suggested by Lazzari et al. (2009) and this is what distinguishes it from transformational or participatory leadership (Lazzari et al., 2009).

Moreover, although the findings provided evidence that there have been changes in people's beliefs about the role of women and their ability to lead, the stereotypical view of women and their role is still influential, consistent with the arguments of previous studies (Eagly & Karau, 2002; Institute of Women's Studies, UN Women & Promundo, 2017;

Phelan & Rudman, 2010). Therefore, the leadership experience was a great challenge for all participants, but it was more challenging for those who faced non-acceptance, as the burden on them increased in terms of completing the tasks or confronting aggressive behaviors towards them, similar to the discussion of other scholars (Blackmore, 2017; Eagly & Karau, 2002; Phelan & Rudman, 2010). A number of women in this study expressed their suffering throughout their leadership of the department, which was represented by quarrels within meetings, lack of cooperation in carrying out various activities and spreading rumors about some of them such as a tomboy, arrogant and superior. However, the findings also revealed that other factors could create conflict within the department or with senior management such as competition for department leadership, having different philosophies or personal interests, and not accepting accountability. Consistent with the feminist perspectives, this means that gender factor intersects with other factors, and influences the selection and support of leaders (Dominelli, 2002; Northouse, 2016; Rasool, 2020).

Furthermore, participants indicated that effective leadership style is not related to being a woman or a man as much as it is related to a leader's beliefs about leadership. In this aspect, the participants revealed their struggles with former women leaders who held masculine beliefs about leadership and referred to positive experiences with male leaders who had a positive understanding of leadership and women. This result is in line with the idea of feminist leadership, which rejects authoritarian leadership practices, whether by women or men alike (Lazzari et al., 2009; Sinclair, 2014).

Finally, the results indicated that all women were satisfied with their performance and had positive self-evaluations about their performance. They all pointed out that this success was due to the support of senior management, some of their colleagues, community organizations, and their families; this is in spite of the challenges and resistances that many of them faced in their roles.

Implications

The results showed that Palestinian women were able to overcome political, social and cultural obstacles, obtain higher education and reach senior administrative positions in Palestinian universities. Not only that, they also developed a clear vision about their leadership roles and confidence in their ability to influence the decisions of the institution. These findings underscore the importance of providing supportive policies and diverse opportunities for women in the fields of education and employment. The results also indicated awareness among women leaders about how to use power and replace it with empowerment, but there was a lack of discussion about the hierarchical structure and power over relationships from senior management in selecting people for senior positions. This accentuates the importance of developing activities that help open discussion on issues of everyone's participation in decision-making, and developing accountability policies in the event that such matters do not occur. Moreover, the challenges facing some women leaders as a result of not being accepted into leadership positions require the development of clear accountability policies for all those who misbehave with women within institutions. In terms of future research, this study emphasizes the importance of conducting research on this topic with other male and female groups such as senior management, faculty, and students to explore their perceptions and experiences of leadership.

References

Anderson-Nathe, B., Gringeri, C., & Wahab, S. (2013). Nurturing "critical hope" in teaching feminist social work research. *Journal of Social Work Education, 49*(2), 277–291.
Ayres, L., Kavanaugh, K., & Knafl, K. A. (2003). Within-case and across-case approaches to qualitative data analysis. *Qualitative Health Research, 13*(6), 871–883.
Blackmore, J. (2017). Educational leadership: A feminist critique and reconstruction. *Deakin Studies in Education Series, 3*, 63–87.
Blome, W., & Safadi, N. S. (2016). Shared vicarious trauma and the effects on Palestinian social workers. *Illness, Crisis & Loss, 24*(4), 236–260.
Christensen, M. C. (2011). Using feminist leadership to build a performance based, peer education program. *Qualitative Social Work, 12*(3), 254–269.
Dominelli, L. (2002). *Feminist social work theory and practice*. Palgrave.
Dunn, D., Gerlach, M. J., & Hyle, A. E. (2014). Gender and leadership: Reflections of women in higher education administration. *International Journal of Leadership and Change, 2*(1), 9–18.
Eagly, A. H., & Carli, L. L. (2003). The female leadership advantage: An evaluation of the evidence. *Leadership Quarterly, 14*, 807–834.
Eagly, A. H., & Karau, S. J. (2002). Role congruity theory of prejudice toward female leaders. *Psychological Review, 109*, 573–598.
Elia, N. (2017). Justice is indivisible: Palestine as a feminist issue. *Decolonization: Indigeneity, Education & Society, 6*(1), 45–63.
Chin, J. L. (2007). Overview women and leadership: Transforming visions and diverse voices. In J. L. Chin, B. Lott, J. K. Rice & J. Sanchez-Hucles (Eds.), *Women and leadership* (pp. 1–17). Blackwell.
Griffin, R. W., Phillips, J. M., & Gully, S. M. (2017). *Organizational behavior: Managing people and organizations*. Cengage Learning.
Hesse-Biber, S. N., & Leavy, P. L. (2007). *Feminist research practice*. Sage.
Hyde, C. (2022). *Feminist macro social work practice*. Encyclopedia of Social Work.
Institute of Women's Studies, UN Women & Promundo (2017). *Understanding masculinities: Results from the international men and gender equality survey (MAGES) – Middle East and North Africa*. https://imagesmena.org/wp-content/uploads/2018/03/Understanding-Masculinities-in-Palestine-English.pdf
Kuttab, E. (2009). The Palestinian women's movement: From resistance and liberation to accommodation and globalization. *Vents d'Est, vents d'Ouest: Mouvements de femmes et féminismes anticoloniaux [online]*. Graduate Institute Publications. https://books.openedition.org/iheid/6310?lang=en
Lay, K., & Daley, J. G. (2007). A Critique of feminist theory. *Advances in Social Work, 8*(1), 49–61.
Lazzari, M. Colarossi, L., & Collins, K. S. (2009). Feminists in social work: Where have all the leaders gone? *Affilia: Journal of Women and Social Work, 24*(4) 348–359. DOI: 10.1177/0886109909343552
Lloyd, D. (2014). It is our belief that Palestine is a feminist issue. *feminists@law, 4*(1). https://journals.kent.ac.uk/index.php/feministsatlaw/article/view/107
Mehrotra, G. (2010). Toward a continuum of intersectionality theorizing for feminist social work scholarship. *Affilia: Journal of Women and Social Work, 25*(4) 417–430.
Northouse, P. G. (2016). *Leadership: Theory and practice* (7th ed). Sage.
Palestinian Central Bureau of Statistics (2020). *Sustainable development goals statistical report, 2020*. Palestinian Central Bureau of Statistics, Sustainable Development Indicators Database. https://unstats.un.org/capacity-development/UNSD-FCDO/palestine/
Phelan, J. E., & Rudman, L. A. (2010). Prejudice toward female leaders: Backlash effects and women's impression management dilemma. *Social and Personality Psychology Compass 4*(10), 807–820.
Rasool, S. (2020). Feminisms. In A. V. Breda & J. Sekudu (Eds.), *Theories for decolonial social work practice in South Africa* (pp. 157–177). Oxford.
Shalhoub-Kevorkian, N., Wahab, S., & Al-Issa, F. (2022). Feminist except for Palestine: Where are feminist social workers on Palestine? *Affilia, 37*(2), 204–214.
Sinclair, A. (2014). A feminist case for leadership. In J. Damousi, K. Rubenstein & M. Tomsic (Eds.), *Diversity in leadership: Australian women, past and present* (pp. 17–35). The Australian National University.

Turner, S. G., & Maschi, T. M. (2015). Feminist and empowerment theory and social work practice. *Journal of Social Work Practice, 29*(2), 151–162.
Tylor, V., Whittier, N., & Rupp, L. J. (2009). *Feminist frontiers* (8th ed.). McGraw-Hill.
Wendt, S., & Moulding, N. (2017). The current state of feminism and social work. *Australian Social Work, 70*(3), 261–262.
Woodley, X. M., & Lockard, M. (2016). Womanism and snowball sampling: Engaging marginalized populations in holistic research. *The Qualitative Report, 21*(2), 321–329.

28
THE CONTRIBUTIONS OF LATIN AMERICAN FEMINISMS TO SOCIAL WORK UNDERGRADUATE ACADEMIC TRAINING IN ARGENTINA

Melisa Campana Alabarce, Laura Lorena Leguizamón and Maria Belén Verón Ponce

Introduction

This chapter aims to analyse the influence of the contributions of Latin American critical Feminisms on the professional training of Argentinean Social Work. We are interested in identifying the changes that have taken place over the last decade, as important advances have been made in our country in terms of the visibility of feminist demands and their incorporation into the public agenda. Examples of this are the Law on Comprehensive Protection to Prevent, Punish and Eradicate Gender Violence (26485/2009), Gender Identity Law (26743/2012), Equal Marriage Law (26618/2010), Law on the Voluntary Interruption of Pregnancy (27610/2021), just to mention a few. Similarly, during this period, there were changes in the curricula of Social Work degrees, which reflect the dialogue between academia and social movements associated with those struggles.

The first section gives an account of the debates within Feminisms and the contributions of critical Feminisms – epistemologically and politically positioned- in the Global South. More precisely, from eco-Feminisms, communitarian Feminisms and Black Feminisms, as social and academic movements that question white Feminisms, as well as recognise the intersectionality of oppressions and the situated standpoint.

Professional training projects in Social Work are reflected in undergraduate curricula. In this chapter, the current curricula of 21 academic units are analysed to recognise the presence of key categories of Latin American feminist theory. The central aim is to identify the impact of the debates and knowledge of feminist movements and epistemologies in the undergraduate training of our profession, as contributions to equality, expansion of rights and depatriarchalisation of our societies.

Recent developments of Latin American feminist theory

Latin American critical Feminisms are in non-Western, situated approaches. Although they are nourished by the Feminisms of equality, they question the idea of the bases of freedom supported by the capitalist economy.

Critical Feminisms are constituted as a reaction to white Feminisms insofar as they highlight a series of oppressions that refer to the experiences of racialised women, peasants, migrants and women geo-politically located in the Global South (Gargallo, 2013; Mendoza, 2014).

The term white feminism refers to those trends framed within classical liberal feminism, that proclaim the rights of "women" as a universal political subject, ignoring the heterogeneity of women's experiences and other identities crossed by multiple oppressions (González, 2020; Lugones, 2021). On the contrary, the concerns of eco-Feminisms, communitarian Feminisms and Black Feminisms relate to how oppressions derived from capitalism, Patriarchy and Colonialism are intertwined in our territories and bodies (Bidaseca & Vázquez Laba, 2011; Paredes, 2010).

This situated position is the starting point for our discussion in this chapter. From this perspective, the contributions of eco-Feminism, communitarian Feminism and Black Feminism are considered as sources of interjection to be explored in the curricula of social work undergraduate training in the public universities of Argentina.

In the first place, eco-Feminisms are positioned in the dialogue between ecology and feminism, placing at the centre of the debate the recognition of life. Although this trend did not emerge in Latin America, it has been taken up critically by social movements in the region. The proposal is to draw attention to the conditions of habitat, ecosystems and care, which are affected by Patriarchy and capitalism, generating ecological, economic and political crises. Eco-Feminisms criticise anthropocentrism and modern rationality based on scientific knowledge, as a guarantee for man's dominance over nature and women and, therefore, define the consequences of this model as a "war against life" (Herrero, Pascual & González Reyes, 2018).

Another contribution of eco-Feminisms is to make visible and denounce the conception of women's bodies as objects of appropriation, exploitation and capitalist commodification. In this sense, Marxian notions have been questioned to warn how in the origins of capitalism, "original accumulation" is related not only to the enclosure of land (private property) but also with the dispossession and appropriation of women's knowledge and labour. For this purpose, it was necessary to delegitimise and persecute these practices under the institution of the "witch-hunt" carried out by the Catholic Inquisition (Federici, 2010).

The category body-territory is thought from eco-Feminisms as a locus where the expropriator violence of capitalism and Patriarchy are manifested: "a prolonged process of stigmatisation and persecution was required for women to lose control over themselves, and the female body was territorialised and turned into a place for the expression of power relations in all orders" (Quiroga & Gago, 2014, p. 9). In this sense, rape as a form of violence is an expression of patriarchal domination over women's bodies, just as territory is invaded under an expropriator logic for the commodification of its resources.

On their part, communitarian Feminisms present itself as an emancipatory, situated and critical proposal. It combats the oppressions of the system imposed by the colony, while recognising pre-colonial oppressions transmitted by the ancestral cosmogonic conception of the world system. As it was stated before, it is a counterproposal to classical (white) feminism. This trend asks about farmers and Indigenous women, whose community life has been made invisible by the feminism of equality and difference. Its standpoint is the Indigenous cosmovision of "good life". As this trend disputes the colonial designations, it takes up the name *Abya Yala* for what is now known as the American Continent. It is both a theoretical and a political proposal, which recreates a world interconnected by different entities of which human beings are only a part (it is worth noting that communitarian feminism is not primarily written but arises from the oral tradition, and the few written references attest to the existence of other ways of communication).

Finally, Black Feminisms start from the interpellation of the negation of slavery and racism, and at the same time, question the appropriation of other societies. This trend speaks not only of women of African descent but also frames women of colour in countries where colonisation imposes a stereotype (González, 2015; hooks, 1984; Oyěwùmí, 2004; Pineda, 2023).

From this position, it opened the door to intersections, analysing the consequences of different oppressions on bodies: race, class and gender are potentiated, skewing existence. This perspective is also concerned with recovering the contributions of African roots in Latin America. Furthermore, at the intersection of class and gender, it contests classical Marxism's analysis of privilege.

Social Work undergraduate academic training in Argentina: current revisions and debates

The Argentinian Federation of Professional Associations of Social Service (FAAPSS) is the national organisation for associations and councils of Social Service and Social Work across the country. One of its goals is the "defence of professional competencies; to defend a policy that contemplates the validity of democracy, public freedoms and full respect for the dignity of the person" (https://trabajosocialargen.wordpress.com). Since the creation of FAAPSS in 1987, there has been a concern to discuss the training of Social Work professionals. Within the country's Social Work training centres, there is great heterogeneity in terms of educational levels, qualifications and curricula, which is why it is proposed to develop a common curriculum, although open to regional particularities and, in some cases, also to a global agenda of Social Work standards.

Likewise, the Argentine Federation of Academic Units of Social Work (FAUATS) groups and coordinates the academic units of Social Work throughout the country. Its objective is to promote undergraduate and graduate training, research and cooperation. In several documents drawn up by FAUATS since 2005, a consensus was reached on general criteria to be considered in successive revisions of the curricula, namely: a minimum of four years' study; a core of classroom-based disciplinary training; supervised field placements; research as the core of training; inclusion of the theoretical-methodological, ethical-political and operational-instrumental dimensions. Based on these agreements, since 2011, it has been necessary to establish professional competencies defined by both federations, which would adapt to changes in the context and, at the same time, receive a regulatory framework to support them.

In December 2014, the National Senate passed the Federal Law on Social Work 27.072, the draft of which was prepared by the FAAPSS, with the participation and consensus of the academic units that make up the FAUATS. This law establishes among its objectives the need to standardise professional practice throughout the national territory; at the same time, it articulates and unifies basic principles for professional practice. There are, therefore, notorious differences between the formulation of the Scope of the Degree before and after the enactment of the National Law, which was then slowly adhered to by the sub-regional states (it should also be noted that none of the documents produced by FAUATS before the enactment of the Federal Law, mentioned the need to incorporate the gender or feminist agenda into the curricula guidelines).

In the curricula prior to 2014, terminology from the 1980s appears, since most of the local (not national but sub-national or regional) normative or laws on professional practice were passed immediately after the recovery of democracy.

In other plans, reference is made to the Draft Project for the Modification of Decree 579/586 of the National Ministry of Education, prepared by FAUATS in 1996, and a clear semantic updating is noted:

> To contribute to the construction of alternatives for the modification, overcoming and/or transformation of problematic situations of individuals, families and groups at the prevention, assistance and promotion levels, valuing the sense of Human Dignity (...) To generate, enhance and/or strengthen processes of community and/or institutional organisation, building spaces in the articulation between the needs and interests of the sectors that participate in them and the objectives and interests of the institutions, tending towards the satisfaction and legitimisation of Social Rights.

Finally, those Plans reformed post-2014 already refer to Article 9 of the Federal Law on Social Work:

> Advice, design, implementation, audit and evaluation of: (a) Public policies related to the different areas of professional practice (...) Integration, coordination, guidance, training and/or supervision of disciplinary, multidisciplinary and interdisciplinary work teams (...) Preparation of social expertise in the field of justice (...) Professional intervention in mediation bodies or programmes (...) Management and performance of undergraduate and postgraduate teaching, extension and research functions in the field of academic units of professional training in Social Work and Social Sciences (...) Management, integration of teams and development of teams in the field of Social Work (...) Management, integration of teams and development of research lines and projects in the social field (...) Participation in advice, design and implementation of new legislation of a social nature, integrating forums and councils for the promotion and protection of rights (...) Management and administration of public and/or private institutions at different levels of operation and decision making in public policies.

These formulations place the discipline in the concert of the Social Sciences and link it to social rights, the production of knowledge, the design of public policies and advocacy in the legislative agenda. These perspectives were missing from previous curricula, which focussed – for instance – on Social Work traditional methods, technocratic aspects of professional intervention, para-medical or para-juridical role of social workers. That is to say that proposals related to the human rights perspective, institutional intervention and research with a clear ethical–political orientation of the stage were incorporated.

It must be said that until 2018, FAAPSS did not have an area for discussion of the gender perspective, even though this was the year in which an initiative of the Gender and Diversity Commission of the Professional Association of Social Service of Cordoba led to the creation of a Permanent Forum on Gender and Sexual Diversity, within the framework of the FAAPSS. Its aim was to undo patriarchal cultural patterns that shape social relations under the hetero-norm and the consequent hierarchisation of bodies (FAAPSS, Permanent Forum on Gender and Sexual Diversity, 2022).

The Forum began its activities in 2019, bringing together representatives from different cities, and proposed to broaden the classic gender agenda with the interests of sex-gender dissidence. While in the past, those who worked on the gender perspective did so from other disciplines, the particularity of the Forum is that its approaches are based on the disciplinary field itself. To date, it has concentrated on three lines of action: advising the professional councils or sub-regional associations to set up their own gender and diversity commissions; drafting pronouncements whenever rights are violated; and organising discussions and debates that allow gender issues to be explored in greater depth (Claudio Barbero, personal communication by zoom, July 2022).

Among the objectives of the Forum, is mentioned the need to discuss with FAUATS an agenda around the revision of the curricula of universities about gender, Feminisms and gender-based dissidence.

The impact of Latin American Feminisms on Social Work curricula

As mentioned above, the chapter analyses the incidence of Latin American feminist theory in undergraduate Social Work training in Argentina, through documentary research carried out mainly for the writing of this chapter. The three researchers who write this report live in different regions of the country and were able to gather the documentary corpus thanks to access to relevant sources of information, such as the national federations of Social Work.

In the first place, the presence of concepts and categories of Latin American feminist theory in the Social Work curricula of 21 public universities throughout the country was identified and surveyed (it is important to note that most of the plans were revised, considering there are 23 academic units recognised by FAUATS). Regarding the survey of professional training projects expressed in curricula, the first task was to identify the place of Latin American feminist theory in disciplinary training, both in the plans (that is to say, the complete curricula content) and in the subjects (that is to say, the courses or seminars that make up the plan) of Social Work degrees in Argentina. For this purpose, an exhaustive systematisation and analysis was carried out of the current plans in 21 academic units belonging to the FAUATS, as well as of the contents of those subjects whose minimum content alluded in some way to key categories of Latin American feminist theory.

If we consider the discussions and recommendations prior to the effective sanctioning of the Federal Law of Social Work, we identify 12 reformed plans between 2009 and the present, from all regions of the country (Buenos Aires, Misiones, San Luis, Santiago, Patagonia and Tandil). Strictly speaking, only six of those plans have been reformed during or post 2014. If only the latter are taken into consideration, the remarkable fact is that all of them correspond to the central region (Cuyo, Rosario, Lanús, Mar del Plata, Moreno and Villa María). We are emphasising on this timeline because it is notorious that the legislative changes implied in the Federal Law relates directly to the Social Work curricula.

A first feature that emerges from the analysis of all the plans surveyed Is that, as far as the Graduate Profile is concerned, they state that it should aim for a solid theoretical-methodological training that enables them to intervene in the multiple expressions of the social question. We can take just one example, from one of the major academic units of the country:

> Social Work, as a profession that forms part of the Social Sciences, has constituted its object of disciplinary intervention for more than 100 years around what we now define as the social question and the social action of the State to confront it. Its field of intervention, therefore, develops from the various manifestations of this social question, which express a set of social inequalities that affect the conditions of material and social reproduction of individual and collective actors.

In a second stage, the minimum contents of the 21 curricula were reviewed. They were organised regarding the contents of each subject, according to the presence of a series of thematic axes. In turn, the following categories or key concepts were outlined: Feminisms, gender studies, Colonialism, post/des/colonial studies, territory, territoriality, situated thought, extractivism. These keywords served as exclusion criteria from which the topics to be reviewed in depth were selected, making a total of 259.

In axis 1, the subjects of Philosophy, Epistemology and Ethics were grouped together. A total of 25 programmes were found whose contents allude to key concepts and categories with themes referring to: women's studies; epistemologies of the south; racism; decolonial thought; Colonialism of knowledge; multiculturalism; Patriarchy.

In axis 2, the subjects of Anthropology, Sociology and Social Theory were grouped together. A total of 56 programmes were found whose contents allude to key concepts and categories with themes referring to: identity; kinship and gender; post-Colonialism; race; eco-territorial turn; situated thought; Intersectionality; inequality and gender; families.

In axis 3, the subjects of Social Policy, Public Policy Analysis, Social Management, Social Problems, Social Structure were grouped together. A total of 43 programmes were found whose contents allude to key concepts and categories with themes referring to: class, ethnic, gender and territorial inequalities; gender and social policy; gender and citizenship.

In axis 4, the subjects of Economics and History were grouped together. A total of 42 programmes were found whose contents allude to key concepts and categories with themes referring to: sexual division of labour; women's work; women and the labour market; suffragism; equal marriage and gender identity; feminist movements in history.

In axis 5, the subjects of Communities, Families, and Territories were grouped together. A total of 44 programmes were found whose contents allude to key concepts and categories with themes referring to: social movements and domestic units; care tasks; families; hetero and homo-parenthood; maternity; gender and human rights; equal marriage; families and Feminisms.

Research Methodology subjects were grouped together in axis 6. A total of nine programmes were found whose contents allude to key concepts and categories with themes referring to: research with a gender perspective; decolonial approach in research; critical, decolonial and feminist perspective of knowledge in Social Sciences.

Axis 7 groups together the subjects of Law and Human Rights. A total of 22 programmes were found whose contents allude to key concepts and categories with themes referring to: gender identity; family law; forms of kinship; gender violence; family and Social Work; gender and human rights.

In axis 8, elective or optional subjects specifically related to gender, feminism, Colonialism and situated thought were grouped together. A total of 17 programmes were found whose contents – or even their names – allude to key concepts and categories, in general, with themes referring to: childhood, family and human rights; family violence; social intervention and Feminisms; gender mainstream; territorial organisation of care; gender–class–race/ethnicity in social intervention.

An interesting aspect to highlight is the specific bibliography proposed by each of the subjects analysed. In this respect, the recurrence of female authors is notorious, as at least two of the following appear in all the aforementioned subjects: the: Judith Butler, Gayatri Spivak, Paul B. Preciado, Virginie Despentes, Kimberlé Crenshaw, Gayle Rubin, Joan Scott, Audre Lorde, bell hook, Cristina Molina Petit, Silvia Federici, Ana María Fernández, Paula Aguilar, Laura Restrepo, Laura Pautassi, Juliana Martínez Franzoni, Claudia Anzorena, Pilar Arcidiácono, Dora Barrancos, Corina Rodríguez Enríquez, Felicitas Elías, Carla Zibecchi, Mariana Carbajal, Roxana Longo, Valle Moreno and Verónica Gago. To this corpus should be added the inclusion of bibliography on strictly Latin American Feminisms in the syllabuses of 28 of the 259 subjects observed: Karina Bidaseca, Eleonor Faur, María Luisa Femenías, María Eugenia Hermida, Marcela Lagarde, Diana Maffía, Marisol Patiño Sánchez, Silvia Rivera Cusicanqui, Rita Segato and Maristella Svampa.

Considering that not all readers are familiar with these authors, below is a table indicating the disciplinary affiliation and main contributions of each of them. Table 28.1 also groups the authors according to whether they are non-Latin American classics, Latin American classics or strictly speaking contemporary Latin American feminists.

Table 28.1 Critical feminist scholarly contributors

Classical non-Latin American	Trend/discipline	Main field/contributions
Judith Butler	Post-structuralist philosophy	Her theory was foundational to queer thought
Gayatri Spivak	Post-colonialist theory and deconstruction	Denounces discursive, totalising and patriarchal homogeneity
Nancy Fraser	Critical theory	Denounces capitalism as an institutionalised social order and neo-liberalism reconfigured from a gender perspective
Paul B. Preciado	Non binarist philosophy	Contributes to queer and post-queer thinking
Virginie Despentes	Contemporary feminist literature	Denounces patriarchal violence against women's bodies
Kimberlé Crenshaw	Critical intersectional theory	Black feminism. Denounces racial and class violence
Gayle Rubin	Cultural anthropology	Defines the gender system
Joan Scott	History and feminism	Postulates gender as a historical category of análisis
Audre Lorde	Critical literature	Black feminism. Denounces and criticises white, heteropatriarchal feminism

(*Continued*)

Table 28.1 (Continued)

Classical non-Latin American	Trend/discipline	Main field/contributions
bell hooks	Feminist philosophy	Denounces the system of race, class, gender oppression
Cristina Molina Petit	Feminist philosophy	Problematises enlightenment feminism
Silvia Federici	Political philosophy and History	Marxist Feminism. Situates Patriarchy and capitalism from historical perspective. Emphasises the exploitation of women
Classical Latin American	Trend/discipline	Main field/contributions
Ana María Fernández	Psychology	Addresses the tensions between psychoanalysis and Feminisms
Laura Restrepo	Literature	Migrant women
Laura Pautassi	Social and political theory	Human Rights approach. Gender and care
Juliana Martínez Franzoni	Social and political theory	Social policies, gender and care
Claudia Anzorena	Sociology	Relations between state and gender. Abortion
Dorra Barrancos	Philosophy and history	History of women. Gender theory
Elizabeth Jelin	Sociology	Gender and citizenship. Work, families and gender
Corina Rodríguez Enríquez	Political economy	Feminist economy
Silvia Rivera Cusicanqui	Sociology and Latin American history	Postcolonial feminism
Rita Segato	Feminist anthropology	Gender violence and new masculinities
Latin American contemporary feminist	Trend/discipline	Main field/contributions
Karina Bidaseca	Sociology	Postcolonial feminism
Eleonor Faur	Sociology	Gender, public policies and families
María Luisa Femenías	Feminist philosophy	Gender and multiculturalism
María Eugenia Hermida	Social Work	Decolonial feminism
Marcela Lagarde	Feminist anthropology	Purposes the category "feminicidio"
Diana Maffía	Feminist philosophy	Gender and diversity. Sexual work and migrations. Gender and science
Marisol Patiño Sánchez	Social Work	Social representations. Migrant women
Maristella Svampa	Sociology	Environmental feminism
Paula Aguilar	History and political theory	Gender and householding
Pilar Arcidiácono	Social and political theory	Social policies, gender and care
Carla Zibecchi	Sociology	Social policies, communitarian organisations and care
Mariana Carbajal	Social communication	Contemporary feminist movements. Abortion.
Roxana Longo	Social psychology	Feminisms, work and care policies
Verónica Gago	Sociology	Gender violence. Communitarian organisations

These set of authors are academic references for critical feminist trends and constitute a necessary source of reference in the prolific bibliographical production of the field. Among the former are the authors who support Latin American critical epistemologies. Regarding classic Latin American authors, there is a heterogeneity of perspectives that include diverse readings, from an institutional perspective, centred on the human rights approach, and which tends to have an impact on public policy, to more critical approaches to institutional and State responses. With respect to the authors' disciplinary inscriptions, there is also a wide range of backgrounds, including Philosophy, Anthropology, Sociology, History, Economics, Political Science, Law and, to a lesser extent, Social Work.

Precisely, if we consider the heterogeneity of disciplinary inscriptions shown in the table and link them to the axes described above, we see how feminist literature has been permeating different subjects of the plans, beyond those specifically referring to Social Work.

Conclusions

Academic and activist Feminisms question the sciences and disciplines from their own spaces of knowledge production and professional intervention. In recent years, social and political changes have taken place as a result of the impact of Feminisms. They have also been present in the recent debates on the epistemological, theoretical and methodological bases of Social Work, which are reflected in the Federal Law on professional practice and in the curricula of the different degree careers.

In this chapter, the contents of 21 plans and 259 programmes on different subjects were analysed to identify the presence of categories, concepts, authors and bibliography that show the influence of Latin American critical Feminisms.

Feminist activism in Argentina had an important political impact in terms of dialogue with academic institutions. For instance, participation in the massive National Women's Meetings held in different cities since 1986 made collective construction possible between the activist and academic sectors. Besides, the massive mobilisations against gender violence around the slogan "Ni Una Menos" (Not One Less) from 2015 onwards, constituted an impulse for the demands in many different institutional spheres (Cabral & Acacio, 2016; Iribarren Martínez et al., 2018).

Before this general or massive process, the interests surrounding gender issues were part of the agendas of research groups and some academic sectors that proposed the debate since the beginning of the 21st century in Social Work bachelor's degrees. In this sense, the text of the Federal Law of Social Work passed after a wide-ranging debate, was crucial because it not only placed but also remarked respect for diversity as a fundamental principle as well as the approach to public gender policies as a main professional competence.

As another milestone, we can mention is the formation of the Inter-University Network for Gender Equality and Against Violence (RUGE) in 2018, with the participation of academics and activists from different universities from Argentina. Parallelly, the FAAPSS set up Gender Forums in 2019. Into Social Work academic units, it can be assured that the RUGE, the Gender Forums and also the Micaela Law (which obliges training on gender issues for all state agents), strengthened the postulates of the Federal Law on Social Work in terms of gender. It can therefore be affirmed that feminist activism nourished the debates on professional training, establishing channels of dialogue based on different institutional strategies.

Although there are differences and particularities between the academic units – due to the trajectories, the institutional contexts in which the degree careers are located and the geographical regions – there is a minimum content base that is present in all the plans. Regarding the findings of this study, the prevalence of elective or optional subjects that address gender or feminism as a "problem", "theme" or "field" of study and intervention is acknowledged. There is no strategic choice for a cross-cutting approach in the curricula yet. The curricular spaces devoted to methodological approaches to research and professional intervention (pre-professional internships) do not show a centrality of problematisations linked to Feminisms; on the contrary, they appear as marginal or accessory themes.

In general, a recurrent trend in the different subjects has been the incorporation of feminist interpellations based on the approach to families and the dynamics surrounding them, such as the sexual division of labour, care tasks, work–family reconciliation, gender roles and the democratisation of families. This shows that the field of interpersonal relations has been an entry point for problematising patriarchal structures in relation to our typical areas of professional intervention. In this sense, it is the white feminist trend or those centred on the perspective of gender equality and human rights that prevail in the subjects. Perspectives linked to eco-Feminisms, communitarian Feminisms or Black Feminisms can be found in the problematisation of intersectionality, the territorial turn, the decolonial approach, post-Colonialism and situated thought, but always to a lesser extent.

From this first approach, questions can be raised about the absence in the plans of a view of the regional expressions of Feminism, based on a political agenda traversed by the effects that Patriarchy and Colonialism impose on the bodies-territories of women and dissidents in Latin America.

New questions are also being raised about the debates, disputes and decisions that take place dynamically in the different academic units and which have a direct impact on undergraduate training. For instance, it is worth asking about the presence of feminist epistemologies in final projects or research dissertations, postgraduate training spaces or the lines of research on the field in the different academic units.

The Initial research carried out for the preparation of this chapter allows a first overview from a federal perspective on the presence of critical feminist epistemologies from the Global South in our academic units. The conclusions provide a first and provisional approximation to the theoretical and methodological options of the academic units in terms of feminist content, which should be further explored in future studies.

If we recognise the commitment to a feminist perspective and think about it as inherent to professional training that claims to be critical, emancipatory and in pursuit of social justice, a profound reflection on our training programmes and practices is an unavoidable starting point.

References

Bach, A. (2010). *Las voces de la experiencia. El Viraje de la filosofía feminista*. Biblos.
Barbero, Claudio. Personal communication. Foro de Género y Diversidad, FAAPSS. On line by zoom, July 16th, 2022.
Bidaseca, K. & Vázquez Laba, V. (2011). "Feminismos y (des) colonialidad. Las voces de las mujeres indígenas del sur". *Revista Temas de Mujeres*, año 7, nro. 7. Nueva Época.
Cabnal, L. (2010). *Feminismos diversos: el feminismo comunitario*. ACSUR-Las Segovias.
Cabral P. & Acacio J. A. (2016). "La violencia de género como problema público. Las movilizaciones por "Ni Una Menos" en la Argentina". *Question* 51, 170–187.

FAAPSS (2022). *Pronunciamientos y piso normativo del Foro Federal de Géneros y Diversidad. Periodo 2018-2022.* https://www.facebook.com/faapssTrabajoSocialArgentina

Federici, S. (2010). *Calibán y la bruja. Mujeres, cuerpo y acumulación originaria.* Traficantes de Sueños.

Foro Permanente de Género y Diversidad Sexual. Documento 1(5) Watch|Facebook (29 Abril de 2019).

Gargallo Celentani, F. (2013). *Feminismo desde Abya Yala. Ideas y proposiciones de las mujeres de 607 pueblos en Nuestra América.* América Libre.

González, L. (2015). "La catégorie político-culturelle d' amefricanité". *Les cahiers du CEDREF* (20). http://journals.openedition.org/cedref/806

González, L. (2020). "Mulher negra". Ríos, M. & Lima, M. (Eds.) *Por um feminismo afrolatinoamericano* (pp. 84–100). Zahar.

Herrero, Y., Pascual, M., & González Reyes, M. (2018). *La vida en el centro: voces y relatos ecofeministas.* Libros en acción.

hooks, b. (1984). *Feminist theory: from margin to center.* Routledge.

Iribarren Martínez, J., Machado Terreno, A., Manzotti, R., & Pérez, C. (2018). "Ni Una Menos: Análisis de la acción colectiva en el ámbito público". *Sociales Investiga*, 5(5), 126–134. http://socialesinvestiga.unvm.edu.ar/ojs/index.php/socialesinvestiga/article/view/165

Lugones, M. (2021). *Peregrinajes. Teorizar una coalición contra múltiples opresiones.* Ediciones del signo.

Mendoza, B. (2014). "La epistemología del sur, la colonialidad del género y el feminismo latinoamericano". Espinosa Miñoso, Y., et al. (Eds.). *Tejiendo de otro modo: Feminismo, epistemología y apuestas descoloniales en Abya Yala.* Editorial Universitaria de Cauca, p.19–36.

Oyĕwùmí, O. (2004). *Conceituando o gênero: os fundamentos epistemología dos conceitos feministas e o desafio das epistemologías africanas.* Codesria Gender Series 1, 1–8.

Paredes, J. (2010). *Hilando fino desde el feminismo comunitario.* El Rebozo.

Pineda E. (2023). *Ser afrodescendiente en América Latina.* Prometeo.

Quiroga Díaz, N. & Gago, V. (2014). Los comunes en Femenino. Cuerpo y poder ante la expropiación de las economías para la vida. *Economía y Sociedad*, 45(19), 1–18.

SECTION 4

The politics of care

29
LIFE-SUSTAINING COMMUNITARIAN WEAVINGS
Feminist interpellations of the approach of community social work[1]

Javiera Cubillos-Almendra

Introduction

This chapter presents three strategies for community social work practice drawn from feminist theory and practice.[2] The first interpellation looks at our understanding of community, which is crucial for promoting reflexivity about who or what we work with. The chapter argues that community is a kind of relationship between people and their environment that is founded on respect, reciprocity and shared responsibility. Women play an indispensable role in forming these relationship connections, which ultimately aim to reproduce social life (Federici, 2004, 2019; Carrasco, 2013; Gutiérrez, 2017; Cruz, 2020). From this perspective, and in line with feminist reflections, caregiving in its material, emotional and symbolic dimensions is a constitutive element of community. As such, it is important to recognize its significance in the on-going collaborative effort to sustain individual and collective life.

Drawing on this concept of community, this chapter outlines three essential points for approaching community social work. First, the notion of *communitarian weavings* (Gutiérrez, 2011, 2017) helps us visualize and redefine the many social connections that we rely on to create and sustain the collective. Though often overlooked, these connections are tightly intertwined with everyday life and critical to sustaining life and shaping the community. The *communitarian weavings* – with all its various characteristics, intensities, extensions and scales – give rise to the community sphere.

Second, the primary purpose of the *communitarian weavings* is caregiving or sustaining the lives of community members. Caregiving does not solely take place within the home or the domestic sphere. It also extends into the closest surrounding spaces generating fundamental – yet often invisible – synergies between what is deemed private (such as the domestic, the family, the individual, the market) and the public (the collective, the commons).

Third, we must recognize that women's leading role in caregiving within the household and in sustaining the community sphere can overburden them with work and undermine their overall well-being. Concepts such as *care debt* (Herrero, 2012) or *patriarchal debt* (Carrasco et al., 2014), *caregiving footprint* (Herrero, 2012) and *time poverty* (Vickery, 1977; Bardasi and Wodon, 2006; Andreozzi et al., 2021) help us understand the social and economic debt that we owe to women. They highlight the importance of acknowledging this debt when working with communities to update processes, so community social workers can avoid rendering women's work invisible and contributing to its expropriation.

The community: a kind of relationship

The first question we should ask ourselves when approaching community social work is how we understand the term community. Community social work aims to identify comprehensive solutions to the problems facing various groups and communities and this implies the existence of a collective agency capable of addressing these issues in a participatory, synergetic and inclusive manner (Ross, 1967; Ander-Egg, 2003; Pastor, 2004, 2013; Duarte, 2017). Thus, one of the first steps is to identify the target community where we plan to work, including its needs, resources, composition and dynamics.

Once we identify the community, we can assess the factors that are important for identifying its strengths and capacities. These are important questions, and revisiting work on *communitarian weavings* by authors like Raquel Gutiérrez (2011, 2017) can help us address them. *Communitarian weaving is a term used to describe* a collaborative network of different types of stable relationship ties such as networks of neighbours or relatives, women's networks, support groups, assemblies and councils. Its objective is to ensure members' well-being. *Communitarian weaving* aims to address and better meet the basic needs of social and collective life by enabling the production and reproduction of human and non-human life[3] (Gutiérrez, 2011, 2017; Gutiérrez and Salazar, 2019).

The notion of *communitarian weaving* is inclusive enough to encompass several types of human networks, even those that may be unfamiliar or that commonly go unnoticed. It is not intended as conceptual closure but to draw attention to practices often undervalued and ignored under market logic and state policy. These practices sustain individual and collective life as well as our capacity to build the commons, a term that goes beyond tangible goods like water or a community garden, to encompass political projects (Federici, 2012, 2019). The relational processes of reciprocity and caregiving (intangible goods or relational goods), which enable the satisfaction of collective needs and the attainment of tangible goods, are also considered commons (Carrasco, 2014; Ramírez-Gallegos, 2019).

One of the primary tasks of community social work is to promote community members' capacity to identify and acknowledge their reciprocity networks and the commons they produce, both tangible (e.g., community gardens, community kitchens, and meeting spaces) and intangible (a sense of belonging, emotional support and care). The challenge is to rediscover the community and focus on the co-action that underpins it without taking it for granted or assuming it to be universally known. Instead, it is important to acknowledge that co-action is a dynamic and often invisible force, closely intertwined with our everyday lives (Tapia et al., 2021).

When we conceive of community social work as centred on collective practice, we recognize a kind of grassroots solidarity that continuously sustains our lives and can serve as a platform for more far-reaching action that contributes to individual and collective well-being. These foundational acts of reciprocity predate any community activation and can be considered pre-reflexive. Therefore, in addition to providing another approach to everyday practices, an initial exercise in collective reflection enables community social workers and the community itself to identify the constructed, constitutive and, particularly, intangible resources of a given community. While shared needs are still important, they can be temporarily set aside to prioritize practices that unite the community and generate a *communitarian weaving*.

Understanding these connections and everyday practices as opportunities can pave the way for internal cohesion and individual and collective empowerment processes (Pastor, 2004, 2013). It reveals how the community responds to everyday needs and contingencies (health, political and economic crises) which may be perceived as private but still require interdependence with others. Even though communities do not always recognize themselves as such, reflective and creative methodologies can be used to promote self-awareness and leverage existing connections to undertake more impactful action. Facilitating reflection processes that lead to action creates the conditions in which communities can recognize and develop their collective capacities (Pastor, 2013). This is especially true in neoliberal and individualistic policy and practice contexts, where the practices of reciprocity in everyday life become less apparent and less significant.

Observing a community's reality from a *communitarian weaving* perspective provides an intricate understanding of the community. This approach allows us to see and value the closest, most essential connections that make life possible and create a sense of belonging. It also helps us understand that the community as a type of relationship has multiple manifestations and is articulated on different scales and spatial contexts. Consequently, we can conceive of it extending beyond the boundaries of the neighbourhood or the local area.

Relational networks of reciprocity are dynamic and ever-changing. They regenerate, strengthen, weaken, or pause depending on the will and objectives of their members but remain flexible enough to adapt to the contexts, contingencies and requirements that arise. By understanding the community as a type of relationship, we can decouple it from the local or group level to understand it in multiple spatial contexts. Practices of reciprocity can be understood as points of convergence for different trajectories, which cross time and scale to weave together a particular locus (Massey, 1994; Soto-Villagrán, 2016; Jirón et al., 2022). Thus, the spatiality of *communitarian weavings* is always open and flexible, unconstrained by pre-determined borders or limits (Cubillos-Almendra et al., 2022). The blurred boundaries between private and public and personal or collective bring us to our second interpellation.

Sustaining life is the mobilizing force for communitarian weavings

The concept of *communitarian weavings* shows how communities are motivated by a *reproductive rationale* (Cendejas, 2017) or by the "natural way" of reproducing life, which emphasizes reciprocity, caregiving and "use value" instead of market logic or state policies (Gutiérrez and Salazar, 2019).

Caregiving is a constitutive element of these *communitarian weavings* that reproduce life and enable us to understand human life in terms of interdependence. They emphasize our reciprocal need for others as we develop our autonomy and make our lives liveable (Benhabib, 1992; Butler, 2004; Carrasco, 2013; Sales, 2016). The practices of reciprocity that these weavings promote include activities, services, goods, relationships and affections. They contribute to the strength and duration of communities by alleviating precariousness experienced by large swaths of the population. This precariousness works in two ways: an existential way (the physical, emotional and psychological fragility inherent to the human condition) and a conditioned way caused, for example, by public policies that have not prioritized social welfare (Butler, 2004; Sales, 2016; Sanchís, 2020).

Paying attention to the caregiving exchanges that produce and reproduce the *communitarian weaving* helps blur the division between the domestic and the collective. In today's pandemic context, the blurring of domestic and community boundaries is even more apparent. Especially in times of crisis (health, political, social, and economic), households are sustained by social networks that extend beyond them, such as a friend or someone who shares common motivations, a neighbour next door or across the street, or people we meet in a park or on the street.

Households are in constant dialogue with their immediate surroundings (both territorialized and non-territorialized) to sustain life in material and symbolic terms. This is always a shared task and difficult to carry out on the basis of privatized logic. The community can be seen as an extension of household connections and caregiving that modifies the structure of both the home and public space (Federici, 2020). The separation between the community and the domestic is analytical and arbitrary. It cannot always capture the synergies between households and the community sphere.

Recent research in geography and human mobility (Jirón et al., 2022; Oriolani, 2022) supports two observations. On the one hand, households are embedded within *communitarian weavings* that constitute and lend meaning through practices that enable, forge and transform people's daily lives (Oriolani, 2022). On the other hand, the complexity of caregiving requires spaces that extend beyond the domestic sphere (Jirón et al., 2022). Many functions taken on by households interface with community space, for example, commuting, communal areas or the homes of relatives, neighbours, and friends. Thus, the interdependence of the household becomes fundamental to sustaining life as people coordinate, negotiate, move and provide the care that makes life possible (Jirón et al., 2022; Oriolani, 2022).

In the context of community social work, reflecting on the daily interdependence that we inhabit and help sustain could promote empowerment processes as communities recognize their potential and their essential role in addressing our society's *caregiving crisis* (Ezquerra, 2011). Such empowerment can enhance community members' well-being, especially in countries with limited public policy to support social well-being (Sanchís, 2020; Zaldúa et al., 2020). Likewise, awareness of everyday interdependence beyond the household helps us understand how intertwined households are with community spaces and the daily bidirectional transformations that take place. As a result, community social work involves politicizing what happens in domestic contexts (domestic and gender violence, lack of essential services, time scarcity, etc.) and understanding how this can facilitate or hinder community action. Debating these issues could create new spaces for reflection that strengthen collective efforts and make community connections and participation more equitable.

As we will see in the next section, limiting the scope of caregiving to only or primarily the family comes with costs. It weakens the *communitarian weaving* and imposes social, emotional and material costs, especially on women who have been overburdened in their social role as caregivers.

Women's protagonism and the patriarchal debt

Another substantial aspect of community social work is recognizing women's fundamental role in weaving community networks through caregiving work. Socially attributed to women and primarily performed within domestic/household spaces, caregiving work is projected into and constitutes the most intimate relational spaces (Federici, 2019; Cruz, 2020).

The gendered division of labour has confined women to the domestic sphere. Caregiving work is often regarded as a labour of love and is therefore expected to be performed freely and invisibly (Jónasdóttir, 1991; Mies, 1999; Federici, 2004; Carrasco, 2014; Soto-Villagrán, 2016; Charmes, 2019). The result is an unjust and unequal distribution of caregiving work among genders and social classes, countries and generations.[4] As the responsibility of ensuring the well-being of a significant portion of the population is relegated to the domestic sphere as a private, family issue, our society's *caregiving crisis* has overburdened women with work.

The feminization of caregiving work is an expression of gender-based power relationships that are intertwined with women's bodies and emotions. These power dynamics manifest themselves in areas of women's lives, such as their overall health, employment opportunities, professional development, political participation and time availability (Federici, 2004, 2012, 2019; ILO, 2018; Vaca Trigo, 2019). Feminist economics has made several efforts to name and politicize the expropriation of women's reproductive work and its repercussions. For example, Carrasco et al. (2014) discuss the concept of a "social debt" owed to women – *care debt* or *patriarchal debt* – which accounts for the large amount of "caregiving work and affective energies that women have historically carried out to maintain life" (49). Applying the notion of *debt* to the realm of caregiving aims to draw attention to "the continuous dispossession of women's time and labour" (Carrasco et al., 2014: 53) that the capitalist system has deemed a free and readily available resource (Mies, 1999). Although men have benefited most from caregiving work without paying for it equitably (Jónasdóttir, 1991; Herrero, 2012; Carrasco et al., 2014), they are not the only "debtors." The state and society as a whole also owe a debt to women, as the state has been ineffective in producing collective well-being and has failed to take on its share of responsibility. These shortcomings result in "offloading it onto the backs of families and households" (Ezquerra, 2014: 54) and further dispossession of caregiving work and its value.

When low-income women cannot afford to outsource care work their dispossession and overwork increases. As a result of the absence of care policies, low-income households, and particularly low-income women, must take charge of all these duties, and sometimes they have to resort to indebtedness to hire some paid help. This deepens their financial vulnerability and, hence, their social vulnerability (Federici, 2021; Federici et al., 2021; Tumini & Wilkis, 2022).

Yayo Herrero (2012) defines *care debt* "as the debt that Patriarchy has contracted with women around the world for the work they do for free" (229). Conceptualizing this debt is a political strategy to raise awareness. Though it is difficult to assess the economic and social consequences of the expropriation of caregiving work, we can attempt to quantify them. An example of quantifying the impact of the sex-based division of labour on social well-being is the concept of *"caregiving footprint"* (Herrero, 2012). This indicator shows the unequal distribution of time, affection and human energy expended by people to attend to their needs and the needs of others to ensure the continuity of life.

The concept of *time poverty* has also contributed to raising awareness of the work overload experienced by women and its repercussions (Vickery, 1977; Bardasi and Wodon, 2006; Andreozzi et al., 2021). It describes the shortage of time available to engage in valued activities such as rest, recreation and leisure, due to the burden of paid or unpaid work. The notion recognizes time as a dimension of well-being and a dimension of poverty. *Time poverty* highlights scarcity that cannot be measured by monetary standards and, thus, would otherwise remain unnoticed (Vickery, 1977; Chatzitheochari & Arber, 2012; Giurge &

Whillans, 2020) along with the people who perform caregiving and the resulting losses in terms of well-being.

By acknowledging that this injustice permeates private and public life, we can reflect on how its invisibility ignores the fundamental role women have played in weaving care-based community networks and the costs they have borne to do so. This exercise could politicize this role since the projection of caregiving work into collective spaces shows that many women have overcome barriers and confinement to the private sphere by forming cooperation networks and exercising leadership in the public sphere. Recognizing the power inherent in the practices that sustain life has the potential to foster individual and collective empowerment among women.

Women have been burdened with caregiving work, and our society has generally been unable to recognize this or provide optimal conditions under which to perform the work. Feminist political action and reflection strive to raise awareness of the importance of caregiving work to trigger processes of reflection in society at large and in the women who primarily perform the work. These actions, which came from the intertwining between the private and the public spheres, have prompted self-valuation and empowerment processes.

Given the relevance of caregiving work in shaping *communitarian weavings* and its costs in women's lives, community social work should neither rely on overburdening women nor take advantage of the unpaid work they do, often at the expense of their personal integrity and well-being. Progress toward repaying the social debt owed to women could begin with encouraging reflection, politicization and collective action around caregiving work, and potentially shifting it away from the family sphere.

Conclusions

Does the community social work we promote benefit from caregiving work that is neither valued nor socially remunerated? Does the community work we encourage identify or seek to repay the *care debt*? Have we contributed to raising awareness of the leading role women have played in sustaining *communitarian weavings*? Do we recognize the life-sustaining interactions between the domestic and community spheres as a fundamental capacity (or resource) of a community? Have we facilitated processes of reflection about the importance and potential of caregiving practices in women and in communities?

In this chapter, we argue that the community sphere needs to be thought of as a dynamic relationship between people and their environment, founded on respect, reciprocity and co-responsibility. This recognizes that: (i) caregiving, or the work of sustaining life, is a constitutive element of community; (ii) women have played an indispensable role in weaving community networks; and (iii) the community would propose logic that differs from market logic and state policy.

This way of understanding community adds complexity to our approach. It leads to three lines of critical reflection on community social work from perspectives that broaden our horizons for social justice by examining the interaction between the private/domestic and the collective spheres. The first strategy is to view the community sphere in terms of *communitarian weavings*, visualizing and redefining the social connections that enable the production and reproduction of the commons, which are often made invisible and undervalued in neoliberal contexts. The concept of *communitarian weaving* is broad and flexible enough to allow professionals and community members to recognize and reflect upon those everyday connections that sustain the community, the tangible and intangible commons and our own capacity to build the commons. These reflections contribute to collective awareness and recognition of the potential within the *communitarian weaving*.

Second, our aim is to view these social networks from a caregiving perspective, recognizing that the primary objective of *communitarian weavings* is to reproduce life in material and symbolic ways. Placing caregiving at the centre of our analysis makes it clear that *communitarian weavings* are motivated by *reproductive rationale* and allows for flexibility in addressing different needs and contingencies. This approach shows that the communal is intertwined with the domestic and that this creates multiple life-sustaining spatial contexts, which contributes to decoupling the community from a local or territorialized space. By understanding the fundamental and often invisible synergies between the private/domestic/individual and the public/common/collective, we broaden our perspective.

Finally, it is essential to recognize the leading role that women have played in sustaining the community sphere, which has led to work overload and undermined their overall well-being. This underscores the importance of creating space for reflection among women and their communities to redefine and revalue caregiving work and promote individual and collective empowerment processes.

While there is still a long way to go, we must forge the paths collectively. These three lines of reflection should help continue the debate, while also adding complexity to our community social work and advancing our understanding of caregiving as collective, collaborative work as we try out ever-fairer ways of performing it.

Notes

1 The chapter is part of the research project "Limitations and possibilities for the constitution of an autonomous community sphere in Chile" (Fondecyt Regular Project N°1220173 – National Agency for Research and Development, Chilean Government).
2 These reflections also draw from the analysis of women's and feminist initiatives during the COVID-19 pandemic.
3 Reflections on the community have broadened the spectrum of links established between people to investigate links with territories, ecosystems and non-human animals. The importance of this reflection is acknowledged, however, given the objectives of this chapter, it will not be explored further.
4 The inequitable distribution of caregiving work merits an intersectional approach that includes gender inequalities intertwined with other social inequalities (race, class and age, among others). Although this is a fundamental perspective, it will not be explored further in this chapter.

References

Ander-Egg, E. (2003). *Metodología y práctica del desarrollo de la comunidad. Tomo I ¿Qué es el desarrollo de la comunidad?* Lumen-Humanitas.
Andreozzi, L., Peinado, G., Giustiniani, P., Geli, M., & Ganem, J. (2021). Género y Pobreza de Tiempo en la ciudad de Rosario, Argentina. *Investigaciones Feministas*, 12(2), 559–574. https://doi.org/10.5209/infe.64113
Bardasi, E. & Wodon, Q. (2006). *Measuring Time Poverty and Analyzing Its Determinants: Concepts and Application to Guinea*. University Library of Munich.
Benhabib, S. (1992). *Situating the Self. Gender, Community, and Postmodernism in Contemporary Ethics*. Polity Press.
Butler, J. (2004). *Precarious Life. The Powers of Mourning and Violence*. Verso.
Carrasco, C. (2013). El cuidado como eje vertebrador de una nueva economía. *Cuadernos de Relaciones Laborales*, 31(1), 39–56.

Carrasco, C. (2014). El cuidado como bien relacional: hacia posibles indicadores. *Papeles de relaciones ecosociales y cambio global*, 128(15), 49–60.

Carrasco, C., Díaz, C., Marco, I., Ortiz, R., & Sánchez, M. (2014). Expolio y servidumbre: apuntes sobre la llamada deuda de cuidados. *Revista de Economía Crítica*, 18, 48–59.

Cendejas, J. (2017). Más allá de la reproducción ampliada de la vida. Una interpelación feminista de la economía social solidaria. *Tesis Psicológica*, 12(2), 116–134.

Charmes, J. (2019). *The Unpaid Care Work and the Labour Market. An Analysis of Time Use Data Based on the Latest World Compilation of Time-Use Surveys*. International Labour Office.

Chatzitheochari, S. & Arber, S. (2012). Class, gender and time poverty: A time-use analysis of British workers' free time resources. *The British Journal of Sociology*, 63(3), 451–471. https://doi.org/10.1111/j.1468-4446.2012.01419.x

Cruz, D. (2020). Feminismos comunitarios territoriales de Abya Yala: mujeres organizadas contra las violencias y los despojos. *Revista Estudios Psicosociales Latinoamericanos*, 3(1), 88–107. https://doi.org/10.25054/26196077.2581

Cubillos-Almendra, J., Tapia-Barría, V., & Monsalve-Marabolí (2021). ¡Entre nosotras nos cuidamos! Sonata sobre un apañe feminista en tiempos de crisis. In V. Tapia, F. Letelier, J. Cubillos & S. Micheletti (Eds.), *Lo comunitario. Alternativas en tiempos de crisis* (pp. 99–128). Ediciones UCM.

Cubillos-Almendra, J., Tapia-Barría, V., & Letelier-Troncoso, F. (2022). Juntas nos cuidamos: Entramados comunitarios feministas durante la pandemia por COVID-19. *Revista de Ciencias Sociales*, 29, 1–25. http://doi.org/10.29101/crcs.v29i0.18749

Duarte, C. (2017). *Trabajo social comunitario: Perspectivas teóricas, metodológicas, éticas y políticas* [Doctoral dissertation, Universidad Complutense de Madrid]. Research Online. https://eprints.ucm.es/id/eprint/42891/

Ezquerra, S. (2011). Crisis de los cuidados y crisis sistémica: la reproducción como pilar de la economía llamada real. *Investigaciones Feministas*, 2, 175–194. https://doi.org/10.5209/rev_INFE.2011.v2.38610

Ezquerra, S. (2014). La crisis o nuevos mecanismos de acumulación por desposesión de la reproducción. *Papeles de relaciones ecosociales y cambio global*, 124, 53–62.

Federici, S. (2004). *Caliban and the Witch. Women, the Body and Primitive Accumulation*. Autonomedia.

Federici, S. (2012). *Revolution at Point Zero. Housework, Reproduction and Feminist Struggle*. PM Press.

Federici, S. (2019). *Re-Enchanting the World. Feminism and the Politics of the Commons*. Autonomedia.

Federici, S. (2020). *Revolution at point zero: Housework, reproduction, and feminist struggle*. PM Press.

Federici, S. (2021). Mujeres, dinero y deuda. Notas para un Movimiento Feminista de Reapropiación. In S. Federici, V. Gago and L. Cavallero (Ed.). *¿Quién le debe a quién?: ensayos transnacionales de desobediencia financiera*. (pp. 19–40). Tinta Limón.

Federici, S., Gago, V., & Cavallero, L. (2021). ¿Quién le debe a quién? Manifiesto por la desobediencia financiera. In S. Federici, L. Cavallero and V. Gago (Ed.). *¿Quién le debe a quién?: ensayos transnacionales de desobediencia financiera* (pp. 141–159). Tinta Limón.

Giurge, L. M., Whillans, A. V., & West, C. (2020). Why time poverty matters for individuals, Organisations, and nations. *Nature Human Behaviour*, 4(10), 993–1003. http://doi.org/10.1038/s41562-020-0920-z

Gutiérrez, R. (2011). Pistas reflexivas para orientarnos en una turbulenta época de peligro. In R. Gutiérrez (Ed.), *Palabras para tejernos, resistir y transformar en la época que estamos viviendo* (pp. 31–55). Pez en el árbol.

Gutiérrez, R. (2017). *Horizontes comunitario-populares. Producción de lo común más allá de las políticas estado-céntricas*. Traficantes de Sueños.

Gutiérrez, R., & Salazar, H. (2019). Reproducción comunitaria de la vida. Pensando la transformación social en el presente. In El Aplante (Ed.), *Producir lo común. Entramados comunitarios y luchas por la vida* (pp. 21–44). Traficantes de sueños.

Herrero, Y. (2012). Golpe de estado en la biosfera: los ecosistemas al servicio del capital. *Investigaciones Feministas*, 2(0), 215–238. https://doi.org/10.5209/rev_INFE.2011.v2.38612

ILO (2018). *Care Work and Care Jobs for the Future of Decent Work*. International Labour Organization.

Jirón, P., Solar-Ortega, M., Rubio, M., Cortés, S., Cid, B., & Carrasco, J. (2022). La espacialización de los cuidados. Entretejiendo relaciones de cuidado a través de la movilidad. *Revista INVI*, 37(104), 199–229. https://doi.org/10.5354/0718-8358.2022.65647

Jónasdóttir, A. (1991). *Love Power and Political Interests. Toward a Theory of Patriarchy in Contemporary Western Societies*. University of Örebro.

Massey, D. (1994). *Space, Place and Gender*. Polity Press.

Mies, M. (1999). *Patriarchy and Accumulation on a World Scale*. Zed Books.

Oriolani, F. (2022). La casa como red. Flujos cotidianos y ensamblajes actorales en un barrio popular. *Geograficando*, 18(1), e109. https://doi.org/10.24215/2346898Xe109

Pastor, E. (2004). La participación ciudadana en el ámbito local, eje transversal del trabajo social comunitario. *Alternativas. Cuadernos de Trabajo Social*, 12(0), 103–137. http://doi.org/10.14198/ALTERN2004.12.6

Pastor, E. (2013). Metodología y ámbitos del Trabajo Social comunitario para impulsar cambios sociales sostenibles y autónomos en el complejo universo relacional en España en el siglo XXI. *Emancipação*, 13(1), 143–158. http://doi.org/10.5212/emancipação.v13i1.5114

Ramírez-Gallegos, R. (2019). Los "bienes relacionales" en la sociología política de la vida buena. Crisol, 9. https://crisol.parisnanterre.fr/index.php/crisol/article/view/171

Ross, M. (1967). *Community Organization. Theory and Principles* (2nd Ed.). Harper & Row.

Sales, T. (2016). Contra la precariedad, con la precariedad; cuidados y feminismo. *Oxímora. Revista Internacional de Ética y Política*, 8, 53–62.

Sanchís, N. (2020). Ampliando la concepción de cuidado: ¿privilegio de pocxs o bien común? In N. Sanchís (Ed.). *El cuidado comunitario en tiempos de pandemia… y más allá* (pp. 9–21). Asociación Lola Mora-Red de Género y Comercio.

Soto-Villagrán, P. (2016). Repensar el hábitat urbano desde una perspectiva de género. Debates, agendas y desafíos. *Andamios*, 13(32), 37–56.

Tapia, V., Letelier, F., Cubillos, J., & Micheletti, S. (2021). *Lo comunitario. Alternativas en tiempos de crisis*. Ediciones UCM.

Tumini, L. & Wilkis, A. (2022). *Cuidados y vulnerabilidad financiera: un análisis a partir de la Encuesta Nacional de Endeudamiento y Cuidados (ENEC) en la Argentina*. Comisión Económica para América Latina y el Caribe (CEPAL).

Vaca Trigo, I. (2019), *Oportunidades y desafíos para la autonomía de las mujeres en el futuro escenario del trabajo*. CEPAL.

Vickery, C. (1977). The time-poor: A new look at poverty. *The Journal of Human Resources*, 12(1), 27–48. https://doi.org/10.2307/145597

Zaldúa, G., Lenta, M., & Longo, R. (2020). *Territorios de precarización, feminismos y políticas del cuidado*. Teseo.

30
INCUBATORS OF THE FUTURE
Motherhood, biology and pre-birth social work in feminist practice

Eileen Joy and Liz Beddoe

Introduction

The last few decades have seen a proliferation of studies on intensive mothering as a sociocultural phenomenon that centres children (Hays, 1996). In social work, we hold the idea of the vulnerable child in relationship with the risky parent (Faircloth & Rosen, 2020). In this conceptualisation, the child is 'at risk' while the parent under scrutiny (usually a mother) poses 'a risk' (Blaxland et al., 2021). Her vulnerability is often not the focus other than how much her parenting is affected by what troubles her. Too often, social work (risk) assessment is focused on scrutiny of parenting practice, and as we shall discuss in depth below, behaviours that earn the label of either protective or negligent. Faircloth (2020) captures succinctly the impact of the collision of the development of ideologies of intensive parenting and the neoliberal obsession with predicting and avoiding future harm, where early childhood vulnerability is assumed in the early years, and a "developmental 'blueprint' can be set during this period, engendering a highly deterministic, heavily loaded understanding of the parenting relationship" (p. 145).

It is this focus on the prediction of harm, and the responsibility of mothers to prevent it, that sits behind our argument that lurking within the contemporary discourses of motherhood is a concerning emphasis on women as the incubator of the future. This inscription of the *woman as uterus* is manifest in exhortations of how pregnant and even pre-pregnant women should behave, what they should consume and why they must avoid exposure to stress, thus ensuring an ideal environment for the foetus. The parenting environment paradoxically expands and contracts by positioning the uterus as the original (in)hospitable environment. Maternal responsibility is shifted back in time, she is responsible for *all* the potential environmental ills that might be experienced (and the resultant successful or unsuccessful child-adult) while the impact of structural conditions- misogyny, racism, poverty, and violence are ignored or minimised. The centring of women in the task of creating an idealised childhood environment in which young model citizens can be manufactured is highly gendered and individualised and can perniciously filter into social policies on parenting and early intervention.

At the heart of these policies, and heavily influencing social work education, are 'knowledges' such as neuroscience, epigenetics, and the developmental origins of health and disease (DOHaD) that have been largely uncritically adopted in the teaching of human development, alongside the traditional application of attachment theory (Joy & Beddoe, 2019; Gillies et al., 2017). To some extent, their rapid uptake reflects a historical weakness in social work identity, seeking validation in science: "At times when social work felt most insecure about its knowledge base and scientific grounding, the profession desperately sought refuge to the rigidity of positivism (biomedical models) and the illusionary authority of pseudo-science (eugenics)" (Ioakimidis & Trimikliniotis, 2020, p. 1896). Over the last decade, this uncritical transfer of knowledge has been valorised widely in social work leading to an unhappy collision of early intervention 'science' and child protection (Featherstone et al., 2013).

Drawing on the intersectional theorisation of reproductive justice, we will argue that this unquestioning application of biological science to social work needs to be problematised. An intersectional approach positions motherhood and parenting within multiple intersecting identities and social locations – gender, race, class, sexualities, geography, culture, health and disabilities—thus situating many people in a precarious position.[1] An intersectionally informed feminist social work is incompatible with a view of those with uteruses (including women, non-binary, gender fluid and trans men, hereafter referred to shorthand as women) as the breeding machine of future children. People who give birth have human rights distinct from their children. Our environmental resources and mental and physical health matter more than just their impact on our current or future children. This re-inscription of biological motherhood additionally normalises cishet relationships and nuclear families. We will argue that a social work that is grounded in a gender/reproductive rights discourse must interrogate these new (yet so old) cultural framings of motherhood and biology and explore the intersections with class and ethnicity.

Social work and reproductive justice

Reproductive justice, and indeed consideration of reproductive rights, has in the past been often ignored or minimised in the social work curricula (Witt et al., 2021) and scholarship (Liddell, 2018) despite the potential for social work advocacy (Beddoe, 2021; Beddoe et al., 2019; Smith, 2017). However, a recent flurry of activity has been observed motivated by increased threats to abortion services worldwide (Beddoe et al., 2023; Goldblatt Hyatt et al., 2022; Gomex et al., 2020). The relative absence of a clear focus on reproductive justice in social work means that social workers risk approaching practice with women preconception and during pregnancy without considering a critical understanding of reproductive rights, healthcare, and justice. The growth of faith-based services in many jurisdictions has increased the number of providers who suppress access to birth control information and abortion (Borrero et al., 2019), and further stigmatise abortion (Kimport, 2019). These attacks on reproductive justice necessitate a firm positioning of reproductive justice in the social work education curriculum (Beddoe, 2021; Witt et al., 2021; Younes et al., 2021).

Reproductive justice is rooted in intersectional feminism when in the 1990s, African American women rejected the narrow focus of white middle-class women on abortion rights. Its foundational principles are: (1) the right not to have a child; (2) the right to have a child; and (3) the right to parent children in safe and healthy environments

(Ross & Solinger, 2017). Ross (2006) also noted the importance of the "necessary enabling conditions to realise these rights" (p. 4), as the ability of any woman to fully determine her own choices is linked directly to her socio-political and socioeconomic environment. Reproductive rights demand individual choice and access to legal, safe healthcare, while reproductive justice lays bare the reality of the unequal opportunities we face in controlling our reproductive choices (Ross, 2006). Grounded in intersectional feminism, reproductive justice recognises how "multiple shifting experiences of oppression differentially shape access and inclusion, social-ecological well-being, bodily self-determination, and deemed parental fitness" (Gomez et al., 2020, p. 2). As we will go on to argue below, considerable tensions arise when people who are subject to systemic misogyny, colonisation and racism experience struggles in their ability to choose whether and when, to have children and face increasing surveillance of their choices (Brown et al., 2022; Le Grice & Braun, 2017; McKenzie et al., 2022). Where women are caught up in the child protection system, pregnancy may be viewed as an obstacle to the custody of their current and future children (Critchley, 2019). A feature of some programmes that support women who have children in care is a requirement that they accept long-acting contraception (Morriss, 2018), while contraceptive prescribing may be shaped by racist assumptions (Higgins et al., 2016). Young women who themselves have been in the child protection system as children experience a shift in focus from their needs and vulnerabilities to a focus on any risk of harm they may pose when they become parents (Blaxland et al., 2021).

In examining reproductive justice, it is critical to understand the experience of Black and Indigenous women (Brown et al., 2022; Le Grice & Braun, 2017; McKenzie et al., 2022). Reproductive justice scholarship and teaching in social work must acknowledge the history of Black and Indigenous people, immigrant communities, and communities of colour, and working-class people who have suffered abuses such as forced sterilisation and assimilation, the large-scale and on-going removal of children by the state, been unwilling research participants in medical trials, and experienced inadequate and inequitable access to sexual and reproductive healthcare (Ross & Solinger, 2017).

In June 2022, the United States Supreme Court ended the constitutional protections for abortion that had been in place for nearly 50 years following the 1973 ruling known as Roe v Wade, a court decision that legalised abortion across the United States. Removing this protection signals a major threat to many of the gains made in reproductive healthcare and turns back the clock on rights.

The implications of the reversal of Roe v wade

Roe v Wade essentially affirmed that every woman had the right to make decisions over her own body. Concern about a possible reversal of Roe v Wade intensified in 2016 as globally, feminists warned about the risk to Roe that would accompany a Trump administration that would support fundamentalist misogynist forces to push back hard-won rights to reproductive justice. Over recent years many states set up 'trigger bans' that would come into law if Roe were reversed. The reversal of Roe has led to abortion bans in roughly half of the US states, and limitations in many others, affecting millions with significant impacts on reproductive health (Guttmacher Institute, 2022). In an editorial for *BJOG: An International Journal of Obstetrics & Gynaecology,* Silver (2022) lists the immediate concerns of many health professionals. These include the potential increase in maternal mortality, and unsafe abortions, noting that limitations to abortion have historically increased the rate of unsafe abortion (Guttmacher Institute, 2009). Silver also notes that increases in unintended pregnancies may also increase the risk of adverse pregnancy outcomes, including impacts on mental health. The quality of care for people who experience ectopic pregnancies or spontaneous pregnancy loss is likely to be affected as health professionals fear prosecution. Adding to this anxiety, the surveillance of 'pre-pregnant' people is intensified: people who take medication for chronic illnesses may find their healthcare provider anxious about the possible teratogenic effects should a pregnancy occur where there are strict abortion bans. A recent editorial in the *Lancet Rheumatology* argued that legal codes were confusing: "murky, often medically ambiguous wording makes exceptions difficult to define, putting physicians in the untenable position of facing criminal liability as a result of serving a patient's medical interests" (2022, np).

An increased active, invasive policing of pregnant (or even might be pregnant) people's bodies using surveillance technology is a sinister outcome of the reversal of Roe v Wade. On social media, soon after the ruling, data justice activists encouraged people to delete period tracking apps and request the deletion of data. People were urged to take stringent measures to avoid searching for information online for fear of being later accused of abortion if they miscarried. Even before the reversal of Roe, miscarrying women have been interrogated, even arrested on suspicion of having procured an abortion. This criminalisation of pregnant people is not confined to the United States. Shanti Das reported that despite a common understanding that abortion access is safe in the United Kingdom, Freedom of Information requests revealed that dozens of women have been investigated by Police for suspected breaches of an 1861 law over the past ten years (Das, 2022). Invasive investigation and surveillance of personal communications in such investigations is cruel and offensive. It is within this climate that we argue that the principles of reproductive justice outlined above are essential if social work is to resist the pernicious ideology of 'woman as incubator' where her rights are subsumed by a surveillant state's obsession with the future as yet unrealised child.

Manufacturing optimal incubators

Notions of how pregnant people can influence the growing foetus are not new. Theories of 'maternal impression' from the 16th through to 19th centuries suggested that women's experiences, thoughts, behaviours, and eating habits during pregnancy were responsible for later child physical and mental characteristics (Ballif, 2019). Such 'impressions' were thought to cause physical 'abnormalities' from birthmarks to more severe conditions. As Ballif (2019) notes, while these ideas faded a little during the latter part of the 19th century as medical discourses became more prominent, more recent research developments in the last few decades indicate a reinvigoration of the impression theory.

The teratogenic effects of substances such as alcohol and drugs have been known for some time—even if the *exact* doses required for them are less certain (Waggoner, 2017). Concern for these effects is most pronounced for the results of substance consumption during the earliest weeks of pregnancy (when a woman may not know she is pregnant), as that is when the most severe teratogenic effects are likely to occur (Waggoner, 2017). Waggoner (2017) notes that the period when women do not know they are pregnant generates the most concern. If the risk of harm to the foetus-child is so very great, foetus-centric logic dictates that anyone capable of becoming pregnant must *always* behave as if they *are* pregnant. This 'anticipatory' work creates specific subject positions requiring women to anticipate being pregnant, imagine what that future (child) might look like and behave 'appropriately' (Ballif, 2022). As an extreme crystallisation of this thinking, in 2021, the World Health Organisation released a draft *Global Alcohol Action Plan,* which recommended preventing the initiation of drinking amongst women of childbearing age, rendering all menstruating people perpetually pre-pregnant (Foster, 2021). Here the nine-month time frame of pregnancy extends backwards to first menses; to be an optimal incubator, one should behave as if one is *already pregnant.*

Concern for the effects of 'substances' on the foetus-child extends beyond public health warnings about alcohol and drugs. Women report precautionary consumption work as a way to minimise foetal exposure to chemicals, highly gendered work that continues after birth as they manage the (potentially harmful) chemical loads contained in breast/formula milk and first foods (Mackendrick, 2014). Research in neuroscience, epigenetics and DOHaD has focused on substance effects via maternal nutrition and stress hormones during and even *before* pregnancy (Gillies et al., 2017). The uterus must be optimised and remain optimised and hospitable, lest it becomes inhospitable and produces less optimal children. For example, in DOHaD research, pregnant people are advised to eat just the right amount of food least their child be programmed with a propensity to overeat through exposure to a uterus likened, in a particularly nasty racialised metaphor, to a 'metabolic ghetto' (Wells, 2010). Further, women, rather than polluting companies, are responsible for eating non-polluted seafood, so the foetus-child remains untainted (Mansfield, 2012). Communities of Indigenous women are caught in the middle; avoid traditional foods or risk the foetus-child. Either choice means a colonised foetal environment/incubator.

Management of the 'ideal' foetal environment for an optimised foetus-child is likely to be stressful—especially for already marginalised women (see: Mackendrick, 2014; Parker & Pausé, 2019)—yet women are *also* advised to avoid stress during pregnancy lest their foetal-children become accustomed to stress in utero resulting in harm to the developing brain (Gillies et al., 2017). Such an exhortation to avoid stress tends to ignore and simplify the lived reality of many people's lives. There is a danger that broader environmental conditions—such as intimate partner violence, precarious housing and/or colonisation—collapse to the uterus rendering the pregnant person the most critical and important environment and ultimately responsible. Mothers must carefully balance their stress levels so there are no impediments to optimal foetal-child neuronal development regardless of what environmental constraints they experience.

At the same time as the environment collapses to the uterus, in neuroscience, it is widened and extended in time through epigenetics. Epigenetics is a more recent development in the broader study of genetics and focuses on changes to gene function (but not genes themselves) due to interactions between genes and environments (McGowan & Szyf, 2010). The science on the inheritance of such effects past maternal grandchildren or paternal children is unclear (see: Heard & Martienssen, 2014; Van Wert et al., 2019); however, that has not prevented media from claims of certainty (Dubois & Guaspare, 2020). Here the theory is that maternal behaviour in the perinatal period is capable of causing epigenetic change affecting generations of subsequent children (Richardson, 2015). Mothers then, like nested Russian dolls, contain their future generations and the consequences of their behaviours on those generations within. Researchers have warned that "exaggerations and over-simplifications are making scapegoats of mothers and could even increase surveillance and regulation of pregnant women." (Richardson et al., 2014, p. 131).

The combination of such knowledges (DOHaD, neuroscience, and epigenetics) in optimising pregnancy (and thus manufacturing the optimal human incubator) expands definitions of 'harm' to (foetus) children and muddies the line between eugenics and euthenics—the latter being the manipulation of the environment to optimise population outcomes. Through a combination of gene and environment optimisation in the uterus, the woman (as the uterus), across all her childbearing years, is situated as a project of euthenics *and* eugenics. Harm elimination, proximity to purity, is the goal so that future generations remain as unsullied as possible.

Troubling the notion of pre-birth social work

Child protection social work is governed by notions of risk, requiring social workers to anticipate what might happen to a child if the 'right' intervention does or does not take place. The work of social workers in protecting children is analogous to (and part of) the anticipatory regime that Ballif (2022) describes as governing pregnancy and parenting. Ballif (2022) explains that pregnant people are increasingly subjectified through an anticipatory logic that encourages a future orientation—all actions before, during pregnancy and parenting, are geared towards anticipating outcomes and imagining a future child. Parents, in particular women, are positioned as "anticipating agents" with pregnant women's autonomy "framed as entire or limited in consideration to the foetus" (Ballif, 2022, p. 4). Here the unborn are presented as the future, and their rights are "extend[ed]... not because foetuses are regarded as children in their own right, but because eventually, they *will* be children" (Ballif, 2022, p. 9). The lines are blurred, and Schrödinger[2] citizen is 'born' – unborn and born, a (non)citizen requiring state protection and potential intervention. As agents of the state tasked with protecting children and anticipating harm, social workers are increasingly drawn into these spaces (Buchner et al., 2022; Critchley, 2021; Keddell et al., 2022; Wise & Corrales, 2021).

Pre-birth social work is the type of anticipatory governance of pregnancy that Baliff (2022) is questioning. For these social workers, the concern is about whether a mother is capable of parenting a child and intervening as soon as possible to protect the future of that foetus-child. Social work planning in such situations is fraught with difficulties as laws can differ between jurisdictions (differences between States and countries), preventing intervention until the foetus-child is *actually* a child with rights (Wise & Corrales, 2021). However, this does not prevent pregnant people from being surveilled by the state with their actions seen as determining both fitness to parent and capacity to harm. Given the increasing influence of the likes of neuroscience, epigenetics and DOHaD in child protection practice (Gillies et al., 2017, Wastell & White, 2017), it is hardly surprising that social workers are assessing harm in the present (to the foetus) *and* future (to the child) through pregnancy and then acting as soon as the foetus-child has been born—often as soon as they are *legally* able to do so.

Such anticipatory social work is problematic as it increases the responsibilisation of mothers, decreases paternal responsibility, obscures structural factors, and often increases existing inequalities and threatens reproductive rights (Buchner et al., 2022; Critchley, 2019, 2021). Gender re- and de-responsibilisation in pre-birth child protection mean that men can at least partially choose their level of engagement with child protection in a way that women cannot. For example, Critchley (2021) noted that while many fathers were not involved in pre-birth child protection social work assessments, many wanted to be and yet were marginalised by social workers. This stance can be partially explained by a reluctance by social workers to engage with men who might be violent; however, it can also function to deprive children of a potentially supportive relationship and increases the maternal burden (Critchley, 2021). It is likely that for many women and men, this focus entrenches societal stereotypes about parental gender roles and may well have knock-on effects resulting in isolated mothering and the transmission of 'traditional' (and suffocating) gender roles to children. Indeed, mothers in these situations have described how they must 'jump through hoops' to perform appropriate parenting work for social workers in a way that fathers rarely have to (Buchner et al., 2022; Critchley, 2019).

Perhaps predictably, given the over-representation of Indigenous families and children in child protection in many colonised countries, pre-birth child protection work has had an alarming focus on Indigenous families (Buchner et al., 2022; Wise & Corrales, 2021). In Aotearoa New Zealand, a policy focus in the mid-2010s on ensuring that children were removed from homes as early as possible has been linked with a 33% increase in the removal of Māori babies aged under three months (Keddell, 2019). The policy documents informing practice over these times relied on 'evidence' that touted the importance of neuroscience and intervening as early as possible to ensure that parents optimised their children while ignoring things like poverty, racism and colonisation (Beddoe & Joy, 2017). However, in July 2019, pre-birth child protection social work in Aotearoa New Zealand was exposed to the public in a way that provides an instructive (and *hopeful*) example of what can happen when child protection social work extends its reach backward into pregnancy and treats the unborn as *born*. Keddell and colleagues (2022) note that this attempted removal, not long after birth, of a Māori baby from its mother became what they call a "sentinel event" (p. 2), opening up space for such practices to be questioned and the possibility of change.

Keddell et al. (2022) note that what became known as the 'Hawkes Bay' case was an unusual example in that media centred attention on the perceived over-reach of state child protection (rather than finding fault with parents) and—surprisingly in a colonised nation—the injustice of the overrepresentation of whānau Māori in child protection cases. Subsequent inquiries, both internal and external to the state agency, found breaches of law and process and arguably led to a substantial *reduction* in the removal of all babies at birth, particularly Māori babies whose rates of removal went from 102 per 10,000 to 39 (Keddell et al., 2022). Unlike other situations where public outcry about the perceived failures of child protection social work has resulted in increased removals (Warner, 2015), the opposite seems to have occurred in Aotearoa New Zealand.

Conclusion

The example of Aotearoa New Zealand provides an interesting case study on the effects of pre-birth child protection and what can happen once such practices are more widely and critically examined. In detailing this case, we are not claiming that child protection social workers in Aotearoa New Zealand no longer work in the pre-birth space, or that child protection social work here has been decolonised. Instead, we wish to show that this work has far-reaching consequences and ways it might be challenged. We would argue that the 'anticipatory' work required in pre-birth social work might best be re-purposed to anticipating how the *state* might best support families, and parents (not just mothers), with adjusting to having a new baby. Such anticipatory social work would be grounded in reproductive justice principles and might include advocacy for and support with housing, employment, migration status and income. More macro-level anticipatory social work could work on 'anticipating' a decolonised, less patriarchal society where social workers do not need to worry about optimising a foetal environment because the structural conditions for the parent, the mother, have been taken care of. This would be a less blaming, more holistic 'incubation' of societal potential than a singular focus on the nexus of the uterus-woman and foetus-child.

Notes

1 An intersectional approach, by definition, encompasses both an individual and a structural analysis; it is about the structures that impact on individuals in specific locations (Collins & Bilge, 2016).
2 Here we are referring to a famous thought experiment popualrly known as 'Schrödinger's cat' where the 'cat' is thought of simultaneously as being dead *and* alive.

References

Ballif, E. (2019). Policing the maternal mind: Maternal health, psychological government, and Swiss pregnancy politics. *Social Politics: International Studies in Gender, State & Society*, 27(1), 74–96.

Ballif, E. (2022). Anticipatory regimes in pregnancy: Cross-fertilising reproduction and parenting culture studies. *Sociology*. https://doi.org/10.1177/00380385221107492

Beddoe, L. (2021). Reproductive justice, abortion rights and social work. *Critical and Radical Social Work*, 10(1), 7–22. https://doi.org/10.1332/204986021X16355170868404

Beddoe, L., & Joy, E. (2017). Questioning the uncritical acceptance of neuroscience in child and family policy and practice: A review of challenges to the current doxa. *Aotearoa New Zealand Social Work*, 29(1), 65–76.

Beddoe, L., Hayes, T., & Steele, J. (2019). Social justice for all!' The relative silence of social work in abortion rights advocacy. *Critical and Radical Social Work*, 8(1), 7–24.

Beddoe, L., Joy, E. Meadows, L., Cleaver, K., & Crichton-Hill, Y. (2023). Reproductive justice: Holding the line and pushing forward. *Aotearoa New Zealand Social Work*, 35(4), 1–12.

Blaxland, M., Skattebol, J., Hamilton, M., van Toorn, G., Thomson, C., & Valentine, K. (2021). From being 'at risk' to being 'a risk': Journeys into parenthood among young women experiencing adversity. *Families, Relationships and Societies*, 1–20. https://doi.org/10.1332/204674321X16297270094275

Borrero, S., Frietsche, S., & Dehlendorf, C. (2019). Crisis pregnancy centers: Faith centers operating in bad faith. *Journal of General Internal Medicine*, 34(1), 144–145. https://doi.org/10.1007/s11606-018-4703-4

Brown, K., Plummer, M., Bell, A., Combs, M., Gates-Burgess, B., Mitchell, A., Sparks, M., McLemore, M. R., & Jackson, A. (2022). Black women's lived experiences of abortion. *Qualitative Health Research*, 32(7), 1099–1113. https://doi.org/10.1177/10497323221097622

Buchner, K., Pearson, T., & Burke, S. (2022). Indigenous women's experiences with child protection at their child's birth. *Practice*, 34(4), 255–272.

Collins, P. H., & Bilge, S. (2016). *Intersectionality*. Polity Press.

Critchley, A. (2019). Jumping through hoops: Families' experiences of pre-birth child protection. In: L. Murray, L. McDonnell, T. Hinton-Smith, N. Ferreira, & K. Walsh (Eds.), *Families in motion: Ebbing and flowing through space and time* (pp. 135–154). Emerald Publishing Limited.

Critchley, A. (2021). Giving up the ghost: Findings on fathers and social work from a study of pre-birth child protection. *Qualitative Social Work*, 1–22. https://doi.org/10.1177/14733250211019463

Das, S. (2 July 2022). Women accused of illegal abortions in England and Wales after miscarriages and stillbirths. *The Guardian*. https://www.theguardian.com/world/2022/jul/02/women-accused-of-abortions-in-england-and-wales-after-miscarriages-and-stillbirths

Dubois, M., & Guaspare, C. (2020). From cellular memory to the memory of trauma: Social epigenetics and its public circulation. *Social Science Information*, 59(1), 144–183.

Faircloth, C. (2020). Parenting and social solidarity in cross-cultural perspective. *Families, Relationships and Societies, 9*(1), 143–159. https://doi.org/10.1332/204674319X15668430693616

Faircloth, C., & Rosen, R. (2020). Childhood, parenting culture, and adult-child relations in global perspectives. *Families, Relationships and Societies, 9*(1), 3–6. https://doi.org/10.1332/204674320X15804876175640

Featherstone, B., Morris, K., & White, S. (2013). A marriage made in hell: Early intervention meets child protection. *British Journal of Social Work.* https://doi.org/10.1093/bjsw/bct052

Foster, A. (2021, June 18). Outrage at WHO's call to prevent 'child-bearing age' women from drinking. *New Zealand Herald.* https://www.nzherald.co.nz/lifestyle/outrage-at-whos-call-to-prevent-child-bearing-age-women-from-drinking/5NEHZZKLNBWULC4VMK6BN3RCNA/

Gillies, V., Edwards, R., & Horsley, N. (2017). *Challenging the politics of early intervention: Who's 'saving' children and why.* Policy Press.

Goldblatt Hyatt, E., McCoyd, J. L. M., & Diaz, M. F. (2022). From abortion rights to reproductive justice: A call to action. *Affilia, 37*(2), 194–203. https://doi.org/10.1177/08861099221077153

Gomez, A. M., Downey, M. M., Carpenter, E., Leedham, U., Begun, S., Craddock, J., & Ely, G. (2020). Advancing reproductive justice to close the health gap: A call to action for social work. *Social Work, 65*(4), 358–367. https://doi.org/10.1093/sw/swaa034

Guttmacher Institute (2009). *Abortion worldwide: A decade of uneven progress.* https://www.guttmacher.org/report/abortion-worldwide-decade-uneven-progress

Guttmacher Institute (2022). *State bans on abortion throughout pregnancy.* https://www.guttmacher.org/state-policy/explore/state-policies-later-abortions

Hays, S. (1996). *The cultural contradictions of motherhood.* Yale University Press.

Heard, E., & Martienssen, R. A. (2014). Transgenerational epigenetic inheritance: myths and mechanisms. *Cell, 157*(1), 95–109.

Higgins, J. A., Kramer, R. D., & Ryder, K. M. (2016). Provider bias in long-acting reversible contraception (LARC) promotion and removal: Perceptions of young adult women. *American Journal of Public Health, 106*(11), 1932–1937. https://doi.org/10.2105/ AJPH.2016.303393

Ioakimidis, V., & Trimikliniotis, N. (2020). Making sense of social work's troubled past: Professional identity, collective memory and the quest for historical justice. *The British Journal of Social Work, 50*(6), 1890–1908. https://doi.org/10.1093/bjsw/bcaa040

Joy, E., & Beddoe, L. (2019). ACEs, cultural considerations and 'common sense' in Aotearoa New Zealand. *Social Policy and Society, 18*(3), 491–497.

Keddell, E. (2019). Harm, care and babies: An inequalities and policy discourse perspective on recent child protection trends in Aotearoa New Zealand. *Aotearoa New Zealand Social Work, 31*(4), 18–34.

Keddell, E., Cleaver, K., Fitzmaurice, L., & Exeter, D. (2022). A fight for legitimacy: Reflections on child protection reform, the reduction of baby removals, and child protection decision-making in Aotearoa New Zealand. *Kotuitui: New Zealand Journal of Social Sciences Online.* https://doi.org/10.1080/1177083X.2021.201249

Kimport, K. (2019). Pregnant women's experiences of crisis pregnancy centers: When abortion stigmatization succeeds and fails. *Symbolic Interaction, 42*(4), 618–639. https://doi.org/10.1002/symb.418

Le Grice, J. S., & Braun, V. (2017). Indigenous (Māori) perspectives on abortion in New Zealand. *Feminism & Psychology, 27*(2), 144–162. https://doi.org/10.1177/0959353517701491

Liddell, J. L. (2018). Reproductive justice and the social work profession: Common grounds and current trends. *Affilia, 34*(1), 99–115. https://doi.org/10.1177/0886109918803646

Mackendrick, N. (2014). More work for mother: Chemical body burdens as a maternal responsibility. *Gender & Society, 28*(5), 705–728.

Mansfield, B. (2012). Gendered biopolitics of public health: Regulation and discipline in seafood consumption advisories. *Environment and Planning D: Society and Space, 30*(4), 588–602.

McGowan, P. O., & Szyf, M. (2010). The epigenetics of social adversity in early life: Implications for mental health outcomes. *Neurobiology of Disease, 39*(1), 66–72.

McKenzie, H. A., Varcoe, C., Nason, D., McKenna, B., Lawford, K., Kelm, M.-E., Wajuntah, C. O., Gervais, L., Hoskins, J., Anaquod, J., Murdock, J., Murdock, R., Smith, K., Arkles, J., Acoose, S., & Arisman, K. (2022). Indigenous women's resistance of colonial policies, practices, and reproductive coercion. *Qualitative Health Research, 32*(7), 1031–1054. https://doi.org/10.1177/10497323221087526

Morriss, L. (2018). Haunted futures: The stigma of being a mother living apart from her child(ren) as a result of state-ordered court removal. *The Sociological Review, 66*(4), 816–831. https://doi.org/10.1177/0038026118777448

Parker, G., & Pausé, C. (2019). Productive but not constructive: The work of shame in the affective governance of fat pregnancy. *Feminism & Psychology, 29*(2), 250–268.

Richardson, S. (2015). Maternal bodies in the postgenomic order. In S. Richardson, & H. Stevens (Eds.), *Postgenomics: Perspectives on biology after the genome* (pp. 210–231). Duke University Press.

Richardson, S. S., Daniels, C. R., Gillman, M., Golden, J., Kukla, R., Kuzawa, C., & Rich-Edwards, J. (2014). Don't blame the mothers. *Nature, 512*(7513), 131–132.

Ross, L. (2006). Understanding reproductive justice: Transforming the pro-choice movement. *Off Our Backs, 36*(4), 14–19.

Ross, L., & Solinger, R. (2017). *Reproductive justice: An introduction.* University of California Press.

Silver, B. (2022). Editorial. *BJOG: An International Journal of Obstetrics & Gynaecology, 129*(10), 1623–1624. https://doi.org/10.1111/1471-0528.17265

Smith, B. D. (2017). Reproductive justice: A policy window for social work advocacy. *Social Work, 62*(3), 221–226. https://doi.org/10.1093/sw/swx015

The Lancet Rheumatology (2022). The demise of Roe v Wade: Ramifications for rheumatology. *The Lancet Rheumatology, 4*(8), e525. https://doi.org/10.1016/S2665-9913(22)00189-8

Van Wert, M., Anreiter, I., Fallon, B. A., & Sokolowski, M. B. (2019). Intergenerational transmission of child abuse and neglect: A transdisciplinary analysis. *Gender and the Genome, 3*, 1–21.

Waggoner, M. R. (2017). *The zero trimester: Pre-pregnancy care and the politics of reproductive risk.* University of California Press.

Warner, J. (2015). *The emotional politics of social work and child abuse.* Policy Press.

Wastell, D., & White, S. (2017). *Blinded by science: The social implications of epigenetics and neuroscience.* Policy Press.

Wells, J. C. (2010). Maternal capital and the metabolic ghetto: An evolutionary perspective on the transgenerational basis of health inequalities. *American Journal of Human Biology: The Official Journal of the Human Biology Association, 22*(1), 1–17.

Wise, S., & Corrales, T. (2021). Discussion of the knowns and unknowns of child protection during pregnancy in Australia. *Australian Social Work, 76*(2), 173–185. https://doi.org/10.1080/0312407X.2021.2001835

Witt, H., Younes, M. K., Goldblatt Hyatt, E., & Franklin, C. (2021). Examining social work students' knowledge of and attitudes about abortion and curriculum coverage in social work education. *Affilia, 37*(2), 215–231. https://doi.org/10.1177/08861099211068241

Younes, M., Goldblatt Hyatt, E., Witt, H., & Franklin, C. (2021). A call to action: Addressing ambivalence and promoting advocacy for reproductive rights in social work education. *Journal of Social Work Education, 57*(4), 625–635. https://doi.org/10.1080/10437797.2021.1895930

31
PARENTING THROUGH MENTAL HEALTH CHALLENGES
Intersections of gender, race, class and power

Rochelle Hine and Hanna Jewell

Introduction

Despite changing social expectations, parenting remains highly gendered. Women are responsible for the majority of parenting tasks and the emotional and cognitive labour that accompanies the role (Daminger, 2019), even when not actively engaged in parenting 'work'. Mental health challenges can add layers of complexity, although they do not change the performance expectations of a 'good' mother (Hine et al., 2018a; Montgomery et al., 2006).

First Nations women with mental health challenges are often subjected to additional sources of discrimination and disadvantage within Australian healthcare systems, including mental health. This is due to the past and on-going atrocities and impacts of colonisation, particularly stolen generations (Wilson, 1997) and the persistently high and growing numbers of First Nations children removed from their parents' custody by child protection services (Australian Institute of Health and Welfare, 2021) as a pillar of patriarchal white sovereignty (Moreton-Robinson, 2015). The social work profession in Australia is implicated in designing and implementing oppressive and discriminatory policies that result in disproportionately high rates of custody loss for both First Nations families, and families where a parent has mental health challenges (Boursnell, 2014; Hunter, 2008; Krakouer et al., 2021). While many of the issues included herein may apply to First Nations mothers, different strengths, resources, challenges and barriers may also be pertinent. As Moreton-Robinson (2015) has articulated, the goals and aspirations of white feminists do not represent the priorities of First Nations women.

This chapter will explore the characteristics of mental health and child protection services in Australia, two sectors in which social workers are employed as frontline staff, managers and policymakers. It will be argued that these sectors create multiple barriers for social workers who operate within feminist approaches which focus on the empowerment of mothers who experience mental health challenges.

The history of social work is fraught with tension between social control and social change orientations. A new feminist paradigm in which social workers collaborate with mothers in participatory processes of solidarity needs to be activated to address the deficits of the current system and promote gender-sensitive, responsive care that meets the complex needs of mothers experiencing mental health difficulties (Heward-Belle et al., 2018). Envisioning this paradigm necessitates a critique of the idealised nuclear family structure as a patriarchal institution and problematising of the assumption that women are ultimately responsible for children. It requires recognition that women often 'fail' to meet culturally defined mothering ideals due to a lack of social and financial resources (Dominelli, 2002). Persistent structural inequalities that oppress women are not determinants, but rather, intentionally designed and studiously maintained systems that can be dismantled.

Overview of the mental health system in Australia

The Australian mental health system is a complex mix of public and private services funded predominantly by state and federal governments. Mental health–accredited practitioners (from a range of disciplines, including social work) provide psychological therapies privately, with the national public healthcare system covering standard costs for those who are referred by a General Practitioner. However, practitioners' fees are usually in excess, leaving a payment gap that must be filled by the individual (Australian Government, 2021). There is also a limit to the risk and complexity of presentation that private practitioners will accept and with a funding and service model that is individually focussed, family-focussed practice and carer support is scant (Dawson et al., 2021). Meadows and colleagues (2015) found inequity in access to psychiatrists shaped by socioeconomic disadvantage and rurality. Choice and service quality are obvious advantages of the private system; individuals can select a practitioner who meets their needs and with the recent broad-scale increase in telehealth use, a wide range of specialist services are more accessible than ever, to those who can afford to pay.

This chapter will focus on the public mental health system, where people with the most severe and enduring mental health challenges and the least access to socioeconomic resources, must go to have their mental health issues assessed and addressed. Issues of choice and power are pertinent here in a system reinforced by entrenched hierarchical bio-medical structures (Scholz et al., 2017). Legislative frameworks that disintegrate individual rights to self-determination and autonomy, practices of surveillance and regulation, and a dominant white, colonial, patriarchal history (Bondi & Burman, 2001), are in conflict with core social work values and approaches.

The public mental health system is overwhelmed, fragmented and crisis-driven, with woefully inadequate resourcing to meet the demands (Productivity Commission, 2020; State of Victoria, 2021). Despite rhetoric about recovery-oriented practice peppering all State and Federal policy documents, after decades of funding erosion, practitioners focus on the basics of crisis response and risk mitigation, relying on medication as the primary form of treatment (State of Victoria, 2021). This leaves limited capacity for the provision of family and carer support or identifying and addressing the needs of children. Being constantly overwhelmed and under-resourced necessitates a triage process that prioritises, individualistically, those most at risk of harm. This means that people are not able to access the service until their needs reach crisis point.

One of the impacts of relentless work demands is that the sustained urgency of individual tasks obscures a broader system view. Individual-based advocacy efforts (e.g. securing housing or supporting a client at a guardianship tribunal hearing) replace larger scale systems advocacy efforts (e.g. the right to safe and affordable housing for women leaving violent relationships). Social work identity and social justice values can be diluted when social workers are employed as generic 'mental health clinicians' and their work becomes consumed by case management tasks.

Gender stereotypes and negative assumptions about the capability of mothers with mental health challenges permeate clinical decision-making if the multidisciplinary team adopts a group thinking process, blurring disciplinary boundaries (Vrklevski et al., 2017). Understanding broader contextual issues relies on practitioners in different parts of the service asking the right questions to ascertain issues that may be important to women and for this information to be understood and explored as part of a clinical review by the treating team. Procedures and legal frameworks take precedence over a critical standpoint that illuminates sources of gender-based oppression and discrimination. Mental health services are the most common source of discrimination for mothers with mental health difficulties (Lacey et al., 2014).

In clinical decision-making, mothers' mental health challenges often overshadow their parenting strengths. Children's risk and vulnerability overshadow their connectedness to family and culture, their agency and the knowledge children have of their parent and their mental health (Gladstone et al., 2006). Fathering is often invisible within mental health systems. While there is an assumption that women will continue to care for children while unwell (and are then blamed and shamed for the transgression when they are unable to), no parallel expectation exists that men will care for children when they are experiencing an episode of illness. Mental health services demonstrate an ambivalence towards fathering (Price-Robertson et al., 2015) and rarely is time dedicated to discuss how mental health challenges impact on parenting or how parenting stress may impact on the mental health of men, thus perpetuating dominant ideologies about families.

A paternalistic narrative which is reinforced by the compulsory treatment sections of mental health acts, results in power differentials between mental health social workers and those who need to use the service, which is compounded by intersectional factors such as gender, race, culture, age, socioeconomic differences and sexuality. This is rarely interrogated amongst social workers within mental health services – when would there be time? Collaborating with other service providers is another element of robust practice that receives inadequate resourcing, thereby mental health services remain siloed. Limited interaction occurs with child protection, family violence, sexual assault, early years or education settings. If a child is removed from their parent's care, that adult may no longer be viewed as a parent and little effort is expended on providing support to increase their parenting resources to regain custody. Children who are removed are rarely given mental health information to understand their parents' behaviour, often leading to children internalising experiences by blaming either themselves or their parents. This can make it difficult for relational repair in the future.

Strengths and vulnerabilities of women experiencing mental health challenges

Parenting with mental health difficulties is common. The Australian Institute of Health and Welfare (AIHW) (2022) estimates that 16% of parents with co-resident children aged 0–14 years experienced poor mental health in the past 12 months. It is accompanied by a myriad of emotions, opportunities and challenges. Being a parent with a mental illness, despite the stigma, can be associated with good mental health outcomes and improved functioning (Mowbray et al., 2001). Parenting is a role that can provide a sense of identity, meaning and purpose (Montgomery et al., 2006). The provision of support for a person's parenting role may constitute a significant part of mental illness recovery (Awram et al., 2017). Mowbray et al. (2000) stated: "women have identified motherhood as a central force keeping them involved with treatment, a key outlet for expression of feelings of care and concern, and a valued, normative social role" (p. 82). Threats to this identity such as being labelled by a practitioner as an inadequate mother, is an outcome that women seek to avoid at all costs.

Children of parents with mental health challenges experience a broad range of outcomes. Some thrive and speak of the beneficial outcomes of their experiences such as developing empathy and emotional intelligence, gaining life skills and feeling more closely connected to their families. Other children experience poorer mental and physical health outcomes contributed to by increased exposure to social and economic adversities including poverty and family violence due to the parent's mental health condition and societies' failure to prevent adversities (Hine et al., 2018b). Gender, overlays all other socio-economic factors to shape the experiences of women and men within families, communities, mental health systems and their broader cultural context. In relation to mental illness, "…the stigma associated with socially standardised and sanctioned gender roles cannot be properly interrogated without recognising the structural role of power and discrimination within which such gender roles exist" (Reupert et al., 2021, p. 16).

Mizock and Brubaker (2021) argue that the unique needs of women are often overlooked in the mental health service system. Western mental health systems have traditionally separated women's mental health assessment and management from their families and children. Treatment is delivered with a bio-medical focus, containing ingrained stigma and often privileges a risk rather than a strength-based lens. This risk lens is bluntly applied to parenting and results in large numbers of child protection notifications (Hollingsworth, 2004; Seeman, 2015). Fear of custody loss presents a barrier to help-seeking and manifests in mothers concealing both their mental health challenges and their parenting difficulties (Montgomery et al., 2006), "the tragedy of lost opportunities" (Nicholson & Biebel, 2002, p. 167). This fear is well-founded. Even when mothers with mental health challenges are actively help-seeking, they often experience judgement and rejection rather than nurturing responses (Hine et al., 2018b).

Within mental health systems, women face other risks - violence and sexual abuse, treatment bias, economic distress, single parenthood, and sexual and reproductive health problems. Women require service responses that are trauma-informed, gender-sensitive, family focussed and include a life span approach. Recognising that women's needs may differ also due to multiple intersecting needs and dimensions of difference is incompatible with a system under strain that has limited capacity for agility.

Maybery and Reupert (2009) identified three layers of mental health systems that are deficient when services fail to address the needs of parents and families. These are management and policy structures, interagency collaboration and clinician attitude, skill and knowledge. Changes to mental health policy and practice to recognise the unique needs of women are slow, hampered by a lack of political will and the enormity of the task of changing longstanding sexist and racist cultures and attitudes. Professional development for the mental health workforce on gender-sensitive practice has been inadequate in both high and low-income countries (Chandra et al., 2019; Mizock & Kaschak, 2015). Innovative women's programs developed in the 1980s have been largely lost under neoliberalism, providing important lessons on the need for vigilance. Prior to deinstitutionalisation, women's and men's psychiatric wards were usually segregated to protect women from sexual assaults perpetrated by male patients or nurses (Vrklevski et al., 2017). Omitting this option from the design of more modern facilities was an intentional decision made in full knowledge of the consequences it would have for women. After multiple state-wide reviews demonstrating the need for women-only spaces, there remains only one women's prevention and recovery facility in the state of Victoria (Victorian Health Building Authority, 2022).

Social workers are in an advantageous position in that they are trained and qualified to develop policy and to understand and redress systemic injustice across all of these areas. Therefore an opportunity exists to contribute to rectifying systemic deficiencies. To address these deficits, government guidelines and directives must be mandated, to create authorising environments and leadership support for the promotion of inclusive family-focused practices as part of everyday mental health work (Allchin et al., 2021). Feminist approaches with adequate resourcing to meet the full range of intersectional needs have not been prioritised in mental health reforms, although the inequities and oppressions that confront women who need to use mental health services have been repeatedly identified (Mizock & Brubaker, 2021; State of Victoria, 2018).

A key social determinant of women's mental health is the experience of trauma (State of Victoria, 2018). A trauma-informed mental health workforce is important to eliminate the risk of women being traumatised or retraumatised (Isobel, 2016). Seclusion and restraint are particularly harmful forms of control that are used in inpatient settings. Non-segregated inpatient units risk exposing women in crisis to aggressive or abusive behaviours from male patients who are themselves experiencing a mental illness episode. The Victorian Mental Health Complaints Commissioner Report (State of Victoria, 2018) details gender-based violence in mental health facilities. Both the Productivity Commission (2020) and the Royal Commission into Mental Health Services in Victoria (State of Victoria, 2021) have recommended changes to facilities and practices. The Victorian Royal Commission identified the need to assess how the lived experience of trauma affects women's support needs including experiences of sexual assault and family violence. Mental health clinicians are tasked with ensuring that disclosures of these past experiences are not met with disempowering responses. Implementing these recommendations in a way that involves women and is informed by their experiences and perspectives is an urgent piece of work still to be achieved so that women can exercise their right to safety within healthcare settings when at their most vulnerable.

As psychiatric units are not safe spaces for women (State of Victoria, 2018), children are often actively discouraged from visiting their parents in the hospital. While day leaves may provide opportunities for mothers to spend time with their children as they recover, this occurs in the community, remote from the view of mental health staff, making it easier for staff to avoid discussion about this critical component of women's recovery, identity and connectedness. Despite evidence that a family-focussed approach is effective in supporting a parent's role and promoting mental health recovery (Victorian Chief Psychiatrist, 2018), it is rarely implemented.

There is strong evidence of positive outcomes for parents and their children when the parenting role together with the parent's mental health management, service collaboration and a whole of family approach is provided (Foster et al., 2019; Goodyear et al., 2018; Thanhäuser et al., 2017). The concept of relational recovery is founded on understanding the importance of connectedness and wider social determinants of mental health (Price-Robertson et al., 2017). It also challenges the expectation that parenting is exclusively the responsibility and domain of mothers, and holds other family and community members accountable for contributing to the wellbeing and care of children. Werner and Smith (2001) found that relationships outside of the nuclear family can make a significant difference in children's outcomes, even in high-risk situations.

Child protection in Australia

Between 2017 and 2021, the number of children on care and protection orders in Australia increased from 10 to 11 per 1000 children, although the number of substantiations of abuse remained stable at nine out of every 1000 children. For First Nations children the numbers increased alarmingly from 60 to 71 per 1000, a rate almost seven times higher (AIHW, 2022). Data on the proportion of these children who have parents with mental health challenges is not reported; however, O'Donnell and colleagues (2015) found that mothers with mental health difficulties had double the chance of being reported to child protection for alleged child maltreatment.

From its evolution in the 1960s, child protection assessments in Australia were grounded in white middle-class gendered and colonial understandings of what constitutes 'good' parenting. An overarching 20th century assumption of the father's rights as head of the family shaped perspectives (Fogarty, 2008), and poverty-induced neglect has always been more visible than family violence. The legacy of this remains evident in the many contemporary cases where mothers lose custody of their children for failing to protect them from the impact of family violence that they are also the victim of (Hartley, 2004; Humphreys et al., 2022). This has led to a collaborative practice framework being established in Victoria to build the workforce capacity of child protection to respond to gendered violence and hold men accountable (Healey et al., 2018). The trauma of family violence brings a significant mental health impact (VicHealth, 2004) and it is well established that a high proportion of women with mental health issues have experienced family violence (Hegarty, 2011).

Bennett et al. (2020) note that the families most likely to encounter the child protection system have longstanding experiences of poverty, mental health challenges, problematic substance use and family violence. In Australia, the parenting of First Nations women is heavily scrutinised and judged through a white lens that fails to detect First Nations families' strengths and resources (Hine & Krakouer et al., 2022). Mental illness is often decontextualised and viewed primarily as a risk within child protection assessments. There is an underdeveloped understanding of recovery, the episodic nature of mental health challenges and the fluctuating impact on parenting capacity. The Productivity Commission (2020) confirmed that women face stigma in seeking support from parenting agencies who may have limited mental health literacy. Evidence of engagement in a mental health service is interpreted as risk rather than proactive help-seeking, often leading to more intrusive monitoring. And yet closure of an episode of care can be interpreted as signifying that the parent has fewer formal supports in place, even when closure is instigated due to the parent's recovery. A mental illness diagnosis is a label that sticks, marking deviance, and 'risk' regardless of evidence of long periods of wellness.

With a mandate to protect children from harm, child protection practice is often blind to gender issues as all parents are viewed as potential perpetrators of abuse. However, while child protection workers spend most of their time scrutinising the behaviour of mothers, fathers are rarely engaged in meaningful ways (Scourfield, 2018). This gender bias is rooted in Westernised ideals and stereotypes about parenting roles and responsibilities.

Social workers make up a component of the Australian child protection workforce but have never been the key profession, even though it is the child protection sector which the general public and the media most commonly associate with social workers (Gillingham, 2016). Child protection systems across Australia are frequently described as being in crisis; cascading demands stem from mandatory reporting requirements for some professional groups, and changes to police responses to family violence due to reforms in that sector (Healey et al., 2018).

The mechanisation of roles, through reforms led by narrow managerial and technical approaches to risk assessment, have stunted the development of a relational approach that accounts for the "messy, indeterminate, complex" (Lonne et al., 2013, p. 1639) circumstances of family difficulties. Blunt tools and templates are designed to identify broad risk factors with little room for nuance or professional judgement. Lonne et al. (2013) "propose that a child protection system preoccupied with risk, social control and proceduralism is preventing the provision of quality social care and positive outcomes for children and their families" (p. 1631). An investigative role that can be reinforced by police presence and has the weight of the legal system to enforce decisions, creates insurmountable power differentials that are only exacerbated by socioeconomic disparities, gender and other social and cultural factors.

Consequently, social workers often find child protection workplaces to be toxic, punitive, overly technical and administratively heavy environments, which are contradictory to the values, culture and philosophy of the social work profession (Gillingham, 2016; Lonne et al., 2013). Moral injury is a constant threat. All of these factors fuel chronic recruitment and retention issues. With constant staff turnover and an inexperienced workforce, practice wisdom and expertise in responding to parents with mental health difficulties is stifled, and collaborative relationships between child protection and mental health services teams cannot be cultivated.

The 'best interests of the child' remains the underpinning framework of child protection services in Australia. However, it is a highly subjective concept, open to broad interpretation and is particularly susceptible to cultural bias (Long & Sephton, 2011). It is often operationalised as pitting mothers' and children's interests against one another (Dominelli, 2002).

Removing a child from their parents' custody and care is a catastrophic event for children, parents and the broader family network. Even when children are not removed, the terror of the intrusion, assessment, scrutiny, monitoring and the constant threat of losing one's children, erodes mothers' mental health and undermines their parenting confidence. Nonetheless, the impact seems to be minimised within the system, with workers becoming desensitised to the pain and trauma created, particularly when it occurs to a family that workers identify as 'different' from their own. Unconscious bias, stigma surrounding mental illness and racism often combine to suppress empathy and justify decisions.

Integrating a strength-based feminist approach with mothers experiencing mental health challenges

Lonne et al. (2013) have suggested that the child protection system could be reformed through a focus on relationship-based and reflective practice, embedding a public health model and developing a new ethical framework. These three actions echo calls in the mental health sector for a relational recovery model (Price-Robertson et al., 2017). Both are grounded in a critique of the risk lens and developing frameworks that privilege connectedness and critical reflection. Integrating a feminist lens would be consistent with this approach, emphasising gender as an overarching social and economic driver of health outcomes and illuminating gendered resource disparity and mechanisms of patriarchy and social control within mental health and child protection systems.

Women and their families bear the burden of diminished health and social outcomes in a health system that does not focus on primary prevention and early intervention (Mental Health Productivity Commission, 2020). The perinatal period is a key opportunity for responsive care, a time of high vulnerability when women are simultaneously motivated to seek support and create positive change in their lives (Hine et al., 2018b). A strengths-based early intervention approach has the potential to build capacity, promote health, improve the quality of nurturing in the early years and positively impact family outcomes. An opportunity for parents with mental health issues to be able to meet their desires to parent competently is overlooked when risk dominates and supports are in short supply. Promoting self-determination in parents with a strengths and vulnerabilities approach embedded within a recovery framework provides benefits for preventive interventions for children (Goodyear et al., 2022). Social workers are in a prime position to lead such practice transformations.

Instead of blaming and shaming women who lack the capacity and resources to be 'good enough' parents during an episode of illness, social workers need to be asking, who is missing in this picture? How can the men of this family take responsibility for caring roles? What resources and supports are available in the community? Where is the village? Feminist social work practice also supports women to identify and resist cohesion and oppression within families and health and social systems that perpetuate cultures of violence. As Dominelli (2002) states, the dominant nuclear family structure serves men and entrenches gender inequality. Australian feminist Clementine Ford (2020) encourages women to leave their husbands, opening up the liberating possibilities of alternative family and parenting models that do not rely on the subservience of women. Social critique is needed that illuminates who the nuclear family status quo benefits and dispels the myths that still proliferate, about the biological propensity of women to perform parenting roles and functions. Critical reflection, engaging in critical discourse and listening deeply to women's experiences and aspirations, reveals other creative solutions to parenting challenges that can centre the needs of women and children.

Re-centring feminism and activism in social work practice

Social work is a vocation that requires a high degree of congruence between one's professional values and behaviour in the workplace. Complex and intense, highly emotional encounters occur on a daily basis, presenting mental health and child protection social workers with a plethora of ethical and moral decisions. Moral injury can occur when professional values are inconsistent with or even contradict one's practice over an extended period of time. The psychological, spiritual and social harms of moral injury can have lasting effects (Haight et al., 2016). These effects include guilt, shame and depression. Over time, moral injury may erode confidence in one's own and/or others' ability to behave in a just and ethical manner (Drescher et al., 2011, p. 9). This can lead to burnout which is characterised by emotional exhaustion and a loss of capacity for empathy and professional self-efficacy (Wagaman et al., 2015).

Moral transgressions for social workers in the mental health sector can be cumulative and may occur when they remain silent and fail to voice their discomfort over multidisciplinary decision-making that fails to take account of social justice issues or that is based on gender stereotypes around parenting. They may be encountered when social workers do not find enough hours in the day to attend collaborative meetings or respond to the parenting needs of their clients. They can occur when a psychiatrist or magistrate overrules their recommendations, or when they are unable to effectively advocate for a mother who loses custody of her children for failing to protect them from witnessing the perpetration of family violence against her.

Public sector employment codes stifle opportunities for systems advocacy including many types of social action. A core role of social work is to challenge this. Entrenching social work principles of strength-based practice (Golightley & Holloway, 2019), equalising power differentials and redressing disadvantage on a broad (rather than individual) scale are needed to seed opportunities for change. Forming alliances of solidarity with mothers who experience mental health challenges may be one way to embed a feminist stance and reclaim the centrality of social work advocacy and activism. With the expanding lived experience workforce, there are opportunities for social workers to empower mothers to take up these roles and use their expertise to develop new policy and practice frameworks that are informed by a gendered lens.

Dedicating time to networking with social workers in child protection services may enhance mutual understanding. Increasing opportunities for critical reflection and discussion within teams and across sectors, of how to operationalise feminist social work values in tightly legislated systems, may spark innovation and creativity. The activism component of social work practice needs to be salvaged and reinvigorated, informed by intersectoral feminisms to support the rights and fulfil the needs of mothers with mental health challenges (Brown, 2021).

Conclusion

The barriers confronted by mothers experiencing mental health challenges are constructed by patriarchy. Parenting as a role and identity is either overlooked completely or scrutinised relentlessly in the mental health system. Westernised middle-class unattainable mothering ideals do not abate when mental health is compromised, and the social sanctions for transgressions are brutal and long-lasting.

The chapter concludes with a call for social workers to reclaim their roles as advocates and catalysts for change, which have been systematically eroded through successive neoliberal government policies. The foundational principles and competencies of the profession mean that social workers are well placed to contribute towards dismantling systems built on gender-blind policies and practices. A feminist approach includes a focus on strengths and relationships as well as identifying and redressing oppression. Prioritising critical reflection is imperative if we are to become consciously aware of the ways that living in a patriarchal society permeates our own practice.

An opportunity exists to work in solidarity with mothers who experience mental health challenges. We need to listen to and amplify their voices, and use the expertise of lived experience to co-create services that are gender-sensitive, trauma-informed, culturally appropriate and safe and family-focussed.

References

Allchin, B., Weimand, B. M., O'Hanlon, B., & Goodyear, M. (2021). A sustainability model for family-focused practice in adult mental health services. *Frontiers in Psychiatry, 12*. https://www.ncbi.nlm.nih.gov/pmc/articles/PMC8804966/

Australian Government, Services Australia. (2021). *Mental Health Care and Medicare.* Available from: https://www.servicesaustralia.gov.au/mental-health-care-and-medicare?context=60092

Australian Institute of Health and Welfare. (2021). *Child Protection Australia 2019–2020.* Available from: https://www.aihw.gov.au/reports/child-protection/child-protection-australia-2019-20/summary

Awram, R., Hancock, N., & Honey, A. (2017). Balancing mothering and mental health recovery: the voices of mothers living with mental illness. *Advances in Mental Health, 15*(2), 147–160. https://www.tandfonline.com/doi/abs/10.1080/18387357.2016.1255149

Bennett, K., Booth, A., Gair, S., Kibet, R., & Thorpe, R. (2020). Poverty is the problem–not parents: so tell me, child protection worker, how can you help? *Children Australia, 45*(4), 207–214. https://www.cambridge.org/core/journals/children-australia/article/abs/poverty-is-the-problem-not-parents-so-tell-me-child-protection-worker-how-can-you-help/A82C6E4B6245E8F5192A724026FF16B7

Bondi, L., & Burman, E. (2001). Women and mental health: a feminist review. *Feminist Review, 68,* 6–33. https://doi.org/10.1080/01417780122133

Boursnell, M. (2014). Assessing the capacity of parents with mental illness: parents with mental illness and risk. *International Social Work, 57*(2), 92–108. https://journals.sagepub.com/doi/full/10.1177/0020872812445197

Brown, C. (2021). Critical clinical social work and the neoliberal constraints on social justice in mental health. *Research on Social Work Practice, 31*(6), 644–652. https://journals.sagepub.com/doi/epub/10.1177/1049731520984531

Chandra, P. S., Saraf, G., Bajaj, A., & Satyanarayana, V. A. (2019). The current status of gender-sensitive mental health services for women—findings from a global survey of experts. *Archives of Women's Mental Health, 22*(6), 759–770. https://doi.org/10.1007/s00737-019-01001-2

Commonwealth of Australia. (2020). *Mental Health Productivity Commissioner Inquiry Report* 30th of June 2020. Available from: https://www.pc.gov.au/inquiries/completed/mental-health/report

Daminger, A. (2019). The cognitive dimension of household labor. *American Sociological Review, 84*(4), 609–633. https://doi.org/10.1177/0003122419859007

Dawson, L., River, J., McCloughen, A., & Buus, N. (2021). 'Should it fit? Yes. Does it fit? No': Exploring the organisational processes of introducing a recovery-oriented approach to mental health in Australian private health care. *Health, 25*(3), 376–394. https://doi.org/10.1177/1363459319889107

Dominelli, L. (2002). *Feminist Social Work Theory and Practice.* Hampshire: Palgrave.

Drescher, K. D., Foy, C., Kelly, A., Leshner, A., Schultz, K., & Litz, B. (2011). An exploration of the viability and usefulness of the construct of moral injury in war veterans. *Traumatology, 17,* 8–13. https://doi.org/10.1177/1534765610395615

Fogarty, J. (2008). Some aspects of the early history of child protection in Australia. *Family Matters, 78,* 52–59.

Ford, C. (2020, September 22). I thought I might do a soft, floaty lewk for this because that's typically how I imagine a romantic aesthetic. [Status update] Facebook. https://www.facebook.com/clementineford/photos/a.620818907995207/3439648289445574/

Foster, K., Goodyear, M., Grant, A., Weimand, B., & Nicholson, J. (2019). Family-focused practice with EASE: a practice framework for strengthening recovery when mental health consumers are parents. *International Journal of Mental Health Nursing, 28,* 351–360. https://onlinelibrary.wiley.com/doi/abs/10.1111/inm.12535

Gillingham, P. (2016). Social work and child protection in Australia: whose job is it anyway? *Practice, 28*(2), 83–96. https://www.tandfonline.com/doi/abs/10.1080/09503153.2015.1074670

Gladstone, B. M., Boydell, K. M., & McKeever, P. (2006). Recasting research into children's experiences of parental mental illness: beyond risk and resilience. *Social Science & Medicine, 62*(10), 2540–2550. https://doi.org/10.1016/j.socscimed.2005.10.038

Golightley, M., & Holloway, M. (2019). From zero to hero? Or a strengths-based approach. *The British Journal of Social Work, 49*(6), 1373–1375.

Goodyear, M. J., Allchin, B., Burn, M., von Doussa, H., Reupert, A., Tchernegovski, P., ... & Maybery, D. (2022). Promoting self-determination in parents with mental illness in adult mental health settings. *Journal of Family Nursing, 28*(2), 129–141. https://journals.sagepub.com/doi/abs/10.1177/10748407211067308

Goodyear, M. J., McDonald, M., von Doussa, H., Cuff, R., & Dunlop, B. (2018). Meeting the intergenerational needs of families where a parent has a mental illness. *Journal of Parent and Family Mental Health*, 3(2). https://doi.org/10.7191/parentandfamily.1011

Haight, W., Sugrue, E., Calhoun, M., & Black, J. (2016). A scoping study of moral injury: identifying directions for social work research. *Children and Youth Services Review*, 70, 190–200. https://doi.org/10.1016/j.childyouth.2016.09.026

Hartley, C. C. (2004). Severe domestic violence and child maltreatment: considering child physical abuse, neglect, and failure to protect. *Children and Youth Services Review*, 26(4), 373–392. https://www.sciencedirect.com/science/article/pii/S0190740904000064?casa_token=-OJVZuqZrRUAAAAA:j3exW0y1ZuOCSOFwYXh9ffzlsv5xfOPd4Pidh3FAqThTRhgH1BmKz8uXpJJGOLHI9w9vQJQyag

Healey, L., Connolly, M., & Humphreys, C. (2018). A collaborative practice framework for child protection and specialist domestic and family violence services: Bridging the research and practice divide. *Australian Social Work*, 71(2), 228–237. https://www.tandfonline.com/doi/abs/10.1080/0312407X.2017.1409777

Hegarty, K. (2011). Domestic violence: the hidden epidemic associated with mental illness. *British Journal of Psychiatry*, 198(3), 169–170. http://doi.org/10.1192/bjp.bp.110.083758

Heward-Belle, S., Laing, L., Humphreys, C., & Toivonen, C. (2018). Intervening with children living with domestic violence: Is the system safe? *Australian Social Work*, 71(2), 135–147.

Hine, R., Krakouer, J., Elston, J., Fredericks, B., Hunter, S. A., Taylor, K., ... & Skouteris, H. (2022). Identifying and dismantling racism in Australian perinatal settings: reframing the narrative from a risk lens to intentionally prioritise connectedness and strengths in providing care to first nations families. *Women and Birth*. Available from: https://www.sciencedirect.com/science/article/pii/S1871519222000749

Hine, R. H., Maybery, D. J., & Goodyear, M. J. (2018a). Identity in recovery for mothers with a mental illness: a literature review. *Psychiatric Rehabilitation Journal*, 41(1), 16. https://psycnet.apa.org/doiLanding?doi=10.1037%2Fprj0000215

Hine, R. H., Maybery, D., & Goodyear, M. J. (2018b). Challenges of connectedness in personal recovery for rural mothers with mental illness. *International Journal of Mental Health Nursing*, 27(2), 672–682. https://onlinelibrary.wiley.com/doi/abs/10.1111/inm.12353

Hollingsworth, L. D. (2004). Child custody loss among women with persistent severe mental illness. *Social Work Research*, 28(4), 199–209. https://academic.oup.com/swr/article-abstract/28/4/199/1657866?login=false

Humphreys, C., Heward-Belle, S., Tsantefski, M., Isobe, J., & Healey, L. (2022). Beyond co-occurrence: addressing the intersections of domestic violence, mental health and substance misuse. *Child & Family Social Work*, 27(2), 299–310.

Hunter, S. V. (2008). Child maltreatment in remote Aboriginal communities and the Northern Territory emergency response: a complex issue. *Australian Social Work*, 61(4), 372–388. https://www.tandfonline.com/doi/full/10.1080/03124070802430700

Isobel, S. (2016). Trauma informed care: a radical shift or basic good practice? *Australasian Psychiatry*, 24(6), 589–591. https://journals.sagepub.com/doi/abs/10.1177/1039856216657698

Krakouer, J., Wu Tan, W., & Parolini, A. (2021). Who is analysing what? The opportunities, risks and implications of using predictive risk modelling with Indigenous Australians in child protection: a scoping review. *Australian Journal of Social Issues*, 56(2), 173–197. https://onlinelibrary.wiley.com/doi/full/10.1002/ajs4.155

Lacey, M., Paolini, S., Hanlon, M-C., Melville, J., Galletly, C., & Campbell, L. E. (2014). Parents with serious mental illness: differences in internalised and externalised mental illness stigma and gender stigma between mothers and fathers. *Psychiatry Research*, 225(3), 723–733. https://doi.org/10.1016/j.psychres.2014.09.010

Long, M., & Sephton, R. (2011). Rethinking the "best interests" of the child: voices from Aboriginal child and family welfare practitioners. *Australian Social Work*, 64(1), 96–112. https://www.tandfonline.com/doi/abs/10.1080/0312407X.2010.535544

Lonne, B., Harries, M., & Lantz, S. (2013). Workforce development: a pathway to reforming child protection systems in Australia. *British Journal of Social Work*, 43(8), 1630–1648. https://academic.oup.com/bjsw/article-abstract/43/8/1630/1692399?login=false

Maybery, D., & Reupert, A. (2009). Parental mental illness: a review of barriers and issues for working with families and children. *Journal of Psychiatric and Mental Health Nursing, 16*, 784–791. https://onlinelibrary.wiley.com/doi/abs/10.1111/j.1365-2850.2009.01456.x

Meadows, G. N., Enticott, J. C., Inder, B., Russell, G. M., & Gurr, R. (2015). Better access to mental health care and the failure of the Medicare principle of universality. *Medical Journal of Australia, 202*, 190–194. https://doi.org/10.5694/mja14.00330

Mizock, L., & Brubaker, M. (2021). Treatment experiences with gender and discrimination among women with serious mental illness. *Psychological Services, 18*(1), 64–72. https://psycnet.apa.org/doiLanding?doi=10.1037%2Fser0000346

Mizock, L., & Kaschak, E. (2015). Women with serious mental illness in therapy: intersectional perspectives. *Women & Therapy, 38*(1–2), 6–13. https://www.tandfonline.com/doi/abs/10.1080/02703149.2014.978209?journalCode=wwat20

Montgomery, P., Tompkins, C., Forchuk, C., & French, S. (2006). Keeping close: mothering with serious mental illness. *Journal of Advanced Nursing, 54*(1), 20–28. https://onlinelibrary.wiley.com/doi/abs/10.1111/j.1365-2648.2006.03785.x

Moreton-Robinson, A. (2015). *The White Possessive: Property, Power and Indigenous Sovereignty.* University of Minnesota Press.

Mowbray, C. T., Oyserman, D., Bybee, D., MacFarlane, P., & Rueda-Riedle, A. (2001). Life circumstances of mothers with serious mental illnesses. *Psychiatric Rehabilitation Journal, 25*(2), 114.

Nicholson, J., & Biebel, K. (2002). Commentary on "Community mental health care for women with severe mental illness who are parents"—The tragedy of missed opportunities: what providers can do. *Community Mental Health Journal, 38*(2), 167–172. https://link.springer.com/article/10.1023/A:1014551306288

O'Donnell, M., Maclean, M. J., Sims, S., Morgan, V. A., Leonard, H., & Stanley, F. J. (2015). Maternal mental health and risk of child protection involvement: mental health diagnoses associated with increased risk. *Journal of Epidemiology and Community Health, 69*(12), 1175–1183. https://jech.bmj.com/content/69/12/1175.short

Price-Robertson, R., Obradovic, A., & Morgan, B. (2017). Relational recovery: Beyond individualism in the recovery approach. *Advances in Mental Health, 15*(2), 108–120. https://doi.org/10.1080/18387357.2016.1243014

Price-Robertson, R., Reupert, A., & Maybery, D. (2015). Fathers' experiences of mental illness stigma: scoping review and implications for prevention. *Advances in Mental Health, 13*(2), 100–112. https://doi.org/10.1080/18387357.2015.1063746

Reupert, A., Gladstone, B., Hine, R. H., Yates, S., McGaw, V., Charles, G., ... & Foster, K. (2021). Stigma in relation to families living with parental mental illness: an integrative review. *International Journal of Mental Health Nursing, 30*(1), 6–26. https://onlinelibrary.wiley.com/doi/abs/10.1111/inm.12820

Scholz, B., Bocking, J., & Happell, B. (2017). Breaking through the glass ceiling: consumers in mental health organisations' hierarchies. *Issues in Mental Health Nursing, 38*(5), 374–380, https://doi.org/10.1080/18387357.2021.1924067

Scourfield, J. B. (2018). *Gender and Child Protection.* Bloomsbury Publishing.

Seeman, M. V. (2015). Schizophrenia and motherhood. In Reupert, A., Maybery, D., Nicholson, J, Gopfert, M., & Seeman, M. (Eds.) *Parental Psychiatric Disorder: Distressed Parents and their Families*, Ch 3, 107–116. Cambridge University Press.

Seeman, M. V. (2012). Intervention to prevent child custody loss in mothers with schizophrenia. *Schizophrenia Research and Treatment, 2012.* https://www.hindawi.com/journals/schizort/2012/796763/

State of Victoria. (2021). *Royal Commission into Victoria's Mental Health System, Final Report, Summary and Recommendations.* Parliamentary Paper No. 202, Session 2018–21. Available from: http://rcvmhs.archive.royalcommission.vic.gov.au/

State of Victoria. (2018). *The Right to be Safe: Ensuring Sexual Safety in Acute Mental Health Inpatient Units. Mental Health Complaints Commissioner Sexual Safety Project Report.* Available from: https://www.mhcc.vic.gov.au/sites/default/files/2021-01/The-right-to-be-safe-sexual-safety-project-report.pdf

Thanhäuser, M., Lemmer, G., de Girolamo, G., & Christiansen, H. (2017). Do preventive interventions for children of mentally ill parents work? Results of a systematic review and meta-analysis.

Current Opinion in Psychiatry, 30(4), 283–299. https://www.ingentaconnect.com/content/wk/yco/2017/00000030/00000004/art00009

VicHealth. (2004). The health costs of violence: measuring the burden of disease caused by intimate partner violence. *A Summary of Findings*. Available from: https://www.vichealth.vic.gov.au/media-and-resources/publications/the-health-costs-of-violence

Victorian Chief Psychiatrist. (2018). Working together with families and carers. Available from: https://www.health.vic.gov.au/sites/default/files/migrated/files/collections/policies-and-guidelines/c/chief-psychiatrist-guideline-working-with-families-and-carers.pdf

Victorian Health Building Authority. (2022). *Construction begins on Victorian first women's prevention and recovery care centre*. Available from: https://www.vhba.vic.gov.au/news/construction-begins-victorian-first-womens-prevention-and-recovery-care-centre

Vrklevski, L. P., Eljiz, K., & Greenfield, D. (2017). The evolution and devolution of mental health services in Australia. *Inquiries Journal, 9*(10). http://www.inquiriesjournal.com/articles/1654/2/the-evolution-and-devolution-of-mental-health-services-in-australia

Wagaman, M. A., Geiger, J. M., Shockley, C., & Segal, E. A. (2015). The role of empathy in burnout, compassion satisfaction, and secondary traumatic stress among social workers. *Social Work, 60*(3), 201–209. https://doi.org/10.1093/sw/swv014

Werner, E. E., & Smith, R. S. (2001). *Journeys from Childhood to Midlife: Risk, Resilience, and Recovery*. Ithaca, NY: Cornell University Press.

Wilson, R. (1997). *Bringing them Home: National Inquiry into the Separation of Aboriginal and Torres Strait Islander Children from their Families*. Sydney: Human Rights and Equal Opportunity Commission. Available from: https://bth.humanrights.gov.au/the-report/bringing-them-home-report

32
SOCIAL WORK AND TWO TYPES OF MATERNALISM
Supporting single mothers through strategic maternalism

Toshiko Yokoyama

Introduction

Maternalism refers to the idea that mothers possess 'maternal affection' by dint of their biological properties as women and that this affection translates into the labour of caring for children regardless of the circumstances or choices of individual women. Maternalism is a norm and set of expectations imposed on all mothers, though they may embrace and/ or resist this overarching social narrative in a variety of ways. Maternalism includes beliefs such as 'women are naturally mothers and so naturally they should bear and raise children' and 'mothers should raise children with love as a matter of course, precisely because they are mothers'.

These beliefs are based on the ideas of gender roles, division of labour, romantic love, maternal love, familial love, and heterosexism. In some industrialised societies such as the one written about here, namely Japan, it is considered natural for men to undertake paid work outside the home, while women remain in the home, doing unpaid housework and raising the children. Though not all classes can afford this idealised heterosexist dynamic, it holds considerable ideological force and remains a central, though not always achievable, norm across all classes. Consequently, many of the social systems and labour customs in modern Japanese societies are designed on the assumption that men should work in the public sphere of paid employment, while women/mothers should perform housework and care in the private sphere of the family. While present-day societies exhibit more diverse thinking about marriage and families due to new stances on gender diversity, and more people are entering marriages and leading family lives not bound by such systems, the family, gender norms, and systems of the 'modern family' still stand firm (Kromydas, 2020).

Feminism has pointed out the issues of social unfairness between the genders in these overall values and norms and re-examined the gender norms that lie at their roots. Differences in income and labour opportunities between the genders (Litman et al., 2020; Oláh et al., 2018); high rates of poverty among women and single mothers (Doblhammer & Gumà, 2018; Maldonado & Nieuwenhuis, 2015); unpaid labour resulting from marriage, pregnancy, or childbirth (Singh & Pattanaik, 2020); domestic violence against women; and heterosexual supremacy are all rooted in gender norms. Among the many topics that involve gender norms, maternalism is particularly important in the study of family-related gender norms, as discussed below.

In this chapter, I reconceptualise maternalism through a focus on single mothers who face numerous challenges and I make practical suggestions for social workers. I raise the following four issues. First, I discuss why maternalism is representative of family-related gender issues. I then take a critical view of conventional maternalism and maternal norms from a feminist perspective. Second, I focus on suggestions from care feminism and re-evaluate the activity of care from the 'ethics of care' perspective. Here, I debate the potential for an alternative maternalism. Third, I compare and contrast essentialist maternalism and strategic maternalism. Fourth, I discuss suggestions for social work based on strategic maternalism.

The background to the emergence of 'strategic maternalism' was the neoliberalism of the 1980s and globalisation of the 1990s that led to the reduction of public welfare under the welfare state system and, in turn, led to the marketisation of welfare and increased dependence on the family for care in Japan. The growing trend is that care issues, such as childcare and nursing care, are once again becoming the personal responsibility of women. 'Strategic maternalism' is positioned as an objection to this trend.

Motohashi (2021) states that essentialist maternalism understands maternal love to be a natural part of a woman's nature as the birthing sex and has strong maternal norms, whereas 'strategic maternalism' states that naturalistic maternalism is a political device that oppresses motherhood. In other words, she views it as problematic that 'motherhood' has been suppressed and made the responsibility of the individual, despite being premised on the concept of the modern 'individual'. Motohashi also believes that motherhood, which is the state of engaging with vulnerable parties through care, holds new political potential for envisioning a society that tolerates diversity and difference.

Marxist feminism first pointed out the oppression of motherhood, and this theoretical contribution is significant. However, it did not lead to an evaluation and review of the value of care itself (Motohashi, 2021). As will be discussed later, the social recognition of care was pointed out by care feminism, an offshoot of Second Wave Feminism that began with the 'ethics of care' proposed by Gilligan (1982). Gilligan re-evaluates care by women, stating that 'motherhood' has been subordinated to the 'individual', despite the fact that care is a premise of the modern 'individual'. As one challenge to 'feminism as having forgotten motherhood' (Stephens, 2011), the discussion in this chapter shares the recognition of the issue of the subjugation of motherhood and discusses social work with single mothers from a 'strategic maternalism' view based on care feminism (Motohashi, 2021).

Female oppression due to maternalism

Why is maternalism an important topic?

The topic of maternalism is an important one in the context of family-related gender norms for two main reasons. First, the strong notion of women as the 'childbearing sex' that is attached to maternalism lies at the heart of the family gender norms which have greatly contributed to women's social oppression (Giles, 2019; Glenn, 2016; Mussida & Patimo, 2021). Many women have been required to live within the bounds of a fixed heterosexual life course through marriage, pregnancy, childbirth, childrearing, and caregiving. Women are also clearly oppressed by being restricted to the private sphere of family and excluded from the public one of paid employment and social participation. While diverse life experiences in work–family balance has been observed in recent years, multiple dimensions of social pressure centred on childrearing have also been noted (Berger et al., 2022). The re-examination and re-conceptualisation of the notion of women as the 'childbearing sex' which is attached to maternalism is key in breaking down family norms.

The second point is the ability to recognise the value of the experiences and thoughts of women who are in charge of the care and to socially approve them. Although all people require care from others at the early and late stages of their lives, and many at numerous other stages, such care is not often highly valued by society. From the theory of the 'ethics of care', social recognition of care could rescue women/mothers/families enduring the greatest difficulties. This chapter discusses this below, using maternalism as a key analytic concept.

Oppression of women through maternalism

In most societies, the oppression of women is through maternalism (Adrienne, 2010), which is derived from heterosexual, patriarchal family and gender norms, which is found in all societal systems, including labour, education, and social security systems. Looking through the lens of female disadvantage, it is difficult to see how women can acquire a stable economic foundation under a valuation biased toward a life course centred on compulsory heterosexuality including marriage to a man, childbirth, and childrearing. This restrictive role and workload make it difficult for women to be socially or financially independent, make decisions freely, and maintain a sense of self-respect. Moreover, women have been predominantly tasked with caring for children, older adults, and people with disabilities inside the home. Overall, society treats this issue of care as part of the private sphere and by extension accepts and sanctions the starkly divided, heterosexist, gender norm-based, micro-level oppressive relations and domestic violence that take place within the home. Butler (2006) noted that gender perspectives are constructed from language, culture and social norms, and identified issues of power relations and oppression.

These issues are highly obvious in the case of single mothers. Although single mothers are under powerful demands from society to both undertake paid work and raise their children, the existing social structures and lack of appropriate supports such as childcare tend to marginalise women within the labour market and by extension single mothers from high-quality, fair waged, full-time, permanent employment. As a result, single mothers often engage in irregular and precarious employment that is more likely to be low-waged and insecure, resulting in the higher proportions of single mothers and their children living in poverty. According to a survey of single-mother households in Japan in 2021, despite an employment rate of 86.3%, the poverty rate was 48.3% (Ministry of Health, Labour and Welfare, 2019). One reason for this was that non-regular employment accounted for 38.8%, which was significantly higher than that among single-father households (4.9%) (Ministry of Health, Labour and Welfare, 2021). The inequalities in women's employment are evident from these results.

Excessive faith in maternalism lies at the base of this kind of social unfairness—that is, the belief that because of their biological capacity in terms of ability to bear children, it is 'natural' that mothers bear and raise children and that they are the most suited for that type of work. Conversely, according to essentialist maternalism, a 'good mother' accepts care duties as her responsibility and can conduct them appropriately. The key problem, however, is that these mothering norms include the oppression of women and their assumption of personal responsibility. From this perspective, the life issues suffered by single mothers constitute female oppression at the intersection of sexual discrimination and family discrimination. Further, because single mothers often internalise essentialist maternalism norms and values, they may not easily recognise their individual negative experiences as problems caused by social structures that oppress women.

The above discussion can be summarised into three points: (1) essentialist maternalism lies at the heart of the oppression of single mothers; (2) the social structures derived from essentialist maternalism are disadvantageous to women; and (3) responsibility for problems resulting from these disadvantageous social systems is attributed to individual women.

Accordingly, against this backdrop of systems and norms, social workers often make excessive appeals to single mothers to play their motherly roles more appropriately or criticise them for lacking the skills to raise their children; they further oppress these women (Polar, 2022). Contributing to critical social work that empowers rather than oppresses its clients, I argue that re-conceptualisation and logical re-examination of maternalism and family norms is needed in social work.

Insights from care feminism

Care feminism appeared in the 1980s as a critical reaction against liberalism and neo-liberalism, making important points about the premises upon which the modern self is based rather than describing how the modern self should be. Care feminism is a feminist theory that draws on the 'ethics of care', which is based on the idea that we are responsible for others and should be considerate of them, as described by Gilligan (1982) in her classic book *In a Different Voice*. The 'ethics of care', in contrast to the 'ethics of justice' (which Gilligan argues is the major ethical bent of modern rationalism), values consideration of interrelationships with others when responding to given situations. The relationships between mother and child, wherein the self and the other cannot be clearly delineated, and the relationship between a woman and other family members requiring care are particularly representative examples. Gilligan argues that actions based on the ethics of care have been rendered invisible and are valued less than actions and reasoning based on the 'ethics of justice' and that women have thus shouldered the work of the ethics of care (unpaid labour). Also contributing to the early care ethics debate, Okin (1999) explored theories of justice from the perspective of gender, arguing that 'until there is justice in the family, women will not be able to gain equality in politics, at work, or in any other sphere' (p. 4).

Writers from the same era, such as Kittay (1999) and Fineman (2004), have focused on the fates of those who require care from others at the early or late stages of their lives and have asserted feminist theories that focus on the ethics of care from an egalitarian perspective that connotes reliance. Their arguments focus on 'mothering', with Kittay (1999, p. 58) writing that 'we are all some mother's child', arguing that societies need to create social structures that legitimise caregiving and view it as the responsibility of society as a whole (Kittay, 2015). Fineman (2004) criticises the structure that assigns unpaid care roles to women and then makes them reliant on social systems when they undertake the assigned roles. Fineman calls this 'secondary reliance', and she unravels its economic and structural background toward seeking social justice that also involves caring for the caregivers.

Similarly, in her book *Maternal Thinking*, Ruddick (1989) analyses the practices of mothering and motherly thinking and considers how mothers coexist with heterogeneous others (e.g. children) while maintaining relationships with them. She argues that maternal thinking which prioritises responding in an ethical and practical way to others who are in a weaker position than oneself can contribute to building peaceful relationships with others at the family level and beyond.

According to Motohashi (2021), four key points of these different kinds of care feminism are as follows:

1 They spotlight aspects of women's experience that have been ignored by existing scholarship.
2 They interpret caring for others, which has been regarded as a form of self-sacrifice, as an ethics of responsibility to others.
3 They reveal that the androcentricity inherent in the public–private dualism, the genderisation of power relationships, have devalued the practice of care.
4 They expose the ways in which women are isolated from their family and care relationships under public–private dualism.

Feminist social work research has incorporated the ethics of care framework into all areas of care research, including social policy analysis (Phillips, 2015). The need for gendered care in social work practice from an ethics of care perspective has been identified (Orme, 2015).

In the next section, I discuss strategic maternalism, which regards the 'ethics of care' and the experiences of women as important.

Two kinds of maternalism

What is strategic maternalism?

In this section, I first contrast and examine two kinds of maternalism to redefine maternalism based on the studies by Motohashi (2021) and Inoue (2013). First, essentialist maternalism, which I have already introduced briefly, refers to the norms imposed on women based on their biological properties dictating that they should be mothers, that they should possess qualities of maternal affection, and that they should love children and raise them. In contrast, care feminism maternalism is 'strategic maternalism', proposed by Motohashi (2021) as a frame of reference for analysing maternalism and resistance to it in Japanese society and for redefining strategic maternalism both theoretically and conceptually. The characteristics of Motohashi's theory of strategic maternalism are as follows:

- It is founded in principles of care feminism and shares with it an awareness of the problems inherent in essentialist maternalism, which has been accepted as ordinary, absolute, and superhistorical. As mentioned in the introduction, this is a perspective of resistance to the reduction of public welfare and making childbearing and childrearing a matter of personal responsibility against the backdrop of spreading neoliberalism in Japanese society and economic globalisation. The living conditions of single mothers exemplify the most typical socio-structural problems.
- It is critical of degenderisation and adopts a stance aligned with mothers' experiences and realities. This is because degenderisation is thought to potentially devalue women/mothers and encourage them to assume sole responsibility for the care of children and others. Starting the discussion on the issue of maternal oppression can lead to social recognition of the value of the maternal experience. The expression 'mother', which is

used as a metaphor, does not limit the provision of care to mothers; it allows for (does not prohibit) the assumption of diverse care providers.
- It believes that mothering is founded in interrelationships that accept the diversity of and differences between humans. Relatedly, it shares thinking on how to coexist with overwhelmingly weaker others without harming them while caring for them, despite the presence of conflict. Such an emphasis on motherhood has been criticised for putting women back into the role of carers, but strategic maternalism believes that such criticism is problematic because it assumes an oppressive dualism of the 'individual/human' (man) and the 'mother'. It has a deep understanding of the social dimensions in which mothers are placed and finds that the value of their experiences is what has the power to transform society. The starting point for the political empowerment of single mothers is this claim.
- It opposes the imposition of full responsibility for bearing and raising children on women and is positioned within a frame of reference that emphasises empowerment and where mothers have and exercise social and political power. In essential maternalism, mothers are subjected to socio-structural oppression in which they engage in care duties, are made personally responsible, and are economically and psychologically oppressed by their unpaid labour. Furthermore, they are politically disempowered. Political empowerment is essential to changing this situation as women form a group identity with peers, acquire empowering perspectives and knowledge, and disseminate those ideas socially based on the belief that 'the personal is political'.

Comparing and contrasting essentialist maternalism and strategic maternalism

First, the theoretical premises are different for each type. Essentialist maternalism understands care as something that women should shoulder full-time in the private sphere and has rendered it invisible, which has maintained and reinforced the patriarchal 'modern family' ideology. By contrast, strategic maternalism properly evaluates the care that mothers shoulder from the perspective of 'ethics of care' feminism and seeks from society and individuals social fairness that includes appropriate care for caregivers.

The key concepts of essentialist maternalism are 'bearing and raising children' and 'loving children', which are understood as natural, individual acts by individual women/mothers, while the key concepts of strategic maternalism are 'ethics of care' and 'social approval of care'. Strategic materialism intends that 'care' will be expanded to include care relationships that are not limited to 'bearing and raising children', and this kind of maternalism seeks recognition from society that all people have an ethical duty to care for others.

These differences naturally lead to different understandings of women's life courses. Essentialist maternalism envisages a life course for women that follows the trajectory of 'marriage, pregnancy, childbirth, and childrearing', states of being granted to the 'childbearing sex'; moreover, essentialist maternalism is characterised by the social approval given to mothers through their paired relationships with children. By contrast, strategic maternalism envisages a diversity of life courses for women and understands 'raising children' as a skill that women can attain through experience and society rather than an innate property of women. It understands that in some cases, the best option is to separate the 'bearing' of the children and the 'raising' (care) of children, and excludes punitive value judgments in such scenarios. Further, strategic maternalism seeks the social recognition of and support for women's care relationship with children.

In terms of theoretical and practical characteristics, essentialist maternalism contributes to the maintenance and reinforcement of the 'modern family' ideology; problems with that ideology include the oppression of women, the gap between the traditional family and breaking away from it, and divergence from the realities of family in the present day. In contrast, strategic maternalism contributes to proper social recognition of women shouldering care and the improvement and resolution of secondary reliance by carers. Problems include the fact that reform is not easy and will take time because essentialist maternalism has pervaded every level of society (Table 32.1).

Table 32.1 Comparison of essentialist maternalism and strategic maternalism

	Essentialist maternalism	Strategic maternalism
Premises	Patriarchal maternalism	Ethics of care and women's liberation
Expectations	'Bearing and raising children', which are essential properties imbued in the childbearing sex	Society and individuals should appropriately care for caregivers in a fair society based on the ethics of care.
Key concepts	Bearing and raising children, loving children	Ethics of care, social recognition of care, broadening viewpoints by expanding care
Women's life courses and relationships with children	1 Envisages a life course that continues through 'marriage, pregnancy, childbirth, childrearing' as a property given to the childbearing sex 2 Mothers gain social approval through their paired relationships with children.	1 Women have diverse life courses that are at the disposal of the individual woman. 2 The ability to 'raise children' is understood not as something innate or essential to women but rather as a skill they can attain through experience or from society. In some cases, 'bearing' and 'raising' (caring for) children may be undertaken by separate individuals. 3 Care relationships with children (care recipients) should be socially recognised.
Contributions	Maintenance and reinforcement of the 'modern family' ideology	Fair social recognition of women who shoulder care Improvement and resolution of secondary reliance by carers
Problems	Female oppression Split between the standard family and breaking away from it Divergence from the realities of family in the present day	Pervasiveness of essentialist maternalism in all levels of society Social change takes time.

Suggestions for social work based on strategic maternalism

The ultimate goal of strategic maternalism is 'the fair social recognition of the women who bear the burden of care'. Dominelli (2002), a leader in feminist social work, argues that in relation to support for children and mothers. She furthermore argues that we should stop dividing women into 'good mothers' and 'bad mothers' according to their childrearing capacity and stop criticising so-called 'bad mothers' and directing them to act in more 'motherly' ways. The dominant discourse that mothers are primarily responsible for the safety, well-being and care of children is routinely enacted in child welfare even when fathers are present and involved (Strega et al., 2008).

As Hays (2007) states, what is required of feminist social work in the future is to provide support from a 'Complexity of Motherhood' perspective, by developing a comprehensive and cultural understanding of individual experiences and social and cultural influences of the power relations and oppression, in understanding motherhood. The concept of 'Strategic Maternalism' in this section may provide the impetus for this. While the concept of intersectionality is important in gender, there are complex social factors that are also involved in understanding motherhood. Further, because views of motherhood are linked to unconscious bias and privilege, there is a need to develop support systems that allow women to recognise and address their unconscious biases (Turner & Krane, 2014). The importance of promoting policies on women's rights and gender equality from a social justice perspective, emphasising women's voices and experiences, and empowering practices for women have also been noted (Lehman & Beale, 2018).

Two practical challenges arise when aspiring to strategic maternalism as per the following questions: (1) What perspective should we take when considering what is best at three levels, that is, what is best for the children, what is best for the mothers/women, and what is best for the entire family; and (2) what can social workers do to create a society that cares for the caregivers? I discuss this here in the context of social work for single mothers.

When determining the optimal point between what is best for children, best for the mothers, and best for the families, it is important that social workers first of all notice the current level of maternal oppression being suffered by the mother due to essentialist maternalism (Polar, 2022). This requires an appreciation of the lifestyles and experiences of mothers and families and an understanding of gender analysis.

Five key points to consider for gender analysis from Miyaji's (2004) gender sensitivity checklist may be useful to social workers. First, consider the kinds of gender norms found in the context of the position of the client, her family, and her larger social circle. Second, consider how gender influences the issue at hand and the woman's life thereafter. Third, consider whether gender biases are present among the mother's supporters, their philosophies and techniques, the aid relationships the mother has, and other similar contexts. Fourth, consider whether the client is conscious of empowerment from a gender perspective in terms of how to live in a gender-biased society. Fifth, the social worker should consider whether the interpretation of the situation would be the same if the genders were reversed. Gender-sensitive assessment skills are essential competencies for social workers.

The second point involves social reform and the development of resources for 'caring for the caregivers' within the community; in doing so, it is necessary to break down mothers' and children's individual needs and improve familiar support regimes for women during pregnancy, childbirth, and child 'rearing' and to strengthen functional collaborations with existing public support services. While looking to the community as a whole to provide support for childrearing is promoted theoretically and philosophically, it is yet to be fully realised, and numerous challenges exist. This paradox is another socio-structural issue of women's oppression. Dowling and Haukin (2009) also, when discussing Work and Poverty among single mothers, stress the importance of coordination between policy-level provisions and supportive practices. Moreover, many practical issues remain ahead in the transformation of fathers and men into 'the other parent'.

Such transformations are also practical issues for social workers, but the most important thing is that they reform the current situation by taking on the role of collaborator with mothers, facilitating mothers' gaining of social and political power. In this sense, social workers must have the skills to expand community-based social work at the meso and macro levels when encountering the difficulties and experiences of women.

Conclusion

In essentialist maternalism based on heterosexist Patriarchy, mothers are subjected to socio-structural oppression, as they are expected to be the primary caregivers. They are exalted/blamed for this by being made personally responsible, and they are economically and psychologically oppressed due to care duties being unpaid labour. Mothers are also politically disempowered. Underlying these social injustices is an excessive belief in essentialist maternalism. To change this situation, maternalism itself must be relativised. The 'strategic maternalism' examined in this chapter is a useful perspective on resistance to Patriarchy. To this end, social workers can undertake the following three things.

First, they must analyse their gender lens: social workers must re-examine their internalised maternalism from the perspective of feminism and gender. Second, rather than demanding essentialist maternalism from individual clients who are mothers, they must commit to the creation of social conditions that make care possible; that is, engage in meso/macro practices. Social workers must shift their support toward empowerment and end complacency regarding maternal oppression. Third, they should create interactive relationships with interested parties, colleagues, and stakeholders and collaborate for social and political empowerment. Reflective practice will provide the circuit to perpetuate their engagement and speak out through their professional associations, such as civic organisations, about resisting the oppression of women and mothers. As various social systems and institutions are gendered, social work requires a collaborative response to structural oppression.

Acknowledgement

This work was supported by JSPS KAKENHI Grant Number JP21K02027.

References

Adrienne, R. (2010). *Of woman born: Motherhood as experience and institution.* W. W. Norton & Company.
Berger, M., Asaba, E., Fallahpour, M., & Farias, L. (2022). The sociocultural shaping of mothers' doing, being, becoming and belonging after returning to work. *Journal of Occupational Science, 29,* 7–20. https://doi.org/10.1080/14427591.2020.1845226
Butler, J. (2006). *Gender trouble: Feminism and the subversion of identity.* Routledge.
Doblhammer, G., & Gumà, J. (2018). Summary and research implications, In G. Doblhammer & J. Gumà (Eds.), *A demographic perspective on gender, family and health in Europe.* Springer Nature.

Dominelli, L. (2002). *Feminist social work*. Palgrave Macmillan.
Dowling, E. M., & Haukin, S. L. (2009). Single mothers, work, and poverty: Assessing the role of policy and practice. *Affilia: Journal of Women and Social Work, 24*(3), 263–274.
Fineman, M. A. (2004). *The autonomy myth: A theory of dependency*. The New Press.
Giles, M. V. (2019). *Mothering, neoliberalism, and globalization*. The Routledge Companion to Motherhood, 1st Edition. Routledge.
Gilligan, C. (1982). *In a different voice: Psychological theory and women's development*. Harvard University Press.
Glenn, E. N. (2016). *Social constructions of mothering: A thematic overview*. Routledge.
Hays, S. (2007). Addressing the complexity of motherhood: Implications for feminist practice and social work education. *Affilia: Journal of Women and Social Work, 22*(4), 431–443.
Inoue, K. (2013). Gendai Nippon No Hahaoya Kihan To Jiko Aidentiti [Maternal Norms and Self-Identity in Modern Japan] [in Japanese], Kazama Shobo.
Kittay, E. F. (1999). *Love's labor: Essays on women, equality, and dependency*. Routledge.
Kittay, E. F. (2015). Le désir de normalité. Quelle qualité de vie pour les personnes porteuses de handicap cognitive sévère? [Quality of life and the desire for normalcy: Problems, prospects, and possibilities in the life of people with severe cognitive disability]. *Alter, 9*(3), 175–185. https://doi.org/10.1016/j.alter.2015.05.003
Kromydas, T. (2020). Educational attainment and gender differences in work–life balance for couples across Europe: A contextual perspective. *Social Inclusion, 8*(4), 8–22. https://doi.org/10.17645/si.v8i4.2920
Lehman, J. S. & Beale, A. T. (2018). Feminist social work practice: Promoting women's rights and empowerment. *Social Work, 63*(2), 125–133.
Litman, L., Robinson, J., Rosen, Z., Rosenzweig, C., Waxman, J., & Bates, L. M. (2020). The persistence of pay inequality: The gender pay gap in an anonymous online labor market. *PLoS ONE, 15*(2), e0229383. https://doi.org/10.1371/journal.pone.0229383
Maldonado, L. C., & Nieuwenhuis, R. (2015). Family policies and single parent poverty in 18 OECD countries, 1978–2008. *Community, Work & Family, 18*, 395–415. https://doi.org/10.1080/13668803.2015.1080661
Ministry of Health, Labour and Welfare. (2019). Overview of the 2019 comprehensive survey of living conditions. https://www.mhlw.go.jp/toukei/saikin/hw/k-tyosa/k-tyosa19/dl/03.pdf
Ministry of Health, Labour and Welfare. (2021). National survey of single-parent households. https://www.mhlw.go.jp/content/11920000/001027800.pdf
Miyaji, N. (2004). Sōron: Torauma to jendā wa ika ni musubitsuiteiru ka [Outline: How are trauma and gender linked?]. In Naoko Miyaji (Ed.), *Torauma to jendā: Rinshō Kara No Koe* [Trauma and gender: Voices from the clinics]. Kongo Shuppan. [in Japanese]
Motohashi, R. (2021). *Bosei no yokuatsu to teikō: Kea no rinri o tōshite kangaeru senryakuteki bosei shugi* [The oppression and resistance of motherhood: Strategic maternalism considered through the ethics of care]. Koyo Shobo. [in Japanese]
Mussida, C., & Patimo, R. (2021). Women's family care responsibilities, employment and health: A tale of two countries. *Journal of Family and Economic Issues, 42*, 489–507. https://doi.org/10.1007/s10834-020-09742-4
Okin, S. M. (1999). *Justice, gender, and the family*. Basic Books.
Oláh, L. S., Kotowska, I. E., & Richter, R. (2018). The new roles of men and women and implications for families and societies. In G. Doblhammer & J. Gumà (Eds.), *A demographic perspective on gender, family and health in Europe*. Springer Nature.
Orme, J. (2015). Gendered care and social work practice. *International Encyclopedia of the Social & Behavioral Sciences, 2015*, 800–805. https://doi.org/10.1016/B978-0-08-097086-8.28034-3
Phillips, R. (2015). Feminist research and social work. *International Encyclopedia of the Social & Behavioral Sciences, 2015*, 935–941. https://doi.org/10.1016/B978-0-08-097086-8.28033-1
Polar, B. (2022). Mother, service user, and social worker. *Journal of the Motherhood Initiative, 13*(1), 107–126.
Ruddick, S. (1989). *Maternal thinking: Toward a politics of peace*. Beacon Press.
Singh, P., & Pattanaik, F. (2020). Unfolding unpaid domestic work in India: Women's constraints, choices, and career. *Palgrave Communications, 6*(1), 1–13. https://doi.org/10.1057/s41599-020-0488-2

Stephens, J. (2011). *Confronting postmaternal thinking: Feminism, memory, and care*. Columbia University Pres.
Strega, S., Fleet, C., Brown, L., Dominelli, L., Callahan, M., & Walmsley, C. (2008). Connecting father absence and mother blame in child welfare policies and practice. *Children and Youth Services Review, 30*, 705–716.
Turner, S., & Krane, J. (2014). Moving beyond 'resilience' in social work practice: Unveiling invisible unconscious bias and privilege in working with women of color. *Affilia: Journal of Women and Social Work, 29*(1), 52–66.

33
MATRICENTRIC FEMINIST SOCIAL WORK

Towards an organising conceptual framework and practice approach to support empowered mothering

Sarah Epstein and Pippa Mulley

Introduction

**Recognition of the ways that patriarchal motherhood undermines gender justice is important for social workers committed to our core values of human rights and social justice. To do this, it is helpful to draw on feminist theorising of patriarchal motherhood grounded in Adrienne Rich's (1976) distinction between motherhood as an institution and mothering as experience and identity. As an institution, motherhood essentialises maternity leaving the mother vulnerable to discursive, structural and material practices that restrict the value of the work, constrains maternal subjectivity and risks reproducing gender inequality. Conversely, feminist maternal theory and practice recognise mothering as activity, simultaneously constituting the maternal subject and centring experiences of mothering.

This chapter reviews the culturally dominant regime of patriarchal motherhood and the constraints and risks that result in people undertaking motherwork. Matricentric feminist theory, pioneered by Andrea O'Reilly (2019) argues mothers are marginalised and oppressed at the intersection of gender identity *and* maternal identity. The authors draw on matricentric feminism to consider the impact of patriarchal motherhood within the social work service context that places motherwork under surveillance and holds mothers accountable to patriarchal ideals about essentialised maternity. Attention is drawn to the tension for social workers, and consequences for service users, when it comes to working with mothers within social work service structures and practices that are shaped by the ideology of patriarchal motherhood. In response, we consider a matricentric feminist-informed framework for social work practice designed to support mothers to mother outside the institution of motherhood and disrupt patriarchal relations of power.

Patriarchal motherhood

The relationship between feminism and motherhood has shifted and turned into a dynamic process, often revealing conflict (Kinser 2010) and demanding repudiation of the patriarchally constructed mother (Friedan 2001). However, there is general agreement that what it means to be a mother, as well as ideas about who can and should carry out the work that mothering entails, is proscribed by a culturally dominant patriarchal motherhood discourse. Feminist maternal scholarship refers to this patriarchal regime as the institution of motherhood (Rich 1976; Green 2019; O'Reilly 2019; 2021). This regime materially and discursively constrains people who mother, as well as their children, as they face distinct obstacles that intersect with their social location as 'mothers', the material and cultural conditions within which they undertake motherwork and by virtue of their gender identity (O'Reilly 2021).

The institution of motherhood shapes the maternal subject through 'her' biological potential for reproduction (Berger et al. 2020; Sinai-Glazer et al. 2020; O'Reilly 2021), the allocation of primary responsibility for 'her' children's well-being (Buchanan and Moulding 2021) and the withholding of social power (Mulkeen 2012). Sequestered away from public life, often economically reliant, unpaid motherwork is afforded little value. Simultaneously, however, the mother is vulnerable to intense public and social surveillance and scrutiny of their child's health, development and behaviour. This is because patriarchal motherhood imposes ideals that establish expectations and allocate duties and responsibilities for children to mothers (Tazi-Preve 2019; Green 2021). Deviation poses risks for anyone undertaking motherwork with 'bad mother' status allocated to any mother who is not constantly present or bearing full responsibility for all the needs of the children (Tazi-Preve 2019). Understanding the social structure that attributes the values to the idea of 'bad mother' is essential to the dynamics of mother-blaming practice (Fleckinger 2022).

Mothers are positioned within a regulatory framework whereby binary measures of the omniscient 'good' and distracted 'bad' mother are constructed according to patriarchal understandings of what a mother can and should do (Allan 2004). Mothers are always at risk of being labelled a 'bad mother' if they are not wholly present or capable of caring for their child or if they are not seen to be doing so with enthusiasm and ease (Fleckinger 2020; Sinai-Glazer et al. 2020). The institution of motherhood is "almost impossible for most mothers to achieve, including those who do conform to social norms" (Filax & Taylor 2021, p. 676). This is to emphasise that the binary cul-de-sac of the good/bad mother privileges patriarchal norms at the expense of the conditions within which mothering occurs.

Social work and patriarchy

Social work and social support sector research have identified the substantial challenges women face when engaged with systems such as Child Protection whereby women are "subjected to the deficit gaze of the state where technocratic risk assessment procedures increasingly construct mothers as 'failing to protect' their children" (De Simone and Heward-Belle 2020, p. 406) Social workers are often at the interface of determining how normative behaviour is defined (Davies et al. 2003; Weinberg 2010). Gendered discourses are used to frame social work responses to mothers particularly those who have experienced domestic violence (Wild 2022), with women framed as "passive victims" who are unable to care for their children (Buchanan and Moulding 2021). Fleckinger (2020) found that social workers often caused secondary victimisation to victim-survivors of domestic violence due to their expectations of the women both as mothers and as victims as delineated by a patriarchal social system. Entrenched patriarchal motherhood ideals within service responses hold people who mother accountable to the good/bad mother dichotomy and so mothers who fail to reach this ideal are expected to access professional support (Buchanan 2016). For example, in child welfare services where mothers are also survivors of domestic violence, social work responses have been criticised for the construction of victim-survivors as 'bad mothers' who are responsible for their partner's violence (De Simone and Heward-Belle 2020). Patriarchal values are also applied within the family court system, whereby perpetrators of domestic and family abuse are labelled as 'good fathers' (De Simone and Heward Belle 2020) and mother victim-survivors are penalised for failing to protect children from abusive partners (Wendt and Moulding 2017). Child well-being issues are often linked to a mother's parenting capabilities; therefore, protective issues are seen as a failure on the part of the mother (Buchanan 2016), while the father's behaviour is often absent from consideration (Arnull & Stewart 2021). Furthermore, victim-survivors of domestic and family abuse who practice motherwork often experience victim blaming due to support services overfocus on the mother's behaviour or mental health (Khaw et al. 2021). Social work practices need to shift focus from mothers' 'failures' and instead focus on the multiple impacts that domestic and family abuse has on family functioning (Lapierre 2010).

Mother blaming is not a new practice because the patriarchal conditions within which motherhood is constructed rest on gender essentialism and therefore the mother (who is female) is considered the 'natural' and 'best' caregiver. This paradigm valorises the impact of mother-child relationships and the importance of attachment and bonding with the mother. This combines to hold mothers accountable to greater scrutiny (Courcy & Des Rivières 2017). Employing mother blame within social work practice is a component of a patriarchal society, with any scrutiny of the impact of gender and power being largely absent (Arnull & Stewart 2021).

Experiences of mothering and associated social work responses are often positioned within neoliberal contexts that operate to discriminate against marginalised mothers who are mothering in challenging situations (Zufferey and Buchanan 2020). For example, mothers who suffer from a mental illness, who are homeless, who experience domestic and family abuse or who are incarcerated are all discriminated against for not fitting into the 'good' mother discourse (Zufferey and Buchanan 2020). Gallardo and Guerra (2021) highlighted that the 'good' mother discourse creates a homogenous vision of motherhood whereby the complexities and diversities of women's lived experiences are rendered invisible. Other aspects of mother's gender identities intersect to compound oppression, for example, Aboriginal women, women from culturally and linguistically diverse backgrounds, disabled women and women who have been incarcerated are at an increased risk of receiving a lower standard of social service care (Heward-Belle 2018). Furthermore, expectations of mothering are built around white cis-gender heterosexual norms which negatively impact both black mothers and LGBTQIA+ mothers (Forbes et al. 2021).

The ways in which social and criminal policies are enacted against people who mother, especially in the context of domestic and family abuse, are principally white-centric and heteronormative with no consideration for the impact of intersecting oppressions or marginalisations (Arnull & Stewart 2021). Intersectionality is unrecognised in child welfare legislation where concepts of motherhood are permeated by racist and cultural stereotypes and biases (Zufferey and Buchanan, 2020). Killeen (2019, p. 624) argues that mothers "who are situated outside of white visions of motherhood face steeper challenges to being seen by the state and society as "good" mothers". Black mothers are disproportionately punished by both the welfare and the criminal justice system, with black women being over-represented in prisons and facing greater obstacles in returning home once freed (Thompson & Newell 2021).

Implications for social work

The dominant narrative of patriarchal motherhood also reflects the experiences of cisgender women and men who are white, heterosexual, able-bodied and middle-class (Fischer 2021). This is problematic for social work service user demographics because the institution of motherhood is regularly reinforced through social discourse, material structures and surveillance mechanisms endemic to social work service systems, policies and practices (Fleckinger 2020). Not only do mothers feel more pressure to take on responsibility for motherwork, but patriarchal motherhood norms also infiltrate all aspects of society making mothers particularly vulnerable to being assessed and surveilled in their care-taking role (Berger et al. 2020). Failure to meet norms has been found to reduce mother's self-determination and impacts their well-being (Berger et al. 2020). The tension for those doing motherwork is related to their sense of obligation to fulfil patriarchally defined motherhood ideals and to subsume any hopes or desires to experience lives not specifically connected to their motherwork (Berger et al. 2020). The essentialising of motherhood as a natural expression of women's innate nurturing capacity (Davies et al. 2003) creates internal conflict and limits mothers' sense of entitlement (Wilcock and Hocking 2015). Internalised expectations to fulfil patriarchal motherhood ideals (Davies et al. 2003) further position mothers' vulnerability to the good/bad mother dichotomy (Sinai-Glazer et al. 2020; O'Reilly 2021).

Disrupting patriarchal motherhood

Feminist maternal scholarship is interested in exploring the multiplicity of mothering experiences to understand the ways that people who mother make choices, exercise values and ideals in, and through their interactions, with their children and in response to diverse socio-cultural contexts. Feminist maternal scholarship has sought to expose the oppressive conditions within which motherwork takes place (Horwitz 2004) and is inclusive of the diverse lived experiences and gender identities of people who mother (Green 2019; Brant & Anderson 2021; Riggs et al. 2021).

Theorising of motherhood and maternal practice has consolidated over the last 30 years into an academic field and an important area of research that uses a feminist standpoint as a framework for people who engage in mothering so that they can normalise, validate and understand their experiences of motherhood as an institution (Green 2019; O'Reilly 2021). This scholarship conceptualises people who mother as agentic and is interested in supporting people who mother to draw on and justify feelings, hopes and expectations that are 'at odds' with dominant motherhood discourse. Within this framework, patriarchal motherhood is destabilised, exposing inconsistencies and rendering visible diverse maternal practices.

Adrienne Rich's ground-breaking 1976 publication "Of Woman Born: Motherhood as Experience and Institution" has been the galvanising call for feminist maternal scholars seeking to centre mothers' lived experiences to understand both the machinations, and impact, of patriarchal expectations of what a mother should and shouldn't feel, do and be (Rich 1976). In making the distinction between motherhood as an institution and the experience of mothering, the foundation was laid for making visible the thinking and doing of motherwork. Because motherhood operates as a patriarchal institution that positions women outside of meaningful social engagement (O'Reilly 2019) any activity that seeks to render the mother visible is antithetical to patriarchal motherhood and is a vital tool for mothers' empowerment. Feminist maternal scholar Andrea O'Reilly (2021) who has spear-headed global research, theory and practice in matricentric feminism over the last few decades argues that of singular import to understanding mothers' lived experiences is that "real change for mothers cannot be achieved if it is always defined as for and about children" (p. 814).

Matricentric feminist social work

As feminist social workers, we have been thinking about the relationship between feminist maternal scholarship and feminist social work theory and practice. We have engaged with social work research literature about mothers and it seems clear that there is a complex and problematic relationship between agency parameters, social work practice response and service users who are also doing motherwork. It appears that often social work responses to people who mother are not successful in enacting socially just transformative practice because they do not resist patriarchal motherhood and therefore cannot support maternal empowerment.

People who mother face distinct obstacles that are connected to their social location as 'mothers', the conditions within which they undertake motherwork and the patriarchal institution of motherhood (Green 2019; O'Reilly 2019; 2021). This has been the context in which Andrea O'Reilly (2016) proposed the importance of feminism for people who mother, and about people who mother (Green 2019). Matricentric feminism is a feminism that recognises that motherwork matters and has been developed in response to O'Reilly's (2021) research into the disavowal and disappearance of mothering in academic feminism and the concern that motherhood remains the "unfinished business of feminism". Matricentric feminism does not question that mother-centred feminism is necessary and "has emerged as a result of, and in response to women's specific identities and work as mothers" (O'Reilly 2021). Matricentric feminism seeks to make visible, and centre, the socially and historically constructed practice of work that is mothering (O'Reilly 2021). Matricentric feminism makes visible maternal ethics of care (Epstein 2015) and works to reinstate authority to motherwork at the same time as revealing the patriarchal constraints and relations of power that are oppressive to people who occupy the social location of a mother (O'Reilly 2021). Importantly, "a matricentric feminism seeks to make motherhood the business of feminism by positioning mothers' needs and concerns as the starting point for a theory and politic on, and for, women's empowerment" (O'Reilly 2021). We would contend that matricentric feminism can also make motherwork the business of feminist social work.

Matricentric feminism is a form of feminist praxis that contributes to the development and practice of feminism by drawing on knowledge of the experiences of mothering against patriarchal motherhood. Drawing from this work and building on feminist social work's commitment to, and understanding of, gender justice, we have started to think about a framework for supporting matricentric feminist social work practice.

A critical appraisal of patriarchal motherhood

Social work, in general, is committed to socially just practice that recognises what service users need to realise their human rights, and, what they are concerned with to exercise self-determination and be empowered in their lives (AASW 2020). Feminist social work takes steps towards ensuring that there are specific needs and human rights risks as a result of service users' gendered social positioning (Epstein et al. 2018). Moreover, Zufferey and Buchanan (2020) have argued that matricentric feminism offers an intersectional theory and politics for mothers whereby they are "oppressed under patriarchy as women and as mothers". Matricentric feminism recognises that the category of mother is distinct from the category of woman and therefore many of the challenges to self-determination (and therefore empowerment) that come with engaging in motherwork are specific to their role and identity as mothers (Green 2019; O'Reilly 2021). This is inclusive of social, economic, political, cultural and psychological realities. We would contend that matricentric feminist social work starts from the understanding that service users who mother are at risk of being oppressed as a result of both patriarchal motherhood (including the gender binary this is predicated on) and a service response paradigm that does not intentionally engage with patriarchal motherhood conditions. Unexamined constructions of the mother as a function of patriarchal motherhood pervade all areas of social work practice (Davies et al. 2003). As long as social work is enacted without a critical appraisal of patriarchal motherhood, we risk reinforcing the patriarchal institution of motherhood as a function of an oppressive gendered regime (Mulkeen 2012).

Avoiding the good mother/bad mother dichotomy

Feminist social workers employ a feminist ethos in understanding the ways that patriarchy shapes women's experiences; supporting practitioners to resist blaming women for experiences of violence. However, research details idealised motherhood, and the bad mother discourse continues to subjugate women's experiences of mothering and blame (Wild 2022) While as women their experiences may be validated, gendered discourses see mothers blamed for family failure and domestic abuse (Wild 2022). Buchanan and Moulding (2021) suggest that the discourse of mother-blame is so prevalent, that practitioners often fail to identify the nuanced ways in which mothers are protecting their children, so that women's motives, emotions and the exercise of their agency to protect are not explored. Emphasis on the way that patriarchal motherhood is oppressive to both women and to mothers is going to support social workers to "interrogate their practice for any ways that encourage stereotypical gender roles and consider the impact of this on their clients" (Allan 2004).

While it may not be wholly possible to enact core social work values and ethics within the neoliberal logics of modern agency operation and function, as well as diminishing resources (Weinberg 2010), it is still possible to enact liberatory practices by operating outside of institutional regimes such as patriarchal motherhood. Patriarchal motherhood reproduces and maintains oppressive structures, including the gender binary and gendered hierarchy, at the same time as setting people who mother up to being judged and surveilled according to patriarchal measures and needs. Social workers who do not recognise and question this institution are at risk of circulating bad mother discourses and this can be conceptualised as problematic ethical practice. Everyday ethical decision-making enables social workers to make choices about the lens through which they make sense of service users lives and it is in these moments where emancipatory possibilities exist (Weinberg 2010). Engaging in matricentric feminist social work creates the opportunity to centre mothers' lives but it also offers social workers the opportunity to undermine and disrupt rigid gender stereotypes. These two actions enable a starting point to operate outside of a structure and institution that undermines maternal agency and authority.

Reinstating agency and authority by documenting mothering experiences and rendering the mother visible

An underlying driver of feminist maternal scholarship is the potential for mothering to be a location for change and empowerment (Green 2021; O'Reilly 2021). According to O'Reilly any theoretical consideration of what empowered mothering looks like "begins by positioning mothers as 'outlaws from the institution of motherhood' and seeks to imagine and implement a maternal identity and practice that empowers mothers" (O'Reilly 2021, p. 608). This starting point has much to offer social work's objectives of social justice through self-determination (AASW 2020) beginning with reclaiming ways for direct practice to seek out mother's experiences. This involves gaining an understanding of the conditions in which maternal practice occurs as well as efforts to invite mothers' accounts of how they have indeed ended up at the social work organisation in the first place.

To avoid complicity in the perpetuation of patriarchal motherhood we can activate a matricentric feminist standpoint that documents "the lived reality of mothering" (O'Reilly 2021, p. 460). This is a reminder for social workers to find ways of understanding what life is like for the service user we are working with. What messages is the mother receiving about motherhood? That is, to what set of rules and norms does the mother believe they are being held accountable to? And, as a result, what is this like for the mother? How does the mother believe they are being seen to measure up to these standards? This too invites the social worker to consider the messages that we, our agency and the agency remit, are projecting onto mothering. Matricentric feminist social work practice finds ways to create space for maternal authenticity to emerge.

If we, and our agency are holding maternal practice accountable to patriarchal motherhood then what opportunities do we have to truly meet the mothers where they are at? If we were, for a moment, to suspend patriarchal surveillance what more might we learn – about the mothering experience, about the obstacles faced and about the potential to change these? How might a matricentric focus position the mother as central to the development of the story we are constructing about her? The contention is that this is not able to happen within a patriarchal motherhood paradigm whereby the children are the focus. What more can be envisioned for the child when the mother's experiences and intentions are part of the story? A matricentric focus can consider the mothers' perspective as the key to going forward. If feminist mothering seeks to challenge and transform the impact that patriarchal motherhood has in reproducing oppressive conditions (O'Reilly 2021) then a feminist social work framework that operates with a matricentric lens needs to consider how this can happen within the practice context.

Activating existing social work practice and remembering how to normalise, validate and universalise

Feminist maternal scholarship emphasises that empowered mothering starts with mothering against patriarchal motherhood. What opportunities might feminist social workers have to be a part of this, and to facilitate opportunities for mothers to do so if we draw on this knowledge? Perhaps it starts with changing the way that we think about motherhood and interrogating assumptions we bring to our work about what mothers can be and should do? Understanding the patriarchal conditions in which the service user is undertaking their motherwork is the key to recognising the assumptions in the first place. However, we can get closer to this by centring mothers' lived experiences and learning about the impact of patriarchal expectations on the service user. This includes the contextual restraints pertaining to culture and society that circulate classist, racist, homophobic, transphobic and gendered stereotypes. In turn, this can dislodge the lens that is being employed by the social worker making it easier to consider practice responses better able to address mother-blaming practices (De Simone and Heward Belle 2020).

Once maternal lived experiences are centred it is also possible to share knowledge about patriarchal motherhood norms, constructs and unrealistic expectations. Social workers are already comfortable with normalising and validating service users' experiences so it may be valuable to extend these practices by drawing on knowledge of the impact and experience of patriarchal motherhood to justify, validate and universalise these experiences and feelings. While mothering experiences are contextually specific, sharing what we know about the normative standards of patriarchal motherhood legitimates their experience and also supports maternal authenticity by consciousness raising around the impossibility of meeting patriarchally defined maternal standards. Further, the social worker contributes to dismantling the institution of motherhood because alternative possibilities dislodge patriarchal truth claims. Both worker and service user are then able to re-orient maternal subjectivity in ways that may be better aligned with maternal goals, hopes and intentions. This is an agentic activity foundational to empowerment.

Conclusion

This chapter draws on the critique of mother blaming and maternal scrutiny prevalent in the social work and social service literature to justify consideration of matricentric feminist social work. Key to socially just social work practice, and feminist social work's objective of achieving gender justice in general, is an understanding of the relations of power that subjugate mothers' lived experiences. Patriarchal motherhood as an institution establishes, and maintains, impossible ideals and standards whereby mothers as women, non-binary and gender diverse folx face double scrutiny. Patriarchal accountability measures permeate society, including social work practice, whereby the conditions in which mothers carry out motherwork are marginalised. Further, mothers are allocated responsibility for children's problems whilst simultaneously being given responsibility for fixing them. It is simply not fair to allocate disproportionate responsibility to the mother for the success of their children without considering the context and conditions within which mothers are expected to do this work. It is also not fair to hold mothers responsible without affording them authority and agency over what to do when something has not gone well. Matricentric feminist social work practice applies a critical lens to idealised motherhood to support social workers to bring mothers in from the margins and build empowering relationships cognisant of gendered dynamics and patriarchal surveillance of their motherwork. Matricentric feminist social work applies a critical gaze to motherhood as an institution and, through the process of rendering the mother visible, is antithetical to patriarchal motherhood and is the key to disrupting this regime. As such it is a potentially liberatory social work practice approach necessary for mothers' empowerment. The chapter reflects our beginning thinking in this practice area and we welcome on-going conversation, debate and discussion going forward.

References

AASW. (2020). *Code of Ethics*. https://www.aasw.asn.au/about-aasw/ethics-standards/code-of-ethics/

Allan, J. (2004). Mother blaming: a covert practice in therapeutic intervention. *Australian Social Work*, 57(1), 57–70. https://doi.org.10.1111/j.0312-407X.2003.00114.x

Arnull, E. & Stewart, S. (2021). Developing a theoretical framework to discuss mothers experiencing domestic violence and being subject to interventions: a cross-national perspective. *International Journal for Crime, Justice and Social Democracy*, 10(2), 113–126. https://doi.org/10.5204/ijcjsd.1561

Berger, M., Asaba, E., Fallahpour, M. & Farias, L. (2020). The sociocultural shaping of mothers' doing, being, becoming and belonging after returning to work. *Journal of Occupational Science*, 29(1), 7–20. https://doi.org/10.1080/14427591.2020.1845226

Brant, J. & Anderson, K. (2021). Indigenous mothering: new insights on giving life to the people. In A. O'Reilly (Ed.), *Maternal theory: essential readings* (pp. 713–734). Demeter Press.

Buchanan, F. (2016). Child wellbeing, mothering, protection. In S. Wendt & N. Moulding (Eds.), *Contemporary feminisms in social work practice* (pp. 196–207). Routledge.

Buchanan, F. & Moulding, N. (2021). Mothering during domestic abuse: protective agency as a force for change. *Qualitative Social Work: Research and Practice*, 20(3), 665–680. http://doi.org/10.1177/1473325020917743

Courcy, I. & Des Rivières, C. (2017). "From cause to cure": a qualitative study on contemporary forms of mother blaming experienced by mothers of young children with autism spectrum disorder. *Journal of Family Social Work*, 20(3), 233–250. https://doi.org/10.1080/10522158.2017.1292184

Davies, L., Collings, S. & Krane, J. (2003). Making mothers visible: implications for social work practice and education in child welfare. *Journal of the Motherhood Initiative for Research and Community Involvement*, 5(2), 158–169.

De Simone, T., & Heward-Belle, S. (2020). Evidencing better child protection practice: Why representations of domestic violence matter. *Current Issues in Criminal Justice*, 32(4), 403–419.

Epstein, S. (2015). Making women visible in boys' lives. In M. Flood & R. Howson (Eds.), *Engaging men in building gender equality* (pp. 234–242). Cambridge Scholars Publishing.

Epstein, S., Hosken, N. & Vassos, S. (2018). Creating space for a critical feminist social work pedagogy. *Aotearoa New Zealand Social Work*, 30(3), 8–18. https://doi.org/10.11157/anzswjvol30iss3id489

Filax, G. & Taylor, D. (2021). Disabled mothers. In A. O'Reilly (Ed.), *Maternal theory: essential readings* (pp. 691–704). Demeter Press.

Fischer, O. (2021). Forging crossroads: the possibilities and complexities of parenting outside the gender binary. In A. O'Reilly (Ed.), *Maternal theory: essential readings* (pp. 811–822). Demeter Press.

Fleckinger, A. (2020). The dynamics of secondary victimization: when social workers blame mothers. *Research on Social Work Practice*, 30(5), 515–523. https://doi.org/10.1177%2F1049731519898525

Fleckinger, A. (2022). The father absence-mother blame paradigm in child protection social work: an Italian feminist single case study. *European Journal of Social Work* [S.I 2022]. https://doi.org/10.1080/13691457.2022.2045259

Forbes, L., Lamar, M. & Bornstein, R. (2021). Working mothers' experiences in an intensive mothering culture: a phenomenological qualitative study. *Journal of Feminist Family Therapy*, 33(3), 270–294. https://doi.org/10.1080/08952833.2020.1798200

Friedan, B. (2001). *The feminine mystique*, Reprint ed. W. W. Norton & Company.

Gallardo, R. & Guerra, K. (2021). Resistant maternities: political-affective resignifications of women activists in the Chilean post-dictatorship. *Propuestas Críticas en Trabajo Social - Critical Proposals in Social Work*, 1(2), 72–94. https://doi.org/10.5354/2735-6620.2021.61156

Green, F. (2019). Practicing matricentric feminist mothering. *Journal of the Motherhood Initiative for Research and Community Involvement*, 10(1/2). https://jarm.journals.yorku.ca/index.php/jarm/article/view/40555

Green, F. (2021). The motherline. In A. O'Reilly (Ed.), *Maternal theory: essential readings* (pp. 659–678). Demeter Press.

Horwitz, E. (2004). Resistance as a site of empowerment: the journey away from maternal sacrifice. In A. O'reilly (Ed.), *Mother outlaws: theories and practices of empowered mothering* (pp. 43–58). Women's Press.

Khaw, L., Bermea, A., Hardesty, J., Saunders, D. & Whittaker, A. (2021). "The system had choked me too": abused mothers' perceptions of the custody determination process that resulted in negative custody outcomes. *Journal of Interpersonal Violence*, 36(9), 4310–4334. https://doi.org/10.1177/0886260518791226

Killeen, K. (2019). "Can you hear me now?" Race, motherhood and the politics of being heard. *Politics & Gender*, 15(1), 623–644. https://doi.org/10.1017/S1743923X18000697

Kinser, A. (2010). *Motherhood and feminism*. Seal Press.

Lapierre, S. (2010). Striving to be 'good' mothers: abused women's experiences of mothering. *Child Abuse Review*, 19(1), 42–57. https://doi.org/10.1002/car.1113

Mulkeen, M. (2012). Gendered processes in child protection: 'mother-blaming' and the erosion of men's accountability. *Irish Journal of Applied Social Studies*, 12(1), 74–88. http://doi.org/10.21427/D7H721

O'Reilly, A. (2016). *Matricentric feminism: theory, activism and practice*. Demeter Press.

O'Reilly, A. (2019). Matricentric feminism: a feminism for mothers. *Journal of the Motherhood Initiative for Research and Community Involvement*, 10(1), 13–26.

O'Reilly, A. (2021). Matricentric feminism: a feminism for mothers. In A. O'Reilly (Ed.), *Maternal theory: essential readings* (pp. 792–821). Demeter Press.

Rich, A. (1976). *Of woman born: motherhood as experience and institution*. W. W. Norton & Company.

Riggs, D., Hines, S., Pearce, R., Pfeffer, C. & White, F. (2021). Trans parenting. In A. O'Reilly (Ed.), *Maternal theory: essential readings* (pp. 823–832). Demeter Press.

Sinai-Glazer, H., Lipshes-Niv, M. & Peled, E. (2020). The construction of maternal identity among Israeli mothers who are welfare clients. *Child & Family Social Work*, 25(1), 28–36. https://doi.org/10.1111/cfs.12709

Tazi-Preve, M. (2019). Unveiling patriarchal motherhood. *Canadian Womens Studies*, 34(1), 163–173.

Thompson, M. & Newell, S. (2021). *Motherhood after incarceration: community reintegration for mothers in the criminal legal system*. Routledge.

Weinberg, M. (2010). The social construction of social work ethics: politicizing and broadening the lens. *Journal of Progressive Human Services*, 21(1), 32–44. https://doi.org/10.1080/10428231003781774

Wendt, S. & Moulding, N. (2017). The current state of feminism and social work. *Australian Journal of Social Work*, 70(3), 261–262. https://doi.org/10.1080/0312407X.2017.1314752

Wilcock, A. & Hocking, C. (2015). *An occupational perspective of health*. Slack Inc.

Wild, J. (2022). Gendered discourses of responsibility and domestic abuse victim-blame in the English children's social care system. *Journal of Family Violence*, 1(1), 1–13. https://doi-org.ezproxy-b.deakin.edu.au/10.1007/s10896-022-00431-4

Zufferey, C. & Buchanan, F. (2020). *Intersections of mothering: feminist accounts*. Routledge.

34
FEMINIZED CARE WORK, SOCIAL WORK AND RESISTANCE IN THE CONTEXT OF LATE NEOLIBERALISM

Donna Baines

Introduction

As an academic discipline and profession, social work has diverse roots and conflicting models of theory, knowledge and practice (Kennedy Kish et al., 2017). Reflecting these divisions, some social workers have sought to increase their status and legitimacy by regulating the use of the title "social worker" and requiring those who use it to be degree-bearing licensed (Hallahan & Wendt, 2019; Jones, 2019). Others have pursued more permeable, inclusive understandings of social workers as a predominantly female, skilled and often social justice-engaged workforce providing care to a highly inequitable, gendered, racialized and classed world (Jennissen & Lundy, 2018; Kennedy Kish et al., 2017). This chapter reflects on the professionalization of social workers and the inequities it reproduces as well as the contrasting conceptualization of social workers as a highly feminized group of workers involved in care and service as everyday practices of resistance and dignity. The chapter begins by problematizing "care" and social work's strategy of distancing itself from care work through professionalization. The analysis turns to the neoliberal, managerialized, marketized and contracted-out contexts of social work. The chapter then argues that social work's closeness to the struggles of service users and the austere conditions of neoliberalism generates gendered forms of resistance that are simultaneously a form of self-exploitation that may inadvertently legitimize neoliberalism and a force for extending social justice. The chapter concludes with additional practices to equip social work with emancipatory strategies in the context of neoliberalism's on-going austerity and inequity.

Care and care work

Joan Tronto (2013) notes that care is generally taken for granted though everyone receives care throughout their lifetimes and most people provide some sort of care to others throughout their lives. However, care is commonly thought to be the unending responsibility of women and as such it is hard to delineate paid care work from what women are expected to do "naturally" as an aspect of being a wife, a mother, a sister, a daughter or even a colleague, neighbour or friend (Daly et al., 2016). Connecting working conditions and pay with many forms of care is seen by some to cast it as a cold economic transaction rather than a whole-hearted, family-based labour of love that requires no reward beyond itself (Bahn et al., 2020; Folbre, 2017).

Tronto (2013 argues further that democracy and social justice require the on-going care and participation of all citizens. Similarly, "an acceptable way to allocate caring responsibilities must be fostered in a way that…achieves the goals of freedom, equality, and justice" (Tronto, 2013, p. 141). Hence, the just and fair allocation of care work extends beyond an individual's need for care as it advances values and practices aimed at building a more caring, socially just and socially-engaged society.

A feminist intersectional analysis assists in understanding care work as a feminized and racialized endeavour that is simultaneously interwoven with other aspects of identity and social location such class, (dis)ability, age, region, sexual identity and orientation (Carbado et al., 2013; Combahee River Collective, 1977; Crenshaw, 2017; Hill Collins & Bilge, 2016), though as Yuval-Davis (2006) notes, we can never fully list the totality of intersecting oppressions and privileges. Intersectional analysis argues that oppressive forces never operate in complete isolation from each other. Instead, they form a complex and constantly changing web of oppressions and privileges depending on the context and the people involved (Hill Collins & Bilge, 2016).

Care work tends to be stratified into better paid female "professions" such as social work and nursing; quasi-professionalized groups such as child care, community support worker and home care workers; and not-professionalized groups such as personal support worker, disability worker, nanny, housekeeper, and so on. Professionalized care workers tend to reflect the privileges of class including university education. It also reflects the segmentations of race meaning that professionalized care workers in the global north are more likely to be white and receive better pay, conditions and job security. In contrast, not-professional care workers are likely to be racialized, have foreign credentials and/or no higher education, may lack citizenship in the country in which they are employed, and experience low status, low pay and high job insecurity and precarity (Wingfield, 2019). Not-professional care work often falls into the category of feminized bodywork or work that "focuses directly on the bodies of others: assessing, diagnosing, handling and manipulating bodies, which thus become the object of the worker's labour" (Twigg et al., 2011, p. 1). This care work is lower waged, labour-intensive, under-valued and more likely to involve care of and proximity to people's bodies.

As part of the process of raising its status and legitimacy, and reflecting its positivist epistemology, social work has distanced itself from the bodywork aspects of "care" as it professionalized (Cohen & Wolkowitz, 2018; Wolkowitz, 2006), erecting firm boundaries prohibiting contact with clients' bodies (such as hugging), and encouraged social workers to maintain psychological and "professional distance" (Taylor & Whittaker, 2020; see also Cameron & McDermott, 2007). As it professionalized in the white-collar image of the objective, detached and rational expert, social work focused on delineating an exclusive body of knowledge, theory and skills. However, as McDonald (2006) notes, most of the skills and knowledge social work lays claim to are also used by other professions and care workers which makes it difficult for professional associations and licensure bodies to police and defend the boundaries of social work practice from other groups of workers.

In labour market theory, registration and licensure are a form of market closure or removing social work from the pressures and forces of the labour market by erecting protections around social work's turf (Kennedy Kish et al., 2017). Claiming exclusive skills and knowledge, market closure allows those within the enclosure to improve wages and conditions. However, it also increases vulnerability for those outside the enclosure who may have deep community ties, lived experience and organic knowledge. These workers are frequently racialized and more likely to be from lower income backgrounds, those unable to secure university education, those with foreign credentials and education, and/or Indigenous people working in First Nations and Métis territories and communities (Castex et al., 2019). Though largely unintended, market closure exacerbates existing inequities and exclusions based on intersecting social relations of race, class, gender, Indigeneity, (dis)ability, sexual identity, region and age (Beddoe, 2014; Castex et al., 2019). In the case of immigrants, it also serves to privilege Western forms of knowledge and education that diminish and denigrate other systems of social work education (Bartley et al., 2012). As Sellick et al. (2002) notes though professionalism seems to function in a common-sense, apolitical system, practices of power are an integral part of professionalization. These practices of power are used as a purportedly neutral and objective way to protect social work jobs; however, they simultaneously reproduce class, race gender and other deep-seeded inequities (Kennedy-Kish et al., 2017; Rosenberg & Rosenberg, 2006; Spolander et al., 2016). Debates about licensure and registration are, in actuality, struggles around how social work as a profession is willing to be governed, how power will be exercised and distributed, and who is to be marginalized and disregarded (Lynch, 2021).

Theorizing care work and social work

Under the welfare state, some feminized care work jobs such as social work experienced increased credibility and higher wages. However, globally, much of the welfare state has been dismantled over the last four decades, replaced by neoliberal policies and management models that seek private market solutions to social problems and systematically reduce public provision through contracting out and funding cuts (Brown & MacDonald, 2020; Morley et al., 2017). For social workers in many countries, neoliberalism is introduced to social service agencies and the lives of service users through government funding contracts stipulating the use of New Public Management (NPM) metrics, outcome targets and performance management (Kennedy Kish et al., 2017). At the level of lived experience, NPM introduces neoliberalism directly into the everyday practice of social work, the conditions of the work experienced by social workers and the experience of care for service users. In effect, NPM is one of the ways that neoliberal power is exercised and distributed in care workplaces, these dynamics in turn shape who is to be under-served and disrespected.

Through the metrics, performance management and outcome targets applied to everyday work, NPM standardizes care practice arguing that it is doing so to attain efficiencies and effectiveness and reduce costs (Hyslop, 2018; Lawler, 2018). Similar to speeding up work on an assembly line where standardized work processes remove wasted time and movement, the standardization of social work permits employers to speed up work and increase caseloads, in effect eliciting more work from the same number of employees, and/or from lower paid or unpaid workers. Workers in sped-up social service contexts frequently report having fewer and reduced interactions with clients, an increase in documentation work to prove that outcome targets have been met, and increased alienation, burn-out and dissatisfaction with their work (Brown et al., 2019).

Standardization means that higher credentialed, better salaried workers can be replaced by lower credentialed, lower salaried or even unpaid workers, such as volunteers. Standardization concomitantly reduces employee autonomy and discretion and removes practices that are difficult to routinize and measure (Daly et al., 2015; Folbre, 2017). In social work, these difficult-to-quantify practices are generally connected to empowering care for and about service users and their communities. They often include building and maintaining open-ended, dignity-based and respect-enhancing relationships; open-ended intake and needs assessments; on-going community engagement and organising; everyday policy analysis; and advocacy and activities aimed at extending equity and social justice in care work (Baines, 2016).

As more collective, community-engaged practices are reduced or removed from the social work practice repertoire, by default the profession is left with practices that focus on the individual as problematic and in need of change. Individually focused interventions fit neatly with the neoliberal preoccupation with practical, measureable, technical, "clinical skills" and solutions. Unfortunately, this also dovetails with the removal or reduction of social justice, critical thinking and community-engaged education and skill development from the curriculum of many social work departments (Brown & MacDonald, 2020). As a result, students now graduate with less experience and confidence in macro-level, community-centered practice and relationship building, undermining engagement and involvement. This provides another example of the way that power is distributed and exercised in social work with interventions increasingly aimed at individual adjustment to social problems rather than at preventing social problems and fostering broad, inclusive solutions and wider social justice.

Though as Stiglitz (2014) notes "No large economy has ever recovered from an economic downturn through austerity", austerity and funding reductions have become an expected part of social service delivery with governments introducing cutbacks regardless of the financial outlook (Clarke, 2017). This means that social workers are continually expected to do more with less and as a further practice of power become the unwilling conduits of systemic constraint and neoliberalism into the lives of service users. Though critical reflection is a central social work skill (Morley & O'bree, 2021), currently social workers report little time to reflect on the changing nature of their work under neoliberalism or to understand its far-reaching impacts (Hyslop, 2018; Lawler, 2018). Nevertheless, as Galper (1980) noted in his 1980 classic, most social workers work closely with those who are marginalized and excluded and are thus well-positioned to understand how oppression operates in everyday practice, to foster strategies of resistance, and to contribute to the building of a more equitable and socially just society. These themes will be developed in the following sections.

Resistance

Bringing a feminist lens to resistance, Aptheker (1989) argued that people resist in the contexts in which they find themselves, hence women's resistance and activism tend to look different than that of men. Given social expectations that they will provide on-going care, women's resistance is often tied up with incremental changes. This includes: ensuring the day-to-day survival of dependent persons such as children, disabled people and the elderly;

nurturing relationships; sustaining communities; and on-going, small changes recognizing the dignity of those with less voice and power in the world. In other words, the activism and resistance of women happens where women happen to be, including care work.

Unlike many professions, critical schools of social work encourage students to advocate for those oppressed and exploited by everyday interactions and larger social systems and to resist and challenge inequities and social justice in policies, practices and theories (Garrett, 2021; Kennedy Kish et al., 2017; Morley et al., 2017). Resistance in social work can take many forms including bending rules, standing up for service users, working for policy change, and frequently, undertaking unpaid care work to fill the gaps in service resulting from funding cutbacks and standardized interventions (Baines, 2018). This unpaid work involves working through lunch and coffee breaks, coming in to work early and/leaving late, bringing goods and resources from home, as well as working on the weekends and holidays. Unpaid work for one's place of employment is a gendered form of resistance in social work as the predominantly female workforce tends to expect it of themselves, each other, and employers (Baines, 2018). However, it bears a striking resemblance to the unending, uncomplaining and unpaid care expected of women in the home and community.

Research confirms that management and funders depend on the unpaid contributions of the care workforce to keep cash-poor agencies afloat and to extend existing and much-needed services (Daly et al., 2015; Baines, 2016; L. D. Fraser, 2016). When management demands unpaid work from their labour force, obviously it is exploitation. However, when social workers expect unpaid work of themselves and connect this work to counter-narratives, oppositional identities and connections with others, it can be a form of resistance to and activism against a larger uncaring society (Baines, 2016; Cunningham, 2008). Reflecting the complexity of gendered resistance in care work, unpaid work in social work contexts is both a form of self-exploitation and a moral project in which workers know they are consciously making compromises that may sustain an under-funded system, but that they hope benefits service users and communities more (Baines, 2016; Baines & Daly, 2021).

Labour process theory argues that workplace resistance includes everything that one is not supposed to be doing or thinking at work (Ackoyd & Thompson, 2022). For social workers and other care workers, unpaid work often provides the opportunity for workers to develop individual and shared oppositional storylines, analysis and identities. Basically, when unpaid work is given oppositional meanings that challenge the unkindness and uncaring of the workplace, it is more than exploitation as it simultaneously forms the nucleus of counter-hegemonic discourses and may spark further resistance (Baines, 2016). Unpaid work is frequently part of a shared identity among care workers who see themselves as standing up to a flawed social system. Social workers often discuss unpaid work and heavy workloads, and through this discussion develop collective analyses of inequitable policies and practices. Sometimes these discussions feed into group actions and build to further shared resistance, drawing in colleagues and even supervisors (Baines, 2016). Sometimes this resistance also involves more formal, collective, participatory strategies involving unions, professional associations, service users and communities (O'Neill, 2015; Rosenburg & Rosenberg, 2005; Smith, 2022).

In the post-WWII period, Richard Titmuss (2018) was one of the key designers of the British welfare state. He referred to these kinds of care-based forms of actions as a gift relationship in which people provide something of value to non-specified others without expectation of payment or personal gain (Titmuss, 2018). This gift relationship was thought to form the bedrock of solidarity and citizenship in a social state. The unpaid work undertaken by care workers and the oppositional storylines attached to it often challenges the market ethics and logic that defines care work in the context of neoliberalism. Instead, they foreground solidarity with others and care for the vulnerable with no thought as to a specific reward for their altruism.

Feminist philosopher Nancy Fraser (2016) argues that care work/social reproduction is the social glue that holds societies together. By undertaking unpaid care work as resistance, social workers are choosing to challenge the way power is distributed in social service organizations and the ways that service users and social workers are ruled within workplaces by austerity and uncaring. Instead they are strengthening the social glue by reweaving the thinning threads of social relations under neoliberalism and providing critical space for incremental change and oppositional thought, identities and practices to grow. Earlier in this chapter, it was noted that professionalism is a series of practices of power. Providing care work beyond the boundaries of the workday shifts practices of power from those adhering to neoliberal technocracy and clearly defined limits on lean and thinned-out care, to a more expansive and inclusive understanding that care cannot be tightly scripted and parsimoniously allotted.

As part of professionalization, social workers distanced themselves from the lived expertise of clients and often their struggles, and erected strong boundaries that made egalitarian relationships and solidarity with service users more difficult. Galper (1980) was cited earlier, arguing that despite the distance imposed by professionalization, social workers' proximity to service users means that they are well-positioned to understand the oppressive conditions of society and to work with service users and communities to challenge and change them. It is this proximity to service users and recognition of their routinely unrecognized and unmet needs that foster unpaid resistance care work among social workers. Unpaid care work as resistance challenges the tight boundaries characteristic of professionals as unmet needs and humanity disrespected become pivotal rather than adhering to tight time allocations such as the 50-minute hour, and tightly scripted interventions that simultaneously alienate workers and systemically neglect care recipients.

Social justice practices

The practices discussed below extend the feminist analysis of social justice as linked to resistance in everyday social work practice. They reflect a form of social work that works within the system for immediate and far-reaching change, while simultaneously working outside the system to dismantle oppressive policies, practices and social relations. As part of a debate on the future of social work, Garrett (2021) recently called on social work to maintain its ethics and social justice values by engaging in dissenting social work or social work that stands outside of oppressive relations, instead building resistance to neoliberalism and advancing a vision of equity and full participation of all members of society (see also, Baines, 2022; Beddoe, 2022). Meshing with long-held feminist values of participation, collectivity and empowerment (Comhahee River Collective, 1977), the following four practices build on the notion of dissenting social work and the analysis of gendered resistance presented above. They include: (1) critical reflexivity; (2) being humble in the face of lived experience; (3) critical ally-ship; and (4) building the capacity to advocate and to mobilize colleagues and others around social justice and social change.

Critically reflexivity

By examining their own actions and social locations within the complex web of power relations that forms social service work, critical reflection helps social workers recognize social work as a set of power practices nested within social policies, norms, knowledges, cultures and practices. Critical reflexivity is a multi-level, intersectional process involving an exploration of one's own actions, knowledge, suppositions and biases in the context of organisation-level and macro-level social policies and practices. Maintaining a keen awareness of larger social relations and systems allows critical reflexivity to have transformative potential and provides a fertile ground for social workers to use their lived experiences and those of service users to develop and refine theory, knowledge and practice (Morley and O'bree, 2021; Tascón & Ife, 2019). Finally, critical reflexivity provides a way for social workers to maintain a degree of autonomy from oppressive state, institutional and social discourses and practices, and thus to preserve a space in which to build individual and collective resistance.

Being humble in the face of lived experience

The concept of lived experience has become popular in recovery communities, peer counselling and phenomenological research. In this chapter, it refers to the unique insights, awareness, choices and opportunities an individual has had as a result of life challenges, and the importance of this first-hand knowledge in developing enriched and effective support services and interventions. Centring people with lived experience requires humility by social workers, recognizing that while theory and academic learning are important, the subjective knowledge of the service user is also a central source of expertise. Similar to the feminist concept of sharing power (Brown, 2021), centring lived experience is pivotal to identifying practices of power and dominance as well as identifying liberatory solutions to the kinds of problems service users encounter.

Critical ally-ship

To sustain proximity to the needs and lived experience of services users and their communities, collaborative alliances between practitioners and service users are essential. Social movements, including feminists, and an expanding academic literature suggest that "ally-ship" is a problematic term that is increasingly used in depoliticized and commercialized corporate contexts. For example, Gates et al. (2021) argue that mainstream ally-ship is not enough given the structural inequities present globally, and the growing social tensions underlying the COVID-19 pandemic. Instead, social workers need to foster strong allegiances with oppressed communities and work in micro and macro ways to redress colonial, capitalist, patriarchal systemic and structural inequities (Gates et al., 2021). In place of ally, concepts like 'co-conspirator' or 'accomplice' may more accurately capture the shift of power and risk required to enact far-reaching social change with and for those who are culturally and structurally oppressed (Clemens, 2017). Some critics prefer the term critical ally-ship (Yomantas, 2020) to emphasize ally-ship's link to critical social work theory and practice, and to differentiate it from its feel-good use in mainstream discourse. Critical ally-ship emphasizes the need for critical reflexivity in everyday practice, underscoring the circular connection between analysis and action. Gates et al. (2021) suggest five elements of critical ally-ship in social work: (1) through critical reflexivity, acknowledge your biases; (2) educate yourself before you engage; (3) understand that systemic racism goes beyond police brutality to the systems in which social workers are employed; (4) target racism, speak up against racism and involve yourself in projects, campaigns and actions challenging racism and oppression and (5) make critical ally-ship and allegiance a research, policy and practice change priority.

The capacity to advocate and to mobilize

Like advocacy, the skills associated with mobilizing colleagues and communities are highly congruent with the central value of social justice in most social work codes of ethics (Spencer et al., 2017). Rather than the individual pathology approach that characterizes much practice under neoliberalism, this approach is closely interlinked with feminist themes such as shared solutions, preventive strategies, and finds its integrity in proximity to service users' lived experiences or unmet or poorly met needs. As analysed earlier, in the context of neoliberalism's focus on easily quantifiable and measurable interventions, open-ended, hard-to-measure social justice practices such as relationship building, mediation, activism, advocacy and community development are increasingly marginal within the institutional landscape of social work practice (Rawsthorne & Howard, 2019). These community-engagement practices are an important skill set rooted in participation, power sharing and social change and as such are obvious tools for feminist social workers and others seeking to build equitable and social justice-based social work practice. As part of community mobilization practices, social workers can shift their individual-pathology approach to instead draw on their group work and communication skills to re-story workplace discourses that may be limiting or oppressive, and in their place build feminist-compatible, collective, inclusive, oppositional, liberation-engaged practice, knowledge and theory.

Conclusion

The chapter has analysed the professionalization of social workers and the intersecting inequities it reproduces in late neoliberalism. It also analysed an alternative view of social workers as a highly feminized group of care workers well-positioned to resist oppressions with and for services user and their communities. The analysis concluded by suggesting that a more useful formulation of social work is as a group of female-majority workers who understand social work as a form of care work that embraces its closeness to those contending with social injustice to advance emancipatory social work practice.

References

Ackoyd, S. & Thompson, P. (2022). *Organisational misbehaviour*. Sage.
Aptheker, B. (1989). *Tapestries of life: Women's work, women's consciousness, and the meaning of daily experience*. University of Massachusetts Press.
Bahn, K., Cohen, J. & van der Meulen Rodgers, Y. (2020). A feminist perspective on COVID-19 and the value of care work globally. *Gender, Work & Organization*, 27(5), 695–699.
Baines, D. (2022). "Without losing what we know": Dissenting social work in the context of epochal crises. *Aotearoa New Zealand Social Work*, 34(3), 8–20.
Baines, D. (2018). Social ethics of care in a context of social neglect: A five country discussion. In B. Pease, A. Vreugdenhil & S. Stanford (Eds.) *Critical ethics of care in social work: Transforming the politics of caring* (pp. 16–26). Routledge.

Baines, D. (2016). Moral projects and compromise resistance: Resisting uncaring in nonprofit care work. *Studies in Political Economy*, 97(2), 124–142.

Baines, D. & Daly, T. (2021). Borrowed time and solidarity: The multi-scalar politics of time and gendered care work. *Social Politics: International Studies in Gender, State and Society*, 28(2), 385–404.

Bartley, A., Beddoe, L., Fouché, C. & Harington, P. (2012). Transnational social workers: Making the profession a transnational professional space. *International Journal of Population* Research. https://doi.org/10.1155/2012/527510.

Beddoe, L. (2022). The formulation of anti-vaccination mandate views in social work: Unpacking dissent. *Aotearoa New Zealand Social Work*, 34(3), 74–83.

Beddoe, L. (2014). Feral families, troubled families: The spectre of the underclass in New Zealand. *New Zealand Sociology*, 29(3), 51–68.

Brown, A. R., Walters, J. E. & Jones, A. E. (2019). Pathways to retention: Job satisfaction, burnout, & organizational commitment among social workers. *Journal of Evidence-Based Social Work*, 16(6), 577–594.

Brown, C. (2021). Critical clinical social work and the neoliberal constraints on social justice in mental health. *Research on Social Work Practice*, 31(6). https://doi.org/10.1177/1049731520984531.

Brown, C. & MacDonald, J. (Eds.) (2020). *Critical clinical social work: Counterstorying for social justice*. Canadian Scholars' Press.

Cameron, N. & McDermott, F. (2007). *Social work and the body*. Bloomsbury Publishing.

Carbado, D. W., Crenshaw, K. W., Mays, V. M. & Tomlinson, B. (2013). Intersectionality: Mapping the movements of a theory. *Du Bois Review: Social Science Research on Race*, 10(2), 303–312.

Castex, G., Senreich, E., Phillips, N. K., Miller, C. M., & Mazza, C. (2019). Microaggressions and racial privilege within the social work profession: The social work licensing examinations. *Journal of Ethnic & Cultural Diversity in Social Work*, 28(2), 211–228.

Clarke, J. (2017). Articulating austerity and authoritarianism: Re6 imagining moral economics? In B. Evans & S. McBride (Eds.) *Austerity: The lived experience* (pp. 20–39). University of Toronto Press.

Clemens, C. (2017). Ally or accomplice? The language of activism. *Teaching Tolerance*. https://www.tolerance.org/magazine/ally-or-accomplice-the-language-of-activism. Accessed June 8, 2021.

Cohen, R. L., & Wolkowitz, C. (2018). The feminization of body work. *Gender, Work & Organization*, 25(1), 42–62.

Comhahee River Collective (1977). The Combahee River Collective statement. South Carolina: Blackpast. https://www.blackpast.org/african-american-history/combahee-river-collective-statement-1977/. Accessed June 7, 2022.

Crenshaw, K. W. (2017). *On intersectionality: Essential writings*. The New Press.

Cunningham, I. (2008). A race to the bottom? Exploring variations in employment conditions in the voluntary sector. *Public Administration*, 86(4), 1033–1053.

Daly, T., Armstrong, P. & Lowndes, R. (2015). Liminality in Ontario's long-term care facilities: Private companions' care work in the space 'betwixt and between'. *Competition & Change*, 19(3), 246–263.

Daly, T., Struthers, J., Müller, B., Taylor, D., Goldmann, M., Doupe, M., & Jacobsen, F. F. (2016). Prescriptive or interpretive regulation at the frontlines of care work in the "Three Worlds" of Canada, Germany and Norway. *Labour/Le Travaille*, 77, 37–71.

Folbre, N. (2017). The care penalty and gender inequality. In S. Averett, L. Argys & S. Hoffman (Eds.) *The Oxford handbook of women and economy* (pp. 1–28). Oxford University Press.

Fraser, L. D. (2016). Invisible hours: Social service work and unpaid labour. *Open Access Library Journal*, 3(3), 1–15.

Fraser, N. (2016). Capitalism's crisis of care. *Dissent*, 63(4), 30–37.

Galper, J. (1980). *The Politics of Social Services*. Prentice-Hall.

Garrett, P. (2021). 'A world to win': In defense of (dissenting) social work—A response to Chris Maylea. *The British Journal of Social Work*, 51(4), 1131–1149. https://doi.org/10.1093/bjsw/bcab009.

Gates, T., Bennett, B. & Baines, D. (2021). Strengthening critical ally-ship in social work education: Opportunities in the context of #BlackLivesMatter and COVID-19. *Social Work Education*, 42, 371–387. https://doi.org/10.1080/02615479.2021.1972961.

Hallahan, L. & Wendt, S. (2019). Social work registration: Another opportunity for discussion. *Australian Social Work*, 1–10.

Hill Collins, P. & Bilge, S. (2016). *Intersectionality*. Polity Press.

Hyslop, I. (2018). Neoliberalism and social work identity. *European Journal of Social Work*, 21(1), 20–31.

Jennissen, T. & Lundy, C. (2018). Theoretical research: Radical women in social work: A historical perspective from North America. *Aotearoa New Zealand Social Work*, 30(3), 45–56.

Jones, E. (2019). Social work regulation in British Columbia: A developmental history 2008-2015. *Perspectives*, Autumn, 4–6.

Kennedy-Kish, B., Sinclair, R., Carniol, B. & Baines, D. (2017). *Case critical. The dilemma of social work in Canada* (7th ed.). Between the Lines.

Lawler, J. (2018). The rise of managerialism in social work. In E. Harlow & J. Lawler (Eds.) *Management, social work and change* (pp. 33–56). Routledge.

Lynch, K. (2021). *Care and capitalism*. John Wiley & Sons.

McDonald, C. (2006). *Challenging social work: The institutional context of practice*. Bloomsbury Publishing.

Morley, C., Macfarlane, S. & Ablett, P. (2017). The neoliberal colonisation of social work education: A critical analysis and practices for resistance. *Advances in Social Work and Welfare Education*, 19(2), 25–40.

Morley, C. & O'bree, C. (2021). Critical reflection: An imperative skill for social work practice in neoliberal organisations? *Social Sciences*, 10(3), 1–17.

O'Neill, L. (2015). Regulating hospital social workers and nurses: Propping up an "efficient" lean health care system. *Studies in Political Economy*, 95(1), 115–136.

Rawsthorne, M. & Howard, A. (2019). *Everyday community practice*. Allen and Unwin.

Rosenberg, J. & Rosenberg, S. (2006). Do unions matter? An examination of the historical and contemporary role of labor unions in the social work profession. *Social Work*, 51(4), 295–302.

Sellick, M. M., Delaney, R. & Brownlee, K. (2002). The deconstruction of professional knowledge: Accountability without authority. *Families in Society*, 83(5), 493–498.

Smith, K. (2022). Occupied spaces: Unmapping standardized assessments. In D. Baines, N. Clarke & B. Bennett (Eds.) *Doing anti-oppressive practice: Social justice social work* (pp. 272–288). Fernwood Press.

Spencer, E., Gough, J. & Massing, D. (2017). *Progressive, critical, anti-oppressive social work: Ethical action*. Oxford University Press.

Spolander, G., Engelbrecht, L. & Pullen Sansfaçon, A. (2016). Social work and macro-economic neoliberalism: beyond the social justice rhetoric. *European Journal of Social Work*, 19(5), 634–649.

Stiglitz, J. E. (2014). Europe's austerity zombies. *Project Syndicate*, September 26.

Tascón, S. & Ife, J. (2019). *Disrupting whiteness in social work*. Routledge.

Taylor, B. & Whittaker, A. (2020). *Professional judgement and decision making in social work: Current issues*. Routledge.

Titmuss, R. (2018). *The gift relationship: From human blood to social policy*, Re-issue. Policy Press.

Tronto, J. (2013). *Caring democracy: Markets, equality, democracy*. New York Press.

Twigg, J., Wolkowitz, C., Cohen, R. L. & Nettleton, S. (2011). Conceptualising body work in health and social care. *Sociology of Health & Illness*, 33(2), 171–188.

Wingfield, A. H. (2019). *Flatlining: Race, work, and health care in the new economy*.University of California Press.

Wolkowitz, C. (2006). *Bodies at work*. Sage.

Yomantas, E. L. (2020). Decolonizing knowledge and fostering critical ally-ship. In L. Parson & C. C. Ozaki (Eds.) *Teaching and learning for social justice and equity in higher education* (pp. 303–328). Palgrave Macmillan.

Yuval-Davis, N. (2006). Intersectionality and feminist politics. *European Journal of Women's studies*, 13(3), 193–209.

SECTION 5

Allyship, profeminisms and queer perspectives

35
SOCIAL WORK RECKONS WITH CISNORMATIVITY & THE GENDER BINARY

Jama Shelton and Courtney Virginia Fox

Introduction

Most Western societies utilize binary constructs to categorize people and organize social systems. Examples include sexual orientation (homosexual/heterosexual), race (person of color/white), sex (female/male) and gender (woman/man). Binary constructs are inherently limiting, in that they offer only two, mutually exclusive ways of being, which contrasts with the vast diversity of the human experience. Further, binary systems of categorization reinforce a hierarchical social order, in which one category is assumed "better" than the other, resulting in systematic oppression and structural discrimination. Embedded in societal structures and tightly bound with systems of oppression, this hierarchical order confirms power and privilege, maintaining a social order rooted in racism, sexism, classism and cis/heterosexism. Not only does this social order limit the mobility of individuals and groups, but it also perpetuates violence and marginalization (Shelton & Dodd, 2021). Adopting a transfeminist lens can expand social work practice beyond binary normativities that are rooted in white, cisgender womanhood (Pyne, 2015).

Social work ethics emphasize promoting social justice, confronting oppression and recognizing the dignity and worth of all people (NASW, 2021; IFSW, 2014). As the profession reckons with cisnormativity and the gender binary, the approach must be intersectional (Shelton et al., 2022). Trans and gender expansive (TGE) voices from all socioeconomic backgrounds, races and ethnicities, abilities and sizes belong in our communities and in our classrooms and deserve equity in all domains of public life (e.g. employment, housing, health access and education). Social workers can elevate these voices and experiences as teachers, researchers, practitioners and advocates by building relationships and creating spaces that prioritize gender diversity and lived experience. To abolish the gender binary, social workers must take a liberatory approach to this work. One theoretical approach for the social work profession to consider is transfeminism.

Transfeminism

Transfeminism builds upon existing feminist scaffolding, which has at times been both radical in seeking liberation from patriarchal oppression and also limited by exclusionary definitional constraints. Inherently intersectional, transfeminism requires recognition of the shared oppression of *all* people who challenge heteronormativity to effectively respond to patriarchal violence (Sharma, 2009). As a critical approach to feminism, transfeminism is closely aligned with feminist submovements such as queer theory/queer feminism, Intersectionality, sex-positive feminism and postmodern/poststructuralist feminism. What these submovements have in common is the adoption of a more nuanced and expansive view of sexism that acknowledges the existence of numerous forms of sexism (heterosexism, monosexism, etc.) compared to the reductive and simplistic notion of sexism as men oppressing women (Serano, 2012). Transfeminism contends that all systems of oppression that police and control people and their bodies must be confronted to achieve gender equity (Shelton et al., 2022).

Key Terms

The terms people use to describe themselves and their experiences vary across cultures and contexts as language evolves. The following definitions represent the way these terms are used herein, at this particular moment in time in the Western context within which the authors work and live.

Cisgenderism

Cisgenderism refers to an oppressive ideology that stigmatizes people who are labelled as, identify as, or presumed to be TGE, as well as those whose gender expression does not align with societal expectations of traditional socially constructed gender norms (Ansara & Hegarty, 2014; Lennon & Mistler, 2014). Cisgenderism can also be understood as critical to the production and maintenance of the oppression and marginalization of TGE individuals and communities. Cisgenderism provides a framework for understanding and addressing the structural oppression of TGE people, rather than focusing on micro-level expressions of bias (Shelton et al., 2019).

Cisnormativity

The concept of normativity refers to the power held by the dominant or majority ideals in contemporary society. Normativities contribute to the maintenance of power, privilege and oppression (Argüello, 2021). *Cisnormativity* presumes that all people are (and should be) cisgender and reinforces the gender binary and the normative gender roles and behavioural expectations associated with each binary category. Cisnormativity informs our entire social context, including the micro level of individual interactions and the macro level of institutions, systems and policies. Thus, cisnormativity contributes to the systematic marginalization and delegitimization of TGE people (Bauer et al., 2009). The widely held belief that being cisgender is the norm results in severe consequences for anyone who does not or cannot subscribe to the gendered demands of cisnormativity (Shelton & Dodd, 2021; Shelton et al., 2019; James et al., 2016).

Sex and gender

The terms sex and gender are often used interchangeably. However, while sex and gender may be related in some instances, they are not synonymous. Sex designation is related to an individual's chromosomes, anatomy and hormones. An individual is typically assigned a binary sex categorization (female or male) at birth, or prior to birth, usually based on the appearance of their external sex organs. Inherent in the notion of the *sex binary* is the presumption that only two sexes exist and that an individual's sex is biologically determined and immutable. The sex binary is an inaccurate and limiting system of classification that disregards the diversity of human bodies and experiences. Not only is it inaccurate and limiting, the binary system of sex classification is also harmful to those who cannot be categorized within it. For instance, intersex babies and children are often subjected to surgical procedures to which they do not consent and are required to take hormones in a medicalized effort to force their bodies to fit within a binary that their bodies prove to be an insufficient system of classification.

The *gender binary* refers to the widely held belief that there are only two, mutually exclusive gender categories – woman/girl or man/boy. This belief often includes the presumption that an individual's gender is predicted by or is correlated with their assigned binary sex at birth, and that one's gender is fixed and will remain stable over time (Hyde et al., 2019). The notion of binary gender is so pervasive and unquestioned in much of contemporary Western societies that it serves as a foundational element of most social systems and structures. From gendered public restrooms to the marketing of hygiene products, the gender binary and accompanying gender roles and behaviours are consistently reinforced. The profession of social work is not immune to this limited and limiting conceptualization of gender. As a profession situated within cisnormative institutions and systems, including education, social service settings and the medical industrial complex (including pharmaceutical and insurance companies), social workers are often participants in the policing of gender and the reinforcement of the gender binary.

While the gender binary is implemented at the societal and structural levels as a tool of oppression, it can take on a different meaning at the individual level. Identifying with a binary gender (e.g. man or woman) can resonate with many people, including transgender men and women. However, the social expectations of what it means to be a "man" or a "woman" can present challenges, distress and discrimination for cisgender and transgender people alike (Eagan, 2005). For these reasons, and for the inclusion of non-binary and gender-expansive individuals, it is important to challenge the ways in which our systems and structures uphold the gender binary. To reiterate, identifying within the gender binary is not in and of itself the problem. The gender binary becomes problematic when a binary classification of gender is imposed and/or when it is a prerequisite for access to and acceptance within social systems and public institutions.

Social work & binary gender

Engaging in social change efforts and working for the liberation of people are foundational values of the social work profession globally. According to the International Federation of Social Workers (IFSW) and the International Association of Schools of Social Work, "Principles of social justice, human rights.....and respect for diversities" are included in the global definition of social work (IFSW website, 2014). Professional organizations in the

United States, such as the National Association of Social Workers (NASW) and the Council on Social Work Education (CSWE), acknowledge gender identity and expression as aspects of diversity that must be recognized in the profession's charge to work for social justice. It is imperative that the social work profession engage in dismantling the unjust and oppressive ideologies of cisnormativity and the gender binary, and to address the ways in which these ideologies impact individuals and communities.

The profession of social work must acknowledge and reckon with its complicity in the oppression of TGE people and communities, particularly in relation to the policing of gender, the pathologization of gender variance, and the reinforcement of the gender binary. Perhaps the most obvious example of this is the profession's endorsement of the DSM, which has continuously pathologized gender variance (Shelton et al., 2019; Markman, 2011). Even if social workers are not responsible for assigning a diagnosis, they are often gatekeepers to gender-affirming care and are thus complicit in the process of requiring TGE people to prove and defend their gender identities. For example, many insurance companies require a letter of evidence from a social worker or other licensed mental health professional to cover gender-affirming healthcare. As such, social workers hold the power to limit an individual's ability to make their own choices about their own body (Shelton et al., 2019).

Structural social work: a framework for addressing cisnormativity & gender binarism

Although in practice, the social work profession has often been complicit in the perpetuation of cisnormativity and the gender binary, social work remains well-suited to focus on dismantling cisnormativity and gender binarism, and to create solidarity between all gender-oppressed groups. Social work embodies the ethical principles and practical skills to embrace gender diversity. As stated above, the values of social work centre liberation and diversity. An understanding of what it means to uphold these values must be expanded to include all gender expressions and identities. Furthermore, social workers are trained with both advocacy and clinical skills that can be applied to broadening the profession's treatment of gender.

For example, as the U.S. experiences an increase in the state regulation of individual bodies and blurred lines between church and state resulting in morality-based legislative proposals, social workers are ethically required to intervene. In fact, if the social work profession fails to incorporate a structural focus in regard to the gender-based oppression faced by TGE people, it is actively reinforcing cis/heterosexism and interrelated oppressive ideologies.

Structural social work is one framework the profession can utilize to expand binary conceptualizations of gender and dismantle cisnormative systems. According to Mullaly (1997), structural social work "is a moral theory. It suggests that the underlying causes for social problems are the differential control of resources and political power inherent in capitalistic societies. The system is viewed as faulty (p. 119)." Emphasizing social transformation, structural social work is aligned with feminist traditions and connects the personal and political through an examination of and strategic action towards the root causes of oppression (George & Marlowe, 2005). Despite an existing tradition of emancipatory theory and practice, the profession of social work has yet to broadly accept structural social work as a practice framework; apprehensions are, in part, based on the notion that focusing on societal transformation will result in an inability to adequately respond to individuals and their needs (Shelton et al., 2019; George & Marlowe, 2005). This is a fair point, in that the profession, as it exists in some countries within the context of privatized healthcare, largely operates within a "neoliberal context of state-mediated service delivery in which the corporate interests of the insurance and pharmaceutical industries directly influence social work practice and social service delivery" (Shelton et al., 2019, p. 112). These industries emphasize measurable outcomes and efficiency, which results in funding directed to organizations that respond to the needs of individuals rather than working to disrupt the societal structures that contribute to individual needs. Such large-scale work can seem nebulous, requires long-term intervention and can be difficult to quantify (Shelton et al., 2019). However, if interventions are employed on the structural level, disparate individual needs should diminish, or even disappear, over time.

The profession of social work must reconnect to the core professional values of social justice, equity and commitment to oppressed populations (NASW, 2021; IFSW, 2014). These values are reflected in transfeminism and also lend themselves to engagement in structural social work practice. For instance, rather than focusing on interpersonal manifestations of cis/heterosexism such as the individual enactment of anti-trans bias – which locates the problem within individual people – a structural approach would locate the problem within the continued enactment of cisnormativity and the rigid boundaries of the binary gender system.

Action steps

The profession of social work is uniquely positioned to dismantle the reliance upon binary gender classifications and the pervasive cisnormativity within public institutions, societal systems and services. In order for the profession to move beyond the gender binary, social work education, research and practice must be examined for the ways in which they may be reliant upon binary gender categorization and perpetuating the gender binary.

Social work education

With regards to social work education, literature suggests that social work education reinforces cisnormativity through both implicit and explicit curricula that invisibilize or pathologize TGE people and administrative practices that are not considerate of TGE people (Kinney et al., 2023; Shelton et al., 2023; Shelton & Dodd, 2020; Austin et al., 2016). By engaging in these cisnormative practices, schools of social work are "endorsing and perpetuating a model of professional socialization that permits students as emerging professionals to maintain cisnormativity in practice (Shelton et al., 2023, p. 66).

Due to historical reliance on the DSM, and the pathologization of trans and gender expansive people, social work education often perpetuates limited conceptualizations of trans and gender-expansive people and communities. To combat this, educators must provide the historical and cultural context of gender-related "mental" diagnoses, and facilitate discussions of both the utility and potential harm of applying gender-related diagnostic criteria in practice. One strategy for ensuring social work students understand the oppressive nature of cisnormativity and the gender binary is to include this content in foundational courses, rather than relegating it to elective courses on LGBTQ+ issues. If part of their required coursework, social work students will gain a robust understanding of gender-based oppression, movements for gender equity, and the nuanced manifestations of patriarchal violence.

In addition to explicit course content, the learning environment also impacts the ability of social work students to learn about TGE individuals and communities and to engage in liberatory practice. Recent studies indicate TGE social work students experience widespread misgendering and transphobic behaviour from both faculty and students (Shelton et al., 2023; Austin et al., 2016). Almost 40% of participants (n = 97) in Austin et al.'s study reported perceiving faculty as possessing and demonstrating transphobic attitudes and beliefs. Nearly one-third (31%) of participants reported an absence of faculty intervention when observing transphobic behaviour among students (Austin et al., 2016). For specific strategies geared towards creating inclusive educational spaces that do not reinforce the gender binary, see Shelton and Dodd (2021).

Social work research

Social work researchers also have a role to play in dismantling cisnormativity and the gender binary. Researchers can work to ensure that all gender categories are valid by practicing intentional inclusion of participants with a range of genders, both in the design of demographic questions and in the interpretation of findings. The following are suggestions for addressing cisnormativity and gender binarism in social work research:

1. When possible, allow respondents to write in their gender when collecting demographic data. If an open-ended question is not possible, include additional response options other than the binary categories of girl/women and boy/man.
2. Use accurate terminology for sex and gender. Surveys often inquire about gender using the categories female and male. Female and male are sex designations, not genders.
3. Include options beyond the binary sex categories of female and male when asking about sex. Include intersex as an option and allow an option for respondents to write in their sex.
4. Avoid collapsing gender into two categories during the analytic process. This erases participants' identities and is reductionist.
5. When interpreting findings, contextualize results within the larger socio-political context of gender identity-based oppression and marginalization. Providing this context will deepen the understanding of the impact of structural oppression, rather than perpetuating a harmful narrative that TGE people are inherently more likely to experience negative mental and physical health outcomes.

Social work practice

In practice, social workers can examine the policies and procedures of their workplaces to identify the ways in which they rely on and reinforce the gender binary and cisnormativity. If institutions have not been intentionally examined through the lens of cisnormativity, it is very likely they reinforce the gender binary and subsequently marginalize anyone who cannot be classified within it. When working with TGE individuals, social workers can also push beyond the narrative of gender dysphoria and engage people in explorations of gender euphoria. Understanding what situations or contexts trigger discomfort in someone's gender identity can be an important part of providing support; but learning what makes them feel joyful and affirmed in their gender is equally, if not more, important. Taking this anti-pathologizing approach to gender is a radical way of pushing back on cisnormativity and defying the historical oppression of the gender binary. Opening up new ways of being through gender exploration, and normalizing this experience rather than pathologizing it, can be transformative for the social work profession and for our society at large.

To further the practice of depathologizing gender expansiveness, social workers must also engage critically and carefully with the diagnostic criteria of gender dysphoria. Not all TGE people who seek gender-affirming healthcare experience gender dysphoria. In some countries, clinicians must navigate a healthcare space wherein a diagnosis is frequently required by third-party payers and insurance companies, if not also medical care providers (Coleman et al., 2022; Perlson et al., 2021). Discussing the utility and application of a diagnosis with TGE individuals and allowing space to process the experience of being diagnosed are essential steps social workers can take to disrupt the assumption that gender variance is pathological. Furthermore, these spaces and conversations can be used to validate the experiences of TGE individuals and build opportunities for empowerment.

Beyond the scope of individual-level work, social workers can also advocate at the policy level to adjust legal standards for insurance. Gender-affirming care can be made available without a diagnosis if we are willing to push for it. The World Professional Association for Transgender Health has moved away from the DSM in their 7th and 8th publications of their Standards of Care, emphasizing that "Gender incongruence is no longer seen as pathological or a mental disorder in the world health community" (Coleman et al., 2022, p. 57). To embrace liberatory and transfeminist principles, social workers must be vocal in advocating for the depathologization of gender.

Conclusion

The gender binary is an inaccurate representation of human biology and psychology (Hyde et al., 2019). Utilizing a binary classification of gender as a way to organize a society creates functional challenges for many TGE people. Building on feminist traditions of addressing patriarchal violence, transfeminism provides an intersectional framework for challenging systems of oppression that police and control people and their bodies. At a systemic level, the gender binary is not only oppressive for TGE people, it is restrictive for all people in that it prescribes specific gender roles and gendered behaviours that pose challenges for all people who are unable to meet cisnormative demands (Eagan, 2005). Thus, dismantling cisnormativity and binary gender is a form of liberatory social work practice with which the profession has an ethical obligation to engage. The profession of social work must engage in a process of aligning research, educational and practice standards with professional values, or we will be complicit in the continued oppression of trans and gender expansive people and communities.

References

Ansara, Y.G., & Hegarty, P. (2014). Methodologies of misgendering: Recommendations for reducing cisgenderism in psychological research. *Feminism & Psychology, 24*(2), 259–270.

Argüello, T.M. (2021). Heteronormativity and social work: The *what* that dare not speak its name. In S.J. Dodd (Ed.), *The Routledge international handbook of social work and sexualities*. London: Routledge.

Austin, A., Craig, S.L., & McInroy, L.B. (2016). Toward transgender affirmative social work education. *Journal of Social Work Education, 52*(3), 297–310.

Bauer, G. R., Hammond, R., Travers, R., Kaay, M., Hohenadel, K. M., & Boyce, M. (2009). "I don't think this is theoretical; this is our lives": How erasure impacts healthcare for transgender people. *Journal of the Association of Nurses in AIDS Care, 20*(5), 348–361.

Coleman, E., Radix, A.E., Bouman, W.P., Brown, G.R., de Vries, A.L.C., Deutsch, M.B., Ettner, R., Fraser, L., Goodman, M., Green, J., Hancock, A.B., Johnson, T.W., Karasic, D.H., Knudson, G.A., Leibowitz, S.F., Meyer-Bahlburg, H.F.L., Monstrey, S.J., Motmans, J., Nahata, L., ... Arcelus, J. (2022). Standards of care for the health of transgender and gender diverse people, Version 8. *International Journal of Transgender Health, 23*(S1), S1–S260.

Eagan, J. (2005). Denaturing fixed identities: A project for feminist public administration practice. *Administrative Theory & Praxis, 27*(2), 407–412.

George, P., & Marlowe, S. (2005). Structural social work in action: Experiences from rural India. *Journal of Progressive Human Services, 16*(1), 5–24.

Hyde, J., Bigler, R., Joel, D., Tate, C., & van Anders, S. (2019). The future of sex and gender in psychology: Five challenges to the gender binary. *American Psychologist, 74*(2), 171–193.

International Federation of Social Workers (IFSW). (2014). *Global definition of social work*. Retrieved from https://www.ifsw.org/what-is-social-work/global-definition-of-social-work/

James, S.E., Herman, J.L., Rankin, S., Keisling, M., Mottet, L., & Anafi, M. (2016). *The report of the 2015 U.S. transgender survey*. Washington, DC: National Center for Transgender Equality.

Kinney, M.K., Cosgrove, D., Swafford, T.R., & Brandon-Friedman, R.A. (2023). "An Institution Can Have Good Intentions and Still Be Atrocious": Transgender and gender expansive experiences in social work education. *The Journal of Sociology & Social Welfare, 50*(1), Article 6.

Lennon, E., & Mistler, B. (2014). Cisgenderism. *TSQ: Transgender Studies Quarterly, 1*(1–2), 63–64.

Markman, E. (2011). Gender identity disorder, the gender binary, and transgender oppression: Implications for ethical social work. *Smith College Studies in Social Work, 81*(4), 314–327.

Mullaly, R. (1997). *Structural social work practice: Ideology, theory, and practice* (2nd ed.). Toronto: Oxford University Press.

National Association of Social Workers. (2021). *Code of ethics*. Retrieved from https://www.socialworkers.org/About/Ethics/Code-of-Ethics/Code-of-Ethics-English

Perlson, J. E., Walters, O. C., & Keuroghlian, A. S. (2021). Envisioning a future for transgender and gender-diverse people beyond the DSM. *The British Journal of Psychiatry, 219*(3), 471–472.

Pyne, J. (2015). Transfeminist Theory and Action: Trans Women and the Contested Terrain of Women's Services. In O'Neill, B., Swan, T., Mule, N. (eds.) *LGBTQ people and social work: Intersectional perspectives*. Canadian Scholars Press.

Serano, J. (2012, April 18). Transfeminism: There's no conundrum about it. *Ms. Magazine*. Retrieved from https://msmagazine.com/2012/04/18/trans-feminism-theres-no-conundrum-about-it/

Sharma, S. (2009). Translating gender: Āzād Bilgrāmī on the poetics of the love lyric and cultural synthesis. *The Translator, 15*(1), 87–103.

Shelton, J., & Dodd, S.J. (2020). Beyond the binary: Addressing cisnormativity in the social work classroom. *Journal of Social Work Education, 56*(1), 179–185.

Shelton, J., & Dodd, S.J. (2021). Binary thinking and the limiting of human potential. *Public Integrity, 23*(6), 624–635.

Shelton, J., Dodd, S.J., Borgan, J., San Emeterio, G., & Wilhelm, A. (2023). A descriptive account of the practicum experiences of trans and nonbinary social work students. *Journal of Sociology & Social Welfare, 50*(1), 3.

Shelton, J., Dunleavy, M., & Kroehle, K. (2022). The transformational potential of transfeminist social work practice. In C. Cocker & T. Hafford-Letchfield (Eds.), *Rethinking feminist theories for social work practice*. Palgrave.

Shelton, J., Kroehle, K., & Andia, M. (2019). The trans person is not the problem: Brave spaces and structural competence as educative tools for trans justice in social work. *Journal of Sociology and Social Welfare, 46*(4), 97–123.

36
MARICA AND *TRAVESTI* INTERPELLATIONS TO CONSERVATIVE SOCIAL WORK PRACTICES

Alejandra Gutiérrez Saracho and Claudio Barbero

Introduction

Cisexist and heteronormative knowledge and practices in social work

*Those of us who practice social work as a profession have been socialized in cisheterosexual environments, we agree with Langarita and Mesquida (2016) who state, (that) we have been educated to share and encourage the cisheterosexualizing project (p. 176). That is why our gaze may well be committed to the erroneous consideration that cisheterosexuality is a natural fact, which takes invariable forms in the lives of the people with whom we intervene and even in ourselves.

We find, in different contexts and realities, social work practices that have not problematized this view. Instead of fostering and encouraging emancipation processes with the populations with whom they intervene, they become neoconservative reinforcements of the hegemonic cisheterosexual order, thus contributing to sustaining forms of violence against dissident sex-gender identities (*maricas*[1], *travesties*, trans, lesbians, non-binary, etc.). In our opinion, and this is what we will try to contribute in this chapter, is that such practices should be unmasked, reviewed, reported and deeply questioned.

When we speak of knowledge related to sexualities that must be questioned, we refer to the ethical-political approaches and positions related to the myth of the stable couple, the supposed legitimacy of certain patterns of reproduction of the species within the framework of "well-constituted" marriage, the traditionalist model of the nuclear family[2], the necessary association of procreation with marriage, as its exclusive and natural destiny, the encouragement of monogamy as the "normal" and only acceptable modality of relationship in couples, the presumption of heterosexuality in all people (except those who state otherwise), among others.

This framework of knowledge sustains professional practices that result in oppression and discomfort, especially in fields of intervention involving children and youth. It also makes invisible multiple dissident expressions of sexuality.

In this same sense, cisexualization as understood by Millet (2020) is another modality of oppressive practice that, based on the idea that cisgender people are more valuable than trans people, provokes strong processes of expulsion from the public space (pp. 40–41). Millet analyses some of these cisgender practices, such as the assumption of gender, the inadequate use of neutral pronouns in dealing with people, and the subalternized marking of (trans) otherness.

This also includes identity reduction ("the trans" as the only descriptive factor of trans people) and the uncritical reproduction of the false idea that both professionals and institutions have no training on trans identity agency, when in fact they do. Rather, the limit is that such training is based on cissexist approaches and content (Millet, 2020, pp. 43–67). These are cissexist practices that also take shape in the processes of professional social work intervention.

Yet another issue that the discipline has not sufficiently addressed is that of pleasure, enjoyment and the erotic as inseparable and legitimate aspects of sexualities. In deep empathy with the *sentipensar*[3] of Perlongher (1997) we could say that in addition to the right to be recognized and respected, all people have the right not only to desire but also to be desired. In other words, we wonder if it would be possible to imagine and test interventions in social work that, in addition to demanding the guarantee of full access of all people to all their rights, also contribute to generate daily environments in which each and every person is encouraged, welcomed and desired.

In our personal lives, many of us have first-hand experience of the oppressive effects of the hegemonic sexual order. We have faced mockery and harassment for not being "normal", we have had to account for our ways of being in the world (if we have not had to hide them for a while), and we have resisted, often in solitude and other times in the shelter of collective action. Those lived experiences are the foundation from which we assume this body-political positioning (Peralta, 2018), from which we identify the presence of oppressive knowledge and practices.

On the other hand, in our interventions in the educational field of compulsory schooling, in the exercise of teaching, research and extension in formal university spaces, in proposals for continuing education linked to our Professional Colleges and Councils, in the multiple opportunities for meetings between colleagues that our profession usually encourages, in all these instances we note the emancipations still called into question about counter-hegemonic sexualities in our disciplinary training (Giribuela, 2020).

We refer to difficulties and/or resistance in expanding the intelligibility in social work of the processes of configuration of dissident sex-gender identities, both at the sociopolitical level (recognizing their processes of struggle and mobilization for access to all rights) and at the subjective level (the singular agencies of dissident identities). Of particular concern are the forms with which these issues enter into undergraduate training (as seminars or optional subjects, as extracurricular activities, as specific training meetings,) but without permeating the curricula in explicit, transversal and substantive ways.

It is critical to make a social science framework explicit for social work professionals. Throughout its history, social work has been challenged and even conditioned by multiple influences. We identify some of them as obstacles to the process of emancipation of the profession, and we have appropriated others for their power to embrace and consolidate what we have been (and what we wish to be) as a discipline.

The role played by bio-medical-legal hygienism at the dawn of social service is worth recalling: it was in aid of goals that were defined for us from outside the discipline. Moreover, in many latitudes of the Global South and as a consequence of the European colonization processes, the Judeo-Christian churches had a strong influence on the configuration and disciplining of the limits of social services. In those scenarios, hygienist and moralist principles placed dissident sex-gender identities in the category of disease (if not crime) and moral degeneration (sin), as seen from colonial morality (Oliva, 2015; Parra, 2001).

Many early social work approaches were influenced by devices of cure, conversion, punishment and disciplining. These influences favored the consolidation of models of intervention with dissident sex-generic populations and used pathological categories of the "abnormal", such as homosexuality, perversion, onanism, nymphomania, and hysteria (among other categories that were placed at the centre of surveillance by the disciplinary regime of Latin American bourgeois society). Social work was not an exception to these developments.

Although the legal frameworks in favour of the recognition and respect of sexualities and their multiple dimensions are evolving (in different ways in different countries and regions of the world), the socio-cultural transformations have not always kept pace, which is why we continue to find vestiges of retrograde practices of disciplining expressions of sexualities. In 2021 the IFSW, following a request made by the Federal Forum on Gender and Sexual Diversity of the Argentine Federation of Professional Associations of Social Service, issued a strong call for social work professionals to support the rights of the community, especially in countries where homosexuality is punished with any form of torture (including the death penalty)[4]. The transformation agenda at the global level also steers the profession towards positive change.

Just as the profession has been influenced by the restrictive and subalternizing effect of hegemonic scenarios and discourses, social work has also had its own forceful irruption – in its principles and agendas – of emancipatory and transforming knowledge and practices. María Eugenia Hermida (2020) formulates the three most significant interruptions/irruptions in the genealogy of social work as readings coming from Marxist thought (1960s/1970s), citizenship perspectives, including the human rights approach and gender perspectives (1980s/1990s) and finally, the third irruption, decolonial theories and Feminisms of the South. Colonial and patriarchal wounds can provide the impetus to think about the oppressions caused by cisheteronormativity, without ignoring other forms of violence due to race, social class, ethnicity and abilities (among others), which also operate in an intersectional way.

In this political exercise of revisioning social work's disciplinary formation, the third irruption proposed by Hermida (2020) brings together the Feminisms of the South with a series of *marica* and *travesti* knowledge, epistemologies, ethics and aesthetics also from the Global South (De Sousa, 2009). This provides the potential for transformation that can be read and (re)appropriated by social work. Extending social works' disciplinary debates with these sources of knowledge and emancipatory practices could deepen effective strategies of feminist coalition (Mattio, 2020), thus strengthening the depatriarchalizing power (Galindo, 2013) in our interventions.

Marica and *travesti* knowledge and practices from the Global South

Even though social constraints have attempted to reduce sex-affective diversity and multiple forms of gender expression to a story of bitterness, grief and suffering, LGBT people have still been able to build their own communities, explore alternative discourses on sexuality and gender and promote other forms of social organization able to overcome the most orthodox views. A renewed perspective that incorporates queer methodologies, allows us to broaden the horizons of social intervention and, above all, find new ways to promote well-being of the people, communities and groups we work with (Langarita and Mesquida, 2016, p. 175).

Boaventura de Sousa Santos (2009) has described the "Global South" both as a metaphor for human suffering caused by the great forms of oppression (capitalism, Colonialism and Patriarchy) as well as for the resistance to overcoming such suffering. A series of discourses and political practices of resistance to a hegemonic order in the economic, social and cultural fields were produced in Latin America. In this region, the reconceptualization movement in social work produced moments of interpellations of new discourses and models of intervention with critical perspectives. The goal of this new thought is to gain a greater understanding of situated territorialities, with the purpose of politicizing the everyday life of subjects.

These "new" forms of intervention are taught in the academic training in social work, in terms of gender and sexualities. However, they continue to reproduce the cissexist view, leaving out and making invisible dissident sexualities, identities that in the 1960s already began a process of claiming rights and denouncing situations of violation and oppression.

The lived experiences of individuals of dissident sexualities have become collective experiences. This included "aesthetics of existences, thus named to the styles of living that resist the depredations of the body and behavior" (Ponce, 2022, p. 136). Oppressed groups set up an agenda of demands and interpellation to the State. This has included the denunciation of police persecution and criminalization of those holding identities of *putos*, *maricas*, *tortas y travestis* in different political contexts. Though this oppression was particularly acute during civil-military dictatorships in Latin America, it continues in democracy, where the provincial police apply to this day in some cases – codes of misdemeanors to persecute and violate dissident sex-gendered populations, with special viciousness to *travestis* and women who practice prostitution.

To carry out a brief genealogy in Foucauldian terms, as Figari (2009) points out, is to access a series of disparate sequences (history of the pieces) that allows us to know the social and political discourses in relation to sexual dissidence. This brief tour provides an opportunity for social workers to make much-needed epistemological revisions. It also provides an opportunity to think through a sort of historical repair of professional intervention with sex-political groups, very much in the sense of what Franco Ortiz (2022) proposes as a reparative social work.

Processes of collective struggle in Latin America began with the first group of homosexual political activism *Nuestro Mundo* (Our world) in 1967. Years later, in 1971, another group formed by intellectuals and activists took the name *Frente de Liberación Homosexual* FLH (Homosexual Liberation Front), which counted anthropologist Nestor Perlongher among its members. "In Brazil in 1978, the *Núcleo de Acción por los derechos homosexuales* NADH (Nucleus of Action for homosexual rights) was organized, which later adopted the name *Somos* in homage to the FLH of Argentina" (Figari, 2009, p. 189). In Chile, the first LGBTI organization *Movimiento de Integración y Liberación Homosexual* MOVILH (Homosexual Integration and Liberation Movement) was formed in 1990, even though the first homosexual demonstration took place in the 1970s. In 1987 the collective *Las Yeguas del Apocalipsis* (The Mares of the Apocalypse) was formed by writer Pedro Lemebel and artist Francisco Casas, and it made a political proposal to denounce the dictatorship (Peña Ruiz Tagle, 2016).

The return of democracy in 1983 in Argentina led other activists such as Carlos Jáuregui to begin to make homoerotic relationships between people of the same sex visible. In 1984 the *Comunidad Homosexual Argentina* CHA (Argentine Homosexual Community) was created. This opened a long debate on equal rights, where the alliance/coalition with Feminisms culminated in 2010 with the passing of Law No. 26618 known as the "equal marriage law". Access to civil marriage materialized as a crucial step in the recognition of the full citizenship of lesbian, gay, bisexual, *travesti*, transsexual, intersexual (LGBTTI) populations, their children and their families (Figari, 2010). This paradigm legitimizes the equality of non-heterosexual couples before the law and has become a central contribution to social work in the intervention in the field of family approaches.

In the 1990s, the collective struggle of the first political organization called *Travestis Unidas* (United *Travestis*) led by Kenny De Michelis began to take shape in Argentina. In 1993 Claudia Pía Baudracco founded the *Asociación de Travestis Argentinas* ATA (Association of Argentine *Travestis*) and in 1996 the *Asociación de Lucha por la Identidad Travesti* ALIT (Association for the Struggle for *Travesti* Identity) was coordinated by activist Lohana Berkins. Lohana's militancy led to two reports entitled *La gesta del nombre propio* (The feat of the proper name) and *Cumbia, copeteo y lágrimas*, writings that show the vulnerable situation of migrant *travestis* and transsexuals in the city of Buenos Aires. These papers became the first reports with statistical data in Latin America, reporting an average life expectancy of *travestis* in the region of between 35 and 38 years. This path of political militancy opened another debate, such as the recognition of self-perceived gender identity, which in 2012 was sanctioned in Argentina by Law No. 26743 on Gender Identity, a law agreed upon by the *travesti* and trans organizations of the country (Fernandez, 2020).

The strength of the oral histories of *travestis* can be translated into what Marlene Wayar (2019) calls a *travesti* epistemology, which is a "good enough" *travesti* theory of everyday lives traversed by conditions of poverty, discrimination, inequality and neglect by the State. These stories, histories, knowledge and experiences contribute to social work insofar as they make visible "other" forms of family existence, "other" ways of inhabiting bodies, respect for self-perceived identities, as well as the defence of the rights of *travestis* and transgender children, in the different intervention approaches (individual, family, group, community, among others). They also provide histories of care, relationship, dignity, strength and loving families among supportive and resourceful, though excluded and oppressed communities.

These trajectories of collective struggles of sexual dissidence[5] guide us to be able to think of more comprehensive and effective intervention strategies, although we must warn that in the field of disciplinary theoretical production, in relation to sex-gender dissidence, there are significant gaps. Langarita and Mesquida (2016, p. 173) point out that these debates are embryonic in social work. The contributions of Feminisms have been strong, but dialogues with the ideas of LGBTIQ+ studies and movements have taken time.

Social work: professional anti-oppressive intervention

Anti-oppressive professional interventions in social work demand an approach that engages with inequalities based on sex/gender, from a human rights-based approach, in dialogue with *travesti* and *marica* knowledge and experiences, and in accordance with the definition of social work proposed by the IFSW and the standards of undergraduate training suggested by the IASSW.

The IFSW (2022) proposes a global definition of what is understood by social work, stating that

> Social work is a practice-based profession and an academic discipline that promotes social change and development, social cohesion, and the empowerment and liberation of people. The principles of social justice, human rights, collective responsibility, and respect for diversity are fundamental to social work. Underpinned by social work theories, social sciences, humanities, and indigenous knowledge, social work engages people and structures to address life challenges and improve well-being.

In defining global standards for academic units that provide training in social work, the IASSW includes an equity and diversity section. It recommends that academic units ensure that educators, students and service users receive equal opportunities to learn and develop, beyond their gender and sexual orientation, among other diversities (IASSW, 2022).

The global definition of social work by the IFSW and the guidelines and recommendations provided by the IASSW do afford recognition and respect for diversities in general (including singularities related to sexuality). While these definitions and guidelines can be adjusted for context, they still fall short of addressing the challenges the profession still faces.

As noted earlier, depatriarchalization of social work is essential for social justice (Hermida, 2020), and this includes recognizing and respecting all sex-gender experiences. This is necessary as a minimum principle but it is also necessary to recognize that diverse non-cis-hetero experiences are valid and valuable, this includes respect for their singularities and an awareness that violence and oppression have too often been part of those same experiences. Ultimately, the political intention of these understandings is for a transformation of the hegemonic social order.

Social workers have been complicit in the reproduction of the oppressive sexual order, given that social work interventions have largely not been aimed at its interruption. This is what Langarita and Mesquida call "exercise of conciliation with the dominant logics" (2016, p. 174). Thus, we consider urgent the call by Facundo Zamarreño "to denaturalize everything, to question and problematize every interstice of our profession, in order to eradicate practices that, although they do not have that purpose, reproduce cis-hetero-normo-patriarchal logics" (2020, p. 5).

The following principles provide a way to review and expand our theoretical and practice knowledge, with the purpose of contributing to depatriachalization of professional interventions:

1 **Critical reflection on ourselves as practitioners**, as one of the most powerful tools for intervention. It is crucial to be able to ask ourselves questions such as: what happens to us when we think about sexuality? Does it connect with something we have studied/read/reflected on in our undergraduate training? What is our own experience and perception of gender? From where do we position ourselves professionally when we intervene in relation to sexualities? How is this connected to policy, social norms, cultural practices and religion?
2 **Expose, denaturalize and denounce concrete oppressive practices**: this implies analysing and questioning the cisheteronormative device as a matrix of discrimination based on sexual orientation, corporeality and gender identity/expression in the institutions we

inhabit (such as school, university, health centre, families, activist or political organizations, Barbero et al., 2021). This recommendation becomes even more relevant when it is our own colleagues who are the protagonists of such practices.

3 **Abandoning the assumption of people's gender** (Millet, 2020), a political decision we can apply in our daily interactions. This implies leaving aside the belief that we can know who a person is by the way they express themselves, dress, and smell (abandoning the "natural" link between genitality, sex, gender and gender expression). We must strive to decis-sexualize our practices, from the use of binary and cissexist forms to the way we deal with the people with whom we work.

4 Contribute to the progressive **expansion of access to rights for sex-gender dissident populations** (in alliance with the struggles of social movements and organizations in their territories). In some regions, there is still no positive recognition (legal normative) of fundamental human rights for LGBTIQ+ people such as civil marriage, gender identity and free expression of affection in public, among other violated rights that threaten the exercise of full sexual citizenship. Social work is not a profession that only seeks to contribute in guaranteeing access to already recognized rights but (and perhaps especially) also contributes to the processes of struggle and advocacy for the recognition and expansion of access to all rights for all people.

5 Develop **a high/strong/loving capacity to listen to dissident sex-gender subjectivities** (Martinez, 2019), housing their anguish and subjective suffering, problematizing institutional discourses that reproduce cisheteronormativity. As professionals, we must have the capacity and tools for when "to intervene is to accompany" (Morandi, 2020). While we are contributing little by little to the desired and necessary depatriarchalization of knowledge and practices, we are also providing the necessary assistance that the people who demand our intervention have a right to.

6 **Dehistoricize and problematize the notion of the patriarchal family** (Pérez Álvarez, 2013), on which many professional practices in social work have traditionally been based. This means incorporating variations in relation to modes of grouping, types of relationships, genders and sexual orientations of people who configure kinship and filiation links not exclusively and/or necessarily based on consanguinity and biology (Morandi, 2020).

7 Preserve enough openness so as **not to "protocolize" or normativize identities**, without undermining the agency that people make of them. Just as there are trans identities, for example, that are directed towards the binary gender opposite to the one assigned at birth, there are also identity experiences that are migrant, on the margins (Anzaldúa, 2016). Both processes of agency are genuine and may require professional accompaniment. In each situation, what we must prioritize is the embrace of the experience over the marking of agency. And in this sense, there will be struggles in which we may have to support visibilizations through the use of categories (LGBTIQNB+ or others). And there will be other struggles in which we will probably problematize and even shed those same categories. And this does not imply any contradiction but is part of the same emancipatory processes that are taking shape in each region and context.

8 **Make ourselves present in the mass media**, with megaphone strategies (Hermida, 2018) to dispute the hegemonic meanings reproduced to exhaustion around sexualities. Cultural changes also require interventions of massive impact, which manage to interpellate what people think and feel. On many occasions, the "urgencies" of the populations we

work with lead us to devote most of our energies and time to individualized intervention. We have the challenge of thinking how, without neglecting individual care, we can take that voice to the mass media. These challenges are collective, that is why we consider that the professional associations and councils of social work can play a direct and active role.

9 Work with trainers to **revise and update the curricula of our discipline.** We need a deep historiographic critique of the disciplinary training, and this would imply, as Figari (2009) says, "doing a political work", which would allow us to review stately frameworks that are still present in undergraduate training in social work (Gutiérrez Saracho, 2021). This revision would not only aim at the discursive inclusion in programs and curricular proposals of the topics referred to in this chapter but would also install monitoring devices for the effective implementation of perspectives and approaches to gender and sex-gender dissidence.

As Langarita and Mesquida (2016) say, we find ourselves in a stage of new redefinitions in social work at regional and global level, which is why we consider that any effort to emancipate our profession from colonial and patriarchal yokes is necessary and urgent. They add:

> If social work is committed to egalitarian relations, these must also be applied in professional practice and overcome the hegemonic sexual perspectives and gender binarism that still inundate professional work. This is why we cannot remain oblivious to the debates that other disciplines are having regarding sexuality and gender expressions, especially because we need to build our own discourse that allows us to guide interventions from a liberating and inclusive conception, capable of recognizing the richness of diversity. The oppressions derived from gender binarism and compulsory heterosexuality are a serious social problem that unequivocally concerns our discipline. This is why it is not only a question of looking for a new professional niche, but of constructing our own view of a reality that unquestionably challenges our profession.
>
> (p. 178)

María Eugenia Hermida (2020) adds that social work today intersects with the interpellations of the decolonial and feminist critical theories of the Global South. One of the challenges of this decolonial social work is precisely the depatriarchalization of knowledge and practice, as a condition for a transformative social intervention in neoliberal times. This calls for a dissident social work, as suggested by Benites and Fernandez (2021, p. 71), that recovers and nourishes itself from collective experiences and strategies, built by LGBTIQNB+ organizations, in the heat of social struggles for access to all rights.

In reality, both the supposed ignorance of these issues and -especially- the resistance to the social implications of the recognition of all rights for all people, within social work would be in connivance and complicity with the fascist and anti-gender positions that lurk worldwide. Let us recover then the *travesti* and *marica* imaginaries as possible repertoires for the revision of our disciplinary practices. In this way, we will be able to realize, together, the emancipations that we lack.

Notes

1 There is a widespread practice of linguistic resistance in the Global South that consists of resignifying the same words that the cisheteronorm uses to insult, displace, violate and even murder people of sex-gender dissidence, thus turning them into political and identity categories that host (each one with singular territorial nuances) the capacity to dispute the oppressive sexual order. "*Marica*" and "*puto*" are resignifications generally used by gay/homosexual populations, "*torta*" by lesbian populations, "*travesti*" by transgender populations, among others.
2   And the consequent use of pejorative categories to allude to any other family format that does not meet that moral standard. Think of notions such as "dysfunctional" families, for example.
3 We understand *sentipensar* from the contributions of Fals Borda (2009) and Walsh (2017) as a way to combat the split reason/affect operated by patriarchal colonial modernity. This implies identifying and valuing the political potency of recognizing ourselves as affected and situated bodies.
4   The statement of the IFSW Human Rights Commission can be viewed here: https://www.ifsw.org/ifsw-rights-commission-highlight-concerns-for-lgbtqi-people/
5   In Argentina, the struggles of transvestite and trans groups and organizations left as a recent legacy the approval of the trans labor quota law (Law 27636 on promotion of access to formal employment for transvestites, transsexuals and transgender people). There are, however, issues still under parliamentary debate: the Comprehensive Trans Law which covers protection from childhood to adulthood; the Historical Reparation Law for survivors of persecution by the state during the military dictatorship and in democracy; and the Anti-Discrimination Law which contemplates sexual dissidence.

References

Anzaldúa, G. (2016). *Borderlands / La frontera. La nueva mestiza.* España: Capitan Swing.
Barbero, C. O., Stival, E. D. y Zanutigh, V. (2021). "Háganse cargo": reflexiones en torno a intervenciones asistenciales con poblaciones travestis-trans. *Conciencia Social. Revista digital de Trabajo Social,* 5(9): 136–152. https://revistas.unc.edu.ar/index.php/ConCiencia Social/article/view/35353
Benites, M. A. y Fernandez, J. N. (2021). *Procesos de acceso a la salud integral de poblaciones travesti-trans: una aproximación al Programa provincial de implementación de políticas de género y diversidad sexual en el Centro de Atención Primaria de la salud Jorge Newbery del Partido de general Pueyrredón. 2020* [Tesis de licenciatura en Trabajo Social no publicada]. Universidad Nacional de Mar del Plata.
De Sousa Santos, B. (2009). *Una Epistemología del Sur. La reinvención del conocimiento y la emancipación social.* Buenos Aires: Siglo XXI Editores, CLACSO.
Fals Borda, O. ([1979] 2009). Cómo investigar la realidad para transformarla. En *Una sociología sentipensante para América Latina.* Bogotá: Siglo del Hombre Editores. CLACSO Editorial. http://biblioteca.clacso.edu.ar/clacso/se/20160308051848/09como.pdf
Fernandez, J. (2020). *La Berkins, una combatiente de frontera.* Argentina: Editorial Sudamericana.
Figari, C. E. (2009). *Eróticas de la disidencia en América Latina. Brasil Siglo XVII y XX.* 1a ed. Buenos Aires: Fundación Centro de Integración, Comunicación, Cultura y Sociedad- CICCUS- CLACSO.
Figari, C. E. (2010). El movimiento LGBT en América Latina: institucionalizaciones oblicuas. En A. Massetti, E. Villanueva y M. Gómez (comps) *Movilizaciones, protestas e identidades colectivas en la Argentina del bicentenario* (pp. 225–240). Buenos Aires: Nueva Trilce.
Galindo, M. (2013). *No se puede descolonizar sin despatriarcalizar. Teoría y propuesta de la despatriarcalización.* Bolivia: Mujeres Creando.
Giribuela, W. (2020). Emancipaciones en duda: las sexualidades contra-hegemónicas en la formación disciplinar. Conciencia Social. *Revista digital de Trabajo Social,* 4(7), 136–149. https://revistas.unc.edu.ar/index.php/ConCienciaSocial/article/view/30752 ISSN 2591-5339
Gutiérrez Saracho, A. G. (2015). *Aportes al trabajo social desde la visión de la diversidad afectivosexual y de género.* Revista A-INTER-VENIR N° 8, II Jornadas Latinoamericanas y VIII Jornadas

Disciplinares de Trabajo Social "Trabajo Social: debates, experiencias territoriales, sentidos y disputas en Latinoamérica" 21, 22 y 23 de Octubre de 2015, San Fernando del Valle de Catamarca, Argentina. Rhttp://editorial.unca.edu.ar/Publicacione%20on%20line/A-INTERVENIR%20ONLINE/PDF/A-INTERVENIR%208/PDF/10%20gutierrezsaracho.pdf

Gutiérrez Saracho, A. (2021). Trabajo Social y Disidencia Sexual, Memorias, olvidos y experiencias de la trayectoria de formación profesional. Material de Cátedra Antropología Social y Cultural-Licenciatura en Trabajo Social. F.H. UNCa.

Hermida, M. E. (2018). *Derechos, neoliberalismo y Trabajo Social. Por una reconceptualización descolonial del enfoque de derechos en la intervención profesional.* En "XXIX Congreso Nacional de Trabajo Social: La dimensión ético-política en el ejercicio profesional: la revisión de las prácticas en la actual coyuntura" organizado por FAAPSS. Santa Fe, Argentina.

Hermida, M. E. (2020). La tercera interrupción en Trabajo Social: descolonizar y despatriarcalizar. *Revista Libertas, Juiz de Fora*, 20(1), 94–119.

Langarita, J. A. y Mesquida, J. M. (2016). Interpelaciones de las sexualidad(es) al Trabajo Social. Apuntes para una praxis renovada. En E. Pastor y E. Raya (eds.), *Trabajo Social, derechos humanos e innovación social* (pp. 171–182). Navarra: Thompson Reuters.

Martinez, S. (2019). *Trabajo Social y Diversidad Sexual*. Buenos Aires: Editorial Espacio.

Mattio, E. (2020). *Una vez más, l*s sujet*s del feminismo*. En Revista Ideas, de filosofía moderna y contemporánea. Año 5 – Número 11. CABA, Argentina. http://ragif.com.ar/revista_ideas/IDEAS-11Dobles.pdf

Millet, A. (2020). *Cisexismo y salud. Algunas ideas desde otro lado. Colección Justicia Epistémica*. Buenos Aires: puntos suspensivos ediciones.

Morandi, M. (2020). Breve historia de cuerpos, sexualidades y militancias que interpelan nuestro oficio cotidiano. *Periódico digital*. www.elciudadanoweb.com. Recuperado de: https://www.elciudadanoweb.com/breve-historia-de-cuerpos-sexualidades-y-militancias-que-interpelan-nuestro-oficio-cotidiano/

Oliva, A. (2015). *Trabajo social y lucha de clases: análisis histórico de las modalidades de intervención en Argentina.* La Plata: Dynamis.

Ortiz, F. F. (2022). *Discursos sobre homosexualidad/gaycidad de les estudiantes en la toma de la Universidad Nacional de Río Cuarto en 2018* [Tesis de licenciatura en Trabajo Social no publicada]. Universidad Nacional de Río Cuarto.

Parra, G. (2001). *Antimodernidad y Trabajo Social. Orígenes y expansión del trabajo social en Argentina.* Buenos Aires: Espacio Editorial.

Peña Ruiz Tagle, J. (2016). Hitos y trayectoria del movimiento de Lesbianas, Gays, Transexuales y Bisexuales (LGTB) en Chile. Tesis de Profesorado de Historia y Ciencias Sociales. Universidad Austral de Chile, Chile.

Peralta, M. (2018). Cuerpo(s), micropolítica y género en Trabajo Social. Reflexiones corporizadas de experiencias profesionales. Colección "La Universidad Pública pública". Paraná, Entre Ríos, Argentina: Editorial Fundación La Hendija.

Pérez Álvarez, A. (2013). Poner el grito en el cielo: Diversidad sexual e identidades de género en familias con prácticas patriarcales en Cartagena de Indias, 2010-2012. *Revista Palobra*, palabra que obra (Universidad de Cartagena), No. 13, Agosto de 2013. https://doi.org/10.32997/2346-2884-vol.13-num.13-2013-80

Perlongher, N. (1997). Prosa Plebeya. Ensayos 1980-1992. Selección y prólogo de Cristian Ferrer y Osvaldo Baigorria. Buenos Aires, Colihue (Colección Puñaladas, ensayos de punta).

Ponce, E. (2022). *Cuentos breves, historias largas. Filosofar situado desde Catamarca*. Argentina: Editorial el Guadal.

Walsh, C. (2017). *Entretejiendo lo pedagógico y lo decolonial: Luchas, caminos y siembras de reflexión-acción para resistir, (re) existir y (re) vivir*. Valle de Cauca: Alternativas.

Wayar, M. (2019). *Travesti. Una teoría lo suficientemente buena*. Argentina: Editorial Muchas Nueces.

Zamarreño, F. M. (2020). El registro como herramienta política para un Trabajo Social desheteronormativizado. En Margen. *Revista de Trabajo Social*, número 96. https://www.margen.org/suscri/margen96/Zamarreno-96.pdf

Sitios web consultados

IASSW (2022). Asociación Internacional de Escuelas de Trabajo Social AIETS. Estándares globales de formación en Trabajo Social. https://www.iassw-aiets.org/wp-content/uploads/2020/11/IASSW-Global_Standards_Final.pdf

IFSW (2022). Federación Internacional de Trabajo Social FITS. Definición global de la profesión del Trabajo Social. https://www.ifsw.org/what-is-social-work/global-definition-of-social-work/

LatFem. (2017). Murió Mariela Muñoz, la primera madre trans de la Argentina. https://latfem.org/murio-mariela-munoz-la-primera-madre-trans-de-la-argentina/

Revista Sudestada. (2020). Cinco años sin la gigante (aniversario del fallecimiento de Mariela Muñoz). https://www.facebook.com/sudestadarevista/photos/a.879790025391544/5118617768175394/?type=3

37
GENERATION OLD AND PROUD
No going back in the closet

Teresa Savage and Jude Irwin

Introduction

As older members of LGBTIQ+ communities, we ourselves experienced stigma and systemic discrimination. We are both older, white cisgender lesbians (Trans Hub, 2021). We include ourselves when writing collectively about older LGBTIQ+ people in this chapter. We use a Trans-Inclusive and intersectional Feminist lens to unpack how experiences of discrimination, ageism, marginalisation and trauma, combined with ignorant, indifferent and even neglectful responses from governments, ageing, health and community organisations, individuals and groups in the broader community, have limited the ways LBGTIQ+ people grow older. We explore ways in which feminist social workers and other practitioners and service providers involved in counselling and advocacy work with individuals, communities, families and groups, as well as policymakers can challenge dominant narratives of sexuality, identity, bodily presentation, sex characteristics and family structures to ensure that older LGBTIQ+ people are treated with dignity and respect and are able to live happy and fulfilling lives.

A trans-inclusive and intersectional feminist approach

Feminists advocate for equality and equity based on gender, gender expression, gender identity, sex, and sexuality. Embedded in this is a broader commitment to work towards a just society by challenging the numerous forms of inequality, exclusion and oppression that some individuals, groups and communities confront in their daily lives (Wendt & Moulding, 2017). Feminism is a commitment to eradicating the oppression of **all** women.

Gender is critical to feminism. Gender identity refers to a person's understanding of their own gender. We argue that gender identity is based on a person's own internal sense of self and their gender and not solely based on their physical sex characteristics, or the sex they were assigned at birth. Non-binary people don't identify with the sex they were assigned at birth, and neither do they feel like a 'girl' or a 'boy' – they don't identify exclusively as male or female. Adopting a trans inclusive and intersectional feminist lens strengthens women's position, protects all women from oppression and brings trans inclusivity into our practice and our organisations. If gender is narrowly understood based solely on physical sex, it does not meet the goals of inclusive feminism and plays a contributing role in reinforcing women's oppression (Kirkland, 2019). A definition of 'woman' that excludes trans women and non-binary people ignores the ways in which patriarchal and misogynistic attitudes impact their lives, particularly when thinking about the lives of LGBTIQ+ older people where gender identity and sexuality intersect with cultural and linguistic diversity. A joint statement released on violence against transgender women at the 47th Session of the Human Rights Council stated 'Studies show that there has been a steady increase in the global number of reported murders of trans and gender non-conforming persons, with at least 3,664 murders documented since 2008, of which 97% had transgender women as victims' (Independent Expert by the Group of Friends of the Sexual Orientation and Gender Identity (SOGI), 2021, p. 1). Including trans women and non-binary people in our feminist analysis of the lives of older LGBTIQ+ people recognises this global injustice.

All older LGBTIQ+ people experience discrimination both as members of the LGBTIQ+ community, and as older people in a society which valorises youth, binary identities and normative sexualities. Intersectionality is an analytical framework that describes how the overlapping or intersecting of identities and social marginalisation impacts experiences of oppression and discrimination (Crenshaw, 2017). An understanding of Intersectionality shows how gender, race, ethnicity, sexuality, disability, class, age, religion, bodily presentation, and geography are interconnected and compound other forms of social exclusion (Miller & Bassett, 2020). Taking an intersectional viewpoint reveals the many ways that structural inequalities influence our lives and recognises the particular forms of oppression that some groups experience and how these create barriers to support (Kostecki & Macfarlane, 2019). Many older LGBTIQ+ people have intersecting identities, both across the LGBTIQ+ spectrum of experience (eg. Transwomen who identify as lesbian) and also across other structurally disadvantaged identities such as living with a disability or being from a particular cultural background or religion.

Experiences of stigma and discrimination often cause us to hide our authentic selves to ensure our safety. However, over the last several decades, activism, initiated and led by members of LGBTIQ+ communities and our allies, has contributed to significant structural, social and cultural change, increasing the visibility of LGBTIQ+ communities and individuals. LGBTIQ+ communities are diverse, incorporating people from different age groups, sexualities, ethnicities, religions, family structures and social, cultural and political backgrounds. In this chapter, we focus on older members of LGBTIQ+ communities in Australia.

History has had a powerful impact on the lives of older LGBTIQ+ people who have lived through very challenging times. To fully understand the lifelong experiences of older LGBTIQ+ people it is important to have some knowledge of the history of discrimination in Australia. We contextualise this chapter by briefly exploring how the beliefs, practices and values generated by the colonist's invasion of Australia have been embedded into our ways of life and how the growth of activism in the Global North in the 1950s and 1960s propelled lesbians, gay men, trans people and later others from all LGBTIQ+ communities to campaign for change. We share stories from older LGBTIQ+ community members that were gathered from consultations held in 2019 and 2020 in response to Australia's Royal Commission into Aged Care Quality and Safety, developed and delivered by LGBTIQ+ Health Australia (formerly LGBTI Health Alliance) (LHA, 2021c). The lived experience of older LGBTIQ+ people, recalling the struggles that we, as a group, have confronted and how these have influenced the way we grow older, creates the opportunity for us to explore ways in which practitioners in the health, human and community services, policymakers, counsellors and advocacy workers can contribute positively to the lives of older people from LGBTIQ+ communities by providing accessible, inclusive and appropriate services and treat us with dignity and respect.

The social, political and cultural context and the impact of history on our lives today

In contemporary discourse there is an assumption that the history of so-called Australia is homogenous, with one dominant narrative. Diversity is not new. While social and liberation movements in the last 50 years have foregrounded the experience, needs and desires of diverse population groups, we know that First Nations people, migrants from non-Anglo countries, gender and sexually diverse people, and those with religious beliefs beyond Christianity all play a part in the history of Australia. Despite this, the values, beliefs and practices of the invaders have had a powerful influence on the Australia we live in today, impacting communities and people in different and complex ways.

The colonial concept of Australia as a homogenous nation denies the fact that diversity existed pre-colonisation. Australia is home to the world's oldest continuous and diverse cultures and is made up of around 250 Aboriginal and Torres Strait Islanders groups, the First Nations people of Australia, each with their own territories, cultural practices and languages (Walsh & Yallop, 1993). The traditional owners of the land thrived for more than 60,000 years before Australia was invaded and colonised by Britain in 1788, stealing the land from the rightful owners. Sovereignty has never been ceded. The invasion led to the devastation of First Nations peoples, who were removed from their lands, their connection to the country, and their spiritual life and subject to a violent war waged against them. Their access to food was compromised and their children were stolen. The devastating effects of this on First Nations people are intergenerational and have an on-going impact (Perkins, 2022).

The invasion marked the beginning of racism and other forms of structural injustice in Australia, legitimising racist politics, practices, values and institutions. The racist and discriminatory treatment and attitudes experienced by immigrants from diverse cultural, ethnic, religious and class backgrounds who came to Australia is an example of the powerful influence of the values, beliefs and practices of the invaders (Lake & Reynolds, 2008; Stratton, 1998). Older Australians have been subject to racist and colonialist systems and structures as part of our everyday experience, and these power imbalances characterise attitudes towards ageing and aged care (Hastings & Rogowski, 2015).

From the 1960s, Australia and other parts of the Western world saw the huge development and growth of social and political liberation movements, with the radicalising of many marginalised and oppressed groups and communities fighting for equality, justice and human rights. In Australia, First Nations people advocated for rights denied them for two centuries and began campaigning for political and cultural recognition. The millions of immigrants who had arrived in Australia after WW2 challenged their economic, social, structural and racial inequalities, second wave feminists advocated for gender equality and rights, lesbian and gay activists began to lay claims for equality, visibility and safety. This growth of social movements led to a new politics of identity, standing for individual freedom to pursue diverse lifestyles, cultural practices and social behaviour.

Generation old and proud

Australia's long history of violence towards people of diverse sexualities and genders, leading to widespread systemic discrimination in many forms, has had an impact on how we, as members of LGBTIQ+ communities, have lived our lives. Surviving and thriving in a society that regularly threatens a healthy sense of self takes its toll. The experience of systemic and individual violence and abuse has been a regular occurrence in the lives of many members of LGBTIQ+ communities. In Australia gay men grew up at a time when homosexuality was illegal, and in some Australian states anal sex was a crime punishable by death (Croome, 2007). Many endured conversion practices to 'cure' their homosexuality. Gay men or men who were perceived as being gay and transgender women were bashed and murdered in Sydney and in Adelaide a gay man was thrown into a river and drowned, allegedly at the hands of the police (Reeves, 2022). A significant number of people from LGBTIQ+ communities were impacted by the violence that occurred at the first Gay and Lesbian Mardi Gras parade in 1978 and the spectre of police assaulting and arresting 58 people (Marsh & Galbraith, 1995). Lesbians were exposed to violence, discrimination and vilification on the street and lesbian mothers regularly lost custody of their children (Jennings, 2012). Intersex infants, unable to give consent, were and are regularly subjected to surgery aimed at establishing medical and social norms of male and female bodies (OII Australia, 2014). Trans people were not recognised as their authentic gender, often being forced to disclose private information, face harassment and regularly denied employment opportunities. Intersex people endured forced coercive medical practices that violated their human rights, and on-going stigmatisation, discrimination, bullying, body shaming and a raft of misconceptions about gender identity and sexuality. Workplace discrimination was rampant with LGBTIQ+ people sharing their stories of systemic and individual discrimination in their workplaces, including being refused employment or denied promotion, having their careers restricted because of their sexual and gender identity with many not reporting this as they did not feel safe (Irwin, 1999).

Changes began to happen slowly, and in 1984, New South Wales decriminalised male acts of homosexuality with the age of consent at 18, despite heterosexual consent remaining at 16 (Bull et al., 1991). In 1992 the federal government removed the ban on same sex attracted women and men serving in the military (Riseman, 2015; *The Conversation*, 2017). In 1997 the High Court of Australia upheld the gay panic defence which was not abolished until 2020 (Equality Australia, 2020). Same sex couples were not entitled to some forms of income supports and other commonwealth government entitlements until 2008, after extended activism by LGBTIQ+ communities and their allies, 84 commonwealth laws that had discriminated against same sex couples and their children in areas including income support, migration, taxation, superannuation, educational assistance and family law and child support were amended (Irwin, 2009).

After a long and bruising struggle, same-sex marriage was legalised in 2018, when many of our cohort were already in their seventies and eighties (Rugg, 2019). In the same year, same-sex couples were allowed to adopt in all jurisdictions of Australia (Human Rights Law Centre, 2018). After another long campaign, transgender people are no longer forced to divorce after changing the gender on their birth certificate (*ABC News*, 2018).

As older members of LGBTIQ+ communities despite our activism and fighting for equality, many of us have lived with unfair practices and various forms of discrimination which has had different impacts on us as individuals and as communities.

What do we know about older members of LGBTIQ+ communities?

Older LGBTIQ+ people are not exempt from the impact of ageism, directed both from mainstream society and from within LGBTIQ+ communities. Within LGBTIQ+ communities an emphasis on young normative bodies, social activities based on physical capabilities, social networks defined by age cohorts and stereotypes of, for example, the 'lonely old queen', are all too common. Inclusive intergenerational activities are rare.

In the final report of the Royal Commission into Aged Care Quality and Safety, Commissioner Lynelle Briggs writes:

... I fear that society as a whole undervalues older people and their contribution. The acceptance of poorer service provision in aged care reflects an undervaluing of the worth of older people, assumptions and stereotypes about older people and their capabilities, and ageism towards them. This must change.
(Royal Commission into Aged Care Quality and Safety: Final Report, 2021, p. 26)

Bringing about change requires having comprehensive knowledge about and from the communities towards which the change is directed. However, capturing the complex experiences of older LGBTIQ+ people is fraught with challenges. The Australian Census does not include questions relating to sexual orientation, gender identity and intersex status, despite considerable lobbying efforts, so the quantitative information available is patchy. However, it is estimated that around 11% of Australians have diverse sexual orientation, sex or gender identity (Wilson et al., 2020).

Obtaining qualitative data about the general well-being, health and life experiences of older LGBTIQ+ people can also pose challenges. We rely on small-scale studies, which use different definitions, different survey techniques and different contexts (Wilson et al., 2020). This is further complicated by older LGBTIQ+ people often choosing not to disclose their gender identity or sexual orientation because of previous negative experiences. However, in January 2021 the Australian Bureau of Statistics released a Standard which, if widely adopted, will enable the consistent collection of data for sex, gender, variations of sex characteristics and sexual orientation. Consistent data will facilitate a much clearer picture of the health and well-being of LGBTIQ+ communities (*ABS*, 2020).

LGBTIQ+ people in Australia are recognised as a priority population for health policy, because we still carry the burden of higher rates of suicide and suicidal ideation than the mainstream community, higher rates of alcohol and other drug use, poorer mental health outcomes, on-going health issues related to HIV/AIDs status, and significant levels of discrimination, stigma, violence and other forms of oppression (LHA, 2021a).

LGBTIQ+ Health Australia produces a regular snapshot of mental health and suicide prevention data. The 2021 edition reports that 19.2% of LGBT people aged 60–89 (21.6% men and 16.7% women) reported having been diagnosed or treated for any mental disorder in the past three years, 19.4% of transgender and gender-diverse people aged 50 and over reported having a major depressive syndrome and 10.2% of transgender and gender-diverse people aged 50 and over reported having an anxiety syndrome (LHA, 2021b). Other studies have reported high levels of suicide in post operative trans women (Wiepjes et al., 2020).

Structural and individualised experiences of stigma and discrimination accumulate across the life span, rendering older LGBTIQ+ people more vulnerable to higher rates of disability, depression, anxiety and loneliness than the mainstream community

(Fredriksen-Goldsen, 2015). It has been shown that older LGBTIQ+ people have fewer social support- networks, including family and particularly children, and are more likely to live alone (Hughes, 2016). A society structured around cisgender, heterosexual, monogamous nuclear families has left many older LGBTIQ+ people socially isolated, with consequent impacts on quality of life, physical and mental health and longevity (WHO, 2021). During COVID-19 while social isolation increased for all older people it was magnified for older LGBTIQ+ people (LHA, 2020a).

In 2018 the Australian government established a Royal Commission into Aged Care Quality and Safety to examine the adequacy of aged care and develop solutions to improve the system, which was seen to be failing older Australians. In response LGBTIQ+ Health Australia (LHA) consulted extensively across the country through face-to-face workshops, and then as COVID impacted, through local online forums, interviews and surveys. Older First Nations LGBTIQ+ people, older LGBTIQ+ Australians, their friends, advocates and families, as well as LGBTIQ+ aged care workers were included in these consultations. LHA made seven detailed submissions to the Commission with 70 recommendations, which addressed the substantial barriers to older LGBTIQ+ people accessing aged care services (LHA, 2021c).

Stigma, discrimination and prevailing heteronormative attitudes combined with strict binary views of gender all conspire to make aged care a potentially dangerous and traumatising place for older LGBTIQ+ people. The lived experiences and reflections on the aged care system used in this chapter originate in these submissions.

Older LGBTIQ+ people's lived experience and views about aged care services and supports

Particular issues arise when older LGBTIQ+ people make the decision to seek aged care services. Many report a fear of losing their autonomy through institutionalised control, prejudice and discrimination (Crameri et al., 2015). This takes many forms.

Discrimination against trans people was referred to frequently. A non-binary regional aged care worker commented (LHA, 2021c, p. 104):

> *A transgender woman I visit never seems to have hair or makeup done as part of a daily 'routine' offered to other women, only when an LGBTI visitor attends to do this care voluntarily.*

The lack of awareness about the lives of LGBTIQ+ people can result in unintentional discrimination. An example is using the incorrect pronouns for trans and non-binary people.

An Aboriginal gay man in his mid-fifties from regional NSW commented (LHA, 2021c, p. 128)

> *It is neglect. In the aged care home I visit there's a transgender lady – they use the wrong pronouns. She stated who she is and the correct pronouns to be used but they don't. She can't articulate, she's had a stroke, but she is aware of her surroundings.*

Some of the participants talked about challenging myths about LGBTIQ+ people that circulate and influence how people could be treated. An older trans woman stated (LHA, 2021b, p. 15)

It's a myth that trans and gender diverse people with dementia want to revert to their gender assigned at birth. It's just an excuse to squash their authentic self.

Assuming and treating older LGBTIQ+ people as though they are heterosexual was common. A 75-year-old lesbian commented (LHA, 2021c)

I've heard staff say to older women, 'he's keen on you' or 'we will make you look nice because there's a new fella in here today'.

Some services proudly assert that they 'treat everybody the same' but many neglect to provide a culturally safe environment, and risk exposing older LGBTIQ+ people to harmful treatment. Older LGBTI+ people can have a realistic fear that they will be forced back into the closet, hiding their sexuality and gender identity to keep themselves safe.

A 72-year-old regional gay man recounted (LHA, 2021c, p. 101)

My friend had known this out gay man for years. The moment he went into this facility, he was told he had to suppress his gay identity. He was told this! He felt he was back in the closet for the first time in 40 years. Some of these hardwired workers need years of therapy to unlearn their homophobia. People may pretend to be very open minded, but when it comes to the crunch [they're] not.

The LGBTIQ+ community is not homogenous and knowledge of how the intersection of different forms of oppression may play out in a person's life is important. An understanding of different cultural practices can make a huge difference in how practitioners work with diverse groups of older LGBTIQ+ people. An Aboriginal urban lesbian in her mid-seventies commented:

Older Brotherboys and Sistergirls will not ask. They need to be told what is being offered to them and given time to think it over. It may take time before people allow themselves to accept support and services.

First Nations people commonly have longstanding, complex and diverse concepts of gender and sexual orientation which integrate difference. In Australia, First Nations people who are trans generally refer to themselves as Sistergirls or Brotherboys. A Sistergirl is a First Nations person who has a female spirit, and who takes on female roles within their community, while Brotherboys have a male spirit and take on male roles in their communities (Trans Hub, n.d.). Sistergirls and Brotherboys make up a significant cohort of First Nations older LGBTIQ+ people. As an older urban Sistergirl commented (LHA, 2020b, p. 12):

As a Sistergirl, it's hard enough to be accepted in society and then at that age having to go into a place that doesn't accept you with other aged care clients that don't accept you.

Many older LGBTI people have been rejected and marginalised by their family of origin. Many do not have children. It is common for LGBTIQ+ people to create their own family-of-choice by forging strong, intimate bonds with friends, who may share experiences of discrimination and who offer help and support and provide a sense of belonging. These families-of-choice are not always recognised and acknowledged, and harmful assumptions can be made about who exactly is important in the life of an LGBTIQ+ person. If family is narrowly constructed as biologically or legally constructed, then decision-making may be offered to people who know little about the life and experience of the LGBTIQ+ person, or who may hold negative views. As an older urban bisexual man commented (LHA, 2021c, p. 103):

Find ways to keep us connected with our support networks, our friends, and the humans who understand us and accept us for who we are without condition.

Some commented on the importance of being listened to, heard and treated with respect. A 72-year-old lesbian recounted (LHA, 2020b, p. 6):

A nurse asked us one day about our relationship. She was a warm person and had shown us lots of kindness. We told her we were partners and she asked us if we were married (we were not). This was not long after marriage equality went through and word about our relationship spread around the home. Everyone was so supportive and welcoming of us. We don't believe in marriage, but we did want to make a formal commitment to each other. This seemed more important now that we were separated (one still at home & the other in residential care). The staff helped us to plan and hold a ceremony at the residential care home, with our family, friends, and other residents. We have been so welcomed and well cared for and we have not only been encouraged but supported to celebrate our relationship(40+yrs).

Some commented on the importance of accessing services that they trusted. A 55-year-old intersex woman commented on the availability of specific services (LHA, 2020b, p. 13);

If possible, I would like to be able to seek out a specialist service or a known, recommended service provider.

The importance of valuing the life experiences and possible contributions of older LGBTIQ+ people is often minimised or dismissed. An older lesbian talked about how valuable her experiences of collective living may be for her as she gets older (LHA, 2020b, p. 4):

Collective living, it is a strength that lesbians bring into ageing, collective living experiences might keep us out of aged care.

Similarly a sixty one year old gay man living in an urban area stated (LHA, 2020b, p. 9):

It's the same as in the 80s. We have experience developing community response to HIV/AIDS. It starts with the community caring –but where's the LGBTI community response to ageing?

Some talked about how feedback can be perceived as problematic when it is meant to lead to positive change. As an older trans man living in regional Australia commented (LHA, 2020b, p. 11):

We don't want to punish people. We want them to see a complaint as a chance to improve.

'Nothing about us without us' is a term borrowed from the disability rights movement, which describes the principle that people from marginalised groups are the experts in their own lives and are central to developing solutions to their own oppression. The same is true for older LGBTIQ+ people. Any new policy, project or service involving the care of older people must include the voices, experience and aspirations of older LGBTIQ+ people. An 80-year-old urban lesbian shared (LHA, 2021c, p. 97):

We want to be part of the role of change not just recipients. I think the government are afraid of a militant ageing population.

Working with older LGBTIQ+ people in a trans inclusive feminist way

Working with older LGBTIQ+ people from a Trans Inclusive and Intersectional Feminist approach means being aware, identifying and challenging all the barriers that can exclude older LGBTIQ+ people from accessing and participating in aged care services and contributing to a rights-based aged care system. Our suggestions to develop and fine-tune inclusive practice, knowledge, skills and values include, but are not limited to, the following:

1 Becoming educated about our LGBTIQ+ history and current issues

To adopt a rights-based and trans inclusive and intersectional feminist approach in working with older LGBTIQ+ people we need to have a comprehensive knowledge of LGBTIQ+ history and how this intersects with other forms of marginalisation and impacts the health and well-being of older LGBTIQ+ people and their willingness to access aged care services. This will be enhanced by remaining updated about current health disparities and contemporary discrimination and stigma.

2 Developing a critical approach

Practitioners need to develop a critical lens, building on their capacity to critically reflect and contest policies, practice, behaviours and values that support and sustain dominance, exclusion and marginalisation of older LGBTIQ+ people. This can mean identifying and challenging existing policies and practices that do not consider the diversity of service users, challenging discriminatory and unjust treatment and behaviour. Developing a critical lens enables practitioners to identify discriminatory processes and contribute to change towards inclusive practice, enhancing their ability to work with older LGBTIQ+ people with care, respect and dignity.

3 Ensuring cultural safety

Inclusive practice can be built around the enhancement of cultural safety, including cultural awareness and cultural sensitivity for older LGBTIQ+ people (Crameri et al., 2015). This includes having an understanding of how the health, well-being and lives of older LGBTIQ+ people are framed by their histories. Inclusive practice can be strengthened by the knowledge of the history of LGBTIQ+ people in Australia and the intersections of other forms of marginalisation, understanding how the needs of older LGBTIQ+ people may differ from other older people, while keeping in mind the diversity within the older LGBTIQ+ communities. For example, in Aboriginal communities, the terms Sistergirls and Brotherboys validate and strengthen the gender identities and relationships of transgender people.

4 Respecting and including families of choice

It is critical to be aware of how important families of choice are too older LGBTIQ+ people in relation to the deep level of connection and emotional and practical support they provide. Take the time to understand exactly who is important in the life of older LGBTIQ+ people, make them feel welcome and include them in decision-making.

5 Using appropriate language

It is important to be sensitive about the use of the term *Queer* with older people. Older LGBTIQ+ people regularly assert that it is a word that can never be rehabilitated from a time when it was used as a cruel slur. Many prefer the term LGBTI. It is always best to consult with older people about how they would like to be described. Similarly, it is a common criticism that "LGBTIQ+" is an unwieldy term, too long and too difficult to remember and subject to continual revision. When working with our communities it is our suggestion to accept current terminology and to remember and acknowledge that while each group under the LGBTIQ+ umbrella has issues and challenges in common, particularly including experiences of legal and social marginalisation on the basis of prevailing social norms around sex, gender and sexuality, each community has its own unique history and contemporary experience of discrimination. This includes those who are not part of the dominant settler culture.

6 Using LGBTIQ+ inclusive language and correct pronouns

LGBTIQ+ inclusive language is a way of acknowledging and respecting the diversity of bodies, genders and relationships. By using LGBTIQ+ inclusive language, we are showing our respect for all LGBTIQ+ people.

Using the correct pronouns is critical as it confirms a person's sense of themselves and builds rapport and trust. Misgendering, either intentionally or accidentally, is when a person is referred to using language that doesn't align with their affirmed gender, for example continuing to speak about a trans woman as 'he'. Dead-naming is when a person is addressed by the name they used before they affirmed their gender. Misgendering and deadnaming stigmatise trans and non-binary people and could potentially run the risk of invading their privacy and exposing them to others who may harass them or discriminate against them. A 2018 study found that when transgender young people were regularly addressed by their chosen name, their risk of depression and suicide decreased (Russell et al., 2018) If you make a mistake, apologise clearly and move on.

7 Becoming an active ally

The most important contribution social workers and other community service practitioners can make to the well-being of older LGBTIQ+ people (if they are not LGBTIQ+ themselves) is to become a powerful and effective ally. Firstly, this involves listening and learning about the history and contemporary struggles of LGBTIQ+ people and thinking deeply about how that lived experience impacts the delivery of aged care services. It also involves being visible in support, including attending events and speaking out against homophobia and transphobia. This can be frightening. Social workers and community service practitioners are in a unique position to watch out for the well-being of older LGBTIQ+ people and provide emotional support. Actively promote the voices of older LGBTIQ people, rather than your own, and facilitate their full involvement in developing best practice solutions. Take every opportunity to speak to others about your knowledge of the challenges facing LGBTIQ+ older people and encourage them to become an ally too.

8 Listening, hearing and understanding

Listening needs to be intentional to be able to hear and understand the meaning of the speaker. Deep listening means listening with an open mind and an awareness of where the speaker is coming from, creating the possibility of strong empathic ties and a trusting and supportive relationship.

9 Collaborating with older LGBTIQ+ people in decision-making at both an individual community and government level

It is critical to collaborate with LGBTIQ+ people in the development of policy, projects or programs or in any decision-making that involves them, rather than creating programs without their involvement or making decisions for them. We are the experts in our own lives and the wealth of our lived experience is invaluable in ensuring that services and programs are targeted to our needs. It is disappointing to note that in Australia, the newly formed Aged Care Council of Elders, a group critical to the success of the reformed aged care system, does not include any publicly acknowledged LGBTIQ+ people (Australian Government Department of Health and Aged Care, 2024).

10 Advocating for the rights of workers in aged care.

If we believe that LGBTIQ+ older people deserve equitable access to high-quality and culturally safe aged care services, then we need to ensure that workers and staff in aged care services have the time, the training, the support, the conditions and adequate remuneration to enable them to provide that care. Appropriate staffing levels that allow time to be spent with individuals would make a huge difference. Positive action to recruit LGBTIQ+ staff, and ensure that the service is a comfortable place to work will enhance the experience of older LGBTIQ+ people (LHA, 2020a). In Australia, the Silver Rainbow project provides support and guidance to service providers and policymakers about how to meet the needs of older LGBTIQ+ people (LHA, n.d.).

Conclusion

'A rights based aged care system which empowers older LGBTIQ+ people to live fulfilled lives free from discrimination.' (LHA, 2020d, p. 4). This was the foundational recommendation in the LHA submissions to the Royal Commission into Aged Care Quality and Safety, a demand for governments and providers at both policy and practice levels to improve the care of older LGBTIQ+ people.

Social workers, policy analysts, advocates, and service providers, working both in and outside the aged care sector have a key role to play in this. Supporting and fighting for a rights based aged care system from a trans inclusive feminist approach will challenge the unjust practices that have re-enforced the inequality that exists in the aged care system, marginalising older LGBTIQ+ people and other groups in the community.

If adopted, the best-practice actions we recommend in this chapter will improve the lives of older LGBTIQ+ people. But these actions also have broad-reaching impacts. If we get it right for older LGBTIQ+ people, including those with intersecting marginalisation, then we'll get it right for everyone (LHA, 2020d, p. 1).

Acknowledgements

We would like to thank Kathy Mansfield and Nancy Worcester for their feedback on earlier drafts of this paper. We are also grateful for the advice and support of Nicky Bath, CEO of LGBTIQ+ Health Australia (LHA), and pay tribute to all the older First Nations LGBTIQ+ people, older LGBTIQ+ community members, their friends, advocates and families, as well as LGBTIQ+ aged care workers who told their stories for LHA's submissions to the Ageing and Aged Care Royal Commission. Your willingness to speak out enables change to happen.

References

ABC News (2018). Queensland Laws Changed for Married Transgender Couples. https://www.abc.net.au/news/2018-06-14/queensland-laws-changed-for-married-transgender-couples/986806

ABS (2020). Standard for Sex, Gender, Variations of Sex Characteristics and Sexual Orientation Variables. https://www.abs.gov.au/statistics/standards/standard-sex-gender-variations-sex-characteristics-and-sexual-orientation-variables/latest-release

Australian Government Department of Health and Aged Care. (2024) Aged Care Council of Elders. https://www.health.gov.au/committees-and-groups/aged-care-council-of-elders

Bull, M., Pinto, S., & Wilson, P. (1991). Homosexual Law Reform in Australia. *Trends and Issues in Crime and Criminal Justice, 19*, 1–10. https://eprints.qut.edu.au/128198/1/7c5c1e7daf802d9c49c6f2e259991d3d0ca8.pdf

Crameri, P., Barrett, C., Latham, J., & Whyte, C. (2015). It is More than Sex and Clothes. *Australasian Journal on Ageing, 34*, 21–25. https://doi.org/10.1111/ajag.12270

Crenshaw, K.W. (2017). On Intersectionality: Essential Writings. *Faculty Books*, 255. https://scholarship.law.columbia.edu/books/255

Croome, R. (2007). Solemnising Same-sex Unions: Why the Australian Capital Territory Do, and the Australian Government Doesn't. *Gay and Lesbian Issues and Psychology Review, 3*(1), 61–64.

Equality Australia. (2020). *Gay Panic Defence Murder Abolished Australia Wide*. https://equalityaustralia.org.au/gaypanicabolished/

Fredriksen-Goldsen, K.I. (2015). Resilience and Disparities among Lesbian, Gay, Bisexual, and Transgender Older Adults. In R.B. Hudson (Ed.) *Integrating Lesbian, Gay, Bisexual, and Transgender Older Adults into Aging Policy and Practice* (pp. 3–7). Public Policy & Aging Report Series. Washington, DC: National Academy on an Aging Society. http://bit.ly/1IeevFv [Cited August 2015]

Hastings, S.J., & Rogowski, S. (2015). Critical Social Work with Older People in Neo-liberal Times. *Challenges and Critical Possibilities, Practice, 27*(1), 21–33. https://doi.org/10.1080/09513193.2014.983435

Hughes, M. (2016). Loneliness and Social Support among Lesbian, Gay, Bisexual, Transgender and Intersex People Aged 50 and Over. *Ageing and Society, 36*(9), 1961–1981.

Human Rights Law Centre (2018). Australia Now Has Legal Adoption. https://www.hrlc.org.au/news/2018/4/20/australia-now-has-adoption-equality

Independent Expert by the Group of Friends of the Sexual Orientation and Gender Identity (2021). 47th Session of the Human Rights Council, Joint statement on Violence against Transgender Women. https://www.dfat.gov.au/international-relations/themes/human-rights/hrc-statements/47th-session-human-rights-council/joint-statement-violence-against-transgender-women-during-interactive-dialogue-independent-gender-identity-sogi-mandate-28-june-2021

Irwin, J. (1999). The Pink Ceiling is too Low' Workplace Experiences of Lesbians, Gay Men and Transgender People. Report of a Collaborative Research Project Undertaken by the Australian Centre for Lesbian and Gay Research and the NSW Gay and Lesbian Rights Lobby. Sydney: Australian Centre for Lesbian and Gay Research.

Irwin, J. (2009). Lesbians and Gay Men: (Un) equal Before the Law? In P. Swain & S. Rice (Eds.) *In the Shadow of the Law: The Legal Context of Social Work Practice* (pp. 192–207). Federation Press.

Jennings, R. (2012). Lesbian Mothers and Child Custody: Australian Debates in the 1970s. *Gender & History*, 24(2), 502–517. https://doi.org/10.1111/j.1468-0424.2012.01693.x

Kirkland, K.L. (2019). Feminist Aims and a Trans-Inclusive Definition of 'Woman.' *Feminist Philosophy Quarterly*, 5(1). https://doi.org/10.5206/fpq/2019.1.7313

Kostecki, T., & Macfarlane, S. (2019). Women and Older Age: Exploring the Intersections of Privelege and Oppresiion across Lifetimes. In D. Baines, B. Bennett, S. Goodwin & M. Rawsthorne (Eds.) *Working across Difference: Social Work, Social Policy and Social Justice*. Red Globe Press.

Lake, M., & Reynolds, H. (2008). *Drawing the Global Colour Line: White Men's Countries and the Question of Racial Equality*. Melbourne University Publishing.

LHA (2020a). *Me, Us and the World: The Impact of COVID-19 on Older LGBTI Australians*. https://d3n8a8pro7vhmx.cloudfront.net/lgbtihealth/pages/425/attachments/original/1595724248/LGBTI_Me__us_and_the_world-_the_impact_of_COVID-19_on_older_LGBTI_Australians_3_%28fix%29.pdf?1595724248

LHA (2020b). Submissions: Royal Commission into Aged Care: Submission Focussing on Specific Communities. https://d3n8a8pro7vhmx.cloudfront.net/lgbtihealth/pages/562/attachments/original/1594616717/RC_Submission_Focusing_on_specific_communities_30Jun2020.pdf?1594616717

LHA (2020d). When My Rights are Respected, Everyone's Rights are Respected: Policy Commitments for Older LGBTIQ+ Australians. https://assets.nationbuilder.com/lgbtihealth/pages/957/attachments/original/1649721810/Policy_statement.pdf?1649721810

LHA (2021a). LGBTIQ+ Health & Wellbeing Policy Priorities 2021. https://www.lgbtiqhealth.org.au/2021_policy_priorities

LHA (2021b). Snapshot of Mental Health and Suicide Prevention Statistics for LGBTIQ+ People. https://www.lgbtiqhealth.org.au/statistics

LHA (2021c). Care, Dignity and Respect. *LHA Submissions and Response to the Royal Commission into Aged Care Quality and Safety*. https://drive.google.com/file/d/1FfWBHr_fmRJN3fQUQveLMKdlhP-Cdud4/view

Marsh, I., & Galbraith, L. (1995). The Political Impact of the Sydney Gay and Lesbian Mardi Gras. *Australian Journal of Political Science*, 30(2), 300–320. https://doi.org/10.1080/00323269508402338

Miller, N., & Bassett, J. (2020). *Intersectionality in the LGBTQIA Community: Defining the Issues and Understanding the History of Systems of Discrimination*. https://icma.org/articles/pm-magazine/intersectionality-lgbtqia-community

OII Australia. (2014). Intersex for Allies. https://ihra.org.au/allies/

Perkins, R. (2022). The Australian Wars, Screen Australia Podcast. https://www.sbs.com.au/ondemand/tv-series/the-australian-wars

Reeves, T. (2022). *The Death of Dr Duncan*. Wakefield Press.

Riseman, N. (2015). Outmanoeuvring Defence: The Australian debates over gay and lesbian military service, 1992. *Australian Journal of Politics and History*, 61(4), 562–575. https://doi.org/10.1111/ajph.12119

Royal Commission into Aged Care Quality and Safety: Final Report. (2021). https://agedcare.royalcommission.gov.au/publications/final-report

Rugg, S. (2019). *How Powerful We Are: Behind the Scenes with One of Australia's Leading Activists*. Hachette.

Russell, S., Pollit, A., Li, G., & Grossman, A. (2018). Chosen Name Use is Linked to Reduced Depressive Symptoms, Suicidal Ideation and Suicidal Behaviour among Transgender Youth. *Journal of Adolescent Health*, 63(4), 503–505.

Stratton, J. (1998). *Race Daze: Australia in Identity Crisis*. Pluto Press.

The Conversation. (2017). Twenty-five Years after the Ban on Lesbians and Gay in the Military was Lifted, there is Much to Celebrate. https://theconversation.com/twenty-five-years-after-the-ban-on-lesbians-and-gays-in-the-military-was-lifted-there-is-much-to-celebrate-87764

Trans Hub. (2021). Health and Gender Affirmation in NSW: What Does CIS Mean? https://www.transhub.org.au/101/cis

Trans Hub. (n.d.). *Trans Mob*. https://www.transhub.org.au/trans-mob

Walsh, M., & Yallop, C. (1993). *Language and Culture of Aboriginal Australia*. Aboriginal Studies Press.

Wendt, S., & Moulding, M. (2017). The Current State of Feminism and Social Work. *Australian Social Work*, 70(3), 261–262. http://doi.org/10.1080/0312407X.2017.1314752

Wiepjes, C., den Heijer, M., Bremmer, M., Nota, N., de Blok, C., Coumou, B., & Steensma, T. (2020). Trends in Suicide Death Risk in Transgender People: Results from the Amsterdam Cohort of Gender Dysphoria Study (1972–2017). *Acta Psychiatrica Scandinavica, 14*(6), 486–491. https://doi.org/10.1111/acps.13164

Wilson, T., Temple, J., Lyons, A., & Shalley, F. (2020). What is the Size of Australia's Sexual Minority Population? *BMC Research Notes, 13*, 535. https://doi.org/10.1186/s13104-020-05383-w

World Health Organisation (2021). *Social Isolation and Loneliness among Older People: Advocacy Brief.* Geneva. https://apps.who.int/iris/bitstream/handle/10665/343206/9789240030749-eng.pdf?sequence=1

38
HETEROPATRIARCHY AND CHILD SEXUAL ABUSE

Contemplating profeminist practice with men victim-survivors

Alankaar Sharma and Amelia Wheeler

Introduction

Sexual abuse of children is a critical global concern. Thanks to decades of diligent and robust feminist scholarship, we know that while child sexual abuse (CSA) might typically happen at interpersonal level, it stems from heteropatriarchal social systems and structures. CSA experiences of men and boys have begun to receive attention within social work scholarship only in the last 15–20 years and remain an under-addressed area in social work practice. In this chapter, we argue that the experience of CSA for men victim-survivors is firmly rooted in norms and practices associated with patriarchy and heterosexism. Given the centrality of heteropatriarchy to men victim-survivors' experiences, we argue that social work practice with victim-survivors needs to be feminism-informed for it to be meaningful and transformative, and suggest profeminism as a constructive site of reflexive engagement with feminism for men victim-survivors and social workers who work with them. We also highlight the importance of racial inequities that have been historically present in both feminism and social work and the importance of profeminist social work with men victim-survivors of CSA to proactively engage with making whiteness visible and addressing racism. Finally, we propose and discuss some initial ideas for profeminist social work practice with men victim-survivors of CSA.

The World Health Organization (WHO, 2014) estimates the lifetime prevalence of CSA to be 18% for girls and women, and 7.6% for boys and men. These statistics point to a basic fact about CSA, that its burden is disproportionately experienced by girl children as compared to boys. Although fewer boys and men experience sexual abuse during childhood, the prevalence of CSA among this population group is not insignificant. The outcomes of CSA for victims and survivors, including men and boys, are potentially serious and may include long-term adverse physical, emotional, and social consequences. Experiencing CSA has been found to be associated with men victim-survivors' increased risk to a wide range of mental health issues, including depression, anxiety, trauma, and low self-esteem (Alaggia & Millington, 2008; Easton, 2014). Men and boys who have experienced CSA are at a higher risk of contemplating or attempting to end their life by suicide (Dube et al., 2005). Exposure to CSA may influence men victim-survivors' behaviours in relation to addictive

DOI: 10.4324/9781003317371-44

alcohol consumption and substance use (Afifi et al., 2012). CSA can potentially influence men victim-survivors' sexual behaviours and may be associated with sexual addiction, inhibition, or avoidance (Chan, 2014; Vaillancourt-Morel et al., 2015).

CSA is heteropatriarchal (including for men and boy victim-survivors)

Decades of feminist writing and scholarship have carefully exposed and indicted CSA as a fundamentally patriarchal practice (see Armstrong, 1994; Bass & Thornton, 1983; Coy, 2019; Namy et al., 2017; Rush, 1980; Seymour, 1998), making the case that sexual violence against children is profoundly influenced by gender and power. Historically, in comparison, CSA of boys has not received similar attention, which is unsurprising since global statistics indicate that girls comprise most of CSA victim-survivors (Barth et al., 2013; Pereda et al., 2009). This has begun to change in the last 15–20 years and CSA of boy children as well as CSA experiences of adult men victim-survivors has begun to receive the attention of social work practitioners, activists, and researchers. What is particularly noteworthy about this change is that the new scholarship on CSA has started to pay attention to gender and patriarchy as key elements of CSA experiences of men and boys (see Alaggia et al., 2019; Chan, 2014; Easton, 2014; Kennath Widanaralalage et al., 2022; Kramer & Bowman, 2021; Sharma, 2022a, 2022b).

Heteropatriarchy refers to a sociocultural climate where heteronormativity and patriarchy are dominant features. Broadly speaking, heteronormativity refers to the socially widespread belief that heterosexuality is the only normal or legitimate form of romantic or sexual interest among people. Patriarchy refers to a social structure that is defined by a range of ideas that relate to gender and power, including but not limited to dominance and supremacy of men over women and people of other genders, gender-binary (i.e. the belief that there exist only two genders – men and women), and normative expectations about individuals' behaviour and expression based on socially-assigned gender. Heteropatriarchy is at the core of CSA not just for girls and women but also boys and men. As we will discuss below, this is evidenced by research from different parts of the world that has examined CSA from the perspective of men and boy victim-survivors and illuminated the ways in which these experiences are rooted in different aspects of heteronormativity and patriarchy (Chan, 2014; Forde & Duvvury, 2017; Sharma, 2022a, 2022b). It is noteworthy that the research cited in this section comes from a wide range of geographic and cultural contexts including the Global South. Heteropatriarchy is nearly universal in its spread although its material manifestations may vary based on regional and social contexts, including which norms and practices are valued, and considered desirable as masculine.

Heteropatriarchal norms and values get in the way of acknowledging that CSA also happens to boy children and/or that it impacts men victim-survivors adversely. Popular cultural constructions of masculinity in patriarchal societies allow little space for men to be acknowledged as experiencing sexual violence, because they are socially perceived as initiators and active agents of sexual contact, not as recipients or as lacking control and autonomy within the context of sexual contact. Consequently, men and boy victim-survivors of sexual violence, including CSA, often have a hard time disclosing their experiences to others and seeking help, as they worry that they may be seen as weak and lacking control (Alaggia & Millington, 2008; Kia-Keating et al., 2005). These gender norms and expectations are clearly a product of patriarchal beliefs and systems that construct men and boys as powerful, always in control, stoic, and emotionally invulnerable.

There are other reasons too why men and boys find it challenging to disclose their abuse experiences. A major reason is the homophobic stigma associated with same-sex sexual contact among men and boys. Most perpetrators of sexual abuse, including against boy children, are men and boys (Burgess-Proctor et al., 2017). When a boy is abused, there is a strong likelihood that the perpetrator is another boy or man. Within a heteronormative environment where same-sex sexual contact among males is often shrouded in secrecy and shame, men and boys who have experienced such contact in the context of abuse worry about being labelled as gay or homosexual if they disclose their abuse experiences (Alaggia & Millington, 2008; Easton et al., 2014; Sharma, 2022a). Regardless of the victim or survivor's actual sexual orientation, this stigma acts as a barrier to disclosure of CSA.

Another reason why some men do not disclose is because they worry that others will minimise or dismiss their experiences (Sharma, 2022a). This is again rooted in heteropatriarchal belief systems that deny all victims and survivors acknowledgement and affirmation of their lived experiences. In addition, as discussed above, patriarchal societies allow little space for men and boys to be acknowledged as victims and survivors of sexual violence, given that men and boys are expected to seek out and always enjoy sexual experiences. Consequently, their sexual abuse experiences with women can get framed as victims 'getting lucky' because of popular social scripts of younger men's sexual attraction to older women as a rite of passage. Also, boys' sexual abuse experiences with other males can fit the popular narrative of 'boys being boys', and although frowned upon as same-sex sexual contact, may get minimised as boys experimenting or being adventurous (Sharma, 2022a). Indeed, when men and boys disclose their abuse experiences, minimisation or dismissal of their experiences is unfortunately a common experience. Such responses to disclosures often emerge from the societal reluctance to accept that boys can be victims of CSA, or belief that CSA is less likely to adversely affect boys (Alaggia & Millington, 2008; Kenneth Widanaralalage et al., 2022; Sharma, 2022a).

Heteropatriarchy not just influences if and how men and boy victim-survivors can disclose their abuse experiences, it also affects how they understand and make meaning of such experiences. CSA is often an experience for men victim-survivors that transgresses or violates the traditional gender norms and practices. As discussed above, within conventional constructions of masculinity, men and boys are typically expected to always desire and enjoy sexual contact. Consequently, some victim-survivors experience disgust or self-blame if their bodies responded to sexual stimulation with arousal or pleasure within the context of CSA (Alaggia & Millington, 2008). CSA may impact victim-survivors' sexual behaviours and may lead to avoidance of sexual activity with their romantic partners (Sharma, 2022b; Vaillancourt-Morel et al., 2015). Some men victim-survivors perceive this as a threat to their masculine identity where virility is considered a prized attribute within the norms of traditional masculinity (Sharma, 2022b). Men victim-survivors also sometimes hold themselves responsible and feel guilty for the abuse they experienced because they believe that as boys they should have been able to stop it from happening (Alaggia & Millington, 2008; Kia-Keating et al., 2005; Kramer & Bowman, 2021; Sharma, 2022b).

Feminism-informed practice with victim-survivors

As we have discussed in the previous section, CSA for men and boy victim-survivors is a profoundly gendered phenomenon that is rooted in patriarchy, traditional masculinity, heteronormativity, and homophobia. Given the centrality of heteropatriarchy to the lived experiences of victim-survivors, it is only logical that close attention to heteropatriarchy needs to be at the front and centre of working with men who have experienced CSA. Considering that feminism offers the strongest refutation and challenge to patriarchal systems and practices, we contend that work with men victim-survivors of CSA needs to be feminism-led and feminism-informed.

There are some clear positives to approaching social work with men victim-survivors through a feminism-informed lens. It would create a framework for the victim-survivors to develop a gender analysis of their own lived experiences and reflect on the role of heteropatriarchal notions that define and influence traditional masculinity. Developing such an analysis would help men victim-survivors, but also other men, see patriarchy as a double-edged weapon that hurts women and people of diverse genders in profound ways but hurts men too, particularly men who are not valued within the rigid confines of traditional masculinity.

While the idea of traditional masculinity is contextual and varies by time and place, in general, there are some aspects of traditional masculinity that are somewhat common across different cultures and societies because most sociocultural contexts are heteropatriarchal. Traditional masculinity privileges certain practices, behaviours, and experiences among men as appropriately masculine whilst simultaneously stigmatising certain other practices, behaviours, and experiences as unmasculine. Within this patriarchal framework, men who are victim-survivors of sexual violence such as rape or CSA are constructed as men with diminished or damaged masculinities. Understanding CSA of boys through a feminism-informed lens therefore allows men victim-survivors to see their emancipation from the oppression of sexual abuse as inextricably tied to heteropatriarchal oppression that damagingly and disproportionately impacts women, girls, and people of diverse gender identities. Finally, it would also allow men victim-survivors to build community and solidarity with other victim-survivors of sexual and gender-based violence with an understanding of the key role that heteropatriarchy plays in the perpetration of such violence.

The potential of profeminism

The question that then becomes important is what men victim-survivors' engagement with feminism might look like. Why is this question important? That is because men's engagement with feminism is contentious, complicated, and anything but simple and straightforward. There is ample scholarship that illuminates the problematic aspects of men's involvement with feminism (see Flood, 2011; Kahane, 1998; Linder & Johnson, 2015). When men get involved in feminist work, there are risks and concerns regarding the dilution of feminist agenda, undermining women's leadership and work, and taking resources away from women's services by men on account of their conferred patriarchal dominance (Flood, 2011). Patriarchal societies tend to socialise men so that they often speak more than they listen, and 'speak over' more than they 'speak with'. When men get involved with feminist work, regardless of their intentions they pose a real risk to the processes and outcomes entailed in such work because of their patriarchal privilege (Macomber, 2018; Sharma, 2019) unless they commit to critically reflecting on their sociopolitical subjectivities in relation to such work and actively addressing multilayered inequities.

So how can men engage with feminism in ways that are respectful and constructive? We suggest that profeminism offers a useful site for men's meaningful engagement with feminism. Profeminism is an ideological and action-oriented space where men make a commitment to being guided by feminism to achieve gender justice for all through dismantling the patriarchal systems and structures that are at the root of gender-based inequities (Ashe, 2007; Pease, 2016). Within this space, men are required to examine their own lives as gendered. People who assume dominant identity positions within systems of power such as gender, class, race, ability and so on are usually oblivious to their own privilege and therefore rarely examine it; this is one of the fundamental features of oppression. As the dominant identity within patriarchal contexts, men seldom see their own experiences and practices as gendered, hence it is a political act for them to do so as profeminist men.

Assuming a profeminist identity can serve as a reminder of two things for men:

> one, that their own emancipation as gendered individuals is invariably linked to a feminist agenda, and two, that their role and place within feminism is not of co-opting and appropriating women's work but to invest in it following women's leadership.
> *(Sharma, 2019, p. 109)*

Profeminism requires men to recognise the importance of being anti-sexist whilst acknowledging that they can never be non-sexist as it is impossible for a man to be truly and completely free of sexism within a patriarchal society (Flood, 2022). To sum up, profeminism is not just pro-feminism, it also "articulates men's contributions to and benefits from feminism" (Brod, 1998, p. 208). In the specific context of social work practice with men, Pease (2003) has suggested that profeminism is consistent with structural, anti-oppressive, and critical social work.

'Which feminism' can or should profeminist men incorporate into their practice approach? This is an on-going debate in scholarship (see Burrell & Flood, 2019). However, much of the existing scholarship explores engaging men and boys in preventing men's violence against women, not specifically how men can be engaged to prevent men's violence against boys, or how men might be engaged in support of male CSA victim-survivors (and for that matter, victim-survivors of other genders). It is important to acknowledge that 'feminism' is not a homogenous set of ideas that can be applied uncritically to profeminist practice. It is of fundamental importance to consider critiques of the feminist movement and the ways in which whiteness is both recognized and made invisible. As we will discuss in the following section, a critique of whiteness is also fundamental to understanding how profeminist social work practice with male CSA victim-survivors may be approached.

Making whiteness visible in feminist and profeminist social work practice

In any discussion of social work practices, we contend that whiteness must be exposed and named. While individual perpetrators and victim-survivors of CSA exist across all racial groups, there is evidence that there are racial disparities in several aspects of CSA, from disclosure, reporting and substantiation of CSA (see Fix & Nair, 2020; Atkinson et al., 2023) to, court proceedings and sentencing outcomes for perpetrators (see Atkinson et al., 2023). Although there is minimal research exploring the impacts of race on child maltreatment outcomes, particularly research that utilises real-life case data (Alaggia et al., 2019; Atkinson et al., 2023), there is evidence that the racial identities of victim-survivor, accused perpetrator/s, and professionals engaged in CSA cases also significantly impact victim-survivor motivation to disclose and their experiences of disclosure (see Fisher et al., 2016).

Some mock juror studies in CSA cases demonstrate that "white defendants accused of rape or sexual assault of a child are found guilty significantly less often and receive shorter sentences than their Black counterparts" (Atkinson et al., 2023, p. 46). Thus, intersections of race and whiteness must be considered alongside gender when exploring profeminist practices with boys and men CSA survivors.

In addition to substantive evidence that race and whiteness impact on the experiences of CSA victim-survivors, we also know that Black, Brown, and Indigenous children and young people are overrepresented in child protection systems across the world. Child protection and out-of-home 'care' systems have been utilised as a tool for colonisation, dispossession, control and genocide of First Nations populations (see Bennett, 2019). Racial disparities with entry into, experiences within, and outcomes following time in the care of the State persist in the present day (Russ-Smith & Wheeler, 2021). Although not all CSA cases come to the attention of the child protection system, it is essential that whiteness is made visible here, beyond simply a focus for white social workers on the identity of the client as the "raced other" (Russ-Smith & Wheeler, 2021, p. 85). Understanding the history and racial legacy of the profession of social work and its unique form in child protection systems, as well as continuous critical reflection on the self-identity of the individual worker, are essential to decolonising practice (see Green & Baldry, 2008; Russ-Smith & Wheeler, 2021; Walter & Baltra-Ulloa, 2019). Making whiteness visible is an important aspect of this process, which we explore directly below.

Making whiteness visible is particularly important when considering feminist and profeminist ways of being and doing social work. Indigenous, Black, and Persons of Colour scholars and practitioners have led and continue to lead the way in exposing whiteness in social work and in feminism (Hamad, 2019; Moreton-Robinson, 2021; Walter & Baltra-Ulloa, 2019). Whiteness is defined as:

> a structure and social phenomenon which derives from and reasserts colonial and Western dominance ... entrenched and manifested through social systems and structures which dictate social truths and rules regarding privilege, power and ownership ... award(ing) structural advantage and privilege to white people and white ways of knowing.
>
> *(Russ-Smith et al., 2023, p. 3)*

Scholars in so-called Australia have long argued that social work is a product of primarily white, Western culture and knowledges, and that race relations exist here within the context of colonisation (Green & Baldry, 2008; Walter & Baltra-Ulloa, 2019; Yassine, 2019). Yet in many spaces the profession of social work resists naming the centrality of its whiteness, focusing on non-white raced 'others' while at the same time claiming anti-racist practice as key to discipline identity (Russ-Smith & Wheeler, 2021; Yassine, 2019). While whiteness remains invisible, its dominance and power are upheld (Hartmann et al., 2009).

The feminist commitment to exposing power and privilege must crucially extend to the analysis of whiteness. Moreton-Robinson (2021) frames whiteness as "a hegemonic ideology centred in feminism" (p. 174), seeing feminism as rooted in white logics and as blind to race. Berenstain (2020) sees white feminism as taking "only a single-axis approach to gender-based oppression, ignoring the intersections of sexist oppression with racism, classism, ableism, cissexism, transphobia, heterosexism, homophobia, and national context" (p. 736). Although an intersectional feminist approach speaks to the impact of multiple oppressions on gendered experience, this can still result in a limited analysis where whiteness is not raced – thereby retaining both the invisibility and the centrality of whiteness.

Hamad's (2019) concept of 'weaponised White Womanhood' demonstrates how white women draw upon "deeply embedded notions of gender and femininity" (p. 14) to deploy violence under the guise of victimhood against People of Colour, and particularly against Women of Colour. Hamad (2019) contends:

> Women of colour are in an abusive relationship with whiteness more broadly but especially with white women, who pivot between professing sisterhood and solidarity with us based on gender identification, and silencing and oppressing us (with) their White Womanhood to keep us boxed into the binary.
>
> (p. 79)

These arguments highlight that violence and oppression can and do exist under the guise of feminist or profeminist 'allyship', and that 'feminist' can be a contentious label that not all in the fight for justice and equality identify with. (Pro)feminist social workers must practice critical reflexivity to expose whiteness, recognising that the on-going colonial project has wide-reaching impacts on gendered norms and identities. The heteropatriarchy *is white*, and it determines what is considered 'appropriate' gendered and raced behaviour and expression. It is important to note here that existing profeminist scholarship is primarily from Western and white perspectives and has minimally engaged with ideas regarding race and racism. This chapter intends to prompt these important discussions and explorations. It is not only conceivable but likely that (pro)feminist social workers must take part in actively building spaces beyond the white heteropatriarchy and beyond white conceptualisations of feminism; spaces of resistance, anger, and healing; spaces where Indigenous, Black, and Brown voices, and gender and sexually diverse voices are primary.

Suggestions for profeminist social work with male CSA victim-survivors

To conclude, we propose some initial thoughts on profeminist social work practice for work with, and work by, male CSA victim-survivors. We want to emphasise that these are just initial thoughts, not an exhaustive list of ideas or a comprehensive framework for practice. While scholars have recently considered in depth some of the key tenets of profeminism, to our knowledge this has not extended to the analysis of CSA. Burrell and Flood (2019) posit nine 'minimum standards' in profeminist approaches to the elimination of men's violence against women. These standards include (but are not limited to): prioritising gender justice in the personal sphere; prioritising consultation with and accountability to specific feminist women and organisations, while recognising women as leaders in the struggle to end gender inequality; being explicit about the kind of feminist theory being drawn upon; evaluating the effectiveness of profeminist work; and recognising and connecting the many different forms of men's violence against women. While this reads as a thoughtful profeminist creed and meaningfully informs our work, it is solely focused on the prevention of men's violence against women and does not integrate a consideration of violence or sexual abuse perpetrated against boys or men.

Along with the ultimate goals of prevention and elimination of CSA, the formation of a pro-disclosure culture where men and boys feel supported and safe to disclose abuse and access support is a key goal. The structural elements of violence, including forms of State and colonial violence and in particular the ways in which Sovereign First Nations, Black, and Brown men and boys are criminalised by white heteropatriarchy, must be named and actively resisted. Profeminist social workers must actively resist whiteness in their practice, honouring First Nations Sovereignty and self-determination, respecting their relationship with Country, and deeply listening to First Nations peoples. Profeminist social workers must also work to expose whiteness, within systems and within selves, working beyond binaries of gender while also sensitively identifying the prominent harms of the heteropatriarchy on child sexual assault victim-survivors.

Given the centrality of heteropatriarchy to men victim-survivors' experiences of CSA, a necessary and minimum requirement of profeminist social work practice with men victim-survivors would be to focus on a gender analysis of CSA and unpack heteropatriarchy and its consequences for survivors. As Pease (2019) argues, it is "necessary for men to understand patriarchy and its influence on their lives if they are to find a way of challenging it" (p. 10). Another important area of profeminist practice with men would be to connect victim-survivors with other victim-survivors as part of a solidarity building process. From a profeminist perspective, it would be a meaningful experience for victim-survivors to build community through solidarity with other victim-survivors. This follows from the idea that collective care through community building based on shared lived experiences is important in feminist praxis, which recognises care as a "relational accomplishment" (Raap et al., 2022, p. 869). As we have discussed earlier, such practice holds the potential of creating opportunities for a gender-based analysis of abuse experiences for men victim-survivors, which could then lead to understanding CSA as inalienably tied to heteropatriarchy, paving the way for men's broader engagement with anti-sexist and anti-heterosexist work.

While these ideas might sound full of promise, some significant potential challenges accompany them. One, within heteropatriarchal contexts men and boys are typically not socialised into building emotional sensitivity and responsiveness towards other men and boys; instead, they are socialised into viewing each other as competitors. For heterosexual men, homophobia is an impediment to developing close and emotionally intimate relationships with other men (Flood, 2022). These factors would pose obvious challenges to developing men victim-survivors' emotional and relational capacity to find companionship and solidarity through mutual vulnerability and connection. Two, given that patriarchal masculinity is built on a foundation of misogyny and subordination of women, there is a worry that when men bond in male-dominant spaces, male-male relationships can devolve into sites of sexist and anti-feminist thought and action (Haywood & Mac an Ghaill, 2003), such as men's rights activism (MRA) groups. It would be important for profeminist men and (pro)feminist social workers who work with them to stay vigilant about such possible developments.

Profeminist social work practice with men victim-survivors of CSA cannot happen in the absence of a meaningful commitment to deconstructing heteropatriarchal masculinities, thus mandating profeminist men's engagement with efforts to end men's violence against women and people of other gender identities. Men's emancipation from oppressive outcomes of heteropatriarchy in their lives as victim-survivors of CSA is not possible without a broader commitment recognising the profound damage that heteropatriarchy causes in the everyday lives of women and people of diverse gender identities, and dismantling heteropatriarchy. This work would require alliance building between men's profeminist groups and feminist groups and organisations. How this alliance happens is an important area of consideration. Earlier in this chapter we have discussed some potential risks that men pose to feminist efforts through their involvement with these efforts. Therefore, it is crucial for profeminist men to contemplate the politics and pragmatics of their allyship practices (Sharma, 2019). It is also important for allies to distinguish between 'critical allyship' and 'performative allyship' and identify ways in which they can move beyond performative allyship and practice critical allyship.

It is also important for (pro)feminist social workers to contemplate their practices in relation to working with and supporting men victim-survivors of CSA. Pease (2001) argues that social workers must navigate a dilemma of connecting with men's experience while not colluding with patriarchal power, calling upon men to "critically reflect upon their own socialisation processes and engage with their own gendered subjectivity" (p. 5). Navigating this dilemma demands critical reflexivity from social workers, where social workers are asked to reflect on their own sociopolitical location and personal and professional experiences within a context of heteropatriarchy, examine their professional practices in terms of whether these practices enhance or diminish heteropatriarchy, and attend to issues of intersectionality with respect to race, ethnicity, class, ability, migrant status and so on. Moreover, it would be important for social workers to consider the nature of services they provide. If (pro)feminist social work services focus only on individual men's behaviours and personal practices in relation to sexism and heterosexism, the broader social relations, systems, and institutions that shape multilayered inequities concerning gender and sexuality will remain unchallenged (Pease, 2020/2001). It is therefore important for (pro)feminist social workers working with men victim-survivors of CSA to fundamentally challenge sexist and heterosexist oppression at socio-structural levels.

We call on social workers who are undertaking this important work with male CSA victim-survivors to continue sharing their practice wisdom, to build upon these initial offerings of profeminist approaches. We speak in different voices, united in our commitment to eradicating violence fuelled by heteropatriarchy against people of all gender identities.

References

Afifi, T. O., Henriksen, C. A., Asmundson, G. J. G., & Sareen, J. (2012). Childhood maltreatment and substance use disorders among men and women in a nationally representative sample. *The Canadian Journal of Psychiatry*, 57(11), 677–686. https://doi.org/10.1177/070674371205701105

Alaggia, R., & Millington, G. (2008). Male child sexual abuse: A phenomenology of betrayal. *Clinical Social Work Journal*, 36, 265–275. https://doi.org/10.1007/s10615-007-0144-y

Alaggia, R., Collin-Vézina, D., & Lateef, R. (2019). Facilitators and barriers to child sexual abuse (CSA) disclosures: A research update (2000–2016). *Trauma, Violence, & Abuse*, 20(2), 260–283. https://doi.org/10.1177/1524838017697312

Armstrong, L. (1994). *Rocking the cradle of sexual politics: What happened when women said incest.* Addison-Wesley.

Ashe, F. (2007). *The new politics of masculinity: Men, power and resistance.* Routledge.

Atkinson, K., Fix, S., & Fix, R. (2023). Racial disparities in child physical and sexual abuse substantiations: Associations with child' and accused individuals' race. *Journal of Child and Family Studies*, 32, 44–56. https://doi.org.10.1007/s10826-022-02403-0

Barth, J., Bermetz, L., Heim, E., Trelle, S., & Tonia, T. (2013). The current prevalence of child sexual abuse worldwide: A systematic review and meta-analysis. *International Journal of Public Health*, 58(3), 469–483.

Bass, E., & Thornton, L. (Eds.) (1983). *I never told anyone: Writings by women survivors of child sexual abuse.* Harper Colophon.

Bennett, B. (2019). The importance of Aboriginal history for practitioners. In B. Bennett & S. Green (Eds.), *Our voices: Aboriginal social work* (2nd ed., pp. 3–30). Red Globe Press.

Berenstain, N. (2020). 'Civility' and the civilizing project. *Philosophical Papers, 49*(2), 305–337. https://doi.org/10.1080/05568641.2020.1780148

Brod, H. (1998). To be a man, or not be a man—That is the feminist question. In T. Digby (Ed.), *Men doing feminism* (pp. 197–212). Routledge.

Burgess-Proctor, A., Comartin, E. B., & Kubiak, S. P. (2017). Comparing female- and male-perpetrated child sexual abuse: A mixed-methods analysis. *Journal of Child Sexual Abuse, 26*(6), 657–676. https://doi.org/10.1080/10538712.2017.1336504

Burrell, S., & Flood, M. (2019). Which feminism? Dilemmas in profeminist men's praxis to end violence against women. *Global Social Welfare, 6*, 231–244. https://doi.org/10.1007/s40609-018-00136-x

Chan, S. T. M. (2014). The lens of masculinity: Trauma in men and the landscapes of sexual abuse survivors. *Journal of Ethnic & Cultural Diversity in Social Work, 23*(3–4), 239–255. https://doi.org/10.1080/15313204.2014.932733

Coy, M. (2019). What's gender got to do with it? Sexual exploitation of children as patriarchal violence. In J. Pearce (Ed.), *Child sexual exploitation: Why theory matters* (pp. 209–230). Bristol University Press.

Dube, S. R., Anda, R. F., Whitfield, C. L., Brown, D. W., Felitti, V. J., Dong, M., & Giles, W. H. (2005). Long-term consequences of childhood sexual abuse by gender of victim. *American Journal of Preventive Medicine, 28*(5), 430–438. https://doi.org/10.1016/j.amepre.2005.01.015

Easton, S. D. (2014). Masculine norms, disclosure, and childhood adversities predict long-term mental distress among men with histories of child sexual abuse. *Child Abuse & Neglect, 38*(2), 243–251. https://doi.org/10.1016/j.chiabu.2013.08.020

Easton, S. D., Saltzman, L. Y., & Willis, D. G. (2014). "Would you tell under circumstances like that?": Barriers to disclosure of child sexual abuse for men. *Psychology of Men & Masculinity, 15*(4), 460–469. https://doi.org/10.1037/a0034223

Fisher, A., Mackey, T., Langendoen, C., & Barnard, M. (2016). Child and interviewer race in forensic interviewing. *Journal of Child Sexual Abuse, 25*(7), 777–792. https://doi.org/10.1080/10538712.2016.1208705

Fix, R., & Nair, R. (2020). Racial/ethnic and gender disparities in substantiation of child physical and sexual abuse: Influences of caregiver and child characteristics. *Child and Youth Services Review, 116*, Article 105186. https://doi.org/10.1016/j.childyouth.2020.105186

Flood, M. (2011). Involving men in efforts to end violence against women. *Men and Masculinities, 14*(3), 358–377. https://doi.org/10.1177/1097184X10363995

Flood, M. (2022). Living a pro-feminist life. In L. Schmidt (Ed.), *Antisexist: Challenge sexism, champion women's rights, and create equality* (pp. 139–148). Bobo Publishing.

Forde, C., & Duvvury, N. (2017). Sexual violence, masculinity, and the journey of recovery. *Psychology of Men & Masculinity, 18*(4), 301–310. https://doi.org/10.1037/men0000054

Green, S., & Baldry, E. (2008). Building Indigenous Australian social work. *Australian Social Work, 61*(4), 389–402. https://doi.org/10.1080/03124070802430718

Hamad, R. (2019). *White tears, brown scars*. Melbourne University Publishing.

Hartmann, D., Gerteis, J., & Croll, P. R. (2009). Empirical assessment of whiteness theory: Hidden from how many? *Social Problems, 56*(3), 403–424. https://doi.org/10.1525/sp.2009.56.3.403

Haywood, C., & Mac an Ghaill, M. (2003). *Men and masculinities: Theory, research, and social practice*. Open University Press.

Kahane, D. J. (1998). Male feminism as oxymoron. In T. Digby (Ed.), *Men doing feminism* (pp. 213–235). Routledge.

Kenneth Widanaralalage, B., Hine, B. A., Murphy, A. D., & Murji, K. (2022). "I didn't feel I was a victim": A phenomenological analysis of the experiences of male-on-male survivors of rape and sexual abuse. *Victims & Offenders, 17*(8), 1147–1172. https://doi.org/10.1080/15564886.2022.2069898

Kia-Keating, M., Grossman, F. K., Sorsoli, L., & Epstein, M. (2005). Containing and resisting masculinity: Narratives of renegotiation among resilient male survivors of childhood sexual abuse. *Psychology of Men and Masculinity, 6*(3), 169–185. https://doi.org/10.1037/1524-9220.6.3.169

Kramer, S., & Bowman, B. (2021). The making of male victimhood in South African female-perpetrated sexual abuse. *Gender, Place & Culture, 28*(6), 829–852. https://doi.org/10.1080/0966369X.2020.1835831

Linder, C., & Johnson, R. C. (2015). Exploring the complexities of men as allies in feminist movements. *Journal of Critical Thought and Praxis*, 4(1). http://lib.dr.iastate.edu/jctp/vol4/iss1/

Macomber, K. (2018). "I'm sure as hell not putting any man on a pedestal": Male privilege and accountability in domestic and sexual violence work. *Journal of Interpersonal Violence*, 33(9), 1491–1518. https://doi.org/10.1177/088626051561894

Moreton-Robinson, A. (2021). *Talkin' up to the White woman: Indigenous women and feminism*. 20th Anniversary Edition. University of Minnesota Press.

Namy, S., Carlson, C., O'Hara, K., Nakuti, J., Bukuluki, P., Lwanyaaga, J., Namakula, S., Nanyunja, B., Wainberg, M. L., Naker, D., & Michau, L. (2017). Towards a feminist understanding of intersecting violence against women and children in the family. *Social Science & Medicine*, 184, 40–48. https://doi.org/10.1016/j.socscimed.2017.04.042

Pease, B. (2001). Developing profeminist practice with men in social work. *Critical Social Work*, 2(1), 1–8.

Pease, B. (2003). Men and masculinities: Profeminist approaches to changing men. In J. Allen, B. Pease & L. Briskman (Eds.), *Critical social work: An introduction to theories and practices* (pp. 124–138). Allen & Unwin.

Pease, B. (2016). Critical social work with men: Challenging men's complicity in the reproduction of patriarchy and male privilege. *Social Alternatives*, 35(4), 49–53.

Pease, B. (2019). *Facing patriarchy: From a violent gender order to a culture of peace*. Zed Books.

Pease, B. (2020). Theoretical issues and political dilemmas in working with men. In B. Pease & P. Camilleri (Eds.), *Working with men in the human services* (pp. 15–24). Routledge. (Original work published 2001)

Pereda, N., Guilera, G., Forns, M., & Gómez-Benito, J. (2009). The prevalence of child sexual abuse in community and student-samples: A meta-analysis. *Clinical Psychology Review*, 29(4), 328–338. https://doi.org/10.1016/j.cpr.2009.02.007

Raap, S., Knibbe, M., & Horstman, K. (2022). Caring neighbourhoods: Maintaining collective care under neoliberal care reforms. *European Journal of Social Work*, 25(5), 867–879. https://doi.org/10.1080/13691457.2021.1997928

Rush, F. (1980) *The best-kept secret: Sexual abuse of children*. McGraw-Hill.

Russ-Smith, J., & Wheeler, A. (2021). A culturally supportive ethics of care: Working with Aboriginal children and young people. In S. Green & B. Bennett (Eds.), *Aboriginal fields of practice* (pp. 79–99). Palgrave Macmillan.

Russ-Smith, J., Farwa, A., & Wheeler, A. (2023). Everything is White: Exposing and deconstructing whiteness as risk in the helping professions. In J. Ravulo, K. Olcoń, T. Dune, A. Workman & P. Liamputtong (Eds.), *Handbook of critical whiteness: Deconstructing dominant discourses across disciplines*. Springer.

Seymour, A. (1998). Aetiology of the sexual abuse of children: An extended feminist practice. *Women's Studies International Forum*, 21(4), 415–427. https://doi.org/10.1016/S0277-5395(96)00068-4

Sharma, A. (2019). Allyship and social justice: Men as allies in challenging men's violence and discrimination against women. In D. Baines, B. Bennett, S. Goodwin & M. Rawsthorne (Eds.), *Working across difference: Social work, social policy and social justice* (pp. 103–119). Red Globe Press.

Sharma, A. (2022a). Disclosure of child sexual abuse: Experiences of men survivors in India. *British Journal of Social Work*, 52(8), 4588–4605. https://doi.org/10.1093/bjsw/bcac073

Sharma, A. (2022b). Men survivors' perspectives on impact of child sexual abuse. *Children and Youth Services Review*, 137, Article 106485. https://doi.org/10.1016/j.childyouth.2022.106485

Vaillancourt-Morel, M., Godbout, N., Labadie, C., Runtz, M., Lussier, Y., & Sabourin, S. (2015). Avoidant and compulsive sexual behaviors in male and female survivors of childhood sexual abuse. *Child Abuse & Neglect*, 40, 48–59. https://doi.org/10.1016/j.chiabu.2014.10.024

Walter, M., & Baltra-Ulloa, J. (2019). Australian social work is white. In B. Bennett & S. Green (Eds.), *Our voices: Aboriginal social work* (2nd ed., pp. 65–85). Red Globe Press.

World Health Organisation (WHO) (2014). *Lifetime prevalence of child sexual abuse (%)*. https://www.who.int/data/gho/data/indicators/indicator-details/GHO/lifetime-prevalence-of-child-sexual-abuse-(-)

Yassine, L. (2019). To know is to exist: Epistemic resistance. In S. Tascon & J. Ife (Eds.), *Disrupting whiteness in social work* (pp. 91–107). Routledge.

39
MAKING MEN ALLIES IN STOPPING MEN'S VIOLENCE VIA PROCESSES OF INTERSECTIONAL IDENTIFICATION
A study of Swedish profeminist men

Keith Pringle, Anna-Lena Almqvist and Linn Egeberg Holmgren

Introduction

Almost 30 years ago, in a British study about men and social welfare, one of us wrote as follows:

> ...working with men may be partly about helping them get in touch with their multiple masculinities to see which ones they would really like to use in particular situations...some men may be able to access alternative, more benign forms of masculinity with greater ease than others: perhaps because they have had particular experiences or because they have been placed in particular situations.
>
> *(Pringle, 1995, p. 209)*

Although we might use other terminology today, the search for isolating, understanding and replicating such experiences and situations remains as urgent now as it was then – in order to encourage men not only to behave in less oppressive ways but also so that more men will actively challenge other men's oppressive and abusive behaviour. Our chapter continues the search. Like this book as a whole, the chapter demonstrates how anti-sexist social welfare practice can be galvanized in important ways through the use of feminist and other critical theoretical frames: and how such frames can themselves be galvanized by the encounter with practice. In our case, we utilize intersectional perspectives to illuminate how individual men's numerous multiple subject positions – both subordinate and superordinate – can offer vital pathways towards profeminist activism: far more pathways than most previous studies have anticipated. In the process, we develop the concept of intersectional identification to assist the analysis of our data. As will be clear throughout, we are very much inspired by the work of previous scholars and in particular Bob Pease on undoing privilege and making men allies (see Pease, 2017, 2021).

For our data, we draw upon a relatively small, but very rich, sample of qualitative interviews with seven Swedish "expert" respondents. These "expert" respondents were gathered by a process of purposive sampling via contacts within anti-sexist Swedish non-governmental organisations. The respondents were all men working professionally/semi-professionally with other men or boys to challenge men's oppressive behaviour toward women (and sometimes children). All three of the chapter authors undertook the interviews which were carried out using a flexible semi-structured framework. All of the interviews occurred face-to-face in a place of the respondents' own choosing and were audio-recorded. Anonymized transcripts were made and the contents of each transcript were approved by the respective respondents for their accuracy and for use by the research team. The transcripts were then coded and analysed repeatedly by each of the three of us, as well as collectively, using an analytical frame inspired by Charmaz's constructivist grounded theory (Charmaz, 2014).

Thus, in effect, our respondents were engaged in vital preventative social work with men and boys, though not in a formal sense: for, in various ways, they were assisting men and/or boys to avoid violent and oppressive behaviours towards women and girls in their current and future lives. This work occurred sometimes in collaboration with the women's shelter movement as well as with local authorities. We wanted their insights into what makes men, including themselves, take up this kind of work. Moreover, we were interested both in the explanations and understandings they offered, and also in any explanations which they did not mention – but which one might have expected to be mentioned given previous research.

It should be noted that our Swedish qualitative interview data is actually part of a larger transnational study, co-ordinated and solely funded from within the United Kingdom, involving a total of 24 qualitative interview respondents and 40 survey respondents, drawn from Spain, Sweden and the United Kingdom. Some aspects of this whole transnational project have been addressed in a recently published book, of which Almqvist and Egeberg Holmgren are co-authors (Westmarland et al., 2021). However, the processes of intersectional identification which are the focus of this chapter, are not addressed to any great extent in that book. Moreover, as already noted, we explore those intersectional identification processes in detail here based solely on our rich data from the Swedish qualitative interviews.

Previous research

Over the last 15 years, attempts to understand the dynamics by which some men come to actively and publicly challenge men's violence against women, children and other men have steadily developed – all with the practical aim of increasing the number of men who will act as allies in stopping such violence. Among the most important studies and commentaries are those by Casey & Smith (2010), Messner et al. (2015), Casey et al. (2017), Peretz (2017), Flood (2019) and Peretz (2020). Over time, these works have built up a reasonably consistent picture of the general dynamics that encourage men to take an active anti-violence stance (see Westmarland et al., 2021 for a more extended commentary). Reaching a position of activism seems to be a process for men through encountering some of the following experiences in their lives:

- The influence of significant others in their lives, especially women: mothers, sisters, daughters, life partners and friends.

- Having experiences either directly or indirectly (e.g. through significant others) of being subject to, and/or of perpetrating, men's violence.
- Frequently a relatively high level of education even if class backgrounds might vary.
- A supportive network of friends and colleagues once they become activists.
- Being aware of other issues of social justice as a bridge to developing an emotional and intellectual challenge to men's violence.
- Being part of some form of organisation or semi-organisational framework working against men's violence.
- Living in a broader social context is conducive to developing challenges to men's violence.

(Messner et al., 2015; Flood, 2019)

To a large extent, the transnational study (Westmarland et al., 2021) confirmed this broad picture, whilst adding some depth in terms of exploring the impact of three different spatial and societal contexts. The qualitative "expert" interview data from the Swedish part of the transnational project also matched with many of those themes. This Swedish interview data provided very dense material allowing a particularly detailed analysis of relational and experiential themes which seemed especially significant. Perhaps the most striking aspect of the present analysis is the way experience from, and awareness of, other forms of oppression – other dimensions of social justice – can act as a bridge for men to appreciate (intellectually and emotionally) the destructive impact of gender oppression, especially in the form of men's violence. We name this process "intersectional identification". It is akin to what Messner et al. (2015, pp. 185–186) term "organic intersectionality". Intersectional identification refers to the fact that any individual man simultaneously occupies numerous subject positions, at any given time, in relation to a range of different intersecting power relations. If a man recognizes at a personal level the social and structural injustice involved in one form of power relations and becomes sensitized to that injustice, then it may help him to become sensitized to injustice associated with another dimension of power – for instance, gender oppression in the form of men's violence against women and/or children. We focus on the processes of intersectional identification in this chapter because we believe such an analysis offers especially crucial strategies for encouraging more men to openly challenge men's violence. Moreover, our material suggests previous studies may have underestimated the scope and significance of intersectional identification as a key strategic tool.

Of course, several previous studies and commentaries have addressed certain intersectional processes to a degree: in particular, Casey and Smith (2010), Messner et al. (2015), Peretz (2017), Christensen & Jensen (2019) and Pease (2021). However, some of these analyses have only touched on intersectional identification processes rather tangentially while focusing on broader issues of intersectionality and the study of men's practices (for instance, Edström et al., 2016; Christensen & Jensen, 2019; Peretz, 2019). Where there has been a more central focus on something akin to intersectional identification (Casey & Smith, 2010; Messner et al., 2015; Peretz, 2017), we contend this focus has been less broad or deep compared to our analysis here. For instance, Casey & Smith (2010) limit themselves to power relations associated with "racism, classism, and sexism" (p. 959) and relatively briefly. Peretz (2017), in a more extended intersectional analysis, limits himself to power relations associated with sexuality, ethnicity and gender. Of previous studies and commentaries, Messner et al. (2015, pp. 114–121) and Pease (2021) provide the broadest and most considered intersectional perspectives.

The present study

What marks out our analysis below are three features. First, we seek to unravel the complex interplay of intersectional identifications arising from a broader range of power relations associated with class, sexuality, disability, ethnicity, animal rights/environmentalism, gender, rural/urban social location and, to a limited extent, age. Second, most studies have focused largely on men who are marginalized in some way and who thereby might identify with the situation of women. By contrast, our data makes clear that intersectional identification can also occur when men recognize their superordinate power positions as well as when they recognize their subordination in relation to various forms of oppression – thereby opening up intersectional pathways to profeminist recruitment for even more men (see also Pease, 2021). Third, we focus on those potential dynamics of intersectional identification which were surprising by their absence in our data and which one might have expected to be there – and on what this absence might tell us.

Intersectionality as a theoretical frame

Before turning to those three defining features of our analysis, we briefly need to discuss how we understand intersectionality – a concept originally developed from within black feminism (Mama, 1995, 2011; Collins, 2019) – as we apply it here. The concept has represented and still represents a terrain of huge academic debate (for instance, see Carbin & Edenheim, 2013) with a plethora of relevant articles still being published in a broad and disparate range of disciplines. A recent commentary on intersectionality and men's practices by Christensen & Jensen (2019) provides a useful summary that closely matches many of our understandings, combining both structural and more postmodern perspectives. The following passage neatly encapsulates some central understandings of intersectionality as we use it in this chapter:

> […]intersectionality claims that categories are not parallel or static, neither on an identity or everyday level nor on a structural level… Gender, race/ethnicity, class, etc. constitute, construct, and re-construct each other and therefore cannot be analysed separately. Furthermore, this mutual constitution takes place as interplay both between different categories and between different levels of the social – and the interplay may often take paradoxical or contradictory forms.
>
> *(Christensen & Jensen, 2019, p. 84)*

Having briefly clarified our theoretical frame, we now address in turn the three features mentioned earlier that make our analysis stand out: the broad range of power relations; exploring processes of identification arising from men's dominant positions as well as their marginalization; exploring what is not in our data and why.

Multiple, overlapping pathways to intersectional identification

For most of our respondents, a variety of intersectional pathways leading to an awareness of sexism were central to taking a public stance against men's violence against women. Here is an example:

> …people have a hard time understanding things that they do not themselves experience first hand […] it's really difficult if those men are, you know, white, middle class.

It's really difficult because they have to have something, I mean, in my case it was *because* of this something that I could make this imaginary leap.

Above, this man is explaining how hard it is, as a man, to apprehend the immensely negative impact of sexism unless – like himself – one has experienced other forms of discrimination that allow one to make an "imaginary (experiential) leap". We conceptualize this as a process of intersectional identification. The quotation is interesting also because this respondent identifies himself as a person of colour, bisexual and disabled from a lower-class social background. In other words, he is explaining that his personal experience of four different, intersecting and reinforcing forms of social marginalization/subordination – "race", sexuality, disability and class – have been vital for him to recognize and take a stand against women's marginalization through men's violence – even though his position in terms of gendered power relations is relatively superordinate. Moreover, it is hard to see how one could analytically separate out from one another the complex interactions of "race", sexuality, dis/ability and class in producing this gender identification. They are mutually constituted (Christensen & Jensen, 2019). We can thus begin to gauge how complex these processes are.

Another respondent (below) similarly illustrates the complex intersectional pathways which some men travel before they take a stand against men's violence against women. In his process towards engagement with men's violence against women, he started out working for an NGO on sexual education. A combination of knowledge, interest and personal experience developed further to a structural and theoretical understanding of gendered power relations, which he now also works with in different ways. His testimony makes clear that the pathways between different forms of oppressive power relations are multi-directional:

And it was also that from an…for a lack of better words, anti-racist perspective interrogating, "Who am I in Swedish society?" Then, lacking other tools, feminism has filled the gap to a certain extent, as an analytical tool of looking at power relations and identity itself [...]So, it was, you know, that kind of very good substitute teacher. Although I've filled in with the bona fide both feminist and anti-racist post-colonial thinkers, et cetera, on top of that.

This respondent, possessing a multi-ethnic background and identifying himself as queer, is describing how he utilized his understanding of gendered power relations to make sense of his racialized and marginalized position in a predominantly white Swedish society. He then supplemented this understanding by academic study.

As we have seen, many of our respondents had experienced multiple forms of marginalization and subordination, as was also the case in the research by Messner et al. (2015). For our study, dimensions of sexuality, ethnicity, disability, environmentalism, animal rights and class (sometimes including rural/urban geographies) all seemed to have a real potential to sensitize men to the impact of sexism. Given this complexity, it is probably futile to try to isolate out the impact of any one dimension of power relations.

Men's Dominance as a pathway to intersectional identification with anti-sexism

In most previous scholarship exploring intersectional pathways (Pease, 2010 being a major exception), focus has primarily been on how marginalization of men can help them to understand, emotionally and intellectually, the injustice to women and children caused by men's violence. As we have seen, there are numerous examples of this in our data too. However, there are also several examples where a recognition by a man of his superordinate position within some other relation of power has helped him to challenge men's superordinate position in terms of gender relations and gendered violence (see Pease, 2021). Perhaps the clearest example was a respondent who, drawing on his own experience, felt that men engaged in environmental activism (like himself) and animal rights activism might be particularly inclined to challenge men's violence against women through the parallel injustice to animals and the natural world by humans (see Pease, 2019 for a detailed exploration of these issues). Dominance may also assist men to follow an intersectional pathway to challenging men's violence in less direct yet important ways. For instance, another respondent described how his middle-class family background was involved in him not seeking the company of, or depending on, men in groups:

> I've always had the space to back off. And that has meant me never being into these, I haven't been...a little bit outside of the kind of hard groups of guys. I have never belonged to a group of lads. And my own theory is that I simply have...[...] I have a little bit of a side view at it. I have definitely...sometimes I've been in, and sometimes [out]...I think it has something to do with my class background too, making me...I've also had the self-confidence, in some kind of way, to sometimes take part in [groups of men/boys]. But then I also have had the confidence to step out.

Here, an intersectionally constructed privilege of gender and class (masculinity and middle-class) enables an equally privileged potential for stepping aside/out of, or refusing groups (for instance men's secret societies) which otherwise would have further enhanced this respondent's already relatively dominant social position. These examples are important, suggesting that intersectional identification among men can sometimes utilize men's dominant positions as well as their marginalizations, thereby widening both the range of strategies available and the pool of men who can be targeted (see Cornwall, 2016; Pease, 2021).

The sounds of silence: age as intersection

Clearly, our data was valuable in exploring a broad range of overlapping intersectional dimensions of privilege and oppression which could offer access for our respondents to grasp the impact of gender oppression. However, we now want to focus on one intersectional dimension of oppressive power relations that was noticeable by its relatively low profile in our data: age in the form of oppressive adult-child relations. For, what is not mentioned in data can be as revealing as what is mentioned.

Implicitly, age was raised to a limited extent by one or two respondents who referred to violent fathers or other older men. Certainly, one source of encouragement for a few men to take a public stance against men's violence was some men's aggression they witnessed during childhood, such as sports coaches, other men in public spaces and, in a few instances, relatives. This was especially the case for one respondent whose father was violent in the home. He contrasted his father with his more gentle and kind older brother who provided an alternative model of how a man could be. Another man described a childhood filled with ostracism at home and school because of his disability and ethnicity.

Apart from these few references, there was only limited suggestion in our data that men as adults might be challenging men's violence as a result of witnessing men's violence against women when they were children. Perhaps even more surprisingly, we heard very little about men as children being subjected to physical abuse by men. Moreover, there was no mention in any of the interviews about respondents becoming opposed to men's violence because they endured child sexual abuse earlier in life – a form of child abuse that is very predominantly (though not exclusively) perpetrated by men and boys (Freel, 2003). These lacunae are striking because there is abundant research internationally demonstrating that those forms of abuse are very common in all societies (Rasool, 2017), not least Swedish society (for children witnessing men's violence against women in the home see Eriksson, 2017; for child sexual abuse see Pringle, 2016).

There are probably numerous reasons why the dimension of oppressive adult-child power relations was less present in our data compared to ethnicity/"race", sexual orientation, disability, animal rights, environmentalism or class. Some are obvious. For instance, we know that discussing any form of abuse in childhood is painfully difficult for most adults. So, there is bound to be a tendency towards silence on these matters in interviews. Moreover, our study consists of "expert" interviews seeking the informed reflections of men largely working professionally/semi-professionally in this field about what makes men, including themselves, take up this kind of work. As such, our semi-structured interviewing was very open-ended: building from a broad structure, we largely relied on respondents to take the interviews where they felt appropriate. So, it is likely that very sensitive personal material might not be mentioned. However, there may be other, less obvious, reasons for the relative absence of the age dimension in our data. For example, it has been suggested that there are features of the specific Swedish social and cultural context that create particular barriers to the open discussion, or indeed even full acknowledgement, of oppressive power relations associated with issues of bodily integrity (Egeberg Holmgren, 2011) – such as violence against women and child abuse, especially child sexual abuse (Pringle, 2010a, 2010b). At the same time, it might also be relevant that the whole field of critical studies on men globally (and especially in the Nordic countries) seems to have largely neglected oppressive adult/child power relations as a site where vital processes of masculinity formation and reformation occur: Messerschmidt (2000) and Pease (2021) are notable exceptions (see Eriksson, 2007; Pringle, 2016). Therefore, it may not be so surprising that men working with men in Sweden also pay less attention to aged power relations when discussing their own pathways to anti-sexist work and activism. Social work in the anglophone countries, as an academic discipline and as practice, has placed a considerable focus on child sexual abuse in the last three decades: and often from some form of feminist perspective. So, it is strange that critical studies on men, even in the anglophone countries, have devoted so little relative attention to child sexual abuse (compared to violence against women) as a prime site for the moulding/remoulding of oppressive forms of masculinity (Pringle, 2016).

Whatever the reasons for the relative absence of oppressive adult-child power relations in our data, this silence around child abuse may actually suggest a future strategy for encouraging more men to challenge men's violence against women – that is, if we interpret the silence as partly a reflection of the public horror aroused by child abuse. Research (for instance Edleson, 1999) has long made clear that there is a very significant overlap between those men who abuse their partners and those who physically and/or sexually abuse children living within those relationships. Consequently, we suggest that institutions and organizations working with men's violence against women might consider emphasizing these links as a way of encouraging more men to take a public stance against such violence. In Sweden, at least, the intense public unacceptability of child abuse may act as a further "spur" to men's opposition to women abuse once they realize how intimately connected are the two forms of abuse. One of our respondents actually hints at this strategy, when he discusses how to work with violent men:

> Unfortunately [...] the way society looks, it is not enough to motivate men by the fact that women are subjected to violence. [...] I know, it's totally damn sick, that this isn't good enough by itself. It's crazy. But I believe...then you have to, I think make sure that there is...you know, use strategies which harness the self-interest of men, or their interest in the rights of children. I've seen those studies, that show that when you need to get men using violence to stop, it doesn't work to talk about what it is doing to his partner, or what it does to him. He's beyond that. No care for himself either. But when it comes to what this does to the children, there is a specific crack opening up for some kind of empathy. That "oh, ok", when they hear how this affects the children. So I believe, I guess...then we'll use that. If that is, like, the chink in the armour of patriarchy that is on offer.

Conclusion

In terms of considering how our research may assist more men to work with men's violence against women, we must first re-iterate that this analysis is drawn from a relatively small qualitative study; we are not offering definitive responses to that question. Nevertheless, our study is highly suggestive of some important possibilities that can be further explored and further acted upon.

As Peretz (2017) in particular has noted, one of the means by which the issue of violence against women could become personalized for men is via their own parallel intersectional experiences of being oppressed (or indeed of perhaps being an oppressor). In our data, all our respondents demonstrated very high levels of emotional and intellectual awareness around sexism and men's privilege.

We suggest that one of the most important reasons for this relatively heightened awareness among the respondents was the marked degree to which they had reflected upon their own personal encounters with a broad range of multiple and intersecting forms of oppression, other than gender – often from a subordinate position but sometimes from a superordinate one. As we have demonstrated, the spectrum of those forms of oppression and privilege was considerably wider than we have found in most previous similar studies. Moreover, the dimensions of oppression in our data – clustered around issues of "race", ethnicity, disability, sexual orientation(s), class, rural/urban social location, environmentalism, animal rights and, to a limited extent, age – possessed a real valency in terms of sensitizing men to the dynamics of gender oppression. In that sense, our study illuminates more than most previous research the centrality and complexity of intersectional identifications which assisted our respondents to apprehend – emotionally as well as intellectually – the horror of gendered violence and the urgent need to oppose it.

In terms of ways forward, our analysis suggests that a broad range of intersecting dimensions of oppression should be considered more carefully as complex and crucial pathways by which some men transit to anti-gendered violence activities (see also Pease, 2021). If further research and development together confirm our analysis, then the next step should be far more concerted efforts to put these insights into practice. Ideally, the aim then should be for relevant organisations (not least social work ones) and individuals at all levels in society to provide as many opportunities as possible whereby men/boys can recognize and discuss their feelings and thoughts about their own subject positions vis-à-vis a broad range of power relations. And then how those feelings and thoughts can be translated to the position of men and women in terms of the former's violence against the latter. These opportunities should also embrace other existing and emerging strategies for helping men to challenge men's violence (Flood, 2019). Those opportunities include diverse social and feminist initiatives, many of which already exist sporadically in many countries but need to be developed more extensively and in a co-ordinated fashion: such as training courses, community campaigns, discussion groups, individual work with men and boys, school and university programmes, local and national publicity campaigns – and international cooperation. Ideally, all of them should be structured to complement one another, harnessing those multiple pathways by which many more men can be encouraged to become profeminist allies in challenging men's violence against women.

These programmes must of course also include extensive training about the dangers which can be present when profeminist men allies seek to support women challenging men's violence – such as men trying to take over, women's voices being drowned out, draining resources for women's work in the field (for further discussion see Pringle, 1995 and Pease, 2017). Such a broad, societal – and international – vision of how to create profeminist allies would require not only further research but also state – local and national – support. Men's violences against women, and to children, constitute massive social and health problems in all societies. They should be addressed as such governmentally, even in the allegedly "welfare paradise" of Sweden (Balkmar et al., 2009). This template for action draws inspiration from scholars such as Bob Pease (2021) and Andrea Cornwall (2016) as well as from Pringle (1995, pp. 204–214). This is an ideal for the future. Meanwhile, partnerships of activists, researchers and welfare practitioners (including social workers) committed to ending men's violence against women and children need to work together wherever they can to use the broad intersectional pathways analysed here through further research and development. At the same time, we urge such partnerships and anti-sexist organisations – large and small – to consider working far more closely and systematically than hitherto with broader alignments of third-sector activists who work against those other forms of oppression which we have identified as intersecting with sexism (see also Pease, 2021; Westmarland et al., 2021): for instance, environmental and animal rights activism, Leftist groups, trade unions, disability rights campaigners, anti-racist organisations and LGBTQ+ groups. We have seen that each dimension of oppression can be challenged via pathways leading from the others. Such a strategy echoes a similar call made by Connell more than 20 years ago in her conclusion to "Masculinities" (Connell, 2005).

We are not suggesting that the very wide range of intersectional pathways – and their complexities – opened up by our small research project is **the** key to creating a broad and widespread profeminist movement. However, our study does suggest that if those pathways are researched and developed more deeply and systematically, they may well offer an extremely important – and considerably untapped – resource for developing such a movement.

References

Balkmar, D., Iovanni, L. & Pringle, K. (2009). A critical re-consideration of two 'welfare paradises': Research and policy responses to men's violence in Denmark and Sweden. *Men and Masculinities*, 12(2), 155–174. doi:10.1177/1097184X08318183

Carbin, M. & Edenheim, S. (2013). The intersectional turn in feminist theory: A dream of a common language? *European Journal of Women's Studies*, 20(3), 233–248. doi:10.1177/1350506813484723

Casey, E. & Smith, T. (2010). "How can I not?": Men's pathways to involvement in anti-violence against women work. *Violence Against Women*, 16(8), 953–973. doi:10.1177/1097184X18805566

Casey, E. A., Tolman, R. M., Carlson, J., Allen, C. T. & Storer, H. L. (2017). What motivates men's involvement in gender-based violence prevention? Latent class profiles and correlates in an International sample of men. *Men and Masculinities*, 20(3), 294–316. doi:10.1177/1097184X16634801

Charmaz, K. (2014). *Constructing Grounded Theory*. Sage. doi:10.7748/nr.13.4.84.s4

Christensen, A. & Qvotrup Jensen, S. (2019). Intersectionality. In L. Gottzen, U. Mellström & T. Shefer (Eds.) *Routledge International Handbook of Masculinity Studies* (pp. 82–91). Routledge. doi.org/10.4324/9781315165165

Collins, P. H. (2019). *Intersectionality as Critical Social Theory*. Duke University Press. doi.org/10.4324/9781315165165

Connell, R. (2005). *Masculinities* (2nd edition). Polity. doi.org/10.4324/9781003116479

Cornwall, A. (2016). Towards a pedagogy of the powerful. *IDS Bulletin*, 47(5), 75–88. doi:10.19088/1968-2016.168

Edleson, J. L. (1999). The overlap between child abuse and woman battering. *Violence Against Women*, 5, 134–154. doi:10.1177/107780129952003

Edström, J., Singh, S. K. & Shahrokh, T. (2016). Intersectionality: A key for men to break out of the patriarchal prison? *Power, Poverty and Inequality, IDS Bulletin*, 47(5), 57–74. doi:10.19088/1968-2016.168

Egeberg Holmgren, L. (2011). *IngenMansLand: om Män som Feminister, Intervjuframträdanden och Passerandets Politik* [No Man's Land: Men as Feminists, Interview Performances and the Politics of Passing]. Uppsala universitet [Uppsala University].

Eriksson, M. (2007). Childhood studies. In M. Flood, J. Gardner, B. Pease & K. Pringle (Eds.) *International Encyclopedia of Men and Masculinities* (pp. 60–63). Routledge. doi.org/10.4324/9780203413067

Eriksson, M. (2017). Children's voices, children's agency, and the development of knowledge about children exposed to intimate partner violence. In M. Husso, T. Virkki, M. Notko, H. Hirvonen & J. Eilola (Eds.) *Interpersonal Violence: Differences and Connections* (pp. 140–152). Routledge. doi:10.4324/9781315628509

Flood, M. (2019). *Engaging Men and Boys in Violence Prevention*. Palgrave Macmillan. doi:10.1057/978-1-137-44208-6

Freel, M. (2003). Child sexual abuse and the male monopoly: An empirical exploration of gender and a sexual interest in children. *The British Journal of Social Work*, 33(4), 481–498. doi:10.1093/bjsw/33.4.481

Mama, A. (1995). *Behind The Masks: Race, Gender and Subjectivity*. Routledge. doi.org/10.4324/9780203405499

Mama, A. (2011). What does it mean to do feminist research in African contexts? *Feminist Review*, 98(1), S1, e4–e20. doi:10.1057/fr.2011.22.

Messerschmidt, J. W. (2000). *Nine Lives: Adolescent Masculinities, the Body and Violence*. Routledge. doi.org/10.4324/9780429037382

Messner, M. A., Greenberg, M. A., & Peretz, T. (2015). *Some Men: Feminist Allies in the Movement to End Violence Against Women*. Oxford University Press. doi.org/10.1093/acprof:oso/9780199338764.001.0001

Pease, B. (2010). Reconstructing violent rural masculinities: Responding to fractures in the rural gender order in Australia. *Culture, Society and Masculinity*, 2(2), 154–164. doi:10.3149/CSM.0202.154

Pease, B. (2017). *Men as Allies in Preventing Men's Violence against Women: Principles and Practices for Promoting Accountability*. White Ribbon Australia.

Pease B. (2019). Recreating men's relationship with nature: Toward a profeminist environmentalism. *Men and Masculinities*, 22(1), 113–123. doi:10.1177/1097184X18805566

Pease, B. (2021). *Undoing Privilege: Unearned Advantage in a Divided World* (2nd edition). Bloomsbury Publishing. doi:10.5040/9781350223738

Peretz, T. (2017). Engaging diverse men: An intersectional analysis of men's pathways to anti-violence activism. *Gender and Society*, 31(4), 526–548. doi:10.1177/0891243217717181

Peretz, T. (2019). Trends and trajectories in engaging men for gender justice. In L. Gottzen, U. Mellström & T. Shefer (Eds.) *Routledge International Handbook of Masculinity Studies* (pp. 498–507). Routledge. doi.org/10.4324/9781315165165

Peretz, T. (2020). Seeing the invisible knapsack: Feminist men's strategic responses to the continuation of male privilege in feminist spaces. *Men and Masculinities*, 23(3–4), 447–475. doi:10.1177/1097184X18805566

Pringle, K. (1995). *Men, Masculinities and Social Welfare*. UCL Press/Taylor and Francis. doi.org/10.4324/9781315072470

Pringle, K. (2010a). Swedish welfare responses to ethnicity: The case of children and their families. *European Journal of Social Work*, 13(1), 19–34. doi:10.1080/13691450903135659

Pringle, K. (2010b). Comparative studies of well-being in terms of gender, ethnicity, and the concept of 'bodily citizenship': Turning Esping-Andersen on his head?: Turning Esping-Andersen on His Head? In E. U. Oleksy, J. Hearn & D. Golanska (Eds.) *The Limits of Gendered Citizenship: Contexts and Complexities* (pp. 137–156). Routledge. doi.org/10.4324/978 0203831533

Pringle, K. (2016). Doing (oppressive) gender via men's relations with children. In A. Häyrén & H. Wahlström Henriksson (Eds.) *Critical Perspectives on Masculinities and Relationalities: In Relation to What?* (pp. 23–34). Springer. doi.org/10.1007/978-3-319-29012-6

Rasool, S. (2017). Adolescent reports of experiencing gender based violence: Findings from a cross-sectional survey from schools in a South African city. *Gender and Behaviour*, 15(2), 9133–9145. eISSN: 1596-9231

Westmarland, N., Almqvist, A-L., Egeberg Holmgren, L., Ruxton, S., Burrell, S. & Valbuena, C. D. (2021). *Men's Activism to End Violence Against Women: Voices from Spain, Sweden and the UK*. Bristol University Press. doi:10.47674/9781447357971

40
MEN, FEMINIST WELFARE, AND ALLYSHIP IN SOCIAL WORK EDUCATION

Goetz Ottmann and Iris Silva Brito

Introduction

Philips (2023) recently commented on an "explosion of interest in feminism in recent years" arguing that feminism has been instrumental in re-shaping welfare policy and practice. Messner (2016) argues similarly that the institutionalisation of feminism has re-shaped welfare and tertiary institutions and that academic disciplines, such as social work, have contributed to the professionalisation of feminism. In this sense, feminism has also impacted on and transformed social work education. Indeed, Jones and Micek (2019) assert that Australian social work education has been shaped by gendered discourses and a critique of patriarchal structures and power dynamics since its inception and that the profession is "feminine-typed due to its congruence with women's normative caring and benevolent role in Western society" (p. 71). Messner argues that feminism has been institutionalised and that this has led to a political flattening in a sense that feminist values and analysis are widespread throughout the welfare sector. However, it is currently difficult to discern an actual feminist movement (Messner, 2016).

Given this context, social work students[1] are confronted with the task to position themselves within this feminist field and to consider whether they are to become feminist allies. The classroom setting can become a testing ground for their attempts to navigate both gender politics and their professional identity within a female-majority profession. It is important to highlight at the outset that the term 'allyship' means different things within different contexts. Within the context of social justice-focused social work, 'allyship' has developmental connotations and is generally associated with an extensive list of characteristics that inform social work at the micro-, meso-, and macro-level (Gibson, 2016). This definition of 'allyship' differs somewhat from the way the term is used within the social movement literature. In this body of work, and particularly within contributions that focus on identity politics, the term 'allyship' refers to contributions members of a dominant group can make by joining members of a disadvantaged group in their struggle for social justice.

We start this chapter by focusing on allyship through a lens of social movements and collective action before delving deeper into social work feminist allyship. We believe that much can be gained from rendering distinct the (a) social movement frame and (b) the developmental social work approach because both the political and socio-developmental aims resonate with the term 'feminist allyship' but engender very different approaches and outcomes. This approach leads us to connect and contrast feminist allyship debates in normative, developmental social work – focused on addressing socio-cultural and behavioural issues – with the strategic aims of social movements: the political mobilisation of potential sympathisers and resources to affect social change. Indeed, when viewed from a social movement perspective, the more prescriptive contributions to the institutionalised, developmental approach to allyship potentially exclude a majority of men (and students more generally) that could be potential 'allies' and thus limits the socio-political potential of the feminist movement. When viewed from the developmental perspective, the collective action perspective gives rise to an allyship that can be perceived as inauthentic and, in the worst case, undermines the feminist cause. We are attempting to highlight these tensions so that they can be brought into focus during critical reflections in the classroom.

Much of the contemporary social work literature focuses on masculinity as a root cause of oppression and, most importantly, violence against women. This conceptualisation has its roots in the feminist movements of the 1970s that took aim at the deeply ingrained gender[2] inequality and the male domination of most social, economic, governmental, and religious institutions and the violence against women (Messner, 2016). In the 1970s, masculinity became synonymous with oppressive gender roles (oppressing women and dehumanising men) which in turn gave rise to men's liberation movements that embraced a more feminine masculinity founded in love, respect for the environment, and the rejection of violence (Vogel, 2015; Messner, 2016). One of the primary objectives of men's liberation movements was to join women in their fight to do away with men's institutionalised privileges and to alter gender-relations to end violence against women (Messner, 2016). In the 1970s, this gentler, more feminine, new age masculinity with its numerous life-style experiments came under pressure (from within and from outside) from a conservative, nationalist, right leaning, or reactionary masculinism that proclaimed that the ideal of manhood was in crisis. "Men had gone soft ..." and nations, as a result were "weaker, more vulnerable and the future less certain" (Vogel, 2015, p. 464).

The ensuing culture war against the inroads of civil rights, feminist, and minority movements and 'domesticated, emasculated men' was aided by a neo-liberal ethics, on the rise from the late 1970s onwards, that defined virtue in terms of grit, tenacity, independence, and successful competition in a tough marketplace (Harvey, 2005). Conservative masculinism sought to guide men back to traditional gender roles, heteronormativity, and the predominance of white men (Vogel, 2015). In other words, attempts to develop new identities have a political context. They form part of what is often referred to as 'culture wars', a struggle for the dominance of particular beliefs and values. They form part of a wider struggle of social justice-motivated movements to create societal structures and cultures that are *more* inclusive, rights-based, supportive, fair, equal, and democratic and *less* discriminatory, authoritarian, and autocratic. However, conservative and neo-liberal forces seek to undo the success of the socially progressive movements in areas such as welfare and social rights and advocate for a return to traditional gender roles and relationships.

It is important to highlight that discussions of feminist allyship must include a discussion of ethics. In this chapter, we are focusing on two basic conflicting ethical frameworks: a neo-liberal and an ethics of care. A neo-liberal ethics emphasises market-solutions (i.e.

privatisation), independence, individualism, and individual responsibility and seeks to transform welfare into a behaviour-management program assigning human services workers a coercive and punitive function. An ethics of care, however, emphasises our obligation to care for others and emphasises reciprocity, compassion, relationships, emotions, inclusion, and connections, placing it at the core of the fight against gendered (and other) injustices and inequalities. Whereas a neo-liberal ethics places virtue in economic self-sufficiency, an ethics of care is about moral development, values, and supportive relationships acknowledging our dependence on others and the desirability of a safety net in the form of welfare (McAuliffe, 2023).

Social movements, allyship, and alliances

It is difficult to over-estimate the impact of the social movements of the 1960s and 1970s on societal values, institutions, and norms. Feminist (and allied) social movements have popularised the idea of equal rights to a point where we have anti-discrimination legislation and the majority of Australians are supportive of eradicating the gender pay gap, sexual harassment, and other gender inequalities (ANROWS, 2023). Although in practice many forms of oppression and discrimination persist (Prime Minister & Cabinet, n.d.), this represents a radical shift in attitudes compared to the 1950s.

To be sure, social change is contingent upon collaboration between groups that benefit differently from existing norms and social structures. It is also a given that individuals will bring different commitments to their involvement with social movements. Many are sympathisers or bystanders. They appreciate the movement's cause and may take its position in dialogue with others on social media, for example. They will contribute to movements from the periphery. They may, on occasions, join in collective action and participate in protest marches, sign petitions, contribute to online discussions, engage in 'clicktivism', or donate money. However, only a few will become more active in the movement. They might donate their time, organise events, participate in regular meetings, or create regular social media content – they become 'upstanders' (Nardini et al., 2020). And a handful will take on leadership functions and become involved in up-scaling to transform individual groups into a networked movement (Diani, 1992). To be sure, social change is dependent on the actions of organisers, members, and bystanders. Change doesn't happen without them.

Within a collective action context, the term 'ally' could be applied to bystanders or upstanders, depending on their social location vis-a-vis the disadvantaged group whose cause they support. The term 'ally' introduces a distinction based on relative privilege where movement supporters that belong to a clearly identifiable group that is societally more advantaged can only be allies. This, in turn, raises the sceptre of authenticity and the possibility of inauthentic 'performative' allyship based on self-serving support and commitment to a cause (McClanahan, 2021). In other words, allies can play a detrimental role that undermines, financially exploits, co-opts, or attempts to take over a movement. Radke and colleagues (2020) highlight that the *motivation* of allies to support a cause is often a matter of concern for movement members as trust is a crucial element in social movements. The issue of trust and alignment with a movement's framing of an issue has been amplified by the pitfalls of online activism (Nardini et al., 2020). This makes the vetting of potential allies desirable (see, for example, Radke et al., 2020; Thai & Nylund, 2023) but is in practice often not possible. Radke et al. (2020) suggest that motivation to join a movement can be

a based on improving the status of a disadvantaged group;
b conditional in the sense that your support of the disadvantaged group should not come at the detriment of your own advantaged group;
c based on utility in the sense that your support is a means to an end that ultimately is of benefit to you; or
d based on a moral imperative to respond to what you perceive as injustice.

They found that motivations based on 'b' and 'c' are met with considerable suspicion and that movement members generally expect a genuine moral or value-based motivations. However, in practice motivational constellations are often more difficult to discern and may involve a combination of the above-mentioned (or other) elements. More importantly, movements may engage in a strategic alliance with a, to some extent, self-motivated ally (to what extent are politicians self-motivated?) because of their capacity to contribute significantly to the success of a movement. Also, the motivation of an ally can often only be grasped after the fact or may change over the course of an alliance. Further, Radke and colleagues (2020) found that even well-intentioned allies have blind spots that will limit their utility and acceptability to movements and their cause. But the same holds true for movement members. Indeed, the inclusion of members and allies into movements and the formation of alliances forms part of the intense and difficult negotiations that end up defining movements. From a collective action perspective, movements must rely on allies (and members, for that matter) irrespective of their motivation, whether they are authentic, or fully aligned with movement objectives.

Allies can open doors providing access to organisations, institutions, or governmental departments. They can also generate solidarity, legitimise claims, reduce isolation and hostility, lend internal support, and/or provide access to resources (Moser & Branscombe, 2022; Thai & Nylund, 2023). Because they are in a privileged position, they may be instrumental in bringing about the desired change while not facing the backlash that members of the disadvantaged group might face advancing the same demands. They might be in a key position where they can access and recruit a wide range of other allies that might be of importance to a movement (Thai & Nylund, 2023).

So far, we have conceptualised feminist allyship as if the feminist movement were any other social movement. If this were the case, biological sex and gender would not matter when determining whether someone is to be an ally or a movement member. That is, women and men in privileged societal positions relative to other women more oppressed by their intersectional subject location would be regarded as allies and not necessarily members. And it would be expected of privileged women to become aware of unearned privilege as much as it would be expected of men and the question of authenticity would be tied to class and status rather than sex and gender.

Developmental feminist allyship

The notion of developmental feminist allyship is in many ways a complicated one. With it resonate some of the strategic essentialisms (i.e. that the categories of 'men' and 'women' are intrinsically distinct) that underpinned feminist social movement frames of the 1970s. Essentialist claims give rise to central questions, such as what makes a male a feminist ally, whether such allyship is actually possible or desirable, and whether other terms might encapsulate better what ought to be demanded of male feminist 'allies'. It also invites prescriptive taxonomies based on behavioural norms. Some authors see the term 'allyship' as an alternative – or perhaps an escape route – for male students uncomfortable with the term 'feminist' (Schmitz & Haltom, 2017) and signal that the terminology accompanying male transition to a new identity harbours complex ontological and political tensions. Some commentators question whether 'allyship' is simply a term for what otherwise might be called 'feminism light' and whether the term should be abandoned all together (Carlson et al., 2020).

Another aspect of strategic essentialisms is the definition of allyship in terms of the moral development of men. The developmental literature on male feminist allyship offers a continuum of requirements ranging from basic, relatively easy to follow behavioural norms to more challenging obligations (Kahn & Ferguson, 2009; Johnson & Smith, 2018; Nash et al., 2021). On the less challenging side of the continuum, some authors see male feminist allies as 'tempered radicals' that are aware that men form an 'advantaged group' enjoying social privileges, that they are committed to building relationships with women, do not engage in sexist behaviour, and are displaying an active commitment to address gender inequities at work and in society (Kahn & Ferguson, 2009; Johnson & Smith, 2018). Nash and colleagues (2021) add to this that men should be educating themselves about their privilege, biases, and the way they unintentionally reproduce a system that discriminates against women and that they should be prepared to learn from their mistakes. Most male students in the classroom would probably be reasonably comfortable with these requirements. Also, there is considerable overlap between these basic requirements and the elements that foster movement cohesion outlined in the social movement literature mentioned above.

This 'light' approach to feminism has attracted the criticism of activists and academics alike. For example, Carlson et al. (2020) foreground the importance of direct involvement in advocacy and consciousness raising, a 'non-self-absorbed' and accountable self-reflection and an openness to criticism. Carlson and colleagues highlight that allyship can have a distinctly undesirable side as privileged male activists often reproduce inequalities through action or ideology potentially causing harm and undermining the wider feminist struggle. They comment on the 'pedestal effects' (receiving disproportionate praise for their minor contribution) and that men's allyship can produce new inequalities. In a more general sense, this critique focuses on the way men's allyship has translated into an identity (it has been institutionalised and professionalised) rather than into (individual and collective) action and emphasises the need to link men's support with their active support encapsulated by concepts, such as 'currently operating in solidarity with', 'accomplice', and 'co-conspirator'. Their work emphasises 'accountability' to the feminist movement, 'self-reflection', and the need to actively challenge established rules and conventions (Carlson et al., 2020). They reiterate Utt's statement that "if someone uses 'ally' as a label they are applying to themselves, they generally aren't" (Utt, 2013). In this sense, this revised version of allyship is about action – not identity. Selvanathan and colleagues (2020) partially agree but focus on the motivation that underpins men's allyship and the disadvantaged groups that accept it.

Flood (2017) largely endorses the above-mentioned critique and issues a list of requirements that must be met if male allies are to make a real contribution to the feminist struggle. Flood advises that the lens through which social problems and corresponding solutions are being defined must be much more robustly feminist. It must be focused on structural, material, and institutional dimensions of gender inequality and problematise masculinities. Furthermore, he asserts that men must be expected to participate in personal and social change, work towards gender-egalitarian identities, practices, interpersonal relations, contribute to community action, do the work of activism, and practise feminism. Flood (2017) transforms the term 'feminist ally' into a badge of honour that men need to work towards and that should be awarded only if deserved.

Focusing on interventions to eradicate Violence Against Women, Burrell and Flood (2019) add additional behavioural standards required of 'pro-feminist men'. The term 'pro-feminist' highlights a qualitative shift in commitment towards and active support of feminist goals bringing about political, economic, cultural, personal, and social equality alongside advocacy to prevent men's violence against women. The term encapsulates an awareness of women's experiences making these the core of the analytic process (Bojin, 2013). Furthermore, Burrell and Flood (2019) introduce the requirements of accountability to, acting in consultation with feminist women and the importance of being knowledgeable about the diversity of women's experiences and feminist theories, the evaluation of interventions in terms of feminist outcomes, and a gendered reflexivity taking into account of the "full continuum of men's violence against women" in prevention work. They also argue that connections need to be made between our everyday lives and professional work and the patriarchal structures that normalise men's violence against women (p. 244).

Clearly, these standards are much more challenging for pro-feminist men (and women and gender-diverse people) than the 'light', liberal feminist allyship outlined at the beginning of this section. It traverses and links the public and private, and it demands a working knowledge of feminist theory (see also Tienari & Taylor, 2019) and reflexive practice. Furthermore, it defers men's decisional authority demanding a consultative approach that is accountable to feminist women. Whereas these more challenging normative and behavioural frameworks, such as outlined by Flood and other colleagues, bring clearly into view a strategic response how men can contribute to the eradication of intimate partner and domestic violence, from a social movement point of view these frameworks are less likely to attract a mass-following that movements rely on to generate social change and a deepening political commitment to welfare.

Which feminism?

Discussions focusing on the qualities of pro-feminist men's allyship are rendered more complex by the considerable breadth of feminism and feminist scholarship (see also Burrell & Flood, 2019). Cree and Dean (2015), for example, outline that social work students' understandings of feminism are diverse incorporating a melange of all four waves of feminism.[3] Their notion of feminism incorporates the negative facets of conditioning within a patriarchal society (both for men and women), the importance of "ensuring equality with men, in all areas of life and includes elements, such as equal pay, equal say and equal opportunity for employment", obtaining rights, fighting oppression, promoting empowerment, and disrupting gender stereotyping, and gender-based violence. Cree and Dean describe two prevailing attitudes towards feminism amongst students: "I'm not a feminist but ... I support women's rights and believe that women should be treated fairly, etc." and "I am a feminist but ... I am not anti-men, segregationalist" (Cree & Dean, 2015, p. 907). Cree and Dean argue that overall the feminism of the students in their study may be less essential and more self-critical but warn against over-simplification. They state that different branches of feminism coexist but might be highly critical of each other; they posit that these divergences are important as they lead to different ways power, agency, and structure are conceptualised not only in the classroom but also in social work practice (Cree & Dean, 2015, p. 917).

Also, Charter (2022) highlights that for women (but also men or gender-diverse people) 'of colour' or from an ethnic minority background, racialised terms such as 'black feminist' may carry greater meaning and provide more conceptual depth for self-identification.

Commentators from the Global South employing a post-colonial analysis have taken issue with Western feminism more generally. For example, Makama and colleagues (2019) posit that a Western-centric, universal feminism has conceptualised dominant masculinity in ways that are too often informed by a moralistic opposition of victim and villain. They argue that feminism should be committed to promoting positive masculinities rather than assigning toxic qualities to masculinities per se.

Alternative masculinities

As mentioned, masculinity has become a synonym for toxic, anti-social behaviour, societal privileged positions, and systemic oppression. For social work students, answering the question how they can contribute to the dismantling of the masculinist/patriarchal system might become more important at this point. Feminist allyship, in many ways, urges them to develop an identity that is not anchored in a majoritarian form of oppressive masculinity. This often presents an important stumbling block for emerging feminist allies. Because masculinity is often tied to men's behaviour traits, a critique of masculinity can lead to a critique of men's way of being a man (Kimmel, 2010; Schmitz & Haltom, 2017). To counter this, Kimmel argues that a critique of masculinity should not lead to a guilt-driven, introvert politics of self-purification and self-negation that is ultimately "relentless and merciless in its denunciation of one's allies" (Kimmel, 2010, p. 11). In other words, the question of whether or how power can or cannot be reconstructed in masculinity and whether masculinity must be rejected is central to whether social work students can become constructive (rather than self-destructive) feminist allies.

Studies of masculinity largely focus on the various ways in which men are collectively privileged, that not all men are equally privileged, and that individual men can occupy subordinate positions (Kimmel, 2010). In her earlier work, Connell (1997) argued that masculinity needs to be regarded as a hierarchical spectrum whose mark of distinction is the capacity to dominate others and particularly women. In this sense, dominant masculinity is heterosexual, aggressive, and competitive and excludes women (and 'lesser' men and gender-diverse people) from its social networks. Dominant masculinity is culturally produced and re-produced through its celebration in neo-liberal entrepreneurialism, social media, books, action movies, and sport. Kimmel and other masculinity scholars make the point that few men actually live a dominant masculinity and are more likely to find themselves in subordinate positions (i.e. they are themselves oppressed by dominant masculinity) (Connell, 1997; Pease, 2000; Kimmel, 2010). Connell argues that this, however, does not mean that they are not complicit in the patriarchal system as they can passively reap the benefits of Patriarchy without directly wielding power (Connell, 1997, p. 8). Clearly, this kind of negatively conceived, 'subordinate' masculinity which on the one hand harbours negative connotations due to its complicity in Patriarchy and on the other denotes victimhood because of its oppression by dominant masculinity produces a less desirable identity that, Schmitz and Haltom (2017) argue, may form a barrier to social movement allyship and, by extension, gender equality.

Indeed, male students tend to adopt particular strategies in their social interactions to manage varied reactions to feminism. Students learn to navigate social relationships by highlighting or downplaying their own masculinity creating what some have called a 'hybrid masculinity' (Schmitz & Haltom, 2017). Using the term 'allies' rather than 'feminist', according to Messner (2016), forms part of such a strategy as it avoids contentious labelling. Anderson argues that labelling is an issue as the term 'feminist man' signifies a loss of stereotypically masculine traits which in turn has more homosexual connotations compared with the term 'man' (Anderson, 2009). Bearing this in mind, Anderson advances the idea of an 'inclusive masculinity', a masculinity purged of its undesirable traits. Similarly, Schmitz and Haltom (2017) suggest that 'hybrid masculinities' are a useful way to understanding men's experiences in feminised contexts and involvement with female-dominated fields, such as social work, that accentuate men's gendered identities.

Post-masculinist feminist allyship

This perspective has been critiqued by some masculinity scholars highlighting that any so-called positive masculinity will always be valued above femininity, thus reinforcing a binary gender hierarchy (R. Connell, 1997; Pease, 2000, 2023b). Authors following this line of argument are adamant that masculinity must be demolished. For example, Connell argues that "[i]n the long run, the democratization of gender will require profound social change, and the dismantling of conventional masculinities" (1997, p. 10). Pease (2000, 2023b) agrees and adds that men must transform their subjectivity and practices *before* they can choose to work collectively against Patriarchy. Pease argues that the rejection of patriarchy can occur from within but that this undertaking hinges on men developing a different, non-sexist self. The strategy that Pease has in mind is focused on the re-construction of men's ideological and discursive position distinguishing between a "traditional 'men's standpoint' and a 'pro-feminist men's standpoint'" (Pease, 2000, p. 59). In other words, the question is no longer one of essential traits that make men men but one of ideology, standpoints, and personal practice. This transformation of masculinity into an ideology (rather than a trait of men) leads to the hindsight that women can also engage in masculinist behaviour (and do it very well). Thus, by turning masculinism into an ideology that can be adopted by anyone irrespective of gender offers new strategic possibilities to combat this ideology.

In his more recent writings, Pease (2023a) uses the language of 'masculinism' (denoting an ideology that legitimates men's dominance) to avoid the essentialising tendencies that often form an undercurrent in gender analyses. Pease affirms the need to develop alternatives to masculinism in the form of new pro-feminist identities that are locally situated. Yet he also stresses that "masculinism and patriarchy often persist in the face of alternative and changing masculinities" and that a serious challenge to masculinism can only emerge if 'men become woman' and embrace a feminist ethic of care (Pease, 2023a). Pease's project is without a doubt subversive as it dissolves gender and erects in its place what Almassi (2022) calls a yet to be defined, but decidedly feminine, androgynous, pro-feminist identity. Ultimately, Pease (2023b) seeks to move beyond masculinism to construct a post-gender subjectivity with the possibility to create new constellations and becoming.

A growing number of feminist philosophers and scholars of masculinity (see, for example, Pease, 2023b; Asberg & Braidotti, 2018; Braidotti, 2022; Grosz, 2017; Cotter, 2013; Deckha, 2012) have used the work of Deleuze and Guttari to elaborate ontological foundations on which new social constellations can be built, to go beyond thinking about what is, but what could be (Grosz, 2017, p. 1). They tend to be concerned with the question "how to act in the present and, most importantly, how to bring about a future different from the present ..." (Grosz, 2017, p. 132). For example, for Grosz, resistance to this masculinist norm is shaped by unpredictable and often uncontrollable events that will result in "becoming other, becoming minoritarian, becoming woman, becoming something in between or neither …" (2017, p. 160). This ethics of becoming then turns into a journey of intense reflection and discovery that leads to 're-cognition'. It is a dangerous journey as it leads into unknown territory that can turn out to be inhospitable or even uninhabitable. For Grosz, the risk is worth taking for it is only at the point at which constellations are no longer familiar, radical change becomes possible.

Post-humanist allyship

Braidotti (2013, 2022) and others (see, for example, Deckha, 2012; Cotter, 2013) take this transformational onto-ethics one step further by dissolving the human at the centre of philosophical conventions replacing it with 'self-constituting matter'. They use the concept of the 'post-human' to link politics and subjectivity in a new way. In doing so, they attempt to overcome "the fixed, dyadic, and hierarchical categories of nature and culture, or the human and the nonhuman, thereby enabling alternative analyses that explore the entanglements and mutual co-constitutions that result [from this]" (Asberg & Braidotti, 2018, p. 6). In other words, post-humanist feminists assist us to strip back idealist claims of the enlightenment that, if accepted un-critically, hide domination and exploitation in plain sight. Feminist post-humanities aim to discover our multi-directional and multi-facetted entanglements with each other involving a plurality of forces and fields. The purpose of such feminist scholarship is to 'stay with the trouble' and inquire how we might be able to live together in more-than-human worlds (Braidotti, 2013). Braidotti argues that the self-reflection, dialogue, and compromise tied up with a post-human analysis can help us to overcome anthropocentrism, racism, parochialism, homophobia, xenophobia, and sexism along other 'bad habits' and move forward without becoming hamstrung by conventional binary, dyadic thinking (Braidotti, 2013).

Concluding summary

In this chapter, we canvassed a wide range of positions that social work students might consider when pondering their positioning vis-a-vis feminist welfare and Feminisms more generally. Although some of these positions sound challenging, upon reflection students will realise that they link up with social work approaches that form part of a canon of Critical and Anti-Oppressive practice. We hope this might stimulate constructive debates in classroom and practice settings in the knowledge that social workers and social work students are expected to develop a professional standpoint that embraces an ethics of care.

Notes

1 We are consciously using gender neutral language. The reason for this should become clearer over the course of this chapter.
2 The use of the term 'gender' here is politically loaded as it erases 'women' and re-constructs the problem as one of gender inequality, which has wider connotations than focusing on the structural disadvantage of women.
3 The concept that feminism constitutes 'waves' has been critiqued on the basis that is over-simplifies a much more complex history involving a plethora of groups and sub-groups that are often at odds with each other J. Reger (2017). Finding a Place in History: The Discursive Legacy of the Wave Metaphor and Contemporary Feminism. *Feminist Studies*, 43 (1), 193–221.

References

Almassi, B. (2022) *Non-toxic: Masculinity, Allyship, and Feminist Philosophy*. Palgrave Macmillan.
Anderson, E. (2009). *Inclusive Masculinity: The Changing Nature of Masculinities*. Routledge.
ANROWS (2023). Attitudes Matter: NACAS, The 2021 National Community Attitudes towards Violence against Women Survey. Sydney, NSW, Australia's National Research Organisation for Women's Safety (ANROWS). https://irp.cdn-website.com/f0688f0c/files/uploaded/NCAS%2021%20Summary%20Report%20ANROWS.2.pdf
Asberg, C., & Braidotti, R. (2018). Feminist Posthumanities: An Introduction. In C. Asberg & R. Braidotti (Eds.) *A Feminist Companion to the Posthumanities*. Springer International Publishing AG.
Bojin, K. (2013). Feminist Solidarity: No Boys Allowed? Views of Pro-feminist Men on Collaboration and Alliance-building with Women's Movements. *Gender & Development*, 21(2), 363–379. https://doi.org/10.1080/13552074.2013.802879
Braidotti, R. (2013). *The Posthuman*. Polity Press.
Braidotti, R. (2022). *Posthuman Feminism*. Polity Press.
Burrell, S. R., & Flood, M. (2019). Which Feminism? Dilemmas in Pro-feminist Men's Practis to End Violence against Women. *Global Social Welfare*, 6, 231–244. https://doi.org/10.1007/s40609-018-00136-x
Carlson, J., CLeek, C., Casey, E., Tolman, R., & Allen, C. (2020). What's in a Name? A Synthesis of 'Allyship' Elements from Academic and Activist Literature. *Journal of Family Violence*, 35, 889–898. https://doi.org/10.1007/s10896-019-00073-z
Charter, M. L. (2022). Predictors of Feminist Identity Utilizing an Intersectional Lens With a Focus on Non-Hispanic White, Hispanic, and African American MSW Students. *Affilia*, 37(1), 97–117.
Connell, R. W. (1997). Men, Masculinities and Feminism. *Social Alternatives*, 16(3), 7–10.
Cotter, J. (2013). Posthumanist Feminism and the Embodiment of Class. In A. L. Brackin and N. Guyot (Eds.) *Stories in Post-Human Cultures* (pp. 27–37). Inter-Disciplinary Press. https://doi.org/10.1163/9781848882713_004
Cree, V., & Dean, J. S. (2015). Exploring Social Work Students' Attitudes towards Feminism: Opening Up Conversations. *Social Work Education*, 34(8), 903–920. https://doi.org/10.1080/02615479.2015.1081884
Deckha, M. (2012). Toward a Postcolonial, Posthumanist Feminist Theory: Centralizing Race and Culture in Feminist Work on Nonhuman Animals. *Hypatia*, 27(3), 527–545.
Diani, M. (1992). The Concpet of Social Movements. *The Sociological Review*, 40(1), 1–25. https://doi.org/10.1111/j.1467-954X.1992.tb02943.x
Flood, M. (2017). The Turn to Men in Gender Politics. *Women's Studies Journal*, 31(1), 48–58.
Gibson, M. (2016). Social Worker Shame: A Scoping Review. *The British Journal of Social Work*, 46(2), 549–565.
Grosz, E. (2017). *The Incorporeal: Ontology, Ethics, and the Limits of Materialism*. Columbia University Press.
Harvey, D. (2005). *A Brief History of Neoliberalism*. Oxford University Press.
Johnson, B., & Smith, D. G. (2018, 12 October). How Men can Become Better Allies to Women. *Harvard Buisenss Review*. https://hbr.org/2018/10/how-men-can-become-better-allies-to-women
Jones, M., & Micek, S. (2019). Gender Dynamics in Social Work Practice and Education: A Critical Literature Review. *Australian Social Work*, 72(1), 62–74. https://doi.org/10.1080/0312407x.2018.1524919
Kahn, J. S., & Ferguson, K. (2009). Men as Allies in Feminist Pedagogy in the Undergraduate Psychology Curriculum. *Women & Therapy*, 33(1–2), 121–139. https://doi.org/10.1080/02703140903404853
Kimmel, M. (2010). *Misframing Men: The Politics of Contemporary Masculinities*. Rutgers University Press.
Makama, R., Helman, R., Titi, N., & Day, S. (2019). The Danger of a Single Feminist Narrative: African-centred Decolonial Feminism for Balck Men. *Agenda*, 33(3), 61–69. https://doi.org/10.1080/10130950.2019.1667736
McAuliffe, D. (2023). An Ethics of Care: Contributions to Social Work Practice. In D. Hoelscher, D. McAuliffe, & R. Hugman (Eds.) *Social Work Theory and Ethics: Ideas in Practice*. Springer.

McClanahan, A. (2021). The Downfalls of Performative White Allyship on Social Media in the #BlackLivesMatter Movement. *Munn Scholars Awards 7.* https://researchrepository.wvu.edu/munn/7

Messner, M. A. (2016). Forks in the Road of Men's Gender Politics: Men's Rights vs Feminist Allies. *International Journal for Crime, Justice and Social Democracy, 5*(2), 6–20. https://doi.org/10.5204/ijcjsd.v5i2.301

Moser, C., & Branscombe, N. (2022). Male Allies at Work: Gender-Equality Supportive Men Reduce Negative Underrepresentation Effect Among Women. *Social Psychological and Personality Science, 13*(2), 372–381. https://doi.org/10.1177/19485506211033748

Nardini, G., Bublitz, M., Peracchio, L., Rank-Christman, T., & Cross, S. (2020). Together We Rise: How Social Movements Succeed. *Journal of Consumer Psychology, 31*(1), 112–145. https://doi.org/10.1002/jcpy.1201

Nash, M., Moore, R., Grant, R., & Winzenberg, T. (2021, 26 July 2021). It's Not about You: How to Be a Male Ally. *The Conversation.* https://theconversation.com/its-not-about-you-how-to-be-a-male-ally-158134

Pease, B. (2000). Political Issues in Working with Men in the Human Services. *Women Against Violence, 8,* 57–64.

Pease, B. (2023a). Disrupting Masculinism in Public Policy Responses to COVID-19: Unmasking the Gendered Dimension of the Pandemic. In G. Ottmann & C. Noble (Eds.) *Post-pandemic Welfare and Social Work.* Routledge.

Pease, B. (2023b). Men Becoming Otherwise: Lines of Flight from 'Man' and Majoritarian Masculinity. In U. Mellstroem & B. Pease (Eds.) *Post-humanism and the Man Question: Beyond Anthropocentric Masculinities.* Routledge.

Philips, R. (2023). *Practising Feminism for Social Welfare – A Global Perspective.* Routledge Taylor & Francis Group.

Radke, H., R. M., Kutlaca, M., Siem, B., Sright, S. C., & Becker, J. C. (2020). Beyond Allyship: Motivations for Advantaged Group Members to Engage in Action for Disadvantaged Groups. *Personality and Social Psychology Review, 24*(4), 291–315. https://doi.org/10.1177/1088868320918698

Reger, J. (2017). Finding a Place in History: The Discursive Legacy of the Wave Metaphor and Contemporary Feminism. *Feminist Studies, 43*(1), 193–221.

Schmitz, R., & Haltom, T. M. (2017). "I wanted to raise my hand and say I'm not a feminist": College Men's Use of Hybrid Masculinities to Negotiate Attachments to Feminism and Gender Studies. *Journal of Men's Studies, 25*(3), 278–297. https://doi.org/10.1177/1060826516676841

Selvanathan, H. P., Lickel, B., & Dasgupta, N. (2020). An Integrative Framework on the Impact of Allies: How Identity-based Needs Influence Intergroup Solidarity and Social Movements. *European Journal of Social Psychology EASP, 50,* 1344–1361. https://doi.org/10.1002/easp.2697

Thai, M., & Nylund, J. (2023). What Are They In It For? Marginalised Group Members' Percpetions of Allies Differ Depending on the Costs and Rewards Associated with their Allyship. *The British Journal of Social Psychology,* 1–22. https://doi.org/10.1111/bjso.12670

Tienari, J., & Taylor, S. (2019). Feminism and Men: Ambivalent Space for Acting Up. *Organization, 26*(6), 948–960. https://doi.org/10.1177/1350508418805287

Utt, J. (2013). *So You Call Yourself an Ally: 10 Things all 'allies' Need to Know.* https://everydayfeminism.com/2015/11/things-allies-need-to-know

Vogel, J. (2015). Freaks in the Reagan Era: James Baldwin the New Pop Cinema, and the American Ideal of Manhood. *The Journal of Popular Culture, 48*(3), 464–486.

41
'MEN' AS SOCIAL WORKERS
Professional identities, practices and education

Fiachra Ó Súilleabháin and Alastair Christie

Introduction

The contradictions, ambiguities and tensions that result from men's positions as social workers and service users help to expose how 'gender' is (re)produced in organisations/ professions, and how patriarchal cultures and structures continue to oppress women, and to provide men with a patriarchal dividend (Connell, 1995). Men's positions in social work both (re)produce and potentially challenge hegemonic forms of masculinity (Carrigan et al., 1985), which are based on idealised forms of masculinity. In this chapter, we argue that individuals and groups of men social workers can stand alongside women colleagues in developing pro-feminist approaches and challenging patriarchal practices and structures. However, there is strong evidence that overall men's employment as social workers directly and indirectly reproduces patriarchal forms of power.

Judith Butler's ground-breaking feminist work, *Gender Trouble* (1990), demonstrates how gender is performative, through continual ritualised performance of gender norms. These norms determine what is acceptable and intelligible within dominant patriarchal hierarchies. While these norms are fixed through a process that Butler calls 'sedimentation', this process is not totalising and subjects can 'inhabit the social categories through which we are constituted in unintended ways, and in so doing change their meaning' (Butler, 1997, p.103). Even within the reiterative performance of gender norms, there is possibility of slippage, of doing it 'wrong' and/or doing it differently. So that the 'task is not to whether to repeat, but how to repeat or, indeed, to repeat and, through radical proliferation of gender, to displace the very gender norms that enable the repetition itself' (Butler, 1990, p.189). 'Men' in social work as professionals, students and service users are constantly (re)created and normalised (Hicks & Jeyasingham, 2016); however, it is not clear whether the context of social worker provides particularly fertile ground for unintended slippages and the 'radical proliferation of gender'.

Theories that highlight intersectionality have identified how the category 'man' is not only gendered but is also racialised, sexualised and classed. An intersectional approach helps to analyse hierarchical power relations between men as well as between men and women (Christensen & Jensen, 2014). Theories on performativity and intersectionality open up new ways of thinking about 'men' as social workers. In this chapter, we use the terms 'man' and 'men' to refer to individuals who identify themselves as men. While we argue here that individuals and groups of men can potentially challenge dominant forms of gender, their employment in social work and their presence as service users directly and indirectly reinforce patriarchal forms of power (Christie, 1998; Cree, 2000; McLean, 2003; Pease, 2011). This chapter is written by two people who identify as men with varying sexualities who have followed a common pattern from social worker, to social work manager and then to social work academic.

While individual men social workers can adopt pro-feminist approaches, their practices and employment settings are often bound by professional and legal frameworks, which reinforce patriarchal forms of gender regulation (Christie, 1998; Cree, 2000; Mc Lean, 2003; Pease, 2011; Pease and Camerilleri, 2001). Men as social workers also live in worlds 'outside' social work. These worlds again are informed by, and reproduce, patriarchal structures and cultures (see Gřundělová & Gojová, 2022). As yet, it is largely unknown the extent to which men social workers pursue pro-feminist practices and counter-hegemonic forms of masculinity in both their personal and professional lives. The extent to which men as social workers can challenge patriarchal gender relations is also questioned (e.g. Pease, 2011). Overall, this chapter seeks to continue the project of 'naming men as men', focusing on what men do as individuals and as a collective group (Hearn, 2004), as well as critically analysing how the subject positions of those who identify as 'men' are reproduced within social work. To start, we consider men's position within the profession of social work.

Social work as a non-traditional occupation for men

Much of the debate on social work, men and masculinities has focused on social work as an occupation. Social work has been identified along with other occupations (e.g. primary school teachers and nursing) as a 'non-traditional' occupation for men (Christie, 1998; Williams, 1993). This definition of social work as a 'non-traditional' occupation for men is supported by employment/registration statistics that show how men comprise less than 20% of social workers in most countries. For example, in Ireland, where the two authors are based, out of a total of 4983 registered social workers, 16% (785) were identified as men and 84% (4198) as women in 2021 (CORU, 2022). In Scotland, in 2016, 85% of those working the social workforce were identified as women and 15% as men (Cree et al., 2020). Similar statics are found in the USA, there were approximately 715,600 social workers in 2020 (Bureau of Labour Statistics, 2020) and in 2017 it was estimated that 17% of social workers were identified as men and 83% as women (Salsberg et al., 2020). In Australia, 79.5% of the membership of the Australian Association of Social Work identified as women and 20.5% as men (Jones et al., 2019). While these statistics only provide an approximation of the total numbers of men and women social workers, they clearly show that there are significantly less men than women employed as social workers. While there is surprising little information on the employment of social workers and their position within organisations in different countries, there appears to be a general trend that men are over-represented as managers, particularly the most senior managers and social work academics (Cree et al., 2020).

Social work is characterised as being predominantly caring, supportive and person-orientated, whereas occupations traditionally associated with men are often characterised as involving physical strength, being competitive, requiring emotional detachment and constraint and work that includes elements of control and discipline (Christie, 2001; Dahlkild-Öhman & Eriksson, 2013; McLean, 2003). As in the applied 'caring professions', social work has been defined as a 'non-traditional occupation for men'. Other features of social work also support the argument that the occupation is 'non-traditional' for men. These include the fact that social workers usually work with women, both as colleagues and service users, and that the issues that social workers focus on often directly and/or indirectly result from violence by men against women and children (Christie, 1998; Gillingham, 2006; Hearn, 2001; Pringle, 2001). While there are a limited number of men who become active service users, usually most of them present in specific areas of social work. In India, most men social workers are employed in industrial and criminology settings (Anand, 2021), whereas in the UK they are employed in mental health and criminal justice services (Christie, 2001). Depending on particular national contexts, men are generally employed in areas of social work that are more specialised, have higher status and where there are more men as service users. Men are often more noted for their lack of engagement with social work particularly in relation to child welfare social work (D'Cruz, 2002). Most men service users in child protection cases are viewed as a risk; however, they can also be a resource and bring benefits to their children (Brandon et al., 2019). Men are often viewed as a risk because in child welfare social work, men have often perpetrated some form of direct/indirect violence against women and children. However, this is not always the case and individual men can be supportive parents. In the UK, the potential for working with fathers, particularly black and minority ethnic fathers, is often overlooked (Gupta & Featherstone, 2016). Research in England, Ireland Norway and Sweden highlighted how social workers are encouraged to respond to men as fathers in more inclusive ways, however, this encouragement often remains at the policy rather than the practice level (Nygren et al., 2019). Even Sweden, which is considered at the forefront of countries that encourage fathers to care for their children, there are large disparities between fathers in the uptake of parental leave. Fathers with higher academic qualifications who live in metropolitan areas are the group with the greatest uptake of parental leave, whereas those men born outside Sweden, with lower academic qualifications and lower incomes are the least likely take up parental leave (Ma et al., 2020). It could be assumed from these findings that working class and black and minority ethnic men are less interested in providing childcare. However, as Ma et al. (2020) point out, there are many explanations why these men are not able to and/or do not chose to take up parental leave, e.g. for not being aware of the availability of parental leave and/or not being in the type of employment that supports men taking up parental leave. Parental leave policies like social work policies that encourage men to participate in child care need to recognise the barriers that exist for working class and black and minority ethnic men providing child care.

In considering all the above features of social work, it is unsurprising that both men and women social workers recognise that there are ambiguities, tensions and contradictions in men being employed as social workers, and this recognition leads to questions about whether and how men should be trained as social workers. While providing overall support for the training and employment of men as social workers, Pringle's (2001) ground-breaking research identifies a range of problems with training and employing men in the profession. These include concerns that men social workers may (consciously or unconsciously) collude with other men social workers and/or service users to reinforce oppressive practices against women, and that men social workers may use their personal and structural positions to abuse services users, particularly children. The sexual harassment of women social workers by men ones remains a largely hidden area; however, early research has shown that like in other occupations, the sexual harassment of women social workers by men ones is not uncommon (Christie, 1999). Elsewhere, there has been support for the training of men as social workers in countries such as Sweden, where the liberal feminist ideal of gender-balanced workplaces has been promoted since the 1960s (Fahlgren, 2013). Gender balance is often measured in terms of 50–50 or 40–60 employment numbers of women and men. Gender balance is supported in terms of gender equity and the creation of a more diverse workforce. In social work, the pursuit of gender balance is also advocated to ensure more effective responses to the diverse needs of services users. However, the goal of gender balance hides gender-based hierarchies within organisations and as men are in short supply within social work, the drive for a gender-balanced workforce often gives them 'added value' within the profession (Fahlgren, 2013, p.29).

With many more women than men being employed as social workers, social work has also been described as a 'female-dominated profession'. McPhail (2004) questions this description and argues that social work is better described as a 'male-dominated female majority profession' (p.325). For McPhail (2004), advocating that social work is 'female-dominated' obscures the continuing sexism within the profession and fails to acknowledge that much of the power to manage social work as well as to define and regulate social work continues to remain in the hands of men who are over-represented in social work academia (education and research) and professional and regulatory bodies (Cree et al., 2020). Even with a growing number of women employed as social workers, this has not inevitably led to women holding most leadership positions within the occupation (Scourfield, 2003). Social work remains a 'non-traditional' occupation in which in most countries there are relatively few men employed and yet can be seen as a very 'traditional' occupation for men as they often occupy senior and/or higher status positions within the profession.

Men social workers in the workplace

These tensions, ambiguities and contradictions often result in men and women social workers 'adopting' specific strategies within their workplaces. Williams (1993) identified how men redefined their work and emphasise 'masculine' elements, often adopting strategies that position themselves as 'different' from women, thus promoting both vertical and horizontal patterns of job gender segregation. Research in Czech Republic, India, Sweden and the UK show in relation to vertical segregation that men are over-represented in managerial positions and senior/specialist positions, and in horizontal segregation that men social workers are employed in areas where there is a higher proportion of men service users (e.g. probation and mental health), greater use of legal powers (e.g. child protection) and less responsibility for providing direct care (e.g. social work with the elderly) (Anand, 2021; Dahlkild-Öhman & Eriksson, 2013; Gŕundělová & Gojová, 2022; McLean, 2003), rather than them performing care roles themselves. Men can also 'reinterpret' their professional practices, so that, for example, caring becomes the facilitation of others to provide care (Cross & Bagilhloe, 2002). While social work can be described as 'non-traditional' for men, men's individual practices and the professional/organisational cultures can promote hegemonic forms of masculinity. Men seek and are encouraged into management, higher status and specialist posts (Mclean, 2003), while women may be discouraged from applying for these posts and, for those women who do become managers/specialists, they often earn less than men in comparable positions (Pease, 2011). Davey (2002) found that most men who were not already managers were interested in becoming managers and that women's reluctance to apply for managerial positions was mostly related to childcare responsibilities. Even while training to become a social worker, men students expected that they would get promoted more quickly than their women peers (Cree, 2000). Pease (2011) has argued that careerism in men social workers can be seen as offsetting concern for their masculinity from choosing a non-traditional profession. While men are over-represented as managers in social work, it is 'white, able-bodied, heterosexual men, or men not disclosing a marginalized status' (Mclean, 2003, p.63) who tend to get promoted. While men social workers benefit from the overall 'patriarchal dividend' within a patriarchal society and workplace cultures, individual men are likely to experience discrimination based on their race, class origins, sexuality and level of ability/disability (Pease and Pringle, 2001).

In some countries, neo-liberal approaches to welfare have resulted in social work being subject to an increasing de-professionalisation due to the growth of managerialism, decline of professional discretion/autonomy and the growth of the private sector in service provision (Malin, 2017; Trappenburg & van Beck, 2019). The growth of a more managerial approach to social work, which claims a rational-technical focus, may make social work a more attractively gendered occupation for men (Orme and Rennie, 2006). While men are over-represented in senior positions in social work, this pattern is not continuing in all countries. For example, in Sweden, a decreasing proportion of men in senior positions in social work, and more men are choosing specialist rather than management positions and choosing to prioritise their role as carers in their families (Nygren et al., 2021). This, of course, is occurring in a state that promotes gender equality in the workplace and encourages men's practices in child care (Nygren et al., 2021). Again, in Sweden, Dahlkild-Öhman and Eriksson (2013) argue that factors such as age, class and ethnicity are becoming as significant as gender in understanding the positions of men within the social work profession.

Gender norms are reproduced in social work through the repetition of practices (e.g. through the allocation of particular work to men or women, and the assumptions made by social workers about families and caring) as well as being framed within specific discourses (e.g. discourses of care). As discussed above, men social workers' practices include gravitation towards working areas of the occupation. In addition, men social workers can also include practices that support men's homosociability. Some men social workers do this in the workplace by creating de facto 'men only' spaces. In Sweden, Fahlgren (2013) describes that while men and women social workers in a family centre assumed that there were few gendered differences in their practices, men actively decided to have coffee breaks by themselves as a group. Fahlgren (2013) argues that this was a way for those who identified as men being able to maintain gender differences and for the women and men not to become '"androgynous" with male gender identify in particular being at risk in a predominantly female occupation' (p.23). Earlier research in England identified how men social workers often socialised together outside the workplace through, for example, participating in sporting activities together (Christie, 1999). Men social work students in Chile described how one of the main motivating factors in pursuing their social education was the 'meaningful relationships constructed among male colleagues' (Labra et al., 2018).

Men as social workers are often described as being 'special' and in some ways 'heroic' in challenging gendered assumptions by working as social workers, by committing themselves to long hours and dealing with potential violent situations (Christie, 2006). Discourse of 'gentle-men' is also used to represent men social workers as being 'gentle' – being able to work at an emotional level as well as help with service users with more practice tasks. Hicks

(2001) found that men social workers were often described as 'soft', 'nice' and sometimes 'gay'. Even though he found that these words were used to explain why particular men became social workers, he also found underlying heterosexism in which 'any sexuality apart from heterosexuality is inappropriate for workers in child care' (Hicks, 2001, p.50). Green (2005), investigating sexual abuse in residential children's homes, found that being sensitive and nurturing was often linked to gay men who were then also ironically and 'erroneously labelled as potential child abusers' (p.473). As well as being 'gentle', the discourse of 'gentle-men' surrounds men social workers, where men social workers are constructed as 'gentlemen' with 'higher' sets of moral values than other men, and they are contrasted in particular with men service users (Christie, 2006) who are often stigmatised and described in pejorative terms within child welfare (Scourfield & Coffey, 2002). This serves to valorise men's presence in social work, and Cree (2001) argues that men social workers are more likely to be praised for both their attitudes and their behaviours than women social workers. For us, the authors, we have both experienced at times being consider 'special men', different from 'other men' in our abilities to work with women as colleagues and service users as well as with children.

Social work cannot be defined by a fixed set of practices and in different contexts, social workers adopt a range of different methods e.g. individual work, group work and community work. There are constant changes in how social work is defined and the conditions under which social workers are employed. Social work has evolved across diverse national welfare regimes (Christie, 2001). While regulatory bodies attempt to 'fix' the types and levels of knowledge and skills required to qualify as a social worker, how social workers are trained and the types of work they undertake vary over time and in different national and international contexts. Therefore, how 'men' and masculinities are reproduced within social work is constantly changing and needs to be examined within particular contexts.

Educating men to become social workers

The tensions, contradictions and ambiguities that exist in men's employment as social workers also exist in the training of men to become social workers. Given that social work is a 'female majority profession' (McPhail, 2004), it is hardly surprising that there are usually many more women than men students in social work education. For example, in the USA, between 2017 and 2019, only 10% of students completing a Master in Social Work (MSW) course were men (Salsberg *et al.*, 2020). Women accounted for 83.3% of a cross-sectional study of social work students on the island of Ireland (McCartan et al., 2022). With this relatively low number of men social work students, questions are often asked about why so few men apply for social work courses and/or why so few are chosen to be trained as social workers. Pease (2011) asks 'what constitutes "good practice" for men' and urges that there is a need to be 'aware of the dangers and problems, as well as the possibilities that are associated with increasing men's presence in social work' (p.414). Cree (2001) argues that it is not surprising that men are asked about their choice to train as social workers because while 'women's choice to become a social worker is seen as supporting gender norms, men making a similar choice appear to be "going against the grain"' (p.153). Perhaps some of these men who chose to train as social workers had already experienced 'going against the grain', as Cree (2001) found that men social work students often described themselves as 'unconventional men'. The explanation for these men's interest in social work was related to their experiences of providing care for family members, having a significant loss in childhood, and having close relationships with their mothers and women friends. While men social work students may have had these experiences, questions could be asked about why other men who have had similar experiences do not apply? The lack of men as social work students appears to be the case in most European, Northern and Southern American countries and Australasia; however, it is not true of India. India produces the highest number of qualified social workers in the world, within 2018–2019, 67,086 students enrolled on a Bachelor of Social Work (BSW) and 395,561 on an MSW. Precisely 53.38% of students enrolled on the BSW and 54.55% on the MSW were identified as men (Bhatt, 2021). Other occupations in India such as nursing and teaching continue to be undertaken by a majority of women. It is not clear why India has such a night percentage of men social work students. The employment conditions of social workers may result in social work having an actual and/or perceived high status compared to other occupations. Perhaps the gendered definitions of caring and the family encourage more men to enrol on social work courses and/or perhaps the roles of social worker are viewed differently in India by men who chose to train as social workers. As yet, these questions remain unanswered.

Three types of arguments are often used to support increasing the number of men social workers: men social workers provide positive gender roles for boys/men services users, employing men promotes great gender diversity within the profession, and increasing the number of men social workers will improve the status of the profession. For Pease (2011), none of these arguments justify training and employing more men to become social workers. Pease (2011) critiques the 'role model' justification by asserting its reliance on essentialist notions of masculinity and stereotypical differences between men and women, reinforcing dominant assumptions about masculinity rather than challenging gendered hierarchies. In relation to the gender diversity argument, Pease (2011) argues that in relation to diversity, if the number of men training as social workers increases, this will most likely increase the number or men social work managers and do little to improve the diversity of social workers. Lastly, Pease (2011) argues that while employing more men as social workers might change the working conditions for both men and women social workers, it is likely to further reinforce gendered hierarchies within the profession. Debates on the position of 'men' as social workers and the need for greater gender 'equality' in the number of men and women employed as social workers fail to recognise the ways in which social work is gendered and how those who identify themselves as men exclude themselves from the profession.

Even if more men were to become social work students, this would not automatically result in more men qualifying as social workers, as more men than women fail to complete social work qualifying courses (Furness, 2012). It is not clear why more men than women fail to complete social work training, but Furness (2012) suggests that men may place higher expectations on themselves to take on leadership roles, resolve issues of conflict and contribute at meetings. However, from our experience it is not clear that those who identify as men place higher expectations on themselves to take on leadership roles in educational settings where they are a minority. Nevertheless, we would agree with Furness (2012) that the 'social construction of men's "assumed authority" and competence can work against them and prevent them from being able to voice their fears and admit their failings or mistakes as a student in a work setting' (p.495). While men may face additional questions about their own gendered identities and their work as social workers, the failure of men to complete social work training may also raise concerns about the suitability of individual men who are selected for social work training and whether selection procedures favour the inclusion of those who identify as men. Furness (2012) found that black and minority ethnic men students were more likely to fail than white men. More recent research in a university in England (Liu, 2017) found that men students were more likely to fail than women students, and while earlier research had shown that black men with any type of disability were less likely to complete professional social work training at the first attempt, in this research 'black female students with learning disabilities have a higher risk of failing' (p.235) than other students. Unfortunately, there is no comparative data presented on black men students with learning disabilities. This research shows that gender is not the only factor that needs to be considered and that men and women who experience various forms of oppression are disadvantaged within social work education and have a higher risk of failing to qualify as social workers.

Increasing the number of men as social work students is often related to the types of access provided for mature students. Internationally, there are widely differing routes and qualifications required to become a social work student, with national academic and professional bodies requiring different academic standards for entry onto courses. In the UK, McLean (2003) found that many men had worked previously in different forms of social care before becoming social workers. Working in social care had often not been their first choice of work, but once they were employed as social care workers, the next upward career move was to train as a social worker. McLean (2003) argues that men social work students were often uncertain about their career paths but usually saw social work as providing secure employment, especially during periods of economic uncertainty. Others have suggested that men's choices are motivated by political ideals (such as social justice), rather than being interested in the day-to-day practices of being a social worker (Christie & Kruk, 1998). Men's choice to become a social worker also reflects men's classed and racialised positions in society as well as general labour market conditions. For some men, training as a social worker can be viewed as a means of upward class mobility. In some countries, men's presence on social work courses seems to rely heavily on the availability of access routes into universities/colleges for working class and mature students, with men often entering social work to pursue a second career.

The places where men and women learn to become social workers – universities and colleges – also require feminist analysis. These institutions have had a long history of excluding and discriminating against women. They reflect wider societal gender disparities and are 'traditional bastions of male privilege' (Cree, 2001 p.149). Persistent and enduring gender inequalities and cultures that support the reproduction of hegemonic masculinities clearly exist within higher education (Maxwell et al., 2018), with gender inequalities prevailing in salaries, employment security, rank and progression and in roles and responsibilities (Cree et al., 2020). Social work education, like education provided for other 'caring' professions such as nursing, is usually taught by a higher proportion of women than men academics. However, men academics are over-represented in senior positions at school level and even more over-represented within the higher levels of the university administration. Cree et al. (2020) who recently examined social work academia in Scotland found that while women represented 58% of the total social work academic posts in Scotland, men outnumbered women in professorial posts by six to four. When men represent less than 20% of the general population of social workers, these figures highlight some of the basic gender inequalities in social work education. Given the widespread structural discrimination against women in higher education, it is hardly surprising that what is taught is 'neutral or non-gendered is often based on white Western, male, heterosexist assumptions'

(Cree, 2001, p.150). With social work education, or at least the academic/classroom part of social work education, being provided in institutions that largely reflect and reproduce societal gender inequalities and hegemonic forms of masculinity, it remains an uphill task for social work educators to ensure that all students, particularly men students, engage with feminist approaches to social work which includes a critical examination of men and masculinities (Pease, 2011).

Conclusion

While the total number of social workers is likely to grow internationally, as governments respond to new and multiple societal 'crises', the percentage of men as social workers in most countries is not increasing. Even in India, where there are more men than women social work students, the percentage to men students compared to women has reduced between 2010 and 2019 by approximately 6% on BSW and 10% on MSW programmes (Bhatt, 2021). Recent discussions about 21st century men have referred to 'hybrid masculinities' (Bridges & Pascoe, 2014; Eisen & Yamashita, 2017), where men actively construct themselves as 'caring' and distance themselves from hegemonic forms of masculinity. While this seemingly 'new' way of being men and doing masculinities may appear as transformative, research indicates that the practice of 'hybrid masculinities' may be a 'veneer', which serves to 'fortify existing social and symbolic [gendered] boundaries' (Bridges & Pascoe, 2014, p.246). There are some signs that some men are becoming more engaged in housework and that child care is becoming a normalised activity for men within some communities (Roberts, 2018), and there is also research that identifies how men social workers in Sweden are prioritising caring for family members over seeking career promotion. However, currently there is very little critical research on men as social workers and how they live their professional and domestic lives. Perhaps as Butler (1990) suggests there are possibilities of 'slippage' where dominant gender norms are transformed. Ostensibly, social work provides spaces where men social workers practice with women ones and services users and are therefore likely to be aware of the everyday operation of patriarchies. However, it remains unclear what 'slippages' occur in particular national and international contexts and how these 'slippages' impact on 'men' as social workers. The critical study of 'men' as social workers and social work students remains important, as it provides important opportunities to examine how masculinities become normalised through professional activities and reproduced in a variety of national and global contexts.

References

Anand, M. (2021). Gender and social work practices in India: The changing feminist discourses, 33(1), 65–77. https://doi.org/10.1080/09503153.2019.1685084

Bhatt, S. (2021). Students enrolment in social work courses in Indian higher educational institutions: An analysis. 9(2), 50–64. https://doi.org/10.20896/saci.v9i2.1214

Brandon, M., Philip, G., & Clifton, J. (2019). Men as fathers in child protection. *Australian Social Work*, 72(4), 447–460.

Bridges, T., and Pascoe, C. J. (2014). Hybrid masculinities: New directions in the sociology of men and masculinities. *Sociology Compass*, 8(3), 246–258. https://doi.org/10.1111/soc4.12134

Bureau of Labor Statistics, U. S. (2020). Department of Labor, *Occupational Outlook Handbook*, Social Workers. Retrieved July 09, 2022, from https://www.bls.gov/ooh/community-and-social-service/social-workers.htm

Butler, J. (1990). *Gender trouble: Feminism and the subversion of identity*. Routledge.

Butler, J. (1997). *The psychic life of power: Theories in subjection*. Stanford University Press.
Carrigan, T., Connell, B., and Lee, J. (1985). Toward a new sociology of masculinity. *Theory and Society*, 14(5), 551–604. https://doi.org/10.1007/BF00160017
Christensen, A., and Jensen, S. Q. (2014). Combining hegemonic masculinities and intersctionality. *NORMA: International Journal of Masculinity Studies*, 9(1), 60–75. https://doi.org/10.1080/18902138.2014.892289
Christie, A. (1998). Is social work a 'non-traditional' occupation for men? *British Journal of Social Work*, 28(4), 491–510. https://doi.org/10.1093/oxfordjournals.bjsw.a011363
Christie, A. (1999). *Men social workers: Questions of professional and gendered identities* [PhD Thesis University of Manchester]. Manchester.
Christie, A. (2001). Gendered discourses of welfare, men and social work. In A. Christie (ed.), *Men and social work: Theories and practices* (pp. 23–35). Bloomsbury.
Christie, A. (2006). Negotiating the uncomfortable intersections between gender and professional identities in social work. *Critical Social Policy*, 26(2), 390–411. https://doi.org/10.1177/0261018306062591
Christie, A., and Kruk, E. (1998). Choosing to become a social worker: Motives, incentives, concerns and disincentives. *Social Work Education*, 17(1), 21–34. https://doi.org/10.1080/02615479811220031
Connell, R. (1995). *Masculinities*. Polity Press.
CORU. (2022). *Health and Social Care Professionals Council Annual Report 2021*. Retrieved from https://coru.ie/files-publications/annual-reports/coru-annual-report-2021.pdf.
Cree, V. E. (2000). Why do men care? In K. Cavanagh & V. E. Cree (eds.), *Working with men: Feminism and social work*. Routledge.
Cree, V. (2001). Men and masculinities in social work education. In A. Christie (ed.), *Men and social work: Theories and practices* (pp. 147–163). Palgrave Macmillan.
Cross, S., and Bagilhole, B. (2002). Girls' jobs for the boys? men, masculinity and non-traditional occupations. *Gender, Work & Organization*, 9(2), 204–226. https://doi.org/10.1111/1468-0432.00156
Cree, V., Morrison, F., Mitchell, M., and Gulland, J. (2020). Navigating the gendered academy: Women in social work academia. *Social Work Education*, 39(5), 650–664. https://doi.org/10.1080/02615479.2020.1715934
Dahlkild-Öhman, G., and Eriksson, M. (2013). 'Inequality regimes and men's positions in social work'. *Gender, Work & Organisation*, 20(1), 85–99. https://doi:10.1111/j.1468-0432.2011.00572.x
Davey, B. (2002). Management progression and ambition: Women and men in social work. *Research Policy and Planning*, 20(2), 21–34.
D'Cruz, H. (2002). Constructing the identities of 'responsible mothers, invisible men' in child protection practice. *Sociological Research Online*, 7(1), 147–171. https://doi.org/10.5153/sro.705
Eisen, D., and Yamashita, L. (2017). Borrowing from femininity: The caring man, hybrid masculinities, and maintaining male dominance. *Men and Masculinities*, 22(5), 801–820. https://doi.org/10.1177/1097184x17728552
Fahlgren, S. (2013). The paradox of a gender-balanced workforce: The discursive construction of gender among Swedish social workers. *Affilia: Journal of Women and Social Work*, 28(1), 19–31. https://doi.org/10.1177/0886109912475162
Furness, S. (2012). Gender at work: Characteristics of 'failing' social work students. *British Journal of Social Work*, 42(3), 480–499. https://doi.org/10.1093/bjsw/bcr079
Gilligham, P. (2006). Male social workers in child and family welfare: New directions for research. *Social Work*, 52(1), 83–85. https://doi.org/10.1093/sw/51.1.83
Green, L. (2005). Theorizing sexuality, sexual abuse and residential children's homes: Adding gender to the equation. *British Journal of Social Work*, 35(4), 453–481. https://doi-org.ucc.idm.oclc.org/10.1093/bjsw/bch191
Gřundělová, B., and Gojová, A. (2022). Gendered practices of family social workers: The case of the Czech Republic. *International Social Work*, 65(4), 622–637. https://doi.org/10.1177/0020872820911678
Gupta, A., and Featherstone, B. (2016). What about my dad? Black father and the child protection system. *Critical and Radical Social Work*, 4(1), 77–91. https://doi.org/10.1332/204986015X14502659300361

Hearn, J. (2001). Men, social work and men's violence to women. In A. Christie (ed.), *Men and social work: Theories and practices*. (pp. 69-88). Basingstoke: Palgrave Macmillan.

Hearn, J. (2004). From hegemonic masculinity to the hegemony of men. *Feminist Theory*, 5(1), 49–72. https://doi.org/10.1177/1464700104040813

Hicks, S. (2001). Men social workers in children's services: 'Will the "real man" please stand up? In A. Christie (ed.), *Men in social work. Theories and practices* (pp. 49–62). Palgrave.

Hicks, S., and Jeyasingham, D. (2016). Social work, queer theory and after: A genealogy of sexuality theory in neo-liberal times. *British Journal of Social Work*, 46(8), 2357–2373. https://doi.org/10.1093/bjsw/bcw103

Jones, M., Mlcek, S. H. E., Healy, J. P., and Bridges, D. (2019). Gender dynamics in social work practice and education: A critical literature review. *Australian Social Work*, 72(1), 62–74.

Labra, O., Chamblas, I., Turcotte, P., and Dubé, N. (2018). Is it a man's world? An exploratory study of male students in social work: Experiences from Chile. *British Journal of Social Work*, 48(3), 769–786. https://doi.org/10.1093/bjsw/bcx065

Liu, B. C. (2017). Intersectional impact of multiple identities on social work education. *Journal of Social Work*, 17(2), 226–242.

Malin, N. (2017). Developing an analytical framework for understanding the emergence of de-professionalisation in health, social care and education sectors. *Social Work & Social Science Review*, 19(1), 66–162. https://doi.org/10.1921/swssr.v19i1.1082

Maxwell, N., Connolly, L., and Ní Laoire, C. (2018). Informality, emotion and gendered career paths: The hidden toll of maternity leave on female academics and researchers. *Gender, Work & Organization*, 26(2), 140–157. https://doi.org/10.1111/gwao.12306

Ma, L., Anderssson, G., Duvander, A., and Evertsson, M. (2020). 'Fathers' uptake of parental leave: Forerunners and laggards in Sweden, 1993–2010. *Journal of Social Policy*, 49(2), 361–381. https://doi.org/10.1017/S0047279419000230

McCartan, C., Byrne, J., Campbell, J., Coogan, D., Davidson, G., Hayes, D., Kirwan, G., MacDonald, M., McCaughren, S., McFadden, P., McGregor, C., Montgomery, L., Peentaraki, M., Roddy, S., Roulston, A., Shore, C., and Wilson, E. (2022). Social work students on the island of Ireland: A cross-sectional survey. *Social Work Education*, 41(2), 228–247. https://doi.org/10.1080/02615479.2020.1832060

Mclean, J. (2003). Men as a minority: Men employed in statutory social care work. *Journal of Social Work*, 3(1), 45–68. https://doi.org/10.1177/1468017303003001004

McPhail, B. A. (2004). Setting the record straight: Social work is not a female-dominated profession. *Social Work*, 49, 323–326. https://doi.org/10.1093/sw/49.2.323

Nygren, K., Walsh J., Ellingsen, I. T., and Christie, A. (2019). What about the fathers? The presence and absence of the father in social work practice in England, Ireland, Norway, and Sweden – A comparative study. *Child & Family Social Work*, 24(1), 148–155. https://doi.org/10.1111/cfs.12592

Nygren, K., Walsh J., Ellingsen, I. T., and Christie, A. (2021). Gender, parenting and practices in child welfare social work? A comparative study from England, Ireland, Norway and Sweden. *British Journal of Social Work*, 51(6), 2116–2133. https://doi.org/10.1093/bjsw/bcaa085

Orme, J., & Rennie, G. (2006). The role of registration in ensuring ethical practice. *International Social Work*, 49(3), 333–344.

Pease, B. (2011). Men in social work: Challenging or reproducing an unequal gender regime? *Affilia: Journal of Women and Social Work*, 26(4), 406–418.

Pease, B., & Pringle, K. (Eds.). (2001). *A man's world?: changing men's practices in a globalized world*. ZED Books.

Pringle, K. (2001). Men in social work: A double-edged sword. In A. Christie (ed.), *Men and social work: Theories and practices* (pp. 35–48). Palgrave Macmillan.

Roberts, S. (2018). Domestic labour, masculinity and social change: Insights from working-class young men's transitions to adulthood. *Journal of Gender Studies*, 27(3), 274–287. https://doi.org/10.1080/09589236.2017.1391688

Salsberg, E., Quigley, L., Richwine, C., Sliwa, S., Acquaviva, K., and Wyche, K. (2020). *The social work profession: Findings from three years of surveys of new social workers*. Alexandria, VA: The Fitzhugh Mullan Foundation, George Washington University, Council on Social Work Education and the National Association of Social Workers.

Scourfield, J. (2003). *Gender and child protection*. Palgrave Macmillan.

Scourfield, J., and Coffey, A. (2002). Understanding gendered practice in child protection. *Qualitative Social Work*, *1*(3), 319–340. https://doi.org/10.1177/1473325002001003644

Trappenburg, M., and van Beek, G. (2019). 'My profession is gone': How social workers experience de-professionalization in the Netherlands. *European Journal of Social Work*, 22(4), 676–689. https://doi.org/10.1080/13691457.2017.1399255

Williams, C. L. (Ed.) (1993). *Doing "Women's Work", men in nontraditional occupations*. Sage.

42
ALLY WORK AT THE INTERSECTIONS

Theorising for practice and practicing for theory

Glenda Kickett, Antonia Hendrick and Susan Young

Locating our 'selves'

Drawing on Aboriginal and pan-Indigenous protocols, before describing a framework for Ally work and how it may assist in the field of feminist social work, we three authors need to locate ourselves and our social positionings, for these affect how we frame, view and progress our work. We all identify as women, while acknowledging that in this contemporary world, gender is no longer a simple binary, if indeed ever it was. Our identifications however encompass more than our assigned gender and in acknowledging the intersectionality of positioning, we are also very aware of the power infused in claiming and declaring identities. This is particularly so when recalling that white people have not had to defend their identity, while First Nations peoples have had to resist the removal of identity. Similarly women have had to claim identity space in the androcentric sphere.

One of the three, Glenda, identifies as Whadjuk Nyungah yorga, belonging to the Nyungah Nation of the South West of Western Australia, one of the Aboriginal and Torres Strait Islander Nations of Australia. Glenda is writing from her country. The other two authors, Antonia and Susan, are both white with Antonia being Australian born and Susan a migrant. Antonia and Susan have learned about the being of white on stolen land, a learning which has not ended but has led to formulating ways of being on these lands with its First Nations peoples, a practice being developed with Glenda as feminists in Ally work.

As social work educators, our interactions with students and practitioners are to help develop better understandings and knowledges for working more culturally responsively (Bennett, Redfern, & Zubrzycki, 2018) with Indigenous peoples. We are aware of the critique of allyship (Blair, 2021; Kluttz, Walker, & Walter, 2020; Spanierman & Smith, 2017), with some calling for a 'critical allyship' (Bennett, Uink, & Martin, 2022), and try to mitigate some of these in our practice, which we hope strengthens and makes more useful the framework for feminist allyship practice we will describe here. Without wanting to appropriate knowledge or practice, the two white authors note that our work is informed by Indigenous world views drawn from personal and academic interactions in Australia and other parts of the world and pay tribute to the Indigenous peoples who were here before us, and to contemporary Indigenous people who continue to practice their customs and beliefs. We do this with humility.

As women, we all acknowledge and pay tribute to feminist scholarship and practice, in whose debt we are. None of us would occupy the positions we do without those hard-fought battles for equality. However, we also acknowledge that we occupy those positions differently; being white women differs significantly from being an Indigenous woman (Moreton-Robinson, 2013).

The framework discussed below was devised to assist in finding a way of decolonising work with Aboriginal and Torres Strait Islander peoples that was productive, not laden with guilt or avoided because of the fear of getting it wrong. We are particularly interested in this feminist exploration of Ally work with Aboriginal and Torres Strait Islander peoples, especially, but not only, because the Whadjuk lands of the Nyungah Nation have a matrilineal heritage and these practices continue in this 'women's place'.

The Ally Framework is drawn from and contributes to decolonial theorising (Hendrick & Young, 2017, 2019) and has proven to be a useful guide for our practice as educators and mediators. Ally work necessitates self-reflection and interrogation of positions for white people and this has led Susan & Antonia to further conceptualise 'being White' and thence to Whiteness theorising, a prominent concept (Hendrick & Young, 2023; Young, 2008) in this Ally Framework.

Central to the development of the Ally framework to guide our collective work has been the relationships between white and Australian Indigenous peoples. This has necessitated self-reflections and identifications of these many identities we portray. Realisations that there is an inseparability between the personal and the political in asking the 'who benefits' question apply as equally in the racial sphere as it did in the 1960s as part of the 'mushrooming independent women's liberation movement' (Hanisch, 1969, p. 1). While the beneficiaries of the gender divide of that time were men, the beneficiaries in a white majority nation such as Australia are white people. Thus an important component in the Ally Framework is addressing unearned white privilege and for Antonia & Susan in much the same way we imagine that some pro-feminist men have tried to dismantle their privilege. This might take the form of other frameworks for practice starting with an acknowledgement that 'unearned male privileges exist and that they are reproduced by the practices of men' (Pease, 2010, p. 107). Working with the question of 'who benefits' requires us to turn the political and personal gaze on those of us who are the beneficiaries as well as working alongside those whose 'personal problems are political problems' (Hanisch, 1969, p. 4).

Similar to other white settler countries, being part of the white majority population in Australia to whom benefits and privileges flow unearned and often un-acknowledged consequently forms a central plank for how white people need to somehow counter these privileges if they are to work with Indigenous peoples in Australia. So it is with this understanding and some appreciation that Antonia & Susan can understand the questioning from pro-feminist men and feminists who ask, is it possible for men to work with women, given the divisive history of social organisation which has advantaged men over women in ways that have nothing to do with ability or effort.

The framework therefore is adapted here to extend our collective thinking and application across sectors. Rather than apply it only to feminism, this adaptation takes its starting point from intersectional understandings, about which much in this collection addresses and so will not be covered here.

Intersectionality Allyship (Helena, 2021; IWDA, 2016; McGloin, 2016; Olsen, 2018) notes that for the most part, most people are not defined by one identity, and that their circumstances are circumscribed by more than one indicator. There are as many differences as similarities between people who have multiple identities and social locations which place them in advantaged and disadvantaged positions at the same time, though they may experience those circumstances differently in different contexts. An impoverished white single parent has financial stresses because of income but still finds a daily life free from racial discrimination. An educated and successful professional Indigenous person may be free from financial stresses but still has to ask a white colleague to assist in navigating the rental housing market to secure a house, a circumstance experienced by one of the authors. It also remains the case that some people experience discrimination because they are a woman, a Black woman, a Black woman living with a disability even at the same time as holding a respected professional position. It is a case of both/and rather than an either/or situation.

Introducing a practice framework

Practice frameworks are commonly used in social work (Howe, 2017; Parton & O'Byrne, 2000) with authors making the clear link between theories that explain situations and what theories inform the strategies to be applied. For example, explanations of why people from minority backgrounds experience discrimination in the workplace may lead to strategies to address inclusion or affirmative action. Institutional or systemic racism could be the explanation, and anti-oppressive theory could be the intervention or practice approach. An anti-oppressive intervention (Dalrymple & Burke, 2006) might employ the process of challenging the way people are recruited, re-writing employment guidelines and ensuring their enforcement, running cultural responsiveness workshops for staff, ensuring pay equity, etc.

A framework for expanding the theory-practice nexus follows. Figure 41.1 includes our worldviews, the explanatory and intervention theories which most align with those perspectives and an Ally model for practice. It is not suggested that these listed theories encompass all that might be possible but a selection of those that we regularly use in our work. The worldviews, however, while describing our positioning at present and deriving from between us 80 years of experience, are always in the process of change, an outcome of continually reflecting on our 'selves' and our places in the world.

The Ally Framework described at Figure 42.1 is adapted from an original framework designed to illustrate social policy theory and practice for social work and initially taught to social work students in Aotearoa New Zealand (Shannon & Young, 2004). Because of its appearance, students labelled it the 'Eggs' framework.

The 'Eggs' present a sequential trajectory from Worldviews to Explanatory Theory, followed by Intervention Theory and Models. A relatively recent adaptation (Young, McKenzie, Omre, Schjelderup, & Walker, 2014, p. 897) of the Shannon and Young (2004) framework recognises Indigenous peoples' ways of knowing, being and doing as having 'epistemological equality' (Young et al., 2013). However, in this inclusion, we also acknowledge that care needs to be taken that Indigenous knowledges are accurately attributed and not appropriated as well as seeking the correct permissions for any use (Dei, 2000; Young, 2005).

The sequencing asks practitioners to identify their own worldviews or perspectives illustrative of their values and beliefs as these will influence the explanations they provide

Glenda Kickett et al.

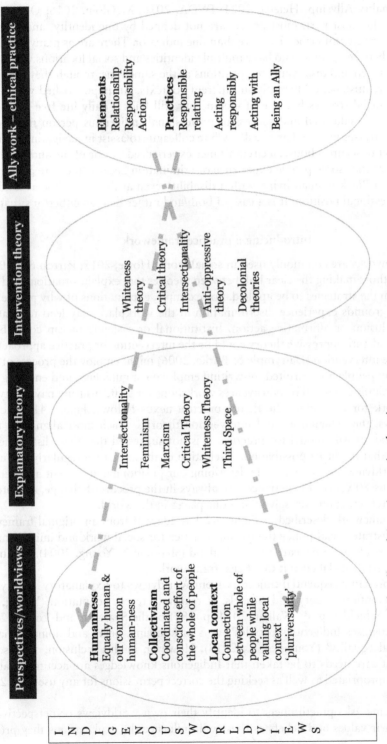

Figure 42.1 A framework for ally work in an intersectional setting
Source: Adapted from Shannon and Young (2004)

for the situations they encounter. These explanations will then influence their decisions and choices of appropriate interventions. The interventions themselves are drawn from theories. Lastly practitioners select the tools, or models, to undertake the practical work. In presenting this framework to students, we caution that 'theory' and 'model' especially are variously and sometimes interchangeably used in texts.

We illustrate this depiction with case examples. For example, we might use as illustration an impoverished Aboriginal mother of an infant and two year old whose partner uses drugs and is sometimes violent. The child welfare authorities warn her that if she does not leave him, they will remove the children for their own safety. The mother has no family living locally and having just moved into the area no social supports. Neither does she have independent income or other material resources. But she also maintains that her partner is engaged in a drug rehabilitation programme and has not been violent recently.

Workers here have some choices, often shaped by the agency for which they work, the policies and procedures of which are also informed by some prevailing socio-political as well as personal values and beliefs. One option is to take a risk averse (Lonne, Parton, Thomson, & Harries, 2008) approach – act first and support later. This reflects beliefs that individuals are responsible for their own choices and that other possible mitigating factors only play a minor role in what individuals choose to do. Another option is to work with the strengths shown by the mother and the partner and provide the necessary resources to support this family. Some of the options might include the mother's Aboriginality, while others might ignore it, preferring instead to apply an 'equality' principle. All these options rely on what values and beliefs influence the practitioner or underpin the policies and procedures of an organisational mandate and consequently how the circumstances are explained – often, but not always, reducible to the individual responsibility/system failures binary.

Gender and feminism as analytical tools have long been reported in the literature concerning child protection settings, which seeks to counter-act the somewhat simplistic binary sometimes found in child protection decision-making. What is often missing are the practice applications of these analyses where studies repeatedly show that gender and ethnicity have undue impact on decision-making (Crawford & Bradley, 2016; Middel, López López, Fluke, & Grietens, 2020, 2022). These offer much more nuanced interpretations as well as clearly showing the ongoing tendency for practitioners to repeat the societal stereotypes which blame mothers and especially mothers from ethnic minorities for the harms and risks to which children are exposed instead of holding perpetrators accountable. Encouragingly though are the emerging practices from feminist researchers and practitioners who seek to go beyond these binaries and envision inclusive practices (Lorenzetti & Walsh, 2022).

Feminism and intersectionality therefore may provide useful explanatory theory for practitioners to assist in working out what they think might be contributing to the situation. Neither are reducible to one position, although feminism can be seen 'as a framework for social justice activism' (Phillips, 2023, p. 1) despite the complexities attendant on location and context. Intersectionality theory has a similar qualification (Collins & Bilge, 2020, p. 3). Practitioners then need to identify which of these most usefully explain the circumstances to enable appropriate interventions to be applied. Depending on the specific circumstances, such as the complexity of the relationships or the structural or systems influences, such as limited income, few social supports or resources, practitioners will need to seek out interventions appropriate to those circumstances. Again feminist and/or intersectional theory can provide some guides to actions.

Intervention theory follows closely from the choice of explanation as it provides the operational foundations for action, without it being that action itself – that is left to the choice of model. Explanatory theory 'gives us goals to aim for' (Shannon & Young, 2004, p. 25) or what needs to be done based on the explanation provided. Intervention theory assists in helping to provide guides to how the identified change can be made. If feminism and/or intersectionality provide the explanation, then they also lead to the choice of practice theories available to try to advance that change. In the example above, if the woman's situation is explained using feminism and intersectionality, that is, her circumstances must be informed by her identity, her relationship with her partner and her wishes for this relationship, as well as the surrounding elements of lack of resources, social supports and others – the simplicity of taking a risk perspective as the first option is not appropriate under this explanation, although the safety of the children is paramount. Here child rights considerations come into play. The risk option usually cites Article 3 of the United Nations Convention on the Rights of the Child as needing to act in the best interests of the child. But taking into account other articles such as Articles 7, 8, 18 and 19 which relate to identity, the relationship with parents, and importantly the requirement that the state provides the support and programmes to assist parents to care for their children are also necessary to include.

The options for Intervention theory will need to take these factors into account. Practitioners may decide that the lack of resources is the first major issue and draw from critical theory and anti-oppressive theory which identifies power differentials and resource allocation deficits. Or they could take the Whiteness and Decolonial theory perspectives which again address power imbalances but focus on the contextual contributions that Indigenous knowledges provide. Having identified what they think contributes to the situation for this woman and using understandings of what might lead to change in her circumstances, the choice of model, or the tools to carry out the work, remains to be done.

There are any number of models from which practitioners can draw, case management, advocacy, education programmes and others and these are often guided by the specific agency in which the practitioners work, and by legislative requirements. The presence of violence and drug use often combine and result in child removal as the sole model and in the above case practitioners would likely find themselves pressured by their organisations to do so. However, feminist analyses have pointed to the continued 'mother-blaming' and lack of perpetrator accountability (Humphreys & Absler, 2011; Mulkeen, 2012; Skinner et al., 2021) in such situations. The model we propose here is of Ethical Practice of Allyship.

An ethical model for ally practice

We expand on the elements listed in Figure 42.1 which have their roots in Decoloniality, described as paying attention to common human-ness, the collective effort of all and valuing the local in the context of the connection to the global, all of which are transgressed by colonial practices (Figure 42.2).

Equal humanness acknowledges shared humanity on equal terms, when so much of past actions have elevated one group of humans above another, or others. The androcentric positioning of men as people and women as gendered illustrates this different construction (Bailey, LaFrance, & Dovidio, 2020). This does not ignore the continuing oppressions and disadvantages experienced by oppressed peoples but rather provides an ethical imperative to strive towards equal humanness when so much of the past has constructed 'White's' 'others' as less than human (Fanon, 1963) and women as somehow lesser than men.

Ally work at the intersections

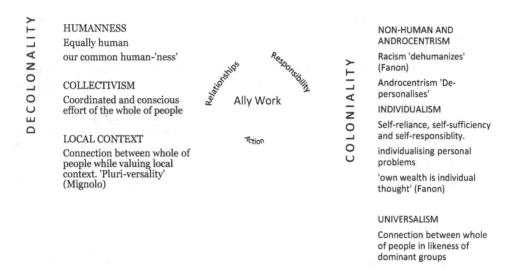

Figure 42.2 Ethical Practice: Allyship
Source: Adapted from Hendrick and Young (2023)

Collectivism represents the valuing of joint collaborative relational work and rejects the attribution of sole responsibility for own's own individual circumstances with consequent blaming, invoking the perspective of the personal is political (Hanisch, 1969). And local context recognises the wisdom and knowledge of the local people, yet at the same time acknowledging the connectedness that joins peoples of different places, what Mignolo (2012) terms 'pluriversality'.

Ally work is intended to act as a decolonial mediator to counter ongoing colonial practices and involves the ethical practices of responsibility which are enacted in the personal sphere; relationship in the interpersonal sphere and action which is a public activity. The micro practices involve a range of activities, including listening quietly, asking honestly, asking permission, refusing appropriation, acting politically with self-understanding, understanding and working with power with not power over, maintaining hope, and taking time – all of which are expected practices for social work with all groups, not just those from marginalised and dispossessed backgrounds. These relational, change-related and collaborative practices are commonly understood and applied in feminist work as demonstrated in this handbook and other applications (for example as found in Belser, 2022; Cooney & Rogowski, 2017; Goodmark, 2018).

The ethics of responsibility, relationships and action as key features of the Ally Framework necessitate considering the 'whole of the people' without neglecting the local context. The examples mentioned above indicate the importance of considering the local conditions at the same time as shining an intersectional and/or gender lens on those conditions.

Applying the Ally Framework

The Ally Framework described here was initially conceived as being applicable for social work students working with Aboriginal and Torres Strait Islander peoples. As educators, we recognised the necessity of being able to work in culturally appropriate and responsive ways with Aboriginal and Torres Strait Islander peoples. In enacting this work, recognising the nature of the relationships Aboriginal and Torres Strait Islander peoples have with the land depends on knowing the local protocols and ensuring these are respected. A recent example in our University is to ensure that all students have an opportunity to be introduced to the culture of the local land on which the University sits and a male Elder has been engaged to do this. Other groups of Elders have pointed out that it is proper that these ceremonies are performed by the proper custodians, both male and female as they have different roles, and especially given the matrilineal heritage of this place. This correction has now been done but was only made possible by the relationship two of the writers have with the Elders and to bring this to the attention of the decision makers to effect this change.

On-Country visits are valued too. Elders and family introduce participants to their country and help them to see it in ways not previously experienced or understood. On one occasion, one of the authors noticed how community rather than individual roles were enacted. For instance, when a baby cried, several family members took a role in picking the child up, comforting, feeding and entertaining, with no expectations as to whose 'proper' role that was. The child was connected to everyone; teenage boy, older woman, uncle, the community. This challenged many stereotypes held of the caring role defaulting to the 'mother' as well as recognising the collective connections, rather than ownership of and to land, beings and spirituality. Embracing the context and being willing to challenge one's own preconceived notions, all contribute to the emerging Ally work practice.

The ethical work for allies of responsibility, relationships and action includes using the skills of listening and knowing when to be silent, unlearning what has previously been taken as accurate learning and helping others to understand the effects of oppression, among others. These come together in the common human-ness, through collective engagement and the pluriversal at the same time as not reducing the individual positionings to the 'commonalities'. Feminist practice requires just the same care.

Seeking to achieve change through working with these elements, while seemingly simple, is not without its problematics. Indigenous peoples as well as women find themselves in positions not of their own choosing, subject to other impositions of expectations, perspectives and judgements as to how they should lead their lives. Nowhere is this more evident than in the juxtapositioning of Aboriginal and Torres Strait Islander peoples with child protection and family violence.

The Northern Territory Emergency Response (NTER), otherwise referred to as the Intervention, illustrates these complexities. The Intervention was enacted in 2006 as a response to emerging serious concerns about violence to children and women in remote Aboriginal communities. It imposed blanket restrictions on welfare payments, prohibited alcohol and pornography and mandated health checks for children. None of these were done in consultation or engaging with the local people, involving them in the solutions, especially the women or in considering the context and local situation. There were, and continue to be, very mixed views amongst Aboriginal people as to the appropriateness of the Intervention with some supporting it to protect women and children, while others saw it as an extension of patriarchal oppression of all Aboriginal people (Maddison & Partridge, 2014, p. 40). It was very clear in the public discourse and prohibitions that Aboriginal people were held as being unable to be responsible and so others had to take responsibility for them. Recalling the previous discussion of 'mother-blaming' here Aboriginal people as a whole were blamed.

In a separate analysis of a different situation, Bacchi and Eveline (2010, p. 311) suggest that taking account of context and to 'rethink assumptions about the obviousness of gender as an analytical priority' might be necessary in order to come to the 'doing' of intersectionality. In the case of the Intervention, where many of the women in those communities welcomed increased services which had for so long been absent, there was also widespread condemnation of the way the Intervention was implemented without any consultation or involvement of the communities themselves.

Applying a 'one size fits all' to very different communities in order to protect women and children continued an oppressive racially based policy (Maddison & Partridge, 2014, p. 40). The complexities of what in another context has been called the 'toxic trio' (Skinner et al., 2021) do not lend themselves to simple solutions and Maddison and Partridge's assessment of the varied and oppositional responses from some white feminists echo Howe's (2009, p. 47) criticism that the failure to speak about the issue of violence in Aboriginal communities is an abrogation of responsibility. Even though violence to women and children was the stimulus for the NTER, resultant analyses moved the blame and responsibility onto the people themselves in a similar way to the allocation of responsibility to mothers for their perceived failure to protect their children when the men in their lives directly impose risk. Here very much more nuanced analyses and approaches are needed.

It is the responsibility of an Ally to act politically with self-understanding (Land, 2015) which means earning the right to speak. This is no easy task and is an ongoing journey for an Ally who in the very act of speaking risks getting it wrong. Taking the guidance of the ethics of personal responsibility, interpersonal relationships and public action may go some way to undertake this work.

Ally work and feminist social work

As is shown in this handbook, feminist and gender analyses of the social world have greatly benefited social work practice and theory. It is no longer acceptable to provide social work tuition without applying the feminist and gender lens to the complexities of social life, even though the resultant analyses have themselves become more complex to include the multi dimensions of people's lives. Similarly intersectionality as a theoretical perspective has a lengthy history, although its application in social work has more recent application (Ortega & Faller, 2011).

In our Ally work, we have focussed specifically on working with social work students to encourage them to learn about being allies with Aboriginal and Torres Strait Islander peoples. For in the acknowledgement that Aboriginal and Torres Strait Islander peoples still experience a gap in all the social indicators of healthy wellbeing, it is evident that the wider society is not attending to closing those gaps quickly or effectively enough. Allies will not provide the panacea but can contribute if they earn the trust of Aboriginal and Torres Strait Islander peoples sufficiently to be given tasks that Aboriginal and Torres Strait Islander peoples believe can assist, however, and whatever they may be.

However, contributing to this handbook has given us the opportunity to extend our vision to consider how this work can speak to its connection to feminist social work. To do this, we have taken an intersectional approach as we have long understood, but perhaps not articulated sufficiently well enough, that there are multiple dimensions and identities present within the scope of Ally work. Feminist and intersectional scholarship as drawn upon here reinforces, among others, the importance of highlighting oppression and privilege in our teaching (Simon, Boyd, & Subica, 2022) and particularly white privilege (Belser, 2022); the importance of and strength in building coalitions (Draper & Chapple, 2023) to foster greater inclusion; and extends our focus on Decoloniality to learn more from 'southern feminisms' (Martínez & Agüero, 2023). Practices found in feminist work such as building relational collaborative ways of working, deep listening, collaboration and empathy are also central to Ally work, at the same time as warning against falling into the trap of considering women to be emotionally focussed and men the rational beings.

Through all this exploration of what constitutes Ally work and its connection to feminist social work is to carefully examine the associated critiques, many of which appear in this handbook. Especially important for our ally work is to heed the critical questions of inclusive and exclusive practices which may go unnoticed by well-established groups, well described by Draper and Chapple (2023) in relation to transgender and non-binary people but equally applies for our work with Aboriginal and Torres Strait Islander peoples who do not 'look' Aboriginal.

Another key example is that of restorative justice which is also present in the Aboriginal and Torres Strait Islander environment. Some feminist and Aboriginal and Torres Strait Islander approaches to restorative justice particularly in relation to violence against women hold that restorative justice has previously been resisted in feminist work as explored by Goodmark (2018, p. 373) who, citing Ptacek, 2009, raises concerns of safety, accountability and against the tendency to relegate violence against women again to the private sphere. There are similar critiques in relation to Indigenous peoples (McNamara, 2000; Nancarrow, 2006). So while new or alternative approaches to working with people may appear attractive, casting an appropriate critical lens across them to identify potential disadvantages and harms is essential.

In our theorising of Ally work, we follow bell hooks' (2000) argument that the work of addressing racism is everyone's business. In particular, in a country like Australia, for those of us who are beneficiaries of white systems of privilege, it is all of our business to work towards dismantling racism. We consider that allyship is one way to do this especially through trying to find that Third Space (Bhabha, 1990) in which to form and maintain the relationships necessary for addressing the inequities and injustices perpetrated on those who are not white.

It is not only in the momentous changes that need to happen, such as to recognise Aboriginal and Torres Strait Islander peoples and provide a Voice to Parliament in the Australian Constitution, a proposition from the Uluru Statement from the Heart in 2017 (2017). But it is also important in the little things, the everyday endeavours of human interaction, kindness, paying attention and listening to those voices that have for so long been silenced that allyship is also necessary. Third Space theory (Bhabha cited in Zubrzycki et al., 2014, p. 30) is a valuable space in which to enact this work, even when, as will happen, the white ally is rejected and refused. Here we maintain are strong connections to feminist practice and, we hope, contributions from Ally work to that practice.

Conclusion

We position ourselves in this chapter, acknowledging we each hold many identities, and conclude that it is in our humanness together that responsible relating best serves our common aim of seeking social justice and rights based practice. Within Ally work, we offer a theoretical framework in which the ethics of relationship, responsibility and action are important bedrocks of our collective efforts. Our chosen illustrations, of which there are many more, help to illuminate the imperfect nature of Ally work; a theory and practice at once offering opportunities to develop improved ways of being human together and aiming to establish the 'pluriversal', or common connection of difference. Paying tribute to the adage 'there is nothing so practical as good theory' (Lewin & Cartwright, 1952), we suggest that our practice has benefited from good theory, at the same time as we propose that our practices can contribute to the theory of allyship.

The principles described with their examples are not unfamiliar in feminist practice, which emphasis empathetic and relational skills. But further they are designed to create change in those oppressive and oppressing spaces experienced by people to whom allies and feminist practitioners offer their support and assistance in whatever way the people identify for themselves is needed. While the situations and experiences are complex, we take a lead from bell hooks who has distilled the complexity to its simplicity as the problem is 'sexism'. As hooks (2000) argues, 'Imagine living in a world where there is no domination, where females and males are not alike or even always equal, but where a vision of mutuality is the ethos shaping our interaction' (hooks, 2000, p. xiv). This could so easily apply to that other intersectional experience – that of racism, where the goal of defeating racism is to have mutuality infuse all our interactions, in the ethics of relationship, responsibility and action. In this stand against racism, we hope that allyship is one step towards that goal.

References

Bacchi, C., & Eveline, J. (2010). *Gender mainstreaming or diversity mainstreaming? The politics of 'doing'*. Adelaide: University of Adelaide Press, pp. 311–334.
Bailey, A. H., LaFrance, M., & Dovidio, J. F. (2020). Implicit androcentrism: Men are human, women are gendered. *Journal of Experimental Social Psychology*, 89, 103980.
Belser, J. W. (2022). Consider the container: Critical reflections on norms as feminist practice. *Journal of Feminist Studies in Religion*, 38(1), 67–69.
Bennett, B., Redfern, H., & Zubrzycki, J. (2018). Cultural responsiveness in action: Co-constructing social work curriculum resources with aboriginal communities. *The British Journal of Social Work*, 48(3), 808–825. https://doi.org/10.1093/bjsw/bcx053
Bennett, R., Uink, B., & Martin, G. (2022). Cultural studies and critical allyship in the settler colonial academe. *Continuum*, 36(5), 723–739.
Bhabha, H. (1990). The third space. Identity, community, culture, difference. *London: Lawrence and Wishart. Commonwealth Eastern Caribbean Community. Current Issues in Tourism*, 6(4), 267–308.
Blair, K. (2021). Empty gestures: Performative utterances and allyship. *Journal of Dramatic Theory and Criticism*, 35(2), 53–73.
Collins, P. H., & Bilge, S. (2020). *Intersectionality*. John Wiley & Sons.
Cooney, L., & Rogowski, S. (2017). Towards a critical feminist practice with children and families: Child sexual exploitation as an exemplar. *Practice*, 29(2), 137–149.
Crawford, B., & Bradley, M. S. (2016). Parent gender and child removal in physical abuse and neglect cases. *Children and Youth Services Review*, 65, 224–230. https://doi.org/10.1016/j.childyouth.2016.04.013
Dalrymple, J., & Burke, B. (2006). *Anti-oppressive practice: Social care and the law*. McGraw-Hill Education.
Dei, G. J. S. (2000). Rethinking the role of indigenous knowledges in the academy. *International Journal of Inclusive Education*, 4(2), 111–132.
Draper, S. C., & Chapple, R. (2023). Resistance as a foundational commons: Intersectionality, transfeminism, and the future of critical feminisms. *Affilia*, 88610992311657. https://doi.org/10.1177/08861099231165788
Fanon, F. (1963). *The wretched of the Earth*. New York: Grover, 2004, 62.
Goodmark, L. (2018). Restorative justice as feminist practice. *International Journal of Restorative Justice*, 1, 372.

Hanisch, C. (1969). *The personal is political.* Personal correspondence. https://webhome.cs.uvic.ca/~mserra/AttachedFiles/PersonalPolitical.pdf

Heart, U. S. f. t. (2017). Uluru Statement from the Heart. Retrieved from https://ulurustatement.org/the-statement/view-the-statement/

Helena. (2021). 6 Practices for Meaningful Intersectional Feminist Allyship. Retrieved from https://disorient.co/intersectional-feminist-allyship/

Hendrick, A., & Young, S. (2017). Decolonising the curriculum, decolonising ourselves: Experiences of teaching in and from the 'third space'. *Advances in Social Work and Welfare Education, 19*(2), 9–24.

Hendrick, A., & Young, S. (2019). Decolonising the curriculum; Decolonising ourselves. Working towards restoration through teaching, learning and practice. *Recognition, Reconciliation and Restoration: Applying a Decolonized Understanding in Social Work and Healing Processes,* 251–270. https://www.orkana.no/wp-content/uploads/2020/06/part4.2-decolonising-the-curriculum-decolonising-ourselves-working-towards-restoration-through-teaching-learning-and-practice.pdf

Hendrick, A., & Young, S. (2023). Ally work, decoloniality, and the problematics of resisting white privilege. In *Handbook of critical whiteness: Deconstructing dominant discourses across disciplines* (pp. 1–14). Springer.

hooks, b. (2000). *Feminism is for everybody: Passionate politics*: Pluto Press.

Howe, A. (2009). Addressing child sexual assault in Australian Aboriginal communities—The politics of white voice. *Australian Feminist Law Journal, 30*(1), 41–61.

Howe, D. (2017). *An introduction to social work theory.* Routledge.

Humphreys, C., & Absler, D. (2011). History repeating: Child protection responses to domestic violence. *Child & Family Social Work, 16*(4), 464–473.

IWDA. (2016). How to Be a Feminist Ally. Retrieved from https://iwda.org.au/decolonising-solidarity-what-does-it-mean-to-be-a-feminist-ally/

Kluttz, J., Walker, J., & Walter, P. (2020). Unsettling allyship, unlearning and learning towards decolonising solidarity. *Studies in the Education of Adults, 52*(1), 49–66.

Land, C. (2015). *Decolonizing solidarity. Dilemmas and directions for supporters of Indigenous struggles.* London: Zed Books.

Lewin, K., & Cartwright, D. (1952). *Field theory in social science: Selected theoretical papers by Kurt Lewin.* London: Tavistock.

Lonne, B., Parton, N., Thomson, J., & Harries, M. (2008). *Reforming child protection.* Routledge.

Lorenzetti, L., & Walsh, C. A. (2022). Feminist participatory action research with men to prevent intimate partner violence. *Action Research, 20*(2), 122–143.

Maddison, S., & Partridge, E. (2014). Agonism and intersectionality: Indigenous women, violence and feminist collective identity. In Woehrle, L. (ed). *Intersectionality and social change* (Vol. 37, pp. 27–52). Emerald Group Publishing Limited.

Martínez, S., & Agüero, J. (2023). Cartography of Southern Feminisms: Contributions of decolonial feminisms and community feminisms. *International Social Work, 66*(3), 842–854.

McGloin, C. (2016). Critical allies and feminist praxis: Rethinking dis-ease. *Gender and Education, 28*(7), 839–850.

McNamara, L. (2000). Indigenous community participation in the sentencing of criminal offenders: Circle sentencing. *Indigenous Law Bulletin, 5*(4), 5–10.

Middel, F., López López, M., Fluke, J., & Grietens, H. (2020). The effects of migrant background and parent gender on child protection decision-making: An intersectional analysis. *Child Abuse & Neglect, 104,* 104479–104415. https://doi.org/10.1016/j.chiabu.2020.104479

Middel, F., López López, M., Fluke, J., & Grietens, H. (2022). Racial/ethnic and gender disparities in child protection decision-making: What role do stereotypes play? *Child Abuse & Neglect, 127,* 105579–105579. https://doi.org/10.1016/j.chiabu.2022.105579

Mignolo, W. (2012). *Local histories/global designs: Coloniality, subaltern knowledges, and border thinking.* Princeton University Press.

Moreton-Robinson, A. (2013). Towards an Australian Indigenous women's standpoint theory: A methodological tool. *Australian Feminist Studies, 28*(78), 331–347.

Mulkeen, M. (2012). Gendered processes in child protection: 'Mother-blaming' and the erosion of men's accountability. *Irish Journal of Applied Social Studies, 12*(1), 7.

Nancarrow, H. (2006). In search of justice for domestic and family violence: Indigenous and non-Indigenous Australian women's perspectives. *Theoretical Criminology, 10*(1), 87–106.

Olsen, T. A. (2018). This word is (not?) very exciting: Considering intersectionality in Indigenous studies. *NORA-Nordic Journal of Feminist and Gender Research, 26*(3), 182–196.

Ortega, R. M., & Faller, K. C. (2011). Training child welfare workers from an intersectional cultural humility perspective. *Child Welfare, 90*(5), 27–49.

Parton, N., & O'Byrne, P. (2000). *Constructive social work. Towards a new practice*. Basingstoke: Macmillan.

Pease, B. (2010). *Undoing privilege: unearned advantage in a divided world*. London: Zed Books.

Phillips, R. (2023). *Practising feminism for social welfare: A global perspective* (1 ed.). London: Routledge, Taylor & Francis Group.

Shannon, P., & Young, S. (2004). *Solving social problems: Southern perspectives*. Dunmore Press.

Simon, J. D., Boyd, R., & Subica, A. M. (2022). Refocusing intersectionality in social work education: Creating a brave sSpace to discuss oppression and privilege. *Journal of Social Work Education, 58*(1), 34–45. https://doi.org/10.1080/10437797.2021.1883492

Skinner, G. C., Bywaters, P. W., Bilson, A., Duschinsky, R., Clements, K., & Hutchinson, D. (2021). The 'toxic trio'(domestic violence, substance misuse and mental ill-health): How good is the evidence base? *Children and Youth Services Review, 120*, 105678.

Spanierman, L. B., & Smith, L. (2017). Roles and responsibilities of White allies: Implications for research, teaching, and practice. *The Counseling Psychologist, 45*(5), 606–617.

Young, S. (2005). Moving beyond the "double bind" Indigenous language and culture learning as an emancipatory project. *Asia Pacific Journal of Social Work and Development, 15*(1), 5–16.

Young, S. (2008). Indigenous child protection policy in Australia: Using whiteness theory for social work. *Sites, 5*(1), 102–123.

Young, S., Zubrzycki, J., Green, S., Jones, V., Stratton, K., & Bessarab, D. (2013). "Getting it right: Creating partnerships for change": Developing a framework for integrating Aboriginal and Torres Strait Islander knowledges in Australian social work education. *Journal of Ethnic and Cultural Diversity in Social Work, 22*(3–4), 179–197.

Young, S., McKenzie, M., Omre, C., Schjelderup, L., & Walker, S. (2014). Practicing from theory: Thinking and knowing to "do" child protection work. *Social Sciences, 3*, 893–915. https://doi.org/10.3390/socsci3040893

Zubrzycki, J., Green, S., Jones, V., Stratton, K., Young, S., & Bessarab, D. (2014). Getting it right: Creating partnerships for change. Integrating Aboriginal and Torres Strait Islander knowledges in social work education and practice. Australian Government Office for Learning and Teaching.

43
BEYOND ALTERNATIVE MASCULINITIES AND MEN'S ALLYSHIP

Troubling men's engagement with feminisms in social work and human services practice

Bob Pease

Introduction

More than 25 years ago, in one of the few feminist social work texts on men and masculinities, Cree and Cavanagh (1996) argued that men have to change if there is to be an improvement in the lives of women and girls. They also expressed concern about whether men in social work could be trusted to engage in ways that supported women. They argued that women needed to set the agenda for working with men and be part of any evaluation of its effectiveness. Women should not just assume that men's support for feminism in social work and the human services will necessarily advantage women.[1]

The aim of this chapter is to draw upon feminist theories to critically interrogate key aspects of work with men and masculinities in social work and the human services. I analyse two common themes in the literature, fostering alternative masculinities and men becoming allies with women, to illustrate some of the dilemmas and problems associated with engaging men in violence prevention and support for gender equality. In the title of the chapter, I use the language of troubling as a verb to explore ways in which alternative masculinities and men's allyship can be troubled or disturbed in the context of men's engagement with feminisms in the profession and the wider society.

It is a feminist and Indigenous convention to position oneself in systems of power and to locate one's theoretical argument in personal stories of political engagement (Kelly, 2005; Beuchamps, 2021). I do so here as a white heterosexually presenting cisgendered, temporarily able-bodied and able-minded older academic man currently living and working on Wurundjeri Aboriginal land in Australia. I have been involved in profeminist activism, education and writing in and outside of social work since the 1970s. Profeminism involves a sense of responsibility for men's own and other men's sexism and a commitment to work with women to end men's violence and abuse (Pease, 2016).[2]

I have noted the dangers and problems, as well as the possibilities associated with increasing men's presence in social work (Pease, 2011). I argue that if men in social work are not actively promoting profeminist practices, they will reproduce an unequal gender regime within the profession. In this chapter, I focus on the two specific themes of alternative masculinities and men's allyship to ground a wider discussion of men's engagement with feminisms and what it might mean for the presence of men in feminism and in feminist social work and human services practice.

Engaging men and masculinities in feminism

Much of the literature in social work seeking to understand men's experiences and role within the profession neglect a nuanced engagement with the complexities and contradictions of feminist theories. Instead, this literature is over-reliant upon psychological accounts of men and masculinities and is often focused on the so-called disadvantages faced by men (Kosberg, 2002; Baum, 2016). Hicks (2015) argues that social work theory tends to treat gender as a static category. When gender is taken for granted, it tends to naturalise gender differences.

It is important to see gender beyond white cisgendered men and women and binary understandings that perpetuate gendered and other inequalities (Kroehle et al., 2020). Gender is more often than not theorised in an individualistic way that is more compatible with liberal forms of feminism and it largely fails to engage with materialist, post-structuralist, intersectional and new materialist feminist accounts of gender or to engage with gender as a practice.

In social work, as in some masculinity studies writing, there is a gap between feminist scholarship, and theories informing men and masculinities. When men say that their practice is informed by feminism, which feminism are they referring to? (Burrell & Flood, 2019). Many feminist theories are incompatible with each other and different feminisms pose different challenges and dilemmas for profeminist men. Consequently, just as there are many feminisms, so too are there many perspectives within profeminism.

Feminists are divided on the issue of whether or not there is any place for men in feminism and this flows on to the place of men in feminist social work and human services practice. The politics of men's engagement with feminisms will thus depend upon which forms of feminism with which men are connecting (Giri, 2022). As I have noted elsewhere (Pease, 2000), men's engagement with feminism is often focused on those forms of feminism that are most sympathetic to men and their issues.

Liberal feminisms, with their focus on equal opportunity and affirmative action, present the most optimistic strategies for men, suggesting that men can transform their masculinities and change their relationships with women without having to change the structures of Patriarchy. We see liberal feminism in such initiatives as Male Champions of Change where men in positions of power commit themselves to take action to support gender equality in their workplaces (Prasad et al., 2021). The language of male champions confers a heroic status on men as women's saviours who are seen to advocate for women's interests. This type of activism can involve men's appropriation of feminism and can end up reproducing men's dominance.

Radical feminisms are less concerned with changing masculinities and are more focused on transforming men's practices and patriarchal structures (Jensen, 2017). Their material and structural analyses of gender are useful in interrogating the gendered structure of social work as a state-based profession and resulting gendered inequality in status and salaries between men and women (Pease, 2011).

Radical feminists are more sceptical or critical of there being a place for men in feminism. Some radical feminists argue that feminism is for women only and that men, even if well intentioned, cannot contribute positively to feminism because of their complicity in Patriarchy (Kremer, 1990). Such radical feminisms which are premised upon women's experiences will see men's understanding as being limited, whatever their level of political commitment to feminism. Crowe (2013) argues that men who seek to support feminism for their own benefits will only be peripherally involved in the feminist movement. For men, to fully support feminism, they must put their own interests aside and adopt a women-centred view of the world. Men informed by radical feminism are more likely to aspire to being profeminist and accountable to women, rather than identify themselves as feminists. Funk (1997), for example, argues for the language of profeminism to avoid minimising the unique experiences of women who claim a feminist identity.

Beasley (2013) accuses profeminist theorists of reinforcing essentialist gendered categories. In her view, profeminist masculinity studies are predominantly modernist in its approach to gender inequality and it has largely ignored or dismissed the post-modern and post-structural turn in feminist theories. In post-structural accounts of men and masculinities, we shift the focus from gender as a category of being to gender as a discursive practice. Discursive and post-structural approaches to gender focus more on the doing of gender and gender performance (West & Zimmerman, 1987; Butler, 1990). Such approaches are sometimes pitted against radical materialism in the form of a critique, emphasising the importance of discourse, language and representation over realism and the material world. However, as profeminist men and masculinities theorist Jeff Hearn (2014) points out, the more nuanced radical feminist-informed accounts involve an expansion of materialist understandings in the form of what Hearn calls the materialist-discursive. The enactment of gender is located in the context of larger structures and social arrangements and the doing of gender reproduces these wider structures (Pease, 2022).

Intersectional feminists emphasise the importance of seeing race, gender and class as 'interlocking systems of oppression'. These feminist perspectives grounded in the diversity of women's lives explore the interconnections between class, gender, race and other social divisions, as they are experienced by women in specific contexts (Collins, 1991; Crenshaw, 1991). Just as intersectional feminists have acknowledged difference to ensure that they serve all women, so too profeminists must deal with the intersecting class, racial, sexual and religious identities of men (Peretz, 2017).

When we work with men who are marginalised by class, race, ethnicity, sexuality and other social divisions, we must address their hybrid status of being both privileged by gender and oppressed by other forms of domination. Messner (1997) argues that profeminist men should place multi-racial feminism with its respect for difference, as well as structural and discursive analyses, at the centre of their strategies. This involves men listening to Indigenous and racialised women and men, and being open to decolonising themselves. While there are certainly examples of profeminist men's work in the Global South (Welsh, 2001; Wu, 2011; Ratele, 2015; Colpitts, 2017) and among men who are marginalised by race and class (Murdolo & Quiazon, 2016), it is nevertheless the case that with few exceptions, the profeminist men's movement comprises overwhelmingly white, heterosexual, cisgendered men in the Global North, and it is these men who are still the focus of most programs engaging men (Flood, 2017).

Some feminists suggest that we need to move beyond gender categories. Deluezian feminists advocate the process of 'becoming' to destabilise capitalist and patriarchal structures. Becoming-woman is an important way for women to exit from majoritarian forms of domination (Grosz, 1994; Braidotti, 2012). Braidotti (2012) argues that men can pursue this strategy as well, albeit from different subjectivities and positionings. However, while more nuanced understandings of gender and the category of 'woman' have developed over the last 50 years since the second wave of feminist scholarship began, the concept of 'man' has not been as interrogated or deconstructed to the same extent (Pease, 2023; Pease & Mellstrom, 2023).

If we are to move beyond the binaries of masculinity and femininity and men and women, we will need to dismantle the concept of gender itself. We know the dangers of universalising the categories of woman and man and how they have historically excluded, exploited and marginalised some people (Eide, 2016). However, to do away with the categories of man and woman will understandably encounter some resistance, not only from men but also from many feminist women. While it is important to reject essentialism theoretically, it is strategically important at times to utilise gender categories such as women and men to achieve political goals. Feminist mobilisations are based on women's gendered and sexed experiences. It is here Spivak's (1996) notion of strategic essentialism, where gender categories with all of their limitations are used strategically to defend women's rights in particular contexts.

It is against this backdrop of multiple feminisms and their different implications for men that I explore the potential and limitations of fostering alternative masculinities and encouraging men's allyship in feminist practice with men.

Beyond alternative masculinities

Cree and Cavanagh (1996) argued in their historic feminist text on working with men that the language of masculinities is the best way to understand men. This would now seem to be an accepted truism in the field of gender politics. Much of the scholarship in masculinity studies and in debates about men and masculinity in social work and popular culture are concerned with how men (implicitly cisgendered men) understand and deal with toxic and abusive forms of masculinity (Thompkins-Jones, 2017).

The concept of 'toxic masculinity' defines a particular type of masculinity that is seen to encourage homophobia, misogyny, domination of women and sexual violence (Watts, 2019). It involves physical conflict as a way of resolving disputes and validates an aggressive expression of masculinity. Proponents of the term emphasise that it is only a particular form of masculinity that is problematic and that there are many diverse expressions of masculinity that are healthy for men. Such proponents want to assure men that there is nothing inherently wrong about being male, and that some forms of male socialisation are inherently useful (Flood, 2018).

However, while notions of alternative masculinity are used to encourage men to challenge men's violence and promote gender equality, they reinforce men's investment in masculinity and manhood (Pease, 2014). Hearn, as far back as 1996, argued that it was preferable to move away from masculinities to focus on men's practices (Hearn, 1996). McMahon (1999) further argued that masculinity is a form of idealism, in that men's behaviour and actions are seen to flow from their masculinity. It was always unclear how changing conceptions of masculinity relate to changing the material practices of men or the social relations of gender.

Schwalbe (2014) critiques the concept of multiple masculinities for obscuring men's privileged positioning and hiding the oppression involved in what he calls 'manhood acts'. For men informed by radical feminism, masculinity and its plural variants have always been problematical. Stoltenberg (1993), for example, argues that masculinity and manhood are so infused with dominance and oppression, that men should exit masculinity and refuse to be a man by committing themselves to moral selfhood in solidarity with women on the basis of respect for difference. Notwithstanding Alcoff's (2016) caution that membership of privileged groups and identities associated with them are not easily exited, I argue, along with Hearn, Schwalbe and Stoltenberg, that we should encourage men to disinvest in masculinity and manhood to challenge both the hierarchical gender binary, which is based on the false premise that there are only two genders, and the use of gender to police normative identities (Pease, 2022).

Dube (2018) argues that alternative and liberated masculinities are limited in their representation of what transformation in men might entail. In his view, all masculine ideals, including the alternative versions, constrain fluidity and mobility. He turns to Braidotti's (2012) notion of nomadic subjectivity to consider what this might mean for masculinity. Nomadic subjectivities create more possibilities for men to shift their subjectivity from adherence to some form of masculine ideal towards multiple and fluid ways of being and becoming, some of which may be gendered and some of which may not. They depart from static idealised notions of masculinity that limit the possibilities for transformation. Focusing on mobile, relational and changing subjectivities does not limit the possibilities of what men can become. Thus, profeminism for men needs to move beyond masculinities in disengaging men from the dominant axes of power (Pease, 2021).

In the context of my work with diverse men in Australia, I would often ask them: 'When do you most feel like a man? Do you feel like a man at every waking moment, or are there particular contexts and experiences when your gendered identity as a man comes to the fore?' Men's responses confirm that their gendered experiences are context-specific and that they move in and out of experiencing themselves as a man. There are some situations when being a man or woman will be central and many other situations when it will just be one subjectivity among many others.

Qualities such as empathy, compassion, caring and emotional vulnerability, which are usually associated with women and femininity, are often reframed as 'healthy masculinity' (Roberts et al., 2019). Yet, to reframe these qualities as masculine discourages men to engage with femininity and ends up reproducing the gender hierarchy that privileges masculinity above femininity. It thus reinforces the gender binary, devalues what is seen as feminine and appropriates human traits as masculinity specific (Waling, 2019). Why are these qualities deemed to be masculine rather than qualities of an ethical human being? Why should we locate these qualities as a kind of masculinity (or femininity) as opposed to important human qualities that all men, women and non-binary people should aspire to (Almassi, 2015)?

To the extent that masculinity can be represented as a diverse and at times contested set of traits and behaviours, the set does not solely belong to men. They are also enacted by women, trans, non-binary and gender non-conforming people as well (Halberstam, 1998; Laporte, 2019). Men, masculinities and being male are too frequently used interchangeably. Thus, discussion of men and masculinity tends to reinforce the link between the male sex category and gendered performance and practice. So, it is hard to see how the practice of changing masculinity, based on traits and behaviours, can avoid the reinforcement of essential gender differences. It follows then that to restrict the discussion of men and masculinity in social work to white heterosexual cisgendered, men would largely reinforce cis-normative and essentialist assumptions about masculinity, race and sexuality (Kroehle et al., 2020).

Beyond men's allyship

In a second dominant strain in the literature, many suggest that the aim of profeminist social work should be to recruit men in social work as feminist allies (Casey, 2010; Gibson, 2014; Betts, 2017). I have written previously about my own involvement as an ally in challenging men's sexism and violence against women (Pease, 2017). I co-founded Men Against Sexual Assault in 1991 to encourage other men to take responsibility for combating men's violence against women[3] and I have conducted numerous Patriarchy Awareness Workshops to examine the impact that Patriarchy has on the lives of women, men and non-binary people. When I talk to men about women's agency in struggling against sexism and men's violence, I also talk about the historical role of profeminist men in feminist politics.

I noted in my earlier work that in acting as allies to women, profeminist men face a number of challenges. When men become involved with women's campaigns, they often move into positions of authority. There is a thin line between being a constructive ally and taking over another group's struggle. Even when men are sensitive to these issues, their involvement is more likely to be acknowledged and praised. I have also acknowledged that in spite of their best intentions, allies sometimes perpetuate the oppression they are challenging. It is inevitable that allies will sometimes 'get it wrong'. They must overcome fear of making mistakes by being willing to learn from oppressed groups and committing themselves to challenge their own internalised domination. Ongoing challenges that allies face include figuring out when to speak, when to listen and when to remove themselves from the activist space. It should be remembered that members of oppressed groups should be the ones to determine who constitutes an ally or not (Edwards, 2006).

In my earlier work, I referred to myself as an aspiring ally to acknowledge that it is a process involving action and reflexivity and that it is never fully attained (Pease, 2017). I am now more uncomfortable with the language of allies. While I noted the dangers of becoming allies above, I did not question the premises upon which much allyship rested. Indigenous Action Media (2014) highlighted these issues in their critique of what they call 'the ally industrial complex', whereby self-proclaimed allies have developed careers out of their allyship work and have turned allyship into an identity that is disconnected from mutuality and solidarity with oppressed people. McKenzie (2015) similarly talks about 'ally theatre', whereby 'allies' perform their allyship on social media and other public spaces where they have an audience for their performance of activism. Kalina (2020) refers to unhelpful and harmful allyship as 'performative allyship'. It is more often associated with hashtag activism where you can publicly declare your stand against some form of injustice without having to sacrifice anything.

Klutttzet al. (2020) emphasise the importance of decolonising and unsettling our assumptions about allyship to enable us to recognise colonial privilege. The privilege that allies possess is rarely acknowledged. Allies are honoured and praised for taking a stand and paraphrasing the issues that oppressed people struggle with every day and they are able to largely avoid being dismissed as too emotional or angry (Patton & Bondi, 2015). Klutttz et al. (2020) argue that the language of being an ally suggests that it is an identity that can be achieved and that such an identity encourages a 'move to innocence', allowing allies to ignore their complicity in ongoing inequalities. One of the limitations of the language of allies is that it does not encourage us to see how members of privileged groups are implicated and complicit in the ongoing reproduction of oppressive systems. Allies are seen as somehow outside the systems of exploitation and oppression (Russo, 2017).

In spite of these critiques, the terminology of allies and allyship are still commonly used in social justice work and social work (Carlson, et al., 2019). Russo (2019) identifies a number of alternative terms, including co-strugglers, collaborators, co-conspirators and accomplices. The latter term, usually associated with complicity in a crime, in the social justice context means cooperation and sense of community with those who are oppressed.

Clemens (2017) distinguishes accomplice work from ally work by suggesting that ally work is focused on individuals, while accomplice work is focused on addressing complicity in structures. McKenzie (2015) talks about 'acting in solidarity with'; the concept of solidarity and willingness to take risks in working alongside people rather than on their behalf is what distinguishes accomplice work from allyship (Powell & Kelly, 2017). The language used by progressive members of privileged groups is important in acknowledging their relationship to power and the ways they are implicated in systems of privilege and oppression. This has important implications for profeminist men, especially in their work alongside women in challenging men's violences (Pease, 2017).

So, is there a place for men in feminism and feminist social work and human services practice?

The place of men in feminism continues to be a source of ongoing controversy. This is not only the issue of whether men can be feminists or not. I argue that men should aspire to becoming profeminist in their practice and not define themselves as feminists. However, there is a more important question of whether men can work towards the goals of feminism, and if they can, how can the dangers of men diverting attention back to themselves be best addressed? It is essential for men to acknowledge their privilege and complicity with Patriarchy, if this danger is to be avoided.

It is argued by many feminists that feminism will benefit from men's participation (Tarrant, 2009; van der Gaag, 2014). It is agreed that men can challenge other men's misogyny, sexism and violence. Silver et al. (2019) argue that including men more fully in feminism will benefit the overall feminist movement. As far back as 1987, Sandra Harding argued that men could create feminist knowledge through critically interrogating their experiences as men in Patriarchy (Harding, 1987). Men are more limited in their capacity to understand privilege and power because they benefit from it, albeit unequally through differential access to the patriarchal dividend (Connell, 1987). Notwithstanding this limitation, as I have argued elsewhere, I believe it is possible for men to understand Patriarchy and challenge their complicity within it (Pease, 2019). In this view, it should be the practice and the interests served by it that defines whether social work and human service work is feminist or not, and not the sex or gender identity of the practitioner.

Many women's concerns about men's involvement in feminism are well founded, however. There are too many examples of men who profess their support for feminism who do not walk the talk. I know from personal experience that it is easier to reject socialisation in our heads than it is in our hearts and our behaviour. Intellectual understanding of feminism is only a first step towards the necessary transformation that men must experience. If men are to live by feminist principles, they must detach themselves from the distanced and so-called objective stance of the neutral observer or scientist. As a man, it has been challenging for me to make myself vulnerable in my writing where I share my personal struggles and dilemmas. I have often had to push back against academic reviewers who have taken me to task for writing in the first person about my experiences.

It is the capacity to be vulnerable that is so important for men's inner transformation (Pease, 2021). Some of the strategies to engage men as allies in addressing issues like men's violence against women, for example, involve diluting feminist analysis or avoiding it completely to make the issue more appealing to men and to discourage them from feeling guilty or uncomfortable about their privilege and complicity in reproducing Patriarchy (Flood, 2018). For example, Silver et al. (2019) suggest that efforts should be made to ensure that men's engagement with feminism should not pose a threat to their masculinity. However, by engaging men in ways that avoid making them uncomfortable, there seems little hope for any significant change. Allies or accomplices must be prepared to face the moral discomfort and epistemic anxiety that acting against injustice as an outsider entails (Sunderman, 2021).

McGloin (2016) argues that members of privileged groups need to experience discomfort, or what she describes as dis-ease, to enable a transformation of the self that is able to recognise complicity in the oppression of others. While McGloin (2016) is discussing the dis-ease of white women scholars struggling with the tensions between their commitment to anti-colonialism and anti-racism and their own privileged subject positions, the language is also useful for addressing the tensions and contradictions experienced by profeminist men engaging with feminist practice. Russo (2019) similarly encourages us to experience what she calls 'brokenheartedness' as we come to accept our complicity in systems of dominance and oppression. Of course there is a danger that when people feel destabilised as a result of recognition of their complicity, they will be paralysed and not feel motivated to take action. However, in my experience, it is more often than not a catalyst for people to initiate change (Pease, 2022).

All members of privileged groups live with internalised and externalised pressures to conform to dominant ideologies. To the extent that we succumb to those pressures, we are less likely to be able to acknowledge the suffering and pain of those who are oppressed (Russo, 2017). Forming respectful and trusting relationships with feminist women is essential for men to increase their understanding and knowledge of feminism. It is not uncommon that men who have a positive engagement with feminism have been in close relationships with feminists who have had a significant influence on their theories, politics and personal practices (Wojnicka, 2012).

Conclusion

When feminism includes men, it complicates the strategies of gender politics and presents new challenges for feminism. Whatever alignments men might feel to feminism, it remains that men gain material advantages from Patriarchy, whether they consciously exploit them or not. Consequently, some feminists will understandably remain sceptical or critical of men's engagement with feminisms. For some feminists, any form of work with men will be seen as being complicit with Patriarchy. Hence, they would prefer to always work in women-only groups (Wiley & Dunne, 2019).

We must acknowledge that bringing men into feminism can de-centre women, as men often dominate in mixed gender social movements. Furthermore, men have used feminism instrumentally to further their own status and career. However, I argue that it is possible, and important for feminism to inspire men's anti-patriarchal practices, without men defining themselves as feminists. While there are feminist methodologies that may rely upon women's embodied experiences of oppression, I argue that men can be actively involved in supporting feminism and can practice feminism in social work and the human services, if they are alert to the dangers and problems discussed here, listen to women's experiences and challenges and if they make their practice accountable to feminist women. Hence, I suggest there is a place, albeit a contradictory and precarious one, for men in feminist social work and human services practice.

Acknowledgements

I would like to thank Kelley Johnson, Marie Brennan, Shelley Hewson-Munro, Shahana Rasool and an anonymous reviewer for their insightful and constructive comments on an earlier version of this chapter.

Notes

1 When I refer to men and women in this chapter, I am meaning cisgendered men and women who identify with the gender assigned to them at birth. This gender designation does not work for many people, including transgender, non-binary and gender fluid people. I focus on cisgender men in this chapter because they are the perpetrators and perpetuators of the most of the violence against cisgendered women, men and gender diverse people.
2 Throughout this chapter, I spell profeminist and profeminism without a hyphen. While there are different linguistic conventions in relation to the use of the hyphen as in pro-feminist and pro-feminism, there are also political differences for many. Brod (1998), for example, distinguishes between pro-feminist men who support feminism and profeminist men who aim to develop feminist politics by men. While the latter includes pro-feminism, it goes further to argue that men must find their own stake in advancing a feminist agenda in solidarity with feminist women.
3 While the focus of my early activist violence prevention work was on men's violence against women, in more recent years, I have been arguing that men's violence prevention should be extended to men's violence against boys and men, as such violence by men is also gendered. See, for example, Gendering men's public violence against men, Chapter 8 of *Facing Patriarchy* (Pease, 2019).

References

Alcoff, L. (2006). *Visible identities: Race, gender and the self*. Oxford University Press.
Almassi, B. (2015). Feminist reclamations of normative masculinity: On democratic manhood, feminist masculinity, and allyship practices. *Feminist Philosophy Quarterly, 1*(2), 1–22.
Baum, N. (2016). The unheard gender: The neglect of men as social work clients. *British Journal of Social Work, 46*(5), 1463–1471.
Beasley, C. (2013). Mind the gap? Masculinity studies and contemporary gender/sexuality thinking. *Australian Feminist Studies, 28*(75), 108–124.
Betts, R. (2017). *From violent inequity to allyship: What is to be gained by men's discomfort?* Unpublished paper. McGill University, Montreal.
Beuchamps, M. (2021). Doing academia differently: Loosening the borders of our disciplining writing practices. *Millennium: Journal of International Studies, 49*(2), 392–416.
Braidotti, R. (2012). *Nomadic theory: The portable Rosi Braidotti*. Columbia University Press.
Brod, H. (1998) To be a man, or not to be a man: This is the feminist question. In T. Digby (Ed.) *Men doing feminism* (pp. 197–202). Routledge.
Burrell, S. & Flood, M. (2019). Which feminism? Dilemmas in profeminist men's praxis to end violence against women. *Global Social Welfare, 6*, 231–244.
Butler, J. (1990). *Gender trouble: Feminism and the subversion of identity*. Routledge.
Carlson J., Leek, C., Casey, E., Tolman, R. & Allen, C. (2019). What's in a name? A synthesis of 'allyship' elements from academic and activist literature. *Journal of Family Violence, 39*, 889–898.
Casey, E. (2010). Strategies for engaging men as anti-violence allies: Implications for ally movement. *Advances in Social Work, 11*(2), 267–281.

Clemens, C. (2017). Ally or accomplice? The language of activism. *Learning for Justice*. Retrieved from https://www.learningforjustice.org/magazine/ally-or-accomplice-the-language-of-activism

Collins, P. (1991). *Black feminist thought: Knowledge, consciousness and the politics of empowerment*. Unwin Hyman.

Colpitts, E. (2017). Engaging men and boys to prevent gender-based violence in South Africa: Possibilities, tensions and debates. *Canadian Journal of Development Studies, 40*(3), 423–439.

Connell, R. (1987). *Gender and power: Society, the person and sexual politics*. Allen and Unwin.

Cree, V. & Cavanagh, K. (1996). Men, masculinism and social work. In K. Cavanagh & V. Cree (Eds.) *Working with men: Feminism and social work* (pp. 1–8). Routledge.

Crenshaw, K. (1991). Mapping the margins: Intersectionality, identity politics and violence against women of color. *Stanford Law Review, 43*(6), 1242–1299.

Crowe, J. (2013). Can men be feminists? University of Queensland TC Beirne School of Law Research Paper No. 13-08. Available at SSRN: https://ssrn.com/abstract=2345526 or https://doi.org/10.2139/ssrn.2345526.

Dube, S. (2018). The violence of the masculine ideal: A case for nomadic masculinities. *HTS: Theological Studies, 74*(2), 1–9.

Edwards, K. (2006). Aspiring social justice ally development: A conceptual model. *NASPA Journal, 43*(4), 39–60.

Eide, E. (2016). Strategic essentialism. In N. Naples (Ed) *Wiley Blackwell encyclopedia of gender and sexuality studies*. John Wiley and Sons. https://doi.org/10.1002/9781118663219.wbegss554.

Flood, M. (2017). Addressing intersections of social disadvantage and privilege in engaging men in violence prevention. Crime and Justice in Asia and the Global South: An International Conference, Cairns, July 10–13.

Flood, M. (2018). *Engaging men and boys in violence prevention*. Palgrave.

Funk, R. (1997). The power of naming: Men in feminism. Retrieved from http://web.archive.org/web/20061021094917/www.feminista.com/archives/v1n4/malefem.html.

Gibson, P. (2014). Extending the ally model of social justice to social work pedagogy. *Journal of Teaching in Social Work, 34*, 199–214.

Giri, K. (2022). Can men do feminist fieldwork and research? *International Studies Review, 24*(1), https://doi.org/10.1093/isr/viac004.

Grosz, E. (1994). *Volatile bodies: Towards a corporeal feminism*. Indiana University Press.

Halberstam, J. (1998). *Female masculinity*. Duke University Press.

Harding, S. (1987). Is there a feminist method? In S. Harding (Ed.) *Feminism and methodology: Social science issues* (pp. 1–14). Indiana University Press.

Hearn, J. (1996). Is masculinity dead? A critical account of the concepts of masculinity and masculinities. In M. Mac an Ghaill (Ed.) *Understanding masculinities: Social relations and cultural arenas* (pp. 202–217). Sage.

Hearn, J. (2014). Men, masculinities and the material(-)discursive. *International Journal for Masculinity Studies, 9*(1), 5–17.

Hicks, S. (2015). Social work and gender: An argument for practical accounts. *Qualitative Social Work, 14*(4), 471–487.

Indigenous Action Media (2014). Accomplices, not allies: Abolishing the ally industrial complex. Retrieved from https://www.indigenousaction.org-complex.org/.

Jensen, R. (2017). *The end of patriarchy: Radical feminism for men*. Spinifex.

Kalina, P. (2020). Performative allyship. *Technium Social Sciences Journal, 11*, 478–481.

Kelly, L. (2005). Racism in legal education special: A personal reflection on being an Indigenous academic. *Indigenous Law Bulletin, 19*. Retrieved from http://classic.austlii.edu.au/au/journals/IndigLawB/2005/5.html.

Klutttz, J., Walker, J. & Walter, P. (2020). Unsettling allyship, unlearning and learning towards decolonising solidarity. *Studies in the Education of Adults, 52*(1), 49–66.

Kosberg, J. (2002). Heterosexual males: A group forgotten by the profession. *Journal of Sociology and Social Welfare, 29*(3), 51–70.

Kremer, B. (1990). Learning to say no: Keeping feminist research for ourselves. *Women's Studies International Forum, 13*(5), 463–467.

Kroehle, K., Shetton, J., Clarke, E. & Seelman, K. (2020). Mainstreaming dissidence: Confronting binary gender in social work grand challenges. *Social Work, 65*(4), 368–377.

Laporte, J. (2019). *Disrupting the toxic vs healthy masculinity discourse: An autoethnographic study.* Master of Arts, University of Massachusetts, Lowell.

McGloin, C. (2016). Critical allies and feminist praxis: Rethinking dis-ease. *Gender and Education,* 28(7), 839–850.

McKenzie, M. (2015). How to tell the difference between real solidarity and 'ally theatre'. Retrieved from http://www/blackgirldangerous.com/2015/11/allytheatre/.

McMahon, A. (1999). *Taking care of men: Sexual politics in the public mind.* Cambridge University Press.

Messner, M. (1997). *The politics of masculinities: Men in movements.* Sage.

Murdolo, A. & Quiazon, R. (2016). *Key issues in working with men from immigrant and refugee communities in preventing violence against women.* White Ribbon Research Series. White Ribbon Australia.

Patton, L. & Bondi, S. (2015). Nice white men or social justice allies?: Using critical race theory to examine how white male faculty and administrators engage in ally work. *Race, Ethnicity and Education* 18(4), 488–514.

Pease, B. (2000). *Recreating men: Postmodern masculinity politics.* Sage.

Pease, B. (2011). Men in social work: Reproducing or challenging an unequal gender regime? *Affilia: Women and Social Work,* 1–13. Advanced Access, https://doi.org/10.1177/08861099114281099 11428207.

Pease, B. (2014). Reconstructing masculinity or ending manhood? The potential and limitations of transforming masculine subjectivities for gender equality. In A. Carabi & J. Armengol (Eds.) *Alternative masculinities for a changing world* (pp. 17–34). Palgrave.

Pease, B. (2016). Engaging men in feminist social work. In S. Wendt & N. Moulding (Eds.) *Contemporary feminisms in social work practice* (pp. 287–302). Routledge.

Pease, B. (2017). *Men as allies in preventing violence against women: Principles and practices for promoting accountability.* White Ribbon Research Series, White Ribbon Australia.

Pease, B. (2019). *Facing patriarchy: From a violent gender order to a culture of peace.* Zed.

Pease, B. (2021). Fostering non-anthropocentric vulnerability in men: Challenging the autonomous masculine subject in social work. In V. Bozalek & B. Pease (Eds.) *Post- anthropocentric social work: Critical posthuman and new materialist and perspectives* (pp. 108–120). Routledge.

Pease, B. (2022). *Undoing privilege: Unearned advantage and systemic injustice in an unequal world,* second edition. Zed Books/Bloomsbury.

Pease, B. (2023). Men becoming otherwise: Lines of flight from majoritarian masculinities and 'Man'. In U. Mellström & B. Pease (Eds.) *Posthumanism and the man question: Beyond anthropocentric masculinities* (pp. 222–235). Routledge.

Pease, B. & Mellstom, U. (2023). Introduction: Posthumanism and the man question. In U. Mellström (Ed.) *Posthumanism and the man question: Beyond anthropocentric Masculinities* (pp. 1–18). Routledge.

Peretz, Tal (2017). An intersectional analysis of men's pathways to antiviolence activism. *Gender and Society,* 31(4), 526–548.

Powell, J. & Kelly, A. (2017). Accomplices in the academy in the age of Black Lives Matter. *Journal of Critical Thought and Praxis,* 6(2), 42–65.

Prasad, A., Centeno, A., Rhodes, C., Nisa, M., Taylor, S., Tienari, J. & Alakavuklaar, O. (2021). What are men's roles and responsibilities in the feminist project for gender egalitarianism? *Gender, Work & Organization.* Retrieved from https://onlinelibrary.wiley.com/doi/epdf/10.1111/gwao.12573.

Ratele, K. (2015). Working through resistance to engaging boys and men towards gender equality and progressive masculinities. *Culture, Health and Sexuality,* 17, 144–158.

Roberts, S., Bartlett, T., Ralph, B. & Stewart, R. (2019). *Healthier masculinities scoping review.* Victorian Health Promotion Foundation.

Russo, A. (2017). Brokenheartedness and accountability. *Journal of Lesbian Studies,* 21(3), 289–305.

Russo, A. (2019). *Feminist accountability: Disrupting violence and transforming power.* New York University Press.

Schwalbe, M. (2014). *Manhood acts: Gender and the practices of domination.* Paradigm.

Silver, E., Chadwick, S. & van Anders, S. (2019). Feminist identity in men: Masculinity, gender roles and sexual approaches in feminist, non-feminist and unsure men. *Sex Roles,* 80, 277–290.

Spivak, G. (1996). Subaltern studies: Deconstructing historiography?" In D. Landry & G. MacLean (Eds.) *The spivak reader* (pp. 203–237). Routledge.
Stoltenberg, J. (1993). *The end of manhood*. Dutton.
Sunderman, Z. (2021). *Can a man condemn himself? The existential dilemmas of white allyship*. New School.
Tarrant, S. (2009). *Men and feminism*. Seal Press.
Thompkins-Jones, R. (2017). Toxic masculinity is a macro social work issue, *The New Social Worker*, Summer, socialwork.com.
van der Gaag, N. (2014). *Feminism and men*. Zed.
Waling, A. (2019). Rethinking masculinity studies: Feminism, masculinity, and poststructural accounts of agency and emotional reflexivity. *Journal of Men's Studies*, 27(1), 89–107.
Watts, G (2019). Stop scolding men for being toxic. *The Conversation*, April 29th, theconversation.com.
Welsh, P. (2001). Unlearning machismo: Men changing men in post-revolutionary Nicaragua. In B. Pease & K. Pringle (Eds.) *A man's world? Changing men's practices in a globalized world* (pp. 177–190). Zed Books.
West, C. & Zimmerman, D. (1987). Doing gender. *Gender and Society*, 1(2), 125–151.
Wiley, S. & Dunne, C. (2019). Comrades in the struggle? Feminist women prefer male allies who offer autonomy, not dependency-oriented help. *Sex Roles, 80,* 656–666.
Wojnicka, K. (2012). The Polish profeminist movement. *Gender,* 4(3), 25–40.
Wu, J. (2011). From benevolent patriarchy to gender transformation: A case study of Pakistan's 'We can end violence against women program. In E. Ruspini, J. Hearn, B. Pease & K. Pringle (Eds.) *Men and masculinities around the world: Transforming men's practices* (pp. 219–231).

SECTION 6

Social movements, engaging with the environment, and the more-than-human

44
DELIBERATE DEMOCRACY AND THE METOO MOVEMENT

Examining the impact of social media feminist discourses in India

Akhila K. P. and Jilly John

Introduction

The emergence of new media platforms has significantly influenced contemporary feminist activism in India (Jain, 2020). The millennial feminists in India have been at the forefront of this movement, utilising social media to organise and mobilise exclusive feminist movements such as the "Slut Walk" of 2011 and the "Bekhauf Azadi" of 2017, which have made a profound impact on the Indian film, media, and print industries (Rejer, 2015; Bhatia, 2022). The social media feminist movements have a transnational and global character, and their reactive nature has had a considerable impact on feminist discourse across borders (Tella, 2018). Therefore, it is important to explore the role of new media platforms in facilitating these exclusive feminist movements in India and their impact on feminist activism globally. It is in this background this chapter aims to address the impact of the #MeToo movement in India, a popular social media mobilisation that addresses sexual harassment against women.

The impact of the #MeToo India Movement has been significant, with many high-profile individuals in the media, academia, entertainment, and political spheres facing accusations of sexual harassment and abuse (Suk et al., 2021; Tahan, 2021). The movement has also sparked a wider conversation about gender-based violence in India, leading to increased awareness and scrutiny of the issue. However, the chapter notes that there are also criticisms of the #MeToo India Movement from different feminist perspectives. Some scholars argue that the movement has been too focused on individual cases and has failed to address the systemic and structural issues that contribute to gender-based violence in India. Others have criticised the movement for its lack of inclusivity and for failing to centre the experiences of marginalised communities. The chapter stresses the relevance of deliberative democracy in addressing the challenges and concerns raised by the #MeToo movement in India. Deliberative democracy can promote a more nuanced understanding of the social and cultural factors that contribute to gender-based violence in India by offering a platform for survivors of sexual violence and harassment to share their experiences and enabling diverse voices to be heard. Through informed and inclusive dialogue, the movement can work towards creating a more comprehensive and effective response to gender-based violence and harassment.

The chapter argues that while social media has transformed feminist activism in India, it alone may not be enough to address all the challenges and concerns raised by the #MeToo movement. Other strategies and approaches, such as legal reforms, policy changes, and collective action, may also be necessary to create meaningful and lasting change. However, deliberative democracy can play a vital role in bringing these different approaches together and facilitating informed and inclusive dialogue among different stakeholders.

Feminist mobilisation in India

Feminist mobilisation in India has been driven by violence against women for centuries, with the movement against Sati being one of the earliest instances of organised feminist activism (Sharma, 2015). This practice was prevalent in certain regions of India until the early 19th century and was seen as emblematic of patriarchal and oppressive social order. Upper class women's movements emerged during the colonial period to challenge this practice and lobby for legal reforms, but it is important to acknowledge that there have been numerous other movements over the past two centuries seeking to challenge oppressive and discriminatory ideologies (Pande, 2018), including the women's suffrage movement, the women's labour movement, the Dalit women's movement, and the Muslim women's movement, to name a few (Chakravarti, 1993; Ahmed-Ghosh, 2012; Krishnan, 2018). These movements have had a significant impact on Indian society, contributing to changes in laws and policies, and advancing the rights and status of women in India. Despite progress, challenges remain, and feminist activism continues to be a crucial force for social and political change in India (Ray, 2018).

The first wave of Indian feminism emerged in the late 19th century during British colonial rule, with prominent women like Savitri Bhai Phule, Pandita Ramabai, Tarabai Shinde, and Tarabai Modak advocating for women's education and employment and fighting against social evils like child marriage, sati, and dowry (Pandey, 2019; Mohanty, 2022; Pandey, 2022; Rajgopal, 2022). The suffragette movement, led by women such as Sarojini Naidu and Kamaladevi Chattopadhyay, demanded political rights for women, including the right to vote, and was part of the wider struggle for India's independence (Cobb, 1975). The suffragette movement played a significant role in India's struggle for independence, and women's participation in the movement was instrumental in breaking down gender barriers and creating a more inclusive society. The first wave of feminism in India was crucial in laying the foundation for women's rights and gender equality. The movement paved the way for subsequent waves of feminism, and its legacy continues to inspire feminist movements in India and beyond.

The second wave of feminism in India, influenced by the global feminist movement of the 1970s, focused on issues such as violence against women, reproductive rights, and economic empowerment, with leaders such as Urvashi Butalia and Kamla Bhasin (Nair, 2008). During the second wave of feminism in India, feminists challenged the societal norms that placed restrictions on women's autonomy and agency. They advocated for greater reproductive rights, including access to safe and legal abortion, as well as for better healthcare and education for women (Pande, 2018). Additionally, they fought for economic empowerment for women, recognising that economic dependence was a significant barrier to gender equality (Patel & Khajuria, 2016).

The third-wave feminists in India have focused on a range of issues, including gender-based violence, sexual harassment, workplace discrimination, reproductive rights, and LGBTQ+

rights (Thakur, 2012). They have also pushed for greater representation of women in politics and media and advocated for changes to cultural attitudes that perpetuate gender inequality. One notable example of third-wave feminism in India is the "Pinjra Tod" (Break the Cage) movement, which began in 2015 as a student-led campaign to challenge restrictions on women's mobility and autonomy on college campuses. The movement has since grown into a larger feminist collective that addresses a range of issues, including gender-based violence, sexual harassment, and police brutality against women (Lepcha, 2019).

Contemporary feminist mobilisation in India, known as the fourth-wave feminism, a relatively recent phenomenon and is still evolving, focuses on various issues, including sexuality, caste discrimination, environmental degradation, selective abortion, and women's health (Kurian, 2018). It is characterised by the use of social media and technology to amplify feminist voices, challenge gender norms, and demand social justice for all genders, races, and sexual orientations (Peroni, 2020). In India, fourth-wave feminism has gained momentum in recent years, particularly in response to incidents of gender-based violence and discrimination. One of the key issues that fourth-wave feminists in India have been addressing is the pervasive culture of rape and sexual violence against women (John, 2020). The movement has called for changes to legal and social structures that perpetuate gender inequality, including reforms to rape laws and the criminal justice system. Social media has been an important tool for fourth-wave feminists in India to connect with each other and amplify their message. Hashtags such as #MeToo and #NotAllMen have been used to share personal stories of sexual harassment and violence, challenge gender stereotypes, and demand accountability from those in positions of power.

The emergence of social media feminism in India

Over the past decade, the emergence of new media platforms has played a significant role in shaping contemporary feminist activism in India (Jain, 2020). This has led to a new kind of conversation on issues related to women's rights, challenging traditional patriarchal norms in India (Loiseau & Nowacka, 2015). Feminist social media movements such as "Slut Walk" and "Bekhauf Azadi" (freedom without fear) have been influential in raising awareness about the impact of sexual violence and harassment on women in India. These movements have sparked discussions and debates about the need to challenge patriarchal norms and practices that perpetuate gender-based violence in Indian society. The Slut Walk movement, which originated in Canada, has resonated with Indian women who have also faced victim-blaming and slut-shaming after experiencing sexual assault. The movement has inspired Indian women to speak out against sexual violence and harassment and to demand justice and accountability from the authorities (Reger, 2015; Davis, 2018). Similarly, the Bekhauf Azadi (freedom without fear) campaign has empowered women to break the culture of silence and fear surrounding sexual violence in India (Baxi, 2016). By using social media platforms, these feminist movements have been successful in creating a community of women who support and advocate for each other's rights. The impact of these movements can be seen in Indian film, media, and print industries, which have started to reflect a more nuanced and inclusive portrayal of women's experiences and struggles. These movements have created awareness of the challenges faced by women in India, challenged the status quo, and connected women across different parts of the world (Powell, 2018).

Social media feminism or the fourth wave of feminism has led to a new kind of activism in India well before the recent feminist resurgence in the US (Munro, 2013).

The #WhyLoiter movements are examples of social media movements led by women in India, which challenged restrictions on women's mobility and violence against them in public spaces. The #PinjraTod movement began in 2015, in response to the imposition of discriminatory hostel rules on women students in Delhi University. The name "PinjraTod" means "break the cage" in Hindi, and the movement seeks to challenge restrictions on women's mobility and autonomy. The movement has since expanded to address a range of issues related to women's safety and freedom, including sexual harassment and violence, and discrimination in educational and workplace settings (Lepcha, 2019). The #Why Loiter movement was founded in 2011, by a group of women in Mumbai who wanted to challenge the notion that public spaces are inherently unsafe for women. The movement encourages women to reclaim public spaces by simply "loitering" – spending time in public spaces without a specific purpose – and challenges the idea that women should only be in public spaces for certain acceptable reasons. The movement has since spread to other cities in India and has inspired similar movements around the world. Both movements use social media and online activism to raise awareness about issues affecting women, and to mobilise support for their causes. They have been instrumental in changing public attitudes towards gender-based violence and discrimination and have helped to create a more inclusive and empowering public discourse around issues of gender and sexuality in India (Phadke, Ranade & Khan, 2009).

The #pinjratod and #whyloiter movements are powerful examples of the ways in which social media can be used to promote social change and challenge societal norms and expectations that perpetuate gender inequality and discrimination. They serve as a reminder of the power of collective action and the importance of using social media and other tools to promote social change and fight for gender equality. These movements amplified the voices of marginalised communities, including Dalit women and LGBTQ+ individuals, and helped to shift the narrative around sexual violence, challenging victim-blaming attitudes and highlighting the systemic nature of the issue.

The social media campaigns mentioned, including #pinjratod and #whyloiter, represent a new wave of feminist activism in India that leverages technology and social media platforms to challenge gender-based violence and discrimination (Kumar, 2020). These campaigns provide a platform for marginalised communities, including Dalit women and LGBTQ+ individuals, to have their voices heard and to challenge the societal norms that perpetuate gender inequality (Srinivasan, 2019). By sharing personal experiences and stories, these movements help to shift the narrative around sexual violence and harassment, challenging victim-blaming attitudes and highlighting the systemic nature of the issue (Vijayan, 2018). Social media is used as a tool for organising and mobilising support for their causes and has been instrumental in changing public attitudes towards gender-based violence and discrimination, creating a more inclusive and empowering public discourse around issues of gender and sexuality in India.

The Delhi Rape case of 2012 was also a pivotal moment in raising awareness about sexual violence and harassment against women in India (Maity, 2022). The brutal gang-rape and murder of a young woman on a bus shocked the nation and triggered nationwide protests, highlighting the pervasive issue of gender-based violence in Indian society. This case not only led to changes in laws but also sparked public discussions about the need for continued efforts to address the root causes of such violence. Social media played a significant role in organising protests, sharing information about support services for survivors, and holding public figures and institutions accountable for their role in perpetuating gender inequality (Belair-Gagnon, Mishra, & Agur, 2014).

The #MeToo movement in India

At the end of 2017, the Indian feminist community was captivated by an unexpected and intense controversy that arose in the wake of the global #MeToo movement, which brought longstanding generational conflicts to the forefront. Raya Sarkar, an Indian graduate student at the University of California, Davis, published a list of sexual predators in Indian academia on Facebook. The cautionary list initially contained 60 prominent male academics located in leading Indian institutions as well as in North America (Roy, 2018). The list provided no context, details, incidents, or explanation of the alleged crimes. The creation of this digital archive exploded the public secret of sexual harassment in the academy.

The #MeToo movement in India can be considered as significant part of the fourth-wave feminist movement, which has been using social media to raise awareness and bring attention to the pervasive culture of sexual harassment and violence against women in India. The movement gained momentum in India in 2018 when multiple women accused prominent figures from various industries, including media, entertainment, and politics, of sexual harassment and abuse. The #MeToo movement has been a powerful force for change in India, shedding light on the issue of sexual harassment and assault and empowering women to speak out against abuse (Dey & Mendes, 2022). The movement began in 2006 when American activist Tarana Burke started using the phrase "Me Too" to raise awareness about sexual violence and abuse.

What sets #MeToo apart from previous movements is its widespread use of social media to amplify the voices of survivors and provide a platform for them to share their stories. It also challenged the notion that sexual harassment and assault are rare occurrences or the fault of individual perpetrators, highlighting the systemic nature of the problem and the need for broader societal change. The movement has inspired similar movements around the world and has been instrumental in shifting public attitudes towards gender-based violence and discrimination (Cho & Boyle, 2019; Kilby, 2020; Jane & Fraley, 2021).

Social media played a crucial role in the #MeToo India Movement by providing a platform for women to speak out about their experiences and share their stories with a wider audience. The movement also brought attention to the power dynamics at play in industries where harassment is rampant, where women often face retaliation and blacklisting for speaking out against powerful men. Social media served as a tool for survivors to break their silence, share their stories, and hold those in power accountable for their actions. The movement raised awareness about the prevalence of sexual harassment in India and highlighted the urgent need for stronger laws and policies to protect women from such abuse (Austin, Wong & Owens, 2022).

The impact of the #MeToo movement in India has been significant, with several high-profile individuals resigning from their positions after being accused of sexual misconduct. The movement has sparked a nationwide conversation about sexual harassment and assault, providing a platform for women to speak out about their experiences (Carlsen et al., 2018). It has also led to some positive changes, such as the implementation of workplace harassment policies.

Despite the long history of feminist mobilisation in India, the #MeToo movement has brought renewed attention to the issue of gender-based violence and discrimination (Braileanu et al., 2021). The movement has demonstrated the power of collective action and solidarity in effecting change and represents a significant moment in the on-going struggle for gender equality and justice in India. While there is still much work to be done, the #MeToo movement has provided a platform for women to speak out against abuse and demand accountability and change (Maier, 2023). Through continued collective action and advocacy, it is possible to create a safer and more equal society for all.

Critiques on the #MeToo movement in India

The #MeToo movement has sparked important conversations about feminism in India, highlighting the diverse perspectives and experiences of women in the country. One of the key debates within the movement has been the role of legal redress and due process versus extrajudicial interventions (Gash & Harding, 2018). Some feminist voices argue that legal channels are the most effective means to achieve gender justice, as they provide a framework for holding perpetrators accountable and ensuring that victims receive justice (Fielding-Miller et al., 2020). However, others point out that the legal system in India has significant limitations, including lengthy delays, high costs, and a lack of sensitivity to the needs of survivors (Neuman, 2013). This has led some to advocate for extrajudicial interventions, such as social media campaigns and boycotts, as a means of exposing perpetrators and holding them accountable. Another important issue raised by the #MeToo movement is the need for a more intersectional approach to feminism in India. Many critics have pointed out that the movement has been dominated by the voices of middle-class and metropolitan women, including journalists, actors, and other professionals, who may not be representative of the experiences of all Indian women. They argue that a truly intersectional approach to feminism would address the multiple vulnerabilities faced by most Indian women, including those from lower socio-economic backgrounds, marginalised communities, and rural areas (Roy, 2018; Nanditha, 2022).

While the movement has been successful in raising awareness about the prevalence of sexual harassment and assault, many have argued that it failed to address the structural inequalities that underpin such violence (Prothero & Tadajewski, 2021). This has led to concerns that the movement is promoting an individualistic form of feminism that is disconnected from the larger social and political context in which sexual violence occurs.

In the Indian context, taking #MeToo as individualist feminism is indeed an irrational idea. Women's experiences of sexual violence are deeply entwined with the larger structures of Patriarchy, caste, class, and religion that shape social relations in the country. Addressing these structural inequalities requires a collective approach that goes beyond individual acts of resistance or personal narratives of trauma. Moreover, the transnational and global nature of the #MeToo movement raises questions about its relevance in the Indian context. While the movement has inspired women to speak out about their experiences of sexual violence, it is important to acknowledge the unique cultural, social, and political factors that shape gender relations in India. This requires a commitment to amplifying the voices and experiences of women from diverse backgrounds and building coalitions that can challenge the structural inequalities that underpin sexual violence. Only then can one hope to create a more just and equitable society for all women in India.

There has been a growing critique of what some have termed "new feminisms" in India, which are perceived to reflect and embody the consumer-oriented, individualistic, and entrepreneurial values of metropolitan middle-class Indian women (Roy, 2018). This form of feminism has been referred to as "neo-liberal feminism" and has been criticised for its limited scope and exclusivity. The movement's emphasis on individual empowerment and self-expression is seen as reflective of a broader cultural shift towards neoliberalism, which prioritises the individual over the collective and the market over the state. In addition, there have been accusations of elitism and Westernisation levelled against these new feminisms. Critics argue that the focus on individual empowerment and self-expression reflects a Western model of feminism that may not be relevant to the Indian context. Moreover, the emphasis on consumerism and entrepreneurship is seen as reflecting a neoliberal ideology that is out of step with the needs and aspirations of most Indian women (Chakraborty, 2018).

The #MeToo movement in India also has been criticised for its limited reach and exclusivity. Furthermore, the feminist movement in India has been criticised for being limited to English-speaking individuals, which excludes those who do not have access to social media or who primarily communicate in regional languages. This has been a challenge for earlier activism as well. As a result, there is a need for the movement to become more inclusive and intersectional, and to reach out to women from diverse linguistic and cultural backgrounds (Bajoria, 2020; Chakraborty, 2021a, 2021b).

The failure of feminists to respond in a unified voice to sexual violence can have significant consequences, both in terms of the movement's effectiveness and its vulnerability to external pressures. When feminists are divided in their response to sexual violence, they become vulnerable to heightened opposition from patriarchal forces, which may seek to undermine their efforts or discredit their message. Patriarchal forces may use these divisions to delegitimise the movement or to argue that the problem of sexual violence is exaggerated or not as pervasive as feminists claim. Moreover, the failure of feminists to speak with a unified voice can also make the movement vulnerable to being co-opted by external actors, such as the state, the market, neo-liberal capitalism, and right-wing nationalisms. These actors may seek to instrumentalise feminist demands for their own purposes, such as by promoting a market-oriented form of feminism that emphasises individual empowerment and consumerism, rather than collective action and structural change. This co-optation can undermine the feminist movement's ability to achieve its goals and may lead to a watering down of its demands. It may also make it more difficult for feminists to build alliances with other social movements and to challenge the broader forces of Patriarchy and capitalism that shape gender relations in society.

Leveraging deliberative democracy and collective action

Deliberative democracy is an approach to decision-making that values open and inclusive dialogue and debate (Fishkin, 2011). By prioritising a diverse range of perspectives and experiences, this democratic process allows for a more comprehensive and nuanced understanding of complex issues (Deveaux, 2018). In the context of the #MeToo movement in India, deliberative democracy can be a powerful tool for addressing the criticisms and challenges that have been raised. One of the key criticisms of the #MeToo movement in India is that it has lacked clear leadership and direction, which has made it difficult to translate the momentum of the movement into concrete policy changes or legal reforms. Deliberative democracy can help to address this challenge by providing a structured framework for engaging in dialogue and decision-making. Through inclusive and informed discussions, the movement can work towards identifying and prioritising specific policy changes and legal reforms that will have a meaningful impact on survivors of sexual violence and harassment. Additionally, the #MeToo movement has highlighted the need for a more comprehensive and nuanced understanding of the social and cultural factors that contribute to sexual violence and harassment in India. Deliberative democracy can provide a platform for survivors of sexual violence and harassment to share their experiences and for diverse voices to be heard.

By providing a platform for survivors of these crimes to share their experiences and for diverse voices to be heard, this includes engaging with a wide range of stakeholders, including survivors, activists, policymakers, law enforcement officials, and members of the broader community. By creating a safe and open space for discussion, deliberative democracy can help build greater trust and understanding between these stakeholders, enabling them to work together more effectively towards a common goal. This can involve developing new policies and strategies to prevent and respond to sexual violence and harassment, as well as advocating for greater awareness and education around these issues.

While deliberative democracy is an important tool in the fight against sexual violence and harassment, it is important to recognise that it may not be sufficient on its own to address all the challenges and concerns raised by the #MeToo movement in India. Other strategies and approaches, such as legal reforms, policy changes, and collective action, may also be necessary to create meaningful and lasting change. For example, legal reforms and policy changes may be necessary to ensure that survivors of sexual violence and harassment have access to justice, support, and resources. This could include measures such as strengthening laws against sexual violence and harassment, providing greater support for survivors through the legal process, and improving access to healthcare and counselling services. It is also important to ensure that woman's collectives and intersectional feminist movements are at the forefront of the fight against sexual violence in India, amplifying the voices and experiences of women from diverse backgrounds and building coalitions that can challenge the structural inequalities that underpin sexual violence. Only then can we hope to create a more just and equitable society for all women in India.

Collective action is also an important strategy for creating change. This could include organising protests, boycotts, and other forms of direct action to demand accountability from those responsible for perpetrating sexual violence and harassment, as well as from those in positions of power who have failed to take action.

Research has shown that collective action can be a powerful tool in bringing about social and political change (Stekelenburg & Klandermans, 2013). Collective action can help raise awareness about the prevalence and impact of sexual violence and harassment and can create pressure on individuals and institutions to take action (Thomas, 1990). Through collective action, survivors of sexual violence and harassment can also find strength and support in the solidarity of others who have experienced similar forms of harm (Garcia-Moreno et al., 2006).

The use of collective action has been a key strategy in the #MeToo movement, both globally and in India. In India, activists have organised protests and demonstrations to demand justice for survivors and to call for systemic changes to prevent sexual violence (Sharma, 2020). These actions have helped raise awareness about the prevalence of sexual violence and harassment in India and have created pressure on institutions to take action. However, it is important to note that collective action is not without its challenges.

Effective collective action requires strong leadership and coordination, as well as a clear and compelling message that resonates with a diverse range of individuals and communities (McAdam & Paulsen, 1993). There may also be risks associated with participating in collective action, such as the potential for violence or repression by authorities (van Stekelenburg & Klandermans, 2022).

In order for collective action to be an effective strategy for creating change, it must be used in conjunction with other approaches, such as legal and policy reforms, and must be sustained over the long term (Garcia-Moreno et al., 2006). By combining collective action with other strategies, such as deliberative democracy and policy reforms, stakeholders can work towards creating a safer and more equitable society for all.

While the #MeToo movement has created a space for deliberative democracy to thrive in India, the movement's lack of clear leadership and direction has presented challenges. The viral nature of social media has enabled people to express their views, exchange ideas, and engage in informed debate, but it has also created a climate of online harassment and intimidation that makes it difficult to translate the momentum of the movement into concrete policy changes or legal reforms. As such, it is important to recognise that while deliberative democracy is an important part of the solution, it must be combined with other strategies and approaches to create real change. This requires clear leadership and direction, as well as a commitment to sustained and coordinated action by all stakeholders involved. By working together in this way, we can create a safer, more just, and more equitable society for all.

Conclusion

The impact of the #MeToo movement in India cannot be fully understood by viewing it solely as a global movement, as the movement in India has its own unique context and set of challenges. The movement in India is influenced by a range of factors, including the country's complex history of caste, class, and gender relations, as well as its diverse cultural and linguistic landscape. Additionally, the movement is shaped by the specific political and social conditions of India, such as the widespread use of social media and the complex relationship between the state and civil society. Furthermore, the movement is not just a singular act but rather a long-term process of building awareness, mobilising support, and advocating for change. The impact of the movement can only be fully understood by examining its various stages and the different actors involved, including survivors, activists, journalists, lawyers, and policymakers. By acknowledging the complexities of the #MeToo movement in India, one can gain a deeper understanding of the various factors that contribute to its success, as well as the challenges that must be overcome to achieve lasting change. This requires a commitment to listening to and centring the voices of marginalised communities and to addressing the broader structural inequalities that underpin sexual violence in Indian society. Only by recognising the diversity and complexity of the movement can we effectively challenge patriarchal power structures and build a more equitable and just society.

Deliberative democracy is a powerful tool in addressing the criticisms and challenges of the #MeToo movement in India. This approach values open and inclusive dialogue and debate, prioritising a diverse range of perspectives and experiences to allow for a more comprehensive and nuanced understanding of complex issues (Deveaux, 2018). Deliberative democracy can help address the movement's lack of clear leadership and direction by providing a structured framework for engaging in dialogue and decision-making (Warren, 2008). It can also provide a platform for survivors of sexual violence and harassment to share their experiences and for diverse voices to be heard, promoting a more nuanced understanding of the social and cultural factors that contribute to the prevalence of these crimes (Mansbridge, 2014). By engaging with a wide range of stakeholders, including survivors, activists, policymakers, law enforcement officials, and members of the broader community, deliberative democracy can help build greater trust and understanding between these groups, enabling them to work together more effectively towards a common goal (Salmon, 2001). While it may not be sufficient on its own to address all the challenges and concerns raised by the movement, deliberative democracy can be combined with other strategies and approaches, such as legal reforms, policy changes, and collective action, to create meaningful and lasting change. Clear leadership and direction, as well as sustained and coordinated action by all stakeholders involved, are necessary to create a safer, more just, and more equitable society for all.

References

Ahmed-Ghosh, H. (2012). *Women and gender in Islam: Historical roots of a modern debate*. Yale University Press.

Austin, J. T., Wong, N., & Owens, A. C. (2022). The hashtag heard around the world: Social media users' perceptions and responses to the #MeToo hashtag. *Atlantic Journal of Communication*, 1–15. https://doi.org/10.1080/15456870.2022.2083136

Belair-Gagnon, V., Mishra, S., & Agur, C. (2023) Reconstructuring the Indian public sphere: News-work and the social media in the Delhi G Rape. *Journalism, Theory, Practice, Criticism*, 1–17

Bajoria, J. (2020). *No #MeToo for women like us*. Human Rights Watch.

Baxi, P. (2016). Impractical topics, practical fields: Notes on researching sexual violence in India. *Economic and Political Weekly, 51*(18), 80–88. Retrieved from http://www.jstor.org/stable/44004239

Bhatia, R. (2022). 'Feminism in the virtual space: The Indian context. *Vantage: Journal of Thematic Analysis, 32*–45. https://doi.org/10.52253/vjta.2022.v03i02.04

Braileanu, M., Edney, E., Azar, S., Lazarow, F., Mogensen, M. A., Tuburan, S., Kadom, N., & Phalke, V. (2021). Radiology, sexual harassment, and the #MeToo movement. *Academic Radiology, 28*(4), 564–571. https://doi.org/10.1016/j.acra.2020.04.036

Carlsen, A., Salam, M., Miller, C. C., Lu, D., Ngu, A., Patel, J. K., & Wichter, Z. (2018, October 23). #MeToo brought down 201 powerful men. Nearly half of their replacements are women. *The New York Times*. Retrieved from https://www.nytimes.com/interactive/2018/10/23/us/metoo-replacements.html

Chakraborty, R. (2018). 'Lean in' and its limits: Rethinking corporate feminism and the possibilities of resistance. *Work & Organization, 25*(5), 514–528.

Chakraborty, D. (2021a). *Feminism in India: A short introduction*. Oxford University Press.

Chakraborty, R. (2021b). Online feminism in India: Challenges and opportunities. *International Journal of Humanities and Social Science Research, 9*(1), 1–6.

Chakravarti, U. (1993). Conceptualising Brahmanical patriarchy in early India: Gender, caste, class and state. *Economic and Political Weekly, 28*(14/15), WS19–WS33.

Cho, H., & Boyle, M. P. (2019). Social media and # MeToo: Analyzing the impact of the campaign on Twitter. *Communication Studies, 70*(4), 450–466.

Cobb, B. (1975). Kamaladevi Chattopadhyaya. *Bulletin of Concerned Asian Scholars, 7*(1), 67–72. https://doi.org/10.1080/14672715.1975.10406367

Davis, K. (2018). SlutWalk. Feminism, activism and media Kaitlynn Mendes. *Feminism & Psychology, 28*(2), 300–302. https://doi.org/10.1177/0959353517701492

Deveaux, M. (2018). *Deliberative democracy and multiculturalism* (A. Bächtiger, J. S. Dryzek, J. Mansbridge, & M. Warren, Eds.). Oxford University Press.

Dey, A., & Mendes, K. (2022). 'It started with this one post': #MeToo, India and higher education. *Journal of Gender Studies, 31*(2), 204–215. https://doi.org/10.1080/09589236.2021.1907552

Fielding-Miller, R., Hatcher, A. M., Wagman, J., Swendeman, D., & Upadhyay, U. D. (2020). Gender, justice and empowerment: Creating the world we want to see. *Culture, Health & Sexuality*, 22(sup1), 1–12. https://doi.org/10.1080/13691058.2020.1736843

Fishkin, J. S. (2011). *The voice of the people: Public opinion and democracy*. Yale University Press.

Garcia-Moreno, C., Jansen, H. A. F. M., Ellsberg, M., Heise, L., & Watts, C. H. (2006). Prevalence of intimate partner violence: Findings from the WHO multi-country study on women's health and domestic violence. *Lancet*, 368(9543), 1260–1269. https://doi.org/10.1016/S0140-6736(06)69523-8

Gash, A., & Harding, R. (2018). #MeToo? Legal discourse and everyday responses to sexual violence. *Laws*, 7(2), 21. https://doi.org/10.3390/laws7020021

Haber, H. F. (1994). *Beyond postmodern politics: Lyotard, Rorty, Foucault*. Routledge.

Jain, S. (2020). The rising fourth wave: Feminist activism and digital platforms in India. *ORF Issue Brief No. 384*, Observer Research Foundation. Retrieved February 25, 2023, from https://www.orfonline.org/research/the-rising-fourth-wave-feminist-activism-on-digital-platforms-in-india

Jane, E. A., & Fraley, R. C. (2021). #MeToo and the politics of social media: A feminist analysis. *Feminist Media Studies*, 21(3), 438–442.

John, M. E. (2020). Feminism, sexual violence and the times of #MeToo in India. *Asian Journal of Women's Studies*, 26(2), 137–158. https://doi.org/10.1080/12259276.2020.1748259

Kilby, S. J. (2020). The #MeToo movement and its implications for feminist activism in the digital age. *Communication, Culture & Critique*, 13(4), 515–532.

Krishnan, A. (2018). The Dalit women's movement in India. *Women's Studies International Forum*, 71, 96–104.

Kumar, A. (2020). #MeToo in India: A turning point? *Journal of Gender Studies*, 29(2), 113–123.

Kurian, A. (2018, May 22). #MeToo campaign brings the rise of 'fourth-wave' feminism in India. *The Wire*. Retrieved from https://thewire.in/gender/metoo-campaign-brings-the-rise-of-fourth-wave-feminism-in-India

Kurian, A. (2021). *Theoretical imaginings on the fourth wave feminism in India*. Washington.edu. Retrieved February 27, 2023, from https://jsis.washington.edu/southasia/wp-content/uploads/sites/12/2021/10/DecolonizingTheBody_AlkaKurian.pdf

Lepcha, N. (2019). A cage broken: 'Pinjra Tod', a movement in progress. *International Journal of Research in Social Sciences*, 9(5), 604–610. Retrieved from https://www.indianjournals.com/ijor.aspx?target=ijor:ijrss&volume=9&issue=5&article=041

Loiseau, E., & Nowacka, K. (2015). *Can social media effectively include women's voices in decision-making processes?* Oecd.org. Retrieved February 27, 2023, from https://www.oecd.org/dev/development-gender/DEV_socialmedia-issuespaper-March2015.pdf

Maier, S. L. (2023). Rape victim advocates' perceptions of the #MeToo movement: Opportunities, challenges, and sustainability. *Journal of Interpersonal Violence*, 38(1–2), NP336–NP365. https://doi.org/10.1177/08862605221081929

Maity, A. (2022). Media representations of the 2012 Delhi gang rape. *Media Asia*, 1–6. https://doi.org/10.1080/01296612.2022.2148915

Mansbridge, J. J. (2014). A systemic approach to deliberative democracy. In J. Parkinson & J. Mansbridge (Eds.), *Deliberative systems: Deliberative democracy at the large scale* (pp. 1–26). Cambridge University Press.

McAdam, D., & Paulsen, R. (1993). Specifying the relationship between social ties and activism. *American Journal of Sociology*, 99(3), 640–667. https://doi.org/10.1086/230319

Mohanty, H. (2022, March 30). *Maniben Amin: The gentle yet fierce educator and freedom fighter*. Feminism in India. Retrieved from https://feminisminindia.com/2022/03/31/maniben-amin-vibhuti-patel-educator-and-freedom-fighter-128774/

Munro, E. (2013). Feminism: A fourth wave? *Political Insight*, 4(2), 22–25. https://doi.org/10.1111/2041-9066.12021

Nair, J. (2008). The troubled relationship of feminism and history. *Economic and Political Weekly*, 43(43), 57–65. Retrieved from http://www.jstor.org/stable/40278103

Nanditha, N. (2022). Exclusion in #MeToo India: Rethinking inclusivity and intersectionality in Indian digital feminist movements. *Feminist Media Studies*, 22(7), 1673–1694. https://doi.org/10.1080/14680777.2021.1913432

Neuman, S. (2013). *The issue of sexual violence against women in contemporary India*. Linnaeu University. Retrieved from https://www.divaportal.org/smash/get/diva2:634833/FULLTEXT01.pdf

Pande, R. (2018). The history of feminism and doing gender in India. *Estudos Feministas, 26*(3). https://doi.org/10.1590/1806-9584-2018v26n358567

Pandey, R. (2019). Locating Savitribai Phule's feminism in the trajectory of global feminist thought. *The Indian Historical Review, 46*(1), 86–105. https://doi.org/10.1177/0376983619856480

Pandey, R. (2022). Two distant feminist standpoints in nineteenth-century India: Case studies of Savitribai Phule and Pandita Ramabai. *The Indian Historical Review, 49*(1_suppl), S96–S119. https://doi.org/10.1177/03769836221105796

Patel, V., & Khajuria, R. (2016). *Political feminism in India an analysis of actors, debates and strategies*. Fes.de. Retrieved March 1, 2023, from https://library.fes.de/pdf-files/bueros/indien/12706.pdf

Peroni, C. (2020). Introduction. The fourth wave of feminism: From social networking and self-determination to sisterhood. *Oñati Socio-Legal Series, 10*(1S), 1S–9S. https://doi.org/10.35295/osls.iisl/0000-0000-0000-1160

Phadke, H., Ranade, S., & Khan, S. (2009). Why loiter? Radical possibilities for gendered dissent. In *Dissent and cultural resistance in Asia's cities*. Routledge.

Powell, C. (2018, June 18). *How social media has reshaped feminism*. Council on Foreign Relations. Retrieved from https://www.cfr.org/blog/how-social-media-has-reshaped-feminism

Prothero, A., & Tadajewski, M. (2021). #MeToo and beyond: Inequality and injustice in marketing practice and academia. *Journal of Marketing Management, 37*(1–2), 1–20. https://doi.org/10.1080/0267257x.2021.1889140

Rajgopal, S. S. (2022). "Fiery sparks of change": A comparison between first wave feminists of India and the U.S. *Journal of International Women's Studies, 24*(2), 3. Retrieved from https://vc.bridgew.edu/jiws/vol24/iss2/3/

Ray, R. (2018). Feminist movements in India: A brief overview. *Social Change, 48*(4), 571–586.

Reger, J. (2015). The story of a slut walk: Sexuality, race, and generational divisions in contemporary feminist activism. *Journal of Contemporary Ethnography, 44*(1), 84–112. https://doi.org/10.1177/0891241614526434

Roy, S (2018). #MeToo is a crucial moment to revisit the history of Indian feminism. *Economic and Political Weekly, 53*(42). Retrieved from https://www.epw.in/engage/article/metoo-crucial-moment-revisit-history-indian-feminism

Salmon, P. (2001). Effects of physical exercise on anxiety, depression, and sensitivity to stress: A unifying theory. *Clinical Psychology Review, 21*(1), 33–61. https://doi.org/10.1016/s0272-7358(99)00032-x

Sharma, I. (2015). Violence against women: Where are the solutions? *Indian Journal of Psychiatry, 57*(2), 131–139. https://doi.org/10.4103/0019-5545.158133

Sharma, K. (2020, December 28). Protests in India against rape and violence against women. *BBC News*. Retrieved from https://www.bbc.com/news/world-asia-india-55451007

Srinivasan, A. (2019). India's transgender community fights back against discrimination. Retrieved from https://www.aljazeera.com/news/2019/3/30/indias-transgender-community-fights-back-against-discrimination

Suk, J., Abhishek, A., Zhang, Y., Ahn, S. Y., Correa, T., Garlough, C., & Shah, D. V. (2021). #MeToo, networked acknowledgment, and connective action: How "empowerment through empathy" launched a social movement. *Social Science Computer Review, 39*(2), 276–294. https://doi.org/10.1177/0894439319864882

Tahan, L. (2021). *#MeToo movement: A sociological analysis of media representations*. Retrieved from https://digitalcommons.ric.edu/cgi/viewcontent.cgi?article=1342&context=etd

Tella, K. K. (2018). #MeToo: An international conversation on sexual violence impacting feminist discourse across borders. *Economic and Political Weekly, 53*(43), https://www.epw.in/engage/article/metoo-international-conversation-sexual-violence-feminist-discourse-impact

Thakur, D. N. (2012). Feminism and women movement in India. *Research Journal of Humanities and Social Sciences, 3*(4), 458–464. Retrieved from https://rjhssonline.com/HTMLPaper.aspx?Journal=Research%20Journal%20of%20Humanities%20and%20Social%20Sciences;PID=2012-3-4-8

Thomas, R. R. (1990). From affirmative action to affirming diversity. *Harvard Business Review*, 68(2), 107–117.

van Stekelenburg, J., & Klandermans, B. (2022). Individuals in movements. In D. A. Snow, D. della Porta, D. McAdam, & B. Klandermans (Eds.), *The Wiley Blackwell encyclopedia of social and political movements* (2nd ed., pp. 687–695). Wiley-Blackwell.

Vijayan, R. (2018). Section 377 and LGBTQ+ rights in India: A long road to equality. Retrieved from https://www.amnesty.org/en/latest/news/2018/09/section-377-and-lgbtq-rights-in-india-a-long-road-to-equality/

Warren, M. E. (2008). Deliberative democracy and climate change: Insights from theory and practice. In S. J. Dryzek, R. B. Norgaard, & D. Schlosberg (Eds.), *The Oxford handbook of climate change and society* (pp. 297–311). Oxford University Press.

45
"WE CAN'T JUST SIT BACK AND SAY IT'S TOO HARD"

Older women, social justice, and activism

Tina Kostecki

Introduction

The concerns, perspectives, and lives of older women are often marginalised or invisibilised because of deep age discrimination normatively embedded in our psyche and materially in our social contexts. Social justice activism tends to be viewed as a public activity which is often associated with younger generations (Sawchuk, 2009). Older women's activism across a range of contexts can be seen in contradistinction to stereotypes of ageing women as frail, weak, objects of ridicule, fear and pity, dependant, and detached (Chazan & Kittmer, 2016; Gullette, 1997, 2004) as well as the 'decline ideology' (Gullette, 2011, p. 6).

This chapter draws upon feminist gerontology to frame and argue that activism among older women can exist in everyday actions and is clearly apparent in older women's involvement with significant political and social movements (Chazan et al., 2018). The title of this chapter quotes a woman who participated in my own study where all participants were over the age of 57 years (Kostecki, 2015). I argue that her activism mirrors quieter unacknowledged social justice activities such as the "…work of educating, organizing, advocating, creating, mentoring and record-keeping…" (Chazan et al., 2018, p. 7) and constitutes a subversion of the compounded silences in relation to stigmatised experiences such as, for instance in this example, sexual abuse (Kostecki, 2015). Importantly, social justice participation by ageing women is instructive for social work as an opportunity to inform critical theory practices and program delivery.

Feminist gerontology: theorising older women's lives

Critical gerontology informed by feminism has guided my research practice for many years assisting to understand the complexity of the age and gender matrix, including the intersections of race, sexuality, and diverse abilities (Chazan, 2020; Kafer, 2013; Sandberg & Marshall, 2017), as well as anti-ageist approaches in social work practice (Chonody & Treater, 2016; Hafford-Letchfield, 2022; Kostecki, 2016). The many expressions of feminism combine to understand the diverse lives of older women by providing the analytical tools to explore patterns of advantage/disadvantage, the gendered nature of power and provide a strong direction for social justice endeavours by actively redressing systemic inequality. Assumptions which are central to a feminist methodology and analysis are "... the existence of structural oppression of women by patriarchal systems and gendered social patterns" (Lauve-Moon et al., 2020, pp. 318–319). Moreover, deepened understandings of context-dependant commonalities and differences are accomplished via theories of intersectionality where "...the understanding that the intersection of two or more social positionalities produces a distinctly different social positionality and experience of oppression" (Lauve-Moon et al., 2020, p. 320). Validating and valuing the diverse lived experiences of older women aligned to the feminist goals of social justice, women's community building, and empowerment (Black, 2017) is a powerful motivation for me as a feminist researcher in social work.

Feminism and critical gerontology share a common concern with the intersection between gender and age and theorise the impact of the gender/age intersection, including issues of oppression (Laws, 1995), the gendered nature of social, political and economic contexts of ageing (Calasanti & Slevin, 2001, 2006; Estes, 2001, 2006), cultural constructions and narratives of ageing (Gullette, 2004), the gendered ageing body (Twigg, 2004), the nexus between feminism and critical age studies (Marshall, 2006), and empowerment perspectives (Garner, 1999a, 1999b). A gender analysis of ageing reveals how power relations are institutionalised, expressed, and govern the daily lives of older women.

Feminist gerontology continues to evolve and respond to the crucial need for inclusive practices. For example, queer and crip studies (Kafer, 2013; Sandberg & Marshall, 2017) provide lenses to deepen an intersectional understanding of the diversity in the lives of older women as well as contesting colonial normativity (Chazan, 2020). Understanding older women's multiple and dynamic identities across a range of social contexts alongside cumulative disadvantage (Kostecki & Macfarlane, 2019) requires intersectional analyses of oppression and privilege axes, including the influence of gender, race, religion, sexuality, dis/ability, class, and ethnicity in shaping and constructing late life experiences. For example, Chazan et al. (2018, p. 7) submit that "... settler Colonialism needs to be contested as it continues to influence the legitimacy given to different ways of knowing, and doing aging, gender, and social change". Furthermore, by engaging with the complex experiences and life expressions of older women, feminist gerontology supports liberational social change, a core ethic, and commitment in the social work profession (AASW, 2020).

Older women, agency, and activism

Gender is a political space (Connell, 2003) and so I would argue, is age. The influence of age discourse, socially and culturally on identity, bears upon many aspects of our sense of 'self' (Gullette, 1997, 2004, 2011). Moreover, the experience of ageing is gendered (Chambers, 2004) with late life precarity aligned to inequalities arising from social and structural barriers such as gender, race, and class across a range of life experiences such as health, employment, and immigration status (Grenier et al., 2020). Women in later life are more likely than older men to experience poverty and income inequality (AGWGEA, 2015), living alone (Chambers, 2004), insecure housing and homelessness (Osborne-Crowley, 2015), make greater use of health and social services, and live longer than men with chronic morbidity or disability (Kalache et al., 2005). In terms of agency, the intersection of age and gender is notably coined as a 'double jeopardy' for women (Krekula, 2007).

Considering this context, the perspectives of older women, including their experiences of personal and systemic violence, and especially their acts of activism, are often absent, marginalised, or hidden, and we need to hear those stories. Privileging diverse voices of older women is a political act which challenges,

> ... taken-for-granted hegemonies to show how subjugated lives are edited, experience is shaped, and social interaction is constrained.
>
> *(Warner, 2009, p. 71)*

Activism tends to be conceived of as a public activity. In truth, it can be infinitely expressed, publicly and privately, collectively, or not, and as an everyday undertaking. Emerging as a key theme and consideration in my earlier research (Kostecki, 2015), I argue that activism can exist in the 'territories of the everyday' (Rose, 1999, p. 280) and notwithstanding that many older women are certainly public resisters, rebels, and activists, they are also involved in unseen, hidden insurrections, and quiet revolutions against considerable forces in their daily lives. Their stories of activism are powerful and are productive deeds of activism. Extending the sense of what constitutes 'activism' represents recognition of diverse social justice actions and "...the inclusion of different knowledges and expressions of knowledge possible" (Chazan et al., 2018, p. 9).

Older women's activism tends to be underestimated, poorly researched, and often equated with younger women (McHugh, 2012; Sawchuk, 2009). Yet Charpentier et al. (2008), in analysing the motivations for social justice involvement with a group of older women in Quebec (average age 70), found that for women of this generation, activism and 'participative citizenship' have been prominent features of their collective social history. As younger women, these women were engaged with several key social change movements, especially those related to gender justice and equality, including the Women's Liberation movement. Despite changes in their activist collaborations, "the values that these women champion have remained the same" (Charpentier et al., 2008, p. 355).

Significantly, for older women in our current Western milieu, the social and cultural contexts in which they have aged are often characterised by ongoing carer responsibilities such as for elderly parents, adult children who have experienced rising rates of divorce and separation and grandchildren, and accordingly, have been described as the 'sandwich generation' (Charpentier et al., 2008, p. 355). So, alongside their ongoing social justice involvements and awareness of gender inequality, they have continued to sustain social justice commitments and "take care of their grandchildren in order to allow their own daughters to become liberated..." (Charpentier et al., 2008, p. 355).

Patently the history of older women engaging in social justice activism is formidable and often their achievements have been the lodestar for subsequent efforts. Globally, older women from Indigenous communities have occupied places of protest in every epoch of forced colonisation. In Australia, women from Aboriginal and Torres Strait Islander communities have sought and fought for justice, continuing to speak up to issues of discrimination, racism, civil rights, land rights and land theft, Native Title, forced removal of children, exploitation in the workforce, intergenerational trauma, and social and emotional wellbeing concerns (Dudgeon & Bray, 2016).

Well-known American activist Maggie Kuhn, after facing imposed and involuntary retirement at the age of 65 in 1970, co-founded the renowned *Grey Panthers* and was convenor from 1972 to 1995. Inspired by Marx, Weber, and Comte (Estes & Portacolone,

2009, p. 16) during her time studying sociology, she embarked on 24 years of activism which not only sought to address structural ageism but poverty, racism, nuclear disarmament and peace, sexism, inequitable health care access, retirement policy, government spending priorities, and unfair tax regimes favouring the rich (Sorrel & Kolenc, 1982, p. 5). She also formed coalitions with young people believing that "...the fates of young and old were inextricably linked..." (Estes & Portacolone, 2009, p. 16).

In another example, the Older Women's League in San Francisco as well as other chapters nationally are not for profit, non-partisan, and committed to responding to issues of concern for older women such as health care, quality of life, housing, transport, aging in place, care giving, and financial (in)security and represent an example of collective agency. A commitment to addressing issues for women in later life informs four key priorities being,

> 1) health care (e.g., universal health care, research on conditions that affect women over 50), 2) economic security (e.g., workplace parity), 3) quality of life (e.g., affordable housing, women's right to control their own life and destiny), and 4) improving the image of older women.
>
> *(McHugh, 2012, p. 287)*

Likewise, other significant groups in North America include the grassroots organisation, *The Raging Grannies*, who are now "more than 100 'gaggles' of Raging Grannies worldwide" (McHugh, 2012, p. 286). Established in 1980 in Canada and the US, the Grannies are non-hierarchical and aim to debunk stereotypes and the dismissal of older women (McHugh, 2012, p. 286) engaging powerfully as social change agents (Chazan & Kittmer, 2016, pp. 297–298). Their activism incorporates action on "...environment, mining, nuclear power, militarism, clear-cut logging, poverty, corporate greed, racism, sexism, and any forms of social and economic injustice..." (Narushima, 2004, p. 24). The 'Grannie psyche' embraces, "... feminist values, creativity, rebelliousness, empathy, risk-taking, spirituality and humour" (Narushima, 2004, p. 24).

Similarly, a prominent organisation in Australia is Older Women's Network established in the early 1990s. They advocate for reform in relation to issues which affect older women (or future older women) such as discrimination, decision-making participation in public decision-making and policy, health, income security, education, and the provision and support of community-based programs which contribute to women's wellbeing. Mears (2015) provides a comprehensive discussion on the New South Wales chapter and their successful campaign, including research, to raise awareness and prevent violence against older women.

Rawsthorne et al. (2017, p. 34) describe their experience of working alongside older women in Glebe, Sydney, and *Concerned Older Women*, a local group who are, "an 'activist' group rather than a 'social group'". Their activism includes "accessibility, mobility, safety, and health and dignity related issues" (Rawsthorne et al., 2017, p. 34) at the local and national level. Challenging ageist stereotypes as reflected in their moniker (Rawsthorne et al., 2017, p. 35), invisibility and providing leadership are predominant in their social justice activities.

Given that activism among older women is poorly researched, *Aging Activists* in Canada is an online, virtual community that aims to "... investigate why and how activists of varied ages, abilities, backgrounds, and genders work for social and political change across diverse movements and across their lives, and how they tell, curate, and circulate their stories of resistance" (http://www.agingactivisms.org/). Moreover, research highlights how diverse older women through 'activist herstories' (Chazan et al., 2016, p. 23) challenge notions of "mothering or grandmothering as incompatible with political engagement or radical action" (Chazan et al., 2016, p. 3). This supports the idea that activism in later life is inextricably connected to personal experiences of discrimination, not only in later life, but over the life course and that later life activism is often a time of "new and renewed activism" (Chazan et al., 2016, p. 3).

By way of example, Chazan and Kittmer (2016) have reported on the Canadian *Grandmothers to Grandmothers* campaign, a powerful engagement with social justice that aims to work at the local, national, and international level with Sub-Saharan grandmothers in Africa who "... strive to sustain their families and communities in the wake of the HIV/AIDS pandemic" (http://grandmothersadvocacy.org/about-us). Priorities include addressing access to education, affordable medicines, and ending violence against women and girls. The reach of the *Grandmothers to Grandmothers* campaign is wide-ranging engaging some "10,000 Canadian women and an estimated three times as many women from across sub-Saharan Africa..." (Chazan & Kittmer, 2016, p. 297) and raising more than 9 million dollars (CAD). This group is one example of how agency is reconstructed and reproduced as a collective endeavour to counter ageist stereotypes but importantly demonstrate how older women are "producing themselves as political subjects at the global level... community builders, lifelong learners, social justice advocates, and key actors in the global fight against HIV/AIDS" (Chazan & Kittmer, 2016, p. 306). Most recently, a particular example of continuing activism over a lifetime is Merle Hoffman (2012) who, at 76 years of age, has reignited a decades long quest for abortion rights in the US helping to establish the organisation, 'Rise Up 4 Abortion Rights' (https://riseup4abortionrights.org/) in the context of the decision to overturn *Roe v Wade* (Coen-Sanchez et al., 2022).

Feminist gerontology and social work

Achieving social justice is a key ethical practice commitment for the social work profession and therefore appreciating the contributions of older women to social change and dismantling ageism is foundational to critical social work practice. Early crucial work by social work feminist theorists such as Browne (1998), and Garner (1999b), provided tools of analysis via the development of comprehensive social work frameworks for policy/research studies and approaches informed by feminist gerontology. Hooyman, Browne, Ray (the only non-social worker), and Richardson (2002, p. 6), motivated by the hitherto absence of age as a key consideration for gender-based concerns, developed a model which is "... critical to social reformation from a feminist gerontological framework". This approach, intended as a heuristic technique to encourage 'new thinking', included the domains of diversity, oppression, political, and structural change. The intention was to reveal the problematics of cumulative disadvantage due to gender-based role expectations, the impact of 'familism' on material life experiences for women, contesting social denigration of older women, and to spotlight in non-stereotypical ways, older women's experiences, developing inclusiveness and transformation through understanding intersecting identity positions, and adopting feminist methodologies to produce change-focused research (Hooyman et al., 2002, pp. 6–10; also see Netting, 2011, p. 241).

Nuanced intersectional understandings of the lived reality of older women are critical for social work practice given that social justice and equity are upheld as core values. More broadly, emancipatory practice in social work as an approach which aims "to improve the life of communities and their children into the future, to address discrimination and disadvantage via structural means" (Phillips, 2018, p. 5) builds on collective social justice action by social movements shaped by "...feminism; anti-racism; anti-ableism and the LGBTQI movement" (Phillips, 2018, p. 6). If social work as a profession seeks to critically engage with issues and concerns in ways that actualise positive social change, then I emphatically agree with Phillips (2018, p. 6) who argues, "In relation to ageing, social work should also aim to be at the core of an anti-ageism movement". This is essential to remedy normative, deeply embedded ageist beliefs in our social contexts of which social work students, social workers, and educators are a part (Allen et al., 2009; Kostecki, 2016; Phillips, 2018), develop anti-ageist models of service delivery, theory, research, and policy change, address late life precarity, and to support older women advocates and activists who work for social change.

The need for an anti-ageist movement in social work which includes critical gerontological frameworks and approaches is relevant for all levels of practice, especially in the context of welfare state decline, extended working lives, late life care giving/receiving patterns, as well as new social contexts arising from the pandemic and migration. As Chambers (2004) explains:

> It is crucial if health and social care workers are to work sensitively and in partnership with older women, that they have access to knowledge, policies and practices which enable them to develop their awareness of both age and gender, and its impact over the life course. Critical social gerontology would seem to fit the bill well.
>
> (p. 756)

Hastings and Rogowski (2015) have discussed how critical social work practice drawing on critical gerontology theory can not only problematise ageism but also provide real-world directions/solutions in service delivery contexts that are firmly established in neo-liberal contexts. Beyond interpersonal practice, they urge collective action from social workers to advocate for change where unjust practices and policies impact lives.

Hulko et al. (2019) provide guidance for anti-oppressive social work practice working with older adults across practice fields, including building inclusive communities, awareness of critiques regarding 'age-friendly' cities and places, engaging in policy and planning change, daily practice with older adults and critical engagement with concerns, including violence, care, trauma, mental health, dementia, and citizenship, through the lens of lived experience. Appreciation of interlocking oppressions using an intersectional lens and foregrounding lived experience is a way to improve access to services and promote age-related equity (Hulko et al., 2019, pp. 258–260).

By way of example in terms of micro practice, for women who have experienced childhood sexual abuse and/or family violence, appropriate assistance and adequate service provision is key. Duncan and Mason (2011) have discussed group work (mezzo practice) as an effective model for working with older women who have experienced sexual violence. The value of a critical feminist gerontological lens is foregrounded by Bows (2018) who, in exploring practitioner views working with older women experiencing sexual violence, found that the impacts mirror the double jeopardy of gender and age due to the stigmatised experience of sexual violence and being older.

Furthermore, critical gerontology at the micro level can enhance and inform issues for older people such as in end of life, depression, dementia, and care. Chonody and Teater (2016, p. 270) discuss feminist gerontology and its relevance for micro social work practice in terms of building awareness of the impact of ageism, consciousness raising, advocacy, and building social networking. Hafford-Letchfield (2022, pp. 210–211) demonstrates how a critical feminist gerontology can apply in social work practice via "… the development of social consciousness about inequities, utilisation of theories and methods that accurately depict life experiences, and the promotion of change in conditions that negatively affect older women".

At the macro level, the need for social policy advocacy and engagement is also important and includes understanding the diversity of ageing experiences within generational cohorts, reconstruction of 'retirement' discourse, and opening imaginations to create improved possibilities for later life (Ferguson & Schriver, 2012). Considering global differences, understanding the landscape of precarity in later life is integral to a critical analysis of circumstances and critical social work responses (Grenier et al., 2020; Hafford-Letchfield, 2022). Invigorating the role of advocacy aimed at policy reform and analysis and including perspectives that support and engage with coalitions of older people and carers are crucial.

Existing systemic inequalities across race, social isolation, ethnicity, and poverty as well as unequal access to health care associated with age have coalesced to create a recognised greater vulnerability for older people globally during the Covid-19 pandemic (Cox, 2020). For social work, Cox (2020) proposes a social justice approach which includes advocacy in relation to caregiver supports, technology in the home, improved policy approaches to address transitions to nursing home care, programs to address social isolation, support for caregivers and grandparents who are carers, as well as research that provides evidence for interventions in relation to barriers to services and inform service provision regarding access (Cox, 2020, p. 621).

Teaching anti-ageist social work practice is a form of activism at the structural level. Given that culturally and socially reinforced age stereotypes are developed and deeply embedded from early childhood through adolescence and into adulthood (Mason et al., 2015), social work students (Allen et al., 2009) often hold ageist assumptions that act as a barrier to developing skills which are embedded in critical social work practice skills (Kostecki, 2015).

Phillips (2018, pp. 6–7) argues for emancipatory practice as a core theoretical perspective in teaching anti-ageist practice to students, including student engagement with practice issues such as,

> … ageism; the dominance of the medicalisation of older age; how gerontology theories have influenced popular ideas about ageing, the role of older people in the workforce and aged care policies; the imposition of risk and assessment on ageing; the complex construction of care and carers and the impact of institutional practice as oppression.

Key characteristics of an anti-ageist teaching practice embedded in critical pedagogy includes the development of analytical skills to deconstruct theory, practice, and research, as well as exploring personal assumptions and belief systems (Phillips, 2018, p. 19). Critical pedagogy with the aim of transformational learning in social work curricula is an important way to support the preparation of students for anti-ageist social work practice.

For me, listening to and learning from older women is the touchstone for a critical feminist gerontology and for anti-ageist social work practice. Tusasiirwe (2019, p. 75) critiques the teaching of social work for its omission in considering culturally relevant contexts "… shaped by local ways of doing and knowing" and provides a wonderful example of decolonising practice by learning from older women in Uganda. The women in this study work in an evolving collective to respond to social issues in alignment with Obuntu philosophies which include "…working collectively, caring, sharing, cooperating and consensus decision making"

(Tusasiirwe, 2019, p. 84). Relevant to social work practice and education is the adoption of language and approaches that support existing initiatives such as the approach embraced by the older women in the study where knowledge is "...passed on from generation to generation through stories, proverbs, taboos and totems, all embedded in the oral tradition" (Tusasiirwe, 2019, p. 84). Reflexively listening to and learning about older women's relevant knowledge practices in culturally diverse communities is a wellspring for decolonised social work practice.

Conclusion

Older women, historically and across a range of diverse social contexts, engage in social activism in ways that demonstrate agency, resistance, and reconstruction. Chazan and Baldwin (2016) contest assumptions which underlie the 'waves' narrative of feminist social action and discuss how this metaphor can marginalise older women's contributions by an inherent 'youthing' of feminist history, privileging of public protest and the inference of intergenerational conflict. Following Chazan and Baldwin (2016), activism of older women is often lifelong, generationally relevant, diverse, public and private, global and local, complex, seen and unseen, nuanced, engaged, and produced every day.

Negative age and gender stereotypes diminish the complexity and nuance in the lives of older women. By recognising older women's social activism in the past and presently, we understand how they politicise social concerns despite age and gender oppressions. Social work must be involved in reflexively listening and learning from older women in all contexts, joining with older women's activism, to redress later life age and gender disparities at the practice, policy level, and as educators to strengthen anti-ageist social work in the profession.

Being now the same age as some of the women in my earlier study (Kostecki, 2015), my appreciation of their contributions has burgeoned. Listening to and writing about their experiences from a reflexive perspective informed by critical theory analysis is one form of my own social justice activism. Reflecting on this, Haraway's (2016, p. 1) chronicle for how to manage current contemporary global issues is an apt metaphor to assist the development of feminist gerontology in social work, "Our task is to make trouble, to stir up potent response to devastating events, as well as to settle troubled waters and rebuild quiet places".

Acknowledgement

My many thanks are extended to Associate Professor May Chazan for providing reflections and comments on early drafts of this chapter.

References

Allen, P. D., Cherry, K. E., & Palmore, E. (2009). Self-reported ageism in social work practitioners and students. *Journal of Gerontological Social Work*, 52(2), 124–134.

Australian Association of Social Workers (AASW) (2020). Code of ethics. https://www.aasw.asn.au/document/item/13400

Australian Government Workplace Gender Equality Agency (AGWGEA). (2015). *Women's economic security in retirement.* https://www.wgea.gov.au/sites/default/files/PP_womens_economic_security_in_retirement.pdf

Black, S. (2017). KNIT+ RESIST: Placing the Pussyhat Project in the context of craft activism. *Gender, Place & Culture*, 24(5), 696–710.

Bows, H. (2018). Practitioner views on the impacts, challenges, and barriers in supporting older survivors of sexual violence. *Violence Against Women*, 24(9), 1070–1090.

Browne, C.V. (1998). *Women, feminism and aging.* Springer Publishing Company.
Calasanti, T. & Slevin, K.F. (2001). *Gender, social inequalities & aging.* Alta Mira Press.
——— (2006). *Age matters: Realigning feminist thinking.* Routledge.
Chambers, P. (2004). The case for critical social gerontology in social work education and older women. *Social Work Education: The International Journal*, 23(6), 745–758.
Charpentier, M., Quéniart, A. & Jacques, J. (2008). Activism among older women in Quebec, Canada: Changing the world after age 65. *Journal of Women & Aging*, 20(3–4), 343–360.
Chazan, M. (2020). Unsettling aging futures: Challenging colonial-normativity in social gerontology. *International Journal of Ageing and Later Life*, 14(1), 91–119.
Chazan, M. & Baldwin, M. (2016). Understanding the complexities of contemporary feminist activism: How the lives of older women activists contest the waves narrative. *Feminist Formations*, 28(3), 70–94.
Chazan, M., Baldwin, M. & Evans, P. (Eds.). (2018). *Unsettling activisms: Critical interventions on aging, gender, and social change.* Canadian Scholars' Press.
Chazan, M., Baldwin, M. & Whattam, J. (2016). Activisms across women's lives: Rethinking the politics of (grand)mothering: Preliminary analysis of activist oral histories, 2013–15. Retrieved from http://www.agingactivisms.org/activisms-report
Chazan, M. & Kittmer, S. (2016). Defying, producing, and overlooking stereotypes? The complexities of mobilizing "grandmotherhood" as political strategy. *Journal of Women & Aging*, 28(4), 297–308.
Chonody, J. & Teater, B. (2016). Constructing gender: Feminist gerontology and social work practice. In *Contemporary Feminisms in Social Work Practice* (pp. 263–274). Routledge.
Coen-Sanchez, K., Ebenso, B., El-Mowafi, I.M., Berghs, M., Idriss-Wheeler, D. & Yaya, S. (2022). Repercussions of overturning Roe v. Wade for women across systems and beyond borders. *Reproductive Health*, 19(1), 1–5.
Connell, R.W. (2003). *Gender and power: Society, the person and sexual politics* (digital ed.). Polity Press.
Cox, C. (2020). Older adults and Covid 19: Social justice, disparities, and social work practice. *Journal of Gerontological Social Work*, 63(6–7), 611–624.
Dudgeon, P. & Bray, A. (2016). Women's and feminist activism in aboriginal Australia and Torres Strait Islands. In R. Sharp (ed.), *The Wiley Blackwell Encyclopedia of gender and sexuality studies.* Wiley Blackwell.
Duncan, J., & Mason, R. (2011). Older women reconnecting after sexual violence through group work. *Women Against Violence: An Australian Feminist Journal*, 23, 18–28.
Estes, C.L. (Ed.). (2001). *Social policy and aging: A critical perspective.* Sage Publications.
——— (2006). Critical feminist perspectives, aging and social policy. In J. Baars, D. Dannefer, C. Phillipson & A. Walker (Eds.). *Aging, globalization and inequality: The new critical gerontology.* (pp. 81–101). Baywood Publishing Company Inc.
Estes, C. & Portacolone, E. (2009). Maggie Kuhn: Social theorist of radical gerontology. *International Journal of Sociology and Social Policy*, 29(1/2), 15–26.
Ferguson, A. J., & Schriver, J. (2012). The future of gerontological social work: A case for structural lag. *Journal of Gerontological Social Work*, 55(4), 304–320.
Garner, J.D. (1999a). Feminism and feminist gerontology. *Journal of Women & Aging*, 11(2/3), 3–12.
——— (Ed.). (1999b). *Fundamentals of feminist gerontology.* The Haworth Press.
Grenier, A., Phillipson, C. & Settersten, R.A. (Eds.). (2020). *Precarity and ageing: Understanding insecurity and risk in later life.* Cambridge University Press.
Gullette, M.M. (1997). *Declining to decline.* University Press of Virginia.
——— (2004). *Aged by culture.* University of Chicago Press.
——— (2011). *Agewise: Fighting the new ageism in America.* University of Chicago Press.
Hafford-Letchfield, T. (2022). Invisible women: Critical perspectives on social work and gender in later life. In C. Cocker & T. Hafford-Letchfield (Eds.) *Rethinking feminist theories for social work practice.* Palgrave Macmillan. doi:10.1007/978-3-030-94241-0_12
Haraway, D.J. (2016). *Staying with the trouble: Making kin in the Chthulucene.* Duke University Press.
Hastings, S. J., & Rogowski, S. (2015). Critical social work with older people in neo-liberal times: Challenges and critical possibilities. *Practice*, 27(1), 21–33.

Hoffman, M. (2012). *Intimate wars: The life and times of the woman who brought abortion from the back alley to the boardroom*. The Feminist Press.
Hooyman, N., Browne, C.V., Ray, R. & Richardson, V. (2002). Feminist gerontology and the life course. *Gerontology & Geriatrics Education*, 22(4), 3–26.
Hulko, W., Brotman, S., Stern, L. & Ferrer, I. (Eds.). (2019). *Gerontological social work in action: Anti-oppressive practice with older adults, their families, and communities*. Routledge.
Kafer, A. (2013). *Feminist, queer, crip*. Indiana University Press.
Kalache, A., Barreto, S.M. & Keller, I. (2005). Global ageing: The demographic revolution in all cultures and societies. In M.L. Johnson (Ed.) *The Cambridge handbook on age and ageing* (pp. 30–46). Cambridge University Press.
Kostecki, K. (2015). *Resistance and reconstruction: Older women talk about childhood sexual abuse*. (Unpublished doctoral dissertation). Deakin University.
Kostecki, T. (2016). Developing anti-ageist practice in social work. In *Doing critical social work* (pp. 241–253). Routledge.
Kostecki, T. & Macfarlane, S. (2019). Women and older age: Exploring the intersections of privilege and oppression across lifetimes. In *Working across difference social work, social policy and social justice* (pp. 120–136). Red Globe Press.
Lauve-Moon, K.R., Enman, S. & Hentz, V. (2020). Mainstreaming gender: An examination of feminist methodology in social work research. *Social Work*, 65(4), 317–324.
Laws, G. (1995). Understanding ageism: Lessons from feminism and postmodernism. *The Gerontologist*, 35(1), 112–118.
Krekula, C. (2007). The intersection of age and gender: Reworking gender theory and social gerontology. *Current Sociology*, 55(2), 155–171. doi: 10.1177/0011392107073299
Marshall, L. (2006). Aging: A feminist issue. *NWSA Journal*, 18(1), vii–xiii. doi:10.1353/nwsa.2006.0014
Mason, S.E., Kuntz, C.V. & McGill, C.M. (2015). Oldsters and Ngrams: Age stereotypes across time. *Psychological Reports*, 116(1), 324–329.
Mears, J. (2015). Violence against older women: Activism, social justice, and social change. *Journal of Elder Abuse & Neglect*, 27(4–5), 500–513.
McHugh, M.C. (2012). Aging, agency, and activism: Older women as social change agents. *Women & Therapy*, 35(3–4), 279–275.
Narushima, M. (2004). A gaggle of raging grannies: The empowerment of older Canadian women through social activism. *International Journal of Lifelong Education*, 23(1), 23–42.
Netting, F.E. (2011). Bridging critical feminist gerontology and social work to interrogate the narrative on civic engagement. *Affilia*, 26(3), 239–249.
Osborne-Crowley, L. (2015). Homelessness and older women: The accumulation of a lifetime of inequality. *Women's Agenda*. https://womensagenda.com.au/latest/homelessness-older-women-the-accumulation-of-a-lifetime-of-inequality/
Phillips, R. (2018). Emancipatory social work with older people: Challenging students to overcome the limitations of ageism and institutional oppression. *Social Work & Policy Studies: Social Justice, Practice and Theory*, https://openjournals.library.sydney.edu.au/SWPS/article/view/11733.
Rawsthorne, M., Ellis, K. & de Pree, A. (2017). Working with COW: Social work supporting older women living in the community. *Journal of Gerontological Social Work*, 60(1), 32–47.
Rose, N. (1999). *Powers of freedom: Reframing political thought*. Cambridge University Press.
Sandberg, L.J. & Marshall, B.L. (2017). Queering aging futures. *Societies*, 7(3), 21.
Sawchuk, D. (2009). The raging grannies: Defying stereotypes and embracing aging through activism. *Journal of Women & Aging*, 21(3), 171–185.
Sorrel, L. & Kolenc, S. (1982). Panthers blow the whistle. *Off Our Backs*, 12(1). http://www.jstor.org/stable/25774187
Tusasiirwe, S. (2019). Decolonising social work through learning from experiences of older women and social policy makers in Uganda. In *Disrupting whiteness in social work* (pp. 74–90). Routledge.
Twigg, J. (2004). The body, gender, and age: Feminist insights in social gerontology. *Journal of Aging Studies*, 18(1), 59–73. doi:10.1016/j.jaging.2003.09.001
Warner, S. (2009). *Understanding the effects of child sexual abuse: Feminist revolutions in theory, research and practice*. Routledge.

46
FEMINIST SOCIAL WORK RESPONSES TO INTERSECTIONAL OPPRESSION FACED BY ETHNIC MINORITY WOMEN IN JAPAN

Osamu Miyazaki

Introduction

For feminist social work, it is critical to consider the plurality of women. This is vital in today's globalised world, where population movements and diversity of values and cultures are increasing on a global scale. Women are by no means monolithic; they are defined by both personal and social differences, and the problems they face and the needs to be met by social work interventions are multiple. However, the recognition of these issues remains insufficient in the field of social work in Japan, particularly regarding the experiences of women with roots in former colonies. Although a national qualification for social workers was established in 1987, it did improve the social status of social workers to some extent. However, their practice tended to remain confined within the legal system framework, leading to increased control by the state. Unfortunately, Japan's social welfare system fails to address the unique challenges faced by individuals with roots in former colonies.

Social work practice in Japan has long been focused on micro-level interventions, thus lacking a comprehensive perspective that considers minorities as a collective group. Moreover, since the early 2000s, the influence of neoliberal policies has given rise to managerialism, further emphasising the tendency to view service users as isolated individuals rather than part of a larger community.

This chapter focuses on the intersectional oppression of Zainichi Korean (ethnic Korean residents in Japan) women, one of Japan's leading ethnic minority groups, from a postcolonial feminist perspective. The purpose is to show the reality of their oppression and resistance and contribute to the search for solidarity with these women within the field of social work. This discussion will lead to a fundamental rethink of social work in Japan, in addition to considering directions for addressing various forms of intersectional oppression faced by women. First, a postcolonial feminist perspective, particularly 'intersectionality' and 'subaltern', is applied in the analysis of this chapter. Subsequently, using these perspectives as clues, the reality of oppression against Zainichi Korean women and their resistance is examined. Finally, issues and strategies for social work are presented.

Zainichi Koreans (ethnic Korean residents in Japan)

Zainichi Koreans are those who immigrated from the Korean Peninsula to Japan before and after Japan's colonial rule, which began with the Japanese annexation of Korea in 1910 and continued until the end of the Pacific War in August 1945, those who immigrated to Japan immediately after the war and during the Korean War, and their descendants living in Japan. They left the peninsula because of land grabbing and poverty or were forced to come to Japan to make up for the labour shortage. Approximately 600,000 Zainichi Koreans live in Japan due to various reasons. If we include those who have acquired Japanese citizenship, there are even more of them. They are one of the representative minority groups in a vulnerable position in Japan.

Zainichi Koreans have been oppressed in various ways in Japanese society. With the end of the war in 1945, Japanese soldiers were demobilised, and the Japanese civilians withdrew from the former colonies, resulting in a rapid increase in the industrial population in Japan. Consequently, Zainichi Koreans were forced out of their workplaces and unemployment increased. However, with the San Francisco Peace Treaty coming into effect in April 1952, the Japanese government stipulated that Zainichi Koreans had 'lost' their Japanese nationality and were excluded from the framework of social security and social welfare. For example, in the past, they were excluded from the public pension system; thus, even now, many elderly Zainichi Koreans without pensions struggle to make ends meet. In addition, ethnic organisations created by Zainichi Koreans for mutual aid have been often suppressed by the Japanese government (Kim, 2022; Shoya & Nakayama, 1997).

There is also exclusion from newly created systems. For example, the Japanese government continues to exclude Zainichi Korean high school students from its free high school education program, which began in 2010. The Japanese government cites diplomatic issues between the Democratic People's Republic of Korea and Japan as the reason, but this is discrimination against students attending Korean schools. Human rights bodies such as the United Nations Commission on the Elimination of Racial Discrimination have repeatedly recommended including Zainichi Korean students in free high school programs when reviewing Japan's human rights situation, but the Japanese government has not complied.

Furthermore, hate crimes and hate speech targeting Zainichi Koreans in Japan occur frequently. In August 2021, an arson incident occurred in the Utoro area (Uji City, Kyoto Prefecture), one of the areas where Koreans are concentrated. The houses of Zainichi Koreans and the materials scheduled to be exhibited at the Utoro Peace Memorial Museum, which was being prepared for its opening, were destroyed by fire. The culprit stated, 'I have suspicion and disgust towards Zainichi Koreans'. Thus, this incident is an 'extremely vicious hate crime based on discriminatory motives aimed at Zainichi Koreans' (Hyun, 2022, p. 45). In April 2022, there was also a hate crime in which the Korea International Academy, where students with diverse cultural backgrounds, including Zainichi Koreans, attended school, was set on fire. Negative discourses about them are widespread among the public. Demonstrations and intimidation by racist groups with hate speech against Zainichi Koreans are frequent. Discriminatory words and deeds against Zainichi Koreans are not limited to blatant racist behaviour. The mass media and the Internet are dominated by discourses that attack Zainichi Koreans. Even in daily conversations among Japanese people, we can hear prejudiced comments making fun of Zainichi Koreans or linking them to crimes.

The exclusion and oppression of Zainichi Koreans are deeply rooted in Japanese society, and they tend to be placed on the fringes of society. Not only do they suffer institutional exclusion and overt violence, but they are also denied access to a positive identity. Although some social workers have practised solving such problems, it is not regarded as a vital issue in Japanese social work overall, largely dominated by the Japanese. In some cases, Zainichi Koreans are subject to discriminatory behaviour by Japanese social workers (Miyazaki, 2018).

Perspectives on oppression of Zainichi Korean women

Postcolonial feminism

The oppression of Zainichi Korean is rooted in colonial rule. Therefore, this chapter attempts to capture the oppression of Zainichi Korean women from the perspective of postcolonial feminism. Here, we refer to the arguments of Mohanty et al. and discuss the issues raised by postcolonial feminism.

In her 1984 book *Under Western Eyes: Feminist Scholarship and Colonial Discourses*, Mohanty criticised Western feminist discourse for colonising the lives and struggles of Third World women and insisted on their agency. In particular, Mohanty (1984) criticised the Western-centeredness of feminism, saying, 'I am attempting to draw attention to the similar effects of various textual strategies used by particular writers that codify Others as non-Western and hence themselves as (implicitly) Western' (p. 334).

What Mohanty (1984) criticises is 'the strategic location or situation of the category "women" vis-a-vis the context of analysis' (p. 336). She argues that

> the assumption of women as an already constituted, coherent group with identical interests and desires, regardless of class, ethnic or racial location or contradictions, implies a notion of gender or sexual difference or even patriarchy (as male dominance—men as a correspondingly coherent group) which can be applied universally and cross-culturally.
>
> *(pp. 336–337)*

Mohanty (1984) makes this criticism because she feels 'the urgent political necessity ... of forming strategic coalitions across class, race, and national boundaries' and thinks that the colonialist analytic principles 'distort Western feminist political practices and limit the possibility of coalitions among (usually White) Western feminists and working class and feminists of colour around the world' (p. 334).

Discussions on postcolonial feminism have been referenced in Japan. Kazuko Takemura (2001), a prominent feminist theorist in Japan, discusses the intersection of postcolonialism and feminism and emphasises,

> in postcolonial studies, colonialism is not considered one "grand narrative", but as a number of "little narratives". Phenomena that until then were overlooked as trivial or obvious and were not subject to criticism are regarded as the cultural medium that supports and fosters colonialism behind the scenes, and they are taken up as a point of discussion for criticism.
>
> *(p. 44)*

Furthermore, she argues,

> naturally, postcolonialism squarely addresses issues of gender and sexuality that have existed within the institution of colonialism, but that have been viewed as external to, or as a partial component of, the system despite being an inherent part of the system itself.
>
> *(p. 44)*

In the field of social work, it is crucial to understand and acknowledge what Takemura referred to as 'phenomena that until then were overlooked as trivial or obvious and were not subject to criticism'. In the broader context, it can be argued that social work in Japan should reconsider its omission of discussions on Colonialism and the experiences of ethnic minority women. However, that alone is not enough. It is necessary to ask ourselves whether research and social work practice aimed at overcoming Colonialism have resulted in a uniform view of perceiving women, colonising them, and depriving them of agency. To do so, it is necessary to carefully place each woman's story of life, livelihood, and resistance as unique – but without ignoring their links to social, cultural, and historical contexts.

Intersectionality

Colonial oppression is not reducible to one factor but is complex. Intersectionality is a concept used to analyse the complexity of oppression. Intersectionality was used by the Black feminist Kimberlé Williams Crenshaw in her 1989 paper to explain how the experience of Black women differed from those of Black men and white women. According to Akiko Shimizu (2021), this is 'a perspective that questions the identity of the category of "women" and consciously seeks to address the plurality of "women" in feminist politics' (pp. 151–152). This concept has also been introduced into social work and has become one of the key concepts that characterise anti-oppression social work (Kojima, 2019).

Intersectionality is a concept that explains the oppression experienced by complex minority people as a structural and multifactorial combination. Shimizu (2021) states that intersectionality 'can be said not to be a perspective that encourages attention to a limited and special area where multiple discriminations overlap' (p. 156). She argues that within a categorical group, 'it is not a task of continuing to narrow the focus to the more marginalised and underrepresented group'. Analysis that considers intersectionality is 'rather than a process of narrowing the focus, it may be a process of refocusing and broadening the field of view to include areas that have been carefully excluded from the field of view' (p. 157).

Subaltern

It is highly challenging to grasp the reality of intersectional oppression stemming from a colonialist background. This is because people who are subjected to colonialist oppression are subaltern. Subaltern is a concept used to refer to those labelled as subsidiary, secondary, and underlayer in the social relations created and reproduced by the domination in which Colonialism is inescapably embedded. This concept was made famous by Spivak. In 'Can the Subaltern Speak?', Spivak (1988) attempts a critique of 'epistemic violence' in which intellectuals carry out 'the remotely orchestrated, far-flung, and heterogeneous project to constitute the colonial subject as Other' (p. 76).

'Can the Subaltern Speak?' does not imply that the subaltern cannot speak. Later, Spivak (1996) explained that

> so, "the subaltern cannot speak" means that even when the subaltern makes an effort to the death to speak, she is not able to be heard, and speaking and hearing complete the speech act. That's what it had meant, and anguish marked the spot.
>
> *(p. 292)*

What kind of situation is this? Spivak (2006) maintains:

> Subalternity is not a pathetic thing about subaltern folk. It is a description of a political or social position. The subaltern speaks for themselves. So what is the difference between them and any other human being? The problem is not that they are deprived of interior life. They have as much of interior life as anyone else. It is not that they are people incapable of feelings, or less than the others, let's say me. So the problem is not located in their being deprived of interior life but in having the access to the public sphere so that their resistance can be recognised as such.
>
> *(pp. 72–73)*

Spivak's argument denounced a structural problem of lack of communication in a one-sided power relationship. What can we learn from these discussions? Social work with people under postcolonial oppression is not about helping them by defining them as pitiful and inferior people. It is not about preparing a place for them to speak, or speaking for them, by regarding them as people who do not have words to speak. Such practices are nothing more than new forms of oppression. Instead, it is necessary to recognise the oppression that exists right now against them as oppression and to recognise their resistance as resistance. Furthermore, if oppression and resistance are not recognised, then clarifying what type of social foundation exists there is what social work is required to do.

Intersectional oppression and resistance of Zainichi Korean women

The reality of oppression and resistance

Based on the above perspectives, we approach the reality of the oppression of Zainichi Korean women. In other words, we perceive the oppression of these women as rooted in Colonialism and use the concepts of intersectionality and subalternity as clues to decipher them. They suffer oppression at the intersection of race/ethnicity and gender. Research by Zainichi Korean women themselves has revealed this reality. It is one form of resistance to clarify the current state of one's oppression and show it to society, and it is also an experience of being empowered through it.

One example is the issue of employment discrimination. Lee (2022) analysed data from the 2020 census and found that Zainichi Koreans were in precarious employment situations. The percentage of Zainichi Koreans who are non-regular employees or family employees amounts to 65.37%. Zainichi Korean women have a higher ratio of unstable employment by 38.0 points than Zainichi Korean men. Even compared to Japanese women, Zainichi Korean women are in a more unstable position by 7.7 points. Even if they are 'the same Zainichi Koreans', the employment situation of Zainichi Korean women is more unstable than that of their male counterparts. This indicates that this reality is overlooked if we discuss oppression only in terms of one factor, such as the 'oppression of Zainichi Koreans' or 'oppression of women' (p. 38).

Apeuro: The Network of Zainichi Korean Women Creating the Future (2019), a group of Zainichi Koreans, surveyed Zainichi Koreans and determined the reality of oppression. More than 40% of Zainichi Korean women reported experiencing discrimination or disadvantage based on their ethnicity, nationality, or gender. However, the largest number of women responded that they 'did not consult anyone' regarding any of their experiences of discrimination. Thus, this group argues that there is an urgent need to establish an effective relief organisation (p. 10).

In addition, women activists of the Committee on the Elimination of Discrimination based on Gender and Sexuality, Human Rights Association for Korean Residents in Japan, conducted a survey on harassment against Zainichi Korean women. The results were compiled and published in a booklet titled 'Breaking Through the Inner Walls: Harassment Cases of Zainichi Korean Women' (2020). The booklet contains the voices of 45 Zainichi Korean women who have suffered sexual, power, maternity, racial, and sexual orientation and gender identity (SOGI) harassment. It was an epoch-making initiative in Japan for Zainichi Korean women to expose a part of the intersecting oppression they were suffering.

Kyong-Hee (2021), one of the members involved in the survey, said,

> In the fight against ethnic discrimination, various forms of discrimination based on gender, age, place of origin and educational background have long been ignored and trivialised. Victims' voices continued to be silenced by words such as "such voices are what divides communities" and "it's just a trifle", and disappointed people left the community one after another.
>
> (p. 66)

Wooki Park-Kim (2021), also one of the members, said, 'I felt that the difficulty of speaking up after being harassed reflects the issue of multiple discrimination, that is, the intersection of the standpoints of 'racism and sexism are intertwined' that Zainichi Korean women are placed in'. She points out that the following is behind the situation in which Zainichi Korean women cannot speak out even if they are victims of harassment:

> First, there is the social alienation of Zainichi Koreans, such as being excluded from the free high school education system and being targeted by various forms of ethnic discrimination and violence such as hate speech. And in such a situation, the community of Zainichi Koreans where they can maintain our identity as Zainichi Koreans has become a valuable place to belong.

Further, she added, 'I thought that this kind of "difficulty speaking up" after being victimised reflects the vulnerability and anguish of the position of Zainichi Korean women, who stand at the intersection of ethnic and gender discrimination'.

The structure that creates oppression is also connected to the difficulty of speaking up and consequently, their subalternity. It is Zainichi Korean women themselves who have clarified this reality. It is difficult to obtain a realistic understanding of the reality of oppression in the lives of individual Zainichi Korean women. However, Dalrymple and Burke (2006) state, 'It is from the experiences of people who have been marginalised, who have their rights denied or violated, that we can understand what is meant by oppression' (p. 39). Although we should be cautious about generalising individual experiences, they reflect social structural oppression. The reality of oppression becomes apparent only through the resistance of those involved. Hence, social workers must listen to the voices of Zainichi Korean women themselves to expand their work.

Colonialism and sexism

In the background of the issue of oppression of Zainichi Korean women, there is a deeply rooted history of intricately intertwined Colonialism and sexism. In Japan, there is a tendency to focus only on the oppression by Zainichi Korean men when mentioning the oppression of Zainichi Korean women. The prevailing view in Japan is that the Zainichi Korean community is deeply patriarchal and extremely male-dominated; accordingly, Zainichi Korean women are oppressed within that structure. However, this is a one-sided view, and it regards Zainichi Korean women only as victims, and moreover, victims of Zainichi Korean men. This indicates overlooking the structures of Colonialism, racism, and sexism in Japanese society. Assuming that Zainichi Korean women are not oppressed in Japanese society leads to drowning out their voices.

Colonialism and sexism are closely related, and the oppression of Zainichi Koreans has been embedded in history. The colonial legacy continues to this day. Thus, when thinking about the issues of gender norms and Patriarchy in Zainichi Korean society, it is necessary to consider how they were strengthened when Japan ruled the Korean Peninsula as a colony. The most symbolic example is that during the period of colonial rule, the Japanese military and government created a system of licensed prostitution to manage and control women's sexuality and the related Japanese military sexual slavery system and transplanted it to the Korean Peninsula. Such a system strengthened gender norms and Patriarchy on the Korean Peninsula and considerably impacted the Zainichi Korean community (Park-Kim, 2021).

After the end of Japan's colonial rule of the Korean Peninsula in 1945, the sexism that remained within the Zainichi Korean community was closely related to the impact of Japanese colonial rule and subsequent ethnic discrimination. From immediately after the end of the war to the 1950s, many Zainichi Koreans were forced to live in poverty because they could not find employment. A mutual aid organisation for Zainichi Koreans, formed to resist it, was branded as anti-social and forcibly disbanded by the Japanese public authorities. At times, blatant political violence was used. Oun-ok Song (2005) notes,

> since the living space of Zainichi Koreans was under the social and economic conditions of the suzerain country Japan, which was exclusionary and discriminatory, it was also an inevitable side to strengthen gender norms and patriarchy in order to protect family, religion, and community. In other words, the social and economic conditions that Zainichi Koreans faced after the liberation of Japan became the ground for further strengthening gender discrimination.
>
> *(pp. 262–263)*

Thus, it is necessary to carefully examine such historical backgrounds and contexts, as well as their influences that continue today.

The damage done to women who were forced to become 'comfort women' (sexual slavery by the Imperial Japanese Army) became apparent because they raised their voices (Yamashita,

2008, pp. 35–51). Making the history of damage visible in society is inextricably linked with the act of resistance (Park-Kim, 2012). Therefore, denying their testimony is not only denying historical facts and affirming Colonialism and sexism but also denying their resistance and empowerment. They are not just 'victims' who need unilateral support and sympathy. They represent an agency that speaks to society about their experiences, solidarises with people, confronts the state, and fights to restore its own lost dignity.

As the tide of historical revisionism intensifies in Japan, the testimonies of women forced to become 'comfort women' are about to be erased. Conservative politicians, religious rightists, and racist groups allege that their testimony was a lie and that there was no coercion by the Japanese state. The oppression of these women has also led to the oppression of those campaigning for the Japanese government to apologise and compensate them. Zainichi Korean women have played a critical role in such movements (Kim, 2011, pp. 198–203). They build solidarity with people, convey the voices of victims, and actively engage in lobbying activities both at home and abroad. The issue of Japanese military sexual slavery concerns them as well. This is because the denial of the existence of those forced to become 'comfort women' denies the existence of Colonialism and sexism that still cause the oppression of Zainichi Korean women today.

Gender discrimination also exists within the Zainichi Korean community, but it is not the only community that discriminates against women. It is not that the Zainichi Korean community is inherently sexist, but that its structure was brought about by Japanese colonial rule and has been reproduced in history. In the first place, Japanese society oppresses Zainichi Korean women. However, the history of colonial rule and the problems of Japanese society are covered up to suggest that only Zainichi Korean men oppress them. If the oppression of women is tied only to ethnic attributes, then it is a manifestation of the oppression of Zainichi Koreans. Hence, it is essential to understand that the oppression of these women was created through various contexts throughout the history of colonial rule and is still intertwined with issues of sexism and racism in Japanese society as a whole (Park-Kim, 2021).

Discussion

Considering the complex oppression of Zainichi Korean women, what types of prospects can be considered for social work? The reality of intersectional oppression of these women and their resistance, which is the focus of this chapter, is not shared in Japanese society, nor is it considered in social work, mostly carried out by Japanese people. Thus, they are beings characterised by subalternity. As Spivak (1996) noted, 'Subalternity is not a pathetic thing about subaltern folk. It is a description of a political or social position' (p. 72).

The unrecognised oppression and resistance faced by Zainichi Korean women can be attributed to a framework that attempts to explain oppression by considering only a single factor. It is crucial for social work in Japan to adopt the concept of intersectionality instead of relying on this limited framework. Although intersectionality has only recently gained attention in Japan, it holds immense potential. By embracing this concept, there is an opportunity to re-evaluate Japanese social work practices and shed light on the intersecting forms of oppression experienced by Zainichi Korean women.

Conservative social work practices in Japan often confine themselves to the framework of the social welfare legal system, focusing on isolated aspects of individuals' lives. This approach obscures the complex realities and overlooks the existence of those who do not fit neatly into that framework. Consequently, their oppression and resistance are obscured as well. Furthermore, the introduction of managerialism into social work through neoliberal policies has made it increasingly challenging to grasp the structural difficulties faced by individuals. Understanding the origins of the current situation requires a critical examination of the history of Colonialism, racism, and sexism. By utilising the concept of intersectionality, Japanese social workers can better comprehend the structural mechanisms that contribute to the hardships faced by Zainichi Korean women.

However, there are other points to be aware of. Zainichi Korean women face a different reality of oppression than both Zainichi Korean men and Japanese women, and it is necessary to focus on them from the perspective of intersectionality. Nevertheless, if we were to emphasise only that point, we would 'victimise' Zainichi Korean women as 'people who are more oppressed' and end up intervening in their life with a colonialist attitude. That would result in social workers agreeing to introduce a 'hierarchisation based on the degree of oppression'. To avoid that, we must also look at the reality of the resistance of Zainichi Korean women. Social workers are not the 'disabling profession' nor 'victimising profession'. As the global definition of social work suggests, social workers should seek to work with them rather than for them.

As evident from the preceding discussion, Zainichi Korean women have demonstrated resilience and solidarity in the face of oppression, bravely shedding light on the realities of their experiences and actively challenging the norms of mainstream society. To make it easier for the voices of Zainichi Korean women to be heard in Japanese society, it is the responsibility of social workers to work with them to create a structure in which they do not remain subaltern.

Postcolonial feminist social work emphasises that alternative solutions emerge from the collective experiences of oppressed women and their leadership (Deepak, 2019). In the context of Zainichi Korean women, this chapter explores the issue of their employment. Their empowerment stems not only from gaining regular employment but also from the opportunity to expose society to the reality of their oppression and collectively advocate for equality. Social workers need to learn from them and fight alongside them, rather than fighting on their behalf. The valuable insights gained from their research can be integrated into social work education, leading to a better understanding of their experiences and fostering solidarity with them.

Moreover, it is essential to collaborate with Zainichi Korean women and fellow social workers to challenge the oppressive structures in society. This entails bringing awareness of the oppression and resistance of Zainichi Korean women to our colleagues in the field and engaging in social actions that appeal to society as a whole. Participatory action research, which involves working collaboratively with them to effect societal change, is also necessary. As Spivak (2006) cautioned, 'once a woman performs an act of resistance without an infrastructure that would make us recognise resistance, her resistance is in vain' (p. 62). Therefore, social workers must actively create an infrastructure for change through practices like those mentioned above. That is vital for amplifying the voices of Zainichi Korean women and making a meaningful impact in society.

Conclusion

In this chapter, we used the perspective of postcolonial feminism to reveal the reality of the intersectional oppression of Zainichi Korean women and their resistance and discussed the possibility of solidarity with them in feminist social work. From a perspective that attempts to view oppression as emanating from only one factor, Zainichi Korean women are relegated to remain out of sight. Thus, social workers must acquire a perspective of intersectionality. In addition, contempt and prejudice towards Zainichi Koreans are deeply rooted in Japanese society, and social workers themselves are not free from them. Therefore, it is imperative to conduct an in-depth exploration of the history and current manifestations of Colonialism, racism, and sexism. Understanding how these oppressive forces have influenced social work is crucial in order to address and overcome these issues effectively.

However, there are additional challenges that need to be addressed. If Zainichi Korean women are solely perceived as clients, they will continue to be marginalised and relegated to a subordinate position. Social workers must confront their own colonial mindset, which views individuals merely as victims and seeks to intervene in their lives. Instead, social workers must actively pursue solidarity with Zainichi Korean women at every possible opportunity and work towards establishing a platform that amplifies their voices in society. Accomplishing this requires a fundamental shift in the attitude of conservative social work and a concerted effort to counter the prevailing trends of neoliberal policies.

References

Apeuro: Network of Zainichi Korean Women Creating the Future. (2019). *2nd survey of Zainichi Korean women: Questionnaire on difficulty in life* (Digest version). https://imadr.net/wordpress/wp-content/uploads/2020/07/Apro_report_digest_2020.pdf

Committee on the Elimination of Discrimination based on Gender and Sexuality, Human Rights Association for Korean Residents in Japan. (2020). *Breaking through the inner walls: Harassment cases of Zainichi Korean Women*.

Dalrymple, J., & Burk, B. (2006). *Anti-oppressive practice: Social care and the law* (2nd ed.). Open University Press.

Deepak, A. C. (2019). Postcolonial feminist social work. In S. A. Webb (Ed.), *The Routledge handbook of critical social work* (pp. 182–189). Routledge.

Hyun, J. (2022). Report on activities as a defense lawyer for victims of the "Arson case in Utoro". *Human Rights and Life, 55*, 44–49.

Kim, P. (2011). *Continuing colonialism and gender*. Seorishobo.

Kim, K. (2022). *Accumulating discrimination and poverty: Zainichi Korean and public assistance system*. Hosei University Press.

Kojima, A. (2019). On the use of concept of intersectionality and the significance of critical reflection in anti-oppression social work practice (AOP). *Women's Studies, 26*, 19–38.

Kyong-Hee, H. (2021). Thoughts on publishing a collection of examples of harassment against Korean women in Japan. *Human Rights and Life, 52*, 66–68.

Lee, H. (2022). Considering intersectionality and multiple discrimination for Korean women in Japan. *Buraku Liberation, 830*, 37–47.

Miyazaki, O. (2018). Exclusion and the values of social work. *Social Work Studies, 44*(3), 43–50.

Mohanty, C. T. (1984). Under Western eyes: Feminist scholarship and colonial discourses. *Boundary 2, 12*(3), 333–358. https://doi.org/10.2307/302821

Park-Kim, W. (2012). Interview with Hyeonok Kim: With a desire to resolve the Japanese military "comfort women" issue and to unify North and South Korea. *Human Rights and Life, 35*, 36–45.

Park-Kim, W. (2021). *Because I want to improve the Zainichi Korean community better*. Hurights Osaka. https://www.hurights.or.jp/japan/multiple-discrimination-and-women/voices/2022/02/post-2.html

Shimizu, A. (2021). The hope of not being the "same women": Feminism and intersectionality. In K. Iwabuchi (Ed.), *Dialogue with diversity: What promoting diversity makes visible* (pp. 145–164). Seikyusha.

Shoya, R., & Nakayama, T. (1997). *Elderly Zainichi Koreans in Japan*. Ocyanomizusyobo.
Song, Y. (2005). Who are Zainichi Korean women? In M. Iwsaki, M. Okawa, T. Nakano & L. Hyoduk (Eds.), *Continuing colonialism: Gender, ethnicity, race and class* (pp. 260–275). Seikyusha.
Spivak, G. C. (1988). Can the subaltern speak? In C. Nelson & L. Grossberg (Eds.), *Marxism and the interpretation of culture* (pp. 271–313). University of Illinois Press.
Spivak, G. C. (1996). Subaltern talk: Interview with the editors. In D. Landry & G. Maclean (Eds.), *The Spivak reader: Selected works of Gayatri Chakravorty Spivak* (pp. 287–308). Routledge.
Spivak, G. C. (2006). *Conversations with Gayatri Chakravorty Spivak*. Seagull Books.
Takemura, K. (2001). Feminism and postcolonialism. In S. Kang (Ed.), *Postcolonialism* (pp. 43–49). Sakuhinsha.
Yamashita, Y. (2008). *From a crack in nationalism: Another perspective on comfort women*. Akashishoten.

47
THE CONTRIBUTION OF FEMINIST NEW MATERIALISM TO SOCIAL WORK

Vivienne Bozalek

The contribution of feminist new materialism to social work

Feminism is a broad field which has made major contributions to social work over many years, since the inception of the profession in the United States and in the United Kingdom, for example, the work of Jane Addams (1860–1935) and her establishment of Hull House in Chicago, and Mary Wollstonecraft's activism in the United Kingdom. The different strands of feminist theory, such as liberal, radical, Marxist, Black, poststructuralist Indigenous and ecofeminist traditions, have impacted on social work theorising and practice across geopolitical contexts. Feminist new materialism (FNM), however, has not been well-documented in social work with the exception of a few recent texts (see, for example, various chapters in the edited collection by Bozalek & Pease, 2021; Stephen Webb's (2021) article on social work and agential realism; and more peripherally, Natasha Mauthner's (2021) article on using Karen Barad's work to theorise and study family relationships; and most recently, Raewyn Tudor's (2023) article on a diffractive experiment in trauma-informed practice, and Mona Livholts' (2023) book which also addresses the post-anthropocentric condition of social work). There is thus a need to engage more closely with these starting conversations about what FNM has to offer social work, which this chapter intends to address through offering an introduction to the FNM by considering common misconceptions in relation to it – what it is assumed to be but what it is not. In so doing, it is hoped that readers will be given some understanding firstly of what FNM entails, and secondly, how social work might be reconfigured using FNM.

As will be seen in the chapter, FNM requires a major reconsideration and reworking of basic assumptions underlying social work. It is premised on a relational ontology where relationships precede entities, with entities only coming into being through relationships. FNM also proceeds from the notion that politics, ethics, ontology and epistemology are inextricably entangled and cannot be separated from each other. FNM builds on poststructuralist and material feminisms, as well as Indigenous sensibilities which foreground the importance of the material-discursive and eschew binary thinking. These approaches challenge human-centred views of the world as well as Western Cartesian assumptions of binary oppositions nature/culture, human/animal, mind/body, which are present in most social and political thought.

The chapter makes no assumptions about familiarity with FNM and its potential contribution to social work as a discipline, practice and a field. In order to acquaint readers with FNM and to argue for the contribution that it can make to reconfiguring social work as a discipline, the chapter is structured around the consideration of common misconceptions about FNM. Although there are a number of major theorists associated with FNM, such as Karen Barad, Rosi Braidotti, Vinciane Despret, Donna Haraway, Erin Manning, Deborah Bird Rose and Isabelle Stengers, this chapter focuses largely on the work of the US queer quantum physicist and philosopher, Karen Barad as a major scholar in the field. Karen Barad is one of the most influential theorists in new materialism and their[1] innovative, rich work has shaken the political, ethical, ontological and epistemological foundations of many disciplines (see, for example, Brown, Siegel & Blom, 2020). Their agential realist framework was developed from a diffractive reading of Niels Bohr's quantum physics through queer theories and poststructuralism. Agential realism is rapidly gaining traction across disciplines in higher education (see, for example, Bozalek & Pease, 2021; Juelskjær, Plauborg & Adrian, 2021; Livholts, 2023; Murris & Bozalek, 2023). Juelskjær et al. (2021, p. 2) explain the importance that agential realism has for FNM in their Dialogues on Agential Realism:

> Agential realism resonates with, and drives, a growing interest in material agency and theories of ontological relationality within the social sciences and humanities. It is specifically embedded in, and stems from, debates concerning the status of materiality in feminist theorizing, feminist politics and feminist science studies.
> *(e.g., Alaimo & Hekman, 2008; Coole & Frost, 2010; Dolphijn & van der Tuin, 2012)*

Research inspired by agential realism can be challenging and difficult to access and this chapter is an attempt to provide accessible ways of engaging with Barad's FNM. This chapter focuses on common misconceptions of FNM through Barad's work. Barad's work is useful for examining these misconceptions in that it provides a clear exposition of the philosophical underpinnings of FNM. More specifically, this chapter concentrates on just three frequent misconceptions about FNM – firstly, that entanglement is about how things and people interact with each other, as individually bounded entities; secondly, that FNM is about uncertainty and different ways of knowing (epistemology); and thirdly, that FNM is supportive of reflexivity, reflection and critique. It is hoped that in clarifying these three misconceptions about agential realism, social work readers might gain fresh insights into complex and contentious concepts which underpin FNM.

First misconception – FNM is about how things and people *interact* with each other

As noted earlier, FNM is predicated upon a relational ontology which holds that entities do not pre-exist, but come into being through relationships. This has a further implication – that entities cannot be assumed to be pre-given, and there are no prior subjects or objects. Such an understanding might be quite difficult for those in the social work profession, or indeed, anyone to come to terms with. It requires much attention, and Barad (2007) spends a great deal of time explaining this and re-turning to these explanations, in their major text *Meeting the Universe Halfway*.

With regard to relational ontology, Karen Barad has developed the neologism *intra-action* in order to distinguish it from interaction. Interaction assumes that entities are given and exist in the world and have a reciprocal influence on each other. In other words, as Barad observes in an interview on intra-action (Kleinman, 2012), interaction assumes the existence of independent individually constituted entities that act upon each other. Intra-action disrupts this metaphysics of individualism, holding that individuals are not determinate and do not exist *a priori* but materialise through intra-action. Individuals only exist in *phenomena* which in Barad's agential realism are "the entanglement—the ontological inseparability—of intra-acting agencies. (Where agency is an enactment, not something someone has, or something instantiated in the form of an individual agent.[2])" (Kleinman, 2012, p. 77).

So to summarise the points made thus far, in Barad's agential realist framework, individuals only exist in phenomena, which in quantum physics is the entanglement of intra-acting agencies. Individuals materialise through specific intra-actions called *agential cuts* where boundaries and properties of individuals become determinate. For example, in the field of disability studies, a cane can be used as a prosthetic device to assist a visually impaired person to grasp and negotiate the terrain – in this instance the agential cut is the personcane – the cane is seen as an extension of the human. It could also, however, be used by the visually impaired person to examine the contours of the cane itself – in this case the agential cut would be visually impaired person and the cane – as separate from each other. The cane is not inherently part of the visually impaired person but, when used to scan the environment, becomes subject and object. When examined by the visually impaired person, it becomes the object, showing that there is no fixity between subject and object (Barad, 2007).

An agential cut is contrasted with a Cartesian cut which is dichotomous and takes for granted inherent distinctions – for example, between subject and object (cane and person), whereas an agential cut effects a contingent subject and object within the phenomenon (personcane or person cane). This means that subjects and objects do not exist prior to the agential cut – they only become determinate contingently through the agential cut. Agential cuts cut together/apart (Barad, 2014) in that they make *contingent boundaries* but are simultaneously *entangled* – this is known as agential separability, which is an enactment of boundaries known as *"exteriority-within-phenomena"* (Barad, 2007, p. 140). In social work, this would mean that there is no absolute separation between social worker and client, observer and observed, subject and object, self and Other, but that these are part of phenomena and contingently come into being through agential cuts. This is also extended to the more-than-human, where human and more-than-human are always already entangled. Stacy Alaimo's (2016) concept "trans-corporeality" is useful for social work, in that it stresses the inseparability of humans and the world, with a radical openness in constant becoming-with the environment through intra-action. This means being "composed, re-composed, and decomposed by other bodies" (p. 77). Here the Cartesian finished product which assumes an individualised fixed and finalised identity is troubled. Alaimo's trans-corporeality is a useful concept for social work as it shows how it is impossible to separate flows of substances and the "economic, political, cultural, scientific, and substantial" from an "ostensibly bounded human subject" (Alaimo, 2016, p. 111). For social work, the entanglement of all these forces and flows is a useful way of conceptualising the world as a complex multiplicity rather than reducing this complexity. Cultivating an attentiveness to such multiplicities is an important sensibility for living and dying on what is now a damaged planet (Haraway, 2016). FNM in the form of agential realism eschews both absolute exteriority and absolute interiority, as well as determinism and free will (Barad, 2007). For example, "culture" is not an external force in social work which acts on nature as a passive force – in other words, "nature" doesn't pre-exist "culture" and vice versa. Rather, they are inseparably material-discursive[3] and affect each other as natureculture – where neither are prioritised and nor pre-exist the other. Intra-actions make some things possible and exclude others, in terms of enabling constraints (Manning, 2020), thus eschewing both determinism and free will, but keeping the future open to new possibilities and new exclusions through intra-active reconfigurations.

That agency does not reside in individual humans or solely in human actions, but rather in the performance of worlding – the way in which part of the world makes itself intelligible to another part of the world, would have significant implications for social work. Liberal humanist traditions which see agency as a human attribute often indirectly inform social work theories and practices. If agency is not an attribute that someone or something has, but an enactment, this needs to be taken into account in the ways in which social work practice, education and research are *done*. This puts the responsibility on social workers to be aware of how particular intra-actions reconfigure some possibilities for change whilst excluding others. Social workers also need to be aware of the iterative possibilities of change through boundary-making processes and reconfigurations of material-discursive conditions. In a similar vein, social workers also need to take cognisance of the fact that the other is always already co-constituted and entangled with the self (so there is no Self-Other dichotomy). This understanding would assist in ethical sensibilities of response-ability (the ability to respond) and responsibility (accountability for) in social work (see Bozalek & Hölscher, 2023 for more about social work posthuman or feminist new materialist sensibilities).

Social work as a profession has taken relationships into account, in contrast to psychology, which focuses primarily on the inner psyche of the individual. However, from a feminist new materialist position of relational ontology, social work's focus on relationships does not go far enough. This is because social work is still informed by a Cartesian individualism and individualist human rights perspective, where the focus is on interconnection or interaction of separate entities or individuals, not intra-action, where the other is threaded through the self rather than being separated from the self. Being predicated on a relational ontology, the focus shifts away from the *subject* and *object* to their co-constitution or entanglement (Barad, 2007). In social work, this would mean becoming-with each other as accomplices through collaborative processual acts of creative experimental practice, potentially capacitating all involved in accessing potential. In this way all are transformed, we are all rendered capable, rather than just the client or the object of change. For example, in a project dealing with forced removals in the area of District Six, in the centre of Cape Town, South Africa, relatives of those who had been forcibly removed during the 1960s were invited to take a walk with the researchers so that all could learn through walking-as-research. Both the relatives of those who had been forcibly removed from District Six and the researchers became aware of how the societal problems in South Africa today can be hauntologically connected to the social and material effects of the apartheid past. In this way, issues of land, recuperation and Otherness become apparent to all involved in a form of embodied transdisciplinary and transgenerational activism (Motala & Bozalek, 2022).

Second misconception – FNM is about *uncertainty*

Another very common misconception about FNM is that it is concerned with uncertainty, rather than indeterminacy. In their major work *Meeting the Universe Halfway*, Barad (2007) goes into fine detail about how uncertainty and indeterminacy differ from each other and what the implications of this are. In this section of the chapter, I will outline these differences and consider the implications of these for social work as a discipline.

Uncertainty has to do with *epistemology* (knowledge), in that it is about not being certain or not knowing whether a state of affairs is or is not. For example – whether it is here or there, now or then. Indeterminacy, on the other hand, is about *ontology* (being or becoming) in that it holds that the world does not consist of individually existing *determinately* bounded entities which have inherent properties or characteristics. Rather, the world consists of phenomena which are always in a state of becoming, of radical openness. In this case, it is not here or there, now or then, but there is no determinate fact of the matter, whether it is here or there, now or then.

Thus, uncertainty assumes that inherent properties of entities exist prior to their measurement, but indeterminacy does not. Barad (2007) uses the work of the quantum physicist Niels Bohr to show how atoms possess an inherent indeterminacy. Barad gives the example of how an electron can sometimes be a particle and at other times be a wave, depending on the material arrangements of the apparatus with which it is measured. In other words, the identity is in an indeterminate state prior to being measured and it has no inherent properties. Particles and waves therefore do not pre-exist intra-actions such as measurement. When something is measured, certain properties become determinate and others are excluded. This means that the ontology or the very nature of the entity changes, depending on the measuring apparatus used.

Barad (2007) provides another example of this in quantum physics – position and momentum, which are known as complementary states, as the one excludes the other – you could never have position and momentum simultaneously. Since concepts like position and momentum are defined by the circumstances required for their measurement, it becomes clear that concepts are not ideational from an FNM position but are dependent on specific physical or material arrangements. In this way, they are material-discursive. For example, position can only be measured if a fixed plate or platform is used in an apparatus, and momentum as a concept comes into being through an apparatus which consists of moveable parts or a platform on a spring. These are said to be complementary states as the one excludes the other – you cannot have position and momentum simultaneously – only one or the other is determinate. Here it is indeterminacy rather than uncertainty that is at stake, as the reciprocal relation between momentum and position is semantic and ontic, not epistemic. Epistemic implies that something is given but one does not know it, it is a case of unknowability. With indeterminacy, on the other hand, it is not possible to know something definite about something which does not have inherent properties or boundaries. It is only through particular material or physical arrangements that something becomes determinate.

If the world is indeterminate rather than uncertain, and concepts are material-discursive, becoming meaningful and semantically determinate in physical arrangements, then this has major implications for social work. In their book *Meeting the Universe Halfway*, Barad (2007) shows how, in a Calcutta jute mill in India, identity categories such as gender, class, and caste are not separately determinate attributes of individual workers but materialise through and are enfolded into one another. How these materialise is also dependent on the spatiality and temporality of the factory floor, and the human power relations which create differential patterns of mattering. Mattering here is used in the double meaning of the word – as matter and as something which comes to matter or is of concern. In the jute factory, workers, management and machines are phenomena which are entangled and co-constitute each other. Using this notion of an entangled phenomenon, the nested notions of society, community and self or local, national and global which are commonly used and taken-for-granted in social work would need to be critically examined and reworked. As Barad (2007, p. 245) puts it:

> different scales of individual bodies, homes, communities, regions, nations, and the global are not seen as geometrically nested in accordance with some physical notion of size but rather are understood as being intra-actively produced through one another.

In a similar vein, is Barad's proposition that theorising is part of the world and is a performance which is not disembodied and does not necessarily involve humans, but:

> The world theorizes as well as experiments with itself. Figuring, reconfiguring. Animate and (so-called) inanimate creatures do not merely embody mathematical theories; they do mathematics. But life, whether organic or inorganic, animate or inanimate, is not an unfolding algorithm. Electrons, molecules, brittlestars, jellyfish, coral reefs, dogs, rocks, icebergs, plants, asteroids, snowflakes, and bees stray from all calculable paths, making leaps here and there, or rather, making here and there from leaps, shifting familiarly patterned practices, testing the waters of what might yet be/ have been/could still have been, doing thought experiments with their very being.
>
> *(Barad & Gandorfer, 2021, p. 15)*

Barad (2007) uses the example of the brittlestar, an oceanic creature, to challenge social work's assumptions of Cartesian knowledge-making that the world exists only in a self-contained rational human subject's mind. Brittlestars intra-act with their oceanic environment without brains or eyes (their body is made up of multiple visual apparatuses) in entangled material practices of knowing and being. They avoid predators by moving away and dropping their limbs, thus reworking their bodies. Self and other are undone – there are no given bodies with inherent boundaries, but rather intra-actions which differentially constitute subjects. Here knowing is part of a response-ability, an ability to respond to what matters and what is excluded from mattering. As Barad (2007, p. 379) points out – "'I think, therefore I am' is not the brittlestar's credo. Knowing is not a capacity that is the exclusive birthright of the human." Knowledge is rather a distributed practice, including the larger material environment, and if the human is involved in practices of knowing, this happens "as part of the larger material configuration of the world and its ongoing open-ended articulation" (Barad, 2007, p. 379). For social work, theorising as radical openness makes it possible to think differently, to ask questions "all the way down" (Barad & Gandorfer, 2021, p. 18). This is also not an individualised activity but an intra-active one, where all are affected. For example, in relation to writing Barad (2007, p. xi) notes, "there is no singular point of time that marks the beginning" of writing and no "I" that wrote the book from beginning to end and no "I" that can claim credit for writing the book. Rather, as they eloquently put it:

> it is not so much that I have written this book, as that it has written me. Or rather, "we" have "intra-actively" written each other ("intra-actively" rather than the usual

"interactively" since writing is not a unidirectional practice of creation that flows from author to page, but rather the practice of writing is an iterative and mutually constitutive working out, and reworking, of "book" and "author")

(Barad, 2007, pp. x–xi)

Indeterminacy thus has major implications for social work in that it completely unsettles the notions of self and other, being and non-being, undoing the notion of identity upon which much social work theorising and practice is based. In FNM, therefore, identity is not given, but is performed and comes into being through relationality. Identity, such as gender, race, sexuality, class or caste, is not an essence in a human but is a doing. It is not something that someone chooses, but it is a performance. In the same way, able-bodiedness is not a natural state of being but

a specific form of embodiment that is co-constituted through the boundary-making practices that distinguish "able-bodied" from "disabled." Focusing on the nature of the materiality of able bodies as phenomena, not individual objects/subjects, makes it clear what it means to be able-bodied: that the very nature of being able-bodied is to live with/in and as part of the phenomenon that includes the cut and what it excludes, and therefore, that what is excluded is never really other, not in an absolute sense, and that in an important sense, then, being able-bodied means being in a prosthetic relationship with the "disabled."

(Barad, 2007, p. 158)

Thus, it can be seen that identity or ontology is never fixed, it is indeterminate and open to both future and past reworkings. In addition to identity, space and time are also not pre-givens but come into being through intra-action and the emergence of phenomena. In the same way that Cartesian thought assumes that the world is populated by independent bounded objects with determinate characteristics; it also assumes that these move around in a "container called "space" in step with a linear sequence of moments called "time". But the evidence indicates that the world does not operate according to any such classical ontology" (Barad, 2012, p. 43). Space is not a given volume in which events happen and time is not about a series of moments as in clock time. Space and time thus do not exist outside phenomena but are intra-actively produced in the making of phenomena. This also impacts significantly on social work as it brings to the fore temporal and spatial indeterminacy which queer our notions of time and space, and which also have ethical implications for how social work is practiced. There are obligations for social work to rework the material effects – the sedimentations and marks on bodies of the past and the future, which are "written into the flesh of the world" (Barad, 2012, p. 47) and to understand social work's complicity in these (see, for example, Bozalek & Hölscher, 2022 for an example of hauntology and social work's complicity in colonial practices).

Third misconception – FNM encourages reflexivity, reflection and critique

Social work practice has paid a great deal of attention to reflection and reflexivity, with critical reflexive/reflective practice playing a prominent influence in professional practice in recent decades (e.g., D'Cruz, Gillingham & Melendez, 2007; Ewing, Waugh & Smith, 2022; Fook, 2015, 2016; Fook & Gardner, 2007; Morley, 2014; Morley & Stenhouse, 2020).

FNM alerts us to the problems with reflexivity and reflection through its reliance on representationalist thought. Representationalism according to Barad (2007) is the belief that words, ideas, concepts etc. accurately mirror or reflect the things to which they refer. This gives rise to the belief that it is possible to turn the mirror back on oneself in a reflexive methodology. Thus, one of the problems of reflexivity is that it is founded on representationalist thought.

> Reflexivity takes for granted the idea that representations reflect (social or natural) reality. That is, reflexivity is based on the belief that practices of representing have no effect on the objects of investigation and that we have a kind of access to representations that we don't have to the objects themselves. Reflexivity, like reflection, still holds the world at a distance. It cannot provide a way across the social constructivist's allegedly unbridgeable epistemological gap between knower and known, for reflexivity is nothing more than iterative mimesis: even in its attempts to put the investigative subject back into the picture, reflexivity does nothing more than mirror mirroring. Representation raised to the nth power does not disrupt the geometry that holds object and subject at a distance as the very condition for knowledge's possibility. Mirrors upon mirrors, reflexivity entails the same old geometrical optics of reflections.
>
> *(Barad, 2007, pp. 87–88)*

Reflection does not work in a relational ontology, as we are part of the world and cannot observe it from a distance. We thus have direct access to the material world as well as to our own ideations of it.

Feminist science scholars in the 1990s became dissatisfied and began to express their misgivings with reflexivity as they saw it as being grounded in representationalism – Donna Haraway was one such scholar (1992, 1997), who began to consider how reflexivity may be inadequate for bringing the self into visibility in relation to situated knowledges (Haraway, 1988). Haraway (1988) developed the notion of situated knowledges, by which she meant a particular and embodied perspective of the knower and their social networks, as she was critical of the limits of scientific universal views of the world. Haraway (1997) proposed diffraction as an alternative methodology to reflexivity. While reflexivity remains caught up in sameness, displacing the same elsewhere because of its mirroring of fixed positions, diffraction is specifically attuned to differences and their effects on knowledge-making practices. Haraway (1992) defined diffraction as "a mapping of interference, not of replication, reflection, or reproduction. A diffraction pattern does not map where differences appear, but rather maps where the effects of difference appear" (p. 300). Importantly, with diffraction, difference is seen in an affirmative light, as a tool of creativity rather than as separation and lack. This is important for social work, as difference is often seen as the abject other, or as less than, and to be included in the mainstream. Difference from within is seen as a means of becoming-with (Haraway, 2016), as noted before in the discussion of exteriority-within, self is threaded through the other and vice versa. Barad (2007) built on Haraway's notion of diffraction as a methodology for affirmative reading.

But what is diffraction? Diffraction is a physical phenomenon which is unique to wave behaviour. It happens when waves (sound, light or water) combine and overlap – and bend and spread out and when they encounter an obstacle. In contrast to reflecting apparatuses like mirrors, which produce images which are the exact replica of the objects in front of them, reflecting sameness, diffraction patterns mark differences in amplitude and phase of the individual waves as they combine. Diffractive patterns also reveal that there is light in darkness and dark in lightness, in this way providing an understanding of how binaries can be queered, and how differences exist both within and beyond boundaries (Barad, 2014).

Barad (2007) built on Haraway's ideas of diffraction as a metaphor, proposing diffraction as a methodology, using ideas from Niels Bohr's quantum physics to focus on difference and the entanglement of matter and meaning. Diffraction requires being accountable for the entanglements which we find ourselves as being part of, as well as the ability to respond, response-ability, in a yearning for social justice (Barad, 2007) and for some worlds and not others (Haraway, 2016). Diffraction is an entanglement of epistemological, political, ontology and ethical domains – Barad refers to it as a politico-ethico-onto-epistemological approach (Barad, 2019).

Both reflection and diffraction are optical phenomena. For Haraway and Barad, diffraction becomes a useful counterpoint to reflection, a well-worn and pervasive trope for thinking and doing in social work. Diffraction is not caught up in sameness as reflection is, but rather is about patterns of difference that matter – the small but consequential differences that are produced. Rather than starting from the assumption of the givenness of things and binaries, diffraction enables a tracing how the material conditions in which boundaries are produced – a thinking about thinking otherwise (Barad & Gandorfer, 2021).

In social work, it would be possible to shift our thinking from reflection to diffraction through an understanding that we are always already part of the world, and it is impossible to extricate ourselves from it in order to hold whatever we are examining from a distance. Reflection requires that we hold objects at a distance in order to reflect on them (this is part of representationalist thought). For social work, a performative understanding of material-discursive practices would challenge the representationalist belief of words to represent pre-existing things. A performative understanding of the world does not position us as above or outside of what we are writing, thinking, observing or theorising. Rather we are part of the world and our practices are always already engaged and entangled with it, inside the other. For example, in conducting home visits, social workers should not come with presuppositions about who or what they might find but should hold the possibility open for letting those who are visited intra-actively shape what happens. In this way, through cultivating a genuine curiosity and openness, surprises may be in store, rather than an unfolding of taken-for-granted assumptions. Thinking diffractively with regard to critique and criticality makes us aware that since we are entangled with whatever is the focus of the critique, it is problematic to speak of a critique *of* something – since that implies that it is at a distance (Barad & Gandorfer, 2021).

In social work, in addition to revisiting the taken-for-granted value of reflexivity and reflective practice, we would have to re-examine the notions of critical, critique and criticality, with the understanding that we are always already entangled with and inseparable from whatever we are focusing on, all the way down. Here epistemology is not enough, but a politico-ethico-onto-epistemology is called for to understand material-discursive entanglements in which intra-action takes place. A diffractive practice of attending to the entanglements of social work as a discipline means that there is no individual self that precedes the encounter in a self-reflexive epistemological way, but a response-ability from with/in the discipline to iteratively read insights through one another, and in this way, an ongoing process of opening up and reconfiguring social work to new ways of thinking, being and doing.

A diffractive reading is an affirmative reading of one text, theory, approach, oeuvre through another, rather than pitting one against another by holding one as stable, pre-existing or primary and comparing it to another. Diffraction does not fix subject and object in advance as separate entities in a relation to absolute exteriority, Barad's framework of agential realism was developed by reading Bohrian quantum physics through Butler and Foucault's poststructuralism, thus thinking the natural and cultural together and looking for inventive insights. As Barad aptly explains the process

> Like the diffraction patterns illuminating the indefinite nature of boundaries-displaying shadows in "light" regions and bright spots in "dark" regions-the relationship of the cultural and the natural is a relation of "exteriority within." This is not a static relationality but a doing-the enactment of boundaries-that always entails constitutive exclusions and therefore requisite questions of accountability.
>
> *(Barad, 2007, p. 135)*

Social work would benefit from seeing itself not as a separate entity with absolute exteriority but as being in touch with the liveliness of other practices and worldings which can be read through each other for patterns of resonance and dissonance in order to gain new insights and a richer perspective. A collaborative approach would assist in developing such insights, where no one discipline is held as primary or as instructive for another, but they are read through each other. An example of a collaborative project of transdisciplinary work with social work, psychology and occupational therapy students across a historically advantaged/white and a historically disadvantaged/Black higher education institution had the effect of getting students and lecturers to re-examine their own disciplinary and institutional boundaries and assumptions in relation to community, self and identity (Carolissen & Bozalek, 2017; Leibowitz et al., 2012).

Diffraction involves reading insights through one another in a detailed reading, paying attention to the specificities of a text, and also being attuned and responding to the differences and how they matter. Differences that our knowledge practices make in the world (Barad, 2007, p. 72), rather than reading against some fixed target. This would change the conventional way that literature reviews are conducted in social work, where the work of one theorist or researcher is usually used as a fixed target, against which another's work is compared, contrasted or juxtaposed. A diffractive reading does not assume a metaphysics of individualism and thus does not take "this" or "that" as separate or given, but rather as in relation to each other, so it is not possible to compare them. For a social work literature review, what would be important would be to interrogate how theories and ideas materialised and how they became sedimented in the profession.

Conclusion

This chapter has provided a number of provocations for breaking out of persistent habits of uncritically embracing representational and humanist logics and imaginaries, which are far more pervasive in social work scholarship, practice and theorising than realised. There are such texts which are now starting to emerge in the discipline, which provide the impetus for doing social work differently (see the contributions in Bozalek & Pease's [2021] book, Tudor's [2023] and Livholt's [2023] work, for example). We need to see what is sedimented in the metaphysics of individualism informing social work and bring this to the surface, so that it can be opened up for reworking and for reconfiguring the field (Barad & Gandorfer, 2021). Moving away from this representationalist trap would require a diffractive rather than reflective methodology. This would require the cultivation of close attentiveness to fine details and a sense of response-ability to opening up the profession. This is not a once-off practice, but one that is ongoing and iterative. Social work needs to be understood from a material-discursive perspective – both in its materiality and in the discourses which have been instrumental in forming it and maintaining it through various geopolitical contexts and eras.

The three common misconceptions which are elucidated in this chapter were used to bring to the forefront important aspects of FNM which have major implications for how we think, practice and theorise social work as a discipline and field. According to Karen Barad, the core principle of agential realism is ontological indeterminacy not epistemological uncertainty. FNM refuses the givenness of a humanist metaphysics of individualism, and social work needs to reconsider its methodologies which undermine a relational ontology of entanglement such as reflexivity, critical reflection, comparison and critique. Where critique operates in a mode of distance and exposure of pathologies, diffraction offers social work an affirmative methodology of reading insights through one another to come to new provocations for the discipline. The world's ongoing dynamism is part of this indeterminacy – differentiating/entangling. Ontology, materiality, discursivity, agency, space and time are completely rethought in FNM, producing new understandings of how social work might be reconfigured.

Space, time and matter cannot be taken as givens in a social work informed by FNM – it is necessary to ask about their production and how the ongoing iteration of spacetimemattering unfolds. The ongoing touching which is ontological indeterminacy results in the world reconfiguring itself. Humans are part of this world and can never extricate themselves from it.

This chapter has attempted to invite the reader to engage with agential realism as a critical practice in social work for making a difference to the world. As social workers, we need to think about which differences matter and to whom they matter. Agential realism allows us to think about phenomena in the world and how we are all part of the world's becoming. Practices of knowing involve social workers playing their part in reconfiguring the world as part of the world, and that is both responsive to and responsible for our past, present and future contributions to the world.

Notes

1 Karen Barad uses the pronouns they/their.
2 This comment in brackets occurs in the interview between Kleinman and Barad and is an important aside, as in most social work feminist texts, agency is assumed to be internal to, or reside in the individual. This might then be seen as another misconception about FNM.
3 Barad (2007) uses discourse in a similar way to Foucault. It does not refer to written words in language or linguistic systems but to what enables or constrains what can be said in a particular era. For example, child abuse only became known and diagnosable in a specific time period in the 19th century – it didn't exist before then. Discourses produce rather than describe subjects and objects of knowledge-making practices.

References

Alaimo, S. (2016). *Exposed: Environmental politics and pleasures in posthuman times*. University of Minnesota Press.
Alaimo, S. & Hekman, S. (Eds.). (2008). *Material feminisms*. University of Indiana Press.
Barad, K. (2007). *Meeting the universe halfway: Quantum physics and the entanglement of matter and meaning*. Duke University Press. https://doi.org/10.2307/j.ctv12101zq.
Barad, K. (2012). Nature's queer performativity. *Kvinder, Køn & Forskning*, 1–2, 25–53.
Barad, K. (2014). Diffracting diffraction: Cutting together-apart. *Parallax*, 20 (3), 168–187.
Barad, K. (2019). After the end of the world: Entangled nuclear colonialisms, matters of force, and the material force of justice. *Theory and Event*, 22 (3), 524–550.
Barad, K. & Gandorfer, D. (2021). Political desirings: Yearnings for mattering (,) differently. *Theory & Event*, 24 (1), 14–66.
Bozalek, V. & Hölscher, D. (2022). From imperialism to radical hospitality: Propositions for reconfiguring social work towards a justice-to-come. *Southern African Journal of Social Work and Social Development*, 34 (1), 1–20.
Bozalek, V. & Hölscher, D. (2023). Reconfiguring social work ethics with posthuman and post-anthropocentric imaginaries. In D. Hölscher, R. Hugman, & D. McAuliffe (Eds.), *Social work theory and ethics*. Social Work. Springer. https://doi.org/10.1007/978-981-16-3059-0_20-1
Bozalek, V. & Pease, B. (Eds.) (2021). *Post-anthropocentric social work: Critical posthumanism and feminist new material perspectives*. Routledge.
Brown, S., Siegel, L., & Blom, S. (2020). Entanglements of matter and meaning: The importance of the philosophy of Karen Barad for environmental education. *Australian Journal of Environmental Education*, 36 (3), 219–233. https://doi.org/10.1017/aee.2019.29
Carolissen, R. & Bozalek, V. (2017). Addressing dualisms in student perceptions of a historically white and black university in South Africa. *Race Ethnicity and Education*, 20 (3), 344–357. https://doi.org/10.1080/13613324.2016.1260229
Coole, D. & Frost, S. (Eds.). (2010). *New materialism: Ontology, agency, and politics*. Duke University Press.
D'Cruz, H., Gillingham, P., & Melendez, S. (2007). Reflexivity, its meanings and relevance for social work: A critical review of the literature. *British Journal of Social Work*, 37, 73–90
Dolphijn, R. & van der Tuin, I. (2014). *New Materialism: Interviews & Cartographies*. Open Humanities Press.
Ewing, R., Waugh, F., & Smith, D. L. (Eds.) (2022). *Reflective practice in education and social work: Interdisciplinary explorations*. Routledge.
Fook, J. (2015). Reflective practice and critical reflection. In J. Lishman (Ed.), *Handbook for practice learning in social work and social care: Knowledge and theory* (pp. 440–454), 3rd ed. Jessica Kingsley.
Fook, J. (2016). *Social work: A critical approach to practice*. SAGE.
Fook, J. & Gardner, F. (2007). *Practising critical reflection: A resource handbook*. Open University Press.
Haraway, D. (1988). Situated knowledges: The science question in feminism and the privilege of partial perspective. *Feminist Studies*, 14 (3), 575–599.
Haraway, D. (1992). The promises of monsters: A regenerative politics for inapproporiate/d others. In L. Grossberg, C. Nelson, & P. A. Treichler (Eds.), *Cultural studies* (pp. 295–337). Routledge.
Haraway, D. (1997). *Modest_Witness@Second_Millenium: FemaleMan_Meets_OncoMouse: Feminism and technoscience*. Routledge.
Haraway, D. (2016). *Staying with the trouble: Making kin in the Chthulucene*. Duke University Press.
Juelskjær, M., Plauborg, H. & Adrian, S. W. (2021). *Dialogues on Agential Realism: Engaging in Worldings through Research Practice*. Routledge.
Kleinman, A. (2012). Intra-actions. *Mousse*, 34, 76–81.
Leibowitz, B., Swartz, L., Bozalek, V., Carolissen, R., Nicholls, L. & Rohleder, P. (Eds.) (2012). *Community, self and identity: Educating South African students for citizenship*. Cape Town: HSRC Press.
Livholts, M. (2023). *The body politics of glocal social work: Essays on the post-anthropocentric condition*. Routledge. https://doi.org/10.4324/9781003193593

Manning, E. (2020). *For a pragmatics of the useless.* Duke University Press. https://doi.org/10.1515/9781478012597.
Mauthner, N. S. (2021). Karen Barad's posthumanist relational ontology: An intra-active approach to theorising and studying family practices. *Families, Relationships and Societies, 10* (1), 33–49. https://doi.org/10.1332/204674321X16111601839112
Morley, C. (2014). *Practising critical reflection to develop emancipatory change: Challenging the legal response to sexual assault.* Ashgate.
Morley, C. & Stenhouse, K. (2020). How might critical reflection enable critical social work practice in mental health? *Social Work Education, 40*, 80–94.
Motala, S. & Bozalek, V. (2022). Haunted walks of district six: Propositions for counter-surveying. *Qualitative Inquiry, 28* (2), 244–256. https://doi.org/10.1177/10778004211042349
Murris, K. & Bozalek, V. (2023). *In conversation with Karen Barad: Doings of agential realism.* Routledge.
Tudor, R. (2023). 'Making cuts that matter' in social work: A diffractive experiment with trauma-informed practice. *Ethics and Social Welfare.* https://doi.org/10.1080/17496535.2023.2198774
Webb, S. A. (2021). Why agential realism matters to social work. *The British Journal of Social Work, 51* (8), 2964–2981. https://doi.org/10.1093/bjsw/bcaa106

48
ECO-FEMAGOGY
A red-green perspective for transforming social work education in the post-covid world

Susan Hillock

Introduction

Despite reams of anti-oppressive rhetoric and the fact that social work is a "…female-majority, male-dominated profession" (McPhail, 2004, p. 325), feminist content, analyses, and curriculum is not yet centred in any significant way in Canadian schools of social work (Bussey, 2008; Wilkin & Hillock, 2015). As a result, students may graduate with limited exposure to, and superficial understandings of, the dynamics underpinning gender-based oppression and systemic inequality, root causes of violence/trauma, or feminist analyses of these issues. The same can be said in terms of social work education content and material related to climate change/justice, environmentalism, and sustainability, which leaves social work practitioners unprepared to handle current and upcoming climate disasters/crises and with inadequate knowledge and skills to help populations who are most vulnerable to their impacts. To fill these gaps, the author presents a new educational approach called *eco-femagogy*. This critical red-green perspective encourages interdisciplinary teaching/learning centres Indigenous, eco-feminist, intersectional/critical race, and socialist/Marxist knowledges and analyses; mobilizes colleagues, students, and citizens towards social and environmental change; and supports social and climate justice/action. Recommendations for improving social work education are detailed. Using concrete examples, the author details how this innovative approach offers a progressive post-covid framework to transform our teaching, curricula, and methods.

The gaps

Minimal feminist content

As mentioned previously, minimal feminist content, analysis, and curriculum are evident in Canadian schools of social work (Bussey, 2008; Wilkin & Hillock, 2015). For example, in Wilkin and Hillock's (2015) review of websites of the 23 accredited Canadian schools of social work's offering Master of Social Work (MSW) programmes, only four schools offered courses specifically dealing with trauma, four offered courses on issues of abuse in families or violence against women, and four offered courses on feminist practice/therapy. Virtually all explicitly feminist and trauma-focused coursework was contained within nine

MSW programmes. Over half of the schools (12 out of 23) offered no courses at that specifically focused on trauma intervention, violence, or feminist practice. To the author, this means that as of 2015, most Canadian schools were still teaching dominant clinical models such as cognitive-behavioural therapy, psychodynamic, and systems theory with little integration of feminist, Indigenous, critical race, or queer critiques of these models. This was a particular surprising finding, as the preceding 1980s and 1990s era had seen an expansion of critical anti-oppressive theories and perspectives in social work (Baines, 2017).

Today, one would hope that after decades of discussion about anti-oppressive practice approaches, identification of gender as a central axis of intersectional oppression, and inclusion of gender-based content in textbooks and journals, this would have led to the inclusion and development of feminist analyses and courses within social work curricula as well as progressive changes in students' attitudes about feminism. However, this may not be the case (Black et al., 2010; Lazar Charter, 2015; Makofane, 2014; Tseris, 2013).

As a result, the author argues that social work education, although slowly evolving in terms of adding mandatory anti-oppressive (i.e. critical race, queer, Indigenous, and gender-based) analysis/content, still tends to be dominated by masculine, as well as white, cis-gendered, and heterosexist constructions of knowledge production, research, and teaching (Hillock, 2021; Light et al., 2015; McMahon et al., 2013). Additionally, within schools that do offer feminist coursework, these courses tend to be only offered at the Masters' level and/or mainly as electives (Wilkin & Hillock, 2015). This sends the message that issues of gender-based oppression and violence directed at women are superfluous and unnecessary material, compared to the vital and important content being explored in core courses.

Furthermore, Goodrich and Silverstein (2005) explain that feminist content and training are only integrated into programmes if a feminist faculty member initiates and sustains them; otherwise, they are not prioritized. Since social work education faculties have historically been made up of mostly white men, the inclusion of feminist courses in the curriculum requires men (and white people) to examine and dismantle their domestic, institutional, and professional privilege and their use of power, authority, and violence, an undertaking requiring a level of awareness that does not seem present at the majority of Canadian schools (Lazar Charter, 2015; Light et al., 2015). This does not only happen in social work. Crabtree and Sapp (2003) have noted a cross-disciplinary resistance to critical feminist pedagogy precisely because it requires faculty to be explicitly accountable to areas of personal privilege and challenges and subverts traditional systemic and educational power hierarchies.

As a result, Canadian social work students may graduate with a superficial understanding of, and limited exposure to, the dynamics underpinning gendered oppression and systemic inequality, root causes of violence/trauma, and/or feminist analyses of these issues (Wilkin & Hillock, 2015).

Environmental awareness missing

One could say the same about a lack of environmental awareness within the social sciences and helping professions. Although social work has an established history of using the person-in-environment approach (Germain & Gitterman, 1980), the notion of environment has been narrowly defined and primarily focused on social environments. Thus, for the most part, the flora, fauna, and planet, and violence towards them, have historically been ignored. Additionally, although social work, "...might be expected to play a leadership role in the planning stages of any new environmental state...we have generally been silent on the serious threats to human well-being and continued existence" (Zapf, 2009, pp. 17–18). As discussed earlier, this has led to significant gaps in social work education in terms of content and material related to climate change, environmentalism, and sustainability.

For instance, until very recently in Canada, its' various codes and standards of professional conduct have not included much about the natural and/or built environments as domains of assessment and intervention. Moreover, there have never been accreditation standards from our national guiding body, the Canadian Association For Social Work Education-L' Association Canadienne Pour La Formation En Travail Social (CASWE-ACFTS), on this topic. This has resulted in a lack of direction for schools of social work in terms of changing/upgrading their curricula. Of course, without relevant standards or rules, there has also been no way of enforcing the topic's inclusion. However, more recently and perhaps indicative of a global seed change in terms of social work's ecological literacy, there has now been a significant update to the Canadian national standards, as the CASWE-ACFTS (2021) has finally moved to adding an environmental standard, called *Environmental Sustainability and Ecological Practice*, which states the following:

Social work students shall have opportunities to...

a understand the need to create ecologically sustainable communities, economies, and natural and built environments, in which all life forms and eco-systems can survive and thrive;
b identify and challenge environmental injustice and racism, i.e. the inequitable burdens borne by those who are socially and economically marginalized in relation to environmental degradation and hazards;
c advance environmental sustainability across individual, organizational, and professional contexts; and,
d embrace the role of social workers in advocacy for public policies and social practices that will ensure ecological health and environmental sustainability at local, regional, national, and global levels (p.16).

It is hoped that the implementation of this new standard will lead to meaningful change.

Eco-femagogy

To fill these gaps in social work education, this author has developed an innovative approach that she calls *eco-femagogy*. It combines feminist and environmental perspectives to offer a critical red-green interdisciplinary educational framework for transforming teaching, curricula, and methods. Although the author has developed this approach within a Canadian context and social work education, it has application internationally and across various disciplines. This new approach builds upon intersectional feminist theory/analysis and women's (and other marginalized groups') ways of knowing, Indigenous knowledges, as well as, critical race, and socialist/Marxist perspectives and highlights the need for environmental awareness/literacy.

Femagogy: the feminism part

Feminism

Over the last century, an analytical and conceptual framework has emerged that can be labelled as distinctly feminist. Although there is much debate about the meaning of the term, Epstein et al. (2018) explain feminism as a way of analyzing social, economic, and political structures to," ... understand the complex cultural discourses and multiple structural systems that women interact with and through which women's lived experiences are shaped (Clegg & David, 2006)" (as cited in ibid, p. 12) that also "...help make visible the nature of violence, power, domination, patronage, exploitation, and hegemony from the standpoint of women and their subjectivities" (Pandya, 2014, p. 499). Accordingly, feminist theory seeks to decode and dismantle patriarchy (Enge, 2013), racism, classism, and heterosexism/homophobia and assesses how these intersectional forces, which can be viewed as a politic of domination, oppress marginalized groups (hooks, 2014).

Although united in terms of looking at gender inequality as a primary cause of oppression, feminism is not monolithic in terms of its goals, beliefs, values, analyses, and recommendations, and not all approaches have incorporated sustainability as a major theme. As such, there are many variations of feminism including Black (Collins, 2000); green/eco-feminism (Isla, 2019); queer (Hillock & Mulé, 2016); and anarchist, liberal, socialist, Marxist, and radical (Archer Mann, 2012).

Feminist goals

In terms of common goals, most feminists support dismantling systems of dominance and working towards building a society free from violence, exploitation, discrimination, and inequality (Light et al., 2015). Feminists also emphasize the importance of using feminist theory in education and research to explain how social, political, and economic factors influence people's lives (Flynn Saulnier, 2008). To do this, feminists critique the way societies choose to organize and distribute power, status, privilege, and wealth and analyze how these choices privilege dominant groups and oppress marginalized groups. Seeking allies and joining with others to build feminist organizations and participate in social action are also seen as essential to the feminist movement.

Eco-feminism

According to Isla (2019), eco-feminists analyze the problematic nature of white and, "... male domination of women and nature" (p. 19). They have been at the forefront in terms of pointing out the similarities between violence against women and vulnerable peoples as colonial objects to be used, exploited, and sold for the dominant group's enjoyment, consumption, and labour and violence towards the planet, animals, and habitats for similar reasons and purposes. Prominent eco-feminist, Silvia Federici, describes this as, "... the systematic subjugation and appropriation of women, nature, bodies, and labour" (as cited in ibid, p. 20). An eco-feminist lens also recognizes and celebrates women's traditional caretaking/food provision roles and close relationships with those who are most vulnerable including the flora, fauna, and planet (Bozalek & Pease, 2021).

Femogogy

Based on the concepts above, the author first developed a new term, *femagogy* (Hillock, 2021), as a way to describe the more collaborative, adult and affective learning-based, inclusive, and environmentally conscious approaches that she had been experimenting with in class and in response to what she saw as gaps in pedagogical (child-based) and andragogical (man-based) approaches to social work education. Frankly, she was also tired of teaching male-centred social work history, research, and theories to mostly female students and was very concerned about the planet. As a result, she defined femagogy as an approach to teaching and education that emphasizes feminist-centred teaching theory, knowledges, methods, and practice (e.g. Dominelli's [2002] and Webb et al.'s [2002] principles) and seeks to uncover, explore, and emphasize women's ways of knowing, doing, relating, and being (Belenky et al., 1997).

Women's ways of knowing. The term "women's ways of knowing", with its underlying modernist assumptions related to the notion that people share common experiences and that there are monolithic structural forces at the root of people's suffering, maybe problematic for some. To be sure, this term originated in the late 1980s and early 1990s may be era of identity politics, long before postmodernism and intersectional analysis became the standard in academia. There is a need to be careful here, given that the subject category of "woman" is highly contested as well as socially constructed, dynamic, diverse, and highly individual, thus, "woman" is not a homogenous classification. The author's argument runs the very real risk here of essentializing or claiming some universal truth about that which is "female" or "woman". That is not her intent.

Intersectionality and critical race theory

Consequently, the author wants to be clear that when she refers to the concept of "women's ways", she is intentionally including all "othered" voices, knowledges, and identities that have been historically dismissed and marginalized; for instance, people who identify as queer, non-binary, and transgender, those living with disability and racialized individuals (Razack et al., 2010). Essentially then, femagogy offers educators a theoretical and practical framework for active resistance to social and cultural manifestations of misogyny, racism, classism, and other manifestations of oppression (Hillock, 2021). To achieve these ends, femagogy uncovers, and centres on, all that is *not* white, male, able-bodied, cisgendered, and straight and deliberately seeks to disrupt traditional education by introducing and exploring approaches to teaching and learning that emphasize women's ways of knowing, doing, relating, and being, as well as feminist-centred theories, methods, and research (Klemmer & McNamara, 2020).

Eco: the green part

Like feminism, social work and environmentalism are congruent as a major part of our work includes an ethic of care, human rights and social justice approaches, community organization, a moral/ethical mandate to serve vulnerable populations, and an assessment paradigm that rests on a person-in-environment approach. If social workers truly support serving vulnerable populations, dismantling oppression, and promoting justice for all – what the author sees as essential parts of our professional identity – then saving the planet must become our mission. Eco-social work, or what Dominelli (2012) calls "green social work", provides a way forward.

Consequently, the author believes that to "green" social work, that is, to ensure that the protection of the flora, fauna, and planet become primary concerns, it is essential that social workers understand climate change and the relevant science to develop ecological literacy and effectively teach this content.

Climate change

Burning carbon-based fossil fuels produces carbon dioxide, a greenhouse gas that overheats the planet. If we are unable to keep global temperature under 1.5°C (which is now extremely unlikely), a series of cascading catastrophic climate events is likely to occur. Although climate change warnings started as early as the 1960s, and key international documents like the Kyoto Protocols (1997) and the Paris Agreement (2015) have been signed by multiple countries, there has been limited action/enforcement. As a result, the current situation is dire; emissions are still on the rise and the window of opportunity to save the planet is closing, as corporations, in a desperate bid for increased profit margins, turn to more extreme extraction options such as the Alberta tar sands oil projects and natural gas fracking, further poisoning the land, water, and air. Of serious concern also Also of serious concern is that Indigenous peoples around the world, especially in Canada's North, are losing the land, animals, plants, and ecology that are part of their spiritual, cultural, and cosmic existence.

Former U.S. Vice president Al Gore, in his 2006 documentary, *An Inconvenient Truth*, "...declared the environmental crisis to be a 'planetary emergency'" (as cited in Zapf, 2009, p. 16). Even the World Bank (2012), known for its conservative views, has warned that we are "...on track for a 4°C warmer world (by century's end) and marked by extreme heat waves, declining global food stocks, loss of ecosystems and biodiversity, and life-threatening sea level rise" (as cited in Klein, 2014, p.13). Indeed, as activist Greta Thunberg exclaimed, in her passionate speech at the World Economic Forum in Davos Switzerland on January 25, 2019, "...our house is on fire" (The Guardian, 2019). Moreover, "...we don't have to do anything to bring about this future. All we have to do is nothing" (Klein, 2014, p. 4).

A feminist issue

Not only was it a woman, Eunice Foote, who in 1856 first, "studied the greenhouse effect..." (Suzuki, 2020, para. 2), but as discussed earlier, eco-feminists have long contended that exploitation, control, and "mastery" of nature, for the purposes of the economy and profit-making (i.e. structural forces of patriarchy, racism, colonialism, and capitalism), go hand-in-hand with the exploitation, and domination of women and racialized peoples (Isla, 2019; Noble, 2021; Waldron, 2018). Because of systemic inequality, women (and children) are the most vulnerable to environmental degradation as they make the least money; have the least assets; are blocked from education resulting in literacy and numeracy issues; often do not have the right to say no to unwanted sex, early marriage, and pregnancy; lack affordable and accessible contraception, and thus, bear the burden of most child-rearing and home care; and, globally, have limited economic and political power, voice, and representation (Williams et al., 2018). Women are also more likely than men to need to visit ER for asthma and respiratory related conditions during wildfires"; experience reproductive issues as "...extreme weather events are associated with greater risks of low birth weight and preterm births"; and be excluded from the climate conversation as "...women make up only 19% of people interviewed, featured or quoted in climate-related news coverage" (Sierra Club, 2020a, para. 3).

Environmental racism

Climate change and disasters negatively impact some groups more than others, particularly those, who because of systemic structural inequality are more likely to experience pollution, unemployment/underemployment, extraction work, residences near factories, poverty, unsafe water and air, migrant refugee status, as well as food/housing insecurity. To describe the differential and unjust impact of intersecting forces of environmental degradation, poverty, and racism, Bullard (1990) coined the term "environmental racism", defined as "... the process whereby black and other disenfranchised minority communities bear [sic] a disproportionate share of the effects of environmental pollution..." (as cited in Dominelli, 2012, p. 97). Vulnerable groups, already under stress, have the least resources to avoid damage and recover from extreme weather events and (hu)man-made and natural disasters (Hetherington & Boddy, 2013). Accordingly, eco/green social work must work towards achieving gender, class, and race equality and consider these as "...a crucial nexus at which climate resilience must be built" (Sierra Club, 2020b, para. 3).

Critical lenses: the red part

To be effective and relevant, this chapter makes the case that eco/green social work must be intersectional, anti-racist, and feminist and, as such, support and promote anti-oppressive feminist values, beliefs, and approaches, as well as women's ways of knowing (Klemmer & McNamara, 2020). To this eco-feminist and anti-racist green lens, the author suggests that a red lens must be added. If we are truly concerned with the root causes of human suffering and eradicating oppression, then the author suggests that we have much to learn from the left ("the Reds"), that is, structural/radical feminist, critical race, and socialist/Marxist theorists. As such, these critical theories have been instrumental in pointing out that most forms of education have been complicit in supporting neo-liberalism, "...perpetuating unsustainable environmental practices" (Shepherd, 2010, p. 15), and acting as a training ground for capitalism, patriarchy and colonialism (Bigelow, 1996). Incorporating a socialist/Marxist view (Wallace, 2018), which means identifying and dismantling the structural forces that harm humans (and more-than-humans), eco/green social work challenges the way we look at the world such as the; need for expansion and progress at all cost; "man's" innate right to control and commodify the planet; view of humans and animals solely as objects/labourers/consumers; for-profit mindset at the expense of all others; and reliance on fossil fuels (Dominelli, 2018; Fogel, Barkdull, & Weber, 2016; Gray, Coates, & Hetherington, 2013; Närhi & Matthies, 2018).

Indigenous leadership

Central to this new world view, that is quintessentially feminist, anti-racist, and socialist, are Indigenous understandings of stewardship, wholism, interdependence, and connectedness in terms of our relationships with each other, nature, and the Earth (Isla, 2019; Skwiot, 2008). Some have described this as "walking the red road" (Spirit Horse Nation, 2022). Taking this path requires educators to centre Indigenous approaches; implement Canada's Truth and Reconciliation Commission's *Calls To Action* (2015); embrace elder traditions; employ "the 5 Rs - relationship, respect, responsibility, reciprocity and restoration" (Evering and Longboat, 2013, p.245); and learn from/adapt Indigenous ways of knowing and being (Rich, 2012).

Table 48.1 Applying eco-femagogy

1	Regularly engage with students in discussions/assignments about the environment, sustainability, climate change/crises, and social and environmental justice/action.
2	Critique capitalism, globalization, neo-liberalism, and corporatization.
3	Discuss structural oppression, systemic inequality, intersectionality, and environmental racism.
4	Critically examine dominant narratives and teach progressive critical approaches.
5	Expand understandings of the person-in-environment model to include more-than-humans.
6	Teach transformative, human rights, and justice approaches to help build democratic citizenship.
7	Value affective learning domains, an ethic of caring, and the importance of relationships.
8	Bring "...gender [race, class, and climate] justice to the classroom" (hooks, 2000, p. 23) and explicitly discuss violence against humans, animals, habitats, and the planet.
9	Recognize spiritual connections to land, identify/know the status of local land treaties, push teaching/learning exercises, assignments, and opportunities beyond the walls of the university, and explore nature/wilderness therapies.
10	Invite Indigenous leaders and climate activists to guest lecture/co-teach (and pay them).
11	Integrate culturally relevant participatory teaching/learning methods.
12	Create innovative assignments including green and oppression-based case studies and roleplays.
13	Provide practical participatory action opportunities and community-based work.
14	Share examples of successful social justice/climate action strategies/campaigns.
15	Review environmental/discrimination policies and practices in agencies/institutions/schools.
16	Prepare for future social work by teaching about climate action, social justice, and disaster work and developing green field placements.
17	Adopt an interdisciplinary and community-based approach to research, curricular design, and teaching.
18	Network with colleagues, students, unions, and community partners to encourage universities/organizations/agencies to: divest from fossil fuels; develop green technologies, policies, and practices; build alternative power structures; and create the conditions necessary for social change.
19	Become climate justice/action leaders by entering climate justice/action arenas, joining resistance movements, and taking on environmental leadership.

Source: Adapted from Baines (2017), Baskin (2011), Besthorn (2018), Bigelow and Swinehart (2014), Campbell and Baikie (2012), Cohee (2004), Dominelli (2002), hooks (2014), Hillock (2021, 2023), Jones (2018), Light et al. (2015), Mathieson (2002), Mezirow (2009), Miller and Hayward (2013), Okaka (2016), Richardson and Langford (2022), Shepherd (2010), Waldron (2018), and Webb et al. (2002).

Eco-femagogy: the post-Covid world

The world changed forever, in 2020, with COVID-19 which has led to a rise in fascism including climate change denial and backlash against physical distancing/masking, reliance on remote learning and employees working from home, as well as increased rates of infection and death, social inequality, isolation, family disruption, and mental health and addiction issues. substance misuse issues Simultaneously, global warming, climate migration, destruction of natural habit and species extinction, environmental racism, and natural/human-caused disasters remain unchecked. In many ways, the Covid pandemic can be viewed as Mother Nature's early warning system as it not only highlights significant global social and economic inequalities and points out those who are most vulnerable but also provides hope that humanity can act in concert to make necessary change. Another hopeful sign is the burgeoning of a massive grassroots mobilization to stop extreme extractivism, reliance on fossil fuels, and global ecocide. Consequently, the author believes that, before it is too late, now is the time for educators to enter en masse into climate justice arenas and incorporate environmental awareness into all education levels.

Recommendations

To accomplish this, she recommends building interdisciplinarity, pivoting academia, and applying eco-femagogy to education. Because social work education is still in the initial stages of trying to mainstream environmental content and develop ecological literacy, we can benefit a great deal from partnering with and learning/adapting from Indigenous leaders, academic colleagues, and community activists. For instance, Indigenous and gender studies, education, and environmental sciences have developed specific technological and pedagogical expertise in terms of *what* to teach and *how* to teach this content (Vincent et al., 2015).

However, this does not mean that social work, in return, has nothing of value to contribute, that we are passive recipients, empty vessels, as it were. Just as social workers might ask themselves, "what do we know about science, pollution, or responding to disasters", scientists would be well advised to ask themselves what they know about community organizing, dealing with mental health issues, and building individual and community resilience (Dominelli, 2018; Fogel et al., 2016; Zapf, 2009).

Furthermore, the author proposes that in order for social work as a profession, and for that matter universities/academia in general, to remain relevant, we must pivot immediately to throw all of our knowledge, skills, expertise, and resources at: fighting climate change; divesting from fossil fuels; creating green technologies; mitigating climate catastrophes; eradicating environmental racism; and dismantling systems of hierarchy and oppression, preparing for disasters, and helping communities that are most vulnerable.

Furthermore, teaching social work students how to be "masters of empathy" (Brown, 1988, p. 130) and "...comfort victims of social issues..." (Mullaly, 2006, p. 145) is simply not adequate preparation for these coming times (please see Hillock, 2023). Instead, what is required is a radical shift, far away from conventional, individualistic, clinical approaches like Cognitive Behaviorial Therapy (CBT), systems, and psychoanalysis to social work education that centres Indigenous knowledge, sustainability, climate action/justice, renewable energy, and critical approaches that challenge the basic tenets of capitalism, patriarchy, and colonialsim. Moreover, the social work profession (and educators generally) must establish a new moral imperative, one that holds the Global North and multi-national corporations responsible for causing extensive damage and joins the demand that wealthy countries rectify the damage by paying for a massive cleanup (Gray et al., 2013; Klein, 2014; Zapf, 2009). Congruently, advances in this area include the recent global biodiversity agreement at the COP15 United Nations Biodiversity Conference in Montreal in December of 2022 that includes a,

> ...pledge to reduce subsidies deemed harmful to nature by at least $500 billion by 2030, while having developed countries commit to providing developing countries with at least $20 billion per year by 2025, and $30 billion per year by 2030.
> (CBC News, 2022, para. 6)

Eco-femagogy: practical application

Teaching from a critical red-green theoretical perspective, challenging neo-liberalism, capitalism, and colonialism, and rethinking the nature of our relationships with all humans, more-than-humans, and the planet are central components to greening social work education. Accordingly, Table 48.1 above suggests ideas for applying eco-femagogy to social work education.

Conclusion

Given the current contexts of teaching and learning, educators must help students navigate ever increasing complexity and uncertainty, as well as environmental and systemic threats, with minimal assured paths to personal, social, and systemic change. In addition, changes in the COVID era point to the need, now maybe more than ever, for social work educators to develop innovative pedagogies, practice approaches, and ways of thinking about social work in the post-Covid world. Applying eco-femagogy with its critical red-green perspective actively encourages interdisciplinary teaching and learning, centres Indigenous, feminist, anti-racist, and socialist knowledge and analyses, mobilizes colleagues, students, and citizens towards social and environmental change, and supports social and climate justice/action.

Referencess

Archer Mann, S. (2012). *Doing feminist theory: From modernity to postmodernity*. Oxford University Press.
Baines, D. (Ed.). (2017). *Doing anti-oppressive practice: Social justice social work* (3rd ed.). Fernwood Publishing.
Baskin, C. (2011). *Strong helpers' teachings: The value of Indigenous knowledges in the helping professors*. Canadian Scholars' Press Inc.
Belenky, M. F., McVicker, C. B., Goldberger, N. R., & Tarule, M. J. (1997). *Women's ways of knowing: The development of self, voice, and mind* (10th Anniversary Ed). Basic Books.
Besthorn, F. H. (2018). Radical ecologism: Insights for educating social workers in ecological activism and social justice. *Critical Social Work, 4*(1), 66–107.
Bigelow, B. & Swinehart, T. (2014). *A people's curriculum for the Earth teaching climate change and the environmental crises*. A Rethinking Schools Publication.
Black, B. M., Weisz, A. N. & Bennett, L. (2010). Graduating social work students' perspectives on domestic violence. *Afflia, 25*(2), 173-184.
Bozalek, V. & Pease, B. (2021). *Post-anthropocentric social work: Critical posthuman and new materialist perspectives*. Routledge.
Brown, C. (1988). Social work education as empowerment. In E. Chamberlain (Ed.), *Change and continuity in Australian social work* (pp. 129–141). Longman Cheshire.
Bussey, M. C. (2008). Trauma response and recovery certificate program: Preparing students for effective practice. *Journal of Teaching in Social Work, 28*(1–2), 117–144.
Campbell, C. & Baikie, G. (2012). Beginning at the beginning: An exploration of critical social work. *Critical Social Work, 13*(1), 67–81.
CASWE-ACFTS. (2021). *Accreditation Standards*. https:// caswe-acfts.ca/wp-content/uploads/2021/04/EPAS-2021.pdf
CBC News. (Dec. 19, 2022). Biodiversity agreement to protect planet reached at UN conference in Montreal. *The Canadian Press*. https://www.cbc.ca/news/science/cop15-montreal-biodiversity-agreement-1.6690667
Cohee, G. (2004). Feminist pedagogy. *The Teaching Exchange, 9*(1), 1–4.
Collins, P. H. (2000). *Black feminist thought: Knowledge, consciousness, and the politics of empowerment* (2nd ed.). Routledge.

Crabtree, R. D., & Sapp, D. A. (2003). Theoretical, political, and pedagogical chal-lenges in the feminist classroom: Our struggles to walk the walk. *College Teaching, 51*(4), 131–140.

Dominelli, L. (2002). *Feminist social work theory and practice*. Palgrave.

Dominelli, L. (2012). *Green social work: From environmental crises to environmental justice*. Polity Press.

Dominelli, L. (Ed.). (2018). *The Routledge handbook of green social work*. Routledge.

Enge, Jacqueline. (2013). Social workers' feminist perspectives: Implications for practice. Retrieved from Sophia, the St. Catherine University repository website: https://sophia.stkate.edu/msw_papers/174

Epstein, S. B., Hosken, N., & Vassos, S. (2018). Creating space for a critical feminist, social work pedagogy. *Aotearoa New Zealand Social Work, 30*(3), 8–18.

Evering, B., & Longboat, D. R. (2013). An introduction to Indigenous environmental studies: From principles into action. In A. Kulnieks, D. R. Longboat & K. Young (Eds.), *Contemporary studies in environmental and Indigenous pedagogies: A curricula of stories and place* (pp. 241–258). Sense Publishers.

Flynn Saulnier, C. (2008). Incorporating feminist theory into social work practice: Group work examples. *Social Work with Groups, 23*(1), 5–29.

Fogel, S. J., Barkdull, C., & Weber, B. (2016). *Environmental justice: An issue for social work education and practice*. Routledge.

Germain, C., & Gitterman, A. (1980). *The life model of social work practice*. Columbia University Press.

Goodrich, T. J. & Silverstein, L. B. (2005). Now you see it, now you don't: Feminist training in family therapy. *Family Process, 44*(3), 267–281.

Gray, M., Coates, J., & Hetherington, T. (2013). *Environmental social work*. Routledge.

Hetherington, T., & Boddy, J. (2013). Ecosocial work with marginalized populations: Time for action on climate change. In M. Gray, J. Coates, & T. Hetherington (Eds), *Environmental Social Work* (pp. 46–61). Routledge.

Hillock, S. (2021). Femagogy: Centreing feminist knowledge and methods in social work teaching. In R. Csiernik & S. Hillock (Eds.), *Teaching social work: Reflections on pedagogy & practice* (pp. 39–55). University of Toronto Press.

Hillock, S. (Ed.). (2023). *Greening social work education: Caring sustainability*. University of Toronto Press

Hillock, S. & Mulé, N. J. (Eds.). (2016). *Queering social work education*. UBC Press.

hooks, b. (2014). *Feminism is for everybody*. Routledge.

hooks, b. (2000). *Feminist theory: From margin to centre* (2nd Ed.). South End Press.

Isla, A. (2019). *Climate chaos: Ecofeminism and the land question*. Inanna Publications & Education Inc.

Jones, P. (2018). Greening social work education: Transforming the curriculum in pursuit of eco–social justice. In L. Dominelli (Ed.), *The Routledge handbook of green social work* (pp. 558–568). Routledge.

Klein, N. (2014). *This changes everything*. Vintage Canada.

Klemmer, C. L. & McNamara, K. A. (2020). Deep ecology and ecofeminism: Social work to address global environmental crisis. *Journal of Women and Social Work, 35*(4), 503–515.

Kyoto Protocols. (1997). https://unfccc.int/kyoto_protocol.

Lazar Charter, M. (2015). Feminist self-identification among social work students. *Journal of Social Work Education, 51*(1), 72–89.

Light, T. P., Nicholas, T., & Bondy, R. (2015). *Feminist pedagogy and higher education: Critical theory and practice*. Wilfrid Laurier University Press.

Makofane, Mdn, (2014). The relevance of feminism in modern social work education. *Social Work/Maatskaplike Werk, 39*(2). DOI:10.15270/39-2-367

Mathieson, G. (2002). Reconceptualizing our classroom practice: Notes from an anti-racist educator. In N. Nathaniel Wane, K. Deliovsky, & E. Lawson (Eds.), *Back to the drawing board: African Canadian feminisms* (pp. 158–174). Sumach Press.

McMahon, S., Postmus, J. L., Warrener, C., Plummer, S. & Schwartz, R. (2013). Evaluating the effect of a specialized MSW course on violence against women. *Journal of Social Work Education, 49*(2), 307–320.

McPhail, B. A. (2004). Setting the record straight: Social work is not a female-dominated profession. *Social Work, 49*(2), 323–326.

Mellor, M. (1997). *Feminism and ecology*. New York University Press.

Mezirow, J. (2009). Transformative learning theory. In J. Mezirow & E. W. Taylor (Eds.), *Transformative learning in practise: Insights from community*. Jossey-Bass.

Miller, S. E. & Hayward, R. A. (2013). Social work education's role in addressing people and a planet at risk. *Social Work Education: The International Journal, 33*(3), 1–16.

Mullaly, B. (2006). Forward to the past: The 2005 CASW code of ethics. *Canadian Social Work Review/Revue canadienne de service social, 23*(1/2), 145–150.

Närhi, K. & Matthies, A. L. (2018). The ecosocial approach in social work as a framework for structural social work. *International Social Work, 6*(4), 490–502.

Noble, C. (2021). Ecofeminism to feminist materialism: Implications for Anthropocene feminist social work. In V. Bozalek & B. Pease (Eds.), *Post-anthropocentric social work: Critical posthuman and new materialist perspectives* (pp. 95–107). Routledge.

Okaka, W. T. (2016). *Developing green university curriculum innovations for sustainable education in Africa*. https://www.google.com/search?rls=en&source=univ&tbm=isch&q=Okaka,+W.+T.+(2016).+Developing+green+university+curriculum+innovations+for+sustainable+education+in+Africa,&client=safari&sa=X&ved=2ahUKEwiG67C0oobyAhUEac0KHcVdAsAQjJkEegQIIRAC&biw=1252&bih=745

Pandya, S. P. (2014). Feminist social work: An Indian lens. *Affilia, 29*(4), 499–511.

Paris Agreement. (2015). https://unfccc.int/process-and-meetings/the-paris-agreement/the-paris-agreement.

Razack, S., Smith, M., & Thobani, S. (2010). *States of race: Critical race feminism for the 21st century*. Between The Lines.

Rich, N. (2012). Introduction: Why link Indigenous ways of knowing with the teaching of environmental studies and sciences? *Environmental Studies and Sciences, 2*(4), 308–316.

Richardson, B., & Langford, R. (2022). Care-full pedagogy: Conceptualizing feminist care ethics as an overarching critical framework to interrupt the dominance of developmentalism within post-secondary early childhood education programs. *Contemporary Issues in Early Childhood, 23*(4), 408–420.

Shepherd, K. (2010). Higher education's role in 'education for sustainability', *Australia Universities' Review, 52*(1), pp. 13–22.

Sierra Club (March 2, 2020a). *Landmark report highlights the critical need for gender-base climate policies in US*. https://www.sierraclub.org/press-releases/2020/03/landmark-report-highlights-critical-need-for-gender-based-climate-policies-us.

Sierra Club (March 2, 2020b). *How research on gender will help us craft climate justice policy*. https://www.sierraclub.org/articles/2020/03/how-research-gender-will-help-us-craft-climate-justice-policy.

Skwiot, R. (2008, Fall). Green dream: Environmental justice is emerging from the shadows. *Social Impact*. https://openscholarship.wustl.edu/cgi/viewcontent.cgi?article=1020&context=socialimpact.

Spirit Horse Nation. (2022). *The Red Road*. https://www.spirithorsenation.org/the-red-road.

Suzuki, D. (2020). The woman who discovered global warming – in 1856! *Science Matters*. Davidsuzuki.org. https://davidsuzuki.org/story/the-woman-who-discovered-global-warming-in-1856/.

The Guardian. (January 25, 2019). *Greta Thunberg speech*. https://www.theguardian.com/environment/2019/jan/25/our-house-is-on-fire-greta-thunberg16-urges-leaders-to-act-on-climate.

Truth and Reconciliation Commission of Canada. (2015). *Calls to action*. http://trc.ca/assets/pdf/Calls_to_Action_English2.pdf

Tseris, E. J. (2013). Trauma theory without feminism? Evaluating contemporary understandings of traumatized women. *Affilia, 28*(2), 153–164.

Vincent, S., Roberts, J. T., & Mulkey, S. (2015). Interdisciplinary environmental and sustainability education: Islands of progress in a sea of dysfunction. *Journal of Environmental Studies and Sciences, 6*(2), 418–424.

Waldron, I. R. G. (2018). *There's something in the water: Environmental racism in Indigenous and Black communities*. Fernwood Publishing.

Wallace, V. (2018). *Red-green Revolution: The politics and technology of eco-socialism*. Political Animal Press.

Webb, L. M., Allen, M. W., & Walker, K. L. (2002). Feminist, pedagogy: Identifying, basic principles. *Academic Exchange, 6*(1), 67–72.

Wilkin, L. & Hillock, S. (2015). Enhancing MSW students' efficacy in working with trauma, violence, and oppression: An integrated feminist-trauma framework for social work Education. *Feminist Teacher, 24*(3), 184–206.

Williams, L., Fletcher, A., Hanson, C., Neapole, J., & Pollack, M. (2018). Women and climate change: Impacts and action in Canada. *Work in a warming world and adapting Canadian work and workplaces to respond to climate change project.* SSHRC-CURA.

Zapf, M. K. (2009). *Social work and the Environment: Understanding people and Place.* Canadian Scholars Press.

Zosky, D. L. (2013). Wounded healers: Graduate students with histories of trauma in a family violence course. *Journal of Teaching Social Work, 33*(3), 239–250.

49
INTERSECTIONALITY, FEMINIST SOCIAL WORK, ANIMALS AND THE POLITICS OF MEAT

Heather Fraser and Nik Taylor

To some if not many, it may seem unusual to link social work to the politics of meat in a book that focusses on Feminisms and social work (Figure 49.1). In part, this is due to the pervasive humanism that underpins the majority of social work and feminist perspectives (Fraser & Taylor, 2019). This humanism has, for many decades, normalised distinguishing between humans and other animals in a binary mode of thought that situates humans as superior to all other nonhuman animals and thus underpins the idea that it is acceptable to eat them. As we shall demonstrate below, this binary has important ramifications for social work (as well as other disciplines), particularly for a social work that aims to be feminist, politicised, intersectional and anti-oppressive. We start this chapter with a very

Figure 49.1 Animals, meat and social work
Source: Heather Fraser (2022).

brief overview of the burgeoning field of animal studies, as this has – at least begun to – legitimate the inclusion of animals in disciplinary fields including social work. We then turn to a consideration of how social work(ers) have begun including other animals in their theories and in fields of practice. Our aim in these sections is to introduce readers to areas that might be unfamiliar to them to contextualise our later argument that social work especially purports to use a species-inclusive intersectionality, must face the politics of meat.

Animal studies and social work

Animal studies is a field that has grown considerably in the last three decades or so, and it continues to do so. Animal studies scholars conduct a wide variety of research on subjects related to animals. Accordingly, offering a definitive history and outline of it is not possible as its parameters continue to move and fluctuate as knowledge grows and as different fields add their own specific flavour. Our own belief is that animal studies in its broadest form rests upon an interest in human-animal relationships and is informed by multiple disciplines from the social sciences, arts and humanities (DeMello, 2012; Taylor, 2013). However, as the field has grown, we have seen the development of specific ideological and epistemological positions within it. Wilkie (2015, p. 212) points out that these positions reflect tensions within the field that in turn reflect "(1)…the extent to which nonhuman animal scholars should be engaged with emancipatory-type research and (2) the emergence of the "animal as such–animal as constructed" axis". This is often reflected in the names scholars choose to use for their work. More mainstream (or animal welfare rather than rights) positions like Anthrozoology, for example, lean towards a scientific and positivist ideology that rests upon and leaves untroubled anthropocentric notions of "animals". Work in this area considers issues such as human attitudes towards animals (e.g., Hopwood, Stahlmann & Bleidorn, 2023) or the welfare of humans who work with animals (Paul et al., 2023).

Alternatively, there are critical approaches that seek to highlight, understand and eradicate power differences between humans and other species (Taylor & Sutton, 2018). Many working within this paradigm self-identify as "critical animal studies" scholars and argue that praxis – reflected in activism on behalf of other animals – is key (e.g., Nocella et al., 2014). Also key to critical animal studies is the idea of interconnected oppressions, an idea that is based on earlier ecofeminist work that pointed to the ways in which women and nature (inclusive of other animals) are similarly oppressed under masculinist, Westernised post-Enlightenment categories of thought (e.g., Plumwood, 1993). We are critical animal studies scholars and return to this later in the chapter.

The discipline and profession of social work in both Australia and New Zealand have been slow to include animals. Western Enlightenment thinking, still conveyed through conventional science, mainstream Christianity and global capitalism, encourages us to define the social only in human terms, and to view all other animals as natural subordinates, if not usable objects readily commodified and consumed at our pleasure (Fraser, Taylor & Riggs, 2021). Empathy and social justice are reserved for humans. To quote Walker et al. (2015, p. 24), "Social work is traditionally human-centred in practice, even though for many the bond between humans and animals is the most fundamental of daily-lived experiences". However, growing evidence from not only animal studies but also other disciplines (such as psychology and sociology) show there are many and diverse benefits that humans can experience from their interactions with animals. This has led to work that has, for example, shown how animals can be "conduits to social work assessment" (Evans & Gray, 2012, p. 603) or how animals are subjected to domestic violence (Taylor & Fraser, 2019).

There are also increasing incentives to include domesticated animals in the delivery of social programmes, including those related to disaster recovery, domestic violence and young offenders (see for example Taylor, Fraser, Signal & Prentice, 2016). This may help explain why more social workers are acknowledging the importance of animals in their own lives, the lives of clients and the wider community, and are interested in advancing areas such as animal-assisted social work (Fraser et al., 2021).

Social work codes of ethics reflect our collective values and priorities. In 2019, the Aotearoa New Zealand Association of Social Workers code of ethics included the following: "We recognise the sentience of animals and ensure that any animal engaged as part of our social work practice is protected" (ANZASW, 2019, p. 11). The following year animals were mentioned for the first time in the Australian Association of Social Workers' *Code of Ethics* (AASW, 2020). This does not, however, necessarily mean that all animal-inclusive programmes work from an ethical basis, with Evans and Grey (2012) noting that while animal-inclusive programmes have potential, animals may be harmed by clients and may find the work stressful. These risks are exacerbated when programmes are underpinned with speciesist attitudes that position animals as "tools" to help humans recover and thrive and ignore the needs and interests of the animals. Further still, as Hagena et al. (2022, p. 95) point out

> By framing it only in a social work practice setting, it seems the association is either dismissing the capacity of other sentient beings from feeling pain, pleasure, fear and other emotions outside of this strict framework or it is suggesting to social workers that it is ethically okay to dismiss and disregard all these very complex emotions altogether when they are interacting with non-human beings outside of their work settings.

Nevertheless, the growth in animal-assisted interventions has also forced the discipline to consider the roles of animals in social work (Taylor et al., 2016; Taylor, Fraser, & Riggs, 2020), although it still remains the case that in many countries no professional training is offered to social workers wanting to include animals in their practice (e.g., Yeung, Robertson, & Sandford-Reed, 2020). We are aware of only two social work programmes, both based in the United States, that certify education in animal social work. And, as we discuss below, their framing is problematic in terms of the argument that we present in this chapter: that social work can, and should, address the intersections of animal oppression and the politics of meat-eating.

Animal-assisted social work at the University of Denver

The University of Denver started its Animal-Assisted Social Work programme in 1996 and now hosts the *Institute for Human-Animal Connection* (IHAC), which offers a series of certified training programmes and a diverse range of engagement and advocacy projects. Philip Tedeschi, a professor in social work, is the original founder and one of IHAC's priorities is to prepare social work graduates for practice. This preparation spans a wide array of activities such as

- canine, equine and other animal-assisted programmes for different human populations;
- humane education (also see Arbour, Signal & Taylor, 2009), which involves evoking empathy in humans for animals;
- the Colorado LINK Project, which educates about the links between animal and human abuse (also see Becker & French, 2004) and

- conservation social work, involving education about the illegal wildlife trade and other anti-cruelty efforts.

From our reading of the IHAC website, the theoretical underpinnings of their programmes and projects seem mixed. On the one hand, there is talk of them "...ask[ing] critical questions to understand how power, privilege, and oppression affect human-animal-environment interactions" (IHAC, n.d.). On the other hand, IHAC notes being "informed by a systems view of social problems...", which is a theoretical perspective that does not centre questions of power, privilege and oppression. This matters because our theoretical perspectives greatly influence how we theorise about animals and social work; whether or not we are likely to ask hard questions about the role of animals and of social work in the context of capitalism and large-scale animal agriculture; and whether we are serious about power, privilege and oppression – for humans and animals. Ultimately, IHAC emphasises animal welfare (rather than animal rights), which fits with their purported use of systems theory.

Veterinary social work at the University of Tennessee

The Veterinary Social Work (VSW) programme at the University of Tennessee (UoT) started in April 2001. Initiated by Elizabeth Strand, a professor in social work, and in partnership with UoT Medical School, the VSW programme centres on four pillars: (1) Animal-assisted interventions; (2) The link between human and animal violence; (3) Animal-related grief and bereavement and (4) Compassion fatigue and conflict management. While we could find no reference to animals in disasters, the VSW graduate competencies are listed as,

- Describe and discover research on human-animal interactions that is salient to ethical-social work practice.
- Develop and demonstrate self-awareness and self-management regarding animal welfare issues.
- Intervene on behalf of human beings in the context of human-animal interactions through micro and macro levels of practice, paying particular attention to underserved and oppressed populations.
- Develop and implement animal-related programmes in existing social work agencies, in stand-alone programmes or in host settings, according to the NASW Code of Ethics and existing veterinary animal welfare protocols.
- Develop and demonstrate psycho-educational, mediation and team-building skills (VSW, 2022).

The stated intention of VSW is "Attending to human needs at the intersection of veterinary and social work practice". All incoming students must pledge an oath to "tend to the human needs that arise in the relationship between humans and animals". They are to do so "From a strengths perspective and using evidence-based practice" while "they...uphold the ethical code of [their] profession, respect and promote the dignity and worth of all species, and diligently strive to maintain mindful balance in all of [their] professional endeavors" (VSW, 2022). As this shows, the VSW at UoT is unreservedly focussed on human needs, from an exclusively human strengths-based approach rather than a critical perspective, perhaps reflecting its geographical location and medical social work origins.

Our position is that social justice cannot be so narrow as to assume that animals' existence relies on the utility they provide to humans; that their needs are not written explicitly into the work. We must recognise that animals' lives and habitats are important in and of themselves, as is their diversity. Recognising the subjectivity and sentience of animals is – or at least should be – a cornerstone of anti-oppressive practice: one that aims to liberate humans and other animals through seeing their oppressions as linked and part of the dynamics of oppression and privilege. Critical social work has a respected subversive and critical history and offers frameworks (albeit in need of adaptation) to achieve this vision.

Women, feminist intersectionality and animals

Social work is gendered and normative gender relations help to reproduce speciesism, or the assumed supremacy of humans over all other animals. Women's numerical domination in the profession has a long history in Australia (Mendes, 2020), and 84% of current social workers in Australia are women (Australian Government, 2021). Women's subordinate social status has always been a challenge for the status of the profession. The inclusion of animals in social work – both in practice and in academic thought – while growing, is not without resistance. Earlier we identified that this is due to the humanism that underpins the discipline where a focus on "clients" has come to mean human clients exclusively (Ryan, 2014). But there are other factors also at play such as concern that any consideration or inclusion of them might further feminise and thus delegitimise a profession already seen as (problematically) feminised (Abrams & Curran, 2004; Alston, 2018; Fraser & Seymour, 2017; Huppatz & Goodwin, 2013; Jones, Mlcek, Healy & Bridges, 2019; O'Connor, 2020). To quote Decka (2013, 50),

> ...the animal advocacy movement should be regarded as a women's movement as it gives rise to gendered, class, racialized practices that impact the lives and experiences of its primarily female membership. Accordingly, the animal advocacy movement, including its central attention to species difference, should be of feminist and intersectional concern.

And as Fraiman (2012, p. 100) notes, when considering the field of animal studies "proximity to this feminized realm may even induce a degree of gender/species anxiety I am tempted to call (with a nod to Eve Sedgwick) pussy panic".

Intersectionality, species and animalisation

Intersectionality is now a common term with diverse meanings and applications. Originally coined by the Comahachee Women's Collective (1971), and brought into scholarly use by Kimberle Crenshaw (1989), feminist intersectionality describes the structures and systems that create and maintain discrimination and oppression that occur across other socially overvalued and devalued identity categories associated with sexuality, race, class, ability and gender. Deckha (2013, p. 48) defines feminist intersectionality as "...a theory and methodology that instructs its adherents to examine the mutually generative and integrative nature of social identities as well as the power relations and the structures and hierarchies of difference to which they give rise". While discrimination and oppression manifest at micro levels (through, for example, the individual abuse of animals), they are inextricably linked to macro processes and structures (such as the normalisation of the subordinated status of other animals). We argue for the inclusion of animal oppression in the conceptualisation of intersectionality, largely by building on early ecofeminist philosophy,

> ...ecofeminism has been from its outset about theorising an intersection between the co-positioning of 'women' and 'nature', but then also developed into a more multi-dimensional account of intersectionality ... The agenda of ecofeminists such as Carol J. Adams and Josephine Donovan in juxtaposing 'animals' and 'women' is not the debasement of women but the explication of relations of power that intersect gender and species.
>
> (Twine, 2010, pp. 399–400)

A few points before we expand on this argument. We recognise the debates over the definitions, breadth, utility, application and ownership of feminist intersectionality. First, there is the problem of intersectionality being founded on distinctly human experience. Speciesism was not part of the original conceptualisation of intersectionality and anthropomorphism, or the tendency to attribute human values and behaviours to other animal species is a common criticism of using humancentric terms such as intersectionality (see Deckha, 2008, 2013). Associated criticisms are that including animal rights in intersectionality does a disservice to animals given the framework prioritises human oppression, and many members of marginalised human groups eat meat, work in animal agriculture or associated industries and are not animal rights advocates. Another important criticism relates to intellectual ownership of intersectionality. We take the view that due acknowledgement should be given to the origins of the theory, the uptake of the theorising Intersectionality is a welcome sign and that we might do as Davis (2020, p. 13) advises, "treat the travels of intersectionality as an occasion for dialogue rather than a contest over ownership". While we recognise the criticisms, we argue that including species oppression in the framework of intersectionality is useful because the animalisation process applies to oppressed human and animal populations.

To animalise is to dehumanise. To declare a human being an animal is to deny any rights they may have as humans, to render them uncivilised or as objects with no proper recognition within the law. Consider for example how people of colour have so often been represented as animals, sometimes dangerous, wild animals. To quote Baumeister (2021, p. 952),

> The historical degradation of Blacks to subhuman, less-than-human, or barely-human status, indispensable to Western colonial domination of the subaltern world, parallels the emergence and ascendency of the concept of Black animality in Western philosophical and scientific discourse.

Sainz et al. (2020) focus on the dehumanisation of working-class or low-income groups; how describing them as "primitive" opens the door to animalisation by justifying behavioural control and reductions in support,

> Animalistically dehumanized groups are unable to control how they behave...In general, animalistic dehumanization can reduce support for welfare policies and increase

the perception of the need for governmental control by creating perceptions that low SES groups waste their money.

(Sainz et al., 2020, p. 10)

Auckland-based social work educator Liz Beddoe (2014), for example, writes about how the trope of "feral families" can be used so punitively against working class and racialised New Zealanders. With reference to people with disabilities, O'Brien (2003, p. 332) makes the case that "Of all marginalized groups, surely those with severe cognitive impairments are among the most vulnerable to being 'animalized' ... [noting that historically] in many cultures idiots were classified as brutes, or animals". However, women across the lines of difference have a long history of being castigated as cows, chicks, hens, ducks, snakes and dogs; animalistic metaphors are still used to convey sexist hostility (Tipler & Ruscher, 2019). Fernández (2022) adds that women, who are much more likely to be vegan than men, may be subject to intense hostility if they are fat vegans, challenging two prized cultural norms, slimness and meat-eating.

The politics of meat

For decades, ecofeminists have shown how gender and animal oppression intersect, especially Carol Adams' 1990 *Sexual Politics of Meat...* (Adams, 2015) and her more recent (2020) book *The Pornography of Meat*. The politics of meat refer to the power and privilege associated with meat-eating, the meat industry and the normative discourses still circulating about the necessity of humans to consume meat. Meat-eating culture reproduces the injunction that meat is essential to good health, strength and masculinity. The annual lamb adverts in Australia are classic examples of this (see Zhou, 2018). Real men are supposed to eat meat, so the cultural injunction goes. Historically this was first applied to upper-class men, then to men across classes and more recently to women as women's economic and social status in countries like Australia and New Zealand has improved (Adams, 2020). Joy refers to this as the ideology of carnism and Potts (2016, p. 19) argues that "If carnism is the ideology, then 'meat culture' is all the tangible and practical forms through which the ideology is expressed and lived". This includes the positioning of animals as inferior and for our use, whether that use is consumption of their body parts or the instrumentalisation of their labour through their *use* in animal-related social work activities. Because one of the goals of this chapter is to get social work to face the politics of meat, we now offer a brief overview of some of the known harms of the meat industry.

Harms to animals

Many meat and dairy consumers live in (wilful) ignorance about the treatment of animals in contemporary animal farming, not helped by the secrecy of slaughterhouses (hidden away in fringe locations in windowless buildings), the cultural injunction to carnism (meat-eating) and the withholding of information by the meat and dairy industries from consumers, if not deliberate misinformation signalled through packaging showing happy cows, pigs and sheep in green pastures (Fitzgerald & Taylor, 2014; Tuhovak, 2022). Meat and dairy consumers rarely know that 90% of the pigs, cows, sheep and deer they eat are from intensive animal agriculture (Animals Australia, 2022). The vast majority of animals grown for meat and dairy live very short miserable lives inside cramped pens that prohibit natural movement. The (Australian) *Farm Transparency Project* (2012), which aimed to draw attention to the barbaric conditions in which the animals are kept, and the painful husbandry practices involved in their mass confinement including the customary teeth cutting, tail removal and castration done without pain relief; the forced impregnation and offspring removal days if not hours after birth and the squalid conditions within which so many animals live.

The stark reality is that these intensively farmed animals are killed in protracted, painful circumstances. The way pigs are killed in gas chambers is one example. Spy cameras secretly installed by Raven Deerbrook and her Californian activist group *Direct Action* showed that, while the industry boasts of pain-free, animal-friendly deaths through "humanely accredited" gas chambers, the truth is a far cry from this (Kristof, 2023). And, were it even possible to have some form of cruelty-free meat and dairy production, our position is that the act of eating and killing other animals undermines an intersectional approach by assuming humans have the right to such practices. As Carol Adams notes,

> To accept that animals want their deaths, we have to believe a rather ludicrous contradiction: animals have no will or legitimate desires with which we need to concern ourselves, yet animals have the desire to be our food.
>
> *(Adams, 2020, p. 130)*

Harms to the environment

The meat and dairy industries are now well documented as two of the largest producers of anthropogenic greenhouse gas emissions and this is likely to worsen as demand for meat and dairy grows (Potts, 2016). One of the most widely cited reports on this issue, *Livestock's Long Shadow: Environmental Issues and Options* (Steinfeld et al., 2006) also noted it is "the largest of all anthropogenic land uses" occupying around 70% of all agricultural land on the planet and often being the main reason for deforestation. Its water use is intense and unsustainable, and one of the main reasons for water pollution (Steinfeld et al., 2006). Such is the impact on the environment of animal agriculture that recent reports (e.g. Willett et al., 2019) have promoted diets that are fully or mainly plant-based, discussed further below.

Harms to humans

The politics of meat refers to the harms caused to humans as well as animals. Carnism (or meat-eating culture) reifies the notion of human supremacy and reproduces toxic forms of masculinity, forming a barrier to gender equality (Adams, 2015, 2020; Potts, 2016). The hierarchy reproduced through the speciesism that meat-eating relies on, and flows through to human populations.

Before it is plastic-wrapped and ready for supermarkets, meat needs to be taken from the bodies of animals. Slaughterhouse workers do this dangerous, dirty and relatively poorly paid work (Leighton, 2021). The exposure to violence by slaughterhouse workers can affect their psychological and emotional well-being. However, it is often these frontline workers who are stigmatised for doing the dirty work of killing and dismembering the animals (Leighton,

2021). In Australia, slaughterhouse workers should be paid around $27 an hour; totalling half of the average weekly earnings (ABS, 2022). However, many of the workers are paid much less. Pacific Islanders, for example, who are brought into Australia in growing numbers to do "meat processing" are paid $753 a week but after labour-hire companies deduct their airfares and accommodation and are left with only $9 per hour, or $310 a week (Baker, 2021). In Australia and New Zealand, many if not most public welfare clients are from low-income if not impoverished backgrounds. Of these, some will work in slaughterhouses and other meat and dairy processing plants. Recognising the harms these workers face is part of facing up to the politics of meat. Similarly, research has demonstrated that there is a "spillover" of violence into human communities situated in close proximity to slaughterhouses. For example, Fitzgerald, Kalof and Dietz (2009) found that slaughterhouse employment increased arrests for violent crimes, rape, sex offenses and overall total arrest rates compared to employment in other industries and Richards, Signal and Taylor (2013) found slaughterhouse workers had a higher propensity for aggression, female slaughterhouse workers in particular.

Vegan, intersectional possibilities

We agree with Lundström (2019) that major changes to the global food economy will occur in the future but not for a couple of decades. Lundström (2019) notes that agrarian scientists have estimated that by 2050 the meat industry will be (finally) condemned for its unsustainable use of resources (land, water, labour) to grow cereals to feed animals rather than human populations. However, we also recognise that justice for animals is so marginalised in and beyond the profession that even mentioning the connection between global warming and meat and dairy eating may prompt some if not many to shut down, turn away or trivialise the issues; sometimes using worn-out "jokes" in the process, such as "bacon—yum!" At the very least, it is likely to prompt some to recount the details of how they only buy organic, "humane meat", uncaged eggs and milk from local dairies – none of which seriously addresses the core problems of animal suffering and environmental degradation. Beyond advocating for vegan social work – or a social work that deploys an expanded version of intersectionality to oppose the exploitation and consumption of animals – what can we do? In Table 49.1 below, we make 13 suggestions of how we can learn about and support existing organisations already doing some of this work.

Concluding comments

For decades, ecofeminists have shown how gender and animal oppression intersect, including Carol Adams' 1990 *Sexual Politics of Meat…* In more recent years, critical animal studies scholars have mapped the connections between human and animal abuse and exploitation, showing not only how speciesism is an axis of oppression (for animals) and privilege (for humans), but also how the subjugation of animals relates to the oppression of human groups. In this chapter, we focussed on the politics of meat from an expanded interspecies intersectional feminist perspective.

To engage with a more fulsome understanding of social justice, an expanded version of feminist intersectionality can help us put animals into the frame. Our central argument has been that intersectional social work is not complete without a consideration of animals and speciesism.

Table 49.1 Vegan-friendly, "real-world" intersectional examples

Actions	Category of animals	Examples
1 Include animals in social work's definition of the "social" (Ryan, 2014).	Farmed animals Wild animals Domesticated animals	*Social Work for Advancing the Human-Animal Bond* Website example: (6) Social Workers Advancing the Human Animal Bond (SWAHAB) | Facebook
2 Appreciate that companion animals are only one category of animals who need protecting (DeMello, 2012).	Farmed animals Wild animals Domesticated animals	*Royal Society of the Prevention of Cruelty to Animals* Website example: RSPCA Australia | For all creatures great & small
3 Join social media groups disseminating scholarly information about animals, including the impact of animal agriculture on the climate crisis (Blattner, 2020).	Farmed animals Wild animals Companion animals	*Animals Studies Scholar Advocacy Facebook Group* Website example: (6) Animals in Society: Animal Studies Scholar Advocacy | Facebook
4 Learn about the real treatment of animals used to produce meat and dairy (Farm Transparency Project, 2012).	Farmed animals Farmed animals who can be forcibly impregnated	*Voiceless* Website example: Voiceless Animal Cruelty Index (VACI) | Voiceless
5 Learn about the risks to humans consuming red and processed meats related to obesity, high cholesterol, diabetes and cancer, especially colon cancer (Qian, Riddle, Wylie-Rosett & Hu, 2020).	Farmed animals Humans	*Cancer Council* Website example: Red meat, processed meat and cancer | Cancer Council NSW
6 Help animal farmers transition away from animal agriculture (Blattner, 2020).	Humans Farmed animals	*Farm Transitions Australia* Website example: Why Transition? | Farm Transitions Australia
7 Substitute plant-based food and other plant-based products wherever possible, which are increasing in range and quality (Qian et al., 2020).	Farmed animals Humans	*Vegan Australia* Website example: Vegan grocery guide - Vegan Australia
8 Support colleagues, friends and family members who are vegetarian or vegan (Taylor, Fraser, Stekelenberg & King, 2022).	Humans Farmed animals	*Vegan New Zealand* Website example: Home - The Vegan Society of Aotearoa, New Zealand

(*Continued*)

Table 49.1 (Continued)

Actions	Category of animals	Examples
9 Support colleagues, community groups and political parties that put animal welfare and rights on the legislative agenda (Gelber & O'Sullivan, 2021).	Farmed animals Wild animals Companion animals	*Animal Justice Party* Website example: Animal Justice Party Australia
10 Support the end of animal factory farming (Fitzgerald & Taylor, 2014).	Farmed animals and many fish populations (e.g. salmon)	*Open Cages*, New Zealand Website example: How will we end factory farming? 4 key areas of action I Open Cages
11 Oppose the criminalisation of animal rights advocates and activists (Gelber & O'Sullivan, 2021).	Humans	*Animal Liberation Australia* Website example: Animal Liberation I Compassion without compromise
12 Oppose government subsidies for animal agriculture (Wills, 2021).	Humans Farmed animals	*Farm Transparency Project* Website example: Cease government subsidies for animal agriculture I Animal Liberation Queensland (alq.org.au)
13 Recognise the exploitation and harms caused to slaughterhouse workers (Leighton, 2021).	Humans	Meat workers union?

References

AASW. (2020). *Code of ethics*. 1201 (aasw.asn.au). Accessed 20.2.2023.

Abrams, L. S., & Curran, L. (2004). Between women: Gender and social work in historical perspective. *Social Service Review*, 78(3), 429–446.

ABS. (2022). Average Weekly Earnings, Australia, November 2022 I Australian Bureau of Statistics (abs.gov.au)

Adams, C. J. (2015). *The sexual politics of meat: A feminist-vegetarian critical theory*. Bloomsbury Publishing USA.

Adams, C. J. (2020). *The pornography of meat: New and updated edition*. Bloomsbury Publishing USA.

Alston, M. (2018). Working with women: Gender-sensitive social work practice. In: Alston, M., & McKinnon, J. (eds.), *Social work: Fields of practice* (2nd ed., pp. 19–31). Oxford University Press

Animals Australia. (2022). *Dairy factory farms on the rise – Australian cows face life in intensive indoor 'barns'*. I Animals Australia. https://animalsaustralia.org/latest-news/dairy-factory-farms-australia/. Accessed 17.2.2023.

ANZASW. (2019). *Code of ethics 2019*. 1–15. https://anzasw.nz/wp-content/uploads/Code-of-Ethics-Adopted-30-Aug-2019.pdf

Arbour, T., Signal, T., & Taylor, N. (2009) Teaching kindness: The promise of humane education. *Society & Animals*, 17(2), 136–148.

Australian Government. (2021). *Social workers* I Labour Market Insights. Retrieved 17/5/23.

Baker, R. (2021). *Pacific island meat workers on $9 per hour after wage deductions* (smh.com.au) Retrieved 18/5/23.

Baumeister, D. (2021). Black Animality from Kant to Fanon. *Theory & Event*, 24(4), 951–976.
Becker, F. & French, L. (2004). Making the links: Child abuse, animal cruelty and domestic violence. *Child Abuse Review*, 13, 399–414.
Beddoe, L. (2014). Feral families, troubled families: The spectre of the underclass in New Zealand. *New Zealand Sociology*, 29(3), 51–68.
Becker, F. & French, L. (2004), Making the links: Child abuse, animal cruelty and domestic violence, Child Abuse Review, 13: 399-414.
Blattner, C. (2020). Just transition for agriculture? A critical step in tackling climate change. *Journal of Agriculture, Food Systems, and Community Development*, 9(3), 53–58.
Crenshaw, K. (1989). Demarginalising the intersection of race and sex: A black feminist critique of antidiscrimination doctrine, feminist theory and antiracist politics. *University of Chicago Legal Forum*, 139—167.
Davis, K. (2020). Who owns intersectionality? Some reflections on feminist debates on how theories travel. *European Journal of Women's Studies*, 27(2), 113–127.
Deckha, M. (2008). Intersectionality and posthumanist visions of equality. *Wisconsin Journal of Law, Gender, & Society*, 23, 249.
Deckha, M. (2012). Toward a postcolonial, posthumanist feminist theory: Centralizing race and culture in feminist work on nonhuman animals. *Hypatia*, 27(3), 527–545.
Deckha, M. (2013). Animal advocacy, feminism and intersectionality. *Deportate, esuli, profughe*, 23, 48–65.
DeMello, M. (2012). *Animals and society: An introduction to human-animal studies*. Columbia University Press.
Evans, N., & Grey, C. (2012). The practice and ethics of animal-assisted therapy with children and young people: Is it enough that we don't eat our co-workers? *The British Journal of Social Work*, 42(4), 600–617.
Farm Transparency Project. (2012). *Aussie Pigs – Campaigns – Farm Transparency Project*. https://www.farmtransparency.org/campaigns/aussie-pigs. Accessed 17.02.2023.
Fernández, L. (2022). Fattening solidarity beyond species: The rebellious (body) politics of fat veganism. In Cudworth, E., McKie, R., & Turgoose, D. (Eds.), *Feminist Animal Studies* (pp. 185–202). Routledge.
Fitzgerald, A. J., Kalof, L., & Dietz, T. (2009). Slaughterhouses and increased crime rates: An empirical analysis of the spillover from "The Jungle" into the surrounding community. *Organization & Environment*, 22(2), 158–184. https://doi.org/10.1177/1086026609338164
Fitzgerald, A. J., & Taylor, N. (2014). The cultural hegemony of meat and the animal industrial complex. In: Taylor, N., & Twine, R. (Eds.), *The rise of critical animal studies: From the margins to the centre* (pp. 185–202). Routledge.
Fraiman, S. (2012). Pussy panic versus linking animals: Tracking gender in animal studies. *Critical Inquiry*, 39(1), 89–115.
Fraser, H., & Seymour, K. (2017). *Understanding violence and abuse, an anti-oppressive practice perspective*. Fernwood Press.
Fraser, H., & Taylor, N. (2019). Women, anxiety and companion animals: Toward a feminist animal studies of interspecies care and solidarity. In Gruen, L., & Probyn-Rapsey, F. (eds.), *Animaladies: Gender, animals, and madness* (pp. 155–172). Bloomsbury Academic.
Fraser, H., Taylor, N., Damien, W., & Riggs, D. W. (2021). Animals in disaster social work: An intersectional green perspective inclusive of species. *The British Journal of Social Work*, 51(5), 1739–1758.
Gelber, K., & O'Sullivan, S. (2021). Cat got your tongue? Free speech, democracy and Australia's 'ag-gag'laws. *Australian Journal of Political Science*, 56(1), 19–34.
Hagena, K., Hagena, A., & Arevalo, L. (2022). For the future of all life, the Code of Ethics is the key. *Aotearoa New Zealand Social Work*, 34(2), 94–99.
Hopwood, A., Stahlmann, G., & Bleidorn, W. (2023). *Personality and compassion for animals*. Anthrozoös, 36(1), 69–81.
Huppatz, K., & Goodwin, S. (2013). Masculinised jobs, feminised jobs and men's 'gender capital' experiences: Understanding occupational segregation in Australia. *Journal of Sociology*, 49(2–3), 291–308.
Institute for Human-Aniamal Collaboration (IHAC) (n.d.). Retrieved from https://socialwork.du.edu/humananimalconnection/about-institute-human-animal-connection

Jones, M., Mlcek, S. H., Healy, J. P., & Bridges, D. (2019). Gender dynamics in social work practice and education: A critical literature review. *Australian Social Work*, 72(1), 62–74.

Joy, M. (2010). *Why we love dogs, eat pigs and wear cows: An introduction to carnism.* Conari Press.

Kristof, N. (2023). Opinion | Spy Cams Show What the Pork Industry Tries to Hide - The New York Times (nytimes.com).

Leighton, P. (2021). The harms of industrial food production: How modern agriculture, livestock rearing and food processing contribute to disease, environmental degradation and worker exploitation. In: Davies, P., Leighton, P., & Wyatt, T. (Eds.), *The palgrave handbook of social harm. Palgrave studies in victims and victimology.* Palgrave Macmillan. https://doi.org/10.1007/978-3-030-72408-5_9

Lundström, M. (2019). The political economy of meat. *Journal of Agricultural and Environmental Ethics*, 32(1), 95–104.

Mendes, P. (2020). Tracing the origins of critical social work practice. In *Critical social work* (pp. 17–29). Routledge.

Nocella, A., J. Sorensen, K. Socha and A. Matsuoka (2014). *Defining critical animal studies: An intersectional social justice approach for liberation.* Peter Lang

O'Brien, G. V. (2003). People with cognitive disabilities: The argument from marginal cases and social work ethics. *Social Work*, 48(3), 331–337.

O'Connor, L. (2020). How social workers understand and use their emotions in practice: A thematic synthesis literature review. *Qualitative Social Work*, 19(4), 645–662.

Paul, N., Cosh, S., & Lykins, D. (2023). A love–hate relationship with what I do: Protecting the mental health of animal care workers, *Anthrozoös*, online first.

Plumwood, V. (1993). *Feminism and the mastery of nature.* Routledge.

Potts, A. (Ed.). (2016). *Meat culture.* Brill.

Qian, F., Riddle, M. C., Wylie-Rosett, J., & Hu, F. B. (2020). Red and processed meats and health risks: How strong is the evidence? *Diabetes Care*, 43(2), 265–271.

Richards, E., Signal, T., & Taylor, N. (2013). A different cut? Comparing attitudes toward animals and propensity for aggression within two primary industry cohorts—Farmers and meatworkers. *Society & Animals*, 21(4), 395–413. https://doi.org/10.1163/15685306-12341284

Ryan, T. (Ed.). (2014). *Animals in social work: Why and how they matter.* Palgrave Macmillan.

Sainz, M., et al. (2020). Dehumanization of socioeconomically disadvantaged groups decreases support for welfare policies via perceived wastefulness. *International Review of Social Psychology*, 33(1): 12, 1–13. https://doi.org/10.5334/irsp.414

Steinfeld, H., Gerber, P., Wassenaar, T. D., Castel, V., Rosales, M., Rosales, M., & de Haan, C. (2006). *Livestock's long shadow: environmental issues and options.* Food & Agriculture Org.

Taylor, N. (2013). *Humans, animals and society: An introduction to human-animal studies.* Lantern Press.

Taylor, N., & Fraser, H. (2019). *Companion animals and domestic violence: Rescuing me, rescuing you.* Palgrave Macmillan.

Taylor, N., Fraser, H., & Riggs, D. (2020). Companion-animal-inclusive domestic violence practice: Implications for service delivery and social work. *Aotearoa New Zealand Social Work*, 32(4), 26–39.

Taylor, N., Fraser, H., Signal, T., & Prentice, K. (2016). Social work, animal-assisted therapies and ethical considerations: A programme example form Central Queensland, Australia. *The British Journal of Social Work*, 46(1), 135–152.

Taylor, N., Fraser, H., Stekelenburg, N., & King, J. (2022). Barbaric, feral, or moral? Stereotypical dairy farmer and vegan discourses on the business of animal consumption. In Tallberg, L., & Hamilton, L. *The Oxford handbook of animal organization studies: A critical reader in ethics, business and society.* Oxford University Press.

Taylor, N., & Sutton, Z. (2018). For an emancipatory animal sociology. *Journal of Sociology* 54(4), 467–487.

Tipler, C. N., & Ruscher, J. B. (2019). Dehumanizing representations of women: The shaping of hostile sexist attitudes through animalistic metaphors. *Journal of Gender Studies*, 28(1), 109–118.

Tuhovak, N. (2022). Breaking the faux transparent glass wall: how animal activists can fight back against the Agricultural Industry through undercover investigations and Federal protections. *Animal L.*, 28, 265.

Twine, R. (2010). Intersectional disgust? Animals and (eco)feminism. *Feminism & Psychology*, 20(3), 397–406.

Veternary Social Work (VSW) (2022). Retrieved from https://vetsocialwork.utk.edu/
Walker, P., Aimers, J., & Perry, C. (2015). Animals and social work: An emerging field of practice for Aotearoa New Zealand. *Aotearoa New Zealand Social Work*, 27(1–2), 24–35.
Wilkie, R. (2015). Academic "dirty work": Mapping scholarly labor in a tainted mixed species field. *Society & Animals*, 23(3), 211–230.
Willett, W., Rockström, J., Loken, B., Springmann, M., Lang, T., Vermeulen, S., & Murray, C. J. (2019). Food in the Anthropocene: the EAT–Lancet Commission on healthy diets from sustainable food systems. *The Lancet*, 393(10170), 447–492.
Wills, J. (2021). Animal Agriculture, the Right to Food and Vegan Dietary Solutions. In Rowley, J., & Prisco, C. (Eds.), *Law and Veganism: International Perspectives on the Human Right to Freedom of Conscience*,121–142. Rowman & Littlefield
Yeung, P., Robertson, N., & Sandford-Reed, L. (2020). Aotearoa New Zealand social workers and their views of inclusion of animals in social work practice – A descriptive study. *Aotearoa New Zealand Social Work*, 32(4), 8–25.
Zhou, N. (2018). 'Going vegan': Australia's latest lamb ad doesn't quite cut it with viewers. *The Guardian*. https://www.theguardian.com/media/2018/jan/11/going-vegan-australias-latest-lamb-ad-doesnt-quite-cut-it-with-viewers. Accessed 07.02.2023.

50
ECOFEMINISM AND THE POPULAR SOLIDARITY ECONOMY IN LATIN AMERICAN SOCIAL WORK

Resistance to the patriarchal and capitalist system

Juana Narváez Jara

Introduction

Ecofeminism challenges the prevailing human-nature relationship that is based on dominance, and instead proposed a shift towards a vision that ensures a good quality of life, known as Buen Vivir, within the framework of the popular solidarity economy (EPS).

Embracing an anti-capitalist and decolonial perspective, social work within the popular social solidarity economy actively supports collective struggles, community organisation and cooperativism as forms of resistance to the extractivist and patriarchal system. These efforts aim to address gender gaps and empower women in the economy of the peoples. The analysis presented in this chapter acknowledges that Patriarchy, capitalism and the new social question are the driving forces shaping our current reality. Capitalism and the new social question lead the management of nature based on interventionist approaches tied to economic development, as well as the implementation of public policies aimed at fostering productive activities to combat poverty and establish life projects in harmony with Mother Earth.

It is crucial to recognise Pachamama, or Mother Earth, as a rights-bearing entity. In this context, individuals, communities, peoples and nationalities have the right to benefit from the environment and natural wealth that enable them to live in a state of well-being. This principle is enshrined in Article 74 of the 2008 Political Constitution of Ecuador, which states: "Individuals, communities, peoples and nationalities shall have the right to benefit from the environment and natural wealth that allow them to live well. Environmental services shall not be subject to appropriation" (Constitution, 2008).

The capitalist, colonial and patriarchal system, under the guise of economic development, rationalises the exploitation of natural resources. This leads to destruction of ecosystems, the encroachment upon ancestral territories and the disregard for cultural diversity. It also undermines the role of women as true custodians of natural resources and Mother

Earth herself. The destruction of the environment would signify the annihilation not only of human beings but also of all other species.

Here are some themes for analysis and reflection within the context of Critical Social Work, the social question and the EPS, approached through an ecofeminist lens with a decolonial, anti-patriarchal and anti-capitalist perspective.

The EPS and the social question

The EPS gained prominence in the 1970s in response to the economic crisis that marked the second half of the 20th century, caused by exploitative capitalism and the unjust appropriation of natural resources. During this time, the social question surrounding the means of production became important.

The social question arose from a growing awareness of the living conditions of a population who were victims of capitalist exploitation. It highlighted the deepening inequalities perpetuated by unequal social relations, distinguishing it from previous forms of impoverishment. It is therefore necessary to begin with an analysis of the socio-economic, political and cultural events that have allowed the capitalist system to thrive under the guise of neoliberal policies and deceptive claims of "economic growth".

The changes that unfolded in the social and economic spheres had various consequences including the diminished capacity of nation states to stimulate the economy, regulate industries and create better opportunities. As a result, individuals turned to strengthening solidarity networks and self-employment to address emerging social needs in a democratic way, as José Luis Coraggio (2011) points out.

Three decades of neoliberalism have exposed the structural character of the social question inherent to capitalism: massive exclusion from employment, the erosion of wages and social rights, the increased concentration of wealth, the liberation of a globalised market that is fierce in its punishment of those who cannot compete and the expansion of a so-called informal sector that is self-aggrandising due to the savage competition for survival. The new social question encompasses these material foundations, which amplify exclusion, structural poverty and a web of contradictions. Addressing it requires a political response (Coraggio, 2011, p. 11).

It is important to separate the two strands that exist within the social economy: first, the market strand refers to traditional entities dedicated to satisfying the needs of its members, made up mainly of cooperatives, as well as labour or limited liability companies; and second, the non-market strand, made up of non-profit organisations, private entities, mostly associations and foundations. These entities usually integrate market logic alongside solidarity and redistribution principles and adopt internal management structures that may resemble those of commercial companies or traditional civic associations (Pérez, Enekoitz, & Guridi, 2009, p. 10).

José Paulo Netto says the nature of poverty underwent significant change with the advent of bourgeois society. In previous societies, poverty was a consequence of scarcity (a framework determined to a very large extent by the level of development of the material and social productive forces). However, in bourgeois society, poverty became intertwined with a framework that aimed to reduce scarcity. The intensified and widespread poverty experienced in the early 19th century, known as pauperism, emerged as something new precisely because it was the product of the very same conditions that should have led to its reduction, or even eradication (Netto, 1992).

The impulse behind the EPS stems from the historical development of the social economy, which represents a distinct concept and practice aiming to redefine economic relationships based on principles of justice, cooperation, reciprocity and mutual aid. In a society dominated by the commodification of the public and private spheres and the pursuit of profit, the structures of the solidarity economy have been institutionalised, often challenging their core values.

The solidarity economy represents a theoretical and practical exploration of alternative economic approaches, grounded in solidarity and labour. Its fundamental principle is the introduction of increasing levels of solidarity in economic activities, organisations and institutions, encompassing enterprises, markets and public policies (Razeto, 2010, p. 47a).

The solidarity economy is seen as a just and humane form of economic organisation; its development can effectively contribute to overcoming the serious problems that negatively impact our societies. It provides women and families with new opportunities for participation, development and empowerment based on their gender identities (Razeto, 2010, p. 48b).

The solidarity economy advocates for a new type of alternative, comprehensive, human scale and sustainable development, with an emphasis on local and territorial aspects. It critically and profoundly challenges to existing structures of society. Margarita Rozas, in her book *Professional Intervention in Relation to the Social Question* (2012), says neoliberalism is the product of the contradictions of capitalism after the so-called "golden age" under the dominance of the United States after the Second World War. During this period, the Welfare State achieved a balance between capital and labour through the development of social policies. However, social inequalities persisted, particularly in Latin America, due to income and wealth disparities. The author suggests that professional intervention in Latin America is institutionalised within the framework of the capitalist state, which assumes responsibility for addressing the "social question" (Rozas, 2012, p. 24).

From this perspective, the social question in Latin America today demands a critique of the action of individuals and the historical-structural processes that have shaped the societies of the continent. This question is closely related to the long-standing historical factors that continue to influence it, such as colonisation, struggles for independence, different forms of state, development plans and social policies.

The solidarity economy strives to produce and distribute sufficient material wealth to ensure self-managed and sustainable development for all people and the planet itself (Pérez, Enekoitz, & Guridi, 2009, p. 13).

However, in our current reality, these principles of the EPS are not respected. The rights of nature and productive units continue to be violated by financial capital. It is therefore important to foster national sovereignty and promote Latin American unity through mechanisms of resistance to the colonial and capitalist system. Moreover, a new form of social intervention should be developed, one that redefines the conditions of professional intervention with a pragmatic, decolonial and anti-capitalist character.

Social work in Latin America

From the critical Latin American Social Work movement, the profession is being reexamined within its historical context as a specialisation of collective work in capitalist society. However, neoliberalism has distorted this original meaning to align it with the current needs of the system. This perspective leads us to perceive social work as a segment of the impoverished class, experiencing similar circumstances but in unique ways. Social workers, as a professional category, undergo the same process of deteriorating working conditions imposed by neoliberalism, either through flexible forms of contracting and relative unemployment, or by the shrinking state response to the "social question".

The administration and management of the process of the neoliberal trend shape the demand for social work. Restructuring capitalism demands a redefinition of the profession's functionality and social significance. This redefinition marks the shift from the profile of and "agent of transformation" to that of an administrator or manager of the "social question". This shift is evident in the field of professional training, where the legacy of the reconceptualisation process is being confronted by visions of "conservative modernisation", which seek to regain prominence within social work (Mamblona & Matusevicius, 2019)

Capitalism and income distribution

In her work "Social Service and Division of Labour", Marilda Iamamoto (1995) urges us to analyse the inherent inequality in the current organisation of capitalist society, social work as well as the private appropriation of the conditions and rewards of labour. This appropriation translates into the growing valorisation of capital and the increasing misery of the worker, as has occurred in neoliberal economies subjected to the policies of the International Monetary Fund. These policies further deepen existing inequalities. In the 21st century, inequality persists in income distribution due to arbitrary and unsustainable features of a predatory capitalism that facilitates dispossession. The accumulation process within this system restricts the possibilities of fair distribution and accessibility of goods and services, undermining the socio-political foundations of equality (p. 24).

The world is going through a period of authoritarianism, deteriorating living conditions for marginalised social sectors and the impoverishment of the middle classes. Public policies are regressing, while a few individuals accumulate and concentrate wealth without bounds. The resulting damage to people's lives and the social fabric is nearly irreparable. This challenge extends beyond the realm of the social sciences. Social work leads us to systematically organise information and construct our research to bring visibility to the vulnerabilities of the social fabric. We must understand who the other is, with whom we work – an other who possesses the status of a citizen with rights, whose social, economic and political rights require profound care and attention.

The challenge is to rethink the discourse from a transformative perspective. We must be aware that neoliberalism is a destroyer of social subjects. Our professional interventions have always aimed for equality, justice and human rights. However, we face setbacks due to failed governments that exploit the people for their own interests.

In recent years, the EPS has gained momentum. It combines and uses fundamental principles of women's participation in both the family economy and in the economy of the state. It is women who sustain their households by fulfilling various roles – productive, reproductive and community-orientated. Rural women in particular, face disadvantages in relation to men, as their subordination is evident. Both women and nature have endured over-exploitation.

Good living

Community social work calls for the incorporation of the objectives of the EPS productive units at a national level. The aim is to achieve Sumak Kawsay or Good Living within communities and in their economic units, within a common framework of popular and solidarity-based financial systems. Public institutions should play a steering role in this endeavour. It is worth mentioning that Ecuador, for example, has a legal body, the Superintendence of the EPS, which determines regulations and principles that make it up: "search for Good Living and the common good; priority of work over capital and collective interests over individual interests; fair trade and ethical and responsible consumption; gender equity; respect for cultural identity" (SEPS, 2012, p. 3).

Preserving ancestral territories free of mining and oil exploitation is crucial. Promoting cultural diversity and maintaining a healthy and sustainable environment ensures equitable, permanent and quality access to water, air and soil, subsoil resources and natural heritage for individuals and communities.

The EPS emphasises work and prioritises human beings above monetary gain. This alternative approach improves the living conditions of vulnerable groups, moving away from the traditional model where the accumulation of capital in competitive markets benefits only specific sectors. In the social sphere, the popular economy serves as a guiding principle for local development that takes into account community commercialisation for informal sectors historically excluded from economic opportunities.

Professionals in the EPS contribute to the creation of employment opportunities and empower collectives to foster a sense of belonging. They promote social participation and work towards transforming society into a more just and equitable place through practices of cooperation, socio-organisational strengthening and environmental responsibility, among others. The popular and solidarity economy shares similar objectives in promoting an alternative development model that values the role of agents of change in improving quality of life, utilising their own opportunities, capacities and resources.

The structure of the social economy offers a redesigned framework for the contemporary financial system that aligns with the realities of local territories. It also strengthens the intervention of addressing the social question. Experiences from processes of struggle and resistance can contribute to discussions on feminist social work. From a Latin American and decolonial perspective, it is women who are the true guardians of water, of their bodies, and of their rights. They are the ones who work for a life project in harmony with Pachamama or Mother Nature.

The State, meanwhile, recognises and guarantees the right to property in its public, private, communal, associative, cooperative and mixed forms, and it is expected to fulfil its social and environmental function in this regard. However, these rights are being violated by the State itself, which has been exploiting natural resources, and even invading the land native peoples – as in the case of the Amazon, where thousands of hectares of previously state-protected forest is in the hands of mining companies that pollute the environment, and contribute, ultimately, to the climate crisis.

Aníbal Quijano (2014) reminds us of the consequences of the system of colonial and Eurocentric domination that usurps lands, and strips people of our roots. Territories and territorially based political organisations, whether partially or totally colonised or uncolonised, were classified in the Eurocentric pattern of modern colonial capitalism (p. 32). Rescuing Pachamama implies recognising that the human being is part of the same nature whose destruction would represent the nature itself, the destruction of which would represent the annihilation of the same being and of all species.

For the Andean cosmovision, nature is sacred, it is life itself. There is an appreciation that Pachamama sustains us; therefore, territories must be respected and cared for.

Boaventura de Sousa Santos invites us to seek alternative mechanisms to the capitalist market such as community organisations, cooperatives, popular and solidarity economy organisations. In his book *Sociologies of Absences and Emergencies from the Epistemologies of the South*, he analyses the world of monocultures: Against the productivist monoculture of capitalist orthodoxy, which prioritises the objectives of accumulation over those of distribution, he defends the ecology of social productions and distributions, i.e. the need to recover and give value to other alternative systems of production, such as workers' cooperatives, "fair trade", self-managed enterprises, popular economic organisations and the solidarity economy (De Sousa, 2006 p. 16).

Ecofeminism and the EPS: resistance to the patriarchal and capitalist system

For activists Vandana Shiva and Maria Mies, ecofeminism submits key concepts of our culture to revision. These include economy, progress and science, and it shows how these hegemonic notions are incapable of leading people to a dignified life. It also highlights the urgency of adopting a new paradigm that puts a stop to this declared war on life.

Ecofeminism objects to the exclusion of the immanence of human life and ecological limits from the concerns of economics and development. This critique challenges the fundamental pillars of the capitalist and patriarchal economic paradigm. Shiva and Mies make a powerful critique of the current social, scientific, economic and cultural model. They propose an alternative view of everyday reality and politics, giving value to elements, practices and subjects that have been designated by hegemonic thought as subaltern, and which have been made invisible. They emphasise the material importance of women's links and relationships; highlighting the inseparable nature of production and reproduction within the economic process. It is necessary to recognise how the capitalist economy sustains itself by destroying nature and exploiting women's labour in households and subsistence economies. The ecological and feminist dimensions are integral to transforming the conception and management of territory (Shiva & Mies, 1997).

In addition to Shiva, other important voices that act as representatives of ecological economics and the defence of the environment include Alicia Puleo, Anna Bosch, Yayo Herrero, the Latinas Berta Cáceres, Tránsito Amaguaña and Dolores Cacuango.

From 1985 to the present, there has been an analytical focus on macroeconomics, which involves discussions around the design of economic policies, the centrality of the market and the analysis of key concepts in economic discourse such as productivity, efficiency and development. In the late 1990s and early 2000s, within Latin America's resistance to neoliberalism, feminism produced a set of structural analyses of capitalism. Alicia Puleo (2011) argues that for feminism – or Feminisms – to maintain its internationalist character, it must think in ecological terms as well. This is particularly relevant because women in the so-called "South" are the first victims of the destruction of their natural environment, which occurs to facilitate the expropriation of products later consumed in the West. Thus, rural Indian or African women living in subsistence economies have tragically seen their quality of life decrease with the arrival of the erroneously termed "rational" exploitation for the international market (Puleo, 2011).

The planet has physical limits, as studied by the science of ecology. These limits necessitate an immediate change in our economic and civilisational model for its own sustainability. Feminisms continue to contemplate the notion of living standards, a complex concept that incorporates the satisfaction of biological and social needs, as well as the satisfaction of emotional and affective needs. Meeting these multifaceted needs requires material resources and contexts and relationships of care and affection, which is often provided through unpaid work, predominantly carried out in the home by women.

Families, in the conventional view, are often considered nothing more than mere units of consumption, which disregards the significant work they contribute to household labour and subsistence. However, the unpaid work carried out by women is essential for the care of life, the body and human existence. By challenging the false boundaries traditionally imposed by economics, feminism and environmentalism find common ground. Both movements highlight that the socio-economic system has two characteristics: it is an open system in relation to nature, and it relies on various activities and work – both paid and caregiving – for its own sustenance (Bosch, Carrasco & Grau, 2005).

It was in 1974 that the French woman Françoise d'Eaubonne first coined the term ecofeminism, to represent the power of women in contributing to the feminist project of a non-sexist and non-patriarchal society through the solidarity economy. Ecofeminism involves an analysis of the economy as a social construct, uniting feminist and ecological consciousness. It aims to address environmental issues from the perspective of women, gender, androcentrism, sexism, care, Patriarchy and more (Puleo, 2011). By bringing together these two movements, ecofeminism highlights shared interests and expands the scope of feminist claims. It integrates the concern about the impact of human activities on nature, while incorporating a gendered vision of humanity that recognises the subordination and oppression experienced by women.

Yayo Herrero (2012) proposes an economy that prioritises human life, recognising the dependence of all life on the biosphere, its materials and processes, and the great amount of work and energy involved in taking care of vulnerable bodies. The intersection of ecological and feminist perspectives can contribute to the emergence of a paradigm that places the preservation of a dignified human life in harmony with nature at the forefront of interest (Herrero, 2012, p. 1).

Ecofeminism acknowledges that environmental issues must be integrated into the feminist agenda.

Tragically, the Honduran Berta Cáceres, an Indigenous Lenca ecofeminist and social activist for the rights of Indigenous Peoples, lost her life in a world that suppresses those who rebel against the chains of developmentalism, capitalism, racism and Patriarchy. Cáceres denounced the hegemonic extractivist development model that promotes a utilitarian view of nature focused solely on generating economic benefits that benefit particular groups at the expense of not only other social groups – in this case Indigenous Peoples – but also of the environmental balance (Portocarrero, 2016, p. 2).

In our Abya Yala, the history of Indigenous and peasant communities, ancestral peoples, is marked by a continuous dispossession of their territories that began with the conquest and colonisation and persists to this day. Indigenous women Dolores Cacuango and Tránsito Amaguaña (1896–1990) led social struggles for land rights, decent work and bilingual education. They fostered awareness of their identity in the face of racism and the patriarchal system. These visionary leaders, considered pioneers of the Ecuadorian left and community ecofeminism in the early 20th century, confronted the ongoing acts of usurpation and violent dispossession of Indigenous Lands and communities since the late 15th century. This dispossession has resulting in ethnic, social and economic discrimination, as well as illness, death and the constant threat of cultural and physical extermination, as Aníbal Quijano argues in his work on the Coloniality of power, Eurocentrism and Latin America.

America, as the first space/time of a new power paradigm, emerged as the initial identity of modernity. This formation of America was shaped by the convergence of two historical processes that became intertwined in the production of this space/time, establishing themselves as the fundamental axes of the new power pattern. One of these processes involved the codification of differences between conquerors and the conquered through the concept of race, which propagated the notion of a supposedly inherent biological distinction that placed one group in a natural state of inferiority in relation to the other (Quijano, 2014).

In the present day, we find ourselves in an oppressive neo-colonial stage, characterised by a subtler and more extractive form of domination than in the past. Our lands, rich in natural resources and biodiversity, are being relentlessly exploited and polluted by transnational companies. The Andean region, in particular, plays a large role in sustaining industrial capitalism. America has emerged as a provider of cheaper and faster resources to the world. Advances in technology have reduced the need for labour, resulting in the virtual production of goods primarily for the purpose of trade. However, this has led to a collapse in the rate of profit and has forced the world economy to confront not only unemployment and poverty but also the reconfiguration of a colonial capitalist system that has been imposed worldwide under the guise of globalisation.

Methodology

The methodology used in this qualitative research project is rooted in the descriptive-narrative approach. It involved conducting interviews with leaders from cooperative development, socio-organisational strengthening and resistance against the capitalist and patriarchal system, as well as the analysis of secondary sources from the contribution of ecofeminists and Latin American Social Work professionals from the academy and who work in the territory. The focal point of the analysis was the EPS from an anti-capitalist and decolonial ecofeminist perspective.

The research is structured in three parts. The first offers a theoretical exploration that delves into historical analysis, objectives and principles of the EPS. Secondly, as part of the theoretical analysis, we considered the different views and contributions of ecofeminists in the EPS and the relationship between the EPS and nature, as well as the link between Ecology and Feminisms. Finally, the research also looks at participation of community leaders who confront market capitalism and the hegemonic power of transnational corporations.

Results

One significant factor that stands out from the research is the presence of extractivist companies that dispossess peoples of their territories, forcing them to migrate to the cities or to other countries in search of better opportunities. Justino Piaguage, an Amazonian leader, highlights the effects of mining in the territories, linking it to neoliberal policies. The Cofan people, in particular, have experienced the destructive impacts of mining extractivism, and that impact includes the assassination of their leaders, illnesses caused by mining activities, restricted movement within their territories, and the contamination of natural resources. The latter has also deprived the older generation from dedicating themselves to ancestral medicine because of contamination. Rather than bringing development, mining companies bring destruction and death, and the inhabitants of the Cofán people are increasingly displaced from their territories.

There have been large mobilisations in defence of nature, but they have been criminalised under the label of "subversive" groups. The women of Cofán have raised their voices because they do not have weapons. They demand the ability to walk through their territories, they ask for respect for mother earth, they denounce the contamination of their waters, that is why in the social outburst of 2019 thousands of Amazonian women and women from the Sierra region took to the streets, They are frustrated that they cannot fight on equal terms as other groups do. They are discriminated against because of their race, gender, ethnicity and social class; The 52 mining concessions continue to pollute the waters of the Aguarico River, the source of life for the Cofán and Secoya nationalities. Likewise, the Sicopae nationality, a cross-border people between Ecuador and Peru, still engages in acts of resistance, and its community leaders are frank about the situation of its inhabitants.

Community leader Justino Piaguage says:

> Our nationality is the conformation of states in two countries, with a population that does not exceed 2,000 inhabitants, with a territory that is increasingly reduced by oil exploitation and palm monoculture. We have a long history of resistance. As a people facing various oil exploitation activities and the incursion of agribusiness, we want to return to our ancestral territory to an indigenous worldview. The central problems are reduced territorial space. We subsist on fishing, the grandfathers and grandmothers go fishing in canoes. We resist the cultivation of palm trees, the sale of timber, and the contamination of rivers that affects human health. We also survived the conflict of 1941, where our families were divided. We have lost our historical memory, our knowledge and ancestral wisdom. We are under the laws of the Ministry of Environment and Water where the communities are pressured by oil activity, palm cultivation, agro-industry, the violation of rights, and the inequitable distribution of territories. We see large pieces of land being handed over to other groups that are not ancestral, yet barely 2% of us have territory.
>
> *(Interview with Piaguage on 5 October 2022)*

The Montubio people of Canton Muisne located on the Ecuadorian coast have been engaged in struggles to protect the mangroves that provide food for thousands of families. One of their leaders, ecofeminist Ruth Cortez tells us that she has been collecting shells since she was young, She and her community have taken part in marches to defend their rights before national and international courts. In 2000, she travelled to Spain to ask for support for the defence and life of the mangroves.

She says: "Since I was nine years old I have been a shrimp farmer. The shrimp industry has affected the mangroves since 1980. We fought with all our strength, we made complaints for more than 18 years we have been fighting for the defence of our mangroves. We marched to Quito to defend what is left of the 350,000 hectares. Only 800 hectares remain. The mangrove is an important barrier against natural disasters such as earthquakes and floods.

Indigenous and peasant organisations across the Coast, Highlands and Amazon have united in their demands for food sovereignty, the defence of their territories, water sources, mangroves and moorlands. They prioritise the family and peasant economy as an alternative to mining extractivism.

Food sovereignty is an important issue for the EPS, and the Agrarian Collective was formed in November 2007 during the government of Rafael Correa, with the aim of reflecting on and collaborating with technical contributions to social organisations on the issue. The research project involved contacting 86 rural women's associations dedicated to agriculture. Only 12% use agroecological practices; however, a training plan has been implemented to support participatory diagnostics, socio-organisational development and the promotion of productive entrepreneurship. Collaboration with international NGOs has been crucial because small producers face challenges in accessing markets and ensuring that process are fair, due to their exclusion from the public procurement portal.

Conclusions

The research highlights the urgent need for an anti-capitalist proposal of the EPS to address inequalities, poverty and unemployment. A new way must emerge from collective organisation, from community social work as an alternative and alternative model. There is a need for the democratisation of the economy to include the unprotected social classes. The struggle against mining extractivism and the promotion of agroecology must also include support for cooperative work, and an ethical-political, economic-cultural commitment, where the cycles of nature are respected. Only then will communities see a future where healthy food is a product of social equity, where both men and women, boys and girls, young people, older adults, ancestral peoples have access to the use and control of resources in an equitable way. Greater investment in research into environmental impact, agro-production, and the EPS is crucial. The role of social organisations in community work, association and sustainability is of utmost importance and facilitates commercialisation and fostering collective identity and exchange. The ultimate goal is to move towards an economy that prioritises life and wellbeing for all.

References

Bosch, A., C. Carrasco, & E. Grau. (2005). *Verde que te quiero violeta. Encuentros y desencuentros entre feminismo y ecologismo. La historia cuenta* (pp. 321–346). Barcelona: Ediciones El Viejo Topo.
De Sousa, B. (2006). Sociología de las ausencias y de las emergencias desde las epistemologías del sur. Buenos aires, Argentina: Clacso.
Constitución. (2008). Derechos de la Naturaleza. En A. Nacional. Quito.
Coraggio, J. L. (2011). *La Economía Social y Solidaria: El Trabajo antes que el capital* (Vol. 1). (A. Alberto, Ed.) Quito, Pichincha: Abya Yala.
Iamamoto, M. (1995). Servicio Social y División del Trabajo: Un análisis Crítico de sus Fundamentos. En Cortez (Ed.). Brasil: Biblioteca Latinoamericana de Servicio Social.
Herrero, Y. (2012). Propuestas Ecofeministas Para un Sistema Cargado de Deudas. *Ecologistas en Acción*, p.25.
Mamblona, C., & Matusevicius, J. (2019). Luchas Sociales, sujetos colectivos y trabajo social en América Latina. Puka (Ed.). Buenos Aires, Argentina.
Netto, J. P. (1992). *Capitalismo monopolista e Serviço Social*. São Paulo: Cortez. País.
Pérez, J., Enekoitz, E., & Guridi, L. (2009). *Economía Social, Empresa Social y Economía Solidaria: diferentes conceptos para un mismo debate*. En R. d. Solidaria (Ed.) Bilbao, España.
Portocarrero, A. (2016). Feminismo y ecología: El rol de las universidades frente a la crisis ambiental. (Encuentro, Ed.) 8.
Puleo, A. (2011). *Ecofeminismo para otro mundo posible*. Madrid: Ed. Cátedra.

Quijano, A. (2014). *Colonialidad del poder, Eurocentrismo y América Latina*. Buenos Aires: Colección Antologías.
Razeto, J. L. (2010). *¿Qué es la economía solidaria?* Obtenido de https://base.socioeco.org/docs/que_es_la_economia_solidaria_l.razeto.pdf.
Rozas, M. (2012). *Intervención Profesional en Relación con la Cuestión Social* (O. Dubini, Ed.) Buenos Aires: Espacio.
Shiva, V., & Mies, M. (1997). *Ecofeminismo: Teoría, crítica y perspectivas*. Obtenido de Ecofeminismo teoría, crítica y perspectivas: https://traficantes.net/sites/default/files/pdfs//9788498886924.pdf
Superintendencia, E. (2012). *Objetivos de la Economía Popular y Solidaria*. Quito. Ecuador

# 51

THE FUTURES OF WRITING *WITH* POSTHUMAN FEMINISM IN SOCIAL WORK

Mona B. Livholts and Fanny Södergran

A chapter of three floors in a wave-shaped building: writing with assemblages

This chapter is composed as a space of three floors, inspired by the public library of Oodi, situated in urban Helsinki, Finland. The library takes the physical form of a wave-shaped building of steel, wood and glass, constituting a space for creativity, imagination, reading, play and collective gathering. Oodi was built in 2018 after a co-design process that engaged citizens and designers for more than a decade. The process included peoples' sharing of dreams, and ideas to shape the spaces and functions of the library through a participatory budget which gave citizens access to part of the resources. The library is a centenary visualisation of independent Finland's autonomy from Russia in 1917 and the location at Kansalaistori (Citizens' Square) opposite Parliament House is described by the city of Helsinki to 'symbolize[s] the role of the library as an organ of citizens' (Helsinki City Library Oodi, 2023).

The multiple meanings of embodiment in this building visualise how we situate our conversations and practices of writing in relation to the open-ended concept of assemblages, as we write with multiple forms of both human and non-human embodiment and agency, such as architecture, animals, plants and water. DeLanda (2016, pp. 20–21) writes that assemblages are constructed through heterogeneous components, including people, material and symbolic objects. Emphasising relationality, Braidotti (2022, p. 238) sees assemblages as 'stretching across sexes, genders, classes, ethnicities and racialized locations, but also across non-human species'. As a concept, assemblages recognise complex processes of otherisation and exclusion of 'women and LGBTQ+ people (sexualised others), Black and Indigenous people (racialized others) and the animals, plants and earth entities (naturalized others)' that have had their symbolic and social existence denied (Braidotti, 2022, pp. 18–19). In this chapter, we also address the structural power of writing and textual shaping, seeking to challenge dichotomies of 'nature/culture, subject/object, human/animal, man/woman', which Bozalek and Pease (2021, p. 1) describe as central for critical posthuman social work. We draw on feminist, Indigenous and postcolonial writers that have used creative and art-based forms of expressivity to transform textual shaping to include more

DOI: 10.4324/9781003317371-58

The futures of writing with *posthuman feminism in social work*

Figure 51.1 Photograph of Oodi Library, Helsinki, Finland
Source: Retrieved: 11.1.2023, from https://www.oodihelsinki.fi

than human agency and have renewed approaches to intersectionality (e.g., Mayor & Pollack, 2022; Guttorm et al., 2021; Tsing et al., 2017; Livholts, 2019, 2022, 2023; Ulmer, 2017, 2018; Anzaldúa, 1981/2015). Mayor and Pollack (2022, p. 383; see also Livholts, 2021) demonstrate how creative writing in the context of the COVID-19 pandemic makes it possible to visualise 'how all levels of social work are complicit with or can work to disrupt systems of white supremacy, hetero/sexism, colonialism, and classism'. At the heart of this view on power lies a transformative philosophical engagement of embodiment in social work that 'situates humans as interdependent and interconnected with all other living things and the material world' (Bell, 2021, p. 65). By entering a conversation on the practices of writing, a deeper reflexivity emerges as an alternative to the distance and expertise infused by colonial and neoliberal academia. Mayor and Pollack (2022, p. 385) critically reconsider a decolonising practitioner's approach to reflexivity to 'engage the whole self: where we are from; how we see the world; our emotional, physical, cognitive, and spiritual wellbeing; and accountability to ancestors, land, and community'. Through engaging in a dialogue with Indigenous story-telling practices and non-human agency, Guttorm et al. (2021, p. 117) see this as the co-authoring and undoing of 'the injustices of intellectual colonialism'.

In our conversation, the limits of reflexivity are intimately intertwined with making writing part of our practice as researchers and educators seeking to carve critical, creative and dialogical spaces for writing in social work that include diverse knowledges and life forms, textually, materially and visually. Tsing et al. (2017, p. 2) discuss how knowledge can be reshaped through movement between genres, where 'we begin with a literary essay […] but later move to a scientific report on the very long history of human-caused extinctions and an anthropological guide on how to read landscape history in the shapes of trees'. Diversi et al. (2020) present collaborative writing *with*, as a way of linking together different aspects of writing, critical thinking and processes of becoming. Bozalek (2022) considers how reading, writing and thinking with feminist posthuman philosophy are important but often neglected as a methodological tool in research and supervision. In social work, Livholts (2013, 2019, 2022, 2023) conceptualises genre-transgressive narrative life writing as a situated intersectional methodology. By using feminist fiction, and narrative life writing genres such as diaries, letters, memory work, poetry and photography, university cultures of engagement, inclusivity, situatedness and imagination can be developed.

The aim of our chapter is to think and write with moments from our conversations on the futures of writing with posthuman feminism in social work. Drawing on posthuman, feminist and postcolonial scholarship, we use creative narrative life writing genres such as diaries, letters, poetry and photography to write *with* assemblages, where diverse intersecting inequalities through the embodiment of humans, multi-species agencies, materiality and nature are entangled with temporal and spatial locations. We are white cisgender women of different ages and nationalities that grew up in rural landscapes with Swedish as our mother tongue. Mona Livholts is a Swedish academic who immigrated to Finland and Fanny Södergran is a doctoral researcher born in Finland who belongs to the Finland-Swedish minority population. Our writing is situated and framed by specific personal, cultural and geographical contexts. We hope that readers, who all have their own diverse histories, locations and intersections, find a resonance with their own way of shaping feminist social work through writing that critically and creatively engages with embodied entanglements and intersections beyond human boundaries.

Part I: The peaceful upper floor

Academic non-belonging

It was in November 2021 when we first met outside the Oodi library under the arched roof of the main entrance. The library's three entrance doors are not easily detected, but they are all illuminated, and one entrance announces its presence by means of music. During our first visit, we walk across the wooden floors and take the escalator to 'the peaceful upper floor'. We talk about how we understand the complex relationship between thinking and writing and how it is shaped by our surroundings. It is on this floor that our conversation about academic non-belonging takes us deeper into the architecture of academia, to reflect on how mainstream textual shaping is often a language of human categorisation in social work.

I want to work with people.

Are the practices of categorisation in social work so dominant that they are a condition of being included in the field? In social work, Bozalek and Pease (2021, p. 2) problematise how the dominant influence of Western humanism devalued 'lesser humans' and created the disconnection and disembodiment of humans from the natural environment. Our conversation evolves around the frequently taken for granted commitment to create academic belonging by speaking and writing with other humans and how it silences interconnection to non-human life and agency (Livholts, 2023; Guttorm et al., 2021; Ulmer, 2017). In *Borderlands/La Frontera: The New Mestiza*, Gloria Anzaldúa (1981/2015) writes about how growing up as a 'border woman' entails living with multiple identities, languages and psychological, physical, sexual and spiritual translations and movements across landscapes. Anzaldúa demonstrates how shifting between languages is a way of keeping memories alive, the voicing of a marginal space, of fears and anger, the wind and images of flowers. Anzaldúa's language is multi-lingual; it shifts between personal and historical, geographies of memory and imagination, poetry and academic prose. When writing is creative and open to interconnections with more-than-human worlds, it becomes a methodological movement in which the writer is enmeshed in deeply embodied, spatial and sound practices.

Monday 4.1.2021 Beneath all this winter (FS)

I recently read Negar Naseh's novel Under all denna vinter *(Beneath All This Winter, 2014), where the second part consisted of a working diary written parallel to the novel. What fascinated me was how Naseh addressed the difficulty of actually writing, and how she ascribed the objects in her story agency as co-authors in the text. Naseh articulated a virtual fear of starting to put the story down on paper. She was afraid of interrupting the free flow she experienced when just 'thinking her story'. The real work with her novel was what came before actually writing anything down – living 'with' the story and letting it shape her as it took its own way.*

Naseh's method was working with a kind of memory palace, where different objects, characters, moods and images slowly started to populate a room. She developed strategies for remembering the pillars that were to outline the story, objects coming and going, gradually re-composing her narrative. Naseh thought that articulating the story at too early a stage would block the novel's own direction. She needed to spend time with the objects and let them create their own space. The objects in the story had agency of their own; they were working with Naseh, writing the novel as much as she was.

The major activity surrounding Naseh's 'thinking the story forward' was reading – a passionate and hungry reading – leading her closer and closer to the core. Reading that I myself cherish in my academic work but still can't seem to find enough time for, maybe because it's not seen as productive. I feel the need to materialise and display something graspable – write drafts that account for where I am in my process. Still, this imagined productiveness often seems to hurry something that needs to take time (the sheer embarrassment of trying to articulate something still in its beginning). When writers block is experienced, maybe it's merely a condition of not being done thinking yet.

The reading that Naseh did shaped a foundation so subtle that its outcome isn't fully revealed to the reader until the last dramatic chapter. For me, reading is a gathering phase, where I immerse myself and take detours. I don't know why I'm reading a certain text at that time, but I still can't seem to stop. Months later, I return to something I have read and feel as if everything suddenly falls into place. Naseh's trust in the story growing through the processes of reading and thinking intrigues me. It says something about the complexity of writing. It honours the multiple actors and seemingly 'unproductive' practices of thinking, re-contextualising it as the main event of intellectual processes. The merging of loose ends and gathered fragments, witnessing the backbone emerge from all of the mess – sensing when you are ready to start.

Thursday 17.3 and 10.11.2022 Letter of the Sea (ML)

It is mid-March and the time of the ice thaw in Helsinki when I begin to write this letter. It is a time when I often walk to the seafront; listening to the clashing of ice blocks; the seeping sound of slush ice; the slowness of water movements. I perceive water during these moments as a source of spiritual recovery; this water also has meaning for me on a personal level, suggesting connectivity and (be)longing; and at the same time, the sea is a political and economic space for fishing, shipping, trading, travelling. At this beach I think with the ice thaw, the sound of water and ice-blocks in movement. Even when I cannot feel the wind, and ice blocks cover most of the surface, there is always movement.

> *Am I floating,*
> *in the sun beams,*
> *of the spring sea,*
> *the surface of ice and open water?*
> *Am I floating, towards open sea,*
> *ice-blocks clashing,*
> *slow water movements,*
> *asking me to listen?*
> *Am I floating,*
> *in this moment,*
> *of intense sunlight,*
> *with the sea of the Gulf of Bothnia,*
> *water, ripples,*
> *the heart beats of clashing ice blocks*
> *of the Sea,*
> *connecting and separating*
> *Finland and Sweden?*

Many years ago, I wrote about water when I sought to understand on a deeper level the exclusionary practices concerning writing about social work that marginalised my texts (Livholts, 2013, 2019). I reflected on how water is part of human embodied selves and the earth and how it can visualise the complexity of understanding social change through memories and stories. Sara Ahmed (2017, p. 3) writes about how the diversity of feminist movements can be understood as 'ripples in water, a small wave, possibly created by agitation from weather; here, there, each movement, making another possible'. I imagined that I joined a movement of water writers. Writing water provided the possibility of seeing and listening beyond the human self to raise awareness of different histories and everyday realities and materialities understood from the basis of inequalities. I say somewhere in my text that I was always writing water as a way out of metaphoric captivity and alienating textual structures in academia. However, writing this letter to the sea from a posthuman viewpoint of assemblages brings in alternative critical understandings. My first scenario with the ice thaw and spiritual recovery co-exists with the realities of the human destruction of waters. I write with a polluted sea. Re-thinking the interconnections between humans and the Baltic Sea, means writing with a polluted embodiment; toxic substances from industries, ships, and agriculture, overfishing and algal blooming; a sea where large areas at the bottom suffer from lack of oxygen. Re-writing actualises the complex extended embodiment of multi-species dependency, writing this letter, writing with the ice-thaw, writing with toxic fish and algal blooming.

Part II: The active ground floor

Embodied-fleshed-more-than-human childhoods

We both have strong sensory perceptions from our childhoods; through smells, sounds and visions, memories are embodied and can be felt in the flesh, enabling us to re-connect with landscapes across temporalities and spatialities. When sharing childhood memories, our conversations brought forth the entanglements of life and death, our own bodies, animal bodies, bodies of waters, forests, and plants, and how all of these are interwoven in the fabric of our knowledges. Guttorm et al. (2021, p. 114) argue that to be able to express the relationship with the natural world, we need to stretch the boundaries of what it means to write an academic text and invite more-than-human agents as narrators and co-authors into the text. We need 'to think like the forest, and to write with these ontologically different epistemologies, where [do] the non-words get translated into words in our writing process?' Our conversation brought forth such contrasts and entanglements of the human working body in the field of crops, to care for the farm animals during their short lifetime, feeding, cleaning the pigs' pen and the sheep's barn, the naming of animals, to witness parts of animal bodies in the freezer or on the ground after slaughter. Permeability with the livelihood – the worn-out backs, the soil and plants staining the skin, adding a new layer on top of it – a rash, something to scratch.

Thursday 20.5.2021 Visits to the Mire (FS)

I'm in the forests of my childhood, walking along the dirt road leading to the mire. A wolf was seen just around here yesterday afternoon. People in the village say that it doesn't belong here, that it's moving too close to populated areas. They say it's not normal behaviour for a wolf, as if it was for them to decide.

The usual route towards the mire is blocked by spruce that have fallen in a storm. The road has been impassable for a long time already, because the firefighter that owned the woods died a couple of years ago. The other way to get to the mire is by following muddy tractor ruts, passing two clear cuts. The mire nowadays consists of perfectly shaped rectangles, demarcated by ditches that have been dug to dry the mire out. This is done to promote the growth of trees so that they can be sold in the future. The years have slowly started to change the habitat of the mire to a resource to be harvested.

It's the month of May. It strikes me that I've never before visited the mire this time of year. Smells of wet peat, moss, bog rosemary and marsh labrador tea. Insects are buzzing around some cloudberry flowers; they look like small white midsummer roses. I've picked their berries countless times in August, but I haven't experienced them blossom before. The most beautiful flowers I have ever seen, rising from the black peat exposed by the heavy weight of the tractors.

Figure 51.2 Cloudberry blossoms in tractor ruts
Source: Photograph by Fanny Södergran

Monday 20.6.2022 Picking Stones, Sowing Barley (ML)

Every time I pass a ploughed field or a field with barley in rural space on a warm summer day, I imagine how I used to walk behind the tractor with my sisters each year to pick stones from the earth in preparation for the sowing. It was hot in the sun, and we wore tall rubber boots. I tried to keep the side of my face towards the tractor to avoid breathing the dust that swirled up from the earth. We were trained to choose the right sized stones; not too large, not too small, but middle sized, stones we were strong enough to pick and carry with us in our buckets, allowing the field to breathe and yet regenerate the growth of the earth. There was a particular rhythm in the movements, leaning forward, picking the stones, moving the bucket, and a clicking sound, 'clock', 'clock', 'clock', could be heard as another stone was dropped in the bucket. This memory is from the seasonal work on the farm where I grew up in rural Sweden in a white patriarchal family. I worked with and cared for the animals: horses, pigs, sheep and our dog. I sometimes sneaked out early in the morning to check the traps for mink and fox that my stepfather had set in the forest. I pleaded that the farm animals, who were my closest friends, should be spared from slaughter. I felt loss and grief for long periods after their death. All memories from this childhood brings with them embodied sensory perceptions of the landscape; the heat when walking behind the tractor; the sound of stones; the smell when cleaning the stables. The sensory perceptions of how my thinking and knowledge are entangled with the forest, the sound of the wind, the companionship of the large birch tree next to the gravel road each morning when I waited for the school bus, the snow each winter that covered the landscape and brought silence, the crunching sound of my horse eating, the fear I felt in an encounter with an elk in the forest, and learning to swim and trust my body in the cold water of a creek. It was an odd feeling of awakening when I realised that some of the discomfort and alienation I felt in academia was caused by the way my embodied experiences and emotions of growing up in a rural environment was not acknowledged as part of urban Western academic knowledge.

(Livholts, 2023, p. 82)

Figure 51.3 Barley
Source: Wikimedia commons, 2023

Part III: The in-between floor

Writing with the Middle

In the in-between floor, we share thoughts on writing our ongoing research projects on exhaustion (ML) and climate activism (FS). Braidotti (2013, p. 186) reminds us that

> the posthuman predicament enforces the necessity to think again and to think harder about the status of the human, the importance of recasting subjectivity accordingly, and the need to invent forms of ethical relations, norms and values worthy of the complexity of our times.

We talk about how practices of situated and slow writing challenge practices of non-linear narration that allow movement, sensory perceptions, visualities and sound. Situated writing takes an interest in questions such as why writing can lead to a better understanding of diversity, power and experiences of becoming writers through an 'artistic practice that takes artefacts as pieces of text as well as visual images, creating mo(ve)ments for change' (Livholts, 2019, p. 4). We argue that posthuman feminist thinking requires situated and slower modes of observing details, soundscapes, images and meanings in the local environment. For Tsing (2015, p. 22), there is a need to reshape imaginaries of progress: 'As long as we imagine that humans are made through progress, nonhumans are stuck within this imaginative framework too.' Ulmer (2017, 2018) writes about doing thought-based practice through a slower mode of writing and photographing that attends to 'the role of local places, natural environmental surroundings, and material landscapes in daily life' (2017, p. 203). Tiainen et al. (2020, p. 219) discuss how as a process of becoming from the perspective of more-than-human agency, intersectionality can be better understood as a process in the *middle*. This process challenges difference and inequality 'not only as a matter of structures, systems and already-existing possibilities for being, but also as open-ended relationalities happening across social, material, discursive, human and more-than-human areas of activity'. Thinking with each other, writing with assemblages in the environments of our research projects, allows for deeper critical reflexive practices.

Saturday 4.4 and Monday 11.5 Writing Exhaustion during the Pandemic (ML)

4th April 2020: Closer to Things

Figure 51.4 Bark skin/*Barkhud/Kuoren iho*. Stockholm, Sweden, 2020
Source: Photograph by Mona Livholts

The futures of writing with posthuman feminism in social work

Dear Diary, The last weeks have gradually infused a different rhythm into my life. I spend more time alone, I read more, I avoid going to the grocery store if it is not necessary, and I keep a distance between myself and other people. I watch TV more often to keep up-to-date with news about Covid. Every morning I talk to my 78-year-old mother, who lives in isolation. The epidemic has brought an increased awareness to my daily life, an uncertainty, sometimes a sense of failure. I use the camera to photograph my surroundings. I feel a renewed attachment to windows, buildings, furniture, trees, flowers and parks. It is as if the social distancing between people brings me closer to things, makes me attentive to all forms of life, materials and architecture. I take a photo of the window in the room where I most often work at home. I have always loved this window, but I now see it as more than a window. I see it as an extension of the flat intertwined with the large trees outside, with the ivy that climbs and embraces the tree trunks.

Tiredness/*trötthet/väsymys*
My heart beats pounding in my ears
The chorus of a *whistling/susande/sipinä/* sound
Restlessness, insomnia, dreams, shivers
Dots with red legs, dancing in the *darkness/mörkret/pimeys*
Spring *trees/vårträd/kevätpuita*
Arms and legs of bark skin
Stretching out, touched by the wind
Rooted in the earth/*jorden/maa*
My skin/*min hud/minun iho*
The largest organ of the body
Breathing/*andas/hengitä*
Connecting with all other bodies/*kroppar/kehot*
(Livholts, 2021, p. 55)

11th May 2020: Reflexive bridges, Traces of Rust and Exhausted Things

Dear Diary, This morning I photographed shadows under the bridge. It felt like I too was made of water, stone and mud. The sun beams broke through the water movements, created shadow patterns on the vaulted concrete passage under the bridge. I called this moment reflexive bridges.

I continued my walk and unexpectedly saw traces of rust on the bridge by the waterfront. I smelled something rusting, of mud, and passed a container filled with steel garbage. Beside it was a row of shopping carts. At first, I just passed, but when I came back, I took a photo; I understood then that traces of rust came from bikes, and shopping carts that had been brought up from the bottom of the lake. I thought there was something hopeful about the scene. I thought it should be made a permanent exhibition; an invitation for people to think and re-think their relationships to things.

Figure 51.5 Exhausted Things/*Utmattade saker*/*Uupuneet asiat*, Stockholm, Sweden, 2020
Source: Photograph by Mona Livholts

Tuesday 10.8.2021 The smallness of what I am (FS)

Back at work after summer leave. A quiet feeling of crisis has been hovering over me. The longest heat wave in Finnish history took place this summer. I've avoided the news and social media, because it feels as if a sudden awakening has happened. The country's biggest newspaper has reported about climate change almost daily and yesterday another IPCC report, which I couldn't bring myself to read, was published.

I feel triggered and at the same time paralysed. It's a paradox of the body and mind. I sit inside during the hottest hours, my mind working at full speed. The amount of time I've spent reading and writing about the social injustices of the climate crisis – but I'm not doing anything now, not even writing. My own activism is in hibernation, I'm just sitting with it, with the fear and anxiety. At the same time I'm fortunate, as this extreme weather is merely a contrast to my daily life.

The heat is permeating my flesh, making daily tasks slow. I'm at the seaside but can't cool off in the sea due to an outbreak of toxic algae. They say the toxins can find their way into the liver and the nervous system, where it slowly affects the functions of the body. Just as human-made toxins have found their way into the sea and manipulated ocean ecologies. Swimming is something I've always taken for granted. It's been part of who I am all my life and not being able to be in the water for long periods each summer feels like an emotional and physical loss. It feels like preparing for grief.

I connect to the ocean,
its cold and soft body carries the weight of me.
While floating on my back, I let go.
Sinking down into the dark matter, then rising back to the surface,
as my chest inflates and deflates.
My ears tucked under the water register what's in me.
My pulse, the smallness of what I am.
Beneath me, primal ocean murmurs,
abstract sounds of a world where I am only a guest.

Part IV: Revisiting the Peaceful Upper Floor
Another future is possible

As we return to the peaceful upper floor, we share the letters, memories, diary notes, photographs and readings, carving a space to write with the futures of posthuman feminism in social work. The choice of the Oodi public library in Helsinki as the architectural space for our conversations, for the composing of our texts inspired by the floors and their in-betweenness, is important as a critical reflective engagement with the architecture of the university and the question of the futures of Feminisms. Thinking and writing with this wave-shaped building created a space that makes a break with linear time and other boundaries, opening up alternative rhythms and connections. If bodies are to be understood beyond human domination, diversity and intersectionality need to take on renewed philosophies and relationalities that attend to the middle of human and more-than-human entanglements (Livholts, 2022, 2023; Puar, 2012). A key aspect that we have returned to during our conversations on the futures of writing with posthuman Feminisms is what Ulmer (2017, p. 202) describes as not 'a slower way of doing scholarship, but how we can find a slower way of scholarly being'. Isabelle Stengers (2018, p. 106) critically argues that 'another future is possible', but also that 'the future is 'coming towards us at full speed'. This other future depends on a change from within the university, the courage to express doubt and time to think. This requires a commitment to move away from the ideal of neoliberal academia's fast science and towards the knowledge economy. As academics we have a specific position of responsibility to 'envisage, feel, think or imagine', as Stengers (2018, p. 107) puts it. The plea for a slow science leads the way towards reclaiming and changing the structural conditions in academia through responsible agency. Stengers (2018, p. 124) refers to slow science as 'the name for a movement in which many paths for recovery might come together'. Bozalek (2022, p. 56) emphasises awareness of creative and transformative practices of reading, writing and thinking and writes: 'In the encounter with writing and thinking, we need to keep ourselves open to how we are being changed by the text or the conversation.' Our memories, letters, diary notes and photographs express diverse intersecting embodiments of humans, multi-species agencies, materiality and nature. They offer the reader slow, close and creative practices in which writers enter into their own conversations, writings and readings. We hope that the dynamic understandings of time and space, incorporating more-than-human agents and bodies, pave the way for intersectional relationality and permeability in the futures of writing with posthuman feminism in social work.

Monday 16.5.2022 Staying in place (FS)

In these times of crisis and rapid change, it does not seem purposeful for academia to reflect hurried temporalities or repeat unsustainable patterns. I would like to think that this condition, on the contrary, calls for careful thought, creative reflection and even rest. What would it mean to resist the continuous measuring, or the engagement in large numbers of projects, producing as much as the mind and body can only just bear?

When Haraway invites us to 'stay with the trouble' (2016), I imagine taking a seat, comfortably staying put even when responsibilities and commitments call for my attention, trusting that I know where my focus should be. I try to see myself in relation to everything else, my surrounding environments and what's beyond me. How small and indifferent the routines and timetables of the everyday life then seem: 'Urgencies have other temporalities, and these times are ours. These are the times we must think; these are the times of urgencies that need stories.'

(Haraway, 2016, p. 40)

In dialogue, Alaimo writes '[t]hinking as the stuff of the world entails thinking in place, in places that are simultaneously the material of the self and the vast networks of material worlds.' (2016, p. 187). Sometimes in the middle of my carefully Timecon-clocked workday, I tie on my shoes and just walk right out into the forest. It feels forbidden, and that invigorates me. Thinking and writing – slowly – consciously registering feelings of discomfort (that might well be 'the trouble' talking), making room and staying in place, is both resistance and trusting what the process will hold.

> *I let my fingertips run along the fauna,*
> *smelling, tasting and listening.*
> *I think it does something to me,*
> *something still resting within.*
> *A piece waiting to fall into place.*

Thursday 19.5.2022 Wave-Shaped Futures of Writing (ML)

When we walk
across the ground floor
and the in-between volume
of more specific functions,
I hear the rush
of the dark green forests
of my childhood.
When we walk,
across the wave-shaped floor
of the peaceful upper floor,
I float with the cold water
in the creek of my childhood,

where I learned to swim.
When we are situated
on the wave-shaped roof,
I hear
the heart beats
of ice blocks
of the spring sea.

Open-ended reflections and questions to inspire your own writing

In this chapter, we have argued that how we write shapes the possibilities to engage *with* more-than human assemblages, that allow for entanglements between humans, the natural world, buildings, forests, waters and animals. We demonstrate how an open-ended, genre-transgressive methodology such as writing memories, diary notes, letters, poetry and photography is useful for this purpose. Thus, situating the writer through acts of reading, seeing, listening, creates slow forms of scholarship that promote creative, responsible and more-than-human knowledges. We bring with us to this last section the idea brought forth by Ahmed (2017, p. 3) that the diversity of feminist movements can be understood as 'ripples in water, a small wave, possibly created by agitation from weather; here, there, each movement, making another possible'. It is in this spirit that we wish to share open-ended reflections and questions to inspire readers' own writing.

~ ~ ~ ~

Our first reflection is related to *creating spaces for thinking and writing with assemblages.* For us, the architectural formation of the wave shaped building of the library of Oodi embodied a physical, material and imaginative space to think and write with the more-than-human. The conversations surfaced multifaceted experiences and memories that promoted a critical re-thinking of the human-centredness and categorisations that tends to dominate social work. We suggest that these questions can be used as a starting point: How do you understand writing with more-than-human assemblages, in comparison to human-focused writing? What possible architectural, material, natural real and/or imagined environments can spur conversations with yourself, other humans and more-than-human subjects?

~ ~ ~ ~

A second set of reflections are related to how *different narrative genres* can be used when focusing on the theme of more-than-human assemblages to situate the writer in different temporal and spatial locations and offer diverse forms of expressivity. For those who wish to read and better understand the characteristics and usefulness of each of these diverse genres Livholts (2019, 2023) work on situated writing and the post-anthropocentric essay can be used as inspiration.

We suggest that you elaborate with *writing short memory scenes* (not more than half a page) where you attend to detail, sensory perceptions, and emotions to narrate specific moments of lived experience. Inspired by this chapter you could work with the question: What are the first memories that comes to your mind related to the environment of your childhood? You are encouraged to use the third person (he, she, they or your own or invented name). If you wish to use the methodology of memory work as a process, read the memory aloud (record it or read to a colleague or friend) and use active listening. How did you perceive the memory when you listened to it? Did it mediate what you thought about when you wrote it? Were there particular details, words, impressions from this memory that were particularly interesting to spur further writing or reading?

We also recommend that you try the practice of *writing a diary* (dated entrances) and/or to *write letters* (dated and directed to a receiver) over a period of two to three weeks on a chosen theme of relevance for your own project. Diaries and letters are blurred genres for life writing that in the context of posthuman social work are formed by the way the writer create communicative acts with self and other humans and the natural world. In our chapter, the diary is used as a form of writing to document everyday insights and thoughts from our projects on exhaustion and environmental activism.

Poetry allows for mediating experiences that are often otherwise silenced and we perceive poetic expressivity to be important to give voice to gaps and in-betweenness and emotions related to embodied entanglements. *Photography* visualises ways of seeing and promote ecological consciousness in the process of writing with diverse forms of embodiments in the intersection of feminism and posthuman social work. As Livholts (2019, p. 39) describe the theory and practices of using life writing genres, she regards it as shaping 'a self-portrait with a performative and life-shaping role, whereby geographical space and nature are part of the writing body.' You are encouraged to create your own use of poetry and photography of relevance for your interest. In our chapter, different ways of engaging with water illustrate this writing. Imagine how the multiple forms of water can be an inspiration to shape your writing. Pay attention to the sensory perceptions and shaping of knowledge by using poetry.

~ ~ ~ ~

For us, the futures of writing with posthuman feminism in social work are characterised by textual practices of shifting genres, that allows for expressing sensory perceptions, images, sounds, smells and nuances. We propose that writers embrace care, trust, creativity and imagination as a way to transform wording and image making towards material-discursive transgressions between humans, multi-species and the natural world. By sharing thoughts from our conversations, written and photographic illustrations and the open-ended reflections and questions in this final section, we hope to inspire you as a reader to pay attention to your own stories, locations and intersections to critically and creatively write with embodied entanglements beyond human boundaries.

References

Ahmed, S. (2017), *Living a Feminist Life*. Duke University Press.
Alaimo, S. (2016). *Exposed: Environmental Politics and Pleasures in Posthuman Times*. University of Minnesota Press.
Anzaldúa, G. (1981/2015). *Borderlands/La Frontera: The New Mestiza* (4th edition). Aunt Lute Books.
Bell, K. (2021). A Philosophy of Social Work beyond the Anthropocene. In V. Bozalek & B. Pease (Eds.), *Post-Anthropocentric Social Work: Critical Posthuman and New Materialist Perspectives* (pp. 58–67). Routledge.
Bozalek, V. (2022). Doing Academia Differently: Creative Reading/Writing-With Posthuman Philosophers. *Qualitative Inquiry*, 28(5), 552–561. https://doi.org/10.1177/10778004211064939
Bozalek, V., & Pease, B. (Eds). (2021). *Post-Anthropocentric Social Work: Critical Posthuman and New Materialist Perspectives*. Routledge.
Braidotti, R. (2013). *The Posthuman*. Polity Press.
Braidotti, R. (2022). *Posthuman Feminism*. Polity.

DeLanda, M. (2016). *Assemblage Theory*. Edinburgh University Press.
Diversi, M., Gale, K., Moreira, C., & Wyatt, J. (2020). Writing with: Collaborative Writing as Hope and Resistance. *International Review of Qualitative Research*, 14(2), 1–11.
Guttorm, H., Kantonen, L., Kramvig, B., & Pyhälä, A. (2021). Decolonized Research-Storying: Bringing Indigenous Ontologies and Care into the Practices of Research Writing. In P. K. Virtanen, P. Keskitalo & T. Olsen (Eds.), *Indigenous Research Methodologies in Sámi and Global Contexts* (pp. 113–143). Brill Sense.
Haraway, D. J. (2016). Staying with the Trouble: Anthropocene, Capitalocene, Chthulucene. In J. W. Moore (Ed.). *Anthropocene or Capitalocene? Nature, History, and the Crisis of Capitalism* (pp. 34–76). PM Press.
Helsinki Central Library Oodi. Retrieved January 11, 2023, from https://design.hel.fi/en/design-stories/central-library-oodi/
Livholts, M. B. (2022). Decolonising Writing in Post-Anthropocentric Social Work. *SocialDialogue* #26. https://socialdialogue.online/sd26/05_article.html
Livholts, M. B. (2023). *The Body Politics of Glocal Social Work. Essays on the Post Anthropocentric Condition*. Routledge.
Livholts, M. B. (2021). Exhaustion and Possibility: The Wor(l)dlyness of Social Work in (G)local Environment Worlds During a Pandemic. *Qualitative Social Work*, 20(1–2), 54–62. https://doi.org/10.1177/1473325020973314
Livholts, M. B. (2019). *Situated Writing as Theory and Method. The Untimely Academic Novella*. Routledge.
Livholts, M. B. (2013). Writing Water. An Untimely Academic Novella. In Stanley, L. (Ed.) *Documents of Life Revisited: Narrative and Biographical Methods for a 21st Century of Critical Humanism* (pp. 137–148). Ashgate.
Mayor, C. and Pollack, S. (2022). Creative Writing and Decolonizing Intersectional Feminist Critical Reflexivity: Challenging Neoliberal, Gendered, White, Colonial Practice Norms in the COVID-19 Pandemic. *Affilia: Feminist Inquiry in Social Work*, 37(3), 382–395. https://doi.org/10.1177/08861099211066338
Naseh, N. (2014). *Under all denna vinter*. Natur och kultur.
Puar, J. K. (2012). "I would rather be a cyborg than a goddess": Becoming-Intersectional in Assemblage Theory. *philoSOPHIA*, 2(1), 49–66. https://muse.jhu.edu/article/486621
Stengers, I. (2018). *Another Science is Possible. A Manifesto for Slow Science*. Polity Press.
Tiainen, M., Leppänen, T., Kontturi, K., and Mehrabi, T. (2020). Making Middles Matter: Intersecting Intersectionality with New Materialisms. *NORA – Nordic Journal of Feminist and Gender Research*, 28(3), 211–223. https://doi.org/10.1080/08038740.2020.1725118
Tsing, A., Swanson, H., Gan, H., and Bubant, N. (Eds). (2017). *Arts of Living on a Damaged Planet: Ghosts and Monsters of the Anthropocene*. University of Minnesota Press.
Tsing, A. (2015). *The Mushroom at the End of the World: On the Possibility of Life in Capitalist Ruins*. Princeton University Press.
Ulmer, J. B. (2018). Minor Gestures: Slow Writing and Everyday Photography. *Qualitative Research in Psychology*, 15(2–3), 317–322. https://doi.org/10.1080/14780887.2018.1430016
Ulmer, J. B. (2017). Posthumanism as Research Methodology: Inquiry in the Anthropocene. *International Journal of Qualitative Studies in Education*, 30(9), 832–848. https://doi.org/10.1080/09518398.2017.1336806
Wikimedia Commons. Retrieved January 11, 2023, from https://commons.wikimedia.org/wiki/File:Hordeum_vulgare_(6-row_barley,_Gerste)_dry_specimens_(2019-08-07).jpg

52
ECO-FEMINIST RESPONSES TO CLIMATE CHANGE AND ITS GENDERED IMPACTS

Leah Holdsworth and Jennifer Boddy

Introduction

The Intergovernmental Panel on Climate Change [IPCC] defines climate change as any change in climate over time, either due to human impact or natural variation. It is considered a threat to the health of global civilisation and is therefore a shared responsibility to address collectively (IPCC, 2022; Tanyanyiwa & Mufunda, 2019). Climate change has been steadily increasing, mostly caused by the increased concentration in Earth's atmosphere of greenhouse gases, in turn, triggered primarily by the burning of fossil fuels such as coal, oil, and gas (IPCC, 2022). Alarmingly, climate change models predict that stronger storms, heavier precipitation, flooding, heatwaves, and droughts will increase in the future, leading to increased natural disasters (IPCC, 2022).

Yet, remarkably, there is no genuine commitment to significant climate change reflected within policies and dominant narratives on a global scale. For instance, David Harvey (2011) argues that while climate change concerns are on the one hand included in global policy debates, in actuality global policy reflects no genuine commitment to meaningful change. This, Harvey (2011) points out, is because capitalism itself both engages and co-opts analysis, modifying policy in a purely symbolic way, and only as much as necessary to create an illusion of the promise of change; however, in reality, the minimal changes that are promised merely maintain the current social order of hegemonic rule and dominance, and the power of the elites. Harvey (2014) uses carbon trading as an example of how global policy lacks real dedication to climate change, noting how it has achieved little to limit overall global carbon emissions. Additionally, Peck and Theodore (2010) highlight the need to challenge strategy that uncritically adopts inconsequential policy, rather than adopting policy that aligns to the needs and circumstances of people and ecosystems. Critique of neoliberal environmental climate change policy is therefore important to show how the outcomes generated could truly show commitment to global environment outcomes for all, including the most vulnerable.

In particular, the focus in this chapter is on women, many of whom are disproportionately affected by changes to the climate (Hetherington & Boddy, 2013; Jerneck, 2018; Nyahunda, 2021; Tanyanyiwa & Mufunda, 2019).

It will examine the ongoing and increasing impacts of climate change on women, actions already taken by feminist and pro-feminist scholars and activists and provide an overview of why an inclusion of the feminist ethics of care, which focuses on the interdependence of humans and the natural environment (Gilligan, 2011), must become integral within social work practice surrounding climate change. It will conclude with recommendations for further climate change policy, practice, and research areas.

Gendered impacts of climate change

The World Health Organisation [WHO] (2019) defines gender as socially constructed roles and behaviours fulfilled by women and men within society. This also includes attitudes that shape female and male roles and interactions that are not only socially determined but also historically, culturally, and contextually bound (Alston, 2012). Gender roles infuse laws, institutions, and frameworks, creating power imbalances between men and women, making it difficult for women to achieve gender equality in both public and private spaces (Alston, 2012). For this reason, women in Australia, and globally, are less likely to own land, assets, and resources, have less influence in decision-making processes including when recovering from environmental disasters related to climate change, are more negatively affected than men in terms of wellbeing, and find expressing their needs and experiences difficult (Nyahunda, 2021).

Climate changed-induced stress can also result in increased instances of domestic violence, again largely impacting women (Boetto, 2016). This gendered vulnerability to climate change is related to women's higher risk due to reproductive and productive labour in different socioeconomic factors and associated burdens related to poverty, and oftentimes poorer access to education, property, and income sources, and is ultimately due to patriarchal dominance (Nyahunda, 2021).

Men are also affected by the impacts of climate change. For example, men's ability to continue their gendered role as primary family breadwinner and decision-maker, the continued dominant narrative around masculinity in many Western countries, is negatively impacted when roles cannot be met due to extreme weather events (Alston, 2012). This then tends to result in men internalising blame, including blame connected to climate change, with many experiencing increased levels of stress and anxiety, and additional mental and physical health concerns (Alston, 2012; Parkinson & Zara, 2016). Indeed, suicide is a higher risk factor for men who experience stress from climate change consequences, and their privilege, power, and influence do little to stop men feeling isolated (Alston, 2012; Pease, 2014).

However, more than any other minority or group, women in rural communities globally, particularly in developing countries, are disproportionately impacted by the ongoing effects of climate change especially when struck by climate-related disasters such as floods, droughts, fires, cyclones, and heat waves (Nyahunda, 2021). As is the case globally, this situation is due to women's lack of access to and control of assets and can lead to water scarcity and food insecurity, energy resource depletion, poor health, and climate-induced migration and conflict (Nyahunda, 2021). For example, across rural South Asia, women look after livestock, run households, take care of children and the elderly, tend to the sick, and cannot own or inherit land or property (Sultana, 2014). In these communities, when disasters occur, there is a greater mortality rate for women and girls; when crops and homes are destroyed, there is little chance of income which results in starvation becoming a real concern particularly for women, as men tend to migrate in search of livelihoods, therefore increasing the vulnerability of women left behind (Sultana, 2014). During relief-work, where women-headed households are left to recover, they tend to receive inadequate information, assistance, shelter, and rehabilitation materials, and women's and girl's needs are likely to be overlooked for this reason alone (Sultana, 2014). Additionally, recovery and reconstruction become complex and difficult when flooding occurs almost annually making it difficult for households to build resilience and worsen vulnerability to the next event (Sultana, 2014).

Due to the specific gender-based vulnerabilities of socio-economic origins, women and girls also have higher mortality rates and instances of violence following natural disasters (Tanyanyiwa & Mufunda, 2019). In the Philippines, for example, following Typhoon Haiyan in 2013, gender-based violence against women and girls highlighted how pre-existing inequalities, rooted in gendered roles, led to vulnerability to further violence following natural disasters (Nguyen, 2019). More so, the death rate of women and girls is higher than men in some communities, and when surviving disasters, they then face a greater risk of gender-based and sexual violence during disaster recovery (True, 2013). Ashraf and Azad (2015) point out that the reasons for women's higher mortality and violence rates involve social and cultural organisations of divisions of labour such as continuing gendered caring-roles for the elderly and children. Additionally, gender-based preconceptions that see women as weak and passive victims needing rescuing in disaster situations, and men as strong and capable who require least assistance are spurious at best (Ashraf & Azad, 2015). In actuality, women are not just victims and often play an active role in disaster recovery; women are survivors who can help countries recover more quickly from natural disasters and conflict (True, 2013).

Feminism and climate change

Eco-feminism is strongly connected to the challenges of climate change and to helping address the climate crisis due to the recognition of the interconnectedness of social, political, economic, and environmental perspectives (Gilligan, 2011). By locating issues within a feminist ethic of care, resistance to the injustices that are inherent in Patriarchy can be addressed (Gilligan, 2011). Ultimately, people are interconnected with the natural environment and should therefore be equally valued, as being fundamentally a part of it (Bozalek & Pease, 2021). From an eco-feminist perspective, a shift must be made from species hierarchy, and a movement towards addressing the intersectionality of posthumanism and post-anthropocentrism (Bozalek & Pease, 2021). Rethinking power dynamics around dwindling natural resources in the age of the Anthropocene becomes a radical act (Tramel, 2018).

Governments, societies, and our globalised world must collectively work in compassionate and caring ways, recognising that humanity is interdependent on nature and not in binary opposition to it; in this way, ecofeminism asserts that there needs to be a move away from internalised, dichotomised frameworks (human versus animal, and man versus women) as such hierarchal ways of thinking ultimately legitimise oppression and mastery of nature (Bozalek & Pease, 2021). From the binary, oppressive framework, the ideal human as male, white, heterosexual, young, and able boded, is distinguished from other 'lesser' humans, as well as other animals, and nature, granting some humans (i.e. white heterosexual males) more rights than others, and allows domination and oppression to continue between humans, and between humans and animals (Bozalek & Pease, 2021).

An ecofeminist epistemology calls for a more nuanced understanding of the power imbalance within climate change discourse, with individual action leading to sufficient climate change action and behaviour change being illogical thinking (Bee et al., 2015). Neoliberal climate polices effectively target some nations, and benefit others, and ultimately place responsibility on the individual, thus yet again shifting responsibility from the state (Bee et al., 2015). From an ecofeminist perspective, climate change policies must become more inclusive of understanding beyond the realms of technical and scientific knowledge, and begin to become inclusive of collective action, and the experiential, embodied, non-scientific forms of knowledge – to focus on the inequalities surrounding climate change (Søndergaard et al., 2022).

A feminist ethic of care focuses on the interdependence of humans, the natural environment, and the importance of care; for a society to be morally just, it must provide adequate care for all, including the most vulnerable (Bozalek & Pease, 2021). According to Gilligan (2011), care involves five key elements: caring about, caring for, caregiving; care receiving; a sense of ongoing responsibility and awareness of importance to partake in caregiving; consideration of the care-receiver's response; and finally, a commitment to justice, equality, and freedom. To apply this to climate change, ignorance of its effects on marginalised groups is viewed as unethical confirming that we have a moral responsibility to explore the effects of neoliberalism on environmental degradation and pay attention to meaningful change, responding to climate change activism through creating a healthy, sustainable, and caring environment for all people. It is morally imperative for governments and people alike to ensure adequate care is taken of the environment and to mitigate climate change effects and ensure this is completed competently, with policies from well-grounded research undertaken.

A feminist ethic of care should be the focus for climate change policies, practices, and interventions. Developing ethical theories based on the lived experiences of locals who have experienced first-hand the effects of climate change is critical, not just from a theoretical perspective, as it has the power to potentially shift the focus of ethical reflection and insight (Allison, 2017). For example, case studies of Indigenous communities who have experienced climate change so far share values with feminist care ethics, including the valuing of collective action (moving to a new location all together), extending care to nonhuman surroundings, critique of the economic valuing over resource management, elevating the value of water, and emphasis on strong relationships and communities (Allison, 2017).

Building a climate change narrative from specific socioecological locations becomes key to the feminist ethics of care perspective and becomes grounded in local narratives, with rich local detail, offering tangible, entangled, interconnected and comprehensive guidelines for ethical insight, and tying into Indigenous and traditional societies, who share knowledge with one another about environment (Allison, 2017). The social goal of climate change response would ideally be to mitigate environmental change responses synergistically with food insecurity, inequality, and poverty levels (Jerneck, 2018). Politicians, policymakers, and practitioners would therefore need to take gender into consideration when considering material distribution of rights, risks and responsibilities that lead towards transformative potential of increased sustainability (Jerneck, 2018).

Feminist social change

Feminist scholars and activists are advocating, lobbying, and mobilising for further social and climate change action; at the micro level, women are often at the forefront of influencing the reduction of household carbon emissions through consumer choices and recycling (Hosseinnezhad, 2017; Williams et al., 2018). At the macro level, intersectional networks of feminist and Indigenous women's activism at local, national, and global levels influence the reframing of climate challenges and actions through Indigenous perspectives and knowledge, and leading Western feminists to activate discourse around gender-bias and suggest equality-based policy (Hosseinnezhad, 2017). The narrative of women being assertive caretakers of the planet and its natural resources has gained traction since the World Women's Congress for a Healthy Planet in 1991, followed by the Earth Summit on Environment and Development (UNCED) in 1992, and the Beijing Women's Platform for Action in 1995; these events have become moments connecting the official discourse surrounding ecofeminism (Resurrección, 2013).

There are now resistance movements in the global North and South working to reduce fossil fuel industries, and these movements are largely led by women (Perkins, 2017). In fact, women are between 60% and 80% more involved with grassroots environmental organisation memberships, and environmental reform projects overall (Gaard, 2019). For example, one of the first examples of women defending nature comes from India, with Indigenous women's protections of trees from mass logging, as part of the Chipko movement (Resurrección, 2013). In Africa, women have been at the forefront of the resistance to corporate globalisation and neoliberalism and have contributed significantly to the ecofeminist politics of resistance heavily since the 1980s (Brownhill & Turner, 2019). Today, these movements exist as resistance to fossil fuels as the main source of energy, and a movement towards reliance on nature, with integration of Indigenous knowledge, seeds, practices, food production methods, and alternative energy technologies key (Brownhill & Turner, 2019).

Similarly, in Pakistan, where there is land erosion, deforestation and pollution, volunteers, many of whom are women, promote environmental conservation, tree planting, recycling, and gardening, and the Global Youth Climate Strike Movement organised a walk in 2014 that led to the banning of plastic bags in some shopping malls (Haq et al., 2020). In another rural area of Pakistan, women who have been affected by the reoccurring floods have begun tackling the challenges in the areas of domestic animals, dairy production, forestry, fishing, and health issues (Haq et al., 2020).

In the face of imminent climate crisis, women activists and their networks increasingly claim that ecofeminist action and system change are connected, with a dramatic shift in gender power structures seen as being essential for system change (Perkins, 2017). The Asia Pacific Forum on Women, Law and Development, for example, used Feminist Participatory Action Research (FPAR) to strengthen the women's activism movements, at a grassroots level, focusing on capacity-building, generating new knowledge and understanding of the impacts of climate change on women, and sharing tools and resources and impactful advocacy (Godden et al., 2020). Through FPAR, empowered action for structural change occurs through subversion of the power relationships between researcher and subject; the goal being to engage in critical dialogue, in order to fuel understandings of systemic injustice and mobilise as activists (Godden et al., 2020).

Women must be valued for their knowledge that can enhance climate adaptations and technological advances in areas related to energy, water, food security, agriculture and fishers, biodiversity services, health, and disaster risk management (Perkins, 2017). Although currently underrepresented in dominant discourse, women, through their paid and unpaid roles and responsibilities within society, are local experts and have first-hand experience of the impacts of climate change and ways of adapting to its effects (Godden et al., 2020).

Implications for social work practice

Increasingly, there is awareness overall for our need to be regularly connected with nature (in other words, landscapes and ecosystems not completely exploited and overcome by people) for our physical and mental wellbeing; (Cleary et al., 2017). Human-nature connections can be broadly understood as the interaction between nature and human beings, which has been shown to have intrinsic and psychological value (Cleary et al., 2017). Some argue that the decline of our connections to the natural environment has affected our mental health, whereby our separation of nature from everyday human existence leads to mental illness such as grief, despair, depression, and anxiety (Divya & Naachimuthu, 2020). There are important decolonising steps that should be taken to follow Indigenous worldviews acknowledging the interrelated nature of the physical environment and humans; Indigenous peoples see themselves as part of nature and caretakers of the natural world (Klemmer & McNamara, 2020).

A holistic view for social workers should include a philosophical underpinning of the interdependence of life, global citizenship, wellbeing including environmental engagement and adoption of values around sustainability being incorporated into ethical practice (Boetto, 2016), based on a critical feminist ethics of care (Boddy, 2017). Interdisciplinary teams must also work together to promote ecological and environmental justice, and a united effort is required to fight the ongoing effects of climate change and the aftermath of disasters that should start to cause transformational societal change.

While social workers consider environmental issues already in practice and education, more work must be incorporated into bringing environmental justice into mainstream social work. Currently, there are too few examples of a 'green' environmentally friendly social work practice (Ramsay & Boddy, 2017), and too little education around climate change and sustainability is incorporated into mainstream education overall (Harris & Boddy, 2017). Part of the responsibility of social work practice must therefore be to challenge the dominant neoliberal ideology in which social work exists, through valuing, protecting, and caring for our environment and fighting poverty simultaneously. Social workers can do so by utilising a feminist ethics of care perspective and working alongside communities affected by climate change, disasters, and environmental degradation.

The literature identifies three phases following a catastrophic disaster: the immediate crisis period; the medium-term recovery stage; and long-term social work responses (Alston et al., 2016). Australia serves as a useful example, therefore, as much of the literature on environmental social work has explored the impacts of Australian environmental disasters on its people and communities, the implications for social work practice and social work education, and the impacts of droughts (Alston, 2017), bushfires and floods (Shevaller & Westoby, 2014), climate change and disasters (Appleby et al., 2017; Harms et al., 2022; Hetherington & Boddy, 2013). Rawsthorne, Howard, and Joseph (2022) point out that in both national and global policy there is a move away from State-level responsibly for disaster preparedness to community-led responses.

Rural women need to contribute to the discussion about interventions given that women are amongst the most vulnerable to the ongoing impacts of climate change; social workers need to enhance empowerment and liberation of women in order for them to contribute to discussions on the effects of climate change (Nyahunda, 2021). A social work empowerment model, that recognises the oppression and power imbalances that contribute to vulnerability, would assist by creating guidelines for climate change interventions, alongside a feminist ethics of care, such as those that focus on the importance of community and the natural environment (Nyahunda, 2021). Programmes and policy developments, and the incorporation of a gendered lens in climate change interventions in mainstream service delivery would acknowledge and address the ongoing roles of women and men as a mechanism for closing the gap between inequalities impacting disproportionally on women in climate change (Nyahunda, 2021).

Recommendations for future climate change policy, practice and research for social work practice

Responses to climate change must be addressed from a feminist ethic of care perspective by all stakeholders including social workers and the wider community, which would affect citizens, policymakers, researchers, and governments alike, with the understanding of the natural environment being everyone's collective responsibility. Care should be integral to discussions around policies, legislation and interventions, and humanity must collectively work in compassionate ways with others, and nature. From an ecofeminist lens, masculinity must be reframed to include care for others, and be inclusive of the natural environment. In turn, those with power must become aware of their responsibility to provide care for others, and as an extension of this, to the natural environment.

Regardless of the perceived gender differences between women and men, climate protection policies tend to be dominated by men, especially in the areas of energy, transport, and urban planning (Gaard, 2019). On a political level, responses must shift from the market-based to the needs of others and their environment, acting responsibly, and exercising competence in care, be responsive to the care-receiver's needs and within a commitment to justice, democracy, and freedom. The increased scarcity of raw materials and resources, loss of biodiversity, overfishing and shortage of water and soil mean that governments urgently need to act as role models. They need to be creators of demand for sustainable products and environments, with a move towards a green economy being key, as well as focusing on social policies with a particular focus on justice (Gaard, 2019).

The two main policy areas for climate action include reduction of greenhouse gas emissions and the adaption strategies to mitigate the ongoing impacts of climate change (Terry, 2009). Gender equalities must be addressed within these policy areas, such as through enabling women to earn a living through renewable energy services, and/or as part of mitigation pathways (Terry, 2009). When considering the refugee crisis and migration that will occur due to climate change outcomes, policy must also consider how around 80% of the world's population in the global South accounts for around 20% of the greenhouse gases emitted, which compares to the global North being responsible for around 80% of the greenhouse gases (Gaard, 2019).

The United Nations has made recommendations on the need for governments to increase their focus on capacity-building and empowerment of women and girls, to ensure greater climate resilience and equal share and control of resources. Other key recommendations made for governments include a transition away from reliance on fossil fuel economies, a shift in the use of economic and social progress to include the valuing of non-market domains including unpaid care and ecosystem services, the expansion of care services with support for unpaid caregivers (UN Women, 2021). Gender-sensitive climate action includes climate policies that consider women's land rights, inclusion of gender issues in national climate plans, and supporting rural women across Africa and Asia, and globally, to build climate resilience, including identifying risks and potential solutions, and supporting women's leaderships in the disaster management sector (UN Women, 2021).

Additionally, more social work practice grounded in ecofeminist ethics of care approaches must become more visible; this could occur through educational opportunities within higher education. Literature gaps exploring the effects of climate change on marginalised communities will impact on the social work profession being able to contribute to curricula and practice, leading to reliance on other disciplines for future social workers, creating issues with evidence-based knowledge, advocacy, and interventions (Rawsthorne et al., 2022). The next generation of social work researchers and academics must be fostered in their passion for this area of practice, and mentors must encourage interdisciplinary approaches to research, mentorship, and the future creation of collaborative research, and in the field and between disciplines (Bexell et al., 2019). Specific future directions for empirical research, and resources and strategies for overcoming interdisciplinary research would also foster further focus and knowledge growth (Bexell et al., 2019).

Conclusion

Government responses to climate change have been slow and for the most part, ineffective. This is becoming alarmingly clear, as environmental disasters continue to increase globally, impacting the most vulnerable within society with the most devastating and ongoing effects. Urgent action must be taken to reduce greenhouse gas emissions and to implement policies surrounding support for those most affected by climate change. These actions must be underpinned by a feminist ethic of care to address the ongoing unequal distribution of power, ultimately linked to living within the patriarchal system. There is a need to introduce a feminist ethic of care, collectively, at the social and community level in order to attain gender equality in disaster-related socio-political discourse. This can be achieved through increasing women's involvement and recognition in roles such as in community leadership, management, and decision-making as it is at the community level that the effects of climate change are evident (Allison, 2017).

Research in the crucial area of climate change must address how we can shift the dominant narrative away from consumerism and the neoliberal perspective towards a paradigm that facilitates the creation of a healthy relationship with the natural environment and to other animals, and to mitigate further impacts to our collective Earth, with post-humanist ways of thinking forming part of the future ways of ethical considerations (Karkulehto et al., 2019). A shift in [patriarchal] power must transform from serving the 1% to the 99% of people (with Indigenous women at the bottom) who currently face dispossession and selling their labour for survival, thus creating a more just, respectful, equal, inclusive, and healthy world (Perkins, 2017).

References

Allison, E. (2017). Toward a feminist care ethic for climate change. *Journal of Feminist Studies in Religion*, 33(2), 152–158.

Alston, M., Hazeleger, T. & Hargreaves, D. (2016). Social work in post-disaster sites. In J. McKinnon & M. Alston (Eds.) *Ecological social work: Towards sustainability* (pp. 158–174). London: Palgrave.

Alston, M. (2012). Addressing the effects of climate change on rural communities. In J. Maidment & U. Bay (Eds.) *Social work in rural Australia: Enabling practice* (pp. 204–217). Crows Nest: Allen and Unwin.

Alston, M. (2017). Ecosocial work: Reflections from the global south. In A. L. Matthies & K. Närhi (Eds.) *The ecological transition of societies: The contribution of social work and social policy* (pp. 91–104). Abingdon: Routledge.

Appleby, K., Bell, K. & Boetto, H. (2017). Climate change adaptation: Community action, disadvantaged groups and practice implications for social work. *Australian Social Work*, 70(1), 78–91.

Ashraf, M. & Azad, A. (2015). Gender issues in disaster: Understanding the relationships of vulnerability, preparedness, and capacity. *Environment and Ecology Research*, 3(5), 136–142.

Bee, B. A., Rice, J., & Trauger, A. (2015). A feminist approach to climate change governance: Everyday and intimate politics. *Geography Compass*, 9(6), 339–350.

Bexell, S. M., Decker Sparks, J. L., Tejada, J. & Rechkemmer, A. (2019). An analysis of inclusion gaps in sustainable development themes: Findings from a review of recent social work literature. *International Social Work*, 62(2), 864–876.

Boddy, J. (2017). The Politics of Climate Change: The Need for a Critical Ethic of Care. In B. Pease, A. Vreugdenhil, & S. Stanford (Eds.) *Critical Ethics of Care in Social Work: Transforming the Politics of Caring.*

Boetto, H. (2016). A transformative eco-social model: Challenging modernist assumptions in social work. *British Journal of Social Work*, 47(1), 48–67.

Bozalek, V. & Pease, B. (2021). *Post-anthropocentric social work.* Abingdon: Taylor & Francis.

Brownhill, L. & Turner, T. E. (2019). Ecofeminism at the heart of ecosocialism. *Capitalism Nature Socialism*, 30(1), 1–10.

Cleary, A., Fielding, K. S., Bell, S. L., Murray, Z., & Roiko, A. (2017). Exploring potential mechanisms involved in the relationship between eudaimonic wellbeing and nature connection. *Landscape and Urban Planning*, 158, 119–128.

Divya, C., & Naachimuthu, K. P. (2020). Human nature connection and mental health: What do we know so far?. *Indian Journal of Health and Well-being*, 11(1–3), 84–92.

Gaard, G. (2019). Out of the closets and into the climate! Queer Feminist climate justice. In K. Bhavnani, J. Foran, P. A. Kurian, & D. Munsh (Eds.) *Climate Futures: Re-imagining Global Climate Justice*, 92–99.

Gilligan, C. (2011). *Ethics of care.* Interview, 21 June 2011.

Godden, N. J., Macnish, P., Chakma, T. & Naidu, K. (2020). Feminist participatory action research as a tool for climate justice. *Gender & Development*, 28(3), 593–615.

Harms, L., Boddy, J., Hickey, L., Hay, K., Alexander, M., Briggs, L., ... & Hazeleger, T. (2022). Post-disaster social work research: A scoping review of the evidence for practice. *International Social Work*, 65(3), 434–456.

Harris, C. & Boddy, J. (2017). The natural environment in social work education: A content analysis of Australian social work courses. *Australian Social Work*, 70(3), 337–349.

Harvey, D. (2014). *Seventeen contradictions and the end of capitalism.* Oxford: Oxford University Press.

Harvey, D. (2011). The future of the commons. *Radical History Review*, 109, 101–107.

Haq, Z., Imran, M., Ahmad, S. & Farooq, R. (2020). Environment, Islam, and women: A study of eco-feminist environmental activism in Pakistan. *Journal of Outdoor and Environmental Education*, 23, 275–291.

Hetherington, T. & Boddy, J. (2013). Ecological work with marginalised populations: Time for action on climate change. In M. Gray, J. Coates & T. Hetherington (Eds.) *Environmental social work* (pp. 46–61). Abingdon: Routledge.

Hosseinnezhad, F. (2017). Women and the environment: Ecofeministic approach to environmental attitudes and behavior in Iran. *European Journal of Sustainable Development Research*, 1(1), 1–7.

Intergovernmental Panel on Climate Change [IPCC] (2022). *Climate change: A threat to human well-being and health of the planet. Taking action now can secure our future.* IPCC, 28 February. Accessed: 22 January 2024 from https://www.ipcc.ch/2022/02/28/pr-wgii-ar6/

Jerneck, A. (2018). What about gender in climate change? Twelve feminist lessons from development. *Sustainability*, 10(3), 627–647.

Karkulehto, S., Koistinen, A. K., Lummaa, K. & Varis, E. (2019). *Reconfiguring human, nonhuman and posthuman in literature and culture.* New York: Routledge.

Klemmer, C. L., & McNamara, K. A. (2020). Deep ecology and ecofeminism: Social work to address global environmental crisis. *Affilia*, 35(4), 503–515.

Nguyen, H. T. (2019). Gendered vulnerabilities in times of natural disasters: maLe-to-female violence in the Philippines in the aftermath of super Typhoon Haiyan. *Violence Against Women*, 25(4), 421–440.

Nyahunda, L. (2021). Social work empowerment model for mainstreaming the participation of rural women in the climate change discourse. *Journal of Human Rights and Social Work*, 6(2), 120–129.

Parkinson, D., & Zara, C. (2016). Emotional and personal costs for men of the Black Saturday bushfires in Victoria, Australia. In *Men, masculinities and disaster* (pp. 81–91). Routledge.

Pease, B. (2014). Hegemonic masculinity and the gendering of men in disaster management: Implications for social work education. *Advances in Social Work and Welfare Education*, 16(2), 60–72.

Peck, J. & Theodore, N. (2010). Mobilizing policy: Models, methods, and mutations. *Geoforum*, 41(2), 169–174.

Perkins, P. E. (2017). *Sustainable commons governance and climate justice: Ecofeminist insights and indigenous traditions*. Doctoral dissertation, Colorado State University.

Ramsay, S. & Boddy, J. (2017). Environmental social work: A concept analysis. *British Journal of Social Work*, 47(1), 68–86.

Rawsthorne, M., Howard, A. & Joseph, P. (2022). Normalising community-led, empowered, disaster planning: Reshaping norms of power and knowledge. *OÑATI Socio-Legal Series*, 12(3), 506–521.

Resurrección, B. P. (2013). Persistent women and environment linkages in climate change and sustainable development agendas. *Women's Studies International*, 40, 33–43.

Shevaller, L. & Westoby, P. (2014). "Perhaps?" and "Depends!" The possible implications of disaster related community development for social work. *Advances in Social Work and Welfare Education*, 16(2), 23–35.

Søndergaard, M. L. J., Kannabiran, G., Chopra, S., Campo Woytuk, N., Gamage, D. Alabdulqader, E. & Bardzell, S. (2022). Feminist voices about ecological issues in HCI. In *CHI Conference on Human Factors in Computing Systems*. Extended Abstracts, 30 April–5 May, New Orleans, LA (pp. 1–7).

Sultana, F. (2014). Gendering climate change: Geographical insights. *The Professional Geographer*, 66(3), 372–381.

Tanyanyiwa, V. I. & Mufunda, E. (2019). Gendered impacts of climate change: The Zimbabwe perspective. In *Climate Action* (pp. 543–555). Cham: Springer International Publishing.

Terry, G. (2009). No climate justice without gender justice: An overview of the issues. *Gender and Development*, 17(1), 5–18.

Tramel, S. (2018). Convergence as political strategy: Social justice movements, natural resources and climate change. *Third World Quarterly*, 39(7), 1290–1307.

True, J. (2013). Gendered violence in natural disasters: Learning from New Orleans, Haiti and Christchurch. *Aotearoa New Zealand Social Work*, 25(2), 78–89.

United Nations [UN] Women (2021). UN women strategic plan 2022–2025. United Nations Headquarters.

World Health Organization [WHO] (2019). *Ten threats to global health in 2019*. Geneva.

INDEX

Note: **Bold** page numbers refer to tables; *italic* page numbers refer to figures and page numbers followed by "n" denote endnotes.

abolition 61, 228–231
abolition feminism 61
Aboriginal and Torres Strait Islanders 60, 61, 428; approaches to restorative justice 494; decolonising work with 486; social work students working with 491–493
Aboriginal and Torres Strait Islander scholars 311–312
'Aboriginal Feminism and Gender' (Coleman) 59
Aboriginal women *see* Indigenous women
abortion: bans 352–353; rights 351–352
Abrahamic religions 29
Abya Yala 4, 69, 72, 73, 77n1, 330, 593; *see also* Latin America(n)
academic: capitalism 292, 294, 295, 297, 300, 301; extractivism 272, 277, 278; feminism 336
Action Plan for Further Improvement of Medical Services (2018–2020) 258
action research 258–269, 275
activist feminism 336
acuerpamiento 104, 109
Adams, Carol 578, 579, 580, 581; *Pornography of Meat, The* 579; *Sexual Politics of Meat...* 579, 581
Affilia: Feminist inquiry in social work (journal) 281–283, 285
Africa: culture 26, 27, 118, 165, 169; feminist identity 168–169
African feminisms (AFs) 22–26, 28, 166, 168, 237

African womanism 25–28, 118, 168, 237
African women: care and motherhood as status symbols 29; invisibility in feminism 23–24; leadership in pre-colonial societies 24; in liberation struggles and political activities 24; lived experiences as source of knowledge 234, 237, 238
Africentric approach 147
"Against Our Will" (Brownmiller) 177
Aged Care Council of Elders 436
agential cuts 549
agential realism 547, 548, 549, 550, 556, 557
Aging Activists 529
Agrarian Collective 596
Agrarian Reform 95
Ahmed, S. 151, 159, 602, 611
"Aint I a Woman: Black Women and Feminism" (hooks) 22, 177
Ajayi, C. E. 194, 197
Alaimo, Stacy 549, 610
allies 1, 4, 177, 242, 451–459, 463, 563
ally theatre 503
alternative masculinities 468–469, 498, 501–502
Alvesson, M. 284, 287
Amaguaña, Tránsito 592, 593
Amazonian women 595
Anderson, E. 248, 469
Andrade, C. 295; *Del biombo a la catedra* 295
androcentric bias of science 273–274
animal(s) 4, 573–583, 618
animal advocacy movement 577

animal-assisted social work 573–581; animal studies and 574–575; intersectionality, species and animalisation 577–579; politics of meat (*see* politics of meat); at University of Denver 575–576; Veterinary Social Work programme at University of Tennesse 576–577; women, feminist intersectionality and 577
Animal-Assisted Social Work programme 575–576
animalisation 577–579
animalistic dehumanisation 578–579
animal rights activism 456, 459
ante-colonial feminism 22–25
ante-colonialism 23; *see also* anti-colonialism
anthropomorphism 578
Anthrozoology 574
anti-carceral feminism 228–232
anti-colonial feminism 23–25
anti-colonialism 3, 23, 56, 59, 74, 505
Anti-Discrimination Law 423n5
anti-feminism 14–15, 22
anti-gender movement 15, 18
anti-imperialism 80–89
anti-racism 45, 47, 48, 51, 56, 61, 70, 89, 236, 445, 455, 505, 531, 566, 569
The Anti-Social Behaviour, Crime and Policing Act (2014) 46
Anzaldúa, Gloria 72, 601; *Borderlands/La Frontera: The New Mestiza* 601
Aotearoa New Zealand Association of Social Workers 575
apartheid systems 139, 140, 166, 170, 319, 550
Apeuro: The Network of Zainichi Korean Women Creating the Future 541
Arab 125–127
Araucanian Federation 95
Araucanian Women's Association Yafluayin 95
Ardley, Emily 203, 206, 208, 209–212
Argentine Federation of Academic Units of Social Work (FAUATS) 330–332
Argentinian Federation of Professional Associations of Social Service (FAAPSS) 330, 332, 336
The Asia Pacific Forum on Women, Law and Development 618
Asociación de Lucha por la Identidad Travesti (ALIT, Association for the Struggle for *Travesti* Identity) 418
Asociación de Travestis Argentinas (ATA, Association of Argentine *Travestis*) 418
Association of Indigenous Women of Santa Maria 103
Association of University Women 295
Australia India Society of Victoria Taskforce against Domestic Violence 224

Australian Association of Social Workers 310; *Code of Ethics* 575
Australian Bureau of Statistics 430
Australian Crime and Violence Prevention Awards 181
The Australian Institute of Health and Welfare (AIHW) 362
Australian Migration and Settlement Awards 182
Australian mothers and parenting, with mental health challenges 360–368; child protection 365–366; feminism and activism in social work practice 367–368; integrating strength-based feminist approach for 366–367; mental health system 361–362; parenting of First Nations women 360, 365; strengths and vulnerabilities 362–365
Australian print media representations, of Indian men's sexual violence 215–225; colonial discourses 216–217, 219–220, 222–223; cultural problem on Indian women 217, 219–220; gendered discourses 217, 221–223; intersectional feminist analysis of 224–225; methodology and sampling 218; Nirbhaya case 216; not acknowledging violence against First Nations peoples 222; patriarchal culture 215–221; sexual violence as global social problem 223; women experiencing intimate partner violence 224
Australian Social Work (journal) 285

Bacchi, Carol 215, 217, 492
"Bad Feminist" (Gay) 178
Ballif, E. 353, 355
Barad, Karen 153, 547–549, 551, 552, 554–557, 557n3; *Meeting the Universe Halfway* 547, 548, 551
"The Beauty Myth" (Wolf) 178
Beauvior, Simone de 178; "The Second Sex" 178
Beddoe, Liz 112, 116, 579
Beijing Women's Platform for Action 618
Bekhauf Azadi 513, 515
biased media 114
Biglia, B. 276, 278
Bilge, S. 70, 72
binary power relations 2
Birinxhikaj, M. 152, 159
BJOG: An International Journal of Obstetrics & Gynaecology 352
Black animality 578
Black feminisms 26, 55, 83, 233, 272, 328–330, 337, 454
Black feminist epistemology 273, 274, 277
Black Lives Matter 113
Black Marxism 83, 89

Index

Black men: labour trafficking of 145; media representation of body 221; racist oppression of 28–29

Black women 12, 16, 18; activism 12; as domestic workers 86; gendered socialisation processes of 145; income of 84; poverty 84; racialised sexual stereotypes of 146; unemployment rate 85

Black women bodies: objectification of 154, 156, 329; sexualisation of 154, 156; staging of sexual fantasies on 155–157

body-territory-daily life 102–109

Bohr, Niels 548, 551, 555, 556

Borderlands/La Frontera: The New Mestiza (Anzaldúa) 601

Bozalek, V. 153, 598, 600, 609

Brah, A. 154, 156

Braidotti, R. 470, 500, 502, 548, 598, 605

Brazil: forced sterilisation processes in 88; Marxism in 80; poverty rate in 84; racist state violence in 87–88; social work in 81; transgender murders in 87; women domestic workers in 86

Brazilian Communist Party 70

Brazilian Constitution (1980s) 80

Brazilian Social Workers Congress 80

'Breaking Through the Inner Walls: Harassment Cases of Zainichi Korean Women' 541

breast cancer survivors, in China 258–269; classification of treatment stages 261–263; cultural discourse 263, 266, 267, 269; decreased/lack of intimate relationships 265–266; feminist participatory action research as methodology 260–261; impact on personal relationships 263–264; mastectomy scar 264; oppression and construct them as "bad luck" 266–267; overview 258; sampling and data collection 261; self-identity 264–265; women empowerment 267–268; women's experience and medical social work 259–260

Britain: colonisation of Nigeria (1884) 189

British Social Work (journal) 285

Brotherboys 432, 434

Brown feminism 272

Brownmiller, Susan 177; "Against Our Will" 177

Buen Vivir 587

Bunston, Wendy 178–181

Burke, M. C. 138, 541

Burkina Faso 27

Burrell, S. R. 446, 467

Butler, Judith 11, 12, 142, 146, 155, 157, 160, 251, 294, 473; *Gender Trouble* 473

Cabnal, Lorena 103, 104, 105, 108

Cacuango, Dolores 592, 593

Calls To Action 566

Canadian Association For Social Work Education-L'Association Canadienne Pour La Formation En Travail Social (CASWE-ACFTS) 562

'Can the Subaltern Speak?' (Spivak) 539–540

capital/capitalist accumulation 82, 86–88

capitalism 11, 75, 80–83, 98, 329, 337; Black/Indigenous women experience of violence 87–88; and income distribution 590; social division of labour in 83–84

capitalist ethical system 83

Carballo, Azpiazu 275, 276

carceral expansion 228, 230, 231

carceral feminism 61

carcerality 228–232

carceral services 230

carceral state 228–231

care and care work 394–395

care debt 341, 345

care feminism 374, 376–377; maternalism (*see* strategic maternalism)

caregiving: crisis 344, 345; feminisation of 345; women role in 341, 344–347; *see also* community social work

caregiving footprint 341, 345

Caribbean: femicide rates in 88; feminisms 21, 23

Caribbean women: domestic and care work of 86–87; experience of violence 87–88; poverty of 84

Carstensen, G. 152, 159

Casey, E. 452, 453

Catholic Church 93

Catholic Inquisition 329

Catholic University Social Work School 80

Causa Justa feminist group 115

Chamallas 233

change agents 125, 529

Charter, M. L. 183, 468

Chazan, M. 527, 530

child protection system 114, 116, 185, 352, 445; in Australia 365–366

child sexual abuse (CSA) 440–448; feminism-informed practice with victim-survivors 442–443; as heteropatriarchal practice 440–442; profeminism 443–444; profeminist social work with male victim-survivors 446–448; in Sweden 457–458; whiteness in feminist and profeminist social work practice 444–446

Chile: intersectionality and decolonial feminism in 68–69; social movements 75

Chile, public policies in 92–99; decolonial proposals and depatriarchalisation for social work 97–99; expropriation of Mapuche

lands 92, 95; implementation of State's Internal Security Law 96; Indigenous feminisms and Mapuche feminist movements 93, 97, 99; integrationist and colonial dispossession policies 92–93, 95; military dictatorship 96; monoculturalist and patriarchal logics 93–94, 98; Pacification of Araucania 95; Spanish conquest, Mapuche territorial and political autonomy 92, 99; struggles of Mapuche women 94–97; visibilisation of non-hegemonic knowledge 93
Chipko movement 618
cisnormativity 407–413
Ch'ixi 273
choice feminism 283
Christensen, M. C. 453, 454
Christian feminism 21
cisgenderism 55, 57, 83–85, 272, 408; knowledge and social work practices 415–417
cis-hetero-androcentric normativity 273, 277
cisnormativity and gender binary 407–413; cisgenderism 408; definition 408, 409; sex *vs.* gender 409; social work education 411–412; social work practice 412–413; in social work profession 409–410; social work research 412; structural social work 410–411; transfeminism 408
civil death 230
climate change 565; definition 614; feminism and 616–617; gendered impacts of 615–616
coalition politics 75–76, 301
Coates, J. 12, 13, 167
code of ethics 575
Código de Ética do/a Assistente Social (Brazilian Social Workers Ethical Code) 81–82
Cofán women 594–595
cognitive extractivism 276, 278
Coleman, Claire 59; 'Aboriginal Feminism and Gender' 59
Collins, P. H. 249–252, 274, 275, 277, 307
colonial feminism 55, 58, 59, 62; colonially constructed social work in 57–58
colonialism 12, 23, 28, 34, 40, 42, 57, 75, 98, 166, 216, 542–543
colonial media discourses 216–217
colonisation 24, 55, 57, 132, 133; Palestine's women challenges and resistance against 132–133, 135, 136; power on Indigenous peoples and culture 58–59
Columbian women: decriminalising abortion 115; reproductive rights of 115
Comahachee Women's Collective 577
Combahee River Collective Statement 75
Commercial Sexual Exploitation of Children (CSEC) 144

Committee on the Elimination of Discrimination based on Gender and Sexuality 541
commodification 82, 83, 86, 154, 156, 329
communalism 26
communitarian feminism 272, 328–330, 337
community 26, 102–109, 341–347, 367
community feminism 102–104, 106
community social work 341–347; community, community weaving and 342–343, 346–347; sustaining life and community weavings 343–344; women's protagonism and patriarchal debt 344–346
community weavings 341–344, 346–347
Comprehensive Trans Law 423n5
Comunidad Homosexual Argentina (CHA, Argentine Homosexual Community) 418
Concerned Older Women 529
Connell, R. W. 468, 469
conscientisation 16, 126, 136, 181, 239, 283
conservative 11, 15, 80, 114, 115, 225, 415–423
conservative Catholicism 115
conservative politics 15, 113, 114
Constitution of the Republic of South Africa 165
consubstantiality 273
contemporary feminism 233, 308–309; problems 15–16; theory 13
context-driven intersectionality 73–74
Coordinadora Arauco Malleco 96
COP15 United Nations Biodiversity Conference 568
Cortina, L. M. 152, 156, 158
cosmogonic heterosexuality 104
Council on Social Work Education (CSWE) 410
COVID-19 pandemic 119
Crawford, Fran 175, 176
Cree, V. E. 467, 478, 480, 501
Crenshaw, Kimberlé Williams 11, 70, 71, 75, 105, 106, 178, 216, 539, 577
criminalisation of pregnant women 353
criminal legal system 229, 231
critical ally-ship 400–401, 448, 485
critical animal studies 574
Critical Edge Women (CrEW) 308, 309, 313; as space for feminist activism 309
critical feminisms 329
critical feminist social work pedagogy 305–314, 561; benefits of intersectionality 306, 313; collective nourishment to imagine, hope and imperfection 310, 313; contemporary feminist analysis 308–309; Critical Edge Women (CrEW) as space for feminist activism 308, 309; definition 311; feminism in social work education 309–310; integration of activism in pedagogical activity

308–309; mutual engagement and power of collectivity 312–313; within neoliberalism 305–307, 313; safety, collective nourishment to imagine, hope and sharing ideas 310; as space for feminist activism 309; success in neo-liberal academy 308; whiteness of Australian social work and Aboriginal social work academics 311–312; women's lived experiences and gendered positioning 312
critical gerontology 526, 527, 531
critical pedagogy 16, 17, 307
critical race feminist rights (CRFR): approach 139, 141–143, 146–148; theory 141–142, 147
critical race theory (CRT) 47, 138, 140, 564
critical social work 68, 80, 112, 113; definition 311
Cuban Revolution 80
Cubillos, A. J. 235, 239, 240
cultural competency 147, 168
cultural humility, definition 51
culture wars 114, 463
Cumbia, copeteo y lágrimas 418
Curiel, Ochy 70, 71, 273, 275, 278

Dalit women 516
"Damned Whores and God's Police" (Summers) 177
Davis, Angela 72, 82, 83
Deakin University 209–211
decolonial feminism 12–14, 22–25, 251, 272, 273, 277; *see also* intersectionality and decolonial feminism to Latin American social work
decoloniality/decolonisation 13, 22, 23, 40, 58, 218, 283; of social work knowledge 41, 42
degenderisation 377
Del biombo a la catedra (Andrade) 295
deliberative democracy 513, 519–521, 519–522
Deluezian feminism 500–501
democracy 96, 116, 513–522, 620
depatriarchalisation 69, 93, 97, 98, 105, 106, 108, 328, 420
development 80, 182, 233–242, 321, 329–330, 428, 465–467
developmental feminist allyship 465–467
developmental origins of health and disease (DOHaD) 351, 354, 355
dialogue 3, 68–77, 328, 336, 513, 519, 578, 610
Dialogues on Agential Realism (Juelskjær) 548
diffraction 554–556
Direct Action 580
Diretrizes Gerais Para o Curso de Serviço Social (Brazilian General Guidelines for Professional Training in social work) 80

disability 17, 45–52, 116, 203–213
disparities 84, 292–301
Djerriwarrh Health Services 180
The Doctrine of Discovery 57
dominant masculinity 468
Dominelli, Lena 113, 118, 234, 235, 367, 380; *Feminist Social Work* 234
dualistic worldview 56

Earth Summit on Environment and Development (UNCED) 618
echoed knowledges 62
eco-femagogy 560–569, 567; climate change 565; critical red-green perspective 566; development 562; eco-feminism 563; environmental racism 565–566; feminism in 562–563; feminist goals 563; feminist issue 565; femogogy 563–564; "green" social work 564; Indigenous leadership 566; intersectionality and critical race theory 564; lack of environmental awareness 561–562; minimal feminist content, analysis, and curriculum 560–561; in post-Covid world 567–568; practical application 569; recommendations 568; red part 566; women's ways of knowing 564
eco-feminism 13–14, 21, 328, 329, 337, 563, 578
eco-feminism, in climate change 614–621; challenges and crisis 616; feminist ethic of care and resistance to injustices 616–617; gendered impacts 615–616; policy, practice and research 620–621; resistance movements against fossil fuel industries 618; social change 617–618; social work practice 619–620
ecofeminism, in Latin America 587–596; capitalism and income distribution 590; extractivist companies and forcing people to migrate 594–596; Good Living 590–592; methodology 594; popular solidarity economy (EPS) and social question 588–589; resistance to patriarchal and capitalist system 592–594; social work and neoliberalism 589–590
ecofeminist epistemology 617
education 10, 16–18, 47, 93, 208, 288, 306–308, 411–412, 416, 462–470, 541, 619
emotional labour 185, 288
environment/environmental: activism 13, 18, 456, 459; justice 2, 13, 14, 619; racism 565–566; sustainability 13, 18, 562
epigenetics 351, 354, 355
epistemic justice/injustice 251–253
epistemic privilege 250, 275
epistemic violence 252, 539

epistemologies/epistemology 3, 16, 76, 247–254, 272–278, 282, 617
epistemologies action research 260–261
Equality Act (2010, England) 50
Equal Marriage Law (26618/2010) 328, 418
Espinosa, Yuderkys 71, 72
essentialist maternalism 374–379, 374–381, 379, 381
estallido social (2019, Social Revolts) 75
ethical valuation/devaluation 83, 84, 87, 88
ethico-onto-epistemological approach 555
ethics of care 374, 376–378, 388, 463, 464, 469, 617
ethics of justice 376
ethnic essentialism 104, 105
eugenics 355
European Union: anti-racism action plan (2020–2025) 51
euthenics 355
exteriority-within-phenomena 549

Fakunmoju, S. B. 194, 195
Farm Transparency Project 580
Federal Constitution (1988) 80
Federal Forum on Gender and Sexual Diversity of the Argentine Federation of Professional Associations of Social Service 417
Federal Law on Social Work 330–331, 336; Article 9 331
Federal Ministry of Women Affairs 198
feminazis 15
femininity 4, 15, 217, 259, 265, 446, 469, 501, 502
"Feminism and the Mastery of Nature" (Plumwood) 178
feminism: Australian second-wave 176, 183; ethical-political dimension 272, 277; generations of 233; institutionalisation of 462; political-epistemological dimension 273, 277; theoretical-epistemological dimension 273, 277; theoretical-methodological dimension 273, 277; waves of 21–23; *see also individual entries*
feminism light approach 466
feminist abolition 231
feminist activism 10, 23, 119, 336; Critical Edge Women (CrEW) as space for 308, 309, 313
feminist corpo-biography 276, 278
feminist critical scholarship 16–17
feminist economics 345
feminist epistemologies 247–254, 278; Black and lesbian 252; concerned with epistemic injustice 252–253; and feminist research 247–248; and gender oppression 250–252; gender oppression and 250–252; notion of situated knowledge 249–250; power struggle 253; reflexivity 253; research from anti-foundational position 248–249; for social work research 254
feminist fractured foundationalism 249
feminist gerontology 526–533; activism 526–530; agency 527–530; experience of ageing 527–528; involvement of older women 526; and social work 530–533; theorising older women's lives 526–527
feminist inquiry 281–284, 289
feminist leadership theory 319–320; *see also* women leaders, in Palestinian universities
feminist man 469
feminist materialism 14
feminist maternal scholarship 385, 387, 390
Feminist May 295
Feminist Movement in Nigeria 24
feminist narrative biographical approaches 276, 278
feminist new materialism (FNM) misconceptions 13–14, 547–557; contributions to social work 547–548; reflexivity, reflection and critique 553–556; relational ontology, intra-actions and interaction 548–550; uncertainty 551–553
Feminist Participatory Action Research (FPAR) 618
feminist politics 2, 9, 10, 16–18, 503, 539, 548
feminist postcolonial scholarship 153, 161
feminist rights-based approach (FRBA) 141, 148
feminist schools of thought 234
feminist social work 111–113; emancipatory practices and citizens' rights 112, 113, 119; gender equality and inclusivity 113; in Palestinian context 319; social justice and 111, 113; theory 318–319; *see also individual entries*
Feminist Social Work (Dominelli and McLeod) 234
feminist social work research (FSWR) queries 281–289; academic journals 281–283; analysis 283–284; data collection 285; gap-spotting and challenges 284, 286–288; implications and recommendations 288–289; limitations 289; marginalisation of feminist inquiry 282, 283; question/statement of purpose 286; sampling 284–285; social work education, scholarship/publication, and practice 287–288; types 284; women and their issues 286
feminist standpoint theory 249, 250
feminist student mobilisations (2018) 69, 75
feminist theories 9–14, 16–18, 55; Black womanist feminism 12; colonial subject as other in 41–42; gender performativity 11–12; intersectionality 11; liberal

feminism 10; postmodern feminism 11; poststructural feminism 11; radical feminism 10; socialist feminism 11; and social work practice 17–18
feminised care work 394–401; care as women's responsibility 394–395; community-engaged practices, removal of 397; in context of neoliberalism 394, 396, 399, 401; registration and licensure 396; social justice practices 399–401; and standardisation of social work 396–397; women as professionalised and not-professionalised care workers 395–396, 399, 401; women's resistance and activism 397–399
femogogy 563–564
first intifada (1987) 125
First Nations people: colonisation and imposing non-Indigenous culture on 114; cultures 59; knowledge 93
First Nations women: in Australian prison 184; non-Indigenous authors as allies 177
Flood, M. 446, 452, 466, 467
food sovereignty 595, 596
forced marriage: definition 46
The Forced Marriage Unit 46, 48
Foreign, Commonwealth & Development Office, United Kingdom 46
47th Session of the Human Rights Council 426
FOS Feminista 115
Foucault, M. 11, 556, 557n3
Frente de Liberación Homosexual (FLH, Homosexual Liberation Front) 418
Furness, S. 479, 480
füta warria 95

Galper, J. 397, 399
Gansen, H. M. 191, 196
Garett, P. M. 152, 399
Gay, Roxanne 178; "Bad Feminist" 178
Gay and Lesbian Mardi Gras parade (1978) 429
gender: balance 476; definition 615; dysphoria 412, 413; equality 14–15, 27, 29, 111, 233, 234, 311; equity 231, 295, 298, 301, 310, 408; euphoria 412; identity 21, 410, 426, 429, 434; non-conformity 230, 272; norms 17, 130, 145, 154, 157, 373–375, 380, 441, 442, 473, 477, 515; performativity 11–12, 153–154, 473–474; progressivism 217; relations 11, 22, 29, 58, 158, 215, 234, 236, 456; sex *vs.* 409
Gender and Diversity Commission of the Professional Association of Social Service of Cordoba 331
gender-based violence (GBV) 222, 295, 456; in India 220; on South African women 138–140, 143
gender binary 2, 234, 235, 410–411; definition 409; in social work profession 409–410; *see also* cisnormativity and gender binary
gender disparities 292–301
gender disparities and academia, in Chile 292–301; career trajectories 292–294, 296–297, 301; concept of "glass ceiling" 293–294, 300; extreme exhaustion/depletion 299–300; female academics' voices and their relation to male peers 298–299; gendered bodies and intersections with motherhood and care 298; intersectional analysis 293, 296–297, 301; lack of women in positions of power 293, 297; social work education 296; in universities 294–295
gendered educational system 16
gender empowerment 125–136
gender equality, in Australia 175–185; allyship with non-Indigenous allies authors 177; experiences of social work supervision 184–185; feminism and teaching social work 182–184; feminist social work activism 180–181; homemade feminist social work practice and 176; methodology and participants 177–179; positionality and privilege 176–177; social constructivism 176; women-specific groups 179–180; women's voices and feminist services 181–182
Gender Forums 336
Gender Identity Law (26743/2012) 328
gender, in Palestine: hierarchies and role in youth work 129–131; impact of equality, structure and dynamics on women's empowerment 125–127, 129–131, 135, 136; political context reinforcing hierarchies 131, 136; 131, 136
gender-neutrality 126, 260
Gender Trouble (Butler) 473
geocentric feminism 14
Gillard, J. 178; "Not Now, Not Ever" 178
Gilligan, C. 178, 374, 376, 617; "In A Different Voice" 178
Gilliland, Alisha 203, 206, 208–212
Gippsland Centre Against Sexual Assault (GCASA) 209, 210
Gippsland SL&RR network 209
Global Alcohol Action Plan 354
Global Estimates of Modern Slavery report 139
Global Gender Gap index 184
globalisation 16, 374, 377
Global North 3, 59, 70, 116, 139, 179, 234, 239, 273, 285, 427, 568, 618
Global North scholarship 70
Global South 13, 28, 42, 118, 328, 417–419, 441

Index

global South women: contribution to decolonial work 24; invisibility in feminism and resistance to patriarchy 23–25; liberation of 41; oppression of 28
Global Youth Climate Strike Movement 618
'go-around' Patriarchy 27
Google Form 192, 199
Gore, Al 565; *Inconvenient Truth, An* 565
Gramsci, A. 34; notion of subaltern 34; theory of hegemony 11
Grandmothers to Grandmothers campaign 530
Gray, M. 12, 13, 167
Green, L. 260, 478
green social work 14
Grey Panthers 528
Grosz, E. 179, 469, 470; "Volatile Bodies" 179
Guggisberg, M. 152, 159
Guttorm, H. 599, 603

Haraway, Donna 153, 249, 532, 548, 554, 555, 610
Harding, Sandra 249, 273, 504
Hargraves, Kay 177; "Women and Work" 177
Harms-Smith, L. 237, 238, 282, 283
Hartsock, N. C. M. 249, 250
"Having Families" (Richards) 177
'Hawkes Bay' case 356
healthy masculinity 502
Hearn, Jeff 152, 500, 502
Hendrick, Antonia 485, 486
Hermida, María Eugenia 417, 422
Herrero, Yayo 345, 592, 593
heteronormativity 15, 21, 153, 154, 156, 157, 160; knowledge and social work practices 415–417
Hicks, S. 477–478, 499
Hill-Collins, Patricia 70, 75
Hispanic feminisms 73
historical-dialectical materialism 80, 81
Historical Reparation Law 423n5
Holland, K. J. 152, 156, 158
homemade feminism 175, 185
homemade social work 175, 176, 185
homophobia 11, 17, 37, 155, 391, 432, 435, 442
homosexuality 59, 417, 429, 442
hooks, bell 16, 22, 72, 154, 176, 177, 221, 494, 495; "Aint I a Woman: Black Women and Feminism" 22, 177
Hull House 547
human rights 63, 115, 119, 141, 142, 151, 168, 310
Human Rights Association for Korean Residents 541
Human Sciences Research Council 164
human services 112, 464, 498–506

human trafficking 87, 139–141; *see also* sex trafficking, of South African women
hybrid masculinity 468–469, 481
hyper-criminalisation 228

Iamamoto, Marilda 590; "Social Service and Division of Labour" 590
IFSW General Meeting (2014) 93
implicit memories 48
"In A Different Voice" (Gilligan) 178
inclusion/exclusion 126, 127
inclusive masculinity 469
Inconvenient Truth, An (Gore) 565
Independent Expert by the Group of Friends of the Sexual Orientation and Gender Identity (SOGI) 426
Indian feminisms 21, 23
'Indigena' as public life 58
Indigenous Action Media 503
Indigenous culture 59, 60
Indigenous feminism 56–57, 63, 272; anti-colonial understanding of gender 59; colonial ideologies and decolonisation in 58, 60
Indigenous homosexuals/homosexuality 57, 59
Indigenous identity 13, 25
Indigenous knowledge/wisdom 13, 55, 56; privileging of 63
Indigenous languages 59, 60
Indigenous Lore 61
Indigenous non-binary people 57, 59, 61
Indigenous people 12–14, 55–63, 60; anti-exploitative practice for social work 62–63; collaboration of non-Indigenous actors with 63; colonial system of law and violence against 57, 61–62; concept of disability/impairment in 58–62; harm caused by social work, colonisation and feminism 57–58; imperialist criminal justice system on 60–62; understanding of gender and sexuality 58–62; wisdom of 55, 56
Indigenous trans people 57, 59–61
Indigenous women 18, 55–56; activism 57; experiencing patriarchy and colonisation 57, 58; exploitation of knowledges and experiences 62; poverty 84; protest of older 528; social justice and equity for 57
Indigenous worldviews 56; *vs.* Western dualistic worldview 56–57
inequality 2, 72, 76, 117, 293, 318, 333, 436, 590
infidelity in Nigeria 190, 195, 198
information deprivation 51
Institute for Human-Animal Connection (IHAC) 575–576
Institute of traditional leadership 165–167
institutional racism 487

Index

Institutional Review Board 297
intellectual disability (ID) 45
intellectually disabled women 45–52; case study 46, 49–50; challenges 213; feminism and 204; impact of racism on 50–52; individual learning 212; intersections of gender, disability and race 46–49; IQ assessment 46–49; mutual learning 212; oppression and discrimination against 45, 49, 51, 52, 205; participants and their life stories 206, 211; as peer educators 210–213; sexual abuse and violence 205, 212, 213; sexuality and respectful relationships 205, 210–211, 213; sexual lives of 206–208; sexual rights 205; social work and 204–205; workshops, training and building skills 208–210
intelligence, definition and measuring 46–47
Intergovernmental Panel on Climate Change (IPCC) 614
interlocking oppressions 1, 50, 51, 73, 75, 500
International Agency for Research on Cancer 259
International Association of Schools of Social Work (IASSW) 93, 409, 419, 420
International Federation of Social Workers (IFSW) 239, 310, 409, 417, 419, 420
International Monetary Fund 118, 590
intersectional feminism 16, 113, 272, 351, 352, 445–446, 500
intersectional identification and Swedish profeminist men 451–459; age as intersection 456–458; intersectionality as theoretical frame 454; men's dominance with anti-sexism 455–456; pathways and awareness of sexism 454–455; present study 454; previous research 452–453; profeminist activism 451; qualitative interviews 452
intersectionality 11, 45, 49, 57, 105–107, 117, 143–145, 176–178, 205, 216, 231, 233, 236–237, 273, 293, 306, 380, 408, 426, 473–474, 539, 564, 577–579
intersectionality allyship 485–495; Ally Framework application 486, 487, 491–493; claiming identity space 485–487; ethical model 490–491, *491*; and feminist social work 493–494; practice frameworks 487, 488, 489–491
intersectionality and decolonial feminism to Latin American social work 68–76; in Chile 68–69, 75; coalition politics promotion 75–76; feminist knowledge production in higher education 69; importance of robust, contextualised, and situated analyses 72–74; problematisation of gender, class, ethnicity, disability, and sexuality 74–75; tensions and dialogues between perspectives 69–72
intersex people 56, 103, 419, 429, 430

Inter-University Network for Gender Equality and Against Violence (RUGE) 336
intifada 125
intimate partner violence (IPV) 190, 198, 354
intra-actions 548–550
Isiugo-Abanihe, U. C. 190, 194
Islamic feminism 21
Israeli colonisation army 125
izzat (honour) 220

Jackson, A. 241; "Taking Back the Narrative: Gendered Anti-Blackness in Predominantly White Schools of Social Work" 241
Jensen, S. Q. 453, 454
Jewish feminism 21
Jiangmen Maternity and Child Health Care Hospital (JMCHCH) 261
Johnson, Kelley 203, 206–207
Jones, M. 112, 462
Journal of Social Work (journal) 285
Juelskjær, M. 548; Dialogues on Agential Realism 548

"Kaaek" (traditional bread) 133
Kabeer, N. 127, 135
Korean War 537
Kuhn, Maggie 528–529
Kyoto Protocols (1997) 565

labour: non-commodified 83, 84; process 398; social division of 80, 82–84
labour power: as commodity 83, 86; by people of colour 85; reproduction 82; valuing and pricing based on race and gender 84–86; white woman and 84–86
La gesta del nombre propio (The feat of the proper name) 418
Lancet Rheumatology (journal) 353
Langarita, J. A. 415, 419, 420, 422
Las Yeguas del Apocalipsis (The Mares of the Apocalypse) 418
Latina feminisms 21, 23
Latin America(n): anti-colonial thought 72, 77n1; Colonialism and coloniality in 69, 73; corporate-military dictatorship (1964–1985) in 80; femicide rates in 88; feminists 9, 70, 72; feminist social movements in 68; gender-based violence in 88; *see also* intersectionality and decolonial feminism to Latin American social work
Latin American critical epistemologies 336, 337
Latin American critical feminism 328–336; developments of 329–330; impact on social work curricula 332–334, 336; scholarly contributors **334–335**; to social

work undergraduate academic training in Argentina 330–332
Latin American Reconceptualisation Movement 80
Latin American women: experience of violence 87–88; poverty 84; struggles for reproductive rights 117; unpaid domestic and care work of 86–87
La Trobe University 207
Law No. 26743 on Gender Identity, Argentina 418
Law on Comprehensive Protection to Prevent, Punish and Eradicate Gender Violence (26485/2009) 328
Law on the Voluntary Interruption of Pregnancy (27610/2021) 328
Lean In (Sandberg) 15
legal/legislative initiatives 228
LGBTI Health Alliance (LHA) *see* LGBTIQ+ Health Australia
LGBTIQA+ communities 11, 417, 421, 426, 429–432, 516
LGBTIQ+ Health Australia 426, 430, 431, 436
LGBTIQNB+ organisations 422
liberal feminisms 10, 21, 499
Liberation Catholicism 115
Livestock's Long Shadow: Environmental Issues and Options (Steinfeld) 580
Livholts, M. 547, 600, 612
Living Safer Sexual Lives (LSSL) 203, 205–208, 211–213
Lorde, Audre 72, 310
Lugones, María 73, 75, 76, 273

MacLure, Carrie 178, 182, 183
Male Champions of Change 499
Mapuche political prisoners 96
Mapuche society: gender relations and sexuality in 93, 97; violence experienced by families 96
Mapuche women: celebrations of puberty 93; displacement and settlement of 95; feminist movements 97, 99; gender violence against 96–98; obstetric violence on 94; political resistance 94–97; as racialised women 97–99; reproductive health, pregnancy and childbirth 94; struggle for gender equality, class and race 98; in trade and labour 97–98; visibilisation as active political agents 97
Mapumachos 97
marginalisation 9, 11, 17, 18, 51, 57, 58, 126, 138, 141, 143, 144, 147, 148; interpersonal 143, 144; structural intersectional 143, 144; and young women empowerment in Palestine 126, 127, 129–131, 134
marica and *travesti*: anti-oppressive professional interventions in social work 419–422; knowledge and practices from Global South 417–419
marijuana, legalisation/criminalisation of 229
Marxism 80–89, 115; accessing of goods and rights by working class 81; Black/Indigenous women experience of violence under capitalism 87–88; in Brazil 80; class contradictions 82; crisis and totality of social reproduction 80–83; inseparable dimensions of racial, binary-gendered and territorial division of labour in capitalism 83–84; perspective in anti-racist, feminist and anti-imperialist struggle 89; reconceptualisation of social issue 80–81; unrecognising domestic and care workload of women of color as legitimate labour 86–87; value and price of labour power based on race and gender 84–87
Marxist feminism 21, 374
Marxist theory 196
Marxist Theory of Dependence 83, 89
mass incarceration/imprisonment 228–230, 288
maternal impression 353
maternalism 373–381; care feminism 374, 376–377; essentialist *vs.* strategic maternalism 374, 378–379, *379*; oppression of women through 375–376; overview 373–374; reasons for significance 374–375; social work based on strategic maternalism 380–381; strategic maternalism 377–378
Maternal Thinking (Ruddick) 376
matricentric feminism 384, 388, 389
matricentric feminist social work 384–391; empowered mothering 390; good mother/bad mother dichotomy 386, 387, 389; matricentric feminism and 388, 389; patriarchal motherhood 384–385, 387–389, 391; patriarchy and social work 385–386; social work practice and normalise, validate and universalise mothering experiences 390–391
matricentric feminist standpoint 390
Mayan-Xinka community feminism, in Guatemala 102–109; acuerpamiento, concept of 104, 109; conception of body as political body 104–105; cosmogony of suspicion 104, 108; emergence 103; feminist, decolonial and emancipatory social work 107–109; intersectionality of body-territory-daily life as theoretical category 105–107, 109; liberation and emancipation of women bodies and depatriarchalisation 105–109; patriarchy, coloniality and oppression of women 102–108; as political-epistemic project 105, 107–109; struggle against neoliberalism and imperialism 102

McKenzie, M. 503, 504
McKinzie, A. 72, 73, 74
McLeod, Eileen 113, 234; *Feminist Social Work* 234
meat 573–583
Meeting the Universe Halfway (Barad) 548
Men Against Sexual Assault 503
men and masculinities, in feminist social work 498–506; engagement and forms of feminism 499–501, 504–505; as feminist allies 503–504; positive relationships with feminist women 505; profeminist men challenges 503–504; toxic, alternative and multiple masculinities 501–502; women's concerns 504
men feminist allyship, in social work education 462–470; aspects of strategic essentialisms 465–466; definition 462–463; developmental feminist allyship 465–467; dominant masculinity 468; feminist social movements and alliances 464–465; hybrid masculinity 468–469; inclusive masculinity 469; post-humanist allyship 470; post-masculinist allyship 469–470; subordinate masculinity 468; waves of feminism and students' attitudes towards feminism 467–468
men social workers 473–481; in child welfare social work 475; discourse of 'gentle-men' 477–478; education 478–481; parental leave policies 475; patriarchal forms of power 473; and sexual harassment of women social workers 475–476; social work as non-traditional occupation 474–476; in workplace 476–478
men's rights activism (MRA) groups 447
The Mental Capacity Act (2005) 46
mental health 114, 178, 229, 353, 360–368, 475
The Mental Health Services Conference Inc. 181
Mesquida, J. M. 415, 419, 420
Messner, M. A. 452, 453, 455, 462, 469, 500
method/methodological/methodology 71, 107, 128, 142, 153–155, 177–179, 192, 206, 217–218, 260–261, 272–278, 284–285, 320–321, 594
#MeToo India Movement: critiques on 518–519; impact of 513–514, 517–518, 520–521; significance in fourth-wave feminist movement 517–518
#MeToo movement 113, 151, 152, 156–157, 160, 183, 217
Micaela Law 336
migrant social workers: experiencing discriminatory practices 39; reasons for hiring 37–38
Millet, A. 415, 416
mining extractivism 594–596
modernisation 13, 590

modernity 13, 72, 73, 594
Modjeska, D.: "The Orchard" 179
Mohanty, C. T. 251, 538; *Under Western Eyes: Feminist Scholarship and Colonial Discourses* 538
monoculturalism 93–94, 98
Montubio people of Canton Muisne 595
moral injury 366, 367
more-than-human 87
Moreton-Robinson, Aileen 177, 360, 445; "Talkin up to the White Woman" 177
Morley, Louise 178, 182, 184, 185
mother-blame 385, 386, 389, 490
Motohashi, R. 374, 377
Moulding, N. 183, 389
movement(s) 4–5, 513–522, 526, 563, 580, 602
Movement for Emancipation of Women in Chile (MEMCH) 95, 295
Movimiento de Integración y Liberación Homosexual (MOVILH, Homosexual Integration and Liberation Movement) 418
Moylan, C. 152, 159
multiple masculinities 501–502
multi-racial feminism 500
Murabitat 133

narrative 35, 38, 76, 142–144, 151–161, 237, 242, 287, 426, 600, 617
National Action Plan to Reduce Violence against Women and their Children: First Action Plan (2010–2013) 208
National Association of Social Workers (NASW) 410
National Disability Insurance Agency 210
The National Gender Policy 189
National Health and Family Planning Commission and State Administration of Traditional Chinese Medicine 258
National Medium and Long-term Talent Development Plan (2010) 258
National Ministry of Education 331; Draft Project for the Modification of Decree 579/586 331
nego-feminism 22, 25, 27, 28, 197
nego-feminism in KwaZulu-Natal (KZN), South Africa 164–172; commitment to African feminist identity 168–169; community structures of oppression and negotiation skills 170–171; conceptualisation of 166–167; Eurocentrism 166; interviews and study with senior women traditional leaders 166–171; male hegemonic attitudes in rural traditional communities 166, 171; patriarchal marginalisation 165–167, 169, 170; women abuse and violent attacks 164, 165, 166, 168–171

neocolonialism 42, 191
neo-liberal capitalism 15, 301
neo-liberal economy 16, 118, 590
neo-liberal ethics 463–464
neo-liberal feminism 519
neoliberalism 15, 81–82, 111, 118, 277, 282, 283, 374, 519
neoliberalisation 68, 74
neoliberal marketing 113
neo-liberal policies 126, 127, 396, 536, 544, 588, 594
Network for Social Work Researchers 295, 296, 301
neuroscience 351, 354, 355
new feminisms 519
New Public Management (NPM) 396
NewsBank database 218
New Wave Gippsland 209
Nigerian women, in premarital relationships 189–199; aggressive behavior and violence 196, 198; Britain colonisation 189–190; economic marginalisation 196; female submission 194, 197, 198; gender inequality in 189, 193–194, 197; impact of patriarchy and male privileges 189–191, 197, 198; infidelity 190, 195, 198; limitation 199; male leadership in 189, 192–193, 197; methodology 192; proving marriageability 194–195, 198
Nirbhaya Delhi gang-rape case (2012–2017) 215–218, 220, 222, 223, 516
Nnaemeka, O. 27, 168–170, 197
no-ego approach 166
nomadic subjectivities 502
non-binary people 426, 431
non-binary politics 16, 17
non-Indigenous feminism 59
North American postcolonial discourse 70
Northern Territory Emergency Response (NTER) 492, 493
"Not Now, Not Ever" (Gillard) 178
Núcleo de Acción por los derechos homosexuales (NADH, Nucleus of Action for homosexual rights) 418
Nuestra America 84
Nuestro Mundo (Our world) 418

"Of Woman Born: Motherhood as Experience and Institution" (Rich) 384, 387
Okeke-Ihejirika, P. E. 195, 197
older LGBTIQ+ people 426–436; ageism, well-being, health and suicide 430–431; lived experience and views about aged care services and supports 431–434; social, political and cultural context and impact of history on 428–429; trans-inclusive and intersectional feminist approach 426–427, 434–436
Older Women's League 529
Older Women's Network 529
Oodi Library 598, 599, 609, 611
oppression 536–545, 575, 581, 616
"oppression Olympics" 76
optimal incubators 353–355
"The Orchard" (Modjeska) 179
O'Reilly, Andrea 152, 384, 388, 390
organic intersectionality 453
Orientalism 216, 222
Orr, Liz 177, 179, 180, 184
Oslo Peace Accord 125, 126
"othered" 13, 34, 36, 41
Oxfam International 87

Pachamama (Mother Earth) 587, 591–592
Pacification of Araucania 95
Palermo Protocol 139, 140
Palestinian Authority (PA) 136n1
parents accepting responsibility – kids are safe (PARKAS) 180–182
Paris Agreement (2015) 565
patriarchal capitalism 13, 14, 16, 97
patriarchal debt *see* care debt
patriarchal motherhood 384–385, 387–389
patriarchy 2, 10, 13, 15, 23, 24, 69, 98, 329, 337; concept of 215; definition 103, 190; influence on Palestine's women 128–129, 135, 136; *see also specific entries*
Patriarchy Awareness Workshops 503
patriarchy in Nigeria: colonisation and 189–190; culture and unequal power relations 191; practice 190; premarital relationships and 190–191; socialisation 191
patricentric religion 57
pauperism 588
Payne, M. 21, 235
Pease, Bob 447, 448, 452, 453, 457, 459, 469, 477–479, 598
pedagogy 16, 17, 19, 305–314, 561
The Peek a Boo Club 180
Peretz, T. 452, 453, 458
performative allyship 448, 503
Perlongher, Nestor 416, 418
Permanent Forum on Gender and Sexual Diversity 331
Personal Safety Survey (2021–2022) 183
Phillips, R. 144, 462, 532
Phoenix, A. 154, 156
Piaguage, Justino 594, 595
#PinjraTod movement 515, 516
Plumwood, Val 178; "Feminism and the Mastery of Nature" 178

pluriversality 491, 495
politic(s) 4, 10, 14, 102, 111–119, 573, 579
Political Constitution of Ecuador (2008): Article 74 587
politico-ethico-onto-epistemology 555
politics of meat 579–581; harming animals 579–580; harms to environment and humans 580–581; vegan and intersectional possibilities 581, **582–583**
popular feminism 272
popular solidarity economy (EPS) 587–592, 588–589, 594, 596
Pornography of Meat, The (Adams) 579
The Portfolio Committee on Social Development 165
post-colonial feminism 22–25, 34, 47, 272, 273, 538–539; colored demarcations in 33–42 (*see also individual subalterned entries*)
post-colonialism 23, 41
post human 550, 598–612
post human ethics 14
post-human feminism and futures of writing 598–612; academic non-belonging 600–603; 'another future is possible' 609; assemblages 598–600, 611; diaries and letters 607–609, 612; embodied-fleshed-more-than-human childhoods 603–605, 611; exhaustion and climate activism 605–606; narrative genres 611; during pandemic 606–607; photography 609–610, 612; poetry 610, 612; short memory scenes 611; situated writing 605; slow science 609–610
post-humanist allyship 470
post-masculinist feminist allyship 469–470
post-modern/post-structuralist feminism 11, 408
post-structuralism 556
Pourmokhtari, N. 139, 141
power relations 2, 9–11, 14, 16, 29, 75, 76, 152, 153, 345
power struggles 247–254
pre-birth child protection social work 355–356; in Aotearoa New Zealand 356
Prevention and Combating of Trafficking in Persons (PACOTIP) Act: No. 7 (2013) 140
Pringle, K. 459, 475
prison-industrial complex (PIC) 61, 228
Prison Nation, buildup of 228–231
privilege (male) privileging 10, 11, 17, 18, 189, 190–191, 197, 198, 221, 486
Productivity Commission 364, 365
profeminism 443–444, 498, 499, 500, 502
profeminist activism 451
profeminist men 444, 447, 448, 459, 467, 499, 500, 503–505; *see also* men and masculinities, in feminist social work; men

feminist allyship, in social work education; men social workers
profeminist social work practice: with male CSA victim-survivors 446–448; whiteness in 444–446
Professional Intervention in Relation to the Social Question (Rozas) 589
progressive social work 147, 311
ProQuest database 218
Public Health England 50
public policies 92–99, 331, 336, 587

Qualitative Social Work (journal) 282, 285
quantum physics 548, 549, 551, 555, 556
queer/cuir feminism 21, 272, 408
Quijano, Aníbal 591, 594

race 2, 4, 10, 45–52, 55, 60, 82, 138–148, 249, 272, 360–368, 527, 595
racialisation 22, 25, 28, 47, 48, 51, 73, 83–84
racial slurs 37
racism 12, 26, 28, 47, 57, 98, 119, 146, 494, 495; definition 51; institutional 141, 230; ranks in social work 38–40; scientific 85; and sexism 144; structural 88; systemic 36, 38, 58, 141, 487
radical feminisms 10, 112, 499–500, 501
radical materialism 500
radical theorising 3
The Raging Grannies 529
Raquel Gutiérrez 342
Rasool, S. 218, 237, 282, 283
reciprocity practices 342
relational ontology 547, 548–550
religious socialisation 191, 198
#Reporting worries (Orosanmälan) 151, 153, 154, 157–159
representationalism 554
reproductive health 10, 29, 94, 115, 116
reproductive justice and social work 351–352
reproductive rationale 343, 347
reproductive rights 10, 115–117, 119, 234, 351, 352, 353, 514
research 3–4, 192, 216, 247–254, 258–269, 273–277, 281–289, 292, 333, 354, 412; *see also* epistemologies action research
restorative justice 230, 494
Rettig Report 96
Rich, Adrienne 384, 387; "Of Woman Born: Motherhood as Experience and Institution" 384, 387
Richards, Lyn 177; "Having Families" 177
Richards, P. 72, 73, 74
Rise Up 4 Abortion Rights 530
Roe *v* Wade 281, 530; reversal of 352–353

Index

Royal Commission into Aged Care Quality and Safety 426, 430, 431
Rozas, Margarita 589; *Professional Intervention in Relation to the Social Question* 589
Ruddick, S. 376; *Maternal Thinking* 376
rural African traditional communities 165, 166, 168, 171

Sandberg, J. 284, 287
Sandberg, Sheryl 15; *Lean In* 15
School of Social Service, Chile 296
Schwalbe, M. 501, 502
scientific epistemology 306
The Scottish Association of Social Workers (SASW) 39
"The Second Sex" (Beauvior) 178
second-wave feminism 9, 374
sedimentation 473
settler Colonialism 230, 527
sexism 12, 17, 26, 55, 60, 86, 111, 454–455, 495, 542–543; and ageism 154, 155; and racism 144
sex-positive feminism 408
sex trafficking, of South African women 138–148; causes and vulnerability 141, 142; critical race feminist rights approach and its limitation 139, 141–143, 146–148; exploitation and 138–142; implications for social work practice 146–147; influence of traumatic childhood experiences 144–145; intersectionality of race and gender 139, 141, 143–147; labels and silenced narratives of lived experiences 139, 141–143, 146, 147; marginalisation and stigmatisation 138, 141, 143, 144, 147, 148; negative portrayal as willing participants 145–146; oppression and gender-based violence 138–140, 143; qualitative research approach 142; sexual abuse in family relations 144–145; social construction 139, 141, 145–146; statutory and common law legislations and policies against 140, 146; and substance use 146
sexual harassment, definition 151, 159
sexual identity 114, 395, 396
sexuality 11, 58–62, 59, 60, 74–75, 157, 429
Sexual Lives & Respectful Relationships (SL&RR) 203, 205, 206, 208, 209, 211, 212
Sexual Politics of Meat... (Adams) 579, 581
sexual violence 14, 61, 88, 114, 152, 155, 215–225, 513, 516, 531, 616
Silver, B. 352, 353, 504, 505
Sistergirls 432, 434
situated feminisms to social work research 272–278, 273–277; cartographies 272–273; ethical-political-epistemological perspective 272–275, 277; theoretical-political-methodological perspective 275–277
situated knowledges 34, 249–250, 252, 274, 275, 554
slavery 85, 86, 88
Slut Walk 513, 515
Smith, Dorothy 176, 195, 307
Smith, T. 452, 453
snail-sense feminism 22, 168, 197
social approval of care 378
Social Characterisation Survey (CASEN) 97
social debt 345
social identities 143, 234–235
Socialist Camp 81
socialist feminism 11
social justice 14, 17, 57, 63, 76, 111, 113, 115, 119, 141, 154, 231, 233, 234, 310, 311, 395
social justice activism 489, 526, 528, 533
social justice and gendered resistance 399–401; advocacy and mobilizing skills 401; critical ally-ship 400–401; critical reflexivity 400; humility and lived experience 400
social media feminism, in India 513–522; contemporary feminist activism 513, 514; critiques on #MeToo India movement 518–519; deliberative democracy and collective action 513, 519–522; emergence 515–517; feminist mobilisation and waves 514–515; feminist social media movements and campaigns 515–517; impact of #MeToo India Movement 513–514, 517–518, 520–521
social policy: of government 115; politics in development and implementation 111; and social work 111
Social Reproduction Theory (SRT) 82–83, 89
"Social Service and Division of Labour" (Iamamoto) 590
social work: amplifying women's voices and agency 238–239; anti-exploitative practice for 62–63; Catholic Church in 115; contemporary 2, 3, 12, 113; education 16–17; emancipatory and anti-oppressive 117–118; gender and feminist perspectives on 233–235; gendered nature of social work construction 235–236; global south feminist's ways of knowing and understanding social world 237–238; intersectionality and diversity 236–237; as "Othering" profession 40; political nature of 113–117; and reproductive justice 351–352; structural 410–411; unequal power relations in 239–242; *see also individual entries*
Social Work (journal) 285
Social Work Grand Challenge 287–288

Index

social work practice: impact of politics on 117–119; neoliberalism on 118; *see also* individual entries
Sociologies of Absences and Emergencies from the Epistemologies of the South (Sousa Santos) 592
solidarity 16, 129, 184, 282, 587–596
Sousa Santos, Boaventura de 418, 592; *Sociologies of Absences and Emergencies from the Epistemologies of the South* 592
The South African Constitution: Act 7 (1996) 140
South African women: domestic and sexual violence against 114; *see also* sex trafficking, of South African women; women of color
Southern Cross University Impact Award for Social Justice 182
Southern feminisms 27, 272, 274
Southern Metropolis Daily 258
speciesism 577–579, 581
Spivak, G. C. 34, 252, 274, 501, 539–540, 543; 'Can the Subaltern Speak?' 539–540; geographies of postcolonialism 36; subalternity 34, 35, 540, 543
Stanley, L. 247, 248, 250–253
Statistics South Africa 168
Steinfeld, H. 580; *Livestock's Long Shadow: Environmental Issues and Options* 580
Stengers, Isabelle 548, 609–610
strategic essentialism 465–466
strategic maternalism 381; essentialist *vs.* 378–379, **379**; Motohashi's theory of 377–378; social work based on 380–381
structural marginalisation 126
structural oppression 103, 113, 142, 542, 527
subaltern 539–540
subalterned ghetto: locating 35–38; as site of oppositional knowledge 40–41; strategies in collective resistance 42; in systemic racism 38–40
subalterned people and their status 33–35, 40
subalterned social worker 35; discriminatory practices in workplace 37; harassment and bullying on 37; intergenerational experience of Colonialism 40
subalterned women 40, 42; *see also* women of color
subalternity 543
subjugated voice 33–34
subordinate masculinity 468
suffragette movement 514
Sumak Kawsay (Good Living) 104, 590–592
Summers, Anne 177; "Damned Whores and God's Police" 177
survival sex 144
Sustainable Development Goal 140

Suttee practice 41
Swedish social work, sexual harassment in 151–161; culture legitimise and normalise sexualising jargon, threats and fear 157–159; cultures of violence and silence 158–159; diffractive intersectionality as narrative methodological tool 153–154, 160–161; power of written biographical stories to promote change 160–161; #Reporting worries 151, 153, 157–159; staging of sexual fantasies on pregnant, young and racialised bodies 155–157; testimonies and ethical considerations 154–155
SWHelper 118

Takemura, Kazuko 538–539
"Taking Back the Narrative: Gendered Anti-Blackness in Predominantly White Schools of Social Work" (Jackson) 241
"Talkin up to the White Woman" (Moreton-Robinson) 177
Temuco Criminal Court 96
Tenancy Law Reform 184
tensions 3, 68–77, 117, 143, 475, 505
teratogenic effects 353
territorialisation 83–84
Third Space theory 494
"Third-world" women 73
3Es to Freedom: Education, Empowerment, Employment 181, 182
three-system Model of Emotions 48
time poverty 341, 345–346
Total Communication 47–48
toxic masculinity 501
traditional leaders 27, 164–172
traditional masculinity 442, 443, 463
trafficking in persons (TIP) 138–141, 146; definition 139; as gendered crime 139–140; *see also* sex trafficking, of South African women
trans and gender expansive (TGE) people 407, 408, 410–413
trans-corporeality 549
transfeminism 407, 408
transfeminist feminism 272
transgenderism 59
transgender people 409, 434
transgenerational activism 550
trans-inclusive feminism 16
trans labor quota law 423n5
trans-national feminism 21, 63, 251
transphobic behaviour 412
trans women 426, 429, 431
travesti epistemology 418
Travestis Unidas (United *Travestis*) 418
Tronto, Joan 394, 395

Truth and Reconciliation Commission 566
Tsing, A. 599, 605
Tumblr 154
Twitter 151

Ubuntu 26–27, 29, 112, 118, 165, 169
Ulmer, J. B. 606, 609
Uluru Statement from the Heart (2017) 494
UN Convention on the Rights of Persons with Disabilities (CRPD) 203, 204; Article 3 204; Article 23 204
Under Western Eyes: Feminist Scholarship and Colonial Discourses (Mohanty) 538
United Nations Commission on the Elimination of Racial Discrimination 537
The United Nations Convention Against Transnational Organised Crime Protocol to Prevent, Suppress and Punish Trafficking in Persons, Especially Women and Children 139
United Nations Convention on the Rights of the Child: Article 3 490; Article 7 490; Article 8 490; Article 18 490; Article 19 490
universal womanhood 23
University of Santiago de Chile 71
University of Tennessee (UoT) 576–577
Utoro Peace Memorial Museum 537

vegan 581, 582–583
Veterinary Social Work (VSW) programme 576–577
The Victorian Mental Health Complaints Commissioner Report 364
Victorian Royal Commission into Family Violence 181
Victorian Royal Commission into Mental Health Service 364
violence 215–225, 451–459
Viveros, Mara 70, 73
Voice to Parliament in the Australian Constitution 494
"Volatile Bodies" (Grosz) 179

Wallmapu 94–96
waves of feminisms 21, 22–23, 467, 514
weaponised White Womanhood 446
Weeks, W. 176, 178; "Women Working Together" 179
welfare state model 117–118
Western culture 93, 445
Western education 189–190
Western Eurocentric feminism/white feminism 9, 24–25, 27, 58, 59, 69, 102, 252, 272, 329, 468, 519
Western feminist movements 25, 40, 61
Western humanism 600
Western knowledge 93–94, 445

Western mental health systems 363
Western Region Service Against Sexual Assault 182
WhatsApp 192
'What's the Problem Represented to be?' (WPR) approach 215, 217, 223
Whitaker, Louise 178–182
white fragility 57
whiteness 18, 62, 140, 177, 444–446
white supremacy 38, 39, 62, 282
white victimhood 57
white women: labour power and 84–86; privilege 17; struggle against patriarchy 55
#WhyLoiter movements 516
Wiccan feminism 21
Wilson, Elizabeth 177; "Women and the Welfare State" 177
Wise, S. 248, 249, 251, 252
witch-hunt 329
'wokeness' 113
Wolf, Naomi 178; "The Beauty Myth" 178
womanism 12, 22
women: access to housing rights 117; in caregiving and domestic work 85–86; domestic and family violence on 116–117, 119; experiences of 'racialised as Black' 25; gendered oppression 113, 116; labour participation 10; liberation 17, 23; reproductive rights 10, 115–117, 119; rights 9; sexual violence on 116, 119; subordination of 10, 17; working class 12; *see also individual entries*
women abuse 27, 164–172
"Women and the Welfare State" (Wilson) 177
"Women and Work" (Hargraves) 177
women leaders, in Palestinian universities 317–325; attitudes toward gender equality 317, 318, 320; data analysis 321; effectiveness of leadership experience 324; feminism, feminist social work and theory 318–319; implications 325; leadership style and gender differences 322, 323, 325; leadership theories 319–320; method 320; motivation and vision 321; participation in labor force 317; perceptions toward 320; positive and negative views 322–323; sampling, data collection and participants 321
women of colour: attack on transgender in USA 119; dehumanisation of 84, 87; experiencing discriminatory practices 39; feminisms 231; non-commodified reproductive work of 84; patronizing in workplace 36–37; in social work 35, 38, 39, 42; unrecognising domestic and care workload as legitimate labour 86–87

Index

Women's Justice Network 181
"Women Working Together" (Weeks) 179
Wood, L. 152, 159
World Bank 118
World Health Organisation (WHO) 88, 224, 259, 354, 440, 615
World Health Organisation Ethical and Safety Recommendations for Interviewing Trafficked Women 142
The World Professional Association for Transgender Health 413
World War II 9, 589
World Women's Congress for a Healthy Planet 618
Wuyi University 258

Young, Susan 485–487
young women empowerment, in Palestine 125–136; challenges and resistance against colonisation 132–133, 135, 136; family influence and patriarchal structures on 128–129, 135, 136; gender role and hierarchies in youth work 129–131; image of youth as political activists 125; impact of gender equality, structure and dynamics on 125–127, 129–131, 135, 136; importance of mentorship 135; inclusion/exclusion discourse and 126–127; marginalisation and 126, 127, 129–131, 134; participation as pathway to 134; political context reinforcing gender hierarchies and limiting women's mobility 131, 136; qualitative approach 128; selection 134–135; social and neoliberal policies 126, 127; structural and institutional biases impact 135; task divisions 134; women leaders as power figures 131–132, 134, 135; youth organisations and programmes for 125–130, 134, 136
youth development 126
youth empowerment 126, 127, 131

Zainichi Korean women oppression, in Japan 536–545; colonialism and sexism 542–543; employment discrimination 540–541, 544; exclusion and hate speech 537–538; gnder discrimination 543; intersectionality 539, 540, 543; postcolonial feminism 538–539, 544; and resistance 540–544; subalternity 539–540
Zarallo, V. C. 235, 239, 240
Zufferey, C. 117, 389
Zulu society 25